P9-CLK-508

THE HANDBOOK OF LIFE-SPAN DEVELOPMENT:

SOCIAL AND EMOTIONAL DEVELOPMENT

VOLUME 2

THE HANDBOOK OF LIFE-SPAN DEVELOPMENT:

SOCIAL AND EMOTIONAL DEVELOPMENT

VOLUME 2

Volume Editors

MICHAEL LAMB

UNIVERSITY OF CAMBRIDGE

ALEXANDRA FREUND

UNIVERSITY OF ZURICH

Editor-in-Chief

RICHARD M. LERNER

TUFTS UNIVERSITY

John Wiley & Sons, Inc.

This book is printed on acid-free paper. ♾

Published by John Wiley & Sons, Inc., Hoboken, New Jersey.
Published simultaneously in Canada.

For general information on our other products and services please contact our Customer Care Department within the United States at (800) 762-2974, outside the United States at (317) 572-3993 or fax (317) 572-4002.

Wiley also publishes its books in a variety of electronic formats. Some content that appears in print may not be available in electronic books. For more information about Wiley products, visit our web site at www.wiley.com.

Library of Congress Cataloging-in-Publication Data:

The handbook of life-span development / editor-in-chief, Richard M. Lerner.
p. cm.
Includes author and subject indexes.
ISBN 978-0-470-39011-5 (v. 1 : cloth); ISBN 978-0-470-39012-2 (v. 2 : cloth); ISBN 978-0-470-39013-9 (set : cloth); 978-0-470-63433-2 (ebk); 978-0-470-63434-9 (ebk); 978-0-470-63435-6 (ebk)
1. Developmental psychology. 2. Maturation (Psychology) 3. Aging–Psychological aspects. I. Lerner, Richard M.
BF713.H3648 2010
155–dc22 2009049300

Printed in the United States of America

10 9 8 7 6 5 4 3 2 1

Contents

VOLUME 2: Social and Emotional Development

Preface

Until the early 1960s, the field of human development was dominated by either descriptions of the behavioral or psychological phenomena presumptively unfolding as a consequence of genetically controlled timetables of maturational change (e.g., see the chapters by Hess and by McClearn in the third edition of the *Handbook of Child Psychology*; Mussen, 1970) or by descriptions of the behaviors presumptively elicited in response to stimulation encountered over the course of early life experiences (e.g., see the chapters by Stevenson or by White in the same edition of the *Handbook*). Framed within a Cartesian dualism that split nature from nurture (Overton, 2006), developmental science focused in the main on the generic human being (Emmerich, 1968) and on the earliest years of life or, at most, the years surrounding the stages of pubertal change. These periods were regarded as the portions of ontogeny in which the fundamental processes of human development emerged and functioned to shape the subsequent course of human life (Brim & Kagan, 1980).

Today, the study of development has evolved from a field embedded within the domain of developmental psychology to an area of scholarship labeled *developmental science* (Bornstein & Lamb, 2005, 2010; Magnusson & Stattin, 1998, 2006). Substantively, developmental science is a field that conceptualizes the entire span of human life as potentially involving developmental change. The possibility of developmental change across life exists because the basic process of development is seen as involving mutually influential relations between an active organism and a changing, multilevel ecology, a relation represented as individual ↔ context relations (Lerner, 2006). These relations provide the fundamental impetus to systematic and successive changes across the life span (Brandtstädter, 1998; Overton, 1973, 2003; Lerner, 2006).

Thus, the contemporary study of human development involves placing postmodern, relational models at the cutting edge of theoretical and empirical interest (Overton, 2006). These models consider all levels of organization—from the inner biological through the physical ecological, cultural, and historical—as involved in mutually influential relationships across the breadth of the entire life course (Bronfenbrenner & Morris, 2006; Riegel, 1975, 1976). Variations in time and place constitute vital sources of systematic changes across ontogeny—even into the 10th and 11th decades of life—and, as such, human life is variegated and characterized by intraindividual change and interindividual differences (Baltes, Lindenberger, & Staudinger, 2006; Elder, Modell, & Parke, 1993). Accordingly, because ontogenetic change is embodied in its relation to time and place (Overton, 2006), contemporary developmental science regards the temporality represented by historical changes as imbued in all levels of organization, as coacting integratively, and as providing a potential for this systematic change—for plasticity—across the life span.

In short, as a consequence of the relational coactions of changes at levels of organization ranging from the biological and the psychological and behavioral to the sociocultural, designed and natural physical ecological, and through the historical (see Gottlieb, 1997; Overton, 2006), processes of development are viewed in contemporary developmental science through a theoretical and empirical lens that extends the study of change across the human ontogenetic span and, as well, through generational and historical time (Elder, 1998; Elder et al., 1993). The variations in the actions of individuals on their contexts and contexts on individuals integratively propel and texture the course of life (Baltes, Freund, & Li, 2005; Brandtstädter, 2006; Freund & Baltes, 2000 Freund, Li, & Baltes, 1999). As a result, the breadth of the life span and all levels of organization within the ecology of human development must be considered to fully describe, explain, and optimize the course of intraindividual change and of interindividual differences in such change (Baltes et al., 2006; Baltes, Reese, & Nesselroade, 1977).

There exist both historical (Baltes, 1979, 1983; Cairns & Cairns, 2006), philosophical, and theoretical (Lerner, 1984; Overton, 1973, 1975, 2006) accounts of the nature and bases of the evolution of developmental science. These accounts document that the field changed from one dominated by psychological, environmental, or biological reductionist, split, and age-period-restricted conceptions of human development processes to become a field focused on relational, systems, and life-span developmental models. As Edwin G. Boring (1950, p. ix) noted, Hermann Ebbinghaus once remarked that "psychology has a long past, but only a short history." In many ways, the same statement may be made about the evolution of the life-span view of human development.

A BRIEF HISTORY OF THE LIFE-SPAN DEVELOPMENTAL PERSPECTIVE

The life-span ideas that we today summarize as "the" life-span perspective began to emerge in the United States in the mid-1960s and early 1970s. However, the conception that was forwarded was neither a newly created perspective of human development nor the only extant conception of life-span development present at the time (or even now). To a great extent, the history of the emergence and refinement of this life-span perspective arose through the discussions at, and the subsequent edited volumes derived from, a series of conferences held in the late 1960s and early to mid-1970s at the University of West Virginia in Morgantown. The conferences were held under the aegis of the Department of Psychology, which was chaired by K. Warner Schaie. As Baltes (1979, 1983) and Cairns and Cairns (2006) explained, the roots of the approach that began to crystallize in Morgantown can be traced to 19th-century scholarship in the United States and to philosophical ideas forwarded about 200 years earlier in Europe. In turn, although there was a different concentration of empirical attention paid to successive portions of human ontogeny (with most attention paid to infancy and childhood and comparatively less work devoted to studying people as they aged into the adolescent and adult periods), many U.S. developmental psychologists might argue that the study of human life within the social and behavioral sciences has always included a focus on behavior across the breadth of ontogeny. Despite the fact that the label *life-span developmental psychology* was not used, there was, at least since G. Stanley Hall's work on senescence (1922), attention paid in some way to periods of life beyond childhood and adolescence.

Nevertheless, despite any claims made that developmental science has been concerned for at least 90 years with development across life, the structure and function of academic work would contradict such assertions. Indeed, it was not until the 1970s and early 1980s, when the term *life-span developmental psychology* became popular in developmental psychology (e.g., Baltes & Schaie, 1973; Goulet & Baltes, 1970; Nesselroade & Reese, 1973), that many departments began offering life-span development courses.

Moreover, most people involved in teaching these courses were trained in infancy, childhood, or, in a few cases, adolescence. They taught what they knew most and, as such, courses were mostly modestly revised child development courses with a few lectures at the end of the course devoted to "adult development and aging." The textbooks that were written for use in these courses—in the main by colleagues also not involved in the study of developmental change across the breadth of human ontogeny—reinforced the approach taken by classroom instructors. Texts were in fact slightly revised child development books with a couple of chapters (and in some cases only one chapter) added about adult development and aging; at the time, the late adult years were still not seen as a part of the process of development. In short, authors wrote these books, and publishers structured them, to meet the "needs" of the instructors, which were to present mostly infancy and childhood, perhaps a chapter on adolescence (puberty, the identity crisis, and problem behaviors were in large part the focus of such chapters) and, finally, "adulthood and aging."

When the work of the key scholars studying the latter portion of the life span, for instance, developmental scientists such as Paul B. Baltes, James Birren, John R. Nesselroade, or K. Warner Schaie, among others, were cited, this scholarship was reduced to the fact that these scholars had promoted the idea of studying development across the life span. Therefore, because the existence of such life-span work required some treatment in the textbook, the author of the textbook would commence to present such topics as the life tasks of adulthood (as discussed, for instance, by Robert Havighurst, 1951), some ideas about intellectual decline with aging, and "death and dying." What was wrong with such approaches to life-span human development?

THE VIEW FROM THE HILLS

These early textbooks in life-span development missed the points being made by the scholars who were gathering in Morgantown, West Virginia, and who were shaping quite a different approach to the study of development across the life span. The work of Baltes, Schaie, Nesselroade, and other major contributors (e.g., scholars such as Nancy Datan, Lawrence Goulet, Willis Overton, Hayne Reese, and Klaus Riegel) to the foundation of the approach to life-span development that has evolved to frame developmental science had, at best, been misinterpreted and, at worst (and in fact most of the time), trivialized. What, then, were the ideas being developed by the scholars meeting in Morgantown? Answering this question is central to the present work: The ideas that began to be developed in the West Virginia hills provide the foundation of the scholarship represented in this *Handbook*. Indeed, one cannot overestimate the impact on developmental science theory and methodology of the books that were derived from the West Virginia conferences (Baltes & Schaie, 1973; Datan & Reese, 1977; Goulet & Baltes, 1970; Nesselroade & Reese, 1973) and from a subsequent series of "annual" advances volumes, *Life-Span Development and Behavior*, first edited by Paul Baltes (1978); then by Baltes and Orville G. Brim, Jr. (1979, 1980, 1982, 1983, 1984); by Baltes, David L. Featherman, and Richard M. Lerner (1986, 1988a, 1988b, 1990); and by Featherman, Lerner, and Marion Perlmutter (1992, 1994). These works pushed the study of human development beyond the split and reductionist conceptual boundaries to which the field had accommodated (Overton, 2006).

As Baltes (1987; Baltes et al., 2006) explained, the life-span view of human development was associated with the integration of a set of ideas, each of which could be found as "stand-alone" concepts within the developmental literature; however, when taken as an integrated or, in fact, a fused, or relational, whole, these ideas changed the conceptual landscape of the field. As such, the set of concepts introduced in the late 1960s and early 1970s at the University of West Virginia life-span development conferences embodied an approach to the study of the human life span that stood in sharp contrast to the simplistic, additive approach to development found in the early textbooks and associated courses in life-span development. Although these "West Virginian" ideas have of course evolved across the ensuing decades and were refined and extended by the their originators and by those who were influenced or trained by them, the fundamental character of these ideas remains the same and constitutes at least a sea change, if not a true paradigm shift, in the nature of thinking about human development.

First, development was seen as a process, one that began at conception and continued through the end of life. For example, developmental processes were conceptualized as involving systematic and successive changes in the organization of relations within and across the levels of organization comprising the ecology of human development (e.g., Bronfenbrenner, 1979; Bronfenbrenner & Morris, 2006; Lerner, 2002, 2006; Overton, 1973, 1978, 2006; Overton & Reese, 1981; Reese & Overton, 1970). There were both qualitatively and quantitatively continuous and discontinuous facets of this process. Accordingly, mutidirectionality of development (increases, decreases, curvilinearity, smooth or abrupt change, etc.) were all possible forms for a developmental process, and the shape or form of a developmental trajectory for an individual or group was a matter of theory-predicated empirical inquiry (Wohlwill, 1973).

In addition, because variation in the form of developmental trajectories may occur for different people (e.g., people who vary with regard to age, sex, race, birth cohort, etc.), living in different settings, or in different historical eras, developmental process may take a different form at different points in ontogeny, generational time, or history across individuals or groups. Thus, diversity—with regard to within-person changes but also to differences between people in within-person change—rose to the level of substantive significance (as opposed to error variance) within the life-span view. For instance, as explained by Bornstein (1995), in regard to his "specificity principle" of infant development "specific experiences at specific times exert specific effects over specific aspects of infant growth in specific ways" (p. 21). In turn, a similar idea was advanced by Freund, Nikitin, and Ritter (2009), albeit one focused at the other end of the life span. Underscoring the importance of viewing the developmental process across the breadth of ontogeny, Freund et al. noted that a person's development during a historical period of extended life expectancy is likely to have important implications for development during young and middle adulthood.

Accordingly, although it would make sense from a life-span developmental perspective to study individuals and groups within (as well as across) ontogenetic "age periods," an age period–specific focus should not be adopted because of the mistaken belief that the developmental process that occurs in childhood or adolescence is somehow a different developmental process than the one that occurs in adulthood and late adulthood. Rather, the life-span developmental scientist has the task of describing and explaining and, as noted again later in this preface, optimizing the form of such change across life. He or she must detail the ways in which changes within one period are derived from changes at earlier periods and affect changes at subsequent periods.

As well, explanations of continuities and discontinuities across life, and of the form (the shape) of the developmental trajectory and of its rate of change, involve a very different theoretical frame than the ones that had been dominant in other approaches to the study of development (i.e., the split and reductionist approaches of past eras). As explained by Overton, both in his prior work (e.g., 1973, 2006) and in the chapter that introduces Volume 1 of the present *Handbook*, a relational metamodel frames the contemporary, cutting-edge study of human development within and across all portions of ontogeny. The use of this relational perspective emerged through the influence of Overton and other developmental scientists (e.g., Sameroff, 1975), including those studying infancy (e.g., Bornstein, 1995; Lamb, 1977; Lewis, 1972; Lewis & Rosenblum, 1974; Thelen & Smith, 1998), as well as through the contributions of comparative scientists (e.g., Gottlieb, 1997; Greenberg & Tobach, 1984; Kuo, 1976; Schneirla, 1957) and biologists (e.g., Novikoff, 1945a, 1945b; von Bertalanffy, 1933, 1968). This scholarship resulted in the elaboration of several variants of a developmental systems theoretical model of development (e.g., Ford & Lerner, 1992; Lerner, 2002); more recently, by explicitly incorporating a relational perspective, these models have been termed *relational developmental systems* models of development (Lerner, 2006; Lerner & Overton, 2008).

Because it may seem counterintuitive that the scholarship of developmental scientists studying infancy was integral in the foundation of the life-span approach to human development, it is useful to illustrate briefly the contributions of such work to the life-span approach. The scholarship of Michael Lewis (e.g., 1972; Lewis & Lee-Painter, 1974) built on the insights of Bell (1968), about the potential presence in correlational data about socialization, of evidence for the bidirectional influences between parents and children. Lewis and his colleagues launched a program of research that provided a new, relational model of infant–parent interaction. In *The Effect of the Infant on Its Caregiver* (Lewis & Rosenblum, 1974), a volume that represents a watershed event in the history of the study of human development through the use of person↔context relational models, Lewis and colleagues argued that "Not only is the infant or child influenced by its social, political, economic and biological world, but in fact the child itself influences its world in turn" (Lewis & Rosenblum, 1974, p. xv) and maintained that "only through interaction can we study, without distortion, human behavior (Lewis & Lee-Painter, 1974, p. 21). Envisioning the relational, developmental systems models that would come to the fore in the study of human development a quarter century later, Lewis noted that a

> relational position not only requires that we deal with elements in interaction but also requires that we not consider the static quality of these interactions. Rather, it is necessary to study their flow with time.... Exactly how this might be done is not at all clear. It may be necessary to consider a more metaphysical model, a circle in which there are neither elements nor beginnings/ends. (Lewis & Lee-Painter, 1974, pp. 46–47).

Lewis's scholarship fostered an intellectual climate among other infancy researchers that resulted in a reconceptualization of phenomena of infant development within the sorts of relational, individual ↔ context relational models he forwarded. I noted earlier in this preface the contributions of Marc Bornstein (1995) in this regard. Here, too, however, we should point out another, foundational instance of the contributions of infancy researchers to the life-span perspective, found in the work of Michael Lamb. For instance, Lamb and his colleagues (e.g., Lamb, 1977; Lamb, Thompson, Gardner, & Charnov, 1985; Thompson & Lamb, 1986) approached the study of infant attachment within the context of the assumptions that (a) children influence their "socializers" and are not simply the receptive foci of socializing forces, (b) early social and emotional/personality development occurs in the context of a complex family system rather than only in the context of the mother–infant dyad, and (c) social and psychological development are not confined to infancy or childhood but involve a process that continues from birth to death (Lamb, 1978, p. 137; cf. Riley, 1979).

Within this conceptual framework, Lamb and his colleagues found that prior interpretations of infant attachment, which included "an emphasis on the formative significance of early experiences, a focus on unidirectional influences on the child, a tendency to view development within a narrow ecological context, and a search for universal processes of developmental change" (Thompson & Lamb, 1986, p. 1), were less powerful in accounting for the findings of attachment research than an interpretation associated with person↔context relational models. Accordingly, in a review of attachment research conducted through the mid-1980s, Lamb and colleagues concluded that "reciprocal organism–environment influences, developmental plasticity, individual patterns of developmental change and broader contextual influences on development can better help to integrate and interpret the attachment literature, and may also provide new directions for study" (Thompson & Lamb, 1986, p. 1).

Lamb's work challenged the field of infancy to move the study of the early years of life beyond the use of narrow, split, or reductionist conceptions of the exclusive influences of heredity or early experiences or of simplistic views of proximal dyadic relationships acting in isolation from the fuller and richer ecology of human development. He provided instead a relational vision for the understanding of infancy as part of the entire life span, of the life-span development of the other people in the infant's world, and of the complex set of infant ↔ social context relations as reciprocal exchanges in and with a multilevel and dynamic context (e.g., see Lamb, 1977; Lamb et al., 1985).

In short, as exemplified by the work embedding the study of infancy within a life-span approach to human development, the theoretical approaches that emerged in the 1970s from the impetus given developmental science by the scholars gathering in the hills of West Virginia constituted an integrative approach to variables across the levels of organization within the relational developmental system. As such, these models rejected as counterfactual the split conceptions, theories, and metatheories that partitioned the sources of development into nature and nurture. Rejected as well were "compromise" views that, although admitting that both of these purportedly separate sources of influence were involved in development, used problematic (i.e., additive) conceptions of interaction (conceptualized much as are interaction terms in an analysis of variance or in other instantiations of the general linear model; see Gottlieb, Wahlsten, & Lickliter, 2006). Instead, the theoretical models promoted by the scholars contributing to the foundation and evolution of the life-span perspective stressed that the basic process of human development involves developmental regulations—that is, individual ↔ context relations that link all levels of the ecology of human development within a thoroughly integrated, or "fused" (Tobach & Greenberg, 1984), dynamic, relational system.

For instance, these levels of the ecology involve ecological systems within the person (i.e., biosocial influences) or most proximal to him or her (what Bronfenbrenner [1979] termed the *microsystem*), extend to the set of contexts within which the individual interacts (the *mesosystem*; Bronfenbrenner, 1979) and to the systems in the ecology within which components of the mesosystem (e.g., parents) interact (e.g., the workplace) that may not directly involve the person but nevertheless may have an impact on him or her. In addition, the ecology includes the *macrosystem*—the broadest level of the ecology; the macrosystem influences all other systems and includes social policies, major intuitions of society (such as education, health care, and the economy), the designed and natural physical ecology, and, ultimately, history. As noted, this latter level of organization within the relational, integrated developmental system provides a temporal component for all other facets of the developmental system and creates the potential for systematic change, for plasticity, in individual ↔ context relations.

One recent instantiation of such relational, developmental systems thinking in regard to the dynamics of the person's exchanges with his or her ecology involves the work of Freund and colleagues in regard to the nature of the goals that individuals pursue within their changing context (e.g., Freund, 2007; Nikitin & Freund, 2008). Freund argues that the interplay of different levels of organization is important not only at the levels of person, family, and society (or other nested levels) but also for understanding the role of specific constructs—in this case, goals—for development. Extending action-theoretical concepts that have tended to view goals as primarily personal constructs, Freund explained that goals are located at multiple levels of the developmental system and that mutually influential relations among these levels need to be assessed to understand fully the nature and role of goals in human development. These levels involve social norms and expectations that inform about age-related opportunity structures and goal-relevant resources; personal beliefs about the appropriate timing and sequencing of goals; personal goals that are influenced by social norms, personal beliefs, the individual's learning history, and external (e.g., social and physical environment) and internal (e.g., talent) resources; and nonconscious goals and motives that might be particularly influential in times of transition or in times of routine.

CONCLUSIONS

A relational developmental systems model of human development constitutes the approach to studying the life span that evolved from the ideas developed among the scholars gathering in the formative conferences at the University of West Virginia (Baltes & Schaie, 1973; Datan & Reese, 1977; Goulet & Baltes, 1970; Nesselroade & Reese, 1973). It is this dynamic, relational perspective that constitutes a radical departure from approaches that study nature, or nurture, or additive, linear (or even curvilinear) combinations (even if cast as "interactions") between the two. Because of the emphasis on the dynamics of relations between the multiple levels of organization involved in the individual and the multiple levels of organization that are part of the ecology of human development, we need to adopt an ontogenetically all-encompassing—a fully life-span—approach to studying relational developmental processes. Such a conceptual frame is required if we are to understand the import of individual ↔ context relations for fostering specific changes, for a specific individual or group, living in a specific context, at a specific point in history (Bornstein, 1995). Clearly, such scholarship requires a multidisciplinary integrative (truly interdisciplinary) approach to the study of human development. Indeed, this need for collaboration across disciplines is in large part why developmental psychology has been transformed into developmental science (Lerner, 2006).

In addition, the concepts of developmental regulation and plasticity integral to a developmental systems framing of the study of development across the life span have another quite important implication for the conduct of developmental science. These concepts in combination afford optimism about the possibility of finding or instantiating individual ↔ context relations that may increase the probability of positive developmental change. Indeed, the life-span approach to developmental science suggests that applications of relational, theory-predicated research findings (in the form of policies or programs) may promote more positive courses of development across life. Efforts to optimize the course of human life through the application of relationally framed developmental science provide, then, an opportunity to test developmental systems ideas about the impact of changes in individual ↔ context relations. As well, such applied efforts constitute a way for developmental scientists to contribute to the improvement of human life among diverse people and their settings. Ultimately, then, such applications of developmental science may contribute to the enhancement of social justice (Lerner & Overton, 2008).

THE GOALS OF THIS *HANDBOOK*

The innovative ideas associated with a developmental systems–framed approach to the study of life-span development is coupled with an admittedly ambitious agenda of basic and applied developmental science devoted to studying and optimizing processes of individual ↔ context relations across the life span. Nevertheless, despite the methodological complexities of adopting this relational approach to developmental science, the past 40 years have provided depth and breadth of empirical evidence in support of the usefulness of these ideas in framing methodologically rigorous and substantively significant developmental science.

As such, one might think that numerous scholarly references exist for scholars to draw on to understand the state-of-the art of the study of life-span development. However, such resources have not existed before the present *Handbook*. Because of this absence, there was no single reference work that developmental scientists or their students could consult to find a thorough, integrative presentation of the breadth of scholarship documenting the use of the relational, developmental systems ideas that frame the life-span study of human development. There was no single high-level reference that provided discussions of the usefulness of relational concepts in integrating and extending the range of substantive areas involved in studying development across the life span.

Instead, to date, the key reference works available to developmental scientists and their students about the nature and scope of life-span change processes have been—paradoxically—age-segmented resources (e.g., Damon & Lerner, 2006; Lerner & Steinberg, 2009). In short, despite the important and rich theoretical and substantive work that is framed by perspectives on human development that encompass the life span, there has been no single reference work that presents the top-tier developmental science work pertinent to such processes.

The goal of this *Handbook* is to provide such a scholarly resource. It is the first-ever reference work to present—through the top-tier scholars in developmental science—the accumulated knowledge about the description, explanation, and implications for optimizing applications (i.e., applications that have the potential to maximize the chances for positive human development) of development across the life span. My fellow editors and I have the aspiration that this *Handbook* will constitute a watershed event in the development of life-span developmental scholarship. With the publication of this *Handbook*, we believe a compelling scholarly alternative will exist to counter both split depictions of developmental processes (e.g., studying childhood and adulthood as if they were composed of distinct, completely discontinuous processes) and split explanations of the changes that occur across the life span.

We hope that this first edition of the *Handbook* will serve as a touchstone for current and future researchers and instructors. As such, future editions of the *Handbook* may provide an even richer depiction of the course of development across the breadth of the life span than is possible in this edition. Given that developmental science has had for so long an age-specific focus, several topics discussed across the two volumes of this *Handbook* remain underexplored, perhaps particularly with respect to the later adult years. When the literature was not available to discuss a particular topic in depth with regard to a portion of the life span, the authors point to this situation and suggest ways to expand the topic more fully across the life span. We believe that their ideas for future scholarship are persuasive—indeed, compelling. As such, our ultimate hope is that future editions of the *Handbook* will reflect the continued theoretical, methodological, and empirical refinement of the concepts about development that began to coalesce in the hills of West Virginia more than four decades ago.

ACKNOWLEDGMENTS

There are numerous people to whom the editors of this *Handbook* owe enormous thanks for their contributions. Clearly, we are deeply grateful to the colleagues who contributed to this work, both for their superb scholarly contributions and for their commitment to working collaboratively to produce this *Handbook*. We also appreciate greatly the unflagging support of our superb editor at John Wiley & Sons, Patricia Rossi. Her commitment to the vision of this *Handbook* and her support for the quality of contribution we sought to make to developmental science were essential, indeed invaluable, assets throughout our work. We are also grateful to Leslie Dickinson and Jarrett M. Lerner, successive Managing Editors at the Institute for Applied Research at Tufts University, for their superb editorial work. Their commitment to quality and productivity, and their resiliency in the face of the tribulations of manuscript production, are greatly admired and deeply appreciated. I am also grateful to the National 4-H Council, the Philip Morris Smoking Prevention Department, the John Templeton Foundation, the Thrive Foundation for Youth, and the National Science Foundation for supporting my work during the development of this project.

Finally, my co-editors and I dedicate this *Handbook* to Paul B. Baltes, one of the pillars of 20th century developmental science and, across the last third of the 20th century, the key intellectual and professional force involved in establishing and enabling the flourishing of theory and research about life-span development. His intellect, leadership, generosity, kindness, and wisdom are warmly remembered and sorely missed.

Richard M. Lerner
Medford, MA
October 1, 2009

REFERENCES

Baltes, P. B. (Ed.). (1978). *Life-span development and behavior* (Vol. 1). New York: Academic Press.

Baltes, P. B. (1979). On the potential and limits of child development: Life-span developmental perspectives. *Newsletter of the Society of Research in Child Development*, 1–4.

Baltes, P. B. (1983). Life-span developmental psychology: Observations on history and theory revisited. In R. M. Lerner (Ed.), *Developmental psychology: Historical and philosophical perspectives* (pp. 79–111). Hillsdale, NJ: Erlbaum.

Baltes, P. B. (1987). Theoretical propositions of life-span developmental psychology: On the dynamics between growth and decline. *Developmental Psychology, 23*, 611–626.

Baltes, P. B., & Brim, O. G. (Eds.). (1979). *Life-span development and behavior* (Vol. 2). New York: Academic Press.

Baltes, P. B., & Brim, O. G. (Eds.). (1980). *Life-span development and behavior* (Vol. 3). New York: Academic Press.

Baltes, P. B., & Brim, O. G. (Eds.). (1982). *Life-span development and behavior* (Vol. 4). New York: Academic Press.

Baltes, P. B., & Brim, O. G. (Eds.). (1983). *Life-span development and behavior* (Vol. 5). New York: Academic Press.

Baltes, P. B., & Brim, O. G. (Eds.). (1984). *Life-span development and behavior* (Vol. 6). New York: Academic Press.

Baltes, P. B., Featherman, D. L., & Lerner, R. M. (Eds.). (1986). *Life-span development and behavior* (Vol. 7). Hillsdale, NJ: Erlbaum.

Baltes, P. B., Featherman, D. L., & Lerner, R. M. (Eds.). (1988a). *Life-span development and behavior* (Vol. 8). Hillsdale, NJ: Erlbaum.

Baltes, P. B., Featherman, D. L., & Lerner, R. M. (Eds.). (1988b). *Life-span development and behavior* (Vol. 9). Hillsdale, NJ: Erlbaum.

Baltes, P. B., Featherman, D. L., & Lerner, R. M. (Eds.). (1990). *Life-span development and behavior* (Vol. 10). Hillsdale, NJ: Erlbaum.

Baltes, P. B., Freund, A. M., & Li, S.-C. (2005). The psychological science of human aging. In M. Johnson, V. L. Bengston, P. G. Coleman, & T. B. L. Kirkwood (Eds.), *The Cambridge handbook of age and ageing* (pp. 47–71). Cambridge, England: Cambridge University Press.

Baltes, P. B., Lindenberger, U., & Staudinger, U. M. (2006). Lifespan theory in developmental psychology. In R. M. Lerner (Ed.) *Handbook of child psychology: Vol. 1. Theoretical models of human development* (6th ed., pp. 569–664). Editors-in-chief: W. Damon & R. M. Lerner. Hoboken, NJ: Wiley.

Baltes, P. B., Reese, H. W., & Nesselroade, J. R. (1977). *Life-span developmental psychology: Introduction to research methods.* Monterey, CA: Brooks/Cole.

Baltes, P. B., & Schaie, K. W. (Eds.). (1973). *Life-span developmental psychology: Personality and socialization.* New York: Academic Press.

Bell, R. Q. (1968). A reinterpretation of the direction of effects in studies of socialization. *Psychological Review, 75*, 81–95.

Boring, E. G. (1950). *A history of experimental psychology* (2nd ed.). New York: Appleton-Century-Crofts.

Bornstein, M. H. (1995). Parenting infants. In M. H. Bornstein (Ed.), *Handbook of Parenting* (Vol. 1, pp. 3–39). Mahwah, NJ: Erlbaum.

Bornstein, M. H., & Lamb, M. E. (Eds.). (2005). Developmental *science: An advanced textbook* (5th ed.). Mahwah, NJ: Erlbaum.

Bornstein, M. H., & Lamb, M. E. (Eds.). (2010). *Developmental science: An advanced textbook* (6th ed.). New York: Psychology Press/Taylor & Francis.

Brandtstädter, J. (1998). Action perspectives on human development. In R. M. Lerner (Ed.), *Handbook of child psychology: Vol. 1. Theoretical models of human development* (5th ed., pp. 807–863). Editor in chief: W. Damon. New York: Wiley.

Brandtstädter, J. (2006). Action perspectives on human development. In R. M. Lerner (Ed.), *Handbook of child psychology: Vol. 1. Theoretical models of human development* (6th ed., pp. 516–568). Editors-in-chief: W. Damon & R. M. Lerner. Hoboken, NJ: Wiley.

Brim, O. G., & Kagan, J. (Eds.). (1980). *Constancy and change in human development*. Cambridge, MA: Harvard University Press.

Bronfenbrenner, U. (1979). *The ecology of human development*. Cambridge, MA: Harvard University Press.

Bronfenbrenner, U., & Morris, P. A. (2006). The bioecological model of human development. In R. M. Lerner (Ed.), *Handbook of child psychology: Vol. 1. Theoretical models of human development* (6th ed., pp. 793–828). Editor in chief: W. Damon. Hoboken, NJ: Wiley.

Cairns, R. B., & Cairns, B. D. (2006). The making of developmental psychology. In R. M. Lerner (Ed.), *Handbook of child psychology: Vol. 1. Theoretical models of human development* (6th ed., pp. 89–165). Editors-in-chief: W. Damon & R. M. Lerner. Hoboken, NJ: Wiley.

Damon, W., & Lerner, R. M. (Editors-in-Chief). (2006). *Handbook of child psychology* (6th ed.). Hoboken, NJ: Wiley.

Datan, N., & Reese, H. W. (Eds.). (1977). *Life-span developmental psychology: Dialectical perspectives on experimental research*. New York: Academic Press.

Elder, G. H., Jr. (1998). The life course and human development. In R. M. Lerner (Ed.), *Handbook of child psychology: Vol. 1. Theoretical models of human development* (5th ed., pp. 939–991). Editor in chief: W. Damon. New York: Wiley.

Elder, G. H., Modell, J., & Parke, R. D. (Eds.). (1993). *Children in time and place: Developmental and historical insights*. New York: Cambridge University Press.

Emmerich, W. (1968). Personality development and concepts of structure. *Child Development*, *39*, 671–690.

Featherman, D. L., Lerner, R. M., & Perlmutter, M. (Eds.). (1992). *Life-span development and behavior* (Vol. 11). Hillsdale, NJ: Erlbaum.

Featherman, D. L., Lerner, R. M., & Perlmutter, M. (Eds.). (1994). *Life-span development and behavior* (Vol. 12). Hillsdale, NJ: Erlbaum.

Ford, D. H., & Lerner, R. M. (1992). *Developmental systems theory: An integrative approach*. Newbury Park, CA: Sage.

Freund, A. M. (2007). Differentiating and integrating levels of goal representation: A life-span perspective. In B. R. Little, K. Salmela-Aro, J. E. Nurmi, & S. D. Phillips (Eds.), *Personal project pursuit: Goals, action and human flourishing* (pp. 247–270). Mahwah, NJ: Erlbaum.

Freund, A. M., & Baltes, P. B. (2000). The orchestration of selection, optimization, and compensation: An action-theoretical conceptualization of a theory of developmental regulation. In W. J. Perrig & A. Grob (Eds.), *Control of human behaviour, mental processes and consciousness* (pp. 35–58). Mahwah, NJ: Erlbaum.

Freund, A. M., Li, K. Z. H., & Baltes, P. B. (1999). The role of selection, optimization, and compensation in successful aging. In J. Brandtstädter & R. M. Lerner (Eds.), *Action and development: Origins and functions of intentional self-development* (pp. 401–434). Thousand Oaks: Sage.

Freund, A. M., Nikitin, J., & Ritter, J. O. (2009). Psychological consequences of longevity: The increasing importance of self-regulation in old age. *Human Development, 52*, 1– 37.

Gottlieb, G. (1997). *Synthesizing nature–nurture: Prenatal roots of instinctive behavior*. Mahwah, NJ: Erlbaum.

Gottlieb, G., Wahlsten, D., & Lickliter, R. (2006). The significance of biology for human

development: A developmental psychobiological systems view. In R. M. Lerner & W. Damon (Eds.), *Handbook of child psychology: Vol. 1. Theoretical models of human development* (6th ed., pp. 210–257). Hoboken, NJ: Wiley.

Goulet, L. R., & Baltes, P. B. (Eds.). (1970). *Life-span developmental psychology: Research and theory*. New York: Academic Press.

Greenberg, G., & Tobach, E. (Eds.) *Behavioral evolution and integrative levels*. Hillsdale, NJ: Erlbaum.

Hall, G. S. (1922). *Senescence: The last half of life*. New York: Appleton.

Havighurst, R. J. (1951). *Developmental tasks and education*. New York: Longmans.

Hess, E. H. (1970). Ethology and developmental psychology. In P. H. Mussen (Ed.), *Carmichael's manual of child psychology* (3rd ed., pp. 1–38). New York: Wiley.

Kuo, Z.-Y. (1976). *The dynamics of behavior development: An epigenetic view*. New York: Plenum.

Lamb, M. E. (1977). A reexamination of the infant social world. *Human Development*, *20*, 65–85.

Lamb, M. E., Thompson, R. A., Gardner, W. P., & Charnov, E. L. (1985). *Infant–mother attachment*. Hillsdale, NJ: Erlbaum.

Lerner, R. M. (1984). *On the nature of human plasticity*. New York: Cambridge University Press.

Lerner, R. M. (2002). *Concepts and theories of human development* (3rd ed.). Mahwah, NJ: Erlbaum.

Lerner, R. M. (2006). Developmental science, developmental systems, and contemporary theories of human development. In R. M. Lerner (Ed.), *Handbook of child psychology: Vol. 1. Theoretical models of human development* (6th ed., pp. 1–17). Editors-in-chief: W. Damon & R. M. Lerner. Hoboken, NJ: Wiley.

Lerner, R. M., & Overton, W. F. (2008). Exemplifying the integrations of the relational developmental system: Synthesizing theory, research, and application to promote positive development and social justice. *Journal of Adolescent Research, 23*, 245–255.

Lerner, R. M., & Steinberg, L. (Eds.). (2009). *Handbook of adolescent psychology* (3rd ed.). Hoboken, NJ: Wiley.

Lewis, M. (1972). State as an infant–environment interaction: An analysis of mother infant behavior as a function of sex. *Merrill-Palmer Quarterly*, *18*, 95–121.

Lewis, M., & Lee-Painter, S. (1974). An interactional approach to the mother–infant dyad. In M. Lewis & L. A. Rosenblum (Eds.), *The effect of the infant on its caregivers* (pp. 21–48). New York: Wiley

Lewis, M., & Rosenblum, L. A. (Eds.). (1974). *The effect of the infant on its caregivers*. New York: Wiley.

Magnusson, D., & Stattin, H. (1998). Person–context interaction theories. In R. M. Lerner (Ed.), *Handbook of child psychology: Vol. 1. Theoretical models of human development* (5th ed., pp. 685–759). Editor in chief: W. Damon. New York: Wiley.

Magnusson, D., & Stattin, H. (2006). The person in context: A holistic–interactionistic approach. In R. M. Lerner & W. Damon (Eds.), *Handbook of child psychology: Vol. 1. Theoretical models of human development* (6th ed., pp. 400–464). Hoboken, NJ: Wiley.

McClearn, G. R. (1970). Genetic influences on behavior and development. In P. H. Mussen (Ed.), *Carmichael's manual of child psychology* (3rd ed., pp. 39–76). New York: Wiley.

Mussen, P. H. (Ed.). (1970). *Carmichael's manual of child psychology* (3rd ed.). New York: Wiley.

Nesselroade, J. R., & Reese, H. W. (Eds.). (1973). *Life-span developmental psychology: Methodological issues*. New York: Academic Press.

Nikitin, J., & Freund, A. M. (2008). Hoping to be liked or wishing not to be rejected: Conflict and congruence of social approach and avoidance motivation. *Applied Psychology: An International Review*, *57*, 90–111.

Novikoff, A. B. (1945a). The concept of integrative levels and biology. *Science*, *101*, 209–215.

Novikoff, A. B. (1945b). Continuity and discontinuity in evolution. *Science*, *101*, 405–406.

Overton, W. F. (1973). On the assumptive base of the nature–nurture controversy: Additive versus interactive conceptions. *Human Development, 16*, 74–89.

Overton, W. F. (1975). General systems, structure and development. In K. Riegel & G. Rosenwald (Eds.), *Structure and transformation: Developmental aspects* (pp. 61–81). New York: Wiley Interscience.

Overton, W. F. (1978). Klaus Riegel: Theoretical contribution to concepts of stability and change. *Human Development, 21*, 360–363.

Overton, W. F. (2003). Development across the life span: Philosophy, concepts, theory. In R. M. Lerner, M. A. Easterbrooks, & J. Mistry (Eds.), *Handbook of psychology: Vol. 6. Developmental psychology* (pp. 13–42). Editor in chief: B. Weiner. New York: Wiley.

Overton, W. F. (2006). Developmental psychology: Philosophy, concepts, methodology. In R. M. Lerner (Ed.). *Handbook of Child Psychology: Vol. 1. Theoretical models of human development.* Volume 1 of (6th ed.) (pp. 18–88). Editors-in-chief: W. Damon & R. M. Lerner. Hoboken, NJ: Wiley.

Overton, W., & Reese, H. (1981). Conceptual prerequisites for an understanding of stability–change and continuity–discontinuity. *International Journal of Behavioral Development, 4,* 99–123.

Reese, H. W., & Overton, W. F. (1970). Models of development and theories of development. In L. R. Goulet & P. B. Baltes (Eds.), *Life-span developmental psychology: Research and theory* (pp. 115–145). New York: Academic.

Riegel, K. F. (1975). Toward a dialectical theory of human development. *Human Development, 18*, 50–64.

Riegel, K. F. (1976). The dialectics of human development. *American Psychologist, 31*, 689–700.

Riley, M. W. (Ed.). (1979). *Aging from birth to death.* Washington, DC: American Association for the Advancement of Science.

Sameroff, A. (1975). Transactional models in early social relations. *Human Development, 18*, 65–79.

Schneirla, T. C. (1957). The concept of development in comparative psychology. In D. B. Harris (Ed.), *The concept of development: An issue in the study of human behavior* (pp. 78–108). Minneapolis: University of Minnesota Press.

Stevenson, H. W. (1970). Learning in children. In P. H. Mussen (Ed.), *Carmichael's manual of child psychology* (3rd ed., pp. 849–938). New York: Wiley.

Thelen, E., & Smith, L. B. (1998). Dynamic systems theories. In R. M. Lerner (Ed.), *Handbook of child psychology: Vol. 1. Theoretical models of human development* (5th ed., pp. 563–633). Editor in chief: W. Damon. New York: Wiley.

Thompson, R. A., & Lamb, M. E. (1986). Infant–mother attachment: New directions for theory and research. In P. B. Baltes, D. L. Featherman, & R. M. Lerner (Eds.), *Life-span development and behavior* (Vol. 7, pp. 1–41). Hillsdale, NJ: Erlbaum.

Tobach, E., & Greenberg, G. (1984). The significance of T. C. Schneirla's contribution to the concept of levels of integration. In G. Greenberg & E. Tobach (Eds.), *Behavioral evolution and integrative levels* (pp. 1–8). Hillsdale, NJ: Erlbaum.

von Bertalanffy, L. (1933). *Modern theories of development.* London: Oxford University Press.

von Bertalanffy, L. (1968). *General systems theory.* New York: Braziller.

White, S. H. (1970). The learning theory tradition and child psychology. In P. H. Mussen (Ed.), *Carmichael's manual of child psychology* (3rd ed., pp. 657–701). New York: Wiley.

Wohlwill, J. F. (1973). *The study of behavioral development.* New York: Academic Press.

Contributors

Carolyn M. Aldwin
Oregon State University
Corvallis, Oregon

Toni C. Antonucci
University of Michigan
Ann Arbor, Michigan

Kenneth E. Barron
James Madison University
Harrisonburg, Virginia

John E. Bates
Indiana University
Bloomington, Indiana

Kira Birditt
University of Michigan
Ann Arbor, Michigan

Daria K. Boeninger
Arizona State University
Tempe, Arizona

Catherine E. Bowen
Jacobs University
Bremen, Germany

Molly R. Butterworth
University of Utah
Salt Lake City, Utah

C. Sue Carter
University of Illinois at Chicago
Chicago, Illinois

Dante Cicchetti
University of Minnesota
Minneapolis/St. Paul, Minnesota

John Colombo
University of Kansas
Lawrence, Kansas

David E. Conroy
The Pennsylvania State University
University Park, Pennsylvania

Keith S. Cox
Northwestern University
Evanston, Illinois

Lisa M. Diamond
University of Utah
Salt Lake City, Utah

Andrew J. Elliot
Rochester University
Rochester, New York

Christopher P. Fagundes
University of Utah
Salt Lake City, Utah

Katherine L. Fiori
Adelphi University
Garden City, New York

Constance A. Flanagan
The Pennsylvania State University
University Park, Pennsylvania

Alexandra M. Freund
University of Zurich
Zurich, Switzerland

G. John Geldhof
University of Kansas
Lawrence, Kansas

Jackson A. Goodnight
Indiana University
Bloomington, Indiana

Daniel Grühn
North Carolina State University
Raleigh, North Carolina

Daniel Hart
Rutgers university
Camden, New Jersey

Melissa Hines
University of Cambridge
Cambridge, England

Lisa M. H. Jackey
University of Michigan
Ann Arbor, Michigan

Gisela Labouvie-Vief
University of Geneva
Geneva, Switzerland

Michael E. Lamb
University of Cambridge
Cambridge, England

Peter Levine
Tufts University
Medford, Massachusetts

Marc D. Lewis
University of Toronto
Toronto, Ontario

Todd D. Little
University of Kansas
Lawrence, Kansas

Dan P. McAdams
Northwestern University
Evanston, Illinois

Kou Murayama
Tokyo Institute of Technology
Tokyo, Japan

Stephen W. Porges
University of Illinois at Chicago
Chicago, Illinois

W. George Scarlett
Tufts University
Medford, Massachusetts

Alice C. Schermerhorn
Indiana University
Bloomington, Indiana

Ursula M. Staudinger
Jacobs University
Bremen, Germany

Joseph Studer
University of Geneva
Geneva, Switzerland

Rebecca Todd
University of Toronto
Toronto, Ontario

Amy Eva Alberts Warren
Tufts University
Medford, Massachusetts

Xiaowen Xu
University of Toronto
Toronto, Ontario

Loriena A. Yancura
University of Hawaii, Manoa
Honolulu, Hawaii

James Youniss
Catholic University
Washington, D.C.

Jonathan F. Zaff
Tufts University
Medford, Massachusetts

CHAPTER 1

Introduction

Social and Emotional Development across the Life Span

ALEXANDRA M. FREUND and MICHAEL E. LAMB

There are numerous handbooks on various aspects of psychology, covering topics as diverse as emotion, motivation, or social psychology. Handbooks of psychology typically include a volume on development, and there also exist two age-defined handbooks about development, the *Handbook of Child Psychology,* the sixth edition of which was edited by William Damon and Richard M. Lerner (2006), and the *Handbook of Adolescent Psychology*, the third edition of which was edited by Richard M. Lerner and Laurence Steinberg (2009). Although some of the finest chapters on life-span development were published in these handbooks, there was no high-level reference work reviewing theory and data about all aspects of psychology across the entire life span until the publication of the present *Handbook.* Our efforts to commission and edit the current volume were predicated on the assumption that a complete and satisfying understanding of any area of functioning requires adoption of a life-span perspective.

Most research and theory in developmental psychology is still clearly concerned with specific phases of the life span. This specialization by researchers has a pragmatic rationale; to work across the full age spectrum would require so much technical and methodological expertise and an understanding of so many different, topic-specific paradigms that one laboratory would not be capable of mastering them all. In addition, the training we provide students of developmental science militates against the acquisition and development of such integrative, life-span knowledge even today. Lecture classes or seminars typically deal with one phase of development, such as "emotional development in childhood" or "self and identity in adolescence." This focus implies that separate age phases constitute meaningful units for studying development. Moreover, most students (especially at the postgraduate level) are likely to study either child development or adult development and aging, giving them expertise regarding one phase of development but not of the entire life span. With this *Handbook of Life-Span Development*, we hope to begin breaking that pattern by commissioning thorough overviews of development in various functional domains across the entire life span.

When conceptualizing this *Handbook,* we first took seriously the idea that development is a lifelong phenomenon. To the extent permitted by the knowledge base within each substantive area of focus included in this volume, the contributors have documented how the processes of development—despite qualitative or quantitative discontinuities (as well, of course, as continuities in these dimensions)—begin in utero and extend across the entire ontogenetic span, ending only with death. Unfortunately, however, variations in the extent to which this orientation to life-span developmental processes has come to characterize the study of different aspects of social and emotional development ensure that there are differences in the degree to which the areas of research reviewed in this volume have been studied across the life span.

As one might expect in a field that tends to describe and study development in such discrete age-graded phases as infancy, childhood, adolescence, adulthood, or old age, our requests of the contributors were daunting and demanding. Most had expertise regarding one or two phases, rather than the entire life span. Although readers will be impressed by how well the contributors have mastered the tasks assigned to them, they will also notice a tendency for many chapters to include more detailed analyses of some phases of life than others. To the extent that these differences in amount of detail reflect differences in the amount of research that has been conducted, we hope that the evident gaps will prompt students and scholars of development to embrace perspectives that encompass the entire life span in their future research and conceptualization.

Second, we have tried in this volume to cover all the diverse topics that comprise the field of social and emotional development. Of course, domains of development can be partitioned in many ways. In the end, the choices we made were largely dictated by the extent to which different topics had been conceptualized and studied, and the chapters included in the volume include different levels of analysis, ranging from the molecular focus on peptides, genes, hormones, and the neurological bases of development, to the macro-level analysis of such constructs as the development of self-efficacy and developmental psychopathology.

Third, when charting the terrain of emotional and social development across the life span, we also sought to cover different experiential or functional aspects of development, including emotions, motivation, and temperament, as well as social and intimate relationships. We do not want to imply that these functional domains are separate; they are not. Humans experience emotions in social contexts, and these experiences are influenced by their motivations as well as their temperaments, for example. However, the focus on different functional domains makes a project like this *Handbook* feasible, while helping to create a holistic understanding of development.

AN OVERVIEW OF THIS VOLUME

Our vision for this volume is instantiated in the chapters that it comprises. The chapters are organized into several areas of scholarship pertinent to social and emotional development.

Emotional Regulation across the Life Span

In the second and third chapters in this volume, Porges and Carter (Chapter 2) and Lewis, Todd, and Xu (Chapter 3) place considerable emphasis on the neurobiological factors that influence or control individual behavior across the life span.

Porges and Carter focus on the neurobiological factors that make social bonding and social interaction possible across the life span. The phylogenetic perspective they introduce draws extensively on research conducted using social animals, including voles, as well as research on individuals whose intrinsic characteristics make it easier to understand the underlying processes, either because they are especially young and immature or because they have conditions such as autistic spectrum disorders that compromise their capacities. Porges and Carter proceed to document the role of neuropeptides in promoting the development of social relationships, in part by inhibiting tendencies to reject or aggress against strangers (including offspring) and also explain how and why the brain, using the vagus nerve, modulates psychological reactions to different social stimulus. Interestingly, as they show, the same basic processes mediate interactions between individuals and their environments, especially but not exclusively their social environments, across the life span. Evidence regarding the ability of this model to explain key aspects of social behavior in childhood should, these authors hope, prompt more extensive research on the interface between neurobiological processes and social behavior at other stages of the life span.

Lewis, Todd, and Xu's approach to emotional regulation, as presented in Chapter 3, also focuses on fundamental processes, including those that determine both the extent and nature of emotional arousal. Lewis and colleagues make clear that the underlying neural mechanisms tend to be quite immature at birth. Furthermore, although developmental change is rapid in the early years, changes continue to take place more or less across the life span, with mature or optimal function emerging only in early adulthood and with neurological changes underlying declines in behavioral function in later adulthood and old age. Thus, the capacity to regulate emotions, especially in response to challenges posed by intrinsic (e.g., pain, illness) and extrinsic (e.g., fear-provoking stimuli or separation from a source of comfort) factors, develops gradually, with significant individual differences attributable to variation in the behavior of others (especially parents and care providers) during the phase of life when regulatory capacity and control shift from extrinsic to intrinsic control.

As with Lewis and his colleague's examination of emotional regulation, Labouvie-Vief, Grühn, and Studer's analysis of the dynamic integration of emotion and cognition (Chapter 4) adopts a dynamic systems approach to the understanding of emotional development. Labouvie-Vief and colleagues present a model of emotional development inspired by Piaget's seminal work on child development in two ways: by acknowledging the importance of striving for equilibrium in developing systems and by taking seriously the intricate interplay and connectedness of emotion and cognition. Their model seeks to explain how people develop by navigating between the needs for safety and well-being on one hand and the need for increased mastery and control on the other. According to their model, the opposing needs create a tension between resting in an equilibrium state and venturing into disequilibrium to develop more complex integrations of emotion and cognition. This model is a true life-span model of emotional development because it describes and explains how the contextual and cultural demands as well as biological changes across the life span interact in shaping the codevelopment of emotion and cognition. In this way, Chapters 3 (Lewis and colleagues) and 4 (Labouvie-Vief and colleagues) nicely complement each other.

Turning to self-regulation, Geldhof, Little, and Colombo (Chapter 5) present an organizing heuristic for the structures and elements of self-regulation that serves as a theoretical model for understanding the development of self-regulation. This heuristic integrates elements from various models developed in the rich literature on self-regulation and thereby helps structure a broad and somewhat confusing field that has produced not only many theoretical accounts of self-regulation but also a variety of rather disconnected empirical findings. Moreover, like both Lewis and colleagues and Labouvie-Vief and colleagues, Geldhof, Little, and Colombo invoke a multilevel approach to self-regulation that encompasses biological and neurocognitive as well as social–psychological and motivational constructs, in the process highlighting the importance of attention, cognitive schemas, expectancies, and immediate and future gains for self-regulation. Taking a developmental perspective highlights the extent to which the elements of self-regulation and their interaction change over time. Moreover, Geldhof and colleagues also review the outcomes of self-regulation, adopting the action-theoretical notion that individuals are not just the products but also the producers of development (Lerner & Busch-Rossnagel, 1981). Self-regulation is one of the hot topics in current psychological research because it is related to performance in many areas of functioning, including emotion, motivation, and cognition, and there is little doubt that the heuristic presented in Chapter 5 will help scholars and researchers gain a better understanding of self-regulation and its development across the life span.

Self, Identity, and Personality across the Life Span

Describing and structuring the development of self and identity across the life span, McAdams and Cox, the authors of Chapter 6, take us on a voyage through historical time and ontogenetic development, clearly demonstrating that any static analysis of self and identity obscures essential elements of these constructs because self and identity are both inherently subject to change as well as being agents of change and development. In their wide-ranging analysis, McAdams and Cox highlight the extent to which the concepts of self and identity are culturally embedded and have self-related and social functions that vary depending on whether the selves are actors, agents, or authors. From the perspective of the self as an author, for instance, telling people who you are communicates what others can expect from you in future interactions, thereby making social relationships more predictable and allowing people to shape their social relationships effectively. Telling their life stories, however, also helps individuals to make meaning of different, perhaps even separate events by drawing them together into a coherent narrative. Moreover, as research on generativity and redemptive life stories has shown, the way people tell their life stories predicts actual behavior, nicely illustrating how different levels of analysis complement one another: Cultural themes such as redemption that shape our sense of self and identity then find expression in life stories that reflect and reconstruct biographical life events and themes, which, in turn, are translated into actions that affect society (such as generative behavior) and foster experiences that transform our sense of self.

Despite a long tradition, research on temperament and personality across the life span typically places considerably less influence on the importance of social context and construction than is done by McAdams and Cox and is substantially less precise about neurobiological mechanisms than either Porges and Carter or Lewis et al.'s chapters; this area of research is eloquently summarized by Bates, Schermerhorn, and Goodnight in Chapter 7. Much of the relevant research is predicated on assumptions (and evidence) that fundamental individual differences in temperament and personality are inherited. Furthermore, there is an increasing body of evidence linking specific aspects of temperament to regulatory processes such as those that control attention (e.g., persistence and distractibility). Recent progress in this respect, as Bates and his colleagues' document, is attributable in large part to consensus regarding at least some of the principal dimensions of temperament and personality. On the other hand, there continues to be a distinction between the major dimensions of temperament studied in infancy and early childhood, as opposed to the dimensions of temperament studied in adulthood, a divergence that has impeded life-span research. In addition, there has been relatively little research on the development of personality and temperament in later life.

Further building on the themes of personality development as well as the concepts of redemption and resilience discussed in the two preceding chapters, Staudinger and Bowen (Chapter 8) examine positive development from a life-span perspective (albeit with a focus on the age phases of adulthood and aging), emphasizing the processes of growth (i.e., improving levels of performance) and adjustment (i.e., maintaining levels of performance). According to Staudinger and Bowen, personality exerts an "executive function," orchestrating the development of other psychological systems (such as cognition or emotion) by allocating resources in response to and in anticipation of a changing balance of gains and losses across the life span. In their view, the self manages and constrains developmental changes, while changing through interaction with the environment. As a result, although personality at the level of traits often appears to involve fixed dispositions that change slightly, if at all, after young adulthood (see Chapter 7), it reacts to and shapes developmental changes that help manage resources and adjustment. In this way, personality processes have fundamental implications for adjustment and growth throughout adulthood and into old age.

Complementing the earlier chapters on positive personality development, self-regulation, and emotion regulation, Aldwin, Yancura, and Boeninger describe the development of coping across the life span in Chapter 9. As their first sentence states and their chapter compellingly shows, "coping and development are inextricably intertwined," with coping both dependent on resources and helping in the maintenance and creation of well-being (see also Staudinger and Bowen, Chapter 8). Echoing Geldhof and colleagues' multilevel approach, Aldwin and her colleagues' analysis of coping and its development across the life span draws on evidence regarding neurocognitive, cognitive, social, and emotional development. Not content to simply list and describe different coping styles and their relative prominence at different points across the life span, Aldwin and colleagues propose that coping should be viewed as self-regulation and problem solving in stressful contexts, with individual capacities developing in response to the interaction among these three factors over time. Because it includes proactive and anticipatory cognitions, coping becomes a process that does not merely involve reactions to stress but also helps individuals to create environments and to influence the world to suit their needs. Like the authors of the preceding chapters, therefore, Aldwin and her colleagues provide an interactive perspective on development, viewing coping as the product of development as well as one of the processes driving development. They illustrate this by reference to the resilience–vulnerability trajectory, describing upward and downward spirals of coping with losses. Their analysis thus raises issues discussed in several other chapters, including Dante Cicchetti's account of developmental psychopathology (Chapter 14), in which resilience is a central concept.

Gender, Friendship, and Intimate Relations across the Life Span

In Chapter 10, Hines discusses the development of gendered behavior across the life span. Echoing Chapters 2 and 3, Hines makes extended references to prenatal biological development, noting that exposure to and uptake of specific compounds at critical biological stages have enduring influences on both anatomy and behavior. It is important to note, however, that these prenatal biological processes are not the sole factors affecting gendered behavior and, at least in some cases, appear to affect members of one gender more than the other. Indeed, as Hines explains, the behavioral dispositions influenced by prenatal hormones are typically reinforced by individual experiences after birth, notably the efforts initiated by parents and reinforced by many others (including peers and teachers) to bring their children's behavior in line with socially prescribed norms. As Hines points out, behavioral differences between males and females are actually much less pronounced than most people think and they are quite varied across cultures and historical eras. Unfortunately, the research literature has focused fairly narrowly on the beginning of the life span, with precious little attention paid to adulthood and old age. As in other cases when the literature is so uneven, we hope that this volume may prompt further research on the "forgotten" phases of the life span.

The need to belong has long been recognized as one of the most central human needs (e.g., Baumeister & Leary, 1995) and thus a fundamental component of life-span developmental science is an understanding of how people form relationships and how both the relationships and the processes develop and change across the life span. Echoing some themes raised by Porges and Carter (Chapter 2), the authors of the next two chapters both address relationship formation. Whereas Diamond, Fagundes, and Butterworth focus on intimate relations (Chapter 11), Antonucci, Fiori, Birditt, and Jackey (Chapter 12) turn to social convoys across the life span.

The first social relationships to develop are, of course, the relationships that infants form with their parents, but the bulk of Diamond and her colleagues' chapter is concerned with what might be called romantic relationships, most of which include sexual intimacy as a key arena for interaction. Diamond and her colleagues show how the characteristics of the first such relationships in adolescence differ with respect to both some defining features as well as their temporal perspective from those established in emerging and later adulthood, when commitment becomes more central. Diamond et al. discuss a growing body of research on the factors associated with both longevity and satisfaction, noting that these appear quite similar across much of the life span as well as in different types of intimate relationships. Unfortunately, there has been much less research on intimate relationships in later as opposed to earlier phases of life, so this remains a fertile area for future research, especially in light of demographic trends that now allow most adults to enter (and terminate) intimate relationships long after the age of reproduction or paid employment.

Clearly, intimate relations are essential for subjective as well as objective indicators of well-being. However, people do not live and develop in close relationships only but typically have networks of family, friends, and acquaintances that constitute important developmental contexts and are, at the same time, subject to development as well. Antonucci, Fiori, Birditt, and Jackey (Chapter 12) review and integrate the literature on the life-span development of social networks or convoys, noting that the structure, function, and quality of these networks all develop over time and vary depending on the larger social and cultural context. The convoy model helps describe as well as explain patterns of change in these social networks, accounting for both stability and change in network compositions and processes. Highlighting the importance of a life-span developmental approach, Antonucci and her colleagues argue that location in the life span crucially affects social relationships (e.g., being the child of one's parents at 3 years of age is very different from being the child at 30 or 60 years of age). Similarly, friendships of 3 years' duration have different qualities and functions than friendships that have lasted 30 years. Only when considering such developmental aspects of social relations can a coherent understanding of social interactions and their functions emerge. The pattern of social relations, as Antonucci et al. further note, not only affects emotional and subjective well-being but also influences physical health and longevity. Thus, a social convoy that moves with people throughout their lives shapes individual development, is shaped by the individual, and can promote—or hinder—individual resilience and growth. Interestingly, as we have already observed, this focus on positive developmental processes reappears in many of the other chapters, representing something of a recurrent theme.

Specific Topics of Life-Span Development: Achievement Motivation, Psychopathology, Civic Engagement, and Religious and Spiritual Development

The focus then shifts in Chapter 13 to motivation, specifically achievement motivation, which is widely seen as an important predictor of the tasks that people select, of the tasks on which they persist, and of how well they perform. The motivational literature has tended not to take a life-span perspective, especially when achievement is concerned, instead focusing on childhood and adolescence. It is not surprising, therefore, that the chapter by Elliot, Conroy, Barron, and Murayama pays considerably more attention to earlier phases of the life span than to adulthood and aging. There is simply not a lot of literature—either theoretical or empirical—on the development of achievement motivation throughout adulthood, pointing to a gap in our knowledge that should be addressed in the future because, as Elliot and colleagues show, achievement motivation plays a crucial role in the development of competence. In their review, Elliot and his colleagues focus on two central constructs. First, approach and avoidance motives (i.e., the need for achievement and the fear of failure) are believed to develop very early in life, even before the acquisition of language, rendering them resistant to change because they are not represented verbally. Second, by contrast, goals develop in childhood when cognitive development is advanced enough that individuals can represent future desired (to be approached) or dreaded (to be avoided) states. Goals change across the life span not only with respect to content but also with respect to such dimensions as time perspective. Elliot and his colleagues present a hierarchical model of achievement motivation that encompasses the dimensions of competence (whether people want to master tasks or perform well) on one hand and valence (approach and avoidance) on the other. Using this well-researched model, Elliot and colleagues show that achievement goals are dynamic and that life-span features of such factors as the time scales relevant to goals need to be considered more fully in future research.

Attention then turns to the development of psychopathology. In his chapter, Cicchetti (Chapter 14) focuses not on the age-graded stages at which specific syndromes or psychological dysfunctions either first emerge or are most likely to impede effective behavior and functioning, but on providing a framework within which the development of both effective and pathological behavior can best be understood. Cicchetti introduces and explains an organizational perspective on development, in terms of which positive early experiences channel development along positive lines of development, whereas adverse experiences (such as maltreatment) set in motion developmental processes that make maladaptive, pathological behavior more likely, both in the present and in the future. Echoing themes mentioned earlier in the book, Cicchetti emphasizes that intrinsic differences among individuals are also important, making some individuals more vulnerable and others more resilient in the face of adverse experiences. Here we thus see an important interaction between inherent differences and the effect of experiences. Indeed, the organizational perspective adopted by Cicchetti proposes that most forms of psychopathology are the result of such interactions between predisposition and life experiences, thereby providing a life-span framework for understanding developmental psychopathology, even though the focus in his chapter is on childhood.

In Chapter 15, Zaff, Hart, Flanagan, Youniss, and Levine discuss a topic of considerable interest to applied social scientists today: the development of civic engagement. Despite its importance, the research on this topic is less extensive than one might assume, with both the life-span approach and research on adulthood conspicuously lacking. Taking a developmental systems framework, however, Zaff and colleagues examine the ways that adolescents develop social responsibility and engagement, illustrating the development of civic engagement by focusing on a group of individuals who are particularly unlikely to engagement in civic activities—namely, adolescents who do not attend college. Civic engagement is a complex and multifaceted phenomenon that requires the integration of cognitive processes, emotion regulation and responsiveness, and actions as well as social relations, structure, and context. Zaff and colleagues carefully explain how these aspects interact in their effect on the development of civic engagement. They argue that civic engagement is not only an outcome but also an influence on development, at least in adolescence. We join them in calling for rigorous research on this important topic and hope that their review of the literature will inspire life-span researchers to study civic engagement at phases of life after adolescence.

Finally, Scarlett and Warren (Chapter 16) address a topic that has received little attention from life-span developmentalists—namely, religious and spiritual development. In a chapter that carefully articulates the conceptual and definitional issues that will have to be addressed by researchers and theorists in the future, Scarlett and Warren make clear how research in this area needs to develop if it is to clarify the important conceptual issues that have often been ignored. As they show, definitions (including the operational definitions of spirituality, religiosity, religious observance, and faith) have especially serious implications for the framing of empirical research questions in this domain; the failure to grapple with these issues has helped impede progress in this area to date. In particular, divergent conceptions of development—notably, the difference between functional and structural models of development—affect such fundamental issues as assumptions regarding the directionality of development and the notion that development necessarily implies growth. Some theories of religious and spiritual development take the view that development occurs in stages and that these stages lead inexorably to "higher" levels of spirituality, thereby adopting views at odds with some of the basic tenets of life span developmental psychology (e.g., Baltes, 1989, 1997)—that development is multidirectional, involving gains and losses, as well as contextual, resulting in heterogeneity rather than universal transitions from one stage to the next. Perhaps an extended dialogue between those studying different aspects of life-span development will help to resolve these issues, promoting a richer understanding of religious and spiritual development in the process.

CONCLUSIONS

To what extent does the *Handbook* include life-span sensitive analyses of all important aspects of social, emotional, and personality development? In truth, we can claim only partial success. The excellent chapters indeed provide deep insights into social and emotional development, but most also reveal incomplete understanding of development as a lifelong process. Our disappointment about this state of affairs is modulated by the hope that awareness of these gaps in the current literature will inspire research to bridge them. In that sense, the thoughtful reviews included in the *Handbook* serve not only to demarcate what we already know but also to direct the future efforts of interested scholars.

There are other sources of disappointment as well. For example, the increased awareness on the part of social scientists that individual differences are the product of interactions between biogenetic factors and experiences is unevenly represented in the volume, with "biological" factors almost entirely unmentioned in some chapters. In addition, some aspects of development, particularly the development of close, nonromantic relationships (such as those within the family) or the development of moral values and attitudes, are not addressed by contributors to this *Handbook*, and their exclusion is disappointing. It is us, the editors, who are to blame for this omission.

On balance, however, we believe that the *Handbook* represents an important step forward. It brings together vast bodies of research that have never been examined so closely, either within individual chapters or within the same volume. We have no doubt that this will have an important impact on developmental science in the next decades, and we are grateful to have been a part of that process.

ACKNOWLEDGMENTS

There are many people we would like to thank. First and foremost, Richard M. Lerner has been enthusiastic, encouraging, and supportive both instrumentally and emotionally. This endeavor would have been impossible without him. Our sincere thanks also go to the colleagues who have written chapters for this volume. They have devoted considerable amounts of their valuable time to craft these richly informative chapters. Taking on the difficult and, in some cases, daunting challenge of applying a truly life-span approach to their fields, many were forced to stretch beyond their comfort zones, risking disequilibrium to integrate the research on diverse age groups. We appreciate their willingness to go beyond the familiar boundaries of more typical age-graded chapters and hope they agree that it was worth the effort. Some of the authors were also willing and able to produce these chapters under adverse circumstances. In this regard, we would like to pay special tribute and thanks to Gisela Labouvie-Vief and her colleagues, as well as Jon Zaff and his colleagues.

Compiling a volume of this sort would not have been possible without the assistance of Jarrett Lerner, who ably coordinated the final preparations and communications with the publishers. Finally, we have benefited from the support and assistance of Tisha Rossi at John Wiley and Sons.

REFERENCES

Aldwin, C. M, Yancura, L. A., & Boeninger, D. K. (2010). Coping across the life span. In A. M. Freund & M. E. Lamb (Eds.), Social and emotional development across the life span: *Vol. 2, Handbook of Life-Span Development*. Editor in chief: R. M. Lerner. Hoboken, NJ: John Wiley & Sons.

Antonucci, T. C., Fiori, K. L., Birditt, K., & Jackey, L. M. H. (2010). Convoys of social relations: Integrating life span and life course perspectives. In A. M. Freund & M. E. Lamb (Eds.), Social and emotional development across the life span: *Vol. 2, Handbook of life-span development*. Editor in chief: R. M. Lerner. Hoboken, NJ: John Wiley & Sons.

Bates, J. E., Schermerhorn, A. C., & Goodnight, J. A. (2010). Temperament and personality through the life span. In A. M. Freund & M. E. Lamb (Eds.), Social and emotional development across the life span: *Vol. 2, Handbook of life-span development* (pp. 208–253). Editor in chief: R. M. Lerner. Hoboken, NJ: John Wiley & Sons.

Baumeister, R. F., & Leary, M. R. (1995). The need to belong: Desire for interpersonal attachments as a fundamental human motivation. *Psychological Bulletin, 117,* 497–529

Cicchetti, D. (2010). Developmental psychopathology. In A. M. Freund & M. E. Lamb (Eds.), Social and emotional development across the life span: *Vol. 2, Handbook of life-span development*. Editor in chief: R. M. Lerner. Hoboken, NJ: John Wiley & Sons.

Damon, W., & Lerner, R. M. (Eds.). (2006). *Handbook of child psychology* (6th ed.). Hoboken, NJ: John Wiley & Sons.

Diamond, L. M., Fagundes, C. P., & Butterworth, M. R. (2010). Intimate relationships across the life span. In A. M. Freund & M. E. Lamb (Eds.), Social and emotional development across the life span: *Vol. 2, Handbook of life-span development*. Editor in chief: R. M. Lerner. Hoboken, NJ: John Wiley & Sons.

Elliot, A. J., Conroy, D. E., & Barron, K. E. (2010). Achievement motives and goals: A developmental analysis. In A. M. Freund & M. E. Lamb (Eds.), Social and emotional development across the life span: *Vol. 2, Handbook of life-span development*. Editor in chief: R. M. Lerner. Hoboken, NJ: John Wiley & Sons.

Geldhof, G. J., Little, T. D., & Colombo, J. (2010). Self-regulation across the life span. In A. M. Freund & M. E. Lamb (Eds.), Social and emotional development across the life span: *Vol. 2, Handbook of life-span development* (pp. 116–157). Editor in chief: R. M. Lerner. Hoboken, NJ: John Wiley & Sons.

Hines, M. (2010). Gendered behavior across the life span. In A. M. Freund & M. E. Lamb (Eds.), Social and emotional development across the life span: *Vol. 2, Handbook of life-span development*. Editor in chief: R. M. Lerner. Hoboken, NJ: John Wiley & Sons.

Labouvie-Vief, G., Grühn, D., Studer, J. (2010). Dynamic integration of emotion and cognition: Equilibrium regulation in development and aging. In A. M. Freund & M. E. Lamb (Eds.), Social and emotional development across the life span: *Vol. 2, Handbook of life-span development* (pp. 79–115). Editor in chief: R. M. Lerner. Hoboken, NJ: John Wiley & Sons.

Lerner, R. M., & Busch-Rossnagel, N. A. (Eds.), *Individuals as producers of their development: A life-span perspective*. New York: Academic.

Lerner, R. M., & Steinberg, L. (Eds.). (2009). *Handbook of adolescent psychology* (3rd ed.). Hoboken, NJ: John Wiley & Sons.

Lewis, M. D., Todd R., & Xu, X. (2010). The development of emotion regulation: A neuropsychological perspective. In A. M. Freund & M. E. Lamb (Eds.), Social and emotional development across the life span: *Vol. 2, Handbook of life-span development* (pp. 51–78). Editor in chief: R. M. Lerner. Hoboken, NJ: John Wiley & Sons.

McAdams, D. P., & Cox, K. S. (2010). Self and identity across the life span. In A. M. Freund & M. E. Lamb (Eds.), Social and emotional development across the life span: *Vol. 2, Handbook of life-span development* (pp. 158–207). Editor in chief: R. M. Lerner. Hoboken, NJ: John Wiley & Sons.

Porges, S. W., & Carter, C. S. (2010). Neurobological bases of social behavior across the life span. In A. M. Freund & M. E. Lamb (Eds.), Social and emotional development across the life span: *Vol. 2, Handbook of life-span development* (pp. 9–50). Editor in chief: R. M. Lerner. Hoboken, NJ: John Wiley & Sons.

Scarlett, W.G., & Alberts Warren, A. E. (2010). Religious and spiritual development across the life span: A behavioral and social science perspective. In A. M. Freund & M. E. Lamb (Eds.), Social and emotional development across the life span: *Vol. 2, Handbook of life-span development*. Editor in chief: R. M. Lerner. Hoboken, NJ: John Wiley & Sons.

Staudinger, U. M., & Bowen, C. E. (2010). Life-span perspectives on positive personality development in adulthood and old age. In A. M. Freund & M. E. Lamb (Eds.), Social and emotional development across the life span: *Vol. 2, Handbook of life-span development* (pp. 254–297). Editor in chief: R. M. Lerner. Hoboken, NJ: John Wiley & Sons.

Zaff, J. F., Hart, D., Flanagan, C. A., Youniss, J., & Levine, P. (2010). Developing civic engagement within a civic context. In A. M. Freund & M. E. Lamb (Eds.), Social and emotional development across the life span: *Vol. 2, Handbook of life-span development*. Editor in chief: R. M. Lerner. Hoboken, NJ: John Wiley & Sons.

CHAPTER 2

Neurobiological Bases of Social Behavior across the Life Span

STEPHEN W. PORGES and C. SUE CARTER

INTRODUCTION AND CONTEXT

The purpose of this review is to provide an analysis of the neurobiology of positive social behaviors, including social engagement, attachment, and bonding. In life-span developmental psychology, social behavior has generally been studied in the context of age-related changes associated with experience, maturation of motor systems, and learned skills. This review takes a different perspective, discussing from phylogenetic, autonomic, and neuroendocrine perspectives the critical role of physiological states in social behavior across the life span.

Personal experiences and observations of others provide many examples in which social behavior is compromised because of the expression of disruptive behavioral states. The behavioral states that disrupt social behavior often have negative labels (such as tantrums or anxiety) and are sometimes used as features of clinical disorders (e.g., attentional-deficit disorders, autism, or anxiety disorders). However, the neurobiology of these states and the biobehavioral systems involved in eliciting or modulating their impact on social behavior are rarely studied and are often minimized in developmental theories. Contemporary subdisciplines of neuroscience tend to focus on the development of affective and social processes, emphasizing the covariation of activity in specific neural circuits with observable behaviors or subjective experiences. In so doing, they have neglected an important domain of human experience.

Many features of social behavior change with development. The underlying explanation is often associated with experience, maturation of motor system, and learned skills. In this chapter, we introduce two dimensions of neurobiological maturation that contribute to individual and developmental differences in social behavior observed throughout the life span. These dimensions are detailed by the morphological and neural regulatory changes in the autonomic nervous system and expression of neuropeptides that modulate both social behavior and autonomic state. The development of the autonomic nervous system in humans follows the phylogenetic history of mammals. Knowledge of phylogeny and ontogeny are used as organizing principles in this review.

Social behaviors can be categorized as either prosocial or agonistic. Important features of positive sociality, which are emphasized in this review, include social engagement, social communication, and social bonds. Both social behavior and social communication rely on evolved physiological processes. Essential to the regulation and expression of social behavior is the autonomic nervous system, which forms a functional physiological platform for the management of social interactions, social communication, and affect regulation. In addition, neurochemical processes, including oxytocin, vasopressin, corticotropin releasing factor (CRF), dopamine, and opioids, help to regulate social behaviors and coordinate the expression of behaviors with other demands, including those necessary for survival and reproduction.

In this chapter, we define social behaviors as positive interactions between two or more individuals. Within this theoretical perspective, selective interactions and long-lasting relationships can be used to operationalize psychological constructs such as social attachments or social bonds.

Aggressive social interactions are less frequently studied in developmental psychology. However, defensive and agonistic behaviors are common features of developmental psychopathologies and as such are discussed. Defensive strategies and agonistic behaviors may be characterized by *mobilized* strategies including avoidance and anxiety, or alternatively by *immobilization* and shutting down.

Although the study of social behavior has a long and distinguished history in developmental psychology, the scientific investigation of a neurobiology of positive social behaviors is recent (Carter, Lederhendler, & Kirkpatrick, 1997). Experimental approaches remain rare in humans, and thus interpreting human social behavior in neurobiological terms often relies on inference from studies measuring physiological correlates of social behavior (e.g., changes in neuroimaging, endocrine, or psychophysiological parameters). Because the neurophysiology of social behavior often requires invasive approaches, the information in this field is typically dependent on inference to humans from studies that are conducted with rodents. For this reason, knowledge of the neural basis of sociality has been largely restricted to nonverbal social behaviors and indirect measures of emotional states. However, using knowledge of mammalian phylogeny, it is possible to develop hypotheses and theories, regarding the origins of processes that underlie positive social behaviors. Even within rodent models, systematic studies of sociality across the life span are rare. In the absence of such research and consistent with the synthesis of E. O. Wilson (1998, p. 8), the approach used here is a "consilience" or "jumping together of knowledge by the linking of facts and fact-based theory across disciplines."

SOCIAL BEHAVIOR IN CONTEXT

Social Engagement, Social Bonding, and the Autonomic Nervous System

Fundamental to sociality are social engagement behaviors, which are most simply measured by the reduction of physical distance between prospective partners. Engagement is followed by recognition of another individual as either familiar or unfamiliar. In time, especially in highly social species, a social preference may be expressed, usually for the familiar partner. Autonomic function is necessary for all forms of affective and emotional experience, including the interactive and contingent behaviors leading to the formation of selective social bonds.

As mammals became increasingly social, they also became dependent on the social engagement system. Social engagement requires the functions of both the central and autonomic nervous system and includes both ancient and comparatively modern adaptations. Conditions that permit social engagement are typically incompatible with those necessary for flight and fight. Thus, enduring social engagement, based on a sense of safety or trust, is necessary for long-lasting and reciprocal relationships.

Definitions of Social Attachment and Bonding in Historical Context

In the analysis of neurobiological mechanisms underlying social behaviors, it is necessary to be aware that constructs, such as attachment and bonding, have colloquial meanings in different behavioral disciplines. Developmental psychologists, following a traditional associated with John Bowlby, have defined *attachment* as a phylogenetically programmed propensity of one person (usually a child) to bond to another who is viewed as stronger and wiser. Bowlby (1969, 1973, 1980) authored several important books dealing with attachment, separation, and the grief of loss. This tradition generated a research field and an experimental approach sometimes termed *attachment theory* (Ainsworth, Blehar, Waters, & Wall, 1978). From this perspective, it is the security of the child's attachment that is considered most relevant, and the mother or other primary caretaker is considered the object of the attachment. This definition of attachment was influenced by the fact that Bowlby was trained in psychoanalysis and strongly influenced by his own experiences and those of Rene Spitz (1945) with children orphaned or separated by war. Bowlby's theories were also affected by ethologists and animal behaviorists of his era. Bowlby merged these perspectives with Freudian theory, and his followers expanded attachment theory to include the "attachment style" of an individual in response to the stress of separation. Reactions to separation were categorized as *secure, insecure, avoidant*, or *disorganized* (Main & Solomon, 1990).

Attachment theory concentrates on the child's relationship with the parent and usually involves children old enough to express behaviorally their preferences and reactions to separation. This approach was later extended to adult attachment styles (Main, Kaplan, & Cassidy, 1985). In this model, other forms of "bonds" are acknowledged but differentiated from "attachments."

The term *bonding* has also been used to describe the emotional relationship between adults and children (Klaus & Kennell, 1982). This point of view focused initially on the development of emotional reactions in a mother toward her child and on events during the postpartum period. Other relationships with children including those between the child and father, adoptive parents, and other caretakers were sometimes ignored. The *maternal bond,* as originally described, seemed to limit the concept of bonding to the relationship between a mother and her biological offspring, creating considerable controversy (Lamb, 1982).

The tendency for limited definitions for both attachment and bonding to not encompass other forms of strong relationships may have slowed the understanding of the mechanisms for these behaviors. In addition, at the time these fields were emerging, knowledge of the neurobiology of behavior was highly limited. Within the past few decades, it has become increasingly clear that at least some of the neural changes associated with birth and the postpartum period extend to other processes, including sociality. In addition, there is now increasing evidence that the same physiological factors that regulate social behaviors and social bonds are also capable of influencing other aspects of health including emotional responses to challenges or stressors. By understanding the causes of sociality, we are also gaining an awareness of the mechanisms through which "social support" is protective against a variety of physical and emotional disorders. Shared physiological substrates and shared experiences are associated with positive social behaviors and help to explain why the same neurobiological systems that are necessary for sociality are also involved in perceived safety, individual survival, and eventually genetic fitness.

Hofer (1987), on the basis of his studies of the development of the maternal and infant dyad, inferred that regulators of physiology were embedded in social behavior. Hofer's concept of regulation focused on the beneficial effects of proximity, especially in terms of how maternal proximity regulated the infant's body temperature. On the basis of the social engagement system model described in detail later in this chapter, other aspects of social behavior are regulators as well. In addition, the anatomical structures involved in the social engagement system have neurophysiological interactions with the hypothalamic–pituitary–adrenal (HPA) axis and neuropeptides, including oxytocin and vasopressin (for overview, see Carter, 1998; Porges, 2001).

In contrast to the narrow definitions of social behavior in the behavioral sciences, biologists working with animal models have tended to use terms such as attachment and bonding interchangeably. Positive social behaviors, such as selective approaches or physical contacts, are often used to measure attachment or a social bond. Responses to separation and reunion, such as vocalizations (assumed to index distress) or attempts to reunite with a partner after separation, also have been used to index social bonding and attachment (Hennessy, 1997). Studies of relatively simple measures of social preferences in animals (Keverne, 2005; Williams, Catania, & Carter, 1992), as well as studies of social isolation (Grippo, Gerena, et al., 2007; Young, Murphy-Young, & Hammock, 2005), have permitted an increasingly detailed analysis of the effects of specific neurobiological systems involved in the presence or absence of social partners. On the basis of these kinds of studies and imaging research in humans, specific neural pathways, sometimes termed the *social nervous system* (Adolphs, 2006), have been implicated in both sociality and emotional reactions.

Behavioral and Ecological Context for Social Behavior

From immature dependent beginnings as infants, most humans continue to have needs for social interaction and companionship throughout the life span. People need people to develop, to survive, and to prosper. Even as adults, humans rely on our families and companions for physical and emotional support. Even when we appear to be alone, society and its economics provide for our needs in the form of food, shelter, energy, and other resources. These commonplace benefits of group living are easily understood, although sometimes noticed only when they are not available. Voluntary isolation or prolonged social withdrawal is frequently viewed as a feature of psychiatric disorders, whereas involuntary or forced isolation is often experienced as a punishment. The absence of a bond between parent and child can be taken as evidence of psychopathology, whereas solitary confinement is considered by many as a punishment worse than death. Thus, the emotional and physical history and state of each individual contributes to sociality. However, it is important to note that social behaviors, and the neurobiology of social behaviors, are inherently "plastic" permitting each individual to use his or her history to predict and adapt to a constantly changing social environment.

The behavioral consequences of exposure to stress or trauma can have consequences across the life cycle. The body's management of stress includes processes that physiologically prepare the individual for difficult or dangerous events to follow. These mechanisms are most clearly identified in early development. For example, trauma in early life may amplify the response to later stressful experiences. Conversely, positive experiences, such as high levels of nurturance in development, may encourage later sociality and support reproduction (Meaney, 2001). In this context, it not surprising that the neurobiology of sociality across the life span is linked to stress and stress management, especially in early life.

In general, social support and social bonds are stress buffering. The mechanisms for these effects are not well identified (Singer & Ryff, 2001). Epidemiological studies have found that indices of social support are strong predictors of vulnerability to or recovery from diseases, including cardiovascular disease, cancer, and mental illness (reviewed Knox & Uvnäs-Moberg, 1998). Both perceived social support and "giving" appear to have health benefits for the recipients and those who give (Brown, Brown, House, & Smith, 2008; Uchino, Cacioppo, & Kiecolt-Glaser, 1996). There is increasing evidence that mechanisms, such as recruiting vagal activity, dampening HPA axis and thus dampening the release of glucocorticoids (such as cortisol), and increasing the release of the central peptide oxytocin are capable of calming bodily states to support health, growth, and restoration. These physiological mechanisms are both facilitatory and a consequence of prosocial behaviors. The neural mechanisms mediating prosocial behavior and the specific physiological states that promote health are bidirectionally interfaced in the mammalian nervous system with the consequence that prosocial behavior promotes health and healthy nervous systems facilitate the expression of prosocial behavior.

Evolutionary Context for Social Behavior

Social behavior and the benefits of sociality are considered central to evolution (Nowak, 2006). The human nervous system is a product of evolution (Harris, 2007; MacLean, 1990; Porges, 2007). Although, our mammalian ancestors did not possess the cortically dominated nervous system and complex behavioral repertoire that we consider typical of modern humans, many aspects of brain function and social and emotional behaviors are shared with other species. Much of social behavior is not occurring at the high levels of the brain that we associated with conscious awareness and voluntary behavior but relies instead on subcortical brain structures, below our conscious awareness. Thus, the voluntary and conscious aspects of social behavior and social engagement behaviors may be directly influenced by the same neural systems, including the central and autonomic nervous systems, that regulate survival and homeostasis. States created by these systems limit the degree to which mammals can be physically approached, communicate, interact, and establish or maintain relationships. Thus, studies of sociality and emotional reactivity in nonhuman animals can inform an understanding of human behavior.

For example, the neuroendocrine processes responsible for mammalian sociality rely on ancient molecules and basic neural processes that are shared among species. A given molecule may serve as both a hormone and a neuromodulator, capable of affecting many aspects of physiology and behavior. However, the specific patterns of hormone synthesis and release, as well as the actions of receptors responsible for social behaviors, show patterns of differences among different species. Knowledge of species-typical mating and social strategies puts the biology of sociality into perspective. For example, comparisons of socially monogamous species versus related, but less social, mammalian species has helped to map the neurocircuitry of sociality (Carter, DeVries, & Getz, 1995; Young & Wang, 2004).

The endocrine systems responsible for sociality contribute to reproductive success, and various reproductive hormones also are implicated in sociality. In addition, the capacity to detect and cope with stressful experiences is integral to sociality, and hormones of the same systems responsible for managing stress, including the HPA axis, also regulate sociality.

Social behaviors are necessary for both individual survival and eventual survival of a species. At the heart of mammalian survival and sociality is the concept of safety and the ability to distinguish whether the environment is safe and whether other individuals are friend or foe. An evolutionary perspective helps to explain why and how social interactions and perceived social support are so essential to our ability both to reproduce and also to manage the "stress of life."

Phylogenetic Perspectives on Social Behavior

Knowledge of the physiological distinctions between reptiles and mammals has provided important clues regarding the origins and neurophysiology of social behavior, as well as insights into the systems that are compromised in disrupted sociality and clinical disorders. When a mammalian mother initially interacts with her offspring, she has usually just given birth and provides nutrition in the form of milk to her newborn. Thus, the onset of maternal behavior is associated with birth and lactation. For this reason, the physiology of birth and lactation have long been assumed to play a role in the mother–infant interaction. More recently, the same neural and endocrine systems that permit birth, lactation, and maternal behavior have been implicated in other forms of positive social experiences, including behaviors that occur in situations extending beyond motherhood to include complex human emotions and relationships.

Neurophysiological and neurochemical systems necessary for mammalian social behaviors emerged during the phylogenetic transition from reptile to mammal. Two mammalian hormones, oxytocin and vasopressin, play a central role in birth and lactation. The genes responsible for these ancient hormones are believed to have evolved more than 700 million years ago, initially to regulate cellular processes such as water balance and homeostasis, with secondary roles in reproduction (Donaldson & Young, 2008). In modern mammals, these neuropeptides (originating primarily in the brain) regulate birth and lactation, as well as related social and sexual behaviors, defensive behaviors, and stress-coping responses. Concurrently, in the evolution of modern mammals and especially primates, changes occurred in the neural regulation of the autonomic nervous system and the regulation of facial and head muscles (Porges, 2007). These systems, including neuropeptides and the autonomic nervous system, are essential components of the neural substrates of sociality and are the focus of much of this chapter.

Major changes in the neural regulation of the autonomic nervous system also provided the unique mammalian capacity to use social interactions as mechanisms to regulate autonomic state and to facilitate growth, health, and restoration. Of special interest to the study of social behavior is the uniquely mammalian feature of a neural convergence between the regulation of autonomic state and the neural regulation of the muscles of the face and head. This convergence enabled prosocial facial expressions, vocalizations, and head gestures to occur in conjunction with physiological states of calmness. Conversely, agonistic expressions are usually associated with agitated physiological states.

Developmental Context and Social Behavior

Social relationships are of particular importance during periods of dependence on others, including early life and in old age. The neurobiological systems responsible for sociality vary developmentally, as a function of experience and between males and females. Both genetic and epigenetic factors interact to regulate the expression of social behaviors (Szyf, Weaver, Champagne, Diorio, & Meaney, 2005). Most research on the causal mechanisms of sociality has been conducted in adult animals. The most common developmental studies involve manipulations of early experience, exposure to stressors, or endocrine manipulations, such as hormonal treatments or gonadectomy. In a limited number of cases, studies of aging animals are available.

Developmental psychobiology tends to focus on age-defined periods or *stages* (Michel & Moore, 1995). This has been particularly true with regard to aspects of sociality that may be affected by endocrine events or experiences that change with maturation. Studies can be generally classified into manipulations or experiences during the perinatal (i.e., prenatal or postnatal) period, those associated with adolescence and puberty, or those of adulthood.

Behavioral and endocrine events associated with the prenatal period are inherently difficult to observe. The reliance of the fetus on maternal factors, especially in placental mammals, complicates the interpretation of this period, although there is a growing literature on the effects of prenatal stress on subsequent sociality.

Most commonly, the analysis of the behavioral neuroendocrinology of sociality begins in the immediate postnatal period. Experimental manipulations may be done in early postnatal life and the consequences examined in later life, typically either after weaning or in adulthood. For example, there is considerable evidence that early malnutrition, abuse, or neglect have the potential to have lifelong consequences for sociality, possibly mediated by long-lasting neuroendocrine changes. Research on the neurobiological mechanisms of aging is rare in the field of social neuroscience. For this reason, we focus on organizing principles and relationships between physiology and behavior, although many of these are untested in older age.

The Absence of Social Interactions Also Has Physiological Consequences

In the context of the shared physiology among social and emotional behaviors, it is not surprising that social interactions and isolation have powerful physiological consequences. The need for social interactions has been documented by a growing body of evidence suggesting that individuals with a perceived sense of social support are more likely to avoid or survive illness and have longer lives than otherwise similar people who live alone or who experience a sense of loneliness (Cacioppo, Hughes, Waite, Hawkely, & Thisted, 2006). Processes that change during perceived isolation are also shared with those implicated in sociality.

Experiments in animals provide an opportunity to examine in more depth the physiological consequences of the absence of a social partner. Highly social mammals offer useful models for examining the effects of social isolation because they share with humans the capacity to form long-lasting social relationships. For example, the socially monogamous prairie vole has a humanlike autonomic nervous system, with high levels of parasympathetic–vagal activity (Grippo, Lamb, Carter, & Porges, 2007a, 2007b). Because the parasympathetic nervous system mediates many of the consequences of social interactions, this aspect of prairie vole biology has helped to explain the high levels of sensitivity to the presence or absence of social experiences in this species. In prairie voles, isolation from a partner for a few weeks produced significant increases in several behavioral measures of "depression and anxiety." Isolated animals were less exploratory, showed increases in anhedonia (indexed by a loss of preference for sweet liquids), and were more likely to show immobility in response to a stressor (such as swimming; Grippo, Cushing, & Carter, 2007; Grippo, Wu, Hassan, & Carter, 2008). In prairie voles, separation from a partner, followed by prolonged isolation, is associated with increases in heart rate, decreases in parasympathetic function, and increased behavioral reactivity to stressors, such as the presence of a social intruder. For example, following a 5-minute social stressor (intruder), isolated prairie voles required an average of more than 15 hours for heart rate to return to baseline. In contrast, animals living in sibling pairs required about 2.5 hours for their heart rate to recover.

In the absence of a social partner, the neuropeptide hormone oxytocin increased in female prairie voles (Grippo, Cushing, et al., 2007). Elevated oxytocin in this context may be protective against the negative consequences of isolation. In the context of personal safety, the release of oxytocin could encourage social interactions including those associated with detecting and responding to the emotions or experiences of others. We also tested this hypothesis by treating isolated or paired prairie voles with exogenous oxytocin. Oxytocin injections were capable of reversing the cardiac and behavioral effects of isolation, including protecting against the anxiety and depression-like changes that typically accompany isolation (Grippo, Trahanas, Zimmerman, Porges, & Carter, 2009).

Life-span approaches to sociality are rare even in rodent models. One unique example comes from the study of death from natural causes including mammary cancer in a female rat from a strain that was especially vulnerable to cancer (Yee, Cavigelli, Delgade, & McClintock, 2008). Social behaviors were measured by behavioral responses of female rats to a mild stressor; reciprocal social interactions were studied in female sibling groups throughout the postpubertal life span. Females that showed high levels of affiliative reciprocity showed lower levels of glucocorticoid responses in aging, had a later onset of mammary tumors, and survived longer. Apparently social reciprocity and affiliative interactions buffered the experience of daily stressors, protecting the more social females. Another longitudinal predictor of mammary tumors in rats was differential exploration or neophobia. Neophobia measured in early life was associated with an earlier onset of palpable tumors. Neophobic females showed a more rapid decline in ovarian function and lower levels of glucocorticoids, suggesting that neither ovarian hormones nor exposure to high levels of "stress" hormones were likely to be responsible for these differences.

THE AUTONOMIC NERVOUS SYSTEM AND SOCIAL BEHAVIOR

Central and Peripheral Components of the Autonomic Nervous System

Knowledge of the autonomic nervous system is important to understanding both the causes and consequences of social behavior. It is common to divide the autonomic nervous system into sympathetic and parasympathetic branches. In turn, the primary nerve of parasympathetic nervous system exits the brainstem as the vagus or tenth cranial nerve. The vagus nerve is actually a bundle of fibers including both motor–efferent and sensory–afferent components. Approximately 80% of the vagal fibers are afferent and carry information from the viscera to a brainstem region known as nucleus tractus solitarius (NTS). Output from the NTS contributes to the regulation of higher brain functions including modulation of arousal and bodily state (Porges, 2007).

The two source nuclei of the efferent motor vagus include the ancient unmyelinated dorsal vagal complex (DVC) and the myelinated portion of the vagus, which originates in the nucleus ambiguous located in a brainstem region known as the ventral vagal complex (VVC). Actions of the VVC allow the reduction in fear and the concurrent emergence of calm states necessary for social engagement and bonding. Also originating in the VVC, the special visceral efferent (SVE) pathways regulate the striated muscles of the face and head. The myelinated SVE system allows dynamic and rapid autonomic input in social interactions, including eye movements and auditory communication, which are necessary for mammalian social engagement. The primary features of emotion and affect (i.e., neural regulation of facial muscles and the heart) are regulated by this system.

Functionally, when the environment is perceived as safe, two important features are expressed. First, the bodily state is regulated in an efficient manner to promote growth, restoration, and visceral homeostasis. This is done through an increase in the more evolutionarily modern and rapid vagal motor pathways on the cardiac pacemaker. When activated, this mechanism slows the heart, inhibits the fight–flight mechanisms of the sympathetic nervous system, and dampens the stress response system of the HPA axis (including cortisol release). In modern mammals, the brainstem nuclei that regulate the myelinated vagus are integrated with the nuclei that regulate the muscles of the face and head. This link resulted in bidirectional coupling between spontaneous social engagement behaviors and bodily states. Specifically, the visceral states that promote growth and restoration are linked neuroanatomically and neurophysiologically with the muscles that regulate components of eye gaze, facial expression, listening, and prosody (Figures 2.1 and 2.2; Porges, 2001, 2007).

The Development of the Autonomic Nervous System Parallels and Permits the Emergence of Social Behavior

The autonomic nervous system functions as a neural platform to support both social engagement behaviors and the regulation of behavioral and physiological state. During early development, the autonomic nervous system rapidly changes, supporting the expanding abilities of an infant to explore within the vast domain of social behavior. Coupled with this ability to engage in social interactions is a change in how the child is able to use others to regulate physiological and behavioral state. As the child develops, neural circuits become differentiated and are specialized to foster the child's engagement with either objects or other humans.

The dynamically changing behavioral repertoire and social-interactive needs of the young infant are served by this system. The newborn has poor self-regulation skills and needs "other" to regulate. As is the case for humans and many other mammals, birth is not a transition into independence but an extension of period of dependence. This early period, characterized by "other-regulation," has three related global features that qualify the contexts and objectives of early social behavior: (a) neural feedback loops for state regulation are not complete, limiting the ability to self-regulate (e.g., fussing, crying, hunger, feeding, thermoregulating) and increasing the demands on others; (b) the infant's nervous system has limited abilities to detect risk, to cue others selectively, and to mobilize to defend, avoid, or reach a place of safety; and (c) the infant's adaptive quest for safety is compromised without the "benevolent" interactions of a caregiver.

These behavioral features are dependent on shifts in the neural regulation of the autonomic nervous system. Until recently, within developmental psychology and behavioral pediatrics—fields in which there has been an emphasis on mother–infant interactions and infant skill attainment—the autonomic nervous system has played a background role. However, the autonomic nervous system is a developing and dynamically changing resource, contributing to the complex repertoire of infant behaviors and, in part, mediating, much of the dynamic interaction that the infant has with both others and objects.

POLYVAGAL THEORY: A NEW BIOBEHAVIORAL CONCEPTUALIZATION OF THE AUTONOMIC NERVOUS SYSTEM

As evolutionary forces molded the human nervous system, new structures were added and older structures were modified that regulate the autonomic nervous system and foster new adaptive social behaviors to support survival. The polyvagal theory (Porges, 1995a, 1995b, 1998, 2001, 2003, 2007), by incorporating an evolutionary approach, provides a strategy to investigate developmental shifts is social behavior from a phylogenetic perspective (Table 2.1; Figure 2.1). The theory provides insights into how developmental shifts in neural regulation of the autonomic nervous system are related to the changing repertoire of adaptive behaviors that either limit or expand the expression of social behaviors. The theory emphasizes the unique features in neural regulation of the autonomic nervous system that distinguish mammals from reptiles and how these features serve as a biobehavioral platform, allowing the emergence of contemporary social behaviors. In addition, the theory provides insights into the biobehavioral mechanisms that are rapidly developing in the young infant. As the neural mechanisms facilitating self-regulation improve, the dependence on others to regulate decreases. Thus, allowing social communication to expand beyond the cueing of basic physical survival needs (i.e., thermoregulation, safety, food) into the realm of prosocial engagements.

The polyvagal theory articulates how each of three phylogenetic stages in the development of the vertebrate autonomic nervous system are associated with a distinct autonomic subsystem that is retained and expressed in mammals. These autonomic subsystems are phylogenetically ordered and behaviorally linked to social communication (e.g., facial expression, vocalization, listening), mobilization (e.g., fight–flight behaviors), and immobilization (e.g., feigning death, vasovagal syncope, and behavioral shutdown). The product of this phylogenetic process is a nervous system with three identifiable circuits that regulate adaptive behaviors and physiological reactions to challenges.

These three circuits can be conceptualized as providing adaptive responses to safe, dangerous, or life-threatening events and contexts. Functionally, when the environment is perceived as safe, two important features are expressed. First, bodily state is regulated in an efficient manner to promote growth and restoration (e.g., visceral homeostasis). This is done through an increase in the influence of myelinated vagal motor pathways on the cardiac pacemaker that slows heart rate, inhibits fight–flight mechanisms of the sympathetic nervous system, dampens the stress response system of the HPA axis (e.g., cortisol), and reduces inflammation by modulating immune reactions (e.g., cytokines). Second, through the process of evolution, the brainstem nuclei that regulate the myelinated vagus became integrated with the nuclei that regulate the muscles of the face and head.

Table 2.1 Polyvagal Theory: Phylogenetic Stages of Neural Control

Nervous System Component	Origins of Lower Motor Neurons	Behavioral Functions	Autonomic Functions
Myelinated vagus *(VVC–ventral vagal complex)*	Brainstem-(Nucleus ambiguus)–unique to Mammals	Social engagement and communication, including vocalizations and listening, facial expression. Self-soothing and calming, inhibiting sympathetic-adrenal functions and reducing fear. Enhanced cognition. The mammalian functions of the face and head (Fig. 2)	Stabilization of autonomic processes, including producing cardiac respiratory sinus arrhythmia (RSA), which protects the heart, stabilizes heart rate, and allows oxygenation of the CNS. Oxytocin and vasopressin may act at this level to coordinate the expression of social behavior.
Sympathetic-adrenal system *(SNS–sympathetic nervous system)*	Spinal cord	Mobilization - Active avoidance including flight/fight responses. Associated with active coping responses to threat or danger.	Activation. Increased heart rate, production of energy, including glucose, and conversion of norepinephrine to epinephrine. Vasopressin and CRF increase SNS activity; oxytocin usually inhibits.
Unmyelinated vagus *(DVC–dorsal vagal complex)*	Brainstem Dorsal motor nucleus of the vagus (DMX)	Immobilization and conservation of energy, including shutdown responses and/or loss of consciousness. Associated with passive coping, defensive freezing, and other immobile responses.	Producing bradycardias (slowing the heart). Oxytocin receptors in the DMX may protect against shutting down, allowing "immobility without fear"

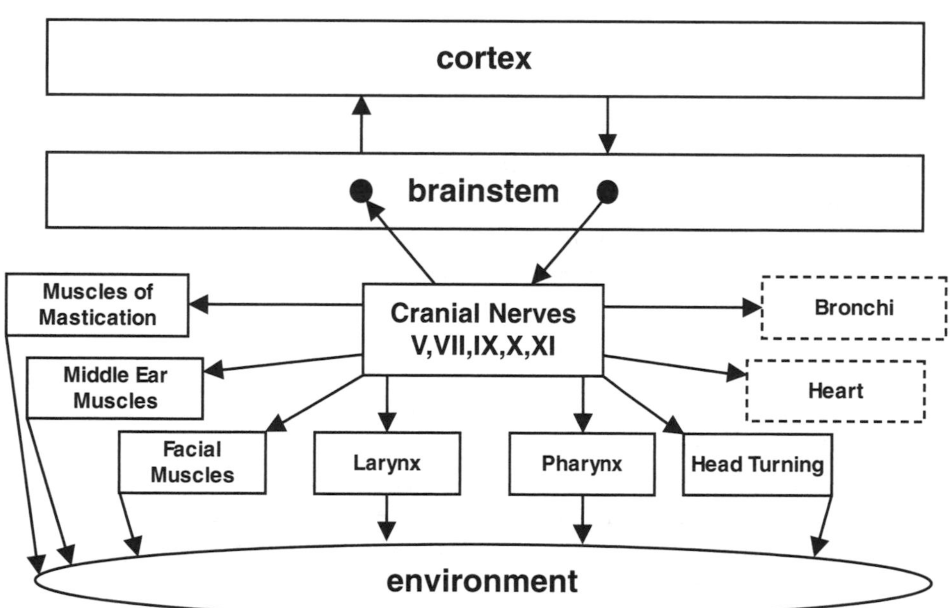

Figure 2.1 The Mammalian *Social Engagement System.* This system involves input from various sensory pathways and the cortex to the brainstem (including the extended amygdala and hypothalamus). The myelinated vagus (arising in the ventral vagal complex in the brainstem) coordinates behavioral and autonomic functions and is a uniquely mammalian system. This is a bi-directional system and permits the dynamic feedback and motor responses necessary for the expression of complex social behaviors. Oxytocin and vasopressin can act at many points within this system.

This link results in the bidirectional coupling between spontaneous social engagement behaviors and bodily states. Specifically, the visceral states that promote growth and restoration are linked neuroanatomically and neurophysiologically with the muscles that regulate eye gaze, facial expression, listening, and prosody.

The polyvagal theory provides a physiological basis to link uniquely mammalian anatomical and physiological circuits involved in visceral state regulation to both the expressive and receptive domains of social communication. The development of these features reflects the phylogenetic distinction between reptiles and mammals and includes a cluster of behaviors dependent on the function of structures that phylogenetically emerged with mammals. Mammals, and not reptiles, have detached middle ear bones, and identification of these in the fossil record is used as the defining feature of mammals. Coincident with the separation of the middle ear bones, the ventral vagal complex (VVC) becomes intertwined with the areas regulating the striated muscles of the face and head, as well as a myelinated vagal system regulating visceral organs located above the diaphragm (i.e., supradiaphragmatic). This system is distinct from an unmyelinated vagal system regulating visceral organs located below the diaphragm (i.e., subdiaphragmatic; DVC; i.e., dorsal vagal complex). This transition permitted a dynamic social engagement system with social communication features (e.g., facial expression, head movements, vocalizations, and listening) which could interact with visceral state regulation.

Unlike reptiles, the mammalian nervous system did not develop solely to survive in dangerous and life-threatening contexts but evolved to promote social interactions and social bonds in safe environments. To accomplish this adaptive flexibility, a new neural strategy for dealing with safe environments emerged, while retaining the more primitive neural circuits to regulate defensive strategies. The response to threat or actual danger involved mobilization, including fight or flight, which required the support of the sympathoadrenal axis. The second and more primitive strategy was to immobilize and conserve energy, which could include freezing behaviors or even death-feigning and relies on the more ancient DVC.

It is important to note that social behavior, social communication, and visceral homeostasis are incompatible with the neurophysiological states and behaviors promoted by the neural circuits that support defense strategies (especially those that involve immobility). Thus, through evolution, the mammalian nervous system has retained three neural circuits, which are in a phylogenetically organized hierarchy. In this hierarchy of adaptive responses, the newest circuit associated with social communication is used first, and if that circuit fails to provide safety, the older survival-oriented circuits are recruited sequentially.

Social communication (see Social Engagement System later in the chapter) involves the myelinated vagus, which serves to foster calm behavioral states by inhibiting the sympathetic influences to the heart and dampening the HPA axis (e.g., Bueno et al., 1989). The mobilization system is dependent on the functioning of the sympathetic nervous system. The most phylogenetically primitive component, the immobilization system is dependent on the unmyelinated vagus, which is shared with all vertebrates. With increased neural complexity due to phylogenetic development, the organism's behavioral and affective repertoire is enriched. The three circuits can be conceptualized as dynamically adjusting to provide adaptive responses to safe, dangerous, and life-threatening events and contexts.

The "Vagal Brake"

The new or mammalian vagus promotes sociality and clear cognitions, while it actively inhibits the sympathetic nervous system influences on the heart and dampens HPA axis activity (Porges, 2001). To facilitate both defensive and social behaviors, the new mammalian vagus enabled rapid adaptive shifts in autonomic state. The mammalian vagus functions as an active vagal brake (see Porges, Doussard-Roosevelt, Portales, & Greenspan, 1996) in which rapid inhibition and disinhibition of the vagal tone to the heart can rapidly mobilize or calm an individual. Vagal influences to the sinoatrial node (i.e., the heart's pacemaker), produce resting heart rate that is substantially lower than the intrinsic rate of the pacemaker. When the vagal tone to the pacemaker is high, the vagus acts as a restraint or brake limiting the rate the heart is beating. When the vagal tone to the pacemaker is low, there is little or no inhibition of the pacemaker. Thus, the vagal brake may be used as a construct to describe the functional modulation of heart rate by the myelinated vagal efferent pathways.

The vagal brake provides a neural mechanism to change visceral state rapidly and permit social behaviors by slowing or speeding the heart rate. Consistent with the assumptions of the polyvagal theory, the vagal brake contributes to the modulation of cardiac output by decreasing the inhibitory vagal control of the heart to speed heart rate and by increasing the inhibitory vagal control of the heart to slow heart rate. Thus, neurophysiologically the vagal brake is removed or reduced to support the metabolic requirements for mobilization and maintained or increased to support social engagement behaviors. The state of the vagal brake can be assessed by quantifying the amplitude of a periodic component in the beat-to-beat heart rate pattern known as respiratory sinus arrhythmia (RSA). RSA is a naturally occurring rhythm in the heart rate pattern at approximately the frequency of spontaneous breathing. The amplitude of RSA can be quantified to provide a sensitive index of the impact of the myelinated vagus on the heart. By assessing RSA during various challenges, it is possible to measure the dynamic regulation of the vagal brake across the life span.

THE NEURAL BASIS OF SOCIAL ENGAGEMENT AND COMMUNICATION

The Social Engagement System

The social engagement system is conceptualized here as a set of neural pathways that control the muscles of the head and face and regulate visceral state through the vagal brake. The social engagement system is composed of a somatomotor component (i.e., pathways that regulate the muscles of the head and face) and a visceromotor component (i.e., the myelinated vagus that regulates the heart and the bronchi). Specifically, the social engagement system includes the regulation of the eyelids (e.g., social gaze and gesture), facial muscles (e.g., emotional expression), middle ear muscles (e.g., extracting human voice from background sounds), muscles of mastication (e.g., ingestion), laryngeal and pharyngeal muscles (e.g., sucking, swallowing, vocalizing, breathing), and muscles of head turning and tilting (e.g., social gesture and orientation). Collectively, these muscles act as filters for social stimuli (e.g., observing facial expression and the detection of prosody in human voice) and allow the expression of the motor behaviors, described earlier, that are necessary for engagement with the social environment.

These sensory and motor system may interact to optimize sociality. For example, the neural pathway that raises the eyelids also tenses the stapedius muscle in the middle ear, which facilitates hearing sounds in the range of human voice while dampening low-frequency background sounds, which may signal danger (Djupesland, 1976). As a cluster, difficulties in behaviors associated with the social engagement system (e.g., gaze, extraction of human voice, flat facial affect, lack of vocal prosody, and head gesture) are common features of children with social communication difficulties (e.g., autism).

The neural control of the muscles necessary for social communication also determines social experiences by changing facial expressions (especially apparent in primates), modulating laryngeal and pharyngeal muscles to regulate intonation of vocalizations, and coordinating both facial and vocal motor tone with respiratory actions. In addition, the frequency of breathing is encoded into the phrasing of vocalizations and may convey urgency by expressing short phrases associated with short exhalations (i.e., rapid breathing) or calmness by expressing long phrases associated with long exhalations (i.e., slow breathing).

Vocal Prosody and Autonomic Regulation: Parallel Outputs of the Social Engagement System

Mammalian vocalization is one component of a conspecific social communication system. This system conveys not only social signals and can signal environmental risk but also information regarding physiological state. In the *Expression of Emotions in Man and Animals*, Darwin (1872/1994) noted that it was well known that several mammalian species modulated acoustic features of vocalizations to signal states of fear and aggression. Pediatricians also interpret the frequency of infant cries as indicators of health state and are especially concerned when infants exhibit high-frequency shrill cries. This covariation between physiological state and the acoustic frequencies of vocalizations is neurophysiologically based. The neural circuits in the brainstem regulating vocalizations (i.e., pathways controlling breath and laryngeal and pharyngeal muscles) are shared with the mechanisms controlling visceral state through the uniquely mammalian myelinated vagus. As described earlier the face–heart connection is part of the integrated social engagement system.

On the basis of the evolved properties of the social nervous system, features of acoustic vocalizations should mirror vagal regulation of the heart. Thus, positive features in both systems are characterized by lower levels (i.e., slower heart rate, lower fundamental acoustic frequency) and a more dynamic neural modulation. The dynamic neural modulation in both systems can be conceptualized as systematic periodic activity. In the heart rate pattern, this is observed as greater amplitude RSA. In the context of vocalizations, this increase in variation is observed as greater modulation of acoustic frequencies. In humans, we label this modulation *prosody*, and research documents that lack of prosody (i.e., lack of acoustic variation) is a risk factor, similar to the lack of RSA. Research with human infants has documented the covariation between the fundamental cry frequency (i.e., pitch) of newborn infants and the influence of myelinated vagus on the heart (see Porter, Porges, & Marshall, 1988).

Middle Ear Structures Regulate the Sensitivity to Conspecific Vocalizations: Implications for Social Communication and Language Development

The neural regulation of the middle ear muscles is also an important component of the social engagement system. These muscles actively attenuate low-frequency sounds. Low-frequency sounds are often associated with predators and the background noises in our environment that make it difficult to hear human voice. The middle ear muscles, when contracted, serve an antimasking function by dampening the background noises and improving the ability of mammals to detect conspecific vocalizations. However, the ability to contract these muscles is state-dependent. Under conditions of threat or danger, physiological states shift to permit mobilization and fight and flight defense strategies. Thus, the physiological state of an angry person or a tantruming child would be incompatible with accessing features of entire social engagement system and would compromise the ability to determine accurately the content of spoken words. In contrast, the ability to access features of the social engagement system is enhanced in a "safe" environment, which by definition is free from the environmental cues associated with fear of predation or other threats.

In a safe environment, contraction of the middle ear muscles enhances social communication by improving the signal-to-noise ratio of human voice over background sounds. These small muscles literally function as a natural amplifier. Thus, conditions of safety provide a sensory advantage for the detection of conspecific vocalizations (vs. social cries of other species). Two physiological mechanisms, selective active antimasking by the middle ear muscles and the passive amplification by the middle ear structures, create species-specific frequency bands in which there is a "perceptual advantage." As a general rule, conspecific vocalizations including the primary vocalizations of humans occupy this frequency band of perceptual advantage.

In general, it is within this frequency band of perceptual advantage that mammalian species produce most of their relevant conspecific vocalizations, and within this frequency range sounds are more easily detected. This frequency band is specific to each mammalian species. In general, smaller mammals have an advantage in the capacity to hear higher frequencies. However, because low-frequency sounds dominate most acoustic environments, the frequency band of perceptual advantage is optimized only when lower frequencies do not overwhelm the acoustic apparatus. Thus, the capacity of middle ear muscle contraction to reduce acoustic energy in the lower frequencies is critical to allowing social communication. If this system is compromised, social interactions that rely on hearing may be difficult or impossible. For example, chronic or repeated ear infections may have lasting implications for social behavior.

Social Communication and Prosody

Although humans and other mammals can vocalize outside the frequency band of perceptual advantage, the within-species social communication is usually characterized by frequency-modulated vocalizations (i.e., prosody) within this frequency band. These frequency-modulated vocalizations reflect prosody in humans and other mammals and convey relevant information about emotional and physiological state. In contrast, danger and pain signals may be shrill cries (i.e., high pitch with diminished frequency modulation) at the upper edge of this frequency band. In addition, aggressive signaling may push vocalizations to lower frequencies outside this band (e.g., the roar of a lion). This preference to vocalize in a social context within the frequencies most easily detected by conspecifics has clear adaptive features, but it also creates challenges. In particular, the frequencies of these vocalizations are dependent on the processing of airborne acoustic energy and are characterized by very short wavelengths that dissipate rapidly with distance from the source. In contrast, low frequencies have long wavelengths that travel over long distances.

Our culture emphasizes the importance of language development in young children and the attainment of language skills as an important benchmark for cognitive function. However, there may be a cost for actively dampening the sensitivity to low-frequency sounds and engaging the neural mechanisms involved in listening to the frequency band of perceptual advantage. Listening to the frequency band of perceptual advantage requires the neural implementation of an active filter that reduces the acoustic information at low frequencies that can reach the brain. Because the sounds associated with predators, especially the movements of larger animals, are characterized by low-frequency sounds, engaging in this active "listening" process has maladaptive consequences by reducing the ability to detect sounds of danger. Thus, the advantage of listening to conspecific vocalization comes with a cost. In dangerous environments, the potential cost of social communication is reduction of the capacity for predator detection. The adaptive consequence of this vulnerability is to restrict or limit listening to vocalizations within the frequency band of perceptual advantage (an important component of social engagement and social communication) primarily in safe environments such as buildings for humans and nests or burrows for other mammals. Interestingly, these adaptive defense mechanisms that efficiently detect predators may be highly tuned in children who are raised in dangerous environments, with the direct consequence of a functional delay in language development.

INTEGRATED COMPONENTS OF THE SOCIAL ENGAGEMENT SYSTEM AND BEHAVIORAL REGULATION

Infant Feeding and Autonomic Regulation

To ingest food properly and efficiently, the infant must have the neural resources to implement the complex sequence of sucking, swallowing, and breathing. This sequence requires the coordination of several structures regulated by the special visceral efferents (i.e., the somatomotor component of the social engagement system). The autonomic support for these muscles is provided by the myelinated vagus (i.e., the visceromotor component of the social engagement system). Thus, similar to the covariation with cry pitch, RSA should covary with changes in sucking behavior. Porges and Lipsitt (1993) tested the gustatory-vagal hypothesis by monitoring sucking frequency, heart rate, and RSA in neonates during manipulations of a sweet gustatory stimulation. In response to increased sweetness, reductions in RSA and increases in heart rate paralleled increased sucking frequency. Moreover, individual differences in RSA were correlated with the magnitude of heart rate reactivity to the gustatory stimulation. These findings clearly demonstrate that the changes in autonomic state and sucking frequency reflect a coordinated response.

Because gustatory-vagal responses can be systematically elicited, the paradigm provides an opportunity to evaluate vulnerability in preterm infants for coordinated physiological–behavioral sequences that require vagal regulation and control of the striated muscles of the face and head. Consistent with the Porges and Lipsitt (1993) findings, studies evaluating the covariation between sucking behavior and RSA have been conducted with high-risk low-birth-weight neonates. In one study, Portales et al. (1997) evaluated RSA before, during, and after bottle-feeding in clinically stable high-risk low-birth-weight neonates. Similar to the full-term infants, RSA decreased during bottle-feeding. In a second study with more compromised infants (Suess et al., 2000), RSA was monitored before, during, and after oral or gastric-tube bolus feedings in preterm infants at approximately 33–34 weeks gestational age. The preterm neonates were categorized into two groups on the basis of gestational age. The earlier-born group had gestational ages less than 30 weeks, and the later-born group had gestational ages greater than 30 weeks. Consistent with the above studies, RSA decreased in both groups during feeding. However, postfeeding RSA increased toward prefeed levels (i.e., recovered) only in later-born infants. The results confirmed the assumption that the higher risk group, independent of corrected gestational age, experienced a compromised vagal regulation during the feeding paradigm.

Vagal Control of the Heart and Behavioral Regulation

Extreme and persistent difficulties in behavioral regulation (i.e., regulatory disorders) have been identified as clinical features of dysfunctions in early life and predictors of later vulnerability. The features of regulatory disorders have been systematically described (Porges, 1993) and include (a) sleep disturbance, (b) difficulties self-consoling, (c) feeding disorders, and (d) hyperarousal. Regulatory disorders often reflect atypical neural regulation of physiological state. An established regulatory disorder reflects persistent problems in several of these dimensions and does not reflect transient problems associated with environmental stress, illness, or early colic that resolves.

Early developmental features of regulatory disorders are related to poor outcomes. DeGangi, DiPietro, Greenspan, and Porges (1991) conducted a prospective study in which age-matched groups of infants with mild or moderate-severe regulatory disorders were evaluated and contrasted with typical infants, assessed at 7 months of age. Problems with self-regulation, including sleep, feeding, state control, self-calming, sensory reactivity, mood regulation, and emotional and behavioral control, were documented during infancy in the two regulatory disorders groups. At 36 months, 60% of the children with mild regulatory disorders did not meet criteria for any clinical disorder, whereas 95% of the infants with moderate-severe regulatory disorders had received diagnoses that fell into two clusters: (a) delays in motor, language, and cognitive development and (b) parent–child relationship problems.

At the core of these clinical features appears to be an inability to appropriately inhibit both behavioral and physiological reactivity in response to environmental demands. Successful accomplishments of several adaptive processes, including sustained attention, require systematic modulation of autonomic state, including cardiac vagal tone (indexed by RSA). Several studies have evaluated whether "regulatory-disordered" infants have an inability to systematically regulate RSA and whether this deficit may precede developmental problems associated with compromised attention skills and emotional control. As described earlier, the ability to regulate the vagal brake systematically has been proposed as a theoretical model to explain the relation between RSA and behavioral regulation (i.e., adaptive and appropriate social and attentional responses to environmental challenges).

Porges et al. (1996) hypothesized that infants who had difficulties regulating RSA during social–attention tasks would have difficulties developing appropriate social interactions requiring reciprocal engagement and disengagement strategies. Infants were assessed for RSA at 9 months of age and tested for behavioral problems at 3 years of age; infants who at 9 months expressed greater decreases in RSA in response to the test situation had fewer overall behavior problems when measured at 3 years. Specifically, infants with more responsive RSA responses had in childhood fewer social withdrawal problems and fewer aggressive behaviors and expressed less depressed behavior. These and other observations support the usefulness of the vagal brake construct to understand how autonomic state serves to support cognitive, affective, and social engagement processes.

Support for the vagal brake hypothesis also comes from DeGangi et al. (1991) in which infants between 8 and 11 months were compared as a function of the presence or absence of an established regulatory disorder. RSA was measured during both sensory and cognitive challenges. In this study, efficient withdrawal of the vagal brake during a challenge occurred only in the normal infants. These findings suggest that vagal regulation of the heart reflects features of the infant's ability to modulate arousal and to mediate complex behavior. Furthermore, deficits in this ability to regulate vagal control of the heart underlie the diagnostic characteristics of the infant with a regulatory disorder. Additional studies have evaluated whether difficulties during infancy in regulating the vagal brake (i.e., decreasing RSA) during social and attentional tasks were related to behavioral outcome. Changes in RSA represent a dynamic adjustment of the inhibitory action of the vagus (i.e., vagal brake) on the heart. Functionally, the removal of the vagal brake provides a physiological state that promotes vigilance as an intermediary and precautionary psychological process to monitor risk in the environment. The outcome of this assessment includes the induction of physiological states in which social behaviors can proceed or in which defensive fight–flight strategies associated with increased sympathetic excitation are necessary. If defensive behaviors are not necessary to maintain or negotiate safety, then the rapid vagal regulatory mechanisms that dampen autonomic state are reinstated, allowing the individual to calm and self-sooth.

Further support for this interpretation can be seen in the infant data in which suppression of RSA is correlated with maternal reports of longer attention spans and being more easily soothed (see Huffman et al., 1998). Consistent with the adaptive functions of the vagal brake in social behavior, Stifter and Corey (2001) reported that 12-month-old infants who suppressed RSA during a challenge were rated by experimenters as more socially approaching. Toddlers with greater externalizing behaviors exhibited less suppression of RSA during laboratory procedures (Calkins & Dedmon, 2000). Moreover, in one of the few studies examining the relation between RSA reactivity and executive function, Blair and Peters (2003) reported that decreases in RSA during a cognitive task were associated with teacher reports of greater on-task behavior in preschool children. Thus, infants and young children who react to a variety of challenges by appropriately reducing RSA appear to exhibit a greater capacity to engage both people (i.e., social engagement behaviors) and objects (i.e., sustained attention). These findings are consistent with the polyvagal theory in which a link between vagal regulatory abilities (e.g., changes in the amplitude of RSA) and adaptive behaviors (e.g., vigilance, mobilization, and social engagement) are mapped.

The ability to suppress RSA contributes to an understanding of physiological mechanisms potentially mediating self-regulation. Thus, both higher baseline RSA and the ability to regulate RSA to challenge (i.e., suppression during attention demands) are characteristics of infants who will have fewer behavioral problems during early childhood.

In contrast, there is a subset of children who have high RSA and lack the ability to regulate RSA via the vagal brake in response to environmental challenges. This subtype of fussy or difficult infants appears to have developmental problems and is hyperreactive to environmental stimuli; however, these children also often have symptoms of a hyperreactive visceral feedback system (e.g., digestive problems). These studies demonstrate two important relations: (a) higher baseline RSA is associated with greater reactivity and (b) greater suppression of RSA in response to challenge is associated with the ability to self-regulate. Data consistently confirm the hypothesis that children with clinical diagnoses differ from nonclinical samples (typical children) in their ability to regulate the vagal brake.

Vagal Regulation and Temperament

Behavioral regulation is a frequently reported feature of temperament. Often the construct of difficultness or negative behaviors is used to capture the features of individual differences in behavioral regulation in young infants. For example, Huffman et al. (1998) found that young infants (i.e., 12 weeks) with higher baseline RSA expressed fewer negative behaviors and were less disrupted by the experimental procedures. Moreover, consistent with the vagal brake concept, the infants who decreased RSA during the laboratory assessment were rated on maternal report temperament scales as having longer attention spans and being more easily soothed.

Porges, Doussard-Roosevelt, Portales, and Suess (1994) reported that at 9 months infants with a more difficult temperament according to maternal reports had greater vagal control of the heart (i.e., higher RSA). Moreover, measures of both RSA and maternal reports of difficultness were relatively stable from 9 months to 3 years (correlations approximately 0.7). Interestingly, higher RSA at 9 months (but not RSA at 3 years) was related to less difficult temperament at 3 years of age. These findings fit with research in which early behavioral reactivity or temperament has been shown to be a precursor of later social behavior (e.g., Calkins & Fox, 1992; Cicchetti, Ganiban, & Barnett, 1991). In another study with 5-month-old infants Bazhenova, Plonskaia, and Porges (2001) demonstrated, during a still-face procedure, that RSA levels paralleled positive affect, whereas decreases in RSA were associated with increases in motor activity and negative affect.

RSA before a challenge (baseline) appears to be an important indicator of self-regulatory autonomic and behavioral responses. However, this relation is not always consistent, and there are individuals with high baseline RSA, who do not suppress or regulate RSA during environmental challenges. Individuals with difficulties in regulating RSA tend to have difficulties regulating their emotions (DeGangi et al., 1991; Porges et al., 1996). Preliminary data suggest that infants with behavioral regulation problems have two important characteristics: high baseline RSA (Porges et al., 1994) and a deficit in the ability to suppress RSA during attention demanding situations (Porges et al., 1996). In addition, measures of behavioral reactivity during infancy can be misleading. For example, fussiness may be an adaptive behavior eliciting appropriate caregiving behaviors. Thus, although fussiness early in infancy may be related to developmental difficulties, it also may predict greater self-regulatory competence later in childhood. Our research supports this speculation. Although higher baseline RSA at 9 months was related to greater "difficultness" measured on the Infant Characteristics Questionnaire (Bates, Freeland, & Lounsbury, 1979) at 9 months, the higher 9-month baseline RSA was also related to less "difficultness" at 3 years of age (Porges et al., 1994). These data suggest that higher infant RSA is associated not only with greater reactivity, interpreted by the mothers at 9 months as difficultness, but also with the self-regulatory skills interpreted by the mothers at 3 years as less "difficultness." These findings are consistent with the polyvagal theory because removal of the vagal brake enables an efficient expression of sympathetic tone and supports mobilization behaviors. Interestingly, the infants exhibiting the most integrated response patterns (i.e., parallel changes in RSA, affect, and motor activity) had the greatest decreases both in positive affect and in RSA in response to a stressor (still face) and were able to recover easily during the social interaction. Another subset of infants that exhibited less coordinated and smaller reactions to the stressor appeared to pay a "biological price" for this conservative response strategy because these children were unable to return to autonomic, behavioral, and affective homeostasis when the stressor was removed.

Vagal Regulation and Disorders of Affect

The outcome of these studies suggests that coordinated regulation of biobehavioral systems characterizes healthy development. In this context, is "dissociation" among response systems an index of vulnerability or risk? The general hypothesis that dissociation among response systems (e.g., heart rate and RSA) can characterize disorders of affect regulation is supported by a number of studies (Blair, Peters, & Granger, 2004; Calkins, 1997). For example, in the adult literature, there is dissociation between RSA and heart rate in the responses to challenge (posture shift) in perpetrators of domestic abuse (Umhau et al., 2002). Posture shift challenges the baroreceptors, which trigger heart rate changes, to maintain blood flow and pressure to the brain when there is an alteration in the relative position of the head and the heart. The vagal regulation of heart rate is a major neural process, mediated by baroreceptor feedback, contributing to the maintenance of blood pressure with posture shift. With most individuals, the shift from sitting to standing, or from supine to standing, will result in reduced RSA and increased heart rate. In the Umhau et al. study, there were significant within-group correlations between the change in RSA and the change in heart rate for subjects within the control groups (consisting of individuals with no history of interpersonal violence). However, within the group of perpetrators of domestic abuse, there was dissociation between the individual changes in RSA and heart rate. A similar dissociation between RSA and heart rate changes was observed in a project investigating adult posttraumatic stress disorder (PTSD; Sahar, Shalev, & Porges, 2001). In the Sahar et al. study, subjects who experienced trauma and developed PTSD were contrasted with subjects who experienced trauma and did not develop PTSD. Both groups had similar levels of RSA. However, individual differences between the heart rate and RSA responses from baseline to the mental arithmetic condition were strongly correlated only in the group that did not develop PTSD ($r = 0.76$). In the group that developed PTSD, the two measures were dissociated ($r = 0.12$). In a study with borderline personality disorder, the same pattern was observed in which changes in heart rate and RSA were not coupled in the borderline group, whereas the control group exhibited a tight covariation between heart rate and RSA (Austin, Riniolo, & Porges, 2007). Similarly, adult women who had a history of child or adult abuse exhibited atypical recovery of vagal regulation of the heart following exercise (Dale et al., 2009). These findings suggest that the neural mechanisms mediating the heart rate response may be different in individuals at risk for or with specific psychiatric disturbances that compromise or limit behaviors associated with the social engagement system.

THE AUTONOMIC NERVOUS SYSTEM AS A NEURAL PLATFORM FOR SOCIAL BEHAVIOR

The Development of Autonomic Regulation

During early development, the autonomic nervous system is rapidly changing and forming a "neural" platform to support the expanding abilities of the child to explore within the vast domain of social behavior. Coupled with this ability to explore is a change in how the child is able to use others to regulate physiological and behavioral states. As the child develops, neural circuits become differentiated that are dedicated to either engaging objects or engaging others.

The conceptualization of the autonomic nervous system as a functional neural platform that supports both engagement behaviors and the regulation of behavioral and physiological state must also take into account the dynamically changing behavioral repertoire and social-interactive needs of the young infant. The infant needs "other" to regulate. As is the case for humans and many other mammals, birth is not a transition into independence but an extension of a period of dependence. Two global features characterize this period of dependence: (a) neural feedback loops for state regulation or self-regulation are not complete with the consequence of state disruptions (e.g., fussing, crying, hunger, feeding) requiring a "benevolent" caregiver for support and (b) the infant's adaptive quest for safety is compromised without the "benevolent" interactions of a caregiver because the immature infant has limited abilities to detect risk, cue others, and mobilize to execute defense strategies.

These behavioral features are dependent on shifts in neural regulation of the autonomic nervous system. However, within the developmental sciences and pediatrics, with an emphasis on mother–infant development and skill attainment, the autonomic nervous system has played a background role. Little concern has been placed on the autonomic nervous system as a developing and dynamically changing resource contributing to the complex repertoire of infant behaviors and, in part, mediating, much of the dynamic interaction that the infant is having with both others and "objects."

On the basis of the polyvagal theory, the development of the mammalian myelinated vagus is critical in the development of both behavior and autonomic regulation. It is through the face–heart connection that social interactions and social engagement behaviors are linked to autonomic regulation. Thus, with more optimal vagal regulation, there are features of more adaptive social behavior. Without a functioning myelinated vagus, social behavior is compromised, and more primitive defensive strategies fight–flight mobilization (e.g., tantrums) and shutdown behaviors are more frequently expressed.

The human infant is not born with a totally functioning myelinated vagal system. The mammalian vagus is only partially myelinated at birth and rapidly develops during the first year postpartum. Morphological studies demonstrate a rapid developmental increase in total myelinated vagal fibers from 24 weeks through adolescence, with the greatest increases observed from approximately 30 to 32 gestational age to approximately 1 month postpartum (see Sachis, Armstrong, Becker, & Bryan, 1982). On the basis of these observations, it is clear that preterm infants born before 30 weeks gestational age are coming into the world without a functioning mammalian vagus. Without a functioning mammalian vagus, the preterm has a limited ability to regulate visceral state and is dependent solely on the sympathetic nervous system and the phylogenetically older unmyelinated vagus. The consequence of this profile of autonomic regulation is that the preterm infant reacts with increases in heart rate via the sympathetic nervous system to support tantrums and mobilization behaviors and is vulnerable to clinically dangerous episodes of bradycardia and apnea (i.e., massive slowing of the heart and cessation of breathing) via the old unmyelinated vagus.

Other features of vagal regulation change during early development. During the first year of life, there is a progressive decrease in the ratio of unmyelinated to myelinated vagal fibers (Pereyra, Zhang, Schmidt, & Becker, 1992). As the ratio of myelinated vagal fibers increases, the infant gains greater control of visceral state, which functionally positions the infant to express improved behavioral regulation and social engagement behaviors.

Human studies monitoring RSA during the preterm period illustrate a monotonic increase in RSA from 32 to 37 weeks gestational age (Doussard-Roosevelt, McClenny, & Porges, 2001; Doussard-Roosevelt, Porges, Scanlon, Alemi, & Scanlon, 1997). This maturational shift in RSA parallels the period of increased myelination of vagal fibers (Sachis et al., 1982). Developmentally, the number of myelinated vagal fibers increases linearly from 24 to 28 weeks gestation until full-term birth, when the number of fibers is comparable to those observed in adolescence (Sachis et al., 1982). More recent neuroanatomical studies suggest that the myelination process is active during the first year of life, particularly during the first 3 months (Pereyra et al., 1992). In longitudinal studies, there is a monotonic increase in RSA from 3 to 13 months (e.g., Fracasso, Porges, Lamb, & Rosenberg, 1994; Izard et al., 1991). Others report an increase in RSA during this period with a trend toward greater stability in the regulation of RSA (e.g., see Alkon et al., 2006). It is possible that although the number of myelinated vagal fibers does not rapidly increase after early development, their function and ability to regulate visceral state (which requires peripheral feedback and central structures) may change developmentally, especially as the ratio of myelinated to unmyelinated vagal fibers increase.

Support for this possibility was observed when basal levels of RSA monitored at 9 months and at 3 years indicated not only significant increases in RSA but also a change in the regulation of the vagal brake when the mean suppression of RSA during mental assessment tasks increased substantially from 9 months to 3 years (Porges et al., 1994). Thus, not only may there be changes in the myelination of the vagus during early development but the function of these myelinated fibers might change and become more "efficient" in regulating visceral state. If visceral homeostasis is challenged and the vagal brake is unable to regulate visceral homeostasis (as might be the case with infants who are persistently crying and fussy), then social engagement behaviors coupled with appropriate behavioral state regulation will be minimized.

In ongoing studies in our laboratory, Senta Furman is investigating this question. In that study, a large sample of infants between 3 months and 3 years of age are being tested in a still-face paradigm. Consistent with previous research, with increasing age there is a monotonic increase in RSA with the steepest slope of increase being observed during the period of 3 to 12 months. When the infants were partitioned into 3- to 6-month and 6- to 12-month groups, the pattern of RSA and heart rate reactivity to the still-face procedure were dramatically different. In the 3- to 6-month group, the still face of the mother disrupted the infants' visceral state, and the infants did not have neural resource to calm and self-regulate. In this young group, not only did RSA drop and heart rate increase to the blank face of the mother, but when the mother's face became animated and she attempted to socially engage and console the infant, the infant did not calm and continued to depress further RSA and increase heart rate. In contrast, when the 6- to 12-month group was confronted with the same still-face procedures, the infants had minimal changes in autonomic state that rapidly recovered when the mother engaged them. These data potentially represent the functional consequence of the developmental changes in the morphology of the vagal system and reflect how the infant is developmentally gaining a greater capacity to "self-regulate" its emotional state.

In parallel with the changing degree of improved vagal regulation of visceral state, the infant develops greater abilities to self-regulate and self-soothe. With the aging process, there appears to be a decrease in the functioning of this system. Cross-sectional research has documented age-associated declines in RSA (e.g., Byrne, Fleg, Vaitkevicius, Wright, & Porges, 1996). Byrne and colleagues studied healthy participants between the ages of 20 and 90 years from the Baltimore Longitudinal Study on Aging. They reported significant correlations between age and RSA of approximately –0.6. This effect was similar when the participants were seated, standing, or in the supine position. In contrast, heart rate was only weakly correlated with age and in only seated or standing postures (i.e., correlations of approximately 0.2–0.3). Interestingly, these age-related changes appear to be the mirror image of the relation between RSA and age during the first 3 years of life in which the positive correlation between age in months and RSA is also approximately +0.6. In both age samples (infants and aging), there are large individual differences. Thus, it is possible that paradigms can be employed to evaluate RSA under a variety of challenges. For example, it may be possible to determine the status of neural development and visceral regulation in typical individuals who are developing or aging, as well as atypical individuals who appear to have behavioral and visceral state regulation difficulties. On the basis of this literature and an understanding of the neural mechanisms of the social engagement system, it is assumed that associated with the decreasing vagal regulation of the heart, there will be difficulties in behavioral and visceral state regulation, and these difficulties will be manifested as compromised social engagement behaviors.

Autonomic Changes During Development Parallel the Phylogenetic History of Mammals

The unique features of the autonomic nervous that support mammalian social behavior start to develop during the last trimester of fetal life. Specifically, the myelinated vagus starts to function and the myelination process rapidly continues during the first year postpartum. This developmental process is observable in parallel developmental changes, which include (a) increases in the amplitude of RSA, (b) improved abilities both to spontaneous engage with others, and (c) the capacity to self-regulate and calm. In this context, the quantification of RSA predicts not only risk for survival in the preterm (Porges, 1992), but also serves as a developmental index of neural maturation that is related to more optimal outcomes. (see Doussard-Roosevelt et al., 1997).

From the phylogenetic perspective presented earlier, there is a greater understanding of the vulnerabilities of the preterm infant. When a preterm infant is born early within the third trimester, the myelinated vagus is not functioning, and the response of the autonomic nervous system to challenge is similar to that of reptiles. As in reptiles, the adaptive defensive responses of the preterm infant are expressed as massive slowing of heart rate (i.e., bradycardia) and cessation of breathing (i.e., apnea). The comparatively smaller and less cerebralized brains of reptiles can function well with limited oxygen. In contrast, the preterm infant's brain circuits are vulnerable to decreased blood flow and oxygenation. Thus, an autonomic response pattern that is adaptive for survival in reptiles predicts risk and vulnerability when seen in preterm infants.

Abundant research in developmental psychobiology has revealed that during the last trimester of gestation and the first year postpartum, child development is characterized by an increase in vagal output to the heart. This increases in vagal control of the heart parallels developmental outcomes.

Convergent with the rapid myelination of the vagus during late gestation and first year postpartum, the ratio of unmyelinated to myelinated vagal fibers decreases. From a physiological perspective, this developmental trend covaries with a more efficient regulation of the vagal brake measured by reliable changes in RSA. Functionally, this increase in myelinated vagal activity allows the healthy infant's ability to self-soothe and calm.

From a behavioral perspective, the functional impact of these developmental changes in vagal regulation on both the heart and behavior can be seen when infants are tested in a still-face paradigm. In the still face paradigm, the mother stops expressing any facial cue or gesture. The sight of the mother's flat affect usually triggers the infant to attempt to elicit engagement behaviors from the mother. When the infant fails to secure the mother's attention and interest, the infant may lose control of behavioral state, followed by fussing or crying. In this paradigm, after a brief period, the mother reengages the infant. Developmentally, there are large differences in the behavior and autonomic reactivity between infants who are 3 to 6 months of age versus infants between 6 and 12 months Young infants typically have less capacity to recruit the inhibitory systems (including the myelinated vagus) to self-soothe and to calm. In contrast, in response to the social overtures of their mother, older infants more readily adjust, respond with positive affect, and can return to the pre-still-face physiological state (i.e., slower heart rate and increases in RSA). These developmental differences in social behavior are paralleled by the maturation of the vagal system and an increase in myelinated pathways. As this system matures neurophysiologically, it provides an enhanced neural platform for the child to regulate physiological and behavioral state and to expand the skills of social behavior. Although, there are large individual differences in these systems, studies have repeatedly demonstrated that both higher amplitude RSA and more systematic regulation of RSA during social and cognitive challenges are related to more prosocial outcomes (see Calkins, Graziano, & Keane, 2007; Hastings et al., 2008; Kennedy, Rubin, Hastings, & Maisel, 2004; Porges et al., 1996).

During older age, the opposite pattern is often observed. With aging both physiological processes and behavior begin to reverse. There is an age-related reduction in the small diameter myelinated vagal fibers and a more limited capacity to self-soothe or calm in the elderly. Thus, the vagal mechanisms that had served the adult well in social settings may no longer be available.

Social support enhances survival and improves behavior, especially in aging populations. This may be explained in part by use or "exercise" of the expanded social engagement system during social interactions. Future research needs to investigate whether opportunities for social interactions among geriatric populations are not only characterized by the expression of facial affect and vocal prosody (via the striated muscles of the face) but also "exercise" the vagal brake, especially under conditions that involve reciprocal regulation of visceral state.

The Social Nervous System Is Involved in Neuroception, Emotion, and Contingent Sociality

Group living is not restricted to mammals but may be especially beneficial to both survival and reproduction in highly social mammals, including humans. Using various techniques, including the methods of classical neurobiology and imaging, evolved neural pathways—functioning together as a social nervous system—have been described (Adolphs, 2006). For example, uniquely mammalian neural circuits exist to allow facial expression and vocal intonation. The social nervous system enables individuals to detect and respond to the features of others as both living and safe, providing a critical component of social emotionality. In addition, the capacity to detect and respond to these features in others permits rapid and contingent responses to the emotional feelings of others (Adolphs, 2006). In addition, specific autonomic and neuroendocrine processes coordinate social behaviors and emotional states (Porges, 2007).

The mammalian nervous system has the ability to signal and to detect social cues in others reflecting states such as pain, distress, or joy. However, social communication is highly species-specific. The primate head and face are unique among mammals. In humans, vocal communication, including language, has special significance for social interactions. The functions of the larynx, pharynx, and middle ear also are species-specific. In humans, these systems are under the control of complex voluntary and autonomic mechanisms. Visual cues are transmitted and received by a defined visual system. The muscles of the upper face, necessary for sending social cues, also are innervated by the autonomic nervous system. Taken together, these coordinated systems provide a "face–heart" connection that is critical to social communication. This system permits a total body response to external social cues as well as forms of threat.

Emotional and visceral states influence how we feel about and react to others, and thus our capacity for sociality. The neural evaluation of risk is rapid and can occur without conscious awareness. For that reason, the term *neuroception* has been introduced to describe how neural circuits, including the autonomic nervous system, function as a safety–threat detection system capable of distinguishing among situations that are safe, dangerous, or life-threatening (Porges, 2003).

Awareness of factors that regulate emotional responses and feelings also lead us to a deeper understanding of the evolved neurobiology of sociality. For example, internal (visceral) sensations make up an important component of our reactivity to others, and thus color our social behavior. Visceral sensations are interpreted as the often vague experience of changes in visceral organs (e.g., heart and gut). This information travels to and from the brainstem through the autonomic nervous system.

Neural and endocrine processes act on sensory, integrative, emotional, and motor systems. It is important to remember that the autonomic nervous system is a bidirectional system, including both sensory and motor components. Brainstem structures involved in the regulation of autonomic state are sentries of visceral states and feelings, but they also convey defensive signals, including emotional cues, to the periphery. The lower brainstem provides a portal through which sensory information related to peripheral sensations, including social cues, contributes to the general activation of higher brain structures including the hypothalamus, amygdala, and cortex. Regulation of the viscera by higher levels is typically not experienced as voluntary. However, social and emotional experiences, perceived at the level of the cortex, are capable of influencing the heart and gut through sensory information transmitted through in brainstem and autonomic nervous system. Brainstem structures convey information to brain regions, such as the insula, that both regulate autonomic state and transmit features of this activation to higher brain structures, where these experiences may be perceived as emotional states or experiences (Critchley, Wiens, Rothstein, Ohman, & Dolan, 2004).

In humans, the evolved modifications, muscles, and peripheral nerves of the face and head took on functions that allowed control over speech and listening. Auditory and visual functions are coordinated with visceral and emotional states through a vagal brake (Porges et al., 1996). The neural regulation of the muscles of the face and head are coordinated by a myelinated component of the parasympathetic nervous system (with faster neural transmission than its unmyelinated counterpart). This faster component of the parasympathetic (vagal) system fosters calm behavioral states and dampens reactivity of the sympathetic nervous system and the HPA axis (Porges, 2007). Through the more recently evolved component of the parasympathetic (myelinated vagal) nervous system, social cues and experiences gain the capacity to overcome threat or fear. Dynamic interactions between safety and fear are at the heart of sociality and relationships.

NEUROCHEMICAL FACTORS COORDINATE AUTONOMIC STATE AND SOCIAL BEHAVIOR

Oxytocin: A Mammalian Hormone Capable of Influencing Positive Social Behavior

The mammalian neuropeptide hormone oxytocin is associated with many positive social interactions (including birth, lactation, parenting, and general affiliation), making its dysregulation a likely target of social bond disruption. Oxytocin and the related neuropeptide vasopressin are also important regulators of the autonomic nervous system (Figure 2.2).

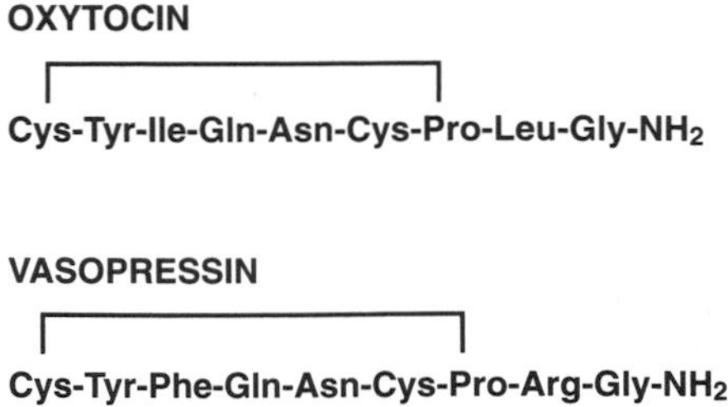

Figure 2.2 OXYTOCIN and VASOPRESSIN are ancient neuropeptides that differ structurally from each other by only 2 of 9 amino acids. Both are released within the nervous system, as well as into the circulation at the posterior pituitary gland. Both can influence social behavior and social bonding, and they interact dynamically with each other. Oxytocin is generally associated with prosocial behaviors, reduced activation, immobility and passive forms of coping, and compensatory or restorative states. Vasopressin is more often associated with mobilization, vigilance, defensiveness and active forms of coping. Sex differences in these neuropeptides within the brain may help to explain sex differences in social behavior.

Oxytocin and vasopressin are synthesized in high concentrations in cells of the paraventricular (PVN) and the supraoptic nuclei (SON) of the hypothalamus. Oxytocin and vasopressin are generally made in separate cells. From the PVN and SON, oxytocin and vasopressin are carried by axonal transport to the posterior pituitary, where they are released into the blood stream. Vasopressin is also synthesized in several other areas, including the medial amygdala and bed nucleus of the stria terminalis (BNST), and is released into the lateral septum (LS; DeVries & Simerly, 2002). Both of these peptides are released into the central nervous system and diffuse through brain tissue, acting on receptors in several target areas. The effects of oxytocin and vasopressin include action on their own receptors and, in some cases, cross-reacting with each other's receptors (Landgraf & Neumann, 2004).

Neuropeptides and Mammalian Evolution

Oxytocin and vasopressin are small peptides, composed of a six amino acid ring, with a three amino acid tail. These peptides differ from each other by two of nine amino acids and may interact with each other to help account for some of the complexity of their behavioral effects. Oxytocin and vasopressin are synthesized primarily in the central nervous system (Landgraf & Neumann, 2004). Oxytocin, released into the blood stream and acting on peripheral tissues, is classically considered a hormone of birth and is essential for milk ejection. Vasopressin is associated with the regulation of blood pressure and other aspects of cardiovascular function. Vasopressin also acts on the kidney to regulate water balance by promoting water retention.

Neuropeptides, and specifically oxytocin, probably played a pivotal role in the evolution of primates and primate cognition. As the central nervous systems and skulls of primates expanded, mechanisms evolved to facilitate birth and postnatal nourishment for the infant (Carter & Altemus, 1997). Oxytocin facilitates the birth process through powerful muscle contraction. It may even protect the fetal nervous system from hypoxia during the birth (Tyzio et al., 2006). Oxytocin also facilitates milk ejection and thus lactation. Lactation in turn permits the birth of immature infants, allowing postnatal cortical and intellectual development in young that are dependent on their mother as a source of both food and caregiving.

Evidence regarding the actions of oxytocin and vasopressin comes from mice made mutant for peptides or their receptors (known as knockout mice; Mantella, Vollmer, & Amico, 2005; Mantella, Vollmer, Li, & Amico, 2003; Nomura et al., 2003; Pedersen, Vadlamudi, Boccia, & Amico, 2006; Ragnauth et al., 2005; Winslow & Insel, 2002). Oxytocin knockout (OTKO) mice are social but show deficiencies in social recognition and social memory. OTKO mice also are less able to manage stressful experiences, especially those with an emotional or social component (Mantella et al., 2005).

Among the consistent effects of exposure to *exogenous* oxytocin are increases in social behavior and reductions in emotionality and reactivity to stressors (Carter, 1998; Pedersen, 1997; Uvnas-Moberg, 1998). The effects of oxytocin include the facilitation of immobile postures, such as lordosis, necessary for mating (Pedersen & Boccia, 2006) and kyphosis, arched back huddling over pups (Bales, Kramer, Lewis-Reese, & Carter, 2004; Stern & Lonstein, 2001). In the context of mammalian reproduction and energy conservation, these behaviors are adaptive.

Oxytocin and Human Social Behavior

The following features of the actions of oxytocin, derived primarily from animal research, help us to understand its role in human social behavior. Treatment with oxytocin quickly facilitates positive social behaviors, including selective partner preferences and parental behavior (Carter & Keverne, 2002). Oxytocin receptors also correlate with positive social behavior. Oxytocin is made in and acts on the brain, especially in the hypothalamus and areas of the nervous system that influence the emotions. Oxytocin is capable of down-regulating or buffering the response to stressors and the reactivity of the autonomic nervous system, including heart rate (Grippo et al., 2009). Oxytocin is released during positive social interactions and may facilitate the ability to be trusting, generous, and socially perceptive and to feel safe and relaxed. Growth and restoration are facilitated by oxytocin (Uvnas-Moberg, 1998). The role of oxytocin is well established in birth, lactation, and parenting, as well as sexual interactions and stress management. In a context of safety, this in turn may feed back on the nervous system, including the autonomic nervous system, to further enhance relaxation.

It can be argued that the biological prototype for mammalian sociality can be found in the mother–infant interaction. Lactation is unique to mammals and relies on oxytocin (among other hormones). The biology of lactation may be highly relevant to human emotion. Women who are nursing their babies experience modifications of the central nervous system and HPA axis. Compared with bottle-feeding mothers, breast-feeding women are buffered from physiological and psychological stress. For example, the levels of HPA axis hormones, including cortisol and vasopressin, released following intense exercise were about twice as high in bottle-feeding versus breast-feeding mothers (matched for other variables; Altemus, Deuster, Gallivan, Carter, & Gold, 1995). Compared with bottle-feeding mothers, breast-feeding women were buffered from physiological and emotional stress (Altemus et al., 2001; Carter, Altemus, & Chrousos, 2001; Redwine, Altemus, Leong, & Carter, 2001). It has also been shown by Heinrichs et al. (2001), in within-subject studies of lactating women, that proximity to an episode of milk letdown (and a presumed pulsatile release of oxytocin) was associated with reduced HPA activity.

The same neuroendocrine processes that are associated with birth and lactation were implicated in maternal behavior and, more specifically, in filial bonding (Keverne, 2005). Among the neuropeptide hormones that have been implicated in maternal bonding, as well as adult sociality and selective pair bond formation, are oxytocin and vasopressin. Oxytocin and vasopressin may act in part by reducing social fear, allowing animals to engage in social interactions and eventually the formation of social bonds. The salience of a relationship may be reinforced by neural mechanisms, involving dopamine, that are shared with reward and pleasure. At the core of the capacity to form selective social bonds are interactions among oxytocin, vasopressin, and hormones of the HPA axis. Social bond formation requires not only systems that rely on dopamine (Aragona et al., 2006) but possibly also the endogenous opioids, through gender-specific and brain-area-specific interactions with oxytocin and vasopressin (Carter & Keverne, 2002).

Rodent Models for Studying the Neurobiology of Adult Sociality and Pair Bond Formation

Understanding of the neurobiology of sociality and the description of the "social nervous system" has arisen primarily from research in nonhuman mammals and especially in rodents. Social relationships have been described in highly social species, and particularly those that (like humans) are either socially monogamous or otherwise capable of developing extended families built around selective social interactions (Carter et al., 1995; Hrdy, 2005).

One approach to understanding the neurobiology of positive social behaviors has been to examine species differences in sociality. Among these the best known are from the rodent genus *Microtus* (voles). On the basis of both field and laboratory data, several species from this genus (including prairie and pine voles) are considered to be socially monogamous, whereas others (including meadow and montane voles) are usually classified as polygamous. Among the defining features of social monogamy in rodents is the capacity of adults to form *selective* social relationships or pair bonds. Comparisons among these closely related voles have provided a new perspective on the behavioral, neuroendocrine, and neuroanatomical basis of social behavior in general and social bonds in particular (Carter, 1998; Carter et al., 1995; Young & Wang, 2004).

The prairie vole (*M. ochrogaster*) lives in grasslands of central North America. Field data, primarily from central Illinois, suggest that in prairie voles the most common family group in nature consists of one adult male and one adult female and their offspring (Getz & Carter, 1996). Within family groups, approximately three fourths of the adult pairs remain together until one member dies. In less than 10% of cases is there evidence that the male has abandoned his female partner. After the death of one member of a pair, fewer than 20% of the survivors acquire a new mate. Thus, in nature a male–female pair bond is at the core of their social organization.

The assumption that environmental factors can influence both the evolution and expression of monogamy provides a clue to the physiological substrates of the social behaviors that define monogamy. Although the overall patterns of social monogamy are species-specific, within-species differences also are common. For example, voles from different habitats may show reliable differences in the traits of social monogamy (Roberts, Gustafson, & Carter, 1997; Roberts, Williams, Wang, & Carter, 1998). Within-species and individual differences (Carter, Boone, Pournajafi-Nazarloo, & Bales, 2009) offer additional insight into the neural mechanisms of social behavior.

Studies in adult prairie voles have implicated vasopressin and oxytocin in pair bond formation. These neuropeptides may be especially important to adaptive behavior and thus vulnerable to change by experience. Adding exogenous oxytocin facilitated pair bonding, especially in females; in contrast, blocking the oxytocin receptor inhibited pair bond formation (Williams, Insel, Harbaugh, & Carter, 1994). Under some conditions, blocking the vasopressin receptor also can interfere with pair bonding in females (Cho, DeVries, Williams, & Carter, 1999). Male prairie voles also rely on oxytocin, but vasopressin appears to be of particular importance, allowing males to develop partner preferences and also defend their partner from other males (Winslow, Hastings, Carter, Harbaugh, & Insel, 1993).

In nature or under seminatural conditions variation in the vasopressin receptor exceeds that observed in the laboratory. These studies also support the notion that variation in the vasopressin system may have an important role in subsequent social behavior and reproductive success (Ophir, Wolff, & Phelps, 2008; Phelps & Young, 2003).

Oxytocin Influences Autonomic Function and Sympathoadrenal Axis

Oxytocin is synthesized in the hypothalamus and acts in both the central and peripheral nervous systems to influence behavior and physiological processes. The hypothalamus is an important site of convergence for neural communication relating to stress, affective disorders, and cardiovascular regulation; thus, it is not surprising that oxytocin influences the HPA axis and autonomic function. This peptide may also play a role in autonomic tone, because oxytocin-deficient mice show disruptions in sympathovagal balance (Mantella et al., 2003, 2005). With regard to endocrine function, oxytocin suppresses the activity of the HPA axis in natural and experimental settings in humans.

Oxytocinergic projections from the PVN to key brainstem regions such as the NTS and the DVC are important in cardiovascular control. The presence of oxytocin binding sites in the DVC has been verified through autoradiography in the rat.

Dynamic Interactions Among Peptides May Influence Approach and Avoidance Behaviors

Dynamic interactions between oxytocin and vasopressin may be of particular importance to the approach and avoidance components of sociality. Intranasal oxytocin facilitates "trust" behavior, as measured in a computer game (Kosfeld, Heinrichs, Zak, Fischbacher, & Fehr, 2005) and the ability to detect subtle cues from pictures of eyes (Domes, Heinrichs, Michel, Berger, & Herpertz, 2007). In the case of autonomic–emotional effects of oxytocin and vasopressin, the actions of these two peptides probably differ in direction and emotional valence (Viviani & Stoop, 2008). Increases in exogenous oxytocin are associated with immobility (Porges, 1998), reduced reactivity to stressors, and reduced responses to fear-eliciting stimuli and pain.

Various brainstem neural systems, including those that rely on peptides such as oxytocin, vasopressin, and CRF, help to regulate emotional states including approach–avoidance reactions and the tendency of mammals to immobilize (Porges, 1998). Oxytocin and vasopressin are synthesized and are particularly abundant in the hypothalamus. However, these neuropeptides have the capacity to move through the brain by diffusion, rather than acting only across a synapse or requiring transport by the circulatory system (Landgraf & Neumann, 2004). For this reason, neuropeptides may have pervasive effects on the central nervous system and may reach distant receptors including those in the cortex and in lower brainstem areas, such as the DVC, responsible for autonomic functions. This property of oxytocin and vasopressin may help to explain their capacity to integrate behavioral and emotional responses.

Social behaviors and social support are critical to the capacity to regulate reactivity to stressors including actions on the HPA axis and the autonomic nervous system. At least some of the consequences of social interactions for other forms of behavior, including coping with a stressor, may be mediated through oxytocin and vasopressin (Carter, 1998).

Vasopressin and CRF are more typically associated with vigilance, mobilization, and increased reactivity to stressors. Vasopressin may increase arousal and has the capacity to synergize with CRF to increase HPA axis activity (Engelmann, Landgraf, & Wotjak, 2004). Active coping and overt defensive behaviors, and possibly anxiety, may rely on vasopressin and CRF, whereas oxytocin is important to behaviors that are characterized by immobility and passive coping strategies, including the behaviors associated with mating, birth, and lactation.

Oxytocin, vasopressin, and CRF receptors are found in many limbic structures, including the extended amygdala. The amygdala and its connections serve a role in the integration of reactions to various kinds of sensory stimuli, including approach and avoidance (Davis, 2006; Viviani & Stoop, 2008). In human males, intranasal administration of oxytocin inhibited the activity of the amygdala and altered downstream connections to brainstem structures involved in the regulation of the autonomic nervous system (Kirsch et al., 2005). Vasopressin and CRF, acting centrally (in areas including the BNST, amygdala, and lateral septum), may elevate vigilance and defensiveness, possibly serving in some cases as an antagonist to the effects of oxytocin. Behaviors mediated by the central amygdala may mediate stimulus-specific fear, whereas the BNST has been implicated in experiences related to anxiety. Other peptides, including CRF, released during "stressful" experiences, may be anxiogenic, acting in the extended amygdala, including the BNST, to influence responses to dangerous or threatening cues (Davis, 2006). At least some of the fear-associated or defensive actions of CRF or vasopressin can be counteracted by oxytocin. Thus, oxytocin may have the capacity to reduce fear and calm the sympathetic responses to stressful stimuli (Viviani & Stoop, 2008).

Receptors for Oxytocin and Vasopressin

Only one oxytocin receptor has been described. The same oxytocin receptor is present in neural tissue and in other parts of the body including the uterus (Gimpl & Fahrenholz, 2001). Three receptor subtypes have been identified for vasopressin. Of these, the V1a receptor, which is found in the brain, has been associated with social behavior (Bales, van Westerhuyzen, et al., 2007) especially in males (Winslow et al., 1993). The V1b receptor has been implicated in endocrine and behavioral responses to stressors and aggression and may play a particularly important role in behaviors that rely on olfaction or olfactory memory (Caldwell, Wersinger, & Young, 2008). The V2 receptor is localized to the kidney and does not appear to be involved in behavior.

Receptors for both oxytocin and vasopressin are localized in areas of the nervous system that regulate social, emotional, and adaptive behaviors; the HPA axis; and the autonomic nervous system (Barberis & Tribollet, 1996). Both individual and species differences in V1a receptor distributions have been identified. Among the sources of these differences are species-typical genetic variations in the promoter region of the gene for the V1a receptor

(Hammock & Young, 2005). The oxytocin receptor also shows species differences in expression (Insel & Shapiro, 1992; Witt, Carter, & Insel, 1991).

Oxytocin and vasopressin and their receptors have broad effects on neuroendocrine and autonomic reactions to threat or danger (Carter, 1998; Koolhaas, Everts, de Ruiter, de Boer, & Bohus, 1998; Porges, 1998, 2001) and may be components of adaptive and sexually dimorphic responses to stressors, especially stressors of a social nature. Both oxytocin and vasopressin receptors are found in brainstem regions, such as the central nucleus of the amygdala, that regulate the autonomic nervous system (Landgraf et al., 1990), including the sympathetic and parasympathetic systems (Porges, 2007; Viviani & Stoop, 2008).

Corticotropin Releasing Factor

A cocktail of hormones and neurotransmitters is probably necessary for pair bonding and other forms of sociality. CRF is another major neuropeptide that has been implicated in social behavior and is also a major component of the HPA axis. CRF is made in the brain and other tissues and plays a complex role in birth, maternal behavior, anxiety, and adult social bonding. CRF receptors distributions are species-specific and sexually dimorphic, which also may contribute to species and sex differences in pair bond formation. The effects of CRF on pair bonding in prairie voles are dose-dependent but thus far have only been studied in males (DeVries, Gupta, Cardillo, Cho, & Carter 2002; Lim et al., 2007). CRF synergizes with vasopressin to promote the release of the adrenal steroid corticosterone. CRF, administered directly into the nucleus accumbens (NAcc), a major site for reinforcement, also facilitated pair bonding in male prairie voles but was not effective in nonmonogamous vole species (Lim et al., 2007).

Increases in CRF gene expression in the NAcc accompanied pair bonding. CRF also modulates (possibly amplifies) the release of dopamine, potentially contributing to the effects of CRF on pair bonding.

CRF also has been implicated in the response to the disruption of social bonds (Bosch, Nair, Ahern, Neumann, & Young, 2009). In prairie voles, separating the male from a sexual partner was followed by increases in passive coping responses, as measured in a forced swim test; these measures are considered indicative of depression. Animals separated from a sibling partner did not show these responses. Infusion of a nonselective CRF receptor antagonist reduced measures of depression, without disrupting the bond itself. Both CRF type 1 and 2 receptors were involved in the emergence of passive stress-coping behavior.

Components of the CRF axis, including the multiple receptors capable of binding CRF and a related peptide (urocortin), also help to down-regulate overreactivity in responses to stressors. For example, activation of the CRF type 2 receptor may serve to decrease anxiety and may be protective against depression-like behaviors (Bale, 2006). Urocortin, with functional relationships to CRF, also may serve as a "stress-coping" peptide.

Dopamine

Dopamine is a catecholamine, synthesized in the brain (as well as the adrenal medulla), that plays a role in behavioral activation and incentive seeking. Of particular relevance to pair bonding are dopamine receptors in the NAcc and the ventral pallidum. Prairie voles have high densities of oxytocin receptors in the NAcc, whereas nonmonogamous montane voles have very low densities of oxytocin receptors in the NAcc. Given the role of dopamine in reward (incentive seeking) and possibly reinforcement, dopamine sensitive regions are attractive candidates for regulating social attachments. For example, infusion of an oxytocin receptor antagonist into NAcc, but not the adjacent caudate putamen, prevents mating-induced partner preference formation (Young et al., 2005). These results suggest that partner preference formation in female prairie voles involves the activation of the mesolimbic dopamine reward circuitry. Dopamine is released within the NAcc in female prairie voles during mating and dopamine receptor antagonists prevent pair bond formation in female prairie voles (Gingrich, Liu, Cascio, Wang, & Insel, 2000).

Brain regions with high levels of dopaminergic input, including the NAcc, have also been implicated in suckling and the emergence of positive response to an infant (Parada, King, Li, & Fleming, 2008). Interactions between oxytocin and dopamine in the NAcc may be necessary to both maternal behavior and pair bonding.

Oxytocin receptors are especially abundant in the NAcc (shell region) in socially monogamous species, including prairie voles, but not in nonmonogamous voles (Insel & Shapiro, 1992). Administration of a general dopamine receptor antagonist in the NAcc blocked mating-induced partner preferences. In contrast, treatment with a dopamine agonist facilitated pair bonding, suggesting an essential role for dopamine in pair bond formation (Aragona et al., 2006). The action of dopamine on social bond formation and maintenance of these bonds is mediated through different subtypes of dopamine receptors. D2 receptors are necessary for pair bond formation. In contrast, D1 receptors play a role in the maintenance of social bonds, including an increase in selective and defensive aggression, which can help to defend and protect the pair bond. So far this work has been done only in males, although both sexes may show "mate guarding."

Vasopressin (V1a) receptors in the lateral septum have been specifically implicated in social recognition in male mice (Bielsky, Hu, & Young, 2005). The lateral septum projects to the dopamine receptor rich NAcc. These studies suggest further mechanisms through which dopamine may serve to reinforce selective social behaviors, such as those necessary for pair bond formation and some aspects of maternal behavior.

The NAcc is also a major input to other brain regions that are rich in dopamine receptors. There is evidence in male prairie voles that vasopressin and dopamine may interact in one of these regions (the ventral pallidum) to facilitate pair bonding (Young & Wang, 2004), possibly by overcoming fear or anxiety and reinforcing social bonds. Prairie voles, compared with nonmonogamous species, have high levels of vasopressin V1a receptors in the ventral pallidum (Insel & Shapiro, 1992; Witt et al., 1991).

Blocking the vasopressin V1a receptor in the ventral pallidum inhibited partner preference formation in male prairie voles. In addition, up-regulation of V1a receptors in the ventral pallidum (using a viral vector) facilitated pair bonding in male prairie voles. Overexpression of the prairie vole V1a receptor in the ventral pallidum of montane voles, a nonmonogamous species, also facilitated partner preference formation in the latter species.

Species-specific microsatellites in the promoter region of the gene for the V1a receptor may alter the expression of this receptor, especially in brain regions necessary for pair bonding. Differences in the colocalization of dopamine, oxytocin, and vasopressin also help to explain species or individual differences in the capacity to form pair bonds.

Opioids and Sociality

Several other neurochemical systems, including those that rely on endogenous opioids, have been implicated in both maternal care and later sociality. In sheep and primates, blocking opioid systems with naloxone in a mother is followed by reductions in these behaviors, although these mothers are still capable of suckling their young. Social interactions in infants also are regulated by opioids, although these effects may be species-specific. In guinea pigs, which are precocial at birth, opiate injection diminished distress vocalizations (Herman & Panksepp, 1978). Because the endogenous opioids also play a role in the regulation of the release of oxytocin and vasopressin (Brunton & Russell, 2008), as well as the HPA axis, they also may influence social behaviors indirectly. The release of oxytocin can be inhibited by endogenous opioids. Complex interactions of oxytocin, vasopressin, and the endogenous opioids are probably important but remain to be described in the context of social behavior.

Stress and Sociality

Because the concept of "stress" or even "stressful stimuli" lacks precision, it is difficult to operationalize in either animal or human research. The term *stress* has been used to describe both certain kinds of stimuli (stressors) and the complex neuroendocrine, autonomic, and behavioral responses to those stimuli (stress responses; Levine, 2005). Despite technical and conceptual issues, a large body of empirical data describes neuroendocrine and autonomic changes in the face of challenges or "stressful" experiences.

Traditional stress research, arising from the pioneering efforts of Selye (1950), has been dominated by studies of the sympathetic-HPA axis and by the related concepts of homeostasis or allostasis (McEwen & Wingfield, 2003). Such studies have centered around the detrimental effects of high levels of or chronic exposure to glucocorticoids. More recently, research in this field has focused on the central nervous system and specific central components of the HPA axis, such as CRF (described earlier), which plays a central role in the regulation of the anterior pituitary and ACTH and also acts directly on the nervous system to affect behavior. CRF, in turn, has been associated with defensive behaviors, anxiety, and negative emotions (Bakshi & Kalin, 2000; Charney & Bremner, 2004; Davis, 2006).

In mammals, the formation of new social bonds is particularly likely during or following periods of perceived vulnerability including birth, lactation and parenting, sexual interactions, and especially in times of stress or distress. The reliability of the mother–child emotional bond, even following the stress of birth, suggested the hypothesis that social bond formation was regulated by biological processes associated with birth, including both peptides associated with birth and lactation (especially oxytocin), hormones of the HPA axis, and catecholamines (including dopamine).

One example of the effects of "stress" on pair bond formation comes again from prairie voles. In male prairie voles, stressful experiences (such as a swim stress) facilitated the formation of a heterosexual pair bond (DeVries et al., 1996). In addition, both corticosterone and CRF (DeVries et al., 2002) were capable of enhancing pair bonding in males. Females, in contrast, responded to stressors or corticosterone treatments by showing a decreased tendency to form a heterosexual pair bond (DeVries, DeVries, Taymans, & Carter, 1995; DeVries et al., 1996). However, a preliminary study suggested that following a stressor, females were capable of showing a partner preference when the choice of a partner was a familiar (vs. an unfamiliar) female, possibly encouraging the formation of same-sex social groups under conditions of adversity. These finding suggest that the effects of stressful experiences on pair bond formation are sexually-dimorphic and also context-dependent (Carter, 1998).

Glucocorticoids (usually cortisol or corticosterone), possibly in conjunction with CRF and vasopressin, play a major role in the regulation of the anterior pituitary as well as affecting social behaviors (DeVries & Panzica, 2006). These same hormones also can mediate sensory perceptions as well as emotional and motivational states and reactivity. Changes in hormones of the HPA axis (most often using blood levels of corticosterone and cortisol), as well as behavior and autonomic responses, are sometimes used to index reactions to social experiences and social stressors—for example, the Trier Social Stress Test (Kirschbaum, Pirke, & Hellhammer, 1993). However, both the basal hormone production and reactions of the adrenal and autonomic system are not highly specific and thus become difficult to interpret in terms of specific social behaviors or emotional states. As just one example, the condition known as PTSD, may be associated with either elevated or reduced basal cortisol (Yehuda & Bierer, 2008).

Neuropepties and Autonomic Nervous System: Defensive Mobilization and Immobility Without Fear

Oxytocin also may regulate the most primitive defensive response system, characterized by immobilization. Under stressful social conditions in which avoidance or escape are not an option, then a more primitive, immobilization strategy, based on ancient neural systems, may emerge. For example, during subordination, the capacity to immobilize and not struggle, or even form social bonds toward a dominant partner, becomes part of an adaptive system. This primitive system is associated with the phylogenetically ancient, unmyelinated vagal pathway that triggers bradycardia, apnea, vasovagal syncope, and defecation as adaptive survival strategies to reduce metabolic demands and feign death. Unfortunately, this system, which functions adaptively for reptiles, amphibia, and fish, can be lethal for mammals. The novel neurophysiological properties of oxytocin, specifically expressed in mammals, also may permit physical immobility without fear in prosocial settings, permitting sleep, digestion, growth, restoration, and reproduction.

Neuropeptide receptors are found in autonomic source nuclei, where they serve to regulate sympathetic and parasympathetic functions, and in this capacity, they can influence social bond formation. For example, oxytocin receptors are abundant in the DVC. The DVC and the unmyelinated vagus have been implicated in various types of conditioning such as taste aversion (e.g., nausea) and passive avoidance. The oxytocin pathways may dampen both sympathoadrenal and DVC (unmyelinated) vagal reactivity, allowing reductions in anxiety and fear and concurrently permitting proximity and social bonds. Within the brainstem, oxytocin may act directly on the source nuclei of the DVC to protect the autonomic nervous system from "surging" and stopping the heart, especially under conditions such as parturition, nursing, or consensual sexual behavior, which require immobility without fear. A sense of safety may be essential to the formation of a social bond. In this context, oxytocin also may change the detection of immobilization from that of life threat to that of safety. In this context of safety, sociality, and eventually reproduction can occur.

Both oxytocin and vasopressin V1a receptors are found in the more modern VVC and may modulate the inhibitory action of the vagus on the heart. This enables the vagus to function as a bidirectional system characterized by dynamically increasing and decreasing the influence of the vagal brake on heart rate and supporting the functions of the SVE without requiring increases in sympathetic activation. Treatment with oxytocin and vasopressin has the capacity to increase sociality in general. However, both oxytocin and vasopressin (in conjunction with other molecules such as CRF and dopamine) may be essential to allow the expression of selective social behaviors including social preferences and the more mobilized states required for defense of a mate. Thus, the combined effects of peptides and other neurochemicals on various brain regions interact to provide physiological "context," which in turn can influence social behavior, emotional states and autonomic functions.

Neuroimaging methods have identified specific neural structures that are involved in detecting risk. These studies suggest that two areas of the temporal cortex, the fusiform gyrus and the superior temporal sulcus, are involved in evaluating biological movement and intention—including the detection of features such as movements, vocalizations, and faces—that contribute to an individual being perceived as safe or trustworthy (Adolphs, 2006). Slight changes in these stimuli can either pose threat or serve to signal safety. Connectivity between these areas of the temporal cortex and the amygdala suggests a top-down control in the processing of facial features that could actively inhibit activity of the structures involved in the expression of defensive strategies.

The amygdala and its connections also play a major role in the integration of autonomic and behavioral reactions to various kinds of sensory stimuli, including approach and avoidance. In human males, intranasal administration of oxytocin inhibited the activity of the amygdala, especially after exposure to fear-associated stimuli; intranasal oxytocin also altered downstream connections to brainstem structures involved in the regulation of the autonomic nervous system (Kirsch et al., 2005). Vasopressin, acting centrally (especially in the amygdala–BNST–lateral septum axis), as well as other peptides, such as CRF, can elevate vigilance and defensiveness. Behaviors mediated by the central amygdala also may mediate stimulus-specific behavioral responses to fear (Viviani & Stoop, 2008), and the BNST has been implicated in experiences related to anxiety (Davis, 2006). At least some of the defensive actions of CRF or vasopressin may be down-regulated by oxytocin acting in the central nucleus of the amygdala. Among the brainstem neural targets for oxytocin are receptors in the paraqueductal gray (PAG), where they may dampen both pain responses and defensive behavioral and autonomic reactions.

Vasopressin is associated with increased mobilization and the management of reactivity to challenge. Under conditions of perceived danger, it may be necessary to increase cardiovascular functions including blood pressure, and vasopressin might play a role in this autonomic mobilization. Vasopressin is elevated following a social challenge in male rats that show active, versus passive, patterns of coping (Landgraf & Neumann, 2004). Vasopressin has the capacity to antagonize the functions of oxytocin, perhaps through direct effects at the oxytocin receptor, as well as through physiological effects of vasopressin on systems associated with behavioral and physiological mobilization (Landgraf & Neumann, 2004). However, oxytocin also may be released under conditions of perceived threat, especially if immobilization is an adaptive strategy. In rats exposed to a swim stressor, oxytocin released into the central nucleus of the amygdala modulates stress-coping behaviors.

In female prairie voles, social isolation increases oxytocin as well as vasopressin, CRF, and corticosterone; oxytocin may help the isolated animal down-regulate arousal. Microinjections of oxytocin into the central nucleus of the amygdala and BNST also can inhibit aggressive behavior in female rats.

In general, central vasopressin has been described as increasing anxiety (i.e., *anxiogenic*; Landgraf & Neumann, 2004). However, the effects of vasopressin can also be *anxiolytic* if injected into the lateral septum (Appenrodt, Schnabel, & Schwarzberg, 1998). Thus, the effects of vasopressin on anxiety or reactions to stressors are likely to be context and gender-specific and probably vary as a function of the site of action, amount of peptide and whether it is experienced acutely or chronically.

The role of oxytocin in reaction to stress or danger may also differ according to gender and conditions of exposure, including whether the peptide is available acutely or chronically. In rats, acute exposure to oxytocin is associated with a transient increase in corticosterone, whereas longer lasting or chronic exposure to oxytocin tends to be followed by reductions in glucocorticoids and blood pressure. These effects of chronic oxytocin are more long-lasting in females than males. The chronic actions of oxytocin may also be mediated by an up-regulation or increase in sensitivity of alpha-2-adrenoreceptors, which could be associated with reduced reactivity to stressors. The effects of oxytocin on reactions to challenge also may involve interactions with other hormones, including CRF.

These studies suggest that among the peptide-sensitive processes in the brain are centers involved in the regulation of the parasympathetic components of the autonomic nervous system and their representations within the CNS (Porges, 2007). Through these actions, central peptides are capable of modulating and in some cases down-regulating the HPA response (Carter, 1998; Landgraf & Neumann, 2004; Uvnas-Moberg, 1998). These neural systems also work in unison with the HPA axis to allow adaptation to various challenges and can set the stage for the emergence of social relationships, which may require both a sense of safety with the partner and the capacity to defend home or family in the face of threat.

Sex Differences

Another clue to the physiology of sociality arises from the observation that the factors responsible for pair bonding differ in males and females. Social behaviors are influenced by sex differences in reproductive demands and may differ in males and females (Young & Carter, 2008). Mammalian reproductive and coping strategies involve either active forms of response, including approach or avoidance, or passive responses, including freezing or immobilization. Although there are many exceptions, males tend to show more active behaviors, whereas the response of females tends to be more physically passive (Koolhaas et al., 1998; Palanza, Gioiosa, & Parmigiani, 2001). These patterns are consistent with sex differences in reproductive functions, including the necessity for female mammals to assume immobile postures, at least briefly, during sexual behavior, birth, and nursing.

Because of its sexually dimorphic occurrence in the amygdala, BNST, and lateral septum (levels are higher in males), vasopressin is an important candidate for a role in explaining sex differences in reactions to social stimuli. Males and females may experience and respond to social cues using different neural pathways. Male prairie voles appear to be more sensitive to the effects of endogenous vasopressin than females. (Insel & Hulihan, 1995; Winslow et al., 1993). Studies in mice of animals knocked-out for the V1a receptor also suggest that males are affected more when this receptor is disrupted (Bielsky et al., 2005).

Although in female prairie voles vasopressin receptor activation does not appear to be necessary for mating-induced pair bonding, exogenous vasopressin is capable of inducing partner preferences in females after a short cohabitation (Cho et al., 1999). Interestingly, partner preferences in this paradigm could be blocked by either an oxytocin or vasopressin antagonist, suggesting that exogenous peptide may be acting to promote selective partner preference formation via both oxytocin and vasopressin receptors. However, either oxytocin or vasopressin may be sufficient to facilitate *nonselective* social behaviors in both sexes (Cho et al., 1999).

The factors regulating endogenous oxytocin synthesis and release are complex and remain incompletely understood. For example, the regulation of systems that rely on oxytocin is sexually dimorphic in some, but not all, cases (Cho et al., 1999). However, in those cases in which sex differences have been measured, oxytocin tends to be higher in females (Kramer, Cushing, Carter, Wu, & Ottinger, 2004). Among the features of the oxytocin system that are at least partially estrogen-dependent are the synthesis of oxytocin and the oxytocin receptor. Oxytocin and the oxytocin receptor respond to transient changes in ovarian status; these effects also are species-specific.

The elevations in oxytocin during periods of isolation in prairie voles are also sexually dimorphic, with females, but not males, showing increases in oxytocin (Grippo, Gerena, et al., 2007). As described earlier, despite the fact that isolated females show increased synthesis and release of oxytocin, isolated females also have the capacity to respond to exogenous oxytocin. Treatment with endogenous oxytocin normalized the behavior and autonomic responses of isolated animals to those seen in paired animals. However, the same treatment with exogenous oxytocin in animals living in pairs did not significantly affect behavior (Grippo et al., 2009). Why this is the case remains to be understood but may be related to the fact that both stressful experiences and increases in specific stressor hormones, such as corticosterone, can (in rats) increase the binding of oxytocin to the oxytocin receptor (Liberzon & Young, 1997).

In postmenopausal women, increases in oxytocin were associated with "gaps in social relationship" (Taylor et al., 2006). The significance of isolation-related elevations in oxytocin in either voles or humans remains to be empirically determined and might be age-dependent. However, it is likely that oxytocin is a component of a self-regulatory process that helps mammals deal with isolation or other stressful experiences. Such responses might also facilitate preparedness for social engagement, functions that could be especially adaptive in females who in nature may be less able than males to live and maintain a family alone.

The most dramatic effects of steroids on oxytocin gene expression in the PVN are seen following hormonal regimens that approximate the circumstances associated with birth and the postpartum period, when individuals may be especially likely to form social bonds. Sequential increases in estrogen and progesterone followed by progesterone withdrawal tend to be followed by release of oxytocin.

Sex differences in the oxytocin receptor depend on the brain region and species under study. In rats, oxytocin does not appear to be sexually dimorphic in some brain regions, such as the central nucleus of the amygdala (Viviani & Stoop, 2008). However, in male rats, oxytocin receptors are more abundant in the spinal cord, and in female rats, the oxytocin receptor is high in the ventromedial hypothalamus (a brain region often implicated in female sexual postures). In female prairie voles, higher levels of oxytocin receptor binding were also observed in the medial prefrontal cortex (Wang, Young, DeVries, & Insel, 1998). Cortical sex differences might be of particular importance in the regulation of both emotion and voluntary behaviors.

Sexually Dimorphic Reactions to Challenge

Behavioral responses to challenge, driven by sex differences in reproductive demands and sexual selection, differ in males and females (Palanza et al., 2001). Mammalian reproductive and coping strategies involve either active forms of response, including approach or avoidance, or passive responses, including freezing or immobilization. If avoidance or escape is not an option, then a more primitive immobilization strategy, based on an ancient neural system, may emerge. Although there are many exceptions, males tend to show more active reactions to challenge, whereas the response of females tends to be more passive. This pattern is consistent with sex differences in reproductive functions, including the necessity for female mammals to remain somewhat immobile during sexual behavior, birth, and nursing. A sex difference in reactivity to either social or emotional challenges might also be important to understand the observed sex biases in certain forms of mental illness, including autism spectrum disorder (ASD; Carter, 2007) and depression (Cyranowski et al., 2008). Knowledge of both endogenous and exogenous influences on systems that rely on oxytocin and vasopressin may be especially helpful in understanding sexually dimorphic developmental disorders, such as ASD, that are characterized by both increased anxiety and deficits in social behavior.

Specific cell populations contain oxytocin and vasopressin and their receptors in the central nucleus of the amygdala (Huber, Veinante, & Stoop, 2005). Electrophysiological measurements in the central nucleus of the amygdala suggest that cell populations containing oxytocin and vasopressin interact to modulate the integration of excitatory information from the other regions of the amygdala and also the cortex. The effects of oxytocin and vasopressin within the central nucleus of the amygdala appear to be in opposite directions, possibly playing a central role in the rapid integration of emotional states and other aspects of visceral functions, such as those necessary for cardiovascular and emotional responses (Viviani & Stoop, 2008).

Models for anxiety or fear may be differentially affected by oxytocin or vasopressin. Although sex differences in amygdala at the level of specific cell populations have not yet been studied, it is likely that males and females might differ in functions of the amygdala. For example, sex differences have been reported in humans in terms of activation of the amygdala in the context of emotional learning (Andreano & Cahill, 2009).

Light-enhanced startle (LES) in rats, which is considered a model for anxiety and reactivity to stress, is typically more pronounced in female versus male rats (Davis, 2006). LES depends on activity in the BNST, which is also known to have many sexually dimorphic components, including androgen-dependent cells that produce vasopressin. Vasopressin in turn has actions in the lateral septum. LES is normally inhibited by androgen, but not estrogen, and this effect depends on the presence of vasopressin. In contrast, fear-potentiated startle, which relies on activity in the central nucleus of the amygdala, is not sexually dimorphic and also not affected by alterations in either testosterone or vasopressin.

Sexual Differentiation

Many aspects of sexual differentiation, including the origins of sex differences in anatomy and behavior, are regulated by gonadal steroid hormones (Becker et al., 2008). Although both sexes produce androgens and estrogens, blood levels of androgen are higher in males, and estrogen levels are generally higher in females. Understanding steroid hormone action is complicated by the fact that testosterone may require conversion to an estrogen for at least some of its "masculinizing" effects on behavior.

Steroid hormones in turn regulate and interact with peptide hormones. For example, endogenous vasopressin is androgen-dependent, especially in brain regions that are necessary for pair bonding. However, the mechanisms through which androgen induces increased central vasopressin synthesis may require conversion to estrogen (De Vries & Simerly, 2002).

Sex steroids also can influence oxytocin and the oxytocin receptor (Gimpl & Fahrenholz, 2001). The effects of steroids on the oxytocin–oxytocin receptor system are species-specific and complicated by the many interactions among steroids and their receptors. However, the findings to date support the general hypothesis that factors affecting vasopressin may be of particular importance to male social behaviors (Carter, 2007). Sex differences in the vasopressin system could have broad consequences for behavior and physiology, forming an underlying substrate for several behavioral processes that are typically attributed to androgens. It is possible that in males both peptide synthesis and receptor functions are primed by early exposure to androgens, including exposure in the early postpartum period (DeVries & Simerly, 2002). Sex differences in central vasopressin may be involved in the capacity of oxytocin manipulations in early life to have differential long-term effects on social behavior in males and females.

Developmental Effects of Experiences in Early Life Are Often Sexually Dimorphic

Genetic differences provide one source of variance in social behavior, including the tendency to form social bonds (Hammock & Young, 2005). However, genetic differences are not sufficient to explain individual variations in social behaviors. An epigenetic model helps to explain the origins of traits, sometimes called *personality* or *temperament,* as well as individual differences in behavior. Understanding of these systems may also offer insights into the origins of pathological or maladaptive behaviors. Among the endocrine systems that have long-lasting effects on gene expression are those that developmentally rely on neuroendocrine systems using oxytocin and vasopressin. In early life, parental interactions with the offspring influence behavioral and emotional systems, allowing young animals to adjust to their immediate environment and also prepare for future social and physical challenges. Oxytocin, vasopressin, and their receptors are components of systems that can be programmed during development, allowing individual behavioral patterns to accommodate change. Genes involved in sociality can undergo long-lasting modifications as a function of early handling and social experiences, mediated in part by maternal stimulation.

Social and emotional behaviors may be especially vulnerable to epigenetic reprogramming. For example, female prairie voles that were deliberately maintained with minimal disturbance during the preweaning period did not in later life form pair bonds, whereas animals that were routinely handled in early life did (Bales, Lewis-Reese, Pfeifer, Kramer, & Carter, 2007). Behavioral effects of exposure to various kinds of handling can be detected in subsequent generations.

Exposure to a single treatment with oxytocin or an oxytocin antagonist on the first day of life had lifelong effects on brain and behavior, at least some of which were associated with increased anxiety and inappropriate social behaviors. After neonatal exposure to high doses of oxytocin, females tested in later life failed to form social bonds and in fact showed a preference for strangers (Bales, van Westerhuyzen, et al., 2007). Males were affected by exposure to exogenous neonatal oxytocin with in general increased sociality in later life. Males treated with an oxytocin antagonist were less social and apparently more anxious in later life. Exposure to these treatments, especially in males, was correlated with changes in vasopressin and the V1a receptor, without measurable effects on endogenous oxytocin or the oxytocin receptor. In males, treatment with an oxytocin antagonist was followed in later life by reductions in both vasopressin and in V1a receptor binding (Bales, Plotsky, et al., 2007; Yamamoto 2004). Conversely, a dose of oxytocin that was associated with increased sociality, also apparently increased V1a receptor binding in the ventral pallidum. As described earlier, the co-occurrence of the V1a vasopressin receptor and dopamine in the ventral pallidum has been implicated in male pair bond formation (Young et al., 2005) and may help to explain this outcome.

Although in female prairie voles the behavioral effects of a low dose of oxytocin were minimal, when females received higher oxytocin doses, pair bonding was no longer facilitated (Bales, Lewis-Reese, et al., 2007). In fact, females that had received the highest dose of oxytocin showed an atypical preference for an unfamiliar partner, possibly suggesting avoidance of familiar partners. Alloparenting was not inhibited by any of the neonatal oxytocin treatments, and even at high doses, females remained comparatively willing to maintain social contact, suggesting that only selective sociality and pair bonding were affected. In female prairie voles, exposure to low doses of either oxytocin or an oxytocin antagonist was associated with an increase in oxytocin in the PVN of the hypothalamus (Yamamoto et al., 2004). In females, and despite comparatively minor effects on behavior of either oxytocin or an antagonist, changes in later life were detected in V1a receptor binding. It is possible that increases in endogenous oxytocin synthesis associated with either neonatal oxytocin or an oxytocin antagonist in females were protective or compensated for the effects of blocking the oxytocin receptor.

Under normal, unmanipulated conditions, sex differences in the effects of early hormones could be adaptive. For example, estrogen, again possibly by increasing oxytocin, might reduce female vulnerability to disorders characterized by social deficits. In contrast, males may have a relatively larger dependence on vasopressin for sociality and emotion regulation. Thus, genetic or epigenetic factors that interfere with either oxytocin or vasopressin might be particularly detrimental to males, possibly contributing to the vulnerability of males to developmental disorders such autism spectrum disorders (Carter, 2007).

Developmental Influences on Sociality and Emotion

Spontaneous parental care in reproductively naïve animals, also known as alloparental behavior, is a dependent variable in many developmental studies and has been used to index the impact of stressful experiences on sociality. A stressful experience immediately before testing increased components of adult male alloparental responses (Bales et al., 2006). In prairie voles, both oxytocin and vasopressin can be released by an intense stressor. Males may require both vasopressin and oxytocin to overcome their fear of the pup and thus show alloparental behavior. Maternal behavior in females appears to be especially dependent on oxytocin (Olazebal & Young, 2006), possibly explaining the almost ubiquitous maternal behavior shown by females at the time of birth. However, the role of vasopressin in females is less clear, and it is possible that high levels of vasopressin would increase anxiety and fear and reduce female sociality. In prairie voles (and possibly other species) females may need high levels of oxytocin, such as those released at birth, to overcome fear and show appropriate maternal behaviors to the newborns.

Neonatal Vasopressin Treatments Also Can Affect Subsequent Social Behaviors

In prairie voles neonatal exposure to vasopressin (in this case, given as seven daily injections in the first week of life) were associated with a later dose-dependent increase in same-sex aggression, especially in males (Stribley & Carter, 1999). In contrast, neonatal exposure to a vasopressin antagonist was associated in later life with very low levels of aggression. Other aspects of behavior including exploration in an elevated plus maze and partner preference formation were not significantly affected by either neonatal treatment. The effects of neonatal vasopressin manipulations on V1a receptor binding have not yet been examined in voles. Moreover, because these studies involved repeated daily injections and handling, the effects of vasopressin cannot be compared directly to those of oxytocin described earlier, in which treatments were typically given only once on the first day of life. Early exposure to gonadal steroids facilitates the response of adult male prairie voles to exogenous vasopressin. In adult male prairie voles, vasopressin plays a major role in pair bond formation (Winslow et al., 1993). However, following neonatal castration, males tested as adults did not form partner preferences in response to centrally administered vasopressin (Cushing, Okorie, & Young, 2003). Neonatal treatment with testosterone restored the ability of castrated male prairie voles to respond to vasopressin in adulthood—in this case, with the formation of a partner preference. Replacement of testosterone in adulthood did not restore partner preference formation in response to vasopressin in neonatally castrated males, suggesting once again that the postnatal period is a time when animals are especially sensitive to hormonal manipulations. Interestingly, in the former study neonatal castration did not affect the distribution of vasopressin V1a receptor, as measured by autoradiography. The lack of an effect of neonatal castration on the V1a receptor is in contrast to the significant and sexually dimorphic effects of neonatal manipulations of oxytocin on the V1a receptor (Bales, van Westerhuyzen, et al., 2007). Changes in peptides in early life, and especially manipulations of oxytocin, may be more relevant than changes in gonadal steroids in regulating later peptide receptor distribution.

Developmental Effects of Hormones

In rats, genes for oxytocin and vasopressin are transcribed as early as Day 16 of intrauterine life. Vasopressin, measured by immunocytochemistry, also is first detected in the SON on Day 16 of gestation. However, oxytocin levels are low during gestation and synthesis of oxytocin is first detected by immunocytochemistry only in the first few days of postnatal life; these findings suggest that the gene encoding oxytocin is regulated at the posttranscriptional level (Lipari et al., 2001). The oxytocin receptor also first appears in the postnatal period (Snijdewint, Van Leeuwen, & Boer, 1989). Thus, the production of oxytocin and possibly its receptor as well (Champagne, Diorio, Sharma, & Meaney, 2001) may be especially vulnerable to postnatal experience. Research first described in rats reveals that peptide manipulations during development (Boer, 1993; Boer, Quak, DeVries, & Heinsbroek, 1994; Swaab & Boer, 1994) can alter the sensitivity of the adult nervous system to subsequent hormonal experiences—sometimes termed *hormonal imprinting*. Early experience, including maternal stimulation, has lifelong consequences for the behavior and physiology of animals (Boccia & Pedersen, 2001; Levine, 2005; Meaney, 2001). For example, high levels of maternal stimulation can both down-regulate the HPA axis and affect gene expression for CRH and vasopressin or their receptors. There is some evidence that oxytocin expression in rats is upregulated by maternal licking and grooming, possibly playing a role in both later behavior and HPA reactivity (Champagne et al., 2001). In female rats, adult oxytocin receptor binding was increased in animals that had received high levels of maternal stimulation during their infancy (Francis, Young, Meaney, & Insel, 2002). There is evidence that maternal licking and grooming alters neuronal survival, whereas social isolation reduces neurogenesis and also long-term potentiation in the hippocampus of rats.

In another example of the possible effects of early neuroendocrine manipulations, male rats treated with vasopressin during the first week of life had lower levels of oxytocin receptor gene expression in the PVN of the hypothalamus in adulthood (Ostrowski, 1998). This finding is of particular relevance because stressful experiences have the potential to release vasopressin in early life and because the PVN is a major neural site for the integration of autonomic and neuroendocrine processes. There is also evidence that oxytocin manipulations in early life change the response of an infant to its mother. Oxytocin injections, given peripherally to the mother, can facilitate nipple attachment by young rat pups (Singh & Hofer, 1978). Rat pups also show preferences for specific odors that are associated with exposure to their mothers. Preferences for the mother do not develop in animals that are pretreated with an oxytocin antagonist (Nelson & Panksepp, 1996). Oxytocin injections can produce rapid effects on the tendency of infants to cry (Insel & Winslow, 1991). Thus, oxytocin may act on both the mother and infant to influence the response of young animals to their maternal environment.

Transforming Effects of Hormones During Development

Oxytocin affects several remarkable cellular transformations including cellular proliferation and differentiation. Recent studies also implicate oxytocin in development and plasticity. For example, oxytocin-producing neurons in the hypothalamus have unusual morphological features compared with other neurons. Oxytocin neurons in adult rats have been described as "immature" with exceptional capacity to change shape and form new synapses, in part through morphological changes in associated glia (Theodosis, 2002; Theodosis, Trailin, & Poulain, 2006). Oxytocin-producing cells are sensitive to oxytocin itself, a form of autocrine feedback that regulates the functions of oxytocin-producing cells. Increases in oxytocin from exogenous sources also can stimulate the production of oxytocin from these cells. Both oxytocin and vasopressin may directly or indirectly influence cellular growth, death or motility, inflammation, or differentiation (Paquin, Danalache, Jankowski, McCann, & Gutkowski, 2002; Theodosis et al., 2006). The potential to remodel the nervous system, especially in early life, offers another process through which oxytocin or vasopressin could have sexually dimorphic affects on physiology and behavior.

Mechanisms of Long-Lasting Effects of Early Experience

Availability or the absence of oxytocin receptors in specific brain regions of the oxytocin receptor may help to account for species and individual differences in sociality and emotionality. The oxytocin receptor is susceptible to epigenetic regulation, for example, by silencing genes via methylation (Kimura et al., 2003; Szyf et al., 2005). The capacity of genes that code for receptors to be silenced or otherwise modified in early life may be particularly relevant to understanding the long-lasting consequences of early experiences, whether originating as behavioral or as hormonal experiences. Effects on early experiences, including prenatal stress and postnatal social interactions, are mediated at least in part by plasticity in peptide receptors, as well as in the neurons that synthesize peptides including oxytocin (Theodosis, 2002).

In rats, prenatal stress can reduce expression of the oxytocin receptor in later life (Champagne & Meaney, 2006). There are also postnatal effects of early parental stimulation on binding to the oxytocin and vasopressin V1a receptor, and these effects are sexually dimorphic (Champagne et al., 2001; Francis et al., 2002). In rats, early experience affected the oxytocin receptor more in females and the vasopressin receptor in males. As described earlier, male mice are more affected than females by genetic disruption of the vasopressin (Bielsky et al., 2005; Lim, Hammock, & Young, 2004). Our work with prairie voles suggests that during critical periods in development, social experiences or manipulations of oxytocin or vasopressin may influence the expression of these same peptides, as well as their receptors, with lifelong behavioral consequences. However, it is not a simple matter to untangle differential functions of oxytocin and vasopressin, especially using available pharmacological tools. Oxytocin and vasopressin can bind to each other's receptors (Barberis & Tribollet, 1996). In addition, the oxytocin antagonist widely used in behavioral studies is not totally selective for the oxytocin receptor and also affects the vasopressin V1a receptor.

Developmental Signaling Consequences of Neuropeptides

There is recent evidence from studies in rats that maternal oxytocin can act as a signaling mechanism between the mother and fetus. Maternal oxytocin, released during birth also triggers a transient switch in gamma-aminobutyric acid (GABA) signaling in the fetal brain from excitatory to inhibitory. *In vivo* administration of an oxytocin antagonist before delivery prevented this switch of GABA activity in fetal neurons and aggravated the severity of hypoxic episodes. Thus, it appears that maternal oxytocin inhibits fetal neurons and increases their resistance to hypoxic insult (Khazipov, Tyzio, & Ben-Ari, 2006). In addition, the birth-related surge in oxytocin also helps to regulate the synchronization of the fetal hippocampal neurons, possibly allowing the transition from prenatal to postnatal life (Crepel et al., 2007). Such changes would be expected to have consequences for both emotional and cognitive functions.

Do Experiences or Hormones in the Prenatal or Perinatal Period Affect Human Behavior?

Changes in vasopressin can be induced by stress but also might be the unintended consequences of process, such as smoking. Smoking (nicotine) is a potent releaser for endogenous vasopressin (Chiodera et al., 1993). There is a well-established link between maternal smoking and behavioral dysregulation in male children (Wakschlag, Leventhal, Pine, Pickett, & Carter, 2006). In addition, early stressors, including medical procedures in pregnancy or infancy, hold the potential to release vasopressin in either the mother or child, with consequences that remain unstudied.

Medical interventions and the effects of differential child rearing practices also hold the potential to influence behavior in later life. For example, compounds of maternal origin may be transmitted to the infant either during the prenatal or postnatal period. Treatments in the prenatal period may alter the duration of pregnancy, the intensity of labor, and postnatal parent–infant interactions, with possible direct or indirect effects on the offspring. In addition, in the postnatal period, maternal milk contains biologically active compounds, including oxytocin (Leake, Weitzman, & Fisher, 1981), as well as prolactin (Grosvenor, Picciano, & Baumrucker, 1993) and cortisol (Glynn et al., 2007). It is likely that these and other hormones in mammalian milk serve to "tune" the developing nervous system.

Exogenous synthetic oxytocin (Pitocin) is widely used to induce or augment labor or prevent postpartum hemorrhage. It has been assumed that Pitocin given to the mother does not pass through the placenta in amounts sufficient to affect the baby. However, this assumption is not well studied, and the placental barrier can be disrupted during birth or by other stressors. In addition, treatment given pregnant women to delay premature labor, such as atosiban, an oxytocin antagonist, could have the potential to affect the offspring's development and perhaps subsequent social behavior. Research on this subject is rare, in part because it is difficult to determine whether these effects are directly due to maternal exposure to oxytocin (oxytocin can alter the strength or duration of uterine contractions) or to indirect effects resulting in differential fetal exposure to hypoxia. Pitocin, especially in conjunction with a surgical birth or anesthesia, also may influence the subsequent ability of the mother to lactate or interact with her offspring in the immediate postpartum period. If findings in animals do generalize to humans, then differential experiences in early life might have long-term behavioral consequences (Meaney & Szyf, 2005).

Oxytocin and Human Development

Research on the developmental consequences of oxytocin has been stimulated by concern for the possible long-term effects of manipulations of this peptide during early life. The concerns expressed here are not new but remain largely unstudied. Implicit in the routine use of oxytocin in humans is the assumption that maternal oxytocin does not cross the placental barrier in amounts that are sufficient to influence the developing fetus; however, the validity of this assumption is not well documented. In addition, effects of peptide manipulations can be indirect, for example, through the consequences of uterine contractions or even through effects on maternal behavior. Proof that the fetus is not influenced by maternal peptides requires functional and *in vivo* measures of the effects of oxytocin. In addition, exogenous oxytocin, oxytocin blocking agents, or other peptides may have effects that differ from those of endogenous oxytocin. Furthermore, the patency of the maternal–fetal barrier could fluctuate during labor and birth, which is the period when medical applications of oxytocin (Pitocin) are most common. Postpartum oxytocin treatments of the mother also are often recommended on the assumption that these will reduce the chances of postpartum hemorrhage, providing another possible opportunity for nursing infants to encounter elevations in oxytocin.

As mentioned earlier, patterns of infant care and feeding also may be translated into peptidergic manipulations. For example, because human milk (Leake et al., 1981), but perhaps not heat-treated baby formulas, contains comparatively high levels of the oxytocin molecule, the decision to bottle-feed an infant also may constitute a manipulation of the peptide history of a child. In addition, breast-fed infants may receive more physical contact, including skin-to-skin contact and oral stimulation, than bottle-fed infants, which may in turn release oxytocin in the infant (or mother; Uvnas-Moberg, 1998).

Translational Consequences of Deficits in Sociality and Emotion Regulation

In many forms of mental illness, including autism, depression, and schizophrenia, a marked decrease in social behavior is a prominent feature of the patients' difficulties (Carter, 2007; Goldman, Marlow-O'Connor, Torres, & Carter, 2008; Skuse & Gallagher, 2009). Episodes of certain mental illness, such as anxiety disorders, depression, and even schizophrenia, may be induced or at least facilitated by social stressors and possibly exacerbated by the absence of social bonds. Furthermore, chronic elevations in sympathoadrenal activity may be detrimental to physical and emotional health, and there is increasing evidence that hormones of the HPA axis have a role in mental illness (Charney & Bremner, 2004). However, mechanisms for the health benefits of positive social behaviors are not widely studied and thus remain largely theoretical and based on animal research.

Autism Spectrum Disorders as a Translational Example

ASD is a developmental disorder characterized by deficits in social behavior and high levels of anxiety. Fearfulness and excessive reactivity to environmental stimuli are core features in the definitions of ASD. For humans, among the most powerful forms of stressors are those related to social interactions. A sense of either trusting or being trusted may be essential to perceived safety. Of particular importance to ASD may be mechanisms for enhancing parasympathetic functions, regulated by myelinated vagal pathways. Vagal activation, either through direct electrical stimulation of the vagus (Murphy, Wheless, & Schmoll, 2000) or the use of behavioral interventions that enhance vagal tone (Porges, 2004), has been associated with improvements in the social features of ASD.

Intranasal oxytocin infusion in men is associated with an increase in "trust" in a computer game (Kosfeld et al., 2005). In addition, intranasal oxytocin reduced neural activation, measured by functional imagine in the amygdala, in response to fear-inducing stimuli; in this same study, oxytocin treatment was associated with reduced coupling of the amygdala to brainstem regions implicated in autonomic arousal and fear (Kirsch et al., 2005). These studies support the larger hypothesis that adaptive systems, including those influenced by the autonomic nervous system, are regulated by dynamic interactions between oxytocin and possibly vasopressin. Dysfunction in any aspect of this system could influence the features of ASD.

In humans, elevations in central vasopressin, experimentally induced by intranasal infusion of this peptide, can have behavioral consequences, potentially by increasing behavioral or emotional reactivity to normally irrelevant stimuli or nonthreatening social stimuli (Thompson, George, Walton, Orr, & Benson, 2006). The behavioral effects of exogenous vasopressin also were sexually dimorphic. Men given additional vasopressin showed increases in activity in corrugator muscles, a component of frowning, and also rated neutral facial expression as more "unfriendly." In contrast, females given an identical vasopressin treatment smiled more and reported more positive, affiliative responses to unfamiliar neutral faces (Thompson et al., 2006). In males (but possibly less so in females), vasopressin-facilitated hypersensitivity to or misinterpretation of social stimuli might exacerbate the features of ASD.

Various lines of evidence implicate the amygdala in defensive behaviors and other features of ASD (Carter, 2007). The extended amygdala, including the BNST, is a region of integration for various kinds of emotional processes, with connections to and from the olfactory system, PVN, and brainstem autonomic centers including those regulating sympathetic and parasympathetic functions. The extended amygdala also is a major target for the behavioral and autonomic effects of oxytocin and vasopressin (Viviani & Stoop, 2008).

The possible effects of early experience or hormonal manipulations also have not been systematically studied in human development. The neural systems that are altered by neonatal peptide manipulations in prairie voles are evolutionarily ancient and have broad behavioral and physiological actions. These systems may be accessible to change and thus vulnerable during development to neural changes that could have long-lasting consequences. Results from animal research suggest the need for a deeper understanding of the mechanisms through which manipulations in endogenous or exogenous peptides might affect neuroanatomy, physiology, and behavior. For example, manipulations in oxytocin could have long-lasting consequences for behavioral endophenotypes, including sociality and reactivity to stressors, that are core to personality types and, in extreme cases, to several psychiatric disorders, including ASD (Carter, 2007), anxiety and depression (Carter & Altemus, 2004) and possibly schizophrenia. Functional sex differences in neuropeptides, including vasopressin and possibly oxytocin, may have particular significance for understanding sexually biased disorders of social behavior (Carter, 2007). Early manipulations of oxytocin can also program various aspects of the body's management of stressful experiences, including measures of behavior, brain activity and chemistry, and stress-related hormones.

Peptides and Development

Neuropeptides, and especially oxytocin and vasopressin, have a different ontogeny than the autonomic nervous system. These neuropeptides are being produced through development and have specific adaptive functions, including water regulation in the fetus. Of particular importance to mammalian social development is the surge of oxytocin during parturition and possibly an enhanced affinity of specific brainstem areas for oxytocin at this time. Relevant to this chapter, a high density of oxytocin receptors are available in the full-term infant in the area of the DVC and the nucleus of the solitary tract. These brain regions permit adaptive physiological states of immobilization, which can occur without fear. During states of immobilization without fear, there is a concurrent, efficient neurobiological state that fosters growth, restoration, and general health. This state is critical to the optimal development of young infants and growing children. However, the neuropeptides necessary for these transitions are primarily generated and released from their source in the hypothalamus of the infant (and, before birth, possibly by the mother).

Future research needs to investigate whether there is a shift during the last trimester from the more primitive vasotocin, found in reptiles and with both oxytocin and vasopressin-like properties, to a well-defined distinction between oxytocin and vasopressin, which occurs near birth. The developmental features of oxytocin and vasopressin have not been well described across the life span. However, we hypothesize that surges or peaks in oxytocin (or functional increases based on changes in the oxytocin receptor) would be expected during developmental periods in which social bonding is occurring. We further speculate that because oxytocin is involved in facilitating a physiological state of immobilization without fear (i.e., recruiting the old unmyelinated vagus to support growth, restoration, and health) and because immobilization without fear is a characteristic of contexts in which social bonds are developed or expressed in close proximity (such as mating behaviors or sleeping together), high levels of oxytocin activity could serve to signal developmental periods in which strong social bonds could be established.

In the early postpartum period, certain biological cues, such as contact, proximity, oral motor activity, and ingestion that dominate the early phases of life, may be efficient triggers for this system in the newborn. After this system is activated, a somewhat unique physiological state and the associated experiences of immobilization without fear may be the framing features of the prototypical *social relation*. Systems regulated by oxytocin probably facilitate the sense of safety and security that is characteristic of the ideal mother–infant bond.

In contrast, the aging process may reflect a dissolution of these integrated systems. It is possible that elderly may not have access to neurobiological resources (i.e., oxytocin or its receptor) to immobilize without fear and thus may find it difficult to feel safe with others and form new social bonds.

The regulation of behavioral state is a critical determinant of the range of social behaviors that an individual can express. The underlying mechanisms mediating behavioral state are tightly linked to the autonomic nervous system and the modulation of the autonomic nervous system by neuropeptides. The investigation of maturational changes in vagal regulation of autonomic state unmasks several of the behavioral features that humans exhibit throughout the life span.

During early infancy an immature vagal system limits the child's ability to self-regulate. Similarly during aging, potentially because of demyelination, the vagal system losses its ability to regulate the vagal brake efficiently. As a consequence of this change in self-regulation, mood state lability compromises the affective repertoire of the aged. In the elderly, the loss of neural regulation of state is mirrored in the loss of neural regulation of the striated muscles of the face and head. Thus, in the aged, the social engagement system (i.e., facial expressivity, vocal prosody, listening, and the vagal brake), which had successfully regulated visceral state through spontaneous social interactions, is no longer efficiently available, leaving the elderly vulnerable to states of anxiety and despair.

From a life-span perspective the ability to regulate state follows a developmental trajectory during the early part of life and a reversed pattern during the latter part of life. As the neural circuits involved in state regulation become more available to the developing child and less available in the elderly, there are parallel opportunities for social engagement behaviors and the development of strong social bonds. Without the efficient myelinated vagus, the infant and the elderly find it is difficult to regulate behavioral state and use the features of the social engagement system (i.e., facial expression, vocal prosody) and cues to recruit others into reciprocal relationships. These developmental limitations in the vagal system may lower thresholds to negative or ambiguous environmental cues with resultant hyperreactivity and severe limitations in the ability to self-soothe and calm.

On the basis of the functional impact of the myelinated vagus on measures of heart rate (i.e., RSA), age trajectories can be observed during functional challenges. Laboratory research illustrates a rapid growth during the last trimester and the first year postpartum, with slower enhancements during the preschool years. With the decrements in behavioral state regulation observed in the aged, there is a parallel decrement in vagal regulation of the heart. During most of adolescent and adult life, the system remains highly functional with only slight decreases in function from age 20 to 65 years. Coupled with the vagal regulation, the neuropeptides of oxytocin and vasopressin contribute to the regulation of physiological state. For example, surges in oxytocin, either in terms of basal levels (e.g., pregnancy) or reactivity to cues in the environment (e.g., romantic settings), may support the establishment of strong social bonds. However, little is known about the developmental shifts in availability and levels of these neuropeptides across the life span.

During most of the life span, the vagal brake and the other features of the social engagement system are readily available and contribute to the numerous opportunities for social learning to occur. Under certain contexts, the ability to self-regulate and to express a calm behavioral state is augmented by the release of oxytocin and strong social bonds are established. However, without the efficient vagal brake turning off the defensive systems (e.g., fight and flight behaviors) and the disruptive manifestations of these systems, prosocial behavior is limited, and opportunities for social learning and social bonding are minimized.

The familiarity of the social environment of home and community provide the social cues for trust and safety that dampen defense reactions and functionally exercise and improve the individual's ability to employ the social engagement system appropriately. In safe environments, social interactions among familiar people trigger the social engagement system, creating reciprocal enduring relationships that, in addition to enhancing prosocial behavior, serve to promote health, growth, and restoration. Life events that change contextual features of the social community, such as changing schools, jobs, or location, require greater vigilance to detect potential risks in novel environments. These contextual changes in the social community, which disrupt the predictable and safe features of the social environment, will also functionally disrupt the regulation of state by removing the vagal brake to foster greater vigilance and lower the threshold for fight–flight behaviors at the expense of developing new social relationships.

The focus of this review has been to emphasize the importance of physiological state as a moderator of social behavior. Understanding the mechanisms and mediators of physiological state provides a different perspective on behavioral states and the role that state may play in either promoting or impeding prosocial behaviors. For example, behavioral tantrums, states of high vigilance, aggressive behavior, or excessive expressed emotional reactivity are incompatible with prosocial behaviors. In the context of social development theory, such behavioral difficulties are often interpreted as a function of learning, experience, maturation of the motor systems, or deliberate attempts to manipulate others. However, in light of neurobiological changes across the life span, it is possible to appreciate the role that the nervous system plays in regulating behavioral state and how state serves as a platform on which complex social behaviors can be shaped by experience and learning (i.e., reinforcement and punishment).

As we look at the timeline of social behavior across the life span, we notice long periods in which self-regulated behaviors, including spontaneous social engagement behaviors, are readily expressed. In contrast, we note that this timeline is anchored on both sides by a dependence on caregivers. It is this dependence that is paralleled by limitations in the neural regulation of autonomic state via the myelinated vagus. Whether the periods of caregiver dependence are modulated by neuropeptides is a question for future research. If oxytocin levels were low during these periods, then the infant and elderly would perhaps be more receptive to bonding and to be soothed by a variety of caregivers. As the neural control circuits develop and there are more opportunities to social engage, perhaps oxytocin plays a more important role in modulating state to promote the establishment of strong social bonds.

SUMMARY

Social behavior and the capacity to manage challenge are coordinate aspects of human physiology. Using animal models chosen for their resemblance to humans, it is possible to gain a deeper understanding of the mechanisms for these functions. There is increasing evidence that ancient neuropeptides, including oxytocin and vasopressin, provide sexually dimorphic neural substrates for both sociality and the beneficial effects of sociality on survival. At least some of the protective actions of oxytocin may be mediated by the actions of oxytocin in the autonomic nervous system. For example, oxytocin plays a role in energy-conserving autonomic functions and can provide mammals with the capacity to "immobilize without fear" (Porges, 1998). Brainstem nuclei associated with primitive shutdown responses, contain high levels of oxytocin receptors, possibly allowing those areas to be coopted for immobilization during reproduction. However, this same mechanism, when it malfunctions, may make women more vulnerable than men to psychiatric disorders such as depression and PTSD. In contrast, the central effects of vasopressin are repeatedly found to be more prominent in males, supporting the capacity of males to show mobilization and a more active reaction to challenge.

An additional life-span benefit of social support may come from the capacity of peptides, such as oxytocin, to buffer against stressors and down-regulate the HPA axis. During aging and especially in the absence of a supportive social environment or in the face of stress or illness, critical developmental processes may be reversed. Autonomic systems may begin to fail, in time reducing the capacity to form new social bonds or to use others to calm or self-soothe.

From a biobehavioral perspective, social behavior is dependent on the ability to regulate behavioral state. The neural circuits involved in the regulation of physiological state are modified throughout the life span. When these circuits are easily available and efficiently functioning, the laws of learning and the impact of experience can shape social behavior. However, when these circuits are not available, either as a function of phase of development or during periods of increased environmental risk, then social behavior is limited, social skills are not easily learned, and social bonds are difficult to establish. Fortunately, through most of our life span, these neural circuits are available and modulated by regulatory neuropeptides, ensuring efficient expression of prosocial behaviors.

REFERENCES

Adolphs, R. (2006). How do we know the minds of others? Domain-specificity, simulation, and enactive social cognition. *Brain Research, 1079,* 25–35.

Ainsworth, M. D. S. (1989). Attachments beyond infancy. *American Psychologist, 44,* 709–716.

Ainsworth, M. D. S., Blehar, M. C., Waters, E., & Wall, S. (1978). *Patterns of attachment: A psychological study of the strange situation.* Hillsdale, NJ: Erlbaum.

Alkon, A., Lippert, S., Vujan, N., Rodriguez, M. E., Boyce, W. T., & Eskenazi, B. (2006). The ontogeny of autonomic responses in 6- and 12-month-old infants. *Developmental Psychobiology, 48,* 197–208.

Altemus, M., Deuster, P. A., Gallivan, E., Carter, C. S., & Gold, P. W. (1995). Suppression of hypothalamic–pituitary–adrenal responses to exercise stress in lactating women. *Journal of Clinical Endocrinology and Metabolism, 80,* 2954–2959.

Altemus, M., Redwine, L. S., Leong, Y-M., Frye, C. A., Porges, S. W., & Carter, C. S. (2001). Responses to laboratory psychosocial stress in postpartum women. *Psychosomatic Medicine, 63,* 814–821.

Andreano, J. M., & Cahill, L. (2009). Sex influences on the neurobiology of learning and memory. *Learning & Memory, 16,* 248–266.

Appenrodt, E., Schnabel, R., & Schwarzberg, H. (1998). Vasopressin administration modulates anxiety-related behavior in rats. *Physiology & Behavior, 64,* 543–547.

Aragona, B. J., Liu, Y., Yu, Y. J., Curtis, J. T., Detwiler, J. M., Insel, T. R., et al. (2006). Nucleus accumbens dopamine differentially mediates the formation and maintenance of monogamous pair bonds. *Nature Neuroscience, 9,* 133–139.

Austin, M. A., Riniolo, T. C., & Porges, S. W. (2007). Borderline personality disorder and emotion regulation: Insights from the Polyvagal theory. *Brain and Cognition, 65,* 69–76.

Bakshi, V. P., & Kalin, N. H. (2000). Corticotropin-releasing hormone and animal models of anxiety: Gene–environment interactions. *Biological Psychiatry, 48,* 1175–1198.

Bale, T. L. (2006). Stress sensitivity and the development of affective disorders. *Hormones and Behavior, 50,* 529–533.

Bales, K. L., Kramer, K. M., Lewis-Reese, A. D., & Carter, C. S. (2006). Effects of stress on parental care are sexually dimorphic in prairie voles. *Physiology and Behavior, 87,* 424–429.

Bales, K. L., Lewis-Reese, A. D., Pfeifer, L. A., Kramer, K. M., & Carter, C. S. (2007). Early experience affects the traits of monogamy in a sexually dimorphic manner. *Developmental Psychobiology, 49,* 335–342.

Bales, K. L., Plotsky, P. M., Young, L. J., Lim, M. M., Grotte, N. D., Ferrer, E., et al. (2007). Neonatal oxytocin manipulations have long-lasting, sexually dimorphic effects on vasopressin receptors. *Neuroscience, 144,* 38–45.

Bales, K. L., van Westerhuyzen, J. A., Lewis-Reese, A. D., Grotte, N. D., Lanter, J. A., & Carter, C. S. (2007). Oxytocin has dose-dependent developmental effects on pair bonding and alloparental care in female prairie voles. *Hormones and Behavior, 49,* 355–342.

Barberis, C., & Tribollet, E. (1996). Vasopressin and oxytocin receptors in the central nervous system. *Critical Reviews in Neurobiology, 10,* 119–154.

Bates, J. E., Freeland, C. A. B., & Lounsbury, M. L. (1979). Measurement of infant difficulties. *Child Development, 50,* 794–803.

Bazhenova, O. V., Plonskaia, O., & Porges, S. W. (2001). Vagal reactivity and affective adjustment in infants during interaction challenges. *Child Development, 72,* 1314–1326.

Becker, J. B., Berkley, K. J., Geary, N., Hampson, E., Herman, J. P., & Young, E. A. (Eds.). (2008). *Sex on the brain: From genes to behavior.* New York: Oxford University Press.

Bielsky, I. F., Hu S-B., & Young, L. J. (2005). Sexual dimorphism in the vasopressin system: Lack of an altered behavioral phenotype in female V1a receptor knockout mice. *Behavioural Brain Research, 164,* 132–136.

Blair, C., & Peters, R. (2003). Physiological and neurocognitive correlates of adaptive behavior in preschool among children in Head Start. *Developmental Neuropsychology, 24,* 479–497.

Blair, C., Peters, R., & Granger, D. (2004). Physiological and neuropsychological correlates of approach/withdrawal tendencies in preschool: Further examination of the behavioral inhibition system/behavioral activation system scales for young children. *Developmental Psychobiology, 45,* 113–124.

Boccia, M. L., & Pedersen, C. A. (2001). Brief vs. long maternal separations in infancy: Contrasting relationships with adult maternal behavior and lactation levels of aggression and anxiety. *Psychoneuroendocrinology, 26,* 657–672.

Boer, G. J. (1993). Chronic OT treatment during late gestation and lactation impairs development of rat offspring. *Neurotoxicology and Teratology, 15,* 383–389.

Boer, G. J., Quak, J., DeVries, M. C., & Heinsbroek, R. P. W. (1994). Mild sustained effects of neonatal AVP and OT treatment on brain growth and behavior of the rat. *Peptides, 15,* 229–236.

Bosch, O. J., Nair, H. P., Ahern, T. H., Neumann, I. D., & Young, L. J. (2009). The CRF system mediates increased passive stress-coping behavior following the loss of a bonded partner in a monogamous rodent. *Neuropsychopharmacology. 34,* 1406–1415.

Bowlby, J. (1969). *Attachment and loss, Vol. I. Attachment.* New York: Basic Books.

Bowlby, J. (1973). *Attachment and loss, Vol. II. Separation. Anxiety and Anger.* New York: Basic Books.

Bowlby, J. (1980). *Attachment and loss. Vol. III. Loss.* New York: Basic Books.

Brown, S. L, Brown, R. M., House, J. S., & Smith, D. M. (2008). Coping with spousal loss: Potential buffering effects of self-reported helping behavior. *Personality and Social Psychology Bulletin, 34,* 849–861.

Brunton, P. J., & Russell, J. A. (2008). Keeping oxytocin neurons under control during stress in pregnancy. *Progress in Brain Research, 170,* 365–377.

Bueno, L., Gue, M., Fargeas, M. J., Alvinerie, M., Junien, J. L., & Fioramonti, J. (1989). Vagally mediated inhibition of acoustic stress-induced cortisol release by orally administered kappa-opioid substances in dogs. *Endocrinology, 123,* 1788–1793.

Byrne, E. A., Fleg, J. L., Vaitkevicius, P. V., Wright, J., & Porges S. W. (1996). Role of aerobic capacity and body mass index in the age-associated decline in heart rate variability. *Journal of Applied Physiology, 81,* 743–750.

Cacioppo, J. T., Hughes, M. E., Waite, L. J., Hawkely, L. C., & Thisted, R. A. (2006). Loneliness as a specific risk factor for depressive symptoms: Cross-sectional and longitudinal analysis. *Psychology of Aging, 21,* 140–151.

Caldwell, H. K., Wersinger, S. R., & Young, W. S. (2008). The role of vasopressin 1b receptor in aggression and other social behaviors. *Progress in Brain Research, 170,* 65–72.

Calkins, S. D. (1997). Cardiac vagal tone indices of temperamental reactivity and behavioral regulation. *Developmental Psychobiology, 31,* 125–135.

Calkins, S. D., & Dedmon, S. A. (2000). Physiological and behavioral regulation in two-year-old children with aggressive/destructive behavior problems. *Journal of Abnormal Child Psychology, 28,* 103–118.

Calkins, S. D., & Fox, N. A. (1992). The relations among infant temperament, security of attachment, and behavioral inhibition at twenty-four months. *Child Development, 63,* 1456–1472.

Calkins, S. D., Graziano, P. A., & Keane, S. P. (2007). Cardiac vagal regulation differentiates among children at risk for behavior problems. *Biological Psychology, 74,* 144–153.

Carter, C. S. (1998). Neuroendocrine perspectives on social attachment and love. *Psychoneuroendocrinology, 23,* 779–818.

Carter, C. S. (2007): Sex differences in oxytocin and vasopressin: implications for autism spectrum disorders? *Behavioural Brain Research. 176,* 170–186.

Carter, C. S., & Altemus, M. (1997). Integrative functions of lactational hormones in social behavior and stress management. *Annals of the New York Academy of Sciences, Integrative Neurobiology of Affiliation, 807,* 164–174.

Carter, C. S., & Altemus, M. (2004). Oxytocin, vasopressin, and depression. In J. A. den Boer, M. S. George, & G. J. ter Horst (Eds.), *Current and future developments in psychopharmacology* (pp. 201–206). Amsterdam: Benecke.

Carter, C. S., Altemus, M., & Chrousos, G. P. (2001). Neuroendocrine and emotional changes in the postpartum period. In E. Ingram & J. Russell (Eds.), *Progress in Brain Research, Vol. 133. The maternal brain* (pp. 241–249). Amsterdam: Elsevier.

Carter, C. S., Boone, E. M., Pournajafi-Nazarloo, H., & Bales, K. L. (2009). The consequences of early experiences and exposure to oxytocin and vasopressin are sexually-dimorphic. *Developmental Neuroscience, 31,* 332–341.

Carter, C. S., DeVries, A. C., & Getz, L. L. (1995). Physiological substrates of monogamy: The prairie vole model. *Neuroscience and Biobehavioral Reviews. 19,* 303–314.

Carter, C. S., & Keverne, E. B. (2002). The neurobiology of social affiliation and pair bonding. In D. Pfaff, A. P. Arnold, A. M. Etgen, S. E., Fahrback, & R. T. Rubin (Eds.), *Hormones, brain and behavior* (pp. 299–337). San Diego: Academic Press.

Carter, C. S., Lederhendler, I. I., & Kirkpatrick, B. (Eds.) (1997). *The Integrative Neurobiology of Affiliation. Annals of the New York Academy of Sciences, 807.* (Rereleased by MIT Press, Cambridge, MA, 1999.)

Champagne, F., Diorio, J., Sharma, S., & Meaney, M. J. (2001). Naturally occurring variations in maternal behavior in the rat are associated with differences in estrogen-inducible central oxytocin receptors. *Proceedings of the National Academy of Sciences, 98,* 12736–12741.

Champagne, F. A., & Meaney, M. J. (2006). Stress during gestation alters postpartum maternal care and the development of the offspring in a rodent model. *Biological Psychiatry, 59,* 1227–1235.

Charney, D. S., & Bremner, J. D. (2004). The neurobiology of anxiety disorders. In D. S. Charney & E. J. Nestler (Eds.), *The neurobiology of mental illness* (pp. 605–627). New York: Oxford Press.

Chiodera, P., Volpi, R., Capretti, L., Bocchi, R., Caffarri, G., Marcato, A., et al. (1993). Gamma-aminobutyric acid mediation of the inhibitory effect of endogenous opioids on the arginine vasopressin and oxytocin responses to nicotine from cigarette smoking. *Metabolism, 42,* 762–765.

Cho, M. M., DeVries, A. C., Williams, J. R., & Carter, C. S. (1999). The effects of oxytocin and vasopressin on partner preferences in male and female prairie voles (*microtus ochrogaster*). *Behavioral Neuroscience, 113,* 1071–1080.

Cicchetti, D., Ganiban, J., & Barnett, D. (1991). Contributions from the study of high risk populations to understanding the development of emotion regulation. In J. Garber & K. A. Dodge (Eds.), *The development of emotion regulation and dysregulation* (pp. 15–48). New York: Cambridge University Press.

Crepel, V., Aronov, D., Jorquera, I., Represa, A., Ben-Ari, Y., & Cossart, R. (2007). A parturition-associated nonsynaptic coherent activity pattern in the developing hippocampus. *Neuron, 54,* 105–120.

Critchley, H. D., Wiens, S., Rothstein, P., Ohman, A., & Dolan, R. J. (2004). Neural systems supporting interoceptive awareness. *Nature Neuroscience, 7,* 189–195.

Cushing, B. S., Okorie, U., & Young, L. J. (2003). The effects of neonatal castration on the subsequent behavioural response to centrally administered arginine vasopressin and the expression of V-1a receptors in adult male prairie voles. *Journal of Neuroendocrinology, 15,* 1021–1026.

Cyranowski, J. M., Hofkens, T. L., Frank, E., Seltman, H., Cai, H. M., & Amico, J. A. (2008). Evidence of dysregulated peripheral oxytocin release among depressed women. *Psychosomatic Medicine, 70,* 967–975.

Dale, L. P., Carroll, L. E., Galen, G., Hayes, J. A., Webb, K. W., & Porges, S. W. (2009). Abuse history is related to autonomic regulation to mild exercise and psychological well being. *Applied Psychophysiology and Biofeedback, 34,* 299–308.

Darwin, C. (1994). *Expression of the emotions in man and animals.* New York: Gryphon Editions. Original work published 1872.

Davis, M. (2006). Neural systems involved in fear and anxiety measured with fear-potentiated startle. *American Psychologist, 61,* 741–756.

DeGangi, G. A., DiPietro, J. A., Greenspan, S. I., & Porges, S. W. (1991). Psychophysiological characteristics of the regulatory disordered infant. *Infant Behavior and Development, 14,* 37–50.

DeVries, A. C., DeVries, M. B., Taymans, S. E., & Carter, C. S. (1995). The modulation of pair bonding by corticosterone in female prairie voles (*Microtus ochrogaster*). *Proceedings of the National Academy of Sciences USA, 92,* 744–748.

DeVries, A. C., DeVries, M. B., Taymans, S. E., & Carter, C. S. (1996). The effects of stress on social preferences are sexually dimorphic in prairie voles. *Proceedings of the National Academy of Sciences USA, 93,* 11980–11984.

DeVries, A. C., Gupta, T., Cardillo, S., Cho, M., & Carter, C. S. (2002). Corticotropin-releasing factor induced social preferences in male prairie voles. *Psychoneuroendocrinology, 27,* 705–714.

DeVries, G. J., & Panzica, G. C. (2006). Sexual differentiation of central vasopressin and vasotocin systems in vertebrates: Different mechanisms, similar endpoints. *Neuroscience, 138,* 947–955.

DeVries, G. J., & Simerly, R. B. (2002). Anatomy, development and functions of sexually dimorphic neural circuits in the mammalian brain. In D. Pfaff, A. P. Arnold, A. M. Etgen, S. E. Fahrback, & R. T. Rubin. (Eds.), *Hormones, brain and behavior* (Vol. 4, pp. 137–192). San Diego, CA: Academic Press.

Djupesland, G. (1976). Nonacoustic reflex measurement: Procedures, interpretations and variables. In A. S. Feldman & L. A. Wilber (Eds.), *Acoustic impedance and admittance: The measurement of middle ear function* (pp. 217–235). Baltimore, MD: Williams & Wilkins.

Domes, G., Heinrichs, M., Michel, A., Berger, C., & Herpertz, S. C. (2007). Oxytocin improves "mind-reading" in humans. *Biological Psychiatry, 61,* 731–733.

Donaldson, Z. R., & Young, L. J. (2008). Oxytocin, vasopressin, and the neurogenetics of sociality. *Science, 322,* 900–904.

Doussard-Roosevelt, J. A., McClenny, B. D., Porges, S. W. (2001). Neonatal cardiac vagal tone and school-age developmental outcome in very low birth weight infants. *Developmental Psychobiology, 38,* 56–66.

Doussard-Roosevelt, J. A., Porges, S. W., Scanlon, J. W., Alemi, B., & Scanlon, K. B. (1997). Vagal regulation of heart rate in the prediction of developmental outcome for very low birth weight preterm infants. *Child Development, 68,* 173–186.

Engelmann, M., Landgraf, R., & Wotjak, C. T. (2004). The hypothalamic-neurohypophysial system regulates the hypothalamic-pituitary-adrenal axis under stress: An old concept revisited. *Frontiers in Neuroendocrinology, 25(3–4),* 132–149.

Fracasso, M. P., Porges, S. W., Lamb, M. E., & Rosenberg, A. (1994). Cardiac activity in infancy: Reliability and stability of individual differences. *Infant Behavior and Development, 17,* 277–284.

Francis, D., Young, L. J., Meaney, M. J., & Insel, T. R. (2002). Naturally occurring differences in maternal care are associated with the expression of OT and AVP (V1a) receptors: Gender differences. *Journal of Neuroendocrinology, 14,* 349–353.

Getz, L. L., & Carter, C. S. (1996). Prairie vole partnerships. *American Scientist, 84,* 56–62.

Gimpl, G., & Fahrenholz, F. (2001). The oxytocin receptor system: Structure, function and regulation. *Physiological Reviews, 81,* 629–683.

Gingrich, B. S., Liu, Y., Cascio, C., Wang, Z., & Insel, T. R. (2000). Dopamine D2 receptors in the nucleus accumbens are important for social attachment in female prairie voles (*microtus ochrogaster*). *Behavioral Neuroscience, 114,* 173–183.

Glynn, L. M., Davis, E. P., Schetter, C. D., Chicz-Demet, A., Hobel, C. J., & Sandman, C. J. (2007). Postnatal maternal cortisol levels predict temperament in healthy breastfed infants. *Early Human Development, 83,* 675–681.

Goldman, M. B., Marlow-O'Connor, M., Torres, I., & Carter, C. S. (2008). Preliminary data on diminished plasma oxytocin in schizophrenic patients with neuroendocrine dysfunction and emotional deficits. *Schizophrenia Research, 98,* 247–255.

Grippo, A. J., Cushing, B. S., & Carter, C. S. (2007). Depression-like behavior and stressor-induced neuroendocrine activation in female prairie voles exposed to chronic social isolation. *Psychosomatic Medicine, 69,* 149–157.

Grippo, A. J., Gerena, D., Huang, J., Kumar, N., Shah, M., Ughreja, R., et al. (2007). Social isolation induces behavioral and neuroendocrine disturbances relevant to depression in female and male prairie voles. *Psychoneuroendocrinology, 32,* 966–980.

Grippo, A. J., Lamb, D. G., Carter, C. S., & Porges, S. W. (2007a). Cardiac regulation in the socially monogamous prairie vole. *Physiology and Behavior, 90,* 386–393.

Grippo, A. J., Lamb, D. G., Carter, C. S., & Porges, S. W. (2007b). Social isolation disrupts autonomic regulation of the heart and influences negative affective behaviors. *Biological Psychiatry, 62,* 1162–1170.

Grippo, A. J., Trahanas, D. M., Zimmerman, II, R. R, Porges, S. W., & Carter, C. S. (2009). Oxytocin protects against negative behavioral and autonomic consequences of long-term social isolation. *Psychoneuroendocrinology, 34,* 1542–1553.

Grippo, A. J., Wu, K. D., Hassan, I., & Carter, C. S. (2008). Social isolation in prairie voles induces behavior relevant to negative affect: Toward the development of a rodent model focused on co-occurring depression and anxiety. *Depression and Anxiety, 25,* 17–26.

Grosvenor, C. E., Picciano, M. T., & Baumrucker, C. R. (1993). Hormones and growth factors in milk. *Endocrine Reviews, 14,* 710–728.

Hammock, E. A., & Young, L. J. (2005). Microsatellite instability generates diversity in brain and sociobehavioral traits. *Science, 308,* 1630–1634.

Harris, J. C. (2007). The evolutionary neurobiology, emergence and facilitation of empathy. In T. F. D. Farrow & P. W. R. Woodruff (Eds.), *Empathy in mental illness.* New York: Cambridge University Press.

Hastings, P. D., Nuselovici, J. N., Utendale, W. T., Couyta, J., McShane, K. E., & Sullivan, C. (2008). Applying the polyvagal theory to children's emotion regulation: Social context, socialization, and adjustment. *Biological Psychology, 79,* 10–21.

Heinrichs, M., Meinlschmidt, G., Neumann, I., Wagner, S., Kirschbaum, C., Ehlert, U., et al. (2001). Effects of suckling on hypothalamic-pituitary-adrenal axis responses to psychosocial stress in postpartum lactating women. *Journal of Clinical Endocrinology and Metabolism, 86,* 4798–4804.

Hennessy, M. B. (1997). Hypothalamic–pituitary–adrenal responses to brief social separation. *Neuroscience and Biobehavioral Reviews, 21,* 11–29.

Herman, B. H., & Panksepp, J. (1978). Effects of morphine and naloxone on separation distress and approach attachment: Evidence of opiate mediation of social effect. *Pharmacology, Biochemistry and Behavior, 9,* 213–220.

Hofer, M. A. (1987). Early social relationships: A psychobiologist's view. *Child Development, 58,* 633–647.

Hrdy, S. B. (2005). Evolutionary context of human development: The cooperative breeding model. In C. S. Carter, L. Ahnert, K. E. Grossman, S. B. Hrdy, M. E. Lamb, S. W. Porges, et al., *Attachment and bonding: A new synthesis* (pp. 9–32). Cambridge, MA: MIT Press.

Huber, D., Veinante, P., & Stoop, R. (2005). Vasopressin and oxytocin excite distinct neuronal populations in the central amygdala. *Science, 308,* 245–248.

Huffman, L. C., Bryan, Y., del Carmen, R., Pedersen, F. A., Doussard-Roosevelt, J. A., & Porges, S. W. (1998). Infant temperament and cardiac vagal tone: Assessments at 12 weeks of age. *Child Development, 69,* 624–635.

Insel, T. R., & Hulihan, T. J. (1995). A gender-specific mechanism for pair bonding: Oxytocin and partner preference formation in monogamous voles. *Behavioral Neuroscience, 109,* 782–789.

Insel T. R., & Shapiro, L. E. (1992). Oxytocin receptor distribution reflects social organization in monogamous and polygamous voles. *Proceedings of the National Academy of Sciences USA, 89,* 5981–5985.

Insel, T. R., & Winslow, J. T. (1991). Central administration of OT modulates the infant rat's response to social isolation. *European Journal of Pharmacology, 203,* 149–152.

Izard, C. E., Porges, S. W., Simons, R. F., Parisi, M., Haynes, O. M., & Cohen, B. (1991). Infant cardiac activity: Developmental changes and relations with attachment. *Developmental Psychology, 27,* 432–439.

Kennedy, A. E., Rubin, K. H., Hastings, P. D., & Maisel, B. (2004). Longitudinal relations between child vagal tone and parenting behavior: 2 to 4 years. *Developmental Psychobiology, 45,* 10–21.

Keverne, E. B. (2005). Neurobiological and molecular approaches to attachment and bonding. In C. S. Carter, L. Ahnert, K. E. Grossman, S. B. Hrdy, M. E. Lamb, S. W. Porges, et al., *Attachment and bonding: A new synthesis* (pp. 101–118). Cambridge, MA: MIT Press.

Khazipov, R., Tyzio, R., & Ben-Ari, Y. (2008). Effects of oxytocin on GABA signaling in the fetal brain during delivery. *Progress in Brain Research, 170,* 243–254.

Kimura, T., Saji, F., Nishimori, K., Ogita, K., Nakamura, H., Koyama, M., & Murata, Y. (2003). Molecular regulation of the oxytocin receptor in peripheral organs. *Journal of Molecular Endocrinology, 30,* 109–115.

Kirsch, P., Esslinger, C., Chen, Q., Mier, D., Lis, S., Siddhanti, S., et al. (2005). Oxytocin modulates neural circuitry for social cognition and fear in humans. *Journal of Neuroscience, 25,* 11489–11493.

Kirschbaum, C., Pirke, K-M., & Hellhammer, D. (1993). *Neuropsychobiology, 28,* 76–81.

Klaus, M. H., & Kennell, J. H. (1982). *Parent–infant bonding*. St. Louis: Mosby.

Knox, S. S., & Uvnäs-Moberg, K. (1998). Social isolation and cardiovascular disease: An atherosclerotic pathway? *Psychoneuroendocrinology, 23,* 877–890.

Koolhaas, J. M, Everts, H., de Ruiter, A. J., de Boer, S. F., & Bohus, B. (1998). Coping with stress in rats and mice: Differential peptidergic modulation of the amygdala-lateral septum complex. *Progress in Brain Research, 119,* 437–448.

Kosfeld, M., Heinrichs, M., Zak, P. J., Fischbacher, U., & Fehr, E. Oxytocin increases trust in humans. *Nature, 435,* 673–676.

Kramer, K. M., Cushing, B. S., Carter, C. S., Wu, J., & Ottinger, M. A. (2004). Sex and species differences in plasma oxytocin using an enzyme immunoassay. *Canadian Journal of Zoology, 82,* 1194–1200.

Lamb, M. E. (1982). The bonding phenomenon: misinterpretations and their implications. *Journal of Pediatrics, 101,* 555–557.

Landgraf, R., Malkinson, T., Horn, T., Veale, W. L., Lederis, K., & Pittman, Q. J. (1990). Release of vasopressin and oxytocin by paraventricular stimulation in rats. *American Journal of Physiology, 258* (1 Pt 2), R155–R159.

Landgraf, R., & Neumann, I. D. (2004). Vasopressin and oxytocin release within the brain: A dynamic concept of multiple and variable modes of neuropeptide communication. *Frontiers in Neuroendocrinology, 25,* 150–176.

Leake, R. D., Weitzman, R. E., & Fisher, D. A. (1981). Oxytocin concentrations during the neonatal period. *Biology of the Neonate, 39,* 127–131.

Levine, S. (2005). Developmental determinants of sensitivity and resistance to stress. *Psychoneuroendocrinology, 30,* 939–946.

Liberzon, I., & Young, L. J. (1997). Effects of stress and glucocorticoids on CNS oxytocin receptor binding. *Psychoneuroendocrinology, 22,* 411–422.

Lim, M. M., Hammock, E. A. D., & Young, L. J. (2004). The role of vasopressin in the genetic and neural regulation of monogamy. *Journal of Neuroendocrinology, 16,* 325–332.

Lim, M. M., Liu, Y., Ryabinin, A. E., Bai, Y., Wang, Z., & Young, L. J. (2007). CRF receptors in the nucleus accumbens modulate partner preference in prairie voles. *Hormones and Behavior, 51,* 508–515.

Lipari, E. F., Lipari, D., Gerbino, A., Di Liberto, D., Bellafiore, M., Catalano, M., et al. (2001). The hypothalamic magnocellular neurosecretory system in developing rats. *European Journal of Histochemistry, 45,* 163–168.

MacLean, P. D. (1990). *The triune brain in evolution: Role in paleocerebral functions*. New York: Plenum Press.

Main, M., Kaplan, N., & Cassidy, J. (1985). Security in infancy, childhood, and adulthood: A move to the level of representation. In E. Bielhartor & E. Waters (Eds.), *Growing points in attachment theory and research. Monographs of the Society for Research in Child Development, 50*, 66–104.

Main, M., & Solomon, J. (1990). Procedures for identifying infants as disorganized/disoriented during the Ainsworth Strange Situation. In M. T. Greenberg, D. Cicchetti, & E. M. Cummings (Eds.), *Attachment in the preschool years: Theory, research and intervention* (pp. 121–160). Chicago: University of Chicago Press.

Mantella, R. C., Vollmer, R. R., & Amico, J. A. (2005). Corticosterone release is heightened in food or water deprived oxytocin deficient male mice. *Brain Research, 1058,* 56–61.

Mantella, R. C., Vollmer, R. R., Li, X., & Amico, J. A. (2003). Female oxytocin-deficient mice display enhanced anxiety-related behavior. *Endocrinology, 144,* 2291–2296.

McEwen, B. S., & Wingfield, J. C. (2003). The concept of allostasis in biology and medicine. *Hormones and Behavior, 43,* 2–15.

Meaney, M. J. (2001). Maternal care, gene expression, and the transmission of individual differences in stress reactivity across generations. *Annual Review of Neuroscience, 24,* 1161–1192.

Meaney, M. J., & Szyf, M. (2005). Maternal care as a model for experience-dependent chromatin plasticity? *Trends in Neuroscience, 28,* 456–463.

Michel, G. F., & Moore, C. L. (1995). *Developmental Psychobiology*. Cambridge, MD: Bradford Book/MIT Press.

Murphy, J. V., Wheless, J. W., & Schmoll, C. M. (2000). Left vagal nerve stimulation in six patients with hypothalamic hamartomas. *Pediatric Neurology, 23,* 167–168.

Nelson, E., & Panksepp J. (1996). Oxytocin mediates acquisition of maternally associated odor preferences in pre-weaning rat pups. *Behavioral Neuroscience, 110,* 583–592.

Nomura, M., Saito, J., Ueta, Y., Muglia, L. J., Pfaff, D. W., & Ogawa, S. (2003). Enhanced up-regulation of corticotropin-releasing hormone gene expression in response to restraint stress in the hypothalamic paraventricular nucleus of oxytocin gene-deficient male mice. *Journal of Neuroendocrinology, 15,* 1054–1061

Nowak, M. A. (2006). Five rules for the evolution of cooperation. *Science, 314,* 1560–1563.

Olazabal, D. E., & Young, L .J. (2006). Oxytocin receptors in the nucleus accumbens facilitate "spontaneous" maternal behavior in adult female prairie voles. *Neuroscience, 141,* 559–568.

Ophir, A. G., Wolff, J. O., & Phelps, S. M. (2008). Variation in neural V1aR predicts sexual fidelity and space use among male prairie voles in semi-natural settings. *Proceedings of the National Academy of Sciences USA, 105,* 1249–1254.

Ostrowski, N. L. (1998). Oxytocin receptor mRNA expression in rat brain: Implications for behavioral integration and reproductive success. *Psychoneuroendocrinology, 23,* 989–1004.

Palanza, P., Gioiosa, L., & Parmigiani, S. (2001). Social stress in mice: Gender differences and effects of estrous cycle and social dominance. *Physiology and Behavior, 73,* 411–420.

Paquin, J., Danalache, B. A., Jankowski, M., McCann, S. M., & Gutkowski, J. (2002). Oxytocin induces differentiation of P19 embryonic stem cells to cardiomyocytes. *Proceedings of the National Academy of Sciences USA, 99,* 9550–9555.

Parada, M., King, S., Li, M., & Fleming, A.S. (2008). The role of accumbal dopamine D1 and D2 receptors in maternal memory in rats. *Behavioral Neuroscience, 122,* 368–376.

Pedersen, C. A. (1997). Oxytocin control of maternal behavior: Regulation by sex steroids and offspring stimuli. *Annals of the New York Academy of Sciences, 807,* 126–145.

Pedersen, C. A., & Boccia, M. L. (2006). Vasopressin interactions with oxytocin in the control of female sexual behavior. *Neuroscience, 139,* 843–851.

Pedersen, C. A., Vadlamudi, S. V., Boccia, M. L., & Amico, J. A. (2006). Maternal behavior deficits in nulliparous oxytocin knockout mice. *Genes, Brain and Behavior, 5,* 274–281.

Pereyra, P. M., Zhang, W., Schmidt, M., & Becker, L. E. (1992). Development of myelinated and unmyelinated fibers of human vagus nerve during the first year of life. *Journal of Neurological Sciences, 110,* 107–113.

Phelps, S. M., & Young, L. J. (2003). Extraordinary diversity in vasopressin (V1a) receptor distributions among wild prairie voles (*microtus ochrogaster*): Patterns of variation and covariation. *Journal of Comparative Neurology, 466,* 564–576.

Porges, S. W. (1992). Vagal tone: A physiological marker of stress vulnerability. *Pediatrics,* 90, 498–504.

Porges, S. W. (1993). The infant's sixth sense: Awareness and regulation of bodily processes. *Zero to Three: Bulletin of the National Center for Clinical Infant Programs, 14,* 12–16.

Porges, S. W. (1995a). Cardiac vagal tone: A physiological index of stress. *Neuroscience and Biobehavioral Reviews, 19,* 225–233.

Porges, S. W. (1995b). Orienting in a defensive world: Mammalian modifications of our evolutionary heritage. A polyvagal theory. *Psychophysiology, 32,* 301–318.

Porges, S. W. (1998). Love: An emergent property of the mammalian autonomic nervous system. *Psychoneuroendocrinology, 23,* 837–861.

Porges, S. W. (2001). The polyvagal theory: Phylogenetic substrates of a social nervous system. *International Journal of Psychophysiology, 42,* 123–146.

Porges, S. W. (2003). The polyvagal theory: Phylogenetic contributions to social behavior. *Physiology and Behavior, 79,* 503–513.

Porges S. W. (2004). The vagus: A mediator of behavioral and visceral features associated with autism. In M. L. Bauman & T. L. Kemper (Eds.), *The neurobiology of autism* (pp. 65–78). Baltimore: Johns Hopkins University Press.

Porges, S. W. (2007). The polyvagal perspective. *Biological Psychology, 74,* 116–143.

Porges, S. W. (2008). The polyvagal theory: New insights into adaptive reactions of the autonomic nervous system. *Cleveland Clinic Journal of Medicine, 75,* S1–S5.

Porges, S. W., Doussard-Roosevelt, J. A., Portales, A. L., & Greenspan, S. I. (1996). Infant regulation of the vagal "brake" predicts child behavior problems: A psychobiological model of social behavior. *Developmental Psychobiology, 29,* 697–712.

Porges, S. W., Doussard-Roosevelt, J. A., Portales, A. L., & Suess, P. E. (1994). Cardiac vagal tone: Stability and relation to difficultness in infants and three-year-old children. *Developmental Psychobiology, 27,* 289–300.

Porges, S. W., & Lipsitt, L. P. (1993). Neonatal responsivity to gustatory stimulation: The gustatory–vagal hypothesis. *Infant Behavior and Development, 16,* 487–494.

Portales, A. L., Porges, S. W., Abedin, M., Lopez, R., Young, M. A., Beeram, M. R., et al. (1997). Vagal regulation during bottle feeding in low-birthweight neonates: Support for the gustatory-vagal hypothesis. *Developmental Psychobiology, 30,* 225–233.

Porter, F. L., Porges, S. W., & Marshall, R. E. (1988). Newborn pain cries and vagal tone: Parallel changes in response to circumcision. *Child Development, 59,* 495–505.

Ragnauth, A. K., Devidze, N., Moy, V., Finley, K., Goodwillie, A., Kow, L-M., et al. (2005). Female oxytocin gene-knockout mice, in a seminatural environment, display exaggerated aggressive behavior. *Genes, Brain and Behavior, 4,* 229–239.

Redwine, L. S., Altemus, M., Leong, Y-M., & Carter, C. S. (2001). Differential immune responses to stress in postpartum women. *Psychoneuroendocrinology, 26,* 241–251.

Roberts, R. L., Gustafson, E. A., & Carter, C. S. (1997). Perinatal hormone exposure alters the expression of selective affiliative preferences in prairie voles. *Annals of the New York Academy of Sciences, Integrative Neurobiology of Affiliation, 807,* 563–566.

Roberts, R. L., Williams, J. R., Wang, A. K., & Carter, C. S. (1998). Cooperative breeding and monogamy in prairie voles: Influence of the sire and geographic variation. *Animal Behaviour, 55,* 1131–1140

Sachis, P. N., Armstrong, D. L., Becker, L. E., & Bryan, A. C. (1982). Myelination of the human vagus nerve from 24 weeks postconceptual age to adolescence. *Journal of Neuropathology and Experimental Neurology, 41,* 466–472.

Sachser, N. (2005). Adult social bonding: Insights from studies in nonhuman mammals. In C. S. Carter, L. Ahnert, K. E. Grossman, S. B. Hrdy, M. E. Lamb, S. W. Porges, et al., *Attachment and bonding: A new synthesis* (pp. 119–136). Cambridge, MA: MIT Press.

Sahar, T., Shalev, A. Y., & Porges, S. W. (2001). Vagal modulation of responses to mental challenge in post-traumatic stress disorder. *Biological Psychiatry, 49,* 637–643.

Selye, H. (1950). *The physiology and pathology of exposure to stress.* London: Oxford Press.

Singer, B. H., & Ryff, C. D. (Eds.). (2001). *New horizons in health: An integrative approach.* Washington, DC: National Academy Press.

Singh, P. J., & Hofer, M. A. (1978). Oxytocin reinstates maternal olfactory cues for nipple orientation and attachment in rat pups. *Physiology and Behavior, 20,* 385–389.

Skuse, D. H., & Gallagher, L. (2009). Dopaminergic-neuropeptide interactions in the social brain. *Trends in Cognitive Sciences, 13,* 27–35.

Snijdewint, F. G. M., Van Leeuwen, F. W., & Boer, G. J. (1989). Ontogeny of AVP and OT binding sites in the brain of Wistar and Brattleboro rats as demonstrated by light microscopical autoradiography. *Journal of Chemical Neuroanatomy, 2,* 3–17.

Spitz, R. (1945). Hospitalism: An inquiry into the genesis of psychiatric conditions in early childhood. *Psychoanalytic Study of the Child, 1,* 53–75.

Stern, J. M., & Lonstein, J. S. (2001). Neural mediation of nursing and related maternal behaviors. *Progress in Brain Research, 133,* 263–278.

Stifter, C., & Corey, J. (2001). Vagal regulation and observed social behavior in infancy. *Social Development, 10,* 189–201.

Stribley, J. M., & Carter, C. S. (1999). Neonatal vasopressin increases aggression in prairie voles. *Proceedings of the National Academy of Sciences USA, 96,* 12601–12604.

Suess, P. E., Alpan, G., Dulkerian, S. J., Doussard-Roosevelt, J. A., Porges, S.W., & Gewolb, I. H. (2000). Respiratory sinus arrhythmia during feeding: A measure of vagal regulation of metabolism, ingestion, and digestion in preterm infants. *Developmental Medicine and Child Neurology, 42,* 169–173.

Swaab, D. F., & Boer, G. J. (1994). Neuropeptides and brain development: Current perils and future potential. *Journal of Developmental Physiology, 5,* 67–75.

Szyf, M., Weaver, I. C. G., Champagne, F. A., Diorio, J., & Meaney, M. J. (2005). Maternal programming of steroid receptor expression and phenotype through DNA methylation in the rat. *Frontiers in Neuroendocrinology, 26,* 139–162.

Taylor, S. E., Gonzaga, G. C., Klein, L. C., Hu, P., Greendale, G. A., & Seeman, T. E. (2006). Relation of oxytocin to psychological stress responses and hypothalamic–pituitary–adrenocortical axis activity in older women. *Psychosomatic Medicine, 68,* 238–245.

Theodosis, D. T. (2002). Oxytocin-secreting neurons: A physiological model of morphological neuronal and glial plasticity in the adult hypothalamus. *Frontiers in Neuroendocrinology, 23,* 101–135.

Theodosis, D. T., Trailin, A., & Poulain, D. A. (2006). Remodeling of astrocytes, a prerequisite for synapse turnover in the adult brain? Insights from the oxytocin system of the hypothalamus. *American Journal of Physiology Regulation, Integrative and Comparative Physiology, 290,* R1175–R1182.

Thompson, R., George, K., Walton, J. C., Orr, S. P., & Benson, J. (2006). Sex-specific influences of vasopressin on human social communication. *Proceedings of the National Academy of Sciences USA, 103,* 7889–7894.

Tyzio, R., Cossart, R., Khalilov, I., Minlebaev, M., Hubner, C. A., Represa, A., et al. (2006). Maternal oxytocin triggers a transient inhibitory switch in GABA signaling in the fetal brain during delivery. *Science, 314,* 1788–1792.

Uchino, B. N., Cacioppo, J. T., & Kiecolt-Glaser, J. K. (1996). The relationship between social support and physiological processes: A review with emphasis on underlying mechanisms and implications for health. *Psychological Bulletin, 119,* 488–531.

Umhau, J. C., George, D. T., Reed, S., Petrulis, S. G., Rawlings, R., & Porges, S. W. (2002). Atypical autonomic regulation in perpetrators of violent domestic abuse. *Psychophysiology, 39,* 117–123.

Uvnas-Moberg, K. (1998). Oxytocin may mediate the benefits of positive social interaction and emotions. *Psychoneuroendocrinology, 23,* 819–835.

Viviani, D., & Stoop, R. (2008). Opposite effects of oxytocin and vasopressin on the emotional expression of the fear response. *Progress in Brain Research, 170,* 207–218.

Wakschlag, L. S., Leventhal, B. L., Pine, D. S., Pickett, K. E., & Carter, A.S. (2006). Elucidating early mechanisms of developmental psychopathology: The case of prenatal smoking and disruptive behavior. *Child Development, 77,* 893–906.

Wang Z., Young, L. J., DeVries, G. J., & Insel, T. R. (1998). Voles and vasopressin: A review of molecular, cellular, and behavioral studies of pair bonding and paternal behaviors. *Progress in Brain Research, 119,* 483–499.

Williams, J. R., Catania, K., & Carter, C. S. (1992). Development of partner preferences in female prairie voles (*microtus ochrogaster*): The role of social and sexual experience. *Hormones and Behavior, 26,* 339–349.

Williams, J. R., Insel, T. R., Harbaugh, C. R., & Carter, C. S. (1994). Oxytocin administered centrally facilitates formation of a partner preference in female prairie voles. *Journal of Neuroendocrinology, 6,* 247–250.

Wilson, E. O. (1998). *Consilience: The unity of knowledge.* New York: Knopf.

Winslow, J. T., Hastings, N., Carter, C. S., Harbaugh, C. R., & Insel, T. R. (1993). A role for central vasopressin in pair bonding in monogamous prairie voles. *Nature, 365,* 545–548.

Winslow, J. T., & Insel, T. R. (2006). The social deficits of the oxytocin knockout mouse. *Neuropeptides, 36,* 221–229.

Witt, D. M., Carter, C. S., & Insel, T. R. (1991). Oxytocin receptor binding in female prairie voles: Endogenous and exogenous oestradiol stimulation. *Journal of Neuroendocrinology, 3,* 155–161.

Yamamoto, Y., Cushing, B. S., Kramer, K. M., Epperson, P. D., Hoffman, G. E., & Carter, C. S. (2004). Neonatal manipulations of oxytocin alter expression of oxytocin and vasopressin immunoreactive cells in the paraventricular nucleus of the hypothalamus in a gender-specific manner. *Neuroscience, 125,* 947–955.

Yee, J. R., Cavigelli, S. A., Delgade, B., & McClintock, M. K. (2008). Reciprocal affiliation among adolescent rats during a mild group stressor predicts mammary tumors and lifespan. *Psychosomatic Medicine, 70,* 1050–1059.

Yehuda, R., & Bierer, L. M. (2008). Transgenerational transmission of cortisol and PTSD risk. *Progress in Brain Research, 167,* 12–135.

Young, L. J., & Carter, C. S. (2008). Sex differences in affiliative behavior and social bonding. In J. B. Becker, K. J. Berkley, N. Geary, E. Hampson, J. P. Herman, & E. A. Young (Eds.), *Sex on the brain: From genes to behavior* (pp. 139–153). New York: Oxford University Press.

Young, L. J., Murphy-Young, A. Z., & Hammock, E. A. (2005). Anatomy and neurochemistry of the pair bond. *Journal of Comparative Neurology, 493,* 51–57.

Young, L. J., & Wang, Z. (2004). The neurobiology of pair bonding, *Nature Neuroscience, 7,* 1048–1054.

CHAPTER 3

The Development of Emotion Regulation: A Neuropsychological Perspective

MARC D. LEWIS, REBECCA TODD, and XIAOWEN XU

Emotion regulation (ER) has been a focus of interest for developmentalists for more than 30 years. Much has been written on normative advances in ER capacities as well as individual differences in ER that appear fundamental to personality and its development. Normative approaches highlight milestones or critical ages at which particular ER capabilities come on line, either as a distinct domain of development (e.g., Kopp, 1989) or as a function of cognitive development more broadly (e.g., Case, 1988; Sroufe, 1996). Approaches concerned with individual differences attempt to explain and/or predict attachment classifications, temperament, personality development, and, at the extreme, developmental psychopathology based on styles of ER (e.g., Bradley, 2000; Eisenberg, Hofer, & Vaughan, 2007; Rothbart & Bates, 1998; Thompson & Lamb, 1984). Unfortunately, however, research on normative advances in ER has remained largely independent of work on individual differences. Moreover, this fragmentation extends to defining ER, determining appropriate paradigms for conceptualizing it, modeling its basic mechanisms, and making sense of the rich and varied phenomena it seems to include. This dissociative—one might even say "dysregulated"—state of affairs is distressing for three interrelated reasons. First, it makes it difficult to conceptualize the critical socioemotional differences that are more or less unique to particular developmental phases or transitions. Second, it makes it difficult to specify and model age-related milestones that remain entangled with individual personality dynamics. Finally, it makes it difficult to move toward a general theory of ER development. If we cannot agree on what it is we're studying, it becomes all the more difficult to explain it.

The absence of a comprehensive, mechanism-based framework may be a principal factor contributing to dysregulation in the developmental study of ER. The goal of this chapter is therefore to try to provide such a framework by approaching the development of ER from a neuroscientific perspective (e.g., Amodio, Master, Yee, & Taylor, 2008; Kim & Hamann, 2007; Marsh et al., 2006; Ochsner & Gross, 2005, 2007). Many fields within psychology, and within developmental psychology more specifically, have benefited from integration with the explosion of knowledge in contemporary neuroscience. The study of the brain, with its emphasis on concrete biological processes and its attention to universal principles of developmental change and consolidation, has been useful for grounding psychological abstractions in firmer terrain. Moreover, by maintaining a macroscopic or system-level perspective, contemporary approaches to the brain have accomplished this grounding without throwing away the richness and relevance of psychological insights. In this chapter, we focus on neuroscientific concepts and techniques that construe the brain as a massive self-organizing system, in which all activity is fundamentally developmental because it arises through interactions among components that continue to change as a result of those very interactions. Our aim is the integration of principles of neural self-organization and self-regulation with constructs from cognitive, personality, clinical, and especially developmental psychology to contribute to a broad-based framework for understanding the development of ER and its impact on individual growth. For a more detailed introduction to self-organizational brain processes, see our earlier publications (Lewis 2005a, 2005b; Lewis & Todd, 2007).

The chapter is organized as follows. We identify two major conundrums for the developmental study of ER—points at which it has gotten bogged down, disjointed, or dysregulated, so to speak. These are construed as metatheoretical problems, inviting resolution at a global scale. Moreover, they characterize central currents in the developmental study of ER, especially in the preschool period, which is when it receives the most attention. In an attempt to resolve these conundrums, we try to pin down the conceptualization of ER by joining the conventional developmental approach with two distinct literatures: the study of *executive function,* the suite of cognitive operations responsible for controlling (or *regulating*) thought, emotion, and behavior (e.g., Blair, Zelazo, & Greenberg, 2005), and the adult literature on self-regulation (e.g., Amodio et al., 2008; Baumeister & Heatherton, 1996), which is sometimes regarded as a distinct domain. We then proceed to a detailed look at the neurobiology of emotion regulation. Neural mechanisms related to cognitive control, emotional processes, and developmental change and crystallization are identified and explained. We address each theoretical conundrum on the basis of those mechanisms, to try to resolve the noted ambiguities and point in new directions for productive theorizing. In the final two sections of the chapter, we introduce two age-specific phenomena that are difficult to explain through psychological approaches to ER development. We extend the neurobiological principles presented in previous sections to help explain each of these phenomena, thus demonstrating the utility of a brain-based analysis for making sense of ER development.

Through this organization we arrive at four conclusions:

1. ER uses cognitive operations neither preceding nor following but integrated with emotional processes; moreover, *cognition* and *emotion* cannot be differentiated in the brain, and self-regulatory activities are best parsed and sequenced according to the functions they serve.
2. Although ER advances in a roughly predictable manner with development, this progression derives from experience-dependent processes of synaptic shaping. In fact, the emotional basis of cortical consolidation locks in individual differences while advancing cognitive capabilities, so that individual elaboration (the emergence of personality styles) and developmental *progress* are deeply intertwined.
3. Despite the increasing sophistication of their cognitive capabilities, adolescents show more negative, dysregulated, or disadvantageous emotional responses, demonstrating the importance of neural maturation for effective and reliable habits of ER.
4. Older adults are prone to more positive emotions despite deficiencies in executive control. This may be facilitated by the recruitment of additional cortical areas for critical functions such as ER to compensate for an overall decrement in cortical efficiency.

WHAT IS EMOTION REGULATION AND WHEN DOES IT OCCUR?

Emotion regulation is generally viewed as a suite or ensemble of cognitive operations that can adjust emotional responses in various ways. These include increasing or decreasing the intensity of emotional feeling states, inhibiting (or disinhibiting) the behaviors that flow from emotions, or changing the form or content of the cognitive, perceptual, and/or motor activities that correspond with various emotions. Emotion regulation can have other meanings as well. It can apply to the modulation of facial expressions or even posture. It can refer to physiological changes that prepare the body to respond to emotional triggers in various ways. Emotion regulation is usually seen to extend along a dimension from rapid, automatic changes to slow, deliberate changes, referred to as *reactive* versus *effortful* control by several theorists (Eisenberg et al., 2007; Kochanska, Murray, & Harlan, 2000), following a distinction initially made by Mary Rothbart (e.g., Rothbart & Derryberry, 1981; Posner & Rothbart, 2000). However, slow or strategic regulatory activities need not be deliberate or even conscious, as in the case of response suppression (Ochsner & Gross, 2007). ER is most often viewed as a cognitive process. However, ER can refer to a much broader set of self-regulatory activities, including physiologial adjustments, fatigue, or social forms of control including reinforcers administered either deliberately (e.g., by parents) or automatically (e.g., in the service of cultural standards). In this chapter, we stick with the idea that ER is cognitive—not because this is completely accurate or inclusive but because it captures the character of adaptive changes that come about through learning, practice, deliberation, and so forth.

When ER is considered as a suite of cognitive activities, ranging from automatic to deliberate, it corresponds closely with another umbrella term: *executive function* (EF). Executive functions include many kinds of cognitive activities that control or change what is going on in thought, perception, emotion, or action. In other words, EFs regulate or control every class of psychological activity. The most familiar executive functions are deliberate or conscious in nature, and they include focused or sustained attention, inhibitory control (which can *help* to sustain attention), switching or choosing one goal or activity over another, self-monitoring or action monitoring, including conflict detection, error monitoring, and so forth, accessing working memory and using it to manipulate and compare possible outcomes, set shifting, and reappraisal or reinterpretation of the meaning or significance of events. This list of activities clearly maps onto the list of operations commonly assigned to ER. We sustain attention to goals to diminish the anxiety of failing to reach them. We inhibit actions such as swearing or shouting when we are angry, and we inhibit feeling states such as sadness and shame simply because they are painful. We switch goals when we anticipate that our efforts are otherwise doomed to failure or because satisfying a present goal (like boasting about our accomplishments) is likely to thwart a superordinate goal (like maintaining others' affection), leading to painful emotions such as shame. We frequently monitor our behavior—for example, our words during an argument—thus modulating the impulses that can invite loss or retaliation, and we are constantly on the lookout for errors, because errors indicate loss of control, which is intrinsically anxiety-inducing. Finally, set shifting is handy for strategic control of emotions (e.g., making light of something), and reappraisal is considered a sophisticated strategy for changing the interpretation that calls up a particular emotion in the first place (e.g., Ochsner & Gross, 2007). As shown by all these examples, the list of executive functions provides a useful chart of many of the cognitive operations recruited for ER. One may even wonder whether executive functions are ever performed *without* modulating some aspect of emotion.

There are other advantages of viewing ER as a specific subclass of EF. First, executive functions have been thoroughly researched through neuroscientific methods, behavioral methods, and formal modeling. They are relatively well understood. Second, a subset of this research has gone into determining the normative developmental timetable at which particular executive functions come on line (e.g., Carlson, 2005; Zelazo, Muller, Frye, & Marcovich, 2003). Third, a number of researchers have paid specific attention to the neural changes that appear to underlie developmental advances in EF (e.g., Bunge & Zelazo, 2006; Lewis, Lamm, et al., 2006; Stuss & Alexander, 2000; Zelazo & Frye, 1997). A neuropsychological timetable for ER is only now being worked out (see Todd & Lewis, 2008), but much can be inferred from the developmental study of EF. We say more on developmental timing in later sections. For now, the important point is that executive functions can be viewed as discreet cognitive acts that alter mental or behavioral states or activities for the sake of some long-term advantage.

However, viewing emotion regulatory activities as discreet cognitive acts introduces the first bottleneck in the study of ER. A discreet cognitive act must come along somewhere in a sequence of mental activity, and this is the case whether it is executed rapidly or extended over time. So the question is this: Where in the sequence of emotional processing do cognitive acts of ER take place? The standard view is that they take place after an unpleasant, challenging, or disruptive emotion has begun to arise. Along comes the unpleasant or challenging emotion and next comes the regulatory activity designed to modify it or to modify the behaviors that emanate from it. However, acts of ER could also precede the target emotion. As long as one anticipates a negative or challenging emotion, one can act to regulate it before it arrives. For example, one could switch attention to focus on something more pleasant and less aversive. In so doing, one could alter one's appraisal so as not to generate the dreaded emotion in the first place. It has been recognized by many researchers that attentional biases can regulate an emotional response before it begins, even in childhood (e.g., Dodge & Somberg, 1987). In fact, one can backtrack even further and consider actions intended to modify an anticipated situation as a form of emotion regulation. If I am about to be introduced to an important or attractive person at a reception and I anticipate feeling shy or incompetent, then I may look beyond the person and hail a familiar face to avoid that helpless feeling of being judged and found inadequate. Notice that, in this example, even such a complex and strategic plan need not be conscious or intentional. One can fall into such behavioral routines rapidly, guided only by the vague anticipation of shame. The upshot is that cognitive acts in the service of emotion regulation can either precede or follow the target emotion, or they can start before the emotion and continue during its activation. Furthermore, these cognitive acts can be conscious or unconscious, deliberate or automatic, short-lived or ongoing. The problem is that behavioral measures and self-report measures are unable to designate where in the sequence of mental operations regulatory acts actually occur. Moreover, there is no way to specify which cognitive acts are geared toward emotion regulation and which are not. As a result, cognitive involvement in emotion regulation cannot be differentiated from the ongoing flow of cognition overall.

These problems of designation, definition, and timing can be quite serious for the study of emotion regulation, because the constituents of emotion regulation appear to have melted completely into the flow of cognitive activity more generally. However, there is a further problem that is specific to the way emotion theorists conceptualize the role of cognition in emotion. In conventional emotion theory, emotions are considered products of cognitive appraisals (here, *cognitive* is interpreted broadly, including *perceptual* activities). An appraisal is simply an interpretation of a situation as being relevant for the self. The sort of interpretation that is constructed then determines the sort of emotion one feels. If a lipstick stain on your husband's collar is appraised as the imprint of a zealous aunt, the emotion of amusement or contempt may follow. If the lipstick is interpreted as resulting from a passionate fling, the emotions of jealousy, anger, fear, or shame may arise instead. The point is that the nature of the emotional response is entirely determined by the cognitive appraisal. Appraisals (despite their name) can be extremely rapid and unconscious (Lazarus, 1995), they can unfold in several steps (Scherer, 1984, 1999; Smith & Kirby, 2001), and they can be altered by deliberate reframing of the situation. In fact it is this alteration that is referred to as *reappraisal*, and it is considered a hallmark of effective emotion regulation. The problem now is that the cognitive appraisals that precede and generate the emotion seem to overlap with the regulatory operations that are designed to *change* the emotion. So not only is ER indistinguishable from the flow of cognitive acts more generally, it is also indistinguishable from the particular set of cognitive acts that cause emotions to happen in the first place (see Campos, Frankel, & Camras, 2004, for a similar argument). Automatic or deliberate cognitive operations generate, specify, and sustain an emotion on one hand, and they modify, inhibit, or terminate the emotion on the other.

In a series of papers from 1995 to about 2005, the first author attempted to resolve this confusion by modeling cognition-emotion interaction as a feedback cycle (e.g., Lewis, 1995, 1996, 1997; Lewis & Douglas, 1998). This model followed the tradition of *process accounts* proposed by other emotion theorists throughout the 1980s and 1990s (e.g., Ellsworth, 1991; Frijda, 1993; Lazarus, 1999; Parkinson, 2001; Scherer, 2001). However, the model took the unconventional tack (also taken by Fogel et al., 1992) of using *dynamic systems* (DS) ideas to explain emotional processes. The DS approach interprets phenomena (in many disciplines) as self-organizing, self-regulating *wholes* that emerge spontaneously from reciprocal interactions among lower order *parts* or *constituents* (e.g., species in an ecosystem, cells in a biological system, molecules in a chemical or physical system). Based on the DS principle of feedback among constituents, the argument was quite straightforward. Instead of trying to designate the cognitive concomitants of emotion as either appraisal or regulation, either pre or post, either generative or constraining, it was proposed that cognitive operations and emotional reactions drive each other in an ongoing feedback process. Start anywhere in the cycle: an element of appraisal (e.g., the sight of the lipstick) induces a flash of emotion (e.g., let's start with anxiety), which elicits a regulatory response from the cognitive system (e.g., focused attention on the dimensions of the lipstick stain: its position, color, shape), which fine-tunes the appraisal of "another woman," which elicits more intense anxiety along with full-fledged jealousy, which calls up regulatory operations such as set switching (this is not about romance but rather about being kissed goodbye by sodden relatives; or, I knew I couldn't trust him: that's the final straw), which modifies the appraisal (or provides a *reappraisal*) of the situation, which alters the emotional state to one of relief or outrage, replacing the helplessness that goes with jealousy. This cycle unfolds as an ongoing set of reciprocal influences, in which the cognitive system is continuously affecting the emotional system and the emotional system continuously affects the cognitive system. Both positive and negative feedback elements are present in the process, as the emotional state and accompanying interpretation continue to shift, to wax and wane in content and intensity, and finally to settle on a particular and lasting interpretation coupled with a fine-tuned, stable emotional state or mood (Lewis, 1996). In dynamic systems terminology, the system has arrived at its attractor, given the particular environmental constraints and psychological conditions applying to this particular individual at this point in time.

This kind of modeling nicely resolves the parsing problem: both the problem of temporal sequencing of cognitive and emotional activities and the problem of designating cognitive activities as either generating or regulating emotion. It also has the advantage of maintaining the character of several discreet cognitive (and emotional) components, which might also be referred to as EFs. This componentiality is useful because it allows investigators to consider the operations of the elements of the system (not just the system as a whole) and to investigate their developmental timetable (see Granic & Lamey, 2002; Granic & Patterson, 2006; Hollenstein, 2007; Hollenstein, Granic, Stoolmiller, & Snyder, 2004; Lewis, Lamey, & Douglas, 1999; Lewis et al., 2004). Problems remain, however. The first problem is that feedback cycles in complex systems can only be analyzed realistically once we have identified their constituents in concrete terms, not abstractions and generalities. Terms such as *appraisal*, *affect*, *operation*, *attention*, and so forth remain highly global, as is typical of psychological constructs. They are not actual constituents with interactions that can be measured over time. It is this kind of problem that has steered post-behaviorist psychologists out of their dedication to cognitive constructs to the study of biological factors, whether in the realm of psychophysiology, genetics, evolutionary psychology, or, of particular importance for this chapter, neuroscience (Thompson, Lewis, & Calkins, 2008). Only by looking to the biological constituents underlying psychological phenomena can one find the precision required for a detailed model—a model that can retain the power and complexity of DS principles such as feedback, coupling, attractors, and so forth, without becoming metaphorical. Thus, in the next section, and again in the latter half of each of the following four sections, we examine the neurobiology of emotion regulation. The goal for the next section is to resolve the ambiguities and contradictions that keep coming up when theorists attempt to explain ER by parsing its cognitive and emotional components. The first and most important point is that cognitive operations and emotional operations simply cannot be distinguished in the brain. It appears that the idea of emotion regulation will have to shed more of its baggage before it can be captured with precision.

NEURAL INVESTIGATIONS OF EMOTION REGULATION

Contemporary investigators of emotion regulation attempt to differentiate cognitive and emotional processes in various ways. For example, they discuss high-level processes versus low-level processes or top-down versus bottom-up processes. This terminology has been used to build an influential model of emotion regulation (Ochsner & Gross, 2005, 2007), with an emphasis on the intermingling of these two kinds of regulatory activities. These models view cognitive functions as "high-level." The problem is that emotional states can also be high-level. They too can affect processing in a top-down fashion, as when depression biases perception, attention, and learning. Moreover, cognitive processes can assemble themselves in a bottom-up direction, as when associations, norm selection, and contextual features are recruited in decision making (e.g., Yeh & Barsalou, 2006). Zelazo and colleagues (e.g., Kerr & Zelazo, 2004) differentiate hot EF from cool EF, the former identified as dealing with emotionally pressing issues and the latter as related to more reflective or abstract reasoning processes. However, these authors have had a difficult time providing a precise delineation and, in the words of Ochsner and Gross (2005, p. 245), regulatory processes used to control emotion are "strikingly similar" to those recruited for "cold" (i.e., cognitive) forms of control.

Neuroscientists find it especially problematic to distinguish cognitive and emotional processes. It is impossible to differentiate cognitive parts of the brain from emotional parts, or cognitive networks from emotional networks, or, worse yet, cognitive functions from emotional functions. For example, it is often said that the amygdala is the emotional center of the brain, and its job is to attach emotional significance to stimuli. However, many theorists see the amygdala as an organ of appraisal, because its function is to evaluate the significance of events through associative memory and similar processes. The same can be said of the orbitofrontal cortex (OFC), a large region of the ventral prefrontal cortex involved in attaching reinforcement contingencies (or expectancies, or, once again, appraisals) to incoming information. In many ways, the OFC performs the same function as the amygdala, but it is able to switch its evaluations on the basis of contextual cues, whereas the amygdala is more rigid in its appraisals. So does the OFC subserve emotion, cognitive appraisal, or both? The hypothalamus orchestrates highly organized response tendencies that correspond with hunger, rage, or sexual pursuit. But are these emotional responses, or are they predesignated motor routines that are switched on or off based on species-specific cues (Barrett et al., 2007)? Feeling tone, affect, and so forth appear to be mediated by the upper brainstem and midbrain (e.g., Damasio, 1999; Panksepp, 1998). Yet the same structures modulate attention, perception, action readiness, and many other functions. Whereas the upper brainstem is essential to emotional responding, it is not at all clear that what the brainstem does can be called *emotional*. Lewis (2005a) made this argument in far greater detail, but one of the main conclusions was that, even if one were inclined to assign an emotional character or a cognitive character to each neural structure or system, brain structures never operate in isolation. As soon as they become activated—or, more precisely, their activation increases from baseline, or changes in mode, firing rate, chemical activity, or any other way—these structures start to work as components in networks composed of many other parts, just as one would expect of a dynamic self-organizing system. Moreover, the resulting networks of activity (recently called *intrinsic connectivity networks*; Seeley et al., 2007) are neither cognitive nor emotional in character. They are always both (Lewis, 2005a). It is more productive to designate these networks according to their functions—such as motor planning, executive control, or stimulus evaluation—and to recognize that different functions have their own unique cognitive and emotional characteristics, according to what works most effectively.

Cognition and emotion are idealized psychological categories, and they refer to processes that are known to operate in tandem. Thus, even theorists who have spent their careers insisting that emotion is a distinct system, not a subtype of cognition, acknowledge that the emotion system works together with the cognitive system in normally functioning animals (Izard, 1993; Panksepp, 1982). In our view, these theorists are absolutely right to insist that emotional systems are not a subbranch of cognitive systems, or cognitive systems plus arousal. Nevertheless, they get bogged down in conceptual contradictions when they try to define emotional systems at the brain level. Brain systems do not correspond well to psychological categories. True, the results of neural activity can be described according to those categories. We do feel emotions and we do think thoughts when our brains are acting properly. But that's because highly specialized networks of brain parts are doing what they're supposed to do, firing when they're supposed to fire, altering their responses to particular inputs in the presence of others, and so forth.

To understand how psychological entities actually derive from a brain, one needs to look at the brain in its own terms (Freeman, 1999; Tucker, 2007). Similarly, if one wants to understand taste in a detailed, mechanistic way, one has to look at the action of molecules on receptors on the tongue and the electrical activity of the cells in which those receptors are embedded. One does not try to describe the tongue's activities in terms of tasting. An aspect of brain activity that is particularly noteworthy is that most communications among neural structures are reciprocal, and this is true from very small scales, such as the flow of signals back to a cell that has just fired, inhibiting its subsequent activity, to the vast two-way traffic routes from the cortex to the brainstem, shipping signals responsible for motor activation, perceptual focus, and inhibitory control downward and neuromodulator flows mediating arousal and attention back upward. Feedback loops are nested in bigger feedback loops. Moreover, each neural feedback loop is incredibly complicated, such that inputs to one structure in the loop can influence outputs from all other structures within the same loop. Furthermore, these loops form self-organizing patterns: that is, many patterns (of activity flow, firing rates, etc.) emerge spontaneously, and they reemerge with greater predictability, time after time, as synapses are sculpted by the outcomes of their own activity. Self-organizing neural "habits" are the essence of learning, memory, and perhaps personality itself (Lewis, 2005b). But back to emotion and cognition. Given the neural principles briefly reviewed here, the substrates contributing to these two psychological categories include a great variety of brain parts, and each is nested in networks that include components (such as the amygdala) involved in *both* cognition and emotion. Thus, it is not surprising that emotion theorists find it difficult to isolate cognitive and emotional events and place them in some sensible sequence. The brain doesn't break down that way.

One of the most interesting implications of neural feedback and reciprocity concerns the timing of neural events. One might think that perception occurs before cognition, and then emotion comes along, and finally action. You have to see the boy take the lunch box, judge that he's stealing it, feel angry as a result, and then give chase (unless he's a lot bigger than you). However, a look at the brain doesn't support this analysis. Perception is guided by judgement and prediction. The perceptual cortices need feedback from frontal or parietal areas to zoom in on relevance, to "know" what to attend to, according to what's likely to make sense. Moreover, the eyes need to know where to look. Emotions are forming and dissolving all the time. So the cognitive judgement concerning stealing may itself be guided by a preexisting mood of resentment against the kids from the rich neighborhoods who bring ostentatious lunches and never share. In this case, emotion regulates appraisal, not the other way around (see P. M. Cole, Martin, & Dennis, 2004, for a discussion of these two fundamental directions of emotion regulation; Lewis & Todd, 2007). In his earlier work, Don Tucker (e.g., 1992) explained that gistlike interpretations mediated by corticolimbic loops invited participation from the sensory areas in the posterior regions of the cortex (e.g., occipital lobe) and generated motor plans in the frontal regions. Tucker's brilliant insight was that the outer layers of cortex, tuned to the world, are constantly resonating with the inner "limbic" areas of cortex, where memory and emotion maintain an ongoing sense of what's personally relevant. To guide perception, limbic relevance tunes the outer layers of the posterior cortex to attend to significant aspects of the external world. To guide action, limbic relevance tunes the outer layers of the frontal and motor cortex to execute specific motor movements in an effective and meaningful sequence. According to this model, sensation does not begin the cycle nor does action end it. Perception and action describe a continuous commerce between the outer brain and the world, and they are continually resonating (or coupling) with the "inner" brain, the limbic cortex, which is in tune with bodily needs, urges, feelings, and meanings (e.g., Tucker, 2001; Tucker, Derryberry, & Luu, 2000). This sort of brain—a brain that works through cyclic time rather than linear time, and which is completely indifferent to the psychologist's breakdown of cognition, emotion, and action—is exactly the right sort of brain to house the mechanics of emotion regulation according to our model (Lewis, 2005b; Lewis & Todd, 2007).

What does this view of the brain mean for emotion regulation? First, because of the brain's preference for parallel rather than sequential time, regulation must be continually embedded in information processing or must be a feature of information processing, rather than a discrete activity that follows or precedes an emotional response. Second, if functional neural activity is always both cognitive and emotional, as mediated by networks connecting diverse regions of cortex, limbic structures, hypothalamus, and brainstem, then one should not think of a cognitive system regulating an emotion system. It may be more correct to say that each network does its own regulating in its own way. A network with the function of tracking and interpreting sensory information must regulate a balance between its openness to novelty and its requirements for vigilance and control. This is not cognitive regulation of emotion per se, yet emotion regulation is certainly a consequence of its functional activity. Thus, third, the different networks, with their unique functions (e.g., perception, action, planning, self-monitoring), would be expected to use (and regulate) emotions in different ways. For example, the sensory appraisal network just described would function most effectively by coloring the meaning of perceptual events with emotions, such as interest or desire in reference to the pursuit of novelty and anxiety signaling the need for vigilance and self-control. Those emotional associations, mediated by structures such as the ventral striatum and amygdala, would derive from the animal's biological makeup and its history of learning, and they would set the occasion for ER in the service of adaptive functioning.

In sum, ER is merely an aspect of emotional processing, and it is embedded in all the major functions of the nervous system—rather than constituting a particular class of cognitive events. Emotion and its regulation can be seen to take on different characteristics according to the functions in which they are embedded, with each function mediated by a distinct network of neural structures working together for some period of time. An implication of this model is that different functional networks may be recruited by particular neural epicenters or hubs (Lewis & Todd, 2007). For example, a perceptual appraisal function would be mediated by a network including the OFC, amygdala, and perceptual cortices. When the animal has the chance to evaluate context in making its appraisals, the OFC may act as an epicenter organizing activity in the other constituents. If emotional intensity is too great or challenge is too immediate, the amygdala may function as the epicenter of the appraisal network. Again, it is not necessary to assign cognitive regulation to one component and emotional activation to another. Rather, the network is responsible for making sense of the world and activating other networks that will respond appropriately. Cognition and emotion are features of this activity, described at the level of global psychological categories. Finally, it becomes possible to designate the temporal sequencing of regulatory events. Although cognitive appraisal does not necessarily precede emotion, and emotion does not always precede cognitive regulation, certain *functions* do precede others, and such sequencing can actually be measured using neural methodologies. For example, a deliberate reappraisal might be activated early in an emotional episode, as mediated by activity in the lateral prefrontal cortex (PFC), whereas the suppression or enhancement of a behavioral response might be activated later, as mediated by other prefrontal areas as well as anterior cingulate cortex. Such temporal sequencing has been hypothesized and tested using event-related functional magnetic resonance imaging (fMRI) methods (Goldin, McRae, Ramel, & Gross, 2008). The implications of this line of research have yet to be worked out, but it is remarkable that a brain-based analysis gets rid of cognition–emotion sequencing and replaces it with a sequence of specific functions that characteristically unfold in a certain order.

As a final consideration, if each functional network is essentially self-regulating, there must be some sort of superordinate interaction of multiple networks in the brain—an interaction that regulates these self-regulating systems. This principle seems to capture the way that bodily systems interact in general. The digestive system regulates itself. The circulatory system regulates itself. The pulmonary system regulates itself. However, these three systems must remain coordinated so that oxygenated blood is most available for action (and not digestion) when the animal is being challenged, yet energy can be extracted from digestive processes and stored for later use when the animal is at rest. Who orchestrates this complex coordination? We often view the brain as the master regulator, but DS thinkers (e.g., Thelen & Smith, 1994) remind us that networks become synchronized spontaneously through their own activities; their orderliness need not be imposed by some master controller. Current work in cognitive robotics and agent-based learning reflects this principle. Thus, we end this section by returning to the idea that emotion regulation involves a heterogeneous suite of processes, as surmised by other theorists (P. M. Cole et al., 2004; Davidson, Putnam, & Larson, 2000; Ochsner & Gross, 2007). Yet these processes should not be viewed as cognitive activities imposed on emotional responses, but as outcomes of self-organizing and self-regulating neural networks responsible for a variety of functions. Because these networks are both independent and cooperative, ER can be highly specialized yet highly coherent, flexible and yet powerful. Finally, self-regulating neural networks do not need to look up to some master regulator to become adaptively synchronized with one another. Rather, they become synchronized spontaneously, in the manner of a hierarchically embedded self-organizing macrosystem, perhaps through mechanisms that have already been studied (e.g., Buzsaki, 1996; Lutz, Lachaux, Martinerie, & Varela, 2002; Thompson & Varela, 2001; Vertes & Kocsis, 1997; von Stein & Sarnthein, 2000; see review by Lewis, 2005a), or perhaps through other mechanisms that have yet to be discovered.

HOW DOES THE NORMATIVE DEVELOPMENT OF EMOTION REGULATION INTERACT WITH INDIVIDUAL DIFFERENCES?

Although theorists are never in complete agreement on the normative timetable of ER development, there is general agreement that such a timetable exists, at least in principle. Moreover, many authors feel that the milestones in ER development provide a basic skeleton for the universal features of emotional development, including the timing of new capacities, sensitive windows for the emergence of social competencies based on these capacities, a guideline for parenting and educational policies based on this timetable, and norms for evaluating what is typical and what is problematic in socioemotional development.

For many theorists, the timetable of ER development reflects the sequencing of cognitive–developmental stages more generally. Since the late 1980s, several leading neo-Piagetian theorists shifted their interests from the traditional domains of cognitive development to the study of social and emotional processes (e.g., Case, Hayward, Lewis, & Hurst, 1988; Fischer, Shaver, & Carnochan, 1990). Other neo-Piagetian theorists have always included emotional regulatory factors in their explanation of cognitive development (Pascual-Leone, 1987). These theorists recognized commonalities between children's solutions to emotional challenges and their solutions to challenges in the more traditional domains of causal or logico-mathematical reasoning, spatial cognition, social or narrative reasoning, and so forth. Others theorists have used different versions of cognitive stage theory to map out a progression of phases of emotional development that includes emotion regulation (e.g., Sroufe, 1979, 1996). Authors who specialize in infant development have proposed more specific regulatory skills that emerge in tandem with milestones of sensorimotor development. These include, for example, the capacity for regulation through intersubjectivity, joint attention, and social referencing, emerging at approximately 9 months (e.g., around the time of Piaget's fourth stage of sensorimotor development—the integration of means and ends—and the age at which infants achieve intentional locomotion; Campos & Barrett, 1984; Sander, 1975; Trevarthen, 1980). Others whose work has focused more exclusively on the development of self-regulation or emotion regulation note a correspondence between specific cognitive advances (such as object permanence, language acquisition, and false-belief understanding) and changes in the style and efficacy of regulatory skills (Carlson, Moses,

& Claxton, 2004; Diamond, 1990; Kopp, 1989, 1992). Older work focusing on more global transitions examined self-understanding (M. Lewis, Sullivan, Stanger, & Weiss, 1989) and self-development (e.g., Kegan, 1982) as leading to advances in the control of emotions, impulses, and behavior more generally.

In sum, theorists who have assembled large-scale models of emotional development (and those who try to unify global theories of cognitive and emotional development) focus on age-related advances in the cognitive regulation of emotion, and they model ER development as a progression of steps of increasing complexity, sophistication, or level of abstraction. However, a more focused approach to the development of ER has been to chart the acquisition of particular regulatory skills, especially in early childhood, rather than viewing ER as an aspect of cognitive change more generally. This approach does not emphasize emotion regulation per se but includes ER under the rubric of self-regulation, and it is this approach that has produced the most impressive empirical progress since the 1990s.

As mentioned previously, the development of self-regulation is often discussed in terms of executive function (EF). We note that EF is most concerned with self-regulatory skills that are deliberate and conscious in nature (Zelazo & Muller, 2002), but EF capabilities may extend to more automatic processes as well. Perhaps the EF that has received the most attention from developmentalists is response inhibition. As children enter the preschool period (3–5 years), they exhibit a marked improvement in inhibitory control, allowing them to inhibit a prepotent response in favor of a more intentional but effortful response option (as seen in their performance of the day–night Stroop task—Diamond, 2006). Other advances in EF include delay of gratification, the capacity to ignore misleading cues or override prepotent response tendencies, set shifting (such as switching rules for categorizing stimuli), and the more general capacity to hold and manipulate information in working memory. All of these capacities go through significant advances between the ages of 3 and 5 years, and they may rely on response inhibition in conjunction with other skills. Using a large sample of children, Carlson (2005) provided the most comprehensive analysis of EF development to date—findings that replicated those of other EF researchers (e.g., Diamond & Taylor, 1996; Frye, Zelazo, & Palfai, 1995). In her studies, EF improved most substantially between ages 3.5 and 5 years, these improvements were generally correlated with age, and this association was independent of language capabilities. Carlson concluded that tasks relying on inhibition and those relying on working memory capacities showed no systematic difference in developmental timing, indicating that EF capacities improve as a cluster rather than as a sequence of specific skills. Most relevant from the present perspective, tasks that tapped "hot" EF capabilities (related to emotional outcomes such as reward vs. punishment) were not developmentally distinct from those that tapped "cool" EF (related to more arbitrary rules and nonemotional outcomes). Both hot and cool EF tasks were found at both the high and low ends of the difficulty spectrum—a finding reminiscent of Ochsner and Gross's (2005) conclusion that regulatory processes applied to the control of emotion are "strikingly similar" (p. 245) to those applied to more strictly "cognitive" performance. Finally, Carlson concluded that variability in the acquisition of particular skills (e.g., inhibition vs. rule learning) was probably a function of individual differences rather than age differences.

This last point introduces the other major approach to research on ER in childhood. Many researchers have been concerned with the impact of ER capacities on development rather than the impact of development on ER capacities. It is well recognized that children differ greatly in their means for controlling their emotions and that these differences both result from and contribute to personality differences. Psychodynamic theories from the first half of the 20th century organized personality styles and clinical outcomes according to the kinds of defenses favored by individuals and the success with which they applied them. For example, more primitive defenses such as splitting and projection foreshadowed a dampened ability to form close, trusting relationships with others, and, in more extreme cases, disposed people toward pathologies such as narcissistic personality disorders and even psychoses (Fairbairn, 1952; Horowitz, 1998). Conversely, defenses that allowed individuals to experience negative emotion, protect others from their own aggression, and remain capable of feeling both affection and aggression predisposed the individual to more mature, complex, and flexible interpersonal relationships (e.g., Weininger, 1989; Winnicott, 1963).

This general association between individual styles of emotion regulation and personality outcomes was incorporated into attachment theory by Bowlby and his followers. Attachment theorists viewed the style and quality of the child's attachment to the caregiver as a result of his or her habitual mode of regulating emotion—especially anxiety. For example, avoidant attachments were considered a result of suppression or denial of anxiety, as indexed by gaze aversion during the reunion episode of the Strange Situation, measured in late infancy (Ainsworth, Blehar,

Walters, & Wall, 1978). Conversely, secure attachments were facilitated by the child's capacity to experience anxiety and seek its resolution in interactions with the parent (Ainsworth et al., 1978). Some of the general conclusions of attachment theory are consistent with other approaches to individual differences, such as associations between inhibition, dispositional avoidance, and physiological markers of chronic stress (Kagan, 1994) and between the ER strategy of suppression and impoverished interpersonal relationships (John & Gross, 2007). However, the stability of attachment outcomes thought to result from early socioemotional habits has never been validated, suggesting a major role for interactions with the social environment rather than the crystalization of an early working model (Thompson, Lamb, & Estes, 1982).

In more recent work, researchers have studied the relations between specific styles of ER and features of personality and social relationships, without the conceptual baggage of attachment theory. In a recent review and overview, Eisenberg et al. (2007) divided the spectrum of individual differences in ER into overcontrolled, undercontrolled, and optimally controlled styles. This breakdown is similar to one we have used in our own work relating overcontrol to overactivation of the ventral PFC and undercontrol to the underactivation of both dorsal and ventral PFC. We return to these neural hypotheses later. In their review, Eisenberg and colleagues first established the stability of individual differences in ER, especially in middle childhood, following the surge in developmental change we discussed earlier. For overcontrolled children, the tendency is to be highly inhibited and less flexible in interpersonal interactions, less relaxed and spontaneous, and more prone to a personality characterized by depressive or anxious concerns. In contrast, undercontrolled children are thought to be low in all kinds of effortful (or executive) control, including inhibition and focused attention, and high in impulsivity and approach behavior, leading to low social competence and a tendency toward aggression. Eisenberg and colleagues also differentiated ER into effortful versus reactive control, the former corresponding with deliberate, conscious regulatory strategies and the latter with more automatic forms of ER. We have used a similar classification scheme to refine parallels between psychological and neurobiological models of ER (Todd & Lewis, 2008). Eisenberg and colleagues report that lower levels of effortful control correspond with poorer social outcomes in general, including poor compliance, more aggression, and poorer overall adjustment (e.g., Calkins, Dedmon, Gill, Lomax, & Johnson, 2002; Kochanska & Knaack, 2003). Thus, effortful control seems to constitute a superordinate form of ER with the greatest impact on developmental outcomes. These findings resonate with earlier work by Rothbart (e.g., Rothbart, Ziaie, & O'Boyle, 1992) demonstrating negative correlations between distress and focused attention even in young infants. Again, however, there appears to be a serious conflation between developmental and individual differences in ER: effortful control is considered a hallmark of ER maturation at approximately 3 years (Posner & Rothbart, 1998, 2000), and yet it is construed as a critical dimension of individual personality and temperament differences with major implications for social developmental outcomes.

Links between ER and individual developmental pathways are perhaps most dramatically exhibited in the study of developmental psychopathology. For some time, clinically significant aggression and anxiety problems have been understood as disorders of emotion regulation (e.g., Bradley, 2000; Calkins, 1994; Calkins & Howse, 2004). Children with these problems have failed to develop the capacity to appropriately modulate their feelings of anger and anxiety and the behaviours that flow from them.

A good deal of research has examined the precursors of aggressive behavior problems. Young children who are less able to focus their attention and inhibit their emotional impulses voluntarily have high levels of aggression, reaching clinical levels, across early and middle childhood (Hill, Degnan, Calkins, & Keane, 2006; Rothbart, Ahadi, & Hershey, 1994). In contrast, young children with good emotional control are able to shift attention away from anger-inducing cues and use nonhostile verbal methods (Eisenberg, Fabes, Nyman, Bernzweig, & Penuelas, 1994), and these associations between self-regulation and healthy social functioning continue into the period of middle childhood (Eisenberg et al., 1997). Finally, inhibitory control contributes to the development of conscience in young school-age children (Kochanska, Murray, & Coy, 1997), and children's emotion regulation fosters awareness of responsibility for their own actions and negative consequences for other people (Derryberry & Reed, 1996).

Anxiety problems have also been linked to ineffective emotion regulation. However, in the case of clinically significant anxiety, research points to excessive and excessively rigid emotional controls. Anxious children are overly fearful and tend to amplify their fears by focusing on stress-inducing stimuli rather than recruiting a flexible repertoire of coping strategies (e.g., problem solving; Bradley, 2000). Vigilance in relation to threatening cues prevents these children from flexibly allocating attention elsewhere, and withdrawal or inhibition are among the only self-regulatory strategies they have available (e.g., Kagan & Fox, 2006; Kagan, Reznick, Clarke, Snidman, & Garcia-Coll, 1984).

We follow Block and Block (1980), and more recently Eisenberg and colleagues (2007), in assigning aggressive versus anxious behavior to opposite poles on a continuum of control. As noted earlier, the dimension ranging from overcontrol to undercontrol provides a useful scheme for predicting and explaining personality differences; however, at the extremes of this dimension, explanations may also be found for distinct typologies of child psychopathology. Externalizing problems and aggressive disorders (such as conduct disorder, oppositional defiance disorder) are linked with emotional undercontrol, whereas internalizing problems including anxiety disorders and clinical depression may stem from emotional overcontrol. This continuum relates the character of various pathologies with specific styles of emotion regulation, and, as noted previously, it has provided a useful working model for our research linking cortical activation profiles to child behavior problems (e.g., Lewis, Granic, & Lamm, 2006).

This brief review highlights the fact that developmental change and individual differences in ER are usually studied independently. Individual styles of ER are generally considered correlates or predictors of child temperament, attachment style, personality dispositions, or developmental psychopathology, although several investigators have looked at the impact of familial factors on ER (Shipman et al., 2007; Spinrad, Stifter, Donelan-McCall, & Turner, 2004). However, another group of researchers ignore these differences and focus on advances in ER skills, generally seen as expressing an underlying cognitive-developmental timetable or a trajectory of improvements in executive function, although a few researchers consider social and cultural factors as well (e.g., Cole, Dennis, Smith-Simon, & Cohen, 2009). Several distinct problems arise from this bifurcation between normative and individual approaches. First, if differences in ER style, such as overcontrol versus undercontrol, have such potent influences on developmental outcomes, it is difficult to imagine that these differences would not affect the timetable of ER acquisition. In fact, children with robust temperamental differences in ER may be developing their self-regulatory abilities according to vastly different schedules. For example, children low in effortful control, who cannot or do not focus their attention deliberately, should progress much more slowly in the development of ER capacities or should branch off from the normative timetable of ER development at an early age. Extending this point, many aspects of social–cognitive development may depend on individual styles of self-regulation, making any normative timetable an exercise in averaging rather than a step toward meaningful modeling. Second, given the profound differences in ER capacities across the early years, individual differences at one age are unlikely to be commensurable with individual differences at another age. Undercontrol at 3 years might have nothing to do with undercontrol at 5 years. Or, to put it differently, because 2- to 3-year-olds are the most aggressive people on the planet, individual differences in impulse control may be irrelevant at this age. Moreover, the impact of ER differences on families, peers, and educational milieus must be mediated by age-specific capacities and the norms that apply to them, which calls to mind the motto that "timing is everything" (Lewis & Granic, 2009). In fact, if self-regulatory capacities change as a function of other developmental acquisitions, such as language development and theory of mind, then each child's profile of social–cognitive advances will have an impact on his or her repertoire of ER capacities. Further, factors that affect this profile, such as family structure and social experience, will further influence ER differences that will, in turn, have an impact on social–environmental variables, providing the foundation for a feedback loop between social experience, social–cognitive capacities, and the style and content of emotion regulation.

From our perspective, the effects of developmental change on individual variation and of individual variation on developmental change must be extremely complex and difficult to disentangle, because these influences are bidirectional, continuous, and cumulative. Individual differences at particular ages may affect developmental change, thus modulating the timing and consolidation of subsequent ER capabilities, and thus further affecting the child's developmental profile. Moreover, these influences are likely to be componential rather than homogeneous, with particular factors for particular individuals weighing more heavily at some ages than others, or in different ways than others, or differently for different individuals at the same ages. For example, at an age when social anxiety is relatively high (e.g., age 4 for many children), an overcontrolled style of ER might enhance certain forms of selective attention, accelerating attention to threatening stimuli, while hindering advances in skills such as self-monitoring, such that inappropriate behavioral tendencies are increasingly difficult to modify. In conclusion, we suggest that normative and individual aspects of ER development are so hopelessly conflated that their interaction cannot be analyzed meaningfully given current methodologies. As a result, investigators may feel obliged to select one or the other perspective as their home base, and ignore the other, to maintain a manageable research program. Dynamic systems (DS) approaches to development attempt to deal with this kind of complexity, investigating reciprocal influences among factors giving rise to unique developmental profiles, or profiles that pass through similar transitional phases yet differ in individual content (e.g., Granic, Hollenstein, Dishion, & Patterson, 2003; Lewis, Zimmerman, Hollenstein, & Lamey, 2004). However, the DS approach to emotional development has not been highly influential, and we share the concern that DS methods continue to lag behind DS principles concerning reciprocal causality and self-organizing developmental outcomes.

DEVELOPMENTAL VERSUS INDIVIDUAL DIFFERENCES IN THE NEURAL UNDERPINNINGS OF EMOTION REGULATION

It is obvious that the brain goes through massive developmental changes, and the emerging field of developmental neuroscience has tried to capture universal trends that describe these changes in meaningful ways. Most developmental accounts examine the cerebral cortex—the layers of cells surrounding limbic and diencephalic (thalamus and hypothalamus) structures and which are held responsible for the most refined levels of perception, action control, attention, planning, and self-regulation. As noted previously, the PFC and the anterior cingulate cortex (ACC, located along its medial walls) are most often singled out in relation to self-regulation. Therefore, change in PFC function should be an important consideration when examining developmental change in self-regulatory capacities. However, there are more general developmental factors that should be considered first. Brain maturation is usually viewed in terms of two complementary processes: changes in the synapses that connect cortical neurons and changes in the white matter (primarily axons) that form the pathways from one cell to the next. In general, developmental change involves the pruning of excess synapses, from an overabundance of synapses in infancy to a diminished and more streamlined synaptic architecture in adulthood. Pruning thins out the cortex in different regions at different ages, with primary sensory and motor regions thinning out first and association areas responsible for more complex cognitive processes thinning out later. The final waves of pruning take place in late adolescence, when the prefrontal cortex begins to assume its adultlike structure. During the pruning process, the axonal network becomes more directed, allowing greater connections across diverse regions, and also more efficient, allowing more rapid transmission of information from one synapse to the next. Taken together, these changes favor the development of a brain that is more streamlined, with fewer connections overall but with dedicated functions served by those connections. Most important, these normative changes in cortical structure are considered the principle engine of cognitive development, broadly conceived. Increases in the efficiency, precision, and scope of information processing allow for increasing cognitive power, cognitive complexity, or cognitive sophistication and coherence—depending on one's theoretical language.

While these global cortical changes are taking place, individual learning experiences continue to build new synapses and strengthen those already in existence, through the process of *synaptogenesis* (as well as guided pruning, e.g., through active inhibition). Thus, the general thinning out of synapses does not preclude novelty and, in fact, contributes to massive restructuring at particular phases of development. The big picture is that new skills are embedded in the ongoing changes taking place in synaptic networks while these networks become more refined and more efficient. In fact, a unitary principle common both to synaptic growth and synaptic pruning is that brain development is always a function of *experience*. In much the same way that the activity of organisms shapes natural selection, the activity of synapses—activity that underpins experience and learning—shapes the selection of the brain's eventual wiring plan. A simple catch phrase that helps keep this in mind was proposed by Donald Hebb more than half a century ago: "What fires together wires together" (Hebb, 1949). Synapses between neurons that are coactivated, when processing information, are strengthened; those between neurons that are rarely coactivated are pruned. Thus, synapses survive and prosper according to their degree of use, and in this they compete with other synapses that process the same information in different ways. This system of competition and elimination has been referred to as *Neural Darwinism* (Edelman, 1987), following earlier work by Changeux (e.g., Changeux & Dahaene, 1989; Changeux & Danchin, 1976) and others.

Yet how does this selectionist framework help us conceptualize the emergence (and consolidation) of individual styles of ER in particular? Isn't there a single "best way" to regulate one's emotions? Or do distinct styles of ER emerge under different circumstances, like diverse species that emerge under different evolutionary pressures? Do these distinct styles compete with each other during the many occasions in which we are required to deal with emotional demands—at least until one or more consolidate within one's personal repertoire?

Greenough (e.g., Greenough & Black, 1992) was one of the first developmentalists to present a model of neural change that addresses the tension between developmental progress and individual differences. His model differentiates *experience-expectant* changes—changes that take place for all members of a species, based on an average, expectable environment—from *experience-dependent* changes—changes that are exclusive to individuals because of their unique experiences. Thus, nearly all humans develop language when exposed to a consistent linguistic environment, due to synaptic modifications in cortical speech areas (although these linguistic advances can seem to evaporate quickly during family arguments at the dinner table). However, only some of us become piano players, based on particular experiences with piano teachers, due to synaptic modifications in areas integrating hand and finger movements with areas representing pitch, rhythm, and so forth. It is handy to point to a principle by which normative and individual changes can be so neatly differentiated, but unfortunately there is no way to track the actual synaptic modifications that would be ascribed to one or the other. That is partly because, even though we all learn how to talk, we all talk differently (especially during heated arguments), and we all learn to regulate our emotions, but never in quite the same way. Now, if so-called normative cognitive capacities—like language—are mediated by varied cortical configurations, then it follows that the more unique cognitive capacities—like a specific style of emotion regulation—must be mediated by even more distinctive configurations. It thus becomes difficult to know where to draw the line between normative and individual acquisitions or how to differentiate experience-dependent from experience-expectant changes.

Synaptic proliferation continues throughout the life span despite ongoing pruning, fashioning a continuous trail of neural footprints on the basis of novel experiences. However, synaptic plasticity is not infinite. As the cortical architecture becomes consolidated with age, there is a corresponding drop in the kind and degree of new capabilities, refinements, and learning that can take place. A well-known example is the inability to learn new languages without an accent after middle childhood or the difficulty most of us have in learning new languages at all after adolescence or early adulthood. Primary skills become embedded in the architecture of the cortex and cannot be easily replaced by alternative skills after a certain age. It is particularly intriguing to consider that normative cognitive advances slow down and perhaps stop at about the same time that individual differences become consolidated and immutable. The reason may be that both cognitive advances and individual variation rely on the same thing: synaptic plasticity. Synaptic plasticity gets used up, across each cortical site according to its function and connectivity, within a more or less typical (normative) developmental window. This principle is related to the principle of sensitive periods: universal age ranges for synaptic plasticity. Each window permits certain kinds of learning to take place as long as it remains open. We have argued in a number of papers that consolidating styles of emotion regulation, and personality dispositions more generally, are subject to age-specific constraints on neural plasticity in PFC and related structures. For example, maximal plasticity in the orbitofrontal cortex is used up by age 10 years and in the ACC a little later, by age 15 or so (Shaw et al., 2008). But how do we approach the question of *what* gets laid down in synaptic networks? According to developmentalist Esther Thelen, the configurations that persist are those that *work*—a simple but profound principle. We would add that the functions served by those configurations also come to *rely* on them, by dint of another simple but profound principle: "What fires together wires together" (Hebb, 1949). The brain does not have the luxury of throwing out the synaptic structures it has dedicated to important functions over years of practice. Thus, by adulthood, it is generally not possible to try on highly novel skills, or strategies, or modes of experience (implying novel cortical configurations), because the brain is already wired up to interpret and respond to the world according to its repertoire of habits (as mediated by its present wiring diagram). Tucker (e.g., 2001) calls this trade-off the stability–plasticity dilemma. The more stability you have achieved, the more you have to lose by rewiring the cortex in the service of novelty. This principle is important for the development of individual styles of emotion regulation, and it can help explain why generations of developmentalists continue to associate personality patterns with individual habits of emotion regulation. ER is such a critical *function* that the basic style of ER laid down in early childhood has probably colonized enough synapses to prevent the development of new strategies. Therefore, the habits of overcontrol or undercontrol (for example), that determine personal functioning in early childhood, have every reason to remain stable, as reported by Eisenberg et al. (2007), based on the early formation of dedicated synaptic configurations.

Synaptic shaping is a broad developmental principle. More than that, however, it is the engine that drives the two kinds of growth that were so difficult to reconcile using the tools of behavioral research: normative development and individual variation. Individual variation, laid down by experience-dependent synaptic shaping, is an inevitable product of cortical development. The progressive elaboration of synaptic networks achieves both increasing efficiency and increasing adaptation to one's own unique environment. Moreover, the principle of synaptic shaping explains diminishing plasticity with age. The elaboration of unique cortical networks uses up the "degrees of freedom" for how the cortex (and limbic system) might become structured. What starts out as an indeterminate process becomes deterministic with time, as is the case in all complex, self-organizing systems. Of specific relevance here, synaptic shaping is the vehicle for normative cognitive advances *and* the consolidation of individual styles of self-regulation. Therefore, strategies or modes of self-regulation embody increasing cognitive skill, but they do so in intrinsically unique ways. When gazing through a fine enough lens, cognitive advancement is never literally normative—it is always, to some degree, unique. Furthermore, the elaboration of individual styles is a kind of cognitive "progress," a movement forward as well as outward from the norm. In sum, individuality and cognitive advancement are both built into the neural flesh, but they are not two interacting processes. Rather, they express one unitary process from two distinct angles. Cortical maturation is entirely dependent on experience: It is experience that produces synaptic change even while it lays down increasingly enduring habits. Yet the nature of experience is to become increasingly specialized and fine-tuned, mediated as it is by increasingly elaborate neural networks. Thus, from a brain's-eye view, developmental progress and individual variability are inseparable.

Lewis and Douglas (1998) presented a global scheme depicting personality development as increasing individuality or increasing specialization with age. This scheme, reproduced in Figure 3.1, shows a branching pathway of developing individual differences. These differences can be conceptualized as attachment styles or temperament differences in the first year or two of life and then increasingly refined personality patterns over subsequent years. Note that the pathway "selected" by the individual during each phase of development constrains the choices for the next developmental juncture. We use the terms *selected* and *choices* metaphorically, with a teleological spin, but of course the individual does not select or choose a developmental path. If anything, the developmental path chooses the individual. More precisely, the developmental path self-organizes through the interaction of many forces. (Perhaps in adulthood we do exert a certain amount of conscious influence over our developmental pathways, but most of personality consolidation has already crystalized by then.) The scheme, although highly global, helps one to picture the synthesis of developmental progress and consolidating individual differences. At each developmental juncture, new pathways emerge, representing both increased individual elaboration of a unique personality style and increased developmental efficacy in cognitive, emotional, and self-regulatory capabilities.

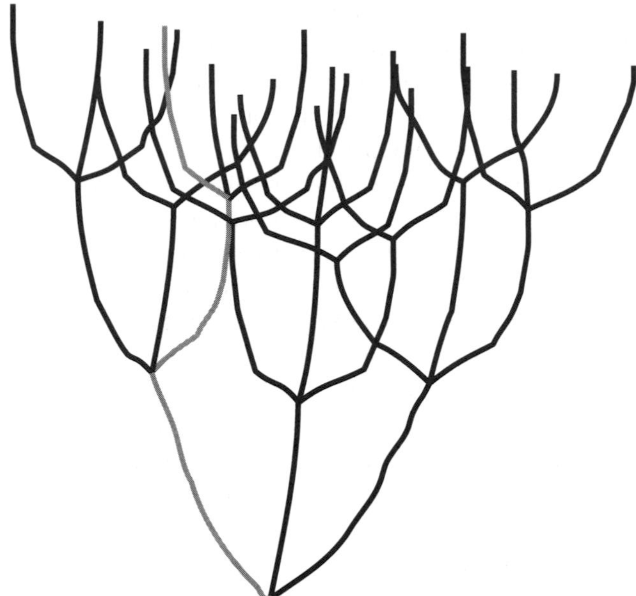

Figure 3.1. A branching pathway of individual styles of emotion regulation, constituting increasingly elaborate and unique constellations of personality development. At each developmental juncture, the pathway "selected" by a given individual is represented against a background of potential pathways. However, each branching "uses up" degrees of freedom in terms of dedicated synaptic circuitry, bringing the individual further along an irreversible developmental journey.

A few details concerning cortical development help to refine this picture further. Data based on a variety of methods indicate that cortical maturation involves three coactive changes: increasing specialization, increasing frontalization, and increasing communication. With development, the cortex becomes increasingly specialized, such that particular regions take on dedicated functions and become more and more proficient at those functions. An aspect of that tendency is that prefrontal systems take on responsibility for self-regulation or self-control—at least the kind emphasized by conventional accounts. All the means by which control is manifested, through response inhibition, decision making, comparison, judgment, planning, and self-monitoring, become specialized in frontal (and anterior cingulate) regions rather than spread throughout the cortex. Finally, specialized cortical regions become better coordinated with each other, forming extensive networks that are highly efficient at a variety of functions (Fair et al., 2009; Johnson, 1999). Thus, rather than relying on multipurpose regions that do many things moderately well, the brain develops into a more efficient processor in which a number of regions (or "modules") each becomes highly specialized. Then it is the coordination of those regions into functional networks that permits more articulated capacities and the rapid and flexible shifting from one function to another.

This kind of portrayal has been articulated most elegantly by Johnson's (1999, 2000) *interactive specialization* approach. In Johnson's model, even the basic "modules" of the cortex are not defined at birth. Rather, they are acquired through the dedication of specific cortical populations to specific functions, on the basis of their structure, their connections, and so forth. For example, the language centers (Broca's area and Wernicke's area) do not start off as language centers—they acquire their dedication to language through competition, pruning, and the other experience-based processes we have reviewed. These basic capacities then become coordinated with each other into larger scale, more elaborate functions, through development, as proposed by a number of theorists, including Johnson. Coordination across specialized cortical regions makes for a processing network that is malleable, plastic, and efficient. Finally, this maturational mechanism may explain the finding that cortical activity necessary for task performance generally decreases with development. More mature brains need to expend less energy than younger brains to do the same task (Casey, Giedd, & Thomas, 2000). They are simply more efficient—at least until we get old.

This brief review has portrayed the developing brain as a system of developing subsystems, each built up through experience, synchronized with each other in real time to take on more and more complex functions with age, but never escaping from its stamp of individual uniqueness. In fact, the principles of cortical pruning, competition, and specialization ensure that each individual assembles his or her own unique cortical architecture, based on recurrent experiences, with each circuit becoming more refined and consolidated, thus locking in individual differences—and resulting in recurring experiences—while supporting a set of increasingly advanced functions that are necessary for living in a shared social world. Through this process, plasticity gets used up, and stability is both the price we pay and the reward for our efforts. The brain is a self-organizing, self-regulating system, as we and other authors have highlighted over recent years. Yet how does this portrayal resolve the conflation between developmental change and individual elaboration specifically in the domain of emotion regulation?

As we have noted, cortical development constitutes the increasing specification of structure, permitting activities that are more organized, more efficient, and more complex. However, there are other parts of the brain that change far less from infancy to old age. Because the cortex is intimately connected with these parts, the circuits that join them also become more elaborated, more efficient, and increasingly shaped by experience. This has particular implications for the neural basis of emotion and its regulation. Developmental reorganization takes place not only within the cortex but also within the larger networks that connect the cortex with the amygdala, thalamus, hypothalamus, brainstem, and striatum—structures that mediate central aspects of emotional feeling, emotionally biased perception, emotional memory, and emotional response tendencies. As a result, ER, construed as cognitive modulation of emotion, develops through the elaboration of connections between cortical and subcortical regions. So what evolve are habits of corticolimbic or corticostriatal connectivity that modulate emotional responses, mediated by a variety of networks that each have their own functions. (Note that some subcortical structures, especially the hippocampus, amygdala, and cerebellum, are highly modifiable and plastic. However, to simplify the present treatment, we highlight plasticity and experience-dependent cortical change in contrast to the relative stability of subcortical—really sublimbic—structures.)

The implications are twofold. First, the fusion between developmental advances and individual habits of processing extends from the cortex to the whole brain. For example, amygdala-mediated associations take on their potency and meaning through interactions with prefrontally mediated expectancies and sensory gestalts supported by the temporal lobes. Thus, the self-regulatory aspects of various networks both advance with cortical efficiency and take on the individual styles of appraisal, reappraisal, associations, and so forth on the basis of synaptic shaping. Second, cortical plasticity itself is hugely influenced by emotion.

Mechanisms of synaptic consolidation such as long-term potentiation (LTP) depend on the state of excitability of the receptive neuron at each synapse. For many authors this implies that the neurochemical excitation that accompanies emotional states is essential for synaptic modifiability and learning (Freeman, 1995; Post et al., 1998; Tucker, 2001). Research demonstrates that neuromodulator arousal facilitates LTP (e.g., Centonze, Picconi, Gubellini, Bernardi, & Calabresi, 2001; Izquierdo, 1997; Izumi & Zorumski, 1999) and that neuropeptide action consolidates synaptic change and enhances memory formation (Adamec, Kent, Anisman, Shallow, & Merali, 1998; Flood, Baker, Hernandez, & Morley, 1990). Moreover, the amygdala may be critical to memory consolidation in various systems, because of its facilitation of brainstem and hypothalamic release of neuromodulators (Packard & Cahill, 2001) and its direct coupling with the hippocampus (Paré, Collins, & Pelletier, 2002). These and related findings suggest that only events that are emotionally significant can maintain arousal and attention long enough for learning to take place (Gallagher & Holland, 1992; Rolls & Treves, 1998; Tucker, 2001). Moreover, emotion regulation is particularly relevant for two reasons: because all lasting emotional states involve regulation and because regulation is the means by which the brain establishes routines for minimizing disruption and maximizing effective functioning. Overall, the activation and regulation of lasting emotional states may be a key ingredient of synaptic plasticity and synaptic change. Thus, both advances in cortical function, through enhanced specialization, and the locking in of individual differences, through variations in experience-dependent synaptic shaping, may depend on emotion regulation.

In sum, the tension between developmental advancement and individual differences was considered a conundrum from the perspective of psychological accounts of ER development. From the perspective of brain science, however, it could hardly be otherwise. Advances in the complexity and effectiveness of ER cannot be separated from the unique ways different brains implement these advances. Children's styles of ER do not have to be similar, or even commensurable, for these advances to fulfill the demands of normative functioning. Rather, such advances cannot help but be embedded in the individual developmental pathways through which synaptic modifications take place. Efficiency derives from recurrent use of particular synaptic configurations, based in pruning, competition, specialization, and coordination, thus consolidating individual styles and promoting more effective solutions to familiar problems. Especially where emotion is concerned, cortical consolidation (or, more accurately, corticolimbic consolidation) drives the self-organization of the entire brain. At the same time, emotion regulation may enhance learning through the release of neurochemicals throughout the cortex, facilitating synaptic plasticity over extended periods.

We conclude this section by introducing the idea of *cascading constraints* as a principle that integrates developmental change and individual variation. According to the idea of cascading constraints (Lewis, 1997), the emergence of structure (e.g., a schema, skill, or belief) at any point in a developmental sequence constrains the characteristics of the structure to emerge next. With respect to emotion regulation, self-regulatory habits established in early childhood constrain the kinds of social roles one assumes a year or two later. In turn, these interpersonal habits set the course for self-concept and social preferences in middle childhood and adolescence. The idea of cascading constraints helps make sense of developmental trajectories. Structures appearing early in development limit the possible features of later structures, then development selects from among those features, further narrowing the path of possibilities.

However, at the psychological level of analysis, cascading constraints remain vague and abstract. At the neural level of analysis, they can be analyzed with considerable detail. For example, the recruitment of specialized functions by specific cortical regions has an impact on synaptic selection, constraining the formation of networks that coordinate those regions. Moreover, the development of neural habits of ER influences neuromodulator flows that continue to facilitate the sculpting of neural networks that mediate individual repertoires. These cascading constraints, self-organizing in their own right, constitute a set of markers along the route of a developmental trajectory, and each plays its part in fashioning and refining that trajectory. However, from this perspective, the path of development can be seen as progressive rather than normative. More refined functions emerge from earlier ones. Moreover, although they are constrained by their origins to lock in individual differences, they are also selected, on the basis of their efficiency, to perform normative functions demanded by a shared world. Brains become increasingly individualistic as neural commitments at one age narrow the field of options for neural commitments at the next age. However, they also become increasingly effective at normative requirements as they advance. With respect to emotion regulation, individual differences in emotional experience get built into the very structure of the networks that do the regulating. Then differences in the structure of those networks reinforce and extend differences in experience. Yet this process of crystalizing uniqueness also establishes progressive stages of mastery over the challenges we all have to face. There is no way to separate out the sequence of increasing regulatory efficiency from individual habits of experience feeding back on themselves.

WHY DO NEGATIVE EMOTION AND PSYCHOPATHOLOGY INCREASE IN ADOLESCENCE?

The cognitive advances of adolescence are well known. Piaget's theory framed these advances in terms of a global stage transition from concrete to formal operations. More recent approaches focus on the development of higher order executive functions, including abstract capacities for rule manipulation, generalization, and insight, and contemporary theories regard adolescent cognitive advances in terms of a suite of executive abilities coordinated through conscious reflection and flexible self-control (Keating, 2004). In the realm of emotion regulation, these advances provide some obvious advantages in the modulation of negative or maladaptive emotional response tendencies. Adolescents have at their disposal a massive suite of cognitive tools that can modify the causes and consequences of emotional arousal in a great variety of ways. In essence, they shift from younger children's reliance on contextual supports and overt behavioral strategies to a cluster of cognitive transformations that can radically change the meaning of emotion-eliciting events and the responses they induce. An excellent list of such strategies was provided by Jennifer Silk (2002), including problem solving, information seeking, cognitive restructuring, catastrophizing, ventilation, acceptance, distraction, avoidance, self-criticism, blaming others, wishful thinking, humor, suppression, social withdrawal, resigned acceptance, denial, alcohol and drug use, seeking social support, and religion or spiritual support (Compas, Connor-Smith, Salzman, Thomsen, & Wadsworth, 1999). According to Holodynski and Friedlmeier (2006), ER skills come to include symbolic comprehension and self-reflection, and Steinberg (2005) noted that these advances rest on changes in social cognition, response inhibition, monitoring, and the capacity for abstract, reflective, multidimensional, and hypothetical thinking.

Yet despite these advances in ER, adolescents show the most emotional dysregulation of the life span (with the possible exception of infants and toddlers). First, adolescents' emotions are all over the map. They are more emotionally reactive, switching moods more frequently and less predictably than adults and probably children as well (Larson & Asmussen, 1991; Larson, Csikszentmihalyi, & Graef, 1980). Second, they experience more intense emotional dynamics than younger children or adults. In particular, experience-sampling methods indicate that they experience higher rates of negative emotions than preadolescents (Larsen & Lampman-Petraitis, 1989) or adults (Larson et al., 1980). However, their interactions with parents appear to be a major source of this negativity (Collins, 1990), whereas interactions with peers are sources of both emotional challenge and interpersonal comfort (e.g., Berndt, 1982). Third, and most important, all major classes of psychopathology rise sharply during adolescence. These include depression, substance abuse, suicide, and antisocial or delinquent behavior patterns (e.g., Kazdin, 1993). Psychopathological profiles that climb steeply in adolescence can be divided into externalizing and internalizing difficulties. Externalizing disorders, including conduct disorders, lying, bullying, criminal behavior, substance abuse, and so forth, are more prevalent in males, whereas depression, anxiety disorders, bulimia, and anorexia are more prevalent in females. Both internalizing and externalizing disorders increase substantially in incidence and intensity between ages 13 and 16 years. The rise of depression and other internalizing disorders, beginning in early adolescence, is particularly troublesome (D. A. Cole et al., 2002; Yap, Allen, & Sheeber, 2007). Fourth, it is well known that adolescents use drugs and alcohol to regulate their moods far more than children or adults (Yap et al., 2007). Of course, these forms of regulation become available to adolescents for the first time, and this fact of life must contribute to their extensive use of drugs before rules and habits of self-control become instantiated. Nevertheless, substance use is not the most effective means of ER, as it tends to heighten negative affect in the long run while relieving it in the short run. Hence, adolescents' reliance on self-regulating substances points toward painful emotions that cannot be easily contained.

The phenomenon that has puzzled developmental psychologists for decades has been familiar to parents and teachers for centuries, and perhaps for millennia. "The young are more troubled by their passions than are their elders," wrote Aristotle (Topics, Book 3, Chapter 2). Yet why should this be so? It is well recognized that adolescents are exposed to major shifts in the expectations imposed on them by their families and social milieus and that their expectations concerning their roles, rights, and responsibilities clash with the social position to which they became accustomed over childhood. They struggle with contradictions between their need for increased autonomy and their reliance on the social support systems they have depended on since infancy. Nevertheless, adolescence isn't all bad. In fact, negative assumptions about the impact of puberty on emotional issues have not been supported by psychological research. Puberty is not the source of any explosion of negative emotion. Although the physical and social changes triggered by puberty increase emotionality (Brooks-Gunn, Graber, & Paikoff, 1994), novel emotional dynamics can be attractive and exciting as much as they are threatening and disorganizing. Adolescence provides a greatly expanded access to positive emotions resulting from intimacy with peers, romantic involvements, and increased opportunities for freedom and exploration, all without the need for financial or social self-sufficiency. It also widens the availability of emotional support systems through the inclusion of peer relations, thus fleshing out sources of emotion regulation that were unavailable to younger children (Gottman & Mettetal, 1986). Why, then, is adolescence characterized as a time of increased emotional lability, increased negative emotion, and dramatically increased incidence of developmental psychopathology?

The answer to this question may lie squarely in the degree of reorganization in the PFC during adolescence. Investigators have found it highly challenging to track age-specific cortical changes, especially because different regions of cortex change at different rates, with inflection points in the trajectory of change observed at different ages. However, a number of principles are generally accepted. After a period of synaptic proliferation in late childhood (Giedd et al., 1999), the PFC goes through a decline in grey matter (or synaptic) density at the same time as a proliferation in white matter (thought to be due to myelination). Spear (2000) reviewed a number of findings suggesting that pruning is the main source of synaptic reduction, although Paus (2005) suggested that myelination may account for the appearance of gray matter thinning. Regardless, most investigators point to massive restructuring of the PFC in adolescence, as more specific regions respond to more specific stimuli while overall efficiency is enhanced by the elimination of redundant synapses. Researchers who study adolescent socioemotional development interpret the reorganization of PFC as both an opportunity and challenge for the adolescent (Dahl, 2003; Steinberg, 2005). This is because the areas that undergo greatest reorganization are those that are associated with self-regulation. In Steinberg's words,

> there is considerable evidence that the second decade of life is a period of great activity with respect to changes in brain structure and function, especially in regions and systems associated with response inhibition, the calibration of risk and reward, and emotion regulation. (p. 69)

Developmentalists note that the increases in emotional intensity and arousal elicited by new forms of social experience in adolescence are out of sync with the consolidation of adultlike modes of self-regulation. In particular, dorsal regions of PFC are among the last to mature (to reach adult levels of synaptic pruning; Gogtay et al., 2004), yet these regions are considered most effective when it comes to response selection and insight-based modes of self-control. In other words, adolescents' difficulties with emotion regulation may derive from novel sources of emotional arousal managed by a brain that is not yet proficient in deliberate self-regulation.

Our own modeling has attempted to flesh out this explanation in greater detail (Lewis, 2005b; Todd & Lewis, 2008). As noted earlier, cortical specialization, frontalization, and coordination increases throughout childhood. By the time children reach early adolescence, the cognitive controls recruited for ER are largely mediated by prefrontal regions. However, different regions of PFC take on particular kinds of regulatory capacities, such that different cortical patterns are associated with specific styles of ER. Our lab has been particularly interested in the discrepancy between ventral and dorsal styles of self-regulation (Lewis, Granic, & Lamm, 2006). Ventral prefrontal regions, such as the orbitofrontal cortex, ventromedial PFC, and ventral ACC, are involved in rapid, stimulus-bound forms of control, associated with the reactive control mechanisms identified by Eisenberg and colleagues (2007). Because of close ties between ventral PFC and the amygdala, ER mediated by this region may also maintain attention to threatening features of situations, such that an excess in ventral prefrontal activation disposes individuals to anxiety or depression. Indeed, anxiety disorders in adolescents and adults and depressive disorders in adulthood have been associated with greater levels of ventral prefrontal activation (Drevets & Raichle, 1998; Mayberg et al., 1999). Moreover, our own research has revealed a significant reduction in ventromedial prefrontal activation for 8- to 12-year-old children diagnosed with internalizing and externalizing symptoms, who improved clinically after a 3-month course of treatment (Lewis et al., 2008). In contrast to ventral regions, dorsal PFC, and particularly the dorsal division of the ACC, is implicated in more deliberate, conscious, or reflective forms of self-regulation, consistent with Eisenberg and colleagues' (2007) notion of effortful control. The recruitment of dorsal prefrontal regions may permit individuals to select appraisal and response options from competing alternatives and distance themselves from the more compelling but threatening features of difficult situations. Indeed, dorsal regions of the ACC are associated with more "cognitive" than "affective" task orientations, and dorsal prefrontal activation has been shown to diminish ventral activation, apparently through direct competition (Bush, Luu, & Posner, 2000; Drevets & Raichle, 1998).

We suggest that the adolescent brain, like any complex self-organizing system, has to go through a phase of disorganization before it can become reorganized. Developmentalists with a dynamic systems orientation have shown that developmental transitions or sensitive periods are marked by increased instability or vulnerability followed by the stabilization of new developmental forms (Ruhland & van Geert, 1998; van der Maas & Molenaar, 1992). Thus, the changes in prefrontal synaptic configuration and white matter volume that typify the adolescent brain may usher in a period in which existing modes of emotion regulation become difficult to maintain, especially in highly distressing situations, promoting a period of corticolimbic instability until more advanced modes of ER have a chance to consolidate. Evidence for the reorganization of prefrontal mechanisms of self-regulation, and the finding that dorsal regions mature later than ventral regions, suggest the possibility of a temporary increase in ventral modes of ER during this period. This ventral regression would tend to maintain negative appraisals mediated by the amygdala, despite ongoing attempts to suppress emotional impulses. As noted by Ochsner and Gross (2007), response suppression is a less effective means of ER than reappraisal, yet a reversion to ventral mechanisms of control may be the only alternative for the adolescent experiencing intense emotional challenges.

This exercise in neural modeling is not meant to be definitive, and the details certainly require empirical validation. However, it would not be surprising if the very fact of cortical reorganization in adolescence was a key causal factor in the emotional dysregulation and increasing rates of psychopathology that characterize this period. As emphasized in a previous section, advances in the development of ER require the laying down of cortical habits, through the consolidation of synaptic networks that are shaped on the basis of recurring experiences. Cortical habits constrain experience, fitting it into familiar and predictable patterns that continue to reinforce particular synaptic configurations, as individual differences become increasingly refined and increasingly functional. Adolescent development may invoke the breakdown of cortical habits of self-regulation, making emotional experience less predictable and consistent, and increasing vulnerability to problematic developmental outcomes. One does not need to look at the brain to see adolescence as a period of instability, but a brain's-eye view helps us to specify critical details about how emotional information is processed and about specific trade-offs between processing efficiency and preferred modes of self-regulation. Thus, a serious consideration of the implications of neural reorganization may help us model the psychological features of adolescent emotional development in new and innovative ways.

WHY DO OLDER ADULTS EXPERIENCE MORE POSITIVE EMOTION?

To date, research on emotion regulation extending into old age has produced a contradictory set of results. On one hand, executive processes and the frontal networks that mediate them show an overall decline with age. On the other hand, a growing body of evidence suggests that older adults are better regulators of negative emotion than young adults. Although the intensity of discrete emotional experiences does not appear to decline with age (Carstensen, Pasupathi, Mayr, & Nesselroade, 2000; Tsai, Levenson, & Carstensen, 2000), the overall experience of negative affect declines relative to positive affect (Carstensen et al., 2000; Charles, Reynolds, & Gatz, 2001). After controlling for chronic illness, rates of anxiety and depression are *reduced* relative to young adulthood (Kunzmann, Little, & Smith, 2000). Despite a wide range of individual differences, there is evidence that, in general, older adults report better control over negative emotion (Gross et al., 1997) and shorter durations for the experience of negative emotion (Carstensen et al., 2000), as well as less distress in response to both daily stress and major stressful life events (Birditt, Fingerman, & Almeida, 2005; Lichtenstein, Gatz, Pedersen, Berg, & McClearn, 1996).

These findings seem to contradict what we infer as psychologists and what we assume as social individuals living in proximity to parents, grandparents, aunts, and uncles. Aren't old people supposed to be more anxious and more grumpy? Doesn't the decline of executive function contribute to a period characterized by poor attention, wandering concerns, and a lack of enthusiasm for daily living? Apparently not. In fact, the observed decrease in negative emotion has been linked to beneficial changes in selective attention, episodic memory, and regulatory strategies (Charles & Carstensen, 2007). For example, there is evidence of a shift in attentional bias with age, but the net effect is the opposite of what we might imagine. Younger adults show greatest attentional capture by negatively valenced images, but older adults show equal capture by positive and negative images (Mather et al., 2004; Rosler et al., 2005). Older adults also differ from young adults in the content of emotional episodic memory (Rahhal, May, & Hasher, 2002) and are more likely than young adults to remember positive than negative events (Charles, Mather, & Carstensen, 2003; Kensinger, Garoff-Eaton, & Schacter, 2007). Older adults may also rely more on explicit regulatory strategies, avoid people and situations likely to elicit negative affect (Carstensen, Gross, & Fung, 1997), and cope differently with negative events (Carstensen, Fung, & Charles, 2003). This shift in both implicit and explicit regulatory processes has been explained in terms of greater emphasis on emotionally meaningful goals, which in turn fosters an emphasis on regulatory strategies that modulate negative affect (Charles et al., 2003). Thus, the data suggest an age-based positivity effect (Charles & Carstensen, 2007). The cognitive changes that correspond with normal aging help rather than hinder one's mood.

Indeed, these findings seem incongruent with the well-known age-related decline in effortful cognitive processes that include episodic memory retrieval (Levine, Svoboda, Hay, Winocur, & Moscovitch, 2002), selective attention and working memory (Lustig, May, & Hasher, 2001; Rowe, Hasher, & Turcotte, 2008; Winocur & Moscovitch, 1983), and inhibitory control (Hasher, Stoltzfus, Zacks, & Rypma, 1991). These cognitive processes are critically important for regulating emotion. Moreover, they belong to the family of executive functions identified with effortful or deliberate control (Eisenberg et al., 2007) as opposed to lower level, stimulus-bound mechanisms that can maintain appraisal of threat-related stimuli. Why doesn't a decline in the efficacy of these mechanisms unleash *more* negative emotion? How can this developmental decline *improve* positive mood?

Looking to the brain does not immediately resolve these contradictions. There is evidence of structural and functional decline in neural processes that should be fundamental to emotion regulation. Grey and white matter deterioration occurs in prefrontal regions that are implicated in strategic emotion regulation processes (Buckner, 2004; Raz et al., 1997). Moreover, age-related deficits are greater in executive tasks that activate dorsal ACC and dorsolateral prefrontal brain regions (MacPherson, Phillips, & Della Sala, 2002), consistent with a decline in effortful rather than reactive control. Further supporting a picture of age-related decline in effortful regulation, a recent fMRI study of brain activation in young, middle-aged, and older adults across several cognitive tasks suggested that networks involved in problem solving become less efficient relative to "default" networks associated with task-free resting states (Grady, Springer, Hongwanishkul, McIntosh, & Winocur, 2006). This study concluded that, with age, we are less likely to engage regions associated with executive function when performing a cognitive task (see also Logan, Sanders, Snyder, Morris, & Buckner, 2002).

In contrast, age-related brain changes appear to enhance several aspects of emotional salience not normally related to self-regulation. Greater relative amygdala activation has been found for positive as opposed to negative pictures in older but not younger adults, consistent with the notion of a behavioral positivity bias (Mather et al., 2004). Other fMRI research demonstrates an age-related change in filtering mechanisms. Older adults show a broadened scope of visual processing regardless of valence (Schmitz, De Rosa, & Anderson, 2008). In other words, they are less inclined to filter out task-irrelevant information on the basis of emotional valence. Hence, they may experience a broadened "attentional spotlight" more generally—as experienced by younger adults only in positive emotional states. Such broadened scope has been linked to enhanced cognitive flexibility, creative problem solving, and overall well-being (Dreisbach, 2006; Fredrickson, 2002; Isen, Daubman, & Nowicki, 1987; Rowe, Hirsh, & Anderson, 2007).

This hodgepodge of findings helps to specify age-related brain changes that may accompany an increasing positivity with old age, but the pattern of data does not point to an obvious mechanism to explain it. Can such a mechanism be inferred by contextualizing brain processes within a developmental framework? We propose that reduced efficiency in effortful control processes has a direct impact on older adults' style of ER. Less efficiency in effortful control suggests increased reliance on reactive control processes mediated by ventral prefrontal mechanisms. The finding of increased amygdala activation across categories of emotional stimuli supports this inference. Reduced effortful control, corresponding with reduced efficiency in dorsal PFC, requires older adults to rely on more primitive modes of ER. Interestingly, this parallels the developmental changes we attributed to adolescence. However, the net outcome for adolescents was increased negativity and emotional dysregulation. It may be that the opposite outcome—increased positivity and more consistent self-regulation—corresponds with the same changes in older adulthood. This is because, rather than feeling thrust into a world of new demands requiring novel self-regulatory habits, older adults live in a world of highly familiar demands. This may permit them to fall back on well-established habits that are moderated by unconscious regulatory processes subserved by ventral prefrontal mechanisms.

According to this explanation, adolescents have not developed a repertoire of sophisticated habits of ER. As a consequence, their poor mastery of dorsally mediated control processes (such as self-monitoring and conscious response selection) induces a struggle to maintain socially appropriate affects and behaviors despite intense emotional perturbations and reactive habits for dealing with them. In contrast, older adults have spent decades acquiring a repertoire of ER habits. They know what they like, what they don't like, what they permit themselves to feel, and what they tend to avoid. For them, the reduction in dorsally mediated control processes may result in a more spontaneous, automatic mode of self-control, based on well-established ventral habits. Thus, the critical role of individual habits of self-regulation, highlighted throughout this chapter, may afford older adults the freedom to feel, think, and act more reflexively than their younger counterparts and to struggle less with negative emotions when they arise.

As an alternative explanation, we note that older adults use more distributed (less localized) cortical networks to mediate higher order information processing, presumably to compensate for the reduced efficacy of local networks (Cabeza, Anderson, Locantore, & McIntosh, 2002). It may be that, rather than using less cortex to do more, as is characteristic of adolescents, older adults use more cortex to do less. This point seems particularly intriguing. If the networks used by older adults are more distributed and less specialized, then ER may be more flexible, simply because it is no longer the province of specialized circuitry. A compelling example is the finding that older adults show less hemispheric specialization when performing cognitive functions such as memory, perception, and inhibitory control (Cabeza, 2002). It follows that regulatory functions localized to the left PFC may now be mediated by frontal networks in both hemispheres. It is possible that this reduction in specialization permits a style of ER that is more flexible and less driven by predictions of negative outcomes or by the strictures associated with normative solutions to emotional problems. This style of ER might therefore be more resilient when it comes to evaluating negative situations and responding to them creatively.

CONCLUSIONS

This chapter attempted to resolve several conundrums stemming from psychological research through the application of insights from developmental neuroscience, in order to ground the developmental study of ER in a comprehensive, mechanism-based framework. The first conundrum was the issue of identification and timing. Are the cognitive operations involved in ER specific to emotion, or do they characterize cognition more generally, and can we determine on the basis of psychological study whether they precede, accompany, or follow emotional processes? We demonstrated that ER uses cognitive operations that neither precede nor follow the generation of emotion but are, rather, integrated with the other components of emotional response. In fact, we view ER as a somewhat arbitrary categorization of a set of processes that inevitably precede and follow from emotional triggers. From a neural perspective, the full articulation of an emotional response cannot help but include self-regulatory processes, because neural processes at every level are intrinsically self-regulating. What's more, *cognition* and *emotion* cannot be differentiated in the brain, because many neural components, and the networks in which they participate, underpin both cognitive and emotional activities. Thus, rather than construe ER as a cognitive operation regulating an emotional operation, it is more accurate to say that different neural networks are self-regulating in their own unique ways. The function of each of these networks determines the sort of regulation required. Moreover, although it is impossible to place abstract terms such as cognition and emotion in a meaningful sequence, the functions subserved by various brain networks (such as appraisal vs. response modulation) can be placed in sequence, and thus the phases of an emotion episode can be described with precision. Finally, self-regulating neural networks need not be controlled in any top-down manner; rather, they may become adaptively synchronized with one another in the manner of a self-organizing system.

When it comes to the study of ER in development, we described a bifurcation between research on developmental change and research on individual differences. One group of investigators considers individual styles of ER as either predictors or correlates of child temperament, attachment style, personality dispositions, or, at the extreme, developmental psychopathology. However, another group ignores these individual differences and focuses instead on developmental advances in ER, considered as outcomes of a cognitive-developmental timetable, a progression of social–cognitive acquisitions, or a sequence of improvements in self-regulation defined in terms of executive function. The bifurcation of these two research approaches has unfortunate consequences for the field: It ignores the likelihood that individual differences in ER affect developmental timing, and the likelihood that developmental timing determines the significance and impact of individual differences in ER. Rather than distinct phenomena, we suggest that developmental timing and individual differences in ER capacities are deeply interwoven, resulting in a set of reciprocal influences that feed back to one another and affect both personality consolidation and developmental sequencing in a cumulative fashion.

To arrive at an integrated approach to ER in development, a neuroscientific perspective may be necessary. The shaping of synaptic networks underlies the two kinds of growth that were so difficult to reconcile from the perspective of developmental psychology. Individual variation is achieved through the unique shaping of synaptic networks, through the impact of experience on cortical development. In fact, these cortical changes are the vehicle by which individual differences consolidate. Yet a progression of increasing specialization, pruning, and communication among cortical regions advances the power and sophistication of ER mechanisms, making them more efficient at dealing with challenges faced by most or all children. The individual nature of cortical development and its reliance on repeated patterns of emotional experience explain why it is so difficult to shift styles of ER, or attachment or personality, once we reach adulthood. The elaboration of unique cortical networks uses up cortical plasticity, along a route of cascading constraints that continue to narrow the options for subsequent outcomes. As a result, we become increasingly specialized users of a unique style of ER that is nevertheless increasingly advanced, efficient, and effective at dealing with normative requirements.

In sum, although cortical development shows common features in its progression, it is individual in its details. What's more, the emotional basis of cortical consolidation locks in individual differences while extending neural plasticity, learning, and developmental progress. We conclude that individuality and normative advances in ER capacities are *both* products of corticolimbic development. However, rather than two interacting processes, they express one unitary process from two distinct angles. Cortical maturation is entirely dependent on experience, whereas the nature of experience is entirely constrained by a cascade of changes in self-regulatory capacities. Moreover, emotional highlighting is a critical contributor both to individual uniqueness and developmental change. Thus, from the perspective of neuroscience, not only emotion and its regulation but also developmental progress and individual variability are inseparable.

In the last two sections of the chapter, we considered two age-specific questions concerning the development of emotion regulation—questions that have not been satisfactorily resolved through the application of psychological modeling and behavioral research findings. First, despite the increasing sophistication of their cognitive capabilities, adolescents show more negative, dysregulated, or disadvantageous emotional responses. Why should this be so? We argued that the reorganization of the PFC that takes place in adolescence may shift the epicenter of ER networks from more dorsal systems (particularly dorsal ACC) to more ventral systems (such as the orbitofrontal cortex). Such a change would shift the style of ER from a more conscious, deliberate mode based largely on response selection to a more stimulus-bound mode that maintains attention to threatening aspects of situations. This shift implies a temporary regression in self-regulatory skills while the PFC is "under construction," and it demonstrates the importance of synaptic consolidation and cortical efficiency for effective and reliable habits of ER. Second, there is ample research demonstrating the counterintuitive tendency for older adults to show more positive emotions, despite deficiencies in their executive control and the deterioration of neural tissue assumed to be responsible. How do older people become more expert in regulating their emotions despite this decline? We suggested two explanations. For one, older adults appear to recruit additional cortical areas for critical functions such as ER, to compensate for the loss of cortical efficiency, particularly in PFC and dorsal ACC. Specifically, they may rely more on ventral PFC, like adolescents undergoing synaptic reconfiguration. However, rather than increase negative mood, as it does with adolescents, this ventral automaticity may result in more intuitive and more efficient habits of ER honed through recurrent individual experiences, and automatic, perhaps unconscious, mechanisms for avoiding negatively valenced events. Our second suggestion was that older adults may use more distributed cortical networks for performing regulatory functions that were previously mediated by specialized circuits. This spreading out of function across more diverse regions might result in ER skills that are more flexible, more resilient, and more reflective of unique individual solutions for normative emotional challenges.

This chapter was intended to introduce new directions for modeling the development of emotion regulation, by integrating neuroscientific and psychological constructs and research findings. We have not attempted a review of age-specific ER acquisitions, because this information can be obtained from other publications (e.g., Todd & Lewis, 2008). However, neurobiological research into emotion regulation is still in its infancy, especially as it pertains to child, adolescent, and particularly life-span development. We hope that the conceptual pathways set out in this chapter will help provide a framework to support productive avenues of research for the next generation of investigators.

REFERENCES

Adamec, R., Kent, P., Anisman, H., Shallow T., & Merali, Z. (1998). Neural plasticity, neuropeptides and anxiety in animals: Implications for understanding and treating affective disorder following traumatic stress in humans. *Neuroscience and Biobehavioral Reviews, 23*, 301–318.

Ainsworth, M. D. S., Blehar, M., Waters, E., & Wall, S. (1978). *Patterns of attachment*. Hillsdale, NJ: Erlbaum.

Amodio, D. M., Master, S. L., Yee, C. M., & Taylor, S. E. (2008). Neurocognitive components of the behavioral inhibition and activation systems: Implications for theories of self-regulation. *Psychophysiology, 45*, 11–19.

Barrett, L. F., Lindquist, K., Bliss-Moreau, E., Duncan, S., Gendron, M., Mize, J., et al. (2007). Of mice and men: Natural kinds of emotion in the mammalian brain? *Perspectives on Psychological Science, 2*, 297–312.

Baumeister, R. F., & Heatherton, T. F. (1996). Self-regulation failure: An overview. *Psychological Inquiry, 7*, 1–15.

Berndt, T. J. (1982). The features and effects of friendship in early adolescence. *Child Development, 53,* 1447-1460.

Birditt, K. S., Fingerman, K. L., & Almeida, D. M. (2005). Age differences in exposure and reactions to interpersonal tensions: A daily diary study. *Psychology and Aging, 20*, 330–340.

Blair, C., Zelazo, P. D., & Greenberg, M. (2005). The assessment of executive function in early childhood: Prospects and progress. *Developmental Neuropsychology, 28*, 561–571.

Block, J. H., & Block, J. (1980). The role of ego-control and ego-resiliency in the organization of behavior. In W. A. Collins (Ed.), *Minnesota symposia on child psychology* (pp. 39–101). Hillsdale, NJ: Erlbaum.

Bradley, S. (2000). *Affect regulation and the development of psychopathology*. New York: Guilford Press.

Brooks-Gunn, J., Graber, J. A., & Paikoff, R. L. (1994). Studying links between hormones and negative affect: Models and measures. *Journal of Research on Adolescence, 4*, 469–486.

Buckner, R. L. (2004). Memory and executive function in aging and AD: Multiple factors that cause decline and reserve factors that compensate. *Neuron, 44*, 195–208.

Bunge, S., & Zelazo, P. D. (2006). A brain-based account of the development of rule use in childhood. *Current Directions in Psychological Science, 15,* 118–121.

Bush, G., Luu, P., & Posner, M. I. (2000). Cognitive and emotional influences in anterior cingulate cortex. *Trends in Cognitive Sciences, 4*, 215–222.

Buzsaki, G. (1996). The hippocampal–neocortical dialogue. *Cerebral Cortex, 6*, 81–92.

Cabeza, E. (2002). Hemispheric asymmetry reduction in old adults: The HAROLD model. *Psychology and Aging, 17*, 85–100.

Cabeza, R. E., Anderson, N. D., Locantore, J. K., & McIntosh, A. R. (2002). Aging gracefully: compensatory brain activity in high-performing older adults. *Neuroimage, 17*, 1394–1402.

Calkins, S. D. (1994). Origins and outcomes of individual differences in emotion regulation. *Monographs of the Society for Research in Child Development, 59,* 53–72.

Calkins, S. D., Dedmon, S., Gill, K., Lomax, L., & Johnson, L. (2002). Frustration in infancy: Implications for emotion regulation, physiological processes, and temperament. *Infancy, 3*, 175–198.

Calkins, S. D., & Howse, R. (2004). Individual differences in self-regulation: Implications for childhood adjustment. In P. Philipot & R. Feldman (Eds.), *The regulation of emotion* (pp. 307–332). Hillsdale, NJ: Erlbaum.

Campos, J. J., & Barrett, K. C. (1985). Toward a new understanding of emotions & their development. In C. E. Izard & J. Kagan (Eds.), *Emotions, cognition and behavior* (pp. 229–263). New York: Cambridge University Press.

Campos, J. J., Frankel, C. B., & Camras, L. (2004). On the nature of emotion regulation. *Child Development, 75*, 377–394.

Carlson, S. M. (2005). Developmentally sensitive measures of executive function in preschool children. *Developmental Neuropsychology, 28*, 595–616.

Carlson, S. M., Moses, L. J., & Claxton, L. J. (2004). Individual differences in executive functioning and theory of mind: An investigation of inhibitory control and planning ability. *Journal of Experimental Child Psychology, 87*, 299–319.

Carstensen, L. L., Fung, H. H., & Charles, S. T. (2003). Socioemotional selectivity theory and emotion regulation in the second half of life. *Motivation and Emotion, 27*, 103–123.

Carstensen, L. L., Gross, J. J., & Fung, H. H. (1997). The social context of emotional experience. In K. W. Schaie & M. P. Lawton (Eds.), *Annual review of gerontology and geriatrics: Focus on emotion regulation* (pp. 325–352). New York: Springer.

Carstensen, L. L., Pasupathi, M., Mayr, U., & Nesselroade, J. R. (2000). Emotional experience in everyday life across the adult life span. *Journal of Personality and Social Psychology, 79*, 644–655.

Case, R. (1988). The whole child: Toward an integrated view of young children's cognitive, social, and emotional development. In A. D. Pellegrini (Ed.), *Psychological bases for early education* (pp. 155–184). New York: John Wiley & Sons.

Case, R., Hayward, S., Lewis, M. D., & Hurst, P. (1988). Toward a neo-Piagetian theory of cognitive and emotional development. *Developmental Review, 8,* 1–51.

Casey, B. J., Giedd, J. N., & Thomas, K. M. (2000). Structural and functional brain development and its relation to cognitive development. *Biological Psychology, 54*, 241–257.

Centonze, D., Picconi, B., Gubellini, P., Bernardi, G., & Calabresi, P. (2001). Dopaminergic control of synaptic plasticity in the dorsal striatum. *European Journal of Neuroscience, 13*, 1071–1077.

Changeux, J.-P., & Dahaene, S. (1989). Neuronal models of cognitive functions. *Cognition, 33*, 63–109.

Changeux, J.-P., & Danchin, A. (1976). Selective stabilization of developing synapses as a mechanism for the specification of neuronal networks. *Nature, 264,* 705–712.

Charles, S. T., & Carstensen, L. L. (2007). Emotion regulation and aging. In J. J. Gross (Ed.), *Handbook of Emotion Regulation* (pp. 307–327). New York: Guilford Press.

Charles, S. T., Mather, M., & Carstensen, L. L. (2003). Aging and emotional memory: The forgettable nature of negative images for older adults. *Journal of Experimental Psychology: General, 132,* 310–324.

Charles, S. T., Reynolds, C. A., & Gatz, M. (2001). Age-related differences and change in positive and negative affect over 23 years. *Journal of Personality and Social Psychology, 80,* 136–151.

Cole, D. A., Tram, J. M., Martin, J. M., Hoffman, K. B., Ruiz, M. D., & Jacquez, F. M. (2002). Individual differences in the emergence of depressive symptoms in children and adolescents: A longitudinal investigation of parent and child reports. *Journal of Abnormal Psychology, 111,* 156–165.

Cole, P. M., Dennis, T. A., Smith-Simon, K. E., & Cohen, L. H. (2009). Preschoolers' emotion regulation strategy understanding: Relations with emotion socialization and child self-regulation. *Social Development, 18,* 324–352.

Cole, P. M., Martin, S. E., & Dennis, T. A. (2004). Emotion regulation as a scientific construct: Methodological challenges and directions for child development research. *Child Development, 75,* 317–333.

Collins, W. A. (1990). Parent–child relationships in the transition to adolescence: Continuity and change in interaction, affect, and cognition. In R. Montemayor & G. R. Adams (Eds.), *From childhood to adolescence: A transitional period? Advances in adolescent development: An annual book series* (pp. 85–106). Thousand Oaks: Sage.

Compass, B. E., Connor-Smith, J. K., Saltzman, H., Thomsen, A. H., & Wadsworth, M. (1999). Getting specific about coping: Effortful and involuntary responses to stress in development. In M. Lewis & D. Ramsay (Eds.), *Soothing and stress* (pp. 229–256). Mahwah, NJ: Erlbaum.

Cunningham, W. A., Van Bavel, J. J., & Johnsen, I. R. (2008). Affective flexibility: Evaluative processing goals shape amygdala activity. *Psychological Science, 19,* 152–160.

Dahl, R. (2003). Beyond raging hormones: The tinderbox in the teenage brain. *Cerebrum: The Dana Forum on Brain Science, 5.*

Damasio, A. R. (1999). *The feeling of what happens: Body and emotion in the making of consciousness.* Fort Worth, TX: Harcourt College.

Davidson, R. J., Putnam, K. M., & Larson, C. L. (2000). Dysfunction in the neural circuitry of emotion regulation: A possible prelude to violence. *Science, 289,* 591-594.

Derryberry, D., & Reed, M. A. (1996). Regulatory processes and the development of cognitive representations. *Development and Psychopathology, 8,* 215–234.

Diamond, A. (1990). Developmental time course in human infants and infant monkeys and the neural bases of inhibitory control in reaching. In A. Diamond (Ed.), *The development and neural bases of higher cognitive functions* (pp. 637–669). New York: New York Academy of Sciences.

Diamond, A. (2006). The early development of executive functions. In E. Bialystok & F. Craik (Eds.), *Lifespan cognition: Mechanisms of change* (pp. 70–95). New York: Oxford University Press.

Diamond, A., & Taylor, C. (1996). Development of an aspect of executive control: Development of the abilities to remember what I said and to "Do as I say, not as I do." *Developmental Psychobiology, 29,* 315–334.

Dodge, K. A., & Somberg, D. R. (1987). Hostile attributional biases among aggressive boys are exacerbated under conditions of threats to the self. *Child Development, 58,* 213–224.

Dreisbach, G. (2006). How positive affect modulates cognitive control: The costs and benefits of reduced maintenance capability. *Brain and Cognition, 60,* 11–19.

Drevets, W. C., & Raichle, M. E. (1998). Reciprocal suppression of regional cerebral blood flow during emotional versus higher cognitive processes: Implications for interactions between emotion and cognition. *Cognition and Emotion, 12,* 353–385.

Edelman, G. M. (1987). *Neural Darwinism.* New York: Basic Books.

Eisenberg, N., Fabes, R. A., Nyman, M., Bernzweig, J., & Pinuelas, A. (1994). The relations of emotionality and regulation to children's anger-related reactions. *Child Development, 65,* 109–128.

Eisenberg, N., Fabes, R. A., Shepard, S. A., Murphy, B. C., Guthrie, I. K., Jones, S., et al. (1997). Contemporaneous and longitudinal prediction of children's social functioning from regulation and emotionality. *Child Development, 68,* 642–664.

Eisenberg, N., Hofer, C., & Vaughan, J. (2007). Effortful control and its socioemotional consequences. In J. J. Gross (Ed.), *Handbook of emotion regulation* (pp. 287–306). New York: Guilford Press.

Ellsworth, P. C. (1991). Some implications of cognitive appraisal theories of emotion. In K. T. Strongman (Ed.), *International review of studies on emotion.* Chichester, England: John Wiley & Sons.

Fair, D. A., Cohen, A. L., Power, J. D., Dosenbach, N. U. F., Church, J. A., Miezin, F. M., et al. (2009). Functional brain networks develop from a "local to distributed" organization. *PLoS Computational Biology, 5,* e1000381.

Fairbairn, W. R. (1952). *Psychoanalytic studies of the personality.* London: Routledge & Kegan Paul.

Fischer, K. W., Shaver, P. R., & Carnochan, P. (1990). How emotions develop and how they organize development. *Cognition and Emotion, 4,* 81–127

Flood, J. F., Baker, M. L., Hernandez, E. N., & Morley, J. E. (1990). Modulation of memory retention by neuropeptide K. *Brain Research, 520,* 284–290.

Fogel, A., Nwokah, E., Dedo, J. Y., Messinger, D., Dickson, K. L., Matusov, E., et al. (1992). Social process theory of emotion: A dynamic systems approach. *Social Development, 1,* 122–142.

Fredrickson, B. L. (2002). The broaden-and-build theory of positive emotions. *Philosophical Transactions of the Royal Society of London, 52,* 1122–1131.

Freeman, W. J. (1995). *Societies of brains: A study in the neuroscience of love and hate.* Hillsdale, NJ: Erlbaum.

Freeman, W. J. (1999). *How brains make up their minds.* London: Weidenfeld & Nicolson.

Frijda, N. H. (1993). The place of appraisal in emotion. *Cognition and Emotion, 7,* 357–387.

Frye, D., Zelazo, P. D., & Palfai, T. (1995). Theory of mind and rule-based reasoning. *Cognitive Development, 10,* 483–527.

Gallagher, M., & Holland, P. C. (1992). Understanding the function of the central nucleus. In J. P. Aggleton (Ed.), *The amygdala* (pp. 307–321). New York: John Wiley & Sons.

Giedd, J. N., Blumenthal, J., Jeffries, N. O., Rajapakse, J. C., Vaituzis, A. C., Liu, H., et al. (1999). Development of the human corpus callosum during childhood and adolescence: A longitudinal MRI study. *Progress in Neuro-Psychopharmacology & Biological Psychiatry, 23,* 571–588.

Gogtay, N., Giedd, J. N., Lusk, L., Hayashi, K. M., Greenstein, D., Vaituzis, A. C., et al. (2004). Dynamic mapping of human cortical development during childhood through early adulthood. *Proceedings of the National Academy of Sciences, 101,* 8174-8179.

Goldin, P. R., McRae, K., Ramel, W., & Gross, J. J. (2008). The neural bases of emotion regulation: Reappraisal and suppression of negative emotion. *Biological Psychiatry, 63*, 577–586.

Gottman, J., & Mettetal, G. (1986). Speculations about social and affective development: Friendship and acquaintanceship through adolescence. In J. Gottman & J. Parker (Eds.), *Conversations with friends: Speculations on affective development* (pp. 192–237). New York: Cambridge University Press.

Grady, C. L., Springer, M. V., Hongwanishkul, D., McIntosh, A. R., & Winocur, G. (2006). Age-related changes in brain activity across the adult lifespan. *Journal of Cognitive Neuroscience, 18*, 227–241.

Granic, I., Hollenstein, T., Dishion, T. J., & Patterson, G. R. (2003). Longitudinal analysis of flexibility and reorganization in early adolescence: A dynamic systems study of family interactions. *Developmental Psychology, 39*, 606–617.

Granic, I., & Lamey, A. V. (2002). Combining dynamic systems and multivariate analyses to compare the mother–child interactions of externalizing subtypes. *Journal of Abnormal Child Psychology, 30*, 265–283.

Granic, I., & Patterson, G. R. (2006). Toward a comprehensive model of antisocial development: A dynamic systems approach. *Psychological Review, 113*, 101–131.

Greenough, W. T., & Black, J. E. (1992). Induction of brain structure by experience: Substrates for cognitive development. In M. R. Gunnar & C. A. Nelson (Eds.), *Minnesota symposium on child psychology, Vol. 24: Developmental behavioral neuroscience* (pp. 155–200). Hillsdale, NJ: Erlbaum.

Gross, J. J., Carstensen, L. L., Pasupathi, M., Tsai, J., Skorpen, C. G., & Hsu, A. Y. (1997). Emotion and aging: experience, expression, and control. *Psychology and Aging, 12*, 590–599.

Hasher, L., Stoltzfus, E. R., Zacks, R. T., & Rypma, B. (1991). Age and inhibition. *Journal of Experimental Psychology: Learning, Memory, and Cognition, 17*, 163–169.

Hebb, D. O. (1949). *The organization of behavior.* New York: John Wiley & Sons.

Hill, A., Degnan, K., Calkins, S. D., & Keane, S. P. (2006). Profiles of externalizing behavior problems for boys and girls across preschool: The roles of emotion regulation and inattention. *Developmental Psychology, 42*, 913–928.

Hollenstein, T. (2007). State space grids: Analyzing dynamics across development. *International Journal of Behavioral Development, 31*, 384–396.

Hollenstein, T., Granic, I., Stoolmiller, M., & Snyder, J. (2004). Rigidity in parent–child interactions and the development of externalizing and internalizing behavior in early childhood. *Journal of Abnormal Child Psychology, 32*, 595–607.

Holodynski, M., & Friedlmeier, W. (2006). *Development of emotions and emotion regulation.* New York: Springer.

Horowitz, M. J. (1998). *Cognitive psychodynamics: From conflict to character.* New York: John Wiley & Sons.

Isen, A. M., Daubman, K. A., & Nowicki, G. P. (1987). Positive affect facilitates creative problem solving. *Journal of Personality and Social Psychology, 52*, 1122–1131.

Izard, C. E. (1993). Four systems for emotion activation: Cognitive and noncognitive processes. *Psychological Review, 100*, 68–90.

Izquierdo, I. (1997). The biochemistry of memory formation and its regulation by hormones and neuromodulators. *Psychobiology, 25*, 1–9.

Izumi, Y., & Zorumski, C. F. (1999). Norepinephrine promotes long-term potentiation in the adult rat hippocampus in vitro. *Synapse, 31*, 196–202.

John, O. P., & Gross, J. J. (2007). Individual differences in emotion regulation strategies: Links to global trait, dynamic, and social cognitive constructs. In J. J. Gross (Ed.), *Handbook of emotion regulation* (pp. 351–372). New York: Guilford Press.

Johnson, M. H. (1999). Cortical plasticity in normal and abnormal cognitive development: Evidence and working hypotheses. *Development and Psychopathology, 11*, 419–437.

Johnson, M. H. (2000). Functional brain development in infants: Elements of an interactive specialization framework. *Child Development, 71*, 75–81.

Kagan, J. (1994). *Galen's prophecy: Temperament in human nature.* New York: Basic Books.

Kagan, J., & Fox, N. (2006). Biology, culture, and temperamental biases. In N. Eisenberg (Vol. Ed.), W. Damon & R. M. Lerner (Series Eds.), *Social, emotional, and personality development: Vol. 3. Handbook of child psychology* (pp. 167–225). Hoboken, NJ: John Wiley & Sons.

Kagan, J., Reznick, S. J., Clarke, C., Snidman, N., Garcia-Coll, C. (1984). Behavioral inhibition to the unfamiliar. *Child Development, 55*, 2212–2225.

Kazdin, A. (1993). Adolescent mental health: Prevention and treatment programs. *American Psychologist, 48*, 127–141.

Keating, D. P. (2004). Cognitive and brain development. In R. M. Lerner & R. Steinberg (Eds.), *Handbook of adolescent psychology* (pp. 45–84). Hoboken, NJ: John Wiley & Sons.

Kegan, R. (1982). *The evolving self: Problem and process in human development.* Cambridge, MA: Harvard University Press.

Kensinger, E. A., Garoff-Eaton, R. J., & Schacter, D. L. (2007). Effects of emotion on memory specificity in young and older adults. *The Journals of Gerontology Series B: Psychological Sciences and Social Sciences, 62*, P208–P215.

Kerr, A., & Zelazo, P. D. (2004). Development of "hot" executive function: The Children's Gambling Task. *Brain and Cognition, 55*, 148–157.

Kim, S. H., & Hamann, S. (2007). Neural correlates of positive and negative emotion regulation. *Journal of Cognitive Neuroscience, 19*, 776–798.

Kochanska, G., & Knaack, A. (2003). Effortful control as a personality characteristic of young children: Antecedents, correlates, and consequences. *Journal of Personality, 71*, 1087–1112.

Kochanska, G., Murray, K., & Coy, K. C. (1997). Inhibitory control as a contributor to conscience in childhood: From toddler to early school age. *Child Development, 68*, 263–277.

Kochanska, G., Murray, K. T., & Harlan, E. T. (2000). Effortful control in early childhood: Continuity and change, antecedents, and implications for social development. *Developmental Psychology, 36*, 220–232.

Kopp, C. B. (1989). Regulation of distress and negative emotions: A developmental view. *Developmental Psychology, 25*, 343–354.

Kopp, C. B. (1992). Emotional distress and control in young children. *New Directions for Child Development, 55*, 41–56.

Kunzmann, U., Little, T. D., & Smith, J. (2000). Is age-related stability of subjective well-being a paradox? Cross-sectional and longitudinal evidence from the Berlin Aging Study. *Psychology and Aging, 15*, 511–526.

Larson, R., & Asmussen, L. (1991). Anger, worry, and hurt in early adolescence: An enlarging world of negative emotions. In M. E. Colten & S. Gore (Eds.), *Social institutions and social change* (pp. 21–41). New York: Aldine De Gruyter.

Larson, R., Csikszentmihalyi, M., & Graef, R. (1980). Mood variability and the psychosocial adjustments of adolescents. *Journal of Youth and Adolescence, 9*, 469–490.

Larson, R., & Lampman-Petraitis, C. (1989). Daily emotional states as reported by children and adolescents. *Child Development, 60*, 1250–1260.

Lazarus, R. S. (1995). Vexing research problems inherent in cognitive-mediational theories of emotion and some solutions. *Psychological Inquiry, 6*, 183–196.

Lazarus, R. S. (1999). The cognition–emotion debate: A bit of history. In T. Dalgleish & M. Power (Eds.), *Handbook of cognition and emotion* (pp. 3–19). Chichester, England: John Wiley & Sons.

Levine, B., Svoboda, E., Hay, J. F., Winocur, G., & Moscovitch, M. (2002). Aging and autobiographical memory: Dissociating episodic from semantic retrieval. *Psychology and Aging, 17*, 677–689.

Lewis, M., Sullivan, M. W., Stanger, C., & Weiss, M. (1989). Self-development and self-conscious emotions. *Child Development, 60*, 146–156.

Lewis, M. D. (1995). Cognition–emotion feedback and the self-organization of developmental paths. *Human Development, 38*, 71–102.

Lewis, M. D. (1996). Self-organising cognitive appraisals. *Cognition and Emotion, 10*, 1–25.

Lewis, M. D. (1997). Personality self-organization: Cascading constraints on cognition–emotion interaction. In A. Fogel, M. Lyra, & J. Valsiner (Eds.), *Dynamics and indeterminism in developmental and social processes* (pp. 193–216). Mahwah, NJ: Erlbaum.

Lewis, M. D. (2005a). Bridging emotion theory and neurobiology through dynamic systems modeling (target article). *Behavioral and Brain Sciences, 28*, 169–194.

Lewis, M. D. (2005b). Self-organizing individual differences in brain development. *Developmental Review, 25*, 252–277.

Lewis, M. D., & Douglas, L. (1998). A dynamic systems approach to cognition–emotion interactions in development. In M. F. Mascolo & S. Griffin (Eds.), *What develops in emotional development?* (pp. 159–188). New York: Plenum Press.

Lewis, M. D., & Granic, I. (2009). *Bed Timing*. Toronto: HarperCollins.

Lewis, M. D., Granic, I., & Lamm, C. (2006). Behavioral differences in aggressive children linked with neural mechanisms of emotion regulation. *Annals of the New York Academy of Sciences, 1094*, 164–177.

Lewis, M. D., Granic, I., Lamm, C., Zelazo, P. D., Stieben, J., Todd, R. M., Moadab, I., & Pepler, D. (2008). Changes in the neural bases of emotion regulation associated with clinical improvement in children with behavior problems. *Development and Psychopathology, 20*, 913–939.

Lewis, M. D., Lamey, A. V., & Douglas, L. (1999). A new dynamic systems method for the analysis of early socioemotional development. *Developmental Science, 2*, 458–476.

Lewis, M. D., Lamm, C., Segalowitz, S. J., Stieben, S., & Zelazo, P. D. (2006). Neurophysiological correlates of emotion regulation in children and adolescents. *Journal of Cognitive Neuroscience, 18*, 430–443.

Lewis, M. D., & Todd, R. M. (2007). The self-regulating brain: Cortical–subcortical feedback and the development of intelligent action. *Cognitive Development, 22*, 406–430.

Lewis, M. D., Zimmerman, S., Hollenstein, T., & Lamey, A. V. (2004). Reorganization of coping behavior at 1 1/2 years: Dynamic systems and normative change. *Developmental Science, 7*, 56–73.

Lichtenstein, P., Gatz, M., Pedersen, N. L., Berg, S., & McClearn, G. E. (1996). A co-twin–control study of response to widowhood. *The Journals of Gerontology Series B: Psychological Sciences and Social Sciences, 51*, P279–P289.

Logan, J. M., Sanders, A. L., Snyder, A. Z., Morris, J. C., & Buckner, R. L. (2002). Under-recruitment and nonselective recruitment: Dissociable neural mechanisms associated with aging. *Neuron, 33*, 827–840.

Lustig, C., May, C. P., & Hasher, L. (2001). Working memory span and the role of proactive interference. *Journal of Experimental Psychology: General, 130*, 199–207.

Lutz, A., Lachaux, J.-P., Martinerie, J., & Varela, F. J. (2002). Guiding the study of brain dynamics by using first-person data: Synchrony patterns correlate with ongoing conscious states during a simple visual task. *Proceedings of the National Academy of Science USA, 99*, 1586–1591.

MacPherson, S. E., Phillips, L. H., & Della Sala, S. (2002). Age, executive function, and social decision making: A dorsolateral prefrontal theory of cognitive aging. *Psychology and Aging, 17*, 598–609.

Marsh, R., Zhu, H., Schultz, R. T., Quackenbush, G., Royal, J., Skudlarski, P., et al. (2006). A developmental fMRI study of self-regulatory control. *Human Brain Mapping, 27*, 848–863.

Mather, M., Canli, T., English, T., Whitfield, S., Wais, P., Ochsner, K., et al. (2004). Amygdala responses to emotionally valenced stimuli in older and younger adults. *Psychological Science, 15*, 259–263.

Mayberg, H. S. (2006). Defining neurocircuits in depression: Strategies toward treatment selection based on neuroimaging phenotypes. *Psychiatric Annals, 36*, 259–268.

Mayberg, H. S., Liotti, M., Brannan, S. K., McGinnis, S., Mahurin, R. K., Jerabek, P. A., et al. (1999). Reciprocal limbic-cortical function and negative mood: Converging PET findings in depression and normal sadness. *The American Journal of Psychiatry, 156*, 675–682.

Ochsner, K. N., & Gross, J. J. (2005). The cognitive control of emotion. *Trends in Cognitive Sciences, 9*, 242–249.

Ochsner, K. N., & Gross, J. J. (2007). The neural architecture of emotion regulation. In J. J. Gross (Ed.), *Handbook of emotion regulation* (pp. 87–109). New York: Guilford Press.

Packard M. G., & Cahill, L. (2001). Affective modulation of multiple memory systems. *Current Opinion in Neurobiology, 11*, 752–756.

Panksepp, J. (1982). Toward a general psychobiological theory of emotions. *Behavioral and Brain Sciences, 5*, 407–467.

Panksepp, J. (1998). *Affective neuroscience: The foundations of human and animal emotions*. New York: Oxford University Press.

Paré, D., Collins, D. R., & Pelletier, J. G. (2002). Amygdala oscillations and the consolidation of emotional memories. *Trends in Cognitive Sciences, 6*, 306–314.

Parkinson, B. (2001). Putting appraisal in context. In K. R. Scherer, A. Schorr, & T. Johnstone (Eds.), *Appraisal processes in emotion: Theory, methods, research* (pp. 173–186). New York: Oxford University Press.

Pascual-Leone, J. (1987). Organismic processes for neo-Piagetian theories: A dialectical causal account of cognitive development. *International Journal of Psychology, 22*, 531–570.

Paus, T. (2005). Mapping brain maturation and cognitive development during adolescence. *Trends in Cognitive Sciences, 9*, 60–68.

Posner, M. I., & Rothbart, M. K. (1998). Attention, self-regulation, and consciousness. *Philosophical Transactions of the Royal Society of London, B, 353*, 1915–1927.

Posner, M. I., & Rothbart, M. K. (2000). Developing mechanisms of self-regulation. *Development and Psychopathology, 12*, 427–441.

Post, R. M., Weiss, S. R. B., Li, H., Smith, M. A., Zhang, L. X., Xing, G., et al. (1998). Neural plasticity and emotional memory. *Development and Psychopathology, 10*, 829–855.

Rahhal, T. A., May, C. P., & Hasher, L. (2002). Truth and character: Sources that older adults can remember. *Psychological Science, 13*, 101–105.

Raz, N., Gunning, F. M., Head, D., Dupuis, J. H., McQuain, J., Briggs, S. D., et al. (1997). Selective aging of the human cerebral cortex observed in vivo: Differential vulnerability of the prefrontal gray matter. *Cerebral Cortex, 7*, 268–282.

Rolls, E. T., & Treves, E. T. (1998). *Neural networks and brain function*. New York: Oxford University Press.

Rosler, A., Ulrich, C., Billino, J., Sterzer, P., Weidauer, S., Bernhardt, T., et al. (2005). Effects of arousing emotional scenes on the distribution of visuospatial attention: Changes with aging and early subcortical vascular dementia. *Journal of the Neurological Sciences, 229–230*, 109–116.

Rothbart, M. K., Ahadi, S. A., & Hershey, K. L. (1994). Temperament and social behavior in childhood. *Merrill-Palmer Quarterly, 40*, 21–39.

Rothbart, M. K., & Bates, J. E. (1998). *Temperament*. Hoboken, NJ: John Wiley & Sons.

Rothbart, M. K., & Derryberry, D. (1981). Development of individual differences in temperament. In M. E. Lamb & A. L. Brown (Eds.), *Advances in developmental psychology* (pp. 37–86). Hillsdale, NJ: Erlbaum.

Rothbart, M. K., Ziaie, H., & O'Boyle, C. G. (1992). Self-regulation and emotion in infancy. In N. Eisenberg & R. A. Fabes (Eds.), *New directions for child development* (pp. 7–23). San Francisco: Jossey-Bass.

Rowe, G., Hasher, L., & Turcotte, J. (2008). Age differences in visuospatial working memory. *Psychology and Aging, 23*, 79–84.

Rowe, G., Hirsh, J. B., & Anderson, A. K. (2007). Positive affect increases the breadth of cognitive selection. *Proceedings of the National Academy of Sciences, 104*, 383–388.

Ruhland, R., & van Geert, P. (1998). Jumping into syntax: Transitions in the development of closed class words. *British Journal of Developmental Psychology, 16*, 65–95.

Sander, L. W. (1975). Infant and caretaking environment: Investigation and conceptualization of adaptive behavior in a system of increasing complexity. In E. J. Anthony (Ed.), *Explorations in child psychiatry* (pp. 129–166). New York: Plenum Press.

Scherer, K. R. (1984). On the nature and function of emotion: A component process approach. In K. R. Scherer & P. Ekman (Eds.), *Approaches to emotion* (pp. 293–318). Hillsdale, NJ: Erlbaum.

Scherer, K. R. (1999). Appraisal theory. In T. Dalgleish & M. Power (Eds.), *Handbook of cognition and emotion* (pp. 637–663). Chichester: John Wiley & Sons.

Scherer, K. R. (2001). Appraisal considered as a process of multilevel sequential checking. In K. R. Scherer, A. Schorr, & T. Johnstone (Eds.), *Appraisal processes in emotion: Theory, methods, research* (pp. 92–120). New York: Oxford University Press.

Schmitz, T. W., De Rosa, E., & Anderson, A. K. (2008). Emotional states differentially modulate the scope of attentional "spotlight" in older and younger adults. Paper presented at the Annual Meeting of the Society for Neuroscience, Washington, DC.

Seeley, W. W., Menon, V., Schatzberg, A. F., Keller, J., Glover, G. H., Kenna, H., et al. (2007). Dissociate intrinsic connectivity networks for salience processing and executive control. *Journal of Neuroscience, 27*, 2349–2356.

Shaw et al. (2008). Shaw, P., Kabani, N. J., Lerch, J. P., Ecksrand, K., Lenroot, R., Gogtay, N., et al. (2008). Neurodevelopmental trajectories of the human cerebral cortex. *Journal of Neuroscience, 28*, 3586–3594.

Shipman, K. L., Schneider, R., Fitzgerald, M. M., Sims, C., Swisher, L., & Edwards, A. (2007). Maternal emotion socialization in maltreating and non-maltreating families: Implications for children's emotion regulation. *Social Development, 16*, 268–285.

Silk, J. (2002). *Emotion regulation in the daily lives of adolescents: Links to adolescent adjustment*. Unpublished doctoral dissertation, Temple University, Philadelphia.

Smith, C. A., & Kirby, L. D. (2001). Toward delivering on the promise of appraisal theory. In K. R. Scherer, A. Schorr, & T. Johnstone (Eds.), *Appraisal processes in emotion: Theory, methods, research* (pp. 187–201). New York: Oxford University Press.

Spear, L. P. (2000). The adolescent brain and age-related behavioral manifestations. *Neuroscience and Biobehavioral Reviews, 24*, 417–463.

Spinrad, T. L., Stifter, C. A., Donelan-McCall, N., & Turner, L. (2004). Mothers' regulation strategies in response to toddlers' affect: Links to later emotion self-regulation. *Social Development, 13*, 40–55.

Sroufe, L. A. (1979). Socioemotional development. In J. Osofsky (Eds.), *Handbook of infant development* (pp. 462–518). Hoboken, NJ: John Wiley & Sons.

Sroufe, L. A. (1996). *Emotional development: The organization of emotional life in the early years*. New York: Cambridge University Press.

Steinberg, L. D. (2005). Cognitive and affective development in adolescence. *Trends in Cognitive Sciences, 9*, 69–74.

Stuss, D. T., & Alexander, M. P. (2000). Executive functions and the frontal lobes: A conceptual view. *Psychological Research/ Psychologische Forschung, 63*, 289–298.

Thelen, E., & Smith, L. B. (1994). *A dynamic systems approach to the development of cognition and action*. Cambridge: MIT Press/ Bradford.

Thompson, E., & Varela, F. J. (2001). Radical embodiment: Neural dynamics and consciousness. *Trends in Cognitive Sciences, 5*, 418–425.

Thompson, R. A., & Lamb, M. E. (1984). Assessing qualitative dimensions of emotional responsiveness in infants: Separation reactions in the strange situation. *Infant Behavior and Development, 7*, 423–445.

Thompson, R. A., Lamb, M. E., & Estes, D. (1982). Stability of infant–mother attachment and its relationship to changing life circumstances in an unselected middle-class sample. *Child Development, 53*, 144–148.

Thompson, R. A., Lewis, M. D., & Calkins, S. D. (2008). Reassessing emotion regulation. *Child Development Perspectives, 2*, 124–131.

Todd, R. M., & Lewis, M. D. (2008). Emotion, cognition and top-down control: The neural underpinnings of self-regulation in development. In J. Reed & J. W. Rogers (Eds.), *Child neuropsychology: Concepts, theory and practice*. London: Blackwell.

Trevarthen, C. (1980). The foundations of intersubjectivity: Development of interpersonal and cooperative understanding in infants. In D. R. Olson (Ed.), The *social foundations of language and thought: Essays in honor of Jerome S. Bruner* (pp. 316–342). New York: Norton.

Tsai, J. L., Levenson, R. W., & Carstensen, L. L. (2000). Autonomic, subjective, and expressive responses to emotional films in older and younger Chinese Americans and European Americans. *Psychology and Aging, 15*, 684–693.

Tucker, D. M. (1992). Developing emotions and cortical networks. In M. R. Gunnar & C. Nelson (Eds.), *Minnesota symposia on child psychology: Vol. 24. Developmental behavioral neuroscience* (pp. 75–128). Hillsdale: Erlbaum.

Tucker, D. M. (2001). Motivated anatomy: A core-and-shell model of corticolimbic architecture. In G. Gainotti (Ed.), *Handbook of neuropsychology: Vol. 5. Emotional behavior and its disorders* (pp. 125–160). Amsterdam: Elsevier.

Tucker, D. M. (2007). *Mind from body: Experience from neural structure*. New York: Oxford University Press.

Tucker, D. M., Derryberry, D., & Luu, P. (2000). Anatomy and physiology of human emotion: Vertical integration of brainstem, limbic, and cortical systems. In J. C. Borod (Ed.), *The neuropsychology of emotion* (pp. 56–79). New York: Oxford University Press.

van der Maas, H. L. J., & Molenaar, P. C. M. (1992). Stagewise cognitive development: An application of catastrophe theory. *Psychological Review, 99*, 395–417.

Vertes, R. P., & Kocsis, B. (1997). Brainstem-diencephalo-septohippocampal systems controlling the theta rhythm of the hippocampus. *Neuroscience, 81*, 893–926.

von Stein, A., & Sarnthein, J. (2000). Different frequencies for different scales of cortical integration: From local gamma to long range alpha/theta synchronization. *International Journal of Psychophysiology, 38*, 301–313.

Weininger, O. (1989). The Differential Diagnostic Technique: A visual-motor projective test: Further research. *Psychological Reports, 65*, 64–66.

Winnicott, D. W. (1963). The capacity for concern. In *The maturational processes and the facilitating environment*. New York: International Universities Press.

Winocur, G., & Moscovitch, M. (1983). Paired-associate learning in institutionalized and noninstitutionalized old people: an analysis of interference and context effects. *Journal of Gerontology, 38*, 455–464.

Yap, M. B. H., Allen, N. B., & Sheeber, L. (2007). Using an emotion regulation framework to understand the role of temperament and family processes in risk for adolescent depressive disorders. *Clinical Child and Family Psychology, 10*, 180–196.

Yeh, W., & Barsalou, L. W. (2006). The situated nature of concepts. *American Journal of Psychology, 119*, 349–384.

Zelazo, P. D., & Frye, D. (1997). Cognitive complexity and control: A theory of the development of deliberate reasoning and intentional action. In M. Stamenov (Ed.), *Language structure, discourse, and the access to consciousness* (pp. 113–153). Amsterdam & Philadelphia: John Benjamins.

Zelazo, P. D., & Muller, U. (2002). Executive function in typical and atypical development. In U. Goswami (Ed.), *Handbook of childhood cognitive development*. Oxford: Blackwell.

Zelazo, P. D., Muller, U., Frye, D., & Marcovitch, S. (2003). The development of executive function in early childhood. *Monographs of the Society for Research in Child Development, 68*, vii–137.

CHAPTER 4

Dynamic Integration of Emotion and Cognition: Equilibrium Regulation in Development and Aging

GISELA LABOUVIE-VIEF, DANIEL GRÜHN, and JOSEPH STUDER

Throughout history and in current psychological theories, the development of emotions is seen as occurring within two modes of regulation. On the one hand, evolution has equipped us with highly automatic response systems that protect individuals from runoff into dangerous levels of stimulation. These processes, termed *primary* by Sigmund Freud, obey homeostatic laws that safeguard the survival of organisms. Such homeostatic laws are strongly hedonically oriented, following an energetic and homeostatic *pleasure–pain* principle of optimizing personal well-being. On the other hand, social and cultural development demands that these response systems be transformed and integrated with *secondary* processes of conscious reflection and effortful control. In this transformation, the *energetic* pleasure–pain principle is tailored: At times it needs to give way to *structural* principles of rational, conscious judgment or the dictates of outer agencies, the aim of which is to constrain the palette of emotions bestowed by nature to specific pathways important to the social system.

Emotional regulation and its development, by consequence, needs to navigate between Skylla and Kharybdis[1]—between two opposite, vital demands or poles. On the one hand, emotional development is supposed to safeguard individuals' survival and well-being. On the other hand, cultural forces guide individuals toward more complex and cognitively demanding forms of control that demand individual sacrifices in the interest of communal well-being. Development often requires that we temporarily venture out into zones of discomfort, endure delay of gratification, and even accept temporary disequilibrium in the interest of further growth.

How individuals integrate these dual demands, then, is at the core of a life-span-oriented account of emotions. Yet how such integration is achieved—or when, in turn,

[1] In Greek mythology, Skylla and Kharybdis (or Scylla and Charybdis) were two sea monsters that sat on two opposite cliffs in the straits of Messina and posed a dangerous threat to passing sailors. They were located in close proximity, so that avoiding Skylla meant passing too closely to Kharybdis, and vice versa.

it fails—is rarely discussed in a unified manner that spans earlier and later portions of life. For example, research on emotional development in later life is often oriented toward hedonic criteria of well-being, such as high life satisfaction, high positive affect, and low negative affect (Charles, Reynolds, & Gatz, 2001; Mroczek & Kolarz, 1998). In contrast, research in early emotional development has been much more interested in outlining dimensions of cognitive reorganization that are at the base of more complex understandings of emotional processes and ultimately guide progressions in emotional development (Harris, 1989, 2008). As a result of these somewhat different theoretical emphases, there is a dearth of integrative theorizing that truly covers the full range of the life span, "from womb to tomb."

In the current chapter, we aim to offer an account of how the two modes or dimensions of emotional development are intertwined and integrated both within single events and across the process of life-span development as a whole. The account we offer is based on recent formulations of dynamic integration theory (Labouvie-Vief, 2003, 2009; Labouvie-Vief, Grühn, & Mouras, 2009; Labouvie-Vief & Marquez, 2004). The theory is consistent with many of Freud's original proposals about the dynamics of transformation of primary to secondary process (see Pribram & Gill, 1976) but includes more recent and up-to-date conceptions from developmental psychology and neuroscience. The specific structure of the current proposal owes profoundly to Piaget's theorizing about cognitive and emotional development (Piaget, 1981). Piaget was one of the first developmental psychologists to reject the traditional division between reason and affect. He suggested that reason and affect are entirely intertwined; whereas affect offers the energetics of cognition, reason provides structure to the energetics of emotion. In this view, "cognition" and "emotion" do not represent two different realms or incorporate two different kinds of representations. Cognition and emotion are two aspects of the same unified system. The parallelism of energetics and structure implies that just as is true for cognitive development in the beginning of life, emotional development can be described as the evolution of complex representations out of simple automatic and biologically hardwired structures. Complex structures, when well-regulated (see later section) are more flexible and adaptive to a wider range of situations than simple structures. Similar to cognitive development, emotional development can thus be described as a series of periods or stages implying cognitive enrichments and transformations of emotions. Specifically, the transformation from simple to more complex emotional structures suggests that the functional range over which equilibrium can be maintained is widened as more stable cognitive–emotional schemas are built. In this view, emotional structures and representations are both cognitive and emotional in nature.

Although highlighting the principle of structure and improved stability of emotion, we do not suggest such complex cognitive–emotional structures function in a static way. Rather, the building of complex structures integrates and maintains basic dynamic laws of equilibrium and homeostasis with their emphasis on inherent fluctuation and context-dependence of behavior. While preserving this core dynamic, a change in complexity effects changes in certain parameters (such as range and thresholds) of the resulting equilibrium systems. In particular, as higher order representations become part of the regulatory equilibrium system, tension thresholds (breakpoints of the system) are expanded so that higher levels of tension can be absorbed. The resulting *crystallized cognitive–emotional structures*, similar to ones in the purely intellectual realm, transform the energetics of emotion regulation through the creation of more complex structures and thereby provide well-automated emotion regulation, the effectiveness of which increases well into midlife. Effective emotion regulation is challenged or even impaired under restraining conditions that bound the effectiveness of complex structures. These conditions include constraints of fluid capacities, high load of cognitive effort, and high emotional activation passing tension thresholds.

The chapter is divided into two sections: one theoretical and one empirical. The first part details how highly automated emotion systems become enriched and enlarged as a result of cognitive processes. Because the theory offers propositions about the transformation of equilibrium processes as a function of development and aging, we begin by discussing simple equilibrium models. These simple models are successively generalized to more complex ones involving higher order cognitive processes. The transformation from simple to complex structures results in changes in the energetic of emotional functioning. We propose general levels of cognitive–emotional functioning, each of which implies a highly dynamic view of emotion regulation. The theory thus provides a discussion of basic and general developmental principles as well as a rich view of the dynamics of functioning as a result of variations in context, stimulation, and individual differences.

In the second part of this chapter, we offer a review of findings on emotion regulation at different stages of the life span. We begin by detailing developmental changes on four core dimensions of cognitive–affective complexity. These components are usually not evident in isolation but contribute toward integrated, complex responses. To give examples of their contribution, we outline their joint presence in the early development of two complex emotion systems: emotional understanding and empathy/compassion. Finally, we address the dynamic nature of the emotion system in later life as it results from a combination of gains and losses brought about by aging.

ENERGETICS, STRUCTURE, AND EQUILIBRIUM IN LIFE-SPAN EMOTIONAL DEVELOPMENT

This chapter's foundation is based on an interest in emotions and life-span development that initially was more closely tied to questions about the development of intelligence than of emotions: Why did Piaget's vision of intellectual development limit itself to the period from childhood to adolescence but neglected that of adulthood and old age? As part of the wide-ranging effort of several writers in defining "postformal" aspects of cognitive development (Commons et al., 1990; Commons, Richards, & Armon, 1984; Commons, Sinnott, Richards, & Armon, 1989), Labouvie-Vief (1980, 1982) proposed that one limitation of Piaget's theory was the focus on highly formal cognitive tasks. This focus may reflect specific tasks and processes of early development but not necessarily of later development. A unique aspect of mature adult thinking seems to be its integration of formal cognition with emotional and intuitive systems. An important aspect of adult thinking is the development and integration of what we refer to as complex emotions.

Complex emotions are emotions that, just like complex cognitions, develop out of biologically based, highly automated emotion schemas originally proposed by Darwin (1872/1998). As an example, take recent work on the development of empathy (Decety & Jackson, 2004; Decety & Meyer, 2008; Singer, 2006). Although Darwin had already speculated on an automatic and biology-evolved base of empathy when describing his infant son's attempt to console his nurse when she faked distress, many developmental psychologists felt that real empathy is a phenomenon of much higher complexity (Harris, 2006). Nevertheless, several recent theories propose that mature forms of empathy do, in fact, build on highly automated forms of empathic resonance. These automated forms of empathy are response systems observable in animals and in very young infants (de Waal, 2008). These forms support automatic perception–action systems or systems of automatic resonance that reflects contagion-like responding to emotions observed in others (Preston & de Waal, 2002). Yet as children develop more complex understandings of the functioning of emotions as well as the difference between emotional states of self and others, the capacities for empathy grow progressively. In advanced forms of development, emotional understanding can reach the capacity to empathize with individuals or groups extremely different from the self (Erikson, 1985). Other examples are the so-called moral emotions, such as guilt or shame (Haidt, 2004). Although based on evolved systems of automatic discrete emotions (Ekman, 1992; Izard, 1977; Tomkins, 1984), in their mature form, moral emotions integrate more complex representations supporting highly differentiated conception of the needs of others and of social rules about right and wrong.

Although it would be an exaggeration to state that Piaget's theory embraced affect with enthusiasm, he offered important metatheoretical discussions about the nature of affect and its relationship to evolving cognitive processes as early as the 1950s. His thinking about reason and affect is gathered in the volume *Intelligence and Affectivity* (Piaget, 1981). He proposed that a developmental course of automatic-to-complex transformation of structures is common to emotional and intellectual development. Consequently, he stated that:

> If our ... hypotheses are correct, we shall be able to parallel, stage by stage, the intellectual structures and levels of emotional development. Since no structure exists without dynamic and since, respectively, a new form of energizing regulation must correspond to any new structure, a certain type of cognitive structures must correspond to each new level of emotional behavior. (Piaget, 1981, p. 10)

This view influenced a large body of research showing progressions consistent with his theory (see Labouvie-Vief & Marquez, 2004). The cognitive–affective schemas that emerge out of ones that are originally sensorimotor, automatic and reactive transform into ones that involve more and more representation, that is, more intentionality, goal-orientation, and temporal and spatial extension and stability. In the process, emotions themselves become transformed from primary ones to more complex ones—emotions that are empowered by cognitive understandings and appraisals not evident in their quasi-reflexive origins. As detailed in the second part of this chapter, individuals acquire more complex understandings of the temporal organization of emotions, of the fact that emotions issue from intentional agents with desires and thoughts, of increasing differentiation of self from others, and of the increasing capacity to accommodate tension between diverse and often opposite emotions.

Hypothesizing that similar movement continued from adolescence to adulthood, Labouvie-Vief and colleagues (Labouvie-Vief, Chiodo, Goguen, Diehl, & Orwoll, 1995; Labouvie-Vief, DeVoe, & Bulka, 1989) began investigating the trajectory of cognitive–emotional complexity across the life span. High cognitive–emotional complexity was defined by "a language that is complex, nonstereotypical, and nondualistic; that tolerates intra- and interindividual conflict; and that appreciates the uniqueness of individual experiences" (Labouvie-Vief, DeVoe, & Bulka, 1989, p. 426). Thus, cognitive–emotional complexity was measured by coding people's understanding of emotions and their description of their self and of other people. Findings showed that from adolescence to middle adulthood, richness of emotional understanding increased dramatically, as evident, among others, by complex historical perspectives supporting more differentiated views of self and others, as well as increased capacity to integrate the tensions between positive and negative emotions related to self and others. These cross-sectional findings about the developmental trajectory of affect complexity have been confirmed in longitudinal studies (R. Helson & Soto, 2005; Labouvie-Vief, Diehl, Jain, & Zhang, 2007).

The results of this research were a great surprise and frankly disappointing. We expected an increase of cognitive–emotional complexity up into old age. Indeed, integration and complexity of emotions showed increases up until middle adulthood. However, they decreased thereafter into old age; this was the disappointing part. Even more surprisingly, the developmental trajectory of cognitive–emotional complexity appeared to be quite independent of hedonic aspects of regulation. The correlation between cognitive–emotional complexity and well-being was actually zero for the total sample; however, the correlation varied widely for different subgroups (Labouvie-Vief & Medler, 2002). I suspected that these patterns had, in part, to do with developmental changes.

The surprising aspect of this puzzle was the independence of criteria of hedonic well-being and cognitive–emotional complexity. Was this independence a part of certain developmental changes? For example, developmental models—such as that of Piaget—embracing disequilibrium as well as equilibrium processes might well imply a changing relationship between complexity and hedonic tone as individuals move through cycles of equilibrium and disequilibrium. An important aspect of Piaget's language of equilibrium and disequilibrium is the proposition that complex and well-integrated representations function to maintain equilibrium. Yet how can we define this relationship more specifically, in a way that is not abstractly intellectual but that involves organismic mechanisms of real emotions' activation and arousal?

To pursue this question, we begin by pointing to the pervasiveness and even generality of the distinction between two systems of regulation at the base of emotion regulation. After defining those, we build on connections between equilibrium processes borrowed from biology and those implied in Piaget's theory of intelligence. From there, we begin with a discussion of basic equilibrium models but gradually extend those to forms that are more and more complex and that involve the types of reorganization of which Piaget spoke in the intellectual realm.

Two Modes of Regulation

Since Freud's (1923/1957) suggestion that the demands of the Id's "pleasure principle" must be balanced by the objective and veridical function of the Ego's "reality principle," many scientists have stressed that affective adaptation implies that we are constituted as dual-mode beings. On one hand, our inborn reflexes, affects, and proclivities compel us toward automatically maximizing personal pleasure while minimizing personal pain by avoiding the buildup of too much tension and negative affect in the system. On the other hand, we are able to endure and even embrace negative affect in the pursuit of growth and the creation of meaning. For Freud, development was based on the tension between two modes of being and of defining reality: primary and secondary process. Primary process is a mode in which an inner world of desires and wishes prevails. Secondary process is, in contrast, a mode striving to find out what is objectively true, what holds in the outer world. It is the developing individual's task to strike a relatively harmonious balance between these two forms of relating to the world.

Piaget proposed as well that the reality to which we adapt is not merely an external given or an objective world "out there." He proposed that what we come to understand as "reality" is based on the organismic ground of our biological and psychological being. Hence, to develop successfully, the individual must not merely internalize the conditions of outer reality, he or she also must find outward expression for his or her inner biological needs and desires and creative tendencies. Piaget explicitly proposed, in fact, that successful development requires that these two movements—inward and outward, assimilation and accommodation—form a balance or dialogue. If one pole predominates, Piaget claimed, adaptation remains disturbed.

Theories of emotion also emphasize that affective regulation requires that we orchestrate two modes. According to such dual-process models (e.g., Chaiken & Trope, 1999; Clore & Ortony, 2000; Damasio, 1995; Epstein & Pacini, 1999; LeDoux, 1996; Schore, 1994; Tucker, 1992), the first mode functions in a highly automatic way involving activation in an all-or-none fashion requiring relatively low resources. In contrast, a second mode is based on systematic, effortful processing in which components of a knowledge structure can be accessed separately through processes of selective facilitation and inhibition, imparting on behavior a higher degree of choice and flexibility. This mode involves more formal meanings that are elaborated through processes of differentiation of already existing knowledge through selective facilitation and inhibition.

Metcalfe and Mischel (1999) referred to these two modes as *hot* and *cool* systems. In the hot system, information of high survival value to the organism is given priority, ensuring quick action in high emergency situations. Hence, information is, in essence, organized hedonically, that is, information is prioritized according to a good–bad or pleasure–pain polarity. In contrast, the cool system involves a process of differentiation by which the automatic activation of inner states is interrupted and information is processed in terms of semantic structures, problem solving, systematic appraisal, and deliberation—the evaluation of emotional information at a relatively conceptual and representational level. The hot system is often associated with the energetics and immediacy of performance, whereas the cold system is associated with its organization and capacity for delay.

Another aspect that differentiates the modes is the way in which they create meaning (Bruner, 1986; Piaget, 1955; Werner, 1955). Hot cognition is inherently tied to personal experience or inner states of the individual. It appears to be especially closely related to the activation of emotions in settings that involve subjective and intersubjective experience that is relatively implicit, such as affective communication through facial gestures or prosodic features (Gianotti, 1999; Tucker, 1992; Vingerhoets, Berckmoes, & Stroobant, 2003). Hence, meanings are inherently ineffable—experiential, nondeclarative, personal, and connotative. Cold cognition, in contrast, is based on denotative and precise meanings. These meanings are relatively formal and decontextualized through semantic structures and propositions. They refer less to intimate personal or interpersonal experience but rather represent experience in terms of relatively impersonal and conventional structures of abstract meaning.

The difference between the personal–interpersonal versus relatively formal nature of meaning also has implications for how the two modes are affected by learning and experience. Although hot cognition implies amygdala-based biological triggers (Metcalfe & Jacobs, 1998; Metcalfe & Mischel, 1999), these triggers can be conditioned to new ones through implicit learning processes that bypass consciousness. LeDoux (1996; LeDoux & Phelps, 2000) suggests that this implies a "low road" route, exemplified in the conditioning of fear reactions to tone. In this case, direct pathways from sensory cortex to amygdala provide subcortical circuits for learning, providing a "quick and dirty" processing road of high survival value in certain emergency situation. At the same time, much of learning and cultural development is based on a "high road" cortical pathway in which prefrontal cortical mechanisms participate in behavior change through processes of inhibition and executive control. As already noted, this route to change has been of special interest to cognitive accounts of emotion (Lazarus, 1966, 1982, 1991; Lazarus, Averillm, & Opton, 1970). Developmental research similarly shows how emotion regulation changes as individuals acquire complex structures of emotion knowledge that involve differentiated logical relations that are explicitly and systematically structured. In the case of "logical learning" (Pascual-Leone, 1991), change is based on explicit principles for which mastery depends on the availability of cognitive resources. The widely held differentiation between more automatic, energy-rich and more controlled, effortful and highly cognitively invested forms of regulation is evident even in recent thinking about the neurobiology of emotion–cognition relations. However, the degrees to which these systems can account for mutual transformation vary greatly on the type of underlying model that specifies their cooperation.

Tension Reduction and Equilibrium Maintenance

The energy end of the energy–structure relationship is best represented by models of regulation that imply the need to maintain low levels of tension to secure the proper functioning of the system. Since Cannon's (1939) introduction of the notion of homeostasis as a core mechanism by which living systems regulate themselves, models of homeostasis and equilibrium have been used as prototypes of such situations and enjoyed great popularity in psychological theories (e.g., Brent, 1978; Carver & Scheier, 1998; H. Helson, 1964). Cannon was primarily interested in the regulation of biological parameters such as body temperature or blood pressure. In the case of body temperature, for example, the system aims at preserving "normal" body temperature of about 98.6° Fahrenheit (37.0° Celsius). If there is significant deviation from this steady state or *end point* in either direction, temperature rises to dangerously high or low levels that increasingly threaten the capacity for integrated functioning. At the extremes, damage or total breakdown and death can result. The body initiates restorative activities that are set in motion in proportion to their deviation from the ideal or end state.

Like Freud's theory before him, Cannon's theory represented a tension reduction model. A homeostatic model with tension reduction features is, in Walker's (1956, p. 63) words, "one which through the operation of a mechanism restores a certain end state unless and until the point of breakdown is reached." Such a system attempts to keep the discrepancy or tension between end state and current state at a minimum. In such a *negative* or *feedback-reducing* system, the vigor of activity increases as a function of discrepancy, and regulation is successful when the homeostatic mechanism itself has come to rest as a result of successfully restoring the end state (Brent, 1978; Walker, 1956). This state of affairs has been depicted in Figure 4.1.

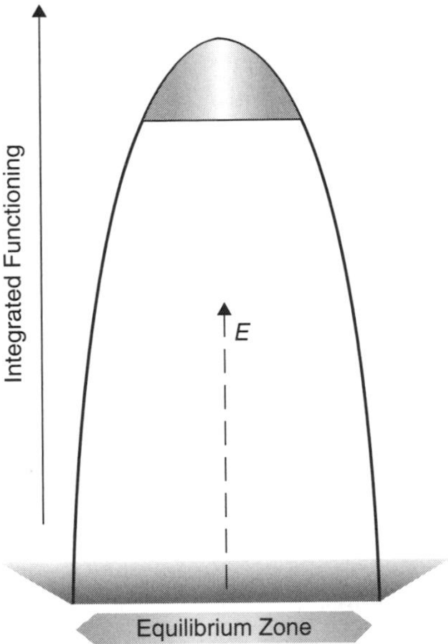

Figure 4.1 A simple equilibrium model showing the relationship between integrated functioning and the range of deviation from the end state (E). Shading from light to dark indicates transition from equilibrium zone (white) to zones of increasing stress and tension and, finally, breakdown (dark). Reprint from Labouvie-Vief (2009) with permission from IOS Press.

Figure 4.1 pictures the relationship between the functioning of the system being regulated (such as temperature regulation) and the discrepancy of the crucial parameter from its end state. The abscissa shows deviations of the critical parameter, such as temperature from its ideal end state—the energetic aspect. The ordinate, in contrast, shows the degree to which the system can function in a way that is integrated and efficient. For example, body temperature affects the organized interplay—the structural aspect—of many systems that need to function in a well-coordinated way to ensure well-being. The well-known inverted-U–shaped relationship between the two specifies the relationship between energetics deviation or tension and structure and organization. The state and organization of the system being regulated depends on the degree of deviation from the ideal end state. In general, functioning is optimal close to the end state (E) but decreases as the discrepancy deviates in either direction. For example, in the case of body temperature, if discrepancies are not too pronounced, the system will function at high levels of efficiency, but increasing deviations from the ideal imply increasing tension for the system. Fever is such a deviation from the ideal. It is a sign of illness that implies two aspects: On one hand, the system is in a state of nonoptimal functioning; on the other hand, the system attempts to restore the end state. With increasing discrepancies from the ideal, the system may reach breakdown points, where compensatory mechanisms to restore the end state fail. Signs of increasing stress are indicated by darkener shading of the range at its edges in Figure 4.1. We can define an *equilibrium zone* as the range of the system under which it is able to function with sufficient efficacy and integrity. In Figure 4.1, the equilibrium zone is the wedge under the apex of this curve.

One aspect that is also implied in homeostatic systems is that they have a capacity for self-repair that is directly related to functioning in the equilibrium zone. First, restorative, self-repair efforts are nonexistent or minimal close to the end zone (that is, at relatively minor discrepancies), when functioning is at its optimum. However, as the system shows increasing deviation from the end zone and experiences increasing tension and stress, its functioning is more and more impaired. With increasing deviations, efforts at restoring the end state and optimal functioning become progressively more vigorous. As restorative efforts reach limits of the system to endure tension, restorative efforts degrade or may even fail. The shading of the equilibrium zone in Figure 4.1 depicts increasing discrepancies from the ideal and increasing degradation of functioning. Right and left from the equilibrium zone, the system breaks down—compensatory efforts are no longer effective. In the example of body temperature, very low or very high body temperatures will result in failure of the system and eventually death.

Tension Amplification and Complex Equilibria

Cannon-type models are termed *tension* or *discrepancy–deviation reduction models* because they imply that living systems ultimately aim at keeping tension at a minimum. The system attempts to minimize feedback activity. Ideally, it aims for rest or inactivity of the homeostatic system altogether. Despite their usefulness, Cannon-type models contain a major drawback as far as psychological systems are concerned. In contrast to the aim of reducing discrepancy, psychological systems often deliberately engage in *feedback amplifying* or *feedforward activities*. At times, psychological systems aim at creating deviation, tension, and novelty. In the long run, deliberate deviations change some of the very parameters and functioning of the equilibrium system, that is, the system shows growth (Brent, 1978; Lewis, 2005). Cannon-type models do not contain this developmental idea that tension might promote growth; Cannon-type models are ultimately stable systems without long-term development.

Based on the simple Cannon-type model, H. Helson (1964) proposed a more complex theory, *adaptation level* (AL) theory. Cannon assumed a relatively fixed steady-state range. For example, body temperature varies around a relatively fixed value of 98.6° Fahrenheit (37.0° Celsius). Helson, in contrast, described systems that can profit from experiences by changing the sensitivity to aspects of stimulation. For example, eyes adapt to environmental light conditions by changing the size of the pupil, thereby regulating the amount of light that enters the eye. Such changes imply a resetting of the ideal set point. In Helson's theory, the ideal end zone is called adaptation level and refers to a level of preferred stimulation for optimal functioning. The resetting of adaptation levels also resets the critical range—or equilibrium zone. Changes of adaptation levels and corresponding ranges may be short-lived for momentary adaptation goals or may represent long-lasting changes in the system. Thus, on the basis of previous experiences, the range of optimal functioning as well as the system's breakdown points may change over time.

There is another significant difference between Helson's theory and Cannon-type models. Cannon-type models assume that the system's ideal point is reached when the system notes no deviation—the system is at rest. In Helson's theory, in contrast, the system's optimal functioning does not actually coincide with the adaptation level. He suggested that the system functions most effectively and with most positive affect at an optimal range that *slightly exceeds* the adaptation level. In this type of system, the assumed ideal state is no longer rest, but implies activity and some level of tension/deviation. Thus, systems initiate activities that drive them slightly away from the end state or set point. In other words, such systems, at junctures to be discussed shortly, use *feedforward* or *positive* feedback aimed at growth rather than stability. However, growth- and stability-oriented processes must be coordinated through a combination of positive and negative feedback. In this way, runoff of positive feedback into dangerous ranges is avoided. The resulting balance between stability and change ensures "intelligible change, which does not transform things beyond recognition at one stroke, and which always preserves invariance in certain respects" (Piaget, 1970, p. 20).

The idea of an optimal range that slightly exceeds a point of neutrality is consistent with neo-Piagetian and dynamic systems views (e.g., Prigogine & Stengers, 1984; Thelen & Smith, 1994; see also Lewis et al., this volume) in which developmental achievements may happen in equilibrium systems at points away, yet not too far away, from the steady state. This idea is also supported by theories of stress and cognition. For example, Selye (1978) proposed that adaptive changes (such as focusing of attention and effort) are initiated at slight levels of stress (i.e., activation). Recent neurohormonal theories of stress have detailed the relation between stress and cognitive functioning (e.g., McEwen & Sapolsky, 1995). At slight levels of activation, cognitive functioning is often facilitated by the effects of glucocorticoids; at very high levels of activation, in contrast, cognitive functioning is impaired, reflecting changing occupancy ratios of Type I and Type II glucocorticoid receptors that determine the direction and magnitude of stress effects on cognitive function (e.g., de Kloet, Oitzl, & Joels, 1999; Lupien et al., 2002).

Helson's propositions are in agreement with modern views of the relationship between energetic and structural changes and are mirrored in recent thinking about the relationship between emotion and cognition. For example, research shows that cognitive functioning actually is enhanced at a level slightly discrepant from the set point, that is, involving a moderate amount of tension, a phenomenon referred to as *emotional facilitation*. For example, there is considerable evidence that arousal enhances memory functioning (Cahill & McGaugh, 1998; McGaugh, 2003). Once discrepancy moves further beyond the adaptation level—the zone of emotional facilitation—individuals begin to engage in more controlled, effortful emotion regulation activities aimed at down-regulating increasing tension. Although emotion regulation is often associated with *down*-regulating affect, in some circumstances, *up*-regulating affect might be required to generate necessary activation internally. For example, when confronted with a difficult or even odious task, imagining the long-term rewards of successfully completing the task might generate enough internal activation for the task. Such *controlled up-regulation* appears to be particularly important at or very close to the end state where the tension necessary for emotional facilitation is not sufficient or entirely absent. Finally, as one moves yet further away from the range of optimal functioning into *zones of increasing effortful regulation* and zones of increasing tension, systems tend to reach a *breakdown zone* in which the efficacy of regulation and coherence of behavior break down altogether. As an example, one might think about emotion regulating during a funeral: At the beginning of a funeral, tension might still be low to medium high, and effortful regulation of preventing an emotional outburst is possible. As the funeral proceeds, high levels of tension might be built, reaching a break down in which effective emotion regulation is no longer possible.

Complex equilibrium models entail another important proposition: Reactivity to external circumstances is altered as organisms implement certain *internal* changes (Brent, 1978). For example, physical exercise is well known to induce many bodily changes (e.g., in muscle, heart, and lungs) diminishing the potentially stressful effects of exercise. Whereas an untrained person may feel quite miserable after running 3 km with many bodily reactions (e.g., sore muscles, wildly racing heart, etc.), a trained person may show only minor bodily reactions. Many psychological theories of development, such as Piaget's theory, involve qualitative reorganizations of system elements, which become more and more complexly interlinked and hierarchically embedded. Simple structures are qualitatively reorganized into complex representations. Thus, the system becomes less reactive by making internal adjustments, in fact, by changing its very structure.

Disequilibrium and Reorganization in Development

While introducing the capacity for change and adaptation into his theory, Helson already incorporated a degree of complexity into the model. Degrees of complexity are also embodied in developmental models that posit changes in equilibria as a function of cognitive development. Piaget's cognitive–developmental theory (see also Chapman, 1988) is a prime example of the four propositions of Helson's theory—*reactivity and equilibrium change* may result in permanent *internal changes* based on *self-initiated feed-forward activity* that occurs at places *away from equilibrium*. For Piaget, the crux of internal changes concerned the complexity and integrative capacity of representations. Piaget thought that the emergence of representations in development had real biological equilibrium functions, as is evident in his writings asserting that intellectual functions are the prime extension of inborn biological ones (e.g., Piaget, 1971). Even though he described such notions as discrepancy and tension in terms that lack the motivational urgency of Darwinian differential emotions or Freudian drives, in his writings on affect, he (Piaget, 1981) refused an easy distinction between cognition on the one hand and emotion on the other hand. Instead, he viewed affect and cognition as interdependent, dynamically related aspects, with cognition forming the structural and structuring aspect of emotions, and emotions forming the dynamic aspect that energizes cognition. Just as intelligence develops from primarily sensorimotor forms to highly elaborated cognitive representations, emotions also develop from primarily reflex-like and simple forms to complex representations of emotions in the self and others as well as moral understanding. Whereas simple emotion structures are easily disequilibrated (i.e., slight activation may result in a break down), complex representations provide more stable organizations through time and context.

In his later works, Piaget (e.g., Piaget, 1976, 1980) carefully described how this expansion from simple to more complex structures occurs and how more complex representations resolve tensions that are evident in simple representations. He described a process of cycles of assimilation and accommodation that involve the reestablishment of new assimilation–accommodation balances. At first, children engage in mere *assimilation*, an automatic process in which reality is affirmed or "seen" in terms of schemas that are activated from moment to moment in response to the stimulus situation. Assimilation is a highly automated process that implies a feedback-dampening mode of information processing in which a current representational framework operates to dampen any deviation. A good example is the conservation task of liquids, in which children will assert that the volumes of liquids are identical as long as the dimensions of the vessel change little. In turn, however, the automatic feedback cycle affirming equality breaks down after the dimensions change dramatically in opposite directions.

At crucial junctures, however, children note inconsistencies resulting from the limits of simple structures and automatic regulations. Piaget referred to this moment as "grasp of consciousness" (Piaget, 1976). This moment initiates a dramatic change in children's behavior: They direct their attention to the problem, begin to explore it, experiment with different ways of resolving it, and generally engage in a sustained and effortful search toward a solution. No longer *assimilating* but in fact inhibiting their assimilatory tendencies, they begin a self-directed process of *accommodation,* in which they engage directly into the conflicting situation with its tension and (momentarily) lack of solution. In general, this process highlights tension amplification, in which feed-forward processes predominate. Piaget (1980) described this period of tension as a period of differentiation and experimentation. Typically, tension is also marked by emotional aspects as it brings a new palette of feelings, such as surprise, interest, and effortful engagement, concern, and even fear (Kreibig, Wilhelm, Roth, & Gross, 2007). A characteristic aspect of this situation is that the child is able to hold tension and engage actively into disequilibrium.

Eventually, the differentiation is integrated within a more complex internal model or representation. Integration at higher levels of integrated complexity implies changes in the organization and hierarchical embedding of the component elements and processes elaborated during the off-equilibrium phase of differentiation. These structures, once highly exercised, greatly increase the range and effectiveness of functioning through space and time, and do so with high efficacy as they restore rapid assimilation of complex information. At the same time, the high automatization implies that the threshold of comfortable complexity has been raised and new cycles of differentiation and disequilibration, and reintegration can commence at yet higher levels.

Such sequences of equilibrium–disequilibration–reequilibration have been well documented in the domain of emotions. Whereas in the "purely cognitive realm," the tension associated with functioning far from equilibrium is more often described through differentiation and lack of coherence, in the emotional realm the tension of disequilibration entails more directly energetic and affective negativity. For example, Sroufe (1996) described newborns' limited capacity for self-regulation, evident in low tension thresholds and distress at low levels of stimulation. Over time, however, infants are able to accept and to engage actively with more complex, dynamic, and intense stimulation. They reset their tension thresholds and begin to tolerate and even prefer more vigorous stimulation (Sroufe, 1996). In a similar fashion, Schore (1994) has suggested that early periods of negativity and shame create stress that can support further development of self-regulation and the internalization of standards (Schore, 1994), as discussed more fully later. At a level yet more advanced, Harter (1999) observed parallel processes in adolescence, when cognitive growth can initiate a period of heightened negative affect as adolescents' advances in differentiation and complexity raise their awareness of conflicts between different self-attributes. At first, this awareness produces tension and an increase in negative emotions but eventually, such opposites are integrated into larger representations as discussed later in this chapter.

From an equilibrium perspective, the integrations just discussed resolve existing tensions with the aid of more complex representations. Thereby they act to expand the range of situations over which individuals can function in an equilibrated way. Thus, complex cognitive–affective structures emerge out of a dynamic interplay between assimilation and accommodation (Labouvie-Vief & Marquez, 2004). This dynamic (which, as already noted, is central to Piaget's theory) parallels the contemporary differentiation between two modes of processing affective information: schematic and conscious processing (Chaiken & Trope, 1999; Clore & Ortony, 2000; LeDoux, 1996; Metcalfe & Mischel, 1999). Assimilation represents a low effort, automatic, and schematic processing mode, in which judgments are framed in a binary fashion of good or bad, right or wrong, and positive or negative. Regulation is oriented at dampening deviations from these binary evaluations. Accommodation, in contrast, involves a conscious and effortful unfolding, elaboration, and coordination of emotional schemas into complex knowledge structures.

Figure 4.2 presents the relation between increasing levels of complexity and an expanding range of optimal functioning over time. Figure 4.2 displays a sequence of three developmental levels of complexity, simply for purposes of illustration. In actuality, the precise number of levels one is willing to postulate is, in part, a matter of convenience and depends on one's purpose and the level of analysis adequate to that level (Brent, 1978). Below, we actually detail different levels of development typically proposed in models of child and adult development. In contrast, the purpose of Figure 4.2 is merely to indicate that accommodation and effortful engagement function to expand the equilibrium zone by extending the breakdown points farther away from

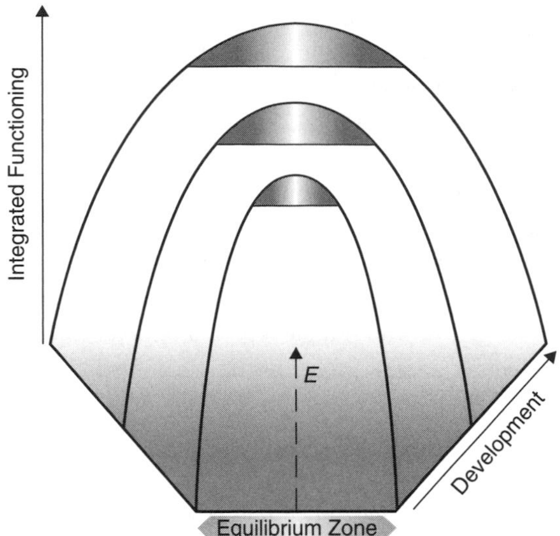

Figure 4.2 A complex equilibrium model indicating broadening of equilibrium zones and elevation of tension thresholds at low, moderate, and high levels of complexity of cognitive–emotional structures. Reprinted from Labouvie-Vief (2009) with permission from IOS Press.

the adaptation level. In this way, individuals can maintain complex functioning and lowered levels of activation and arousal over a broader range of complex and previously negative and disturbing situations.

Developmental Trade-Offs of Energy for Structure

The examples we have outlined thus far exemplify how temporary high-energy and high-effort processes far from equilibrium in simple structures are eventually exchanged for low-energy and low-effort processes in more complex structure and organization. Schore (1994) argued that a critical aspect of this process is the creation of temporary and relatively slight levels of stress that are related to elevated levels of corticosteroid circulation. If these transient stress periods are well regulated—for example, with the aid of the parents or other social support systems who help contain runoff into breakdown zones—they become crucial in supporting neurogenesis and neural rewiring of cortical circuits that support self-regulation and internalization of standards. This process is interlinked with the rapid development throughout childhood of prefrontal cortical areas that provide control structures supporting functions such as planning, reasoning, and gating out distracting information (Tsujimoto, 2008). The rapidity and efficiency of these control structures is supported by the development of representational redescriptions into complex representations for rules, symbols, and language (Karmiloff-Smith, 1992).

How representations come to serve the function of creating more stable systems of regulation has been the focus of speculation ever since Freud's ideas (see Pribram & Gill, 1976). Luria (1932) was probably the first researcher addressing this question in the emotional realm. He demonstrated that symbol systems such as conventional images and words serve to dampen peripheral arousal induced by situations related to high emotional conflict. Using hand tremor as a measure of arousal (well before the implementation of modern methods of assessing arousal), he showed that, when individuals were asked to provide symbols or to use linguistic labels for conflict situations, tremor was greatly reduced. Modern neuropsychological studies found similar effects. When identifying emotionally activating stimuli (e.g., angry or fearful faces) through emotion labels (i.e., *angry* vs. *fearful*) rather than simply viewing the stimuli, amygdala activation was greatly reduced (Hariri, Bookheimer, & Mazziotta, 2000; Lieberman et al., 2007). Such findings support the conclusion that the development of systems implies a trade-off of high-energy and highly reactive emotional processes for highly ordered cognitive–emotional systems that are much more resistant to perturbation. Lewis (Lewis, 2005; Lewis et al., this volume) proposes that the psychological counterpart of such structures be referred to as *emotional interpretations*. In this chapter, we refer to them as complex cognitive–emotional schemas.

These kinds of trade-off processes were first postulated by Freud (see Brent, 1978; Pribram & Gill, 1976), who proposed that developing ego functions "bind" the tension inherent in external stimulation through the development of new representational systems that provide greater stability and resistance to perturbation. Importantly, this process does not entail that vivid emotional experience gives way to or even gets lost in abstractions. Rather, individuals are able to develop new emotional systems that, although more complex, function in an immediate and automatic fashion. This is similar to the frequent differentiation of the mind's abilities into two forms of "intelligence": Intelligence A and Intelligence B by Hebb (1949) or fluid and crystallized intelligence by Cattell (see Cattell, 1971). Fluid intelligence represents a basic adaptive potentiality mediated mainly by the complexity and plasticity of the central nervous system. Crystallized intelligence, in contrast, represents the highly practiced and canalized result of experience and cultural investment. As a result, crystallized abilities are quite resistant to variations that easily perturb fluid abilities. In the cognitive–emotional realm, one should expect that crystallized structures provide similar protection against perturbations to which more basic automatic emotion systems are vulnerable.

The stability provided by crystallized cognitive–emotional structures comes with an additional trade-off. As structures become more orderly, they also become more determined and *deterministic* (Lewis, 2005). Initially, development is based on relatively pure fluid abilities with many degrees of freedom and high susceptibility to perturbation, but as structures become more fully specified and stable, they have fewer degrees of freedom. Hence developmental trajectories themselves become stabilized, with the result that further growth becomes more highly constrained. To say this differently, at the beginning of the life span, when structures tend to be simple and fluid, the system has many opportunities for developmental paths. The simple structure can become practically everything. When structures become more complex and crystallized, the system becomes more restricted in its developmental pathways. Complex structures are already something. With the richness and protection provided by crystallization processes therefore comes a higher degree of specialization and canalization of developmental pathways, with the important implication that flexibility of fluid functioning becomes successively restricted (see also Lewis, 2005; Lewis et al., this volume).

Levels and Directions of Cognitive–Emotional Development

Through a recursive application of cycles of disequilibration and reequilibration, individuals are able to establish successively higher levels of cognitive–emotional development. Figure 4.2 indicates three such levels in a schematic fashion. Many stage theories of development differentiate about four levels of development characterizing the passage from childhood to youth and about three additional levels in adulthood. Before discussing these levels in more detail, there are two important points to keep in mind. First, dynamic integration theory does not necessarily propose a certain fixed number of developmental levels or stages. Reorganization of structures through equilibrium and disequilibrium cycles can occur quite frequently at different rates and different times. Stage theories are, however, helpful in highlighting and defining the nature of major changes in the cognitive architecture that are consistent with dynamic integration theory. Second, these levels are dynamic rather than rigid sequences of steps. For example, individuals can occupy different positions from time to time depending on the context. Hence, many factors other than age or the mere passage of time contribute toward exactly which level is being displayed by a particular individual at a particular time. For example, variations in stimulus intensity, effectiveness of different regulation strategies (Labouvie-Vief & Marquez, 2004), as well as availability of social support (Fischer & Bidell, 2006) can determine the levels expressed by a particular individual. Similarly, circumstances such as unusual stress can cause individuals to display performance lower than those habitually shown. Thus, the levels serve as a rough and flexible guideline, and to describe the level at which an individual functions momentarily requires that one be able to specify the conditions under which the level is assessed.

Directions of Early and Late Development

When talking about development over the life span, some theoreticians propose that the meaning of development takes on somewhat different forms at earlier levels (i.e., in the first part of life) as opposed to later levels (i.e., in the second part of life). One major reason relates to the internal (e.g., genetic–maturational) sources that direct processes of development at earlier and later stages of life. Early growth appears to be regulated by maturational processes that have a strong biological and evolutionary base. There is considerable agreement that evolutionary selection pressures have worked more strongly on the first part of life (see Baltes, 1997; Baltes, Lindenberger, & Staudinger, 2006). The benefits of evolution ensure reproductive success and survival of the species. In later life, similar benefits of evolution grow weaker as reproduction has been passed. As a result, changes in later life often appear less ordered and can be relatively random.

For childhood, for example, the progressive development of fluid cognitive structures that support the formation of crystallization and complex processes of automation, as well as the resulting expansion of equilibrium ranges appears to be strongly driven by biological processes shaped during evolution. In later life, fluid functioning declines tremendously. Effortful regulation processes (see the section "Tension Amplification and Complex Equilibria" earlier in this chapter), the efficacy of which relies greatly on fluid processes, are expected to show similar declines in effectiveness. In contrast, more crystallized function of emotion regulation are rather well protected in old age. Nevertheless, optimal functioning of crystallized structures depends in part on the presence of fluid functioning. Thus, in late life, a decline in fluid processes should result in a decline of the efficiency of crystallized processes as well (Labouvie-Vief, 2009).

Biological processes do not, of course, take place in a cultural vacuum. Different directions of development can be expected because of cultural influences or variations. Early development is strongly oriented by culture's demand that individuals adopt standardized symbol systems, which often come to dominate the more private symbolism inherent in personal experience. In that process of standardization, "meaning systems that originate in the organismic, the sensorimotor, the figurative, the dynamic, and the personal, are gradually displaced by those that are abstract, conceptual, stable, conventional, and impersonal" (Labouvie-Vief, Hakim-Larson, DeVoe, & Schoeberlein, 1989 p. 283). The direction of development is outward and acquisitive with an orientation toward appropriating and even becoming entrenched in conventional linguistic and symbolic worlds. Some authors (e.g., Jung, 1933; Labouvie-Vief, 2008; Stern, 1985) have suggested that early development implies a strong entrenchment in cultural conventions, an entrenchment that implies not only a gain but also a suppression of potentialities (Jung, 1933) and loss of spontaneity and creativity.

Although the advantage of this outer orientation is that the child and novice adult be able to categorize experience in a stable and reliable manner in accordance with cultural needs, the resulting hierarchical structure becomes a liability in adulthood. From the standardization of inner life and the suppression of inner richness springs certain rigidity. Later life offers, however, the opportunity to turn to more integrative themes (Jung, 1933). Mature individuals are able to reinfuse their inner life into more external and formal frameworks. This process of centroversion contrasts with that of extraversion that dominates earlier development. Other authors have also talked of similar processes and suggested that mature individuals recuperate some of the emotional richness of childhood but at a higher level of sophistication (Labouvie-Vief & DeVoe, 1991). This union of emotional richness with intellectual insight has been referred to as a *second naiveté* (Ricoeur, 1970) or an *emancipated innocence* (Chinen, 1989).

As a result of these two sets of influences on development, evolutionary and cultural influences, the life course of cognitive and cognitive–emotional functions is likely to be different for the early and late parts of the life span. Early development is usually described as an upward movement of growth, driven—although not exclusively—by biological maturation. In later life, however, the effects of relative normative declines in fluid functions begin to exert their influence. Whether fluid declines in late life lead to lowered emotion regulation depends on whether individuals are able to bring to bear a stock of highly automated, well-integrated and crystallized cognitive–emotional schemas. If so, individuals can draw on their rich background and give evidence of well preserved and sometimes even superior emotion regulation. Nevertheless, optimal and well-integrated performance depends of the availability of crystallized cognitive–emotional schemas. Performance will show evidence of deterioration when situations draw on more effortful fluid processes, such as in novel situations or high-arousing situations. Therefore, we expect that performance will maintain high levels when based on purely crystallized domains; nevertheless, the equilibrium range will be narrowed. This situation is depicted in Figure 4.3a. It indicates the level of performance that can be maintained or even raised, even when the range becomes narrower and more restricted.

In contrast to the benefits of depending on one's past integration and automation of experiences, situations that fall clearly outside of this facilitative range will show a much more negative outcome. For tasks demanding high involvement of executive resources and high levels of emotional activation well outside of the zone of facilitation, we would predict two consequences: First, we expect a narrowing of the equilibrium zone with lowering of tension thresholds. Second, we expect degradation of performance including lower efficiency and lower overall integrated complexity. This situation is indicated in Figure 4.3b. It shows simultaneous narrowing of the equilibrium range with lowering of level of functioning and integration.

Levels of Cognitive–Emotional Development

As already stated, Piaget proposed parallels between levels of cognitive development and levels of emotional development. Accordingly, his emotional stages follow the same structure as his cognitive stages of development.

The first stage, corresponding to the *sensorimotor period*, is characterized by the beginning transformation of inborn and reflex-like organizations that quickly expand through the sensorimotor period. Feelings and emotions begin to be less characterized by the here and now; they begin to be more explicitly linked to extensions of self and other in time and space. This period also marks increasing engagement and exploration, which results in the extension of thresholds of stimulation and creates a more intentional orientation toward the external world. To be sure, Piaget's

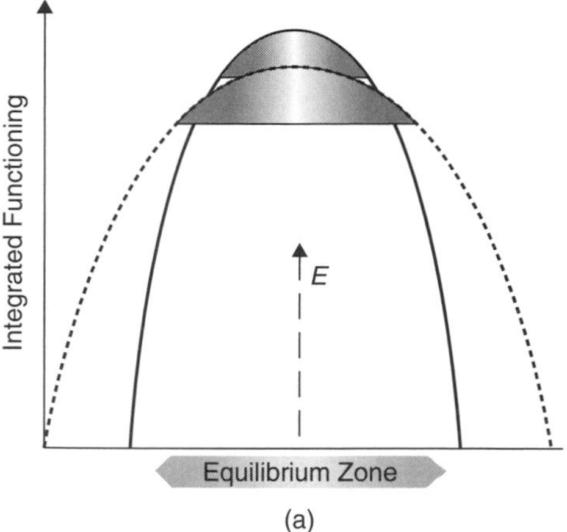

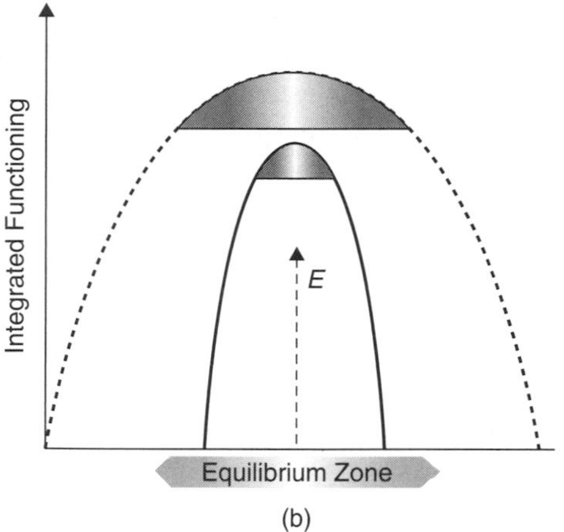

Figure 4.3 A complex equilibrium model showing two types of hypothetical changes from midlife (dotted line) to old age (solid line). (a) This model shows narrowing of the equilibrium zone (range) but maintaining (or even raising) integrated functioning in well-crystallized domains. (b) This model shows narrowing of the equilibrium zone (range) and accelerated lowering of integrated functioning in domains subject to losses in fluidity. Reprinted from Labouvie-Vief (2009) with permission from IOS Press.

hereditary organizations were not explicitly modeled after those primary emotion schemas Darwin had proposed. However, Piaget's theoretical framework can easily be seen as an extension of these primary emotion schemas. A genuine limit of Piaget's approach is his relative disinterest and even devaluation of the interpersonal and intersubjective context of development (Labouvie-Vief, 1996). He tended to see the interpersonal world as derived rather than assuming that from the beginning, emotions are elaborated in shared interpersonal contexts and involve the elaboration of a self in relationships (Labouvie-Vief, 2005).

In the *preoperational period*, children acquire the capacity of internalized action patterns. In the form of representation and language, these patterns permit stabilization and conservation of feelings in memory and imagination. Better understanding of others and their role vis-à-vis the self marks the beginning of morally relevant feelings in an often intuitive form. Piaget called these feelings seminormative because they are not yet clearly stabilized by representations.

During the *concrete period*, representations bring more intentional feelings including the use of the "will" through which feelings can be produced in an autonomous fashion. Children also show keen interest in the development of ordering relationships in the form of social comparisons, social orders, and the moral aspects of justice and injustice.

During the *formal period*, with the capacity to understand abstract systems of laws, adolescents become highly interested in how feelings are coordinated among groups. Ethics and ideals become important in unifying feelings, role of conventions becomes stabilized in terms of abstract ideals and generalized social and interpersonal standards. Similar to Erikson, Piaget saw this period as pivotal in the "formation of personality."

Although Piaget saw development as essentially terminated by late adolescence, the 1980s brought a keen interest in adult development after the formal period. This interest in *postformal levels* was stimulated by the work of Kohlberg. His work on postconventional moral thinking expands the development of stages of intellectual development in which individuals became more critical of conventional abstractions. For example, one limitation of formal thinking is that it can develop abstract systems but lacks the capacity to form systems that compare abstract systems among each other (e.g., Fischer & Bidell, 2006; Labouvie-Vief, 1984). The capacity for such meta-abstraction appears to emerge as relativism and deconstruction of conventional systems, with the aim of establishing intersystemic comparisons. Finally, some individuals arrive at a level at which they attempt to develop unifying ways of thinking about reason, emotion, morality, and life. This level is called *integrated* by Labouvie-Vief and colleagues (Labouvie-Vief, Chiodo, et al., 1995; Labouvie-Vief, DeVoe, Chiodo, & Coyle, 1995) or *metasystematic* by Commons (Commons & Wolfsont, 2002).

Cognitive–Emotional Integration and Its Variations

So far we have assumed that the result of transformation is a well-integrated system, and this assumption is, in fact, inherent in Piagetian theory. In his theory, resolution of a level of complexity is essentially accompanied by integration. However, other theories do not assume that the result of progression and transformation is perfect integration. These theories propose that individuals can develop partial solutions for particular levels or stages. An example is the theory of Erik Erikson (1985). In his theory, a particular integrative theme dominates each stage of the life span; however, the degree to which individuals are able to arrive at well-integrated solutions varies. In particular, Erikson proposed that each stage is characterized by a polarity of a relatively optimal solution and one that is clearly suboptimal. Individuals' resolution of a stage can assume a position either closely to the optimal outcome or closely to a more problematic adaptation.

Bowlby's attachment theory (Bowlby, 1969, 1973) provides a model of how individuals vary in optimal developmental outcomes. As Piaget, Bowlby assumed that individuals develop representational systems that guide more automatic systems. Bowlby used the term *internal working models*. In contrast to Piaget, he proposed that the relationship between representational systems of different levels is not always coherent. Whereas Piaget assumed that each lower level representational model (e.g., sensorimotor schema) becomes transformed within a higher level representation (e.g., for example, the child who masters concrete operations *directly* apprehends that increases in height have been compensated by decreases in width), Bowlby assumed that such transformation-with-integration is not a necessary result. Rather, individuals can develop a "defensive exclusion" through which they attempt to protect themselves from threatening experiences and their memories. Individuals thus can develop two (or more) representational models that coexist: One representation reflects an automatic model of actual painful experiences lived, whereas the other represents experiences that are deformed, for example, as a result of being excluded from child–parent or even cultural discourse, (in the manner already discussed previously). The latter model is often more important for socialization success and becomes the dominant representation. In contrast, the former model is often repressed and no longer accessible to memory. This is the case, for example, in the strategy of attachment avoidance, which results in a discoordination of systems. For example, an individual who has developed automatic and quite unacknowledged fears of close social contacts, rather than being aware of such fears, develops cognitive representations that devalue others and being emotionally close to them; instead, the self is defensively overevaluated to compensate for its fears. Though highly complex, such representations may exist in a state that is entirely unintegrated with the original automatic system, that is, fear.

When are such failures to integrate likely to occur? In general, the DIT proposes (see Labouvie-Vief & Marquez, 2004) that integration is most likely to occur at levels of activation that are close to, but slightly away from, an existing equilibrium set point. This requires that some mechanism be provided that protects from too-high activation that would disrupt integrative processes. For example, Schore (1994) mentions the need for parents to provide such regulatory help as offering repair for temporary escalations of arousal. Many cultural mechanisms also are ideally aimed at providing such optimal regulation of developmental transitions, although in actuality, culture also may provide levels of activation that foster and even fixate failures to integrate. Indeed, we already noted that a degree of disconnection is quite normative with socialization into conventional systems. In contrast, many developmental theorists also propose that such failures are not necessarily irreversible, but can be restored through the coherence provided by therapy or through spiritual and personal experiences that are part of mature adulthood, when conventional pressures relax for some people. In any case, it is important to note that increasing development to higher levels of complexity does not necessarily imply a higher level of integration. We prefer, therefore, to make a specific differentiation between forms of complexity that are not integrated and ones that, in contrast, are integrated in the sequel of this chapter.

Heinz Werner's developmental theory (1957) conveyed this dynamic interplay between complexity and integration. In Werner's theory, *integration* presumes the presence of differentiated substructure. Such integrated structures, we suggest (see Labouvie-Vief, 2009) involve at once a particular level of integrated cognitive-conceptual complexity and a sufficiently positive tone free of excessive stress and negative emotion. In Werner's terms, integration can also occur without complexity (e.g., reflective and complex thinking), in which case it is referred to as *globality*; complexity without integration is *fragmentation*.

In our own work (see Labouvie-Vief & Medler, 2002) we applied this distinction to characterize different forms of defensive exclusion. For example, some individuals give highly positive evaluations of situations (and show, in that sense, apparent signs of emotional integration) without being able to differentiate the aspects and elements of such situations. In fact, sometimes we may make emotionally toned judgments that are simply intuitive without being able to differentiate in any way why we arrive at those judgments. Individuals given to such judgments show a high degree of globality. In turn, other individuals may evolve highly differentiated structures that are not integrated. For example (as in the example of Harter's research we cited), they may vacillate between describing self and others in positive and then negative terms, but be unable to specify any integrative theme. In these individuals, high conceptual differentiation does not go along with integration into a positive emotional self-core; in fact, it is related to raised levels of negative affect and even depression. Yet both these groups are not entirely fragmented but can present a degree of organized and coherent adaptation to their environment that may be functional in their context. In contrast, individuals classified as overwhelmed appear to be truly fragmented, disorganized, and poorly adapted. Individuals classified as integrated stand out against the other three groups. As in Werner's ideal, integrated individuals reflect a balance between integration and differentiation.

An example of these different strategies that has been widely utilized in Bowlby's (1969) formulation of attachment strategies, a formulation that reflects the close dependence between social regulation of fears of separation and need for security on one hand, and the extent to which individuals can regulate such fears in relatively integrated or more fragmented ways. According to Bowlby, persons with a secure attachment style perceive others more positive, have more positive expectations about others, and are more responsive to a romantic partner's needs than persons with an unsecure style (Bartholomew & Horowitz, 1991; Hazan & Shaver, 1987). Their good integration is shown, at the same time, in their capacity to acknowledge negative information and to coordinate it with positive information about self and others. In contrast, other attachment styles are less well integrated. In particular, attachment avoidance is characterized by repression of affective content, especially that related to closeness. Anxious persons, in contrast, focus on others and their own dependence on them, which leads to excessive resonance of others' negative emotions and associated personal distress (Shaver & Mikulincer, 2002).

LIFE-SPAN DEVELOPMENT OF EMOTIONAL SYSTEMS

As we have outlined so far, emotional development along the life span consists, in essence and ideally, of changes in the complexity and integration of emotions. Associated with these changes is a cascade of other changes, in particular, tension thresholds and the implications for well-being and well-integrated functioning. In this section, we offer an empirical review of the complexity of emotions along the life span. First, we outline the relatively normative emergence of complex emotions from basic or primary emotions in the first part of life as well as possible declines in the second part of life. Whereas the first part of the life span tends to show a general pattern of growth, of differentiation, and of increasing resources, the second part of the life span usually also brings a general pattern of biological decline enforcing dedifferentiation and compensation. These changes bear in important ways on the dynamics of the emotional system and its integration with cognition.

Second, consistent with the equilibrium perspective adopted, emotion systems' functioning depends on a set of general principles. The principles are consistent with all phases of the life span, from birth to death. On the basis of contextual variables and individual characteristics, such as individuals' resources, activation levels, and regulations styles, emotional systems may show tremendous variability in their functioning. This aspect is dealt with in a second subsection on the rise and fall of tension thresholds.

Cognitive–Emotional Complexity from Childhood to Adulthood

Early theory and research on emotional development owes a tremendous heritage to Darwin's (1872/1998) work. He postulated the existence of a limited number of highly automated emotions: As a result of evolutionary pressures, emotions represent reliable response systems ensuring vital adaptation of the organism for survival and reproduction. The identification of these differential response systems formed the topic of much earlier research on the development of emotions (see Labouvie-Vief & DeVoe, 1991). As we pointed out, developmental psychologists, including Freud and Piaget, suggested that some of these primary emotions experience dramatic transformations throughout the life span. Such transformations may involve two aspects: On the one hand, existing emotion schemas are linked to new external conditions; on the other hand, new emotional systems can emerge as a result of cognitive changes that affect the organization and representation of emotions. An important facet of such emerging emotional complexity is the capacity of differentiating own states from those of others. This capacity for self–other differentiation forms a crucial aspect of the development of complex forms of emotions as empathy, guilt, and other moral emotions (Haidt, 2004).

There has been some argument about whether what we call complex emotions also have an inborn and automatic base. Darwin proposed that highly automated forms that recognize the states of others as different from the self are already present at birth. For example, he commented on what seemed to him an instinctual form of empathy in his infant son:

> When a few days over six months old, his nurse pretended to cry, and I saw that his face instantly assumed a melancholy expression, with the corners of the mouth strongly depressed; now this child could rarely have seen any other child crying, and never a grown-up person crying, and I should doubt whether at so early an age he could have reasoned on the subject. Therefore it seems to me that an innate feeling must have told him that the pretended crying of his nurse expressed grief; and this through the instinct of sympathy excited grief in him. (Darwin, 1872/1998, p. 359)

In contrast to this view of the instinctual nature of the recognition of others' emotions, developmental psychologists have often emphasized the essential cognitive nature of complex moral emotions (see Harris, 1989). Recent proposals from neuroscience (Decety & Jackson, 2004; Rizzolatti & Arbib, 1998; Singer, 2006) and primatology (Preston & de Waal, 2002) suggest continuity among simpler forms of recognizing emotions to more complex forms, such as mature forms of empathy.

Our approach similarly reflects a more recent tendency to think of the development of emotions in terms of two component processes that highlight two classes of abilities. One reflects the perhaps inborn tendency to resonate automatically with the emotional state of another, prior to any cognitive understanding. This ability constitutes a precursor for developing shared emotional meanings. The other ability reflects cognitive elaboration and representation of others' subjective feeling (Decety & Meyer, 2008). This ability requires additional computational mechanisms beyond the shared representation level. In particular, the distinction of states of the self and the other is beyond basic resonating, including the capacities to inhibit the empathic contagion and distress that may be induced by the suffering of others, to differentiate the state of oneself from that of others, to read and appropriately interpret the state of the other, and to imagine and produce a response appropriate to the others' situation. Along with Piaget's thinking, complex emotional systems such as mature empathy hence seem to emerge from more automatic emotional systems set in place by evolutionary pressures.

Of course, as already discussed in the first section of this chapter, the differentiation of emotions and emotional responses of varying levels of complexity involves more than a binary distinction between automatic and more complex and reflective levels. Complex emotions evolve over the course of development into different forms of complexity. Labouvie-Vief and colleagues (e.g., Labouvie-Vief, Chiodo, et al., 1995; Labouvie-Vief, Hakim-Larson, et al., 1989; Labouvie-Vief & Marquez, 2004) proposed such levels of complexity along the entire life span. They differentiated four general dimensions along which development of more complex and integrated structures proceeds: First, individuals become increasingly aware that emotional states are not merely automatic but intentional. Individuals perceive the self and others as *reflective* agents with inner resources such as intentions, desires, and thoughts. This beginning "theory of mind" (Harris, 2000) gives rise to second-order feelings such as self-evaluative emotions (e.g., embarrassment, shame, guilt) as well as supporting metaemotional skills of reflective self-regulation. A second dimension is *self–other differentiation* that is highly interwoven with perceiving self and others as reflective agents. It is the ability to experience others as individual's distinct from the self (Labouvie-Vief, Chiodo, et al., 1995) yet incorporate the resulting diversity within progressively more abstract and wider intersubjective bonds implying a reciprocity of intentions, thoughts, and values. Pervading these two dimensions is the capacity to embrace the tension between opposites of emotional valence, *the complexity of valence*. Finally, individuals develop complex conceptions of emotions that imply *variation and organization of emotions across time and context*. This organization supports temporal delay as well as a sense of emotional continuity and of individuals' emotional identity and personality in the face of change (Lewis & Ferrari, 2001).

Although these dimensions are interrelated in individuals' responses, the dimensions can be distinguished on conceptual grounds, as well as in the responses of individuals. We provide a more detailed perspective on the development of self–other differentiation and integration of opposites. We then outline the development of emotional functioning and emotional systems in two emotion areas: (a) empathy and compassion and (b) emotional understanding. These two areas function as prime examples of the development of more complex emotional structures from simple and automatic emotional systems.

Self–Other Differentiation and Integration

The dimension of self–other differentiation is important in two respects: First, it reflects that individuals are inherently related to others through bonds of intersubjectivity. Such intersubjectivity lies at the very core of the development of the self in relation to others (see Trevarthen, 1993; Werner & Kaplan, 1963). Second, along the life span, individuals become better and better able to distinguish states of others from those of the self. At the same time, individuals form new understandings of forms of intersubjectivity that tie together human relationships, ensuring both difference between and continuity among self and others (Kohlberg, 1969).

Primary forms of intersubjectivity have been identified at the beginning of life, especially in early forms of mother–child interaction. Mother–child interactions demonstrate the importance of synchronous, mutually contingent responding for the establishment of profiles of emotional responses (Nadel, Carchon, Kervella, Marcelli, & Reserbat-Plantey, 1999). Building in innate tendencies, the infant's ability to use primary forms of intersubjectivity to bridge breaks in continuity and reciprocity is clearly limited. Infants' vulnerability to ruptures in synchrony and continuity in interactions are vast. Therefore, the lion's share of the responsibility of providing a safe space falls clearly on the adult. The adult becomes an important regulator of the child's states and ideally possesses mature capacities to protect the infant from emotions that would break the bond. The child, in contrast, has still-limited capacities to integrate differences between self and other. It is no doubt for this reason that major developmental theories accord great importance to this time as the most formative of all.

Throughout the first year, and hopefully supported by a sensitive parent who can provide good intersubjective continuity, children become better able to bridge differences and even tensions between self and other. This time marks the emergence of an explicit recognition of the self as a separate physical entity. This self-recognition also implies the beginning of self-evaluative emotions such as shame (Schore, 1998). The child can, in an intuitive way, understand that his or her behavior is evaluated by others and can orient behavior accordingly. However, to develop into a mature form of self-evaluative capacity, parents need to repair the temporary stress related to episodes of shame. This will tilt the developing capacity toward healthy moral standards rather than a permanently impaired self-concept (Schore, 1998). For similar reasons, Erikson (1985) located the crucial developmental conflict between autonomy versus shame and doubt into this phase of development.

For theorists such as Freud and Kohlberg, this period of development is characterized by a predominant orientation of the child toward parents. Parents are seen as powerful individuals whom we aim to please. Through approval or gentle critique, parents can serve as a guide toward building healthy feelings related to morality and social cohesion.

The work of Kohlberg has been particularly important in providing extensions of such preliminary forms of intersubjectivity. In middle childhood, children develop a greater independence of judgment and capacity for difference in opinion. For example, children become better able to understand that others have different perspectives and desires and that different emotions can result from those. This permits the development of a sense of reciprocity, which is, however, tied to specific interactions with concrete others. In contrast, the ability to relate to more abstract norms and rules emerges at the conventional level in which viewpoints can be coordinated in terms of social groups. A first evidence of these social rules is a sense that group expectations ("generalized other") take precedence over individual feelings. Somewhat later, a more complex societal perspective emerges in which a more generalized social system perspective of formalized laws takes precedence even over the rules of one's immediate group. Erikson (1985) identified this level with a strong emotional orientation toward ideological values, an association similarly proposed by Piaget (1981).

The conventional and then societal perspectives are important throughout adolescence and early adulthood, but in adulthood, a more complex perspective yet emerges. Now, individuals often turn from the "is" to the "ought." This postconventional perspective is initiated by rising doubts that the laws and truths one has come to accept are, indeed, unalterable, and the suspicion that context and history matter. Such transitional doubt further leads individuals to wonder whether such change and diversity can be orderly and principled. This matures into the conviction that change can come about in an ordered way if individuals integrate their varying perspectives by formal mechanisms of agreement, contract, objective impartiality, and due process. In this way, it is possible to critique the validity of laws in terms of the degree to which they preserve and protect fundamental rights and values. Finally, individuals may adopt a more universalizing perspective affirming the equality and dignity of all human beings, whatever their cultural, ideological, or religious origin. Social agreements then are valid to the extent that they honor such general principles.

One general feature of the progressions outlined is that individuals are able to include more and more diversity and difference into their conceptions of self and others. An important feature of the resulting widened equilibrium is that, with increasing development, negative emotions can be more comfortably integrated with positive ones. The capacity to manage the tension between positive and negative emotions increases systematically from childhood to youth. Newborns' tolerance for high levels of stimulation is limited and evokes distress. Over time, however, infants actively engage with more complex, dynamic, and intense stimulation and as a consequence reset their tension thresholds (Sroufe, 1996). Schore's (1994) analysis of the reorganization of attachment relations in the second year of life is a good example. In this transition, negative experiences are integrated within an overall positive framework. In early infancy, the relation between infant and mother tends to be characterized by mutual attunement. The mother, aware of the limited capacity of the infant, regulates positive exchanges. However, after the age of about 10 months, a qualitative change in mother–infant interaction begins as mothers change from a preponderance of reward to prohibitions. The unexpected lack of cooperation of the mirroring object that may express disapproval or even shame and disgust creates negative feelings. These states, which involve a sudden change from energy mobilizing sympathetic activation to energy-conserving parasympathetic activation, play a critical role in the development of inhibitory systems crucial for self-regulation. Ideally, the mother helps repair such states by reengaging positive communication, permitting transition to sympathetic–dominant arousal. In this way, the child is able to maintain a positively toned relationship with a caretaker, who occasionally acts in a negative and frustrating way.

As mentioned in the first section of this chapter, Harter (1999) observed parallel processes in adolescents' coordination of positive and negative affect. Adolescents' cognitive and social development advance differentiation of the self. However, this development also increases the awareness of conflicts and disagreements between opposite self-aspects. For example, an adolescent may feel "joyful" and "depressed." The awareness of these conflicts between positive and negative self-aspects creates in the beginning heightened negative affect. Eventually, adolescents learn to integrate these opposite self-attributes into a contextual framework. They realize that different aspects of their self are emphasized under different contexts or under different times. They might feel "frank" with their mother but "withdrawn" from their father, or they might feel "sluggish" at school but "active" in their sports club. In a similar vein, King and Hicks (2007) outlined how losses and regrets might promote development in adulthood. They argued that losses and regrets are related to concurrent distress and lowered well-being; however, losses and regrets are also related to heightened levels of complexity. This may in time lead to new and better forms of integration and dealing with difficult situations. Thus, as implied in our proposal of development as cycles of disequilibration and re-equilibration, losses and regrets may even promote complexity, integration, and happiness in the long run.

The increasing capacity to incorporate tension and diversity into one's cognitive-affective structures thus forms an important part of the development of higher levels of complexity and integration. Indeed, in Erikson's (1985) theory of development, this capacity to maintain balance and equilibrium in the face of strong diversity constitutes one of the most important aspects of mature adulthood. For example, children may quite readily accept difference between self and parents or close others, especially ones with whom one shares a bond of liking. However, such integration becomes more and more difficult in the face of increasing difference between self and other. For Erikson, mature adulthood ideally brings the capacity to transcend vast differences, with the capacity to accept even individuals with widely diverging backgrounds of culture and ideology. Nevertheless, he acknowledged that this capacity is by no means an automatic consequence of advancing age, and many individuals may instead develop tendencies to view different others as inherently less complex and acceptable. This tendency to deny and simplify the complexity of life can bring a tendency of excluding others from the very circle of humanity of which the self is considered a part. We will turn to this issue of the development of integrative and empathic responding next.

Empathy and Compassion

Empathy is a complex emotion defined as the naturally occurring subjective experience of similarity between the feelings expressed by self and others without loosing sight of whose feelings belong to whom (Decety & Jackson, 2004). This definition highlights the interaction of two components, an automatic component, the ability to share and resonate with another's emotion, and a more effortful and controlled component, the ability to take the perspective of another and to differentiate between one's own emotion and another's emotion. For mature empathy, the emotional state activated automatically by the perception of another person in distress needs to be regulated and controlled (Decety & Jackson, 2004). A lack of regulation would lead to personal distress—an aversive emotional response such as anxiety or discomfort (Batson, Early, & Salvarani, 1997; Decety & Meyer, 2008).

The capacity to respond to others' emotions in ways that match those emotions is considered to be hardwired and appears early in life (Decety & Jackson, 2004; Decety & Meyer, 2008; Eisenberg & Eggum, 2009; Hoffman, 2000). Several investigators have reported that infants react to the distress of others also with distress of their own (Hoffman, 1978; Nadel & Baudonnière, 1982). For example, sounds of neonatal cries produce reactive crying in newborns (Sagi & Hoffman, 1976; Simner, 1971). Obviously, infant's auditory perception of another's aversive affective state elicits automatically the same distressful emotional reaction. In the following months of development, reactive cries decrease because of the emergence of awareness of themselves as distinct of others (Hoffman, 2000). By 6 months, infants require more prolonged signs of another's distress before feeling distress themselves (Hay, Nash, & Pederson, 1981). Infants' reactions are still highly automatic and resonating responses that reflect a process of "contagion" or spontaneous matching. This process is captured in the perception–action model (Preston & de Waal, 2002; for a more cognitive orientation, see Hommel, Musseler, Aschersleben, & Prinz, 2001): The perception of a given behavior or emotion in another person automatically activates one's own representation of this behavior or emotion. This mechanism activates empathic distress in the observer and provides the affective and motivational base for more complex forms of empathy but is not sufficient for mature forms of empathy (Hoffman, 1982). Toward the end of the first year, infants begin to develop a sense of self as coherent. They react less passively to the distress of others and engage in behavior designed to reduce their own distress (Hoffman, 2000).

The infants' behavior reflects a degree of self-concern (Eisenberg & Miller, 1987) that does not necessarily permit the transformation of emotion into feelings and actions targeted to the situation of the observed individual. The quality of an empathic response is not usually based on purely automatic processes but can reflect the coinfluence of appraisal and regulation processes. These processes permit the individual to respond in ways aiming at transforming responses (e.g., by consoling, comforting, understanding) that are appropriate to the other's condition (e.g., sadness) rather than mirroring the response of the other person. Such empathic responses reflect a perspective-taking capacity, which is based on knowing the state of other and responding to it in ways that alleviate the other's condition. In contrast to the automatic mode, this capacity involves systematic and effortful processing regulating emotional systems and representations. These processes are involved in selective facilitation and inhibition as well as in imparting a higher degree of choice and flexibility on behavior.

The capacity for empathy that involves perspective taking emerges in children as young as about 2 years of age, when children respond with comforting and helping to the distress of others, without necessarily showing signs of emotional resonance (Harris, 1982). Warneken and Tomasello (2006) have shown that children as young as 18 months help others achieving their goals in situations requiring both an understanding of other's goal and an altruistic motivation to help. Eisenberg and Fabes (1998) referred to this form of complex empathy as sympathy. Sympathy reflects the presence of both self–other differentiation and an empathic feeling response. For example, Knafo, Zahn-Waxler, Van Hulle, Robinson, and Rhee (2008) investigated early development of two aspects: empathic concern—the expression of concern for a victim—and hypothesis testing—behavior to comprehend distress and prosocial behavior. Children at 14, 20, 24, and 36 months showed different developmental trajectories for empathic concern and hypothesis testing: Although an increase in empathic concern took place mainly from 14 to 20 months, complex modes of hypothesis testing further increase in the later ages, possibly reflecting children's increased ability for complex, verbal forms of inquiry. Moreover, the relationship between empathy and prosocial behavior was stronger at 24 and 36 months than in younger ages. These results are consistent with Hoffman's view: Development in the second year of life enables children to become less self-oriented and more other-oriented (Hoffman, 2000).

The development of more complex forms of empathy is based on supporting interaction with parents. This development can be disturbed by unstable mother–child interactions. For example, Zahn-Waxler, Kochanska, Krupnick, and McKnew (1990) found that 5- to 6-year-old children of depressed mothers felt more responsible to others' distress than children of nondepressed mothers. This different pattern reversed for 7- to 9-year-old children. In particular, this involvement in others' distress showed an age-related increase in children of nondepressed mothers but no increase in children of depressed mothers. The overinvolvement in parent's problems early in life occurs before children have cognitive, behavioral, and emotional maturity to deal effectively with feelings of responsibility. This results in greater guilt experience and developing tendencies to distance or protect themselves from the distress of others (Zahn-Waxler et al., 1990). The ability to express more complex forms of empathy and prosocial behavior also develops along advances in cognitive abilities, such as effortful control and inhibitory control. For example, Valiente and colleagues (Valiente et al., 2004) investigated 4.5- to 8-year-old children's personal distress and sympathy. Children's effortful control ability was negatively related to their experience of personal distress and positively related to the experience of sympathy; that is, children with high cognitive abilities showed more sympathy and less personal distress than children with low cognitive abilities. The impact of effortful control was particularly important for children exposed to high levels of parental stress. High levels of parental negative emotions tend to disrupt the development of more complex forms of empathy. In these children, cognitive abilities are more important to manage attention and empathic emotion.

With advancing age, children show marked improvements in understanding one's own and another's feeling in distressing situation. Their interpretation of emotional experiences becomes more personal and psychological. For example, Strayer (1993) showed vignettes of children in distressing situations to 5-, 7-, 8-, and 13-year-old children. Children were asked whether they felt an emotion when watching a vignette and to explain why. Nearly all children identified the character's emotions correctly. However, age differences were found in the attribution of children's own emotions: For 5-year-olds, explanations were mostly event- or situation-based; for 7- and 8-year-olds, explanations were mostly focused on the person in the event; and for 13-year-olds, explanations were more focused on the character's inner states. Whereas 5-year-olds interpreted their distressed feelings as based on external events, 7- to 13-year-olds understood that their distressed feelings are caused by the other's situation (Hoffman, 2000). In a longitudinal study, Eisenberg and collaborators (Eisenberg et al., 1987) found that empathy and donating were positively related in children aged 11 to 12 years but not in children aged 9 to 10 years. It seems children before the age of 11 are not able to take into account their empathic emotions for altruistic behavior.

During adolescence, moral reasoning becomes more mature, and new ways of moral thinking develop (Eisenberg, Cumberland, Guthrie, Murphy, & Shepard, 2005; Kohlberg, 1984). The development of moral reasoning is supported by the development of complex empathic skills and perspective taking abilities. For example, Eisenberg and collaborators (Eisenberg et al., 2005) investigated the development of self-reported empathy and moral judgment from adolescence (aged 15–16 years) to young adulthood (aged 25–26 years). During this period, sympathy remained relatively stable, whereas perspective taking increased and personal distress decreased. This finding highlights two aspects: First, from adolescence to young adulthood, individuals turn out to be better able to be other-oriented, to take into account another's perspective. Second, from adolescence to young adulthood, individuals become less susceptible to experience overarousing distress. Thus, the ability to deal with high-arousing situations continues to develop through adolescence into adulthood. In the same time range, moral reasoning also showed marked increases. In particular, prosocial moral reasoning becomes more complex from adolescence to the early 20s and remains stable thereafter.

There are, at the same time, wide variations in forms of empathic development, which do not always end up in integrated forms of regulation. Persons with a mature and functional regulation style are likely to show sympathy to others' needs, transform the response in an appropriate way to the other's condition (e.g., by consoling, comforting, understanding), and are more likely to help others (Eisenberg & Fabes, 1990; Toi & Batson, 1982). In contrast, persons with a dysfunctional regulation style may be overwhelmed by others' negative emotions and react with avoidance (Zahn-Waxler, Cole, Welsh, & Fox, 1995), antisocial behavior (Kochanska, 1993; Miller & Eisenberg, 1988), and even aggressive behavior (Miller & Eisenberg, 1988; Radke-Yarrow, Zahn-Waxler, Richardson, & Susman, 1994). These examples illustrate that automatic precursor forms of empathy do not always develop into mature empathy.

Some life-span developmental psychologists have argued that empathy develops far into old age (e.g., Erikson, 1985; see also McAdams, this volume). Erikson, for example, postulated that one developmental goal of adulthood and old age was to achieve a balance of "understanding the wisdom necessary to being empathic while not condoning selfishness, being helpful while not being intrusive, and being proud but not smug" (Erikson, Erikson, & Kivnick, 1986, p. 58). For Erikson, successful development is associated with a widening of relational circles across the life span, as noted in the previous section. We will return to empirical research dealing with this period of the life span in the next major section of the chapter.

Emotional Understanding

Theory of mind is the ability to attribute mental states to own self and others (Premack & Woodruff, 1972). Emotional understanding begins with infants' awareness of the self and others as reflective agents with intentions, desires, emotions, and thoughts. This initial "theory of mind" builds the foundation for higher order feelings and emotional understanding. Children become aware that others have their own intentions, desires, emotions, and thoughts distinct from children's own (Eisenberg, Murphy, & Shepard, 1996).

Wellman and Woolley (1990) demonstrated that 2-year-olds can already predict actions and reactions related to simple desires. At this age, children are able to understand that others have desires and react emotionally depending on whether desires are achieved. Later, children begin to understand that people have beliefs and that people's beliefs can be different from children's own beliefs (Eisenberg et al., 1996). Typically, between ages 3 and 5 years, children show clear improvements in the ability to perform false belief tasks (Flavell, 2004). At about 6 years, children become able to incorporate another's desires and beliefs when judging another's emotional state (Harris, 1989; Harris, Johnson, Hutton, Andrews, & Cooke, 1989). Between 6 and 7 years, children become able to understand second order false belief tasks (Harris, 2006; Perner & Wimmer, 1985). This kind of task is more complex than standard false-belief task: Children have to assess what one actor would believe about the beliefs of another actor (e.g., Perner & Wimmer, 1985).

Sociocognitive and emotion understanding become more elaborated and flexible throughout childhood (de Rosnay & Hughes, 2006). The development is highly related to the acquisition of language as an instrument of cognitive representation and social communication (Pons, Lawson, Harris, & de Rosnay, 2003). The development of cognitive representations and social communication support false-belief understanding (e.g., Astington & Jenkins, 1999; de Rosnay, Pons, Harris, & Morrell, 2004) as well as emotion understanding (Pons et al., 2003). Throughout childhood, emotion understanding becomes more and more complex, abstract, and reflective. At around 5 years, emotion understanding is related to external aspects of emotions as situational causes or outward expressions. At around 7 years, children understand the mental and inner nature of emotion, the capacity to understand connections between desires and beliefs. Between 9 and 11 years, children understand that one can use strategies to regulate emotions and that one can feel ambivalent feelings (Pons & Harris, 2005; Pons, Harris, & de Rosnay, 2004).

Although emotional understanding has been well studied during the first part of the life span, relatively little is known about how people describe emotions and the self throughout adulthood. How this understanding changes was the topic of a series of studies examining individuals' descriptions of their emotions (Labouvie-Vief, DeVoe, & Bulka, 1989; Labouvie-Vief, Hakim-Larson, et al., 1989) and their self (Labouvie-Vief, Chiodo, et al., 1995) from adolescence through adulthood. This work attempted to continue weaving the picture that had already emerged from studies on children. Specifically, we proposed that as individuals begin to reevaluate and reinterpret aspects of reality as conventionally understood, their understanding of the nature and causes of emotions changes as well. Early development demands that individuals define their emotional lives in accordance with external criteria and to regulate behavior in accordance to externally imposed rules. This process fosters external adaptation. However, it also brings with it a degree of dissociation and alienation from personal meanings in the interest of impersonal, abstract, and collective meanings. In (late) adulthood, we proposed a compensatory movement inward—toward personal meanings. In adulthood, inner dynamics, private experience, and rich emotive content come to the forefront.

The work of Labouvie-Vief and collaborators (Labouvie-Vief, DeVoe, & Bulka, 1989) did, indeed, show such a progression from adolescence to middle adulthood (see Figure 4.4). Younger or less mature individuals used a language of emotions that was almost entirely devoid of felt sense. Feelings were described in terms of an outer conventional language (e.g., "Things were bottled up") rather than in terms of inner feedback. Formal, technical processes and distant, static terms were used as descriptors (e.g., "Your blood pressure rises"). In addition, feelings were described in terms of how one *should* feel, of external rules and standards of conduct rather than organismic feelings (e.g., I was really scared, because I knew that if I didn't play good, that they'd tease me about it").

In comparison, mature adults, around middle adulthood, showed a significantly reorganized emotion language. Feelings were described in terms of a vivid felt process (e.g., "My heart felt like bursting" or "I felt a rush of energy"). Their language was inner and personal rather than outer

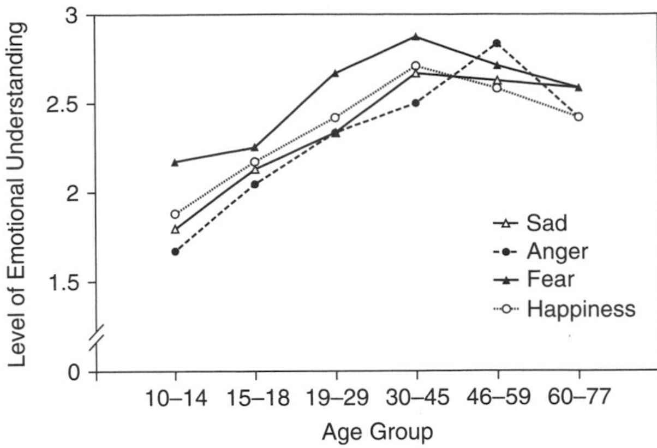

Figure 4.4 Level of emotional understanding for four emotional events by age group. The complexity of emotional understanding increases up until late middle adulthood but declines thereafter. Copyright © 1989 by the American Psychological Association (APA). Adapted with permission from Labouvie-Vief, DeVoe, and Bulka (1989). The use of APA information does not imply endorsement by APA.

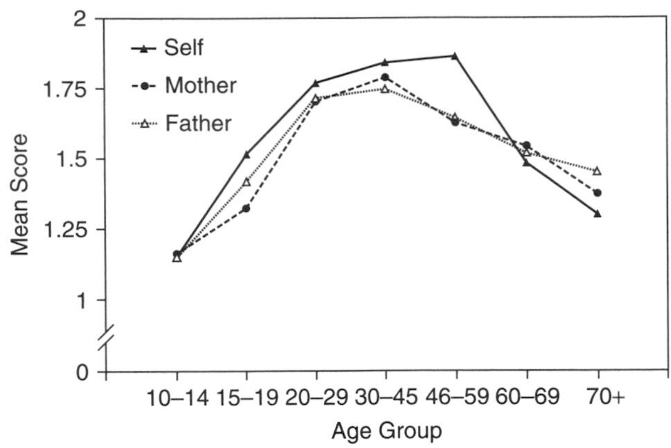

Figure 4.5 Levels of cognitive–emotional development in representations of self, mother, and father by age group. The complexity of self and parents' representations increases up until early midlife and declines thereafter. Adapted from Labouvie-Vief, DeVoe, Chiodo, & Coyle (1995) with permission from Springer Science+Business Media.

and technical. Individuals used metaphors that were dynamic, oriented not toward static states but toward describing process and transformation. This turn toward a more process-oriented emotion language was accompanied by the beginnings of individuals' attempt to differentiate an inner realm of emotional experience from an outer realm of convention. Mature adults thus attempted to deconstruct their conventional views and to reconstruct a self that was felt to be more genuine. They acknowledged that a conflict often existed between these realms, and indicated that they were more willing to accept impulses and thoughts that previously seemed too overwhelming. Instead, emotions are accepted as motivating forces that could be mastered and guided into self-directed growth. In this process, others are much less likely to be blamed for one's own states but seen in a more reciprocal way.

Similar changes were observed focusing on individuals' conceptions of self and others (Labouvie-Vief, Chiodo et al., 1995; Labouvie-Vief, DeVoe et al., 1995). Figure 4.5 provides individuals' level of complexity for the representation of the self, the mother, and the father. Younger and less mature individuals frame self and others in terms of a conventional perspective, that is, an organized, codified, and abstract set of role expectations. These individuals had a static view of the self or others. At later levels, a more transformative language was evident. Institutional values became susceptible to doubt and criticism. For example, individuals felt that conventional values "can be carried too far." Instead, individuals were more likely to use a dynamic language in which descriptions of self and others vividly convey the uniqueness and evolving nature of experience within the context of unique life histories.

Against the predictions of both studies, however, the empirical findings showed declines from late middle adulthood to old age. Thus, older adults showed lower levels of complexity in emotions and self-representations. Although against the original predictions in these studies, this pattern is consistent with the equilibrium model proposed in this chapter. Nevertheless, these aging-related changes showed profound variability in later life, an issue we will discuss more fully in the next major section of this chapter.

Section Summary: Childhood to Adulthood

In this section we provided evidence that cognitive–emotional development during the first part of the life span implies an increase in the ability to endure complex, high intensity information that contains potentially conflicting elements. We refer to this change as a rise in tension thresholds with accompanying widened range over which individuals can change equilibrium and equanimity. This ability is apparent in a deepened ability to understand inner states in self as well as in others, leading to a gradual widening of the circle of individuals with which one can identify and to which one can extend compassionate understanding.

Throughout this chapter, we highlight that these general processes do not happen in a lock-step fashion, and that individuals' actual level of performance may show a high degree of variability. The reason is that cognitive-emotional capacities remain directly dependent on the degree to which the individual has already acquired well-automated cognitive-emotional schemas, as well as the degree to which these function in a more or less integrated fashion. That is, the degree of complexity, the level of novelty versus familiarity, and the level of activation of a given situation are among those factors that may cause systematic changes in tension thresholds and ranges. Thus even in relatively integrated individuals, the capacity for integration has clear limits. And studying variations in individuals' range and level of functioning is at least as important as studying individuals' normal level. This testing-the-limits approach is particularly important in the later part of the life span, to which we will turn next.

Rise and Fall of Tension Thresholds in Later Life: Facilitation, Challenge, and Breakdown

DIT has been particularly strongly influenced by research on emotions in the later portion of the life span, and suggests that the study of the dynamics of emotional functioning becomes particularly important in later life. That is, whereas the general mechanisms outlined so far all remain valid throughout the life span, the importance of dynamic variations becomes particularly important in later life. The reason for this importance of dynamic functioning is that the processing of emotional states of high tension is strongly dependent on cognitive resources that make high demands on resources of executive functions such as inhibition, memory, and integration of complexity and novelty—abilities that imply high fluidity of cognitive functioning. Such fluid abilities are particularly strongly affected with aging and tend to show consistent declines after the age of about 60 years (Baltes & Lindenberger, 1997; Schaie, 1994).

Whether such losses affect emotional processing will depend on the degree to which individuals have in place already highly automated processing systems or strategies—that is, schemas that permit ease of processing even in situations that are objectively judged as difficult. In the relatively purely cognitive realm, such schemas are referred to as crystallized intellectual functions (such as those related to information that has been acquired over a lifetime) and are known to be quite resistant to variations in executive resources. Nevertheless, research shows that this protective functioning of crystallized abilities itself is moderated by fluid functioning, a relationship of dependence that becomes stronger with age in later life. As crystallized abilities thus become more "fluidized," their protective function wanes and formerly automated capacities become more difficult.

Our proposal about cognitive–emotional changes in later life parallels that of changes in the more purely cognitive realm. Accordingly, individuals in later life often show high levels of cognitive–emotional functioning (e.g., Charles & Carstensen, 2007; Labouvie-Vief & Medler, 2002). Nevertheless, with increasing age and loss of fluid cognitive functioning, the capacity to deal with high tension and high complexity emotional information becomes increasingly compromised. These capacities are, of course, related to the general level of cognitive–emotional functioning that individuals have been able to achieve during their lifetime, but in general, with increasing age, DIT expects that this functioning will become more and more strongly compromised. Again, the degree will depend on situational as well as individual factors. In particular, aging is expected to bring increasing difficulty with high arousing and high complexity cognitive–emotional information; in addition, these difficulties will be exacerbated for those individuals who have not developed cognitive–emotional schemas or strategies of a high level of integration.

Although we propose that cognitive–emotional capacities are likely to be compromised in conditions that imply high tension and cognitive effort, this does not apply to situations of low effort. Indeed, much of literature on aging and emotions suggests that automaticity per se remains functional in later life and may even increase in importance (Hess, 2005), aiding good performance in certain emotion regulation tasks (e.g., Blanchard-Fields, 2009). However, whether the preservation of automaticity is an aid depends on whether it is facilitative in a particular task. In tasks where individuals need not inhibit their well-automated cognitive–emotional knowledge to arrive at good solutions and in ones that do not exceed the complexity of the individual, automaticity is likely to aid performance. However in tasks that exceed the individual's complexity level, that require that automated knowledge be inhibited, and/or that require very high levels of arousal, performance is likely to suffer. Accordingly, developmental patterns of later life cognitive–emotional development can include more positive as well as more problematic forms.

Advantages of Increasing Automaticity and Crystallization of Knowledge in Aging

The different patterns of aging implied for automatic and well-exercised processes on one hand and controlled and effortful ones on the other raise the interesting possibility that effects often identified with aging—such as a reduction of cognitive control over emotions—are not always detrimental but actually may also bring positive benefits to the extent that aging individuals may utilize automatic processes to support their performance. We focus on two such reported benefits: Deepened Inner Orientation and Reliance on Personal Meanings.

Deepened Inner Orientation In fact, in the eyes of some theoreticians increases in automatic functioning in later life may bring unique benefits to the aging person. Jung (1933) suggested long ago that with a relaxation of controlled functioning, mid to late adulthood can bring a liberation of unconscious processes and with it, a turn away from preoccupations with the outer world. Instead, the increases in understanding inner components of experience that forms a general dimension of developmental progressions may achieve its height in later life, through a process of "centroversion" toward the inner world (see Labouvie-Vief, 1994). One sign of this inward shift is a general way in which individuals' relationship to information becomes restructured. For the young adult, information is seen as an outer given that one attempts to reproduce in a literal way. In contrast, middle and older adults turn more to the landscape of human motivations and intentions. Hence, they may become experts at the processing of information relating to subjective processes and inner dynamics. Although this symbolic processing style can result in deficits on the literal level, it may imply a richer psychological texture.

This shift from a more text-dependent mode to one that is more interpretive and subjective was shown in a series of studies about individuals' rendition and interpretation of narratives (for review, see Jepson & Labouvie-Vief, 1992). For example, young, middle-aged, and old adults were asked to respond to a series of fable-like stories. The young adults produced detailed, almost verbatim, reproductions of these tales. Older adults, however, were primarily concerned with general meanings that were symbolic, moral, and inner-psychological, such as "a lot of times things that appear to be situations outside ourselves are really things that we need to be conquering inside. But we have to have the outside confrontation to find out who we are and what we're made of" (Jepson & Labouvie-Vief, 1992, p.130).

Similar findings were also reported in a study by Adams (1991) who asked individuals to summarize a Sufi teaching tale. Again, adolescents produced texts that were very detailed and literal. Middle adults' recall focused on the implied psychological and metaphoric meaning of the tales. Older adults, similarly, were interested in the meaning, which they produced in very brief but highly integrative and abstract ways. For example, one 13-year-old adolescent recalled:

"Once there was a stream. The stream made a journey and was stopped by a desert. When the stream tried to pass the desert it was absorbed by the sand. A voice said that the wind had to carry the stream over the desert. The stream doubted it but later agreed to let the wind carry him over. The wind carried the stream over and the stream never forgot what the voice said" (Adams, 1991, p. 333).

In contrast, a 39-year-old participant gave a much more interpretive summary:

"I believe what this story was trying to say was that there are times when everyone needs help and must sometimes make changes to reach their goals. Some people may resist change for a long time until they realize that certain things are beyond their control and they need assistance. When this is finally achieved and they can accept help and trust from someone, they can master things even as large as a desert" (Adams, 1991, p. 333).

Finally, elders gave highly abstract summaries such as "The essence of the story is that in order to accomplish one's goals, one sometimes has to sacrifice one's individuality and join forces with others moving in similar directions" or "Do not be afraid to venture out of your original" and present form for you will also retain your true identity" (Adams, 1991, p. 333). Thus older individuals may continue to develop highly integrated and personally meaningful insights about life's regularities—the hallmark we think, of advanced wisdom.

Reliance on Personal Meanings Similar to research on interpretation of texts rich in symbolic meaning, a considerable body of research suggests that older individuals can perform at high levels if experimental tasks permit them to make use of the inner orientation that draws on rich knowledge of self and psychological processes. For example, several studies suggest that age related differences between young and older adults are diminished or even disappear when older adult can work with personally relevant and value-based information. For example, Blanchard-Fields (2007) reported that older adults often are more affective than young adults in solving interpersonal or emotionally salient problems. Older adults also can be more accurate when making trait inferences and they recall more information about a target that is similar to them in age (Hess, Rosenberg, & Waters, 2001). Finally, older adults' memory deficits were reduced when problems deal with personally relevant issues such as truth or moral character (Rahhal, May, & Hasher, 2002).

The effects of personal relevance and interest on the elderly indicate that they are well able to profit from the empowering effects of emotional facilitation. Yet since much research also suggests that younger adults are able to function well even in the absence of emotional facilitation, they also may suggest that older individuals become more *dependent* on the emotional facilitation that produces such facilitation effects. Without this effect, the burden of processing would be fully placed on the effortful conscious processing system—fluid processes. Thus Labouvie-Vief (2009) recently proposed that such facilitation effects in the elderly suggest that high-level functioning can at the same time go along with a narrowing of the range over which it can be applied. This effect is indicated in Figure 4.3a, which suggests that increases in integrated functioning in later life can go along with a narrowing of contexts which become increasingly restricted to those more personally meaningful.

Loss of Fluidity and Emotion Processing in Later Life

In contrast to the quite circumscribed advantages of crystallization, loss of fluidity is apparent in situations outside of the limited range facilitation and when automated knowledge needs to be inhibited.

High Levels of Arousal Are Experienced as More Aversive with Advancing Age One key dynamic aspect of the equilibrium model is that processing shifts from more complex and differentiated representations to more simple and automatic representations under high activation or limited resources. There is considerable empirical evidence that polarization—that is, black-and-white thinking—is more likely under high activation or limited resources. For example, (young) adults show a more positive and less negative self-concept under high activation or reduced resources (Paulhus, Graf, & Van Selst, 1989; Paulhus & Levitt, 1987). Persons under high activation show also a more negative representation of others and they are less resistant against stereotypes (e.g., Paulhus & Lim, 1994). Thus, persons under stress perceive the world in more simple schemes of good and bad.

From a developmental perspective, older adults with their limited resources should be more vulnerable to high levels of activation. There is initial evidence that older adults perceive high activation as more negative than young adults do. Grühn and Scheibe (2008) investigated young and older adults' evaluations of 504 emotional pictures. Older adults rated pictures generally as more extreme than young adults did. Specifically, older adults rated negative pictures as more negative and more arousing, and they rated positive pictures as more positive and less arousing than young adults did. Thus in general, there was a strong linear association between valence and arousal, but this association was stronger for older adults ($r = -.95$, $R^2 = .90$) than for younger adults ($r = -.85$, $R^2 = .73$). Similarly, Gilet and colleagues (Gilet, Grühn, Studer, & Labouvie-Vief, 2009) examined the evaluations of young, middle-aged, and older adults for 835 French adjectives and found that the linear association between valence and arousal was stronger for older adults ($r = -.85$) than for middle-aged ($r = -.78$) or young adults ($r = -.63$). Figure 4.6 presents separate scatterplots between valence and arousal for young, middle-aged, and older adults. Finally, Keil and Freund (2009) investigated young, middle-aged, and older adults reactions to positive, neutral, and negative pictures and found that older adults' evaluations were more one-dimensional whereas younger adults' evaluations were more two-dimensional (U-shaped): Older adults showed a strong linear association between valence and arousal. Young adults, in contrast, perceived low-arousing material as neutral and high-arousing material as either positive or negative depending on the depicted content. Keil and Freund argued that arousing material becomes more aversive as people get older.

The three studies about young and older adults' reactions to emotional stimuli show high consistency in their findings (Gilet et al., 2009; Grühn & Scheibe, 2008; Keil & Freund, 2009): On the one hand, older adults perceive high-arousing material as more negative and low-arousing material as more positive than young adults. On the other hand, the higher correlation between valence and arousal in older adults, in contrast to younger adults, is suggestive of more simplified and more polarized representations of emotions. Grühn and Scheibe (2008) speculated that this age pattern of findings could be due to a dedifferentiation of the emotional space with age—maybe due to declining cognitive resources. This speculation as well as the empirical findings is consistent with our proposed equilibrium model. With advancing age, the emotional and the cognitive system show a greater interdependence (see also Labouvie-Vief, Chiodo, et al., 1995); thus, declines in the cognitive system (especially in fluid abilities) should imply that the processing and regulation of emotional information gets more and more difficult. Wurm and colleagues (Wurm, Labouvie-Vief, Aycock, Rebucal, & Koch, 2004)

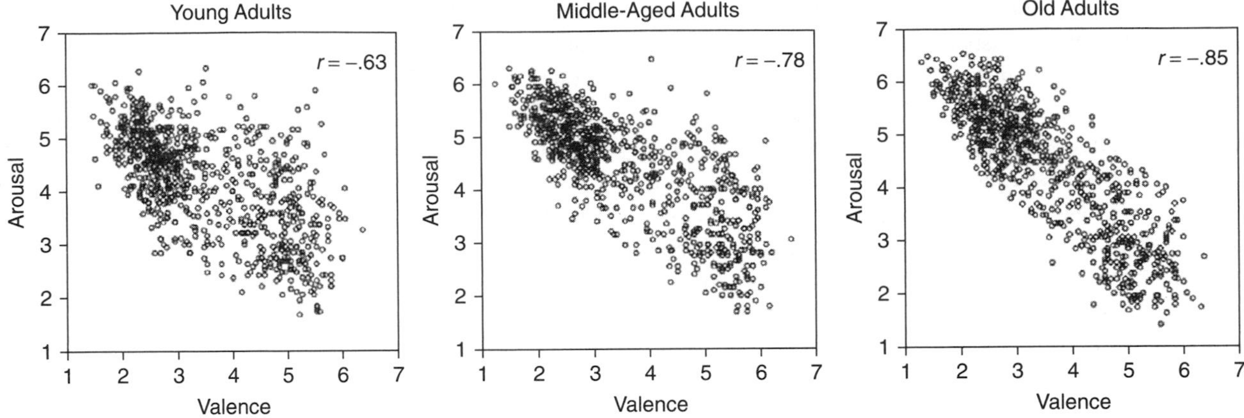

Figure 4.6 Scatterplots between valence and arousal by age group. In older age groups, valence and arousal are more highly associated than in younger age groups.

showed that highly arousing information created more interference in a Stroop task for older but not for younger individuals. Thus in general, these results that suggest that thresholds for tolerating high levels of tension are lowered in later life, compared to younger adult ages.

Tension Thresholds Are Lowered with Advancing Age In general, the results on increasing negativity of high arousal stimuli is consistent with the notion that thresholds for tolerating and processing high levels of tension are lowered in later life (see Figure 4.3b). As a consequence, processing emotional material in ways that are both complex and well-integrated will become more difficult with advancing age and/or decline of fluid type abilities.

Studies that have systematically examined the impact of variations in activation level of the stimulus material on emotion processing are one way to examine the capacity to maintain high level processing in the face of tension as apposed to lowering performance level. Indeed, there is empirical evidence that stimuli's arousal level affects young and older adults differently. In a study using an emotional Stroop paradigm, Wurm and colleagues (Wurm et al., 2004) investigated the effects of low- and high-arousing word material on response latencies. Older adults showed a marked increase in response latencies for high-arousing words compared with low-arousing words. Young adults, in contrast, did not show any differences in response latencies between low- and high-arousing materials. These results indicate that older individuals may have a problem inhibiting high arousal. In two memory experiments, Grühn and colleagues investigated age differences in emotional memory. One experiment used relatively low-arousing material—namely, words (Grühn, Smith, & Baltes, 2005)—whereas the other one used high-arousing material—namely, emotional pictures (Grühn, Scheibe, & Baltes, 2007)—as to-be-remembered material. In both studies, negative material was better remembered than positive and neutral information. However, by comparing young and older adults' memory performance for emotional material, age-related differences were only clearly evident for pictorial rather than verbal material: Young adults recognized more negative than positive and neutral pictures, whereas older adults showed hardly any difference in recognizing positive, negative, and neutral pictures. One interpretation for the different age pattern between studies might be differences in levels of activation, especially for negative information. Thus, arousal may have different effects for young and older adults' memory. Specifically, young adults' performance might profit from arousal, whereas older adults' performance might be hindered.

The interpretation that older adults may have difficulties in remembering high-arousing material is also supported by looking at memorability scores (i.e., how easily a stimulus can be remembered) for individual pictures and their associated arousal levels (Grühn & Scheibe, 2008): Whereas young adults showed no specific associations between memorability and arousal levels (or even a positive association), older adults showed a small but consistent and significant negative relation between memorability and arousal (partial correlations controlled for valence: $-.10 \leq r \leq -.18$). Thus, older adults remembered high-arousing pictures (irrespective of their valence) less well than low-arousing pictures. These findings fit perfectly well with the proposed equilibrium model. It might be that the selected emotional pictures in the study by Grühn and Scheibe represented a range of activation that is in the optimal range of functioning for young adults but already in a range of suboptimal functioning for older adults because of their shrunken zone of equilibrium. This interpretation implies several aspects: First, although older adults' emotion processing is more vulnerable to high activation, young adults' emotion system will also reach suboptimal levels of functioning or even breakdown thresholds if challenged strongly enough. We do not know, however, how strong this level of activation has to be. It might be that we do not reach young adults' thresholds with ethically justifiable laboratory experiments. Second, optimal levels of activation and their range might differ between age groups. Whereas young adults may show optimal emotion systems under a large range of activation levels, older adults may show optimal emotion processing under a smaller and slightly lower range of activation levels.

Our interpretation stressing lowering of tension thresholds is further consistent with research on stress. This literature suggests an age-related increase in physiologic reactivity and especially cardiovascular reactivity to stressful situations (Jennings et al., 1997; Uchino, Holt-Lunstad, Bloor, & Campo, 2005). For example, Jennings and colleagues (1997) examined cardiovascular reactivity to mental challenge in 902 men ranging from 46 to 64 years. Despite the small age range, the authors found a clear age-related increase in cardiovascular reactivity. This cross-sectional pattern was also supported by a longitudinal study. Uchino and colleagues (Uchino et al., 2005) examined cardiovascular reactivity during acute stress in middle-aged and older adults. Independent from other demographic or health-related factors, they found an age-related increase in some indicators of cardiovascular reactivity (systolic blood pressure and respiratory sinus arrhythmia) over a 10-month period. Uchino and colleagues (Uchino, Berg, Smith, Pearce, & Skinner, 2006) argued for a threshold effect: Older adults, in contrast to young or middle-aged adults, show lower reactivity at lower levels of activation (i.e., stress) but stronger reactivity at higher levels of activation. This argumentation is similar to our interpretation that high activation is more problematic for older adults than for young adults. Bäckman and Molander investigated young and older adults' miniature golf performance under training (normal-stress level) and competition (high-stress level): Older adults were more strongly affected by high-stress situations than young adults were (Bäckman & Molander, 1986b), and older adults had deficits in compensating for the negative effects of nonoptimal levels of arousal (Bäckman & Molander, 1986a). In a similar vein, research showed that recovery after a stressful event takes longer with advancing age. This deleterious physiologic effect has been widely documented for cortisol reactivity in rats (Sapolsky, Krey, & McEwen, 1986) and humans (Otte et al., 2005). High sustained levels of cortisol reactivity are dysfunctional and impair cognitive performance (de Kloet et al., 1999). Thus, older adults are also more affected by high levels of stress during recovery than young adults. These studies on stress provide further support for the notion that high levels of arousal are more severe for older adults.

Tension Thresholds in Aging Are Strongly Affected by Preexisting Socio-Emotional Skills As discussed in the previous section, aging is related to a general lowering of tension thresholds. Nevertheless, the degree to which individuals are thus affected, according to DIT, depends on the degree to which they have available already well-integrated cognitive–emotional schemas—or automated skills to deal effectively with tension. To the extent that older individuals lack such skills, their activation levels would be likely to escalate even more strongly and their performance to be affected more strongly than that of young individuals with less effective strategies. For example, older adults with high cognitive–specific anxiety recalled fewer words than older adults with low cognitive–specific anxiety. Young adults, in contrast, performed well irrespective of their anxiety level (Andreoletti, Veratti, & Lachman, 2006). Similarly, older adults showed significant negative associations among anxiety, depression, and withdrawal on the one side and word recall on the other side. Young adults showed slightly positive but nonsignificant correlations between these ratings and word recall (Deptula, Singh, & Pomara, 1993). In these studies, older adults' memory performance was degraded by high internal negative activation, whereas young adults' memory performance was practically unaffected. There are, however, some studies that find a detrimental effect of anxiety on memory performance in both, young and older adults (Cavanaugh & Murphy, 1986; Whitbourne, 1976). In a similar vein, Hogan (2003) investigated young and older adults' performance in a divided attention task. In this study, greater anxiety was related to poorer performance for older but not for younger adults.

Evidence for age-differentiated effect of regulation styles on emotion processing was also found in a study by Jain and Labouvie-Vief (in press). In this research, regulation styles were indicated by attachment classifications, and the core hypothesis was that variation in attachment styles would have much stronger effects on emotion processing and reactivity in older than in younger adults. In general, secure older individuals were expected to show signs of good response integration such as low reactivity and positive affect, but that insecure elders would show problems of overactivataion. Specifically, highly anxious elders were predicted to show signs of overactivation. In contrast, avoidant-dismissing elders who are known for their self-protective efforts at emotion avoidance should show lower levels of reactivity but at the same time, signs that these efforts would show breakdown signs such at particularly high levels of activation. Results provided evidence for these hypotheses in two studies. In an emotion Stroop performance task, elders with a dismissing attachment classification showed generally decreased reactivity but reactivity was heightened for fear and anger words. In contrast, secure individuals showed increased latency for joy words. No attachment style differences were found in young adults. In a second study, heart rate was monitored while adult mother-daughter pairs (ages 25–82) discussed conflict, happy, and neutral emotion events. During conflict discussion, older but not younger dismissing women had highest initial HR and slowest recovery. These results suggest that a dismissing style can serve a partially protective role for older individuals, but a role that breaks down if levels of activation a raised to critical levels.

Aging Brings Declines in Cognitive-Emotional Complexity One of the most crucial propositions of DIT is that tension thresholds are a direct correlate of levels of cognitive–emotional complexity and integration. A direct consequence of lowering of tension thresholds, according to DIT, is therefore that individuals' capacity for integrated complexity is lowered. We already noted evidence of such lowering of complexity in the research of Labouvie-Vief and colleagues (Labouvie-Vief, Chiodo, et al., 1995; Labouvie-Vief, DeVoe, et al., 1995) that indicated that in general, from mid-life to later life, the complexity of emotion understanding was reduced. Such lowering should directly affect the ability to form complex differentiations between the states of self and other. Congruent with this prediction, when older adults are asked to evaluate social relationships or social situations, they tend to rely more on stereotypical information than do younger adults (e.g., Blanchard-Fields, Baldi, & Stein, 1999; Mather, Johnson, & De Leonardis, 1999; von Hippel, Silver, & Lynch, 2000). This suggests that compared with younger adults, older adults tend to make decisions in a more schematic rather than a well-reasoned way. Similarly, older adults' thinking seems to rely more on contextual aspects than does young adults' thinking (Hess, 2005). For example, older adults' likability ratings for abstract symbols (Japanese Kanji characters) were more easily influenced by positive and negative prime words than younger adults (Hess, Waters, & Bolstad, 2000): Older adults liked symbols more after a positive prime word and liked symbols less after a negative prime word. In contrast, young adults' likability ratings were hardly affected by the prime word—the context. Similarly, older adults seem to be more influenced by positive or negative information about others when making interferences about others' behaviors (Hess & Auman, 2001). Thus, older adults' thinking relies more on contextual and schematic cues. Taken together, these lines of research suggest that older adults' view of self and others is less differentiated than that of middle-aged adults. In particular, it is more polarized, and less regulated by deliberate control processes (Labouvie-Vief & Marquez, 2004).

One domain in which self-other differentiation is particularly important, as discussed in the section on earlier development, is that of empathy. In contrast to development of empathy in the first part of life, little is known on how empathy develops from young adulthood to old age or across the adult life span. Some studies suggested that empathy remains stable across the adult life span (Diehl, Coyle, & Labouvie-Vief, 1996; Eysenck, Pearson, Easting, & Allsopp, 1985; Grühn, Rebucal, Diehl, Lumley, & Labouvie-Vief, 2008) whereas other studies indicate a decline of empathy in old age (R. Helson, Jones, & Kwan, 2002; Schieman & Van Gundy, 2000). Grühn and colleagues (2008) investigated self-reported empathy in a 12-year longitudinal study with participants between 10 and 87 years at the first wave. In cross-sectional analyses, older adults reported lower empathy than younger adults. In longitudinal analyses, however, individuals remained fairly stable in their reported empathy—independent from their chronological age. This finding suggests that the observed age differences in cross-sectional analyses are due to cohort effects: Older cohorts reported lower empathy than younger cohorts—maybe because of a stronger infusion of psychological research into everyday life nowadays than 50 years ago.

In sum, there are two conclusions about empathy in adult development: First, the mixed pattern of findings seems to be due to cohort effects. This is surprising; it might be the first reported cohort effect in the emotion domain. Second, levels of empathy seem to remain fairly stable over the adult life span—even into very old age. This stability of empathy in adulthood suggests that some adult forms of empathy are based on highly crystallized and resilient emotion systems.

There is, however, one limitation of this conclusion: Studies in adult development of empathy are primarily based on self-reported empathy rather than real-life situations. Self-report data may differ tremendously from actual behavior. In the context of dynamic integration theory (Labouvie-Vief, 2003, 2008, 2009; Labouvie-Vief et al., 2009), real-life situations may be more arousing and challenging than filling out a questionnaire. Real-life conditions may trigger the emotion system away from the equilibrium zone. Nevertheless, self-reported empathy was positively associated to markers of positive development and to day-to-day social interactions (Grühn et al., 2008): In particular, empathic individuals reported higher subjective and psychological well-being than less empathic individuals. Moreover, in an experience-sampling study, empathic individuals (a) felt more positive about themselves, (b) thought that their interaction partners felt more positive, (c) reported that their interaction partners expressed more positive emotions, and (d) thought that their interaction was more meaningful than less empathic individuals. This is consistent with the idea that empathy is a cornerstone of responsive relationships and of widening social interactions (e.g., Eisenberg, Fabes, Guthrie, & Reiser, 2000; Erikson, 1968; Hoffman, 2000; Singer, 2006).

As already noted, from the perspective of DIT, one problem with much research on empathy in adulthood and later life is that most of these studies consist of self-reported measure of empathy. In particular, they do not differentiate between automatic and controlled components of empathy and the different age trajectories that might result from those. While cognitive functions such as working memory (e.g., Hasher & Zacks, 1988; Mitchell, Johnson, Raye, Mather, & D'Esposito, 2000), inhibition (e.g., Hasher, Stoltzfus, Zacks, & Rypma, 1991), executive control (e.g., Rabbitt & Lowe, 2000) are generally negatively affected by age, one would expect that low resource demanding and more automatic forms of empathy should be preserved with increasing age whereas more complex forms and resources demanding forms of empathy involving controlled processes should be negatively affected with age. Using the Empathy Quotient (EQ; Baron-Cohen & Wheelwright, 2004) a self-reported measure of affective and cognitive empathy Bailey, Henry, and von Hippel (2008) found evidence for such differentiated components: there were no age difference in affective empathy but significant age differences were found in cognitive empathy, with lower scores in older adults than in younger ones. This view finds also support in several recent researches in theory of mind and mentalizing tasks. While some studies using mentalizing tasks found no age differences (Keightley, Winocur, Burianova, Hongwanishkul, & Grady, 2006; MacPherson, Phillips, & Della Sala, 2002) or better theory of mind in older as opposed to younger adults (Happé, Winner, & Brownell, 1998), studies using more complex tasks or varying the level of difficulty of the tasks found age related difficulties (Bailey & Henry, 2008; German & Hehman, 2006; Maylor, Moulson, Muncer, & Taylor, 2002; McKinnon & Moscovitch, 2007; Sullivan & Ruffman, 2004). For example, Bailey and Henry (2008) manipulated inhibitory demands involving either low or high inhibition of the self-perspective in a theory of mind task. There were no age-related differences when inhibitory demand was low but a significant impairment in older when demand was high in a false belief task. Similarly McKinnon and Moscovitch (2007) asked participants to read short stories describing complex social situations and to answer first- (i.e., A feels or thinks X) and second-order (i.e., A thinks B feels or thinks X) ToM questions. They found that older and younger adults performed equally when answering first-order ToM questions. In contrast, older adults performed lower than younger when answering second-order ToM questions. Hence both young and older adults understood each character's perspective of the story separately (i.e., first-order questions) whereas older adults failed when comparison between 2 characters' perspectives is required (i.e., second-order questions).

Implications for Well-Being—Compensatory Strategies of Self-Protection As mentioned in the first part of this chapter, in our research about affect complexity (Diehl et al., 1996; Labouvie-Vief & Diehl, 2000; Labouvie-Vief, Diehl, Tarnowski, & Shen, 2000; Labouvie-Vief, Hakim-Larson, & Hobart, 1987), we found no association between affect complexity and subjective well-being. In particular, older adults reported more positive and less negative affect (i.e., affect optimization) than young adults. At first glance, this seems to argue for the superiority of emotion regulation in older adults (e.g., Charles & Carstensen, 2007) and to contradict the finding of decreased affect complexity in old age. The equilibrium view implies, however, that well-being is achieved at one's equilibrium range and level, thus specific to individual variation in levels of integrated complexity. Well-being is, thus, not linearly correlated with integrated complexity. Thus with lowering of complexity, individuals' capacity for positive well-being will be increasingly challenged; however, individuals can eventually reachieve well-being by lowering the level of complexity and the demands it places in the system (Lawton & Nahemow, 1973). In this way, it is possible to maintain activation within tolerable ranges of the equilibrium zone. And as a consequence, according to DIT, the correlation between well-being and level of integrated complexity is expected to be zero (Labouvie-Vief & Medler, 2002).

This mutual co-regulation of level of complexity and well-being is an entirely adaptive process already implicit in the H. Helson (1964) adaptation level model. Adaptation in that sense does not imply, however, higher levels or stages of development, but rather that developmental processes tend to be regulated in such a way as to aim at well-being. Hence even regression to a lower level is an adaptive process to the extent that it secures well-being and perhaps even survival by switching from a primary concern with complexity to a predominant focus on maintaining sufficient hedonic tone.

In our interpretation, therefore, research on well-being would need to integrate the core question: what is the level of complexity at which the individual can maintain sufficient positive hedonic tones. Specifically, older adults may fall back on simplified emotion schemas to save resources and protect themselves. These simplified emotion schemas may reflect a compensatory strategy that ensures well-being in the face of declining resources. In contrast, if older adults try to maintain high levels of complexity despite declining resources, their emotion system may be more fragile to external stressors. As a consequence, an increase in positive affect in later life is not necessarily a sign of good emotion regulation but may actually indicate a compensatory adjustment to a decline in cognitive resources (see also Blanchard-Fields, 1999; Hess, 1999).

The partial independence of well-being and complexity was demonstrated in the already mentioned research of Labouvie-Vief and Medler (2002) who investigated the impact of regulation styles on emotional functioning. They defined different regulation styles—among others a self-protective group and an integrated group. The *self-protective* group was characterized by low complexity of affect and high positive affect (and low negative affect). These individuals placed low emphasis on personal growth and reported low levels of empathy. They scored high on conformity, denial, and repression and very low on doubt and depression. The *integrated* group was defined by high positive affect but also by high complexity of affect. These individuals were comfortable acknowledging negativity. They reported high well-being, empathy, health, and a secure relationship style. They displayed high tolerance of ambiguity and openness to affect exploration. These integrated individuals differed, in turn, from a *complex* group that also showed signs of high complexity, but at the same time were prone to negativity and depression. Interestingly, the percentage of integrated individuals increased from youth to middle age but then stayed nearly constant (13.5%, 35.2%, and 31.3% of their respective age groups). In contrast, the self-protective group increased from early to late adulthood continuously (13.5%, 21.1%, and 39.6% of their respective age groups), whereas the number of complex individuals declined consistently (29.7%, 22.5%, and 10.4% of their respective age groups) (Labouvie-Vief & Medler, 2002). Hence, consistent with our discussion of maintaining well-being in light of declining resources, older adults seem to engage in more self-protective behavior. This behavior is low in complexity—viewing the world more in polarized terms of good and bad—but ensures high levels of well-being. In contrast, with increasing age it seems to become more difficult to maintain high complexity along with well-being for another subgroup of elderly individuals.

Indeed, longitudinal data provide direct support for this compensatory interpretation (Labouvie-Vief et al., 2007): Over a 6-year period, decreases in affect complexity were significantly related to increases in affect optimization (high positive affect and low negative affect). Consistent with the compensatory interpretation, this effect was only evident among older adults. Older adults who showed reduction in affect complexity were able to maintain high levels of well-being. In contrast, older adults who maintained high levels of affect complexity were more likely to show declines in well-being (see also R. Helson & Soto, 2005).

In sum, individuals' well-being is a function of the ability to maintain emotion systems in tolerable ranges. If well-being is more readily achieved with more simplified and automatic emotion structures because of declining resources, this quasi-regressive process is nevertheless adaptive. It is important, at the same time, to emphasize that these simplified emotion structures are, however, more prone to reach breakdown zones than more complex and well-integrated emotion structures. In light of declining resources, individuals need to compromise between complexity and well-being. In terms of real life adaptive consequences, simplifying emotion structures (for example, in terms of bad/good polarizations) may be an adaptive solution to dealing with everyday problems—even if it means that the *range* of adaptation has been limited.

Section Summary: Rise and Fall of Tension Thresholds in Aging

In this section, we reviewed research on emotion processing and aging. Dynamic integration theory proposes not a single pattern of aging, but rather one that shows systematic fluctuations with variables of contextual and interindividual variation. The view we propose encompasses patterns of continued positive development as well as developmental restrictions. Whether positive or negative, however the integrating theme of aging changes in contrast to those of the earlier part of the life span, sooner or later tension thresholds tend to decline. Even in those cases where individuals have developed rich structures as a function of the life long accumulation of knowledge, we suggest that these structures become quite restricted to one's personal background of experience. However within that restriction of range, individuals often appear to show continued progressive movements in the form of deepening and increasing integration of their knowledge. In contrast, in those cases where one's background of personal knowledge is no longer an advantage and even becomes a disadvantage, much research suggests that elders become increasingly likely to overactivation as a result of stimulation that is increasingly experienced as aversive, stressful, and too complex. As a result, they are often found to develop compensatory tendencies of simplification—tendencies that, although adaptive in the sense of preserving a sense of well-being, give evidence of an increasing restriction of the range and thresholds of stimulation.

CONCLUSION AND OUTLOOK

In this chapter, we formulated a theory of emotional development that proposes a coherent account of the growth and aging of emotions over the total span of life. Borrowing from the equilibrium perspectives of theorists such as Freud and Piaget, dynamic integration theory implies two core propositions. The first is derived from a cognitive–developmental view of affect. This view suggests that affective structures can be ordered in terms of increasing levels of complexity and integration. Emotion systems develop from simple and automatic emotion structures to complex and integrated emotion structures. High levels of complexity and integration of emotion schemas also imply a highly robust and stable pattern of emotion regulation abilities. The second proposition suggests that the efficiency of emotion systems is a dynamic interplay and flexible tradeoff between contextual variables as well as individual characteristics. Three main factors are (a) the strength of activation (i.e., arousal), (b) the cognitive resources available to deal with the emotion, and (c) preexisting and more traitlike regulation styles that may hinder or facilitate the success of emotion regulation. Thus, the outcome of emotion regulation in a given situation depends on the dynamic interaction of these factors at any given time. That is, the optimal range of activation for an individual depends on his or her available resources and regulation styles. The range of activation people can deal with is typically larger for people with more resources and better regulation styles than for people with low resources and dysfunctional regulation styles.

In the equilibrium model, there are two major aims of the emotion system—at whatever level of development. First, they aim to maintain the current state of the system in the zone of equilibrium, that is, in a zone of optimal functioning (see Figure 4.1). Deviations from the optimal end state build up tensions. With increasing deviation from the end state, more and more effortful control processes are recruited to reduce tension. Further deviation will eventually lead to a breakdown zone, where the efficiency of the emotion system is disrupted. The second aim, however, is to drive away from these zones of equilibrium through a focus on tension amplification and effortful engagement in which original automatic emotions systems become integrated and empowered with the regulatory power of cognitive representations. As a result, complex cognitive–emotional structures develop that provide widened ranges of equilibrium and raised thresholds. We outlined the general characteristics of this theoretical view over the life span. In particular, we highlighted the development of more complex emotion representations in two emotion domains: emotional understanding and empathy.

As a result of the increasing linkage and integration of automatic emotion systems with complex representational ones, DIT presents the first part of development as a period of rising tension thresholds and broadening ranges of equilibrium in which individuals are able to not only tolerate, but also work constructively with increasingly more diverse, complex, and dynamic stimulation. This capacity becomes, in part, automated and in this way forms the crystallized basis for positive forms of later life cognitive–emotional development—forms that may bring richness of personal and psychological knowledge and regularities of inner experience. Interwoven with this process of deepening, there are, however, the effects of challenges to complex executive resources that are a part of later life development, which lead to a gradual restriction of homeostatic capacities of emotion regulation and increasing difficulties with emotion regulation. At the same time, DIT stresses the importance of wide individual variations in this general pattern.

Although our equilibrium model is consistent with empirical findings, further work is needed to investigate systematically the mechanisms involved in processing affective information across the life span. To do this, our perspective would encourage resisting simple formulations about growth or decline in emotion regulation capacities at any point of the life span. Instead, we would propose that the focus of future be aimed at more directly describing the dynamic ranges that are characteristic of individuals' emotion regulation skills. Already commonplace in such domains as physical exercise and aging or the determination of cardiac resistance to stress, such work would benefit from focusing on three lines of research as well as their dynamic interrelationships: (a) the experimental manipulation of activation levels, (b) the investigation of neurophysiologic processes underlying age-related differences in processing affective information, and (c) the impact of interindividual differences of cognitive and emotional resources in processing affective material.

REFERENCES

Adams, C. (1991). Qualititative age differences in memory for text: A lifespan developmental perspective. *Psychology and Aging, 6,* 323–336.

Andreoletti, C., Veratti, B. W., & Lachman, M. E. (2006). Age differences in the relationship between anxiety and recall. *Aging & Mental Health, 10,* 265–271.

Astington, J. W., & Jenkins, J. M. (1999). A longitudinal study of the relation between language and theory-of-mind development. *Developmental Psychology, 35,* 1311–1320.

Bäckman, L., & Molander, B. (1986a). Adult age differences in the ability to cope with situations of high arousal in a precision sport. *Psychology and Aging, 1,* 133–139.

Bäckman, L., & Molander, B. (1986b). Effects of adult age and level of skill on the ability to cope with high-stress conditions in a precision sport. *Psychology and Aging, 1,* 334–336.

Bailey, P. E., & Henry, J. D. (2008). Growing less empathic with age: Disinhibition of the self-perspective. *Journals of Gerontology Series B-Psychological Sciences and Social Sciences, 63,* P219–P226.

Bailey, P. E., Henry, J. D., & Von Hippel, W. (2008). Empathy and social functioning in late adulthood. *Aging and Mental Health, 12,* 1–5.

Baltes, P. B. (1997). On the incomplete architecture of human ontogeny: Selection, optimization, and compensation as foundation of developmental theory. *American Psychologist, 52,* 366–380.

Baltes, P. B., & Lindenberger, U. (1997). Emergence of a powerful connection between sensory and cognitive functions across the adult life span: A new window to the study of cognitive aging? *Psychology and Aging, 12,* 12–21.

Baltes, P. B., Lindenberger, U., & Staudinger, U. M. (2006). Life-span theory in developmental psychology. In W. Damon & R. M. Lerner (Eds.), *Handbook of child psychology: Vol. 1: Theoretical models of human development* (6th ed., pp. 569–664). Hoboken, NJ: John Wiley & Sons.

Baron-Cohen, S., & Wheelwright, S. (2004). The empathy quotient: An investigation of adults with Asperger syndrome or high functioning autism, and normal sex differences. *Journal of Autism and Developmental Disorders, 34,* 163–175.

Bartholomew, K., & Horowitz, L. M. (1991). Attachment styles among young adults: A test of a four-category model. *Journal of Personality and Social Psychology, 61,* 226–244.

Batson, C. D., Early, S., & Salvarani, G. (1997). Perspective taking: Imagining how another feels versus imagining how you would feel. *Personality and Social Psychology Bulletin, 23,* 751–758.

Blanchard-Fields, F. (1999). Social schemacity and causal attributions. In T. M. Hess & F. Blanchard-Fields (Eds.), *Social cognition and aging* (pp. 219–236). San Diego, CA: Academic Press.

Blanchard-Fields, F. (2007). Everyday problem solving and emotion: An adult developmental perspective. *Current Directions in Psychological Science, 16,* 26–31.

Blanchard-Fields, F. (2009). Flexible and adaptive socio-emotional problem solving in adult development and aging *Restorative Neurology and Neuroscience, 27,* 539–550.

Blanchard-Fields, F., Baldi, R., & Stein, R. (1999). Age relevance and context effects on attributions across the adult lifespan. *International Journal of Behavioral Development, 23,* 665–683.

Bowlby, J. (1969). *Attachment and loss: Vol. 1. Attachment.* New York: Basic Books.

Bowlby, J. (1973). *Attachment and loss: Vol. 2. Separation: Anxiety and anger.* New York: Basic Books.

Brent, S. B. (1978). Motivation, steady-state, and structural development: A general model of psychological homeostasis. *Motivation and Emotion, 2,* 299–332.

Bruner, J. (1986). *Actual minds, possible worlds.* Cambridge, MA: Harvard University Press.

Cahill, L., & McGaugh, J. L. (1998). Mechanisms of emotional arousal and lasting declarative memory. *Trends in Neurosciences, 21,* 294–299.

Cannon, W. B. (Ed.). (1939). *The wisdom of the body* (Rev. ed.). New York: Norton.

Carver, C. S., & Scheier, M. F. (1998). *On the self-regulation of behavior.* New York Cambridge University Press.

Cattell, R. B. (1971). *Abilities: Their structure, growth and action.* Boston: Houghton Mifflin.

Cavanaugh, J. C., & Murphy, N. Z. (1986). Personality and metamemory correlates of memory performance in younger and older adults. *Educational Gerontology, 12,* 385–394.

Chaiken, S., & Trope, Y. (1999). *Dual-process theories in social psychology.* New York: Guilford Press.

Chapman, M. (1988). *Constructive evolution: Origins and development of Piaget's thought.* New York: Cambridge University Press.

Charles, S. T., & Carstensen, L. L. (2007). Emotion regulation and aging. In J. J. Gross (Ed.), *Handbook of emotion regulation* (pp. 207–327). New York: Guilford Press.

Charles, S. T., Reynolds, C. A., & Gatz, M. (2001). Age-related differences and change in positive and negative affect over 23 years. *Journal of Personality and Social Psychology, 80,* 136–151.

Chinen, A. B. (1989). *In the ever after: Fairy tales and the second half of life.* Willmette, IL: Chiron.

Clore, G. L., & Ortony, A. (2000). Cognition in emotion: Always, sometimes, or never? In R. D. Lane & L. Nadel (Eds.), *Cognitive neuroscience of emotion* (pp. 24–61). New York: Oxford University Press.

Commons, M. L., Armon, C., Kohlberg, L., Richards, F. A., Grotzer, T. A., & Sinnott, J. D. (1990). *Adult development: Vol. 2. Models and methods in the study of adolescent and adult thought*. New York: Praeger.

Commons, M. L., Richards, F. A., & Armon, C. (1984). *Beyond formal operations*. New York: Praeger.

Commons, M. L., Sinnott, J. D., Richards, F. A., & Armon, C. (1989). *Adult development: Vol. 1. Comparisons and applications of developmental models*. New York: Praeger.

Commons, M. L., & Wolfsont, C. A. (2002). A complete theory of empathy must consider stage changes. *Behavioral and Brain Sciences, 25,* 30–31.

Damasio, A. R. (1995). *Descartes' error: Emotion, reason, and the human brain*. New York: Avon Books.

Darwin, C. (1998). *The expression of the emotions in man and animals* (3rd ed.). New York: Oxford University Press. (Original work published 1872)

Decety, J., & Jackson, P. L. (2004). The functional architecture of human empathy. *Behavioral and Cognitive Neuroscience Reviews, 3,* 71–100.

Decety, J., & Meyer, M. (2008). From emotion resonance to empathic understanding: A social developmental neuroscience account. *Development & Psychopathology, 20,* 1053–1080.

de Kloet, E. R., Oitzl, M. S., & Joels, M. (1999). Stress and cognition: Are corticosteroids good or bad guys? *Trends in Neurosciences, 22,* 422–426.

Deptula, D., Singh, R., & Pomara, N. (1993). Aging, emotional states, and memory. *American Journal of Psychiatry, 150,* 429–434.

de Rosnay, M., & Hughes, C. (2006). Conversation and theory of mind: Do children talk their way to socio-cognitive understanding? *British Journal of Developmental Psychology, 24,* 7–37.

de Rosnay, M., Pons, F., Harris, P. L., & Morrell, J. M. B. (2004). A lag between understanding false belief and emotion attribution in young children: Relationships with linguistic ability and mothers' mental-state language. *British Journal of Developmental Psychology, 22,* 197–218.

de Waal, F. B. M. (2008). Putting the altruism back into altruism: The evolution of empathy. *Annual Review of Psychology, 59,* 279–300.

Diehl, M., Coyle, N., & Labouvie-Vief, G. (1996). Age and sex differences in strategies of coping and defense across the life span. *Psychology and Aging, 11,* 127–139.

Eisenberg, N., Cumberland, A., Guthrie, I. K., Murphy, B. C., & Shepard, S. A. (2005). Age changes in prosocial responding and moral reasoning in adolescence and early adulthood. *Journal of Research on Adolescence, 15,* 235–260.

Eisenberg, N., & Eggum, N. D. (2009). Empathic responding: Sympathy and personal distress. In J. Decety & W. Ickes (Eds.), *The social neuroscience of empathy*. Cambridge, MA: MIT Press.

Eisenberg, N., & Fabes, R. A. (1990). Empathy: Conceptualization, measurement, and relation to prosocial behavior. *Motivation and Emotion, 14,* 131–149.

Eisenberg, N., & Fabes, R. A. (1998). Prosocial development. In W. Damon & N. Eisenberg (Eds.), *Handbook of child psychology: Vol. 3. Social, emotional, and personality development* (5th ed., pp. 701–778). New York: John Wiley & Sons.

Eisenberg, N., Fabes, R. A., Guthrie, I. K., & Reiser, M. (2000). Dispositional emotionality and regulation: Their role in predicting quality of social functioning. *Journal of Personality and Social Psychology, 78,* 136–157.

Eisenberg, N., & Miller, P. A. (1987). The relation of empathy to pro-social and related behaviors. *Psychological Bulletin, 101,* 91–119.

Eisenberg, N., Murphy, B. C., & Shepard, S. A. (1996). The development of empathic accuracy. In W. Ickes (Ed.), *Empathic accuracy* (pp. 73–116). New York: Guilford Press.

Eisenberg, N., Shell, R., Pasternack, J., Lennon, R., Beller, R., & Mathy, R. M. (1987). Prosocial development in middle childhood: A longitudinal study. *Developmental Psychology, 23,* 712–718.

Ekman, P. (1992). An argument for basic emotion. *Cognition and Emotion, 6,* 169–200.

Epstein, S., & Pacini, R. (1999). Some basic issues regarding dual-process theories from the perspective of cognitive-experiential self-theory. In S. Chaiken & Y. Trope (Eds.), *Dual-process theories in social psychology* (pp. 462–482). New York: Guilford Press.

Erikson, E. H. (1968). *Identity: Youth and crisis*. New York: Norton.

Erikson, E. H. (1985). *The life cycle completed: A review*. New York: Norton.

Erikson, E. H., Erikson, J. M., & Kivnick, H. Q. (1986). *Vital involvement in old age*. New York: Norton.

Eysenck, S. B., Pearson, P. R., Easting, G., & Allsopp, J. F. (1985). Age norms for impulsiveness, venturesomeness and empathy in adults. *Personality and Individual Differences, 6,* 613–619.

Fischer, K. W., & Bidell, T. R. (2006). Dynamic development of action and thought. In R. M. Lerner & W. Damon (Eds.), *Handbook of child psychology: Vol. 1. Theoretical models of human development* (6th ed., pp. 313–399). Hoboken, NJ: John Wiley & Sons.

Flavell, J. H. (2004). Theory-of-mind development: Retrospect and prospect. *Merrill-Palmer Quarterly, 50,* 274–290.

Freud, S. (1957). The id and the ego. In J. Rickman (Ed.), *A general selection from the works of Sigmund Freud* (pp. 210–235). Garden City, NY: Doubleday. (Original work published 1923)

German, T. P., & Hehman, J. A. (2006). Representational and executive selection resources in "theory of mind": Evidence from compromised belief-desire reasoning in old age. *Cognition, 101,* 129–152.

Gianotti, G. (1999). Emotions as a biologically adaptive system: An introduction. In G. Gianotti (Ed.), *Handbook of neuropsychology: Emotional behavior and its disorders* (2nd ed., Vol. 5, pp. 1–15). London: Elsevier.

Gilet, A.-L., Grühn, D., Studer, J., & Labouvie-Vief, G. (2009). *Valence, arousal, and imagery ratings for 835 French attributes by young, middle-aged, and older adults: The French Emotional Evaluation List (FEEL)*. Manuscript submitted for publication.

Grühn, D., Rebucal, K., Diehl, M., Lumley, M., & Labouvie-Vief, G. (2008). Empathy across the adult lifespan: Findings from a 12-year longitudinal study and an experience-sampling study. *Emotion, 8,* 753–765.

Grühn, D., & Scheibe, S. (2008). Age-related differences in valence and arousal ratings of pictures from the International Affective Picture System (IAPS): Do ratings become more extreme with age? *Behavior Research Methods, 40,* 512–521.

Grühn, D., Scheibe, S., & Baltes, P. B. (2007). Reduced negativity effect in older adults' memory for emotional pictures: The heterogeneity-homogeneity list paradigm. *Psychology and Aging, 22,* 644–649.

Grühn, D., Smith, J., & Baltes, P. B. (2005). No aging bias favoring memory for positive material: Evidence from a heterogeneity-homogeneity list paradigm using emotionally toned words. *Psychology and Aging, 20,* 579–588.

Haidt, J. (2004). The emotional dog gets mistaken for a possum. *Review of General Psychology, 8,* 283–290.

Happé, F. G. E., Winner, E., & Brownell, H. (1998). The getting of wisdom: Theory of mind in old age. *Developmental Psychology, 34,* 358–362.

Hariri, A. R., Bookheimer, S. Y., & Mazziotta, J. C. (2000). Modulating emotional responses: Effects of a neocortical network on the limbic system. *Neuroreport, 11,* 43–48.

Harris, P. L. (1982). Cognitive prerequisites to language? *British Journal of Psychology, 73,* 187–195.

Harris, P. L. (1989). *Children and emotion.* Oxford: Blackwell.

Harris, P. L. (2000). Understanding emotions. In M. Lewis & J. Haviland-Jones (Eds.), *Handbook of Emotions* (2nd ed., pp. 281–292). New York: Guilford Press.

Harris, P. L. (2006). Social cognition. In D. Kuhn & R. S. Siegler (Eds.), *Handbook of child psychology: Vol. 2. Cognition, perception, and language* (6th ed., pp. 811–858). Hoboken, NJ: John Wiley & Sons.

Harris, P. L. (2008). Children's understanding of emotions. In M. Lewis, J. Haviland-Jones, & L. Feldman-Barrett (Eds.), *Handbook of emotions* (3rd ed., pp. 320–331). New York: Guilford Press.

Harris, P. L., Johnson, C.-N., Hutton, D., Andrews, G., & Cooke, T. (1989). Young children's theory of mind and emotion. *Cognition and Emotion, 3,* 379–400.

Harter, S. (1999). *The construction of the self: A developmental perspective.* New York: Guilford Press.

Hasher, L., & Zacks, R. T. (1988). Working memory, comprehension, and aging: A review and a new view. In G. H. Bower (Ed.), *The psychology of learning and motivation: Advances in research and theory* (Vol. 22, pp. 193–225). San Diego, CA: Academic Press, Inc.

Hasher, L., Stoltzfus, E. R., Zacks, R. T., & Rypma, B. (1991). Age and inhibition. *Journal of Experimental Psychology: Learning, Memory, & Cognition, 17,* 163–169.

Hay, D. F., Nash, A., & Pederson, J. (1981). Responses of 6-month-olds to the distress of their peers. *Child Development, 52,* 1071–1075.

Hazan, C., & Shaver, P. (1987). Romantic love conceptualized as an attachment process. *Journal of Personality and Social Psychology, 52,* 511–524.

Hebb, D. (1949). *The organization of behavior: A neuropsychological theory.* New York: John Wiley & Sons.

Helson, H. (Ed.). (1964). *Adaptation-level theory: An experimental and systematic approach to behavior.* New York: Harper & Row.

Helson, R., Jones, C., & Kwan, V. S. Y. (2002). Personality change over 40 years of adulthood: Hierarchical linear modeling analyses of two longitudinal samples. *Journal of Personality and Social Psychology, 83,* 752–766.

Helson, R., & Soto, C. J. (2005). Up and down in middle age: Monotonic and nonmonotonic changes in roles, status, and personality. *Journal of Personality and Social Psychology, 89,* 194–204.

Hess, T. M. (1999). Cognitive and knowledge-based influences on social representations. In T. M. Hess & F. Blanchard-Fields (Eds.), *Social cognition and aging* (pp. 237–263). San Diego, CA: Academic Press.

Hess, T. M. (2005). Memory and aging in context. *Psychological Bulletin, 131,* 383–406.

Hess, T. M., & Auman, C. (2001). Aging and social expertise: The impact of trait-diagnostic information on impressions of others. *Psychology and Aging, 16,* 497–510.

Hess, T. M., Rosenberg, D. C., & Waters, S. J. (2001). Motivation and representational processes in adulthood: the effects of social accountability and information relevance. *Psychology and Aging, 16,* 497–510.

Hess, T. M., Waters, S. J., & Bolstad, C. A. (2000). Motivational and cognitive influences on affective priming in adulthood. *Journals of Gerontology Series B—Psychological Sciences and Social Sciences, 55,* P193–P204.

Hoffman, M. L. (1978). Psychological and biological perspectives on altruism. *International Journal of Behavioral Development, 1,* 323–339.

Hoffman, M. L. (1982). Affect and moral development. *New Directions for Child Development, 16,* 83–103.

Hoffman, M. L. (2000). *Empathy and moral development: Implications for caring and justice.* New York: Cambridge University Press.

Hogan, M. J. (2003). Divided attention in older but not younger adults is impaired by anxiety. *Experimental Aging Research, 29,* 111–136.

Hommel, B., Musseler, J., Aschersleben, G., & Prinz, W. (2001). The theory of event coding (TEC): A framework for perception and action planning. *Behavioral and Brain Sciences, 24,* 849–937.

Izard, C. E. (1977). *Human emotions.* New York: Plenum Press.

Jain, E., & Labouvie-Vief, G. (in press). Compensatory effects of emotion avoidance in adult development. *Biological Psychology.*

Jennings, J. R., Kamarck, T., Manuck, S., Everson, S. A., Kaplan, G., & Salonen, J. T. (1997). Aging or disease? Cardiovascular reactivity in Finnish men over the middle years. *Psychology & Aging, 12,* 225–238.

Jepson, K. L., & Labouvie-Vief, G. (1992). Symbolic processing of youth and elders. In R. L. West & J. D. Sinnott (Eds.), *Everyday memory and aging* (pp. 124–137). New York: Springer.

Jung, C. G. (1933). *Modern man in search of a soul* (W. S. Dell & C. F. Baynes, Trans.). London: Harcourt, Brace & World.

Karmiloff-Smith, A. (1992). *Beyond modularity: A developmental perspective on cognitive science.* Cambridge, MA: MIT Press/Bradford Books.

Keightley, M. L., Winocur, G., Burianova, H., Hongwanishkul, D., & Grady, C. L. (2006). Age effects on social cognition: Faces tell a different story. *Psychology and Aging, 21,* 558–572.

Keil, A., & Freund, A. M. (2009). Changes in the sensitivity to appetitive and aversive arousal across adulthood. *Psychology and Aging, 24,* 668–680.

King, L. A., & Hicks, J. A. (2007). Whatever happened to "What might have been"? *American Psychologist, 62,* 625–636.

Knafo, A., Zahn-Waxler, C., Van Hulle, C., Robinson, J. L., & Rhee, S. H. (2008). The developmental origins of a disposition toward empathy: Genetic and environmental contributions. *Emotion, 8,* 737–752.

Kochanska, G. (1993). Toward a synthesis of parental socialization and child temperament in early development of conscience. *Child Development, 64,* 325–347.

Kohlberg, L. (1969). Continuities and discontinuities in childhood and adult moral development. *Human Development, 12,* 3–120.

Kohlberg, L. (1984). *Essays on moral development: Vol. II. The psychology of moral development.* San Francisco: Harper and Row.

Kreibig, S. D., Wilhelm, F. H., Roth, W. T., & Gross, J. J. (2007). Cardiovascular, electrodermal, and respiratory response patterns to fear- and sadness-inducing films. *Psychophysiology, 44,* 787–806.

Labouvie-Vief, G. (1980). Beyond formal operations: Uses and limits of pure logic in life-span development. *Human Development, 23,* 141–161.

Labouvie-Vief, G. (1982). Dynamic development and mature autonomy: A theoretical prologue. *Human Development, 25,* 161–191.

Labouvie-Vief, G. (1984). Logic and self-regulation from youth to maturity: A model. In M. L. Commons, F. A. Richards, & C. Armon (Eds.), *Beyond formal operations.* New York: Praeger.

Labouvie-Vief, G. (1994). *Psyche and Eros: Mind and gender in the life course.* New York: Cambridge University Press.

Labouvie-Vief, G. (1996). Trapped in the mirror: Psychosocial reflections on mid-life and the queen in Snow White: Comment. *Human Development, 39,* 173–180.

Labouvie-Vief, G. (2003). Dynamic integration: Affect, cognition, and the self in adulthood. *Current Directions in Psychological Science, 12,* 201–206.

Labouvie-Vief, G. (2005). Self-with-other representations and the organization of the self. *Journal of Research in Personality, 39,* 185–205.

Labouvie-Vief, G. (2008). Dynamic integration theory: Emotion, cognition, and equilibrium in later life. In V. Bengtson, M. Silverstein, N. Putney, & D. Gans (Eds.), *Handbook of theories of aging*. New York: Springer.

Labouvie-Vief, G. (2009). Cognition and equilibrium regulation in development and aging. *Restorative Neurology and Neuroscience, 27,* 551-565.

Labouvie-Vief, G., Chiodo, L. M., Goguen, L. A., Diehl, M., & Orwoll, L. (1995). Representations of self across the life span. *Psychology and Aging, 10,* 404–415.

Labouvie-Vief, G., & DeVoe, M. (1991). Emotional regulation in adulthood and later life: A developmental view. In K. W. Schaie & M. P. Lawton (Eds.), *Annual review of gerontology and geriatrics: Behavioral science and aging* (Vol. 11, pp. 172–194). New York: Springer.

Labouvie-Vief, G., DeVoe, M., & Bulka, D. (1989). Speaking about feelings: Conceptions of emotion across the life span. *Psychology and Aging, 4,* 425–437.

Labouvie-Vief, G., DeVoe, M., Chiodo, L. M., & Coyle, N. (1995). Representations of self and parents across the life span. *Journal of Adult Development, 2,* 207–222.

Labouvie-Vief, G., & Diehl, M. (2000). Cognitive complexity and cognitive-affective integration: Related or separate domains of adult development? *Psychology and Aging, 15,* 490–504.

Labouvie-Vief, G., Diehl, M., Jain, E., & Zhang, F. (2007). Six-year change in affect optimization and affect complexity across the adult life span: A further examination. *Psychology and Aging, 22,* 738–751.

Labouvie-Vief, G., Diehl, M., Tarnowski, A., & Shen, J. (2000). Age differences in adult personality: Findings from the United States and China. *Journal of Gerontology: Psychological Sciences, 55B,* P4–P17.

Labouvie-Vief, G., Grühn, D., & Mouras, H. (2009). Dynamic emotion–cognition interactions in development: Arousal, stress, and the processing of affect. In H. B. Bosworth & C. Hertzog (Eds.), *Cognition in aging: Methodologies and applications* (pp. 181–196). Washington, DC: American Psychological Association.

Labouvie-Vief, G., Hakim-Larson, J., DeVoe, M., & Schoeberlein, S. (1989). Emotions and self-regulation: A life span view. *Human Development, 32,* 279–299.

Labouvie-Vief, G., Hakim-Larson, J., & Hobart, C. J. (1987). Age, ego level, and the life-span development of coping and defense processes. *Psychology and Aging, 2,* 286–293.

Labouvie-Vief, G., & Marquez, M. G. (2004). Dynamic integration: Affect optimization and differentiation in development. In D. Y. Dai & R. J. Sternberg (Eds.), *Motivation, emotion, and cognition: Integrative perspectives on intellectual functioning and development* (pp. 237–272). Mahwah, NJ: Erlbaum.

Labouvie-Vief, G., & Medler, M. (2002). Affect optimization and affect complexity: Modes and styles of regulation in adulthood. *Psychology and Aging, 17,* 571–587.

Lawton, M. P., & Nahemow, L. (1973). Ecology and the aging process. In C. Eisdorfer– & M. P. Lawton (Eds.), *The psychology of adult development and aging* (pp. 619–674). Washington, DC: American Psychological Association.

Lazarus, R. S. (1966). *Psychological stress and the coping process.* New York: McGraw-Hill.

Lazarus, R. S. (1982). Thoughts on the relations between emotion and cognition. *American Psychologist, 37,* 1019–1024.

Lazarus, R. S. (1991). Cognition and motivation in emotion. *American Psychologist, 46,* 352–367.

Lazarus, R. S., Averillm, J. R., & Opton, E. M. J. (1970). Toward cognitive theory of emotion. In M. B. Arnold (Ed.), *Feelings and emotion* (pp. 207–232). New York: Academic Press.

LeDoux, J. E. (1996). *The emotional brain: The mysterious underpinnings of emotional life.* New York: Simon & Schuster.

LeDoux, J. E., & Phelps, E. A. (2000). Emotional networks in the brain. In M. Lewis & J. M. Haviland-Jones (Eds.), *Handbook of emotions* (2nd ed., pp. 157–172). New York: Guilford Press.

Lewis, M. D. (2005). Bridging emotion theory and neurobiology through dynamic systems modeling. *Behavioral and Brain Sciences, 28,* 169–245.

Lewis, M. D., & Ferrari, M. (2001). Cognitive-emotional self-organization in personality development and personality identity. In H. A. Bosma & E. S. Kunnen (Eds.), *Identity and emotion: Development through self-organization* (pp. 177–198). Cambridge, England: Cambridge University Press.

Lieberman, M. D., Eisenberger, N. I., Crockett, M. J., Tom, S. M., Pfeifer, J. H., & Way, B. M. (2007). Putting feelings into words: Affect labeling disrupts amygdala activity in response to affective stimuli. *Psychological Science, 18,* 421–428.

Lupien, S. J., Wilkinson, C. W., Briere, S., Menard, C., Ng Ying Kin, N. M. K., & Nair, N. P. V. (2002). The modulatory effects of corticosteroids on cognition: Studies in young human populations. *Psychoneuroendocrinology, 27,* 401–416.

Luria, A. (1932). *The nature of human conflicts.* New York: Liveright.

MacPherson, S. E., Phillips, L. H., & Della Sala, S. (2002). Age, executive function and social decision making: A dorsolateral prefrontal theory of cognitive aging. *Psychology and Aging, 17,* 598–609.

Mather, M., Johnson, M. K., & De Leonardis, D. M. (1999). Stereotype reliance in source monitoring: Age differences and neuropsychological test correlates. *Cognitive Neuropsychology, 16,* 437–458.

Maylor, E. A., Moulson, J. M., Muncer, A.-M., & Taylor, L. A. (2002). Does performance on theory of mind tasks decline in old age. *British Journal of Psychology, 93,* 465–485.

McEwen, B. S., & Sapolsky, R. M. (1995). Stress and cognitive function. *Current Opinion in Neurobiology, 5,* 205–216.

McGaugh, J. L. (2003). *Memory and emotion. The making of lasting memories.* New York: Columbia University Press.

McKinnon, M. C., & Moscovitch, M. (2007). Domain-general contributions to social reasoning: Theory of mind and deontic reasoning re-explored. *Cognition, 102,* 179–218.

Metcalfe, J., & Jacobs, W. J. (1998). Emotional memory: The effects of stress on "cool" and "hot" memory systems. In D. L. Medin (Ed.), *The psychology of learning and motivation: Advances in research and theory* (Vol. 38, pp. 187–222). San Diego, CA: Academic Press.

Metcalfe, J., & Mischel, W. (1999). A hot/cool-system of delay of gratification: Dynamic of willpower. *Psychological Review, 106,* 3–19.

Miller, P. A., & Eisenberg, N. (1988). The relation of empathy to aggressive and externalizing antisocial-behavior. *Psychological Bulletin, 103,* 324–344.

Mitchell, K. J., Johnson, M. K., Raye, C. L., Mather, M., & D'Esposito, M. (2000). Aging and reflective processes of working memory: Binding and test load deficits. *Psychology and Aging, 15,* 527–541.

Mroczek, D. K., & Kolarz, C. M. (1998). The effect of age on positive and negative affect: A developmental perspective on happiness. *Journal of Personality and Social Psychology, 75,* 1333–1349.

Nadel, J., & Baudonnière, P. M. (1982). The social function of reciprocal imitation in 2-year-old peers. *International Journal of Behavioral Development, 5,* 95–109.

Nadel, J., Carchon, I., Kervella, C., Marcelli, D., & Reserbat-Plantey, D. (1999). Expectancies for social contingency in 2-month-olds. *Developmental Science, 2,* 164–173.

Otte, C., Hart, S., Neylan, T. C., Marmar, C. R., Yaffe, K., & Mohr, D. C. (2005). A meta-analysis of cortisol response to challenge in human aging: Importance of gender. *Psychoneuroendocrinology, 30,* 80–91.

Pascual-Leone, J. (1991). Emotions, development, and psychotherapy: A dialectical–constructivist perspective. In J. Safran & L. S. Greenberg (Eds.), *Emotion, psychotherapy, and change* (pp. 302–335). New York: Guilford Press.

Paulhus, D. L., Graf, P., & Van Selst, M. (1989). Attentional load increases the positivity of self-presentation. *Social Cognition, 7,* 389–400.

Paulhus, D. L., & Levitt, K. (1987). Desirable responding triggered by affect: Automatic egotism? *Journal of Personality and Social Psychology, 52,* 245–259.

Paulhus, D. L., & Lim, D. T. (1994). Arousal and evaluative extremity in social judgments: A dynamic complexity model. *European Journal of Social Psychology, 24,* 89–99.

Perner, J., & Wimmer, H. (1985). "John thinks that Mary thinks that . . .": Attribution of second-order beliefs by 5- to 10-year-old children. *Journal of Experimental Child Psychology, 39,* 437–471.

Piaget, J. (1955). *The language and thought of the child.* New York: New American Library.

Piaget, J. (1970). *Structuralism.* New York: Basic Books.

Piaget, J. (1971). *Biology and Knowledge* (B. Walsh, Trans.). Chicago: University of Chicago Press.

Piaget, J. (1976). *The grasp of consciousness: action and concept in the young child.* Cambridge, England: Harvard University Press.

Piaget, J. (1980). *Experiments in contradiction* Chicago, IL: University of Chicago Press.

Piaget, J. (1981). *Intelligence and affectivity: Their relationship during child development* (T. A. Brown & C. E. Kaegi, Trans.). Oxford, England: Annual Reviews.

Pons, F., & Harris, P. L. (2005). Longitudinal change and longitudinal stability of individual differences in children's emotion understanding. *Cognition and Emotion, 19,* 1158–1174.

Pons, F., Harris, P. L., & de Rosnay, M. (2004). Emotion comprehension between 3 and 11 years: Developmental periods and hierarchical organization. *European Journal of Developmental Psychology, 1,* 127–152.

Pons, F., Lawson, J., Harris, P. L., & de Rosnay, M. (2003). Individual differences in children's emotion understanding: Effects of age and language. *Scandinavian Journal of Psychology, 44,* 347–353.

Premack, D., & Woodruff, G. (1972). Does the chimpanzee have a theory of mind? *The Behavioral and Brain Sciences, 4,* 515–526.

Preston, S. D., & de Waal, F. B. M. (2002). Empathy: Its ultimate and proximate bases. *Behavioral and Brain Sciences, 25,* 1–20.

Pribram, K. H., & Gill, M. M. (1976). *Freud's "project" reassessed.* New York: Basic Books.

Prigogine, I., & Stengers, I. (1984). *Order out of chaos.* New York: Bantam.

Rabbitt, P., & Lowe, C. (2000). Patterns of cognitive ageing. *Psychological Research, 63,* 308-316.

Radke-Yarrow, M., Zahn-Waxler, C., Richardson, D. T., & Susman, A. (1994). Caring behavior in children of clinically depressed and well mothers. *Child Development, 65,* 1405–1414.

Rahhal, T. A., May, C. P., & Hasher, L. (2002). Truth and character: Sources that older adults can remember. *Psychological Science, 13,* 101–105.

Ricoeur, P. (1970). *Freud and philosophy: An essay on interpretation.* New Haven, CT: Yale University Press.

Rizzolatti, G., & Arbib, M. A. (1998). Language within our grasp. *Trends in Neurosciences, 21,* 188–194.

Sagi, A., & Hoffman, M. L. (1976). Empathic distress in the newborn. *Developmental Psychology, 12,* 175–176.

Sapolsky, R. M., Krey, L. C., & McEwen, B. S. (1986). The neuroendocrinology of stress and aging: The glucocorticoid cascade hypothesis. *Endocrine Reviews, 7,* 284–301.

Schaie, K. W. (1994). The course of adult intellectual development. *American Psychologist, 49,* 304-313.

Schieman, S., & Van Gundy, K. (2000). The personal and social links between age and self-reported empathy. *Social Psychology Quarterly, 63,* 152–174.

Schore, A. N. (1994). *Affect regulation and the origin of the self: The neurobiology of emotional development.* Hillsdale, NJ: Erlbaum.

Schore, A. N. (1998). Early shame experiences and infant brain development. In P. Gilbert & B. Andrews (Eds.), *Shame: Interpersonal Behavior, Psychopathology and Culture* (pp. 57–77). New York: Oxford University Press.

Selye, H. (1978). *The stress of life* (2nd ed.). Oxford, England: McGraw-Hill.

Shaver, P. R., & Mikulincer, M. (2002). Attachment-related psychodynamics. *Attachment & Human Development, 4,* 133-161.

Simner, M. L. (1971). Newborn's response to the cry of another infant. *Developmental Psychology, 5,* 136–150.

Singer, T. (2006). The neuronal basis and ontogeny of empathy and mind reading: Review of literature and implications for future research. *Neuroscience & Biobehavioral Reviews, 30,* 855–863.

Sroufe, L. A. (1996). *Emotional development: The organization of emotional life in the early years.* New York: Cambridge University Press.

Stern, D. L. (1985). *The interpersonal world of the infant.* New York: Basic Books.

Strayer, J. (1993). Children's concordant emotions and cognitions in response to observed emotions. *Child Development, 64,* 188–201.

Sullivan, S., & Ruffman, T. (2004). Social understanding: How does it fare with advancing years? *British Journal of Psychology, 95,* 1–18.

Thelen, E., & Smith, L. B. (1994). *A dynamic systems approach to the development of cognition and action.* Cambridge, MA: MIT Press.

Toi, M., & Batson, C. D. (1982). More evidence that empathy is a source of altruistic motivation. *Journal of Personality and Social Psychology, 43,* 281–292.

Tomkins, S. S. (1984). Affect theory. In K. R. Scherer & P. Ekman (Eds.), *Approaches to emotion* (pp. 163–196). Hillsdale, NJ: Erlbaum.

Trevarthen, C. (1993). The self born in intersubjectivity: The psychology of an infant communicating. In U. Neisser (Ed.), *The perceived self* (pp. 121–173). New York, NY: Cambridge University Press.

Tsujimoto, S. (2008). The prefrontal cortex: Functional neural development during early childhood. *The Neuroscientist, 14,* 345–358.

Tucker, D. M. (1992). Developing emotions and cortical networks. In M. R. Gunnar & C. A. Nelson (Eds.), *Developmental behavioral neuroscience* (pp. 75–128). Hillsdale, NJ: Erlbaum.

Uchino, B. N., Berg, C. A., Smith, T. W., Pearce, G., & Skinner, M. (2006). Age-related differences in ambulatory blood pressure during daily stress: Evidence for greater blood pressure reactivity with age. *Psychology and Aging, 21,* 231–239.

Uchino, B. N., Holt-Lunstad, J., Bloor, L. E., & Campo, R. A. (2005). Aging and cardiovascular reactivity to stress: Longitudinal evidence for changes in stress reactivity. *Psychology and Aging, 20,* 134–143.

Valiente, C., Eisenberg, N., Fabes, R. A., Shepard, S. A., Cumberland, A., & Losoya, S. H. (2004). Prediction of children's empathy-related responding from their effortful control and parents' expressivity. *Developmental Psychology, 40,* 911–926.

Vingerhoets, G., Berckmoes, C., & Stroobant, N. (2003). Cerebral hemodynamics during discrimination of prosodic and semantic emotion in speech studied by transcranial doppler ultrasonography. *Neuropsychology, 17,* 93–99.

von Hippel, W., Silver, L. A., & Lynch, M. E. (2000). Stereotyping against your will: The role of inhibitory ability in stereotyping and prejudice among the elderly. *Personality and Social Psychology Bulletin 26,* 523–532.

Walker, N. (1956). Freud and homeostasis. *British Journal for the Philosophy of Science, 7,* 61–72.

Warneken, F., & Tomasello, M. (2006). Altruistic helping in human infants and young chimpanzees. *Science, 311,* 1301–1303.

Wellman, H. M., & Woolley, J. D. (1990). From simple desires to ordinary beliefs: The early development of everyday psychology. *Cognition, 35,* 245–275.

Werner, H. (1955). *On expressive language.* Worcester, MA: Clark University Press.

Werner, H. (1957). *Comparative psychology of mental development.* Oxford, England: International Universities Press.

Werner, H., & Kaplan, B. (1963). *Symbol formation.* Oxford, England: John Wiley & Sons.

Whitbourne, S. K. (1976). Test anxiety in elderly and young adults. *International Journal of Aging & Human Development, 7,* 201–210.

Wurm, L. H., Labouvie-Vief, G., Aycock, J., Rebucal, K. A., & Koch, H. E. (2004). Performance in auditory and visual emotional Stroop tasks: A comparison of older and younger adults. *Psychology and Aging, 19,* 523–535.

Yerkes, R., & Dodson, J. (1908). The relation of strength of stimulus to rapidity of habit formation. *Journal of Comparative Neurology and Psychology, 18,* 459–482.

Zahn-Waxler, C., Cole, P. M., Welsh, J. D., & Fox, N. A. (1995). Psychophysiological correlates of empathy and prosocial behaviors in preschool children with behavior problems. *Development and Psychopathology, 7,* 27–48.

Zahn-Waxler, C., Kochanska, G., Krupnick, J., & McKnew, D. (1990). Patterns of guilt in children of depressed and well mothers. *Developmental Psychology, 26,* 51–59.

CHAPTER 5

Self-Regulation across the Life Span[1]

G. JOHN GELDHOF, TODD D. LITTLE, and JOHN COLOMBO

Self-regulation has been the subject of inquiry for more than a century (e.g., James, 1890) and has influenced nearly all domains of psychology. Aspects of self-regulation have been integral to understanding conscious (Mischel & Ebbesen, 1970), unconscious (Fitzsimmons & Bargh, 2004), emotional (Calkins & Johnson, 1998), self-deterministic (Ryan & Deci, 2002; Wehmeyer, 2004), and prosocial (Eisenberg, Wentzel, & Harris, 1998) behaviors, just to name a few. In fact, self-regulation has been portrayed as one of the few core aspects of human functioning (G. E. Schwartz & Shapiro, 1976).

Despite the long and influential history of self-regulation in psychology, Freund (2001) discussed its modern study as rooted in the cognitive revolution of the late 1960s. Behaviorism, the predominant theory at the time, emphasized the environment as the primary predictor of an organism's behavior. The role of the self was virtually eliminated in an attempt to trace all action back to the immutable laws of classical and operant conditioning. As authors such as Mischel (1968) and Bandura (1969) reintroduced the importance of the "self" for predicting human behavior, the serious consideration of self-regulation was made possible. For instance, breaking from the environment-driven behaviorist paradigm allowed for the idea of the self as a proactive agent capable of influencing its own development (e.g., Lerner & Bush-Rossnagel, 1981).

Self-regulation is clearly a broad topic and to cover all aspects of self-regulated behavior in one chapter would be impossible. In this chapter, we coordinate our discussion primarily around an action-theoretical approach to self-regulation with particular emphasis on the development of the agentic individual. Our action-theoretical approach bears on domain-general theories of self-regulation, as well as more nuanced approaches. Although we consider self-regulation broadly and include many of its instantiations, the present chapter should not be regarded as fully comprehensive.

[1] This work was supported in part by grants from the National Institutes of Health (NIH) to the University of Kansas Intellectual and Developmental Disabilities Research Center (Grant No. 5 P30 HD002528). Its contents are solely the responsibility of the authors and do not necessarily represent the official views of the NIH.

The various views on self-regulation expressed in this chapter do not necessarily reflect a consensus across researchers in the field or among the authors of this chapter.

We first provide a definition of self-regulation in action-theoretical terms, paying particular attention to what it means to regulate one's own behavior. We outline how an action-control metatheory pervades many current approaches to self-regulated behavior and in some ways integrates apparently disparate theoretical approaches. We then integrate key aspects of these theories into an organizing heuristic that clarifies the development of self-regulation across the life course. We discuss development in terms of the key components of our heuristic as they are addressed. We summarize our heuristic toward the end of the chapter and close by discussing the theoretical and methodological limitations that the field currently faces. We also address several "burning questions" left unanswered in the current literature.

SELF-REGULATION AND ACTION THEORY

The term *self-regulation* can encompass nearly any behavior produced by an organism. Likewise, action theory is a broad metatheory with a pervasive, yet oftentimes under-appreciated, influence. In our presentation, we provide a brief discussion of how self-regulation can be approached by various action theories and how these approaches are useful for understanding the precursors and effects of self-regulated action across the life span.

Self-Regulation

Self-regulation is often addressed as a singular topic. Instead, self-regulation actually represents two closely related ideas. Scholars who address self-regulation implicitly address two questions: "What is the self?" and "How does the self regulate its actions?" Authors discussing self-regulation often ignore the first question, starting with the a priori assumption that an agentic and active self exists. This assumption often leads researchers to provide either (a) a meta-theoretical framework by which an agentic self *could* regulate its behavior, or (b) a neural basis for self-regulation that describes which neural substrates likely mediate the path between the agentic self and observable behavior. A strictly meta-theoretical framework focuses on the social and environmental inputs that are likely to influence the self's ability to regulate and reflects a fluid organismic perspective. A strictly neural model regards regulation as the interaction among several neural substrates and reflects a more mechanistic perspective.

Assuming the existence of an agentic and active self seemingly reintroduces the concept of the homunculus (see Mischel & Ayduk, 2004, for a discussion). By presupposing a self-regulating agent, self-regulation researchers appear to fall squarely on the side of free will in the free will versus determinism controversy. However, as Wehmeyer (2004, 2005) pointed out, this characterization is not necessarily valid. Locke's (1690) definition of freedom involves an individual's ability to act on volitions without external constraint. Nothing in the Lockean definition requires that the individual's will be free, only that the individual be free to act. A person's will can be fully determined by the forces of nature and nurture, with self-regulation developing through self-organizational principles. In a completely deterministic scenario, the set of possible actions (and from a Lockean perspective, the person's will) still remains free. We promote a Lockean definition of "self-determined," as described by Wehmeyer. This perspective allows researchers to approach agentic self-regulation in a way that is equally applicable to traditional free will and deterministic paradigms.

From the Lockean perspective, we can define the self-determined aspect of self-regulation in a fashion similar to Wehmeyer's causal agency theory (2004). Behavior is self-determined when the individual acts as a causal agent in performing intentional actions. Self-determined behaviors require both the capability to act and some challenge to be met. In Wehmeyer's (2004) terms, the capability to act requires both the ability to cause an effect and the ability to direct behavior toward an end. Challenges require the use of capabilities to derive a desirable outcome when an opportunity arises or to avert threats (see also Little, Snyder, & Wehmeyer, 2006).

A definition of what self-regulation is and is not depends strongly on which aspects of the organism are thought to regulate behavior. From a purely physiological perspective, the vegetative regulation of, for example, respiration and cardiac function by the brainstem qualify as self-regulated. These same behaviors do not qualify from a psychological perspective. Purposeful responses to stimuli and intrinsically motivated actions are considered self-regulated from a psychological perspective. We rely on the idea of "actions" to connote behaviors that reflect self-regulation from a psychological perspective. Actions involve responses that are mediated to some degree by cognitive processes and are therefore regulated by some aspect of the agentic self.

As mentioned, our discussion of self-regulation is not comprehensive. Instead, we limit our approach primarily to agentic (i.e., self-determined) behavior as previously described. Although automatized reactions to environmental stimuli also touch on self-regulated action, they generally fall beyond the scope of our discussion of self-regulation. Admittedly, the demarcation line between agentic and automatized behavior is somewhat arbitrary. At times we deviate from our own definition to address unconscious processes related to self-regulation; automatized behaviors do not necessarily represent "intentional" actions but are still highly germane to this chapter. These deviations are limited and only provide theoretical junctures to which other theories of regulated behavior can be synthesized.

Action Theory

Action theory is more aptly considered as a broad metatheoretical stance. It has pervasively influenced many other theories but makes no distinctly testable hypotheses on its own. All action theories recognize the importance of an individual's actions and his or her control of them. They emphasize that some aspect of behavioral action plays a major role in both theory and hypothesis testing. Although metatheoretical approaches such as action theory somewhat betray the conventional definitions of a theory, a metatheoretical approach does help to clarify how various action-control approaches are inherently related and highlights the breadth of an action-theoretical perspective. In this regard, an action-theoretical approach influences much of the work on self-regulation either implicitly or explicitly.

Action theories make two major assumptions relevant to self-regulation. First, humans are intrinsically driven to produce behavior–event contingencies (Heckhausen & Schulz, 1995; see also White, 1959). In other words, self-regulated behavior aims to influence the environment in some predictable way. Predictably altering the environment to meet one's goals is also considered primary control because it is the primary mechanism of goal achievement (Heckhausen & Schulz, 1995). Primary control can also be considered assimilative (e.g., Brandtstädter & Renner, 1990) because it is the mechanism by which individuals assimilate the environment to their goals.

Action theories also assume humans negatively perceive restrictions and reductions to their ability to produce behavior–event contingencies (Heckhausen & Schulz, 1995). Human behavior is prone to failure and is inherently restricted by resource availability, however. Heckhausen and Schulz (1995) posited the idea of secondary control to buffer inevitable losses and restrictions to primary control. Secondary control facilitates current and future primary control by changing the individual internally. Selecting a limited subset of goals from all possible goals or redefining goals in the face of failure are both instances of secondary control. Secondary control can also be considered accommodative (e.g., Brandtstädter & Renner, 1990) because it accommodates an organism to its environment.

According to the model of primary and secondary control (Heckhausen & Schulz, 1995), the purpose of self-regulation is therefore to influence one's environment such that goals can be achieved. External actions can be performed to alter the environment (primary control), or action can be directed internally to buffer against negative outcomes (secondary control).

Types of Action Theories

Action theories incorporate a wide variety of perspectives, each emphasizing one or several of action's many components. Some theories emphasize structuralist conceptions of action (e.g., Boesch, 1991; Piaget, 1952), whereas others focus variously on the motivation of action (e.g., Eccles, 1983; Metcalfe & Mischel, 1999; Ryan & Deci, 2002), the influence of culture (e.g., Vygotsky, 1978), or the role of previous experience on action choice (e.g., Eccles, 1983). Although a majority of action theories defy categorical definition, Brandtstädter (1998, 2006) classified four archetypal forms of action theories (structural, control-system, motivational, and social-constructivist). We next present each type and discuss how action is emphasized within it.

Structural Structural theories, as the label implies, emphasize the structural components of action, but "structural components" can mean many things. For example, Piaget's theory (1952) focuses on the formal structure of actions and the cognitive operations that underlie them (Brandtstädter, 2006). Structural theorists might approach self-regulation, for instance, by detailing how the processes of assimilation and accommodation result in action schemas that are activated or inhibited by the self.

We expand the definition of the structural approach to include cognitive–developmental theories. Such theories often center on the development of executive function or on neurological development. In both instances, self-regulation is a product of integrating lower order components of cognition or action. The proposed development of temperamental effortful control is a prime example of a structural approach to the development of self-regulation as we define it. Although a property of temperament, effortful control is not a fully articulated process at birth. Effortful control begins as "orienting regulation" in young infants (Garstein & Rothbart, 2003) and becomes truly effortful only after the development of willfully directed attention (an underlying structural component). After effortful control emerges as an articulated process, it becomes a key structural feature of self-regulation.

Another example comes from explanations of the A not B error seen in infants. In the A not B task infants watch as a toy is hidden in one of two identical wells. Infants generally reach for the correct well the first time they see the toy hidden. If on a subsequent trial the toy is hidden in the other of the two wells, however, infants still tend to reach for the toy in the first location. This error occurs despite the fact that the infant watched as the toy was hidden in the new location (e.g., Diamond, 1985). Correct responding in the A not B paradigm is thought to require a certain degree of working memory and the ability to inhibit a dominant response. Both underlying properties are mediated by development in the frontal lobes (Diamond, 1985, 1988; Diamond & Goldman-Racik, 1989).

Control System Control-system theories also focus on the structure of action but draw more heavily from cybernetics and systems theories (e.g., Carver & Scheier, 1981; Mischel & Shoda, 1995; Norman & Shallice, 1986). Control-system approaches explicate the internal dynamics of action. They often rely on the use of hierarchically organized feedback loops that help move a person successively closer to goal attainment. Put simply, a person iteratively compares his or her current state with one or several hypothetical goal states, performing some sort of action meant to reduce the discrepancy between iterations. If an action reduces the discrepancy, it continues. Otherwise, the action is terminated and replaced by a new one.

Compared with structural theories, control-system approaches are better suited to allow actions to influence subsequent behavior. Action is generally considered an integral part of a larger feedback loop. Control-system theories also diverge in the explicit role of self-regulation; control-system approaches often emphasize how actions are controlled to reach some specific goal. This emphasis can be construed as motivated self-regulation. Structural approaches, in contrast, are more descriptive of action, giving less attention to self-directed control.

Motivational Motivational approaches are often similar to expectancy–value models in which action is highly dependent on the expectancies and values of potential outcomes (e.g., Eccles, 1983; Wigfield & Eccles, 2000). In such models, an individual's reinforcement history and aspects of his or her self-efficacy combine to determine which actions are possible and which actions are most likely to result in preferred outcomes. Outcome preference is relative to the personal goals and motivations of the person performing the actions.

In the motivational family of theories, action is emphasized as both directed toward a desired outcome and as a determinant of future actions. Actions directed toward one goal have subsequent effects on future behavior. When the motivational approach is applied to self-regulation, it becomes clear that behavior is regulated by much more than will alone. Assume that one course of action (*a1*) is optimal for attaining some goal. A personal reinforcement history might oppose *a1* and instead promote an alternative response (*a2*). This opposition could arise because the person does not believe he or she is able to perform *a1* or believes that *a1* cannot result in the desired outcome. In either scenario, preference for *a2* is influenced by past action and influences future actions.

Social Constructivist Social constructivist approaches are the final subset of action-control theories and have arisen largely from the work of Vygotsky (1934/1962, 1978). These theories emphasize that action mediates between physical reality and personal consciousness. Social-constructivist theories simultaneously stress the importance of experience on the organization of thought. They emphasize action as a process that helps build a cognitive architecture by providing the individual with conceptualizations of objects, tools, and symbols.

When applied specifically to the study of self-regulation, social-constructivist theories emphasize the importance of objects and symbols with high cultural importance. Objects and symbols help direct behavior in socially expected ways. Regulating behavior in this manner allows individuals to assimilate social norms readily and directs children's attention to the scaffolds provided by older members of society.

Section Summary

The various subtypes of action theories are united in seeing the reasons for and outcomes of *actions* as the cornerstone human behavior. From an action-theoretical perspective, all actions are behaviors but not all behaviors are actions. Action requires meaningful execution of behavior by the self. Although individual theories can be classified solely as representing one subtype of action theory or another, most action-theoretical approaches are not easily classifiable and may span two or more subdomains. We next describe an organizing heuristic that integrates the various action-theoretical approaches. Our heuristic provides a general account of self-regulation that frames a discussion of its development across the life span.

AN ORGANIZING HEURISTIC

Our heuristic clarifies the organization of the action-theoretical views just presented. By expanding the structural theories to emphasize the basic cognitive structure underlying self-regulation, our heuristic allows a hierarchical organization of the action theory subtypes (see Figure 5.1). In our hierarchy, each tier represents self-regulation at a specific level of abstraction, with other levels informing that tier's function. The social-constructivist view is incorporated as a global influence that simultaneously affects all other levels.

A more concrete approach to our heuristic emphasizes two levels of magnification. At the macroscopic level, a person is described as iteratively processing and responding to environmental information (see Figure 5.2). At this level, the individual encodes information from his or her current environment (situation), which is then processed by a system of cognitive and affective schemas and structures (the *cognitive–affective processing system*, e.g., Mischel & Ayduk, 2004; Mischel & Shoda, 1995). The cognitive–affective processing system then produces behavior, which alters the situation and influences external observers. The behavior's influence on observers further influences the situation, which is then reanalyzed. Biological and sociohistorical influences affect processing at all stages.

A more microscopic view of our heuristic details how processing within the cognitive–affective processing system occurs. As discussed by Mischel and colleagues

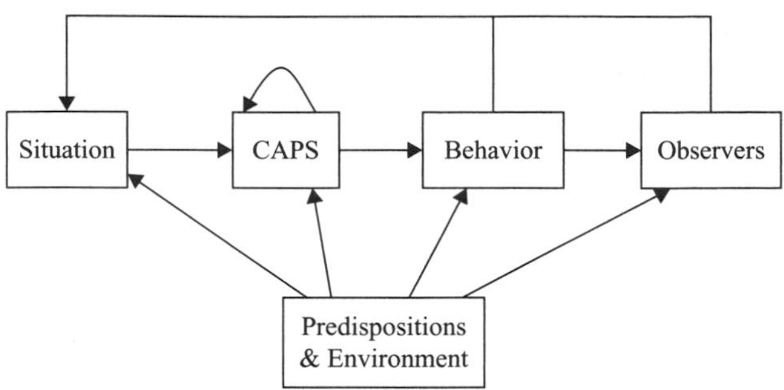

Figure 5.2. The Behavioral System of a Cognitive-Affective Processing System Approach. CAPS is the cognitive-affective processing system. *Source:* Adapted from Mischel & Shoda, 1999.

(e.g., Metcalfe & Mischel, 1999; Mischel & Ayduk, 2004; Mischel & Shoda, 1995), a cognitive–affective processing system is an architecture of informational and emotional–motivational units. These are called cool nodes and hot spots, respectively (see Figure 5.3). In our instantiation of a cognitive–affective processing system, external cues activate cool nodes, which in turn pass activation on to motivational hot spots. Hot spots then initiate action schemas, which are themselves sets of hierarchically organized cool nodes. Upon activation, any given hot spot will pass activation on to several possible action schemas. Selection of a schema is influenced by the expectancy that the schema can be successfully completed and on the overall value that completing the schema is likely to provide (e.g., Eccles, 1983). Polyvalent schemas (i.e., that work toward multiple goals) are preferred over schemas that serve only a single goal, for instance. Schemas then produce behavior, with their progress monitored by a motivational unit.

In the remainder of this chapter, we describe the details of our heuristic, discussing the development of self-regulation by focusing on the developmental features of

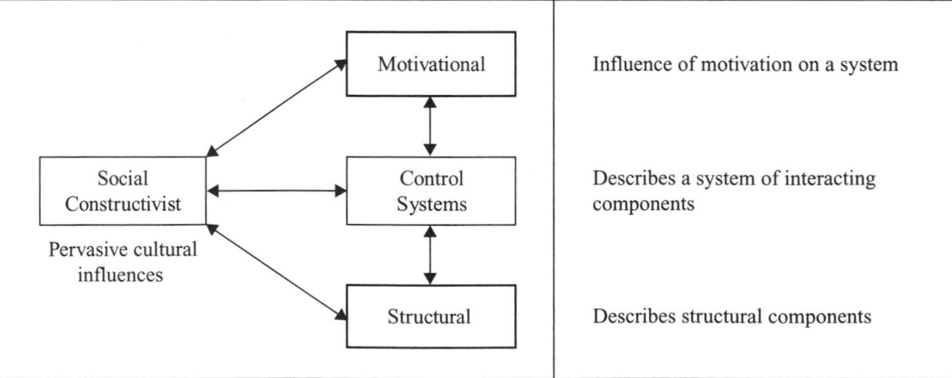

Figure 5.1 A hierarchy of action-control theories of self-regulation.

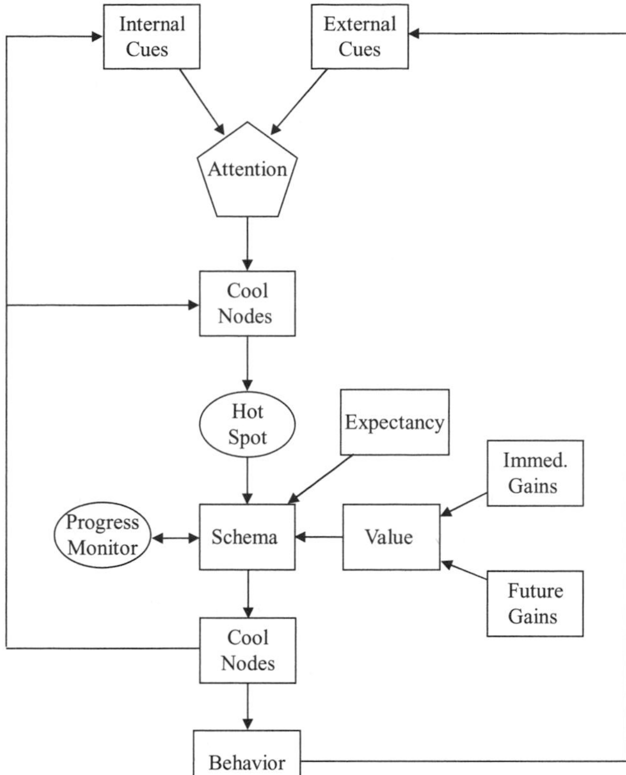

Figure 5.3. An organizing heuristic for the structures and elements of self-regulation.

Note: All components and connections are influenced by the context in which they are imbedded.

the heuristic's key components. Guided by our parameterization of Brandtstädter's four types of action theories, we discuss our heuristic from the bottom up. We first approach the structural basis of self-regulation, followed by the control-system organization to which it gives rise. We then discuss the motivational aspects of self-regulation that the control-systems organization allows for. Finally, we discuss the influence of social constructivist theories. To emphasize the importance of a life-span approach, however, we first discuss the impact of self-regulation across development.

The Importance of Self-Regulation across Development

Hierarchically organized goals serve as guidelines for intentional self-development, which in turn organizes behavior (e.g., Brandtstädter, 1989, 2006). Goal hierarchies also foster the transition from goal to action, allowing for successful goal attainment. Higher order goals are decomposed into smaller and more concrete units, which are then enacted or pursued. Reflecting the importance of self-regulation for goal attainment, studies often find that greater self-regulation is associated with positive developmental outcomes.

The developmental literature is rich in findings that associate positive outcomes with self-regulation. For instance, work by Mischel and colleagues shows a distinct relationship between preschoolers' ability to delay gratification and positive outcomes later in life. In the delay of gratification task, children are asked to choose between waiting for a preferable reward and immediately receiving a less-preferable reward (e.g., Mischel, Shoda, & Rodriguez, 1989). If they choose to wait, children can receive the less preferable reward at any time and end the task. Children who show a greater ability to delay their gratification show greater levels of ego resilience and academic, social, and coping competence during adolescence (Mischel, Shoda, & Peake, 1988). Preschoolers who could better delay in conditions requiring the spontaneous ideation of delay strategies when rewards were present were also better regulated as adolescents and scored higher on the SAT (Shoda, Mischel, & Peake, 1990).

A greater ability to delay gratification in preschool may also serve a protective function. Preschool delay ability largely buffers negative developmental outcomes for adults displaying high rejection sensitivity, for instance. Among adults with high rejection sensitivity, those who could better delay gratification as preschoolers showed greater positive functioning, were more educated, and were less likely to use hard drugs (i.e., crack or cocaine; Ayduk et al., 2000).

Work by Little and colleagues has shown strong relationships between scholastic achievement and higher levels of control expectancy and agency. Control expectancy and agency are both components of self-regulation. *Control expectancy* refers to the belief that a goal can be reached, whereas *agency* refers to the belief that a specific means can be successfully implemented. Although somewhat moderated by cultural factors (e.g., Little & Lopez, 1997), the relationships among agency, control expectancy, and academic performance have been universally positive (Little, Lopez, Oettingen, & Baltes, 2001; Little, Stetsenko, & Maier, 1999). Further, the positive relationship between agency and academic performance may be reciprocal. In one study, children's agency for their own abilities was positively related to academic performance at the end of the school year. School performance then predicted measures of agency obtained during the next school year (Little et al., 1999). Agency also mediates between Deci and Ryan's (e.g., Ryan & Deci, 2002) concepts of intrinsic, identified, and introjected motivation and academic performance (Walls & Little, 2005).

Aspects of self-regulation are further associated with subjective well-being in adults. Commitment to personal goals leads to increased subjective well-being when goal attainability is high. The inverse is true for goals with low attainability (Brunstein, 1993). Likewise, Emmons (1986) has shown that having goals with high personal value, putting effort into goals, and measures of previous goal attainment are all associated with positive affect. Having goals with a low probability of success and having goals about which the actor has low perceived control over or is ambivalent about is associated with negative affect.

Self-regulation is especially related to positive outcomes in older adults (e.g., Wrosch, Dunne, Scheier, & Schultz, 2006). Aspects of goal selection and attainment are positively related to aging satisfaction and well being (Freund & Baltes, 1998; Jopp & Smith, 2006). Personal control over development and subjective developmental attainment are both negatively related to older adults' depressive outlook for personal development (Brandtstädter, 1989).

Because self-regulation is clearly a construct with lifelong effects, it is important to understand its development across the life span. We now implement our heuristic model to organize a discussion of the development of self-regulation, guided by Brandtstädter's four action theory types.

Structural Approaches: Based on Cognitive Neuroscience

Structural action theories attempt to explain the structure and operations necessary for action. Defined as the agentic control of behavior, self-regulated action is fully mediated by executive function. Executive function is itself mediated by neural pathways. Thus, we present the cognitive and neural underpinnings of self-regulation before moving to more classic action-theoretical approaches. Although the cognitive neuroscience of self-regulation is detailed more explicitly by Lewis et al. (Chapter 3, this volume), a general overview of structural theories from a cognitive standpoint is necessary for the completeness of our discussion.

Executive Function

Executive function underlies higher-order cognitive processes in general and is related to self-regulation in particular. There are several underlying components of executive function, and we present the functions of attention, inhibition, long-term memory, and working memory. These components are all intrinsically related to self-regulation.

Attention Executive function is a critical component of self-regulation (Gestsdóttir & Lerner, 2008), and attention may be its most important aspect. Early in life, attention is largely driven by exogenous (i.e., stimulus-based) influences but eventually grows to include the volitionally controlled direction, inhibition, and shifting of attentional focus (see Colombo, 2001; Colombo & Cheatham, 2006). Attention directs the self toward relevant environmental stimuli (James, 1890) and facilitates their detection (Posner & Petersen, 1990; Posner & Raichle, 1994).

As shown more clearly in Figure 5.3, Attention is the lynchpin of self-regulation as we have defined it. Without the ability to direct attention purposefully and intentionally, behavior would be unregulated by the conscious self. The link between voluntary attention and aspects of self-regulation is also supported in the literature; attention plays important roles in both emotional and behavioral regulation. Orienting attention away from aversive stimuli can reduce children's distress levels, for example (Calkins & Johnson, 1998; Harman, Rothbart, & Posner, 1997). In the delay of gratification task, children who are either distracted (i.e., attention is removed from the rewards) or direct their attention to nonmotivating aspects of a reward (e.g., its shape) display increased delay compared with control groups (e.g., Mischel & Moore, 1973).

Early-developing forms of attention are directed by external, as opposed to endogenous, cues (Posner & Rothbart, 1998) and are therefore largely reactive. Earlier forms of attention are therefore not self-regulated in an endogenous sense. These early forms of attention instead develop to give rise to willed attention and control. Colombo and colleagues (e.g., Colombo, 2001; Colombo & Cheatham, 2006) detailed the emergence and development of fully endogenous (self-controlled) attention. In the next sections, we present an overview of the development of volitional attention and its precursors (arousal, orienting, and attention to object features) as discussed by Colombo (e.g., 2001).

Arousal: Even the most rudimentary and exogenously driven forms of attention require that infants first achieve and maintain a state of arousal.[2] In fact, several neural pathways arising from the brainstem, thought to induce an aroused state, are implicated in attention (Robbins, 1998). A newborn human infant spends less than 20% of its time in an aroused–wakeful state, with arousal increasing over the first weeks of development (Wolff, 1965; see also Colombo & Horowitz, 1987). The ability to attain an aroused state therefore represents one of the first substrates of self-regulation to develop.

[2] Here arousal describes an alert state. This should not be confused with the negative arousal described by Kopp (1982), which describes a state of uneasiness.

Orienting: Orienting attention toward objects or locations is a unique component of attention (Posner & Petersen, 1990) and underlies self-regulation. In our heuristic, attention mediates between the external environment and internal processing. Purposeful mediation by attention requires that individuals orient attention to specific components of the environment or the self to modulate an otherwise environmentally determined course of action. The ability to orient attention is subserved by two primary behaviors: orienting to objects and disengaging attention from objects. Both develop in early infancy.

Smooth pursuit and saccades both orient attention to objects and are present early in life (Shea & Aslin, 1990). Smooth pursuit continues to develop over the first few months (von Hofsten & Rosander, 1997). Although these behaviors may at first glance appear to be self-regulatory in nature, orienting in very young infants is predominantly driven by external stimuli and is not self-directed as we have defined self-regulation to be. Self-regulation requires an effortful component.

The ability to disengage attention is the other key component of orienting. If attention remains fixed on an initial stimulus, reorienting becomes difficult if not impossible. Similar to orienting behavior, the ability to disengage attention is present in very young infants (Csibra, Tucker, & Johnson, 1998; Matsuzawa & Shimojo, 1997) and develops rapidly over the first few months of life (Johnson, Posner, & Rothbart, 1991; Matsuzawa & Shimojo, 1997). Disengagement is therefore another early developing component of attention that underlies orienting.

Object-related processes: Attention to specific object features and to clusters of features that distinguish objects has strong implications for the arrangement of units in the cognitive affective processing system. If features are haphazardly associated with latent concepts, the system becomes incapable of streamlined processing. Furthermore, attention to object features allows differentiation between similar yet functionally unique aspects of the environment. Although very young infants are capable of processing basic visual information, research suggests that features are processed individually early in life. Infants are able to process multidimensional stimuli as conjunctive units by the fourth or fifth month (Bushnell & Roder, 1985; Dannemiller & Braun, 1988; Mundy, 1985).

Endogenous attention: The early components of attention develop into rudimentarily functional forms by or around the sixth month. This timeframe is also when the precursory building blocks of endogenous (i.e., self-directed) attention begin to emerge (e.g., Colombo, 2001; Johnson, 1995; Johnson, Posner, & Rothbart, 1994; Richards, 1989). The joint development of the three attentional systems then allows endogenous attention to emerge in its most rudimentary form toward the end of the first year. This primordial aspect of endogenous attention is also related to other advances in language and higher order cognition at that time. Although primordial forms of endogenous attention may be seen late in the first year, it emerges more fully in the second year.

Attentional modulation of emotion: Empirical research examining emotion modulation in infants generally supports the idea that self-regulation develops by the end of the first year. At that time, infants regulate their arousal using two distinct methods. They can initiate behaviors to modulate their own arousal, or they can call on adult caregivers for comfort (see, e.g., the Infant Regulatory Scoring System; Weinberg & Tronick, 1994). Stifter and colleagues similarly describe infant regulation in terms of reorienting, nonnegative vocalizations, self-comforting, avoidance, and looking to an experimenter (Stifter & Braungart, 1995; see also Stifter & Spinrad, 2002). Our present discussion focuses on arousal modulation. We reserve our review of infant–parent interactions for the later consideration of social-constructivist theories.

Orienting attention away from aversive stimuli is one way that infants self-regulate arousal (Harman et al., 1997; Weinberg & Tronick, 1994). Volitional reorienting requires endogenous attention. As noted earlier, the emergence of endogenous attention begins late in the first year (Colombo & Cheatham, 2006; Rothbart, Ziaie, & O'Boyle, 1992) and may also explain an increased use of self-distraction and self-soothing between 6 and 12 months (Manglesdorf, Shapiro, & Marzolf, 1995). Self-soothing behaviors correlate with higher levels of executive attention (Sheese, Rothbart, Posner, White, & Fraundorf, 2008) and are another way infants can modulate negative arousal (e.g., Rothbart et al., 1992). Self-soothing redirects attention to calming behaviors created by and directed toward the self. Self-soothing emerges in the first year (Kopp, 1982; Mangelsdorf et al., 1995; Rothbart et al., 1992). Infants, for instance, might modulate their emotions through thumb sucking, which in early infancy can modulate arousal, but we argue that it only becomes truly self-regulating with the emergence of endogenous attention. Before attention and behavior become endogenous, arousal modulation is more reactive than purposefully enacted.

Self-regulation in toddlerhood is directly tied to mechanisms of attention. Calkins and Johnson (1998), for instance, measured 2-year-olds' reaction to and regulation of distress. Regulation of distress was indicated by children orienting their attention to their mothers, self-distraction, constructive coping, and aggression-venting. The first three were predicted to be indicators of successful regulation, and the last was hypothesized to be an indicator of poor regulatory ability. As hypothesized, displays of frustration were positively related to aggression-venting, indicating that children who show high levels of aggression also poorly modulate their frustration. Further, the inverse was also found: all other self-regulatory behaviors were negatively related to displays of frustration. Work by Kochanska and colleagues supports the relationship between attention-based self-regulation and emotion control in very young children. In their study, effortful control was associated with less intense anger in 22- and 33-month-olds. Effortful control was also associated with less intense anger and joy in 33-month-olds, further indicating emotion-modulation (Kochanska, Murray, & Harlan, 2000).

Inhibition Inhibition is a component of executive function that is deeply connected to self-regulation. The very act of inhibiting implies that behavior has been regulated. Indeed, self-regulation (effortful control) has been defined as "the ability to inhibit a dominant response to perform a subdominant response" (Rothbart & Bates, 1998, p. 137). Inhibition is a principal factor measured by several self-regulation tasks (e.g., Gerstadt, Hong, & Diamond, 1994; Stroop, 1935). Such tasks require one to inhibit automatic responses and replace them with ones that are less salient. In the delay-of-gratification paradigm (e.g., Mischel et al., 1989), for example, children are asked to inhibit their urge to receive an immediate but small reward to obtain a greater reward in the future.

Inhibition plays a major role in motivational theories of self-regulated behavior. Many theories of motivation (e.g., Gray, 1981) have incorporated systems to allow motivators to inhibit initial urges and clear the way for goal-directed behavior. Likewise, inhibition is incorporated into theories that describe the maintenance of goal-directed behavior (Velig & van Knippenberg, 2006). Theories of goal shielding, for example, assert that inhibition must be present to both initiate specific self-regulated behaviors and limit the salience of secondary or novel goals that might compete with active ones (Shah, Friedman, & Kruglanski, 2002). In support of this idea, Velig and van Knippenberg (2006) found longer response times to goal-interfering stimuli than to goal-relevant or control stimuli. Goal-interfering stimuli required more processing and, implicitly, greater inhibition.

Development of inhibition: Children are able to attend willfully to stimuli and are able to modulate their own emotions toward the end of infancy. Endogenous attention and emotion modulation certainly qualify as self-regulation, although they somewhat lack the motivational luster often attributed to self-regulation in older children and adults. Infants might attend to stimuli on the basis of their own interests or regulate their emotions to avoid experiencing negative affect. More mature forms of self-regulation center explicitly on goal attainment and often require inhibition. Children inhibit their behavior to obtain a preferred reward in the delay-of-gratification task, for instance (Mischel & Moore, 1973).

Children show little evidence of intentional inhibitory control before 3 years (Posner & Rothbart, 1998), although there appears to be a link between earlier sustained attention and later forms of self-regulation. Endogenous attention continues to develop throughout the third year and shows a jump in development around 30 months (Posner & Rothbart, 1998). The leap in endogenous attention coincides with increases in effortful control and increased performance on conflict tasks between 24 and 36 months (Gerardi-Caulton, 2000; Rothbart, Ellis, Rueda, & Posner, 2003). Conflict tasks require inhibition, and performance on conflict tasks continues to develop throughout early childhood (Diamond & Taylor, 1996; Gerstadt et al., 1994; Reed, Pien, & Rothbart, 1984).

The development of inhibition is also indicated by young children's ability to attend to multiple facets of a situation. Behavior that requires processing multiple dimensions requires the inhibition of dominant responses activated by a single salient dimension. The inability to process multiple dimensions simultaneously reflects the Piagetian preoperational stage in which children cannot conserve measures of liquid, distinguish reality from appearance, or compare old ideas with new ones (see Diamond & Taylor, 1996). Like more direct measures of error detection and conflict processing, multidimensional processing begins to make gains around the third year.

Behavioral control and compliance both emerge during the third year (Kopp, 1989), and effortful control (which also requires inhibition and attention) develops throughout the toddler and preschool years (Kochanska et al., 2000; Kochanska, Tjebkes, & Forman, 1998). By 33 months, measures of effortful control have consolidated into a single definable construct that is moderately stable across time and is predictable by measures of self-regulation. Effortful control becomes more stable by 45 months. Early effortful control is itself predicted by focused attention during infancy (Kochanska et al., 2000).

The development of inhibition continues throughout early childhood. Switching between two incompatible rules is easier for 5-year-olds than 3-year-olds (Zelazo & Jacques, 1996), for example. Children younger than 3 often fail to report observed errors in dimension-change tasks (Jacques, Zelazo, Kirkham, & Semcesen, 1999), despite being able to detect errors made in unidimensional tasks such as tower construction (e.g., Bullock & Lütkenhaus, 1988). Children younger than 6 also have trouble detecting two separate stimuli when different parts of their body (e.g., face and arm) are touched simultaneously (Fink & Bender, 1953).

In a Simon Says–type paradigm, children are told to follow directions given by one puppet but to ignore (inhibit) directions given by a second puppet. In this task, children show increased reaction times to trials that follow an error between 36 and 44 months (Backen Jones, Rothbart, & Posner, 2003; Posner & Rothbart, 1998; Reed et al., 1984). Increased reaction times are taken to indicate greater error processing. Older preschoolers similarly perform better than younger preschoolers on go–no go and other inhibition tasks (Gerstadt et al., 1994; Livesey & Morgan, 1991), are less distractible, and are capable of ignoring some distractors altogether (Kannass & Colombo, 2007). Older preschoolers are also better able to adapt to rule changes (Zelazo & Jacques, 1996), even if changing rules does not require a different motor response (Jacques et al., 1999). These developments indicate increased inhibition between 3 and 5 years.

Toddlers and preschoolers also develop the ability to delay gratification, such as that seen in Mischel's classic delay of gratification task (Mischel & Moore, 1973). The ability to delay behaviors emerges by 18 months and improves throughout the second and third years (Vaughn, Kopp, & Krakow, 1984; Vaughn, Krakow, Kopp, Johnson, & Schwartz, 1986).

The developmental trend established for the cognitive substrates of self-regulation in early childhood continues into middle childhood with an emphasis on the development of inhibition. By the end of middle childhood, the development of inhibition has largely plateaued, with development in late childhood and adolescence more reflective of fine-tuning than the drastic growth seen at earlier ages.

As already stated, inhibition is needed to examine multiple aspects of a situation simultaneously. Inhibition is therefore also implicated in older children's successful social interaction. Inhibition is required for children to determine the mental state of their peers and to compare peers' mental states with their own (e.g., false-beliefs tasks, Leslie & Polizzi, 1998; theory of mind, Carlson & Moses, 2001). Inhibition is also required for successful emotion regulation during social interactions, which correlates with social competence (Hay, Payne, & Chadwick, 2004). Emotion regulation has important implications for social development throughout childhood and beyond. Self-regulation clearly correlates with children's social and emotional development (J. E. Bates, Bayles, Bennet, Ridge, & Brown, 1991; Eisenberg, Fabes, Guthrie, et al., 1996; Eisenberg, Fabes, Karbon, et al., 1996; Eisenberg et al., 1997; Masten & Coatsworth, 1998; Nigg, Quamma, Greenberg, & Kusché, 1999; see also Thorell, Bohlin, & Rydell, 2004). Prior measures of self-regulation predict first graders' emotion knowledge (Schultz, Izard, Ackerman, & Youngstrom, 2001), and inhibition negatively predicts concurrent and longitudinal measures of non-cooperative behavior in a sample of 7- to 11-year olds (Ciairano, Visu-Petra, & Settani, 2007).

Although inhibition largely reaches mature levels by the end of childhood, performance on more complex tasks continues to increase throughout adolescence and into early adulthood (Daniel, Pelote, & Lewis, 2000; Hooper, Luciana, Conklin, & Yarger, 2004; Lin, Chen, Yang, Hsiao, & Tien, 2000). Adults outperform adolescents on several inhibition-related tasks. Adults are more accurate on go–no-go tasks, and make fewer errors on tasks that involve rule switching (Rubia et al., 2006).

Long-Term Memory Memory might seem somewhat removed from the processes that underlie volitional action, but long-term memory influences and is influenced by self-regulation. Long-term memory provides important information that helps determine the optimal path for goal attainment. Retaining that a particular action has not been successful in the past may lead to a choice not to pursue that action or to qualify its use strongly. Long-term memory also mediates the role of attention on self-regulation by directing attention toward stimuli that were previously relevant in similar situations. Indeed, the choice of appropriate path(s) to problem solving as informed by long-term memory may be one definition of strategic behavior. Long-term memory is in turn affected by attentional and self-regulated processes. Goal-relevant cues are often encoded and stored for later retrieval.

Several theories of self-regulation require the assistance of long-term memory, especially motivational action theories. Eccles and colleagues (e.g., Eccles, 1983), for example, have approached behavior as a function of expectancies and values associated with behavior completion. As discussed earlier, expectancy–value theories see the selection of an action as a function of its expected probability of success and the value of obtaining the desired outcome. Information stored in long-term memory informs an action's expectancy and value attributions, providing a connection between memory stores and self-regulated goal selection. The connection between memory stores and behavior is also present in theories that incorporate action schemas. Piaget, for instance, saw behavior as a series of assimilated schemas that are accommodated to an individual's environment. The ability to enact a schema is fully moderated by the ability to store and retrieve it from memory. Norman and Shallice's (1986) influential model of self-regulation takes a similar approach.

Working Memory Working memory and self-regulation implicitly go hand in hand, and many measures of self-regulation also require working memory. These tasks require participants, often children, to inhibit an initial response to follow some set rule (e.g., Cameron Ponitz et al., 2008; Diamond & Taylor, 1996; Gerstadt et al., 1994; Stroop, 1935). When participants are able to both hold a rule in working memory and apply it to a situation, the resultant behavior is self-regulated.

Empirical studies also support a link among working memory, executive function, and self-regulation in adults. Inhibition positively correlates with working memory (Lehto, Juujärvi, Kooistra, & Pulkkinen, 2003; Stevens, Quittner, Zuckerman, & Moore, 2002), and working memory is positively correlated with attention shifting, an aspect of self-regulation (Lehto et al., 2003). Working memory capacity has been identified as a primary contributor to individual differences in executive attention (Engle, 2002). Ego depletion (in which the self-regulatory mechanism is fatigued, e.g., Schmeichel & Baumeister, 2004) also leads to a subsequent decrease in working memory (Schmeichel, 2007).

Working memory therefore influences self-regulated behavior, but its influence may be more proximal. Working memory allows the self to monitor the moment-to-moment steps that lead to the immediate or imminent attempts to attain a goal. The combination and integration of attention, long-term memory, and working memory may be thought of as the underlying components of an executive system that can use current or past information to guide action toward an optimal resolution. In other words, it is a system capable of regulating behavior toward personal goals. During this synthesis, novel information is assimilated, and the schemas called from long-term memory are accommodated to better match the individual's experience.

Cognitive Decline Cognitive decline during old age has implications for many of the cognitive substrates underlying self-regulation. For instance, fluid cognitive abilities peak in the mid-20s with a gradual decline into old age (e.g., P. B. Baltes, Staudinger, & Lindenberger, 1999). Crystallized abilities remain stable and can possibly increase until very old age (e.g., P. B. Baltes et al., 1999; Beier & Ackerman, 2005). In terms of our heuristic, the cognitive–affective architecture can be seen as crystallized, whereas modulation through attention is fluid. Cognitive decline has also been linked to decreases in processing speed (Park et al., 1996; Salthouse, 1996; see also Li et al., 2004), decreased working memory (Park et al., 1996), and a decreased ability to filter irrelevant stimuli in the environment (inhibition; see Hasher & Zacks, 1988; Hasher, Zacks, & May, 1999), all of which relate to self-regulation in our heuristic.

Neural Substrates

Any theoretical account of self-regulation will benefit from at least a basic understanding of the neurological pathways associated with the executive functions that mediate regulated behavior. Understanding the brain regions that must be coordinated to regulate behavior can provide added support for theoretically sound arguments and also foster the generation of new ideas. We discuss the neuroanatomy of two brain regions (prefrontal cortex, anterior cingulate cortex) and their involvement in self-regulation. Our discussion is not a comprehensive overview but instead is meant to give a general understanding of the how the development of particular brain areas is related to understanding the development of self-regulation across the life span. A sizable percentage of the references in this section refer to work done with nonhuman primates but reflect how the field currently views the anatomy and function of the human brain.

Prefrontal Cortex The prefrontal cortex is particularly associated with self-regulation. Input from several lower order brain systems terminate in the frontal lobes, facilitating intersystem communication (see Colombo & Cheatham, 2006, for a brief discussion). Because of their location and role in cross-communication, the frontal lobes are readily able to modulate (i.e., regulate) neural processes.

The prefrontal cortex receives a great deal of input from the thalamus (Barbas, Henion, & Dermon, 1991), and sensory information via the parietal lobe (Chavis & Pandya, 1976). Output from the prefrontal cortex is directed to midbrain structures, such as the thalamus and hypothalamus (Fuster, 1997; Siwek & Pandya, 1991), and indirectly reaches the motor cortex (J. F. Bates & Goldman-Racik, 1993; Lu, Preston, & Strick 1994). The prefrontal cortex is therefore implicated in pathways that translate sensory input into action and is in direct communication with the diencephalon, which plays a role in autonomic regulation.

The prefrontal cortex has two major circuits: an executive dorsolateral circuit and a motivational ventral circuit (Banfield, Wyland, Macrae, Münte, & Heatherton, 2004). The dorsolateral prefrontal cortex receives information about gaze direction from the parietal lobe (Andersen, 1989) and projects output to the premotor and oculomotor cortices (Passingham, 1993). The dorsolateral portion of the prefrontal cortex is involved in the selection and initiation of actions (Spence & Frith, 1999) and with working memory. The dorsolateral circuit is especially implicated in executive processes such as attention shifting, selective attention, planning, choice, and working memory functions (Banfield et al., 2004). These connections suggest that the prefrontal cortex provides top-down input for task-relevant behavior (see also MacDonald, Cohen, Stenger, & Carter, 2000). As one indication of the role of the dorsolateral prefrontal cortex in self-regulation, studies show that lesioning the dorsolateral prefrontal cortex in primates results in behavior similar to that seen in children who persevere with the A not B error (Diamond, 1990; Diamond & Goldman-Rakic, 1989; see also Passingham, 1993).

Development of the Prefrontal Cortex The prefrontal cortex develops slowly throughout childhood and adolescence (Benes, 2001; Shonkoff & Phillips, 2000) and is implicated in aspects of children's self-regulation (Luciana & Nelson, 1998; Tsujimoto, Yamamoto, Kawaguchi, Koizumi, & Sawaguchi, 2004). The dorsolateral prefrontal cortex is especially linked to behavioral inhibition (Liddel, Kiehl, & Smith, 2001; Tamm, Menon, & Reiss, 2002), and vicariously to endogenous attention. Performance on tasks that involve the dorsolateral prefrontal cortex primarily develop until a child is approximately 7 (e.g., continuous performance task, Kanaka et al., 2000), although later development does occur (e.g., Conners, Epstein, Angold, & Klaric, 2003).

The prefrontal cortex matures more slowly than other brain areas (Casey, Galvan, & Hare, 2005; Gogtay et al., 2004) and develops well into adolescence and early adulthood (Paus et al., 2001; Sowell, Thompson, Holmes, Jernigan, & Toga, 1999; Sowell, Thompson, Tessner, & Toga, 2001). Significant pruning and myelination occur in the prefrontal cortex during adolescence (Luna & Sweeney, 2001; Sowell et al., 1999; Sowell et al., 2001), which results in increased efficiency of brain systems (e.g., Luna & Sweeney, 2001). As will become apparent later, the foundations of self-regulation are largely in place by the onset of adolescence. Development during adolescence and adulthood reflect this increased efficiency as a fine-tuning of an already-present system.

The relative immaturity of the prefrontal cortex during adolescence may predispose adolescents to "dysregulated" or risky behaviors (discussed later). The ventral regions of the prefrontal cortex are especially implicated in self-regulation and development during adolescence. The ventromedial prefrontal cortex and its close associate, the orbital frontal cortex, develop well into the second decade (Segalowitz & Davies, 2004). Similarly, the ventrolateral prefrontal cortex shows signs of immaturity in adolescents as old as 17 (Crone, Donohue, Honomichl, Wendelkin, & Bunge, 2006). Both are related to direct measures of self-regulation. The ventrolateral prefrontal cortex is implicated in the ability to use rules (Brass et al., 2003; Bunge, 2004; Bunge, Kahn, Wallis, Miller, & Wagner, 2003) and is activated during the stop-signal task, which measures inhibition (Rubia et al., 2001). The orbital frontal cortex is implicated in processing reward–punishment information (Critchley, Mathias, & Dolan, 2001; Elliot, Dolan, & Frith, 2000; Elliot, Frith, & Dolan, 1997), and its volume has been positively correlated with measures of adolescent effortful control (Whittle et al., 2008).

Anterior Cingulate Cortex The anterior cingulate cortex interacts with the prefrontal cortex in regulating behavior (Gehring & Knight, 2000). It has been implicated in both emotional and behavioral regulation (Bush, Luu, & Posner, 2000) and in volitional attention (Posner & Rothbart, 1998). Three major brain areas are connected to the anterior cingulate cortex that likely relate to its ability to self-regulate. The anterior cingulate is connected to the motor cortex, the prefrontal cortex, and to the thalamus and brainstem. These connections indicate roles in behavior, cognitive processing, and motivation–arousability, respectively. The overlap of these functions is hypothesized to give rise to a system that is capable of willed control and translating intentions into action (Banfield et al., 2004; Paus, 2001).

The anterior cingulate cortex is also portrayed as an error or conflict-detection system. Activation of the anterior cingulate cortex appears in situations that potentially require conflict monitoring (Posner & Rothbart, 1998) and inhibition (Amodio, Master, Yee, & Taylor, 2008). The anterior cingulate is therefore implicated in actions that require the inhibition of environmentally prompted responses.

In a meta-analysis of anterior cingulate cortex activation studies, Bush et al. (2000) found that the anterior cingulate cortex is part of two competing systems: a dorsal division that involves cognitive processing and a rostral–ventral division that involves affect-related processes. These two systems have similar functions but activate (or deactivate) in response to different stimuli. The cognitive division is involved in error detection, complex or demanding tasks, and modulating the executive functions. The affective division is responsible for assessing the salience of motivating or emotional information and for emotional regulation (Bush et al., 2000). These two circuits compete such that activation of the logical circuit tends to suppress activation of the emotional circuit and vice versa (Bush et al., 2000; Drevets & Raichle, 1998). Their competition implies that the anterior cingulate cortex serves as a weighting mechanism that reweights emotional and cognitive stimuli differentially depending on the situation. These two regions are clearly implicated in the cognitive–affective processing system of regulation depicted in Figure 5.3.

Development of the Anterior Cingulate

The rapid growth of self-regulatory abilities beginning in the third year suggests physical growth in the brain areas related to inhibitory self-regulation. The dorsolateral prefrontal cortex is implicated in inhibition that is driven by memory-related processes (Diamond, 1988, 1990, 1991). Damage to this area results in inhibition errors in humans (Luria, 1973) and disrupts performance on the A not B task in monkeys (Diamond & Goldman-Rakic, 1989). The prefrontal cortex develops slowly throughout childhood and into adolescence (Benes, 2001; Shonkoff & Phillips, 2000).

The anterior cingulate is also implicated in tasks specifically targeting inhibition such as the Stroop task (MacDonald et al., 2000; Pardo, Pardo, Janer, & Raichle, 1990) and is related to control and conflict processing in adults (Bush et al., 2000; Fan, Flombaum, McCandliss, Thomas, & Posner, 2003; MacDonald et al., 2000). A leap in inhibitory ability during early childhood is therefore more likely due to development in the anterior cingulate. Indeed, the anterior cingulate has been linked to conflict tasks in children (Casey et al., 1997).

Diamond and colleagues (Diamond & Taylor, 1996; Gerstadt et al., 1994) found that preschool children make substantial strides on tasks that require inhibition, including the day–night task and an adaption of Luria's (1966) tapping task. In the day–night task, children must inhibit saying "night" when a picture of the moon is shown and instead say "day." The inverse holds for a picture of the sun. In the tapping task, children must tap a dowel twice each time the experimenter taps once, or tap once each time the experimenter taps twice. Both tasks require that children internalize a task-specific rule and inhibit a dominant response. In the day–night task, the dominant response is to say "day" to the sun card and "night" to the moon card. In the tapping task, the children must inhibit the urge to repeat what the experimenter is doing. Both tasks demonstrate continued improvement between 3.5 and 7 years, with initial jumps in performance occurring between 3.5 and 4 years. Development in these tasks implies a developmental trajectory for the anterior cingulate.

The anterior cingulate continues to develop during middle childhood and remains associated with conflict monitoring through adolescence and into adulthood (Casey et al., 1997). Scores on behavioral inhibition tasks such as the day–night and tapping tasks improve during early childhood but begin to asymptote by the time a child is 6 or 7 (Diamond & Taylor, 1996; Gerstadt et al., 1994). Tasks that measure children's ability to filter out task-conflicting information reflect a similar developmental trajectory (Rueda, Fan, et al., 2004; Trick & Enns, 1998). Results from the child version of Fan and colleagues' attention networks task (Fan, McCandliss, Sommer, Raz, & Posner, 2002) also show significant improvements in conflict monitoring between 6 and 7 years but little evidence of development between 7-year-olds and adults (Rueda, Fan, et al., 2004).

Summary of Structural Approaches

Structural action theories of self-regulation place explicit emphasis on regulation's structural components. By describing the brain areas and key aspects of cognitive functioning that mediate self-regulated behavior, we have attempted to build a structural perspective through which other theories of self-regulation can be assessed. In the next section, we move away from structural theories to discuss control-system action-theoretical approaches in which hypothetical systems are used to describe self-regulation. These theoretical approaches can accommodate what we know about the structural components of self-regulation, much as Norman and Shallice (1986) have done with their supervisory attentional system (discussed later).

Control-System Approaches

Control-system theories separate themselves slightly from the basic structural components of regulatory processes by assuming an unspecified set of lower order pieces come together to form various functional units. They make use of these functional units, hypothesizing which functions must be served and how the various functional pieces must interact. Control-system approaches therefore make broad hypotheses about self-regulation and rely on structural approaches to explicate the exact mechanisms that underlie the hypothesized processes. Although there are many important theories of self-regulation that could be categorized as control-system approaches, we limit our discussion to three well-known models: feedback loops, Norman and Shallice's schema activation model, and action-control beliefs.

Feedback Loops

Perhaps the control system account most readily associated with self-regulation is Carver and Scheier's (1981, 1990; see also Carver, 2004) approach to feedback loops. Feedback loops are not original to Carver and Scheier's work (e.g., Wiener, 1948), but they present a comprehensive system in which hierarchically arranged feedback loops influence thought and behavior at various levels of abstraction and whose overall function influences and is influenced by felt emotion. The design of these loops moves a person iteratively closer to some preselected goal state (i.e., regulates behavior toward goals). Each feedback loop contains four elements that are described in terms of their function. The form of these units is largely ignored.

The first necessary element of Carver and Scheier's model is the reference function, or the goal to which action is regulated. This goal can be dynamic, such as the continual desire to be a "good person," or can be static such as the goal to have a document completed by a certain date. Goals can be positive or negative, with positive goals drawing behavior toward them and negative goals (antigoals) repelling behavior away from them (Carver & Scheier, 1990). In either case, progress is monitored by comparing a person's current state with one of these types of goal.

A goal itself cannot direct behavior because goals are simply ideals. Just as a thermostat setting has no direct access to a system's heating and cooling elements, a goal has no direct access to behavior. The influence of the goal must be mediated by a second component, which Carver and Scheier call the comparator. The comparator contrasts current status with the reference function to determine which actions are optimal for goal achievement. In some instantiations (e.g., MacKay, 1966) the comparator is broken into two separate parts, one that serves as a store for potential actions (similar to a long-term memory store of action schemas), whereas the other activates appropriate behaviors based on the current state–reference function comparison. The comparator also plays a role in secondary loops that monitor the performance of primary loops. In the Carver and Scheier approach, secondary loops monitor the progress of goal attainment, comparing it with an expected rate of progress. When progress is unsatisfactory, these monitoring loops produce an emotional output that motivates behavior.

The comparator's function is fully dependant on the final two pieces of the feedback loop: input and output. Input is generally sensory and provides the comparator with information about the current status of the system. Sensory information allows a comparison to occur. The feedback loop is then closed by the output function, which, in terms of self-regulated behavior, is the behavior itself. The output from a given iteration of the feedback loop affects the input of the next iteration, which results in a new assessment by the comparator. The new assessment then enacts a new behavioral sequence, (a) ceasing action because the current state matches the reference function, (b) continuing with the current course of action, or (c) altering behavior in some way. Figure 5.4 presents a graphic representation in which the circular connection of functional elements is made more apparent.

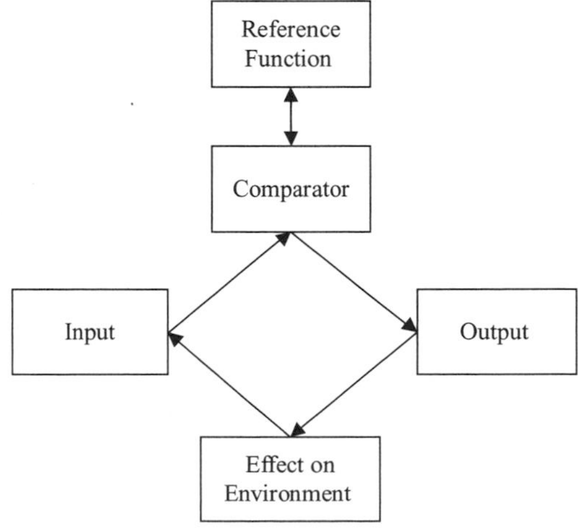

Figure 5.4. A feedback loop. *Source:* Adapted from Carver and Scheier, 2002.

Behavior is ill-described by a series of isolated feedback loops alone. Instead, the complex actions of an organism are better described by a set of hierarchically nested loops that influence behavior at various levels of abstraction. Carver and Scheier (1990) adopt Powers' (1973) approach to hierarchically arranged loops in which the output of one loop alters the reference function for a nested loop. Carver and Scheier discuss, for instance, three nested loops. At the highest (most abstract) level, the reference function is a hypothetical idealized self-image. The idealized image produces "output" in the form of various slightly less abstract things that a person should do to attain the idealized state. For instance, one should be kind. This output of "being kind" in turn serves as the reference function for another loop that outputs actions typifying a kind person. The output of a nested loop might be something like helping someone cross the road or shoveling snow off of a neighbor's walkway. In theory, the output of the lower tier loop should be specific actions reflecting assisting behavior or snow shoveling. Theoretically, these more concrete actions then serve as reference functions for even less abstract loops that specify specific motor output.

Although our overview of Carver and Scheier's more complex theory is cursory, the elements we present provide an example of how the control-system family of action theories can rely on structural components without specifying them. If structural-level work shows that a key element of the feedback loop hypothesis does not exist or does not behave as hypothesized, the control-system theory would be rendered inadequate or require an ancillary prediction correction. Control-systems theories therefore require verification by structural approaches.

Schema Activation

Like the feedback loop hypothesis, the view presented by Norman and Shallice (1986) falls heavily in the category of control-system theories. Their approach describes two interacting systems that regulate behavior by influencing schema activation. The Norman and Shallice model moonlights as a structural theory in that it makes explicit statements about the relationship between the higher and lower order processes involved in regulation (e.g., Cooper & Shallice, 2000) and openly predicts the brain area that provides willed control over the self-regulatory system (Norman & Shallice, 1986; Shallice & Burgess, 1996). Their theory also moonlights as a motivational approach in that it allows prior experiences and each person's unique interpretation of the environment to impact goal selection and schema activation. The Norman and Shallice (1986) model posits two systems that describe both consciously and automatically regulated behavior. By addressing both types of regulated behavior, their approach can account for common action slips and can be applied clinically (e.g., M. F. Schwartz et al., 1995).

Norman and Shallice's first system, the contention scheduling system (1986; Cooper & Shallice, 2000), is presented as a mechanistic setup in which action schemas are automatically activated to produce task-relevant behavior. Schemas are arranged hierarchically (similar to hierarchically arranged feedback loops) and represent behavior at various levels of abstraction (i.e., ranging from general abstraction to specific action). Although similar, schemas contain two components that distinguish them from feedback loops. These components help describe when and how schema activation occurs. Each schema has an internal activation threshold, which is the amount of schema activation necessary for a schema to be selected and implemented. Each activation threshold has an associated activation value, which represents the real-time degree of activation a schema is receiving. A schema is implemented when its activation value meets or exceeds its activation threshold. Surpassing the activation threshold results in either the activation of lower order schemas or in behavior itself. When two schemas require the same resources, they are hypothesized to inhibit each other laterally. Thus, activation of one schema can inhibit activation of other schemas requiring the same resources.

In their refinement of the original model, Cooper and Shallice (2000) described a variety of ways that schemas might be activated. The mechanisms of activation tend to fall along one of two orthogonal dimensions: vertical and horizontal. Vertical activation occurs when activation signals are passed down the schema hierarchy. Here, activation of a higher level schema sends activation signals to its subordinate schemas. The schema for a motor behavior, for example, should not activate until a higher schema dictates that it is appropriate. Horizontal activation arises as a direct response to environmental input. For instance, a person preparing a cup of coffee might activate a higher order schema that simply represents "obtain sugar." Several schemas can satisfy the needs of the "obtain sugar" schema (i.e., grab a sugar cube, open a sugar packet, spoon sugar from the sugar bowl). When only a sugar bowl is present, only the "spoon sugar from the sugar bowl" schema can receive enough horizontal activation to be implemented.

No higher order schema can be completed until all of its component schemas are complete, and these components are often ordered. Lower order schemas are normally ordered in some way, with the specific ordering arising from three sources (Cooper & Shallice, 1990). Ordering can be limited by the physical environment (e.g., you have to have a tool in your hand before you can use it), dictated by the task (e.g., you have to open a jar before accessing its contents), or can arise out of personal preference (e.g., you are used to doing things in a certain way). Preferential ordering can be changed without affecting goal completion.

The contention scheduling system provides an excellent map of how behaviors are selected and activated, but it alone does not account for actions that are influenced by conscious choice, a defining element of self-regulation. To account for volitional behavior, the Norman and Shallice model incorporates a *supervisory attentional system.* The system does not activate schemas or implement behavior; it instead modulates behavior by influencing the operation of the contention orienting system. Motivation supplements the supervisory attentional system.

The supervisory attentional system overlays horizontal activation and influences behavior by directing attention. As implied by our discussion of horizontal activation, attention to environmental stimuli is a strong activator of higher order schemas and a necessary precursor to the basic-level schemas that dictate overt action. If a system mandates that sugar be put into a cup of coffee but no environmental information about what types of sugar are available (or where the sugar is), the "obtain sugar" schema cannot be fulfilled. As Norman and Shallice (1986) noted, the functions of the supervisory attentional system coincide closely with the functions of the prefrontal lobes as described by Luria (1966).

Existence of the supervisory attentional system has been indirectly tested using evidence from patients with prefrontal damage. Damage to the hypothesized supervisory attentional system should not affect routine functions that have been well learned, because these routines would be enacted by the contention scheduling system. Prefrontal damage should impact tasks requiring error correction, planning, overcoming temptation, or novel behavioral sequences. These same behaviors are impaired in patients with prefrontal lesions (Norman & Shallice, 1986; Walsh, 1978).

The Norman and Shallice approach reflects two distinct aspects of self-regulation in our heuristic. First, the contention scheduling system mirrors the architecture of the cognitive–affective processing system. The hierarchically organized action schemas in this approach reflect the hierarchical arrangement of both feedback loops and the architecture of hot spots and cool nodes. The supervisory attentional system, in contrast, reflects the mediating role of attention in our heuristic. In the Norman and Shallice approach, the supervisory attentional system directs attention such that some schemas receive more activation than others. In terms of our organizing heuristic, this differential activation is akin to directing attention such that cool nodes selectively pass activation to goal-specific hot spots.

Because the contention scheduling system is roughly equivalent to the cognitive–affective processing system, we reserve our discussion of its development until we have more fully elucidated what the cognitive–affective processing system is. Similarly, the equivalence of endogenous attention and the supervisory attentional system makes a full discussion of its development redundant. A discussion of endogenous attention and its development is provided earlier in the chapter.

Action-Control Beliefs

The previous two control-system models decompose action at the microscopic level and connect to the cognitive architecture that underlies action. Skinner and colleagues, however, provided a more macroscopic analysis of action and its regulation. Their model describes three basic constituents of action and their observable relationships: actors, means, and outcomes (Chapman, Skinner, & Baltes, 1990; see also Little, 1998; Little, Oettingen, Stetsenko, & Baltes, 1995; Oettingen, Little, Lindenberger, & Baltes, 1994; Skinner, Chapman, & Baltes, 1988;). Existing at a more macroscopic level, action-control beliefs represent cognitions about the relationships between any two components of action (agent, means, or ends), with each intercomponent relationship treated as meaningful and distinct from the other relationships.

Agency beliefs relate the agent and a given means (Little, 1998; Skinner et al., 1988; Vanlede, Little, & Card, 2006). In terms of the motivational theories discussed later, agency for a behavior represents the belief that it can be performed by the agent. The expectancy of success is separated from this definition. When faced with a difficult task, an individual might have high agency for putting forth continued effort even though the agent may not see effort as potentially effective (a means–ends belief). Agency therefore shares similarities with the concept of self-efficacy (e.g., Bandura, 1995; see Little, 1998).

The perceived effectiveness of any given behavior is represented by a means–ends belief; such beliefs connect specific behaviors with potential outcomes without respect to the agent (Skinner et al., 1988; Little, 1998; Vanlede et al., 2006). This definition makes means–ends beliefs agent-general. I might see ability as key for accomplishing good grades (a means–ends belief about ability in general), but I may not believe that I personally possess the requisite ability (an agency belief about my ability).

Control-expectancy beliefs represent the relationship between agent and outcome (Skinner et al., 1988; Little, 1998, Vanlede et al., 2006). Specifically, control expectancy involves the perception that goals are attainable, regardless of means–ends conceptions or the specific agency beliefs. As Skinner and colleagues point out, some may see control expectancy as redundant when means–ends and agency beliefs are combined, but this is not the case. A researcher, for example, might believe that a hypothesis is testable before actually sitting down to design the necessary experiment. The control-expectancy belief in this situation existed before the means were determined. Control-expectancy beliefs also serve as a barometer of changing environmental contingencies, as when a stable social network becomes unstable. In this situation, the control-expectancy belief for making new friends can be undermined, but the agency and means–ends beliefs for making new friends are unaffected (Lopez & Little, 1996).

The discriminant and predictive validities of the action-control belief dimensions have been well established both cross culturally and across the life span (M. M. Baltes & Baltes, 1986; Little, 1998). Agency and control-expectancy beliefs are positively correlated (Karasawa, Little, Miyashita, Mashima, & Azuma, 1997; see also Little et al., 1995), and both are predictive of adaptive functioning, as was discussed earlier (see also Lopez & Little, 1996). Means–ends beliefs, however, are not consistently related to adaptive functioning.

As cognitions about the perceived control of action, action-control beliefs have clear links to control-system approaches to self-regulation. In this regard, self-regulation is not treated as a piecemeal conglomeration of facets. Instead, they are treated as a gestalt system in the development of the agentic self (Hawley & Little, 2002; Little, Hawley, Henrich, & Marsland, 2002; Little et al., 2006). Agentic action reflects all aspects of the action-control beliefs system and describes active self-regulated functioning. Agentic action requires that an agent be aware of goals and the means that can be used to attain them. Agentic action additionally requires that agents pursue goals and select task-appropriate means. Agentic action is therefore an integrated synthesis of the action-control system by which individuals self-regulate their behavior by selecting attainable goals (control-expectancy beliefs), understanding the means needed to attain them (means–ends beliefs), and employ those means one is capable of implementing (agency beliefs).

Summary of Control-System Approaches

The control-system approaches can be thought of as hierarchically superordinate to structural theories, but, in fact, overlap with structural theories to a significant degree. Both models describe the structural components of action. The difference is that the control-system models explicate the interaction of higher order systems while leaving the assumed structural components rather vague. Control-system theories can and should be synthesized with approaches that arise from hierarchically superordinate and subordinate tiers. We have provided a cursory synthesis of the structural and control-system levels, but more explicit synthesis is possible. For instance, the Norman and Shallice approach could be reworded as a system of hierarchically organized feedback loops that are activated through horizontal and vertical activation. The function of these loops is fully dependant on the executive functions, whereas the executive functions rely on specific neural pathways. Agentic action can similarly be seen as a hierarchy of feedback loops that involves agents, means, and goals.

In the next section, we describe agentic self-regulation as it is portrayed by motivational action theories. Behavioral activation in the previous models presupposes that some mechanism helps motivate behavior. The following discussion describes how motivational theories accommodate and validate the theories already discussed.

Motivational Approaches

Many action-theoretical perspectives describe motivation and its relationship to self-regulation. Motivational theories make this relationship a priority. Although we acknowledge the breadth of motivational theories in the literature (e.g., Atkinson, 1957; Kuhl, 1986), we focus only on two approaches. The first theory provides an exemplar for expectancy–value theories, which have made a significant contribution to our understanding of motivation and its influence on action and action control. Second, we discuss the cognitive–affective processing system, which integrates a novel approach to motivation with a larger architecture of cognitive–affective units.

Expectancy–Value Theories

Expectancy–value theories emphasize the fact that self-regulation requires motivation, focusing on two conditions required for behavior to occur. First, a person must have the expectancy that a self-regulated behavior can be performed successfully, similar to the concept of agency described earlier. A certain behavior can be required to attain a goal, but that behavior may not be feasible. If not, that behavior is not likely to be enacted. The value associated with a behavior also influences the likelihood of its initiation. A subjective cost–benefit analysis helps determine whether a behavior is worth doing. The subjective worth of an action is gauged relative to the worth of other behaviors. A determination of the best behavior is then made on the basis of perceptions of expectancy and value.

Eccles and colleagues (Eccles, 1983; Wigfield & Eccles, 2002) presented an expectancy–value theory that exemplifies how motivation affects regulation. Their theory is based on the assumption that experience is subjective and that it affects choice—the outcome of interest—in several ways. Experience tells us what we can do and how well we can do it (Eccles, 1987). The expectancy that one can adequately perform a behavior is directly dependant on a number of factors (Eccles, 1983; Wigfield & Eccles, 2000). A person's perceived ability level is weighed against the perceived difficulty of a task and against the perception of others' expectations. An expectancy judgment also relies on the encoding of past experiences. For instance, someone who has had previous success with a behavior is likely to have a high self-concept of ability for that behavior. Heightened perceptions of ability will not occur if the person has an external locus of control or has otherwise attributed previous success to an external cause (e.g., luck). Similar biases can influence perceptions of enactment difficulty or others' expectations.

A person's evaluation of value also influences choice. People should choose behaviors that lead to the greatest reward and come at the lowest cost. Indeed, the value aspect of expectancy–value theories can be seen as a kind of cost–benefit analysis. Three processes attribute value to a behavior. Attainment value is determined by how important a person sees the behavior as being, intrinsic value is determined by how intrinsically pleasurable the behavior is, and utility value is determined by the extent that a person believes the behavior will serve his or her goals. The subjective value of a behavior is weighed against its cost, which comes from the amount of effort required for success, the psychological cost of potential failure, and consideration of the time required for behavior completion. When a behavior's value is small, the time that it requires might be better spent pursuing other goals.

Expectancy–value theories emphasize the importance of motivation in self-regulation. Motivation results from previous experience and the way that experience is encoded. This type of model helps clarify the influence of the environment on behavior while acknowledging the unique influence of the individual. These perceptions can be brought into the discussion that follows as cognitive–affective units, which highlight the motivational side.

Value Attributions in Adolescence Adolescents are often portrayed as underregulated. The apparent underregulation is likely related to a reweighting of the values associated with long-term versus short-term goals. Long-term goals become preferable later in adolescence. An increased importance of long-term goals in adolescence mirrors the development of a future orientation as described by Nurmi (1989, 1994). Future orientation consists of the interests that people have in the future (motivation), how goals will be realized (planning), and the degree that goals are expected to be realized (evaluation). Studying these constructs cross-sectionally, Nurmi (1989) found that individuals focus their interests away from play and more toward work during adolescence. Concerns about future leisure activities decrease in early adolescence (11–15 years), and interest in future education increases. Interest in future occupation, family, and property increase during middle and late adolescence (15–18 years).

Reweighting of value attributions across adolescence may reflect increased gist processing, as is suggested by fuzzy trace theory. Individuals tend to process the gist of a situation more than the verbatim details with increased age (e.g., Reyna & Farley, 2006). If adults process the gist of a risky behavior as "bad," they will be less likely to engage in that behavior. If adolescents process the details and not the gist, they might determine that the likelihood of the same risky behavior is sufficiently small, relative to the potential benefits. Adolescents would accordingly engage in the risky behavior.

Cognitive–Affective Processing System

The cognitive–affective processing system model of Mischel and colleagues (Metcalfe & Mischel, 1999; Mischel & Ayduk, 2004; Mischel & Shoda, 1995) presents an integrative approach to self-regulation and serves as the foundation for our heuristic. Their theory comes from a mixed control-system and motivational perspective that also accommodates structural perspectives. The cognitive–affective processing system model was originally created as an attempt to account for the rift between many personality researchers and their data. Researchers often search for stable personality traits, whereas their data tend to show intraindividual differences across situations. Traditional models attribute these differences to be error. In the cognitive–affective processing system model, however, intraindividual differences are seen as meaningful variability that informs personality. Drawing from the literature on social and emotional information processing, the cognitive–affective processing system model proposes a system in which mean levels of behavior can be examined in conjunction with overall patterns of behavior to better inform personality. Two children might inhibit behavior equally when compared across situations, but we are better informed if we know that Child A inhibits better when externally motivated, whereas Child B inhibits best when internally motivated. Traditional approaches can easily miss such distinctions.

The cognitive–affective processing system model also accounts for unexpected findings in the delay-of-gratification task discussed earlier in the chapter. In the delay task (e.g., Mischel & Ebbesen, 1970; Mischel et al., 1989), researchers initially hypothesized that children would wait longer when rewards were present during the wait than they would if the rewards were not immediately present. The reward's presence was thought to provide continuous motivation to delay (Mischel & Ebbesen, 1970). Much to their surprise, the opposite occurred. Children were less able to delay when the reward was present, indicating that the reward's presence motivated the need for immediate gratification rather than delay.

Subsequent research showed that children would wait longer when only a photograph of the reward was present, compared with the real reward. Increased delay in the photograph situation indicates that motivation for gratification arises from the actual reward but does not carry over to its informational representation. The motivating factor for gratification must lie in some part of the reward that is not present in a photograph. A marshmallow is tasty and satisfies hunger, for instance, but a photograph does not. These findings suggest that selectively attuning attention to informational aspects of a reward allows for better delay. Accordingly, future work showed that a reward's presence has little or no effect when children attend only to informational aspects of a reward by pretending that the reward is instead only a photograph of itself (Moore, Mischel, & Zeiss, 1976).

In its fullest instantiation (Metcalfe & Mischel, 1999; Mischel & Ayduk, 2004), the cognitive–affective processing system model relies on two intertwined systems, each addressing one of these two issues. The cognitive–affective processing system model initially proposed by Mischel and Shoda (1995) is a predominantly control-system approach that predicts stable situation–behavior contingencies, with personality emerging as consistencies across behaviors. A second component of the cognitive–affective processing system model includes a more motivational account that details the interaction between informational and arousing aspects of stimuli and situations. This motivational aspect accounts for the counterintuitive findings from the delay-of-gratification paradigm (Metcalfe & Mischel, 1999), for example.

A Control-System Organization The predominantly control-system component of a cognitive–affective processing system relies on the organization of cognitive–affective units. Units receive information from other units and the environment, firing to activate yet other units when they receive a certain amount of activation. These units mediate the path between environmental input and behavioral output. They can be any aspect of cognition, including encoded information, goals, values, behavioral expectancies, self-regulatory competencies, or pieces of emotion such as the sweet taste of a marshmallow. The taste of a marshmallow is part of a larger emotion that represents the satisfaction that stems from eating something sweet. In short, cognitive–affective units represent the various processing units that are activated when environmental information is processed. Cognitive–affective units mediate the input–output stream and enact behavioral sequences.

The organization of cognitive–affective units creates interindividual differences within situations and intraindividual differences across situations. Each person's unique organization develops over time and is influenced by several variables. Bio-psychological variables that influence key determinants of behavior (e.g., temperament) should also bias the organization of cognitive–affective units across the life span. Temperamental effortful control predicts concurrent measures of empathy, for instance (Rothbart, Ahadi, Hershey, & Fisher, 2001). Effortful control might therefore bias children's behavior toward being more empathic.

Biological influence alone is not enough to tailor an individual's behavior to his or her unique environment. An experiential component is required and forms an integral part of cognitive–affective processing system development.

Experience plays three roles in a cognitive–affective processing system: it prompts systemwide organization, creates new cognitive–affective units, and acts as a priming agent. As a system organizer, experience effects the connections between experience-relevant cognitive–affective units. Connections are made between units that repeatedly activate together, which is a form of learning.

The environment also influences behavior through the somewhat slow decay of a cognitive–affective unit's activation level. A cognitive–affective unit that was previously activated will slowly become deactivated after the system stops sending it activation signals. A decrease in activation level does not occur immediately but rather decays over time. If a cognitive–affective unit is not fully deactivated when another activation signal flows through the system, activation will occur more readily than if the unit was at its resting level. In other words, immediately prior experience can facilitate the future activation of a cognitive–affective unit by priming it.

The larger organization of various cognitive–affective units results in a semistable system that does not operate reliably across situations. A person who normally adheres to a personal weight-loss regime might overindulge during the holidays, for instance. Behavior instead consists of interconnected "if ... then" situation–behavior relations in which stable behavior is only produced when situations share common features (Mischel & Shoda, 1995). Intraindividual stability across situations emerges out of these relationships from a tendency to favor certain cognitive–affective units. These units tend to send the same types of activation through the cognitive–affective processing system across situations and therefore tend to produce the same types of behaviors.

Preferred units can also become chronically activated. Chronic activation occurs when repeated activation of a unit over time elevates its resting activation level (see also automatization, e.g., Bargh, Gollwitzer, Lee-Chai, Barndollar, & Trötschel, 2001). When chronically activated, less (or no) additional input is required to activate a unit. Chronic activation can bias behavior by predisposing the system toward chronically activated units, which might represent stable personal preferences or chronic goals.

For example, a desire to lose weight might become chronically activated in a dieter. To lose weight, a person might engage in daily workouts, eat healthy foods, and limit the amount of time spent in front of the television. At first, conscious effort is required to engage in most of these behaviors. Further experience should lead to the chronic activation of the weight management goal. Chronic activation could then lead this person to use the stairs instead of the elevator, even if this person did not previously commit to using the stairs more often. The option of using the stairs can become preferable to the elevator because it has the added utility value of serving a chronic goal.

This example also illustrates how new cognitive–affective units can be created through experience. Our hypothetical person had to create the goal "reduce weight" for the goal to be followed. The new goal was likely the result of a series of internal processing dynamics. The person had to first realize that he or she could stand to lose a few pounds. The realization interacted with a cognitive–affective unit that represented the person's agency for weight loss and several other units to form and then pursue the weight management goal. Further, this person's success at weight loss likely increased the strength (chronic activation) of his or her agency for weight management, which would have positive effects on subsequent weight management attempts. The expectancy of success at weight management is thereby increased.

Development of an internalized conscience during early childhood (e.g., Kochanska, 1993; Kochanska, Murray, & Coy, 1997) corresponds closely to the idea of chronic activation.

Conscience represents the degree that a person's cognitive–affective architecture has been molded by repeated exposure to societal expectations.[3] Conscience likely arises from two primary sources: fearfulness and effortful control (e.g., Kochanska, 1993). Internalization requires effortful control because it presupposes that the internalized behaviors were consciously enacted at some point.

Compliance is an early forerunner of an internalized conscience (Lytton, 1977, 1980) and often requires self-regulation. Compliance to caregiver requests is usually effortful, and repeated compliance restructures the cognitive–affective architecture by connecting certain units while chronically activating others. The result is a system that is predisposed to behave the way caregivers previously requested. Two forms of compliance have been described, each with different impacts on the development of conscience (Kochanska, Coy, & Murray, 2001). Committed compliance requires that a child internalizes a caregiver's demand, making the caregiver's desire his or her own. Situational compliance occurs when a child obeys a request but does not internalize the desire to complete the requested task.

---

[3] The idea that morality represents the internalization of society is not new to psychology, cf. Freud (1930, 1923/1961).

Both forms of compliance require children to self-regulate, but committed compliance especially represents the internalization of a behavior (i.e., obeying parents, behaving according to social norms). Conscience, as a form of internalization, has been positively related to committed compliance but negatively or not related to situational compliance (Kochanska, Aksan, & Koenig, 1995; Kochanska et al., 1998; see also Stayton, Hogan, & Ainsworth, 1971). The committed–situational compliance dichotomy represents the difference between simple activation through attention and repeated activation that causes architectural change in the cognitive–affective processing system. Both are relevant to self-regulation and characterize how the development of different pieces of our organizing heuristic influences behavior.

Fearfulness also underlies a developing conscience and is related to some forms of self-regulation and internalization in early childhood (Derryberry & Rothbart, 1997; Kochanska, 1993; Rothbart & Ahadi, 1994; Rothbart, Ahadi, & Evans, 2000; Rothbart & Bates, 1998). Fearful children, for example, display more committed compliance than their less fearful peers (Kochanska et al., 2001). A tendency toward fearfulness, however, does not necessitate a predisposition to cognitive volition. The effect of fearfulness on observed self-regulation is mediated by its effect on the architecture of the cognitive–affective system and might reflect one instance of temperament influencing the cognitive–affective architecture. Dienstbier (1984) similarly hypothesized that anxious children are more easily conditioned to inhibit transgressions.

Internalization as discussed here also reflects Deci and Ryan's (e.g., 2002) approach to intrinsic and extrinsic motivation in older children and adults. In their approach, behaviors range across a continuum of internalization. Completely nonmotivated behaviors lie at one extreme of the spectrum, fully intrinsic motivation lies at the other. Purely intrinsic behaviors are performed simply because of personal interest and the inherent satisfaction gained from doing them. Between these two poles lie various degrees of extrinsic motivation at which behaviors are less-to-more externally motivated. Extrinsic motivation can be highly nonintrinsic (e.g., behavior aimed at avoiding punishment) or nearly intrinsic (e.g., internally motivated behaviors that have been incorporated with personal ideals and goals). In Deci and Ryan's terms, situational compliance is extrinsically motivated, whereas committed compliance tends toward intrinsic motivation.

The Hot–Cool Organization of a Motivational Theory We next discuss the second element of the cognitive–affective processing system, which better reflects motivational theories of action control. The hot and cool systems of the cognitive–affective processing system clarify the functional connections between cognitive–affective units. They also reflect motivational action theories by specifying how action is motivated. Mischel and colleagues (e.g., Metcalfe & Mischel, 1999) used the metaphor of a parallel distributed system to describe the architecture of the cognitive–affective processing system and to explicate the hot and cool systems. The hot system consists entirely of hot spots, or cognitive–affective units that represent fragments of emotion and are immediately associated with motivation. The cool system consists of cool nodes that process nonemotional data. Nonemotional units can be spatial, temporal, or episodic features of a situation, for instance. These two systems are interconnected through the various cognitive–affective units that exist simultaneously in both systems. In the delay of gratification paradigm, a cognitive–affective unit representing the reward is likely present in both systems. A participant simultaneously processes both the logical and emotional–motivating features of the reward.

The two systems are not logical and emotional mirrors of each other. Hot spots are sparsely interconnected. Cool nodes, in contrast, are often deeply interconnected. This discrepancy allows for quick and reflexive responses from the hot system and complex or deliberative responses from the cool system. In a similar vein, the hot system has fewer nodes than the cool system. Nearly every hot spot has a corresponding cool node, whereas cool nodes do not necessitate a corresponding motivational aspect. In the delay of gratification task, informational components of a reward (e.g., the exact dimensions of a marshmallow) are not motivating. Only the corresponding hot spots (e.g., its rich taste) motivate behavior.

Activation of a given cognitive–affective unit is partially dependant on the amount of attention available. Although many automated processes can be simultaneously active (provided they do not interfere with each other), cognitive–affective units that require additional activation from the environment are dependent on the processes of attention and encoding. In this respect, the cognitive–affective processing system is akin to the Norman and Shallice (1986) model already discussed.

A cognitive–affective processing system predicts, similar to Norman and Shallice, that activation is modulated by attention. As a result, a cognitive–affective processing system model predicts that selective activation of cool nodes or irrelevant hot spots can attenuate hot spot activation. In the delay-of-gratification paradigm, for example, attending to informational aspects of rewards should allow greater delay (be less motivating of gratification) than attending to hot or motivational aspects. The motivating cognitive–affective units for gratification receive less activation. Attention to cool representations therefore deprives the hot spots of attentional activation.

In Mischel and colleagues' approach, the hot and cool systems also react differentially to stress. Mild stress enhances the operation of both systems, whereas increased stress attenuates the cool system and strengthens the hot system. This stress relationship means that quick emotional decisions are favored when stress is high. With increased stress, the relevance of quick and reflexive decisions becomes more salient and the relevance of complex reflection and thought decreases. In very high stress situations, this system allows for nearly complete control by fight or flight motivations. A dual-system approach thus has intrinsic utility to the organism.

The hot–cool systems dichotomy is largely motivational in nature but easily accommodates lower tiers of our action-theory hierarchy. From a control-systems perspective, the architecture of hot spots and cool nodes is similar to Norman and Shallice's contention scheduling system. Structurally, the cool system is likely based in the hippocampi, frontal areas, and other brain areas implicated in comprehension and control. The hot system is likely amygdala-based (Metcalfe & Mischel, 1999). The hot–cool dichotomy also reflects the dual functions of the cingulate cortex described earlier. Further work is required to explicate fully the neural pathways of the hot and cool systems, but it is reasonable to expect findings that agree with these hypotheses. Separate neural pathways could also account for the unique operation and developmental trajectories associated with the two systems. The hot system reigns during infancy but gives way to the cool system as the child develops.

Two theories are relevant to the organization and function of the cognitive–affective processing system across development. First, temperament influences the cognitive–affective architecture at birth and continues to influence interunit connections across the life span. Temperamental effortful control is especially relevant to the development of self-regulation. The model of selection, optimization, and compensation (e.g., Freund & Baltes, 2000) is also relevant to the cognitive–affective processing system and provides an example of how the cognitive–affective processing system develops across adolescence and adulthood.

Foundations of the Cognitive-Affective Processing System: Temperament Major theories of temperament have included aspects of self-regulation (e.g., Ahadi, Rothbart, & Ye, 1993; Eysenck, 1967; Gray, 1970; Thomas & Chess, 1977). We previously argued that agentic self-regulation is fully dependant on attentional control, indicating a relationship between attention and temperament. Rothbart's approach to temperament (e.g., Rothbart, Ellis, & Posner, 2004) adequately captures the regulation–attention relationship and provides an example of how temperament is related to self-regulation. Although all three of Rothbart's primary dimensions of temperament are related in some way to self-regulation, we focus explicitly on the construct of effortful control. Effortful control regulates behavior and arises from attention.

Using the Child Behavior Questionnaire, Rothbart and colleagues (2001; Ahadi et al., 1993) identified three primary dimensions of temperament. *Negative Affectivity* is positively represented by shyness, discomfort, fear, anger/frustration, and sadness and negatively represented by soothability and attentional focusing. *Extraversion/Surgency* is positively represented by high intensity pleasure, smiling/laughter, activity level, and impulsivity, and negatively represented by shyness, inhibitory control, and attentional focusing. *Effortful Control* also emerged, being positively represented by smiling/laughter, soothability, inhibitory control, attentional focusing, low-intensity pleasure, and perceptual sensitivity.

Rothbart's structure is consistent with models in which self-regulation is dependant on directed attention. Anger/frustration, which we have previously described as a proxy for dysregulation, loads positively onto *Negative Affectivity*. Markers of self-regulation (attentional focusing and soothability) load negatively. Similarly, impulsivity represents dysregulation, and loads positively onto *Extraversion/Surgency*. Indicators of self-regulation (here, inhibitory control and attentional focusing) load negatively. All indicators of self-regulation additionally load positively onto effortful control, indicating a common foundation.

As might be expected from the development of endogenous attention and inhibition, these findings apply to children 3 years and older. In the absence of directed attention and inhibition, one should not expect to see effortful control as a fully formed construct in very young children. Reflecting the absence of a full self-regulatory system in infancy, Garstein and Rothbart (2003) found three factors of infant temperament that resembled Rothbart and colleagues' previous findings but that lacked a complete analogue of *Effortful Control. Surgency/Extraversion* and *Negative Affectivity* were both found in the infant sample, with *Effortful Control* replaced by a factor of *Orienting/Regulation*. Orienting was indicated by low-intensity pleasure, cuddliness, duration of orienting, and soothability, which, for the most part, are also indicators of *Effortful Control. Orienting/Regulation* lacks an "effortful" component, however. The effortful components of attention control and inhibition are not sufficiently developed in infancy to be meaningful indicators.

In Rothbart's view, the growth of directed attention allows for the development of temperamental effortful control. An individual's level of self-regulation is related to the degree that the components of temperament (e.g., effortful control) have been inherited, providing at least one direct mechanism by which biological differences influence variability in self-regulation. Individual differences in effortful control might in turn be related to neural processing speed or biologically based preferences for certain types of stimuli (e.g., repetitive stimuli, novelty). Biological differences may therefore be linked to the supervisory attentional system, cognitive–affective architecture, or both through temperament.

Selection, Optimization, and Compensation The major structural components of our heuristic model develop primarily between infancy and adolescence. Development of the cognitive–affective architecture, however, occurs across the life span. To accommodate development across the life span, we discuss the model of selection, optimization, and compensation (P. B. Baltes & Baltes, 1990; Freund & Baltes, 2000). The elements of SOC theory are applied (consciously or not) to the context of goal-related action (Freund & Baltes, 2002 Gestsdóttir & Lerner, 2007). SOC therefore concerns self-regulation. Most accounts of self-regulation emphasize the immediate effects of self-regulated action (e.g., resisting a temptation, performing a behavior). Instead, the SOC model focuses on developmentally relevant regulation.

Developmentally relevant regulation consists of behaviors that affect an individual across development. Development in terms of the SOC model occurs over an extended period of time, and gross structural development is not required for selection, optimization, or compensation to regulate behavior. We therefore argue that the processes described by the SOC model represent the slow and steady development of the cognitive–affective architecture across the life span.

The SOC model describes action in response to changes in available resources and can thus be applied to any age group. Humans never reach absolute developmental stasis, and resources dynamically shift across the life course. The first aspect of SOC theory—selection—reflects resource limitations and involves directing and focusing the expenditure of resources to specific domains (Lerner, Freund, De Stefanis, & Habermas, 2001). Resources are never unlimited, and focusing personal resources on a subset of key domains requires that other domains be ignored. From an action theoretic approach, selection means setting personal goals (Freund & Baltes, 2000).

The second element of SOC is optimization. Optimization occurs when behaviors maximize resources (P. B. Baltes & Baltes, 1990), as when behavior is directed toward goal achievement. Practice, persistence, and modeling successful others are all instances of optimization (Freund & Baltes, 2000). Compensation, the final element of SOC, also maximizes selected processes and is goal-directed. Compensation is therefore similar to optimization but differs in that compensation occurs when the individual experiences a loss of resources. When restricted resources limit commonly implemented means, new means are implemented through compensation (Freund & Baltes, 2002). Note that unlike selection, compensation does not redefine or select new goals.

The three processes described in the SOC model easily cohere with our heuristic model of self-regulation. Developmental regulation is in fact derived from the interaction of selection, optimization, and compensation. The shift in focus from short-term to long-term goals during adolescence can be seen as a shift of expectancy–value attributes within the cognitive–affective processing system. Expectancy–value models therefore also connect SOC theory to our heuristic.

The structure of self-regulation is established by adolescence; further refinement of the cognitive–affective architecture is a function of experience. Experience alters and creates the connections between cognitive–affective units. The model of selection, optimization, and compensation provides a control-system-like description of how connecting and reweighting occur. Through experience, the individual learns that it is impossible to apply resources to every possible domain, forcing selection. Goal selection is parallel to focusing attention on select cognitive–affect units (e.g., goals) and allowing the activation levels of nonselected units to dissipate. Nonselected goals therefore take a backseat to the goals that the individual has selected.

The theory of selection, optimization, and compensation accounts for development across the life span, but selection, optimization, and compensation do not meaningfully differentiate until adolescence (Gestsdóttir & Lerner, 2007). SOC theory explains developmental regulation, and it is not surprising that the elements do not differentiate until after childhood. Self-regulation after childhood tends toward longer term goals (Lerner et al., 2001). The development of the SOC strategies is also thought to underlie an increase in truly intentional self-regulation during adolescence (Gestsdóttir & Lerner, 2008).

Although the foundations of self-regulation and the differentiation of selection, optimization, and compensation all occur during adolescence, the development of the prefrontal cortex is far from complete. As implicated already, the lag in cortical development has been offered as one explanation for adolescents' stereotypically dysregulated behavior (Ernst, Pine, & Hardin, 2006; Spear, 2000; see also Steinberg, 2004). We next describe several adolescent behaviors normally portrayed as dysregulated and relate them instead to the predispositions of an incompletely developed system.

Self-regulation during adolescence is commonly discussed in terms of self-regulatory failures. Adolescents tend to be poorer than adults at setting adaptive goals (Byrnes, 2002) and tend to discount the riskiness of their behaviors (Benthin, Slovic, & Severson, 1993). Adolescents therefore have a heightened propensity for risk taking (e.g., Arnett, 1992). Lower self-regulation is related to increased risky sexual behaviors (Raffaelli & Crocket 2003), behavioral problems (Dougherty et al., 2003; Feldman & Weinberger, 1994; Krueger, Caspi, Moffitt, White, & Stouthamer-Loeber, 1996; Wulfert, Block, Santa Ana, Rodriguez, & Colsman, 2002), and aggression (Henry, Caspi, Moffitt, & Silva, 1996; Krueger et al., 1996) in adolescents.

Self-regulation is also associated with resiliency against risk factors (Eisenberg, Smith, Sadovsky, & Spinrad, 2004). Peer pressure is significantly related to risky behaviors (Brown, Clasen, & Eicher, 1986), and self-regulation in adolescence is thought to allow some children to better resist peer pressure than others by fostering attention to long-term over short-term goals. Association with deviant peers is associated with antisocial behavior but not for adolescents with high levels of self-regulation (Gardner, Dishion, & Connell, 2008), for instance. Adolescents who anticipate negative consequences from risky behaviors are also less likely to perform them (Galvan, Hare, Voss, Glover, & Casey, 2007).

As described previously, adolescents are not dysregulated per se but instead likely regulate toward goals differently than adults. Adults process the gist of situations and act based on the general valence of potential outcomes. Adults also tend to regulate behavior toward long-term goals. Adolescents, in contrast, process the details of a situation more fully and make decisions based on the probability of risk. Adolescents are also less likely to regulate toward long-term goals.

The elements of SOC continue to develop during late adolescence and early adulthood, peaking in middle adulthood (Freund & Baltes, 2002). During the period of peak SOC performance, the three components each serve a unique role in directing action. When an individual realizes that resources are necessarily limited, he or she must selectively apply resources to only a small subset of all possible domains (i.e., goals). To do otherwise would be to spread oneself too thin. After specific domains have been selected, applying resources within those domains is optimized. Many behaviors, including planning and forethought, practice, cognitive enrichment, and selection itself, serve this purpose. Further, the mechanisms by which goals can be attained are dynamic. Compensation occurs when one mechanism fails and a secondary mechanism compensates for the loss by taking its place. The process of SOC can be seen as the fine-tuning of the cognitive–affective architecture such that adaptive restructuring of the system equates with self-regulation.

SOC continues to describe self-regulation into later adulthood, when individuals have fewer resources on which to draw (Jopp & Smith, 2006). Resource restriction in later life results in dramatic changes in how self-regulation is applied. The ability to attain goals by influencing the external environment (primary control) increases into adulthood, but declines during old age. Internal mechanisms of goal attainment (secondary control; e.g., changing goals, positive reappraisal), however, grow throughout the life span (Heckhausen & Schulz, 1995). Accordingly, age is negatively correlated with the endorsement of SOC strategies in older adults (Freund & Baltes, 1998), whereas use of secondary control increases with age across adulthood (Heckhausen, 1997).

Changes in self-regulation parallel changes in goal structure during later adulthood. Individuals expect fewer opportunities for goal attainment in late adulthood (P. B. Baltes & Baltes, 1990), and the perceived end of life may make long-term goals appear less meaningful (e.g., Heckhausen

& Schulz, 1998). Decreased resources further limit goal pursuit as decreased resources demand increasingly restrictive goal selection. Goal pursuit is moderated by age-related resource availability (Heckhausen & Shulz, 1998), subjective well-being is greater when resource availability is considered during goal selection (Diener & Fujita, 1995), and emotion regulation goals appear to take precedence over information-seeking goals in old age (e.g., Carstensen, 1995), possibly as a result of resource restriction.

Manifestations of self-regulation tend to be positively related to successful development in late adulthood. For instance, SOC strategy use is associated with successful aging (Freund & Baltes, 1998). Jopp and Smith (2006) found that SOC endorsement, especially of optimization, was positively related to satisfaction with aging during the eighth decade. General well-being is also associated with primary control during early and middle adulthood, whereas secondary control predicts well-being in middle and late adulthood (Wrosch, Heckhausen, & Lachman, 2000). The positive influence of self-regulation in old age moderates the impact and development of several life challenges (Kempen et al., 2003; Wrosch et al., 2006). Greater perceived control is positively related to preventative maintenance in health-related domains (Seeman & Seeman, 1983) and negatively correlates with older adults' depressed outlook (Brandtstädter, 1989). Higher levels of control negatively predict functional declines, including later disability (see Kempen et al., 2005).

The idea that greater *perceived* control mitigates the negative effects of aging is discussed by the model of assimilative and accommodative coping (e.g., Brandtstädter, 1989; Brandtstädter & Renner, 1990). This model draws on aspects of motivational, social constructivist, and control-systems theories to describe self-regulation in older adults. The model of assimilative and accommodative coping is founded on the premise that goal-related action aims to reduce the discrepancy between a person's current state and some referent. In this respect, it is similar to control-systems theories based on feedback loops.

The model of assimilative and accommodative coping emphasizes two mechanisms for reducing the discrepancy between an individual's current standing and a target state. The person can work to alter his or her current state (assimilation) or can accommodate goals to the environment. Individuals generally prefer to actively regulate their environment, and assimilative strategies are more prevalent in younger adults (Brandtstädter & Renner, 1990). As aging-related declines become more apparent, assimilation becomes increasingly difficult and becomes intractable in some domains. Accommodative efforts emerge when assimilation becomes unfeasible and likewise tends to increase throughout adulthood (Brandtstädter & Renner, 1990). Because accommodation occurs only when assimilative efforts fail, the two are conceptualized as antagonistic processes. The more assimilative processes are relied on, the less accommodative processes occur and vice versa.

The model of assimilative and accommodative coping draws from several action theoretical domains, explicating specific limitations and moderators of assimilation and accommodation (e.g., Brandtstädter & Wentura, 1995). Choosing an assimilative action from the larger set of possibilities depends on each action's corresponding expectancy and value attributions. Accommodation depends on the ability to restructure the cognitive–affective architecture effectively, which also partly depends on experience. Other limiting factors include the presence of mitigating cognitions (e.g., optimism) and a person's self-concept (Brandtstädter & Wentura, 1995).

The hypothesis that control beliefs are important in later adulthood because of declines in health and cognition (e.g., Lachman, 1986) necessarily links increasing age with declining function. Theories such as SOC are conditioned on context (Freund & Baltes, 2002), however, and the influence of self-regulation is better examined in the context of resource availability. For instance, Jopp and Smith (2006) found less satisfaction with aging in older adults who had fewer available resources. The positive relationship between SOC strategies and aging satisfaction was also stronger in the low-resource group, indicating that the buffering effect of SOC is stronger when resources are limited.

Social Constructivist Approaches

Experience shapes the connections between cognitive units in our heuristic model. The role of experience implicitly agrees with many of the views held by social constructivist theories. This section provides an overview of social constructivist theory as it applies to action control and self-regulation. Our discussion largely follows the social constructivist approach of Vygotsky (e.g., 1978). We discuss the effects of social context on the development of self-regulation by examining the microsystem effects of parents and peers and the macrosystem effect of culture.

Vygotsky and Action Control

Vygotsky's model relies on symbols, which can be thought of as the mental analogue of tools. A symbol is some cognitive representation (e.g., a word or concept) that brings aspects of the environment together to interact. Preferably, the interaction results in a favorable outcome. A hammer (a tool) and nail might be brought together such that force is applied to the nail, driving it into a piece of wood. A symbol for "clock" brings together perceptions of hands and numbers so the perceiver can recognize the time. Vygotsky made three assumptions about symbols that directly affect the way his theory relates to agentic self-regulation. Symbols are assumed to arise out of culture, mediate action in the individual, and affect the development of higher psychological functions such as perception, choice, and attention. Culture can therefore indirectly influence the processes underlying self-regulation.

Symbols are cultural phenomena that arise from interpersonal interaction. Culture mediates symbol formation. Vygotsky exemplified the role of culture by describing the (hypothetical) development of pointing behavior. When trying to obtain some object, a very young child is likely only to perform externally directed behaviors like grasping. A behavior as limited as grasping can only get the child so far because not all objects that a child can want are easily within reach. When a parent sees a child who is grasping for an out-of-reach object, the parent understands the child's intent and gets him or her the desired object. Grasping now serves both the personal purpose of obtaining objects and the interpersonal purpose of conveying desires. The interpersonal definition of grasping could not have arisen if the parent did not interpret the child's failed reaching as an indication of wanting.

As the child internalizes the interpersonal meaning of (failed) grasping, he or she begins to understand the action as a meaningful gesture. Further, the gesture can be used as the child sees fit, indicating the development of some degree of agency. Through physical refinements, the interpersonally intended use of failed grasping becomes intentional pointing.

We can see how symbols mediate action through the internalization of the pointing gesture. Before internalizing the pointing "symbol," the only possible way for a child to get what he or she wanted was to grab the object and draw it near. The advent of the pointing symbol opens up a whole new variety of behaviors that involve pointing to things that the child wants or, with further development, to things the child wants someone else to pay attention to. These alternative behaviors cannot occur in the absence of a symbolic definition of pointing.

Internalizing symbols can free one from the confines of the environment. Freedom from environmental restraints allows for the development of what Vygotsky called the "higher functions." The transition to symbolically driven (i.e., mediated) behavior results in objects being treated as instruments (i.e., practical intelligence) and allows a perceiver to reconstruct mentally a perceived environment. Reconstructions form the basis of what we call "memory" by incorporating aspects of the present environment with aspects of previous environments. Reconstruction also allows a perceiver to pay attention purposefully to various aspects of the reconstructed environment and results in voluntary attention.

Internalizing symbols restructures psychological activity to be compatible with cultural norms and rules. Internalization shapes the development of self-regulation by influencing the way we perceive and attend to our environment. The effect of socially mediated internalization meshes easily with our organizing heuristic; context pervades the entire system. Social constructivist models such as Vygotsky's explicate at least part of this influence, showing how cultural experience partially determines the growth and definition of cognitive units. Just as our hypothetical child learned the meaning of pointing through social interaction, the arrangement and connections among cognitive units is fully dependant on culturally defined definitions and categories. As a result, the possibility exists that some cognitive–affective units may exist in some cultures, but not in others.

Microsystem

Culturally mediated internalization relies on interaction with others. More experienced people have already internalized culturally defined symbols and transmit these to people with less experience. The people in a child's microsystem represent culture at-large and accordingly exert a strong influence on the development of self-regulation. Agents within a culture are not all homogenous, however, and interindividual differences in children's microsystems can result in differential development of self-regulation. One way these differences have been studied is by comparing mother–child interactions.

Caregivers play two roles in the development of infant self-regulation. First, infants must associate self-regulatory behaviors with their regulatory function. This association is facilitated by social interaction (cf. Stifter & Spinrad, 2002). Caregivers provide the social scaffolds necessary for the development of self-regulated behavior. An infant's cries communicate distress to caregivers who in turn perform actions that help reduce the infant's arousal. An infant's cries convey purposeful intent (i.e., explicitly calling a caregiver) by the 10th month, and repeated exposure to caregivers' arousal-reducing behaviors toward the end of the first year teaches infants that negative affect can be alleviated and that certain behaviors can serve a regulatory role. The development of socially mediated self-regulation therefore also depends on the infant's ability to communicate negative arousal to caregivers (Kopp, 1989; Stifter & Spinrad, 2002).

Caregivers' ability to regulate infant emotions marks a second role for caregivers in the development of infant self-regulation. When an infant's own regulatory mechanisms are inadequate, he or she learns to depend on caregivers to reduce negative arousal. Accordingly, infants often use social referencing as a way to reduce stress (e.g., Diener, Mangelsdorf, McHale, & Frosch, 2002).

Calkins and Johnson (1998) reported findings that support the development of self-regulation through social interaction (see also Calkins, Smith, Gill, & Johnson, 1998). In their study, several maternal behaviors were related to children's ability to modulate their emotions.

Maternal negative control (e.g., telling a child "no") negatively predicted children's distress. Maternal positive guidance (e.g., praise) was positively correlated with children's self-distraction and constructive coping, both measures of self-regulation. Self-distraction and constructive coping were in turn negatively related to children's distress. Maternal interference and children's distress also interacted to predict children's aggression, with distress positively predicting aggression at all levels of maternal interference. The relationship between distress and aggression increased with higher levels of maternal interference (Calkins & Johnson, 1998).

Research further suggests that children with warm and supportive parents develop better self-regulation. Maternal responsiveness and socialization positively predict measures of later self-regulation (Kochanska et al., 2000). Maternal responsiveness may also support the child's autonomy (e.g., Eisenberg et al., 2004). In social constructivist terms, maternal responsiveness facilitates internalizing symbols and leads to greater directed attention. Better directed attention then leads to better self-regulation. Responsiveness may also help children internalize a system of symbols in which the environment is generally seen as safe and able to be reliably manipulated. Such a system of symbols would encourage exploration and reconstruction of the environment, leading to increases in self-regulation.

Peers are an important part of a child's microsystem and contribute to the development self-regulation. Vygotsky's theory, for instance, sees imaginary play as a significant contributor to the development of self-regulation (McCabe, Cunnington, & Brooks-Gunn, 2004; Vygotsky, 1978). A large amount of imaginary play involves peers, thus implicating peers in a child's ability to self-regulate. According to Vygotsky, imaginary play develops during the same period as the realization of unattainable desires and serves a related purpose. When children experience desires that cannot be immediately met, they create an imaginary world where those desires are attainable. A child who wants a pony, for instance, might pick up a stick and pretend that he or she is riding one because the actual object is unattainable. Imaginary play redirects desires, thereby regulating behavior.

Children also create and follow rules to constrain their imaginary situations. Children will often abide by the rules of a game, even if acting against these rules better serves a child's interests. Play can serve as one mechanism by which children learn to consciously direct attention to some, but not other, cognitive–affective units to regulate their behavior. Peers are implicated as moderators to the development of self-regulation because imaginary group play follows rules that are socially constructed (e.g., Piaget, 1932/1965). More imaginary (rule-based) play means more time practicing directed attention.

Although the cognitive development of self-regulation follows a rather clear trajectory across childhood, its behavioral manifestations do not. Social expectations for children change as they transition between early and middle childhood. Qualitatively different expectations require that children show qualitatively different displays of self-regulation.

Middle childhood marks the beginning of school for most children, and classroom performance strongly reflects a child's ability to self-regulate. Greater self-regulation results in better performance in school (Flynn, 1985; Howse, Calkins, Anastopoulos, Keane, & Shelton, 2003; Normandeau & Guay, 1998; see also Keogh, 1992) and may be a stronger predictor of academic success than intellectual functioning (e.g., Normandeau & Guay, 1998).

Just as self-regulation positively affects school performance, deficits in self-regulation can be detrimental. Attention-deficit/hyperactivity disorder (ADHD) is a disorder characterized by poor attentional skills, a hallmark of conscious self-regulation. Other researchers (e.g., Barkley, 1997) have also theorized a link between inhibition and ADHD. A full discussion on the scholastic impacts of ADHD is beyond our scope, but it is sufficient to say that ADHD negatively affects classroom performance (e.g., Deshazo Barry, Lyman, & Klinger, 2002; Rapport, Scanlan, & Denney, 1999).

Social interactions also become more salient as children transition to middle childhood. Self-regulation is positively related to children's social functioning. In their work, Eisenberg and colleagues have found that effortful self-regulation is differentiated from more automatic forms of control such as behavioral inhibition (e.g., Eisenberg & Spinrad, 2004). Effortful self-regulation is especially related to children's social functioning (Eisenberg et al., 1993, 2000, 2007; see also Eisenberg, Fabes, & Murphy, 1995). In fact, effortful regulation and social competence have shown correlations above .90 when measured as latent constructs (Spinrad et al., 2006).

Effortful self-regulation fosters the development of social skills, which may partially explain their profound relationship. Prosocial behavior, for instance, requires that children regulate their own and others' emotions (Bergin, Tallry, & Hamer, 2003). Highly regulated children are better at managing their anger reactions with peers (Eisenberg et al., 2004). Effortful self-regulation also affects the way children deal with others' negative emotions. Self-regulation is positively related to children's expressions of sympathy and negatively related to showing personal distress in sympathy-provoking situations (Eisenberg et al., 1998). Children can begin to focus on others' needs only after they regulate their own emotions (Trommsdorff & Friedlmeier, 1999). Self-regulation and parental expressivity interact to predict personal distress (Valiente et al., 2004), further emphasizing the importance of the social environment.

Less altruistic forms of prosociality (e.g., public prosociality; see Carlo, Hausmann, Christiansen, & Randall, 2003; Carlo & Randall, 2002) also require self-regulation. Children can act prosocially to gain social acceptance and esteem, for instance. The social regard gained through prosociality presumably benefits the children at a later time. Self-serving prosociality is therefore similar to delayed gratification. Children behave against their immediate interests (i.e., prosocially) in anticipation of greater rewards later on.

Macrosystem

The transmission of self-regulation from parent to child is influenced by a variety of sources (e.g., culture, genetic heritability, parent-specific practices). Evidence especially favors a model that includes cultural factors. Keller and colleagues (2004), for instance, found that Cameroonian and Greek parenting styles are related to different levels of self-regulation. Body contact during free play predicted internally motivated compliance (self-regulation) in Cameroonian children. Greek children received lower levels of body contact and showed significantly lower levels of compliance.

Other studies show that the interpretation of self-regulation may even differ by culture. Rothbart and colleagues found that effortful control related differentially to other aspects of temperament in Chinese and American samples (Ahadi et al., 1993). Feldman, Masalha, and Alony (2006) also found that although Israeli and Palestinian children had equivalent levels of overall self-regulation, Israelis were higher on compliance, and Palestinians rated higher on inhibition. Self-regulation in these two samples was also predicted by different factors. Similarly, East Asian and Western college students differed on the focus of self-regulatory goals. East Asian students showed greater focus on negative outcomes (e.g., avoiding failure) and less promotion focus (e.g., achieving success). Asian students raised in a Western context focused on both, indicating a direct effect of the participants' immediate cultural environment, and an indirect effect of their historical culture (Ouschan, Boldero, Kashima, Wakimoto, & Kashima, 2007). In this instance, culture mediates goal selection (e.g., winning a game vs. not losing).

The development of directed attention and self-regulation is mediated by social processes, which in turn mediate cultural factors. Our heuristic accommodates the pervasive influence of culture by allowing it to influence self-regulation at every hierarchical tier. As the research in this section shows, culture can affect the very nature of how we self-regulate (structural level). The influence of culture also has implications for the control-system and motivational levels. Culture helps determine which cognitive–affective units develop and how they interact. Cultural norms also help define the expectancies and values attributed to action.

SUMMARY OF DEVELOPMENT

Our organizing heuristic provides a scaffold for understanding the unfolding of self-regulation across the lifespan. We now adopt a chronological perspective, summarizing the development of self-regulation from infancy to old age. In each section, we discuss both the cognitive changes and behavioral manifestations of self-regulation most germane to development according to our heuristic.

Infancy

The foundations of self-regulation are presumably laid in infancy. Particularly in the early years, the growth of self-regulation evolves from an initially passive–reactive mode to one in which behavior may be self-initiated (Calkins, 1994; Kopp, 1982; Sroufe, 1996). Mischel and colleagues (e.g., Mischel & Shoda, 1995) drew a parallel between this course of development and development of cognitive–affective processing systems. One of the primary goals in developing self-regulation requires movement away from hot-system-dominated responses and toward responses dominated by the cool system.

In terms of our organizing heuristic, the primary force underlying the development of infant self-regulation is attention. Self-regulated behavior in infancy tends to fall into two major categories. Infants can modulate their attention to help them explore their environment or they can modulate negative arousal. Reflecting the transition from hot-system dominance to cool-system dominance, our focus was primarily on the regulation of arousal and its development in infancy. As mentioned, emotion regulation is a subset of self-regulation that relies on the selective engagement–disengagement of attention (see also Rueda, Posner, & Rothbart, 2004). Attention is itself moderated by social phenomena, and we briefly described how social interaction influences the function and development of self-regulation.

Early Childhood

Error detection, conflict-processing, and inhibition are all germane to self-regulation. All emerge during the toddler and preschool years and are linked to development in the anterior cingulate cortex. Emotion-regulating behaviors tend to dominate self-regulation throughout the toddler years, with emotional reactions correlating with self-regulatory strategies. More complex forms of self-regulation such as behavioral inhibition and compliance arise as children enter the preschool years.

More complex instantiations of self-regulation reflect an increased mastery of the child's own cognitive–affective architecture. As we elucidated earlier, inhibition and other forms of self-regulation require attention to select cognitive–affective units such that behavior is successfully modulated.

Middle and Late Childhood

Middle to late childhood is a time when self-regulation continues to develop and begins to affect novel aspects of children's functioning. The neural mechanisms underlying self-regulation are largely developed by the end of middle childhood, and as social interaction becomes more salient during the school years, the influence of self-regulation on development widens. Development during middle and late childhood encompasses three aspects of our organizing model. The supervisory attentional system continues to develop until children are approximately 7 years old, with only minor development beyond that. Experience continues to influence the cognitive–affective architecture, and the interaction between self-regulation and social behavior becomes more pronounced. We specifically addressed the influence of self-regulation on academic performance and social interactions.

Adolescence

As is clear, the development of self-regulation is largely related to the development of attention and inhibition prior to adolescence. Although these processes reach mature levels by the end of childhood, performance on more complex tasks continues to increase throughout adolescence and into early adulthood. Advantages into adulthood indicate protracted development of self-regulation and the continued development of the prefrontal cortex.

The self-regulation literature often portrays adolescents as behaviorally underregulated. Our heuristic posits that adolescents are not necessarily poorly regulated but instead often regulate their behavior to different goals than do adults. Adolescents discount risks and attribute less value to long-term goals than do adults.

Adulthood

The development of self-regulation apparently peaks and plateaus during middle adulthood, making adult self-regulation the benchmark to which regulation at other ages is compared. By middle adulthood, the primary processes underlying our organizing heuristic have become relatively stable and, as Freund and Baltes (2002) have shown, the elements of SOC are being maximally used. In many ways, the development of self-regulation is the protracted development of adultlike self-regulation across infancy, childhood, and adolescence. The development of self-regulation during adulthood (excluding old age) primarily involves fine-tuning of the already existent cognitive–affective architecture.

Later Adulthood

The development of self-regulation during adulthood primarily consists of minor modifications to the cognitive–

affective structure. The transition into old age, however, marks a time of cognitive decline in which self-regulation changes qualitatively as well as quantitatively. Our discussion of self-regulation in adulthood is deeply rooted in the model of selection, optimization, and compensation but is by no means limited to it. Self-regulation moderates the effects of cognitive decline in old age but is not itself immune to declines. Fluid abilities such as the dynamic application of attention decrease in old age. The cognitive–affective architecture is more crystallized, however, and may remain intact well into old age.

SUMMARY OF THE HEURISTIC

We presented an organizing heuristic to synthesize action-theoretical approaches to self-regulation (see Table 5.1 and Figure 5.3). From a structural perspective, self-regulation is mediated throughout the life span by executive function and its underlying neural substrates. The elements of the structural level combine into organized control-systems that describe the processes underlying self-regulated action. In this regard, we highlighted Carver and Scheier's (1981, 1990) feedback loop model, Norman and Shallice's (1986) dual system model, and Skinner et al.'s (1988) action-control model. The control-system models were also synthesized with two motivational theories, Eccles and colleagues' approach to expectancy–value models (Eccles et al., 1983; Wigfield & Eccles, 2002) and Mischel and colleagues' cognitive–affective processing system (Metcalfe & Mischel, 1999; Mischel & Shoda, 1995). Our heuristic incorporates the impact of culture at all levels and is also tied to the model of selection, optimization, and compensation (P. B. Baltes & Baltes, 1990; Freund & Baltes, 2000).

Table 5.1 Key Elements of the Organizing Heuristic Model

Structural	- System is mediated by executive functions
	- Executive functions are mediated by neural pathways
Control Systems	- The organizing system consists of cognitive–affective units
	- Cognitive–affective units must be activated (vertically or horizontally)
	- Activation can be modulated by attention
	- Activation decays slowly over time
	- Cognitive–affective units can become chronically activated to various degrees
	- Cognitive–affective units are arranged hierarchically
	- Schemas are hierarchical chains of cool nodes that are activated by hot spots and result in behavior
	- Schemas represent a series of hierarchically organized feedback loops
	- Cognitive–affective units activate when their activation threshold is exceeded
Motivational	- Progress of feedback loops is monitored by superordinate progress monitoring loops
	- Behavior is motivated by activation of hot spots
	- Schemas have corresponding expectancy and value attributions
	- Expectancy and value attributions influence activation
Social Constructivist	- The organization of cognitive–affective units is arbitrary
	- A person-specific organization arises out of experience
	- Shared cultural experiences can cause groups of individuals to have similar structures
	- Similar structures within a group represent shared symbols, customs, norms of action, etc.
	- The socially mediated organization of cognitive–affective units constrains behavior

Broader Application of the Heuristic

To be a useful reference for understanding the development of self-regulation, any organizing heuristic must adequately account for the nuanced predictions made by other theories. Our heuristic can accommodate more nuanced theories of self-regulation. We now examine five subdomains of the self-regulation literature and discuss how our model captures self-regulation as it is currently portrayed in the field.

Agentic Self-Regulation: Effortful and Automatic Processes

A recurrent issue in the self-regulation literature is the distinction between effortful and automatic processes. Although we have focused on agentic regulation and its development, the heuristic model adequately addresses both willed and automatized forms of behavior. Cognitive–affective units are arranged such that activation can be passed from input nodes to motivational hot spots and then hierarchically down to overt behavior without conscious intervention. Agentic regulation is fully dependant on the individual's ability to direct attention consciously such that the automatic processes can be modulated according to conscious goals. A discussion of whether consciously directed attention is in fact willful or is simply an automatic response that only appears willful (i.e., determinism) is beyond the scope of this chapter. Accordingly, the focus of this chapter was self-regulation as agentically directed attention and actions.

Agentic self-regulation also allows the individual to deal with novel situations and behaviors. Situations requiring novel responses activate hot spots that no existing node or schema can fully satisfy. The lack of an adequate schema leads the system to put continual pressure on the various subordinate nodes, despite the fact that they cannot serve the required purpose.

Personally directed attention can alleviate this pressure through two related processes. First, personally directed attention can activate several lower order nodes by combining candidate nodes (e.g., the ones with the greatest activation values) into a new schema that would be held initially in working memory. The new schema can be thought of as a node with an activation threshold that is proportional to an expected likelihood of success. When a certain combination of nodes is sufficiently likely to result in success, the schema activates its associated nodes. Activation of the new schema results in an attempt at a novel behavior. The new schema is then sent to long-term memory with an associated expectancy for that schema based on the result of its activation.

Influence of Stress

In the Mischel and colleagues' original instantiation of the cognitive–affective processing system, hot spots and cool nodes both feed directly to a behavioral buffer. The behavioral buffer then translates intention into action. Increased stress is hypothesized to heighten the function of the hot system and enhance the function of the cool system at low levels. Stress inhibited the cool system when high. This relationship rests on the assumption that both hot spots and cool nodes could result in motor behavior.

Our heuristic does not require a behavioral buffer but instead allows feedback loops consisting of cool nodes to enact motor behavior. Eliminating the behavioral buffer helps maintain the hierarchical nature of schemas and their related feedback loops. The differential reaction to stress as posited by Mischel and colleagues is important, and a heuristic that does not account for differential behavior during high versus low stress is unsatisfying. To account for behavioral variance related to stress, we propose that stress increases the strength of activation that is output by the hot spots while decreasing the activation thresholds of cool nodes. If stress produces the proposed reaction, the heuristic model can account for the types of behavior seen in varying stress situations. Under low or no stress, the activation values for cool nodes are high, making processes more deliberate. This deliberate processing allows for complex processing. Slightly increasing stress is not likely to alter the eventual output of the system. Instead, it would decrease node activation thresholds enough to result in more efficient processing. Thus, mild stress will enhance performance of the cool system. As stress increases, the hot spots become more demanding, and the activation thresholds of their subservient cool nodes decreases. High levels of stress can therefore lead to nearly immediate activation of the most salient nodes in lieu of deeper processing.

Self-Regulatory Failure

Self-regulation is often portrayed as the ability to choose a course of action and to follow through with it. If a person fails to follow through, he or she has experienced regulatory failure. In our organizing heuristic, no mechanism represents a store of willpower or regulatory energy that can feasibly fail. For example, when a child summons the experimenter to receive the smaller reward in the delay of gratification task, the child has not failed to regulate. Instead, the relative weight of immediate gratification has surpassed the weight of delaying and the child's behavior was regulated accordingly. The fact that cognitive units reweight over time is extraordinarily adaptive, and it is not correct to consider reweighting as a system failure. Without a store of willpower, self-regulative energy, or some similar trigger mechanism, the only way for self-regulation to fail is for the system to shutdown (cf. catatonia). Although it is possible to say that the child failed to regulate his or her behavior toward the initial goal, the child did not fail to self-regulate. The same logic applies for the college student who switches majors because he or she no longer finds an initially pursued degree appealing.

Self-Regulation as a Limited Resource

Work by Baumeister and colleagues (Baumeister, 2002; Baumeister, Bratslavsky, Muraven, & Tice, 1998; Baumeister, Heatherton, & Tice, 1994; see also Schmeichel & Baumeister, 2004) provides evidence that self-regulation consumes some amount of a limited resource. Tapping a limited resource for use in one task consistently reduces the ability to self-regulate in subsequent tasks, consistent with self-regulatory failure as described above.

Our heuristic model does not posit some limited store of willpower, although attention can be depleted by mental fatigue (e.g., Boksem, Meijmna, & Lorist, 2005). As a result, attentional control might be a somewhat limited resource. Baumeister and colleagues showed that rest and pleasurable activities tend to replenish the self-regulatory energy, and it is possible that these activities similarly allow endogenous attention to take a break and replenish itself. Replacing an unspecified pool of energy with attention accommodates Baumeister and colleagues' approach. In terms of Norman and Shallice's approach, when the supervisory attentional system is weakened by fatigue, behavior will be directed by the contention scheduling system. Fatigued individuals will fail to regulate to prespecified goals that require horizontal activation to maintain while the function of the self-regulatory system as a gestalt remains intact.

Emotion Regulation

A significant body of literature focuses specifically on emotion regulation. This literature addresses how we modulate our emotions and how emotions regulate our behavior. A thorough overview of emotion regulation is covered elsewhere (see Lewis et al., Chapter 3, this volume), but we note that our heuristic model accommodates both of the described aspects. Within the hot system, emotions and emotional fragments serve as the motivators of action, showing how emotions can regulate behavior. Conscious self-regulation of emotions is also made possible by the processes of the cognitive–affective processing system model (see also Metcalfe & Mischel, 1999). The influence of an emotional hot spot can be reduced by focusing attention on nonmotivating cool nodes or on competing hot spots. Activation of these alternative cognitive–affective units inhibits activation of the emotional hot spot, hastening the natural decay toward its resting activation level.

Carver (2004) discussed a second function of emotions in the self-regulatory system. Here, emotions monitor progress toward goals, representing satisfaction (or dissatisfaction) with the progress being made. The organizing model accounts for emotional monitoring by assuming second-order feedback loops within hot spots. Activation of a hot spot initiates one feedback loop that directs behavior and a second loop that monitors the first loop's progress. When the first loop is behaving as expected, no output by the second order loop is needed. When the first loop behaves unsatisfactorily, the second loop creates an output function that represents either a negative emotion or additional motivation–activation of the first-order loop. Likewise, when the first-order loop behaves better than expected, the second-order loop can either change its comparator value to match current progress, or it can suppress the lower order loop. Such suppression allows the associated hot spot to coast a little and allows energy to be applied toward other salient goals.

An Alternative Approach

Although our heuristic presents a somewhat novel approach, it is important to acknowledge that other models and heuristics can be equally integrative. One example is the model proposed by Boesch (1991). In discussing Boesch's model, we also discuss the similarities that various integrative models might share by comparing Boesch's approach with our own account. This sampling of Boesch's larger theory is presented to highlight Boesch's historical place in the study of actions and to emphasize that our heuristic is not unique in integrating the various types of action theories.

Structural

Whereas our model predominantly integrates a more cognitive version of structural models (i.e., structure of brain areas, executive function), Boesch's structural roots are more in line with Brandtstädter's (1998) original definition. Boesch's theory is styled after Piagetian constructivism (e.g., Piaget, 1970), which focuses on a child's self-construction of reality and therefore action potential. Boesch's constructivism sees action arising from primarily three parameters: (a) objects and physical laws, (b) cultural rules, and (c) individual propensities. Objects and physical laws construct action through their ability to constrain action or make certain actions possible. A hammer makes it possible to drive a nail into a wall, but this action would be limited were the wall made of concrete. Cultural rules and regulators also construct action, similar to the idea of cultural mediation in social constructivist models. Cultural rules help define which actions are appropriate (or "possible," e.g., the cultural requirement to wear headscarves or not) and mediate the potential outcomes of action. The third constructor of action is personal propensities, be they goals, hopes, or simply preferences. In the delay of gratification task, children only have to delay if they see the larger reward as a preferable goal. Similarly, children may use different strategies for delaying gratification simply because of individual propensities and preferences.

Control System

Although focusing strongly on the personal and cultural features that construct action, Boesch's treatment of symbols, action, and goals is similar to the control-system approaches described previously. Having a theory of cultural psychology, Boesch expanded the control-system structure of action to include both internal structures and structures in the environment (e.g., culture). The whole of an individual's environment is described as an action field. One part of the action field (the action space) pertains to locations in the environment and is defined by the actions performed in them. A professor defines the office as a place to work. A student defines the same location as a place to go for help with an assignment. When individually or culturally imposed goals, conditions, and (nonphysical) limitations are considered within the action space, their sum represents the action field.

Boesch's consideration of symbols, goals, and actions can also be thought of as a control-system approach and mirrors many of the aspects in our model. Like cognitive–affective units, Boesch's symbols are mental representations of objects, ideas, or actions, and carry one or more personal meanings. In fact, symbols are almost always polyvalent (representing many things at once) in a fashion similar to the cognitive–affective unit that connects to and activates many other units simultaneously. Symbols also carry emotional and motivational meanings and are therefore distinguished from what Boesch called signs. Signs only have overt and culturally dictated meanings. When used in its mathematical sense, a plus sign has only one culturally dictated meaning. Extend the bottom bar a little and you have a symbol relevant to many people, a cross.

Motivational

By considering the structure and interaction of symbols, goals, and actions, Boesch's approach takes on the sheen of a motivational theory. In Boesch's account, goals pervade all action, are arranged hierarchically, and are polyvalent. Any given action is performed in the service of some goal, but is also in the service of many other goals. When a young man washes his car, the immediate goal is to have a clean car. Washing the car also serves the purposes of showing off material wealth, impressing the girl he is taking on a date later that night, and appeasing his mother, who has been asking him to wash the car for over a week.

The actions that serve goals are broken into smaller actemes, which are defined as the subactions performed in the service of a larger action. Actions are distinguished from actemes only by the subjective feeling of finality that accompanies the completion of an action. The hierarchical ordering of actions and goals resembles the hierarchically ordered feedback loops described earlier, while acknowledging the motivational aspects of goals. Thus, Boesch's approach to goals and actions is somewhat like a control-system theory.

Boesch's theory also approaches goals in a more "motivational" sense, with goals arising primarily from two sources. First, an individual can perceive a deficit between his or her current or future state and some ideal referent state. Here, discrepancy causes the individual to search out and activate goals that would reduce the perceived difference. Boesch also acknowledged the possibility of Freudian-like drives that accumulate and create pressure to activate a certain goal. In both cases, some situation creates a need, which then activates or creates a complementary goal. When a goal has been created, selected, and activated, the result is the formation of an intention.

Social Constructivist

Boesch's theory is predominantly a social constructivist approach, with clear Piagetian undertones. Boesch saw the constructivist model as a framework for cultural psychology. By acknowledging the various (and by no means small) influences of culture, his approach became less rooted in individual construction. Instead, construction of an individual's reality results from a complex interplay among cultural symbolism, individual symbolism, and experience. In short, culture is both the product of action and a condition for future action.

Culture mediates action at all levels of Boesch's theory (see also Figure 5.1). The impact of culture at the structural level has already been addressed, with culture narrowing the number of acceptable actions from a larger (nearly infinite) range of possibilities. Boesch described the structure of action in terms of its interaction with culture by allowing culture to alter the possibilities in the action field and by influencing the generation of symbols. Just as Vygotsky saw symbol formation as a process of internalizing cultural symbols, Boesch's theory sees symbols as partially representing culturally consistent ideas that are modified by personal experience. Finally, culture interacts with the motivational aspects of Boesch's theory by determining which goals are appropriate and influencing the ways that those goals are achieved.

Boesch's theory therefore encapsulates the various forms of action theories, with a special focus on social construction. His model presents another example of an integrative approach through which the development of self-regulation can be viewed that augments and informs the heuristic presented in Table 5.1 and Figure 5.3.

LIMITATIONS AND BURNING QUESTIONS

Individual theories of self-regulation tend to focus on one or two of the action-control subtypes described by Brandtstädter (1998). The absence of a generally accepted unifying metatheory currently limits theoretical and empirical progress in the study of self-regulation. Integrating across levels of action theories and synthesizing various other theoretical positions, as we have attempted with our organizing heuristic, allows for a broader and more theoretically sound approach to self-regulation. Further integration would greatly benefit the field.

One area in which integration has already been fruitful is the integration of attention and self-regulation. In Mischel's model, for example, cool processing is facilitated by directed attention. Rothbart, Posner, and colleagues have similarly worked attention into their conceptualization of temperamental effortful control, which has led many researchers to acknowledge an attention–regulation link.

The study of temperament should also be expanded to incorporate lower level theories. We previously mentioned that temperament should manifest in biological forms. To our knowledge, the biological correlates underlying increased (or decreased) effortful control have not been fully elucidated. Our organizing heuristic suggests that such correlates should facilitate attention processing or modulate the connections made within the cognitive–affective processing architecture. More work in this area is needed. Integration could also be helpful when studying the conscious–automatic dichotomy of self-regulation. Automatic forms of self-regulation are a recurrent theme in the field, although little work attempts to incorporate both expressly (but see Kochanska, 1993). Automatic and effortful forms of regulation share common roots and should be theoretically synthesized as such. Each form is expected to have a unique influence on development, however (e.g., committed vs. situational compliance), and should be studied as separable constructs. Many measures of behavioral self-regulation unabashedly combine the information related to conscious and automatic processes.

Although direct measures of cognitive inhibition (e.g., go–no go tasks) more or less tap willful processes directly, many parent and teacher report measures do not. A child might be well behaved at school because he or she has excellent self-control, but children with only moderate self-control can behave just as well. Moderate regulators may have strongly internalized standards and simply do not think to misbehave. Little, Jones, Henrich, and Hawley (2003) have divided the variance of aggression into discernable forms and functions using latent constructs. A similar approach could be taken with measures of agentic and automatic self-regulation.

Another potential limitation in the current literature is the application of a deficit model to dysregulation. Problem behaviors are often said to arise because of a lack of self-regulation. Although deficits in attention, working memory, and so on lead to suboptimal behavior, research would be well informed if it simultaneously considered which elements of the self-regulatory system are present in dysregulated children and which aspects cause problematic behavior. Considering low expectancy or value attributions to future rewards may be more helpful than studying a lack of inhibition alone, for instance. Identifying constellations of individuals with similar architectures may prove beneficial, but would require a more person-oriented analysis (e.g., Bergman & Magnusson, 1997).

These limitations and directions deal primarily with issues related to theory integration. Another limitation concerns the continuity of self-regulation across the lifespan. Self-regulation develops in two relatively distinct epochs. The primary components of self-regulation develop through adolescence, whereas the SOC model largely explains development from adolescence to old age. An important goal for future research is to better synthesize the SOC model with self-regulation as it is traditionally studied in childhood (e.g., inhibition, effortful control, agency).

In summary, synthesizing multiple approaches to self-regulation will facilitate theoretical and empirical development in the field. Integration brings new and meaningful questions to the forefront. Addressing the questions that ensue will heighten our understanding of self-regulation, a core aspect of human functioning.

REFERENCES

Ahadi, S. A., Rothbart, M. K., & Ye, R. (1993). Children's temperament in the US and China: Similarities and differences. *European Journal of Personality, 7,* 359–377.

Amodio, D. M., Master, S. L., Yee, S. M., & Taylor, S. E. (2008). Neurocognitive components of behavioral inhibition and activation systems: Implications for theories of self-regulation. *Psychophysiology, 45,* 11–19.

Andersen, R. A. (1989). Visual and eye movement functions of the posterior parietal cortex. *Annual Review of Neuroscience, 12,* 377–403.

Arnett, J. J. (1992). Reckless behavior in adolescence: A developmental perspective. *Developmental Review, 12,* 339–373.

Atkinson, J. W. (1957). Motivational determinants of risk-taking behavior. *Psychological Review, 64,* 359–372.

Ayduk, O., Mendoza-Denton, M., Mischel, W., Downey, G., Peake, P. K., & Rodriguez, M. (2000). Regulating the interpersonal self: Strategic self-regulation for coping with rejection sensitivity. *Journal of Personality and Social Psychology, 79,* 776–792.

Backen Jones, L., Rothbart, M. K., & Posner, M. I. (2003). Development of executive attention in preschool children. *Developmental Science, 6,* 498–504.

Baltes, M. M., & Baltes, P. B. (Eds.). (1986). *The psychology of control and aging*. Hillsdale, NJ: Erlbaum.

Baltes, P. B., & Baltes, M. M. (1990). Psychological perspectives on successful aging: The model of selective optimization with compensation. In P. B. Baltes & M. M. Baltes (Eds.), *Successful aging: Perspectives from the behavioral sciences* (pp. 1–34). New York: Cambridge University Press.

Baltes, P. B., Staudinger, U. M., & Lindenberger, U. (1999). Lifespan psychology: Theory and application to intellectual functioning. *Annual Review of Psychology, 50,* 471–507.

Bandura, A. (1969). *Principles of behavior modification*. New York: Holt, Rinehart & Winston.

Bandura, A. (1995). *Self-efficacy: The exercise of control*. New York: Freeman.

Banfield, J. E., Wyland, C. L., Macrae, C. N., Münte, T. F., & Heatherton, T. F. (2004). The cognitive neuroscience of self-regulation. In R. F. Baumeister & K. D. Vohs (Eds.), *Handbook of self-regulation: Research, theory, and applications.* (pp. 99–129). New York: Guilford Press.

Barbas, H., Henion, T. H. H., & Dermon, C .R. (1991). Diverse thalamic projections to the prefrontal cortex in the rhesus monkey. *Journal of Comparative Neurology, 313*, 65–94.

Bargh, J. A., Gollwitzer, P. M., Lee-Chai, A., Barndollar, K., & Trötschel, R. (2001). The automated will: Nonconscious activation and pursuit of behavioral goals. *Journal of Personality and Social Psychology, 81,* 1014–1027.

Barkley, R. A. (1997). Behavioral inhibition, sustained attention and executive functions: Constructing a unifying theory of ADHD. *Psychological Bulletin, 121,* 65–94.

Bates, J. E., Bayles, K., Bennet, D. S., Ridge, B., & Brown, M. M. (1991). Origins of externalizing behavior problems at eight years of age. In D.J. Pepler & K.H. Rubin (Eds.), *The development and treatment of childhood aggression* (pp. 93–120). Hillsdale, NJ: Erlbaum.

Bates, J. F., Goldman-Rakic, P. S. (1993). Prefrontal connections of medial motor areas in the rhesus monkey. *Journal of Comparative Neurology, 336,* 211–228.

Baumeister, R. F. (2002). Ego depletion and self-control failure: An energy model of the self's executive function. *Self and Identity, 1,* 129–136.

Baumeister, R. F., Bratslavsky, E., Muraven, M., & Tice, D. M. (1998). Ego depletion: Is the active self a limited resource? *Journal of Personality and Social Psychology, 74,* 1252–1265.

Baumeister, R. F., Heatherton, T. F., & Tice, D.M. (1994). *Losing control: How and why people fail at self-regulation.* San Diego, CA: Academic Press.

Beier, M. E., & Ackerman, P. L. (2005). Age, ability, and the role of prior knowledge on the acquisition of new domain knowledge: Promising results in a real-world learning environment. *Psychology and Aging, 20,* 341–355.

Benes, F. M. (2001). The development of prefrontal cortex: The maturation of neurotransmitter systems and their interactions. In C. A. Nelson, & M. Luciana (Eds.), *Handbook of developmental cognitive neuroscience* (pp. 79–92). Cambridge, MA: MIT Press.

Benthin, A., Slovic, P., & Severson, H. (1993). A psychometric study of adolescent risk perception. *Journal of Adolescence, 16,* 153–168.

Bergin, C., Tallry, S., & Hamer, L. (2003). Prosocial behaviours of young adolescents: A focus study group. *Journal of Adolescence, 26,* 13–32.

Bergman, L. R., & Magnusson, D. (1997). A person-oriented approach in research on developmental psychopathology. *Development and Psychopathology, 9,* 291–319.

Boesch, E. E. (1991). *Symbolic action theory and cultural psychology.* Berlin: Springer-Verlag.

Boksem, M. A. S., Meijman, T. F., & Lorist, M. M. (2005). Effects of mental fatigue on attention: An ERP study. *Cognitive Brain Research, 25,* 107–116.

Brandtstädter, J. (1989). Personal self-regulation across development: Cross-sequential analyses of development-related control beliefs and emotions. *Developmental Psychology, 25,* 96–108.

Brandtstädter, J. (1998). Action perspectives on human development. In W. Damon (Series Ed.) & R. Lerner (Vol. Ed.), *Handbook of child psychology: Vol. 1. Theoretical models of human development* (pp. 1029–1144). New York: John Wiley & Sons.

Brandtstädter, J. (2006). Action perspectives on human development. In W. Damon (Series Ed.) & R. Lerner (Vol. Ed.), *Handbook of child psychology: Vol. 1. Theoretical models of human development* (pp. 516–568). Hoboken, NJ: John Wiley & Sons.

Brandtstädter, J., & Renner, G. (1990). Tenacious goal pursuit and flexible goal adjustment: Explication and age-related analysis of assimilative and accommodative strategies of coping. *Psychology and Aging, 5,* 58–67.

Brandtstädter, J., & Wentura, D. (1995). Adjustment to shifting possibility frontiers in later life: Complementary adaptive models. In R. Dixon & L. Bäckman (Eds.), *Compensating for psychological deficits and declines: Moderating losses and promoting gains* (pp. 83–106). Mahwah, NJ: Erlbaum.

Brass M., Ruge H., Meiran N., Rubin O., Koch I., Zysset S., et al. (2003). When the same response has different meanings: Recoding the response meaning in the lateral prefrontal cortex. *NeuroImage, 20,* 1026–1031.

Brown, B. B., Clasen, D. R., & Eicher, S. (1986). Perceptions of peer pressure, peer conformity dispositions, and self reported behavior among adolescents. *Developmental Psychology, 22,* 521–530.

Brunstein, J. C. (1993). Personal goals and subjective well-being: A longitudinal study. *Journal of Personality and Social Psychology, 65,* 1061–1070.

Bullock, M., & Lütkenhaus, P. (1988). The development of volitional behavior in the toddler years. *Child Development, 59,* 664–674.

Bunge, S. A. (2004). How we use rules to select actions: a review of evidence from cognitive neuroscience. *Cognitive, Affective, & Behavioral Neuroscience, 4,* 564–579.

Bunge S. A., Kahn I., Wallis J. D., Miller E. K., Wagner A. D. (2003). Neural circuits subserving the retrieval and maintenance of abstract rules. *Journal of Neurophysiology, 90,* 3419–3428.

Bush, G., Luu, P., & Posner, M. (2000). Cognitive and emotional influences in anterior cingulate cortex. *Trends in Cognitive Science, 4,* 215–222.

Bushnell, E. W., & Roder B. J. (1985). Recognition of color-form compounds by 4-month-old infants. *Infant Behavior and Development, 8,* 255–268.

Byrnes, J. P. (2002). The development of decision-making. *Journal of Adolescent Health, 31,* 208–215.

Calkins, S. D. (1994). Origins and outcomes of individual differences in emotion regulation. In N. A. Fox (Ed.), *Emotion regulation:*

Behavioral and biological considerations: Monographs of the Society for Research in Child Development, 59,* 53–72.

Calkins, S. D., & Johnson, M. C. (1998). Toddler regulation of distress to frustrating events: Temperamental and maternal correlates. *Infant Behavior & Development, 21,* 379–395.

Calkins, S. D., Smith, C. L., Gill, K., & Johnson, M. C. (1998). Maternal interactive style across contexts: Relations to emotional, behavioral and physiological regulation during toddlerhood. *Social Development, 7,* 350–369.

Cameron Pontiz, C. E., McClelland, M. M., Jewkes, A. M., Connor, C. M., Farris, C. L., & Morrison, F. J. (2008). Touch your toes! Developing a direct measure of behavioral regulation in early childhood. *Early Childhood Research Quarterly, 23,* 141–158.

Carlo, G., Hausmann, A., Christiansen, S., & Randall, B. A. (2003). Sociocognitive and behavioral correlates of a measure of prosocial tendencies for adolescents. *Journal of Early Adolescence, 23,* 107–134.

Carlo, G., & Randall, B. A. (2002). The development of a measure of prosocial behaviors for late adolescents. *Journal of Youth and Adolescence, 31,* 31–44.

Carlson, S. M., & Moses, L. J. (2001). Individual differences in inhibitory control and children's theory of mind. *Child Development, 72,* 1032–1053.

Carstensen, L. L. (1995). Evidence for a life-span theory of socioemotional selectivity. *Current Directions in Psychological Science, 4,* 151–156.

Carver, C. S. (2004). Self-regulation of action and affect. In R. F. Baumeister & K. D. Vohs (Eds.), *Handbook of self-regulation: Research, theory, and applications* (pp. 13–39). New York: Guilford Press.

Carver, C. S., & Scheier, M. F. (1981). *Attention and self-regulation: A control theory approach to human behavior.* New York: Springer-Verlag.

Carver, C. S., & Scheier, M. F. (1990). Origins and functions of positive and negative affect: A control-process view. *Psychological Review, 97,* 19–35.

Casey, B. J., Galvan, A., & Hare, T. A. (2005). Changes in cerebral functional organization during cognitive development. *Current Opinion in Neurobiology, 15,* 239–244.

Casey, B. J., Trainor, R. J., Orendi, J. L., Schubert, A. B., Nystrom, L. E., Giedd, J. N., et al. (1997). A developmental functional MRI study of prefrontal activation during performance of a go-no-go task. *Journal of Cognitive Neuroscience, 9,* 835–847.

Chapman, M., Skinner, E. A., & Baltes, P. B. (1990). Interpreting correlations between children's perceived control and cognitive performance: control, agency, or means-ends beliefs? *Developmental Psychology, 26,* 246–253.

Chavis, D. A., & Pandya, D. N. (1976). Further observations on the corticofrontal connections in the rhesus monkey. *Brain Research, 117,* 369–386.

Ciairano, S., Visu-Petra, L., & Settanni, M. (2007). Executive inhibitory control and cooperative behavior during early school years: A follow-up study. *Journal of Abnormal Child Psychology, 35,* 335–345.

Colombo, J. (2001). The development of visual attention in infancy. *Annual Review of Psychology, 52,* 337–367.

Colombo, J., & Cheatham, C. L. (2006). The emergence and basis of endogenous attention in infancy and early childhood. *Advances in Child Development and Behavior, 34,* 283–322.

Colombo J., & Horowitz F. D. (1987). Behavioral state as a lead variable in neonatal research. *Merrill-Palmer Quarterly, 33,* 423–438.

Conners, C. K., Epstein, J. N., Angold, A., & Klaric, J. (2003). Continuous performance test performance in a normative epidemiological sample. *Journal of Abnormal Child Psychology, 31,* 555–562.

Cooper, R., & Shallice, T. (2000). Contention scheduling and the control of routine activities. *Cognitive Neuropsychology, 17,* 297–338.

Critchley, H. D., Mathias, C. J., & Dolan, R. J. (2001). Neural activity in the human brain relating to uncertainty and arousal during anticipation. *Neuron, 29,* 537–545.

Crone, E. A., Donohue, S. E., Honomichl, R., Wendelken, C., & Bunge, S. A. (2006). Brain regions mediating flexible rule use during development. *The Journal of Neuroscience, 26,* 11239–11247.

Csibra, G., Tucker, L. A., & Johnson, M. H. (1998). Neural correlates of saccade planning in infants: A high-density ERP study. *International Journal of Psychophysiology, 29,* 201–215.

Daniel, D. B., Pelote, M., & Lewis, J. (2000). Lack of sex differences on the Stroop color–word test across three age groups. *Perceptual and Motor Skills, 90,* 483–484.

Dannemiller, J. L., & Braun, A. (1988). The perception of chromatic figure-ground relationships in 5-month-olds. *Infant Behavior and Development, 11,* 31–42.

Derryberry, D., & Rothbart, M. K. (1997). Reactive and effortful processed in the organization of temperament. *Development and Psychopathology, 9,* 631–650.

DeShazo Berry, T., Lyman, R. D., & Klinger, L. G. (2002). Academic underachievement and attention-deficit/hyperactivity disorder: The negative impact of symptom severity on school performance. *Journal of School Psychology, 40,* 259–283.

Diamond, A. (1985). The development of the ability to use recall to guide action, as indicated by infants' performance on AB. *Child Development, 56,* 868–883.

Diamond, A. (1988). The abilities and neural mechanisms underlying AB performance. *Child Development, 59,* 523–527.

Diamond, A. (1990). Developmental time course in human infants and infant monkeys and the neural bases of inhibitory control in reaching. *Annals of the New York Academy of Science, 608,* 637–676.

Diamond, A. (1991). Neuropsychological insights into the meaning of object concept development. In S. Carey & R. Gelman (Eds.), *The epigenesis of mind: Essays on biology and knowledge* (pp. 67–110). Hillsdale, NJ: Erlbaum.

Diamond, A., & Goldman-Rakic, P. S. (1989). Comparison of human infants and rhesus monkeys on Piaget's AB task: Evidence for dependence on dorsolateral prefrontal cortex. *Experimental Brain Research, 74,* 24–40.

Diamond, A., & Taylor, C. (1996). Development of an aspect of executive control: Development of the abilities to remember what I say and to "Do as I say, not as I do." *Developmental Psychobiology, 29,* 315–334.

Diener, E., & Fujita, F. (1995). Resources, personal strivings, and subjective well-being: A nomothetic and idiographic approach. *Journal of Personality and Social Psychology, 68,* 926–935.

Diener, M. L., Mangelsdorf, S. C., McHale, J. L., & Frosch, C. A. (2002). Infants' behavioral strategies for emotion regulation with fathers and mothers: Associations with emotional expressions an attachment quality. *Infancy, 3,* 153–174.

Dienstbier, R. A. (1984). The role of emotion in moral socialization. In C. Izard & R. B. Zajonc (Eds.), *Emotions, cognitions, and behaviors* (pp. 484–513). New York: Cambridge University Press.

Dougherty D. M., Bjork J. M., Harper A. R., Marsh D. M., Moeller F. G., Mathias C. W., et al. (2003). Behavioral impulsivity paradigms: A comparison in hospitalized adolescents with disruptive behavior disorders. *The Journal of Child Psychology and Psychiatry, 44,* 1145–1157.

Drevets, W. C., & Raichle, M. (1998). Reciprocal suppression of regional blood flow during emotional versus higher cognitive processes: Implications for interactions between emotion and cognition. *Cognition and Emotion, 12,* 353–385.

Eccles, J. (1983). Expectancies, values, and academic behaviors. In J. T. Spence (Ed.), *Achievement and achievement motives: Psychological and sociological approaches* (pp. 75–146). San Francisco: Freeman.

Eccles, J. S. (1987). Gender roles and women's achievement-related decisions. *Psychology of Women Quarterly, 11,* 135–172.

Eisenberg, N., Fabes, R. A., Bernzweig, J., Karbon, M., Poulin, R., & Hanish, L. (1993). The relations of emotionality and regulation to preschoolers' social skills and sociometric status. *Child Development, 64,* 1418–1438.

Eisenberg, N., Fabes, R. A., Guthrie, I. K., Murphy, B. C., Maszk, P., Homgren, R., et al. (1996). The relations of regulation and emotionality to problem behavior in elementary school children. *Development and Psychopathology, 8,* 141–162.

Eisenberg, N., Fabes, R. A., Karbon, M., Murphy, B. C., Wosinski, M., Polazzi, L., et al. (1996).The relations of children's dispositional prosocial behavior to emotionality, regulation, and social functioning. *Child Development, 67,* 974–992.

Eisenberg, N., Fabes, R., & Murphy, B. C. (1995). Relations of shyness and low sociability to regulation and emotionality. *Journal of Personality and Social Psychology, 68,* 505–517.

Eisenberg, N., Guthrie, I. K., Fabes, R. A., Reiser, M., Murphy, B. C., Holgren, R., Maszk, P., & Losoya, S. (1997). The relations of regulation and emotionality to resiliency and competent social functioning in elementary school children. *Child Development, 68,* 295–311.

Eisenberg, N., Guthrie, I. K., Fabes, R. A., Shepard, S., Losoya, S., Murphy, B., et al. (2000). Prediction of elementary school children's externalizing problem behaviors from attentional and behavioral regulation and negative emotionality. *Child Development, 71,* 1367–1382.

Eisenberg, N., Michalik, N., Spinrad, T. L., Hofer, C., Kupfer, A., Vaiente, C., et al. (2007). The relations of effortful control and impulsivity to children's sympathy: A longitudinal study. *Cognitive Development, 22,* 544–567.

Eisenberg, N., Smith, C. L., Sadovsky, A., & Spinrad, T. L. (2004). Effortful control: Relations with emotion regulation, adjustment, and socialization in childhood. In R. F. Baumeister & K. D. Vohs (Eds.), *Handbook of self-regulation: Research, theory, and applications* (pp. 259–282). New York: Guilford Press.

Eisenberg, N., & Spinrad, T. L. (2004). Emotion-related regulation: Sharpening the definition. *Child Development, 75,* 334–339.

Eisenberg, N., Wentzel, M., & Harris, J. D. (1998). The role of emotionality and regulation in empathy-related responding. *School Psychology Review, 27,* 506–521.

Elliot, R., Dolan, R. J., & Frith, C. D. (2000). Dissociable functions in the medial and lateral orbitofrontal cortex: Evidence from human neuroimaging studies. *Cerebral Cortex, 10,* 308–317.

Elliott, R., Frith, C. D., & Dolan, R. J. (1997). Differential neural response to positive and negative feedback in planning and guessing tasks. *Neuropsychologia, 35,* 1395–1404.

Emmons, R. A. (1986). Personal strivings: An approach to personality and subjective well being. *Journal of Personality and Social Psychology, 51,* 1058–1068.

Engle, R. W. (2002). Working memory capacity as executive attention. *Current Directions in Psychological Science, 11*(1), 19–23.

Ernst, M., Pine, D. S., & Hardin, M. (2006). Triadic model of the neurobiology of motivated behavior in adolescence. *Psychological Medicine, 36,* 299–312.

Eysenck, H. J. (1967). *The biological basis of personality.* Springfield, IL: Charles C. Thomas.

Fan, J., Flombaum, J. I., McCandliss, B. D., Thomas, M. K., & Posner, M. I. (2003). Cognitive and brain mechanisms of conflict. *Neuroimage, 18,* 42–57.

Fan, J., McCandliss, B. D., Sommer, T., Raz, A., & Posner, M. I. (2002). Testing the efficiency and independence of attentional networks. *Journal of Cognitive Neuroscience, 14,* 340–347.

Feldman, R., Masalha, S., & Alony, D. (2006). Microregulatory patterns of family interactions: Cultural pathways to toddlers' self-regulation. *Journal of Family Psychology, 20,* 614–623.

Feldman, S. S., & Weinberger, D.A. (1994). Self-restraint as a mediator of family influences on boys' delinquent behavior: A longitudinal study. *Child Development, 65,* 195–211.

Fink, M., & Bender, M. B. (1953). Perceptions of simultaneous tactile stimulation in normal children. *Neurology, 3,* 27–34.

Fitzsimmons, G. A., & Bargh, J. A. (2004). Automatic self-regulation. In R. F. Baumeister & K. D. Vohs (Eds.), *Handbook of self-regulation: Research, theory, and applications* (pp. 151–170). New York: Guilford Press.

Flynn, T. (1985). Development of self-concept, delay of gratification, and self-control and disadvantaged preschool children's achievement gain. *Early Child Development and Care, 1,* 65–72.

Freud, S. (1923/1961). *The ego and the id.* New York: Norton.

Freud, S. (1930). *Civilization and its discontents.* New York: J. Cape & H. Smith.

Freund, A. M. (2001). Developmental psychology of life-management. In N. J. Smelser & P. B. Baltes (Eds.), *International encyclopedia of the social & behavioral sciences* (Vol. 13, pp. 8827–8832). Oxford: Elsevier Science.

Freund, A. M., & Baltes, P. B. (1998). Selection, optimization, and compensation as strategies of life management: Correlations with subjective indicators of successful aging. *Psychology and Aging, 13,* 531–543.

Freund, A. M., & Baltes, P. B. (2000). The orchestration of selection, optimization, and compensation: An action-theoretical conceptualization of a theory of developmental regulation. In W. J. Perrig, & A. Grob (Eds.), *Control of human behavior, mental processes and consciousness: Essays in honor of the 60th birthday of August Flammer* (pp. 35–58). New York: Erlbaum.

Freund, A. M., & Baltes, P. B. (2002). The adaptiveness of selection, optimization, and compensation as strategies of life management: Evidence from a preference study on proverbs. *Journal of Gerontology: Psychological Sciences, 57B,* P426-P434.

Fuster, J. M. (1997). *The prefrontal cortex: Anatomy, physiology, and neuropsychology of the frontal lobe.* New York: Lippincott-Raven.

Galvan A., Hare T., Voss H., Glover G., & Casey B. J. (2007). Risk-taking and the adolescent brain: Who is at risk? *Developmental Science, 10,* F8–F14.

Gardner, T. W., Dishion, T. J., & Connell, A. M. (2008). Adolescent self-regulation as resilience: Resistance to antisocial behavior within the deviant peer context. *Journal of Abnormal Child Psychology, 36,* 273–284.

Garstein, M. R., & Rothbart, M. K. (2003). Studying infant temperament via the revised infant behavior questionnaire. *Infant Behavior and Development, 26,* 64–86.

Gehring, W., & Knight, R. (2000). Prefrontal cingulate interactions in action monitoring. *Nature Neuroscience, 3,* 516–520.

Gerardi-Caulton, G. (2000). Sensitivity to spatial conflict and the development of self-regulation in children 24–36 months. *Developmental Science, 3,* 397–404.

Gerstadt, C. L., Hong, Y. J., & Diamond, A. (1994). The relationship between cognition and action: Performance of children 3½–7 years old on a Stroop-like day–night task. *Cognition, 53,* 129–153.

Gestsdóttir, S., & Lerner, R. M. (2007). Intentional self-regulation and positive youth development in early adolescence: Findings from the 4-H study of positive youth development. *Developmental Psychology, 43,* 508–521.

Gestsdottir, S., & Lerner, R. M. (2008). Positive development in adolescence: The development and role of intentional self-regulation. *Human Development, 51,* 202–224.

Gogtay N., Giedd J. N., Lusk L., Hayashi K. M., Greenstein D., Vaituzis A. C., et al. (2004). Dynamic mapping of human cortical development during childhood through early adulthood. *Proceedings of the National Academy of Sciences USA, 101,* 8174–8179.

Gray, J. A. (1970). The psychophysiological basis of introversion-extraversion. *Behaviour Research and Therapy, 8,* 249–266.

Gray, J. A. (1981). A critique of Eysenck's theory of personality. In H. J. Eysenck (Ed.), *A model of personality* (pp. 246–276). New York: Springer.

Harman, C., Rothbart, M. K., & Posner, M. I. (1997). Distress and attention interactions in early infancy. *Motivation and Emotion, 21,* 27–43.

Hasher, L., & Zacks, R. T. (1988). Working memory, comprehension and aging: A review and a new view. In G. H. Bower (Ed.), *The psychology of learning and motivation* (Vol. 22, pp. 193–225). New York: Academic Press.

Hasher, L., Zacks, R. T., & May, C. P. (1999). Inhibitory control, circadian arousal, and age. In D. Gopher & A. Koriat (Eds.), *Attention and performance XVII: Cognitive regulation of performance: Interaction of theory and application* (pp. 653–675). Cambridge, MA: MIT Press.

Hawley, P. H., & Little, T. D. (2002) Evolutionary and developmental perspectives on the agentic self. In D. Cervone & W. Mischel (Eds.), *Advances in personality science* (pp. 177–195). New York: Guilford Press.

Hay, D. F., Payne, A., & Chadwick, A. (2004). Peer relations in childhood. *Journal of child Psychology and Psychiatry, 45,* 84–108.

Heckhausen, J. (1997). Developmental regulation across adulthood: Primary and secondary control of age-related challenges. *Developmental Psychology, 33,* 176–187.

Heckhausen, J., & Schulz, R. (1995). A life-span theory of control. *Psychological Review, 102,* 284–304.

Heckhausen, J., & Schulz, R. (1998). Developmental regulation in adulthood: Selection and compensation via primary and secondary control. In J. Heckhausen & C. S. Dweck (Eds.), *Motivation and self-regulation across the lifespan* (pp. 50–77). New York: Cambridge University Press.

Henry, B., Caspi, A., Moffitt, T. E., & Silva, P. A. (1996). Temperamental and familial predictors of violent and nonviolent criminal convictions: Age 3 to age 18. *Developmental Psychology, 32,* 614–623.

Hooper, C. J., Luciana, M., Conklin, H. M., & Yarger, R. S. (2004). Adolescents' performance on the Iowa gambling task: Implications for the development of decision making and ventromedial prefrontal cortex. *Developmental Psychology, 40,* 1148–1158.

Howse, R. B., Calkins, S. D., Anastopoulos, A. D., Keane, S. P., & Shelton, T. L. (2003). Regulatory contributors to children's kindergarten achievement. *Early Education and Development, 14,* 101–119.

Jacques, S., Zelazo, P. D., Kirkham, N. Z., & Semcesen, T. K. (1999). Rule selection versus rule execution in preschoolers: An error-detection approach. *Developmental Psychology, 35,* 770–780.

James, W. (1890). *The principles of psychology*. New York: Henry Holt.

Johnson, M. H. (1995). The inhibition of automatic saccades in early infancy. *Developmental Psychobiology, 28,* 281–291.

Johnson M. H., Posner M. I., & Rothbart M. K. (1991). Components of visual orienting in early infancy: Contingency learning, anticipatory looking, and disengaging. *Journal of Cognitive Neuroscience, 3,* 335–344.

Johnson, M. H., Posner, M. I., Rothbart, M. K. (1994). Facilitation of saccades toward a covertly attended location in early infancy. *Psychological Science, 5,* 90–93.

Jopp, D., & Smith, J. (2006). Resources and life-management strategies as determinants of successful aging: On the protective effect of selection, optimization, and compensation. *Psychology and Aging, 21,* 253–265.

Kanaka, N., Matsuda, T., Tomimoto, Y., Noda, Y., Matsushima, E., Matsuura, M., & Kojima, T. (2008). Measurement of development of cognitive and attention functions in children using continuous performance test. *Psychiatry and Clinical neurosciences, 62,* 135–141.

Kannass, K. N., & Colombo, J. (2007). The effects of continuous and intermittent distractors on cognitive performance and attention in preschoolers. *Journal of Cognition and Development, 8*(1), 63–77.

Karasawa, M., Little, T. D., Miyashita, T. Mashima, M., & Azuma, H. (1997). Japanese children's action control beliefs about school performance. *International Journal of Behavioral Development, 20,* 405–423.

Keller, H., Yovsi, R., Borke, J., Kärtner, J., Jenning, H., & Papaligoura, Z. (2004). Developmental consequences of early parenting experiences: Self-recognition and self-regulation in three cultural communities. *Child Development, 75,* 1745–1760.

Kempen, G. I. J. M., Ormel, J., Scaf-Klomp, W., van Sonderen, E., Ranchor, A. V., & Sanderman, R. (2003). The role of perceived control in the process of older peoples' recovery of physical functions after fall-related injuries: A prospective study. *Journal of Gerontology: Psychological Sciences, 58B,* P35–P41.

Kempen, G. I. J. M., Ranchor, A. V., Ormel, J., van Sonderen, E., van Jaarsveld, C. H. M., & Sanderman, R. (2005). Perceived control and long-term changes in disability in late middle-aged and older persons: An eight year follow-up study. *Psychology and Health, 20,* 193–206.

Keogh, B. K. (1992). Temperament and teachers' views of teachability. In W. Carey & S. McDevitt (Eds.), *Prevention and early intervention: Individual differences as risk factors for the mental health of children* (pp. 246–254). New York: Bruner/Mazel.

Kochanska, G. (1993). Toward a synthesis of parental socialization and child temperament in early development of conscience. *Child Development, 64,* 325–347.

Kochanska, G., Aksan, N., & Koenig, A. L. (1995). A longitudinal study of the roots of preschoolers' conscience: Committed compliance and emerging internalization. *Child Development, 66,* 1752–1769.

Kochanska, G., Coy, K. C., & Murray, K. T. (2001). The development of self-regulation in the first four years of life. *Child Development, 72,* 1091–1111.

Kochanska, G., Murray, K., & Coy, K. C. (1997). Inhibitory control as a contributor to conscience in childhood: From toddlerhood to early school age. *Child Development, 68,* 263–277.

Kochanska, G., Murray, K. T., & Harlan, E. T. (2000). Effortful control in early childhood: Continuity and change, antecedents and implications for social development. *Developmental Psychology, 36,* 220–232.

Kochanska, G., Tjebkes, T. L., & Forman, D. R. (1998). Children's emerging regulation of conduct: Restraint, compliance, and internalization from infancy to the second year. *Child Development, 69,* 1378–1389.

Kopp, C. (1982). Antecendents of self-regulation: A developmental perspective. *Developmental Psychology, 18,* 199–214.

Kopp, C. (1989). Regulation of distress and negative emotions: A developmental perspective. *Developmental Psychology, 25,* 343–354.

Krueger, R. F., Caspi, A., Moffitt, T. E, White, J., & Stouthamer-Loeber, M. (1996). Delay of gratification, psychopathology, and personality: Is low self-control specific to externalizing problems? *Journal of Personality, 64,* 107–129.

Kuhl, J. (1986). Motivation and information processing: A new look at decision making, dynamic change, and action control. In R. M. Sorrentino & E. T. Higgins (Eds.), *Handbook of motivation and cognition: Foundations of social behavior.* New York: Guilford Press.

Lachman, M. E. (1986). Personal control in later life: Stability, change, and cognitive correlates. In M. M. Baltes & P. B. Baltes (Eds.), *The psychology of control and aging* (pp. 207–236). Hillsdale, NJ: Erlbaum.

Lehto, J. E., Juujärvi, P., Kooistra, L., & Pulkkinen, L. (2003). Dimensions of executive functioning: Evidence from children. *British Journal of Developmental Psychology, 21,* 59–80.

Lerner, R. M., & Busch-Rossnagel, N. A. (1981). *Individual as producers of their development: A lifespan perspective.* New York: Academic Press.

Lerner, R. M., Freund, A. M., De Stefanis, I., & Habermas, T. (2001). Understanding developmental regulation in adolescence: The use of the selection, optimization, and compensation model. *Human Development, 44,* 29–50.

Leslie, A. M., & Polizzi, P. (1998). Inhibitory processing in the false belief task: The influence of family ecology and kin relations. *International Journal of Behavioral Development, 19,* 39–52.

Li, S., Lindenberger, U., Hommel, B., Aschersleben, G., Primz, W., & Baltes, P. B. (2004). Transformations in couplings among intellectual abilities and constituent cognitive processes across the life span. *Psychological Science 15,* 155–163.

Liddel, P. F., Kiehl, K. A., & Smith, A. M. (2001). Event-related fMRI study of response inhibition. *Human Brain Mapping, 12,* 100–109.

Lin, C. C. H., Chen, W. J., Yang, H., Hsiao, C. K., & Tien, A. Y. (2000). Performance on the Wisconsin Card Sorting Test among adolescents in Taiwan: Norms, factorial structure, and relation to schizotypy. *Journal of Clinical and Experimental Neuropsychology, 22,* 69–79.

Little, T. D. (1998). Sociocultural influences on the development of children's action-control beliefs. In J. Heckhausen & C. S. Dweck (Eds.), *Motivation and self-regulation across the life span.* (pp. 281–315). New York: Cambridge University Press.

Little, T. D., Hawley, P. H., Henrich, C. C., & Marsland, K. (2002). Three views of the agentic self: A developmental synthesis. In E. L. Deci & R. M. Ryan (Eds.), *Handbook of self-determination research* (pp. 389–404). Rochester, NY: University of Rochester Press.

Little, T. D., Jones, S. M., Henrich, C. C., & Hawley, P. H. (2003). Disentangling the "whys" from the "whats" of aggressive behavior. *International Journal of Behavioral Development, 27,* 122–133.

Little, T. D., & Lopez, D. F. (1997). Regularities in the development of children's causality beliefs about school performance across six sociocultural contexts. *Developmental Psychology, 33,* 165–175.

Little, T. D., Lopez, D. F., Oettingen, G., & Baltes, P. B. (2001). A comparative-longitudinal study of action-control beliefs and school performance: On the role of context. *International Journal of Behavioral Development, 25,* 237–245.

Little, T. D., Oettingen, G., Stetsenko, A., & Baltes, P. B. (1995). Children's action-control beliefs and school performance: How do American children compare to German and Russian children? *Journal of Personality and Social Psychology, 69,* 686–700.

Little, T. D., Snyder, C. R., & Wehmeyer, M. (2006). The agentic self: On the nature and origins of personal agency across the lifespan. In. D. K. Mroczek & T. D. Little (Eds.). *Handbook of personality development* (pp. 61–80). Mahwah, NJ: Erlbaum.

Little, T. D., Stetsenko, A., & Maier, H. (1999). Action-control and school performance: A longitudinal study of Moscow children and adolescents. *International Journal of Behavioral Development, 23,* 799–823.

Livesey, D. J., & Morgan, G. A. (1991). The development of response inhibition in 4- and 5-year-old children. *Australian Journal of Psychology, 43,* 133–137.

Locke, J. (1690). *An essay concerning human understanding.* Retrieved October 10, 2008, from http://www.arts.cuhk.edu.hk/Philosophy/Locke/echu/.

Lopez, D. F., & Little, T. D. (1996). Children's action-control beliefs and emotional regulation in the social domain. *Developmental Psychology, 32,* 299–312.

Lu, M. T., Preston, J. B., & Strick, P. L. (1994). Interconnections between the prefrontal cortex and the premotor areas in the frontal lobe. *Journal of Comparative Neurology, 341,* 375–392.

Luciana, M., & Nelson, C. (1998). The functional emergence of prefrontally guided working memory systems in four-to eight-year-old children. *Neuropsychologia, 36,* 273–293.

Luna, B., & Sweeney, J. A. (2001). Studies of brain and cognitive maturation through childhood and adolescence: A strategy for testing neurodevelopmental hypotheses. *Schizophrenia Bulletin, 27,* 443–455.

Luria, A. R. (1966). *Higher cortical functions in man.* New York: Basic Books.

Luria, A. R. (1973). *The working brain* (B. Haigh, Trans.). New York: Basic Books. (Original work published 1969)

Lytton, H. (1977). Correlates of compliance and the rudiments of conscience in two-year-old boys. *Canadian Journal of Behavioral Science, 9,* 242–251.

Lytton, H. (1980). *Parent–child interaction: The socialization process observed in twin and singleton families.* New York: Plenum Press.

MacDonald, A. W., Cohen, J. D., Stenger, V. A., & Carter, C. S. (2000). Dissociating the role the role of the dorsolateral prefrontal and anterior cingulate cortex in cognitive control. *Science, 288,* 1835–1838.

MacKay, D. M. (1966). Cerebral organization and the conscious control of actions. In J. C. Eccles (Ed.), *Brain and Conscious Experience* (pp. 422–445). Berlin: Springer-Verlang.

Manglesdorf, S., Shapiro, J., & Marzolf, D. (1995). Developmental and temperamental differences in emotion regulation in infancy. *Child Development, 66,* 1817–1828.

Masten, A. S., & Coatsworth, J. D. (1998). The development of competence in favorable and unfavorable environments: Lessons from research on successful children. *American Psychologist, 53,* 205–220.

Matsuzawa, M., & Shimojo, S. (1997). Infants' fast saccades in the gap paradigm and development of visual attention. *Infant Behavior & Development, 20,* 449–455.

McCabe, L. A., Cunnington, M., & Brooks-Gunn, J. (2004). The development of self-regulation in young children: Individual characteristics and environmental contexts. In R. F. Baumeister & Vohs, K. D. (Eds.), *Handbook of self-regulation: Research, theory, and applications* (pp. 340–356), New York: Guilford Press.

Metcalfe, J., & Mischel, W. (1999). A hot/cool-system analysis of delay of gratification: Dynamics of willpower. *Psychological Review, 106,* 3–19.

Mischel, W. (1968). *Personality and assessment.* New York: John Wiley & Sons.

Mischel, W., & Ayduk, O. (2004). Willpower in a cognitive–affective processing system: the dynamics of delay of gratification. In R. F. Baumeister & K. D. Vohs (Eds.), *Handbook of self-regulation: Research, theory, and applications* (pp. 99–129). New York: Guilford Press.

Mischel, W., & Ebbesen, E. B. (1970). Attention in delay of gratification. *Journal of Personality and Social Psychology, 16,* 329–337.

Mischel, W., & Moore, B. (1973). Effects of attention to symbolically presented rewards on self-control. *Journal of Personality and Social Psychology, 28,* 172–179.

Mischel, W., & Shoda, Y. (1995). A cognitive–affective system theory of personality: Reconceptualizing situation, dispositions, dynamics, and invariance in personality structure. *Psychological Review, 102,* 246–268.

Mischel, W., Shoda, Y., & Peake, P. K. (1988). The nature of adolescent competencies predicted by preschool delay of gratification. *Journal of Personality and Social Psychology, 54,* 687–696.

Mischel, W., Shoda, Y., & Rodriguez, M. L. (1989, May 26). Delay of gratification in children. *Science, 244,* 933–938.

Moore, B., Mischel, W., & Zeiss, A. (1976). Comparative effects of the reward stimulus and its cognitive representation in voluntary delay. *Journal of Personality and Social Psychology, 34,* 419–424.

Mundy, P. C. (1985). Compound-stimulus information processing by 3-month-old infants. *Journal of Genetic Psychology, 146,* 357–365.

Nigg, J. T., Quamma, J. P., Greenberg, M. T., & Kusché, C. A. (1999). A two-year longitudinal study of neuropsychological and cognitive performance in relation to behavioral problems and competencies in elementary school children. *Journal of Abnormal Child Psychology, 27,* 51–63.

Norman, D. A., & Shallice, T. (1986). Attention to action: Willed and automatic control of behavior. In R. J. Davidson, G. E. Schwartz, & D. Shapiro (Eds.), *Consciousness and self-regulation: Advances in research and theory* (Vol. 4, pp. 1–18). New York: Plenum Press.

Normandeau, S., & Guay, F. (1998). Preschool behavior and first-grade school achievement: The meditational role of cognitive self-control. *Journal of Educational Psychology, 90,* 111–121.

Nurmi, J. (1989). Development of orientation to the future during early adolescence: A four-year longitudinal study and two cross-sectional comparisons. *International Journal of Psychology, 24,* 195–214.

Nurmi, J. (1994). The development of future-orientation in a life-span context. In Z. Zaleski (Ed.), *Psychology of future orientation* (pp. 63–74). Lublin, Poland: Towarzystwo Naukowe KUL.

Oettingen, G., Little, T. D., Lindenberger, U., & Baltes, P. B. (1994). Causality, agency, and control beliefs in East versus West Berlin children: A natural experiment on the role of context. *Journal of Personality and Social Psychology, 66,* 579–595.

Ouschan, L., Boldero, J. M., Kashima, Y., Wakimoto, R., & Kashima, E. S. (2007). Regulatory focus strategies scale: A measure of individual differences in the endorsement of regulatory strategies. *Asian Journal of Social Psychology, 10,* 243–257.

Pardo, J. V., Pardo, P. J., Janer, K. W., & Raichle, M. E. (1990). The anterior cingulate cortex mediates processing selection in the Stroop attentional conflict paradigm. *Proceedings of the National Academy of Sciences, 87,* 256–259.

Park, D. C., Smith, A. D., Lautenschlager, G., Earles, J. L., Frieski, D., Zwahr, M., et al. (1996). Mediators of long-term memory performance across the life span. *Psychology and Aging, 11,* 621–637.

Passingham, R. (1993). *The frontal lobes and voluntary action.* New York: Oxford University Press.

Paus, T. (2001). Primate anterior cingulate cortex: Where motor control, drive, and cognition interface. *Nature Reviews Neuroscience, 2,* 417–424.

Paus, T., Collins, D. L., Evans, A. C., Leonard, G., Pike, B., & Zjdenbos, A. (2001). Maturation of white matter in the human brain: A review of magnetic resonance studies. *Brain Research Bulletin, 54,* 255–266.

Piaget, J. (1932/1965). *The moral judgment of the child.* New York: Free Press.

Piaget, J. (1952). *The origins of intelligence in children.* New York: Norton.

Piaget, J. (1970). *Structuralism.* New York: Harper & Row.

Posner, M. I., & Petersen, S. E. (1990). The attention system of the human brain. *Annual Review of Neuroscience, 13,* 25–42.

Posner, M. I., & Raichle, M. E. (1994). *Images of mind.* New York: Scientific American Library.

Posner, M. I., & Rothbart, M. K. (1998). Attention, self-regulation, and consciousness. *Philosophical Transactions of the Royal Society of London B, 353,* 1915–1927.

Powers, W. T. (1973). *Behavior: The control of perception.* Chicago: Aldine.

Raffaelli, M., & Crockett, L. J. (2003), Sexual risk taking in adolescence: The role of self-regulation and attraction to risk. *Developmental Psychology, 39,* 1036–1046.

Rapport, M. D., Scanlan, S. W., & Denney, C. B. (1999). Attention-deficit/hyperactivity disorder and scholastic achievement: A model of dual developmental pathways. *Journal of Child Psychology and Psychiatry, 40,* 1169–1183.

Reed, M. A., Pien, D. L., & Rothbart, M. K. (1984). Inhibitory self-control in preschool children. *Merrill-Palmer Quarterly, 30,* 131–147.

Reyna, V. F., & Farley, F. (2006). Risk and rationality in adolescent decision making: Implications for theory, practice, and public policy. *Psychological Science in the Public Interest, 7,* 1–44.

Richards, J. E. (1989). Development and stability in visual sustained attention in 14-, 20-, and 26-week-old infants. *Psychophysiology, 26,* 422–430.

Robbins, T. W. (1998). Arousal and attention: Psychopharmacological and neuropsychological studies in experimental animals. In R. Parasuraman (Ed.), *The attentive brain* (pp. 189–220). Cambridge, MA: MIT Press

Rothbart, M. K., & Ahadi, S. (1994). Temperament and the development of personality. *Journal of Abnormal Psychology, 103,* 55–65.

Rothbart, M. K., Ahadi, S. A., & Evans, D. E. (2000). Temperament and personality: Origins and outcomes. *Journal of Personality and Social Psychology, 78,* 122–135.

Rothbart, M. K., Ahadi, S. A., Hershey, K. L., & Fisher, P. (2001). Investigation of temperament at three to seven years: The children's behavior questionnaire. *Child Development, 72,* 1394–1408.

Rothbart, M. K., & Bates, J. E. (1998). Temperament. In W. Damon (Series Ed.) & N. Eisenberg (Ed.), *Handbook of child psychology: Vol. 3. Social, emotional, and personality development* (pp. 99–166). Hoboken, NJ: John Wiley & Sons.

Rothbart, M. K., Ellis, L. K., & Posner, M. I. (2004). Temperament and self-regulation. In R. F. Baumeister & K. D. Vohs (Eds.), *Handbook of self-regulation: Research, theory, and applications* (pp. 357–370), New York: Guilford Press.

Rothbart, M. K., Ellis, L. K., Rueda, M. R., & Posner, M. I. (2003). Developing mechanisms of temperamental effortful control. *Journal of Personality, 71,* 1113–1143.

Rothbart, M. K., Ziaie, H., & O'Boyle, C. (1992). Self-regulation and emotion in infancy. In N. Eisenberg & R. Fabes (Eds.), *Emotion and its regulation in early development* (pp. 7–23). San Francisco: Jossey-Bass/Pheiffer.

Rubia, K., Russell, T., Overmeyer, R., Brammer, M. J., Bullmore, E. T., Sharma, T., et al. (2001). Mapping motor inhibition: Conjunctive brain activations across different versions of go/no-go and stop tasks. *NeuroImage, 13,* 250–261.

Rubia, K., Smith, A. B., Wooley, J., Nosarti, C., Heyman, I., Taylor, E., et al. (2006). Progressive increase of frontostriatal brain activation from childhood to adulthood during event-related tasks of cognitive control. *Human Brain Mapping, 27,* 973–993.

Rueda, M. R., Fan, J., McCandliss, B. D., Halparin, J. D., Gruber, D. B., Lercari, L. P., & Posner, M.I. (2004). Development of attentional networks in childhood. *Neuropsychologia, 42,* 1029–1040.

Rueda, M. R., Posner, M. I., & Rothbart, M. K. (2004). Attentional control and self-regulation. In R. F. Baumeister & K. D. Vohs (Eds.), *Handbook of self-regulation: Research, theory, and applications* (pp. 283–300). New York: Guilford Press.

Ryan, R. M., & Deci, E. L. (2002). An overview of self-determination theory. In E. L. Deci & R. M. Ryan (Eds.) *Handbook of self-determination research* (pp. 3–36). Rochester, NY: University of Rochester Press.

Salthouse, T. A. (1996). The processing-speed theory of adult age differences in cognition. *Psychological Review, 103,* 403–428.

Schmeichel, B. J. (2007). Attention control, memory updating, and emotion regulation temporarily reduce the capacity for executive control. *Journal of Experimentla Psychology: General, 136,* 241–255.

Schmeichel, B. J., & Baumeister, R. F. (2004). Self-regulatory strength. In R. F. Baumeister & K. D. Vohs (Eds.), *Handbook of self-regulation: Research, theory, and applications* (pp. 84–98). New York: Guilford Press.

Schultz, D., Izard, C. E., Ackerman, B. P., & Youngstrom, E. A. (2001). Emotion knowledge in economically disadvantaged children: Self-regulatory antecedents and relations to social difficulties and withdrawal. *Development and Psychopathology, 13,* 53–67.

Schwartz, G. E., & Shapiro, D. (1976). *Consciousness and self-regulation: Advances in research.* New York: Plenum Press.

Schwartz, M. F., Montgomery, M. W., Fitzpatrick-DeSalme, E. J., Ochipa, C., Coslett, H. B., & Mayer, N. H. (1995). Analysis of a disorder of everyday action. *Cognitive Neuropsychology, 12,* 863–892.

Seeman, M., & Seeman, T. E. (1983). Health behavior and personal autonomy: A longitudinal study of the sense of control in illness. *Journal of Health and Social Behavior, 24,* 144–160.

Segalowitz, S. J., & Davies, P. L. (2004). Charting the maturation of the frontal lobe: An electrophysiological strategy. *Brain and Cognition, 55,* 116–133.

Shah, J. Y., Friedman, R., & Kruglanski, A. W. (2002). Forgetting all else: On the antecedents and consequences of goal shielding. *Journal of Personality and Social Psychology, 83,* 1261–1280.

Shallice, T., & Burgess, P. The domain of supervisory processes and temporal organization of behaviour. *Philosophical Transactions of the Royal Society of London B, 351,* 1405–1412.

Shea, S. L., & Aslin, R. N. (1990). Oculomotor responses to step-ramp targets by young human infants. *Vision Research, 30,* 1077–1092.

Sheese, B. E., Rothbart, M. K., Posner, M. I., White, L. K., & Fraundorf, S. H. (2008). Executive attention and self-regulation in infancy. *Infant Behavior & Development, 31,* 501–510.

Shoda, Y., Mischel, W., & Peake, P. K. (1990). Predicting adolescent cognitive and self-regulatory competencies from preschool delay of gratification: Identifying diagnostic conditions. *Developmental Psychology, 26,* 978–986.

Shonkoff, J. P., & Phillips, D. A. (Eds.). (2000). *From neurons to neighborhoods: The science of early childhood development.* Washington, DC: National Academy Press.

Siwek, D. F., & Pandya, D. N. (1991). Prefrontal projections to the mediodorsal nucleus of the thalamus in the rhesus monkey. *The Journal of Comparative Psychology, 312,* 509–524.

Skinner, E. A., Chapman, M., & Baltes, P. B. (1988). Children's beliefs about control, means–ends, and agency: Developmental differences during middle childhood. *International Journal of Behavioral Development, 11,* 369–388.

Sowell, E. R., Thompson, P. M., Holmes, C. J., Jernigan, T. L., & Toga, A. W. (1999). In vivo evidence for post-adolescent brain maturation in frontal and striatal regions. *Nature Neuroscience, 2,* 859–861.

Sowell, E. R., Thompson, P. M., Tessner, K. D., & Toga, A. W. (2001). Mapping continued brain growth and gray matter density reduction in dorsal frontal cortex: Inverse relationships during postadolescent brain maturation. *The Journal of Neuroscience, 21,* 8819–8829.

Spear, L. P. (2000). The adolescent brain and age-related behavioral manifestations. *Neuroscience and Biobehavioral Reviews, 24,* 417–463.

Spence, S. A., & Frith, C. D. (1999). Toward a functional anatomy of volition. *Journal of Consciousness Studies, 6,* 11–29.

Spinrad, T. L., Eisenberg, N., Cumberland, A., Fabes, R. A., Valiente, C., Shepard, S. A., et al. (2006). Relation of emotion-related regulation to children's social competence: A longitudinal study. *Emotion, 6,* 498–510.

Sroufe, A. L. (1996). *Emotional development: The organization of emotional life in the early years.* New York: Cambridge University Press.

Stayton, D. J., Hogan, R., & Ainsworth, M. D. S. (1971). Infant obedience and maternal behavior: The origins of socialization reconsidered. *Child Development, 42,* 1057–1069.

Steinberg, L. (2004). Risk taking in adolescence: What changes, and why? *Annals of the New York Academy of Sciences, 1021,* 51–58.

Stevens, J., Quittner, A. L., Zuckerman, J. B., & Moore, S. (2002). Behavioral inhibition, self-regulation of motivation, and working memory in children with attention deficit hyperactivity disorder. *Developmental Neuropsychology, 21,* 117–139.

Stifter, C. A., & Braungart, J. M. (1995). The regulation of negative reactivity: Function and development. *Developmental Psychology, 38,* 448–455.

Stifter, C. A., & Spinrad, T. L. (2002). The effect of excessive crying on the development of emotion regulation. *Infancy, 3,* 133–152.

Stroop, J. R. (1935). Studies of interference in serial verbal reactions. *Journal of Experimental Psychology, 18,* 643–662.

Tamm, L., Menon, V., & Reiss, A, L. (2002). Maturation of brain function associated with response inhibition. *Journal of American Academy of Child Adolescent Psychiatry, 41,* 1231–1238.

Thomas, A., & Chess, S. (1977). *Temperament and development.* New York: Brunner/Mazel.

Thorell, L. B., Bohlin, G., & Rydell, A. M. (2004). Two types of inhibitory control: Predictive relations to social functioning. *International Journal of Behavioral Development, 28,* 193–203.

Trick, L. M., & Enns, J. T. (1998). Lifespan changes in attention: the visual search task. *Cognitive Development, 13,* 369–386.

Trommsdorff, G., & Friedlmeier, W. (1999). Motivational conflict and prosocial behavior of kindergarten children. *International Journal of Behavioral Development, 23,* 413–429.

Tsujimoto, S., Yamamoto, T., Kawaguchi, H., Koizumi, H., & Sawaguchi, T. (2004). Prefrontal cortical activation associated with working memory in adults and preschool children: An event-related optical topography study. *Cerebral Cortex, 14,* 703–712.

Valiente, C., Eisenberg, N., Fabes, R. A., Shepard, S. A., Cumberland, A., & Losoya, S. H. (2004). Prediction of children's empathy-related responding from their effortful control and parents' expressivity. *Developmental Psychology, 40,* 911–926.

Vanlede, M., Little, T. D., & Card, N. A. (2006). Action-control beliefs and behaviors as predictors of change in adjustment across the transition to middle school. *Anxiety, Stress, & Coping, 19,* 111–127.

Vaughn, B. E., Kopp, C. B., & Krakow, J. B. (1984). The emergence and consolidation of self-control from 18 to 30 months of age: Normative trends and individual differences. *Child Development, 55,* 990–1004.

Vaughn, B. E., Krakow, J. B., Kopp, C. B., Johnson, K., & Schwartz, S. S. (1986). Process analyses of the behavior of very young children in delay tasks. *Developmental Psychology, 22,* 752–759.

Velig, H., & von Knippenberg, A. (2006). Shielding intentions from distraction: Forming an intention induces inhibition of distracting stimuli. *Social Cognition, 24,* 409–425.

von Hofsten C., & Rosander K. (1997). Development of smooth pursuit tracking in young infants. *Vision Research, 37,* 1799–1810.

Vygotsky, L. S. (1934/1962). *Thought and language*. Cambridge, MA: MIT Press.

Vygotsky, L. S. (1978). *Mind in society: The development of higher mental processes.* Cambridge, MA: Harvard University Press. (Original works published 1930, 1933, 1935)

Walls, T. A., & Little, T. D. (2005). Relations among personal agency, motivation, and school adjustment in early adolescence. *Journal of Educational Psychology, 97,* 23–31.

Walsh, K. W. (1978). *Neuropsychology: A clinical approach.* Edinburgh: Churchill Livingston.

Wehmeyer, M. L. (2004). Beyond self-determination: Causal agency theory. *Journal of Developmental and Physical Disabilities, 16,* 337–359.

Wehmeyer, M. L. (2005). Self-determination and individuals with severe disabilities: Re-examining meanings and misinterpretations. *Research & Practice for Persons with Severe Disabilities, 30,* 113–120.

Weinberg, M. K., & Tronick, E. (1994). Beyond the face: An empirical study of infant affective configurations of facial, vocal, gestural, and regulatory behaviors. *Child Development, 65,* 1503–1515.

White, R. W. (1959). Motivation reconsidered: The concept of competence. *Psychological Review, 66,* 297–333.

Whittle, S., Yücel, M., Fornito, A., Barrett, A., Wood, S. J., Lubman, D. I., et al. (2008). Neuroanatomical correlates of temperament in early adolescents. *Journal of the American Academy of Child & Adolescent Psychiatry, 47,* 682–693

Wiener, N. (1948). *Cybernetics: Control and communication in the animal and the machine.* Cambridge, MA: MIT Press.

Wigfield, A., & Eccles, J. S. (2000). Expectancy-value theory of achievement motivation. *Contemporary Educational Psychology, 25,* 68–81.

Wigfield, A., & Eccles, J. S. (2002). The development of competence beliefs, expectancies for success, and achievement values from childhood through adolescence. In A. Wigfield & J. S. Eccles (Eds.), *Development of achievement motivation* (pp. 92–122). New York: Academic Press.

Wolff, P. H. (1965). The development of attention in young infants. *Annals of the New York Academy of Sciences, 118,* 815–830.

Wrosch, C., Dunne, E., Scheier, M. F., & Schulz, R. (2006). Self-regulation of common age-related challenges: Benefits for older adults' psychological and physical health. *Journal of Behavioral Medicine, 29,* 299–306.

Wrosch, C., Heckhausen, J., & Lachman, M. E. (2000). Primary and secondary control strategies for managing health and financial stress across adulthood. *Psychology and Aging, 15,* 387–399.

Wulfert, E., Block, J. A., Santa Ana, E., Rodriguez, M. L., & Colsman, M. (2002). Delay of gratification: Impulsive choices and problem behaviors in early and late adolescence. *Journal of Personality, 70,* 533–552.

Zelazo, P. D., & Jacques, S. (1996). Children's rule use: Representation, reflection, and cognitive control. In R. Vasta (Ed.), *Annals of child development: A research annal* (Vol. 12, pp. 119–1760). London: Jessica Kingsley.

CHAPTER 6

Self and Identity across the Life Span

DAN P. McADAMS and KEITH S. COX

Northwestern University

There are as many conceptions of self (and identity) as there are behavioral scientists to study them. Indeed, there are more, for the self is a topic that attracts endless speculation and inquiry, both scholarly and not, on the part of philosophers, theologians, novelists, and neuroscientists. Authors of review chapters on *the self*, like this one, often begin by throwing up their hands in mock despair: The topic is too vast; it is impossible to review it all here! For example, Robins, Tracy, and Trzesniewski (2008) reported that their PsychINFO search on the keyword *self* identified 265,161 articles. Rather than read them all, Robins et al. followed the lead of other smart review authors: They narrowed their survey to focus on a few themes that are especially salient within a given field of inquiry. Taking the same approach, Harter (2006) examined the literature on self from the standpoint of *child development*, and Baumeister (1998) did the same for the field of *social psychology*. In these cases, the reviewers implicitly defined *self* and *identity* in terms of their particular academic disciplines. How do social psychologists study self? What do developmental psychologists mean when they use the term identity?

In one sense, this chapter follows the predictable pattern. The central question is this: What should we know about self and identity from the standpoint of *life-span developmental studies*? Just as Baumeister (1998) spoke to and for the field of social psychology, so, too, our chapter aims to frame the study of self and identity for life-span developmental scientists. However, many life-span scholars view their field—the broad study of human development from birth to death—to be an extraordinarily interdisciplinary affair, drawing broadly from psychology, sociology, demography, family studies, cognitive and affective sciences, and a range of other disciplines (e.g., Elder, 1995; Levy, Ghisletta, Legoof, Spini, & Widmer, 2005). Therefore, an adequate review of any topic within this interdisciplinary nexus would require an especially broad and judiciously selective perspective. In keeping with this expectation, this review draws from a relatively large number of intellectual traditions in the study of self and identity, including philosophical treatments of these topics, as well as major frameworks to be found in the traditions of child psychology, cognitive developmental studies, personality and social psychology, life course sociology, social gerontology, psychoanalysis and humanistic psychology, and the recently emergent interdisciplinary field called *the narrative study of lives* (e.g., Josselson & Lieblich, 1993; McAdams, Josselson, & Lieblich, 2006).

The current review differs from most others in a second way, too. The review sketches a new theoretical framework for conceptualizing the self across the life span. With substantial refinement and adaptation, the framework is derived from the first author's three-layered theory of personality (McAdams & Adler, 2006; McAdams & Pals, 2006), which argues that people's internalized life stories are layered over their characteristic goals and values, which are, in turn, layered over their core dispositional traits. Correspondingly, this review aims to integrate disparate topics, findings, and theories regarding the development of self and identity over the life span in terms of three broad metaphors: The self as *actor, agent*, and *author*. These three metaphors specify three fundamentally different and progressively more complex standpoints from which the human self can be seen to operate.

We begin life as social actors, even before a self emerges. The self's first and most fundamental role is to be a social actor. Human beings evolved to live in small groups, competing and cooperating, seeking to get along and get ahead in the environment of evolutionary adaptedness (Buss, 2008; Hogan, 1982). In that gaining some proficiency in the role of social actor is a literal prerequisite for human survival (and reproductive success), it should come as no surprise that human selves are fundamentally oriented toward social performance. We engage our environments first as social actors, equipped with particular performance traits. We know ourselves as social actors before we know anything else about who we are. Self-development in the early childhood years, therefore, reflects the elaboration and maturation of an actor-self who performs on a social stage.

The role of a motivated social agent comes next: A self who desires, plans, schemes, and strives to achieve ends in the social world—an actor with a forward-looking purpose. Whereas even an infant's behavior is goal-directed in some sense, children become more planful and self-consciously goal-oriented as they move into and through elementary school, signaling the emergence of the agent-self. A 3-year-old may define herself as a pretty girl who likes to dance. Six years later, at age 9, she still thinks she is pretty, but her selfhood is now just as much about wanting to get to the next level in her ballet class and striving to get good grades in school. *Self-esteem* has now entered the picture, as well—the agent-self evaluates the discrepancies between what it desires, hopes, and plans it might be on the one hand and what it believes it is at this moment in time on the other. The smaller the discrepancy, the higher the self-esteem.

Eventually, the self becomes an author, too, seeking to tell a story—for its own and others' edification—regarding how I came to be (the past) and where I may be going (the future). The author-self develops offstage for much of childhood and early adolescence, only to make a developmentally grand entrance in the emerging-adulthood years. What Erikson (1963) described as the developmental task of ego identity may be recast as the author-self's struggle to formulate a meaningful story of life, integrating the reconstructed past and imagined future in such a way as to explain why the actor does what it does, why the agent wants what it wants, and who the self really is, as a developing person in time (McAdams, 2008).

In a fundamental sense, the actor exists in the performative present; the agent extends the timeline forward, to look to a motivated future; and the author extends the timeline even more, backward and forward, bringing coherence to the reconstructed past and the imagined future by composing, and then living, a story of self. In the adult years, all three guises of self—actor, agent, and author—are fully operative. As the actor-self, the adult is able to identify and reflect on his or her action traits, aware of himself or herself as an actor who plays characteristic roles and expresses characteristic action patterns ("I am an extravert"; "I shy away from men who remind me of my father"). As the agent-self, the adult is able to articulate and organize his or her life according to long-term plans and goals ("I am working hard to put my children through college"; "I am looking for a man who will love and cherish me"). As the author-self, the adult is able to construct a self-defining life story to provide a narrative meaning for life ("I am living a rags-to-riches story"; "My mother's death was the turning point in my life, from which I will never recover"). The development of self and identity over the human life span is about how the three guises of human selfhood—actor, agent, and author—develop and interact with each other, from infancy through old age.

To put into a broad context our conception of the self as actor, agent, and author, this review begins by tracing some of the most important ideas regarding self and identity as they have appeared in the philosophical tradition, culminating with the seminal contributions of William James. Next, it highlights a range of influential conceptions of self and identity under the headings of psychoanalytic, humanistic, cognitive–developmental, and social–psychological traditions, and in the narrative study of lives. The bulk of the chapter, then, considers contemporary research on self and identity across the life span from the perspectives of the self as actor, agent, and author, picking up on central themes identified in the overview of intellectual traditions.

TRADITIONS OF INQUIRY

As contemporary social and behavioral scientists gaze on the self, they encounter a peculiar social (and linguistic) construction, the historical lineage of which may be traced back a couple thousand years in the Western philosophical tradition. What they see (and often assume to be universal) is what the philosopher Charles Taylor (1989) described as the *modern self*. Among its many taken-for-granted properties, the modern self lists inwardness, reflexivity, and executive control. The modern self is more inside than outside the person, with privileged access to a private world of thought, feeling, and desire. The modern self owns its inner life; the modern self knows that what is inside belongs to the self and not to another. Ideally, this sense of ownership and appropriation of one's subjective experience confers upon the modern self a singular sense of unity and wholeness (Harre, 1998). I think (and feel, and desire, and appropriate all that I think and feel and desire); therefore, I am. In a reflexive fashion, the modern self takes itself as an object of perception and work. The self reflects on itself, and in the modern world the self often works hard to control, develop, enlarge, or improve itself. Shaped by social forces for sure, the modern self nonetheless strives to be autonomous and responsible, and it strives to make commitments to other selves, through which it is (ideally) further defined and enriched. The modern self is the executive force within the person, the ultimate seat of social action, agency, and authorship. The executive should be in control. Therefore, *losing* the self means, among other things, losing autonomy and control. And losing control is rarely a good thing.

The Philosophical Tradition

The problem of self-control was arguably the fundamental conundrum in Plato's vision of the ideal republic and the good life. For Plato, the human soul contains within it both the chaotic forces of desire and the unifying power of reason. Only when reason reigns over the lower appetites can the human soul accomplish the unity and harmony required for living the good life in a well-ordered social community. Aristotle, too, regarded rational thought as the indispensable resource for self-mastery. However, Aristotle's vision was rather more pragmatic and particularized than Plato's. Presaging the modern image of the self as social actor, Aristotle's wise man or woman knows how to behave in ways that best fit any particular social situation. The self seeks to strike a balance between its own inner strivings and the collective aims of the polis, ultimately expressing a kind of practical wisdom. Practical wisdom is an "awareness of order, the correct order of ends in my life, which integrates all my goals and desires into a unified whole in which each has its proper weight" (C. Taylor, 1989, p. 125).

For both Plato and Aristotle, then, the self (soul) is the inner seat of rationality and executive control. With an eye toward the outside world, the self aims to fashion a good life in society. With an eye toward inner experience, the self must *know itself* to achieve the good life. The focus on the vicissitudes of inner experience became much more keenly elaborated, however, in the centuries to follow, especially among certain Christian writers and in the Enlightenment. In his *Confessions*, St. Augustine (354–430 AD) described how the self scrutinizes its own thoughts, feelings, and desires in an effort to find God's truth within. According to C. Taylor (1989), Augustine's turn to radical reflexivity firmly established a first-person standpoint for selfhood and made "the language of inwardness irresistible" (p. 131). The inner light of self-awareness and self-scrutiny "shines in our presence to ourselves." "What differentiates it from the outer light is just what makes the image of inwardness so compelling, that it illuminates that space where I am present to myself" (C. Taylor, 1989, p. 131).

In the 17th century, Descartes described a further separation of the inner from the outer, as the self aims to see itself from a nonmaterial, disembodied, and objective perspective, employing the power of disengaged reason. The same idea is developed further by Locke, who imagined the self as a point from which a fully disengaged observer views itself, in the same manner by which it might observe any object in the world. From Plato to the Enlightenment, then, the Western philosophical tradition tracks an evolving sense of the self's reflexivity, articulating:

> [a] growing ideal of a human agent who is able to remake itself by methodical and disciplined action. What this calls for is the ability to take an instrumental stance to one's given properties, desires, inclinations, tendencies, and habits of thought and feeling, so that they can be *worked on*. (C. Taylor, 1989, pp. 159–160)

The modern self's powers of self-control and self-expression rely on its reflexive nature, its ability to take itself as an object of reflection and instrumental work.

When the self (subject) takes a reflexive and instrumental stance on itself (object), what is the nature of the object toward which the subject aims? What is the self that the self works on? As Robins et al. (2008) argued, most conceptions of the self distinguish between the reflexive *self-awareness* to which Augustine, Descartes, and Locke so effectively turned the Western mind and the mental *self-representations* that are the ultimate products of that awareness. In the modern world, people represent themselves in a multitude of ways. It is common today to delineate a broad range of features that distinguish one self from another. This may not have always been the case. In the traditional and religiously oriented societies that preceded the modern age, the self was typically defined according to a delimited set of (mainly) ascribed characteristics. A craftsman's son might grow up to be a craftsman. A farmer's daughter might marry another farmer. Upward social mobility was rare. The notion that one might adopt a different religious tradition from one's family was virtually inconceivable. According to Baumeister (1986), most people living in medieval Europe typically defined themselves in terms of their geographical home, ancestral family, marriage, job, social rank, gender, age, bodily characteristics, moral goodness, and religious beliefs. One's identity was mainly a matter of assuming clearly defined social roles and conforming to fixed characteristics and constraints. One might "work on" oneself in the sense of trying to become a more productive member of society, a better father, or a more devout Christian; but this kind of reflexive self-work did not usually involve efforts to transform the self into a qualitatively *different kind of person*.

The idea that the self must find or construct an identity that is uniquely suited to itself—that I must discover or construct who I (really and uniquely) am (or will be)—developed gradually in the West. A key figure in its development was the 16th-century philosopher Michel de Montaigne, who argued that self-reflection should focus mainly on discovering one's own unique form. When the self takes itself as an object of reflection and work, it should dig beneath ascribed characteristics, socially mandated roles, and the false conceits of everyday religious life to discover one's true and unique identity. Montaigne helped to inaugurate "a new kind of reflection which is intensely individual, a self-explanation, the aim of which is to reach self-knowledge by coming to see through the screens of self-delusions which passion or spiritual pride have erected" (C. Taylor, 1989, p. 181). Montaigne's project paved the way for the emergence of biography and the novel as Western genres of self-expression, even as Christian writings like Augustine's *Confessions* provided an earlier model of autobiography as spiritual self-transformation. Eventually, a person's unique effort to discover who he or she truly is became a story worth telling and hearing in Western philosophical and literary traditions. Early on, it was the lives of the most distinguished men and women that were deemed most worthy of dramatic representation. By the 19th century, however, the public's appetite extended to stories of self-discovery pertaining even to everyday folk (Gittings, 1978).

The social and economical factors that produced cultural modernity—the decline of religious authority, the democratization of Western societies, the spread of capitalism and the Industrial Revolution, the rise of science and technology, mass communication, global trade and commerce, the proliferation of lifestyle options and choices for the middle class, among others—are the same factors that are typically invoked to explain the problems and the potentialities of the modern self (Baumeister, 1986; Gay, 1986; Giddens, 1991; McAdams, 1996). In traditional societies men and women typically worked at home and had daily contacts with a small group of people who defined their social worlds. In the 19th century, however, more and more adults left home to work in industry, making for a stark separation between the worlds of work and home. Separate worlds could make for separate selves, or the perception that I am one kind of person at work and another kind of person at home. The distinction between the public self and the private self became something of a cultural preoccupation in Victorian England (Gay, 1986), as middle-class adults increasingly came to wonder: Who am I? What is the real me?

The notion of an *identity crisis* appears to be a modernist social construction. Baumeister (1986) reports that it was not until the 19th century that Westerners commonly described periods in their lives wherein they experienced severe confusion in self-definition. Increasingly, modern men and women struggled to define their own *distinctiveness* vis-à-vis each other and to discern the sense of *continuity* within their own complex lives that a satisfying self-identity requires (Erikson, 1963; Giddens, 1991). When it comes to cultural modernity, the upside for the self is that it can be many different things. The downside, however, is precisely the same thing, for amid all the choice and potential, one often seeks to find or make the one kind of self that is just right for me, a self that affirms my individuality while connecting me in meaningful relationships with others (C. Taylor, 1989). Ideally, the self that I reflect on—my conception of who I am—should express the fullness and uniqueness of what my life is about while still committing me to social roles and social communities that give my life meaning and purpose.

The Legacy of William James

The reflexivity of selfhood—the sense wherein the self is able to reflect on itself—marks the famous starting point for William James's (1892/1963) psychological treatment of self:

> The Me and the I—Whatever I may be thinking of, I am always at the same time more or less aware of *myself*, or my *personal existence*. At the same time it is *I* who am aware; so that the total self of me, being as it were duplex, partly known and partly knower, partly object and partly subject, must have two aspects discriminated in it, of which for shortness we may call one the *Me* and the other the *I*. I call these "discriminated aspects" and not separate things, because the identity of *I* with *me*, even in the very act of their discrimination, is perhaps the most ineradicable dictum of commonsense, and must not be undermined by our terminology here at the outset, whatever we may come to think of its validity at our inquiry's end. (James, 1892/1963, p. 166)

James summoned forth a simple grammatical distinction—between the I (subject) and the Me (object)—to capture a fundamental feature of modern selfhood, the philosophical lineage of which can be traced back as far as Augustine. In the terms of Descartes, the I is the thinker, whose very existence is proved by the fact that it thinks. From a Lockean perspective, the I is the disengaged stance from which the self (the Me) may be observed and analyzed. At its rational best, the I is able to adopt the same kind of dispassionate, objective, and coolly analytical stance vis-à-vis the Me that it may adopt toward any object in the world. Thus, the I learns about the Me through self-perception, an idea that struck a resonant chord for many empirical social psychologists in the 20th century (e.g., Bem, 1972). As I repeatedly observe myself acting in friendly ways toward many different kinds of people, I come to learn that I am (in general) a friendly person; that is, the I attributes the trait of friendliness to the Me. Of course, the I does more than merely observe the Me. The I also represents, critiques, manages, controls, edits, reformulates, explores, improves, expands, develops, and, in the most general terms, works on the Me. For the modern I, the Me becomes its pet project.

To the Jamesian I, we may attribute social action, agency, and authorship. It would seem, then, that the I is like a person inside the person, an executive who controls behavior, sets forth a motivational agenda for life, and composes a narrative interpretation of the person's life on the fly. However, like many philosophers and behavioral scientists, James resisted the idea of endowing the person with a kind of redundant homunculus. Instead, the self is like a *stream of consciousness*, James argued. Each thought in the stream serves as the thinker itself, appropriating that which comes before it in such a fluid manner that people typically come to feel that they are the same person (I am I) from one moment to the next. In his memorable example, James asserted that when Peter wakes up in the morning, he virtually never thinks that he is Paul, even though he and Paul talked at great length the night before and even though Paul may indeed be in the very same bed! Peter's morning thoughts connect up to the thoughts he had before he fell asleep, making for a continuously flowing sense of self-continuity. "The thoughts themselves are the thinkers," James famously concluded (1892/1963, p. 198).

Like James, many other scholars have wrestled to develop a conception of the I that evades the problem of the homunculus. Following Locke, Blasi (1988) conceived of the I as the subjective stance from which the world is observed and the Me is appropriated. In a similar vein, Harre (1998) described the I as "a sense of one's point of view, at any moment a location in space from which one perceives and acts on the world, including the part that lies within one's own skin" (p. 4). Adopting a more dynamic metaphor, Loevinger (1976) described the subjective self as a *process*; the I is rather more like a verb (I-ing, self-ing) than a noun (McAdams, 1996). As it flows along, the I makes a Me—indeed, it may be the making of the Me that constitutes what the I fundamentally is.

If the I is like a process, the Me is akin to a product. The Me is the self that the I makes, observes, and works on. In its broadest sense, James contended, the Me is all that a person can or might call his or her own. James demarcated three large regions within the Me—the material, social, and spiritual Me. The latter two have attracted the most interest among social scientists, for they directly concern issues that are central to psychology and social relations. By contrast, the material Me seems rather more mundane, consisting as it does of one's own body, clothing, home, and most cherished material possessions. Nonetheless, some researchers have explored the individual differences people show in the extent to which their very selves are defined by the tangible objects they possess, as well as what those objects may say about their social and spiritual selves (Csikszentmihalyi & Rochberg-Halton, 1982; Gosling, 2008). Oddly perhaps, James also included with the material realm of Me one's spouse, children, and parents—and, in principle, those other *people* in the world (we may also wish to include pets here) for whom one feels a sense of responsibility. According to James, what qualifies these individuals for inclusion within the material Me is the fact that their well-being and success elicit the same feelings that one's own well-being and success might elicit. The material self, therefore, might expand endlessly, should an individual come to feel that an entire nation, say, or even the world writ large consists of *my* people, as might be the case for grandiose delusions or in the lives of such notable selves as Jesus and Gandhi (Erikson, 1969).

In an ambiguous formulation, James wrote: "A man's social me is the recognition he gets from his mates" (p. 168). Throughout his famous chapter on self, James seems to blur together two very different senses of the social Me, or what Harre (1998) identified as Self 2 and Self 3 (for Harre, Self 1 is the I). To the extent that the "recognition" a person "gets" resides solely in the minds of others (and outside the awareness of the person who is being recognized), James's social self equates to one's *reputation* in a social community, or what Harre called Self 3. The person's own understanding of how he or she is recognized in the community, however, may be a very different thing, or what Harre called Self 2. Most social scientists have identified James's social self in this latter, Self 2 sense—as a person's own understanding of how others see him or her.

The idea that a social Me is made up largely of a person's conception of what other people think, say, and feel about him or her was developed further by Cooley (1902), who coined the term *looking glass self*. The metaphor is simple but rather profound: The social world is a mirror (a looking glass), and we learn who we are through the reflected appraisals of others. Mead (1934) elaborated the theme further by emphasizing how the development of a social Me involves the ability to take the role of others in the social world. According to Mead, "the individual experiences himself as such, not directly, but only indirectly, from the particular standpoint of the social group as a whole to which he belongs" (1934, p. 140). Through a series of stages, involving the development in childhood from simple play to organized games, the person's understanding of how others see him or her expands, eventually to encompass a sense of the *generalized other*. This is a personal conception of the general audience or observer of one's social behavior. To adopt the perspective of the generalized other is to imagine how others in general see me. Through such imaginative activity, a person builds and further refines a sense of the social Me.

Finally, the spiritual Me encompasses "the entire collection of my states of consciousness, my psychic faculties, and dispositions taken concretely" (James, 1892/1963, p. 170). The spiritual Me is a person's own understanding of himself or herself as a psychological being, endowed with thoughts, feeling, desires, and dispositions. Put differently, the spiritual Me is *not* literally the mind itself (subject) but rather the mind's understanding of itself (object). Here James located most of the psychological attributions that people make about themselves—their understandings of their own traits, motives, values, beliefs, desires, fears, and so on. Many people feel that the spiritual Me calls on their deepest sense of self. It should come as no surprise, therefore, that those perspectives on selfhood that purport to delve deepest into the psychology of the person typically feature aspects of what James categorized as the spiritual Me. A case in point is Freud and the psychoanalytical tradition.

Psychoanalytical Perspectives on Ego, Self, and Identity

It is fair to say that, in one important sense, Sigmund Freud held James's concept of the spiritual Me in low regard. What does it matter, Freud showed again and again, if the person consciously thinks he or she has one particular set of traits, motives, and desires when his or her unconscious life suggests the operation of quite another? In other words, what the I appropriates as its own psychological life usually turns out to be a deception of consciousness, a defensive ruse designed to disguise the unconscious truth. In another sense, however, Freud held out the hope that psychoanalytical therapy, and in some cases one's own self-analysis, might unearth psychologically critical artifacts from the unconscious and bring them to the light of the conscious self. The talking cure that Freud introduced to Western thought and practice ideally resulted in an expansion of what James regarded as the spiritual Me. For Freud, to gain psychoanalytical insight was to incorporate into one's conscious understanding of self those heretofore unconscious traits, beliefs, desires, and complexes that explain the psychopathology of everyday life—to bring into the self what was nonself—and in so doing to relieve anxiety and pave the way for work, love, and good mental health.

In the Freudian story, the *ego* plays the role of the Jamesian I. The correspondence between the two might be more obvious for English readers had Freud's German words for the ego—*das Ich*—received a more straightforward translation ("the I"). For Freud, the ego (the I) is the center of conscious subjectivity, an agentic and appropriating force that takes itself (the Me) as an object of reflection. Freud's ego is a much more beleaguered agent–process than James ever imagined, however. Freud (1923/1961) conceived of the ego as the great mediator of psychical life, forever striving to effect compromises among the conflicting forces originating from the id, the superego, and external reality. In an odd way, furthermore, the ego is forced to share its reflexive, Me-observing powers with another I-agent—the superego (the "over-I"). From the standpoint of an internalized authoritarian other (parent), the superego observes psychical life and, like the ego, makes reflexive judgments about the Me. Freud was clearer than James could ever be about the possibility that everyday psychological life entails fundamental splits in I-ness, splits that reflect the long history of intrapsychical conflict. Within a given self, there may be more than one actor, agent, and author.

The precariousness of the I is a central theme in one line of psychoanalytical thought that begins with the *object relations theories* of Fairbarin (1952) and Mahler (Mahler, Pine, & Bergman, 1975) and develops into Kohut's (1971) psychoanalytical *self theory*. These theorists argued that one's basic sense of self as an autonomous and self-determining agent in the world emerges in the first few years of life as a product of deeply emotional family relationships (called *object relations*). For Mahler, the infant begins to differentiate from a felt symbiosis with the mother toward the middle of the first year of life. The child typically achieves full separation–individuation of selfhood by age two or three, through which he or she is now able to modulate an emotionally complex relationship with mother and other attachment objects. In Kohut's theory, a young child's *bipolar self* (anchored by ambitions and idealized goals) develops through a mirroring relationship with the mother (who reflects back the child's grandiosity and strength, consolidating ambition) and an idealizing relationship with the father (who serves as a calming model of goodness and value, consolidating goals). Healthy mirroring and idealizing in early object relations paves the way for the development of an empowered and autonomous bipolar self. However, mirroring and idealizing often go awry, Kohut maintained, resulting in the development of numerous pathologies of self. Most common is the problem of narcissism. In Kohut's view, extreme narcissists display an excess of pathological self-love and disregard for others because early object relations in their lives failed to provide them with the deep sense that they are special, worthy, and good.

Following a second theoretical line, the *ego psychologists* of the 1940s and 1950s—Anna Freud, Heinz Hartmann, Erich Fromm, Karen Horney, Erik Erikson, and Robert White, for example—endowed Freud's conception of the ego with greater powers of agency and integration. More optimistic than Freud about the self's ability to overcome adversity and resolve internal divisions, these later theorists described the ego as a masterful, creative, and synthesizing force in the personality. They also turned their attention to the Me. In a major theoretical advance, Erik Erikson (1958, 1963) showed that the I's synthesizing work goes well beyond simply constructing a serviceable Me. Beginning in adolescence, the I must refashion the Me into a new and dramatically different pattern or form that provides the young person with a sense of inner sameness and continuity across situations and over time, that consolidates ideological beliefs and vocational aspirations and that situates the individual within a meaningful niche in the psychosocial ecology of adulthood. The new pattern is what Erikson termed an *identity*; the struggle to formulate the pattern is identity development in the adolescent and adult years; the upheaval and angst that often accompanies such a struggle in modern life is what Erikson famously called an *identity crisis*.

Erikson forever raised the bar for the modern Me. Beginning in late adolescence and young adulthood, Erikson maintained, it is no longer enough simply to have a self that encompasses what James saw to be the central material, social, and spiritual constituents. Given the developmental demands of adulthood and the cultural demands of modern life, the I must arrange the various pieces of the material, social, and spiritual Me into a new pattern that confers upon the Me a unifying and purposeful sense of identity. The new pattern answers the basic identity question: Who am I? The question has little psychosocial meaning or relevance before the adolescent years. Thus, children have Jamesian selves—the childhood I constructs a Me—but they do not yet have Eriksonian identities. This is not because they do not know who they are but rather because they do not understand how the question "Who am I?" could have any meaning. Children do not conceive of identity as a problem; therefore, they do not have it, for Erikson's very definition of identity presupposes the I's awareness that it no longer knows who it is, knows that indeed it could be many things, and knows that it needs to figure out this problem to some degree—ideally sooner rather than later—if life is to move onward in a developmental sense.

For many people in the modern world, identity becomes a problem during the late adolescent years, and it is destined to remain something of a problem for the rest of life, Erikson suggested. To address the problem, the I must take stock of its own traits, skills, habits, beliefs, aspirations, and (most important) its history, and it must judiciously consider the opportunities and constraints provided by culture, particularly its ideology, and the expectations that society has for the self. At the same time, the I should question the validity of both culture and society and the appropriateness of others' perceptions and expectations (Blasi, 1988; Erikson, 1963; Marcia, 1980; McAdams, 1985). This process of questioning and integration should occur around certain critical life areas, such as one's future occupation, sexuality, and religious and political beliefs, and it should ultimately lead to a flexible but durable commitment in these areas, or what Erikson called *fidelity*. Nonetheless, commitments shift gradually, even across the adult years, and identity is probably never set in stone. Erikson's revolutionary conception of identity is the great Pandora's box of self-development. Once the question of "Who am I?" gets out, you can never push it all the way back into the box again.

Humanistic Conceptions

For James, Freud, and Erikson, self-development was something of a balancing act. The I (ego) must monitor what is going on both inside the person and in the person's outside world and then discover or construct some form of dynamic accommodation between the two. Erikson was especially insistent that healthy identity development should entail the young adult's assumption of a psychosocial niche wherein internal needs and external opportunities find their match. The development of the self is about compromise, accommodation, and constructing a Me within a world of constraints. Going back to Rousseau and Emerson, however, a romantic tradition in European and American thought has consistently rejected this approach. Instead, the true self waits deep inside, a seed that must be watered so that it will germinate and grow, an inner light that must be uncovered so that it can shine in the world, even if the world does not appreciate its glow. From the 19th-century Romantic point of view, self-development is about discovering the truth within and living that truth to the fullest. Ralph Waldo Emerson urged his American audiences to cast off their Calvinist constraints and live the self-reliant life, the guide for which is each person's inner light of intuition (McAdams, 2006a). Reject society's norms and encumbrances, Emerson proclaimed, and live true to the good inner self. In the 20th century, *humanistic* conceptions of the self followed the Emersonian line. Good and true selves lay deep inside, yearning to be born and to live free.

The most ardent spokespersons for humanistic conceptions of selfhood in the 20th century were Carl Rogers (1951) and Abraham Maslow (1968). Like the ego psychologists, both theorists underscored the I's capacity to synthesize conscious experience and make meaning in the world. Rogers and Maslow, however, felt no allegiance whatsoever to the Freudian legacy of a dynamic unconscious, psychic conflict, the id, the superego, and all that sort of thing. As an alternative to the inherent tragedy of Freudian life, Rogers and Maslow offered a more optimistic, can-do alternative that featured *self-actualization* as the highest motivation in human living. After our base needs regarding hunger, safety, attachment, and esteem are met, Maslow argued, we are freed up to be all that we can be, to fulfill our inner potential and become the fully functioning person that we were, in some existential sense, meant to become. The process of becoming our true selves requires courage and perseverance, the humanists argued, but it also typically entails experiences of joy and satisfaction. Put simply, being true to the self can feel really, really good! Behavior that grows the self is intrinsically rewarding. It is performed not to obtain external rewards but rather to fulfill inner needs that are believed to be finer and nobler than what the material world has to offer. Incorporating Buddhist themes, the most fully actualized self is sometimes able to lose itself in peak moments of ecstasy and wonder, making for a deeper unity of consciousness. Maslow (1968) wrote:

> In some reports, particularly of the mystic experience or the religious experience or philosophical experience, the whole of the world is seen as unity, as a single rich lived entity. In other of the peak experiences, most particularly the love experience and the aesthetic experience, one small part of the world is perceived as if it were for the moment all of the world. In both cases the perception is of unity. (p. 88)

Among contemporary empirical psychologists, the most loyal heir to the humanistic tradition in the study of self is *self-determination theory*, as articulated by Deci and Ryan (1985, 1991). The theory begins with the observation, obtained from countless research studies, that monkeys, children, college students, and adult humans will often ignore material rewards to perform behaviors that meet basic needs for competence, autonomy, and interpersonal relatedness—intrinsically motivating behaviors that are fundamentally self-determining. Self-determining activities promote the expansion and actualization of the self. They are experienced with "a full sense of choice, with the experience of doing what one wants, and without the feeling of coercion or compulsion" (Deci & Ryan, 1991, p. 253). A broad research literature in personality, social, and developmental psychology has explored the various kinds of family environments, classroom situations, and cultural norms that promote or impede self-determination in human behavior (e.g., Ryan & Deci, 2006; Sheldon & Kasser, 1998).

According to Deci and Ryan, the human infant is endowed with a nascent self—a vital core of I-ness that contains the potential for tremendous expansion. As they put it, "the nature of life is to overtake itself" (Deci & Ryan, 1991, p. 239). The I seeks to overtake its surroundings, to appropriate things, people, ideas, and environments, to make that which is non-Me part of the Me. As the infant masters and synthesizes new experiences, the self becomes more encompassing (it takes in more things) and more integrated (it organizes contents into meaningful systems). Over time, self-determined behavior enhances the development of the self, and as the self develops further, more and more behavior becomes self-determined.

The Cognitive–Developmental Paradigm

Whereas humanistic conceptions celebrate the self's growth potential, they have not traditionally been specific regarding the step-by-step process through which selves grow. Beginning with Piaget (1952), in contrast, a strong tradition of inquiry has focused squarely on stages and sequence in cognitive development, with important implications for understanding self. Epitomized in the work of Piaget himself, Kohlberg (1969), Perry (1970), Selman (1980), Kegan (1982), and Loevinger (1976), the cognitive–developmental paradigm views the individual as an active knower who structures experience in ever more adequate and complex ways. From this broad perspective, development is viewed as a progression through hierarchically arranged stages. Each stage specifies a particular organization or structure through which the individual makes sense of subjective experience. Earlier stages of knowing must be mastered before subsequent stages can be approached. Each stage logically builds on its predecessor and ultimately encompasses all that comes before it. Movement from one stage to the next is a complex product of both internal maturation and external forces, which are in constant reciprocal interaction. Higher stages are better (logically more consistent and encompassing) than lower ones, providing interpretive structures for the world that are more differentiated, integrated, and adequate than those that precede them. Typically, a highest stage represents a psychological ideal for development.

Jane Loevinger's (1976) theory of *ego development* charts a hierarchical sequence of stages that the I follows over time. At the lower stages in Loevinger's scheme, the child interprets the world and the Me in highly egocentric and immediate terms. Impulse control is weak, relationships are viewed as mechanisms for need fulfillment, and the individual is preoccupied with bodily feelings and short-term aims. With time and experience, people typically move into the middle range of ego stages, wherein selves become socialized in terms of conventional norms, values, and rules. The I becomes a cooperative and loyal conformist vis-à-vis family, social groups, and (ideally) society writ large. At the higher stages, the I comes to question many of the "truths" represented in the middle stages and develops a more discerning, principled, and individuated perspective from which to make sense of experience. Most people tap out in the middle stages of development, but for those who reach Loevinger's highest levels, the I strives for reconciliation among opposites, self-fulfillment, and a sense of unity and purpose in life. At the highest stages, the self experiences both autonomy from and interdependence with the social and cultural environment.

Building on the ideas of Cooley (1902) and Mead (1934), cognitive–developmental theories of self typically highlight the increasing sophistication of perspective taking over time. In early childhood, the I begins to see that others have a different perspective from one's own, but it is not until middle childhood that the I observes others observing the Me and can, thereby, coordinate the self's perspectives with those of others. The adolescent I can do more; it shows the ability to step outside the two-person situation and imagine how the self is seen by a generalized other (Selman, 1980). As the I comes to adopt more differentiated and sophisticated perspectives on others, it furthermore comes to construct a more differentiated and sophisticated Me (Damon & Hart, 1982; Harter, 2006). The young child may describe the Me in terms of momentary mood states ("I'm sad") and preferences or aversions ("I like ice cream"). In middle and late childhood, descriptions emphasize such phenomena as knowledge and learned skills ("I can throw a curve ball"; "I'm the smartest kid in the class"). The early adolescent speaks of psychologically related social skills ("I'm a good listener"; "I care for people who are less fortunate than I am"). Finally, in late adolescence and adulthood, the I employs complex descriptions of values, belief systems, and thought processes ("I am a devout Catholic who takes issue with the church on abortion"; "I believe that government should help the needy but also encourage personal responsibility").

Social Psychology

Over the past three decades, experimental social psychologists have generated an endless array of conceptions and findings that claim some relevance to the concepts of self and identity. In that it has become nearly de rigueur in this field to include the word *self* in the titles of most all journal articles and books, providing a comprehensive review of the literature on the social psychology of self is next to impossible (to see valiant efforts: Baumeister, 1998; Baumeister & Bushman, 2008; Robins, Tracy, & Trzesniewski, 2008). Nonetheless, a few broad themes can be discerned, picking up on ideas that fit roughly within James's categories of I and Me.

When contemporary social psychologists address issues that correspond to what James viewed to be aspects of the subjective I, they tend to speak in terms of reflexive *self-processes*. What does the self do (to and for itself)? For starters, the self is, or can be, aware of itself, or at least aware of its own efforts to be aware of itself (Baumeister, 1998). Duval and Wicklund (1972) launched a venerable tradition of research into the sometimes edifying and sometimes distressing effects of becoming especially aware of oneself during social behavior. One of the most interesting findings is that when people are positioned in front of mirrors, which literally reflect the self back on the self, they will cheat less and engage in more socially appropriate and virtuous behavior. It is as if the mirror functions in the same kind of self-monitoring manner as Mead's (1934) generalized other. At the same time, self-awareness can be unpleasant and even maladaptive, as in studies showing that people suffering from depression and severe anxiety often experience heightened states of self-awareness (Ingram, 1990). Under some circumstances and especially in the wake of failure, people will try to escape self-awareness through such tried-and-true means as excessive alcohol consumption, drug abuse, binge eating, and high-risk sexual behavior (Baumeister, 1998) and through more positive mechanisms such as meditation. Focusing too much conscious attention on the self may sometimes compromise decision making and undermine performance, whereas peak performance in athletics, music, and certain other highly demanding tasks is sometimes associated with losing conscious awareness of oneself and either "going with the flow" or focusing unswervingly on the task at hand (Leary, 2004).

Whereas being made aware of oneself may sometimes help to reign in impulses and promote socially appropriate behavior, self-control often requires a much greater effort. Just how much and what kind of effort is involved, what social conditions enhance and undermine such efforts, and what the immediate and long-term effects of these efforts are constitute some of the main questions addressed in the burgeoning social-psychological literature on *self-regulation* (Gailliot, Mead, & Baumeister, 2008). Higgins (1996) contended that regulating itself is the sovereign work that the I does, ultimately generating the most important features of self-knowledge (the Me). Developmentally speaking, among the earliest demonstrations of self-regulation is the ability to delay gratification. By age 5, children have typically developed a number of strategies for delaying gratification in the face of an alluring temptation, such as distracting themselves or persevering at a task that promises longer term benefit. Research suggests that children's relative ability to delay gratification is a significant predictor of social adaptation in adolescence (Mischel, Shoda, & Peake, 1988). Beginning in middle childhood, self-regulation becomes increasingly linked to the manner through which individuals monitor their own behavior in light of personal goals and ideals (Carver & Scheier, 1982). People receive feedback from the environment regarding their own goal pursuits, and they use that feedback to note discrepancies between what they perceive to be their *actual selves* on one hand and their *idealized* and *ought* selves on the other. They then endeavor to change their behavior to minimize the perceived discrepancies (Higgins, 1987). Self-regulation requires considerable psychological work, and work requires energy. As captured in the folk notion of "willpower," exercising one's self-regulatory function may be akin to exercising one's muscles—one needs to rest afterward to recoup the energy expended (Baumeister & Heatheron, 1996).

Although people expend considerable energy in their efforts to control their impulses and live up to ideals, self-regulation is but one arena of psychological work wherein the I is perennially employed. Bigger jobs fall under the motivational headings of *self-enhancement* (S. E. Taylor & Brown, 1988) and *self-consistency* (Swann, 1985). Put simply, the I seeks to enhance the Me—to make it bigger, better, stronger, and more excellent. The I seeks to make the Me consistent, understandable, and predictable. Supporting the first position are hundreds of studies and thousands of years of accrued common sense suggesting that people are strongly motivated to put themselves in the best possible light (e.g., Greenwald, 1980). Among the countless strategies that people employ to make themselves look good and maintain positive self-evaluations (Tesser, 1988) are construing downward social comparisons ("I may not be the world's greatest father, but I am certainly better than my own father was") and constructing positive illusions about the self. Maintaining positive self-esteem may even help to stave off anomie and the terror people may conceivably feel when they sense that their lives have no ultimate meaning (Greenberg et al., 1992). At the same time, many studies show that people seek information that verifies or confirms the self they believe they have, even to the point of sometimes preferring negative (but self-consistent) information over positive information that does not ring true. In this sense, the self may function somewhat like a well-accepted theory, and observations (of self and the world) may be consistently assimilated to its well-established axioms (Epstein, 1973). It is clear that self-enhancement and self-consistency motives can sometimes conflict with each other, and for that reason, among others, social psychologists have long debated about which of these two motivational tendencies of selfhood deserves top billing (Paulhus & Trapnell, 2008; Sedikides, 1993).

As the I endeavors to regulate, enhance, and confirm itself, it eventually builds a structure to comprise the Me. What does the structure look like? Many social-psychological theories suggest that James's self-as-object—variously called the self-concept, self-knowledge, self-schema, self-digest, self-construal—is hierarchically organized, with smaller subselves nested within larger ones (e.g., Martindale, 1980). Kihlstrom and Klein (1994) described a family of situationally-defined selves arranged in a hierarchy, from the most specifically-contextualized selves at the bottom to more general and abstract selves toward the top. Hierarchies vary with respect to differentiation and complexity. Linville (1987) defined *self-complexity* as the number of self-aspects a person generates to organize self-information. A related idea is *self-concept differentiation* (Donahue, Robins, Roberts, & John, 1993), which refers to the tendency to see oneself as having different personality characteristics in different social roles. Interestingly, research suggests that more self-complexity may be linked to higher levels of well-being, but greater self-concept differentiation is linked to poorer social adjustment. Adopting a very different metaphor for the Me, Wyer and Srull (1989) conceived of the self as an especially *non*hierarchical collection of *bins*. Each self-bin is labeled with a header describing a specific domain or experience, such as "self-as-father" or "self-at-parties." Information about the self is deposited in permanent, unlimited capacity, content addressable storage bins, each containing propositions about a person's traits and behaviors as well as other kinds of representations such as images of one's body and autobiographical memories. Bins organize information in a push-down stack. That is, representations are stored in bins in the order they are formed and retrieved through a probabilistic top-down search. Beyond the principle of "last in, first out," the bin contents are unorganized.

Whether hierarchically organized, arranged in storage bins, or designed in some other way, what does the Me contain? Among other things, it is likely to contain *semantic* information about the self as encoded self-descriptive statements of various sorts ("I am an outgoing person"; "my favorite candy is M & M's") and *episodic* information of the sort encoded in autobiographical recollections ("the first time I kissed Rebecca"). It appears likely that the brain organizes semantic and episodic information about the self in very different ways, which suggests that these two sources for the Me may sometimes be curiously unrelated to each other (Klein, Loftus, & Kihlstrom, 1996). Among the Me's most important elements, argued Markus and Nurius (1986), are *possible selves*, or "individuals' ideas of what they might become, what they would like to become, and what they are afraid of becoming" (p. 954). The Me is as much defined by what it might be in the future as by what it may be now. Whereas the I imagines idealized selves to be realized in the future, it also summons forth images of fear and loathing—*undesired selves* that must be avoided at all psychological costs. Ogilvie (1987) showed that the perceived distance between one's actual and undesired selves is strongly predictive of subjective well-being. In other words, the further away I currently am from what I fear I might become, the happier I am at the moment.

Importantly, the Me is differentiated in terms of social categories, such as race, class, gender, and occupation.

Social identity theory postulates that the self-concept is organized into two subsystems, one composed of social categories such as gender, nationality, political affiliation, and so on, and the other of more personal categories such as bodily attributes, psychological characteristics, habits, and tastes (Tajfel & Turner, 1979). M. B. Brewer and Gardner (1996) distinguished among individual, interpersonal, and group selves. Individual selves subsume self-attributed traits; interpersonal selves include important social roles; and group selves specify group prototypes. Robins et al. (2008) divided the Me into four levels, each with its corresponding audience or reference point: (a) personal (private audience: "I am a sensitive person"), (b) relational (intimate audience: "I am Amy's close friend"), (c) social (interpersonal audience: "I am a popular professor"), and (d) collective (communal audience: "I am Irish"). Cultural factors exert a strong impact on the structure and content of selves. For example, North American and Western European societies may encourage the development of *independent* self-construals, whereas the more collectivist societies of East Asia may promote the formation of *interdependent* construals of the Me (Markus & Kitayama, 1991).

The Narrative Perspective

Beginning in the 1980s, scientists and scholars in a number of fields proposed that creating a self is akin to telling a story (Sarbin, 1986). For example, Bruner (1986) and Polkinghorne (1988) asserted that human beings are storytellers by nature, designed to make sense of their own actions and intentions—and indeed their very lives—as stories unfolding over time. By assimilating one's life to a culturally recognized narrative, a person is able to make sense of his or her own behavior and strivings over time and is able to convey the meaning of his or her life to other people whose cultural knowledge enables them to recognize and (ideally) affirm the narrative (Cohler, 1982; Gregg, 1991). Stories provide a culture's ultimate perspective from which to judge both the psychological and the moral value of a life (MacIntyre, 1981; C. Taylor, 1989). Therefore, a person's internalized life story—the broad narrative of the Me that the I composes, edits, and continues to work on—functions to provide a life with some degree of meaning, unity, and purpose (Giddens, 1991; McAdams, 1985). That is, the I achieves some semblance of identity by making the Me into an internalized drama, complete with setting, scenes, characters, plots, and themes. The story does not simply remain inside the mind, however. People constantly tell stories about themselves to each other. People perform narratives according to the behavioral norms and discursive rules that prevail in their own culture (Rosenwald & Ochberg, 1992; Shotter & Gergen, 1989; Thorne, 2000). With each performance, the I gains yet another opportunity, no matter how tiny, to transform the Me into something new.

Recasting Erikson's concept of identity in narrative terms, McAdams (1985) proposed that the I begins to arrange the Me into a self-defining narrative in the late-adolescent and young-adult years. In his *life-story model of identity*, McAdams (1985, 1996, 2006a) argued that identity formation is largely a matter of constructing a life story that integrates the remembered past and imagined future to provide a convincing, unifying, and purposeful account of life. *Narrative identity* is the broad and ideally integrative story that a person begins to work on during emerging adulthood and continues to work on for much of the rest of life—a story that tells how the Me came to be and where the Me may be going within a specified world of work, love, and belief (see also, Hammack, 2008; McLean, Pasupathi, & Pals, 2007; Singer, 2004). The story reflects both the person's evolving conception of himself or herself as well as an implicit understanding of the world wherein the self is situated. Narrative identity is a *psychosocial construction*, a joint production through which a storytelling I works within a cultural, psycho-literary tradition that spells out the kinds of stories that can and should be told if a life is to be seen as good and meaningful (McAdams, 1996). The I works off of a menu of the culture's most favored images, themes, and plots. Appropriating what it is able to appropriate, given the resources at hand, and working within the constraints of gender, race, and social class, the I does its best to make the Me into a more-or-less satisfying, coherent, and meaningful story. At the end of the developmental day, self-authorship is distributed across many sources. I am what I and what my world author Me to be.

Although narrative identity continues to develop across the adult life course, one can obtain a freeze-frame shot at any given developmental moment to examine the story's constituent parts, features, and tendencies. For example, the life story may be grounded in a particular *ideological setting*, or backdrop of belief and value, often religiously informed, that sets forth what a person believes or assumes to be right, good, and true (Gregg, 1991; McAdams, 1985). The story may be punctuated by key *scenes* (McAdams, 1985; Tomkins, 1987), or what Singer and Salovey (1993) describe as *self-defining memories*—episodes that stand out in bold print within the text of the narrative, often depicted as high points, low points, or turning points in the story.

The story may also contain key characters, often portrayed as personified and idealized images of the self, or what McAdams (1985) called personal *imagoes*. Imagoes may interact or conflict over the course of the story, providing the kind of narrative tension that serves to push the plot forward. Life stories may also be characterized in terms of broad *thematic lines*, or recurrent goal-oriented sequences (McAdams, 1985). Whereas narrative identity may be portrayed through as many themes as can be found in the world's greatest literature, many of the most personally consequential thematic lines are variations on the broad psychological tendencies toward *agency* (e.g., autonomy of the self, achievement, power) and *communion* (e.g., connection to others, love, community; McAdams, 1985). Life stories, therefore, may be compared and contrasted with respect to setting, scenes, characters, and themes. Other important dimensions on which narrative identities vary include narrative *complexity* (McAdams, 1985) and *coherence* (Habermas & Bluck, 2000; McAdams, 2006b).

Whereas McAdams's approach to narrative identity examines broad, internalized life narratives that are assumed to provide a person's life with some degree of purpose and integration, a second line of theory and research in the narrative study of lives tends to privilege the smaller, moment-by-moment stories that people enact in daily social behavior (e.g., Bamberg, 1997; Pasupathi, 2006; Shotter & Gergen, 1989). Going back to Goffman's (1959) dramaturgic metaphor for social life, these approaches suggest that people perform many kinds of narratives as they take on different, socially constructed scripts and roles. Contemporary social life is saturated with narratives, argued Gergen (1991). The self is as much out there—in the confusing narrative swirl of postmodern life—as it is inside the head of the person (Holstein & Gubrium, 2000). What do we find inside the head? As much multiplicity and flux as we find outside, maybe more. The Me may be full of stories, but no single narrative proves robust enough to integrate the disparate elements into the kind of unifying and purposeful identity described by Erikson (1963) and McAdams (1985). Under the complex conditions of contemporary social life, the I may find it impossible to construct a coherent Me. Indeed, the whole idea of a single, integrative I-process may itself be a myth (Raggatt, 2006). For example, Hermans (1996) contended that subjective selfhood arises from multiple I-positions, each of which offers its own subjective perspective and its own distinctive voice. The self is an open-ended *polyphonic novel*, Hermans suggests. It is an uneven, decentered set of multiple stories and story fragments, each tale told by a different teller.

Summary

The origins of what C. Taylor (1989) deems the modern self may be traced back in Western philosophical traditions to Plato and Aristotle, who sought to understand the nature of the individual soul or self and its proper relationship with society. The ancient Greeks anticipated the writings of contemporary social psychologists such as Higgins (1996) and Baumeister (1998) in identifying self-control as one of the great problems in social life. They also saw the self as the seat of reason and introspection, an idea that expanded greatly over the next couple thousand years as philosophers explored the nature of reflexivity in human selfhood. From Augustine to William James, Western conceptions of the self highlighted the reflexive manner whereby the subjective I takes itself (the Me) as an object of observation, reflection, and work. James famously delineated three regions within the Me—the material, social, and spiritual selves—that play themselves out in private introspection and public life. Freud provided the I with a more dynamic flavoring, conceiving of the ego (*das Ich*, the I) as an ever-vigilant, Me-observing mediator whose job is to control impulses, defend against conflict and anxiety, and meet the demands of an oppressive social world, while channeling energy into productive work and mature love. Building on Freud, Erikson envisioned a more powerful I, and a more forgiving social world. The I confronts the broad challenge of identity in late adolescence and young adulthood. In modern societies, the young-adult I must reconfigure the Me into a patterned whole that both provides life with meaning and purpose and situates the young adult within a culturally sanctioned psychosocial niche.

The relationship between I and Me has received a good deal of scholarly and scientific attention in the humanistic tradition (e.g., Rogers, Maslow), cognitive–developmental studies, social and personality psychology, and recent narrative perspectives on self and identity. From Rousseau and Emerson to the latest writings in self-determination theory (e.g., Ryan & Deci, 2006), a strong humanistic streak runs through many Western conceptions of selfhood, emphasizing the inherent goodness, uniqueness, and integrity of an autonomous, inner-directed, and intrinsically motivated I—an I whose very reason for being is to realize its full potential. Cognitive–developmental perspectives chart the growth of the I (and the Me) from primitive, simple, and egocentrical childhood versions to the more complex, sociocentric, and principled forms encountered in adolescence and adulthood. By contrast, the field of social psychology has tended to ignore how the self changes and grows over time and has instead examined a range of self-processes, such as self-regulation, self-awareness, self-enhancement, and self-verification. The I imagined by contemporary social psychologists seems to see itself (the Me) as a broad compendium or digest of semantic information—self-schemas, self-aspects, possible selves, social identities, and so on—that may be called on to address a wide range of challenges in social life. Recently developed narrative theories of the self suggest that the compendium includes episodic information as well, such as autobiographical recollections and other stories of the Me, both remembered from the past and imagined for the future. From a narrative perspective, identity itself may be an internalized and evolving story that the I constructs about the Me to provide life with some semblance of unity, purpose, and meaning. The I is (in part) a storyteller, and the Me is (in part) the story that it tells.

THE SELF AS ACTOR

Gathering together initial impressions regarding the behavior of human beings on earth, a visitor from another galaxy finds especially noteworthy the fact that these strange creatures always live in groups wherein they engage in complex and highly ritualized social action. At first, our other-worldly friend cannot do interviews with the objects of her study; she can but observe their behavior from an objective distance, like Locke's punctual perspective from which the I gazes upon the Me. Yet there is so much to see! Human beings constantly interact with each other. They gather together in pairs and groups to discuss just about anything that can be discussed. They work in groups to accomplish difficult, multifaceted tasks. They congregate together to eat, play, learn, and pray. They pay an inordinate amount of attention to their youngest ones, providing care, instruction, and discipline. They cooperate with each other to stage complex social performances. However, they also compete for scarce resources in the environment, be those resources food, land, material possessions, mates, or prestige. They endlessly argue, negotiate, and bargain. There seems to be a tremendous amount of social conflict in and between their groups, which often leads to fighting. They organize themselves as armies to wage war.

It must be the case, the visitor reasons, that human beings evolved to live this way, as social actors performing on a complex and dynamic stage. Of course, she is right. Over the past 1.5 million years of human evolution, the prime challenge for the cognitively gifted, bipedal, tool-making, group-living creature of central interest here is what Goffman (1959) famously named the *presentation of self in everyday life*. Taking Shakespeare's words more seriously than any other social scientist has ever taken them, Goffman asserted that all the world is indeed a stage and all the men and women are but actors and actresses on it. Social actors present themselves to each other through *performances*, in which people play roles, enact routines, and manage impressions. What matters for social actors is the effectiveness of the performance—how well do they play the role, how convincing is their enactment of the part, how skillful are they at managing the impressions of the other actors on stage, who simultaneously play the roles of audience and critic, as we all do, for we are constantly observing each other's performances, evaluating each other's roles, and adjusting our own scripts accordingly.

We never leave the stage, Goffman argued. Human beings never go home to live their real and authentic lives offstage, for the stage *is* home, and we play for keeps. Social performance is the *natural* way we live. In his socioanalytical theory of human behavior, Robert Hogan (1982) provided a clear evolutionary explanation for Goffman's insights. Playacting is part of human nature, Hogan maintained. We evolved to perform as actors in small bands and tribes, hunting and gathering to obtain food, cooperating and competing in an environment of limited resources, perennial threat, and diverse adaptational challenges. Continuously striving for social acceptance (to get along) and social status (to get ahead), we formed alliances and shifting coalitions, we jockeyed for position in different social arenas, we worked the group through persuasion, guile, deception, reputation, and sometimes brute force. We enacted a wide range of roles in group life to protect ourselves from predators, to find food and shelter, to secure mates, to raise the young, and to amass the material wherewithal required to live long enough and well enough in the group such that our genes managed to find their way down the generational line. In the environment of evolutionary adaptedness, those actors who played their roles the best—who were best able to get along and get ahead in the group—were more likely, it is assumed, to survive and reproduce, or were more likely to promote the survival and reproduction of those other social actors with whom they shared genes. In Hogan's view, there was and is nothing more important for human adaptation than the social roles we actors play:

> Self-presentation and impression management are not trivial party games. They are fundamental processes, rooted in our history as group-living animals. They are archaic, powerful, compulsive tendencies that are closely tied to our chances for survival and reproductive success. (Hogan, Jones, & Cheek, 1985, p. 181)

Performative Styles: Temperament as Precursor to Self

There is a sense in which the human infant is like the intergalactic visitor who is sent to earth to observe the group-living species who dominates our planet. The infant observes the social actors on stage to figure out just what human social life is all about. At first it may seem like a blooming, buzzing confusion, but observation leads quickly to imitation, as the infant begins to sort a few things out and assume a rudimentary social role. A sense of an actor-self begins to emerge—a self-contained, embodied source of activity in which performances affect what other actors do. As James suggested, the actor-self reflects back on its own performances, observes itself on stage, and begins to form a conception of just what kind of an actor it is. A great deal of what we know to be true about ourselves derives from our repeated observations of our own behavior in a variety of social situations (Bem, 1972). In principle, this kind of self-knowledge does not require much introspection. We simply observe what we do. We learn about ourselves in the same manner we learn about others, by observing social performances. A shy boy observes that he spends a great deal less time with the other boys on his street than does his more gregarious sibling. A conscientious young girl notices that she keeps her room and her things well organized and she always hands in her homework on time. Each of us develops particular styles of playacting. We find ourselves playing our roles in the same characteristic ways. We observe the patterns and eventually attribute the patterns to the Me. I must be an aggressive person because I am always beating people up! I must be really smart because I keep scoring the highest on the math tests.

Even before the self emerges, characteristic styles of social performance begin to reveal themselves as babies express those inborn patterns of *temperament* that they unwittingly bring to the stage. Temperament refers to broad and basic differences in behavioral and emotional style that show up very early in life, assumed as they are to be largely a product of genetic endowment. Many researchers believe that temperament provides the "early-in-life framework" out of which personality traits eventually develop (Saucier & Simonds, 2006, p. 118). In their authoritative review of the literature on child and adult personality, Caspi, Roberts, and Shiner (2005) suggested that (a) a surgency factor in child temperament (encompassing positive affectivity and positive approach) may herald the development of adult traits traditionally subsumed within the extraversion and positive emotionality domain, (b) temperament dimensions of anxious or fearful distress and irritable distress may foreshadow the development of neuroticism or negative emotionality in adulthood (with irritable distress perhaps also a precursor to low agreeableness), and (c) childhood capacities for focused attention and effortful control, as well as behavioral inhibition in children, may underlie the development of adult traits of conscientiousness, constraint, and aspects of agreeableness. Just how these early differences in temperament eventually morph into adult dispositional traits remains to be determined, although researchers typically assume that the process involves complex and sustained interactions of genes and environments (Krueger & Johnson, 2008). In any case, it is clear that the first glimmerings of basic differences in the ways that human actors characteristically play their roles in social life can be seen in the first few months of life. Some actors seem generally cheerful and smiley; others, distressed. Some actors consistently approach opportunities for social reward; other show marked inhibition.

Temperament does not require a self. At first, the inborn differences in behavioral and emotional style that infants show are *observed* only by *others*—parents and other caregivers mainly, and sometimes researchers. However, temperament will eventually exert strong effects on self in at least two ways. First, basic temperament differences play themselves out in a range of self-processes, especially self-regulation. The manner in which individuals reflexively work on themselves—their efforts to control, manage, improve, and actualize the self—is strongly influenced by temperament. Second, as social actors observe their own, temperament-driven performances, they eventually build up an internalized representation of how they perform. The Me will eventually include my understanding of my own temperament dispositions, based on my observations of my own social behavior. Even before the actor-self emerges, therefore, certain features of its I–Me contours are being laid down. The self is never able to make a clean and fresh start of it. Like the visitor from another galaxy, it shows up on the scene to encounter a well-structured world already in process. It emerges in the middle of a lifelong series of social performances, and it has to figure out not only which roles to play but which roles it has already (unknowingly) been playing.

Self-Awareness: I and Me

Human beings gradually become aware of themselves as independent actors on a social stage during the first 4 to 5 years of development. Synthesizing three decades of research on self-recognition behavior in infants and children, Rochat (2003) charted five levels in the development of human self-awareness. At the first level, manifested at birth to about 2 months of age, infants already show some rudimentary sense of their own body as a differentiated entity in the world. Contrary to the speculations of such psychoanalytical theorists as Mahler et al. (1975), there appears to be no purely symbiotic period in the course of human development—nothing quite akin to what Freud famously described as the oceanic feeling—wherein the self merges completely with the other. Instead, newborns seem to sense a basic distinction between their own bodies and the bodies inhabited by others. The differentiation is shown, for example, in studies demonstrating stronger rooting responses (e.g., turning the face in the direction of a stimulus to the infant's cheek) when the source of stimulation is external (e.g., the experimenter's finger) than when the stimulus comes from the infant's own body (e.g., the infant's finger) (Rochat & Hespos, 1997).

Beginning around 2 months of age, infants show a second level of self-awareness, as they become more actively involved in exploring the consequences of their own behavior. In addition to the self-world differentiation expressed at the first level, infants now show an implicit understanding of how their own body is *situated* in relation to other entities in the environment (Rochat, 2003). Their actions appear now to be guided by an increasingly sophisticated and accurate sense of how they are positioned as an embodied actor on a stage containing other objects and other bodies. Reporting on a series of studies, for example, Rochat (2003) found that 4- to 6-month-old infants' decisions to reach toward an object placed at various distances and locations in front of them were determined by their own sense of situation and postural ability. In the social realm, infants begin to smile and make eye contact with other actors during this time. They engage in face-to-face play, taking turns and sharing basic affective states (I feel excited; I feel distress) with others (Stern, 1985). These proto-conversations play out with gestures, squeals, laughter, and a whole host of nonlinguistic behaviors that reliably solicit the attention and engagement of parents, caregivers, siblings, and the many other actors who enter and exit the infant's social world (Rochat, Querido, & Striano, 1999).

Putting young children in front of mirrors and observing their responses to the reflections they see, researchers have noted that infants appear to recognize features of their own bodies by 5 to 6 months of age. For example, 6-month-olds will respond in different ways to prerecorded videos of themselves and of other, same-aged infants. However, it is not clear that infants this young actually realize that what they are seeing on the TV screen is indeed themselves (Rochat, 2003). Instead, they appear to be expressing recognition of a familiar facial gestalt, the result of previous perceptual learning and exposure to mirrors and reflecting objects.

It is only by about 18 months of age, instead, that unambiguous signs of self-recognition emerge in response to visual reflections (Lewis & Brooks-Gunn, 1979; Rochat, 2003). In many experiments, researchers have surreptitiously placed markings on young children's faces (by applying rouge to the child's nose, for example, or by placing a sticker on the child's forehead), placed the children in front of mirrors, and then observed their reactions. By 18 months of age, children confronted with their altered images in the mirror will engage in a range of self-directed behaviors indicating that they now realize that what they see is a reflection of their own bodies. For example, they will point to the marking on their own face, and they may try to erase or remove it. This kind of advance in self-awareness ushers in Rochat's (2003) third level, wherein the child begins to form a rudimentary sense of the Me. It is during the second year of life, furthermore, that children typically begin to use self-referential words, such as "me" and "mine," and begin to show certain kinds of self-referential emotions, such as pride and embarrassment (Kagan, 1998; Tangney, Stuewig, & Mashek, 2007). To feel pride or shame in response to one's own actions presupposes a sense of the self as an actor whose performances are viewed and evaluated by others in the environment. Therefore, the I emerges as a self-conscious actor shortly before or around the child's second birthday (Harter, 2006; Howe & Courage, 1997). Reflexively, an impression or image of the Me begins to take form as the child begins to take note of his or her own actions and other actors' reactions to those actions.

Although a reflexive I–Me actor-self emerges around age 2, this sense of self is surprisingly unstable and inconsistent in the months following its debut. As one indication of the confusion that sometimes occurs, take Povinelli's (2001) charming example of the 3-year-old Jennifer. Observing a video taken 3 minutes earlier in which she appears with a sticker on her head, Jennifer says, "it's Jennifer . . . it's a sticker," and then adds, "but why is she wearing my shirt?!" (Povinelli, 2001, p. 81). Indeed, 3-year-olds will reach for a large sticker they see on top of their own head while viewing a live video of themselves, but they will not reach for it, even though it is still there, when viewing the replay of the same video taken only 3 minutes earlier

(Povinelli, 2001). Furthermore, when asked who was on TV in the video made minutes before, it is only by 4 years of age that the majority of children say "Me" rather than their proper name, suggesting a first-person stance rather than a third. Even though the young child is aware of itself as an actor on the social stage, he or she may fail to realize that the actor *continues to be me* over time. The I loses track sometimes, failing to make the appropriate first-person attribution (it's me) when the sequence of actions goes on for a while. The consolidation of a sense of the Me as extended in time marks the fourth level in Rochat's (2003) model of self-awareness. Children do not typically reach this level until age 3 or 4.

By the time young children begin to express and recognize themselves as enduring actor-selves, they also begin to show major advances in understanding the behavior of other actors. In their fourth and fifth years, children become able to hold multiple representations and perspectives on objects and people. Relatedly, they begin to show an astute understanding of what goes on in the minds of other actors. As we will see later in this chapter, Rochat's fifth and final level of self-awareness points to features of selfhood that go well beyond the actor role. Children eventually come to understand themselves and others as motivated agents whose desires, wants, beliefs, goals, and plans energize and direct their actions toward future ends. As selves, we human beings are surely more than mere actors, but we begin as actors only.

The Problem of Self-Regulation

One of the prime challenges of being an actor is to learn how to *control* one's performance. As Goffman (1959) suggested, social actors work hard to manage the impressions of others by carefully monitoring and calibrating how they express themselves on the stage. Losing control can sometimes prove disastrous, for not only does the actor thereby ruin the scene, but he or she may also compromise well-being and reputation for the future. Going back to Plato's conception of the Republic, the regulation of the self has proved to be one of the most vexing, if not the most vexing, challenge of self-presentation in social life. Indeed, five of the seven deadly sins of Christian medieval thought involved failures in self-regulation—greed, lust, gluttony, sloth, and wrath (Baumeister, 1998). It is not surprising, therefore, that the most influential social theorists of recent times have typically devoted considerable attention to the problem of self-regulation, articulating its vicissitudes under such headings as "socialization," "social control," "self-control," "impulse control," and the development of "conscience." Freud (1923/1961), for example, imagined the Oedipus complex as the grand solution to the problem of self-regulation. With the internalization of the threatening oedipal authority and the establishment of the superego, the child gains an internal monitoring voice, the lifelong functions of which are to *observe* the self and to keep impulses in check. Mead (1934) put his money on the external social world. As the child becomes increasingly aware of how the social world sees him or her, the child will likely monitor behavior more closely and aim to act in ways that meet the approval of the generalized other. Like many other theorists, Freud and Mead suggested that self-regulation depends on the *observation* of the self. Something or someone must keep watch. Social performances require an audience. When the audience monitors and critiques in effective ways, selves should become regulated.

The importance of observation for the regulation of self brings us back to James's distinction between the I and the Me. In that selves are reflexive, selves (the I) observe (and ideally regulate) themselves (the Me). In keeping with this theme, a number of contemporary theorists maintain that the prime function of self-awareness itself is indeed the regulation of social action (Carver & Scheier, 1982; Higgins, 1996). From this perspective, the great leap forward in the development of self-regulation is the emergence of self-awareness—the acting I's recognition of the Me as an actor—in the second year of life. Once the I is able to take the Me as an object of reflection, the I can begin to control the presentation of self on the social stage. Assisting its efforts are powerful social–moral emotions, such as pride and shame (Tangney et al, 2007). Beginning in the second year, children feel pride when their actions bring the approval of others. In response to the audience's applause, they take a psychological bow. By contrast, they may feel shame, regret, or guilt when their actions bring disapproval, when they fail to live up to a socially mandated standard. In general, developmental psychologists assume that children enjoy feeling pride and obtaining social approval and that they find aversive the experiences of shame, guilt, and the fear they may feel when they anticipate punishment and other forms of social critique. Over time, children learn which behaviors bring social approbation and which bring critique. As they seek to maximize reward and the feel-good experience of pride and to minimize punishment and the feel-bad emotions of shame and guilt, children should gradually become something like the socialized and self-regulated actors that their ever-watchful audiences want them to become.

Researchers have followed three approaches in the study of self-regulation in young children. The first focuses on temperament. For example, some very young children find it extremely difficult to control their impulses, whereas others are able to keep themselves in check in situations in which impulsive behavior could lead to trouble. The temperament dimension of *effortful control* refers to the "child's active and voluntary capacity to withhold a dominant response in order to enact a subordinate response given situational demands" (Li-Grinning, 2007, p. 208). Children with a strong temperamental inclination toward effortful control are able to delay immediate gratification to focus their attention on longer term goals to be achieved and rewards to be obtained. In preschool, they are better able than children with low effortful control to resist candy when told to do so or to focus their attention on a game even if they want to do something else at the moment. In grade school, they may be tempted to watch television after school, but if mom tells them that doing their homework instead will result in their going to the amusement park this weekend, they are able to resist temptation and buckle down. From the first year of life onward, girls tend to show better effortful control than boys. Differences are also linked to social class. Children from more economically deprived families tend to show lower levels of effortful control than do children from more affluent families. Research has shown that high levels of effortful control are predictive of successful interpersonal functioning in childhood, better school grades, and fewer behavioral problems (Li-Grinning, 2007). Effortful control appears to be an important factor in moral development and the consolidation of *conscience* (Kochanska & Aksan, 2006). Being able to control one's impulses at home and preschool may pave the way for rule compliance and the ability to interact with others in a respectful and cooperative manner on a broader social stage.

A second line of research focuses on attachment. Many researchers argue that the quality of attachment bonds established in the first 2 years of life has a strong influence on the development of self-regulation in young children (Sroufe, 1996; Thompson, 1998). For securely attached infants and young children, caregivers infuse into the social arena a pervasive feeling of trust and safety. In the presence of their attachment objects, securely attached children explore the environment with confidence and aplomb. When they sense danger, they will readily find comfort in their caregivers' ministrations. In secure attachment, therefore, the caregiver functions as both secure base and safe haven (Mikulincer & Shaver, 2007). In addition, the caregiver may also play the role of moral guide. Securely attached children check back with their caregivers to determine which kinds of actions are likely to meet with their approval and disapproval. Illustrating this point, Diener, Mengelsdorf, McHale, and Frosch (2002) found that infants who were securely attached to both parents showed greater levels of parent-oriented regulation relative to their peers who were less securely attached to one or both parents. As children develop, they set up in their minds internalized *working models* of attachment relationships (Bowlby, 1969), and they take those models with them from one social situation to the next. As such, actors never enter the stage alone. They come equipped with intrapsychic resources, including the internalized representations of past relationships. These working models are like acting coaches in the head. Ideally, they inspire confidence and urge the actor on to better performance. They may also provide constraints and guidelines, much like Freud's superego. Mother may not literally be on stage with me as I walk into my first-grade classroom, but I am still able to check back with her, in a sense, by unconsciously consulting my working model. Attachment theorists suggest that this kind of consultation serves a self-regulatory function. It helps keep me on message, makes it easier for me to follow the socially valued script and to ignore, hold back, put off, or translate into productive behavior a wide range of potentially distracting impulses.

A third line of research examines how parents continue to provide support, guidance, and scaffolding for the development of self-regulation through the childhood and adolescent years (Dodge & Garber, 1991; Saarni, 2006). A major theme in this literature is that children look to parents and other role models for information regarding how to respond to emotionally ambiguous situations and how to think about and translate into effective action their impulses and their emotions. Children observe themselves, observe their parents, and observe their parents' observing them, and through all the observations, they ideally learn which kinds of performance work well when they feel happy, when they feel sad, and when they feel that they are having a hard time controlling what they feel. It is especially important, argue some researchers, that parents and other role models talk with children about their emotions. In this regard, Gottman, Katz, and Hooven (1997) conceive of parents as socioemotional *coaches*. As such, parents should (a) be aware of their children's emotions, (b) take advantage of their children's emotional expressions as learning opportunities, (c) help their children to label and verbalize their feelings, (d) empathize with and validate their children's emotions, and (e) assist their children in dealing with emotionally difficult experiences. Effective coaches help their children to soothe themselves in tough times, to inhibit negative feelings and behaviors, and to focus attention on the task demands of particularly challenging social and emotional performances.

Building the Self-Concept Through Childhood and Adolescence

Over the course of childhood and adolescence, the I develops through stages of increasing complexity, and as it does so, it builds up an increasingly complex and differentiated Me. Loevinger's (1976) theory of ego development charts the I's passage through early stages of heightened egocentricity and limited perspective taking to more sociocentric stages wherein group norms, values, and conventions help to shape how the I makes sense of itself and the world around it. At higher stages still, the I comes to question societal convention and to develop a more nuanced and dynamic understanding of the relationship between self and society. How the I represents itself—the Me, variously described as a self-representation or self-concept (Damon & Hart, 1982; Harter, 2006)—keeps pace with the development of the I, the inevitable result, as James (1892/1963) underscored, of the self's inherent reflexivity.

Let us trace the development of the Me. Things are simple in the beginning. When asked to describe herself, the 3-year-old tells you right off the bat that she is indeed 3 years old, that she lives in a white house with her parents and older brother, that she has green eyes and brown hair, that she runs real fast, that she owns three Barbie dolls, and that she likes to eat macaroni and cheese. As Harter (2006) showed, the preschool child's self-concept consists mainly of concrete representations of observable features. Self-representations at this early point in development are typically tied directly to behavior ("I run fast") or to tangible objects (houses, macaroni and cheese). The young child is like a demographer or radical behaviorist, focusing all of her attention on the observables in the environment (Harter, 2006). To the extent she reports on what is going on inside, the young child may speak of feeling happy or sad or of wanting certain things and fearing others. However, these internal statements are less about the self as an ongoing entity and more about momentary states and moods. In its early incarnations, then, the actor-Me is all about what the Me looks and sounds like for its imagined audience and what the Me can do in a very concrete sense, as well as what kind of stage the Me acts on—be it a white house, a public park, or the preschool class room.

As children move through elementary school, their self-representations begin to take the form of more general, stable, and comparative attributions about appearance and social performance (Harter, 2006). Social comparison is a key process here. Eight-year-olds will compare their performances to those of other actors in their world. "I am a very good baseball player, but my handwriting is sloppy." "I am pretty popular in my class, but not as popular as Tiffany." "My mother says that I am a very kind and considerate person, but I also know that I can be mean to people when they say mean things to me." Reflecting the I's greater sensitivity to group standards and social norms, the self-concept of grade school adds a whole new set of self-generalizations to those simple representations about "my eyes" and "my Barbie dolls." In the early grades, children use mainly positive generalizations to describe themselves—"nice," "helpful," "funny," "smart." By the time they are in fourth or fifth grade, however, their trait attributions have become more specific and now may include some sharply negative assessments (Harter, 2006). Therefore, 10-year-olds may see themselves as "outgoing," "spontaneous," "open-minded," "a very good listener," "lacking confidence in new situations," "terrible at math," and "happy with my girlfriends but shy around boys."

Over the course of childhood and into adolescence, the I's characteristic manner of describing itself (the Me) comes to rely more and more on the discourse of dispositional *traits* (Harter, 2006; Loevinger, 1976; McAdams, 1998). Trait labels capture general individual differences between social actors with respect to their characteristic thoughts, feelings, and behaviors. Of course, people display some traitlike, cross-situationally consistent differences in social behavior even in infancy, as studies of temperament have convincingly shown. However, infants and young children are not really aware of these differences; they have very little insight into their own temperament dispositions. With development, however, people gain awareness. As Bem's (1972) self-perception theory suggests, actors repeatedly observe their own performances and the performances of other actors, and they eventually come to define themselves in terms of those observations. Over the course of late childhood and adolescence, the actor-self's observations lead increasingly to generalizations, and eventually convictions, regarding his or her own traits and how they compare to the traits of other actors.

Studies that rely on self-report questionnaires designed to assess personality traits show that trait self-ratings become increasingly stable in the preteen years and begin to show the common five-factor structure that has been repeatedly observed among adults (Roberts, Wood, & Caspi, 2008). Following the conventions of McCrae and Costa (1997), the five factors that emerge in study after study with adults—and in culture after culture—may be labeled extraversion (encompassing social dominance, gregariousness, positive affectivity), neuroticism (negative affectivity, emotional instability), conscientiousness (constraint, dependability, perseverance), agreeableness (kindness, cooperativeness, altruism), and openness to experience (imaginativeness, creativity, liberalness). When results from adults' self-ratings of personality traits are factor analyzed, their self-report responses tend to fall into broad categories resembling these five labels. In that this pattern begins to show up in the preteen years, it is not an exaggeration to say that personality traits begin to hijack the actor-self at this time. It is *not* that personality traits begin to form or develop in the preteen years. Nor is it the case that personality traits suddenly begin to exert an influence on behavior at this time. Dispositional traits have been developing all along, as it were, influencing behavior in many ways (Caspi et al., 2005). It is not until the late childhood years, however, that *people begin to see themselves as the owners of their dispositional traits*. In late childhood and into adolescence, the I comes to appreciate the power of trait attributions—their generality, their economy, the way they capture so much about psychologic individuality with so little effort. Call me an extravert! There is great meaning in the trait claim. It tells the world that I am an outgoing, socially dominant, self-assured, and exuberant actor on my social stage. Of course, I am more than this, too. I am other traits, perhaps many traits. But *I am traits*. And my traits are different from yours.

From early childhood into the teenaged years, then, the I evolves from being a radical behaviorist to a trait psychologist. Whereas I was once merely the observable features and behaviors of my social performances, I am now the higher order generalizations and attributions that I am able to make from repeated observations of those performances. Over the course of adolescence, the I continues to refine the discourse of traits, articulating traits in both greater depth and greater detail, and pushing traits as far as they can be pushed. According to Harter (2006), early adolescence is marked by a proliferation of traits and the construction of multiple versions of Me to accommodate an increasingly complex social ecology. The teenager can act in many ways, depending on the demands of situations. He or she can show a host of traits, express a wide range of selves for different roles and audiences. It may be at this point in the life course that James's (1892/1963) famous passage on the social self's multiplicity begins to resonate clearly:

> Properly speaking, *a man has as many social selves as there are individuals who recognize him* and carry an image of him in their mind. To wound any one of these images is to wound him. But as the individuals who carry the images fall naturally into classes, we may practically say that he has as many social selves as there are distinct *groups* of persons about whose opinion he cares. He generally shows a different side of himself to each of these different groups. Many a youth who is demure enough before his parents and teachers, swears and swaggers like a pirate among his "tough" young friends. We do not show ourselves to our children as to our club-companions, as to our customers as to our laborers we employ, to our own masters and employers as to our intimate friends. From this there results what practically is a division of the man into several selves; and this may be a discordant splitting, as where one is afraid to let one set of his acquaintances know him as he is elsewhere; and this may be a perfectly harmonious division of labor, as where one tender to his children is stern to the soldiers or prisoners under his command. (James, 1892/1963, p. 169, italics in original)

James pointed out an obvious fact of social life: Actors must show different traits for different roles. Sometimes the shifting back and forth is easy and smooth, reflecting a "harmonious division of labor." At other times, however, social actors may experience what James called a "discordant splitting." As teenagers move into and through high school, many appear to become increasingly cognizant of the discordant splitting. The contradictions and multiplicities of self-presentation become an increasing source of concern for older adolescents, Harter (2006) suggested. Like the iconic Holden Caulfield in J. D. Salinger's *Catcher in the Rye*, some adolescents may begin to see the multiple roles they play as indicators of just how "phony" social life is. If I swear and swagger like a rap star with my buddies but am demure and self-effacing with my girlfriend's parents, which of these two discordant trait attributions reflects what I "really" am?

One of the startling psychological insights of adolescence is the realization that the self is, and has been all along, merely a social actor. It is as if some teenagers suddenly "get it" when it comes to Goffman's (1959) radical claim that social life is nothing but playacting. However, they do not like Goffman's insight, even if they never heard of the great sociologist. Suddenly, acting seems like artifice, which of course (at some level) it is. There must be more to me than the roles I play, something more real and true. Harter (2006) wrote that it is not until adolescence that individuals begin to set up a contrast between a "meant to be" true self and the many false selves that may be enacted in certain social performances. The actor-self of adolescence begins to critique itself as lacking in authenticity. Yet then it is surely the nature of social acting to take on many roles and to play out many traits, as both Goffman and James maintained. One must continue to act in a complex and multifaceted social world. Yet one begins to search, in adolescence, for a way to represent a level of truth and coherence in the Me that goes beyond, and is in some sense deeper than, the conflicting roles and traits that the actor shows on stage. The I's search for this kind of self-consistency and authenticity in the Me is part of what Erikson (1963) had in mind in describing the adolescent and adult problem of identity.

Identity, Traits, and the Actor-Self in Adulthood

The development of the actor-self in adulthood begins with Erikson's (1963) conundrum of identity. Who am I *really*? What roles am I to assume in adult life? In the emerging adulthood years, the Me expands to encompass a broad range of traits, roles, and relationships. The I looks to find or construct a coherent pattern amid all the things than now comprise the Me. The pattern must make internal sense; it must feel true and authentic. At the same time, other salient actors and audiences must validate the choices that follow from the new identity. The new identity must reflect forms of action, belief, and being that find favor in the minds of other adults. It must situate the person in a productive and meaningful way within a psychosocial niche, paving the way for commitments in the realms of occupation or vocation, family and intimacy, and personal ideology (Marcia, 1980).

A portion of the psychological work that goes into the construction of identity during the emerging adulthood years is trait work. The actor-self elaborates and refines its dispositional profile. In efforts to forge more integration in the Me, the I subsumes narrower self-attributions within broader, higher order categories (Harter, 2006). To achieve a greater sense of self-coherence, it may seek to resolve contradictions among different trait attributions (Donahue, Robins, Roberts, & John, 1993). I am conscientious in situations that really matter to me, but at other times it is fine if I am lazy and don't give a damn. I am kind and caring toward all people who need my help, but for those who rebuff my overtures, I can be cold and heartless. The I tempers its broad and integrative trait attributions with a dose of social psychology; it comes to know and respect the power of situations in the shaping of the Me (Harter, 2006). Moving into adulthood, then, representations of one's internal dispositions and social roles are likely to become both more integrated and more differentiated, showing greater self-complexity (Rafaeli-Mor & Steinberg, 2002).

Gender and ethnicity play important roles in the young adult's efforts to construct a coherent dispositional profile for the actor-self. In adolescence, females detect more contradictions and oppositions among their self-attributions than do males (Harter, 2006). As they move into adulthood, the competing demands of work or schooling on one hand and family and relationships on the other can create even more conflict in the Me, especially for well-educated young women who want both to pursue a career and raise a family. For certain ethnic groups, the self may be split between the performative demands associated with two contrasting cultures. Going back to W. E. B. DuBois's (1903/1989) characterization of double consciousness in *The Souls of Black Folk*, social scientists have analyzed the challenges faced by African American adults who must adapt to the norms of behavior among white Americans while staying true to their identities as people of color. Research with bilingual Mexican Americans and other Latina and Latino groups suggests that some ethnic minorities in the United States feel torn between different self-representations. In one study, for example, bilingual Mexican Americans tended to endorse different personality traits when thinking about themselves in English compared with thinking about themselves in Spanish (Ramirez-Esparza, Gosling, Benet-Martinez, Potter, & Pennebaker, 2006). Benet-Martinez has conducted a number of studies on *bicultural identity integration* (*BII*), which is the extent to which bicultural individuals are able to combine the self-attributions they associate with their different cultures into a coherent whole (e.g., Benet-Martinez & Haritatos, 2005; Benet-Martinez, Leu, Lee, & Morris, 2002). Lower scores on BII indicate greater cultural conflict, and they predict more daily stress for bicultural individuals. By contrast, higher scores on BII are associated with greater psychologic well-being.

In constructing the actor-self, people also differ on just how fixed or malleable they believe their own (and others') attributes to be (Dweck, Chiu, & Hong, 1995; Molden & Dweck, 2006). Individuals who implicitly embrace an *entity theory* of the Me believe that their traits are like self-essences that cannot readily be changed. If I am a neurotic person prone to negative affect, I am fated to be neurotic forever. There is nothing I can really do about it.

By contrast, individuals with an *incremental theory* of the Me believe that their traits can be changed, through work and circumstances. I may be neurotic, but I am working on that trait these days, and I hope to improve myself over time. An incremental theory of the self would appear to hold many psychological advantages over an entity theory, especially in the wake of failures and disappointments. People with an incremental theory may be better able to recover from failures and continue to work on improving themselves for future social performances. As social actors, they know that they are still a work in progress, still becoming better. Entity theorists, by contrast, may feel that they rely mainly on their God-given talents and proclivities. The entity understanding of the Me proves adaptive when the reviews of one's social performances are glowing. When their internal resources prove insufficient for the dramaturgic task, however, entity theorists are left with fewer options for a productive response, because they are skeptical about changing the way they inherently are. In one study, Beer (2002) showed that shy incremental theorists prefer to engage in relatively challenging social interactions that they believe may help them develop new social skills, even though they find these interactions to be difficult. In sharp contrast, shy entity theorists typically take the easier way. They choose to interact only in those comfortable situations that do not challenge their social skills.

Self-representations continue to develop across the adult life course. Even after the I manages to fashion an arrangement of the Me that qualifies for a more-or-less coherent and satisfying Eriksonian identity in young adulthood, James's self-as-object continues to change as life circumstances change. Should the person become a spouse, parent, aunt, uncle, or grandparent, these family roles come to occupy prominent positions in the Me. In a similar manner, changing roles at work and in the community become incorporated into the Me. The actor-self continues to reflect the main activities of life—what I do in the many arenas of social life, and how I do it. Consequently, roles and traits tend to be the main players in the adult's actor-self (Roberts & Pomerantz, 2004). Over time, roles are likely to change in important ways, for people show different kinds of social performances for different audiences and different purposes across the life course. By contrast, trait attributions show more continuity over time (Diehl, 2006). Even though I am doing different things than I used to do, I may be doing them in the same kinds of ways.

The relationship between personality traits and the actor-self during the adult years can be viewed in two different ways. From the first perspective, one may consider the extent to which people naturally or spontaneously include trait attributions in their verbal representations of the Me (Diehl, 2006). For example, McCrae and Costa (1988) used the Twenty Statements Test to examine spontaneous self-representations of adults from aged 32 to 84. They found that younger adults were more likely to produce trait statements (I am a friendly person; I am nervous) when describing the self than were older adults, who were likely to mention age, health status, interests, hobbies, and beliefs as part of their spontaneous self-representations. Nonetheless, trait attributions retain some centrality in self-representations, even among the very old. Freund and Smith (1999) found that old and very old adults, ranging in age from 70 to 103 years, projected a wide range of features into their self-representations, including roles, relationships, interests, and dispositional traits.

A second perspective on traits and the self focuses on self-report responses to personality questionnaires. The logic of this approach contends that even if an adult never writes the statement "I am an extravert" when asked to describe the self, his or her self-reports on an extraversion scale reflect important aspects of self. In other words, if my responses on a self-report scale indicate that I score high on the trait of extraversion, not only must we conclude that I am indeed an extravert, but it must also be true, given that the assessment comes from *self*-report, that I *see myself* as an extravert, or at least I am more-or-less *aware* of my extraversion tendencies. In other words, my self-report score on the trait of extraversion provides information about the actor-Me.

The development of self-report trait attributions over the adult life course may itself be viewed from two angles: temporal stability in individual differences and mean-level change. With respect to the former, longitudinal studies show that people tend to hold their relative positions on self-report trait continua, even over two or three decades in adulthood (Roberts & DelVecchio, 2000). This means that if my self-reports show that I am high on extraversion at age 30, the chances are pretty good, although by no means absolute, that I will score toward the high end of the extraversion continuum at age 50. This is not to suggest that individual differences on self-report traits are set in stone by the time a person reaches middle adulthood. Some shifting around on traits will invariably occur; people do indeed change, sometimes dramatically. Nonetheless, the overall trend is toward increasing stability in individual differences for the basic traits that feature prominently in the actor-self, such as extraversion, neuroticism, and conscientiousness—at least through the early retirement years (Roberts et al., 2008). What happens in old age is less clear. At least one study suggests that individual differences in traits may become less stable in the last years of life (Martin, Long, & Poon, 2002). Declining health and other negative changes of very old age may change, sometimes in unpredictable ways, people's self-representations, including their self-report trait attributions.

When it comes to mean-level change in self-report traits across the adult years, data from cross-sectional and longitudinal studies show some important trends. Although exceptions to the rules can always be found, it appears that self-representations of dispositional traits become more positive over time, as adults become more comfortable with themselves, less inclined to moodiness and negative emotions, more responsible and caring, and less susceptible to extreme risk taking and the expression of unbridled internal impulses. What Caspi et al. (2005) deemed the *maturity principle* in self-attributions states that people come to see themselves as more dominant, agreeable, conscientious, and emotionally stable over the course of adult life, or at least up through late middle age. In terms of self-report assessments of the Big Five, mean-level scores for traits subsumed within the broad domains of conscientiousness and agreeableness appear to increase from adolescence through late midlife, and scores subsumed within neuroticism tend to decrease over that period (e.g., Allemand, Zimprich, & Hertzog, 2007; Helson & Soto, 2005; McCrae et al., 1999; Srivastava, John, Gosling, & Potter, 2003).

Roberts, Walton, and Viechtbauer (2006) conducted a meta-analysis of 92 longitudinal studies analyzing mean scores on dispositional traits by age decades, from age 10 to 70. Most of the studies were from North American samples of participants, with largely White and middle-class samples. Self-report scores on conscientiousness showed mainly a gradual and steady increase across the age span, but the increase in agreeableness was less smooth. Average agreeableness scores crept up slowly (and nonsignificantly) to age 50, showed sharp increase from 50 to 60, and then leveled off again. Neuroticism decreased through age 40 and then leveled off. Self-reports of extraversion showed a mixed picture. Extraversion-spectrum traits related to *social dominance* tended to show increases through age 30, whereas extraversion-spectrum traits related to *social vitality* tended to decrease after age 50.

Roberts et al. (2006) argued that increases in conscientiousness and agreeableness and decreases in neuroticism from adolescence through midlife reflect the I's increasing investment in normative social roles related to family, work, and civic involvement. As the Me becomes increasingly structured around social roles that demand commitment and care, the trait attributions that depict how the actor expresses his or her roles shift accordingly, in the direction of greater conscientiousness and agreeableness and away from tendencies toward emotional instability. By contrast, Costa and McCrae (2006) explained the same trends in self-reports as a product of biological maturation, suggesting that human beings may be genetically wired such that their self-conceptions should mature in the direction shown by research on dispositional traits. In the view of Costa and McCrae (2006), increases in agreeableness and conscientiousness may be correlated with increasing investment in certain social roles, but both developmental trends in the Me—changes in traits and roles—are a function of an unfolding biological program that helps to ensure that adults care for the next generation and take on the social responsibilities that group life among human beings demands. Whether the actor learns new roles as he matures (Roberts et al., 2006) or finds himself or herself naturally taking them on (Costa & McCrae, 2006), social life demands increasingly productive, family-oriented, and civic-minded performances as the actor moves from early adulthood through the middle-adult years. The I continues to reshape, refine, and transform the Me as new challenges present themselves on the social stage.

Summary

Human beings evolved to live in small tribes and bands, competing and cooperating in the face of limited resources, striving to get along and get ahead as social actors whose performances were (and continue to be) prime determinants of their survival and reproductive success. It makes developmental sense, therefore, that the self should debut as a social actor—a self-contained and embodied source of activity whose performances affect what other actors do. Human beings begin to recognize themselves in mirrors, to use the words "me" and "mine," to show self-referential emotions such as pride and embarrassment, and to show other signs of self-awareness around 18 months of age. It is not until the third or fourth year of life that the I develops a sure-footed sense of the Me as a temporally continuous self. Among other things, the I's reflexive awareness of itself promotes self-regulation, much as Freud's conception of the superego and Mead's notion of the generalized other brought outside observers into the actor's head to monitor and critique social performance. Developmental research shows that the temperament dimension of effortful control, secure attachment relationships, and the scaffolding and mentoring influences of parents and other authorities all provide the actor-self with invaluable assistance in the regulation of impulses, emotions, and other unruly internal states. As Plato and Aristotle knew, self-regulation is at the heart of effective social performance.

Over developmental time, the I builds up a representation of itself as an actor-Me. In the early years, these representations are simple and concrete, tied directly to behaviors, tangible objects, and momentary states. Moving through childhood and into early adolescence, however, the I attributes more complex and abstract qualities to the actor-Me, such as personality traits and the roles or situations wherein these traits are expressed. Many adolescents, furthermore, come to see how the many different traits that comprise the actor-Me may conflict with or contradict each other. As Erikson's theory of identity suggests, many adolescents may strive to reconcile the contradictions, launching a search to find "the true self" (the self that was "meant to be"), perhaps, or seeking to resolve inconsistencies by explaining, to themselves and to others, how certain situations call for certain kinds of trait-based performances, whereas others call for others. With even more maturity, the I may become more comfortable with or tolerant of ambiguity and contradiction in the actor-Me.

Gender and ethnicity play important roles in the young adult's efforts to construct a coherent sense of the self as a social actor. Young adults who hold entity theories about the Me see their own characteristics as fixed and immutable, whereas those who think about themselves in more incremental and developmental terms hold out hope that they can improve their traits with effort and circumstances. Performance traits and social roles continue to occupy prime positions in the actor-Me over the adult life span. As people move into middle adulthood, the I tends to see the Me in more conscientious and agreeable terms and as containing fewer neurotic tendencies. The general developmental trend is toward more effective social performances, at least through late middle age. As adults take on and gain proficiency in roles related to work, family, and civic life, they ideally become better social actors—more caring and productive; more dependable, steady, and efficacious; more self-regulated; more flexible; and more astutely aware of themselves as the social actors we all evolve to be.

THE SELF AS AGENT

Selves have secrets that no observers can see. Actors play their roles on a social stage, but no matter how long the audience watches the performance, they can never know for sure what is going on in the actors' heads. Whether the actors themselves even know is the question that Freud asked, but everybody nonetheless agrees to this: *Something* is going on in the actors' heads. Something that the audience can only *infer*. *What does the actor want*? What is the actor *really* trying to accomplish? One answer is this: The actor is trying to accomplish the role. The actor wants to enact the performance that the situation demands. This kind of answer satisfies nobody but Goffman (1959). Even the visitor from another galaxy, assigned to investigate human life on earth, probably expects more. If the visitor is psychologically designed in a manner that even remotely resembles human beings on earth, she will also be left wondering about the motivational secrets that assumedly lie somewhere inside the performers on stage, beyond her view. What is interesting here is not so much that the observers cannot know the secrets inside but rather that they know they cannot know, that observers always expect that there *must* be something beyond their direct observations, something inside the actors' heads, something *motivational*, something about desire and want. We assume that actors want something within and beyond their social performances (Klinger, 1987; Wellman, 1993). We assume that human selves are motivated, goal-directed *agents*. Selves often act not just for the sake of acting. Selves often act to accomplish personal ends. Even when they are not acting, even when it seems that selves are doing nothing at all, they still want something.

Applied to the self, agency means many things. It means that a self has some modicum of *ownership* over subjective experience. As James (1892/1963) repeatedly emphasized, the self appropriates or takes possession of certain thoughts, feelings, desires, memories, things, and people. Peter knows that his thoughts are his, and not Paul's. He virtually never mixes this up. When Peter recalls yesterday's dinner with his sister, he knows that it is he who is recalling it (the I) and that it was indeed he, and again not Paul, who had dinner with his sister yesterday, and that his sister is indeed *his* sister (part of Me) and not Paul's. Agency also suggests some modicum of personal *causation*. Selves not only act; they initiate action (Deci & Ryan, 1991). Selves cause things to happen. If Peter wants to have dinner with his brother tomorrow, he can make it happen. He can send his brother a text message to work out the arrangements. As Peter punches in the words on his BlackBerry, he knows not only that he is the one who is sending the message but also that he (and not Paul, not anybody else) has decided to do this, that he has made a *choice*. After all, Peter could stay in tomorrow evening and watch a movie instead of having dinner with his brother. Why choose his brother over the movie? Because he *wants to*. He wants to tell his brother about the woman he is now dating. He wants to catch up on what has been going on in his brother's life. He wants to share with his brother a *plan* he has to start a new business. He *hopes* his brother will like the plan and agree to loan him some money so that the plan can get off the ground. In Peter's mind, tomorrow night's dinner with his brother will be about more than merely ordering off the menu, exchanging pleasantries, and paying the bill. It will be about a long-term *project* that Peter has worked out, about his *goals* for the future.

Agency is a defining feature of modern selfhood. Agents assume some degree of ownership and control over things, both internally (I control my own thoughts) and externally (I make things happen in the environment). Agents are the sources of self-initiated endeavors, translating their own never-to-be-directly observed wants into plans of (observable) action in the social world. In the ideal Republic, Plato wrote, different strata of society should strive for different aims. Artisans should act to fulfill basic appetites; soldiers should pursue courageous ends to bring glory to themselves and to protect the society; the guardians, or philosopher-kings, should pursue the goals of reason and the good. In Aristotle's view, the mature self aims to achieve the golden mean whereby the fulfillment of personal desires and goals contributes to the good of society as a whole.

Whatever their motivational agendas, agents move forward in life in a self-determined and goal-directed manner. How could it indeed be otherwise? Quite easily, claimed Jaynes (1976), in a provocative historical argument. Listen to the characters in *The Iliad*, as well as the patriarchs of Genesis, explain why they do what they do. Singing of "Agamemnon lord of men and brilliant Achilles," Homer asks, "What god drove them to fight with such fury?" (Fagles, 1990, p. 77). Voices in their heads told these men to go to war, to sire offspring, even to sacrifice their own children. Athene, Apollo, Zeus, the Old Testament God, and a host of other external agents called the motivational shots in these ancient texts, as if the human actors in these stories had not yet become agents. That is because *they were not agents*, Jaynes (1976) insisted, or the authors of these texts, passed down from antiquity, did not originally understand these actors to be agents, perhaps because they did not understand themselves to be agents either. Jaynes (1976) argued that human beings *learned* how to be self-consciously agentic selves sometime during the millennium before the birth of Christ.

Even today, selves lose agency to the extent they feel controlled by external forces. When a capricious or punishing environment fails to support or reinforce goal-directed striving, the self may descend into *learned helplessness* (Seligman, 1975). Sometimes the overwhelming forces come from within, as both James and Freud knew. A person may feel *possessed* by forces over which the self cannot gain supremacy. Sometimes the internal forces are so strong that the self may feel pushed aside or split off from itself, in that parts of the person (things I do, feel, think, and want) seem as if they are not really parts of Me. What may follow is a feeling that the I is depleted, or that the I splits into multiple agencies, as in cases of dissociative identity disorder, more commonly known as multiple personality (Hacking, 1995).

We should not, therefore, take agency too much for granted. Its status is always somewhat tentative and contingent, dependent on a wide range of psychological and cultural factors that shape how and to what extent people feel that they own and control their own experiences. The agent-self emerges slowly in human development, several steps behind the actor. Children appear to be aware of their own social performances before they are consistently aware of their motivations for performing as they do. Even after children understand that they (and other people) are self-determined agents in the world, they still do not, at first, define themselves in terms of their recurrent wants and desires and their long-term goals. But eventually, of course, they do. The agent-self eventually melds into the actor-self as the I attributes goals, plans, and projects to the Me. Indeed, the two—actor and agent—are never separate entities in a literal sense. The human self assumes many guises. It begins as a social actor, but over time it takes on a more self-consciously agential, self-determining guise. Yet the self continues to perform as an actor on the social stage. Much of what it is and does has little to do with agency per se. I may see myself as a friendly person who tends to work hard and who feels dread when I interact with authority figures who remind me of my father. I do not need words that connote desires, goals, and plans—I do not need a language of agency—to convey (to others and to myself) those traitlike features of the Me. Nonetheless, I do need that motivational discourse to convey and understand those aspects of Me that are about what I want in life, what I am striving for, what I want to be (but am not yet), and what, despite my best efforts, I fear I might become in the future.

Precursors to the Agent-Self: Intentionality and Theory of Mind

Like all animals, human beings are designed to pursue goals. We must, in some manner, go out into the environment and identify what we need (to survive and procreate), and we must move our bodies in some manner to get it. As Klinger (1987) pointed out, "goal-striving, and therefore motivation in the larger sense, are integral facets of life as an animal" (p. 337). Even the newborn infant behaves in a goal-directed fashion, turning its head toward the nipple to suck, positioning its body in such a way as to achieve the goal of nursing. Throughout the 20th century, motivational theorists were quick to attribute a wide range of broad goals that infants and young children pursue. For example, baby humans and rhesus monkeys seek the contact comfort and security afforded by a caregiving object, be that object a flesh-and-blood caregiver or a soft-cloth surrogate (Harlow & Harlow, 1962; Sroufe & Waters, 1977). Bowlby (1969) described mother–infant attachment as a goal-corrected system, designed to achieve the immediate goal of mother–infant proximity (to achieve the evolutionary goal of protecting the infant from predators). White (1959) argued that young children, as well as certain other primates, aim to achieve mastery and competence in their behavior. Murray (1938) identified more than 20 psychogenical needs that energize and direct human behavior across the life course, including the needs for play, affiliation, dominance, and order. It is nearly impossible to make psychological sense of human behavior without resorting to the language of goals, needs, motives, and human agency (although some psychologists have tried, e.g., Skinner, 1971).

It is one thing, however, to say that human beings pursue goals (this is so true as to be trivial), and it is quite another to say that the I reflexively conceives of the Me as an appropriating agent who seeks to achieve certain valued goals over time. It requires even more to say, and to show, that the I *evaluates* the Me—confers upon the Me a certain degree of esteem—by determining the extent to which valued goals have been achieved. Newborns may (implicitly, unknowingly) pursue goals, but they are a long way from conceiving of themselves as goal seekers. Human beings take the first steps along that path toward the end of the first year of life, with the emergence of a special interest in *intentionality* (Tomasello, 2000). At approximately 9 months of age, infants will begin to behave in ways suggesting that they understand what others are *trying* to do. They will imitate and improvise on intentional, goal-directed behaviors shown by adults at much higher rates than random behaviors. They will attend to objects and events toward which adults express interest and positive emotions, as if to suggest that they, too, may *want* what others want. They will decode others' behaviors to determine the extent to which the actions are intended or wanted. For example, 9-month-olds (but not 6-month-olds) will express more impatience (e.g., reaching, looking away) when an adult is unwilling to give them a toy (when the adult refuses to give it) than when she is simply unable to give it to them (because she drops or fumbles the toy; Behne, Carpenter, Call, & Tomasello, 2005). In this clever study, the 9-month-olds can tell when the adult intends to keep the toy away from them (which they find to be very annoying) and when the adult unintentionally (it seems) screws up. They are more forgiving of the latter scenario, as if to suggest that trying is what really counts! The researchers concluded:

> Because infants' behavioral responses were appropriately adapted to different kinds of intentional actions, and because the adult's actions sometimes produced results that did not match her goal (when having accidents or failed attempts), these findings provide especially rich evidence that infants first begin to understand goal-directed action around 9 months of age. (Behne et al., 2005, p. 328)

The next big steps on the way to the agent-self can be traced forward in the third and fourth years of life. It is during these years that children develop a folk-psychological understanding of how human minds work, what researchers call a *theory of mind* (Wellman, 1993). The "theory" is simple: People have desires and beliefs in their minds, and they act on those desires and beliefs. Most children now behave in ways to suggest that they do indeed understand that their own behavior, and the behavior of others, is motivated by the particular desires and beliefs that are located in the minds of the actor. Put differently, children now know that they are agents, and that others are agents, too. The achievement of theory of mind corresponds with what we earlier described as Rochat's (2003) fifth and final stage of the development of self-awareness in children. Children are now aware of their own goals and beliefs, and they understand that other people have their own goals and beliefs. As a motivated agent, my actions are the end results of my internal desires, beliefs, and plans. It is the same for you—I now know that you, too, are a motivated agent, that your actions, like mine, result from those particular desires, beliefs, and plans that constitute your mind.

It is hard to imagine what social life would be like if human beings were not endowed with theory of mind. If we did not understand ourselves as mindful agents who strive to put our desires and beliefs into action and if we did not understand others in the same terms, how would human beings be able to cooperate on joint ventures, establish alliances, develop commitments to others and to groups, and predict the future? Yet, according to some researchers, it is just this kind of deficit that may be partly responsible for the odd behaviors and social difficulties shown by some autistic children (Baron-Cohen, 1995; Pellicano, 2007). Research has shown that autistic children often perform poorly on experimental tasks designed to assess theory of mind. They often provide responses suggesting that they do not fully understand the agential mindfulness of other people's behaviors. Case studies of autism, furthermore, sometimes suggest a remarkable lack of personal agency, which can border on a sense of depersonalization. Behavior may follow performance scripts, but it seems to lack an internally generated purpose, as if it were performed by a robot. The actor-self never evolves into the agent-self, or only does so to a limited extent. In extreme cases, not only does the autistic child fail to articulate personal goals and desires, but he or she may find it difficult even to take personal ownership of subjective experience. For example, Sacks (1995) tells the story of Stephen Wiltshire, an autistic prodigy who, despite his extraordinary artistic talents, never seems to develop a sense of personal agency:

> I had the feeling that the whole visible world flowed through Stephen, like a river, without making sense, without being appropriated, without becoming part of him in the least. That though he might, in a sense, retain everything he saw, it was retained as something external, unintegrated, and never built on, connected, revised, never influencing or influenced by anything else. (p. 56)

Autism may strike many people as so strange because it violates a fundamental rule of human selfhood—that rule says that by the time they have reached their fifth birthday, most children find it easy and natural to interpret their own experiences and to imagine the experiences of others in terms of desire, motive, goal, and purpose. The seeds of an early appreciation for human intentionality have now blossomed, by age 5, into a full understanding that human selves are fundamentally intentional, purposeful, goal-directed agents. In fact, many children seem to overdo their newfound understanding of agency, imputing purposeful design in most anything they see and expressing what Kelemen (2004) described as a "promiscuous teleology" (p. 295). They will project agential qualities onto inanimate and even imaginary objects, such as favorite toys and imaginary companions. They will implicitly conclude that artifacts in the environment are the result of the agential activities of others—all things that exist were made by purposeful agents who self-consciously set forth to make them. The idea of an ultimate maker makes good sense to a mind primed to detect agency. Religious accounts of the creation of the world hold special appeal for children at this age, an appeal that often endures, depending on the cultural support it enjoys, for the remainder of the life span. God is imagined as a purposeful agent whose own desires, goals, and beliefs are translated into motivated action. By virtue of their keen appreciation for agency, human beings are "intuitive theists," wrote Kelemen (2004, p. 295). Agent-selves construe the world as populated with and determined by other agent-selves, and all can be traced back to an ultimate Agent, whose own desires, goals, and beliefs set everything into motion.

The Growth of the Agent-Self and the Emergence of Self-Esteem

As the I increasingly appropriates subjective experience from the standpoint of a goal-directed and purposeful agent, it begins to attribute recurrent and salient goals to the Me. In simple English, this means that school-age children begin to define themselves in terms of their most important goals. By age 7 or 8, children have readily identifiable and well-articulated goals, and they see themselves as more-or-less self-determining, goal-directed agents whose aspirations take up increasing space in consciousness and show increasing influence on daily behavior (Walls & Kollat, 2006). Some of the goals developed by school-age children may be expressions or derivatives of the three basic self-needs identified by Deci and Ryan (1991)—needs for autonomy, competence, and relatedness. Some may be grouped into the well-known motivational trichotomy developed by McClelland (1985)—motives for achievement, power, and intimacy and affiliation. Other may reflect spiritual and religious concerns (Emmons, 1999). Still others may be more idiosyncratic and reflective of family, school, neighborhood, and other social influences (B. R. Little, 1999; T. D. Little, Snyder, & Wehmeyer, 2006). Within the

Me, goals may sit side by side with actor-self attributions regarding performance styles and basic dispositional traits, but the goals are not the same things as the traits. I may see myself as a friendly and outgoing person (traits: actor-self), but this self-attribution suggests little regarding my goals and aspirations (motivation: agent-self). A friendly person may set out to become a star athlete, a good student, a popular chum, the teacher's pet, the class clown, a successful entrepreneur, a fashion model, an artist, a scientist, a revolutionary, a good provider, a loyal wife, or president of the United States. A less friendly person might pursue the same goals. A girl who sees herself as a conscientious but emotionally volatile actor on the social stage may privilege power, achievement, intimacy, nurturance, play, or any other motivational domain within which to pursue and develop her agent-self (McAdams & Pals, 2006; Roberts & Robins, 2000). The Me is a big house, and it can readily accommodate the new agential self-attributions who begin to move in and take up residence during the childhood and adolescent years.

The agent-self expresses what Bandura (1989) termed *self-efficacy*. Self-efficacy is a person's belief that he or she can execute goal-directed behavior in a successful manner, especially under challenging or stressful circumstances. A strong sense of self-efficacy encourages the I to set higher goals and standards for the Me, to invest more energy and commitment into goals, to exert greater effort and persistence in goal pursuit, to envision successful outcomes of goal-directed behavior, and to bounce back from defeats with ever-more energized and focused self-strivings. Across the life course, the development of self-efficacy proves to be an important resource for exercising agential control over challenging and threatening situations.

Beginning in the elementary school years, agential self-attributions regarding purpose and long-term goals greatly enrich the content and structure of the Me. However, the agent-self brings with it a new problem. If the Me now consists, in part, of those goals and aspirations that I pursue, then the I cannot resist the temptation to evaluate the progress of goal pursuit. I want to be a good student. OK, how am I doing on that goal? Well, not so well: I got a low grade on my last math test, and my teacher says that my essay on German history was really bad. My current evaluation of my good-student goal is pretty negative, and I feel pretty bad about that. I also want Jessica to like me. Yesterday, she told me that I was cute, and she kissed me. That agential project is looking real good right now, and I feel good about that. As the I evaluates its many goal pursuits, it begins to make attributions—some general and some more domain-specific—about how the Me is doing. These evaluations add up to *self-esteem*.

James (1892/1963) defined self-esteem as a fraction: "success" divided by "pretensions" (p. 175). Pretensions are those goals that we pursue; success is what we feel when we achieve them, or at least make good progress toward achieving them. The implication in James's simple conceptualization is that if people did not have pretensions—if they never held out goals to pursue—they would never have to worry about self-esteem. In other words, self-esteem is strongly linked to the agent-self; it is a logical outgrowth of the I's newfound tendency to set forth goals and then evaluate progress with respect to those goals.

Linking James's conception of self-esteem to the consolidation of an agent-self in mid-childhood fits nicely with Harter's (2006) findings regarding the development of self-esteem in children. Preschool and kindergarten children show few individual differences in self-esteem, her data show. In general, young children see themselves in a positive light. They do not evaluate the self in a critical way. Beginning around age 7 or 8, however, children begin to show sharp and consistent differences in their self-evaluations. Some children show consistently high levels of self-esteem, and some show consistently low levels, and many, of course, fall between the two extremes. In grade school and high school, furthermore, self-esteem will fluctuate in response to how well things are going in different domains of the young person's life. Harter (2006) suggested that these changes result in part from increasing expectations for performance coming from parents and teachers and cognitive–developmental changes that enable older children to compare their own goal-based performance in various domains—from sports to academics to moral behavior—to the performance of others. For the agent-self, the issue here is this: How well am I doing? To answer the question, I take stock of my goals and evaluate my progress toward them. Social comparison facilitates the evaluation. I may look around and conclude that I am doing quite well compared with others. My pretensions may be high, but social comparison suggests to me that my successes are also substantial. Or I may see that I am not doing so well, compared with others in my social environment. In this case, social comparison tells me that the discrepancy between my successes and my pretensions is quite large, leaving me with a distressingly tiny fraction for my self-esteem.

As soon as individual differences in self-esteem begin to show up in middle childhood, girls show lower scores than boys (Harter, 2006). The sex difference persists in varying degrees across much of the rest of the life span, with the largest advantages for males typically showing up in middle and late adolescence (Harter, 2006). From adolescence onward, African Americans tend to score higher on measures of self-esteem than do White Americans (Twenge & Crocker, 2002). Robins et al. (2002) traced the developmental course of global self-esteem from age 9 to 90, employing cross-sectional data obtained from more than 300,000 respondents via the Internet. They found that self-esteem scores tend to be relatively high in childhood, decline markedly in the adolescent years, and then begin a slow but steady improvement in young adulthood, continuing upward to a peak at around age 60. Self-esteem scores then drop again after age 70, with men showing particularly precipitous declines in their later years. These cross-sectional trends held across gender, socioeconomic status, ethnicity, and nationality. The findings from Robins et al. (2002) are generally consistent with other research.

Social psychologists have conducted a wealth of research on the vicissitudes of self-esteem (Baumeister, 1998; Baumeister & Bushman, 2008). What factors enhance or undermine self-esteem? How do people maintain high levels of self-esteem, even when they receive negative feedback? What benefits follow from having high self-esteem, and what negative ramifications follow from low self-esteem? For example, high self-esteem tends to be associated with greater initiative in the pursuit of goals and greater enjoyment of success in goal attainment. Low self-esteem is associated with fear of failure, higher levels of internal conflict and ambivalence, and a cautious, prevention-focused orientation toward life's challenges. At the same time, there is considerable evidence to suggest that high levels of self-esteem may not be all that they are cracked up to be. It is not clear that boosting self-esteem actually improves people's performance on challenging tasks. What seems more likely is that success on challenging tasks boosts self-esteem. Cross-national comparisons suggest that many Americans report unrealistically high levels of self-esteem compared with citizens of other countries. Narcissists and many violent criminals often show very high levels of self-esteem. Further, pursuing self-esteem as an end in itself can be counterproductive, leading to lower levels of well-being and diminished commitments to other people (Crocker & Park, 2004).

Life Goals, Possible Selves, and Identity

Through the articulation of and investment in personal goals, the agent-self extends the Me into the future. What goals do I wish to achieve in the future? Where is my life going? What do I wish to become? As Erikson (1963) suggested, questions like these gather together around the big issue of identity in adolescence and young adulthood. Identity raises the stakes for the agent-self by pushing the I to make choices regarding the *big* goals for life. According to Erikson, identity development involves the young person's broadening of consciousness to encompass a wide range of life goals and the eventual narrowing of consciousness so as to focus on and commit to those goals most worth pursuing. When it comes to identity, you can be many things, but you cannot be everything. In a famous passage, James (1892/1963) described the identity choice that must be made:

> I am often confronted by the necessity of standing by one of my empirical selves and relinquishing the rest. Not that I would not, if I could, be both handsome and fat and well-dressed, and a great athlete, and make a million a year, be a wit, a *bon vivant*, and a lady-killer, as well as a philosopher; a philanthropist, statesman, warrior, and African explorer, as well as a "tone-poet" and saint. But the thing is simply impossible. The millionaire's work would run counter to the saint's; the *bon vivant* and philanthropist would trip each other up; the philosopher and lady-killer could not well keep house in the same tenement of clay. Such different characters may conceivably at the outset of life be alike *possible* to a man. But to make any one of them actual, the rest must more or less be suppressed. So the seeker of his truest, strongest, deepest self must review the list carefully, and pick out the one on which to stake his salvation. All other selves thereupon become unreal, but the fortunes of this self are real. Its failures are real failures, its triumphs real triumphs, carrying shame and gladness with them. (p. 174)

The life goals to which adolescents and young adults must eventually commit themselves fall into the broad identity categories of occupation, ideology, and relationships. Marcia (1980) launched a long and fruitful line of research examining how young adults explore these identity options and make commitments to identity goals. At any given point in adolescence or young adulthood, Marcia showed, a person can be said to exist in one of four *identity statuses*. Individuals operating within the status of *moratorium* are actively exploring various ideologic, occupational, and interpersonal possibilities for identity, but they have not yet committed themselves fully to particular identity goals. Individuals who have passed through moratorium and finally made strong commitments to goals in the areas of occupation, ideology, and relationships operate in the status of *identity achievement*. In Erikson's stage model of development, the identity achievers have successfully journeyed through the fifth stage (identity vs. role confusion) and they are now ready to confront the psychosocial issue of intimacy (vs. isolation, the sixth stage). By contrast, young people who fail to entertain different identity options but instead simply commit to occupational, ideologic, and interpersonal roles and goals set forth for them by parents and other authority figures exist in what Marcia (1980) called the *foreclosure* status. In a fundamental sense, foreclosures have failed the identity challenge; the foreclosed I fails to see the need for the kind of thoroughgoing revision of the Me that constitutes true identity achievement. Finally, individuals who have not yet begun the exploration of identity options and who have not yet made commitments to long-term identity goals show *identity diffusion*. In a fundamental sense, individuals at identity diffusion have not yet entered Erikson's fifth stage of development.

Looking forward to the future, with both hope and trepidation, the agent-self confronts the developmental task of identity by considering what Markus and Nurius (1986) called *possible selves*. Possible selves "represent individuals' ideas of what they might become, what they would like to become, and what they are afraid of becoming." They are "the cognitive components of hopes, fears, goals, and threats and they give the specific self-relevant form, meaning, organization, and direction to these dynamics" (Markus & Nurius, 1986, p. 954). At any point in the life course, the Me may contain a plethora of possible selves—"the successful self, the creative self, the rich self, the thin self, or the loved and admired self," as well as "the dreaded possible selves" such as "the alone self, the depressed self, the incompetent self, the alcoholic self, the unemployed self, or the bag lady self" (Markus & Nurius, 1986, p. 954). Each possible self exists as a concretely articulated and highly personalized motivational image in the Me. At age 25 in law school, let us say, my "lawyer" possible self pictures me in the future as a well-dressed man walking through midtown Manhattan, on my way to meet a famous client, perhaps a politician who has been indicted for corruption. I will strive to be a great litigator, winning many cases in court. I will also defend poor clients who run afoul of the system. I will come home in the evening to a beautiful Italian wife. We will have three children. Their names will be....

Possible selves can be both declarative and subjunctive. Not only do they specify what I hope or fear I will become, but they also spell out what I might have been. King and Hicks (2006) described *lost* possible selves as those images that people develop of what they might have been had things worked out differently in their lives. In a series of intriguing studies, King and Hicks (2006) asked (a) divorced women to describe how their lives might have turned out otherwise had their marriages remained intact, (b) gays and lesbians what their lives might have been like had they been heterosexual, and (c) mothers of Down syndrome children what their experiences as parents might have been like had their children been born without this disability. The researchers discovered that many of the participants in these studies constructed very clear and detailed portraits of their lost possible selves. Individuals at high levels of ego development (Loevinger, 1976) tended to show the most differentiated and fully developed understanding of what might have been. Furthermore, holding a rich and detailed lost possible self at the beginning of the study predicted greater positive change (upward movement) in ego development 2 years later. As King and Hicks (2006) saw it, psychological maturity in adulthood involves the ability to construct a detailed and thoughtful understanding of what one's life is all about now and how life might have been different had certain contingencies prevailed. At the same time, King and Hicks (2006) reported that life satisfaction is unrelated to the level of detail and complexity expressed in lost possible selves. Instead, the most satisfied people in their studies were those who reported that they were able to let go of their lost possible selves and focus most of their energy on current goals. Therefore, maturity and happiness may be expressed in very different ways within the Me (see also Bauer & McAdams, 2004a). The most mature I constructs a psychologically complex Me that expresses a deep understanding of what is, what will be, and what might have been. The happiest people, however, keep their focus on the direct links between who they are now and what they plan to be in the near future.

As the actor-self ascribes performance traits to the adult identity mix, the agent-self fashions and contributes goals, motives, and plans. By the time we enter adulthood, actor-selves have a pretty clear understanding of what kind of a performer we can be on the social stage. As agent-selves, we plan future performances to live out the choices we have made and fulfill our most important goals. Our future plans—short-term and long-term, mundane and exalted—may be captured in the *personal strivings* (Emmons, 1986), *personal projects* (Little, 1999), and *life longings* (Schiebe, Freund, & Baltes, 2007) into which we invest our psychic energies. Like a strategic investment banker, the I chooses to infuse capital into those strivings, projects, and longings that promise a good return in the future. It sets them up for business in the Me, providing them with the Me's best office space and suitable resources so that they can work, grow, and prosper. Their relative success can be measured by how much they ultimately pay back in tax receipts, so as to provide funding for greater psychological well-being, self-esteem, and the like. Research suggests that the Me receives its greatest benefits when personal goals (a) tap into intrinsically satisfying needs such as autonomy and relatedness rather than extrinsic needs such as fame and fortune; (b) work together in harmony rather than creating conflict and ambivalence in the Me; and (c) pose challenges that are difficult enough to be interesting and personally meaningful, and yet manageable enough to afford a reasonably high likelihood of goal success (Brunstein, Schultheiss, & Grassmann, 1998; Emmons & King, 1988; Kasser & Ryan, 1996; Palys & Little, 1983; Riedeger & Freund, 2004).

Across the life course, culture exerts a strong influence on the development of the agent-self, setting parameters for the content and the timing of personal goals (McAdams & Pals, 2006). Individualistic societies like the United States typically place a strong premium on goals that enhance the autonomy, achievement, and power of the individual person, over and against the group. What Markus and Kitayama (1991) described as *independent* self-construals tend to favor values, plans, and goals that make for the separation of the self from others. Each agent-self pursues its own goals, sets forth on its own journey of self-actualization. By contrast, collectivist societies, such as Japan and China, may encourage the development of *interdependent* self-construals. In a collectivist context, the agent-self seeks social harmony and connection to the social context. Personal goals should promote broader group goals. The general distinction between independent and interdependent self-construals, and the cultural contexts that support each, may be something of an exaggeration, for research does not always reveal stark cultural effects (Oyserman, Coon, & Kemmelmeier, 2002). Nonetheless, interesting cultural differences in goal pursuits have been revealed. For example, goals aimed at *avoiding* negative states seem to be rather more common among certain cultural groups than others. Asian Americans, Koreans, and Russians tend to show higher levels of avoidance goals, compared with European Americans (Elliot, Chirkov, Kim, & Sheldon, 2001). By contrast, European Americans show more goals aimed at *approaching* positive states. Avoidance goals suggest social vigilance and caution; the I takes care to construct a Me that does and receives no harm, aimed at achieving security and social harmony. Approach goals, by contrast, may suggest personal entrepreneurship and the uninhibited pursuit of self-fulfillment. The I construes the Me to be a high-stakes risk taker, a restless, intrepid, internally energized, autonomy-seeking, ever-striving agent on the run.

Selfhood and Agency across the Life Course

The development of the self in adulthood reveals continuity and change. Features of the actor-Me—especially self-attributions regarding dispositional performance traits—typically show considerable stability over time, and this becomes increasingly so as adults get older (Roberts & DelVecchio, 2000). However, changes in the agent-self may be more forthcoming (Hooker & McAdams, 2003; McAdams & Pals, 2006). People do change their goals, plans, programs, projects, and possible selves in the adult years, in response to on-time developmental challenges such as retirement and unpredictable off-time events. Historical factors such as war, economical recessions, social movements, and changing societal mores may exert significant effects on the personal goals and strivings that occupy prime positions in identity (Elder, 1995; Stewart & Healy, 1989). In their midlife years, many people may reassess their goal priorities. Although the kind of dramatic *midlife crisis* described by Levinson (1978) may not be as common as the popular press believes, longitudinal data suggest that many adults in their 40s and 50s nonetheless engage in what Stewart and Vandewater (1999) termed *midlife reviews* and *midcourse corrections*. Although few adults may overthrow the entire panoply of choices, values, and commitments that structure their lives, it is quite common for midlife men and women to review where they are going in life, develop new pursuits and shed old ones, change priorities and alter the direction of their strivings to accommodate the changing social ecology within which their agent-self is embedded. Regrets about goals not pursued in the past may motivate significant changes in direction. Stewart and Vandewater (1999) found that midlife women who act on their regrets to change their goal priorities tend to enjoy higher levels of well-being than women who fail to make changes in their goal pursuits but instead ruminate about opportunities missed in the past.

The patterns whereby young adults consider identity options and make commitments to life goals may presage later patterns of continuity and change. Josselson (1996) found that college women classified as identity achievement (having explored identity options and made commitments to identity goals; Marcia, 1980) tended to move forward into midlife as *pathmakers*. In their 30s and 40s, pathmakers enjoyed "a sense of conviction in the basic meaningfulness of their lives" (Josselson, 1996, p. 101). For pathmakers,

> self-doubt was present but not disabling—they were aware that they might have made other choices, that some of their choices had led to pain or dead ends, but these women had the capacity to rally themselves and choose again, hoping to do so with better understanding and insight. (Josselson, 1996, p. 101)

The women who held the moratorium status in college (high exploration, little commitment) continued to act as *searchers* in their 30s and 40s. Compared with the pathmakers, they experienced more self-doubt and self-criticism and reported more vivid emotions and strong spirituality. Nonetheless, most of the searchers managed to make commitments, albeit provisional, to particular occupational and interpersonal goals. Those with foreclosed identities in college (low exploration, high commitment) became *guardians* in midlife, according to Josselson (1996), retaining a good deal of the ideological certitude they expressed as young adults. Nonetheless, many guardians did manage to discover "inner aspects [of themselves] they had long ago buried" (Josselson, 1996, p. 70). Finally, college women classified as identity diffusion (low exploration, low commitment) moved into midlife in a halting and ambivalent manner, as *drifters* whose "checkered and complex" history of goal pursuit left them with a large number of regrets about missed opportunities and lost goals (Josselson, 1996, p. 168).

It is clear that as personal goals change over time, they reflect important developmental trends in self and identity (Cross & Markus, 1991; Freund & Riediger, 2006; Hooker, 1992; Roberts, O'Donnell, & Robins, 2004). Developmental studies of goal constructs have traced the changes in the content and structure of goals over time and changes in the ways people think about, draw upon, pursue, and relinquish goals. Research conducted in modern societies suggests that among young adults goals related to education, intimacy, friendships, and careers are likely to be especially salient. Middle-aged adults tend to focus their goals on the future of their children, securing what they have already established, and property-related concerns. Older adults show more goals related to health, retirement, leisure, and understanding current events in the world (Freund & Riediger, 2006). Goals indicative of prosocial societal engagement—generativity, civic involvement, improving one's community—become more pronounced as people move into midlife and remain relatively strong for many adults into their retirement years (McAdams, de St. Aubin, & Logan, 1993; Peterson & Duncan, 2007; Rossi, 2001). Goals in early adulthood often focus on expanding the self and gaining new information, whereas goals in late adulthood may focus more on the emotional quality of ongoing relationships (Carstensen, Pasupathi, Mayr, & Nesselroade, 2000; Helson, Soto, & Cate, 2006).

The ways in which people manage multiple and conflicting goals may change over time. Young adults seem better able to tolerate high levels of conflict among different life goals, but midlife and older adults manage goals in ways to minimize conflict. In trying to reconcile their goals to environmental constraints, young adults are more likely to engage in what Heckhausen and Schulz (1995) called *primary control strategies*, which means that they try actively to change the environment to fit their goal pursuits. By contrast, midlife and older adults are more likely to employ *secondary control strategies*, which involve changing the Me to adjust to limitations and constraints in the environment (see also Wrosch, Heckhausen, & Lachman, 2006). With some exceptions, older adults seem to approach goals in a more realistic and prudent manner, realizing their limitations and conserving their resources to focus on those few goals in life they consider to be most important (Ogilvie, Rose, & Heppen, 2001; Riediger & Freund, 2006). Compared with younger adults, they are often better able to disengage from blocked goals and to rescale personal expectations in the face of lost goals. As adults move into and through their midlife years, they become more adept at selecting goals that offer the best chances for reward, optimizing their efforts to attain the best payoffs for their projects and strivings, and compensating for their own limitations and losses in goal pursuit (Baltes, 1997).

As adults move into the later years, they may become increasingly focused on how much time they have left to live. In most cases, the I's shifting time perspective leads to further revision of the agent-Me. Freund and Riediger (2006) indicated that a recalibration of future-oriented aspirations is a key factor in successful adaptation to old age. Older adults need to scale back some of their goals and put most of their energy into those that are most immediate—mainly health, family, and immediate social ties. As the ratio of gains to losses in one's life becomes increasingly negative, individuals shift their investment of resources toward the maintenance of functioning and counteracting loss, as opposed to focusing on growth and expansion of the self. Secondary control strategies come to predominate over the more active primary strategies, as older adults recalibrate their expectations and their hopes to carry on as best they can in the face of mounting losses and relentless decline.

Summary

To be an agent is to take ownership of subjective experience and to organize behavior for the future in the service of goals. Like all animals, human beings pursue goals, but they do not become aware of themselves as intentional, goal-directed agents until the fourth or fifth year of life, with the consolidation of theory of mind. At this time in development, children come to realize that other people have minds within which are housed desires and beliefs and that other people, in turn, act on those desires and beliefs to accomplish goals in life. The same insight is applied to the self: I am an agent who possesses desires and beliefs; I determine my own future; I am my goals. As they move into elementary school, children's goals become clearer and more salient within the agent-Me, and children begin to evaluate their own progress in achieving their goals. Evaluations like these, especially as they become the grist for a social comparison mill, figure strongly in the calculation of self-esteem. Individual differences in self-esteem emerge in mid-childhood, with girls showing consistently lower scores than boys. Despite self-esteem's high profile in many developmental and social-psychological theories, research regarding the effects of self-esteem on behavior shows mixed results, with some studies suggesting that high self-esteem may be more of an effect than a cause of successful goal pursuit.

Goals are to the agent-self what trait attributions are to the actor-self. Goals specify strivings, projects, plans, and programs into which the I invests various amounts of capital. In adolescence and young adulthood, the person must make major choices regarding how to distribute that capital into those long-term goals that are most likely to yield good identity dividends. Research on different identity statuses—identity achievement, moratorium, foreclosure, and diffusion—charts the extent to which young adults explore and eventually make commitments to various life goals with respect to occupation, ideology, and other identity arenas. Psychological well-being is enhanced when personal goals tap into intrinsically satisfying needs such as autonomy and relatedness, when goals work in harmony rather than at cross purposes, and when goals provide the agent-I with challenges that are interesting and personally meaningful, and yet realistically achievable given the resources at hand. Different cultures provide different guidelines regarding the content and timing of life goals. The various goals that comprise the agent-Me show both continuity and change over the adult life span. For example, goals regarding generativity and civic involvement appear to rise in importance up through midlife. Goals in early adulthood often focus on expanding the self and gaining new information, but goals in later adulthood may focus more on the emotional quality of ongoing relationships. Whereas young adults appear to tolerate high levels of contradiction and complexity among the goals that make up the agent-Me, older adults aim to achieve a sleeker goal portfolio, investing mainly in a few most highly valued goals, such as those linked to family life.

THE SELF AS AUTHOR

About 300 years ago, a peculiar new literary form emerged in Western Europe. It was called the *novel*. An extended prose narrative that imaginatively depicted human experience through a connected sequence of events involving a group of persons in a specific setting, the novel became a dominant artistic expression in the 19th and 20th centuries. From Daniel Defoe's *Robinson Crusoe* to Toni Morrison's *Beloved*, the power of the novel lay in its ability to explore subjective human experience with extraordinary breadth, depth, and authenticity. The novel conveys the vicissitudes of social performance and human agency, as it chronicles what characters do in social contexts and explores the motivational reasons—the wants, desires, fears, goals, choices, and conflicts—behind their actions. The novel does much, much more, however. By tracking action and agency *over time*, the novel expresses how characters change, as well as how they remain continuous, over the course of seconds, minutes, days, years, and decades. The reader can follow the development and the decline of characters over time, whether it be a single day in the life, as in James Joyce's *Ulysses*, or the full course of a character's entire life, from birth to death. In addition, many novels convey how the characters themselves experience and make sense of their own development or decline (or both). Increasingly through the 20th century and up to today, the modern novel aims to convey what James (1892/1963) described as the stream of human *consciousness* flowing over time (Bruner, 1986; Langbaum, 1982; C. Taylor, 1989). The modern novel asks: How do conscious selves make sense of themselves from one moment to the next and over the long haul? How do people make *meaning* out of their social performances and motivated projects extending over time? How do those meanings shift, evolve, and interact across the sequence of moments, episodes, chapters, and epochs that comprise a human life?

The rise of the novel parallels the historic evolution of the modern self (C. Taylor, 1989). Cultural modernity ushered in an expanded understanding of the self and greater expectations regarding what the I should be able to know and to express about the Me (Baumeister, 1986; Giddens, 1991). Under the conditions of cultural modernity, the I encounters the Me as an extraordinarily complex, even baffling, project into which it must invest a tremendous amount of *work*. Much of that work involves making sense out of the Me, figuring it out, trying to integrate what seem to be its multiple parts and facets into something that seems to have some modicum of meaning, purpose, and wholeness. The modern Me is a multifaceted, multilayered, and dynamic affair. Its many parts exist at many levels, and the whole thing is constantly evolving over time, challenging the I to integrate the many into one, to dig deep to find those aspects that are hidden or obscured, and to discern a pattern that can characterize the relentless flux and flow. The issue of time is critical for the modern Me. In *Being and Time*, Heidegger (1927) described the inescapable temporal structure of being in the modern world—that from a sense of what we have become, among a range of present possibilities, we project our future being. Heidegger's insight is true in the trivial sense that if I know that I am currently standing in line at the bank, I also immediately understand that I got there by walking from my house (the past) and that I will soon leave the bank to pick up my daughter from her oboe lesson (the future). The deeper and more psychological take on Heidegger's insight is that people know *who they are* at any given time in life (the present) by construing the events that explain how they came to be who they are now (the past) and imagining where they will go in an existential sense—that is, who they will *become*—in the future.

How does the I meet Heidegger's challenge? Many scholars argue that the I constructs a Me that makes sense in time in the same way that the novelist achieves the literary goal of conveying the full panoply of subjective human experience as it unfolds over time (Bruner, 1986; MacIntyre, 1981; Ricoeur, 1984; C. Taylor, 1989). That is, the I becomes a storyteller of the self. The I authors a life narrative that integrates the reconstructed past, perceived present, and imagined future in such a way as to explain how the Me came to be what it is and where the Me may be going in the future. Indeed, the story about the Me becomes an integral feature of the Me. The author-I recasts the Me into an autobiographical novel, complete with setting, scenes, characters, plots, and themes. In so doing, the author-I expands the Me backward and forward in time. The novelist is not content merely to chronicle the self's social performances and to announce the self's desires and goals for the future. The novelist must make sense of action and agency by telling a tale about it all, by creating a self-narrative that is both retrospective and prospective, traveling far back in time and far forward, aiming to tell the full story that gives a full life its full meaning.

Under the conditions of cultural modernity, the self typically becomes an author in the late teens and 20s (Habermas & Bluck, 2000; McAdams, 1985, 2008). This period in the human life course, which today is often designated as *emerging adulthood* (Arnett, 2000), is precisely the period wherein, according to Erikson (1963), identity comes to the developmental fore. From the standpoint of the author-self, the major psychosocial challenge of emerging adulthood is the construction of an integrative life story that serves to arrange the Me into a temporal structure that makes psychological sense both to the I itself and to the social world within which the I acts, wants, and narrates (Hammack, 2008; McAdams, 1996, 2006a). To construct in the mind something approaching an outline of the autobiographical novel, even in a rough-draft form, is a monumental achievement in self-development. It is also a signal indication, Erikson (1958) intimated, that I have become *an adult*:

> To be adult means among other things to see one's own life in continuous perspective, both in retrospect and in prospect. By accepting some definition as to who he is, usually on the basis of a function in an economy, a place in the sequences of generations, and a status in the structure of society, the adult is able to selectively reconstruct his past in such a way that, step by step, it seems to have planned him, or better, he seems to have planned *it*. In this sense, psychologically we *do* choose our parents, our family history, and the history of our kings, heroes, and gods. By making them our own, we maneuver ourselves into the inner position of proprietors, of creators. (pp. 111–112)

The Narrating I, Autobiographical Memory, and Children's Stories

In the beginning, the modern self is but an actor. By midchildhood, it has become a social agent as well. It is not until the emerging adulthood years, however, that the self fully exploits the powers of reflexive authorship. Still, authorship does not spring forth fully formed out of the developmental blue. Storytelling evolves for many years before adolescence. The origins of the author-self can be traced back to the preschool years, when children learn how to tell stories, how to listen to them, and how to shape their own experiences, and the experiences of others, into stories (Fivush & Haden, 2003).

The neuroscientist Antonio Damasio (1999) wrote: "Consciousness begins when brains acquire the power, the simple power I must add, of telling a story without words, the story that there is life ticking away in an organism" (p. 30). Damasio seems to be suggesting that subjective consciousness is a matter of mentally taking the position of a narrator. Consciousness involves a continual telling of lived experience, a kind of online stream of narration that flows through the minds of most sentient human beings much of the time. The telling does not require words. Instead, the organism simply takes note of its ongoing, temporally extended experience, perhaps by generating a corresponding stream of sensations and images that *give the feeling* of things happening inside of me as time is passing (see also, Stern, 1985). In the same sense that the infant can act and want long before it is aware of itself as an actor or agent, so, too, the infant may be narrating its own experiences, in a primitive sense, years before the emergence of an author-self.

The same developments that mark steps forward for the actor-self and agent-self have important implications for the development of authorship as well. For example, the 1-year-old's newfound ability to detect intentionality in the activities of others is also a developmental harbinger of storytelling. As Bruner (1986) and many others have noted, stories are fundamentally about the vicissitudes of human intention organized in time. A story typically begins when a motivated character (i.e., an agent) tries to do something, and the plot of the story typically "thickens" when that intention is blocked or deflected in some manner. Therefore, many of the developmental markers for the agent-self—the appreciation of intentionality at age 1, the development of theory of mind at ages 3 and 4—do double duty in laying the groundwork for storytelling. If an individual never developed the folk psychology of human motivation that says human beings formulate intentions, desires, and beliefs and then act on these mental constructs in a goal-directed manner (theory of mind), then that same individual would have a very difficult time constructing and telling intelligible stories about human behavior and experience. Developmentally speaking, agency is something of a prerequisite for authorship, because the main thing that authors do is to construct stories about agents. No agency, no authorship. It is interesting to note, therefore, that some autistic children who show significant deficits in theory of mind (Baron-Cohen, 1995) also encounter problems in comprehending and telling stories about their own (and others') personal experiences (Bruner, 1994; Sacks, 1995).

With the development of language and the emergence of self-recognition behavior in the second and third years of life, children begin to show evidence of basic autobiographical memory (Howe & Courage, 1997). They begin to show the ability to recall particular episodes from the recent past as events within which they played a role. They remember that they were in the event, and they come to consider the memory of that event as their own. At some point before kindergarten, children begin to encode, collect, and tell autobiographical memories, and these become part of the Me. Among the various qualities and features that the I may attribute to the Me at this time—qualities and features such as my name, what I look like, my favorite toys, and so on—are autobiographical episodes that are encoded as narratives, *my* little stories about *me*. Just when autobiographical memory kicks in, however, is a matter of some debate among developmental psychologists (Reese, 2002). Whereas Howe and Courage (1997) argued that the I begins to formulate and hold on to personal episodic memories around age 2, others suggest that autobiographical memory requires a firmer sense of personal continuity over time, something that may not be present until age 4 (Nelson, 1996; Perner & Ruffman, 1995). Children younger than 4 can remember events from the past, but they may have difficulty attaching those events to a temporally stable Me. For this reason, among others, adults typically have very autobiographical memories that date before the age of 3 or 4 (Reese, 2002).

Autobiographical memory and self-storytelling develop in a social context. Parents typically encourage children to talk about their personal experiences as soon as children are verbally able to do so (Fivush & Nelson, 2004). Early on, parents may take the lead in stimulating the child's recollection and telling of the past by reminding the child of recent events, such as this morning's breakfast or yesterday's visit to the doctor. Taking advantage of this initial conversational scaffolding provided by adults, the young child soon learns to take more initiative in sharing personal events. By the age of 3 years, children are actively engaged in co-constructing their past experience in conservations with adults. By the end of the preschool years, they are able to give a relatively coherent account of their past experiences, independent of adult guidance. Yet individual differences in how parents converse with their children appear to have strong impacts on the development of storytelling. For example, mothers tend to encourage daughters, more than sons, to share *emotional* experiences, including especially memories of negative events that produced sadness (Fivush & Kuebli, 1997). Early on, girls use more emotion words than boys in their autobiographical recollections. When mothers consistently engage their children in an elaborative conversational pattern, asking children to reflect and elaborate on their feelings and thoughts, children develop richer autobiographical memories and tell more detailed stories about themselves. Conversely, a more constricted style of conversation on the part of mothers is associated with less articulated personal narratives in children (Reese & Farrant, 2003). Research suggests that mothers of securely attached children tend to use more elaborative and evaluative strategies when reminiscing with their children, compared with mothers of insecurely attached children. Securely attached children may in turn be more responsive than insecurely attached children in the conversations they have with their mothers about personal events (Reese, 2002).

By the time children are able to generate their own narrative accounts of personal memories, they also exhibit a good understanding of the canonical features of stories themselves. Five year olds typically know that stories are set in a particular time and place and involve characters that act on their desires and beliefs over time. They expect stories to evoke suspense and curiosity and will dismiss as "boring" a narrative that fails to live up to these emotional conventions (W. F. Brewer & Lichtenstein, 1982). They expect stories to conform to a conventional *story grammar* (Applebee, 1978) or generic script concerning what kinds of events can occur and in what order. In a simple, goal-directed episode, for example, an initiating event may prompt the protagonist to attempt some kind of action, which will result in some kind of consequence, which in turn will be followed by the protagonist's reaction to the consequence (Mandler, 1984). Stories are expected to have definite beginnings, middles, and endings. The ending is supposed to provide a resolution to the plot complications that developed over the course of the story. If a story does not conform to conventions such as these, children may find it confusing and difficult to remember, or they may recall it later with a more canonical structure than it originally had.

The Emergence of Narrative Identity

The full realization of the author-self requires more than merely telling stories about what happened to me yesterday or last year. To construct a narrative identity, the person must envision his or her entire life—the past reconstructed and the future imagined—as a story that portrays a *meaningful sequence* of life events to *explain* how the person has developed into who he or she is now and may develop into who he or she may be in the future. Reviewing the empirical literature on cognitive development, Habermas and Bluck (2000) have shown how some of the requisite cognitive skills for self-authorship do not typically come online until adolescence. To construct an integrative life story, the person must first know how a typical life is structured—when, for example, a person leaves home, how schooling and work are sequenced, the expected progression of marriage and family formation, what people do when they retire, when people typically die, and so on. These kinds of normative expectations, shaped as they are by both biology and culture, are what Habermas and Bluck (2000) called the *cultural concept of biography*. Children begin to internalize the cultural concept of biography in elementary school, but considerable learning in this domain will also occur in adolescence.

Critical to the ability to explain the development of the Me over time is what Habermas and Bluck (2000) called *causal coherence*. With increasing age, adolescents are better able to provide narrative accounts that explain how one personal event caused, led up to, transformed, or in some way was or is meaningfully related to subsequent events in one's life. An adolescent girl may explain, for example, why she rejects her parents' liberal political values—or why she feels shy around boys, or how it came to be that her junior year in high school represented a turning point in her understanding of herself—in terms of personal experiences from the past that she has selected and reconstructed to make a coherent personal narrative. She will explain how one event led to another, which led to another, and so on. She will likely share her account with others and monitor the feedback she receives to determine whether her attempt at causal coherence makes sense (McLean, 2005; Thorne, 2000). Furthermore, she may now identify an overarching theme, value, or principle that integrates many different episodes in her life and conveys the gist of who she is and what her biography is all about—a cognitive operation that Habermas and Bluck (2000) called *thematic coherence*. In their analyses of life narratives constructed between the ages of 8 and 20 years of age, Habermas and Paha (2001) and Habermas and de Silveira (2008) showed that causal and thematic coherence are relatively rare in autobiographical accounts from late childhood and early adolescence but increase substantially through the teenage years and into early adulthood.

Cognitive development, then, sets the stage for narrative identity. However, as Erikson (1963) emphasized, socioemotional and cultural factors also play important roles in moving the identity agenda forward in the teens and 20s. In modern societies, teachers, parents, peers, and the media all urge the adolescent to begin thinking about who he or she really is and what he or she wants to become as an adult. Social and cultural forces tell the young person that it will soon be time to "get a life" (Habermas & Bluck, 2000). Of course, even children know vaguely that they will become adults someday, and they may wonder what they will be when they grow up. In early adolescence, these wonderings may begin to take narrative form in fantasies, diaries, web postings, and other self-expressions. Elkind (1981) described these early drafts of narrative identity as *personal fables*. Often grandiose and breathless, these tales of personal greatness and personal tragedy (I will write the great American novel; I will play shortstop for the New York Yankees; I will save the world, or maybe destroy it; I will find the perfect love, and my lover will save me; nobody will ever understand how deep and unique my life has been and will be) may spell out a coherent story of life, but it is typically one that is wildly unrealistic. This is (usually) OK, Elkind suggested, putting grossly paranoid and destructive ideation aside. Narrative identity needs to start somewhere. As they mature into later adolescence and beyond, the authors of personal fables edit, revise, and often start the whole thing over, so as to compose life narratives that are better grounded in reality, reflecting a keener understanding of social constraints and a more astute appraisal of personal skills, values, gifts, and past experiences (Elkind, 1981; McAdams, 1985).

Even though most people ultimately abandon their personal fables, narrative identity never completely descends into literal realism. If they are to inspire and integrate, the stories we tell ourselves about who we are and how we came to be must retain their mythical qualities. Like personal fables, they are acts of imagination that creatively select, embellish, shape, and (yes, it is true) distort the past so that it connects causally and thematically to an imaginatively rendered and anticipated future, all in the service of making meaning (McLean et al., 2007; Singer, 2004). The author-I is more like a novelist than a secretary. The job is to tell a good story rather than to report exactly what happened at the meeting. Still, facts are important. A person's narrative identity should be based on the facts of his or her life as they are generally understood in a social community, for credibility is a cardinal criterion of maturity in identity and in social life (McAdams, 1985). Those facts are part of the material—the psycho-literary resources—with which the author works to craft a self-defining narrative. All by themselves, though, facts are devoid of social and personal meaning. A fact of my life may be that I lost a limb in the Iraq War. What do I make of that fact? Marshalling all the resources at my disposal and working within a social community that privileges some kinds of narratives and discourages others, I decide if my loss signals tragedy, irony, romance, redemption, a return to God, a recommitment to family, a loss of faith, or whatever. There are many narrative possibilities, but not an infinite number. Like any novelist, the self-author can work only with the material at hand. Narrative identity draws on the powers of imagination and integration to shape those materials into a good story, empowered and constrained as the author is by the physical, biologic, psychologic, ideologic, economic, historic, and cultural realities in play (Hammack, 2008; McAdams, 2006a; Rosenwald & Ochberg, 1992).

Narrative identity emerges during a period of the life course that will forever retain a special salience in autobiographical memory. One of the most well-documented findings in cognitive psychology is the tendency for older adults (say, over the age of 50) to recall a disproportionate number of life events from the emerging adulthood years (roughly age 15 to 30). What is called the *memory bump* represents a dramatic departure from the linear forgetting curve that one might expect to prevail for autobiographical recollections (Conway & Pleydell-Pearce, 2000; Fitzgerald, 1988). This is to say, that people tend to recall fewer and fewer events as they go back further and further in time. I remember yesterday better than the day before. I remember what happened in 2007 better than what happened in 2003. The research shows that this general trend holds, except for memories of what happened in my emerging adulthood years. For those years, I likely hold many more memories, especially highly emotional memories, than the linear temporal trend predicts. Researchers have proposed many reasons for the memory bump, such as the possibility that this period in the life course simply happens to contain a disproportionate number of objectively momentous life events, such as leaving home, first job, first sexual relationships, and so on. The memory bump may also reflect the emergence of narrative identity, however. As the I begins to author a story of the Me, it invests personal experiences with special meaning and salience. I remember so much about my emerging adulthood years because that was when I began to put my life together into a story.

Narrating Personal Growth and Self-Transformation

As the author-self constructs narrative identity, it features and elaborates on high points, low points, turning points, and other emotionally charged scenes in the story (Singer & Salovey, 1993; Tomkins, 1987). Positive scenes entail emotions such as joy, excitement, and love; negative scenes are about experiences of distress, sadness, fear, anxiety, anger, guilt, shame, and the like. Tomkins (1987) suggested that people tend to organize emotionally positive and negative scenes in their life stories in correspondingly different ways. Scenes built around the positive affects of joy and excitement tend to be construed and organized as *variants*, Tomkins argued. People accentuate variation in their positive scenes, and in so doing their narrative identities affirm the conviction that people can be happy in many different ways. By contrast, scenes built around negative affects tend to be construed and organized as *analogs*. People accentuate the similarities among their negative events, perceiving common patterns and repetitive sequences, as if to suggest that unhappiness tends to happen in the same old way, over and over again. Positive scenes in narrative identity feel like this: "Wow! This is cool!" For negative scenes, it is more like, "Oh no! Here we go again."

There are many reasons to believe that emotionally positive and negative events present correspondingly different challenges and fulfill different functions in narrative identity (Pals, 2006a, 2006b). At a general level, many theories in psychological science link positive emotions to a behavioral approach system in the brain, designed to regulate reward-seeking activities. By contrast, negative emotions may signal avoidance behaviors in response to threat or uncertainty, regulated by a behavioral inhibition system. In her mobilization–minimization theory, S. E. Taylor (1991) underscored the asymmetrical effects of positive and negative events. Negative (adverse or threatening) events evoke strong and rapid physiologic, cognitive, emotional, and social responses, Taylor argued. The organism mobilizes resources to cope with and ultimately minimize the adverse effect of a negative event. Negative events produce more cognitive activity in general and more efforts to engage in causal reasoning, compared to positive events. At the level of narrative identity, positive scenes invite the I to savor and relive what was good (Lyubomirsky, Sousa, & Dickerhoff, 2006), but negative scenes seem to *demand an explanation*. Negative events in the life story challenge the author-self to make narrative sense of the bad thing that happened—to explain why it happened and perhaps why it may not happen again, to explore the consequences of the negative event for later development in the story.

When it comes to life storytelling, there are many ways to narrate negative events. Perhaps the most common response is to discount the event in some way. The most extreme examples of discounting fall under the rubrics of repression, denial, and dissociation. Some stories are so bad that they simply cannot be told—cannot be told to others and, in many cases, cannot really be told to the self. Freeman (1993) argued that some traumatic and especially shameful experiences in life cannot be incorporated into narrative identity because the narrator (and perhaps the narrator's audience as well) lacks the world assumptions, cognitive constructs, or experiential categories needed to make the story make sense. Less extreme are examples of what S. E. Taylor and Brown (1988) called *positive illusions*. People may simply overlook the negative aspects of life events and exaggerate the potentially positive meanings. "I may be sick, but I am not nearly as sick as my good friend's wife." "God is testing my resolve, and I will rise to the challenge." Bonnano (2004) showed that many people experience surprisingly little angst and turmoil when stricken with harsh misfortunes in life. People often show resilience in the face of adversity, Bonanno argued. Rather than ruminate over the bad things that happen in their lives, they put it all behind them and move forward.

In many situations, however, people cannot or choose not to discount negative life events. Instead, they try to make meaning out the suffering they are currently experiencing, or experienced once upon a time. For example, McLean and Thorne (2003) showed that adolescents often find it necessary to discern lessons learned or insights gained in self-defining memories that involve conflict with others. Pals (2006a) argued that autobiographical reasoning about negative events ideally involves a two-step process. In the first step, the author-self explores the negative experience in depth, thinking long and hard about what the experience feels or felt like, how it came to be, what it may lead to, and what role the negative event may play in one's overall understanding of self. In the second step, the author-self articulates and commits to a positive resolution of the event. Pals (2006a) warned that one should not pass lightly over Step 1. When it comes to narrative identity, Pals suggested, the unexamined life lacks depth and meaning. Consistent with Pals (2006a), a number of studies have shown that exploring negative life events in detail is associated with psychological maturity (King & Hicks, 2006; King, Scollon, Ramsey, & Williams, 2000; Pals, 2006b).

Narrative studies of life transitions have also shown that self-exploration and elaboration are associated with higher levels of ego development (Loevinger, 1976). Bauer and McAdams (2004b) examined narrative accounts from people who had undergone major life changes in either work or religion. People high in ego development tended to construct accounts of these difficult transitions that emphasized, learning, growth, and positive personal transformation. The extent to which personal narratives emphasizing self-exploration, transformation, and integration are positively correlated with ego development has also been documented in studies of life goals (Bauer & McAdams, 2004a) and narrative accounts of life's high points, low points, and turning points (Bauer, McAdams, & Sakaeda, 2005). In another study linking development to narrative processing, McLean and Pratt (2006) found that young adults who used more elaborated and sophisticated forms of meaning making in narrating turning points in their lives tended also to score higher on an overall identity maturity index. Analyzing data from the Mills College Longitudinal Study, Pals (2006b) found that the extent to which women at age 52 explored the ramifications of negative life events mediated the relationship between coping style at age 21 and psychosocial maturity at age 61. Women who in early adulthood scored high on self-report scales assessing an open and nondefensive coping style constructed more elaborate and exploratory narrative accounts of difficult life events at age 52, and narrative exploration at age 52 predicted (and accounted for the relationship of coping openness to) clinical ratings of maturity at age 61.

If the first step in making narrative sense of negative life events is exploring and elaborating on their nature and impact, Step 2 involves constructing a positive meaning or resolution (Pals, 2006a). Numerous studies have shown that deriving positive meanings from negative events is associated with life satisfaction and indicators of emotional well-being (e.g., Affleck & Tennen, 1996; McAdams, Reynolds, Lewis, Patten, & Bowman, 2001). For example, in her analysis of longitudinal data from the Mills study, Pals (2006b) found that coherent positive resolutions of difficult life events at age 51 predicted life satisfaction at age 61 and were associated with increasing ego resiliency between young adulthood and midlife.

Finding positive meanings in negative events is the central theme that runs through McAdams's (2006a) conception of *the redemptive self.* In a series of nomothetical and idiographic studies conducted over the past 15 years, McAdams and colleagues have consistently found that midlife American adults who score especially high on self-report measures of generativity—suggesting a strong commitment to promoting the well-being of future generations and improving the world in which they live (Erikson, 1963)—tend to see their own lives as narratives of redemption (Mansfield & McAdams, 1996; McAdams, 2006a; McAdams & Bowman, 2001; McAdams, Diamond, de St. Aubin, & Mansfield, 1997; McAdams et al., 2001). Compared with their less generative American counterparts, highly generative adults tend to construct life stories that feature redemption sequences, in which the protagonist is delivered from suffering to an enhanced status or state. In addition, highly generative American adults are more likely than their less generative peers to construct life stories in which the protagonist (a) enjoys a special advantage or blessing early in life, (b) expresses sensitivity to the suffering of others or societal injustice as a child, (c) establishes a clear and strong value system in adolescence that remains a source of unwavering conviction through the adult years, (d) experiences significant conflicts between desires for agency–power and desires for communion–love, and (e) looks to achieve goals to benefit society in the future. Taken together, these themes articulate a general script or narrative prototype that many highly generative American adults employ to make sense of their own lives. For highly productive and caring midlife American adults, the redemptive self is a narrative model of the *good life.*

The redemptive self is a life-story prototype that serves to support the generative efforts of midlife men and women. Their redemptive life narratives tell how generative adults seek to give back to society in gratitude for the early advantages and blessings they feel they have received. In every life, generativity is tough and frustrating work, as every parent or community volunteer knows. However, if an adult constructs a narrative identity in which the protagonist's suffering in the short run often gives way to reward later on, he or she may be better able to sustain the conviction that seemingly thankless investments today will pay off for future generations. Redemptive life stories support the kind of life strivings that a highly generative man or woman in the midlife years is likely to set forth. They also confer a *moral legitimacy* to life, a life-narrative function that C. Taylor (1989) and MacIntyre (1981) identified as central to the enterprise of self-authorship. Certain kinds of life narratives exemplify what a society deems to be a good and worthy life. Indeed, virtually all life narratives assume some kind of moral stance in the world. Authorselves write from a moral perspective and seek to affirm the moral goodness of their identity quests. C. Taylor

(1989) writes that "in order to make minimal sense of our lives, in order to have an identity, we need an orientation to the good," and "we see that this sense of the good has to be woven into my understanding of my life as an unfolding story" (p. 47).

Culture and Narrative

McAdams's (2006a) conception of the redemptive self brings to attention the crucial role of culture in the construction of narrative identity. The kinds of life stories that highly generative American adults tend to tell reprise quintessentially American cultural themes—themes that carry a powerful moral cachet. Indeed, the stories of highly generative American adults may say as much about the cultural values that situate the story and the teller as they do about the storytellers themselves. McAdams (2006a) argued that the life-story themes expressed by highly generative American adults recapture and couch in a psychological language especially cherished, as well as hotly contested, ideas in American cultural history—ideas that appear prominently in spiritual accounts of the 17th-century Puritans, Benjamin Franklin's 18th-century autobiography, slave narratives and Horatio Alger stories from the 19th century, and the literature of self-help and American entrepreneurship from more recent times. Evolving from the Puritans to Emerson to Oprah, the redemptive self has morphed into many storied forms in the past 300 years as Americans have sought to narrate their lives as redemptive tales of atonement, emancipation, recovery, self-fulfillment, and upward social mobility. The stories speak of heroic individual protagonists—the *chosen people*—whose *manifest destiny* is to make a positive difference in a dangerous world, even when the world does not wish to be redeemed. The stories translate a deep and abiding script of *American exceptionalism* into the many contemporary narratives of success, recovery, development, liberation, and self-actualization that so pervade American talk, talk shows, therapy sessions, sermons, and commencement speeches. It is as if especially generative American adults, whose lives are dedicated to making the world a better place for future generations, are, for better and sometimes for worse, the most ardent narrators of a general life story format as American as apple pie and the Super Bowl.

Different kinds of narrative identities make sense in different kinds of cultures. In Erikson's (1958) classic study of Martin Luther's identity formation, the stories that young man Luther constructed to make sense of his own life—stories about physical encounters with devils and saints—made all kinds of cultural sense in 16th-century Christian Germany, but they strike the modern secular ear as somewhat odd. A member of a rural Indian village may account for his feelings of tranquility this morning as resulting from the cool and dispassionate food he ate last night (Shweder & Much, 1987). His story will make sense to his peers in the village, but it will not fit expectations for life-narrative accounts in contemporary Berlin. Furthermore, within modern societies, different groups are given different narrative opportunities and face different narrative constraints. Especially relevant here are gender, race, and class divisions in modern society. Linking agency to authorship in the self, feminist author Carolyn Heilbrun (1988) remarked that many women have traditionally "been deprived of the narratives, or the texts, plots, or examples, by which they might assume power over—take control of—their own lives" (p. 17). The historical and contemporary life experiences of many African Americans do not always coalesce nicely into the kind of life-narrative forms most valued by the White majority in the United States (Boyd-Franklin, 1989). Narrative identity, therefore, reflects gender and class divisions and the patterns of economic, politic, and cultural hegemony that prevail at a given point in a society's history (Franz & Stewart, 1994; Gregg, 2006; Rosenwald & Ochberg, 1992).

With respect to cultural effects, researchers have noted strong differences in autobiographical memory and self-authorship between East Asian and North American societies. For example, North American adults typically report an earlier age of first memory and have longer and more detailed memories of childhood than do Chinese, Japanese, and Korean adults (Leichtman, Wang, & Pillemer, 2003). In addition, several studies have noted that North Americans' personal memories tend to be more self-focused than are the memories of East Asians (e.g., Wang, 2001, 2006). The differences are consistent with the well-known argument that certain Eastern societies tend to emphasize interdependent construals of the self, whereas Western societies emphasize independent self-conceptions (Markus & Kitayama, 1991). From an early age, Westerners are encouraged to think about their own individual exploits and to tell stories about them. In a more collectivist culture that inculcates interdependent self-construals, by contrast, children may be encouraged to cultivate a listening role over a telling role and to construct narratives of the self that prioritize other people and social contexts.

Wang and Conway (2004) asked European American and Chinese midlife adults to recall 20 autobiographical memories. Americans provided more memories of individual experiences and one-time events, and they focused their attention on their own roles and emotions in the events. In contrast, Chinese adults were more inclined to recall memories of social and historical events, and they placed a greater emphasis on social interactions and significant others in their stories. Chinese also more frequently drew on past events to convey moral messages than did Americans. Wang and Conway (2004) suggested that personal narratives and life stories fulfill both self-expressive and self-directive functions. European Americans may prioritize self-expressive functions, viewing personal narratives as vehicles for articulating the breadth, depth, and uniqueness of the inner self. By contrast, Chinese may prioritize the self-directive function, viewing personal narratives as guides for good social conduct. Confucian traditions and values place a great deal of emphasis on history and respect for the past. Individuals are encouraged to learn from their own past experiences and from the experiences of others, including their ancestors. From a Confucian perspective, the highest purpose in life is *ren*—a blending of benevolence, moral vitality, and sensitive concern for others. One method for promoting *ren* is to scrutinize one's autobiographical past for mistakes in social conduct. Another method is to reflect on historical events to understand one's appropriate position in the social world. It should not be surprising, then, that personal narratives imbued with a Confucian ethic should draw on both individual and historical events to derive directions for life.

Continuity and Change in Narrative Identity

The lion's share of empirical research on narrative identity in adulthood has examined (a) relations between particular themes and forms in life narratives on the one hand and personality variables (such as traits, motives, and defenses) on the other, (b) life-narrative predictors of psychological well-being and mental health, (c) variations in the ways that people make narrative sense of suffering and negative events in life, (d) the interpersonal and social functions of and effects on life storytelling, (e) uses of narrative in therapy, and (f) the cultural shaping of narrative identity (McAdams, 2008). To date, there exist few longitudinal studies of life stories and no long-term efforts, of the sort found in the literature on personality traits, to trace continuity and change in narrative identity over decades of adult development. Nonetheless, the fact that researchers have tended to collect life-narrative data from adults of different ages, rather than focusing on the proverbial college student, provides an opportunity to consider a few suggestive developmental trends.

Because a person's life is always a work in progress and because narrative identity, therefore, may incorporate new experiences over time, theorists have typically proposed that life stories should change markedly over time. Yet if narrative identity is assumed to provide life with some degree of unity and purpose, then one would expect that self-authorship should also show some longitudinal continuity. But how might continuity and change be assessed? By determining the extent to which a person "tells the same story" from Time 1 to Time 2? If yes, does "same story" mean identifying the same key events in a life? Showing the same kinds of narrative themes? Exhibiting the same sorts of causal or thematic connections? In a 3-year longitudinal study that asked college students to recall and describe 10 key scenes in their life stories on three occasions, McAdams et al. (2006) found that only 28% of the episodic memories described at Time 1 were repeated 3 months later (Time 2), and 22% of the original (Time 1) memories were chosen and described again 3 years after the original assessment (Time 3). Despite change in manifest content of stories, however, McAdams et al. (2006) also documented noteworthy longitudinal consistencies (in the correlation range of .35 to .60) in certain emotional and motivational qualities in the stories and in the level of narrative complexity. Furthermore, over the 3-year period, students' life-narrative accounts became more complex, and they incorporated a greater number of themes, suggesting personal growth and integration.

Cross-sectional studies suggest that up through middle age, older adults tend to construct more complex and coherent life narratives than do younger adults and adolescents (Baddeley & Singer, 2007). One process through which this developmental difference is shown is *autobiographical reasoning*, which is the tendency to draw summary conclusions about the self from autobiographical episodes (McLean et al., 2007). Autobiographical reasoning tends to give a life narrative greater causal and thematic coherence (Habermas & Bluck, 2000). Pasupathi and Mansour (2006) found that autobiographical reasoning in narrative accounts of life turning points increases with age up to midlife. Middle-aged adults showed a more interpretive and psychologically sophisticated approach to life storytelling, compared with younger people. Bluck and Gluck (2004) asked adolescents (age 15–20), younger adults (age 30–40), and older adults (age 60 and over) to recount personal experiences in which they demonstrated wisdom. Younger and older adults were more likely than the adolescents to narrate wisdom scenes in ways that connected the experiences to larger life themes or philosophies, yet another manifestation of autobiographical reasoning.

Singer, Rexhaj, and Baddeley (2007) found that adults over age 50 narrated self-defining memories that expressed a more positive narrative tone and greater integrative meaning compared with college students. Findings like these dovetail with Pennebaker and Stone's (2003) demonstration, based on laboratory studies of language use and analyses of published fiction, that adults use more positive and fewer negative affect words and demonstrate greater levels of cognitive complexity as they age. The findings are also consistent with research on autobiographical recollections showing a positivity memory bias among older adults (e.g., Kennedy, Mather, & Carstensen, 2004). At the same time, evidence suggests that older adults tend to recall more general, as opposed to specific, event memories, tending to skip over the details and focus mainly on the memory's emotional gist (Baddeley & Singer, 2007). In our later years, narrative identity may become warmer and fuzzier.

Counselors who work with the elderly sometimes employ the method of *life review* to encourage older adults to relive and reflect on past events (Butler, 1963). In life review, older adults are encouraged to mine their autobiographical memory for specific events that seem to have meaning and value. Life review therapists teach their clients how to reminisce productively about these events and to reflect upon their meaning. Some studies suggest that life review can improve life satisfaction and relieve symptoms of depression and anxiety among older adults (Serrano, Latorre, Gatz, & Montanes, 2004). Even without undergoing formal training or assistance in life review, however, the author-self may draw increasingly on reminiscences as the years go by. Positive memory biases among older people may give narrative identity a softer glow in the later years. The increasing tendency with age to recall more generalized memories may also simplify life stories in old age (Singer et al., 2007).

All good things for the self do, unfortunately, come to an end. With memory loss and increasing frailty, the oldest adults may no longer be psychologically involved in the construction of narrative identity. The author-I may tell fewer and fewer stories and expend less and less energy in the construction of a narrative Me. Dementia undermines the author-self's fundamental function, scrambling and eventually destroying the material out of which narrative identity is to be made (McColgan, Valentine, & Downs, 2000). In very old age, shortly before death, self-authorship may eventually fade away, and so too, perhaps, strong agency, as the oldest old return instead to those most basic issues of living day to day as social actors, conserving energy to focus on the moments left in life, surviving and holding on as best they can, before death closes the door.

Summary

The author-I lies for many years in waiting. It is not until adolescence and young adulthood, that individuals living in modern societies begin to put their lives together into meaningful and purposeful narrative identities—internalized and evolving self-narratives that reconstruct the past and imagine the future as a story that explains how the person came to be and where his or her life is going in the future. Extending the Me back further into the past and forward further into the future, the author-self provides a narrative explanation for what the social actor does and what the motivated agent wants, accounting for how action and agency develop over time in a way that makes sense to the self and to the various audiences that ultimately come to judge the story of a life. Laying the groundwork for self-authorship are many of the same developmental milestones that marked the evolution of the actor-self and agent-self—such as the appreciation of intentionality at age one, the emergence of self-awareness in the second year of life, and the development of theory of mind. Children begin to tell stories about their personal experiences at ages 2 and 3, and parents typically encourage these initial efforts in self-narration according to the norms of culture and gender. Eventually, children internalize a cultural concept of biography as they come to understand how a typical life in their culture develops. In adolescence, they hone cognitive skills that enable them to construct causal sequences in life-narrative accounts and to derive overarching life themes. The first adolescent efforts to construct narrative identity may resemble the fantastical personal fables first noted by David Elkind. Eventually, however, narrative accounts become more realistic and more integrative, as modern young adults face Erikson's identity challenge.

The author-self constructs a life story that contains high points, low points, turning points, and other self-defining scenes. The narration of low points, or negative scenes more generally, has captured the interest of many researchers. Elaborating fully the vicissitudes of negative life events appears to be positively associated with psychological maturity in adulthood, whereas resolving these negative scenes in a positive or redemptive manner tends to be associated with greater psychological well-being and higher levels of generativity. Especially generative American adults—midlife men and women who show high levels of caring and productive behavior and strong commitments to promoting future generations—tend to author especially redemptive life narratives, expressing quintessentially American cultural themes of personal atonement, upward social mobility, emancipation, and recovery. Research on the redemptive narratives of generative American adults illustrates the power of culture to shape narrative identity. Indeed, the I appears to come to terms with culture through the construction of a self-defining life story. Cross-sectional studies suggest developmental trends in narrative identity. Up through midlife, the author-I appears to engage in greater levels of autobiographical reasoning, constructing more and more coherent and psychologically nuanced narrative identities. From midlife into later adulthood, life stories may become more emotionally positive overall and somewhat simpler in structure. However, the onset of dementia and other health crises in very old age may diminish autobiographical memory and ultimately undermine the I's ability to be an author.

CONCLUSION

The life-span perspective on self and identity presented in this chapter draws widely from philosophical treatments of the self and from the disciplines of social and personality psychology, cognitive–developmental studies, motivational psychology, life-span psychology, life course sociology, psychoanalysis, humanistic psychology, and the narrative study of lives, among others. The heir to the philosophical tradition—and the hero of our long, interdisciplinary saga—is what Charles Taylor (1989) called the *modern self*, an inherently reflexive, internalized patterning of psychological individuality most famously captured in William James's (1892/1963) distinction between the I and the Me. Synthesizing ideas from Augustine, Locke, and others, James argued that the self is both subject and object, process and product, the stance from which the world is observed and the mirror reflection that arises from the observation. To depict the essential subjectivity of human selfhood (the I), psychologists and other social scientists have used terms like "ego," "self-awareness," "consciousness," the "phenomenal self," human "agency," the "existential self," and the like. To characterize the other half (the Me), they have generated theories about the "self-concept," "self-schemas," "self-representations," "possible selves," the "objective self," "identity," and so on. How should we conceive of the modern, duplex self? What can we say about its development across the human life span?

We submit that the self can be profitably understood as appearing in three developmentally successive guises—the self as actor, agent, and author. People begin life as social actors; eventually they become goal-directed agents; by early adulthood, they add to their self-repertoire the retrospective (and simultaneously prospective) author. Each of the three guises of human selfhood—actor, agent, and author—may be seen from the standpoint of the I and the Me. The actor-I constructs a sense of itself as a social performer; the agent-I sets forth plans, goals, and projects within the Me, and then pursues them. The author-I constructs a life story to make meaning of it all. We believe that viewing the self as an actor, agent, and author provides an innovative and broad framework that integrates a surprisingly large amount of contemporary research on the self and its development over the human life span.

The first to emerge in development, the actor-self performs on that fundamental social stage for which human beings have evolved first and foremost to perform. The actor-I observes its own performances and the responses to those performances from other actors and audiences, and through self-observation it gradually builds up a sense of itself as an actor—that is, the actor-Me. Among the most important features of the actor-Me are those broad traits and specific roles that the person comes to understand as tending to characterize his or her own social performances. Among the greatest challenges for the actor-self is self-regulation (Baumeister, 1998). How do I control myself to generate the most effective performances in my social world? As Mead (1934), Goffman (1959), Bem (1972), and Hogan (1982) described in brilliant detail, the presentation of the self on the social stage of everyday life is a social game that everybody must play. The stakes are huge—having to do with social acceptance, status, reputation, and other social considerations that, throughout evolution, have served as standards of inclusive fitness for the bipedal, cognitively gifted, group-living creatures we call human beings.

The actor-self becomes more fully elaborated and articulated as the individual moves from childhood, through adolescence and young adulthood, and into the middle-adult years. Self-ratings on certain common dimensions of social performance, furthermore, show developmental trends, with actors seeing themselves as increasingly warm, conscientious, and emotionally stable as they move across the big middle of the human life span, from about age 20 to 70. Self-attributed traits and social performance roles remain important features of the actor-self in old age. Across the human life span, the self never gives up its guise as the actor. The cliché that identifies the human being as a social animal is deeply true. The social actor is first and last what the self is.

However, the self is more than an actor, and it becomes more as we move into the middle childhood years. The agent-self captures the complex sense in which the I takes ownership of subjective experience; makes choices and assumes control; and puts desires, plans, and hopes into play to carry out goal-directed projects in the future. Even newborns are goal-directed strivers in some sense, but agency takes developmental steps forward with the appreciation of intentionality that 1 year olds begin to show and the emergence of theory of mind in the third and fourth years of life. As they move through elementary school, children articulate clear goals and projects and begin to define themselves in terms of what they want to accomplish. As James (1892/1963) intimated and research (Harter, 2006) shows, self-esteem arises in middle to late childhood as a problem in goal pursuit. The I feels good about the Me to the extent that the Me is perceived as actualizing, achieving, or making good progress in the pursuit of its most cherished goals.

The agent-self expands further in adolescence and young adulthood by incorporating longer term goals and possible selves. To consolidate an Eriksonian identity, the agent-self explores various life options with respect to ideology, occupation, and relationships and, in the ideal scenario, chooses what kind of person to become—what to value, what work to do, whom to love, what dream to follow—in the future, reshaping the Me through commitment. Across the adult life course, on-time developmental challenges, unexpected or off-time events, and cultural factors combine to shape choices, commitments, and goals. In the earlier adult years, the agent-self makes room for many goals, even those that may conflict with each other. As the person moves through middle adulthood, however, agency narrows to focus on the most salient, satisfying, or concerning goal arenas, such as family, close friends, and health. Goals regarding generativity and civic involvement may peak in the midlife years. As the adult moves into the later years, primary control strategies eventually give way to secondary strategies wherein the agent-self selects, optimizes, and compensates in the face of declining power and mounting losses.

The author-self is the last to arrive to the party. Whereas children can tell stories about their experiences by the time their parents sign them up for kindergarten, full self-authorship awaits the development of cognitive capacities that do not come online until adolescence. These include the abilities (a) to connect personal events into causal chains that explain how a person has come to be who he or she is and (b) to derive an overarching theme that characterizes that personal development (Habermas & Bluck, 2000). Socioemotional and cultural factors also play prime roles in urging the self to assume the authorship stance in late adolescence and young adulthood, to begin the process of transforming the Me into a temporally integrative life story. As MacIntyre (1981), Ricoeur (1984), McAdams (1985), Sarbin (1986), Bruner (1986), C. Taylor (1989), Giddens (1991), Singer (2004), and many others have argued in recent years, the modern self finds unity and temporal coherence, to the extent these things can be found, by assuming the form of a dynamic life narrative.

Therefore, we may define narrative identity as the internalized and evolving story of the self that the author-I constructs, complete with setting, scenes, characters, plots, and themes. The story integrates a selective and embellished reconstruction of the past with an imaginative rendering of the future. Under the conditions of cultural modernity, narrative identity provides life with some semblance of unity, purpose, and meaning. With culture serving as the ultimate editor and literary agent, the author-self continues to work on the story over the adult life course, revising, updating, and sometimes recomposing from scratch, ever attuned to opportunities for self-transformation. The author-self invests a great deal of energy into the narrative construction of emotionally negative events, sometimes making them into tales of redemption. Up through midlife, narrative identity appears to develop in the direction of increasing complexity and causal coherence. In the later years, life stories may become simpler and happier. In very old age, however, narrative identity may begin to disintegrate, as the author-self loses access to a coherent body of autobiographical memory. Playing out the modern self's scenario up through the last months of a very long and very full life, the author-self may eventually fade away, and also, to a large extent, the goal-directed agent-self may do so as well. Completing the full life span, human beings may end up back where they began—as social actors.

REFERENCES

Affleck, G., & Tennen, H. (1996). Construing benefits from adversity: Adaptational significance and dispositional underpinnings. *Journal of Personality, 64,* 899–922.

Allemand, M., Zimprich, D., & Hertzog, C. (2007). Cross-sectional age differences and longitudinal age changes in personality in middle adulthood and old age. *Journal of Personality, 75,* 323–358.

Applebee, A. N. (1978). *The child's concept of story.* Chicago: University of Chicago Press.

Arnett, J. J. (2000). Emerging adulthood: A theory of development from the late teens through the twenties. *American Psychologist, 55,* 469–480.

Baddeley, J., & Singer, J. A. (2007). Charting the life story's path: Narrative identity across the life span. In J. Clandinin (Ed.), *Handbook of narrative research methods* (pp. 177–202). Thousand Oaks, CA: Sage.

Baltes, P. B. (1997). On the incomplete architecture of human ontogeny: Selection, optimization, and compensation as foundation for developmental theory. *American Psychologist, 52,* 366–380.

Bamberg, M. G. W. (1997). Positioning between structure and performance. *Journal of Narrative and Life History, 7,* 335–342.

Bandura, A. (1989). Human agency in social-cognitive theory. *American Psychologist, 44,* 1175–1184.

Baron-Cohen, S. (1995). *Mindblindness: An essay on autism and theory of mind.* Cambridge, MA: MIT Press.

Bauer, J. J., & McAdams, D. P. (2004a). Growth goals, maturity, and well-being. *Developmental Psychology, 40,* 114–127.

Bauer, J. J., & McAdams, D. P. (2004b). Personal growth in adults' stories of life transitions. *Journal of Personality, 72,* 573–602.

Bauer, J. J., McAdams, D. P., & Sakaeda, A. R. (2005). Interpreting the good life: Growth memories in the lives of mature, happy people. *Journal of Personality and Social Psychology, 88,* 203–217.

Baumeister, R. F. (1986). *Identity: Cultural change and the struggle for self.* New York: Oxford University Press.

Baumeister, R. F. (1998). The self. In D. T. Gilbert, S. T. Fiske, & G. Lindzey (Eds.), *Handbook of social psychology* (4th ed., pp. 680–740). New York: McGraw-Hill.

Baumeister, R. F., & Bushman, B. J. (2008). *Social psychology and human nature.* Belmont, CA: Thomson.

Baumeister, R. F., & Heatherton, T. F. (1996). Self-regulation failure: An overview. *Psychological Inquiry, 7,* 1–15.

Beer, J. S. (2002). Implicit self-theories of shyness. *Journal of Personality and Social Psychology, 83,* 1009–1024.

Behne, T., Carpenter, M., Call, J., & Tomasello, M. (2005). Unwilling versus unable: Infants' understanding of intentional action. *Developmental Psychology, 41,* 328–337.

Bem, D. J. (1972). Self-perception theory. In L. Berkowitz (Ed.), *Advances in experimental social psychology* (Vol. 6, pp. 1–62). New York: Academic Press.

Benet-Martinez, V., & Haritatos, J. (2005). Bicultural identity integration (BII): Components and psychosocial antecedents. *Journal of Personality, 73,* 1015–1050.

Benet-Martinez, V., Leu, J., Lee, F., & Morris, M. (2002). Negotiating biculturalism: Cultural frame-switching in biculturals with oppositional versus compatible cultural identities. *Journal of Cross-Cultural Psychology, 35,* 492–516.

Blasi, A. (1988). Identity and the development of the self. In D. K. Lapsley & F. C. Power (Eds.), *Self, ego, and identity: Integrative approaches* (pp. 226–242). New York: Springer-Verlag.

Bluck, S., & Gluck, J. (2004). Making things better and learning a lesson: Experiencing wisdom across the lifespan. *Journal of Personality, 72,* 543–572.

Bonanno, G. A. (2004). Loss, trauma, and human resilience: Have we underestimated the human capacity to thrive after extremely aversive events? *American Psychologist, 59,* 20–28.

Bowlby, J. (1969). *Attachment.* New York: Basic Books.

Boyd-Franklin, N. (1989). *Black families in therapy: A multisystems approach.* New York: Guilford Press.

Brewer, M. B., & Gardner, W. (1996). Who is this "we"? Levels of collective identity and self-representation. *Journal of Personality and Social Psychology, 77,* 83–93.

Brewer, W. F., & Lichtenstein, E. H. (1982). Stories are to entertain: A structural–affect theory of stories. *Journal of Pragmatics, 6,* 473–486.

Bruner, J. S. (1986). *Actual minds, possible worlds.* Cambridge, MA: Harvard University Press.

Bruner, J. S. (1994). The "remembered" self. In U. Neisser & R. Fivush (Eds.), *The remembering self* (pp. 41–54). New York: Cambridge University Press.

Brunstein, J. C., Schultheiss, O. C., & Grassmann, R. (1998). Personal goals and emotional well-being: The moderating role of motive dispositions. *Journal of Personality and Social Psychology, 75,* 494–508.

Buss, D. M. (2008). Human nature and individual differences: Evolution of human personality. In O. P. John, R. W. Robins, & L. A. Pervin (Eds.), *Handbook of personality: Theory and research* (3rd ed., pp. 29–60). New York: Guilford Press.

Butler, R. N. (1963). The life review: An interpretation of reminiscence in old age. *Psychiatry, 26,* 65–76.

Carstensen, L. L., Pasupathi, M., Mayr, U., & Nesselroade, J. R. (2000). Emotional experience in everyday life across the adult life span. *Journal of Personality and Social Psychology, 79,* 644–655.

Carver, C. S., & Scheier, M. F. (1982). Control theory: A useful conceptual framework for personality–social, clinical, and health psychology. *Psychological Bulletin, 92,* 111–135.

Caspi, A., Roberts, B. W., & Shiner, R. L. (2005). Personality development: Stability and change. In S. T. Fiske & D. Schacter (Eds.), *Annual review of psychology* (Vol. 56, pp. 453–484). Palo Alto, CA: Annual Reviews.

Cohler, B. J. (1982). Personal narrative and the life course. In P. Baltes & O. G. Brim, Jr. (Eds.), *Life span development and behavior* (Vol. 4, pp. 205–241). New York: Academic Press.

Conway, M. A., & Pleydell-Pearce, C. W. (2000). The construction of autobiographical memories in the self-memory system. *Psychological Review, 107,* 261–288.

Cooley, C. H. (1902). *Human nature and the social order.* New York: Scribner's.

Costa, P. T., Jr., & McCrae, R. R. (2006). Age changes in personality and their origins: Comments on Roberts, Walton, and Viechtbauer (2006). *Psychological Bulletin, 132,* 26–28.

Crocker, J., & Park, L. E. (2004). The costly pursuit of self-esteem. *Psychological Bulletin, 130,* 392–414.

Cross, S., & Markus, H. (1991). Possible selves across the lifespan. *Human Development, 44,* 230–255.

Csikszentmihalyi, M., & Rochberg-Halton, E. (1982). *The meaning of things: Domestic symbols and the self.* New York: Oxford University Press.

Damasio, A. (1999). *The feeling of what happens: Body and emotion in the making of consciousness.* Orlando, FL: Harcourt.

Damon, W., & Hart, D. (1982). The development of self-understanding from infancy through adolescence. *Child Development, 53,* 841–864.

Deci, E. L., & Ryan, R. M. (1985). *Intrinsic motivation and self-determination in human behavior.* New York: Plenum Press.

Deci, E. L., & Ryan, R. M. (1991). A motivational approach to self: Integration in personality. In R. Dienstbier & R. M. Ryan (Eds.), *Nebraska symposium on motivation: 1990* (pp. 237–288). Lincoln: University of Nebraska Press.

Diehl, M. (2006). Development of self-representations in adulthood. In D. K. Mroczek & T. D. Little (Eds.), *Handbook of personality development* (pp. 373–398). Mahwah, NJ: Erlbaum.

Diener, M. L., Mengelsdorf, S. C., McHale, J. L., & Frosch, C. A. (2002). Infants' behavioral strategies of emotion regulation with fathers and mothers: Associations with emotional expressions and attachment quality. *Infancy, 3,* 153–174.

Dodge, K. A., & Garber, J. (1991). Domains of emotion regulation. In J. Garber & K. A. Dodge (Eds.), *The development of emotion regulation and dysregulation* (pp. 3–14). New York: Cambridge University Press.

Donahue, E. M., Robins, R. W., Roberts, B. W., & John, O. P. (1993). The divided self: Concurrent and longitudinal effects of psychological adjustment and social roles on self-concept differentiation. *Journal of Personality and Social Psychology, 64,* 834–846.

DuBois, W. E. B. (1903/1989). *The souls of black folk.* New York: Penguin.

Duval, S., & Wicklund, R. A. (1972). *A theory of objective self-awareness.* New York: Academic Press.

Dweck, C. S., Chiu, C., & Hong, Y. (1995). Implicit theories and their role in judgments and reactions. *Psychological Inquiry, 6,* 267–285.

Elder, G. H., Jr. (1995). The life course paradigm: Social change and individual development. In P. Moen, G. H. Elder, Jr., & K. Luscher (Eds.), *Examining lives in context: Perspectives on the ecology of human development* (pp. 101–139). Washington, DC: American Psychological Association Press.

Elkind, D. (1981). *Children and adolescents* (3rd ed.). New York: Oxford University Press.

Elliot, A. J., Chirkov, V. I., Kim, Y., & Sheldon, K. M. (2001). A cross-cultural analysis of avoidance (relative to approach) personal goals. *Psychological Science, 12,* 505–510.

Emmons, R. A. (1986). Personal strivings: An approach to personality and subjective well-being. *Journal of Personality and Social Psychology, 51,* 1058–1068.

Emmons, R. A. (1999). *The psychology of ultimate concerns.* New York: Guilford Press.

Emmons, R. A., & King, L. A. (1988). Conflict among personal strivings: Immediate and long-term implications for psychological and physical well-being. *Journal of Personality and Social Psychology, 54,* 1041–1048.

Epstein, S. (1973). The self-concept revisited: Or a theory of a theory. *American Psychologist, 28,* 404–416.

Erikson, E. H. (1958). *Young man Luther.* New York: Norton.

Erikson, E. H. (1963). *Childhood and society* (2nd ed.). New York: Norton.

Erikson, E. H. (1969). *Gandhi's truth.* New York: Norton.

Fagles, R. (Trans.). (1990). *Homer's The Iliad.* New York: Penguin.

Fairbairn, W. R. D. (1952). *The object relations theory of personality.* London: Routledge & Kegan Paul.

Fitzgerald, J. M. (1988). Vivid memories and the reminiscence phenomenon: The role of a self-narrative. *Human Development, 31,* 261–273.

Fivush, R., & Haden, C. (Eds.). (2003). *Autobiographical memory and the construction of a narrative self: Developmental and cultural perspectives.* Mahwah, NJ: Erlbaum.

Fivush, R., & Kuebli, J. (1997). Making everyday events emotional: The construal of emotion in parent–child conversations about the past. In N. L. Stein, P. A. Ornstein, B. Tversky, & C. Brainerd (Eds.), *Memory for everyday and emotional events* (pp. 239–266). Mahwah, NJ: Erlbaum.

Fivush, R., & Nelson, K. (2004). Culture and language in the emergence of autobiographical memory. *Psychological Science, 15,* 573–577.

Franz, C., & Stewart, A. J. (Eds.). (1994). *Women creating lives: Identity, resilience, resistance.* Boulder, CO: Westview Press.

Freeman, M. (1993). *Rewriting the self: History, memory, narrative.* London: Routledge.

Freud, S. (1923/1961). The ego and the id. In J. Strachey (Ed.), *The standard edition of the complete psychological works of Sigmund Freud* (Vol. 19). London: Hogarth.

Freund, A. M., & Riediger, M. (2006). Goals as building blocks of personality and development in adulthood. In D. K. Mroczek & T. D. Little (Es.), *Handbook of personality development* (pp. 353–372). Mahwah, NJ: Erlbaum.

Freund, A. M., & Smith, J. (1999). Content and function of the self-definition in old and very old age. *Journal of Gerontology: Psychological Sciences, 54B,* P55–P67.

Gailliot, M. T., Mead, M. L., & Baumeister, R. F. (2008). Self-regulation. In O. P. John, R. W. Robins, & L. A. Pervin (Eds.), *Handbook of personality: Theory and research* (3rd ed., pp. 472–491). New York: Guilford Press.

Gay, P. (1986). *The bourgeois experience: Victoria to Freud: Vol. 2. The tender passions.* New York: Oxford University Press.

Gergen, K. J. (1991). *The saturated self: Dilemmas of identity in contemporary life.* New York: Basic Books.

Giddens, A. (1991). *Modernity and self-identity: Self and society in the late modern age.* Stanford, CA: Stanford University Press.

Gittings, R. (1978). *The nature of biography.* Seattle: University of Washington Press.

Goffman, E. (1959). *The presentation of self in everyday life.* Garden City, NY: Doubleday.

Gosling, S. (2008). *Snoop: What your stuff says about you.* New York: Basic Books.

Gottman, J., Katz, L. F., & Hooven, C. (1997). *Meta-emotion.* Hillsdale, NJ: Erlbaum.

Greenberg, J., Solomon, S., Pyszczynski, T., Rosenblatt, A., Burling, J., Lyon, D., Simon, L., & Pinel, E. (1992). Why do people need self-esteem? Converging evidence that self-esteem serves an anxiety-buffering function. *Journal of Personality and Social Psychology, 63,* 913–922.

Greenwald, A. G. (1980). The totalitarian ego: Fabrication and revision of personal history. *American Psychologist, 35,* 603–618.

Gregg, G. (1991). *Self-representation: Life narrative studies in identity and ideology.* New York: Greenwood Press.

Gregg, G. (2006). The raw and the bland: A structural model of narrative identity. In D. P. McAdams, R. Josselson, & A. Lieblich (Eds.), *Identity and story* (pp. 89–108). Washington, DC: American Psychological Association Press.

Habermas, T., & Bluck, S. (2000). Getting a life: The emergence of the life story in adolescence. *Psychological Bulletin, 126,* 748–769.

Habermas, T., & de Silveira, C. (2008). The development of global coherence in life narratives across adolescence: Temporal, causal, and thematic aspects. *Developmental Psychology, 44,* 707–721.

Habermas, T., & Paha, C. (2001). The development of coherence in adolescents' life narratives. *Narrative Inquiry, 11,* 35–54.

Hacking, I. (1995). *Rewriting the soul: Multiple personality and the sciences of memory.* Princeton, NJ: Princeton University Press.

Hammack, P. L. (2008). Narrative and the cultural psychology of identity. *Personality and Social Psychology Review, 12,* 222–247.

Harlow, H. F., & Harlow, M. K. (1962). Social deprivation in monkeys. *Scientific American, 207,* 136–146.

Harre, R. (1998). *The singular self: An introduction to the psychology of personhood.* London: Sage.

Harter, S. (2006). The self. In N. Eisenberg (Ed.) & W. Damon & R. M. Lerner (Series Eds.), *Handbook of child psychology: Vol. 3. Social, emotional, and personality development* (pp. 505–570). Hoboken, NJ: John Wiley & Sons.

Heckhausen, J., & Schulz, R. (1995). A life-span theory of control. *Psychological Review, 102,* 284–304.

Heidegger, M. (1927). *Being and time.* Tubingen, Germany: Neimeyer.

Heilbrun, C. (1988). *Writing a woman's life.* New York: Norton.

Helson, R., & Soto, C. J. (2005). Up and down in middle age: Monotonic and nonmonotonic changes in roles, status, and personality. *Journal of Personality and Social Psychology, 89,* 194–204.

Helson, R., Soto, C. J., & Cate, R. A. (2006). From young adulthood through the middle ages. In D. K. Mroczek & T. D. Little (Eds.),

Handbook of personality development (pp. 337–352). Mahwah, NJ: Erlbaum.

Hermans, H. J. M. (1996). Voicing the self: From information processing to dialogical interchange. *Psychological Bulletin, 119,* 31–50.

Higgins, E. T. (1987). Self-discrepancy: A theory relating self and affect. *Psychological Review, 94,* 319–340.

Higgins, E. T. (1996). The "self digest": Self-knowledge serving self-regulatory functions. *Journal of Personality and Social Psychology, 71,* 1062–1083.

Hogan, R. (1982). A socioanalytic theory of personality. In M. Paige (Ed.), *Nebraska symposium on motivation: 1981* (pp. 55–89). Lincoln: University of Nebraska Press.

Hogan, R., Jones, W. H., & Cheek, J. M. (1985). Socioanalytic theory: An alternative to armadillo psychology. In B. R. Schlenker (Ed.), *The self and social life* (pp. 175–198). New York: McGraw-Hill.

Holstein, J. A., & Gubrium, J. F. (2000). *The self we live by: Narrative identity in a postmodern world.* New York: Oxford University Press.

Hooker, K. S. (1992). Possible selves and perceived health in older adults and college students. *Journal of Gerontology, 47,* P85–P95.

Hooker, K. S., & McAdams, D. P. (2003). Personality reconsidered: A new agenda for aging research. *Journal of Gerontology: Psychological Sciences, 58B,* P296–P304.

Howe, M. L., & Courage, M. L. (1997). The emergence and early development of autobiographical memory. *Psychological Review, 104,* 499–523.

Ingram, R. E. (1990). Self-focused attention in clinical disorders: Review and a conceptual model. *Psychological Bulletin, 107,* 156–176.

James, W. (1892/1963). *Psychology*. Greenwich, CT: Fawcett.

Jaynes, J. (1976). *The origin of consciousness in the breakdown of the bicameral mind.* Boston: Houghton Mifflin.

Josselson, R. (1996). *Revising herself: The story of women's identity from college to midlife.* New York: Oxford University Press.

Josselson, R., & Lieblich, A. (Eds.). (1993). *The narrative study of lives* (Vol. 1). Thousand Oaks, CA: Sage.

Kagan, J. (1998). Is there a self in infancy? In M. Ferrari & R. J. Sternberg (Eds.), *Self-awareness: Its nature and development* (pp. 137–147). New York: Guilford Press.

Kasser, T., & Ryan, R. M. (1996). Further examining the American dream: Differential correlates of extrinsic and intrinsic goals. *Personality and Social Psychology Bulletin, 22,* 280–287.

Kegan, R. (1982). *The evolving self: Problem and process in human development.* Cambridge, MA: Harvard University Press.

Kelemen, D. (2004). Are children "intuitive theists"? *Psychological Science, 15,* 295–301.

Kennedy, Q., Mather, M., & Carstensen, L. L. (2004). The role of motivation in age-related positivity effect in autobiographical memory. *Psychological Science, 15,* 208–214.

Kihlstrom, J. F., & Klein, S. B. (1994). The self as a knowledge structure. In R. S. Wyer, Jr., & T. K. Srull (Eds.), *Handbook of social cognition: Vol. 1. Basic processes.* (2nd ed.). (pp. 153–208). Hillsdale, NJ: Erlbaum.

King, L. A., & Hicks, J. A. (2006). Narrating the self in the past and future: Implications for maturity. *Research in Human Development, 3,* 121–138.

King, L. A., Scollon, C. K., Ramsey, C., & Williams, T. (2000). Stories of life transition: Subjective well-being and ego development in parents of children with Down syndrome. *Journal of Research in Personality, 34,* 509–536.

Klein, S. B., Loftus, J., & Kihlstrom, J. F. (1996). Self-knowledge of an amnesic patient: Toward a neuropsychology of personality and social psychology. *Journal of Experimental Psychology: General, 125,* 250–260.

Klinger, E. (1987). Current concerns and disengagement from incentives. In F. Halisch & J. Kuhl (Eds.), *Motivation, intention, and volition* (pp. 337–347). Berlin: Springer-Verlag.

Kochanska, G., & Aksan, N. (2006). Children's conscience and self-regulation. *Journal of Personality, 74,* 1587–1617.

Kohlberg, L. (1969). Stage and sequence: The cognitive–developmental approach to socialization. In D. A. Goslin (Ed.), *Handbook of socialization theory and research* (pp. 347–480). Skokie, IL: Rand McNally.

Kohut, H. (1971). *The analysis of the self.* New York: International Universities Press.

Krueger, R. F., & Johnson, W. (2008). Behavior genetics and personality: A new look at the integration of nature and nurture. In O. P. John, R. W. Robins, & L. A. Pervin (Eds.), *Handbook of personality: Theory and research* (3rd ed., pp. 287–310). New York: Guilford Press.

Langbaum, R. (1982). *The mysteries of identity: A theme in modern literature.* Chicago: University of Chicago Press.

Leary, M. (2004). *The curse of the self.* New York: Oxford University Press.

Leichtman, M. D., Wang, Q., & Pillemer, D. B. (2003). Cultural variations in interdependence: Lessons from Korea, China, India, and the United States. In R. Fivush & C. Haden (Eds.), *Autobiographical memory and the construction of a narrative self* (pp. 73–97). Mahwah, NJ: Erlbaum.

Levinson, D. J. (1978). *The seasons of a man's life.* New York: Knopf.

Levy, R., Ghisletta, P., Legoff, J. M., Spini, D., & Widmer, E. (Eds.). (2005). *Towards an interdisciplinary perspective on the life course: Advances in life course research* (Vol. 10). London: Elsevier.

Lewis, M., & Brooks-Gunn, J. (1979). *Social cognition and the acquisition of self.* New York: Plenum.

Li-Grinning, C. P. (2007). Effortful control among low-income preschoolers in three cities: Stability, change, and individual differences. *Developmental Psychology, 43,* 208–221.

Linville, P. W. (1987). Self-complexity as a cognitive buffer against stress-related illness and depression. *Journal of Personality and Social Psychology, 52,* 663–676.

Little, B. R. (1999). Personality and motivation: Personal action and the conative evolution. In L. A. Pervin & O. John (Eds.), *Handbook of personality: Theory and research* (2nd ed., pp. 501–524). New York: Guilford Press.

Little, T. D., Snyder, C. R., & Wehmeyer, M. (2006). The agentic self: On the nature and origins of personal agency across the life span. In D. K. Mroczek & T. D. Little (Eds.), *Handbook of personality development* (pp. 61–79). Mahwah, NJ: Erlbaum.

Loevinger, J. (1976). *Ego development.* San Francisco: Jossey-Bass.

Lyubomirsky, S., Sousa, L., & Dickerhoff, R. (2006). The costs and benefits of writing, talking, and thinking about life's triumphs and defeats. *Journal of Personality and Social Psychology, 90,* 692–708.

MacIntyre, A. (1981). *After virtue.* Notre Dame, IN: University of Notre Dame Press.

Mahler, M. S., Pine, F., & Bergman, A. (1975). *The psychological birth of the human infant.* New York: Basic Books.

Mandler, J. M. (1984). *Stories, scripts, and scenes: Aspects of schema theory.* Hillsdale, NJ: Erlbaum.

Mansfield, E. D., & McAdams, D. P. (1996). Generativity and themes of agency and Communion in adult autobiography. *Personality and Social Psychology Bulletin, 22,* 721–731.

Marcia, J. (1980). Identity in adolescence. In J. Adelson (Ed.), *Handbook of adolescent psychology* (pp. 159–187). New York: John Wiley & Sons.

Markus, H., & Kitayama, S. (1991). Culture and the self: Implications for cognition, emotion, and motivation. *Psychological Review, 98,* 224–253.

Markus, H., & Nurius, P. (1986). Possible selves. *American Psychologist, 41,* 954–969.

Martin, P., Long, M. V., & Poon, L. W. (2002). Age changes and differences in personality traits and states of the old and very old. *Journal of Gerontology: Psychological Sciences, 57B,* P144–P152.

Martindale, C. (1980). Subselves: The interpersonal representation of situational and personal dispositions. In L. Wheeler (Ed.), *Review of personality and social psychology* (Vol. 1, pp. 193–218). Beverly Hills, CA: Sage.

Maslow, A. (1968). *Toward a psychology of being* (2nd ed.). New York: D. Van Nostrand.

McAdams, D. P. (1985). *Power, intimacy, and the life story: Personological inquiries into identity.* Homewood, IL: Dorsey Press.

McAdams, D. P. (1996). Personality, modernity, and the storied self: A contemporary framework for studying persons. *Psychological Inquiry, 7,* 295–321.

McAdams, D. P. (1998). Ego, trait, identity. In P. M. Westenberg, A. Blasi, & L. C. Cohn (Eds.), *Personality development: Theoretical, empirical, and clinical investigations of Loevinger's conception of ego development* (pp. 27–38). Hillsdale, NJ: Erlbaum.

McAdams, D. P. (2006a). *The redemptive self: Stories Americans live by.* New York: Oxford University Press.

McAdams, D. P. (2006b). The problem of narrative coherence. *Journal of Constructivist Psychology, 19,* 109–125.

McAdams, D. P. (2008). Personal narratives and the life story. In O. P. John, R. W. Robins, & L. A. Pervin (Eds.), *Handbook of personality: Theory and research* (3rd ed., pp. 242–262). Washington, DC: American Psychological Association Press.

McAdams, D. P., & Adler, J. (2006). How does personality develop? In D. K. Mroczek & T. Little (Eds.), *Handbook of personality development* (pp. 469–492). Mahwah, NJ: Erlbaum.

McAdams, D. P., Bauer, J. J., Sakaeda, A. M., Anyidoho, N. A., Machado, M. A., Magrino, K., White, K. W., & Pals, J. L. (2006). Continuity and change in the life story: A longitudinal study of autobiographical memories in emerging adulthood. *Journal of Personality, 74,* 1371–1400.

McAdams, D. P., & Bowman, P. (2001). Turning points in life: Redemption and contamination. In D. P. McAdams, R. Josselson, & A. Lieblich (Eds.), *Turns in the road: Narrative studies of lives in transition* (pp. 3–34). Washington, DC: American Psychological Association Press.

McAdams, D. P., de St. Aubin, E., & Logan, R. L. (1993). Generativity among young, midlife, and older adults. *Psychology and Aging, 8,* 221–230.

McAdams, D. P., Diamond, A., de St. Aubin, E., & Mansfield, E. D. (1997). Stories of commitment: The psychosocial construction of generative lives. *Journal of Personality and Social Psychology, 72,* 678–694.

McAdams, D. P., Josselson, R., & Lieblich, A. (Eds.). (2006). *Identity and story: Creating self in narrative.* Washington, DC: American Psychological Association Press.

McAdams, D. P., & Pals, J. L. (2006). A new Big Five: Fundamental principles for an integrative science of personality. *American Psychologist, 61,* 204–217.

McAdams, D. P., Reynolds, J., Lewis, M., Patten, A., & Bowman, P. J. (2001). When bad things turn good and good things turn bad: Sequences of redemption and contamination in life narrative, and their relation to psychosocial adaptation in midlife adults and in students. *Personality and Social Psychology Bulletin, 27,* 472–483.

McClelland, D. C. (1985). *Human motivation.* Glenwood, IL: Scott Foresman.

McColgan, G., Valentine, J., & Downs, M. (2000). Concluding narratives of a career with dementia: Accounts of Iris Murdock at her death. *Ageing and Society, 20,* 97–109.

McCrae, R. R., & Costa, P. T., Jr. (1988). Age, personality, and the spontaneous self-concept. *Journal of Gerontology: Social Sciences, 43,* S177–S185.

McCrae, R. R., & Costa, P. T., Jr. (1997). Personality trait structure as a human universal. *American Psychologist, 52,* 509–516.

McCrae, R. R., Costa, P. T., Jr., de Lima, M. P., Simoes, A., Ostendorf, F., Angleitner, A., et al. (1999). Age differences in personality across the adult life span: Parallels in five cultures. *Developmental Psychology, 35,* 466–477.

McLean, K. C. (2005). Late adolescent identity development: Narrative meaning making and memory telling. *Developmental Psychology, 41,* 683–691.

McLean, K. C., Pasupathi, M., & Pals, J. L. (2007). Selves creating stories creating selves: A process model of self-development. *Personality and Social Psychology Review, 11,* 262–278.

McLean, K. C., & Pratt, M. W. (2006). Life's little (and big) lessons: Identity statuses and meaning-making in the turning point narratives of emerging adults. *Developmental Psychology, 42,* 714–722.

McLean, K. C., & Thorne, A. (2003). Late adolescents' self-defining memories about relationships. *Developmental Psychology, 39,* 635–645.

Mead, G. H. (1934). *Mind, self, and society.* Chicago: University of Chicago Press.

Mikulincer, M., & Shaver, P. (2007). *Attachment in adulthood: Structure, dynamics, and change.* New York: Guilford Press.

Mischel, W., Shoda, Y., & Peake, P. K. (1988). The nature of adolescent competencies predicted by preschool delay of gratification. *Journal of Personality and Social Psychology, 54,* 687–696.

Molden, D. C., & Dweck, C. S. (2006). Finding "meaning" in psychology: A lay theories approach to self-regulation, social perception, and social development. *American Psychologist, 61,* 192–203.

Murray, H. A. (1938). *Explorations in personality.* New York: Oxford University Press.

Nelson, K. (1996). *Language in cognitive development: The emergence of the mediated mind.* New York: Cambridge University Press.

Ogilvie, D. M. (1987). The undesired self: A neglected variable in personality research. *Journal of Personality and Social Psychology, 52,* 379–385.

Ogilvie, D. M., Rose, K. M., & Heppen, J. B. (2001). A comparison of personal project motives in three age groups. *Basic and Applied Social Psychology, 23,* 207–215.

Oyserman, D., Coon, H. M., & Kemmelmeier, M. (2002). Rethinking individualism and collectivism: Evaluation of theoretical assumptions and meta-analysis. *Psychological Bulletin, 128,* 3–72.

Pals, J. L. (2006a). Authoring a second chance in life: Emotion and transformational processing within narrative identity. *Research in Human Development, 3,* 101–120.

Pals, J. L. (2006b). Narrative identity processing of difficult life events: Pathways of personality development and positive self-transformation in adulthood. *Journal of Personality, 74,* 1079–1109.

Palys, T. S., & Little, B. R. (1983). Perceived life satisfaction and the organization of personal project systems. *Journal of Personality and Social Psychology, 44,* 1221–1230.

Pasupathi, M. (2006). Silk from sows' ears: Collaborative construction of everyday selves in everyday stories. In D. P. McAdams, R. Josselson, & A. Lieblich (Eds.), *Identity and story: Creating self in narrative* (pp. 129–150). Washington, DC: American Psychological Association Press.

Pasupathi, M., & Mansour, E. (2006). Adult age differences in autobiographical reasoning in narratives. *Developmental Psychology, 42,* 798–808.

Paulhus, D. L., & Trapnell, P. D. (2008). Self-presentation of personality: An agency-communion framework. In O. P. John, R. W. Robins, &

L. A. Pervin (Eds.), *Handbook of personality: Theory and research* (3rd ed., pp. 492–517). New York: Guilford Press.

Pellicano, E. (2007). Links between theory of mind and executive function in young children with autism: Clues to developmental primacy. *Developmental Psychology, 43,* 974–990.

Pennebaker, J. W., & Stone, L. D. (2003). Words of wisdom: Language use over the life span. *Journal of Personality and Social Psychology, 85,* 291–301.

Perner, J., & Ruffman, T. (1995). Episodic memory or autonoetic consciousness: Developmental evidence and a theory of childhood amnesia. *Journal of Experimental Child Psychology, 59,* 516–548.

Perry, W. C. (1970). *Forms of intellectual and ethical development in the college years.* New York: Holt, Rinehart and Winston.

Peterson, B. E., & Duncan, L. E. (2007). Midlife women's generativity and authoritarianism: Marriage, motherhood, and 10 years of aging. *Psychology and Aging, 22,* 411–419.

Piaget, J. (1952). *The origins of intelligence in children.* New York: International Universities Press.

Polkinghorne, D. (1988). *Narrative knowing and the human sciences.* Albany: State University of New York Press.

Povinelli, D. J. (2001). The self: Elevated in consciousness and extended in time. In C. Moore & K. Lemmon (Eds.), *The self in time: Developmental perspectives* (pp. 75–95). Mahwah, NJ: Erlbaum.

Rafaeli-Mor, E., & Steinberg, J. (2002). Self-complexity and well-being: A research synthesis. *Personality and Social Psychology Review, 6,* 31–58.

Raggatt, P. T. F. (2006). Multiplicity and conflict in the dialogical self: A life-narrative approach. In D. P. McAdams, R. Josselson, and A. Lieblich (Eds.), *Identity and story: Creating self in narrative* (pp. 15–35). Washington, DC: American Psychological Association Press.

Ramirez-Esparza, N., Gosling, S., Benet-Martinez, V., Potter, J. P., & Pennebaker, J. (2006). Do bilinguals have two personalities? A special case of cultural frame switching. *Journal of Research in Personality, 40,* 99–120.

Reese, E. (2002). Social factors in the development of autobiographical memory: The state of the art. *Social Development, 11,* 124–142.

Reese, E., & Farrant, K. (2003). Social origins of reminiscing. In R. Fivush & C. A. Haden (Eds.), *Autobiographical memory and the construction of a narrative self* (pp. 29–48). Mahwah, NJ: Erlbaum.

Ricoeur, P. (1984). *Time and narrative* (Vol. 1; K. McGlaughlin and D. Pellauer, Trans.). Chicago: University of Chicago Press.

Riediger, M., & Freund, A. M. (2004). Interference and facilitation among personal goals: Differential associations with subjective well-being and goal pursuit. *Personality and Social Psychology Bulletin, 30,* 1511–1523.

Riediger, M., & Freund, A. M. (2006). Focusing and restricting: Two aspects of motivational selectivity in adulthood. *Psychology and Aging, 21,* 173–185.

Roberts, B. W., & DelVecchio, W. F. (2000). The rank-order consistency of personality traits from childhood to old age. *Psychological Bulletin, 126,* 3–25.

Roberts, B. W., O'Donnell, M., & Robins, R. W. (2004). Goal and personality trait development in emerging adulthood. *Journal of Personality and Social Psychology, 87,* 541–550.

Roberts, B. W., & Pomerantz, E. M. (2004). On traits, situations, and their integration: A developmental perspective. *Personality and Social Psychology Review, 8,* 402–416.

Roberts, B. W., & Robins, R. W. (2000). Broad dispositions, broad aspirations: The intersection of personality traits and major life goals. *Personality and Social Psychology Bulletin, 26,* 1284–1296.

Roberts, B. W., Walton, K. E., & Viechtbauer, W. (2006). Patterns of mean-level change in personality traits across the life course: A meta-analysis of longitudinal studies. *Psychological Bulletin, 132,* 1–25.

Roberts, B. W., Wood, D., & Caspi, A. (2008). The development of personality traits in adulthood. In O. P. John, R. W. Robins, & L. A. Pervin (Eds.), *Handbook of personality: Theory and research* (3rd ed., pp. 375–398). New York: Guilford Press.

Robins, R. W., Tracy, J. L., & Trzesniewski, K. H. (2008). Naturalizing the self. In O. P. John, R. W. Robins, & L. A. Pervin (Eds.), *Handbook of personality: Theory and research* (3rd ed., pp. 421–447). New York: Guilford Press.

Robins, R. W., Trzesniewski, K. H., Gosling, S. D., Tracy, J. L., & Potter, J. (2002). Global self-esteem across the life span. *Psychology and Aging, 17,* 423–434.

Rochat, P. (2003). Five levels of self-awareness as they unfold early in life. *Consciousness and Cognition, 12,* 717–731.

Rochat, P., & Hespos, S. J. (1997). Differential rooting response by neonates: Evidence for an early sense of self. *Early Development and Parenting, 6,* 150.1–150.8.

Rochat, P., Querido, J., & Striano, T. (1999). Emerging sensitivity to the timing and structure of protoconversations in early infancy. *Developmental Psychology, 35,* 950–957.

Rogers, C. R. (1951). *Client-centered therapy.* Boston: Houghton-Mifflin.

Rosenwald, G. C., & Ochberg, R. L. (Eds.). (1992). *Storied lives: The cultural politics of self-understanding.* New Haven, CT: Yale University Press.

Rossi, A. (Ed.). (2001). *Caring and doing for others.* Chicago: University of Chicago Press.

Ryan, R. M., & Deci, E. L. (2006). Self-regulation and the problem of human autonomy: Does psychology need choice, self-determination, and will? *Journal of Personality, 74,* 1557–1585.

Saarni, C. (2006). Emotion regulation and personality development in childhood. In D. K. Mroczek & T. D. Little (Eds.), *Handbook of personality development* (pp. 245–262). Mahwah, NJ: Erlbaum.

Sacks, O. (1995, January 9). Prodigies. *The New Yorker,* pp. 44–65.

Sarbin, T. (Ed.). (1986). *Narrative psychology: The storied nature of human conduct.* New York: Praeger.

Saucier, G., & Simonds, J. (2006). The structure of personality and temperament. In D. K. Mroczek & T. D. Little (Eds.), *Handbook of personality development* (pp. 109–128). Mahwah, NJ: Erlbaum.

Schiebe, S., Freund, A. M., & Baltes, P. B. (2007). Toward a developmental psychology of *Sehnsucht* (life longings): The optimal (utopian) life. *Developmental Psychology, 43,* 778–795.

Sedikides, C. (1993). Assessment, enhancement, and verification determinants of the self-evaluation process. *Journal of Personality and Social Psychology, 65,* 317–338.

Seligman, M. E. P. (1975). *Helplessness: On depression, development, and death.* San Francisco: Freeman.

Selman, R. L. (1980). *The growth of interpersonal understanding.* New York: Academic Press.

Serrano, J. P., Latorre, J. M., Gatz, M., & Montanes, J. (2004). Life review therapy using autobiographical retrieval practice for older adults with depressive symptomatology. *Psychology and Aging, 19,* 272–277.

Sheldon, K. M., & Kasser, T. (1998). Pursuing personal goals: Skills enable progress, but not all progress is beneficial. *Personality and Social Psychology Bulletin, 24,* 1319–1331.

Shotter, J., & Gergen, K. J. (Eds.). (1989). *Texts of identity.* London: Sage.

Shweder, R. A., & Much, N. C. (1987). Determinants of meaning: Discourse and moral socialization. In W. M. Kurtines &

J. L. Gerwitz (Eds.), *Moral development through social interaction* (pp. 197–244). New York: John Wiley & Sons.

Singer, J. A. (2004). Narrative identity and meaning-making across the adult lifespan: An introduction. *Journal of Personality, 72,* 437–459.

Singer, J. A., Rexhaj, B., & Baddeley, J. (2007). Older, wiser, and happier? Comparing Older adults' and college students' self-defining memories. *Memory, 15,* 886–898.

Singer, J. A., & Salovey, P. (1993). *The remembered self.* New York: Free Press.

Skinner, B. F. (1971). *Beyond freedom and dignity.* New York: Alfred A. Knopf.

Srivastava, S., John, O. P., Gosling, S. D., & Potter, J. (2003). Development of personality in early and middle adulthood: Set like plaster or persistent change? *Developmental Psychology, 84,* 1041–1053.

Sroufe, L. A. (1996). *Emotional development.* Cambridge, England: Cambridge University Press.

Sroufe, L. A., & Waters, E. (1977). Attachment as an organizational construct. *Child Development, 48,* 1184–1199.

Stern, D. N. (1985). *The interpersonal world of the infant.* New York: Basic Books.

Stewart, A. J., & Healy, M. J., Jr. (1989). Linking individual development and social changes. *American Psychologist, 44,* 30–42.

Stewart, A. J., & Vandewater, E. A. (1999). "If I had it to do over again . . .": Midlife review, midcourse corrections, and women's well-being in midlife. *Journal of Personality and Social Psychology, 76,* 270–283.

Swann, W. B. (1985). The self as architect of social reality. In B. R. Schlenker (Ed.), *The self and social life* (pp. 100–125). New York: McGraw-Hill.

Tajfel, H., & Turner, J. C. (1979). An integrative theory of intergroup conflict. In W. J. Austin & S. Worchel (Eds.), *The social psychology of intergroup relations* (pp. 33–48). Monterey, CA: Brooks-Cole.

Tangney, J. P., Stuewig, J., & Mashek, D. J. (2007). Moral emotions and moral behavior. In S. Fiske & D. Schacter (Eds.), *Annual review of psychology* (Vol. 58, pp. 345–372). Palo Alto, CA: Annual Reviews.

Taylor, C. (1989). *Sources of the self: The making of the modern identity.* Cambridge, MA: Harvard University Press.

Taylor, S. E. (1991). Asymmetrical effects of positive and negative events: The mobilization-minimization hypothesis. *Psychological Bulletin, 110,* 67–85.

Taylor, S. E., & Brown, J. D. (1988). Illusion and well-being: A social psychological perspective on mental health. *Psychological Bulletin, 103,* 193–210.

Tesser, A. (1988). Toward a self-evaluation maintenance model of social behavior. In L. Berkowitz (Ed.), *Advances in experimental social psychology* (Vol. 21, pp. 181–227). San Diego, CA: Academic Press.

Thompson, R. A. (1998). Early socio-personality development. In W. Damon & N. Eisenberg (Eds.), *Handbook of child psychology: Vol. 3. Social, emotional, and personality development* (5th ed., pp. 25–104). New York: John Wiley & Sons.

Thorne, A. (2000). Personal memory telling and personality development. *Personality and Social Psychology Review, 4,* 45–56.

Tomasello, M. (2000). Culture and cognitive development. *Current Directions in Psychological Science, 2,* 37–40.

Tomkins, S. S. (1987). Script theory. In J. Aronoff, A. I. Rabin, & R. A. Zucker (Eds.), *The emergence of personality* (pp. 147–216). New York: Springer Publishing Company.

Twenge, J. M., & Crocker, J. (2002). Race and self-esteem: Meta-analyses comparing Whites, Blacks, Asians, and American Indians and comment on Gray-Little and Hafdahl (2000). *Psychological Bulletin, 128,* 371–408.

Walls, T. A., & Kollat, S. H. (2006). Agency to agentic personalities: The early to middle childhood gap. In D. K. Mroczek & T. D. Little (Eds.), *Handbook of personality development* (pp. 231–244). Mahwah, NJ: Erlbaum.

Wang, Q. (2001). Culture effects on adults' earliest recollections and self-descriptions: Implications for the relation between memory and the self. *Journal of Personality and Social Psychology, 81,* 220–233.

Wang, Q. (2006). Earliest recollections of self and others in European American and Taiwanese young adults. *Psychological Science, 17,* 708–714.

Wang, Q., & Conway, M. A. (2004). The stories we keep: Autobiographical memory in American and Chinese middle-aged adults. *Journal of Personality, 72,* 911–938.

Wellman, H. M. (1993). Early understanding of mind: The normal case. In S. Baron-Cohen, H. Tager-Flusberg, & D. J. Cohen (Eds.), *Understanding other minds: Perspectives from autism* (pp. 10–39). New York: Oxford University Press.

White, R. W. (1959). Motivation reconsidered: The concept of competence. *Psychological Review, 66,* 297–333.

Wrosch, C., Heckhausen, J., & Lachman, M. E. (2006). Goal management across adulthood and old age: The adaptive value of primary and secondary control. In D. K. Mroczek & T. D. Little (Eds.), *Handbook of personality development* (pp. 399–421). Mahwah, NJ: Erlbuam.

Wyer, R. S., Jr., & Srull, T. K. (1989). *Memory and cognition in social context.* Hillsdale, NJ: Erlbaum.

CHAPTER 7

Temperament and Personality through the Life Span

JOHN E. BATES, ALICE C. SCHERMERHORN, and JACKSON A. GOODNIGHT

Thousands of words describe personality differences (Goldberg, 1993), suggesting that distinctions among patterns of behavior are a major interest of society. Many of the words used for making personality distinctions, along with their underlying concepts, have been used for a very long time. Moreover, such distinctions have long been addressed from a philosophical perspective. The familiar four humors typology—sanguine, choleric, phlegmatic, and melancholic—has its roots in ancient Greek and Roman thought (Kagan & Fox, 2006; Rothbart & Bates, 2006). The four humors, blood, yellow bile, phlegm, and black bile, are mixed, or tempered to varying degrees, and thus, we have the concept of temperament. During the final stage of the 2008 campaign for the U.S. presidency, a cover of *Time Magazine* asked the question, "Does Temperament Matter?" In previous presidential elections, personality dimensions had been widely considered. During the 2008 campaign, however, perhaps because it was marked by fairly widespread perception of crisis, news articles about the candidates frequently mentioned the concept of temperament. Because temperament is regarded as the core part of personality, *Time*'s temperament question implies a resurgence of interest in the most core parts of personality, the bedrock on which one might predict performance in many possible circumstances.

The authors of this chapter believe that temperament does matter, and this chapter tries to explain how it matters. We ask how the concept of temperament should be defined, how it is related to and different from the concept of personality, how temperament and personality traits develop, how they remain stable, and how they change. The chapter also asks how temperament and personality are related to social adaptations. This is consistent with the large part of temperament research that focuses on differences in social adaptation, including psychopathology. Many researchers have the goal that temperament and personality research will provide ways to improve interventions (Bates, 1989b; Chess & Thomas, 1984; McClowry, 2003). The authors of this chapter do try to apply temperament concepts, in an experimental way, in clinical work with families with oppositional children. One recent case illustrates some of the temperament issues to be addressed in this chapter:

In the first weeks of a family's work with us we learned that Heather was a 4-year-old girl who was highly oppositional to her parents. She often failed to comply with their demands until they became harsh with her. She frequently engaged in tantrums, which sometimes involved her crying for 45 minutes or longer. She went to sleep quickly when put to bed, but often woke up extremely early. Heather's parents clearly cared about her and took their parenting roles seriously. At the same time, they were often resentful of Heather. They found her domineering attitude repellant, and they felt that they were often walking on eggshells, trying to avoid her coercive screaming. When she was playing on her own, they would often avoid interacting with her. When she demanded holding, they often provided it in a passive or ambivalent way. They loved Heather, but they found very little joy in her. They were intelligent and educated people. Even before coming to our clinic, the parents had consulted with professionals and read parenting literature. Unfortunately, however, they did not show much evidence of successfully using information and professional support in ways that worked to improve their daughter's behavior. In the first part of our work with the family, the parents tried new techniques in a grudging or desultory way, found little satisfaction in successes, and quickly became discouraged.

This case could be seen in terms of conventional categories of psychopathology in the child and the parents, as well as in terms of conventional theories, including dynamic (e.g., parental rejection) and behavioral (e.g., coercive family process) models. However, in the specific context of this chapter, what is interesting about this case is that the temperament of the child has particular implications for the behavior patterns of the parents and the ecology of the family. And the temperament and personality characteristics of the parents also raise questions. Heather had a notable streak of dominance. This is an aspect of positive emotionality—Heather liked to produce attention and action from her parents and others—her expressions were often positive when she had people following her directives. She did not like to surrender much control to her parents. She often experienced and expressed frustration in control struggles with her parents. These are aspects of the broad dimensions of positive emotionality and dysregulation. Another dimension was also salient in Heather: She had a tendency to experience distress easily and perhaps anxiety as well, both forms of negative emotionality. In her tantrums, her frustrated anger appeared to merge into a more general distress. The parents were not only high in negative emotionality but also deficient in self-regulation, particularly effortful control of attention. Most striking, and most challenging for treatment, was their low level of positive emotionality traits. Can core personality or temperament traits change? Under what circumstances? Can they remain in place but have less pernicious impact on the development of the child and development of the parents? How? Research on temperament and personality traits, their changes over development, and their interactions with stressors and environmental characteristics may shed some light on these questions.

CONCEPTS

Temperament

Basic Definition

The term *temperament* is most often used as a summary term for biologically based individual differences in reactivity and self-regulation (Rothbart & Bates, 2006; Zentner & Bates, 2008). The most fundamental biological basis is genetic, and current research is showing how specific dimensions of temperament are related to specific genes and the neurotransmitters they produce, such as a disposition to be impulsive being related to genes affecting dopamine signaling (Forbes et al., 2009). Biological models of temperament also refer to brain organization, and current research is also showing how temperament is related to the morphology and activity of brain regions, such as relatively high activity in the right frontal regions being associated with a disposition to experience high levels of negative affect (Davidson, Ekman, Saron, Senulis, & Friesen, 1990). The term temperament is applied to traits that appear relatively early in development. However, it is important to note that these traits' appearance depends on development. For example, in the domain of negative emotionality, early differences on a rather global dimension of negative emotionality appear in early infancy (Rothbart & Bates, 2006), but with neural and psychological development, in later infancy, negative emotion becomes differentiated into fear and anger, and ratings of distinct fear and anger dispositions become more feasible. An even more striking example of development is in the domain of self-regulation via effortful control, which requires neural and psychological developments that are especially notable in the second year (Rothbart & Bates, 2006). Therefore, individual differences in effortful control are not meaningfully assessed, typically, until after age 18 months. The term temperament also refers to a core personality (Zuckerman, 1991) that is relatively stable. Stability is most evident from age 3 years (Lemery, Goldsmith, Klinnert, & Mrazek, 1999), but even then, it is not perfectly stable. Evidently, there may be change in temperament variables, at least at the level they are measured. It may be useful to think of temperament as a concept that has multiple levels (Bates, 1989a). At the most basic level, the genetic basis of temperament, high levels of stability would be expected, although it is possible for genetic aspects of temperament to change, especially when one considers that a gene's activity is a function of its chemical environment, which is a product of the actions of other genes and the person's ongoing experience. At an intermediate level, temperament's basis in the brain's organization and action, less stability would be expected than at the genetic level, but there still would be considerable stability. Neural organization and function change with development and environmental circumstances, but these systems are still rather conservative. At the top level, the patterns of behavior that comprise temperament, one would expect even more changeability. Not only are there frequent opportunities to learn from the consequences of behavior, but there are also cognitive and social controls on behavior. For example, a child with the genetic and neural dispositions to be fearful in novel situations might come to construe many ostensibly novel situations as safe, and thus the behavioral index of inhibition would change. Later, we more explicitly consider processes that might explain change in temperament and personality.

Specific Constructs

The general concept of temperament can be a useful rubric (Goldsmith & Reiser-Danner, 1986), but the main usefulness is in specific trait constructs under that rubric. We describe two main foundations for the constructs: recognition of patterns of behavior and advances in description of neural systems.

First, we consider the "pattern recognition" foundation. In work that stimulated much of the modern interest in temperament, especially in developmental science, Thomas and Chess and their colleagues (Thomas, Chess, Birch, Hertzig, & Korn, 1963) studied detailed notes on the behaviors of a sample of infants, described by parents, followed across development. With the help of their clinical skills, Thomas et al. derived nine dimensions of behavioral differences between the infants (Rothbart & Bates, 2006; Thomas et al., 1963). Thomas, Chess, and Birch (1968) combined five of these in their concept of "difficult temperament," low rhythmicity (of daily cycles), low adaptability, predominantly negative mood, high intensity of emotional reactions, and low distractability (from negative moods). Subsequently, researchers used the patterns detected by Thomas et al. and other early temperament researchers to derive more precisely defined trait dimensions. On the basis of a large amount of research using parent-report questionnaires, the most general, broad factors of temperament in childhood are negative emotionality, surgency or extraversion, high-intensity pleasure, effortful control or self-regulation, and, relatively recently identified, the concept of agreeableness or adaptability (Rothbart & Bates, 2006). We discuss subdimensions of these broad constructs as they become relevant later. Although these dimensions are similar to those found in infancy, they are understandably more differentiated from one another than those of infancy.

The second foundation for specific constructs of temperament is knowledge about neural systems (Rothbart & Bates, 2006). Neural models both converge with and enrich the factor-based models of behavioral traits. For example, to consider reactive aspects of temperament, brain research has shown that the irritability and fear components of the broad negative emotionality construct are related to different neural systems. In Gray's (1991) highly influential model, irritability is associated with a brain system for processing information about potentially rewarding stimuli, leading to approach or reward-seeking behavior and to frustration when blocked, associated with a system for responding to unconditioned punishments and nonrewards. Fear is associated with another system that processes information about potentially punishing or nonrewarding stimuli, leading to inhibition. To consider self-regulatory aspects of temperament, Rothbart's model of effortful control, based on the brain's executive attention system (Rothbart, Derryberry, & Posner, 1994; Rothbart & Bates, 2006), has been seminal. In addition, there are neural models for agreeableness–manageability traits, involving brain opiates and the neuropeptide oxytocin (see Rothbart & Bates, 2006). In these and other neural models of temperament, individual differences in the activity, density, and connectivity of neurons in the relevant brain structures would be associated with temperamental differences in these domains.

Measurement

This chapter is not the place to consider measurement issues in detail. However, because what we know depends on how we know it, we do need to make a few points about how temperament is operationally defined. It is useful to bear in mind the nature of measures in evaluating the theoretical meaning of findings. This chapter emphasizes the constructs and organizing principles that we find most clear, but ultimately, we recognize that the empirical meanings of measures are not necessarily the same as these constructs and organizing principles. Humans are highly complex, and temperament is simply a tool for organizing this complexity. As we mentioned, we define temperament at multiple levels, so any single measure cannot fully capture the nature of the individual. Moreover, each of the main approaches to measuring temperament—caregiver and self-reports on questionnaires and structured laboratory observations, both of behavior and psychophysiology—has demonstrated considerable validity but also many shortcomings (Kagan & Fox, 2006; Rothbart & Bates, 2006). Questionnaires can inexpensively sample from many behavior settings, including ones that are infrequent and hard to observe directly, and they have repeatedly demonstrated modest to moderate levels of convergence across reporters and with observational measures. However, they also have potential inaccuracies because of the inability to recall or see the relevant behaviors and because of various kinds of response bias. Observational measures, now typically involving structured situations, have high degrees of objectivity but may fail to capture behavior in highly diagnostic but rare situations, may be too brief to provide a reliable sample of behavior, may be of questionable relevance to natural behavioral ecology, and are expensive. See Rothbart and Bates (2006) for other strengths and concerns of various kinds of measure. So, although each kind of measure provides useful information, for example, in which the temperament measure predicts socially relevant outcomes in development to at least a moderate degree, it is perhaps ideal, where feasible, to have multiple measures (Kagan & Fox, 2006; Ozer & Benet-Martinez, 2006; Rothbart & Bates, 2006).

The most important property of a measure is its validity, that is, the ways in which the measure converges with other relevant measures and diverges from irrelevant measures. Validity is often thought of as how well a tool measures what it is supposed to measure, but we tend to think of validity as an emergent truth. Validity is a tool for evaluating both the meaning of the measure itself and the network of constructs that comprise theory. This property shifts dynamically as research proceeds and theory develops. We think of validity as an open-ended, complex, and provisional property of a measure. We try to keep in mind the qualities of measures that are the source of any conclusions emerging from research, while making some assumptions that allow a sense of progress in understanding. In other words, we try to be aware of the forest, not merely the trees.

Personality

Basic Definition

Personality is a broader construct than temperament, at least for most who write about it. It includes, in addition to the constitutionally based core components we call temperament, many specific aspects of how people come to think about themselves and others and organize their adaptations to the world (Caspi, 1998; Rothbart & Bates, 2006). McAdams and Pals (2006) described a hierarchy of three levels of traits: At the most basic level, there are dispositional traits, which include the typically considered personality dimensions, such as extraversion, and which McAdams and Pals describe as a sort of framework for the personality. At the next level are characteristic adaptations, which include cognitive and motivational patterns that derive in some ways from the more basic dispositional traits but that, more important, derive from transactions with the social environment. Examples include attachment security, social goals, and defense mechanisms. We would also place in this category social information processing characteristics (Crick & Dodge, 1994), such as biases to attribute hostile intent in ambiguous social conflict situations and characteristic ways of evaluating possible responses (Fontaine, Yang, Dodge, Bates, & Pettit, 2008). At the final level, there are integrative life narratives, which are stories that one uses to imbue one's life with meaning.

Although we believe that the McAdams and Pals approach to defining personality is heuristic (and recommend the McAdams et al. chapter in this volume), in our chapter, we take another approach—the dimensional taxonomy approach—which appears more compatible with our strong interest in temperament concepts and more parsimonious for the purpose of considering the developmental questions of the present chapter. Dimensional taxonomies, such as the Big Three or Big Five models, use factor analysis to summarize larger numbers of personality dimensions. The most standard Big Three model includes negative emotionality, positive emotionality, and constraint (Tellegen, 1985; Watson & Clark, 1992). These correspond roughly to the major dimensions of temperament, as discussed earlier. The most standard Big Five model includes neuroticism, extraversion, agreeableness, conscientiousness, and openness to experience (McCrae & Costa, 1999). As with the Big Three list of personality constructs, the Big Five list also resembles that of the most general temperament factors mentioned earlier. The Big Three and Big Five dimensional structures have had enormous impact on the field of personality, providing a coherent framework for summarizing the thousands of possible descriptors of individual differences in attitudes, cognitions, and behavior, and providing conceptual linkages between the myriad operational measures used in research. We chose to employ this dimensional framework in this chapter not only because it has become the most widely used in the literature but also because it would be convenient for comparison of studies describing developmental continuity and change. This is especially true for charting how early temperament characteristics transform, over development, into personality characteristics (Caspi, 1998; Rothbart & Bates, 2006). We considered the possibility that we would be omitting some important aspects of personality in the McAdams and Pals (2006) scheme—such as social cognitive variables (e.g., one's bias to interpret another's ambiguous behaviors as hostile) or life narratives. However, as we reflected further on these ostensibly non–Big-Five-type personality characteristics, we thought it likely that such characteristics will themselves eventually be summarized in Big Five–type language.

Specific Constructs

The foundations for the Big Three and Big Five constructs are essentially the same as for temperament constructs—initially, observation of many individual behavior traits, followed by factor analysis, and increasingly, by collation of dimensions of behavior with neural structures and processes. Given the substantial convergence between personality factors and temperament factors (Caspi & Shiner, 2006), this is not surprising. Moreover, just as temperament, especially in the form of behavioral phenotypes, can change as a result of development, personality is also regarded as somewhat responsive to developmental forces. Because the Big Three is subsumed, essentially, in the Big Five, we summarize the specific constructs in the Big Five. *Extraversion* involves social outgoingness, high activity, enthusiastic interest, and assertive tendencies. At the negative end of the dimension, descriptors include socially withdrawn and constricted. This dimension relates to the temperament construct of positive emotionality. *Neuroticism* involves negative affect tendencies, especially fear, worry, and irritability. At the opposite pole are poised and self-confident traits. This dimension relates to the temperament notion of negative emotionality. *Agreeableness* involves trusting, cooperative, helpful, caring behaviors and attitudes toward others. Someone at the negative end of the dimension is seen as "difficult" in the most common sense of the term—unhelpful, oppositional, and stingy. *Conscientiousness* involves tendencies to be responsible, task-oriented, and planful. Someone at the negative pole tends to be irresponsible, inattentive, and impulsive. This dimension relates to the effortful self-regulation component we discussed under temperament. Finally, *Openness* refers to how apparent one's intellect is and how open one is to experience, ranging from curious, self-aware, and explorative to intellectually and esthetically disinterested and uncreative. This last trait seems less easily mapped onto the core temperament dimensions than the others. Perhaps it springs more from one's upbringing than other traits do. Perhaps it also has to do with some distinctly non-temperament-like cognitive functioning abilities. However, some characteristics measured in infancy and very early childhood, such as Rothbart's concept of low-intensity pleasure, may prove to converge with Openness (Rothbart & Bates, 2006).

Measurement

The points we made about measurement of temperament apply to measurement of personality, at least personality as we are using the concept here. In the past, there was considerable dispute about whether it was meaningful to speak of personality traits as existing in individuals at all as opposed to being essentially an artifact of situational pressures, but it was eventually established, through the convergence of reports of knowledgeable informants, such as self and friends, that personality traits do exist (Kenrick & Funder, 1988). In principle, self- or other-rated personality traits could be measured in structured or naturalistic laboratory tasks, just as temperament traits sometimes are. However, in practice, there has been little interest in developing observational measures of personality. Personality research seems to have a more fundamental acceptance of questionnaire measures. Nevertheless, the questions we raised earlier with regard to temperament measures would also apply to personality questionnaires. We think of the personality constructs at multiple levels—genetic, psychophysiological, and behavior patterns—in the same way we think of temperament constructs. Ultimately, it might be of value to have measures that combine multiple perspectives and levels, just as has been often recommended for the measurement of temperament.

Environmental Contexts for Temperament and Personality

Behavior has meaning only with respect to environmental circumstances. For example, a fearful response to a novel situation would mean something different as an index of temperament or personality than would a fearful response to a previously encountered situation. Conversely, one would not expect individual differences in the trait of behavioral inhibition to be evidenced to the same degree in familiar situations as in novel situations. This is why all constructs of temperament and personality consider psychological and behavioral events in relation to environmental contexts. Sometimes the environmental contexts are specified in great detail, as in structured tasks to measure temperament in the laboratory; sometimes more generally, as in typical questionnaire measures of temperament or personality in which a context is loosely described; and sometimes merely implied, as in adjective checklist measures of personality.

Despite the vital importance of environmental context to the understanding of behavior and individual differences in behavior, however, there has been relatively little systematization of constructs of the environment (Little, Snyder, & Wehmeyer, 2006; Magnusson & Stattin, 2006). Developmental science has indeed described many qualities of the environment, in many different contexts, especially in terms of caregiver and teacher–child interactions and peer interactions but also in terms of stressors and affordances. Noted developmental scientists have offered some conceptual systems of the wider range of environmental contexts (Bronfenbrenner & Morris, 1998; Lerner & Kaufman, 1985; Sampson, Raudenbush, & Earls, 1997; Wachs, 2000), pointing out how one context of the environment, such as parenting, is functionally embedded in other contexts, such as neighborhood. Nevertheless, we have not seen a systematization of context that even begins to approach the empirical and theoretical systematization of temperament and personality. As Little et al. (2006) expressed it,

> Current theoretical models that outline the levels of contextual influence . . . have slid to the periphery of mainstream inquiry, even though few would consider contextual influences to be unimportant. . . . [T]he most likely explanation [of this neglect] is that the methodological and statistical analyses required to model the contextual influences on development are rather daunting in their complexity. (p. 75)

The current chapter aims to keep environmental contexts in mind, of course. However, a major task for future research is to organize constructs of context for the sake of theoretical comparisons among the many concepts and measures of the environment.

Developmental Contexts for Behavioral Individuality

One particularly relevant aspect of the complexity of environment concepts is that environmental contexts differ at different stages of development. For example, it is only after the infant's brain has physically developed to the point at which familiar and unfamiliar social objects can be readily distinguished that individual differences in responses to strangers would have theoretical importance. The myriad transactions between the person's developing competencies and emerging changes in demands and affordances of the environment would influence not only the meanings of individual differences in behavior, but also, quite likely, the ways in which behavioral phenotypes are related to core personality traits. We would expect that dynamically emerging, developmental, person–environment transaction processes affect the expression, continuity, and change of personality traits, just as they do cognitive and motor abilities (Adolph, 2008; Thelen & Smith, 2006). From an *organizational* perspective (e.g., Sroufe, 1979), social development involves a succession of life tasks, such as acquiring basic bonds to other people, skills for regulating attention and behavior, and understanding of others' viewpoints, as well as skills for working in cooperative groups, competing, and pair bonding. We assume that the development of a social behavior involves some kind of active "exercise," which would include basic and advanced forms of learning and the attendant creation of and pruning of neural pathways, just as in acquisition of perceptual, motor, and cognitive skills. Development of individual differences in such behaviors would involve individuality in the particular "exercise" and learning that occur.

As development proceeds, there are normative changes in the settings and affordances for acquiring and strengthening social skills and individual differences in the skills. For example, a 4-year-old might, because he or she has or can now easily learn the basic self-regulation and social–relationship skills, be placed in a new, relatively structured, group with peers and teachers. This presents the child with some types of opportunities and stressors that he or she might seldom see in the family. The child's developmental changes in the external context are accompanied by changes in the child's internal context. For example, the child who has language has a useful tool for regulating emotional responses, for example, by self-cueing a redirection of attention away from an attractive but forbidden object—"Just think about other things for awhile"—or whatever way they have learned the formula from their parents and siblings. Children with more advanced language are more likely to show more well-regulated responses. Such developmental considerations lead us not to expect simple correspondences between personality traits at one stage and a later stage. We do expect some forms of continuity, however, based on the power of learned habits and the ability of people to select and shape their environments (Caspi, 1998). Nevertheless, we also expect some discontinuities, based on the reorganization possibilities accompanying the external and internal changes that constitute development. To some extent, the discontinuities should be lawful (Sroufe, 1979), such as when a neglectful or highly stressful environment is ameliorated, and a child's levels of emotional reactivity become less pronounced.

CONSISTENCY AND CHANGE IN TEMPERAMENT AND PERSONALITY

Concepts of Consistency and Change

Our conceptualizations of change have been influenced considerably by theories of development. To help bridge the gap between developmental and personality perspectives, we draw connections between developmental terminology and terms in the personality literature when possible.

One major conceptualization of change involves change within an individual—comparing the individual to himself or herself over time. Baltes and Nesselroade (1979) referred to change conceptualized this way as *intraindividual change*. For example, returning to the case of Heather, we might compare Heather's level of negative affect right now with her level of negative affect when she was a toddler. In the personality literature, this type of change is typically referred to as *mean-level* or *normative* change (or its opposite, *absolute continuity*; Caspi & Roberts, 2001), referring to normative, developmental change in the average level of a characteristic in the population (Caspi & Shiner, 2006; Roberts, Walton, & Veichtbauer, 2006). Because both intraindividual and mean-level change refer to change within individuals or samples without consideration of variation between individuals, both intraindividual change and mean-level change refer to the valence and magnitude of typical or normative change. However, they differ from one another statistically. Intraindividual change is typically calculated using growth curve modeling to compare each individual's scores across three or more time points, and then identifying the average change in the sample. In contrast, mean-level change has historically been calculated using repeated measures analysis of variance, although recent work has used growth curve modeling to examine average change (Caspi & Roberts, 1999).

A contrasting conceptualization of change focuses on individual differences—differences between people. This conceptualization extends to differences between individuals in patterns of change, referred to by Baltes and Nesselroade (1979) as *interindividual patterns of intraindividual change*. This type of change is referred to in the personality literature as *differential continuity* (Caspi & Shiner, 2006) and as *rank-order consistency* (Roberts et al., 2006). This conceptualization of change involves comparing people with each other, and examining how differences between people change over time. For example, Heather may have more negative affect than her peers now, but that may change over time; perhaps, with help from her parents, she may have less negative emotionality—down the road she could even have less negative affect than the average child. In this chapter, we refer to mean-level or intraindividual change as *discontinuity*, interindividual differences in change as *instability*, and we use the terms *change* and *consistency* in a general way to refer to either comparisons within individuals or comparisons between individuals.

Rutter (1984) distinguished between various forms of continuity. *Absolute invariance* is a complete absence of change; for example, after the cognitive skill of object permanence is attained, the child does not lose it. In terms of temperament and personality development, this form of consistency—for example, engaging in a temper tantrum in the exact same way with the same frequency over the entire life course—is rare, partly because environmental provocations and demands change over the life course, and partly because of improved coping with the environment as a function of maturation. However, we may see consistencies in behavior over time, even if not absolute constancy. Consistent with this idea, Rutter (1984) described continuity in the underlying structure but not necessarily in the surface representations of that structure, and the corresponding term in the personality literature is *personality coherence* (Caspi & Shiner, 2006). An important further distinction is made in the personality literature between homotypic continuity, or consistency in phenotypic attributes over time, and heterotypic continuity, or consistency in the genotypic attribute underlying differing phenotypic behaviors (Kagan & Moss, 1962). Returning to our example of Heather, if she stops having temper tantrums but grows up to be an adult who angrily criticizes others on a daily basis, that would reflect coherence in her personality. She would be showing consistency in frequently experiencing and expressing negative emotions; in both cases using her negative emotions to try to influence others' behavior.

Ipsative stability, or *ipsative continuity* in the personality literature (Caspi & Roberts, 2001; Caspi & Shiner, 2006), is a persistent pattern or configuration of characteristics within an individual (Rutter, 1984). An example of ipsative stability would be if Heather remains high in extraversion and negative affectivity (or neuroticism) and also low in effortful control (or conscientiousness) from preschool age to adulthood. A consistent pattern or configuration of characteristics at the group-level is known in the personality literature as *structural continuity*, referring to consistency in the interrelationships among personality characteristics in the population (Caspi & Roberts, 2001).

Consideration of time scale is important in concepts of consistency and change. Change occurs in "real time" (moment-by-moment) processes, "developmental time" (long periods of time), and intermediate time scales. Processes unfolding in one time scale may influence processes unfolding in another time scale (Thelen, 1995). Much of the empirical literature has focused on relatively long time scales. One notable exception is Lewis's (2002) distinction between emotions and cognitions at a micro level, moods at a meso level, and personality at a macro level. Relatedly, Walls and Kollat (2006) described development of agency over short time scales and development of agentic personality characteristics over moderately long time scales. Mroczek and Almeida (2004) examined daily stress and negative affect among adults ranging in age from 25 to 74 years. For older adults, the association between stress and negative affect was stronger than for younger adults, particularly for older adults high in neuroticism. We would like to see more studies like these. By examining dynamic phenomena involving reactivity and regulation over varying time scales, these research designs offer a glimpse into the development of the patterns of individual differences we term temperament and personality.

In the next section, we discuss and try to reconcile differing views regarding the extent to which temperament and personality change, and we review the empirical literature on this question, as well as on typical developmental patterns of change in temperament and personality. We then turn to another form of continuity, one that Rutter (1984) identified: predictable patterns of associations between experiences at one phase of development and change in temperament and personality at a later point in development. We then review the empirical literature on such patterns of association, such as temperament × environment interactions producing personality development.

THE LITERATURE ON CONSISTENCY AND CHANGE IN TEMPERAMENT AND PERSONALITY

Conceptual Considerations

The degree to which temperament and personality show consistency versus change has been the subject of considerable debate. Some perspectives have emphasized consistency as a central feature of temperament and personality, whereas others explicitly accommodate change and development in temperament and personality. Reviewing the empirical literature, Caspi and Roberts (2001, p. 62) argued that "when pitted against one another, the forces of consistency outweigh the forces of change, and with time and experience the battle between change and consistency is won out by the forces of continuity." Although they acknowledged the contributions of the environment to personality change, they suggested that, through increasing age and accumulated experience, people learn to interact with the environment in ways that make their personalities more consistent.

In contrast, because of low interrater agreement, and on the basis of low consistency of behavior from one context to another, Lewis (2001) argued that there is little evidence of consistency in personality. Notably, the inference of low consistency was based largely on ratings of child depression, rather than ratings of temperament or personality, and several studies have found moderate levels of consistency in ratings of temperament and personality (see McCrae, 2001, for a review). In any case, Lewis (2001) explained what he described as limited consistency of behavior across time, observer, and context as being due to interactions between the individual and the environment. Thus, he argued that consistency in temperament and personality are present to the extent that consistency is present in the context. This is a notion that we can more readily endorse. Similarly, some have suggested that consistency emerges when the context provides the necessary stimulus to elicit the expected (trait-consistent) response (Shiner, Tellegen, & Masten, 2001). We suspect that consistency depends partly on the context but also partly on the individual, including the individual's efforts to select environments (niche picking; Scarr & McCartney, 1983) that contribute to greater consistency because they actively elicit or, at the very least, do not challenge the individual's typical behavior patterns. Moreover, we would argue that studies showing that some children appear distressed by contexts that are only mildly threatening (Buss, Davidson, Kalin,

& Goldsmith, 2004) highlight the degree of consistency of temperament across contexts. That is, comparing an individual's behavior in a given context to behavior norms in that context reveals striking trait-related consistencies (Paunonen, 2001).

Rothbart and Ahadi (1994) suggested that, to understand consistency and change, perspectives on temperament and personality development should emphasize the interrelatedness of the parts (e.g., neurological, behavioral) of an individual, with traits being part of the organization of the whole individual. Rothbart and Ahadi also argued that such perspectives must recognize the dynamic, continuous nature of development, as the individual reacts and adapts to the environment—a process that involves reciprocal relationships between the individual and the environment. Such perspectives must evaluate similarities and dissimilarities in an individual's behavior at different ages and in different contexts with an eye to how the behavior functions within the overall organization of the individual (Rothbart & Ahadi, 1994).

There is considerable evidence that personality change is possible at any point in the life span, but there is some debate regarding just how much personality develops beyond age 30. Caspi and Roberts (2001) argued that personality change does not end by early adulthood, but personality does become increasingly consistent across the life span, with personality change leveling off around age 50. McCrae (2001) argued that even by age 30, personality is quite stable and that mean-level changes are modest. However, it has also been found, for most dimensions of personality, that studies examining relatively longer time periods have found more change (Roberts et al., 2006); in other words, individuals show more change in personality traits over longer periods of time than over shorter periods of time.

In the following subsections, we consider change and consistency in the major eras of development. We focus our discussion on the major, higher order dimensions of temperament and personality. Findings of studies investigating lower level dimensions are interesting as well, but they are also less consistent than for the higher order dimensions (see Caspi, Roberts, & Shiner, 2005, for a review). Patterns of change in these dimensions for each era of development are summarized in Table 7.1.

Continuity and Stability of Childhood Traits

Extraversion

There is considerable evidence of change in behaviors in the domain of extraversion in childhood. In young infants, normative rates of smiling increase between 2 and 4 months (Werner, 1985), vocalization increases around

Table 7.1 Change in the Big Five Dimensions of Temperament/Personality over the Life Span

Big Five Dimension	Childhood	Adolescence	Adulthood
Extraversion	Extraversion increases over first year, and decreases from early to middle childhood.	Social dominance increases and shyness decreases; other dimensions of extraversion, and extraversion as a whole, do not change.	Some mixed findings, but overall extraversion decreases over the course of adulthood, particularly beginning in the early 20s.
Negative emotionality and neuroticism	Negative emotionality decreases.	Findings are mixed; some studies suggest neuroticism does not change, and others suggest it decreases. There is also some evidence that neuroticism may increase in young adolescent girls prior to age 14.	Neuroticism decreases beginning in late adolescence/early adulthood, with some evidence of an increase in old age.
Agreeableness	—	Agreeableness shows relatively little change during adolescence.	Agreeableness increases across adulthood.
Effortful control and conscientiousness	Effortful control increases.	Conscientiousness mainly appears to decrease, but there is some evidence of no change, and a little evidence of an increase.	Conscientiousness increases across adulthood.
Openness	—	Openness primarily increases, but there is some evidence of no change or even decreases.	Openness increases in early adulthood, and decreases in later adulthood.

3 to 4 months (Bradley, 1985; Rothbart, 1986), and positive affect continues to increase across the first year of life (Rothbart, 1981, 1986). Interestingly, though, some infants who are highly approaching at age 5 or 6 months become much more inhibited in their approach to stimuli around the end of the first year (Rothbart, 1988; Schaffer, 1974). These findings suggest that individual differences in extraversion may not mean the same in early infancy as those after inhibition in the presence of novelty develops around the end of the first year of life. After the emergence of behavioral inhibition, individual differences in extraversion and inhibition show consistency over time (Kagan & Snidman, 1991).

Although activity level does not show stability from the newborn period to age 3–4 months, it does show stability from age 4 weeks to later points (Birns, Barten, & Bridger, 1969). Activity level has been found to be linked to both positive and negative emotional reactivity; in newborns, activity level is often associated with negative affect (Escalona, 1968; Korner, Hutchinson, Koperski, Kraemer, & Schneider, 1981), but later in infancy, it is often associated with positive affect (Kistiakovskaia, 1965; Wolff, 1965). However, newborn nondistress motor activity predicted high activity and approach at ages 4 to 8 years (Korner et al., 1985), and at 4 months of age, activity co-occurring with negative affect predicted later behavioral inhibition (Fox, Henderson, Rubin, Calkins, & Schmidt, 2001; Kagan, 1998), whereas activity co-occurring with positive affect predicted later uninhibited behavior (Calkins & Fox, 1994; Fox et al., 2001). In other research, stability of activity level was not found using actometer measures from 7 to 36 months, but monozygotic twins were more similar in their activity levels and in their changes in activity over this period compared with dizygotic twins (Saudino & Eaton, 1995), suggesting that some consistency may be present and may be due to genetic factors.

Lemery et al. (1999) compared two statistical models of stability in positive emotionality and activity level during infancy and toddlerhood. One of the models, an autoregressive model, posits that the level of a trait at one point in time influences the level of that trait at the next time point; high levels of a trait at one time point have no association with the levels of that trait at a later time point, except through the intermediate time points. This model suggests progressive, developmental change from one time point to the next, with, for example, levels of the trait at Time 2 fully mediating associations between those at Time 1 and Time 3. The other model, a common factor model, posits that there is a core, underlying trait that is measured (imperfectly) at each time point (the measurements from each of the time points all load on the common factor, and their factor loadings are roughly equal); any apparent changes in the trait are actually the result of measurement error, rather than true developmental change. In this model, measurements at each time point are associated with one another only through the common factor. Lemery and her colleagues found that the autoregressive model fit well for positive emotionality and for activity level during infancy (3–18 months), but the common factor model fit well for activity level in toddlerhood (24–48 months; positive emotionality was not assessed in toddlerhood). In addition, correlations between assessments of activity level at different time points were larger in toddlerhood than in infancy, even though the time points were spaced farther apart in toddlerhood. This pattern of findings suggests that activity level fluctuates considerably during infancy but becomes stable by toddlerhood.

There is also evidence of continuity of social inhibition from toddlerhood through age 7.5 years (Kagan, 1989). Children who had consistently been either inhibited or uninhibited in the laboratory in toddlerhood or early childhood were assessed again at age 7.5 years. Correlations with age 7.5 inhibition were quite strong (r = .67) for the children initially tested in toddlerhood and also fairly strong (r = .39) for the children initially tested in early childhood. In addition, three fourths of the children retained their earlier classifications. However, inhibition does appear to change somewhat. For example, some of the children in Kagan's study changed from earlier classifications as uninhibited to an age 7.5 classification as very inhibited. Furthermore, one study found that inhibition at 2 years shows relatively low levels of consistency across situations (Rubin, Hastings, Stewart, Henderson, & Chen, 1997). However, other work has found surprising consistency in inhibition; individuals who had been classified as inhibited at 4 to 6 years of age showed significantly more inhibition at 23 years of age than controls (Asendorpf, Denissen, & van Aken, 2008). Although children who had been undercontrollers (uninhibited) at age 4 increased in shyness by age 23 and children who had been overcontrollers (inhibited) at age 4 increased in aggression by age 23, those who had been overcontrollers as children remained more shy as adults than either undercontrollers or resilient (adaptive) participants (Dennissen, Asendorpf, & van Aken, 2008). Thus, there was some discontinuity at the intraindividual level, with members of both groups becoming less extreme. At the same time, individual differences appeared to remain fairly stable, even across a period of the life span in which rapid developmental change occurs in many domains.

Another set of studies considers continuity in an underlying "ease of evoking arousal" (Arcus, 2001, p. 46). Studies have examined associations between reactivity to stimuli in early infancy and later fearfulness or inhibition (shyness or timidity in new situations). In one study, 3-year-olds with the highest levels of inhibition were found to have been, at 1 year of age, both high in negative emotionality and low in positive emotionality (Park, Belsky, Putnam, & Crnic, 1997). In another study, 4-month-old infants showing less motoric and crying reactivity to stimuli showed less fearful responses to unfamiliar events at 14 months than those who had previously been classified as high reactive (Kagan & Snidman, 1991). In a separate sample of children, reactivity at 4 months was associated with fearfulness at 14 and 21 months of age (Arcus, 1994), and modest associations were found between reactivity at 4 months and inhibition at 4.5 years (Kagan, Snidman, & Arcus, 1998). It is interesting that responses early in infancy that are more outwardly noticeable (greater reactivity) are associated with diminished responses (social inhibition) later in infancy (Kagan, 1989). It may be the case that inhibited children become inhibited because they have stronger biological reactions to environmental stimuli. It is worth emphasizing, however, that the overall pattern of results does not indicate a particularly high level of continuity in behavior over this 4-year period. Kagan and his colleagues offered two possible explanations of these findings: One is that there are subgroups of children in the high and low reactive groups who would be expected to show continuity. Alternatively, it may be that experiences with the environment shape inhibition, leading to the observed findings of relatively modest continuity in inhibition. We return to these ideas in a later section when we discuss factors that promote temperament and personality development.

Overall, studies suggest extraversion, positive emotionality, and activity are fairly consistent by early to middle childhood. Meta-analysis of 152 longitudinal studies by Roberts and DelVecchio (2000) revealed moderate (statistically significant) levels of stability in approach and activity level during childhood (primarily before age 12). The study by Pedlow, Sanson, Prior, and Oberklaid (1993) provides an example of the overall pattern: Pedlow et al. found that approach was moderately stable from infancy to toddlerhood, and highly stable from toddlerhood to age 8 years. As another example, Asendorpf and van Aken (2003b) found consistency in extraversion from age 4–6 years to age 12 years.

Extending these findings to another aspect of extraversion, positive emotionality, Vaughan Sallquist et al. (2009) found stability in parent- and teacher-reported positive emotional intensity over a 6-year period that began between kindergarten and third grade and also found normative (mean-level) decline in positive emotional intensity. Interestingly, children who had higher initial levels of positive emotional intensity were concurrently rated by teachers as less socially skilled and showed a greater decline in their social skills compared with their peers.

Negative Emotionality

As with behaviors and traits in the extraversion domain, behaviors and traits in the negative emotionality domain, as well as their topography and regulation, also develop with age. For example, when 3- to 6-month-old infants who were distressed by a stimulus were presented with a soothing stimulus, their distress disappeared (Harman, Rothbart, & Posner, 1997). However, when the soothing stimulus was removed and the distressing stimulus reappeared, the infants returned to their previous levels of distress. Although the outward signs of distress had disappeared, the underlying distress apparently had not. Infants as young as 6 months of age can disengage their attention from distressing stimuli; at 13 months of age, disengagement of attention is associated with less concurrent negative affect (Rothbart, Ziaie, & O'Boyle, 1992). Considerable additional empirical work indicates a connection between regulation of attention and coping with distressing experiences (see Rothbart & Bates, 2006, for a review). Thus, there appear to be two control systems—an emotional reaction system and self-regulatory system—and the reactive system appears to develop earlier than the self-regulatory system (Rothbart & Bates, 2006).

As with the previously mentioned models of continuity in dimensions of extraversion, Lemery et al. (1999) found that for distress–anger and fear, the best-fitting model in infancy (3–18 months) was the autoregressive model, but the best-fitting model in toddlerhood (24–48 months) was the common factor model. Although other models tested by Lemery and colleagues suggested that stability in these dimensions of temperament results at least partly from continuity through the intermediate time points, the overall pattern of findings suggests that temperament stabilizes by the beginning of the toddler period.

Across studies, negative emotionality and neuroticism show stability in childhood (Roberts & DelVecchio, 2000). As examples, Pedlow et al. (1993) found high levels of stability in irritability from infancy through age 3 years, and Asendorpf and van Aken (2003b) found consistency in neuroticism from age 4–6 years to age 12 years. Negative emotional intensity also shows consistency for both parent and teacher reports across a 6-year period beginning in early elementary school (Vaughan Sallquist et al., 2009).

In addition, negative emotionality also shows change during early and middle childhood. Negative emotional intensity shows a significant mean-level decline from the period of early elementary age through the ensuing 6-year period (Vaughan Sallquist et al., 2009). Decreases in mean-level neuroticism have also been found over a 36-month period beginning at age 10–11 years (De Fruyt et al., 2006).

Agreeableness

As with extraversion and neuroticism, agreeableness also shows stability across studies (Roberts & DelVecchio, 2000). Pedlow et al. (1993) found high levels of stability in cooperativeness from infancy through age 3 years, and Asendorpf and van Aken (2003b) found stability in agreeableness from age 4–6 to age 12 years.

Effortful Control

There is evidence that executive attention begins to emerge toward the end of the first year (Kochanska, Murray, & Harlan, 2000). The development of effortful control appears to be associated with a child's executive ability to focus attention. Sustained attention increases from 12 to 18 months and increases further between 24 and 30 months (Krakow, Kopp, & Vaughn, 1981). Similarly, inhibitory control is considerably greater in 30-month-olds than in 18-month-olds (Krakow & Johnson, 1981), and other work suggests that individual differences in self-control become established during the second and third years of life (Vaughn, Kopp, & Krakow, 1984). Moreover, focused attention at 9 months predicts later effortful control; effortful control is related to anger regulation at 22 and 33 months and joy at 33 months (Kochanska et al., 2000). Regulation of anger and joy, as well as fear-related inhibition at 22 months, are associated with higher subsequent levels of effortful control (Kochanska & Knaack, 2003). Effortful control shows increasing stability from 22 to 45 months. Control over attentional shifting and inhibitory control also appears to increase over the period from age 4 to 12 years (Murphy, Eisenberg, Fabes, Shepard, & Guthrie, 1999).

Several studies have also found evidence of consistency in effortful control and conscientiousness in middle childhood. Roberts and DelVecchio's (2000) meta-analysis revealed moderate levels of stability in task persistence. Pedlow et al. (1993) found high levels of stability in task persistence from toddlerhood through age 8 years, and Asendorpf and van Aken (2003b) found consistency in conscientiousness from age 4–6 to age 12 years.

Other Dimensions

Several studies have found consistency in other dimensions of temperament and personality, including openness to experience, from age 4–6 to age 12 years (Asendorpf & van Aken, 2003b) and rhythmicity, threshold, and inflexibility, from infancy or toddlerhood to age 8 (Pedlow et al., 1993; Roberts & DelVecchio, 2000). Vaughan Sallquist et al. (2009) found stability in parent- and teacher-reported emotional expressivity (which could involve both positive and negative emotions). They also found a mean-level decline in emotional expressivity over a 6-year period, beginning around kindergarten to third grade, which suggests growth in self-regulation skills.

Person-Oriented Approaches

Person-centered approaches to personality allow examination of continuity and change in the overall configuration of personality attributes. One person-centered approach to the study of continuity in personality involves correlating individuals' Q-sorts of personality, cognitive, and social attributes over time. This approach revealed considerable continuity in the configuration of personality attributes across ages 3, 4, 7, 11, 14, and 18 years (Ozer & Gjerde, 1989). Correlating Q-sorts by teachers at ages 4 and 6 years and Q-sorts by mothers and teachers at ages 10 and 12 years in a Dutch sample, also revealed continuity (Asendorpf & Van Aken, 1991).

Children's scores for the particular configurations called resilience, overcontrol, and undercontrol demonstrated modest, but statistically significant, levels of continuity between the ages of 4–6 and 10 years (Asendorpf & Van Aken, 1999) and in early adulthood (Asendorpf, Borkenau, Ostendorf, & Van Aken, 2001). Similarly, consistency was found for children classified at age 3 years as undercontrolled, inhibited, well adjusted, confident, or reserved to behavior patterns at age 18 years (Caspi & Silva, 1995).

Interestingly, higher levels of resilience were associated with greater consistency in Q-sorts (Asendorpf & Van Aken's, 1991, 1999). These findings suggest that more desirable characteristics become reinforced over time by contingencies in the environment, such as positive responses from parents, teachers, and peers, whereas undesirable characteristics are discouraged, a pattern observed many years ago by Kohlberg, Lacrosse, and Ricks (1972). Although it seems likely that developmental processes would generally operate to increase desirable characteristics and decrease undesirable characteristics, Caspi and Silva (1995), however, found somewhat stronger evidence of consistency for undercontrolled and inhibited children than for the other classifications, including well-adjusted and confident classifications. We consider this a further reminder that the laws of psychology are not yet fully established.

Genetic and Environmental Contributions to Consistency and Change

Studies have examined genetic and environmental contributions to consistency and change during childhood in various temperament domains. Genetic factors have been found to contribute to consistency from age 14 to 20 months in a wide range of temperament dimensions, including behavioral inhibition, task orientation, emotionality, sociability, shyness, and negative mood; environmental factors have been found to contribute to continuity in shyness and positive emotionality (Plomin et al., 1993). Moreover, Plomin and his colleagues found that genetic factors contribute to change in activity level, positive mood, and negative emotionality, and environmental factors contribute to change in positive emotionality. In other research, from age 14 months to age 36 months, genetic contributions to empathy increased, and shared environmental contributions decreased (Knafo, Zahn-Waxler, Van Hulle, Robinson, & Rhee, 2008). Whereas genetic factors contributed to both consistency and change in empathy, the shared environment contributed primarily to consistency and the nonshared environment contributed primarily to change. This pattern of findings is fairly consistent across studies; more details on findings regarding genetic and environmental contributions to consistency and change in temperament are reviewed in Saudino (2005).

Summary

The literature reveals consistency in dimensions of temperament during childhood, but it also suggests an interesting pattern of development of temperament during childhood. Extraversion shows increases over the first year of life, followed by decreases from early to middle childhood. However, what appear to be increases in extraversion may simply be the appearance for the first time of social behaviors, which emerge as part of biological maturation. Negative emotionality decreases over childhood, which seems likely to have much to do with the complementary finding that effortful control increases in the same developmental era.

Continuity and Change in Adolescence

Extraversion

Overall, findings suggest that extraversion shows stability in adolescence, from age 12 to age 16 or 17 years (Asendorpf & Van Aken, 2003a; McCrae et al., 2002).

Findings on mean-level changes in extraversion are more mixed. Allik, Laidra, Realo, and Pullmann (2004) found no meaningful age differences in extraversion among 12- to 18-year-olds using cross-sectional data. McCrae et al. (2002) also reported no significant age differences in extraversion in cross-sectional samples of 14- to 18-year-olds and 12- to 18-year-olds.

However, pursuing this question further, Roberts et al. (2006) conducted a meta-analysis of mean-level change in personality traits beginning at age 10 years. They found that one dimension of extraversion, social dominance, increases from age 10 to 18 years—that is, individuals become more socially dominant over the course of adolescence. This was moderated by a cohort effect; cohorts born in 1940 or more recently showed greater increases in social dominance during adolescence than earlier cohorts. In contrast to the results from the meta-analysis, a recent longitudinal study across age 11 years to 17 years found intraindividual declines in extraversion (Branje, Van Lieshout, & Gerris, 2007). However, separate tests based on adolescent gender indicated that levels of extraversion decreased for boys and increased for girls. Ganiban, Saudino, Ulbricht, Neiderhiser, and Reiss (2008) found that shyness decreases from early to mid-adolescence, but activity level and sociability do not change significantly. A methodological strength of the Ganiban et al. study was the multi-informant (mother and father), repeated assessment of temperament. Thus, findings from various studies point to the need to consider specific facets of extraversion in looking for converging evidence across the empirical literature.

Neuroticism

Previous studies have also found stability in neuroticism during adolescence (Asendorpf & Van Aken, 2003a; McCrae et al., 2002), but they offer mixed findings regarding whether there is also significant change in neuroticism during adolescence. Using meta-analytic techniques, Roberts et al. (2006) found increases in emotional stability (the inverse of neuroticism) from age 10 to 18. Similarly, decreases in mean-level neuroticism have been found from age 12–13 to age 15–16 years (De Fruyt et al., 2006). Allik et al. (2004) found no meaningful age differences in neuroticism in their sample of 12- to 18-year-olds. However, a series of studies by McCrae and colleagues (2002), using three samples of adolescents, yielded different findings. In one sample, which consisted of adolescents from age 12 to age 16, McCrae et al. (2002) found increases in neuroticism for girls (but not for boys). However, in a separate cross-sectional sample of 14 to 18 year olds, McCrae and his colleagues (2002) found no significant age differences in neuroticism, although girls had higher levels of neuroticism than boys at age 14 only. In a third cross-sectional sample of adolescents ranging in age from 12 to 18 years, older girls had higher levels of neuroticism than younger girls, but there were no age differences for boys (McCrae et al., 2002). Together, McCrae and colleagues' findings suggest that neuroticism may increase in girls by mid-adolescence. Partially consistent with that, Ganiban et al. (2008) found increases in negative emotionality from early to mid-adolescence for their sample as a whole (controlling for both gender and the gender × age interaction). However, examining intraindividual change from age 11 to 17 years, Branje et al. (2007) found no change in neuroticism for either boys or girls. Given that Branje et al. examined change beginning at age 11, we would have expected to find increases in neuroticism for girls over the course of the study. Moreover, because Branje et al. used longitudinal data to examine within-person change, a stronger methodological approach, we can have more confidence in their findings, that is, of no change in neuroticism for either adolescent boys or girls. Thus, at this point, there is not converging evidence regarding gender-related differences in developmental change in neuroticism.

Agreeableness

Agreeableness shows stability during adolescence (Asendorpf & Van Aken, 2003a; McCrae et al., 2002). There is relatively little change in agreeableness during adolescence. Using three separate samples of adolescents (samples ranged from 12 to 18 years of age), McCrae et al. (2002) found no significant age differences in agreeableness, although girls showed significantly higher levels of agreeableness than boys. Across ages 11 to 17 years, Branje et al. (2007) found no intraindividual change in agreeableness for boys but intraindividual increases in agreeableness for girls. In contrast, Allik et al. (2004), however, found substantially lower levels of agreeableness among older adolescents compared with younger adolescents in their sample of 12- to 18-year-olds.

Conscientiousness

Research suggests conscientiousness is also stable during adolescence (Asendorpf & Van Aken, 2003a; McCrae et al., 2002). Mean-level changes do occur. In their longitudinal study, McCrae et al. (2002) found significant decreases in conscientiousness from age 12 to 16, but no significant change when boys' and girls' data were examined separately. This latter test split the sample roughly in half, reducing power to detect mean-level change. Moreover, Allik et al. (2004) found that levels of conscientiousness were significantly higher among younger adolescents than among older adolescents, in their sample of 12- to 18-year-olds. Similarly, De Fruyt et al. (2006) found decreases in mean-level conscientiousness from age 12–13 years to age 15–16 years. Decreases in conscientiousness during adolescence are somewhat surprising, considering the significant brain development and associated improvements in self-management. Perhaps expectations for self-management are increasing at a faster rate during this period than brain development, which might contribute to the appearance of decreases in conscientiousness. Another possibility is that opportunities and rewards for risk taking are increasing. Interestingly, in separate cross-sectional samples of 14- to 18-year-olds and 12- to 18-year-olds, no significant age differences in conscientiousness were found (McCrae et al., 2002). Across ages 11 to 17 years, Branje et al. (2007) found no intraindividual changes in conscientiousness for boys, but *increases* in conscientiousness for girls.

Openness to Experience

As with the other dimensions, openness to experience shows stability during adolescence (Asendorpf & van Aken, 2003a; McCrae et al., 2002). McCrae et al. (2002) found significant increases in average levels of openness to experience from age 12 to 16 for both boys and girls. Similarly, in a separate cross-sectional sample of 14- to 18-year-olds, McCrae et al. (2002) found that levels of openness were significantly higher for older adolescents than for younger adolescents and that girls had higher levels of openness, but boys appeared to increase more in openness than girls did. Note, however, that this inference is drawn from cross-sectional rather than longitudinal data, limiting conclusions to age differences, rather than age-related change. In a third cross-sectional sample (with ages ranging from 12 to 18 years), McCrae et al. (2002) found that older children had higher levels of openness than younger children, and this finding held for both boys and girls. However, although Branje et al. (2007) found intraindividual increases in openness for girls across ages 11 to 17 years, they found intraindividual decreases in openness for boys over this period. In addition, Allik et al. (2004) found no meaningful age differences in openness in their sample of 12- to 18-year-olds. However, De Fruyt et al. (2006) found decreases in mean-level imagination (related to openness) over a 36-month period beginning at age 12/13 years.

Person-Oriented Approaches

Examining changes in the constellation of personality traits during adolescence (ages 10–20 years), Akse, Hale, Engels, Raaijmakers, and Meeus (2007) found that the most common change was from undercontroller to overcontroller. In addition, changes in anxiety were associated with changes in personality; adolescents who changed from overcontrollers to resilients experienced a decrease in anxiety, whereas adolescents who changed from resilients to overcontrollers experienced an increase in anxiety.

Genetic and Environmental Contributions to Consistency and Change

Given the complex array of findings, one important question concerning temperament and personality in adolescence involves the degree to which consistency and change result from genetic or environmental influences (or both). Using a large sample of adolescent sibling pairs, Ganiban et al. (2008) found that both genetic and nonshared environmental factors contributed to variability in activity level, shyness, and sociability (all related to extraversion) and to variability in negative emotionality (related to neuroticism). Change in levels of these characteristics, which were reassessed approximately 2.5 years later, was explained by both genetic and nonshared environmental factors, but stability was explained primarily by genetic factors. In addition to this study, Gillespie, Evans, Wright, and Martin (2004) examined genetic contributions to change in the Big Five during adolescence. They found that genetic factors underlie changes between age 12 and age 16 years in psychoticism (low agreeableness and low conscientiousness), neuroticism, and extraversion, including some changes between ages 14 and 16. Notably, behavior genetic studies of change and consistency in temperament during adolescence are rare, so further investigation is needed.

Summary

All of the major dimensions of temperament and personality show stability during adolescence, but there are also complex changes during this era. The empirical literature also suggests that extraversion as a whole, and many of the facets of extraversion, do not change but that social dominance increases and shyness decreases during adolescence. Agreeableness appears not to change. Findings regarding neuroticism and negative emotionality are rather mixed, with some studies suggesting neuroticism does not change, and others suggesting it decreases. One finding that has received support from several studies is that neuroticism may increase in girls by early adolescence. Overall, conscientiousness appears to decrease and openness appears to increase, but findings are somewhat mixed for both of these dimensions. Mixed findings during adolescence may result partly from individual differences in rates of biological development during adolescence, as well as differing experiences in relationships with peers and family, a subject we return to in a later section.

Continuity and Change in Adulthood

Extraversion

There are modest to moderate levels of consistency in extraversion in adulthood. This includes findings of significant rank-order stability in extraversion from age 18 or 19 to age 21 or 22 (Robins, Fraley, Roberts, & Trzesniewski, 2001), and stability in extraversion, positive affect, and shyness (Vaidya, Gray, Haig, Mroczek, & Watson, 2008), stability in positive emotionality over a 10-year period, beginning around 20 years of age (McGue, Bacon, & Lykken, 1993), and considerable stability for both middle-aged and older adults over a 4-year period of observation (Allemand, Zimprich, & Hertzog, 2007), and across the period from 33 to 42 years of age (Rantanen, Metsapelto, Feldt, Pulkkinen, & Kokko, 2007).

In addition to indicating that extraversion shows consistency during adulthood, research fairly consistently suggests that extraversion decreases over the course of adulthood. However, the findings from some studies reveal a more nuanced picture of development in this trait. Terracciano, McCrae, Brant, and Costa (2005) found mean-level declines in extraversion across adulthood, including old age. After first establishing measurement invariance across ages 16 to 91 years, Allemand, Zimprich, and Hendriks (2008) also found older adults had lower levels of extraversion than did younger adults, consistent with the findings of Terracciano et al. Because measurement invariance was established, we can have greater confidence that this finding is indicative of true structural differences in extraversion, rather than being an artifact of measurement problems resulting from developmental changes. We would like to see more studies testing for measurement invariance. Interestingly, Allemand et al. (2007) found that although older participants were less extraverted than middle-aged participants, neither older nor middle-aged participant groups showed significant change in extraversion over the 4-year period of longitudinal follow-up (after establishing measurement invariance in the middle-aged and older adult groups). Nonconverging findings come from McGue et al. (1993), who found no significant mean-level change in positive emotionality during the 10 years beginning around age 20, and Rantanen et al. (2007), who found mean-level increases in extraversion for both men and women from ages 33 to 42. In addition, Carstensen, Pasupathi, Mayr, and Nesselroade (2000) found no age differences in the experience of positive affect, and Robins et al. (2001) found no mean-level change in extraversion from age 18 or 19 to age 21 or 22. Furthermore, Robins et al. found that personality traits showed a significant level of structural stability (i.e., consistency in the intercorrelations among the traits across people) and ipsative stability (i.e., the relative ordering of traits within an individual) across this age period, suggesting a high level of consistency in extraversion in early adulthood.

Nevertheless, more reports exist of decreases in extraversion. Cross-sectional tests of age differences suggest that extraversion declines beginning in mid- to late adolescence through age 50+ across samples from Germany, Italy, Portugal, Croatia, and South Korea (McCrae et al., 1999), the United Kingdom, Spain, Czechoslovakia, and Turkey (McCrae et al., 2000), as well as American, Russian, Japanese, and Estonian samples (Costa et al., 2000). We are struck by the consistency of this pattern across cultures. In a sample of older adults, aged 70 to 103 years, Staudinger, Freund, Linden, and Maas (1999) found no significant correlations between age and the frequency of experiencing any of 10 positive emotions; however, when the 10 positive emotions were averaged together, the average correlated negatively with age, suggesting fewer overall positive emotions with increasing age in this group of older adults.

Providing further clarification, Roberts et al. (2006; see also Roberts, Robins, Trzesniewski, & Caspi, 2003, for a related literature review) conducted a meta-analysis of levels of Big Five traits over the course of adulthood. They found that levels of one dimension of extraversion—social vitality—increase from age 18 to age 22, decrease from age 22 to age 30, then remain fairly steady until age 60, after which point they decrease further from age 60 to age 70. Another dimension of extraversion—social dominance—was found to continue its increase in adolescence, increasing from age 18 to age 22, 22 to 30, and 30 to 40. These increases were moderated by a cohort effect, with more recent-born cohorts showing greater increases in social dominance. A more recent study, using longitudinal data, found mean-level increases in extraversion from age 18 to 21, after which point it leveled off (Vaidya et al., 2008). In addition, mean levels of positive affect increased steadily, and shyness decreased from ages 18 to 21 before leveling off. Moreover, growth curve analyses revealed intraindividual increases in extraversion and positive affect (Vaidya et al., 2008).

Neuroticism

Robins et al. (2001) found rank-order stability in neuroticism across the period from age 18–19 to age 21–22, and McGue et al. (1993) found moderate levels of stability in negative emotionality over a 10-year period, beginning around 20 years of age. From ages 18 to 24 years, Vaidya et al. (2008) found moderate levels of stability in neuroticism; stabilities were greater from age 21 to age 24 than from age 18 to age 21. In addition, Rantanen et al. (2007) found high levels of stability in neuroticism across the period from 33 to 42 years of age. Measures of negative affect also show stability during early adulthood (Vaidya et al., 2008).

Roberts et al.'s (2006) meta-analysis revealed increases in emotional stability (decreases in neuroticism) from ages 18 to 22, 22 to 30, and 30 to 40, with some evidence of an increase from age 50 to age 60. In their literature review, Roberts, Robins, et al. (2003) similarly reported that most studies report an increase in or no change in emotional stability over the life span. Consistent with that, Terracciano et al. (2005) found mean-level declines in neuroticism across adulthood until age 80, but beginning around age 80, neuroticism showed mean-level increases. Consistent with this curvilinear pattern, Carstensen et al. (2000) found that the frequency of negative emotions declined from early adulthood (age 18 years) to around age 60, after which point change in negative emotions leveled off. Interestingly, they also found that emotional experience becomes more differentiated and complex with increasing age. For example, experiencing negative and positive emotions at the same time occurs more frequently among older adults. In contrast, in their sample of adults ages 70–103 years, Staudinger et al. (1999) found a negative correlation between specific negative emotions and age, suggesting a decline in the experience of negative emotion.

With regard to cross-cultural consistency of findings, levels of neuroticism decline from middle to late adolescence to age 50 in samples from Germany, Italy, Portugal, Croatia, and South Korea (McCrae et al., 1999), in samples from the United Kingdom, Spain, Czechoslovakia, and Turkey (McCrae et al., 2000), and in American and Japanese samples, but not in Russian or Estonian samples (Costa et al., 2000).

In more recent work, Allemand et al. (2008) found fluctuations in neuroticism across adulthood, but no consistently increasing or decreasing patterns of age-related differences in neuroticism. In contrast, Allemand et al. (2007) found that middle-aged participants showed less neuroticism than older participants and that both age groups showed declines in neuroticism across the 4-year period of observation. Vaidya et al. (2008) found intraindividual decreases in neuroticism and negative affect from age 18 to age 24. Rantanen et al. (2007) found mean-level decreases in neuroticism for both men and women during this period.

Agreeableness

Several studies have documented stability in agreeableness over portions of adulthood. For example, Vaidya et al. (2008) found significant levels of stability in agreeableness between ages 18 to 24 years, with greater stability found between ages 21 and 24 years than between 18 and 21 years. Compared with other Big Five traits, however, agreeableness demonstrates relatively lower levels of stability (Allemand et al., 2007). Rantanen et al. (2007) found high levels of stability in agreeableness across the period from 33 to 42 years of age. In a study of college students, Robins et al. (2001) found significant rank-order stability in agreeableness from age 18/19 to age 21/22.

In terms of patterns of developmental change, the Roberts et al. (2006) meta-analysis revealed that agreeableness increased across the age period from 50 to 60 years. Although significant change in agreeableness was not found in other discrete age periods during adulthood, the overall pattern was one of increasing agreeableness across the life span (Roberts et al., 2006; Roberts, Robins, et al., 2003). This increase in agreeableness was moderated by a cohort effect, with cohorts born before 1930 or after 1960 showing greater increases in agreeableness. Similarly, Vaidya et al. (2008) found mean-level increases in agreeableness from age 18 to age 24. Rantanen et al. (2007) found mean levels of agreeableness increased for both men and women from age 33 to 42, and women had higher levels of agreeableness than men at both time points. Terracciano et al. (2005) found mean-level increases in agreeableness across adulthood, from age 30 to age 90. Allemand et al. (2007) found that older participants were more agreeable than middle-aged participants, and middle-aged participants showed significant increases in agreeableness over the 4-year period of follow-through. Similarly, across ages 16 to 91 years, Allemand et al. (2008) found that levels of agreeableness were greater at older ages, although the oldest age group in their sample suggested a leveling off of this pattern.

Patterns suggesting higher agreeableness in older, compared with younger, adults from middle to late adolescence to age 50 years appear to generalize across samples from Germany, Italy, Portugal, Croatia, and South Korea (McCrae et al., 1999), samples from America, Russia, Japan, and Estonia (Costa et al., 2000), and samples from the United Kingdom and Spain, but there was less clear evidence of this in Czech and Turkish samples (McCrae et al., 2000).

Conscientiousness

Several studies have found considerable stability in conscientiousness as well. For example, Robins et al. (2001) found significant stability in conscientiousness from age 18–19 to age 21–22, and Vaidya et al. (2008) found moderate levels of stability in conscientiousness between ages 18 to 24 years. In addition, McGue et al. (1993) found moderate levels of stability in constraint over a 10-year period, beginning around age 20 years, and Rantanen et al. (2007) found high levels of stability in conscientiousness across the period from age 33 to 42 years.

Terracciano et al. (2005) found mean-level increases in conscientiousness from age 30 to about 70, after which point conscientiousness appears to stabilize and even shows slight declines. In their meta-analysis, Roberts et al. (2006) found that conscientiousness increased from ages 22–30, 30–40, 40–50, and 60–70. As with agreeableness, the increase in conscientiousness was moderated by a cohort effect, with cohorts born before 1930 or after 1960 showing greater increases in conscientiousness. A literature review by Roberts, Robins, et al. (2003) described a similar pattern of increasing conscientiousness, particularly during early adulthood.

Using cross-sectional data from samples ranging in age from mid-adolescence to over 50 years, conscientiousness was somewhat higher among older adults than among younger adults, and this pattern was consistent across American, Russian, Japanese, and Estonian samples (Costa et al., 2000); across samples from Germany, Italy,

Portugal, Croatia, and South Korea (McCrae et al., 1999); and across British, Spanish, Czech, and Turkish samples (McCrae et al., 2000).

More recently, in a sample of adults ages 16 to 91 years, Allemand et al. (2008) found that older adults had higher levels of conscientiousness than younger adults, but Allemand et al. (2007) found neither age-related differences in conscientiousness nor significant change in conscientiousness for either middle-aged or older participants. However, Vaidya et al. (2008) found conscientiousness increased steadily from age 18 to age 24, and Rantanen et al. (2007) found mean-level increases in conscientiousness for both men and women from 33 to 42 years of age.

Openness to Experience

Robins et al. (2001) found significant stability in openness from age 18–19 to age 21–22, and Vaidya et al. (2008) found considerable increasing stability in openness to experience from ages 18 to 24 years. Rantanen et al. (2007) found high levels of stability in openness across the period from 33 to 42 years of age.

In terms of developmental change in levels of openness to experience, Roberts et al. (2006) found increases in openness from age 18–22, and decreases from age 60–70. Roberts, Robins, et al. (2003) described more mixed findings in their literature review but described the overall pattern of change as one of increasing openness in early adulthood, followed by a leveling off. Across cultures, openness appears to be higher in younger than in older adults in samples from Germany, Italy, Portugal, Croatia, and South Korea (McCrae et al., 1999); the United States (although not statistically significant); Russia, Japan, and Estonia, (McCrae et al., 2000); and Spain, Czechoslovakia, and Turkey (McCrae et al., 2000). However, openness was not higher in younger adults than in older adults for samples from Britain or Germany (McCrae et al., 2000).

Furthermore, Terracciano et al. (2005) found mean-level declines in openness across adulthood, including old age. Allemand et al. (2008) also examined age differences in autonomy, which is somewhat similar to openness to experience. They found age-related, nonsignificant decreases in autonomy, although the decreases in the oldest age groups (beginning with age 60 years) did approach significance. Similarly, Allemand et al. (2007) found that older participants were less open than middle-aged participants, but neither group showed significant change in openness across the 4-year period of the study. Middle-aged participants showed more variability in openness than did older participants. Vaidya et al. (2008) found mean-level increases in openness from age 18 to age 21 and from age 21 to age 24, and Rantanen et al. (2007) found openness showed mean-level increases for both men and women during the period from 33 to 42 years of age, and women had higher levels of openness.

Person-Oriented Approaches

In a sample of older adults (average age at the beginning of the study was 78 years), measures of cognitive functioning, self and personality functioning (e.g., neuroticism, extraversion), and social integration at the beginning of the study were used to test for the presence of subgroups (Gerstorf, Smith, & Baltes, 2006). Three groups were found: (a) an overall positive profile, characterized by above-average functioning in all three domains; (b) an overall average profile, characterized by average functioning in all three domains; and (c) a high cognition, low self and personality functioning, low social integration profile. Membership in the groups showed continuity over time, with the majority of the sample remaining in the same group 6 years later. However, there was also change in group membership for a sizable proportion of the sample. Changes in group membership were associated with poorer health, older age, and steeper decreases in cognitive functioning and in self and personality functioning. Changes in group membership were also associated with greater likelihood of dying within 10 years of the beginning of the study. In addition, individuals who were in the overall positive group at the beginning of the study had higher levels of psychological well-being (e.g., life satisfaction) 6 years later and less likelihood of dying within 10 years, compared with the other groups.

Genetic and Environmental Contributions to Consistency and Change

In a sample of twins who were approximately 20 years of age at the first assessment, McGue et al. (1993) found that changes in positive emotionality, negative emotionality, and constraint over the ensuing 10 years were largely due to environmental factors, although genetic factors also contributed somewhat to change. Stability in all three dimensions of personality was explained primarily by genetic factors. Relatedly, Viken, Rose, Kaprio, and Koskenvuo (1994) found evidence of decreasing heritability, and increasing environmental effects, for both extraversion and neuroticism, from 18 through 59 years of age. For extraversion, whereas new environmental effects were found at various ages, genetic factors were primarily associated with the maintenance of individual differences. For neuroticism, both genetic and environmental factors contributed to both stability and change, including new genetic contributions to neuroticism even at 40 years of age, but the primary contribution of genetic factors was to stability rather than change. Genetic factors were the main source of stability in neuroticism for women, but genetic and environmental factors contributed about equally to stability in neuroticism for men. In early adulthood, genes appear to contribute primarily to consistency in traits related to both behavioral inhibition and behavioral approach, whereas the environment appears to contribute to both change and consistency (Takahashi et al., 2007).

Summary

The empirical literature documents significant consistency of personality during adulthood. Although findings regarding patterns of change are somewhat mixed, overall, extraversion decreases over the course of adulthood, particularly beginning in the early 20s. Neuroticism also decreases beginning in late adolescence or early adulthood, with some evidence of an increase in old age. In contrast, agreeableness and conscientiousness increase across adulthood. Additionally, openness to experience increases in early adulthood but decreases in later adulthood.

Consistency and Change across Age Periods

As noted earlier, person-oriented behavioral classifications of 3-year-olds as undercontrolled, inhibited, well adjusted, confident, or reserved are consistent with behavior at 18 years of age (Caspi & Silva, 1995). In a longitudinal study beginning at about age 6, Hampson and Goldberg (2006) found that personality traits showed less stability up to about age 11 than during adulthood (approximately 40 years later). Moreover, returning to our earlier discussion of conceptualizations of change and consistency, recent work indicates that associations among different dimensions of temperament do not change significantly from age 16 to age 91 years (Allemand et al., 2008), providing new evidence of structural continuity across the life span. A few studies have focused specifically on consistency of personality from adolescence to adulthood. Donnellan, Conger, and Burzette (2007) examined personality from approximately age 17 to age 27 and found that the average correlation for measures of the same trait across this period was .47, indicating a moderate level of consistency. This level of stability is comparable to the stability coefficients found within adolescence (e.g., McCrae et al., 2002; Asendorpf & Van Aken, 2003a). Donnellan et al. (2007) found a small decrease in positive emotionality, a large decrease in negative emotionality, a medium increase in constraint, and a medium decrease in absorption (which is related to openness to experience). The magnitudes of these changes are roughly comparable to those reported within early adulthood (Roberts et al., 2006). Similarly, Johnson, Hicks, McGue, and Iacono (2007; see also Blonigen, Carlson, Hicks, Krueger, & Iacono, 2008) examined personality from age 14 to 24 and found that alienation (high neuroticism and low agreeableness) and aggression (low agreeableness) decreased, whereas control (conscientiousness) and harm avoidance (avoidance of excitement and adventure) increased. Stress reaction (high neuroticism) increased somewhat from age 14 to age 17 and then returned to age-14 levels by 24 years of age. Well-being (low neuroticism and high extraversion) was quite stable, aside from a small decrease from ages 14 to 17. Thus, these studies suggest considerable change from adolescence to adulthood—Blonigen et al. (2008) found that 94% of their sample of 17- to 24-year-olds showed reliable change on at least one personality trait. In addition, Donnellan et al. (2007) found that although mean-level change in traditionalism was nonsignificant, there were considerable, opposing changes in traditionalism at the individual level. Approximately 25% of the sample increased in traditionalism and approximately 25% decreased, reflecting interindividual differences in intraindividual change.

Roberts and DelVecchio (2000) also used meta-analytic techniques to examine stability across childhood through adulthood age periods, in traits considered to reflect adult personality dimensions (i.e., the Big Five). They found moderate levels of stability in extraversion, agreeableness, conscientiousness, neuroticism, and openness to experience across the life span. Furthermore, they found that, across traits, stabilities increased from childhood to early adulthood, increasing further by age 30 years, and increasing further between ages 50 and 70 years, before leveling off. Across many studies reviewed here, personality change has been found to occur in middle age and into old age. The fact that there is change in personality into old age supports the life-span developmental perspective (Lerner, 2004). Baltes (1997) suggested that although change is possible throughout the life span, it is also limited.

Overall Patterns of Change over the Life Course

We would like to comment on some interesting patterns of change in temperament and personality over the life course. During childhood, while effortful control increases, extraversion decreases, as does negative emotional reactivity. Thus, one possibility is that initially higher levels of extraversion and negative emotional reactivity in infancy and early in childhood (or at least their outward expression) may be reined in by increasing self-regulatory abilities as children get older.

Neuroticism during adolescence shows a mixed pattern, so we will wait for further evidence. Agreeableness appears to be unchanging in adolescence, although individual differences in patterns of change may contribute to the appearance of constancy, if some individuals' increases offset other individuals' decreases. Extraversion does not change much, but adolescents do become more socially dominant and less shy. This coincides with, and might be related to, increases in openness and decreases in conscientiousness. That is, decreasing conscientiousness may contribute to more impulsive, socially outgoing behavior, which may in turn expose adolescents to new experiences and to people with differing viewpoints, which may increase openness to experience.

Agreeableness and conscientiousness increase during adulthood, perhaps prompted by increasing responsibilities related to work and family. At the same time, extraversion declines, especially from the early 20s—a point in the life span at which many people enter serious romantic relationships. Numerous biological and social developments could explain decreasing extraversion, such as the increased energy expended on raising children. Openness increases in early adulthood; perhaps exposure to more varied experiences—through college, new friends, work experiences—promotes openness. Around the same time, neuroticism decreases. One possible explanation for this decrease may be that increasingly stable romantic and occupational situations reduce external stressors that make negative emotionality salient. There is also some evidence of an increase in neuroticism in old age, which may result partly from the growing losses and stresses of this time of life. In addition, openness decreases in later adulthood. Consistent with this decrease, later adulthood may be a time of pruning back one's investments, rather than branching out (Baltes & Baltes, 1990; Carstensen, 1995), as we discuss in the next section.

FACTORS CONTRIBUTING TO TEMPERAMENT AND PERSONALITY DEVELOPMENT

Conceptual Considerations

Development occurs within a broad context. In our efforts to understand social development, we consider the interplay between multiple interacting factors—the individual's temperament or personality traits, characteristics of the broader environment, and aspects of developmental, familial, and historical time—and then seek to identify which of these things, in which combinations, produce which outcomes (Jelicic, Theokas, Phelps, & Lerner, 2007; Rothbart & Bates, 2006; Shiner, 1998). Wachs has articulated a highly influential model of the differential effects of the same environmental characteristic on children with different temperaments, or organismic specificity (Wachs & Gruen, 1982). We return to our example of Heather: Because she is both demanding and easily frustrated, she is more likely to experience interactions with her parents as anger-provoking than a more agreeable child might. Thus, temperament provides a filter through which the environment is experienced, and therefore contributes probabilistically to individual differences in development over the course of the life span. Although temperament and personality clearly have a basis in biology, they are not determined solely by genes (Wachs, 1994). Rather, probabilistic models of reciprocal influence between genes, other biological processes, the environment (including family, peers, broader contexts), and behavior also must be considered in a description of the course of temperament and personality development. An excellent discussion of genetic and environmental contributions to personality development can be found in Caspi and Shiner (2006).

Baltes and Baltes (1990) identified three processes that together make up an effective strategy of maximizing functionality over the course of development: selection, optimization, and compensation (SOC). *Selection* refers to identifying one's goals, committing to them, and limiting oneself to a smaller number of tasks or activities from among all of the available options; *optimization* refers to directing one's effort, energy, time, and other resources toward one's chosen goals; and *compensation* involves efforts directed at overcoming one's limitations or lack of resources (Baltes, 1997). Lerner, Freund, de Stefanis, and Habermas (2001) provided one example of the use of this SOC approach: They recommended consideration of what adolescents do in "identifying, organizing, and deciding to pursue goals" (p. 35, selection); "developing knowledge and skills to pursue goals and to recruit social and physical resources to facilitate reaching one's goals" (p. 36, optimization); and "developing the ability to deal with the diversity of outcomes that their actions will produce and, of special importance for adaptive functioning across adolescence and into the adult years, with failure" (p. 37, compensation). Carstensen provides another example: Her socioemotional selectivity theory suggests that, over the life course, individuals intentionally devote energy to the social relationships that maximize their social and emotional gains and minimize social and emotional risks (Carstensen, 1992). According to the theory, selectively reducing social contacts as one ages is adaptive (Carstensen, 1995). Empirical work indicates that frequency of interaction with acquaintances and close friends declines over the life course but that frequency of interaction with spouses and siblings increases, as does emotional closeness with relatives and close friends (Carstensen, 1992), and older adults' perceptions that time is limited appear to underlie these changes (Carstensen, Isaacowitz, & Charles, 1999). Older adults persist more at compensation tasks, whereas younger adults persist more at optimization tasks (Freund, 2006). Interestingly, when individuals perceive time to be limited, younger and older adults equally prioritize relationships that meet emotional needs (Carstensen et al., 1999).

In another approach to questions of how temperament and personality develop, Scarr and McCartney (1983) presented the notion of *niche picking*, or the individual's selection of environments that provide a good fit to the individual. Even in childhood, individuals select environments that will reinforce or exercise existing behavioral tendencies. For example, a child high on assertiveness and physical activity might engage in sports, which would increase the value and the strength of the assertiveness and activity traits. Scarr and McCartney (1983) also pointed out that children *evoke* particular responses from the environment because of their unique characteristics and behavior. For example, an irritable child might elicit more hostility, which in turn amplifies the tendency to be irritable. Others have endorsed and expanded on the Scarr and McCartney ideas. Shiner and Caspi (2003; Caspi & Shiner, 2006) identified *environmental construal*, the process by which temperament contributes to individual differences in children's interpretations of the environment, and *learning processes*, the influence of temperament on what and how children learn from reinforcement and punishment (see also Rothbart & Ahadi, 1994). Moreover, Shiner and Caspi pointed out that temperament influences how children act on their environments (*environmental manipulation*), children's choices of environments (*environmental selection*), the responses children elicit from others (*environmental elicitation*), and children's comparisons of themselves with others (*social and temporal comparisons*).

Some authors have concluded that there is little empirical evidence of environmental influence on personality (McCrae et al., 2000). In contrast, Roberts and his colleagues (Roberts & Wood, 2006; Roberts, Wood, & Smith, 2005) have emphasized the roles of several factors in contributing to consistency and change. They developed several principles to explain patterns of change and consistency. First, the *cumulative continuity principle* suggests that individuals increase in consistency for all personality traits as a typical part of the aging process, and that developing, committing to, and maintaining an identity, as well as committing to social roles, lead to increasing consistency (Roberts & Wood, 2006). Second, the *maturity principle* suggests that, in addition to this pattern of increasing consistency, age-related increases in social dominance, agreeableness, conscientiousness, emotional stability, openness to experience, and social vitality before late adulthood facilitate becoming more effective in close relationships and work, and becoming healthier (Roberts & Wood, 2006). Third, according to the *corresponsive principle*, life experiences serve to strengthen the very personality characteristics that draw people to those life experiences (Roberts & Wood, 2006). Roberts and Wood (2006) have also discussed factors that prevent personality from changing more than it does, such as individual difference characteristics that may buffer or enhance susceptibility to environmental influence (see also Fraley & Roberts, 2005, for a formal mathematical model of the processes driving consistency and change). In addition, Boyce and Ellis (2005; Ellis & Boyce 2008; Ellis, Essex, & Boyce, 2005) have suggested that there is a U-shaped relationship between the quality of the environment and children's development of biological sensitivity to context. That is, children in either high quality, supportive environments or stressful, adverse environments are more likely to be more reactive to the environment than children in more moderate environments. This is because reactivity enables children who are in high-quality environments to benefit more from those environments and enables children who are in adverse environments to protect themselves more from risk in those environments.

We believe that life experiences, especially interpersonal experiences, are important shapers of temperament and personality. Life experiences alter the connections between emotional reactions to events, conceptualizations of events, and strategies for coping with events (Rothbart & Bates, 2006). For example, children's exposures to arguments between their parents may shape their emotional reactions to and conceptual understandings of subsequent interparental conflict, as well as their choice of coping strategies (Davies & Cummings, 1994). In addition, the interconnections among children's emotional reactivity, conceptualizations, and coping strategies may be influenced by experiences with interparental conflict. Repeated exposure to hostile interparental conflict might cause strong emotional responses, which themselves might influence how children interpret conflict. For example, when hearing a disagreement between her parents, a child who is old enough might think to herself, "Mom and Dad are having a fight. I'm scared and sad. Maybe they'll get a divorce." Such an emotional–conceptual process might also influence selection of a coping strategy, perhaps causing the child to get involved in the conflict in some way, for example, to try to resolve the conflict directly or to draw attention to herself through misbehavior.

Empirical Findings of Factors in Change and Consistency

Next we discuss the empirical literature on factors that are associated with change and consistency in temperament and personality, such as relationships and workplace experiences.

Relationships

Among infants who were highly reactive at 4 months of age, the infants whose mothers were more responsive when they showed signs of distress and less firm in setting limits for behavior showed more inhibition in the laboratory at 14 months of age (Arcus, 2001). Arcus suggested that setting firm limits and responding less to distress signals may aid infants' development of self-regulatory skills. Similarly, in another study, parental supportiveness (high sensitivity and low intrusiveness) were associated with higher levels of inhibition at 3 years of age, especially for children with high levels of negativity in infancy (Park et al., 1997). Belsky, Hsieh, and Crnic (1998) also found that fathers' intrusive parenting was associated with lower levels of behavioral inhibition in toddlers who were rated as high in fear and frustration but was not associated in toddlers who were rated as low in fear and frustration. In another study, maternal oversolicitousness, or high levels of warmth and control coupled with insensitivity, was associated with higher levels of inhibition in 2-year-olds, particularly for children high in fearfulness (Rubin et al., 1997). Maternal oversolicitousness was operationalized in terms of intrusive control (cleaning up toys their child had been asked to clean up), unresponsiveness toward the child, physical affection and positive affect with the child, and attempts to assist the child at times when the child did not appear to need assistance. Thus, the findings of Rubin and colleagues seem at least partly counter to the findings from Arcus's and Park et al.'s studies. However, it is possible that the parenting pattern Rubin et al. described was overchallenging to children rather than optimally challenging (Rothbart & Bates, 2006). With the possible exception of Rubin et al.'s findings, then, there are suggestions that children who are high in negative emotionality and fearfulness may benefit from being at least moderately challenged by their parents, perhaps because well-managed exposure to stress helps such children to develop effective emotion-regulation skills (Arcus, 2001; Rothbart & Bates, 2006).

Crockenberg, Leerkes, and Lekka (2007) found a different pattern of relations in their examination of associations between marital aggression and infant withdrawal (disengagement from the environment), which is considered a maladaptive response to stress because it precludes learning from the environment. The positive association between marital aggression and withdrawal in 6-month-old infants was strongest for infants higher in temperamental distress to novelty—that is, infants whose mothers described them as more reactive to novel experiences. Crockenberg and her colleagues observed that infants high in distress to novelty were more likely to withdraw from the challenge of a novel stimulus if they showed a lot of physical activity when shown the novel stimulus but were less likely to withdraw if they looked away, presumably allowing themselves to regulate their levels of arousal (Crockenberg & Leerkes, 2004).

According to the dominant, transactional models of development, parenting might shape children's phenotypical temperament. However, few longitudinal, transactional studies have examined the influence of parenting on temperament (Bates & Pettit, 2007). In one exception, maternal inconsistent discipline during middle childhood was associated with subsequent increases in children's fearfulness and irritability (Lengua & Kovacs, 2005). However, another study found no influence of parenting at age 2 on temperament at age 4 (Rubin, Nelson, Hastings, & Asendorpf, 1999). Further study of the influence of parenting on temperament, using more sensitive measures and more powerful designs, is needed (Bates & Pettit, 2007). In addition to limitations due to cross-sectional designs, findings from previous studies (including longitudinal ones) could actually be due to some quality of the parents that is reflected in their parenting and in their child's temperament—perhaps passive gene–environment correlation or an active process of parent behavior shaping child behavior that operationally defines child temperament (Bates & Pettit, 2007).

During adolescence, in contrast, Big Five personality characteristics do influence relationships. However, relationships do not appear to predict significant change in Big Five personality characteristics over the course of adolescence (Asendorpf & Van Aken, 2003a). Specifically, conscientiousness predicted increases in paternal support and extraversion predicted increases in peer support, but neither kind of support predicted change in extraversion, emotional stability, agreeableness, conscientiousness, or culture (openness to experience).

A number of studies have examined the role of relationships in adults' personality development. Among a sample of newlyweds followed over a 2-year period, Watson and Humrichouse (2006) found that spouses had differing perceptions regarding each others' personality change. Whereas women's self-ratings revealed decreases in neuroticism and increases in agreeableness and conscientiousness and men's self-ratings revealed increases in conscientiousness, their spouses' ratings did not confirm these changes. In fact, husbands reported that their wives had decreased in extraversion, openness, and agreeableness and had not changed in neuroticism; wives reported that their husbands had decreased in agreeableness and conscientiousness. Interestingly, spouse-reported personality change was associated with change in marital satisfaction, but self-reported personality change was not. Declines in satisfaction are often observed in the first few years of marriage. It is interesting to speculate that these either stem from or cause negative perceptions of marital partners' personality. Moreover, these findings remind us of the limitations of using only self-report of personality.

Part of the answer regarding the timing of associations between personality and relationship quality comes from a longitudinal study by Clausen and Jones (1998) beginning in adolescence and continuing over the course of 40 years. The experience of divorce predicted less stability of personality Q-sorts in women (but not men). Relatedly, Sturaro, Denissen, Van Aken, and Asendorpf (2008) found that experiences in several kinds of close relationships at age 17 years were associated with change in personality over the ensuing 6-year period, but age 17 personality did not predict subsequent change in relationships. Conflict with parents or best friends was associated with decreases in emotional stability and extraversion, despite the general trend for increases in emotional stability and extraversion during this developmental era. Conflict with fathers was associated with particularly large personality changes (e.g., with negative effects on emotional stability and conscientiousness), even though there is a normative trend toward less contact with parents in early adulthood (Neyer & Lehnart, 2007). Interestingly, Sturaro et al. (2008) found that perceptions of support in relationships were generally unrelated to personality change, except that support in a best-friend relationship was associated with large increases in extraversion.

Using cross-domain latent growth curve modeling, Neyer and Lehnert (2007) studied associations between change in personality and relationship functioning across multiple domains. They found moderate associations between decreases in insecurity in peer and family relationships and concurrent decreases in neuroticism. Although insecurity, closeness, conflict, and contact in relationships at the beginning of the study did not appear to underlie change in personality, individuals who had high initial levels of neuroticism experienced less decrease in conflict over the ensuing 8 years. In addition, increases in neuroticism were strongly associated with decreases in peer contact and increases in family and peer insecurity. However, high initial levels of neuroticism predicted reduced growth in family insecurity and conflict with one's family, and were associated with earlier onset of serious romantic relationships in young adulthood. In addition, moderate concurrent associations were found between conscientiousness and both family closeness and absence of family conflict. In addition, agreeableness was concurrently and moderately associated with increased peer closeness and decreased family conflict. However, predictive associations were not found.

One major life transition that often occurs during early adulthood is childbearing. Recent work suggests that having children (especially two or more children) is associated with increases in negative emotionality, particularly for individuals with high initial levels of emotionality (Jokela, Kivimaki, Elovainio, & Keltikangas-Jarvinen, 2009). In addition, having children is associated with subsequent increases in sociability for men with high initial levels of sociability and with decreases in sociability for men with low initial levels of sociability.

We think it may be the match (or mismatch) of personalities that produces change. Empirical hints of this are found in Sturaro et al.'s (2008) work in which adult personality change was predicted by conflict, especially with fathers. The presence of conflict may be an index of a mismatch between personalities. In contrast, support and relationship satisfaction (indicative of personalities that mesh well together) are associated with increases in extraversion. Perhaps success in one relationship provides the motivation and self-confidence to pursue additional relationships, as suggested by increasingly extraverted behavior.

The Workplace and Other Institutions

As would be expected, traits such as conscientiousness and agreeableness are associated with occupational success

(Clausen & Jones, 1998; Roberts, Caspi, & Moffitt, 2003), but relatively little research has considered the effects of work experiences on personality. Scollon and Diener (2006), however, did examine associations between personality and work satisfaction. In their sample of 16- to 70-year-olds, there was evidence of reciprocal effects between extraversion and work satisfaction, in that extraversion predicted increases in work satisfaction over the ensuing 8 years, and work satisfaction also predicted increases in extraversion. In addition, although neuroticism predicted decreases in work satisfaction, work satisfaction did not predict decreases in neuroticism.

One study examined college students' personality development as a function of person–environment fit, which was defined in terms of the match between students' values and resources provided by the university environment (Roberts & Robins, 2004). Fit between the individual student and his or her own ratings of the environment, as well as fit between the individual student and overall, consensus ratings of the environment, were assessed. Better person–environment fit was associated with more personality consistency over the 4 years of college. In addition, students who were less agreeable or less neurotic were more likely to have a good fit with their demanding, competitive, unsupportive environment and that good fit was associated with a subsequent decrease in both agreeableness and neuroticism.

As with relationships, a match between the individual and the work or college environment may underlie personality stability and positive personality changes. This idea is suggested by findings that work satisfaction predicts increases in extraversion (Scollon & Diener, 2006) and that good fit predicts more personality consistency, as well as decreasing agreeableness and neuroticism (Roberts & Robins, 2004).

Sociodemographic Risk Factors

Lower levels of effortful control at age 3.5 years are associated with an early history of poverty, geographic relocation, and family mental health or legal problems (Lengua, Honorado, & Bush, 2007). High levels of maternal limit setting and scaffolding (adjusting support to meet the child's needs) reduce this association, but maternal warmth does not. In the National Longitudinal Survey of Youth, from age 3–4 to age 5–6 years, associations between socioeconomic risk factors and change in resilience, undercontrol, and overcontrol were examined (Hart, Atkins, & Matsuba, 2008). Maternal education and cognitive stimulation and emotional support in the home were positively related to increases in resilience, and neighborhood poverty was associated with decreases in resilience, particularly for neighborhoods with a high ratio of children to adults. The latter finding held even though other family characteristics, Head Start participation, maternal depression, and maternal trust in the neighborhood were statistically controlled.

Thus, stressors such as poverty and legal problems may serve as a catalyst for less adaptive personality development. In contrast, greater family resources (e.g., maternal education) may facilitate positive personality development. Moreover, these findings point to the possible role of neighborhoods in shaping personality development, even among young children.

Although the literature on patterns of change in temperament and personality is already rich, and attention has recently focused on external factors associated with personality change, additional work is needed, especially in areas in which inconsistent findings have emerged. Methodologically, more longitudinal studies are needed. Ideally, such studies would include tests of measurement invariance for the personality constructs. In addition, questions regarding issues of timing and developmental transitions for change in temperament and personality remain largely unanswered.

Child Competence

Consistent with the suggestions that change in personality may pertain to individuals' fit with their environments and with their regulatory abilities, it is reasonable to expect that intellectual and other social competencies could affect how personality develops. There is little research on this, but Asendorpf (1994) provided some support: High levels of social competence at age 4 and intelligence at ages 4, 5, 7, and 9 have been associated with decreases in inhibition with strangers and in class (i.e., with peers) across ages 4 to 9.

LINKS BETWEEN PERSONALITY AND ADJUSTMENT

This section reviews evidence for effects of personality on adjustment in childhood and adulthood. These effects are summarized in Table 7.2. Although we consider findings from cross-sectional studies, we emphasize findings from longitudinal studies that rule out confounds, including reciprocal effects of maladjustment on personality. We

Table 7.2. Outcomes/Correlates of Temperament and Personality in Childhood and Adulthood

Big Five Dimension	Childhood and Adolescence	Adulthood
Extraversion	Extraversion associated with high levels of externalizing behaviors; also associated with reduced risk for depression; mixed evidence for prediction of low academic achievement.	Mixed evidence for association between extraversion and high levels of antisocial behavior; associated with good relationship and occupational functioning; also associated with effective coping that reduces risk for depression; also associated with fathers' cognitively stimulating and affectively positive parenting; also associated with high levels of life satisfaction in older adults.
Negative Emotionality and Neuroticism	Irritability predicts high levels of externalizing behaviors; fearfulness predicts low levels of externalizing behaviors; irritability and fearfulness both predict high levels of internalizing problems.	Mixed evidence for association with antisocial behavior and reduced work satisfaction; associated with increased risk for depression and anxiety disorders; also predicts low relationship satisfaction and high levels of affectively negative and intrusive parenting; also associated with poorer social functioning and greater impairments in daily living in older adults.
Agreeableness	Low agreeableness (e.g., callous-unemotionality) associated with early appearing, persistent, and severe forms of externalizing behaviors; also predicts low academic achievement.	Strongest personality correlate of antisocial behavior in adulthood; low agreeableness associated with increased antisocial behavior, reduced peer closeness, and high levels of family conflict; high agreeableness predicts mothers' nurturing parenting.
Conscientiousness (Self-Regulation Traits)	Self-regulation traits predict low levels of externalizing behaviors and high levels of academic achievement.	Self-regulation traits associated with low levels of antisocial behavior, low levels of family conflict, and high levels of family closeness; also predict good occupational functioning (e.g., job performance, salary); also associated with fewer impairments in daily living in older adults.
Openness	Mixed evidence that openness predicts high levels of academic achievement.	Associated with decreased likelihood of choosing highly conventional (rule-regulated) careers.

discuss several major domains of adjustment, including externalizing and internalizing problems and academic achievement in childhood, and antisocial behaviors, internalizing problems, occupational functioning, relationship functioning, and well-being in adulthood.

Personality has the potential to influence maladjustment through several pathways, reflecting direct and indirect processes that are expressed as main, mediation, and interaction effects in statistical models. Previous reviews of personality and temperament effects have described five models that capture these diverse processes (Clark, Watson, & Mineka, 1994; Krueger & Tackett, 2003; Rothbart & Bates, 1998; Widiger, Verheul, & van den Brink, 1999). In the *spectrum* model, maladjustment is an extreme form of personality, and personality and maladjustment stem from common factors but do not necessarily influence one another. This kind of association would be expressed as a main effect in a statistical model. In the *vulnerability* model, personality traits increase exposure to factors that contribute to individual differences in maladjustment, allowing for the possibility for direct pathways from personality to maladjustment and indirect pathways via other, more proximal, factors. This kind of association would be expressed as main and mediation effects in statistical models. In the *resilience* model, personality traits moderate susceptibility to factors, such as deviant family environment, that contribute to maladjustment, suggesting that personality traits could have a sizeable effect on the development (or prevention) of maladjustment without having a direct association. This association would be expressed as a moderation (i.e., interaction) effect. In the *pathoplasty* (or maintenance) model, personality traits influence the manifestation and course of maladjustment but are not directly involved in its etiology. This kind of association would be expressed as a main effect. Finally, in the *scarring* (or complication) model, individual differences in adjustment lead to changes in personality. In this model, individual differences in personality result from, but do not necessarily affect, the development of maladjustment. This kind of association would be expressed as a main effect in cross-sectional models but would be expressed as a noneffect in longitudinal models that control for continuity in adjustment over time.

These models do not describe mutually exclusive processes. Rather, it has been suggested that these models often must be combined to provide accurate descriptions of complex associations between personality and maladjustment (Krueger & Tackett, 2003). Unfortunately, statistical models rarely identify the process(es) underlying a personality effect, so findings are typically consistent with several process models. Some studies, however, use designs that rule out some possibilities. For example, as mentioned earlier, longitudinal studies that control for continuity in adjustment rule out the possibility that a given statistical effect indicates a scarring process.

Main Effects

We first consider main and mediation effects consistent with the spectrum and vulnerability models. Some of these effects may also reflect scarring processes in studies that fail to control for reciprocal effects. Potential mechanisms of influence are discussed when theoretical models apply or when evidence is available. We consider these questions first for children and adolescents and then, later for adults.

Children and Adolescents

Self-Regulation Traits as Predictors of Adjustment.

Conduct problems Self-regulatory deficits (e.g., resistance to control, low effortful control) reflecting impulsivity and low executive control predict the development of conduct problems in early childhood. Bates and colleagues (Bates, Bayles, Bennett, Ridge, & Brown, 1991; Bates, Maslin, & Frankel, 1985; Lee & Bates, 1985), using parental ratings of infant and toddler temperament, found that both difficultness (primarily negative emotionality) and resistance to control were modestly predictive of later occurring externalizing behaviors. However, resistance to control, which is conceptually related to effortful control and impulsivity, demonstrated the most specificity in predicting externalizing maladjustment. Other researchers have found similar trends in relations between temperament and externalizing behavior (Rothbart & Bates, 2006). For example, Caspi and Silva (1995), using aggregated parental ratings of temperament, found a predictive relationship between early childhood "lack of control" and both late childhood and early adolescent externalizing behavior. Wertlieb, Wiegel, Springer, and Feldstein (1987) found that low levels of manageability, a construct similar to resistance to control, were more predictive of externalizing than internalizing behavior.

Murray and Kochanska (2002) found that toddlers' effortful control, assessed by laboratory tasks, was negatively related to preschool age externalizing behavior. In addition to finding links with attention focusing (described earlier), Kochanska et al. (2000) found that greater levels of effortful control assessed at age 22 months were related to lower levels of anger both concurrently and at age 33 months. Also, at age 33 months, greater levels of effortful control were related to lower levels of deviation from their mothers' rules. Eisenberg and her colleagues have found that regulatory difficulties in middle childhood, assessed through parent and teacher ratings of impulsivity, attentional control, and a laboratory measure of difficult task persistence, are concurrently and prospectively associated with high levels externalizing behavior (Eisenberg et al., 1996; Eisenberg et al., 2000; Valiente et al., 2003).

Similar childhood self-regulatory effects have been reported by others. For example, Hughes, White, Sharpen, and Dunn (2000) found a relationship between executive control and preschoolers' anger, antisocial behavior, and reduced compliance. Possibly shedding light on specific deficits in executive function that contribute to externalizing maladjustment, Hughes, Dunn, and White (1998) found that hard-to-manage preschoolers showed normal working memory and attentional set-shifting but showed reduced performance on assessments of planning and inhibitory control. Olson, Schilling, and Bates (1999) found that impulsive characteristics, measured by low levels of executive control, delay of gratification, and sustained attention and effort at ages 6 and 8, were positively related to concurrent and adolescent externalizing behavior after controlling for earlier maladjustment. In addition, Nigg, Quamma, Greenberg, and Kusche (1999) found that early executive control deficit was predictive of childhood teacher-rated externalizing maladjustment. Also, Moffitt and Henry (1989) found that childhood executive control was related to self-reported adolescent externalizing behavior.

Other researchers have tested effects of self-regulatory traits measured in adolescence. Pursell, Laursen, Rubin, Booth-LaForce, and Rose-Krasnor (2008) found that conscientiousness was concurrently associated with aggression and delinquency. In addition, Romero, Luengo, and Sobral (2001) found that approach traits predicted the development of aggression and delinquency in adolescence. Controlling for concurrent antisocial behavior, impulsivity had a small but significant positive effect on later antisocial behavior.

Deficient self-regulation could lead to the development of externalizing problems by means of its effects on emotion regulation and decision making. Poorly regulated children might be unable to inhibit aggressive responses during conflict. They also might be less able to anticipate the negative consequences of antisocial behavior (e.g., a parent's disciplinary response) or attend too strongly to reward cues for antisocial behavior (e.g., a deviant friend's laughter). Miller and Lynam (2001) suggested that deficient self-regulation leads to antisocial behavior through evocative processes. They suggest that children who are low in conscientiousness or resistant to control are likely to evoke harsh and coercive parenting behaviors, reduced efforts by parents to socialize their children, and peer rejection, and these processes result in externalizing behavior problems.

Academic achievement A number of studies have found links between self-regulatory traits and academic achievement. O'Connor and Paunonen (2007) found in their meta-analysis that conscientiousness was the strongest personality correlate of academic success, with an average attenuation-corrected correlation of .24. Laidra, Pullman, and Allik (2007) found that conscientiousness predicted grade point average (GPA) in grades 6 through 12, even controlling for the effects of IQ. Similarly, Noftle and Robins (2007) found that conscientiousness predicted GPA in high school and college. Impressively, conscientiousness remained a significant predictor of college GPA even when high school GPA and SAT scores were statistically controlled. They also found that academic effort and perceived academic achievement mediated the effect of conscientiousness.

How might academic effort stem from high levels of conscientiousness? One possibility is that students who are high in conscientiousness may be better able to focus attention and sustain effort on academic tasks (while simultaneously resisting the urge to participate in preferred activities) than students who are low in conscientiousness. This ability would likely be especially important for academic success in college, when there is increased independence and reduced access to previously available time-management aids (e.g., parents and home routines). Another possibility is that conscientious individuals select friends and environments, such as academically oriented student housing, that provide extra support for academic effort and success.

Positive Emotionality Traits as Predictors.

Externalizing behavior problems High levels of positive emotionality have also been linked with externalizing maladjustment. Romero et al. (2001) found that experience seeking (in male adolescents) and extraversion (in female adolescents) predicted conduct problems when controlling for preexisting levels of conduct problems and the effects of other personality traits. However, these variables were less predictive than self-regulatory variables. A meta-analysis of associations between Big Three personality traits and antisocial behavior found that extraversion had a weak positive association with antisocial behavior that was smaller than effects for disinhibition and neuroticism (Cale, 2006). In addition, the effects of extraversion were stronger for children than for adults.

Academic achievement Petrides, Chamorro-Premuzic, Frederickson, and Furnham (2005) found that extraversion weakly but significantly predicted boys' reduced academic performance over a 2-year period, controlling for previous academic performance, neuroticism, psychoticism, and verbal reasoning. This effect was strongest for boys who were low in verbal reasoning. Noftle and Robins (2007) found in one sample that extraversion was also predictive of lower college GPA, controlling for effects of SAT scores, high school GPA, and other Big Five personality traits. However, they were unable to replicate this finding in other samples. Similarly, a meta-analysis conducted by O'Connor and Paunonen (2007) found mixed evidence for an effect of extraversion.

Depression Low levels of positive emotionality are widely regarded as a risk factor that differentiates the etiology of depression and anxiety. Much research has demonstrated effects of low levels of positive emotionality on depression (see reviews by Clark et al., 1994; Watson, 2005). Recent evidence reaffirms this finding. Moffitt et al. (2007) found that low levels of extraversion at age 18 were associated with increased risk for diagnosis of major depressive disorder, but not generalized anxiety disorder. Anderson and Hope (2008) reviewed additional evidence for an inverse association between positive affect and depression in childhood and adolescence. However, they also reviewed evidence suggesting that positive and negative affect are less separable (as evidenced by higher intercorrelations) in childhood than in adulthood.

Other research suggests that positive affect may be related to the maintenance, but not etiology, of depression. Yang, Chiu, Soong, and Chen (2008) studied effects of personality on depressive episodes in a nonclinical sample of adolescents. They found that low levels of extraversion increased youths' risk for experiencing more than one depressive episode but did not increase risk for experiencing an initial depressive episode, controlling for stressful life events and neuroticism. Clearly, additional research is required to determine the exact role of positive emotionality in the development of depression.

Negative Emotionality Traits as Predictors. Negative emotionality is a multidimensional construct that taps dispositions to experience both frustration and anxious distress. Research on the development of psychopathology in childhood suggests that these subcomponents have shown differential linkages with externalizing and internalizing problems.

Externalizing behavior problems Difficult temperament measured in infancy and toddlerhood has reliably predicted mother-reported externalizing problems in preschool and childhood in the Bloomington Longitudinal Study (Bates & Bayles, 1988; Bates et al., 1991, 1985; Lee & Bates, 1985). Supporting a positive link between negative emotionality and externalizing problems, Morris et al. (2002) found that irritability was associated with high levels of externalizing problems in first and second graders, and Mun, Fitzgerald, Von Eye, Puttler, and Zucker (2001) found that negative emotionality in early childhood predicted externalizing behavior problems several years later. Gilliom and Shaw (2004) also found this. Other studies are reviewed in Rothbart and Bates (2006).

Fearfulness would be expected, on the basis of theory (Rothbart & Bates, 2006), to predict internalizing symptoms. Evidence that this is so will be reviewed in the next section. However, it turns out that fearful temperament also has shown, measured by both parent reports and laboratory tasks, *inverse* links to levels of externalizing problems. Rothbart, Ahadi, and Hershey (1994) found that fearfulness assessed in infancy using laboratory measures predicted lower levels of aggression 5 to 6 years later. Shaw, Gilliom, Ingoldsby, and Nagin (2003) found that age 2 fearlessness predicted high levels of conduct problems from age 2 to 8. Sanson, Oberklaid, Prior, Amos, and Smart (1996) found that inhibition assessed at 3 to 4 years of age predicted lower levels of externalizing problems at 11 and 12 years of age. Likewise, Schwartz, Snidman, and Kagan (1996) found that early-childhood inhibition was associated with lower levels of externalizing maladjustment in adolescence. Other studies showing the same effect include Gilliom and Shaw (2004) and Keiley, Lofthouse, Bates, Dodge, and Pettit (2003).

Internalizing problems Research has revealed a different pattern of associations between the two forms of negative emotionality and internalizing problems. Difficultness is a positive predictor of internalizing problems in preschool and early childhood, just as it is for externalizing problems (Bates & Bayles, 1988; Bates et al., 1991; Lee & Bates, 1985). However, whereas fearfulness is negatively linked to externalizing problems, it is positively linked to internalizing problems. Multiple studies have documented this pattern of effects (positive effects for both difficultness and fearfulness). Keiley et al. (2003) found that both difficultness (negative emotionality and demandingness) and unadaptability (distress in the context of novelty) predicted high, stable levels of internalizing problems measured from age 5 to 14 years using parent and teacher reports. Lemery, Essex, and Smider (2002) also found that early fear and sadness assessed at ages 3 and 4 predicted high levels of parent-reported internalizing problems at age 5.

Agreeableness and Openness as Predictors.

Externalizing behavior problems Frick and White (2008) reviewed evidence suggesting that a dimension called callous-unemotional, found to be specifically associated with low levels of agreeableness (Lynam et al., 2005), is a unique predictor of extreme and persistent forms of antisocial behavior, even when other core psychopathy traits (e.g., impulsivity) are considered. For example, Christian, Frick, Hill, Tyler, and Frazer (1997) found that the callous-unemotional dimension was uniquely associated with early appearing disruptive behavior disorder diagnosis, and Caputo, Frick, and Brodsky (1999) found that the callous-unemotional dimension was uniquely associated with sex offenses among incarcerated adolescents. Furthermore, Frick and Dickens (2006) reviewed studies showing that the callous-unemotional dimension is also associated with higher severity of conduct problems.

Measures of the trait of agreeableness are also associated with externalizing behavior problems. John, Caspi, Robins, Moffitt, and Stouthamer-Loeber (1994) found that low levels of agreeableness were associated with higher levels of adolescents' self-reported delinquency and teacher-rated externalizing (but not internalizing) problems. In addition, Gleason, Jensen-Campbell, and Richardson (2004) found that low agreeableness was concurrently associated with high levels of self-reported aggression in adolescence, controlling for effects of other personality dimensions. In a second sample, Gleason et al. (2004)

found that low agreeableness was uniquely associated with high levels of peer-reported aggression. However, given the cross-sectional design of these studies, one cannot rule out the possibility that low agreeableness is a developmental product of aggression rather than a cause of it.

Academic achievement Laidra et al. (2007) found that agreeableness was the strongest personality correlate of primary school GPA in analyses controlling for effects of IQ. Openness was also significantly associated with GPA. Interestingly, although openness remained a significant correlate of GPA in secondary school, agreeableness did not. Laidra et al. suggested that agreeableness may be related to academic achievement by means of its role in maintaining positive relationships with peers and teachers (Hair & Graziano, 2003).

Noftle and Robins (2007) found that openness was associated with SAT verbal test scores even after controlling for gender and concurrent grades. In contrast, openness was not associated with SAT math scores or with college grades. O'Connor and Paunonen's (2007) recent meta-analysis of personality effects on post-secondary academic performance found mixed evidence for openness. They reported a mean correlation of $r = .06$, with associations ranging from small negative values to moderate positive values. They suggested that this wide variation in effect may be due to unidentified moderating factors. O'Connor and Paunonen also reported mixed evidence for an effect of agreeableness on academic performance. They reported a mean correlation of $r = .06$, with a 90% confidence interval ranging from $r = .01$ to $r = .11$.

Adulthood

Self-Regulation Traits as Predictors.

Externalizing and antisocial behavior Self-regulation personality traits are also linked with several domains of functioning in adulthood. Miller and Lynam's (2001) meta-analytic review found that conscientiousness was a robust, inverse correlate of antisocial behavior. They noted the compatibility of their finding with Gottfredson and Hirschi's (1990) notion of poor self-control as being a core feature of criminal personality. Cale's (2006) meta-analysis found that impulsivity–disinhibition had a moderate positive association with antisocial behavior, and that impulsivity–disinhibition was a stronger correlate than either extraversion–sociability or neuroticism–emotionality. However, Cale suggested that this association may partly reflect content overlap in the assessment of impulsivity–disinhibition and antisocial behavior. Longitudinal studies are needed to evaluate the possibility that antisociality contributes to the development of impulsivity, too.

Relationship functioning As noted earlier, Neyer and Lehnart (2007) found moderate concurrent associations between conscientiousness and both family closeness and family conflict. High levels of conscientiousness were positively associated with closeness and negatively correlated with conflict.

Occupational functioning Barrick and Mount's (1991) meta-analysis of associations between personality and job performance found that conscientiousness was the most robust correlate. It was the only personality characteristic found to be positively associated with job performance and productivity, training performance, and personnel data (e.g., tenure, salary) for all occupational groups (professionals, police, managers, sales, skilled–semiskilled). Barrick and Mount speculated that the effects of conscientiousness on job performance might be due to its links to dependability and motivation. They suggested that these characteristics are important for success in any occupation, whereas other personality traits may be important for specific types of occupations only.

Judge, Higgins, Thoresen, and Barrick (1999) used three longitudinal, intergenerational samples to study how personality in childhood and adulthood predicted extrinsic (income and occupational status) and intrinsic (job satisfaction) success at least 10 to 20 years later. Controlling for general mental ability, conscientiousness was the only personality characteristic to predict both extrinsic and intrinsic success. The association was moderate-to-large in size. Interestingly, childhood personality predicted later occupational success even after adult personality was statistically controlled.

Health and well-being Chapman, Duberstein, and Lyness (2007) found in a sample of older adults (65 years or older) that conscientiousness was positively correlated with physical activity and fewer impairments in daily living activities even when statistically controlling for age, gender, depression, and physician-rated medical morbidity.

Positive Emotionality Traits as Predictors.

Antisocial behavior Miller and Lynam (2001) reported mixed findings in their meta-analysis, with estimates ranging from nonsignificant to weak but statistically significant. They suggested that positive findings may result from content overlap with impulsivity in some questionnaires and that no unique association exists between positive emotionality and antisocial behavior. Cale (2006) also found in his meta-analysis that extraversion and sociability showed the weakest personality effects on antisocial behavior. Furthermore, Krueger, Hicks, and McGue (2001) found that positive emotionality was associated with altruism but not antisocial behavior. This finding suggests that positive emotionality is important for positive adjustment, but may not be for antisocial behavior.

Relationship functioning As noted earlier, Scollon and Diener (2006) found associations between change in personality and relationship functioning across multiple domains, including positive emotionality and extraversion.

Occupational functioning Multiple domains of occupational functioning have been studied. Scollon and Diener (2006) examined longitudinal associations between personality and occupational satisfaction. In their cross-lagged model, they found that extraversion predicted increased work satisfaction. Also, in their cross-domain growth curve model, they found large positive associations between growth in extraversion and growth in work satisfaction. Studies of occupational success have reported context and outcome-specific effects of positive emotionality. Judge et al. (1999) found that extraversion predicted extrinsic, but not intrinsic, job success. Barrick and Mount (1991) found that extraversion was associated with improved job performance for occupations involving social interactions only. Also, Barrick and Mount (1993) found that extraversion correlated with supervisor-rated job performance only for managers who were in high-autonomy positions. They hypothesize that high-autonomy jobs exert less pressure for conformity relative to low-autonomy jobs, allowing individual differences in personality to be more readily expressed in behavior.

Depression Clark et al. (1994) concluded from their review that low levels of positive emotionality increase vulnerability to depression and risk for poor prognosis. They suggested that the behavioral activation system (Gray, 1982), which relates brain systems to approach behaviors, affect, pleasure seeking, and reward responsivity, may link low extraversion and depression. However, Kendler, Gatz, Gardner, and Pederson (2006) found in a population-based longitudinal study that the inverse effect of extraversion on later development of major depressive disorder became nonsignificant after controlling for the effects of neuroticism. Findings from McCrae and Costa (1986) suggest the possibility that effects of positive emotionality on coping may partially explain the link between positive emotionality and depression. They found in two independent samples of adults that self- and other-rated extraversion was associated with "mature coping," which included high levels of rational action, perseverance, positive thinking, restraint, and self-adaptation. High levels of mature coping were associated with high levels of well-being, suggesting that coping mediates the link between positive emotionality and resilience to stressful life events that increase risk for depression.

Health and well-being Mroczek and Spiro (2005) found in a long-term longitudinal study that extraverted men showed higher, more stable trajectories of life satisfaction during late adulthood than nonextraverted men. In contrast, Chapman et al. (2007) found no link between extraversion and social functioning in a sample of adults between the ages of 65 and 97. These differences in effects may be due to differences in the determinants of life satisfaction versus social functioning, which are related, but not identical, constructs. Moreover, among older adults (age 70–103), a surplus of positive emotions relative to negative emotions is associated with greater satisfaction with one's own aging (Staudinger et al., 1999). Aging satisfaction is related positively to extraversion. Age is negatively related to aging satisfaction, but extraversion does not moderate that association.

Parenting Belsky, Crnic, and Woodworth (1995) found that fathers' self-reported extraversion positively predicted observer ratings of their child-directed cognitive stimulation and positive affect. In addition, his findings suggested that these effects were mediated by transient mood; high levels of positive mood mediated the effect of extraversion on cognitive stimulation, whereas low levels of negative mood mediated the effect of extraversion on positive affect. Extraversion was not associated with mothers' parenting. Kochanska, Clark, and Goldman (1997), however, tested personality effects on observed and self-reported maternal parenting behaviors and found that sociability–affiliation, a subcomponent of extraversion, predicted high levels of self-reported power assertion. However, it did not predict any observed or any other self-reported parenting behaviors. Kochanska et al. noted that their lack of an effect for sociability–affiliation could suggest that positive emotionality may be primarily responsible for effects of extraversion on parenting. Returning to our case, Heather's parents may exemplify this pattern: Their primary affect regarding both problems and successes was neutral to negative. For example, a sticker chart they set up to communicate to Heather that they would like her to stay in bed until a more normal hour worked wonderfully, but they took little encouragement from it as they worked on their other issues with Heather. In other cases, where parents are more normal or even high in positive affectivity, such a success would likely have created steeper growth in expressions of self-efficacy.

Negative Emotionality Traits as Predictors.

Externalizing and antisocial behavior Negative emotionality temperament scales, such as difficultness, have been repeatedly found to predict children's externalizing behavior problems (Rothbart & Bates, 2006). However, in considering personality and later outcomes in adults, Miller and Lynam's (2001) meta-analysis found mixed results for an association between negative emotionality and antisocial behavior, with effects ranging from negative to positive. They suggested that negative emotionality may be a consequence of antisocial behavior rather than a cause. If true, the association would emerge after antisocial behavior develops, and statistical effects would depend on the age of the sample being studied. Another reason for irregularity in the association between negative emotionality and antisocial behavior is offered by Burt and Donnellan (2008), who found that high stress reaction was associated with aggression, whereas low self-control was associated with rule breaking. They suggest that the association between personality and antisocial behavior may be domain-specific, meaning that components of antisocial behavior must be studied separately to more clearly explicate the roles of negative emotionality. According to this argument, variations in measurement of antisocial behavior across studies could account for variability in the effects of negative emotionality.

Internalizing problems Negative emotionality measures of temperament have been found in many studies to predict children's internalizing problems (Rothbart & Bates, 2006). Clark et al. (1994) reviewed evidence suggesting that, unlike positive emotionality, negative emotionality is a common factor in both depression and anxiety. More recent research confirms this finding. For example, Kendler et al. (2006) found that neuroticism was a strong predictor of major depressive disorder 25 years later. Furthermore, they found that this link was primarily due to shared genetic risk factors. Other studies (Fanous, Gardner, Prescott, Cancro, & Kendler, 2002; Hettema, Neale, Myers, Prescott, & Kendler, 2006; Hettema, Prescott, & Kendler, 2004) also found that common genetic factors accounted for a substantial portion of the association between neuroticism and several internalizing disorders including major depression and several anxiety disorders.

Occupational functioning Scollon and Deiner (2006) found in their cross-lagged models that neuroticism had a small but significant inverse effect on work satisfaction. They also found in their cross-domain latent growth curve models that growth in neuroticism and growth in work satisfaction had a moderate-to-large inverse association. Judge et al. (1999) found that neuroticism negatively predicted future extrinsic (income and occupational status) but not intrinsic (job satisfaction) career success when effects of general mental ability and other personality traits were controlled. However, in their meta-analysis of personality–occupation success studies, Judge, Heller, and Mount (2002) did not find a consistent link between neuroticism and occupational success. Surprisingly, Judge et al. found a small positive association between neuroticism and job performance among professionals. They suggested that higher than average levels of worrying and nervousness may be advantageous for some job functions. They also consider the possibility that the demands associated with professional jobs may cause increased levels of neuroticism. Because this study relied on cross-sectional evidence, directionality of effect cannot be established.

Relationship functioning Neyer and Lehnart (2007) found that neuroticism was associated with a number of dimensions of close relationship functioning, as discussed earlier. For example, decreases in neuroticism were associated with concurrent decreases in insecurity in peer and family relationships. In addition, Scollon and Diener (2006) found in their longitudinal analyses that neuroticism predicted reductions in relationship satisfaction.

Parenting Kochanska et al. (1997) found that negative emotionality predicted reduced levels of mother-reported "adaptive parenting," which was constructed from self-reported responsiveness and power assertion (reversed), but links were not as clear for observed parenting. Interestingly, mediational analyses suggested that low levels of adaptive parenting partially mediated the effect of maternal negative emotionality on child adjustment.

Similarly, Belsky et al. (1995) found that neuroticism was the most robust personality predictor of observation-based ratings of parenting of boys in early childhood. Personality was assessed at 10 months, and parenting, transient mood, and daily hassles were assessed at 15 and 21 months. In univariate analyses, mothers who were high in neuroticism displayed high levels of affectively negative and intrusive parenting behaviors and low levels of positively affective, cognitively stimulating, and sensitive parenting behaviors. The same associations were observed for highly neurotic fathers, along with the finding that fathers' neuroticism was also associated with high levels of detachment toward their sons. Multivariate analysis in which all personality traits were considered simultaneously indicated that neuroticism uniquely predicted higher levels of negative affect and intrusiveness for mothers and lower levels of cognitive stimulation for fathers. Effects were generally moderate in size.

Prinzie et al. (2004) also studied associations between parental personality and parenting. They found that high levels of emotional stability (negative emotionality reversed) were associated with low levels of parent-reported overreactive (i.e., authoritarian and coercive) parenting. They also found that parental overreactivity partially mediated the association between parental emotional stability and child externalizing behavior problems. Unfortunately, the cross-sectional design of this study prevents a clear determination of the direction of effect between personality and parenting.

Health and well-being Chapman et al. (2007) considered effects of personality on functioning in older adulthood. They found that neuroticism correlated with lower social functioning, poorer physical self-maintenance, more impairment in daily living, and increased effects of emotional problems on work and other activities. Although these analyses were cross-sectional, they statistically controlled for several potentially confounding variables, including age, gender, depression, and physician-rated medical morbidity. Mroczek and Spiro (2005) studied associations between personality and change in well-being from middle to late adulthood. Participants were male and age 45 or older at the beginning of the study and were tracked for up to nine occasions over the next 22 years. Neuroticism was not associated with rate of change in self-reported life satisfaction, but it was associated with lower average levels of life satisfaction across the study period. This finding suggests that neuroticism has a lasting negative impact on life satisfaction that begins in middle adulthood or perhaps earlier but does not lead to an accelerated decline in life satisfaction during late adulthood. However, among very old adults (aged 70–103 years), aging satisfaction is negatively associated with neuroticism and with age, but neuroticism does not moderate the aging satisfaction-age association (Staudinger et al., 1999).

Agreeableness and Openness Predictors.

Antisocial behavior Miller and Lynam's (2001) meta-analysis found that agreeableness was the most consistent and strongest personality correlate of antisocial behavior. The association was moderate in size. Providing further support for this link, Miller, Lynam, and Jones (2008) found in a sample of undergraduates that agreeableness was moderately associated with low levels of substance use, antisocial behavior, risky sex, and aggression. Miller and Lynam (2001) speculated that hostile social attributions might explain this link, and Miller et al. (2008) found evidence to support this possibility. They found that agreeableness was inversely associated with hostile social attributions as well as decreased delay discounting (agreeable individuals chose larger, delayed rewards) in a laboratory decision-making task. It is also possible that self-centeredness and lack of empathy partially explain this link. In addition, Lynam, Leukefeld, and Clayton (2003) found that agreeableness as measured in adolescence was moderately predictive of antisocial behavior and substance use in early adulthood.

Relationship functioning As we discussed earlier, Neyer and Lehnart (2007) reported concurrent associations between agreeableness and increased peer closeness and decreased family conflict, but predictive associations were not found.

Parenting Belsky et al. (1995) found differences in links between agreeableness and observed parenting for mothers and fathers of young boys. In analyses that statistically controlled for effects of extraversion and neuroticism, agreeableness was the most robust personality predictor of mothers' parenting, with links to sensitivity, positive affect, cognitive stimulation, detachment, and negative affect. In fathers' parenting, in contrast, agreeableness did not uniquely predict any dimension of parenting. Belsky et al. speculate that mothers, more than fathers, act to meet the needs of their children and provide them comfort when distressed and that agreeableness contributes to nurturing behaviors such as these. In contrast to these findings, Prinzie et al. (2004) found a small, positive, concurrent association between parental agreeableness and coercive (harsh or authoritarian) parenting for both fathers and mothers in an analysis that controlled for effects of other parent and child personality characteristics. This association partially accounted for an association found between parental agreeableness and child externalizing behavior.

Occupational functioning Judge et al. (1999) found that openness was positively associated with career success. However, after entering all five personality traits into a regression analysis, openness was not a significant predictor. Nonetheless, openness decreased the likelihood of choosing highly conventional (rule-regulated) careers and increased the likelihood of choosing artistic careers in regression analyses that controlled for effects of other personality traits.

Temperament by Environment Interaction Effects

Self-Regulation Moderators

Parenting. In recent years, increasing numbers of studies have considered interactions between self-regulatory dispositions and parenting characteristics, especially as they relate to the development of conduct problems (see

Bates & Pettit, 2007, for a recent review). One pattern of findings that has emerged is an increased susceptibility to the positive effects of firm, consistent discipline among children who exhibit poor self-regulation. Bates, Pettit, Dodge, and Ridge (1998) tested the interaction between temperamental resistance to control and externalizing behavior problems in two independent samples. Controlling for preexisting externalizing behavior problems, they found that resistance to control predicted future externalizing behavior more strongly when parents were low in active, direct child management actions than when parents were high in such actions. That is, the child's level of resistant temperament predicted level of externalizing adjustment more accurately when the mother was seen to be low in control efforts than when the mother tried relatively hard to control the child. Also supporting this general pattern, in a sample of children from recently divorced families, Lengua et al. (2000) found that inconsistent discipline was more strongly concurrently associated with depression and conduct problems in children who were high in impulsivity than in children who were low in impulsivity. In addition, using one of the samples from Bates et al. (1998), Goodnight, Bates, Pettit, and Dodge (2007) found that parents' mindful attempts to reduce their children's conduct problems by increasing limit setting and involvement predicted steeper declines in future conduct problems for children high in resistance to control than for children low in resistance to control. Finally, Pederson and McCarthy (2008) found in cross-sectional analyses that youth-reported impulsivity was more strongly associated with increased risk for self-reported drinking-and-driving for youths receiving low levels of parental monitoring than for youths receiving high levels of parental monitoring.

Positive, supportive parenting also seems to be more influential for poorly self-regulated children's regulation. For example, Goodnight, Bates, Kuwabara, et al. (2006) found that positive parenting was more strongly predictive of reduced levels of conduct disorder symptoms in youths who showed strong attention to reward cues than in youths who showed strong attention to punishment cues. Similarly, Stice and Gonzalez (1998) found in cross-sectional analyses that supportive and involved parenting was more strongly associated with reduced conduct problems and drug use in youths who scored low in temperamental self-control than in youths who were high in self-control. In addition, Prinzie et al. (2003) found that coercive parenting (likely indicating low levels of supportive parenting) was more strongly related to conduct problems for youths who were low in conscientiousness. Also, in a sample of juvenile delinquents, Jones, Cauffman, and Piquero (2007) found that involved and supportive parenting was more strongly associated with low levels of conduct problems in youths who rated themselves as being high in risk taking and impulsivity than in youths who were low in risk taking and impulsivity. Finally, Wright, Caspi, Moffitt, and Silva (2001) found that "family ties," which included measures of intimacy and involvement with parents during late adolescence, were more strongly predictive of low levels of criminal activity in early adulthood for youths low in self-control than for youths high in self-control. Self-control was assessed using self, parent, teacher, and observer reports of impulsivity, hyperactivity, inattention, physical response to conflict, and risk taking, and thus represented a broad definition of impulsivity.

These studies suggest that impulsive youths benefit more than nonimpulsive youths from having parents who place limits on their behavior, closely supervise their activities, and use positive parenting to encourage good behavior. Increased susceptibility to this constellation of parenting behaviors is consistent with recent theoretical accounts of impulsivity. Specifically, it is thought that impulsive youths have difficulty attending to cues for punishment–especially ones peripheral to the rewards that are focused on–and thus impulsive youths require greater levels of external regulation (Newman & Wallace, 1993). It is also thought that impulsive children attend strongly to cues for reward and thus learn better from incentives than punishment (Dadds & Salmon, 2003; Kochanska, 1991, 1995, 1997; O'Brien & Frick, 1996), and that they enjoy participating in risky activities and thus are aided by efforts to prevent them from spending time in high risk, antisocial environments (Lynam et al., 2000).

Peers. Goodnight, Bates, Newman, Dodge, and Pettit (2006) investigated the moderating effects of impulsivity on the association between deviant peer affiliation and the development of conduct problems in middle adolescence. They found that deviant peer affiliation was more strongly predictive of self-reported conduct problems for youths who were strongly focused on reward cues during a card-playing task than for youths who were strongly focused on punishment cues. They suggested that "reward-dominant" youths attend more to reward cues than to punishment cues in their social environments and thus are strongly influenced by the reward contingencies provided by their peers. Gardner, Dishion, and Connell (2008) reported similar findings using a multi-informant measure of self-regulation. They found that friend deviance was predictive of antisocial behavior for youths who were rated as low or medium in self-regulation but not for youths scoring high in self-regulation. These studies suggest that high levels of self-regulation enable youths to consider longer term, potentially negative, consequences of their behavior and, as a result, be less susceptible to immediate reinforcement contingencies provided by peers.

Neighborhood. Self-regulatory traits have also been studied in the context of neighborhood risk. Lynam et al. (2000) investigated whether census-determined neighborhood poverty moderated the effects of impulsivity on boys' antisocial behavior in early and late adolescence. Cross-sectional analyses at age 13 indicated that neighborhood poverty increased the positive association between impulsivity and antisocial behavior. Longitudinal analyses conducted with only African American boys from the same sample provided an internal replication: Impulsivity was a strong predictor of antisocial behavior at age 19 for boys living in poor neighborhoods, whereas impulsivity was not a predictor of antisocial behavior at age 19 for boys living in better-off neighborhoods. These analyses controlled for age 13 antisocial behavior. Meier, Slutske, Arndt, and Cadoret (2008) tested the moderating effects of neighborhood collective efficacy (degree of informal monitoring and involvement provided by neighbors) on the concurrent association between impulsivity and delinquency in adolescence. They found that impulsivity had a strong positive effect on self-reported delinquency for youths reporting low collective efficacy and a moderate positive effect on delinquency for youths reporting high collective efficacy. Gender differences were observed in the interaction, such that the interaction effect was larger for girls. Impulsivity effects were large for both genders when collective efficacy was low, but larger effects were found for boys than for girls when collective efficacy was high, although effects remained significant for both groups. Vazsonyi, Cleveland, and Wiebe (2006) tested interactions between neighborhood risk and impulsivity and found the pattern reported by Lynam et al. (2000) and Meier et al. (2008) for females, but not for males.

Sleep. Interactions between self-regulatory traits and sleep have recently been described. Bates, Viken, and Williams (2003), building on models created in Bates, Viken, Alexander, Beyers, and Stockton (2002), studied the moderating effects of resistance to control on the influence of mother-reported child sleep disruption on teacher-reported adjustment. They found that sleep disruption was strongly associated with poor preschool adjustment in children who were rated as being high in resistance to control but was only weakly associated in children who were low in resistance to control, even after family management and stress were statistically controlled.

Goodnight, Bates, Staples, Pettit, and Dodge (2007) investigated whether a similar pattern would emerge in later childhood. Using cross-domain latent growth curve modeling, Goodnight, Bates, Staples, et al. (2007) found that growth in mother-reported sleep problems was moderately associated with growth in teacher-rated externalizing behavior problems for children high in resistance to control but was not associated for children moderate and low in resistance to control.

Positive Emotionality Variables as Moderators

In one of the few studies examining the moderating effects of positive emotionality, Lengua, Wolchik, Sandler, and West (2000) found that positive emotionality served as a protective factor in children of divorce. More specifically, maternal rejection was associated with increased depression and conduct problems but only among children who were low in positive emotionality. Lengua et al. suggested that children who are high in positive emotionality, in comparison to children low in positive emotionality, may be better able to focus on positive aspects of their environment or may have more positive relationships with other individuals, either of which could buffer the negative effects of parental rejection.

Negative Emotionality Variables as Moderators

Parenting. Several replicated interactions between negative emotionality and parenting have been reported. Kochanska (1991, 1995, 1997) has shown that fearfulness moderates the link between parenting and children's development of conscience. For fearful children, gentle parenting predicted high levels of conscience. In contrast, for fearless children, secure attachment and positive, fun parent–child relationships predicted high levels of conscience. Colder, Lochman, and Wells (1997) found a similar pattern of associations when predicting individual differences in children's aggression. Specifically, harsh parenting was more strongly associated with aggression at school for fearful children than for fearless children.

Seemingly in contrast with these findings, other studies have shown that fearful children may benefit from challenging parenting. Tschann, Kaiser, Chesney, Alkon, and Boyce (1996) found that family conflict was associated with decreased social withdrawal for children who were low in approach but was associated with increased social withdrawal for children who were high in approach. In addition, Bates (2003) found that children's fearful temperament was more predictive of later internalizing problems in families in which parental control was low than in families where parental control was high. Also, Lengua et al. (2000) found that parental rejection was more strongly associated with depression for children who were high in negative emotionality.

Other Personality Traits as Moderators

Parenting and Neighborhood Associations with Conduct Problems. Agreeableness has been studied as a moderator of parental influence. Wootton, Frick, Shelton, and Silverthorn (1997) found that callous–unemotionality moderated the concurrent association between ineffective parenting and conduct problems (combined parent and teacher ratings) in late childhood. They found that ineffective parenting was associated with increased conduct problems only for youths without high levels of callous–unemotionality. Oxford, Cavell, and Hughes (2003) replicated this finding when using teacher and peer-reports of conduct problems. Oxford et al. suggested that high callous–unemotional children are unresponsive to parents' disciplinary efforts because they do not experience sufficient anxious arousal during disciplinary events to learn from them. However, this does not mean that high callous–unemotional youths are completely insensitive to social environments: Meier et al. (2008) found that the callous–unemotional dimension was more strongly related to high levels of delinquency for youths who lived in high risk (low collective efficacy) neighborhoods than in low-risk (high collective efficacy) neighborhoods.

Temperament by Temperament Interaction Effects

In contrast to the many studies testing temperament × environment interaction effects on adjustment, few studies consider interactions between personality characteristics. Eisenberg et al. (2000) studied interactions between self-regulation and negative emotionality as predictors of externalizing behavior problems over a 2-year period in childhood. Low levels of attentional control were more strongly associated with concurrent externalizing behavior problems for children who were high in negative emotionality than for children who were low in negative emotionality. Eisenberg et al. speculated that the moderating effect of negative emotionality may be related to individual differences in the need to regulate frustration. Unlike children who are in high in negative emotionality, children who are low in negative emotionality are unlikely to experience frustration and thus do not require strong attentional control to prevent its manifestation in aggressive behavior.

Similarly, Lonigan and Phillips (2002) hypothesized that neuroticism was not a sufficient trait to develop anxiety problems, because children who have sufficient regulatory abilities would be able to limit their negative reactivity and thus prevent the development of anxiety pathology. Lonigan, Vasey, Phillips, and Hazen (2004) reviewed studies showing that negative affectivity, attentional regulation, and the interaction between the two traits were all associated with anxiety symptoms in adolescence. For example, Vasey (2003) found that negative affectivity was associated with high levels of anxiety if youths were low in attentional control. In contrast, negative affectivity was associated with low levels of anxiety if youths were high in attentional control. In addition, Lonigan et al. (2004) reviewed their own unpublished findings that suggest that high levels of effortful control may reduce the effects of negative affectivity by reducing attentional bias to threatening stimuli. In their data, negative affectivity was associated with attentional bias to threat-relevant words only among youths with low levels of effortful control. Derryberry and Reed (2002) reported a similar interaction in adults. Trait-anxiety was linked with an anxiety-related threat bias only among individuals who were low in self-reported attentional control.

Muris, Meesters, and Blijlevens (2007) found that self-reported effortful control and negative emotionality interacted to predict self-reported internalizing and externalizing problems in a sample of children age 9 to 13. Complementary to the pattern found in research described in the previous paragraph, effortful control was more strongly associated with externalizing and internalizing problems in youths who were high in negative emotionality. The authors suggest that children with high levels of effortful control more effectively modulate negative reactivity and cope more effectively to stressful life events, thereby reducing the expected effects of negative emotionality on psychopathology.

In another related study, Colder and Stice (1998) investigated the interaction between anger and impulsivity as they relate to externalizing behaviors in a sample of high school seniors assessed two times over a 9-month period. Anger was concurrently associated with high levels of delinquency when impulsivity was high but not when impulsivity was low. However, the effect was not found in longitudinal analyses.

A temperament × temperament interaction involving positive emotionality was reported by Colder et al. (1997), who found that impulsivity interacted with positive emotionality to predict alcohol use and impairment in adolescence. Low levels of positive affectivity were concurrently associated with high levels of alcohol use and impairment for impulsive youths but unrelated for nonimpulsive youths. Colder et al. speculated that low levels of positive affectivity lead youths to seek out experiences that they believe will increase positive affect. Among impulsive youths, this experience seeking might lead to involvement in risky activities, such as underage drinking. In contrast, among nonimpulsive youths who are better able to anticipate negative consequences, this experience seeking will lead to involvement in low-risk activities.

Empirically based typologies of personality provide an alternative, configural approach to studying interactions between personality traits. However, the effects of a particular typology could reflect the unrecognized main effect of a component personality trait or simple, additive effects rather than or in addition to true interaction of multiple traits, a possibility that should be considered in future research. Recent factor-analytic approaches (Caspi, 1998; Caspi & Silva, 1995; Robins, John, Caspi, Moffit, & Stouthamer-Loeber, 1996) have identified three personality types in childhood: resilients, with above-average scores on all five factors (conscientiousness, agreeableness, emotional stability, extraversion, openness to experience); overcontrollers, with high scores on agreeableness and very low scores on emotional stability (the inverse of neuroticism) and extraversion; and undercontrollers, with very low levels of conscientiousness and agreeableness and low levels of emotional stability and openness to experience. Robins et al. (1996) studied the relationship between these three personality types and several forms of adjustment. Undercontrollers had lower IQs, lower school performance (even controlling for IQ), worse school conduct, and higher levels of delinquency. Overcontrollers were the most likely to have clinically significant internalizing problems, undercontrollers were most likely to have clinically significant externalizing problems, and undercontrollers were most likely to have comorbid internalizing and externalizing problems. Asendorpf et al. (2001) found support for this typology in children and adults for stability of classification over time and for its differential pattern of associations with externalizing and internalizing characteristics. In addition, Caspi and Silva (1995) and Caspi, Moffitt, Newman, and Silva (1996) reported that the differential associations with externalizing and internalizing characteristics continued into adulthood.

CONCLUSION

This chapter has described temperament and personality in a life-span developmental framework. The traits that are described under the rubric of temperament are conceptually and empirically related to traits that are described under the rubric of personality. They are also related to traits described under the rubric of adjustment or psychopathology. Moreover, temperament and personality show similarities in their patterns of continuity and change. For example, measures of personality traits and of temperament dimensions both show significant consistency (Roberts & DelVecchio, 2000). In addition, studies using measures of the personality trait of neuroticism (McCrae et al., 2002) and of the temperament trait of negative emotionality (Ganiban et al., 2008) both reveal increases in negativity–neuroticism during early adolescence. Progress is being made toward understanding whether there are genetic components to continuity and change of temperament and personality, as well as to specifying the mechanisms by which they work. For example, during adulthood, genetic factors are primarily associated with stability of extraversion (Viken et al., 1994). As this is being written, the field is increasingly considering evidence of interactions between specific gene variants and specific qualities of environments. The trend in findings is for gene × environment moderator effects that conceptually resemble temperament × environment moderator effects (e.g., see Dick et al., 2009). Sometimes, when a gene's functional significance is well understood, precise hypotheses can be made regarding its interactions with environmental characteristics. For example, Rutter (2008) explained that the monoamine oxidase A (MAOA) polymorphism was hypothesized to interact with maltreatment in predicting antisocial behavior on the basis of its association with reactivity to threat and its metabolizing effects on neurotransmitters in the brain. Indeed, consistent with their hypothesis, maltreatment was strongly predictive of the development of antisocial behavior among individuals with low MAOA activity but not among individuals with high MAOA activity (Caspi et al., 2002). The Caspi et al. study illustrates the general point that the developmental implications of exposure to a particular environment are best understood when dispositional factors (such as temperamental reactivity) affecting responsiveness to that environment are also considered. Progress is also being made toward describing the processes by which environments influence continuity and change. Environments can influence continuity in that they have been selected to match core personality traits of the individual—selected by the individual (niche picking) and also by the individual's social networks (typecasting). They might also influence change in personality, for example, as in a positive best-friend relationship associated with increasing extraversion (Neyer & Lehnart, 2007).

We cannot say that we have an empirically solid model of how a minority of individuals show significant changes in personality and how the majority of individuals have relatively high levels of continuity. However, it does appear that developmental tasks could be involved in normative age-related changes, such as increasing agreeableness and decreasing neuroticism in early adulthood. Further, year-to-year stability in rank order on a temperament or personality trait may itself be moderated by developmental stage. In the first few years of childhood, the stabilities are relatively limited but in later years are stronger.

The traits that we have been talking about can be envisioned in more than one way. They might be thought of as relatively fixed biases in the probabilities of various kinds of behavior (given particular environments). Or they might be thought of as varying from time to time in how they are activated, whether because of environmental changes, advances in self-regulation (which would include the products of learning from consequences of actions), or both. The former view has the advantage of keeping already-complex models a little bit simpler than the latter view would allow. The latter view, however, is probably closer to how we perceive the dynamic process of an individual's or family's life. The biological processes that we place under personality or temperament are more likely to be probabilistic, like almost all other biologically based functions, than absolute and mechanical. Environmental incentive conditions are likely to be perceived by the individual actor in probabilistic ways. Even if we had precise characterization of the incentive dimensions of an environmental situation, an individual would be likely to recognize the conditions differently on different occasions. Thus, although there obviously is considerable stability, we should never expect to see extremely high levels of stability in temperament- or personality-related behavior. One force toward stability is that environments tend to remain stable, both because social systems are conservative and because individuals seek out environments consistent with their personalities. However, on some occasions, there are openings for change in the incentive dimensions of environments, such as with normative transitions in development or when there are therapeutic or educational interventions. On these occasions, self-regulatory actions may also be changed, which could change the implications of the more basic personality traits—in effect changing the individuals' internal, cognitive, and emotional environments.

This brings us back, one last time, to Heather: The clinical team made a number of efforts to help the family reduce ambient levels of negative affect and to increase levels of positive exchanges. The aims were to encourage parental cognitive and affective self-regulation, reduce conflict and stress, and increase supportive, warm, and fun interactions. Efforts consisted of both standard and nonstandard interventions. Standard interventions included eliciting more mutual support between the parents and a special, responsive play session between a parent and Heather every day. Nonstandard interventions included the sleep intervention, described previously, which served to reduce stress for child and parents, even if it did not bring joy to the parents. The parents came back, week after week. They resisted recommendations, and they tried them. The most critical point was when they accepted training to recognize when their daughter's tantrum was past the demanding stage and to the dysregulated distress stage, and they accepted the training to respond to this in a way that was supportive but maintained an individuation between parent and child. For example, if, after some minutes, Heather is still crying, despite the supportive presence (Frankel & Bates, 1990) of the mother, and the mother needs to attend to another task, she tells Heather what she is doing, lets her know that she can follow her if she likes, and then goes about her business, maintaining sufficient but not full contact with her distressed daughter.

Heather's noncompliance and tantrums declined markedly, especially after the midpoint of the course of sessions. At the end of treatment, she was behaving much more normally, like a somewhat oppositional girl of her age. Her parents were not fearing her tantrums nearly as much, and she was not having nearly as many. She seemed more secure. The parents had found ways to reduce the likelihood of noncompliance and ways to increase the likelihood of compliance. The parents were confident that they had tools to use when they ran into new difficulties with their daughter. The parents displayed comfortable affection with one another and their daughter. They were playful with one another. They expressed warm gratitude to the therapists. Given the initial levels of dysfunction in the family, this was a striking outcome. Did the parents' and child's temperament or personality change in the course of treatment? We do not think so. We think that the core dispositions are still present but that they represent reaction ranges (Gottesman, 1963). Our intervention targeted negative emotionality dispositions of the family by helping them find ways to reduce the stresses they so frequently experienced, including the standard cognitive–behavioral coaching and the more novel lengthening of the girl's sleep and increasing parents' supportive presence during the girl's meltdowns. Our intervention also targeted positive emotionality to build both behavioral activation and positive bonds by including the fun, responsive play sessions, with assignments of enjoyable activities during the week, and with the upbeat tone the clinicians modeled in their interactions with the family. Self-regulation of negative affect becomes easier when stressors have been reduced. Likewise, positive emotionality is relatively responsive to environmental circumstances (Goldsmith, Buss, & Lemery, 1997; Plomin et al., 1993). Nevertheless, even though we do not think that the basic personalities of the family members changed, we do think it is possible that the changes that have occurred may cascade into others in the family, and indeed, as the development of the child and her parents proceeds, perhaps there will come to be some stable changes to the core personality traits of the parents and the child.

The future of the research area we have reviewed is promising. The numbers of studies that are longitudinal is increasing. The richness of possible descriptions of personality and its referents is increasing—gaining an organized grid of behavioral phenotypes and a growing array of genetic and brain processes. As crucial qualities of environment are better understood, and perhaps as self-report personality measures are more often complemented by other measurement sources, our understanding of how personality develops through the life span will become richer than it is now.

REFERENCES

Adolph, K. E. (2008). Learning to move. *Current Directions in Psychological Science, 17,* 213–218.

Akse, J., Hale, W. W., Engels, R. C. M. E., Raaijmakers, Q. A. W., & Meeus, W. H. J. (2007). Stability and change in personality type membership and anxiety in adolescence. *Journal of Adolescence, 30,* 813–834.

Allemand, M., Zimprich, D., & Hendriks, A. A. J. (2008). Age differences in five personality domains across the life span. *Developmental Psychology, 44,* 758–770.

Allemand, M., Zimprich, D., & Hertzog, C. (2007). Cross-sectional age differences and longitudinal age changes of personality in middle adulthood and old age. *Journal of Personality, 75,* 323–358.

Allik, J., Laidra, K., Realo, A., & Pullmann, H. (2004). Personality development from 12 to 18 years of age: Changes in mean levels and structure of traits. *European Journal of Personality, 18,* 445–462.

Anderson, E. R., & Hope, D. A. (2008). A review of the tripartite model for understanding the link between anxiety and depression in youth. *Clinical Psychology Review, 28,* 275–287.

Arcus, D. (1994). Biological mechanisms and personality: Evidence from shy children. *Advances, 10,* 40–50.

Arcus, D. (2001). Inhibited and uninhibited children: Biology in the social context. In T. D. Wachs & G. A. Kohnstamm (Eds.), *Temperament in context* (pp. 43–60). Mahwah, NJ: Erlbaum.

Asendorpf, J. B. (1994). The malleability of behavioral inhibition: A study of individual developmental functions. *Developmental Psychology, 30,* 912–919.

Asendorpf, J. B., Borkenau, P., Ostendorf, F., & Van Aken, M. (2001). Carving personality description at its joints: Confirmation of three replicable personality prototypes for both children and adults. *European Journal of Personality, 15,* 169–198.

Asendorpf, J. B., Denissen, J. J. A., & Van Aken, M. A. G. (2008). Inhibited and aggressive preschool children at 23 years of age: Personality and social transitions into adulthood. *Developmental Psychology, 44,* 997–1011.

Asendorpf, J. B., & Van Aken, M. A. (1991). Correlates of the temporal consistency of personality patterns in childhood. *Journal of Personality, 59,* 689–703.

Asendorpf, J. B., & Van Aken, M. A. (1999). Resilient, overcontrolled, and undercontrolled personality prototypes in childhood: Replicability, predictive power, and the trait-type issue. *Journal of Personality and Social Psychology, 77,* 815–832.

Asendorpf, J. B., & Van Aken, M. A. G. (2003a). Personality–relationship transaction in adolescence: Core versus surface personality characteristics. *Journal of Personality, 71,* 629–666.

Asendorpf, J. B., & Van Aken, M. A. G. (2003b). Validity of Big Five personality judgments in childhood: A 9 year longitudinal study. *European Journal of Personality, 17,* 1–17.

Baltes, P. B. (1997). On the incomplete architecture of human ontogeny: Selection, optimization, and compensation as foundation of developmental theory. *American Psychologist, 52,* 366–380.

Baltes, P. B., & Baltes, M. M. (1990). Psychological perspectives on successful aging: The model of selective optimization with compensation. In P. B. Baltes & M. M. Baltes (Eds.), *Successful aging: Perspectives from the behavioral sciences* (pp. 1–34). New York: Cambridge University Press.

Baltes, P. B., & Nesselroade, J. R. (1979). History and rationale of longitudinal research. In J. R. Nesselroade & P. B. Baltes (Eds.), *Longitudinal Research in the Study of Behavior and Development.* New York: Academic Press.

Barrick, M. R., & Mount, M. K. (1991). The Big Five personality dimensions and job performance: A meta-analysis. *Personnel Psychology, 44,* 1–26.

Barrick, M. R., & Mount, M. K. (1993). Autonomy as a moderator of the relationships between the Big Five personality dimensions and job performance. *Journal of Applied Psychology, 78,* 111–118.

Bates, J. E. (1989a). Concepts and measure of temperament. In G. A. Kohnstamm, J. E. Bates, & M. K. Rothbart (Eds.), *Temperament in childhood* (pp. 3–26). Chichester, England: John Wiley & Sons.

Bates, J. E. (1989b). Applications of temperament concepts. In G. A. Kohnstamm, J. E. Bates, & M. K. Rothbart (Eds.), *Temperament in childhood* (pp. 3–26). Chichester, England: John Wiley & Sons.

Bates, J. E. (2003, April). *Temperamental unadaptability and later internalizing problems as moderated by mothers' restrictive control.* Presented at meeting of Society for Research in Child Development, Tampa, FL.

Bates, J. E., & Bayles, K. (1988). The role of attachment in the development of behavior problems. In J. Belsky & T. Nezworski (Eds.), *Clinical implications of attachment* (pp. 253–299). Hillsdale, NJ: Erlbaum.

Bates, J. E., Bayles, K., Bennett, D. S., Ridge, B., & Brown, M. M. (1991). Origins of externalizing behavior problems at eight years of age. In D. Pepler & K. H. Rubin (Eds.), *Development and treatment of childhood aggression*. Hillsdale, NJ: Erlbaum.

Bates, J. E., Maslin, C. A., & Frankel, K. A. (1985). Attachment security, mother–child interaction, and temperament as predictors of behavior problem ratings at age three years. In I. Bretherton & E. Waters (Eds.), *Growing points in attachment theory and research* (pp. 167–193).

Bates, J. E., & Pettit, G. S. (2007). Temperament, parenting, and socialization. In J. E. Grusec & P. D. Hastings (Eds.), *Handbook of Socialization: Theory and Research* (pp. 153–177). New York: Guilford Press.

Bates, J. E., Pettit, G. S., Dodge, K. A., & Ridge, B. (1998). Interaction of temperamental resistance to control and restrictive parenting in the development of externalizing behavior. *Developmental Psychology, 34,* 982–995.

Bates, J. E., Viken, R. J., Alexander, D. B., Beyers, J., & Stockton, L. (2002). Sleep and adjustment in preschool children: Sleep diary reports by mothers relate to behavior reports by teachers. *Child Development, 73,* 62–74.

Bates, J. E., Viken, R. J., & Williams, N. (2003, April). *Temperament as a moderator of the linkage between sleep and preschool adjustment.* Presented at meeting of Society for Research in Child Development. Tampa, FL.

Belsky, J., Crnic, K., & Woodworth, S. (1995). Personality and parenting: Exploring the mediating role of transient mood and daily hassles. *Journal of Personality, 63*(4), 905–929.

Belsky, J., Hsieh, K., & Crnic, K. (1998). Mothering, fathering, and infant negativity as antecedents of boys' externalizing problems and inhibition at age 3 years: Differential susceptibility to rearing experience? *Development and Psychopathology, 10,* 301–319.

Birns, B., Barten, S., & Bridger, W. (1969). Individual differences in temperamental characteristics of infants. *Transactions of the New York Academy of Sciences, 31,* 1071–1082.

Blonigen, D. M., Carlson, M. D., Hicks, B. M., Krueger, R. F., & Iacono, W. G. (2008). Stability and change in personality traits from late adolescence to early adulthood: A longitudinal twin study. *Journal of Personality, 76,* 229–266.

Boyce, W. T., & Ellis, B. J. (2005). Biological sensitivity to context: I. An evolutionary–developmental theory of the origins and functions of stress reactivity. *Development and Psychopathology, 17,* 271–301.

Bradley, B. S. (1985). Failure to distinguish between people and things in early infancy. *British Journal of Developmental Psychology, 3,* 281–291.

Branje, S. J. T., Van Lieshout, C. F. M., & Gerris, J. R. M. (2007). Big Five personality development in adolescence and adulthood. *European Journal of Personality, 21,* 45–62.

Bronfenbrenner, U., & Morris, P. A. (1998). The ecology of developmental processes. In W. Damon & R. M. Lerner (Eds.), *Handbook of child psychology: Vol. 1. Theoretical models of human development* (5th ed., pp. 993–1028). New York: John Wiley & Sons.

Burt, S. A., & Donnellan, M. B. (2008). Personality correlates of aggressive and non-aggressive antisocial behavior. *Personality and Individual Differences, 44,* 53–63.

Buss, K. A., Davidson, R., Kalin, N. H., & Goldsmith, H. H. (2004). Context-specific freezing and associated physiological reactivity as a dysregulated fear response. *Developmental Psychology, 40,* 583–594.

Cale, E. M. (2006). A quantitative review of the relations between the "Big 3" higher order personality dimensions and antisocial behavior. *Journal of Research in Personality, 40,* 250–284.

Calkins, S. D., & Fox, N. A. (1994). Individual differences in the biological aspects of temperament. In J. E. Bates & T. D. Wachs (Eds.), *Temperament: Individual differences at the interface of biology and behavior* (pp. 199–217). Washington, DC: American Psychological Association.

Caputo, A. A., Frick, P. J., & Brodsky, S. L. (1999). Family violence and juvenile sex offending. *Criminal Justice and Behavior, 26*(3), 338–356.

Carstensen, L. L. (1992). Social and emotional patterns in adulthood: Support for socioemotional selectivity theory. *Psychology and Aging, 7,* 331–338.

Carstensen, L. L. (1995). Evidence for a life-span theory of socioemotional selectivity. *Current Directions in Psychological Science, 4,* 151–156.

Carstensen, L. L., Isaacowitz, D. M., & Charles, S. T. (1999). Taking time seriously: A theory of socioemotional selectivity. *American Psychologist, 54,* 165–181.

Carstensen, L. L., Pasupathi, M., Mayr, U., & Nesselroade, J. R. (2000). Emotional experience in everyday life across the adult life span. *Journal of Personality and Social Psychology, 79,* 644–655.

Caspi, A. (1998). Personality development across the life course. In W. Damon (Ed.), *Handbook of Child Psychology* (5th ed., pp. 311–388). New York: John Wiley & Sons.

Caspi, A., McClay, J., Moffitt, T. E., Mill, J., Martin, J., Craig, I. W., et al. (2002). Role of genotype in the cycle of violence in maltreated children. *Science, 297,* 851–854.

Caspi, A., Moffit, T. E., Newman, J. P., & Silva, P. (1996). Behavioral observations at age 3 years predict adult psychiatric disorders: Longitudinal evidence from a birth cohort. *Archives of General Psychiatry, 53,* 1033–1039.

Caspi, A., & Roberts, B. W. (1999). Personality continuity and change across the life course. In L. A. Pervin & O. P. John (Eds.), *Handbook of personality: Theory and research* (2nd ed., pp. 300–326). New York: Guilford Press.

Caspi, A., & Roberts, B. W. (2001). Personality development across the life course: The argument for change and continuity. *Psychological Inquiry, 12,* 49–66.

Caspi, A., Roberts, B. W., & Shiner, R. L. (2005). Personality development: Stability and change. *Annual Review of Psychology, 56,* 453–484.

Caspi, A., & Shiner, R. L. (2006). Personality development. In W. Damon & R. Lerner (Series Eds.) & N. Eisenberg (Vol. Ed.), *Handbook of child psychology: Vol. 3. Social, emotional, and personality development* (6th ed., pp. 300–365). New York: John Wiley & Sons.

Caspi, A., & Silva, P. A. (1995). Temperamental qualities at age three predict personality traits in young adulthood: Longitudinal evidence from a birth cohort. *Child Development, 66,* 486–498.

Chapman, B., Duberstein, P., & Lyness, J. M. (2007). Personality traits, education, and health-related quality of life among older adult primary care patients. *Journal of Gerontology: Psychological Sciences, 62B,* 343–352.

Chess, S., & Thomas, A. (1984). *Origins and evolution of behavior disorders: From infancy to early adult life.* New York: Brunner/Mazel.

Christian, R. E., Frick, P. J., Hill, N. L., Tyler, L., & Frazer, D. R. (1997). Psychopathy and conduct problems in children: II. Implications for subtyping children with conduct problems. *Journal of the American Academy of Child and Adolescent Psychiatry, 36,* 233–241.

Clark, L. A., Watson, D., & Mineka, S. (1994). Temperament, personality, and the mood and anxiety disorders. *Journal of Abnormal Psychology, 103,* 103–116.

Clausen, J. A., & Jones, C. J. (1998). Predicting personality stability across the life span: The role of competence and work and family commitments. *Journal of Adult Development, 5,* 73–83.

Colder, C. R., Lochman, J. E., & Wells, K. C. (1997). The moderating effects of children's fear and activity level on relations between parenting practices and childhood symptomatology. *Journal of Abnormal Child Psychology, 25,* 251–263.

Colder, C. R., & Stice, E. (1998). A longitudinal study of the interactive effects of impulsivity and anger on adolescent problem behavior. *Journal of Youth and Adolescence, 27,* 255–274.

Costa, P. T., McCrae, R. R., Martin, T. A., Oryol, V. E., Senin, I. G., Rukavishnikov, A. A., et al. (2000). Personality development from adolescence through adulthood: Further cross-cultural comparisons of age differences. In V. J. Molfese & D. L. Molfese (Eds.), *Temperament and personality development across the life span* (pp. 235–252). Mahwah, NJ: Erlbaum.

Crick, N. R., & Dodge, K. A. (1994). A review and reformulation of social information-processing mechanisms in children's social adjustment. *Psychological Bulletin, 115,* 74–101.

Crockenberg, S. C., & Leerkes, E. M. (2004). Infant and maternal behaviors regulate infant reactivity to novelty at six months. *Developmental Psychology, 40,* 1123–1132.

Crockenberg, S. C., Leerkes, E. M., & Lekka, S. K. (2007). Pathways from marital aggression to infant emotion regulation: The development of withdrawal in infancy. *Infant Behavior & Development, 30,* 97–113.

Dadds, M. R., & Salmon, K. (2003). Punishment insensitivity and parenting: Temperament and learning as interacting risks for antisocial behavior. *Clinical Child & Family Psychology Review, 6,* 69–86.

Davidson, R. J., Ekman, P., Saron, C. D., Senulis, J. A., Friesen, W. V. (1990). Approach-withdrawal and cerebral asymmetry: Emotional expression and brain physiology: I. *Journal of Personality and Social Psychology, 58,* 330–341.

Davies, P. T., & Cummings, E. M. (1994). Marital conflict and child adjustment: An emotional security hypothesis. *Psychological Bulletin, 116,* 387–411.

De Fruyt, F., Bartels, M., Van Leeuwen, K. G., De Clercq, B., Decuyper, M., & Mervielde, I. (2006). Five types of personality continuity in childhood and adolescence. *Journal of Personality and Social Psychology, 91,* 538–552.

Dennissen, J. J. A., Asendorpf, J. B., & Van Aken, M. A. G. (2008). Childhood personality predicts long-term trajectories of shyness and aggressiveness in the context of demographic transitions in emerging adulthood. *Journal of Personality, 76,* 67–99.

Derryberry, D., & Reed, M. (2002). Anxiety-related attentional biases and their regulation by attentional control. *Journal of Abnormal Psychology, 111,* 225–236.

Dick, D. M., Latendresse, S. J., Lansford, J. E., Budde, J. P., Goate, A., Dodge, K. A., & Bates, J. E. (2009). Role of *GABRA2* in trajectories of externalizing behavior across development and evidence of moderation by parental monitoring. *Archives of General Psychiatry, 66,* 649–657.

Donnellan, M. B., Conger, R. D., & Burzette, R. G. (2007). Personality development from late adolescence to young adulthood: Differential stability, normative maturity, and evidence for the maturity-stability hypothesis. *Journal of Personality, 75,* 237–263.

Eisenberg, H. M., Fabes, R. A., Guthrie, I. K., Murphy, B. C., Maszk, P., Holmgren, R., et al. (1996). The relations of regulation and emotionality to problem behavior in elementary school children. *Development & Psychopathology, 8,* 141–162.

Eisenberg, H. M., Guthrie, I. K., Fabes, R. A., Shepard, S., Losoya, S., Murphy, B. C., et al. (2000). Prediction of elementary school children's externalizing problem behaviors from attentional and behavioral regulation and negative emotionality. *Child Development, 71,* 1367–1382.

Ellis, B. J., & Boyce, W. T. (2008). Biological sensitivity to context. *Current Directions in Psychological Science, 17,* 183–187.

Ellis, B. J., Essex, M. J., & Boyce, W. T. (2005). Biological sensitivity to context: II. Empirical explorations of an evolutionary–developmental theory. *Development and Psychopathology, 17,* 303–328.

Escalona, S. K. (1968). *The roots of individuality: Normal patterns of development in infancy*. Chicago: Aldine.

Fanous, A., Gardner, C. O., Prescott, C. A., Cancro, R., & Kendler, K. S. (2002). Neuroticism, major depression and gender: A population-based twin study. *Psychological Medicine, 32,* 719–728.

Fontaine, R. G., Yang, C., Dodge, K. A., Bates, J. E., & Pettit, G. S. (2008). Testing an individual systems model of response evaluation and decision (RED) and antisocial behavior across adolescence. *Child Development, 79,* 462–475.

Forbes, E. E., Brown, S. M., Kimak, M., Ferrell, R. E., Manuck, S. B., & Hariri, A. R. (2009). Genetic variation in components of dopamine neurotransmission impacts ventral striatal reactivity associated with impulsivity. *Molecular Psychiatry, 14,* 60–70.

Fox, N. A., Henderson, H. A., Rubin, K. H., Calkins, S. D., & Schmidt, L. A. (2001). Continuity and discontinuity of behavioral inhibition and exuberance: Psychophysiological and behavioral influences across the first four years of life. *Child Development, 72,* 1–21.

Fraley, R. C., Roberts, B. W. (2005). Patterns of continuity: A dynamic model for conceptualizing the stability of individual differences in psychological constructs across the life course. *Psychological Review, 112,* 60–74.

Frankel, K. A., & Bates, J. E. (1990). Mother–toddler problem-solving: Antecedents in attachment, home behavior, and temperament. *Child Development, 61,* 810–819.

Freund, A. M. (2006). Age-differential motivational consequences of optimization versus compensation focus in younger and older adults. *Psychology and Aging, 21,* 240–252.

Frick, P. J., & Dickens, C. (2006). Current perspectives on conduct disorder. *Current Psychiatry Reports, 8,* 59–72.

Frick, P. J., & White, S. F. (2008). Research review: The importance of callous-unemotional traits for developmental models of aggressive and antisocial behavior. *Journal of Child Psychology & Psychiatry, 49,* 359–375.

Ganiban, J. M., Saudino, K. J., Ulbricht, J., Neiderhiser, J. M., & Reiss, D. (2008). Stability and change in temperament during adolescence. *Journal of Personality and Social Psychology, 95,* 222–236.

Gardner, T. W., Dishion, T. J., & Connell, A. M. (2008). Adolescent self-regulation as resilience: Resistance to antisocial behavior within the deviant peer context. *Journal of Abnormal Child Psychology, 36,* 273–284.

Gerstorf, D., Smith, J., & Baltes, P. B. (2006). A systemic-wholistic approach to differential aging: Longitudinal findings from the Berlin Aging Study. *Psychology and Aging, 21,* 645–663.

Gillespie, N. A., Evans, D. E., Wright, M. M., & Martin, N. G. (2004). Genetic simplex modeling of Eysenck's dimensions of personality in a sample of young Australian twins. *Twin Research, 7,* 637–648.

Gilliom, M., & Shaw, D. S. (2004). Codevelopment of externalizing and internalizing problems in early childhood. *Development & Psychopathology, 16,* 313–333.

Gleason, K. A., Jensen-Campbell, L. A., & Richardson, D. S. (2004). Agreeableness as a predictor of aggression in adolescence. *Aggressive Behavior, 30,* 43–61.

Goldberg, L. R. (1993). The structure of phenotypic personality traits. *American Psychologist, 48,* 26–34.

Goldsmith, H. H., Buss, K. A., & Lemery, K. S. (1997). Toddler and childhood temperament: Expanded content, stronger genetic evidence, new evidence for the importance of environment. *Developmental Psychology, 33,* 891–905.

Goldsmith, H. H., & Reiser-Danner, L. (1986). Variation among temperament theories and validation studies of temperament assessment. In G. A. Kohnstamm (Ed.), *Temperament discussed* (pp. 1–10). Lisse, the Netherlands: Swets & Zeitlinger.

Goodnight, J. A., Bates, J. E., Kuwabara, M., Newman, J. P., Pettit, G. S., & Dodge, K. A. (2006 March). *Positive parenting and adolescent adjustment: The moderating effect of reward sensitivity.* Paper presented at the biennial meeting of the Society for Research in Adolescence. San Francisco.

Goodnight, J. A., Bates, J. E., Newman, J. P., Dodge, K. A., & Pettit, G. S. (2006). The interactive influences of friend deviance and reward dominance on the development of externalizing behavior during middle adolescence. *Journal of Abnormal Child Psychology, 34,* 573–583.

Goodnight, J. A., Bates, J. E., Pettit, G. S., & Dodge, K. A. (2007). Parents' campaigns to reduce their children's conduct problems: Interactions with temperamental resistance to control. *European Journal of Developmental Science, 1,* 212–271.

Goodnight, J. A., Bates, J. E., Staples, A. D., Pettit, G. S., & Dodge, K. A. (2007). Temperamental resistance to control increases the association between sleep problems and externalizing behavior development. *Journal of Family Psychology, 21,* 39–48.

Gottesman, I. I. (1963). Genetic aspects of intelligent behavior. In N. Ellis (Ed.), *The handbook of mental deficiency* (pp. 253–296). New York: McGraw-Hill.

Gottfredson, M. R., & Hirschi, T. (1990). *A general theory of crime.* Stanford, CA: Stanford University Press.

Gray, J. A. (1982). *The neuropsychology of anxiety: An inquiry into the function of the septohippocampal system.* New York: Oxford University Press.

Gray, J. A. (1991). The neuropsychology of temperament. In J. Strelau & A. Angleitner (Eds.), *Explorations in temperament: International perspectives on theory and measurement* (pp. 105–128) New York: Plenum Press.

Hair, E. C., & Graziano, W. G. (2003). Self-esteem, personality and achievement in high school: A prospective longitudinal study in Texas. *Journal of Personality, 71,* 971–994.

Hampson, S. E., & Goldberg, L. R. (2006). A first large cohort study of personality trait stability over the 40 years between elementary school and midlife. *Journal of Personality and Social Psychology, 91,* 763–779.

Harman, C., Rothbart, M. K., & Posner, M. I. (1997). Distress and attention interactions in early infancy. *Motivation and Emotion, 21,* pp. 27–43.

Hart, D., Atkins, R., & Matsuba, M. K. (2008). The association of neighborhood poverty with personality change in childhood. *Journal of Personality and Social Psychology, 94,* 1048–1061.

Hettema, J. M., Neale, M. C., Myers, J. M., Prescott, C. A., & Kendler, K. S. (2006). A population-based twin study of the relationship between neuroticism and internalizing disorders. *American Journal of Psychiatry, 163,* 857–864.

Hettema, J. M., Prescott, C. A., & Kendler, K. S. (2004). Genetic and environmental sources of covariation between generalized anxiety disorder and neuroticism. *American Journal of Psychiatry, 161,* 1581–1587.

Hughes, C., Dunn, J., & White, A. (1998). Trick or treat?: Patterns of cognitive performance and executive function among "hard to manage" preschoolers. *Journal of Child Psychology & Psychiatry, 39,* 981–994.

Hughes, C., White, A., Sharpen, J., & Dunn, J. (2000). Antisocial, angry, and unsympathetic: "Hard-to-manage" preschoolers' peer problems and possible cognitive influences. *Journal of Child Psychology & Psychiatry, 41,* 169–179.

Jelicic, H., Theokas, C., Phelps, E., & Lerner, R. M. (2007). Conceptualizing and measuring the context within person ← → context models of human development: Implications for theory, research and application. In T. D. Little, J. A. Bovaird, & N. A. Card, (Eds.), *Modeling contextual effects in longitudinal studies* (pp. 437–456). Mahwah, NJ: Erlbaum.

John, O. P., Caspi, A., Robins, R. W., Moffitt, T. E., & Stouthamer-Loeber, M. (1994). The "Little Five": Exploring the nomological network of the five-factor model of personality in adolescent boys. *Child Development, 65,* 160–178.

Johnson, W., Hicks, B. M., McGue, M., & Iacono, W. G. (2007). Most of the girls are alright, but some aren't: Personality trajectory groups from ages 14 to 24 and some associations with outcomes. *Journal of Personality and Social Psychology, 93,* 266–284.

Jokela, M., Kivimaki, M., Elovainio, M., & Keltikangas-Jarvinen, L. (2009). Personality and having children: A two-way relationship. *Journal of Personality and Social Psychology, 96,* 218–230.

Jones, S., Cauffman, E., & Piquero, A. R. (2007). The influence of parental support among incarcerated adolescent offenders: The moderating effects of self-control. *Criminal Justice and Behavior, 34,* 229–245.

Judge, T. A., Heller, D., & Mount, M. K. (2002). Five-factor model of personality and job satisfaction: A meta-analysis. *Journal of Applied Psychology, 87,* 530–541.

Judge, T. A., Higgins, C. A., Thoresen, C. J., & Barrick, M. R. (1999). The big five personality traits, general mental ability, and career success across the life span. *Personnel Psychology, 52,* 621–652.

Kagan, J. (1989). Temperamental contributions to social behavior. *American Psychologist, 44,* 668–674.

Kagan, J. (1998). Biology and the child. In W. Damon (Editor-in-Chief) & N. Eisenberg (Vol. Ed.), *Handbook of child psychology: Vol. 3. Social, emotional and personality development* (5th ed., pp. 177–235). New York: John Wiley & Sons.

Kagan, J., & Fox, N. A. (2006). Biology, culture, and temperamental biases. In N. Eisenberg, W. Damon, & R. M. Lerner (Eds.), *Handbook of child psychology: Vol. 3. Social, emotional, and personality development* (6th ed., pp. 167–225). Hoboken, NJ: John Wiley & Sons.

Kagan, J., & Moss, H. A. (1962). *Birth to maturity.* New York: John Wiley & Sons.

Kagan, J., & Snidman, N. (1991). Infant predictors of inhibited and uninhibited profiles. *Psychological Science, 2,* 40–44.

Kagan, J., Snidman, N., & Arcus, D. (1998). Childhood derivatives of high and low reactivity in infancy. *Child Development, 69,* 1483–1493.

Keiley, M. K., Lofthouse, N., Bates, J. E., Dodge, K. A., & Pettit, G. S. (2003). Differential risks of covarying and pure components in mother and teacher reports of externalizing and internalizing behavior across ages 5 to 14. *Journal of Abnormal Child Psychology, 31,* 267–283.

Kendler, K. S., Gatz, M., Gardner, C. O., & Pederson, N. L. (2006). Personality and major depression. *Archives of General Psychiatry, 63,* 1113–1120.

Kenrick, D. T., & Funder, D. C. (1988). Profiting from controversy: Lessons from the person–situation debate. *American Psychologist, 43,* 23–34.

Kistiakovskaia, M. I. (1965). Stimuli evoking positive emotions in infants in the first months of life. *Soviet Psychology and Psychiatry, 3,* 39–48.

Knafo, A., Zahn-Waxler, C., Van Hulle, C., Robinson, J. L., & Rhee, S. H. (2008). The developmental origins of a disposition toward empathy: Genetic and environmental contributions. *Emotion, 8,* 737–752.

Kochanska, G. (1991). Socialization and temperament in the development of guilt and conscience. *Child Development, 62,* 1379–1392.

Kochanska, G. (1995). Children's temperament, mothers' discipline, and security of attachment: Multiple pathways to emerging internalization. *Child Development, 66,* 597–615.

Kochanska, G. (1997). Multiple pathways to conscience for children with different temperaments: From toddlerhood to age 5. *Developmental Psychology, 33,* 228–240.

Kochanska, G., Clark, L. A., & Goldman, M. S. (1997). Implications of mothers' personality for their parenting and their young children's developmental outcomes. *Journal of Personality, 65,* 387–420.

Kochanska, G., & Knaack, A. (2003). Effortful control as a personality characteristic of young children: Antecedents, correlates, and consequences. *Journal of Personality, 71,* 1087–1112.

Kochanska, G., Murray, K. T., & Harlan, E. T. (2000). Effortful control in early childhood: Continuity and change, antecedents, and implications for social development. *Developmental Psychology, 36,* 220–232.

Kohlberg, L., LaCrosse, J., & Ricks, D. (1972). The predictability of adult mental health from childhood behavior. In B. B. Wolman (Eds.), *Manual of Child Psychopathology*. New York: McGraw-Hill.

Korner, A. F., Hutchinson, C. A., Koperski, J. A., Kraemer, H. C., & Schneider, P. A. (1981). Stability of individual differences of neonatal motor and crying patterns. *Child Development, 52,* 83–90.

Korner, A. F., Zeanah, C. H., Linden, J., Kraemer, H. C., Kerkowitz, R. I., & Agras, W. S. (1985). Relation between neonatal and later activity and temperament. *Child Development, 56,* 38–42.

Krakow, J. B., & Johnson, K. L. (1981, April). *The emergence and consolidation of self-control processes from 18 to 30 months of age.* Paper presented at the meeting of the Society for Research in Child Development, Boston, MA.

Krakow, J. B., Kopp, C. B., & Vaughn, B. E. (1981, April). *Sustained attention during the second year: Age trends, individual differences and implications for development.* Paper presented at the meeting of the Society for Research in Child Development, Boston, MA.

Krueger, R. F., Hicks, B. M., & McGue, M. (2001). Altruism and antisocial behavior: Independent tendencies, unique personality correlates, distinct etiologies. *Psychological Science, 12,* 397–402.

Krueger, R. F., & Tackett, J. L. (2003). Personality and psychopathology: Working toward the bigger picture. *Journal of Personality Disorders, 17,* 109–128.

Laidra, K., Pullmann, H., & Allik, J. (2007). Personality and intelligence as predictors of academic achievement: A cross-sectional study from elementary to secondary school. *Personality and Individual Differences, 42,* 441–451.

Lee, C. L., & Bates, J. E. (1985). Mother–child interaction at age two years and perceived difficult temperament. *Child Development, 56,* 1314–1325.

Lemery, K. S., Essex, M. J., & Smider, N. A. (2002). Revealing the relation between temperament and behavior problem symptoms by eliminating measurement confounding: Expert ratings and factor analyses. *Child Development, 73,* 867–882.

Lemery, K. S., Goldsmith, H. H., Klinnert, M. D., & Mrazek, D. A. (1999). Developmental models of infant and childhood temperament. *Developmental Psychology, 35,* 189–204.

Lengua, L. J., Honorado, E., & Bush, N. R. (2007). Contextual risk and parenting as predictors of effortful control and social competence in preschool children. *Journal of Applied Developmental Psychology, 28,* 40–55.

Lengua, L. J., & Kovacs, E. A. (2005). Bidirectional associations between temperament and parenting and the prediction of adjustment problems in middle childhood. *Journal of Applied Developmental Psychology, 26,* 21–38.

Lengua, L. J., Wolchik, S. A., Sandler, I. N., & West, S. G. (2000). The additive and interactive effects of parenting and temperament in predicting problems of children of divorce. *Journal of Clinical Child Psychology, 29,* 232–244.

Lerner, R. M. (2004). Diversity in individual ← → context relations as the basis for positive development across the life span: A developmental systems perspective for theory, research, and application. *Research in Human Development, 1,* 327–346.

Lerner, R. M., Freund, A. M., De Stefanis, I., & Habermas, T. (2001). Understanding developmental regulation in adolescence: The use of the selection, optimization, and compensation model. *Human Development, 44,* 29–50.

Lerner, R. M., & Kauffman, M. B. (1985). The concept of development in contextualism. *Developmental Review, 5,* 309–333.

Lewis, M. (2001). Issues in the study of personality development. *Psychological Inquiry, 12,* 67–83.

Lewis, M. D. (2002). Interacting time scales in personality (and cognitive) development: Intention, emotions, and emergent forms. In N. Granott & J. Parziale (Eds.), *Microdevelopment: Transition processes in development and learning* (pp. 183–212). New York: Cambridge University Press.

Little, T. D., Snyder, C. R., Wehmeyer, M. (2006). The agentic self: On the nature and origins of personal agency across the life span. In D. K. Mroczek & T. D. Little (Eds.), *Handbook of Personality Development* (pp. 61–80). Mahwah, NJ: Erlbaum.

Lonigan, C. J., & Phillips, B. M. (2002). Temperamental basis of anxiety disorders in children. In M. W. Vasey & M. R. Dadds (Eds.), *The developmental psychopathology of anxiety* (pp. 60–91). New York: Oxford University Press.

Lonigan, C. J., Vasey, M. W., Phillips, B. M., & Hazen, R. A. (2004). Temperament, anxiety, and the processing of threat-relevant stimuli. *Journal of Clinical Child and Adolescent Psychology, 33,* 8–20.

Lynam, D. R., Caspi, A., Moffitt, T. E., Raine, A., Loeber, R., & Stouthamer-Loeber, M. (2005). Adolescent psychopathy and the Big Five: Results from two samples. *Journal of Abnormal Child Psychology, 33,* 431–443.

Lynam, D. R., Caspi, A., Moffit, T. E., Wikstrom, P. H., Loeber, R., & Novak, S. (2000). The interaction between impulsivity and neighborhood context on offending: The effects of impulsivity are stronger in poorer neighborhoods. *Journal of Abnormal Psychology, 109,* 563–574.

Lynam, D. R., Leukefeld, C., & Clayton, R. R. (2003). The contribution of personality to the overlap between antisocial behavior and substance use/misuse. *Aggressive Behavior, 29,* 316–331.

Magnusson, D., & Stattin, H. K. (2006). The person in context: A holistic-interactionistic approach. In R. M. Lerner & W. Damon (Eds.), *Handbook of child psychology: Vol. 1. Theoretical models of human development* (6th ed., pp. 400–464). Hoboken, NJ: John Wiley & Sons.

McAdams, D. P., & Pals, J. L. (2006). A new Big Five: Fundamental principles for an integrative science of personality. *American Psychologist, 61,* 204–217.

McClowry, S. G. (2003). *Your child's unique temperament: Insights and strategies for responsive parenting.* Champaign, IL: Research Press.

McCrae, R. R. (2001). Traits through time. *Psychological Inquiry, 12,* 85–87.

McCrae, R. R., & Costa, P. T. (1986). Personality, coping, and coping effectiveness in an adult sample. *Journal of Personality, 54,* 385–405.

McCrae, R. R., & Costa, P. T., Jr. (1999). A five-factor theory of personality. In L. Pervin & O. P. John (Eds.), *Handbook of personality* (2nd ed., pp. 139–153). New York: Guilford Press.

McCrae, R. R., Costa, P. T., Jr., Ostendorf, F., Angleitner, A., Hrebickova, M., Avia, M. D., et al. (2000). Nature over nurture: Temperament, personality, and life span development. *Journal of Personality and Social Psychology, 78,* 173–186.

McCrae, R. R., Costa, P. T., Jr., Pedroso de Lima, M., Simoes, A., Ostendorf, F., Angleitner, A., et al. (1999). Age differences in personality across the adult life span: Parallels in five cultures. *Developmental Psychology, 35,* 466–477.

McCrae, R. R., Costa, P. T., Jr., Terracciano, A., Parker, W. D., Mills, C. J., De Fruyt, F., & Mervielde, I. (2002). Personality trait development from age 12 to age 18: Longitudinal, cross-sectional, and cross-cultural analyses. *Journal of Personality and Social Psychology, 83,* 1456–1468.

McGue, M., Bacon, S., & Lykken, D. T. (1993). Personality stability and change in early adulthood: A behavioral genetic analysis. *Developmental Psychology, 29,* 96–109.

Meier, M. H., Slutske, W. S., Arndt, S., & Cadoret, R. J. (2008). Impulsive and callous traits are more strongly associated with delinquent behavior in higher risk neighborhoods among boys and girls. *Journal of Abnormal Psychology, 117,* 377–385.

Miller, J. D., & Lynam, D. (2001). Structural models of personality and their relation to antisocial behavior: A meta-analytic review. *Criminology, 39,* 765–798.

Miller, J. D., Lynam, D., & Jones, S. (2008). Externalizing behavior through the lens of the five-factor model: A focus on agreeableness and conscientiousness. *Journal of Personality Assessment, 90,* 158–164.

Moffitt, T. E., Caspi, A., Harrington, H., Milne, B. J., Melchior, M., Goldberg, D., et al. (2007). Generalized anxiety disorder and depression: Childhood risk factors in a birth cohort followed to age 32. *Psychological Medicine, 37,* 441–452.

Moffitt, T. E., & Henry, B. (1989). Neuropsychological assessment of executive functions in self-reported delinquents. *Development & Psychopathology, 1,* 105–118.

Morris, A. S., Silk, J. S., Steinberg, L., Sessa, F. M., Avenevoli, S., & Essex, M. J. (2002). Temperamental vulnerability and negative parenting as interacting of child adjustment. *Journal of Marriage & Family, 64,* 461–471.

Mroczek, D. K., & Almeida, D. M. (2004). The effect of daily stress, personality, and age on daily negative affect. *Journal of Personality, 72,* 355–378.

Mroczek, D. K., & Spiro, A. (2005). Change in life satisfaction during adulthood: Findings from the veterans affairs normative aging study. *Journal of Personality and Social Psychology, 88,* 189–202.

Mun, E. Y., Fitzgerald, H. E., Von Eye, A., Puttler, L. I., & Zucker, R. A. (2001). Temperament characteristics as predictors of externalizing and internalizing child behavior problems in the contexts of high and low parental psychopathology. *Infant Mental Health Journal, 22,* 393–415.

Muris, P., Meesters, C., & Blijlevens, P. (2007). Self-reported reactive and regulative temperament in early adolescence: Relations to internalizing and externalizing problem behavior and "Big Three" personality factors. *Journal of Adolescence, 30,* 1035–1049.

Murphy, B. C., Eisenberg, N., Fabes, R. A., Shepard, S., & Guthrie, I. K. (1999). Consistency and change in children's emotionality and regulation: A longitudinal study. *Merrill-Palmer Quarterly, 45,* 413–444.

Murray, K. T., & Kochanska, G. (2002). Effortful control: Factor structure and relation to externalizing and internalizing behaviors. *Journal of Abnormal Child Psychology, 30,* 503–514.

Newman, J. P., & Wallace, J. F. (1993). Diverse pathways to deficient self-regulation: Implications for disinhibitory psychopathology in children. *Clinical Psychology Review, 13,* 699–720.

Neyer, F. J., & Lehnart, J. (2007). Relationships matter in personality development: Evidence from an 8-year longitudinal study across young adulthood. *Journal of Personality, 75,* 535–568.

Nigg, J. T., Quamma, J. P., Greenberg, M. T., & Kusche, C. A. (1999). A two-year longitudinal study of neuropsychological and cognitive performance in relation to behavioral problems and competencies in elementary school children. *Journal of Abnormal Child Psychology, 27,* 51–63.

Noftle, E. E., & Robins, R. W. (2007). Personality predictors of academic outcomes: Big Five correlates of GPA and SAT scores. *Journal of Personality and Social Psychology, 93,* 116–130.

O'Brien, B. S., & Frick, P. J. (1996). Reward dominance: Associations with anxiety, conduct problems, and psychopathy in children. *Journal of Abnormal Child Psychology, 24.*

O'Connor, M. C., & Paunonen, S. V. (2007). Big five personality predictors of post-secondary academic performance. *Personality and Individual Differences, 43,* 971–990.

Olson, S. L., Schilling, E. M., & Bates, J. E. (1999). Measurement of impulsivity: Construct coherence, longitudinal stability, and relationship with externalizing problems in middle childhood and adolescence. *Journal of Abnormal Child Psychology, 27,* 151–165.

Oxford, M., Cavell, T. A., & Hughes, J. N. (2003). Callous/unemotional traits moderate the relation between ineffective parenting and child externalizing problems: A partial replication and extension. *Journal of Clinical Child and Adolescent Psychology, 32,* 577–585.

Ozer, D. J., & Benet-Martinez, V. (2006). Personality and the prediction of consequential outcomes. *Annual Review of Psychology, 57,* 401–421.

Ozer, D. J., & Gjerde, P. F. (1989). Patterns of personality consistency and change from childhood through adolescence. *Journal of Personality. Special Issue: Long-term stability and change in personality, 57,* 483–507.

Park, S-Y., Belsky, J., Putnam, S., & Crnic, K. (1997). Infant emotionality, parenting, and 3-year inhibition: Exploring stability and lawful discontinuity in a male sample. *Developmental Psychology, 33,* 218–227.

Paunonen, S. V. (2001). Inconsistencies in the personality consistency debate. *Psychological Inquiry, 12,* 91–93.

Pederson, S. L., & McCarthy, D. M. (2008). Person–environment transactions in youth drinking and driving. *Psychology of Addictive Behaviors, 22,* 340–348.

Pedlow, R., Sanson, A., Prior, M., & Oberklaid, F. (1993). Stability of maternally reported temperament from infancy to 8 years. *Developmental Psychology, 29,* 998–1007.

Petrides, K. V., Chamorro-Premuzic, T., Frederickson, N., & Furnham, A. (2005). Explaining individual differences in scholastic behaviour and achievement. *British Journal of Educational Psychology, 75,* 239–255.

Plomin, R., Emde, R. N., Braungart, J. M., Campos, J., Corley, R., Fulker, D. W., et al. (1993). Genetic change and continuity from fourteen to twenty months: The MacArthur Longitudinal Twin Study. *Child Development, 64,* 1354–1376.

Prinzie, P., Onghena, P., Hellinckx, W., Grietens, H., Ghesquiere, P., & Colpin, H. (2003). The additive and interactive effects of parenting and children's personality on externalizing behaviour. *European Journal of Personality, 17,* 95–117.

Prinzie, P., Onghena, P., Hellinckx, W., Grietens, H., Ghesquiere, P., & Colpin, H. (2004). Parent and child personality characteristics as predictors of negative discipline and externalizing problem behaviour in children. *European Journal of Personality, 18,* 73–102.

Pursell, G. R., Laursen, B., Rubin, K. H., Booth-LaForce, C., & Rose-Krasnor, L. (2008). Gender differences in patterns of association between prosocial behavior, personality, and externalizing problems. *Journal of Research in Personality, 42,* 472–481.

Rantanen, J., Metsapelto, R.-L., Feldt, T., Pulkkinen, L., & Kokko, K. (2007). Long-term stability in the Big Five personality traits in adulthood. *Scandinavian Journal of Psychology, 48,* 511–518.

Roberts, B. W., Caspi, A., & Moffitt, T. E. (2003). Work experiences and personality development in young adulthood. *Journal of Personality and Social Psychology, 84,* 582–593.

Roberts, B. W., & DelVecchio, W. F. (2000). The rank-order consistency of personality traits from childhood to old age: A quantitative review of longitudinal studies. *Psychological Bulletin, 126,* 3–25.

Roberts, B. W., & Robins, R. W. (2004). Person–environment fit and its implications for personality development: A longitudinal study. *Journal of Personality, 72,* 90–110.

Roberts, B. W., Robins, R. W., Trzesniewski, K., & Caspi, A. (2003). Personality trait development in adulthood. In J. T. Mortimer & M. J. Shanahan (Eds.), *Handbook of the life course* (pp. 579–598). New York: Kluwer/Plenum.

Roberts, B. W., Walton, K. E., & Viechtbauer, W. (2006). Patterns of mean-level change in personality traits across the life course: A meta-analysis of longitudinal studies. *Psychological Bulletin, 132,* 1–25.

Roberts, B. W., & Wood, D. (2006). Personality development in the context of the neo-socioanalytic model of personality. In D. Mroczek & T. Little (Eds.), *Handbook of personality development* (pp. 11–39). Mahwah, NJ: Erlbaum.

Roberts, B. W., Wood, D., & Smith, J. L. (2005). Evaluating five factor theory and social investment perspectives on personality trait development. *Journal of Research in Personality, 39,* 166–184.

Robins, R. W., Fraley, R. C., Roberts, B. W., & Trzesniewski, K. H. (2001). A longitudinal study of personality change in young adulthood. *Journal of Personality, 69,* 617–640.

Robins, R. W., John, O. P., Caspi, A., Moffit, T. E., & Stouthamer-Loeber, M. (1996). Resilient, overcontrolled, and undercontrolled boys: Three replicable personality types. *Journal of Personality and Social Psychology, 70,* 157–171.

Romero, E., Luengo, M. A., & Sobral, J. (2001). Personality and antisocial behaviour: Study of temperamental dimensions. *Personality and Individual Differences, 31,* 329–348.

Rothbart, M. K. (1981). Measurement of temperament in infancy. *Child Development, 52,* 569–578.

Rothbart, M. K. (1986). Longitudinal observation of infant temperament. *Developmental Psychology, 22,* 356–365.

Rothbart, M. K. (1988). Temperament and the development of inhibited approach. *Child Development, 59,* 1241–1250.

Rothbart, M. K., & Ahadi, S. A. (1994). Temperament and the development of personality. *Journal of Abnormal Psychology, 103,* 55–66.

Rothbart, M. K., Ahadi, S. A., & Hershey, K. L. (1994). Temperament and social behavior in childhood. *Merrill-Palmer Quarterly, 40,* 21–39.

Rothbart, M. K., & Bates, J. E. (1998). Temperament. In W. Damon & N. Eisenberg (Eds.), *Handbook of child psychology* (5th ed., Vol. 3, pp. 105–176). New York: John Wiley & Sons.

Rothbart, M. K., & Bates, J. E. (2006). Temperament. In N. Eisenberg, W. Damon, & R. M. Lerner (Eds.), *Handbook of child psychology: Social, emotional, and personality development* (6th ed., Vol. 3, pp. 99–166). Hoboken, NJ: John Wiley & Sons.

Rothbart, M. K., Derryberry, D., & Posner, M. I. (1994). A psychobiological approach to the development of temperament. In J. E. Bates & T. D. Wachs (Eds.), *Temperament: Individual differences at the interface of biology and behavior* (pp. 83–116). Washington, DC: American Psychological Association.

Rothbart, M. K., Ziaie, H., & O'Boyle, C. G. (1992). Self-regulation and emotion in infancy. In N. Eisenberg & R. A. Fabes (Eds.), *Emotion and its regulation in early development: Vol. 55. New directions for child development—The Jossey-Bass education series* (pp. 7–23). San Francisco: Jossey-Bass.

Rubin, K. H., Hastings, P. D., Stewart, S. L., Henderson, H. A., & Chen, X. (1997). The consistency and concomitants of inhibition: Some of the children, all of the time. *Child Development, 68,* 467–483.

Rubin, K. H., Nelson, L. J., Hastings, P., & Asendorpf, J. (1999). The transaction between parents' perceptions of their children's shyness and their parenting styles. *International Journal of Behavioral Development, 23,* 937–958.

Rutter, M. (1984). Continuities and discontinuities in socio-emotional development: Empirical and conceptual perspectives. In R. N. Emde & R. J. Harmon (Eds.), *Continuities and discontinuities in development* (pp. 41–68). New York: Plenum Press.

Rutter, M. (2008). Biological implications of gene–environment interaction. *Journal of Abnormal Child Psychology, 36,* 969–975.

Sampson, R. J., Raudenbush, S. W., & Earls, F. (1997). Neighborhoods and violent crime: A multilevel study of collective efficacy. *Science, 277,* 918–924.

Sanson, A., Oberklaid, F., Prior, M., Amos, D., & Smart, D. (1996, August). *Risk factors for 11–12 year olds' internalising and externalising behaviour problems.* Paper presented at the biennial meeting of the International Society for the Study of Behavioural Development, Quebec City, Quebec, Canada.

Saudino, K. J. (2005). Behavioral genetics and child temperament. *Developmental and Behavioral Pediatrics, 26,* 214–223.

Saudino, K. J., & Eaton, W. O. (1995). Continuity and change in objectively assessed temperament: A longitudinal twin study of activity level. *British Journal of Developmental Psychology, 13,* 81–95.

Scarr, S., & McCartney, K. (1983). How people make their own environments: A theory of genotype à environment effects. *Child Development, 54,* 424–435.

Schaffer, H. R. (1974). Cognitive components of the infant's response to strangeness. In M. Lewis & L. A. Rosenblum (Eds.), *The origins of fear* (pp. 11–24). New York: John Wiley & Sons.

Schwartz, C. E., Snidman, N., & Kagan, J. (1996). Early childhood temperament as a determinant of externalising behaviour in adolescence. *Development & Psychopathology, 8,* 527–537.

Scollon, C. N., & Diener, E. (2006). Love, work, and changes in extraversion and neuroticism over time. *Journal of Personality and Social Psychology, 91,* 1152–1165.

Shaw, D. S., Gilliom, M., Ingoldsby, E. M., & Nagin, D. S. (2003). Trajectories leading to school-age conduct problems. *Developmental Psychology, 39,* 189–200.

Shiner, R. L. (1998). How shall we speak of children's personalities in middle childhood? A preliminary taxonomy. *Psychological Bulletin, 124,* 308–332.

Shiner, R., & Caspi, A. (2003). Personality differences in childhood and adolescence: Measurement, development, and consequences. *Journal of Child Psychology and Psychiatry, 44,* 2–32.

Shiner, R. L., Tellegen, A., & Masten, A. S. (2001). Exploring personality across childhood into adulthood: Can one describe and predict a moving target? *Psychological Inquiry, 12,* 96–100.

Sroufe, L. A. (1979). The coherence of individual development: Early care, attachment, and subsequent developmental issues. *American Psychologist, 34,* 834–841.

Staudinger, U. M., Freund, A. M., Linden, M., & Maas, I. (1999). Self, personality, and life regulation: Facets of psychological resilience in old age. In P. B. Baltes & K. U. Mayer (Eds.), *The Berlin Aging Study: Aging from 70 to 100* (pp. 302–328). Cambridge, England: Cambridge University Press.

Stice, E., & Gonzales, N. (1998). Adolescent temperament moderates the relation of parenting to antisocial behavior and substance use. *Journal of Adolescent Research, 13,* 5–31.

Sturaro, C., Denissen, J. J. A., Van Aken, M. A. G., & Asendorpf, J. B. (2008). Person–environment transactions during emerging adulthood: The interplay between personality characteristics and social relationships. *European Psychologist, 13,* 1–11.

Takahashi, Y., Yamagata, S., Kijima, N., Shigemasu, K., Ono, Y. & Ando, J. (2007). Continuity and change in behavioral inhibition and activation systems: A longitudinal behavioral genetic study. *Personality and Individual Differences, 43,* 1616–1625.

Tellegen, A. (1985). Structures of mood and personality and their relevance to assessing anxiety, with an emphasis on self-report. In A. H. Tuma & J. D. Maser (Eds.), *Anxiety and the anxiety disorders* (pp. 681–706). Hillsdale, NJ: Erlbaum.

Terracciano, A., McCrae, R. R., Brant, L. J., & Costa, P. T., Jr. (2005). Hierarchical linear modeling of analyses of the NEO-PI-R scales in the Baltimore Longitudinal Study of Aging. *Psychology and Aging, 20,* 493–506.

Thelen, E. (1995). Time-scale dynamics and the development of an embodied cognition. In R. F. Port & T. van Gelder (Eds.), *Mind as motion: Explorations in the dynamics of cognition* (pp. 69–100). Cambridge, MA: The MIT Press.

Thelen, E., & Smith, L. B. (2006). Dynamic systems theories. In R. M. Lerner & W. Damon (Eds.), *Handbook of child psychology: Vol. 1. Theoretical models of human development* (pp. 258–312). Hoboken, NJ: John Wiley & Sons.

Thomas, A., Chess, S., & Birch, H. G. (1968). *Temperament and behavior disorders in children.* New York: New York University Press.

Thomas, A., Chess, S., Birch, H. G., Hertzig, M. E., & Korn, S. (1963). *Behavioral individuality in early childhood.* New York: New York University Press.

Tschann, J. M., Kaiser, P., Chesney, M. A., Alkon, A., & Boyce, W. T. (1996). Resilience and vulnerability among preschool children: Family functioning, temperament, and behavior problems. *Journal of the American Academy of Child and Adolescent Psychiatry, 35,* 184–192.

Vaidya, J. G., Gray, E. K., Haig, J. R., Mroczek, D. K., & Watson, D. (2008). Differential stability and individual growth trajectories of Big Five and affective traits during young adulthood. *Journal of Personality, 76,* 267–304.

Valiente, C., Eisenberg, H. M., Smith, C. L., Reiser, M., Fabes, R. A., Losoya, S., et al. (2003). The relations of effortful control and reactive control to children's externalizing problems: A longitudinal assessment. *Journal of Personality, 71,* 1171–1196.

Vasey, M. W. (2003). [Effortful control as a moderator of the relation between anxiety and attentional bias for threat in youth.] Unpublished raw data, Ohio State University. Columbus.

Vaughn, B. E., Kopp, C. B., & Krakow, J. B. (1984). The emergence and consolidation of self-control from 18 to 30 months of age: Normative trends and individual differences. *Child Development, 55,* 990–1004.

Vaughan Sallquist, J., Eisenberg, N., Spinrad, T. L., Reiser, M., Hofer, C., Zhou, Q., Liew, J., & Eggum, N. (2009). Positive and negative emotionality: Trajectories across six years and relations with social competence. *Emotion, 9,* 15–28.

Vazsonyi, A. T., Cleveland, H. H., & Wiebe, R. P. (2006). Does the effects of impulsivity on delinquency vary by level of neighborhood disadvantage? *Criminal Justice and Behavior, 33,* 511–541.

Viken, R. J., Rose, R. J., Kaprio, J., & Koskenvuo, M. (1994). A developmental genetic analysis of adult personality: Extraversion and neuroticism from 18 to 59 years of age. *Journal of Personality and Social Psychology, 66,* 722–730.

Wachs, T. D. (1994). Fit, context, and the transition between temperament and personality. In C. F. Halverson, G. A. Kohnstamm, & R. P. Martin (Eds.), *The developing structure of temperament and personality from infancy to adulthood* (pp. 209–220). Hillsdale, NJ: Erlbaum.

Wachs, T. D. (2000). *Necessary but not sufficient: The respective roles of single and multiple influences on individual development.* Washington, DC: American Psychological Association.

Wachs, T. D., & Gruen, G. E. (1982). *Early experience and human development.* New York: Plenum Press.

Walls, T. A., & Kollat, S. H. (2006). Agency to agentic personalities: The early to middle childhood gap. In D. K. Mroczek & T. D. Little (Eds.), *Handbook of personality development* (pp. 231–241). Mahwah, NJ: Erlbaum.

Watson, D. (2005). Rethinking the mood and anxiety disorders: A quantitative hierarchical model for DSM-V. *Journal of Abnormal Psychology, 114,* 522–536.

Watson, D., & Clark, L. A. (1992). On traits and temperament: General and specific factors of emotional experience and their relation to the five-factor model. *Journal of Personality, 60,* 441–476.

Watson, D., & Humrichouse, J. (2006). Personality development in emerging adulthood: Integrating evidence from self-ratings and spouse ratings. *Journal of Personality and Social Psychology, 91,* 959–974.

Werner, E. E. (1985). Resilient offspring of alcoholics: A longitudinal study from birth to age 18. *Journal of Studies on Alcohol, 47,* 34–40.

Wertlieb, D., Wiegel, C., Springer, T., & Feldstein, M. (1987). Temperament as a moderator of children's stressful experiences. *American Journal of Orthopsychiatry, 57,* 234–245.

Widiger, T. A., Verheul, R., & van den Brink, W. (1999). Personality and psychopathology. In L. A. Pervin & O. P. John (Eds.), *Handbook of Personality* (2nd ed., pp. 347–366). New York: Guilford Press.

Wolff, P. H. (1965). The development of attention in young infants. *Annals of the New York Academy of Sciences, 118,* 8–30.

Wootton, J. M., Frick, P. J., Shelton, K. K., & Silverthorn, P. (1997). Ineffective parenting and childhood conduct problems: The moderating role of callous-unemotional traits. *Journal of Consulting and Clinical Psychology, 65,* 301–308.

Wright, B. R. E., Caspi, A., Moffitt, T. E., & Silva, P. (2001). The effects of social ties on crime vary by criminal propensity: A life-course model of interdependence. *Criminology, 39,* 321–352.

Yang, H., Chiu, Y., Soong, W., & Chen, W. J. (2008). The roles of personality traits and negative life events on the episodes of depressive symptoms in nonreferred adolescents: A 1-year follow-up study. *Journal of Adolescent Health, 42,* 378–385.

Zentner, M., & Bates, J. E. (2008). Child temperament: An integrative review of concepts, research programs, and measures. *European Journal of Developmental Science, 2,* 7–37.

Zuckerman, M. (1991). *Psychobiology of personality.* New York: Cambridge University Press.

CHAPTER 8

Life-Span Perspectives on Positive Personality Development in Adulthood and Old Age

URSULA M. STAUDINGER and CATHERINE E. BOWEN

A LIFE-SPAN APPROACH TO PERSONALITY DEVELOPMENT

Informed by the classical biological model, traditional conceptualizations of human development conceive of a monolithic, unidirectional pathway exclusively characterized by gains and biological maturation during childhood and adolescence and by losses or senescence during adulthood and old age (e.g., Baltes, 1987; Baltes, Reese, & Lipsitt, 1980). In this chapter, we illustrate how taking a life-span approach to personality development, whereby development is at all times characterized by both gains and losses, can open up the view on the potential for positive development across the life span—in particular, during later adulthood and old age.

The process of how we as humans develop—both within our own lifetimes and across generations—has been described as a process of *selective adaptation* (Baltes, 1987). The life-span model differs from the traditional biological model in that selective specialization with its associated gains and losses continues across the life span, although the overall ratio of gains to losses gradually becomes less favorable. As a function of this changing potential for gains and losses, in youth resources (biological, psychological, and cultural) are predominantly invested in growth, or behaviors aimed at reaching higher levels of functioning or adaptive capacity (Staudinger, Marsiske, & Baltes, 1995). As the individual ages, he or she must increasingly invest resources in the adaptive tasks of maintenance, resilience, and the regulation of loss; behaviors respectively aimed at maintaining levels of functioning in the face of threat and challenge, returning to previous levels after a loss, and behaviors that organize adequate functioning at lower levels when maintenance or recovery are no longer possible (e.g., Baltes, Lindenberger, & Staudinger, 2006).

Central to the life-span perspective on development is the concept of plasticity (Baltes, 1987; Lerner, 1984). Plasticity denotes the range of possibilities (and limits) of development. As an index of an individual's change potential, plasticity reflects how flexible and robust an individual might be in dealing with challenges and demands. The degree of plasticity is contingent on an individual's reserve capacity, which is constituted by internal (e.g., cognitive capacity, physical health) and external (e.g., social network, financial status) resources available to the individual at any given point in time (Staudinger et al., 1995). Thus, development has both fixed and variable components. Fixed components refer, for instance, to the limitations of the human species (e.g., limitations on human sensory perception). Variable components are reflected in interindividual differences, intraindividual modifiability, and cross-cultural differences, as well as historical relativity (e.g., life expectancy). Importantly, an individual's plasticity is itself subject to modification (i.e., meta-plasticity). Just as resources are expended in pursuit of growth, maintenance, and resilience, as well as the regulation of loss, so, too, can resources be replenished. Investing in each of the goals of growth, maintenance, and resilience can result in what was formerly a drain becoming a new resource and vice versa (cf. Staudinger et al., 1995). For instance, coming to terms with one's life as lived or unlived, that is, successfully integrating one's life as described in the last of Erikson's psychosocial crises (Erikson, 1959), requires investment of resources in self-reflection and avoiding negative emotions (e.g., regret). If successful, however, achieving life integration can replenish resources by helping to maintain subjective well-being.

According to the life-span perspective, personality, in the sense of the self-system, has an orchestrating or executive function with regard to other psychological subsystems (e.g., cognition)—and the developmental changes occurring in these subsystems (e.g., Baltes et al., 2006; Erikson, 1959; Waterman & Archer, 1990). The self-system manages (selects)—within the biologically based limits—where resources are directed and invested. For instance, it "decides" to channel motivation to making social contacts, which results in behaviors that in turn are categorized as indexing the personality characteristic *extraversion*. As developmental changes occur in other subsystems (e.g., cognition), the personality system has to react and manage such changes. Given our conceptualization, the personality system is the foundation of how the individual manages (proactively as well as retrospectively) changes in all other subsystems. Of course, such orchestration is not necessarily conscious. Thus, understanding positive development as a whole entails understanding positive development of the orchestrating function of the self-system, that is, the metalevel of personality functioning.

Moreover, we find personality development a particularly illustrative domain given that traditional approaches to personality downplay the possibility of personality change across adulthood and into old age (let alone plasticity of personality development), while at the same time, the development of wisdom and personality maturity are among the few positive aspects of aging common in lay stereotypes. Until relatively recently (and even now), many researchers considered adult personality development an oxymoron, going so far as to say that personality past young adulthood is "set like plaster" (Costa & McCrae, 1994, 2006). Freud believed that personality change was virtually impossible past the age of 50 (Freud, 1953). Eysenck (1967) and Cattell (1982) regarded personality structure as invariant from a very early age onward. However, other age theorists offered important alternative views. For instance, Erikson (1959) outlined a life-span model of continued personality development (or at least the potential for it) by specifying age-specific psychosocial dilemmas. Jung (1969) believed that personality maturation was unlikely to occur before the middle years of adulthood (40s–50s) when the individual's psyche becomes individuated. Maslow (1962) theorized that individuals are unable to self-actualize (i.e., reach their full, individual potential) until a person is past the period of youth. Recent writings indicate a more dynamic views of personality development throughout adulthood (e.g., Roberts & Mroczek, 2008; Srivasta, John, Gosling, & Potter, 2003; Staudinger, 2005). In sum, we can conclude that indeed personality continues to change throughout adulthood and old age. Therefore, it is of interest to look more closely which types of changes can be oberserved. Certainly, there are dysfunctional changes as they are treated in clinical psychology. In this chapter, however, we focus on the positive side of personality development and distinguish two different kinds of positive personality development in later adulthood and old age, namely personality *growth* and *adjustment*.

Before we go into more detail of how personality growth and adjustment are defined, we need to attend to the notion of *positive development* itself which is not self-explanatory, particularly in the personality domain. Using the life-span notion of development, successful or positive development has been defined as the maximization of gains and the minimization of losses (Baltes, 1987; Baltes & M. Baltes, 1990; M. Baltes & Carstensen, 1996; Brandtstädter & Wentura, 1995; Marsiske, Lang, Baltes, & Baltes, 1995). This definition of course requires one to specify what constitutes a gain and a loss. Some areas of psychological functioning lend themselves to definitions of more objective criteria relative to others. In the cognitive domain, it seems obvious that faster or more accurate problem solving is better than slower or less accurate problem solving, or that remembering more is better than remembering less. Still, even within the cognitive domain, one can imagine contexts in which less accuracy or remembering less might in fact be more advantageous. For instance, remembering fewer instances of past failure before a performance situation would seem more advantageous than remembering more instances of failure.

Defining gains within the personality domain is even more difficult (e.g., Staudinger et al., 1995). Is there just one ideal end state of personality development or many, potentially incompatible positive end states? We argue that not all personality changes occurring across adulthood reflect increases in maturity or growth. It is not enough to grow older to grow and mature as a person. In this chapter, we delineate two positive objectives against which personality changes can be measured. On one hand, personality development can be evaluated relative to whether personality changes reflect increases or decreases (i.e., gains or losses) in the individual's ability to master the challenges of everyday life and the maintenance of one's subjective well-being. On the other hand, personality development can be evaluated relative to whether personality changes reflect an advance toward or retreat from personal wisdom. We refer to these dimensions as personality adjustment and personality growth, respectively (Staudinger & Kessler, 2009; Staudinger, Dörner, & Mickler, 2005; Staudinger & Kunzmann, 2005). Not necessarily do gains in adjustment indicate gains in personal wisdom—thus although both dimensions reflect positive objectives that are not juxtaposed or independent of each other, we nevertheless suggest that it may be useful to start to consider development along the two dimensions separately.

In the following section, personality *adjustment* and *growth* and present empirical evidence from a wide range of personality research to substantiate the usefulness of this distinction. We discuss how age-related changes in indicators of personality growth and adjustment suggest that aging, in modern industrialized societies, so far normatively optimizes adjustment but not growth. Furthermore, in line with this evidence and with a contextualistic perspective on development (Baltes et al., 2006; Kessler & Staudinger, 2006), we argue whether the potential for personality change actually unfolds also depends to a large degree on (social) contextual influences. In particular, a person's willingness and access to a multitude of contexts can help promote positive personality development along both the adjustment and growth trajectories. We therefore discuss in an exemplary and more detailed fashion two contextual influences that affect positive (personality) development: age stereotypes and the work context.

PERSONALITY ADJUSTMENT AND GROWTH

We argue that adult personality development can follow two interrelated but distinct trajectories of positive development: development aiming at *adjustment* and development aiming at *growth*. Both personality adjustment and growth represent positive forms of development. The ability to adapt to changing circumstances and feel positive about life (i.e., adjustment) represents a fundamental human strength. However, positive personality development has additional dimensions that are not captured by positive feelings or everyday competence.

Therefore, we have defined *personality adjustment* as the extent to which an individual is able to manage changing opportunities and constraints that arise from history-graded, age-graded, and idiosyncratic developmental contexts (Staudinger & Kessler, 2009). In other words, this form of positive development encompasses making the most of a given situation with regard to achieving, maintaining, or regaining well-being and quality of life.

Freud's theory of personality development is a prototypical example of an ontogenetic theory of adjustment (Freud, 1953). Personality adjustment can be measured subjectively or objectively. The prototypical subjective criterion of adjustment is how good one feels about one's self in a world of others. This facet of positive development has also been labelled *socioemotional well-being* (Bauer & McAdams, 2004). Feeling good about the self is typically operationalized as subjective well-being, an umbrella term for the experience of positive and negative affect as well as the cognitive evaluation of life satisfaction. More objectively, adjustment represents the degree to which an individual, according to societal norms, is successful in negotiating and mastering societal and biological demands. Objective indicators of adjustment thus include measures of everyday effective functioning (e.g., independent living) and longevity.

Personality growth refers to changes in the personality system that aim at the transcendence of given circumstances (within oneself, others, and society) for accomplishing a greater good for oneself and others (Staudinger & Kessler, 2009: Staudinger & Glück, in press). To make progress on this trajectory changes in cognition, emotion, and motivation are necessary to coincide. In the cognitive realm better insight into oneself, others and the world are needed. Emotion regulation needs to become more complex in the sense of recognizing the emotional ambivalence of many life circumstances as well making constructive use of the dialectics between positive and negative emotions (rather than regulating negative emotions down to feel better). In terms of values and priorities, personality growth involves a gradual transcendence of ego-centeredness.

The empirical study of personality growth has been hampered in the past as self-report questionnaires seem not ideally suited for assessing personality growth due to social desirability and performance measures usually being quite labor-intensive to assess. Advances toward personal wisdom, or toward the ideal outcomes of personality development described by other authors (e.g., Erikson, 1959; Kohlberg, 1963; Labouvie-Vief, 1982; Loevinger, 1976; Staudinger et al., 2005), require new, challenging experiences that force individuals to reconsider and reevaluate how they see themselves and the world. Ideally this process engenders an emancipation of thought and feeling and transcendence of the structures within which we have been socialized (e.g., Chandler & Holliday, 1990)—being aware of societal "rules" but at the same time being able to imagine and judge the self separately from them. By exposing himself or herself (or by being exposed) to such challenging situations, the individual can discover core aspects of the self that are relatively stable and other aspects that are more sensitive to contextual influences, and thus arrive at a more objective image of the self and a more advanced state of self-relativism whereby one understands that any version of the self is just one of many possible versions.

As with personality adjustment, personality growth or maturity[1] can be measured according to subjective as well as objective criteria. The subjective facet of personality growth is indexed by the degree to which an individual reports to experience and strive for personal growth as well as to transcend oneself and given circumstances and strive towards a greater good. The personal growth dimension of Ryff's (1989a) conceptualization of psychological well-being prototypically describes the subjective aspect of personality maturity. More "objectively," personality growth can be measured by the extent to which an individual exemplifies personal wisdom. Personal wisdom performance has been operationalized by coding individuals' responses to difficult personal problems according to the five personal-wisdom criteria: The two basic criteria are exhibiting deep, broad and balanced self-knowledge and having heuristics or strategies of growth and self-regulation. These basic criteria are necessary, but not sufficient, aspects of personal wisdom. There are three meta-criteria: interrelating the self, self-relativism, and tolerance of ambiguity. These criteria are more specific, require more complex judgmental processes, and are more difficult to acquire (Mickler & Staudinger, 2008).

Other personality models have distinguished between the adjustment-type dimension and "other" forms of positive development but have generally focused on the cognitive, emotional, or motivational component rather than focusing on all three facets conjointly. For instance, they have differentiated between other-orientation and self-orientation (Helson & Wink, 1987) or between emotional and cognitive functioning (Labouvie-Vief & Medler, 2002), or between personal growth and environmental mastery (Helson & Srivastava, 2001; Ryff, 1989a). Labouvie-Vief (e.g., 2003) has distinguished between affect optimization—that is, adults' ability to maintain and enhance levels of subjective well-being and personal happiness—and affect complexity—that is, a person's ability and willingness to understand, differentiate, and integrate emotional experiences (affective), including their dynamics, causes, and consequences (cognitive). Different from these models, we conceive of adjustment and growth as meta-goals at the level of the personality system itself, which guides functioning in all other subsystems (e.g., cognition, emotion, and motivation). Thus, according to our conceptualization, all three facets are coordinated and must be analyzed conjointly.

Relationship between Personality Adjustment and Growth

Personality adjustment and growth are distinct concepts, although not entirely independent of each other. Rather, we assume that at least a threshold level of adjustment is a necessary, but insufficient, condition for growth.[2] Usually only the resources left over after achieving a threshold-level of adjustment can be devoted to growth. *Too much* challenge to adjustment most likely subtracts from the potential to grow. Thus, opportunities for personality growth are unequally distributed. The ease with which an individual can meet biological and cultural imperatives not only affects the amount of resources left over for potential growth including the willingness of the individual to seek out the kind of challenging contexts that promote growth: When a person feels confident that he or she will be able to manage a challenging situation, he or she is also more likely to approach such a context. However, neither does objective ability nor confidence in one's ability to adjust necessarily imply that an individual will invest resources in pursuit of personality growth or seek out new, challenging situations.

[1] We use the term *personality growth* to refer to the process and the term *personality maturity* to refer to the ideal end state of this kind of personality development.

[2] Similarly, Deci and Ryan (2000) argued that meeting basic psychological needs (autonomy, competence in the sense of internal and external environments, and relatedness) is a necessary precondition for personal growth.

Furthermore, optimizing adjustment in the short-term requires avoidance of negative emotions and challenging contexts, both of which, however, are necessary preconditions for growth. Thus, "optimal" life circumstances in which the individual meets few challenges to his or her adjustment at the same time offer little facilitation of personality growth. It seems that one crucial way to make progress on the road toward personality growth is to experience challenges to adjustment; challenges to the used ways of mastery or new challenges for which mastery still has to be ascertained and developed. Such challenges may be mastered by readjusting and thus regaining adjustment, or they may be mastered by recognizing the influences of extant circumstances on a given problem constellation and consequently trying to develop ways to transcend those and thereby continuing on a personality-growth trajectory. Most likely such attempts often lead to a at least temporary loss of subjective well-being, for instance, if the analysis is not shared by others and consequently the individual is marginalized or even repressed. Also, recognizing that a certain context negatively influences oneself, but being unable to escape the context and feeling powerless to do anything against it, can lead to feelings of depression and hopelessness. Facing such feelings and working on the anlysis of this situation has the potential to eventually contribute to growth but in the short term drastically reduces well-being.

As much as challenging situations may initially threaten adjustment, such situations also offer opportunities to practice and potentially improve his or her ability to adjust to a greater range of contexts, creating new resources for future adjustment. Furthermore, experiencing negative emotions (an integral part of personality maturity) might actually improve individual's ability to experience positive emotions (e.g., Aldwin & Stokols, 1988), and the self-transcendent values associated with personality growth have also been associated with measures of well-being (Chan & Joseph, 2000; Schmuck, Kasser, & Ryan, 2000; Sheldon & Kasser, 2001; Sheldon, Ryan, Deci, & Kasser, 2004).

And indeed, some authors with a background in (positive) mental health have viewed adjustment as one important component of maturity (Allport, 1961; Freud, 1923/1961; Ryff, 1989a; Sullivan, 1972). However, there is also another tradition that views adjustment as unrelated to personality maturity (Bauer & McAdams, 2004; Helson & Wink, 1987; Loevinger, 1976) or even negatively related with maturity (e.g., Mead, 1934). Fromm (1941) considered adjustment as the most universal form of neurosis. These conflicting perspectives can be resolved by acknowledging that they are built on different notions of maturity. Fromm's notion focuses on the emancipatory aspect of personality maturity and the former models define maturity as the highest form of adjustment.

According to the latter notion, maturity as the highest form of adjustment is achieved by actively attending to, reconciling, and integrating antagonizing motivations and emotional experiences by developing a tolerance of multiple (dialectic) activations. Adjustment, in the sense of functional solutions, can also be achieved by reducing internal and external conflicts through avoidance or repression—for instance, by reducing the number of available self-conceptions, identity aspects, goals, or priorities or by accentuating the positive while ignoring the negative. As an example, establishing an identity within a romantic partnership entails conflict between the individual's affiliated and autonomous identities. An individual can react to this challenge by actively confronting the antagonistic strain. He or she can attempt to tolerate the conflict and continue to invest in both his or her autonomous identity *and* his or her affiliated identity. Alternatively, an individual can react by choosing (consciously or not, and independent of whether the partnership formally continues) to pursue either an autonomous *or* affiliated identity, and discontinuing investment in the antagonizing identity. The former reaction may cause conflict within the individual and within couple—a conflict that may not be resolved. However, if it can be resolved, the former strategy (relative to the latter) will result in a more stable resource base that will ease adjustment to future life events, such as dissolution of the partnership through divorce or death of the partner or loss of important aspects of the autonomous self, such as the loss of a job.

Empirically, the relationship between growth and adjustment is not easy to ascertain, particularly given the range of definitions and operationalizations of adjustment-related and growth-related personality development. Longitudinal studies are needed to assess the reciprocal relationship between the two trajectories.

Differences in the Individual and Social Imperative for Adjustment and Growth

Both personality adjustment and growth represent positive forms of development, and we do not imply a hierarchy between the two types of development. The ability to adapt successfully to changing circumstances (i.e., adjustment) represents a fundamental human strength and perhaps the prototypical feature that distinguishes humans from other species. The ability to conform and adapt to environmental demands, both natural and man-made (such as the rules, norms, and expectations of communal living), go hand in hand with higher levels of well-being and represent an important outcome for both the individual as well as the community (Helson & Wink, 1987; Staudinger & Kessler, 2009; Staudinger & Kunzmann, 2005). It is in fact personality adjustment that makes communal living possible. The success of any human community depends on a high "incidence rate" of adjustment. If too many people fail to live up to the demands of a given society, the society will collapse; if too many people fail to meet basic personal imperatives (including happiness), political unrest may arise. Indeed, societies take precautions to ensure that its members are equipped with the appropriate tools needed to meet the demands and expectations of the society. Schooling is one example of how societies attempt to equip its members with the necessary resources for meeting societal obligations (e.g., holding a job, participating in society). Societies also expend significant effort to design and implement reward and punishment systems that encourage adjustment. For instance, in modern industrialized countries, successfully adjusting (or not) to a societal demand to be productive is rewarded (or punished) by material enjoyment (or lack thereof). Welfare systems have the function of providing the basic resources needed to maintain basic levels of adjustment in times of crises. For individuals, failing to achieve a threshold level of adjustment can result in emigration or negative mental and physical health consequences. Adjustment can even be a question of survival, when one considers life under a harsh dictatorship or, as a less radical example, the predictive relationship between negative emotions and health (Kiecolt-Glaser, McGuire, Robles, & Glaser, 2002).

As several personality researchers as well as philosophers agree, positive personality development has dimensions that are not captured by the successful mastery of *given* constraints but rather imply their transcendence. The transcendence of given circumstances is the essence of wisdom which since the beginning of humankind, has been described as the ideal endpoint of human development (Baltes & Staudinger, 2000). We have argued elsewhere that personality growth, in the sense of personal wisdom, is one important ingredient in achieving (general) wisdom (Staudinger et al., 2006). The relative invariance in the meaning and cultural importance of wisdom gives rise to the assumption that wisdom, too, has an evolutionary purpose. Transcendence of the given rules coupled with an investment in others allows for progress, allowing communities as a whole to adapt to changing circumstances—if the advice of the individuals who have achieved such an advanced state is heeded. The innovativeness of a society, and therefore its long-term success, depends on a certain percentage of individuals achieving personality maturity (in the sense of wisdom)—that is, a certain percentage of individuals who not only master and negotiate the given rules, norms, and expectations but are also able to transcend the given rules to improve the society to better fit changing circumstances (Staudinger & Kessler, 2009).

On both the individual and societal level, investment in personality growth, however, represents an *optional* task, as opposed to an *obligatory* task (for the distinction between obligatory and optional tasks, see Schindler & Staudinger, 2008; Staudinger & Kessler, 2009). Whereas biological and cultural imperatives *require* a certain obligatory level of adjustment, transcendence of the current situational rules is not necessary for survival on the individual level and nor on the societal level, at least in the short term. As such, modern industrialized societies invest much less in growth as compared with personality adjustment. For instance, schools do not typically reward or punish the attainment of social skills beyond a basic threshold; children are not necessarily encouraged to move beyond fundamental social imperatives such as basic cooperation and aggression control. Skeptics might argue that the continuance of some societal structures actually depends on the incidence rate of personality maturity staying rather low—that certain rules and structures can only be maintained by their rather uncritical acceptance. By design or not, some societal structures may indeed hinder personality growth. For example, an overly exhaustive work schedule takes time away from the kind of critical self-reflection necessary for growth; authoritarian cultures train people to accept societal structures without questioning.

In line with the differing individual and societal imperatives for adjustment and for growth, we argue that aging, as we observe it here and now in modern industrialized nations, seems to be focused on the optimization of personality adjustment more than on personality growth. Despite the increasing constraints in and decreasing opportunities for replenishment of societal and material as well as biological resources across adulthood, the ability to maintain high levels of subjective well-being (i.e., maintaining or achieving adjustment)—at least into "young" old age—is a core finding indicative of the resilience of the aging self (Staudinger et al., 1995). Empirical research has demonstrated that adults maintain a good sense of well-being well into old age (Diehl, Coyle, & Labouvie-Vief, 1996; Diener, 1996; Mroczek & Kolarz, 1998; Ryff, 1989a; Staudinger et al., 1995), an indication that people maintain an ability to adjust to life circumstances increasingly characterized by challenge and threat (e.g., managing work and family responsibilities) and later by loss. Although aging individuals are increasingly faced with challenge, threat, and loss, normative increases (or at least maintenance) of certain personal resources such as crystallized intelligence, professional skills, social support, competence in everyday problem solving, and adjustment-related self-regulation (e.g., increase in accommodative coping strategies) support the aging individual's capacity for adjustment. In addition, the age-related increase in the awareness of life's finitude seems to provide a strong motivational resource for adjustment, at least in the sense of maximizing positive and minimizing negative emotions (Charles & Carstensen, 1999). In contrast to adjustment, age-related increases in personality maturity are a relatively rare event (Mickler & Staudinger, 2008; Staudinger, Dörner, & Mickler, 2005). The absence of facilitative societal structures likely contributes to the low incidence rates of personality growth. In the following section, we present the empirical basis for this argument.

EMPIRICAL EVIDENCE ON PERSONALITY GROWTH AND ADJUSTMENT TRAJECTORIES

The distinction between personality adjustment and growth only becomes meaningful after we have developed a sense of self in time (cf. Habermas & Bluck, 2000) and the ability to choose among life priorities, that is, late adolescence. Up to that point in development, the necessary preconditions for adjustment and growth are acquired. During these years, biological maturation, social interactions, and societal structures (e.g., schooling) equip us (with varying degrees of success) with the resources needed to master adult life. It is during this stage of life that we establish our identity (Marcia, 1980), a self-concept and self-esteem (Harter, 1999), as well as a set of self-regulatory mechanisms that help us to preserve and defend them (e.g., Brandtstädter & Greve, 1994). In line with this proposition, we found in a study of wisdom in adolescence that even up to the age of 25, normative and steep progress is made in acquiring basic knowledge about life and its vicissitudes, which is needed for both personality adjustment and growth (cf. Pasupathi, Staudinger, & Baltes, 2001). Thus, in the remainder of this chapter that is concerned with the developmental trajectories of personality adjustment and personality growth, we focus on adulthood and old age rather than infancy, childhood, and adolescence.

Interestingly, research shows that most mean-level changes in personality (traits) occur between the ages of 20 and 40—not, as commonly supposed, between 10 and 20 (Roberts & Mroczek, 2008). This is also the time period when the trajectories of adjustment and growth begin to diverge. In young adulthood, societal (e.g., work) and biological (e.g., parenthood) imperatives force individuals to choose between different self-aspects to pursue (see also Helson, Kwan, John, & Jones, 2002). The "social investment" that occurs during this period—such as investment in roles associated with one's career, family, and community—is thought to stimulate personality change (e.g., Roberts, Wood, & Smith, 2005). However, after making important decisions at the beginning of adulthood, such as which career path to follow, choosing a romantic partner, becoming a parent, and deciding where to live, on average, we tend to be exposed (and expose ourselves to) fewer new contexts (including new roles) as we age and thereby have a lower likelihood of being confronted with experiences that contradict our expectations (see also Cohn, 1998). The latter, however, is one important precondition for continued growth.

We propose and present evidence that personality adjustment, but not personality growth, normatively increases with age across adulthood. In support of this claim, we draw on empirical findings from different areas of personality research. We relate constructs and findings from both the structural and process-related approaches of personality to our definitions of personality adjustment and growth and integrate the developmental findings to illustrate how the trajectories for these two forms of positive development diverge. As a first step, we present evidence on structural indicators of adjustment and growth from personal-wisdom performance—a measure we designed to measure personality growth as we have defined it here (Mickler & Staudinger, 2008). In addition, we present evidence from more established structural indicators of adjustment and growth, including the Big Five traits, Ryff's psychological well-being, self-concept structure and self-concept maturity, and ego development.

Structural developmental personality research looks at how the structure (e.g., traits, self-conceptions) of personality changes over time (Funder, 2001; Staudinger & Pasupathi, 2000). Such structural approaches to personality typically do not consider the underlying processes or dynamics that lead to a certain disposition nor do they focus on the interplay between dispositions and particular situations (Mischel & Shoda, 1999). For instance, people who exemplify certain traits tend seek out certain situations that reinforce these traits (e.g., Diener, Larsen, & Emmons, 1984). Therefore, the structural approach to personality development may fail to appreciate the *potential* for personality change, because what appears to be *stability* is actually the result of a complex process of self-regulation. Process-related personality development research, in contrast, attempts to unravel the personality processes that underlie changes (or stability) in personality structure. Understanding such processes is essential for understanding how people encode and respond to different situations and how contexts can differentially stimulate positive development (Mischel & Mendoza-Denton, 2003), including personality adjustment and growth. We therefore present evidence on process-related indicators of adjustment and growth, including values, coping strategies, systemic regulatory processes (selective optimization with compensation), and emotion regulation.

Tables 8.1 and 8.2 display the indicators of personality adjustment and personality maturity included in the review. Please note that some of these indicators were originally conceptualized as indicators of positive functioning, whereas others were not. Furthermore, some indicators represent direct, global operationalizations of adjustment or maturity, and others represent specific facets. The indicators also vary in whether they represent antecedents or consequences of personality adjustment or growth.

Table 8.1 Summary of Structural Indicators of Personality Adjustment and Growth

Personality Concepts	Indicators of Adjustment	Indicators of Personality Growth/ Maturity
Personality Characteristics	Emotional stability, agreeableness, conscientiousness	Openness to experience
Personal Wisdom	Medium scores on: • Self-insight • Heuristics for growth Low scores on: • Interrelating the self • Self-relativism • Tolerance of ambiguity	High scores on all five criteria
Psychological Well-Being	Environmental mastery, self-acceptance, purpose in life, autonomy	Personal growth, purpose in life
Self-Concept Structure	Medium level of complexity, high level of self-concept integration	High level of complexity, medium level of self-concept integration
Self-Concept Maturity	Medium complexity, high integration in content and valence, self-enhancing values, high self-esteem	High complexity, medium integration in content and valence, self-transcendent values, moderate self-esteem
Ego Development	Stage 3 (Conformist level) Stage 4 (Self-aware level) Stage 5 (Conscientious)	Stage 7 (Individualistic) Stage 8 (Autonomous)

Table 8.2 Summary of Process-Related Indicators of Adjustment and Personality Growth

Personality Concepts	Indicators of Adjustment	Indicators of Personality Maturity
Coping	Large repertoire of coping styles Coping styles applied flexibly depending on context Coping directed at repairing individual well-being and solving problems	Large repertoire of coping styles Coping styles applied flexibly depending on context Coping directed at increasing insight and furthering the good of others
Systemic Regulatory Processes (SOC)	SOC use with an overarching adjustment goal	SOC use with an overarching growth goal
Values and Personal Strivings	Ego-centered values (e.g., achievement, stimulation, conformity)	Self-transcendent values (e.g., universalism, benevolence, "true" generativity)
Emotion Regulation	Limited affective complexity More positive than negative affect Down-regulation of negative emotions	High affective complexity Balance between positive and negative emotions Coactivation of positive and negative affect

Structural Markers of Personality Adjustment and Maturity

The Big Five

The Big Five model of personality (Costa & McCrae, 1980) is one of the most widespread structural models of personality. According to this model, five dimensions describe the central features of personality: neuroticism (anxiety, hostility, depression), extraversion (warmth, assertiveness, activity), openness to experience (fantasy, aesthetics, ideas), agreeableness (trust, compliance), and conscientiousness (discipline, achievement striving, dutifulness).

The Big Five traits are differentially associated with adjustment and growth (see also Digman, 1997). Of the Big Five traits, emotional stability (i.e., the absence of neuroticism), agreeableness, and conscientiousness best represent personality adjustment. The absence of neuroticism represents the ease or success with which a person is able to maintain well-being. Across studies, neuroticism shows consistently strong links with negative affect (Costa & McCrae, 1980; Diener & Fujita, 1995; Watson & Clark, 1992). Neuroticism has often been viewed as the dispositional underpinning of negative affect and has even been used as an indicator of (poor) mental health. Conscientiousness, as the tendency to fulfill obligations, and agreeableness, the tendency to cooperate with others, represent a person's tendency, desire, or ability to meet social obligations. There are clear parallels between these traits and our concept of adjustment as successful adaptation to societal demands. Indirectly, agreeableness and conscientiousness also seem to be instrumentally associated with adjustment by creating facilitative conditions that help to maintain subjective well-being, for instance, by engendering harmonious social interactions. In fact, agreeableness and conscientiousness have been shown to predict subjective well-being over and above neuroticism (McCrae & Costa, 1991).

Openness to experience, in contrast, is related to personality growth. Openness is the Big Five trait that best represents an individual's interest in pursuing challenging contexts, the kind of contexts and experiences that can stimulate personality growth. Openness to new experience has been discussed as the most central concomitant of personality maturity (Compton, 2001; Schmutte & Ryff, 1997; Staudinger, Lopez, & Baltes, 1997). In this vein, openness to experience shows strong associations with the "personality growth" dimension of Ryff's psychological well-being scale, as defined later (Schmutte & Ryff, 1997). Openness is also positively correlated with ego development (Hogansen & Lanning, 2001; Kurtz & Tiegreen, 2005; McCrae & Costa, 1980), emotional complexity (Kang & Shaver, 2004), maturity of coping strategies (Costa, Zonderman, & McCrae, 1991), general and personal wisdom (Mickler & Staudinger, 2008; Staudinger et al., 2005), and various other constructs related to personality growth (McCrae & Costa, 1997). At the same time, openness to new experience is not significantly correlated with indicators of adjustment such as subjective well-being (Costa et al., 1987). However, there is some indication that openness to new experience might comprise of subdimensions, one related to internal experience ("fantasy, aesthetics, and feelings") and the other to external experience (actions, values, and ideas; Jang, Livesley, Angleitner, Riemann, & Vernon, 2002). Initial research suggests that openness to internal experience is associated with depression and neuroticism whereas openness to external experience is negatively correlated with neuroticism and positively associated with well-being (or lack of depression; Carrillo, Rojo, Sanchez-Bernardos, & Avia, 2001; Wolfenstein & Trull, 1997). New external experiences may be exciting and increase positive affect, but being willing to question and doubt oneself may, at least temporarily, challenge an individual's well-being. The opposing relationships of these two subfacets with well-being may explain the lack of correlation between overall openness scores and subjective well-being.

The relationship of extraversion with growth and adjustment is more difficult to interpret. Digman (1997) provided evidence that openness to experience and extraversion both load onto the same higher order, personality growth-related factor. Indeed, extraversion would seem to be related to an individual's willingness and tendency to zealously explore new (social) contexts, which characterize and can potentially foster personality growth. Likewise, many studies have demonstrated the close relationship between extraversion and the experience of positive emotions (Eid, Riemann, Angleitner, & Borkenau, 2003), one aspect of adjustment. Given the partial overlap between adjustment and growth, it should not come as surprising that the Five Factor model does not conceptually neatly split into a two factor solution. Still, it has been suggested that extraversion is comprised of two subfacets; namely, social assurance and social vitality (Helson & Kwan, 2000). Social assurance (e.g., dominance, norm adherence, independence) shows fit with our notion of personality adjustment in the sense of environmental mastery, although independence is a criterion for both adjustment and growth. Social vitality (e.g., sociability, empathy, social presence) seems to be important for both successful adjustment and personality growth. Social vitality would seem to contribute to or reflect an individual's sense of belonging (adjustment) as well as exploration of the kind of social contexts that can foster personality growth.

The age trajectories of the adjustment-related Big Five traits are in line with our hypothesis that aging, as it is currently observed, optimizes personality adjustment. Specifically, neuroticism decreases across adulthood (Mroczek & Spiro, 2005; Roberts, Walton, & Viechtbauer, 2006; Terracciano, McCrae, Brant, & Costa, 2005), including the transition from young-old age to old-old age (Allemand, Zimprich, & Martin, 2008), although it may show some increase again very late in life (Small, Hertzog, Hultsch,

& Dixon, 2003).[3] Agreeableness increases linearly with age (Helson & Kwan, 2000; Roberts & Mroczek, 2008; Terracciano et al., 2005). Generally, research has shown that conscientiousness normatively increases during adulthood (Helson & Kwan, 2000; Roberts & Mroczek, 2008), although recent research suggests that the relationship between age and conscientiousness is actually curvilinear, with scores on this trait peaking between midlife and young-old age (Donnellan & Lucas, 2008; Terracciano et al., 2005). Together, the mean-level decrease in neuroticism and the increases in agreeableness and conscientiousness have been described as reflecting an increase in social adaptation in the sense of becoming emotionally less volatile and more attuned to social demands (Baltes et al., 2006; Helson & Wink, 1987; Staudinger, 2005; Whitbourne & Waterman, 1979). The age-related increase in the social assurance dimension of extraversion (Helson & Kwan, 2000) fits well with this interpretation, although an age-related decrease in *overall* extraversion has been observed in several studies (e.g., Terraciano et al., 2005).

In contrast to this age-related increase in the indicators of personality adjustment, mean levels of openness to new experience tend to decline after age 60 (Costa, Herbst, McCrae, & Siegler, 2000; Donnellan & Lucas, 2008; McCrae et al., 1999; Roberts, Walton, & Viechtbauer, 2006). This finding supports our hypothesis that personality growth across adulthood is not a normative phenomenon. The age trajectory of the social vitality dimension of extraversion further supports this interpretation, because this trait also decreases with age (Helson & Kwan, 2000). Similar patterns of change were found in longitudinal samples using indicators of norm adherence (self-control, good impression) and openness (flexibility) from the California Psychological Inventory: Mean levels of self-control and good impression increased across adulthood, and flexibility decreased (Helson et al., 2002).

Notably, these mean-level trait changes (i.e., decreases in neuroticism and openness, increases in agreeableness and conscientiousness) seem to be roughly equivalent across cultures, gender, and cohort. In a cross-sectional study comparing samples between age 14 and 83 years from Korea, Portugal, Italy, Germany, Czech Republic, and Turkey, McCrae and colleagues (McCrae et al., 2000) found a highly similar pattern of mean-level age differences within these different cultures. In each country, self-reported conscientiousness and agreeableness were higher in older participants than in younger participants, whereas the reverse was true for extraversion and openness. Interestingly, the results for neuroticism were mixed. In Germany, Portugal, and Korea, older participants reported less neuroticism than younger participants, whereas there were no age differences in Italy and Croatia. Helson and colleagues compared data from two longitudinal studies of different cohorts (born in the 1920s and the late 1930s) and found equivalent patterns of personality change for men and women as well as for the different cohorts, despite significant changes in historical conditions (e.g., women's participation in the labor force; Helson et al., 2002).

Psychological Well-Being

Another approach that provides helpful evidence with regard to personality growth and adjustment is Carol Ryff's conception of "psychological well-being" (Ryff, 1989a; Ryff & Keyes, 1995). This measure, based on models of personality development, encompasses six dimensions, including *environmental mastery* (choosing or creating environments suitable to one's psychic conditions; managing one's surrounding world), *self-acceptance* (holding positive attitudes toward oneself), *autonomy* (having an internal locus of evaluation), *positive social relations* (ability to form warm, trusting interpersonal relations), *personal growth* (continuing to develop one's potential, to grow and expand as a person), and *purpose in life* (beliefs that give one the feeling there is purpose in and meaning to life; having and pursuing life goals).

Our concept of adjustment corresponds with being able to meet social obligations while maintaining a positive, autonomous sense of self (in a world of others). With the exception of personal growth, each of the dimensions of the Ryff scale reflect adjustment-related achievements or is a prerequisite of adjustment. Environmental mastery, self-acceptance, autonomy, purpose in life, and positive social relations relate to an individual's ability to meet personal imperatives successfully (positive sense of self, sense of belonging, sense of importance) within the society—in other words, his or her successful adjustment to external circumstances. The personal growth dimension, however, better reflects (perceived) further development of the personality system itself and hence represents personality growth. Conceptually, purpose in life is related to both personality adjustment and growth. The extent to which

[3] Interestingly, analysis of large cross-sectional German and British samples indicates that there may be cultural differences in the age trend for neuroticism. Namely, neuroticism was higher in older respondents in the German sample. The trend for the British sample was in line with previous findings: older respondents had lower scores for neuroticism than younger respondents.

an individual perceives *having* a purpose in life, as measured in the Ryff scale, seems to be most relevant for his or her adjustment. The *content*, as opposed to the strength, of an individual's purpose in life would yield better clues about the differentiation between growth and adjustment. Perceiving rather a hedonistic purpose in life (e.g., to enjoy oneself) would indicate personality adjustment, whereas perceiving a rather altruistic purpose (e.g., to improve the life situation of others) would indicate personality growth. The Ryff scale does not, however, offer information about the content of individual's purpose in life.

Some factor analyses of psychological well-being support the existence of two factors consistent with adjustment and growth. For instance, environmental mastery and self-acceptance load on the same factor conjointly with indicators of adjustment such as life satisfaction and positive–negative affect, whereas purpose in life and personal growth loaded onto a separate factor (Compton, 2001; Keyes, Shmotkin, & Ryff, 2002; Mickler & Staudinger, 2008). Other work has found close relations between the personal growth dimension and other indicators of personality growth such as personal wisdom and self-concept maturity (Dörner & Staudinger, 2010; Mickler & Staudinger, 2008). A recent factor analysis found that self-acceptance, purpose in life, autonomy, and environmental mastery loaded onto an Agency subfactor of adjustment along with the adjustment indicators of conscientiousness and emotional stability (neuroticism). Positive relations loaded onto a Social Mastery subfactor of adjustment, along with extraversion and agreeableness. Personal growth, however, loaded onto a separate personality maturity factor. Notably, these studies show that purpose in life has been found to load onto both an adjustment-related factor (Staudinger & Dörner, 2006) and a growth-related factor (e.g., Compton, 2001; Keyes et al., 2002; Mickler & Staudinger, 2008), consistent with the conceptual overlap of this dimension on both factors.

Cross-sectional analyses suggest that autonomy and environmental mastery generally increase from young adulthood to middle age and then remain stable. In contrast, purpose in life and personal growth tend to show negative age differences, with older adults scoring lower than either middle-aged or young adults (Ryff, 1989a; Ryff & Keyes, 1995; Ryff, Keyes, & Hughes, 2003; regarding environmental mastery only, Frazier, Newman, & Jaccard, 2007). The small downward trend in purpose in life was also replicated in a meta-analysis of 70 studies that used various operationalizations of this construct (Pinquart, 2002a). The age trends for positive relations and self-acceptance are less clear. Certainly, we echo previous cautions that cross-sectional data on psychological well-being may confound developmental processes with stable cohort differences (Keyes et al., 2002).

The age-related decrease in personal growth is consistent with our hypothesis that aging, as we currently observe it, does not normatively support personality growth. The apparent age-related increases and later stability in autonomy and environmental mastery partially support our hypothesis that individuals maintain a capacity for adjustment across the life span. The apparent age-related decrease in purpose in life would seem to contradict this hypothesis. However, we argue that the negative age trend for purpose in life is more indicative of a structural lag in Western industrialized societies than of ontogenetic processes per se. Societies have yet to "catch up" with the rapid and dramatic increase in life expectancy that has occurred over the past century. As such, there is currently a lack of opportunities for older adults to pursue meaningful goals and to continue to contribute to society.

Personal Wisdom

The personal-wisdom construct was developed to capture the essence of personality growth as we have defined it in this chapter (Mickler & Staudinger, 2008). On the basis of an extensive review of the wisdom literature as well as the literature on personality maturity (e.g., Allport, 1961; Baltes et al., 1992; Bühler, 1968; Erikson, 1968; Freud, 1917/1993; Jung, 1934; Labouvie-Vief, 1982; Maslow, 1994; Rogers, 1961), Mickler and Staudinger (2008) defined five criteria of personal wisdom. The two *basic* criteria are exhibiting deep, broad and balanced self-knowledge and having heuristics or strategies of growth and self-regulation. These basic criteria are necessary, but not sufficient, aspects of personal wisdom. There are three *meta*-criteria: interrelating the self, self-relativism, and tolerance of ambiguity. These criteria are more specific, require more complex judgmental processes, and are more difficult to acquire.

The first basic criterion of personal wisdom is *rich self-knowledge*, that is, deep insight into oneself. A self-wise person should be aware of his or her own competencies, emotions, and goals and has developed a sense of meaning in life. The second basic criterion stipulates that a person has available *heuristics for growth and self-regulation* (e.g., how to express and regulate emotions or how to develop and maintain deep social relations). Humor is an example of an important heuristic that helps one to cope with various difficult and challenging situations. These two aspects of personal wisdom are considered a necessary basis of successful adjustment because they represent the basic self-awareness and self-management skills necessary to reach adjustment-related goals.

Interrelating the self, the third criterion, refers to an individual's ability to reflect on and have insight in the possible causes of one's behavior, feelings, or both. Such causes can be age-related, situational, or linked to personal characteristics. Interrelating the self also implies that the individual acknowledges his or her embeddedness, including his or her dependency on others as well as the context-dependency of the self—that is, that the self as currently known is in part the product of historical and other contextual features of his or her biography. The fourth criterion is called *self-relativism*. People high on self-relativism are able to evaluate themselves as well as others with a distanced view. They critically appraise their own behavior without losing a basic sense of self-acceptance. They also have a high tolerance for others' values and lifestyles, as long as the balance between their own good and that of others is not disturbed. Finally, *tolerance of ambiguity* involves the ability to recognize and manage the uncertainties in one's own life and one's own development in the past, present, and future. It is reflected in an awareness that one's past and present is never fully known as well as an awareness that life is full of uncontrollable and unpredictable events, including death and illness, as well as the capacity to deal with this ambiguity.

Personality growth, by definition, is indicated by high scores on each of the five dimensions of personal wisdom—that is, self-insight, heuristics for growth and self-regulation, interrelating the self, self-relativism, and tolerance of ambiguity. Personality adjustment, in contrast, is represented by a different constellation of scores. A certain level of self-insight and heuristics for growth and self-regulation is necessary for adjustment, whereas the three meta-criteria are not necessary for everyday functioning. Therefore, medium scores on the two basic criteria in combination with low scores on the three meta-criteria indicate personality adjustment.

In a first study, personal wisdom was measured by using a thinking-aloud task based on an adapted version of the Berlin general wisdom paradigm (Baltes et al., 1992). Specifically, participants were asked to think about themselves as a friend and asked to describe their typical behaviors, their strengths and weaknesses, how they act in difficult situations, why they act the way they do, and what they would like to change about themselves as a friend. Answers were recorded and then rated according to the five criteria of personal wisdom. This performance measure of personal wisdom was positively correlated with other performance measures of personality maturity such as Loevinger's (1976) ego development and self-concept maturity (described shortly; Dörner & Staudinger, 2010), as well as with self-report measures of personality growth, such as Ryff's personal growth. Openness to experience and psychological mindedness, a construct measuring interest in thoughts and feelings of other people (Gough, 1957), were both significantly correlated with personal wisdom. Furthermore, the measure was uncorrelated with indicators of adjustment, such as life satisfaction and negative or positive emotions. Importantly, we were able to show that although personal wisdom performance was correlated with general wisdom performance, personal wisdom had unique characteristics not captured by general wisdom (Mickler & Staudinger, 2008).

In a first study, young adults (20–40 years old) and older adults (60–80 years old) completed both a personal wisdom and a general wisdom task. In line with other research (Staudinger, 1999), general wisdom performance was comparable between the two age groups. However, age differences in personal wisdom seem to be less favorable (Mickler & Staudinger, 2008). Overall, older adults scored lower on personal wisdom. Separate analysis of the basic criteria and meta-criteria revealed differential trends: older adults performed better than the young adults on the basic criteria (self-knowledge, self-regulation) but worse than the young adults on the meta-criteria (interrelating the self, self-relativism, and tolerance of ambiguity). Thus, older adults performed better than younger adults on the criteria related more closely with aspects of personality adjustment (e.g., self-knowledge and knowing how to reach one's goals) and worse than younger adults on the three uniquely growth-related criteria. These cross-sectional results are in line with our hypothesis that aging, as it is currently observed, optimizes personality adjustment but not personality growth.

Self-Concept Structure and Self-Concept Maturity

A long research history has investigated the relationship between the structure of the self-concept and positive personality functioning. The structure of the self-concept is often investigated in terms of (a) its *complexity* and (b) its *integration* (e.g., Campbell, Assanand, & Di Paula, 2003). Unfortunately, different authors tend to define complexity quite differently, which complicates a review of the findings (for a review of the different conceptualizations, see Rafaeli-Mor & Steinberg, 2002). *Complexity* has been defined as the number of factors, perspectives, and roles involved in one's thoughts and actions (Allport, 1961); the interlocking of multiple psychological functions (such as emotion, cognition, and motivation, e.g., Labouvie-Vief, 1982); and the level of abstraction and reasoning underlying one's self-descriptions (Loevinger, 1976; Maslow, 1994). We refer to self-complexity as the number of perspectives an individual adopts with regard to himself or herself, as indicated by the number of nonredundant self-aspects or content categories of the self-definition (Linville, 1987). *Integration* is typically defined as the similarity of self-aspects. Integration is typically operationalized as the correlation of trait ratings across domains of the self-concept (Donahue, Robins, Roberts, & John, 1993). High similarity between self-aspects indicates high self-concept integration (Diehl, Hastings, & Stanton, 2001). Importantly, self-concept complexity and integration appear to be independent dimensions (e.g., G. Brown & Rafaeli, 2007; Constantino, Wilson, Horowitz, & Pinel, 2006; Rothermund & Meiniger, 2004).

How do self-concept complexity and integration relate to personality adjustment and growth? We argue that it is important to consider both together (see also G. Brown & Rafaeli, 2007; Rothermund & Meiniger, 2004). With regards to adjustment, empirical evidence all in all confirms a linear association between self-concept integration and psychological health and well-being (Campbell et al., 2003; Diehl et al., 2001; Lutz & Ross, 2003). Interestingly, first results indicate that self-concept integration is most strongly predictive of well-being for older adults (Diehl et al., 2001). Indeed, seeing continuity of one's identity over one's lifetime at the end of life is a major developmental challenge for the end of life (cf. Mickler & Staudinger, 2008).

As for complexity, having a rich variety of self-defining concepts enables individuals to be more flexible in selecting and prioritizing goals and investments that best fit current conditions of living and is considered part of a person's developmental reserve capacity (Riediger, Freund, & Baltes, 2005; cf. Staudinger et al., 1995). Higher self-complexity can, at least theoretically, *prevent* stress because individuals can draw on a larger pool of self-resources to match the situation. Self-complexity is thought to have a buffering effect, such that high self-complexity will prevent negative occurrences related to one or several self-aspects from spilling over to other self-aspects or more global self-esteem (e.g., Linville, 1985). Having a complex self-structure also allows for efficient self-regulation, such that higher levels of self-complexity seem to facilitate activation of self-aspects that allow for positive reappraisal (Rothermund & Meiniger, 2004).

Indeed, a number of studies have found that a higher number of self-aspects can have a buffering effect against stress (Coleman, Antonucci, & Adelmann, 1987; Dietz, 1996; Helson, Elliot, & Leigh, 1990; Rothermund & Meiniger, 2004; Thoits, 1986; Vandewater, Ostrove, & Stewart, 1997). However, the specifics of the buffering hypothesis have yet to be confirmed (e.g., Solomon & Haaga, 2003), and many studies have failed to confirm the buffering hypothesis (e.g., Freund, 1995; Freund & Smith, 1999). Meta-analysis revealed equivocal relationships between self-complexity and measures of well-being (see Raefeli-Mor & Steinberg, 2002). Overall, the relationship between self-complexity and measures of well-being was slightly negative, although the inconsistent results in this literature might also be reflective of variations in operationalizations more than anything else (Koch & Shepperd, 2004). Possibly the mixed results arise from a trade-off between high level of self-complexity and a consistent sense of self (Assagioli, 1978/1989; Block, 1961; Erikson, 1968; James, 1890/1948; Rogers, 1961). Indeed, having a high level of self-complexity frequently goes along with intense self-reflection, which in turn is more likely to induce negative affect, self-doubts, and uncertainty (J. D. Brown & Dutton, 1995; Silvia & Gendolla, 2001; Wicklund & Eckert, 1992; Wilson & Dunn, 2004). A very large number of self-aspects can also be indicative of role strain or identity uncertainty (Block, 1961). The mixed results about the relationship between complexity and well-being might also arise from investigating self-complexity as a main effect, rather than as an interaction with integration. For instance, perceived control over self-aspects was found to moderate the relationship between self-concept complexity and well-being in a young adult student sample (McConnell et al., 2005). Similar results were found for men and women in terms of the number of roles they had: Middle-aged men and women's sense of control moderated the positive relationship between the number of occupied roles and psychological well-being (Chrouser Ahrens & Ryff, 2006). Presumably, feelings of control over a self-aspect are related to the extent that an individual feels the self-aspect represents his or her "true" self—and should, therefore, correlate with measures of integration. In fact, many studies report that well-being tends to increase with the number of self-aspects (e.g., Chouser Ahrens & Ryff, 2006; Lutz & Ross, 2003; Martire, Stephens, & Townsend, 2000), given certain constraining conditions such as the positivity (vs. negativity) of the self-aspects (e.g., Woolfolk, Novalany,

Gara, Allen, & Polino, 1995), a lack of conflict among the self-aspects (e.g., Donahue et al., 1993), and some cohesive sense of self (e.g., Campbell et al., 2003).

All things considered, a medium level of complexity paired with a high level of integration best represents personality adjustment. The adjusted (but not mature) personality[4] has limited tolerance of ambiguity, therefore, we expect that such individuals have relatively undifferentiated self-aspects (i.e., high integration) and fewer self-aspects such that the sense of self is not threatened. Still, a medium level of self-complexity seems necessary for satisfying basic needs such as autonomy and affiliation as well as for buffering the effects of everyday stress (Dörner & Staudinger, 2010).

A different balance between self-concept complexity and integration characterizes personality maturity. Relatively high self-concept complexity is also an important facet of personality maturity according to several approaches (e.g., Allport, Maslow, Loevinger, Heath, Labouvie-Vief). The few empirical studies on the association of self-complexity and personality maturity support this assumption, although these studies used very different operationalizations of self-concept complexity than we do here.[5] The very conflict stimulated by a high number of (inconsistent) self-aspects can stimulate growth in terms of encouraging more complex emotion regulation and a broader insight into the self and the world. In line with the buffering hypothesis, self-complexity can enable individuals to learn from their failure by reducing the threat of negative feedback. In one study, it was demonstrated that self-complexity moderated the effect of negative feedback on self-focus: Individuals with higher self-complexity demonstrated increased tolerance for self-awareness, whereas individuals with lower self-complexity tended to escape and avoid self-focus (Dixon & Baumeister, 1991). It seems that self-complexity helps people to deal constructively with negative feedback—something necessary for personality growth to occur. For these different reasons, high complexity characterizes personality growth. As for integration, exposing oneself to a variety of challenging situations should lead to an expansive view of the self and recognition that the self is different in different situations. Therefore, the mature personality is characterized by high complexity paired with a medium level of integration, such that the individual maintains a sense of self but is simultaneously able to recognize the context-dependency of the self and tolerate the ambiguity aroused by dialectical self-descriptions (e.g., positive and negative aspects). These latter qualities indicate that there is a ceiling level as to how much integration the mature personality will exhibit. Empirical research recently supported this hypothesis: High complexity combined with only a moderate degree of integration was indicative of personality maturity as defined in this chapter (Dörner & Staudinger, 2010).

With regard to self-concept integration, it is widely assumed that the adolescent conflicts raised by conflicting self-aspects tend to alleviate around the onset of adulthood, and the self-structure becomes more and more integrated across adulthood (Arnett, 2000; Moneta, Schneider, & Csikszentmihalyi, 2001). Most theories and evidence covering adulthood expect this trend to continue linearly over the rest of the life span (Markus & Herzog, 1991; Neugarten, Havighurst, & Tobin, 1961). When it comes to empirical research, in one of the few studies on this topic, cross-sectional data indicate an inverted U-shaped relationship between self-concept integration and chronological age for the age range from 20 to 88 years, with the peak (i.e., the highest degree of self-concept integration) occurring in middle adulthood (Diehl et al., 2001). Dörner and Staudinger (2010) found that the degree of integration of self-aspects was higher for older adults (60–80 years) than for younger adults (20–40 years), corresponding with the increase in identity certainty across adulthood (Cramer, 2004; Sheldon & Kasser, 2001; Stewart & Ostrove, 1998). No information about midlife was provided in this study.

Empirical evidence substantiates our hypotheses regarding personality adjustment and maturity. In contrast to widely held theoretical assumptions about age trajectories in self-concept complexity, the empirical evidence neither illustrates an increase (as suggested by Markus & Herzog, 1991; Neugarten, 1968; Perlmutter, 1988) nor a decrease

[4] Given the hypothesized relationship between adjustment and growth, it is possible for a person to be adjusted but not mature, neither adjusted nor mature, mature but not adjusted, as well as adjusted and mature. Here we describe what we expect the self-structure to look like for individuals who are adjusted but not mature.

[5] For example, self-complexity as measured by open self-descriptions was positively related to ego development (Labouvie-Vief et al., 1995). Self-complexity operationalized as the relative complexity of rating patterns across self-descriptive attributes and a number of self-relevant contexts was positively related to ego development in an adolescent sample (Hauser, Jacobson, Noam, & Powers, 1983). Self-concept complexity operationalized as the similarity among reactions to various self-relevant scenarios was positively related to the maturity of psychological defenses (Evans, 1994) and ego development (Evans, Brody, & Noam, 2001).

(as suggested by disengagement theory, e.g., Cummings & Henry, 1961) in the number of self-aspects across the life span. Instead, the number of self-aspects seems to remain relatively stable throughout adulthood, although empirical evidence is scarce. For example, in a cross-sectional study conducted by Mueller, Wonderlich, and Dugan (1986), college students and older adults were asked to select self-descriptive attributes from a large set of descriptors. No age differences were found in the number of selected attributes. Dörner and Staudinger (2010) recently yielded a similar result. Using an adapted version of the Linville self-complexity measure (Linville, 1985), they found no difference in number of self-aspects between younger and older adults (20–40 years old and 60–80 years old, respectively). Circumstances seem to change somewhat when we look at very old age. There a reduction in number as well as multifacetness of self-aspects has been found (Freund, 1995). Nevertheless, it seems fair to conclude that the structure of the self-definition is relatively insensitive to age-graded changes in the external life circumstances, at least given the currently-used empirical paradigms.[6]

In sum, self-concept structure (complexity, integration) is highly relevant to our notions of personality adjustment and maturity. Empirical evidence on age trajectories, particularly with regard to self-concept integration, is equivocal. This is probably at least partly due to variation in measurement within the self-structure literature. Still, the finding that self-concept complexity remains stable while integration increases throughout adulthood supports our assumption that personality adjustment normatively increases. The pattern concerning personality growth are less clear but are at least not in conflict with our contention that personality growth does not normatively occur. The finding that self-concept complexity remains stable throughout adulthood supports our assumption that personality growth does not normatively increase across adulthood, but we restate the need to consider integration and complexity conjointly.

Recently, Dörner and Staudinger (2010) developed *self-concept maturity* as a measure of personality maturity based on the self-concept literature. In addition to simultaneously considering both self-complexity and self-integration, this measure also considered emotional and motivational facets of the self-concept. In other words, the measure assessed the cognitive, emotional, and motivational facets reflective of personality maturity as they apply to the self-concept. Specifically, the measure assessed self-concept complexity and self-concept integration (as defined above), balance of self-related affect (e.g., evaluative integration, Showers, 1992), self-esteem, and value orientation. A specific configuration of traits was defined to index personality maturity. As previously described, personality maturity was indicated by high complexity paired with medium integration, along with a balanced experience of positive as well as negative self-related emotions, self-transcending values and a medium level of self-esteem.[7] Personality adjustment was indicated by medium complexity, high integration, more positive than negative self-related emotions, self-enhancing values, and high self-esteem. Cross-sectional comparisons of older adults (aged 60–80) and younger adults (aged 20–40) revealed no age differences for self-concept maturity. However, relative to the younger adults, significantly more of the older adults demonstrated self-concept adjustment (Dörner & Staudinger, 2010). These findings are in line with the hypothesis that aging, as observed here and now, optimizes adjustment but not maturity. However, without longitudinal evidence, we cannot exclude the possibility that the older adults reached higher levels of adjustment through growth-related means (e.g., complex emotion regulation could theoretically also help to integrate negative emotions into an overall positive whole).

Ego Development

Jane Loevinger's (1976, 1997) stage-model of ego development has gained much prominence as an indicator of personality growth. Analogous to Piaget's model of cognitive development, Loevinger described eight progressive stages of ego development that lead to psychological maturity (impulsive, self-protective, conformist, self-aware, conscientious, individualistic, autonomous, integrated). Certainly, modern notions of development do not embrace

[6] Studies that conceptualized complexity on a more global level, taking into account the degree of abstractness, self-reflection, ambiguity tolerance, and multidimensionality (e.g., motivation, emotion, cognition) in self-descriptions as rated by trained judges or as engagement in multiple spheres (Neugarten, 1968) indicate a quadratic rather than a linear trajectory across adulthood. The pattern of this indicator of self-complexity was an inverted U-shape over an age range from 11 to 85 years old (Labouvie-Vief et al., 1995). However, this conceptualization of self-complexity is hardly comparable to the notion of self-concept complexity as used in this chapter.

[7] In this study, self-esteem was operationalized as the proportion of positively valenced self-descriptions. Other operationalizations of self-esteem might have different relationships with personality growth and adjustment.

the stage approach to development as proposed by Piaget, Leovinger, or Erikson, but what remains enticing about her work is the definition of different phases and levels in ego development.

In the impulsive phase, usually observable by early childhood, the individual has achieved awareness of the self as a separate person. He or she spontaneously acts on his or her impulses as a verification of that "selfhood" and has little control over his or her actions. The emotional range is small. In the self-protective phase, individuals exert some control over their impulses. They are egocentrically motivated and preoccupied by control, either exerting control over others or being controlled by others. The emotional range is still quite limited. These phases are generally outgrown by childhood or adolescence. When an adolescent or adult remains at the impulsive phase, he or she will be unable to master adult life and is in some cases psychopathic. Adolescents and adults remaining at the self-protective phase can sometimes still succeed in the adult world.

In the conformist phase, the individual has progressed to the point of identifying with a social group. He or she has respect for rules and is able to exert control over his or her behavior to conform to group norms. At the self-aware phase, the individual is still basically a conformist but is aware that he or she does not always live up to the group norms. He or she demonstrates some awareness and acceptance that there are allowable contingencies and exceptions for straying from group standards. The individual is more aware of the self as separate from the group and may be somewhat troubled by loneliness or self-consciousness. At the conscientious phase, the person lives by his or her own ideals as opposed to merely seeking group approval. The individual has long-term goals and ideals. By this phase, the individual has a rich vocabulary for expressing shades of emotion. These three phases can be interpreted as indicators of personality adjustment. He or she is able to master adult life within his or her society while demonstrating (to varying degrees, depending on the phase) self-acceptance. In other words, he or she is capable of feeling good about his or her self in a world of others—the prototypical marker of personality adjustment. Empirically, most people rank between the third and fifth phases (Holt, 1980; Loevinger, 1997),

At the individualistic phase, the individual has some awareness of the paradoxes and contradictions in life. People at this phase begin to become aware of development as a process and of the complexities and context contingencies of their own development. They are able to take a broad view of life as a whole. The development of these characteristics continues in the autonomous phase. People at the autonomous phase have transcended dialectical cognitive organizations, such as viewing life choices as good versus bad. Individuals at this phase demonstrate awareness of the multifaceted complexity of life choices. They often display existential humor that plays with the irony of life situations. Above all, there is respect for other people and their need for autonomy. There is a growing tendency to see one's own life as embedded in humanity. Development of these traits continues into the highest phase, the integrated phase. At this point, the individual is able to strike a balance between his or her own good with that of the wider society. Using Maslow's terminology, he or she has self-actualized. The final two phases, the autonomous and the integrated phases, best tap into our notion of personality growth. People at these phases recognize the multifaceted complexity of life (including their *own* life). They can tolerate ambiguity (e.g., by seeing humor in life's ironies) and are able to manage dialectical cognitions and emotions. Finally, they have a motivational orientation that balances their desire and striving for self-fulfillment with the needs of others. In short, people in the last two phases of ego development demonstrate the cognitive, emotional, and motivational facets of personality growth. The highest level of ego development is rarely observed in random samples (Loevinger, 1997).

Ego level correlates positively with psychometric indicators of personal growth such as personal wisdom (Staudinger et al., 2005). Furthermore, evidence from the Mills Study demonstrated that ego level was related to the appreciation of the others' individuality and the individuality and conscious development of a personal philosophy of life (Helson & Roberts, 1994), as assessed by the revised California Psychological Inventory (Gough, 1957). In sum, theoretical as well as empirical evidence supports the use of ego level as one global operationalization of personality maturity.

Loevinger (1976) proposed that there is stability in ego development across adulthood and into old age. After adolescence, individuals typically know enough about the human condition to meet the contextual demands of the adult world; contextual demands are therefore less prone to challenge personality functioning. Furthermore, Loevinger argued that most people proactively select their environments according to their own ego level, thereby inhibiting personality growth. Indeed, empirical results show no age differences in ego level between 25 and 80 years (Cohn, 1998; McCrae & Costa, 1980), with the self-aware phase as the single mode for late adolescents and adult life (Holt,

1980; Loevinger, 1997). Overall, these results support our proposal that aging, at least under current circumstances, does not normatively produce personality growth. Rather, it seems that once people reach the threshold-level of personality adjustment necessary for mastering adult life, further personality growth stops.

Process-Related Markers of Personality Adjustment and Growth

Coping Strategies

Coping is defined as the use of cognitive or behavioral strategies for dealing with actual or anticipated challenges and serves both a homeostatic and a transformational function (Aldwin, 1994). Most coping research has focused on the homeostatic function of coping by which individuals manage their emotions and return to a normal state (i.e., adjustment). However, coping is also the process by which individuals learn from challenges and negative experiences and underlies the process by which a stressful experience can become a catalyst for personality growth.

Generally, individuals who are equipped with (a) a repertoire of different coping strategies and (b) an adaptive algorithm that allows them to flexibly apply the strategy that best fits a given situation are most able to adjust successfully (P. B. Baltes et al., 2006). This "algorithm" can be set to achieve either personality adjustment or personality growth. Adjustment-related coping efforts focus on repair of one's own emotional state. When individuals cope with the goal of adjustment, they try to manage their emotions and return to a normal state of functioning. Most coping research has focused on this homeostatic function of coping. However, coping is also the process by which individuals learn from challenges and negative experiences—and underlies the process by which a stressful experience can become a catalyst for personality growth. The goal of growth-related coping endeavors is the facilitation of a greater good which most often extends beyond the coping individual and may actually also entail discomfort and pain for the respective person. For instance, coping under the auspices of personality growth entails efforts to see both one's self and one's environment realistically (Allport, 1961; Haan, 1977; Maslow, 1994), including open analysis of how circumstances and personal weaknesses have led up to a stressful situation. Thus, coping behavior that takes advantage of negative experiences as opportunities to learn about one's self and the world contributes to personality growth.

When we consider the knowledge and algorithmic facets of coping, we again expect some overlap between personality adjustment and growth. A greater repertoire as well as a flexible algorithm is conducive to both adjustment as well as growth. The critical difference is the goal toward which this repertoire is applied; either the maintenance or regaining of subjective well-being or the mastery of everyday problems or the transcendence of a given situation for the sake of a greater good extends beyond the target person.

Indeed, a greater repertoire of coping responses is related to better mental health (i.e., one indicator of adjustment; Forster & Gallagher, 1986). Possessing a flexible "algorithm" has also been related to adjustment: older individuals who reported selective flexibility in coping (endorsing some coping styles strongly and others not at all) also demonstrated high levels of subjective well-being (Staudinger & Fleeson, 1996). There is, however, no simple answer regarding what kind of coping strategies best optimize adjustment. Whether a coping strategy represents an adaptive response depends entirely on the context: on who does it, in response to which stressor, and in which situation the behavior occurs (e.g., Brandtstädter & Greve, 1994; Filipp, 1999; Heckhausen & Schulz, 1995; Lazarus, 1996; Staudinger et al., 1995).

We expect that personality maturity is characterized by an even richer catalogue of coping strategies and even greater flexibility in application. In particular, we expect that the mature personality copes with stressful experiences by being open to new experiences and using the experience to expand his or her insight, openly tolerating and working through negative and conflicting emotions as well as relying on his or her basic trust in others. In other words, one could say that the mature personality copes with negative experiences with further personality growth. Obviously, acknowledging, experiencing, and working through negative emotions (as opposed to successfully repressing, denying, and/or avoiding them) is a necessary part of growth-related coping. However, at least in the short run, this kind of coping may be detrimental to subjective well-being. In terms of primary and secondary control strategies (i.e., coping strategies that attempt to create better fit between personal strivings and the environment by acting on the environment versus adapting the self), growth-related coping involves a wise judgment about whether to accept the circumstances as they are and change oneself or whether to attempt to change circumstance and continue to strive for one's original goal (cf. Morling & Evered, 2006). In other words, personality maturity implies, efficient deployment of yielding as well as assimilative strategies—with the essential feature that their employment is governed by an algorithm that aims to further the good not only one's own self but also that of others.

Evidence concerning coping behavior suggests that people maintain their capacity for adjustment throughout much of adulthood. In contrast to stereotypical views of the elderly as rigid, older adults seem to be more flexible in adapting their coping response to the characteristics of the situation than do younger adults (Aldwin, 1991). This capacity for adaptation may find its limits in extreme situations, such as the challenges of advanced old age (Baltes & Smith, 2003; Smith & Baltes, 1999). Generally, however, people become increasingly better at adjusting to losses and negative events up until very old age—for example, by disengaging from blocked goals (Wrosch, Scheier, Carver, & Schulz, 2003), rescaling personal expectations to the given situation (Rothermund & Brandtstädter, 2003), or letting go of self-images that do not fit the actual self anymore (Freund & Smith, 1999). Younger adults, on the contrary, are more likely to adhere to their established goals, even if these goals are no longer obtainable (Brandtstädter & Renner, 1990).

Concerning the type of strategy used, reviews of the literature suggest that older adults generally employ fewer escapist and avoidant coping strategies (Aldwin, 1994). The overall use of mature coping mechanisms (e.g., humor, altruism) appear to increase with age, whereas the use of maladaptive and immature coping mechanisms (e.g., passive aggression, acting out) appears to decrease with age (Diehl et al., 1996; Segal, Coolidge, & Mizuno, 2007; Whitty, 2003; Vaillant, 2000). Studies also typically find that yielding strategies (i.e., accommodative, secondary-control, or emotion-focused coping) increase with age (Brandtstädter & Rothermund, 2002; Wrosch, Heckhausen, & Lachman, 2000). That is, in comparison to younger adults, older adults tend to demonstrate an accommodative coping style (i.e., accepting the situation and adjusting the self) in the face of adversity or failure. Findings with respect to the development of assimilative strategies (i.e., acting on the environment, tenaciously pursuing goals) are not completely consistent, but most authors speak, for instance, of stable or even increasing primary control across adulthood (Staudinger, Freund, Linden, & Maas, 1999; Wrosch et al., 2000), including investment of resources such as effort, time, and skills to achieve a chosen goal (although see Brandtstädter & Renner, 1990, for an exception). All in all, however, differences in the endorsement of coping mechanisms seem to be more a function of the type of stressful event (e.g., reversible or irreversible) than of age per se (e.g., McCrae, 1989).

Overall, although coping strategies are clearly involved in the attainment of both adjustment and growth, the age trajectories of coping strategies cannot be easily interpreted in terms of adjustment and growth. The flexibility with which people implement coping strategies seems to increase, and, in addition, older adults report using more mature coping strategies than younger adults. Both of these age trends suggest an increased ability to adjust to changing life circumstances and increase in certain mature qualities. However, it is difficult to say how the increased reliance on yielding strategies fits in with this picture. On one hand, both adjustment and growth require that an individual accept what cannot be changed and to accept that sometimes it is necessary to give up on certain goals in order to allocate resources to more important goals. The importance of yielding strategies for adjustment seems to increase with age, as letting go of important goals and roles becomes a pragmatic response to the declines in the mechanics of life (Schindler & Staudinger, 2005). With increasing age, depressive symptoms are hypothesized to arise as a result of difficulties in relinquishing blocked goals (Brandtstädter & Rothermund, 2002). Indeed, older adults who expressed more accommodative thoughts in structured interviews also reported greater satisfaction with their aging, had a more positive attitude toward their biography, and found more continuity and meaning in their life (Brandtstädter, Rothermund, & Schmitz, 1997). On the other hand, the increased use of yielding strategies might be reflective of an increasing tendency to avoid the kind of identity-challenging contexts that stimulate growth, at least partly stemming from a pragmatic response to shrinking resources and the primacy of adjustment-related goals. It seems likely that the apparent stability of acting-on-environment (i.e., assimilative, primary-control, problem-solving) strategies reflects the unchanging importance of adjustment-related goals such as health and happiness across the life span, whereas the threshold for yielding versus tenacious goal pursuit in domains not essential for a basic level of adjustment (e.g., growth-related goals) is normatively lowered over time.

In sum, although coping strategies are clearly relevant for personality adjustment as well as growth, it is difficult to interpret age-related differences in coping behavior in terms of these two trajectories of positive personality development because coping research is typically more interested in the functionality of coping in regaining or maintaining well-being as opposed to copers' overarching goal(s) (e.g., repairing one's own well-being vs. furthering a greater good). Still, at the very least, the empirical research does not contradict our overarching hypotheses concerning the relative incidence rates of personality adjustment and growth. The increase in so-called mature coping strategies and stability in acting-on-environment coping strategies reflect the impressive ability of aging individuals to adjust to circumstances outside of their control. However, we suspect that this increase in accommodation may at the same time interfere with reaching growth-related goals.

Systemic Self-Regulation: Selective Optimization with Compensation

Selective optimization with compensation (SOC; Baltes & Baltes, 1990) is a general self-regulatory mechanism by which, according to life-span psychology, individuals proactively manage their development. Freund and Baltes (1998) defined the strategies as follows. *Selection* refers to the process by which individuals give direction to their behavior by choosing to allocate resources to certain goals in a nonrandom manner. *Elective selection* (ES) refers to goal selection guided primarily by preference or social norms—for instance, someone decides to study biology rather than chemistry or decides to have go to university instead of getting a job. *Loss-based selection* (LS) occurs when an individual is pressured to change his or her goals (or goal hierarchy) by the loss of some internal (e.g., physical strength) or external resource (e.g., time). For instance, a person decides to retire from a physical job because of health constraints or decides against taking on extra hours at work because he needs to take care of his children. *Optimization* (O) refers to the acquisition, refinement, and deployment of resources to achieve a selected goal. General categories of optimization include persistence, practice, learning new skills, modeling successful others, as well as dedicating time and energy to reach a goal. Finally, *compensation* (C) concerns the acquisition and use of alternative means to maintain a desired level of functioning in the face of actual or anticipated decrease in resources. For example, hiring someone else to buy groceries may help to maintain independent living when health constraints limit mobility. Taken together, using SOC strategies reflects the process by which the individual directs his or her energy to achieve to more meaningful, quality experiences as opposed to general busyness and experience quantity.

It has been argued that the coordinated use of the SOC strategies can (a) increase one's pool of resources, (b) help maintain functioning in the face of life's challenges, and (c) help regulate impending losses in resources. These strategies are supposed to be particularly useful whenever demands require performance near reserve capacity—for instance, when developmental losses predominate over gains and older adults begin in to experience declines in biological, mental, and social reserve capacity (Baltes & Baltes, 1990). Initial self-report and observational studies lend support to the assumption that individuals show higher levels of personality adjustment, both short-term and long-term, when they engage in selective optimization with compensation (Baltes et al., 2006). For example, both cross-sectional and longitudinal studies indicate that romantic partners who reported more frequent use of SOC-related behaviors to manage work-life conflicts also perceived higher levels of well-being (Baltes & Heydens-Gahir, 2003; Wiese, Freund, & Baltes, 2002). Similar findings were obtained with regard to the challenges faced by college students (Wiese & Schmitz, 2002). As another example, older people suffering from osteoarthritis successfully managed their illness by use of behaviors that are consistent with selection, optimization, and compensation (Gignac, Cott, & Badley, 2002).

It has also been argued that selection, optimization, and compensation are central processes for both the acquisition and behavioral expression of wisdom-related knowledge (Baltes & Freund, 2003; Freund & Baltes, 2002). For instance, to grow, the individual must select challenging contexts and dedicate resources to optimizing personality growth—even when it means sacrificing short-term adjustment goals. As for expression of personality growth, the mature individual actively selects to invest in the goals that are most personally meaningful based on his or her self-insight and is willing to seek alternative means to attain his or her goal with a sense of openness. More specifically, he or she will select goals in line with his or her motivation to improve the well-being of others and optimizes goals only to the extent that personal rewards are not gained at the expense of others. However, SOC strategies can also be used to optimize egoistic or even violent goals. Even mafia bosses can expertly use SOC strategies to run criminal operations efficiently. Clearly, SOC strategy use would not be reflective of personality maturity in such a case, again underlying the importance of an individual's overarching developmental goal for differentiating between growth-related and adjustment-related self-regulation.

Conceptually, SOC strategy use is related to both personality adjustment and growth. Using the SOC strategies can help an individual optimize his or her development. In this sense, SOC strategies can be viewed as (proactive) coping mechanisms and as such they do not include a decision about what "optimized development" is. Whether SOC strategies are used to achieve adjustment or growth is a separate decision and rests on individual preferences and overarching developmental goals.

Across adulthood and into old age, cross-sectional data suggest age-related increases in elective selection from young to middle and from middle to later adulthood (Freund & Baltes, 2002). According to the authors, this result points to the fact that whereas young adults experience a high need to explore many pathways of life, by middle and especially later adulthood, pathways of life are more or less set and subsequently pursued (Baltes & Baltes, 1990; Freund & Baltes, 2002). There were no age differences in loss-based selection. Data also suggest increases in optimization and compensation from young to middle adulthood and a decrease in later adulthood (Freund & Baltes, 2002). Despite such declines in the frequency of self-reported optimization and compensation, the elderly do continue to use SOC strategies, and if they do so, they display higher levels of well-being (M. Baltes & Lang, 1997; Freund & Baltes, 1998; Joop & Smith, 2006). Cross-sectional comparison of young-old and old-old adults did not reveal any differences in SOC strategy use, although an interesting age interaction was observed such that SOC strategy use had a direct effect on aging satisfaction independent of resource availability for the young-old, but no direct effect for the old-old. Only the old-old adults characterized by low availability of resources profited from SOC use (Joop & Smith, 2006).

The age-associated patterns of SOC strategy use bear some relevance with regard to the trajectories of personality adjustment and growth. It appears that older adults select more while optimizing and compensating less than younger adults. This fits well with our interpretation of coping trajectories: With age, it seems that adults perceive fewer goals as worth the effort of optimizing and compensating, leading to disengagement from nonessential goals and increased focus (i.e., selection) on the individual's most highly prioritized goals. We suspect that these most highly prioritized goals are likely adjustment related. Only if individuals have resources left over after achieving a basic level of adjustment (which can be aided by using SOC strategies) *and* has an overarching growth-goal to advance insight and better understand themselves and the world will they select goals that foster personality maturity. The pattern in SOC employment is also consistent with age-related increases in accommodative coping strategies, as older adults downgrade the personal importance of domains in which developmental losses have occurred and increasingly select domains in which gains seem possible (Brandtstädter et al., 1998). These accommodative processes help to neutralize the negative affect that is associated with an aversive situation and eventually lead to adjustment. However, the more one selects (i.e., concentrates on a few important goals), the less likely he or she is to experience new and challenging contexts that are necessary for growth to occur.

The greater endorsement of selection strategies and reduced endorsement of optimization and compensation strategies suggests that older adults increasingly react to developmental challenges by narrowing their focus ever more on a few high-priority goals. Although it is important to consider that SOC strategy use can be used to foster both adjustment and growth, depending on the individual's developmental agenda, we posit that this pattern may represent one of the underlying mechanisms underlying normative decreases in personality growth because fewer new contexts and alternative ways to attain goals do not seem to be explored. However, as with coping behavior, this probabilistic argument can only be confirmed by studying personality-process mechanisms conjointly with the developmental goals guiding their use.

Values and Personal Strivings

Research regarding values and personal strivings offers further clues about the trajectories of adjustment and growth. Values, defined as cognitive representations of desirable, abstract goals that motivate actions (Rokeach, 1973; Schwartz, 1992), as well as the degree to which they are realized by an individual, have been described as important antecedents of adjustment (Sagiv & Schwartz, 2000). Furthermore, the values we endorse influence both the (social) goals we select and the means deemed appropriate to achieve them (Achenbaum & Orwoll, 1991; Allport, 1961; Orwoll & Perlmutter, 1990). Therefore, an individual's values may or may not direct behavior and cognition in a mature direction. Several personality theorists have described specific types of values associated with personality maturity, including Rogers' (1961) notion of "organismically" based values, Fromm's (1947) conception of "being" value orientation, and Kasser and Ryan's (1996) notion of "intrinsic" values.

Within the values literature, the differentiation between *self-enhancing* and *self-transcending* values according to Schwartz (1992) best captures the difference in motivational orientations underlying personality adjustment and growth. Self-enhancement values reflect a self-serving and self-gratifying attitude, as indicated not only by hedonism, achievement, and power but also by more "substantial" values such as health and community to the extent that the individual acts on such motives primarily to increase his or her own well-being. Such ego-centered values underlie adjustment. According to our definition, personality growth is characterized by a motivational orientation that transcends self-interest such that the well-being of others and the world is at least as important as one's own happiness. This motivational orientation is reflected in self-transcending values, which according to Schwartz (1992) reflect both universalism (i.e., preference for social justice and tolerance and appreciation of beauty and nature) and benevolence (i.e., preference for the welfare of others with whom one has personal contact). This is in line with several other theories of personality growth (i.e., Maslow, Allport, Erikson, Heath) that personality maturity is characterized by an altruistic motivational orientation invested in the well-being of others.

Ego-centered values have been associated with measures of well-being. Studies have shown that one of the main differences between happy and unhappy people is a hedonic orientation: People who are happy frequently name it as a conscious goal to enjoy their lives, seek positive experiences, and look for stimulation and sensual pleasure (Diener & Fujita, 1995; Lyubomirsky, 2001; Sheldon et al., 2004). A study examining the associations between value priorities and well-being found that those with high levels of affective well-being are more likely to adhere to values related to achievement, self-direction, stimulation, tradition, conformity, and security (Sagiv & Schwartz, 2000). Valuing financial success, physical appearance, and social recognition have been associated with lower levels of well-being, whereas aspirations concerning physical health, the community, and self-acceptance were positively related with well-being (Chan & Joseph, 2000; Schmuck et al., 2000; Sheldon & Kasser, 2001; Sheldon et al., 2004). This latter set of aspirations reflects more substantial (vs. superficial) values, although they still reflect a certain degree of self-centeredness. The relationship between endorsing self-transcending values, such as those concerning community and social relations, and self-enhancing rewards illustrates that personality maturity need not imply that one completely sacrifices personal well-being.

Empirical evidence for the values associated with personality growth comes from studies on personal as well as general wisdom. General wisdom-related performance was found to be positively associated with other-related values (i.e., values relating to the well-being of friends, societal engagement) and self-related values that are oriented toward self-actualization and insight into life in general (Kunzmann & Baltes, 2003). Simultaneously, general wisdom was uncorrelated to values revolving around a pleasurable life. Furthermore, using Schwartz's value scale (1992), Mickler and Staudinger (2008) found that personal wisdom was positively correlated with universalistic and benevolent values and uncorrelated to motives such as power, achievement, and hedonism.

Age-related differences in values have been primarily investigated in terms of value stability and conservatism (e.g., Glenn, 1980). Unfortunately, there is little evidence on age differences in self-enhancing versus self-transcending values. Older adults endorsed fewer hedonistic (i.e., ego-centered) values than younger adults (Kunzmann & Baltes, 2003). In a recent study using the Schwartz value scale, older participants (aged 60–80 years) reported a higher degree of self-transcending values than young adult participants (aged 20–40 years; Dörner & Staudinger, 2010). This result held true for both the universalism scale and benevolence subscales. Such findings are somewhat at odds with the result that universalism has been shown to be strongly associated with openness to experience, at least for young adults (Roccas, Sagiv, Schwartz, & Knafo, 2002), given the age-related decrease in this trait. This seeming contradiction might be related to age differences regarding the adaptive values of universalistic views, because endorsing universalistic values seems to be related to both prosociality as well as a reaction to mortality salience (Joireman & Duell, 2005). In any case, given that values are particularly sensitive to cultural influences, it seems especially important to replicate these results in longitudinal studies and with other cohorts (Bauer & McAdams, 2004; Sheldon, 2005).

The empirical results on age differences in value endorsement suggest that older people in general might adhere more strongly to values that represent self-transcendence compared with younger people (see also Ryff & Baltes, 1976). This pattern suggests that the motivational facet of personality growth, that is, the endorsement of self-transcendent values, shows a normative increase across adulthood. Age trends in self-transcending values parallel findings on generative strivings (McAdams, de St. Aubin, & Logan, 1993; Midlarsky & Kahana, 1994; Sheldon & Kasser, 2001). Thus, the value facet of personality growth may be one of the few elements of personality maturity that actually show normative increases with age. Still, we cannot reject the possibility that the apparent increase in self-transcendent values with age does not arise from ego-centered motives in reaction to mortality salience as opposed to the "true" transcendence (i.e., "belief in the species," Erikson, 1963) associated with personality growth. For instance, the three main motives that drive generative behavior are thought to be (a) a desire to achieve symbolic immortality by leaving behind a personal legacy, (b) a "need to be needed," and (c) cultural norms that adults should take an active role in parenting and the community (McAdams & de St. Aubin, 1992). Notably, these three criteria are all remarkably ego-centered and norm driven—in other words, related to adjustment and not so much personality maturity.

Affect Balance and Emotion Regulation

Emotion regulation refers to the processes of up- and down-regulation of negative and positive affective states. Affect balance refers to the proportional experience of negative and positive emotions. Positive and negative affect independently contribute to a range of outcomes related to adjustment and growth. There is considerable empirical evidence that positive affect plays an extremely important role in adaptation. Isen (2003; Isen, Daubman, & Nowicki, 1987) suggested that moderate positive affect promotes problem solving as well as perseverance and success in decision making. Across the life span, positive affect is described as fostering the integration of experience and the restoration of social, cognitive, and physical resources (Fredrickson, 2000, 2001). Negative affect promotes realistic, analytic thinking, but exhausts energy and debilitates adaptive coping with uncontrollable events (e.g., Cole, Michel, & Teti, 1994). Research has consistently linked negative emotions such as depression, anxiety, loneliness, hostility and anger, as well as neuroticism, with (negative) physical and mental health outcomes (e.g., Kiecolt-Glaser, McGuire, Glaser, & Robles, 2002).

Negative affect can be considered a challenge to personality adjustment, at least in the short run. Therefore, adjustment is primarily dependent on an individual's ability to down-regulate negative emotions and is reflected in the overall experience of proportionately more positive affect relative to negative affect. The ability to inhibit (negative) emotions is considered an important skill among healthy adults (Tomkins, 1984). Certainly, it is a positive, adaptive trait to ignore minor irritations. However, extremely high levels of positive affect are not always a sign of good adaptation and may even be diagnostic of adaptive problems (Showers & Kevlyn, 1999; Showers & Kling, 1996). Ignoring or suppressing negative affect, especially when faced with more extreme stressors, is not always the most beneficial for indicators of adjustment (e.g., Spiegel, Bloom, Kremer, & Gottheil, 1989). Furthermore, negative emotions can act as a benchmark and enable individuals to better recognize, appreciate, and strive toward more favorable emotional states (Aldwin & Stokols, 1988). In short, some level of negative affect is indispensable for long-term adjustment.

Whereas personality adjustment is reflected in an ability to down-regulate negative affect and a positively biased affect balance, the experience of negative affect is an integral part of personality growth. Negative affect stimulates the kind of reflection and critical thinking that leads to deeper insight into the self and the world and is conducive for forming transcendent goals and a sense of integrity. Personality maturity, then, is best reflected by a balance of positive and negative emotions and complex emotion regulation, in the sense that the individual can tolerate the ambiguity aroused by the coactivation of positive and negative emotions; the acknowledgment that positive and negative emotions are not two opposite ends of a single dimension (see also Kessler & Staudinger, in press). Personality growth entails affective complexity—defined as a high degree of affective differentiation and the coactivation of positive and negative emotions. Growth theorists have described affective complexity as a central prerequisite of the capacity to view the self in an open and tolerant fashion (e.g., Loevinger, 1976).

Although the ambivalence associated with coactivation of positive and negative affect is unstable, disharmonious, and unpleasant (i.e., a challenge to adjustment in the short term; Cacioppo, Gardner, & Berntson, 1999; Larsen, Hemenover, Norris, & Cacioppo, 2003), the ability to manage emotional dialectics "may allow individuals to make sense of stressors, gain mastery over future stressors, and to transcend traumatic experience" (Larsen et al., 2003; p. 213) and thereby increase the likelihood that one will be able to work through future major life stressors. Once again, the trajectories of growth and adjustment are clearly intertwined, with growth being detrimental to adjustment in the short run. However, if individuals can master the discomfort and tolerate the ambivalence aroused by the coactivation of positive and negative affect, growth can become a resource for future adjustment.

In sum, a more positive balance of positive affect relative to negative affect and down-regulation of negative affect indicate personality adjustment, whereas relatively equal levels of positive and negative affect and affective complexity represent personality maturity. Previous work has consistently found that these two measures (i.e., valence and complexity criteria) are essentially uncorrelated (Labouvie-Vief, 1999).

A review of the emotion-regulation literature concluded that older adults, relative to younger adults, are more concerned with the down-regulation of negative emotions (Consedine & Magai, 2006). These conclusions were made on the basis of self-reports but also experimental data demonstrating that older individuals are more likely to self-regulate their negative emotions following negative emotional inductions, even in relation to implicit cognitive measures (Blanchard-Fields, Stein, & Watson, 2004; Kessler & Staudinger, 2009; Magai, Consedine, Krivoshekova, Kudadjie-Gyamfi, & McPherson, 2006; Mather & Carstensen, 2003; Watson & Blanchard-Fields, 1998).

Indeed, with a few exceptions, findings suggest that younger adults have a higher level of overall negative affect compared with successive age groups; the negative age trend levels off in early old age (Carstensen, Pasupathi, Mayr, & Nesselroade, 2000; Gross, Carstensen, Pasupathi, Hsu, Tsai, & Skorpen, 1997; Mroczek & Kolarz, 1998; Pinquart, 2001). Data also indicate that age differences in negative emotion are stronger than age differences in positive emotion (Griffin, Mroczek, & Spiro, 2006; Kunzmann, Little, & Smith, 2000). Age differences in implicit affective paradigms disfavor negative stimuli to a greater extent than they favor positive stimuli (Grühn, Smith, & Baltes, 2005; Wood & Kisley, 2006). As for positive affect, older adults seem to experience more low arousal, positive affect (e.g., contentment) than younger adults, but similar levels of high arousal, positive affect (Kessler & Staudinger, 2009). Meta-analysis suggests that across adulthood through advanced old age there is a weaker decline of positive affect and affect balance and a stronger decline of negative affect in representative samples than in nonrepresentative samples (Pinquart, 2001). All in all, these results support a view that older adults tend to avoid negative information (Mather & Carstensen, 2003), unless the information is threatening or extremely aversive (Mather & Knight, 2006), are better able than younger ones to down-regulate negative emotions (Kessler & Staudinger, 2009) as well as remember a lower proportion of negative stimuli than younger adults (Charles, Mather, & Carstensen, 2003)—a trend also apparent in older adults' autobiographical memories, which tend be positively biased (e.g., Kennedy, Mather, & Carstensen, 2004).

Findings from the few studies that have investigated developmental trajectories in affective complexity have been less conclusive, probably due to the variation in paradigms. Affective complexity has been studied using at least two approaches, one building on the covariation of self-reported positive and negative emotions (Carstensen et al., 2000; Larsen & Cutler, 1996; Ong & Bergeman, 2004), the other building on the complexity of adults' self-statements in self-narratives (Labouvie-Vief, DeVoe, & Bulka, 1989; Loevinger, 1976). Within the first approach, affective complexity is based on the self-reported frequency of emotions using an event-sampling method. Affective complexity is then operationalized as (a) the number of dimensions characterizing a person's intraindividual emotional experience and by (b) the average intraindividual correlation between positive and negative affect within a (short) sample period of time. A higher number of dimensions has been interpreted as a high degree of differentiation between different kinds of emotions, whereas high intraindividual correlation between positive and negative affect on the same occasion has been interpreted as "poignancy," or, in other words, coactivation of positive and negative affect. Using this approach, Carstensen et al. (2000) concluded that affective complexity increased with age, as more dimensions were required to reflect the structure of older participants' emotions relative to the younger participants'. Furthermore, although the average correlation between positive and negative affect within a sampled moment was negative at all ages (i.e., people tended to report positive *or* negative emotions), the negative correlation was increasingly smaller at older ages. The authors interpreted the decreasing negative correlation as greater coactivation of positive and negative affect. However, from this study it is not possible to exclude the possibility that older people used positive emotions more often to "undo" negative emotions (e.g., Fredrickson, 2001). Interestingly, the measure of affective complexity used in this study was also negatively associated with negative affect, neuroticism, and daily stress (see also Ong & Bergeman, 2004)—three adjustment-related variables, suggesting that the adjustment interpretation is quite likely.

Research from Labouvie-Vief and colleagues further substantiates the adjustment (rather than the growth) interpretation. In this work, affective complexity is operationalized in a way that more closely taps into the emotional facet of personality maturity. Analysis of the conceptual complexity, openness and multivalence of adults' self-representations has revealed that older adults self-representations are characterized by a low degree of emotional blendings and high levels of repression (Labouvie-Vief, Chiodo, Goguen, Diehl, & Orwoll, 1995; Labouvie-Vief & Medler, 2002). These results suggest that emotion-regulation resources in older people seem to be oriented less toward personality growth and more toward optimizing personality adjustment.

Overall, it seems that as the current cohorts age, individuals become more concerned with and are better at down-regulating or avoiding negative emotions as well as demonstrate less affective complexity. The balance of positive over negative affect seems to increase, while the aging system becomes more self-protective against overactivation (Kessler & Staudinger, 2009; Labouvie-Vief, 2003). The ability to adjust successfully to changing life circumstances seems to reach its limits in very old age because of the tremendous increase in losses and negative events. Older adults between the ages of 74 and 103 years reported increasingly negative affective states with age (Smith & Baltes, 1997) and a longitudinal study over a period of 22 years indicated that life satisfaction peaked at 65 and declined in the seventh decade (Mroczek & Spiro, 2005). These results suggest an increase (at least until the oldest ages) in personality adjustment. In contrast, the decrease in affective complexity and the decrease in negative emotional experience points to a normative decrease in personality growth.

Our interpretation of the developmental trends in emotion regulation (increase in adjustment, decrease or stability in growth) is in line with motivational, cognitive, experiential, and biological theories of emotional development and aging. Socioemotional selectivity theory (SST) posits that shrinking perceptions of one's time left to live lead aging adults to shift their priorities gradually toward optimizing emotional experience (Carstensen, 1991; Carstensen, Isaacowitz, & Charles, 1999). SST predicts that people increasingly structure their lives to maximize positive affect and avoid negative affect—in other words, that aging individuals increasingly gear their lives toward realizing this emotional facet of personality adjustment. Our conclusion is also in line with Labouvie-Vief's (2003) cognitive–affective theory of development that older adults seek to optimize their emotional states relative to younger adults in part because they may have difficulties conceptualizing their emotions in mixed affective terms. Although separate to our separate to our discussion of *to which end* people regulate emotions (i.e., to optimize their own positive affect or to increase self and world insight or further a common good), experiential models suggest that affect regulation may improve as people age due to learning and practice (Lawton, 1996). For instance, some researchers suggest that older individuals might be better able to cope in anticipation with emotion-laden situations (Gross, 1998; Gross et al., 1997; Magai, 2001) because of an increase in the richness and effectiveness of available emotion schemas. Older people also report a better ability to control their emotions and to maintain a neutral emotional state (Gross et al., 1997; Lawton, Kleban, & Dean, 1993), and a recent study found that the (self-reported) ability to regulate affect in the face of difficulties or threatening situations completely mediated the relationship between age and affect (Kessler & Staudinger, 2009). It needs to be noted, however, that experimental evidence as to whether the ability to regulate emotions improves with age—most likely due to differences in paradigm—is inconclusive (e.g., Consedine & Magai, 2006; Kunzmann, Kupperbusch, & Levenson, 2005; Westphal & Bonanno, 2004). Because the constructive function of negative affect plays an important role in personality growth, this sort of expertise in avoiding negative affect contributes to the progress along the adjustment trajectory and challenges further progress along the personality growth trajectory. Also, the biological basis of aging plays a role. Negative emotions are more draining (relative to positive emotions), and therefore may be avoided. This effect is observable in functional magnetic resonance images of the brain: Aging seems to support an adaptive shift toward more controlled processing of negative emotion and less controlled processing of positive emotion involving the medial prefrontal cortex (Williams et al., 2006). Age-related cognitive declines in executive functioning have been associated with the same prefrontal areas that are related to the processing of negative emotions. Therefore, it cannot be excluded that reduced negative emotions may also be a correlate of age-related declines based on the biology of the brain (Dolge, Godde, Voelcker-Rehage, & Staudinger, 2010).

Summing Up: Personality Adjustment and Growth across the Life Span

Our review has provided ample evidence for one of the central assumptions of life-span psychology—namely, that there is dynamic and continued personality change throughout the adult life span (Baltes et al., 1980; Erikson, 1963). Such changes are multidimensional and result from biological, experiential, and motivational changes that occur across adulthood. Furthermore, we have shown that it is theoretically as well as empirically useful to group such changes under the heading of two types of positive personality change across adulthood—personality adjustment and personality growth (Staudinger & Kessler, 2009; Staudinger & Kunzmann, 2005).

This integrative overview of empirical results on personality-related measures indicates that there appear to be normative gains in personality adjustment through at least young old age and a flattening of the personality-growth trajectory during adulthood. Depending on the measure used, personality maturity seems to peak in midlife or shows a stable trajectory throughout adulthood (cf. Staudinger et al., 2005). The age-related increase in self-transcendent values and generative strivings might be regarded as preliminary evidence that the normative stability in personality growth is primarily due to restrictions in the cognitive and the emotional facets of personality growth rather than the motivational facet. These findings point to an untapped potential that may be realized if individuals were provided with the appropriate challenges as well as resources throughout life for developing deeper insight into the self and the world, for more tolerantly accepting the coexistence of apparently antagonistic emotions and truths and for striving towards transcending given circumstances. Apart from not being age-graded, acceptance of the dialectics inherent in human existence may also be at odds with Western logic that trains individuals to think in terms of "either/or" instead of "and" (Peng & Nisbett, 1999).

Although we define adjustment as consisting of well-being as well as fulfilling social norms, most of the evidence we have presented concerns the former. Interestingly, initial evidence on the internalization of social duties over the life course has also been found. Two cross-sectional survey studies found that older and middle-aged Americans were found to feel more autonomous while performing such social duties as voting, tipping, and paying taxes and in their work and citizenship roles relative to young American adults. A third cross-sectional study found that older Singaporeans felt more autonomous while obeying authorities, helping distant relatives, and staying politically informed (Sheldon, Kasser, Houser-Marko, Jones, & Turban, 2005). These studies suggest that older adults are able to reframe social duties as autonomous actions. Such a reframing certainly helps to optimize personality adjustment. However, longitudinal data are needed to draw firm conclusions; we suspect that the cohort effects in fulfilling social obligations are likely to be large.

Clearly, personality adjustment and maturity are not entirely independent. Rather, a certain level of personality adjustment seems to be a necessary precondition for the pursuit of personality growth. However, we argue that optimizing personality adjustment in the short term excludes the possibility of also making progress on the growth trajectory. Reciprocally, pursuing a growth trajectory may lead to more short-term disruptions in adjustment but also leads to strategies and knowledge that would seem to increase the likelihood for maintaining well-being over the long term (see Labouvie-Vief, 2008, for a similar argument). In support of this argument, Labouvie-Vief and Medler (2002) found that the integrated group—that is, those scoring high on both affective complexity (an indicator of the emotional facet of personality growth) and overall positive hedonic tone (an indicator of the emotional facet of personality adjustment)—displayed the most positive adjustment-related outcomes, including high well-being, empathy, health, secure relationship style, high tolerance of ambiguity, and openness to affect exploration. However, this relationship could be explained by our proposition that those most able to attain at least a certain threshold of adjustment also have the most resources to devote to growth, as opposed to a directed causal relationship between adjustment and growth per se. Furthermore, relationships between the emotional facets of personality adjustment and growth will not necessarily extrapolate to the relationship between the full-three facet definitions of adjustment and growth. In short, we stress that adjustment and maturity are two distinct dimensions that do not necessarily occur together. Of course, this is an empirical question. More systematic and longitudinal research is clearly needed to understand the interplay and interrelationship between subjective well-being and meeting contextual demands and the pursuit of personal wisdom and maturity.

The currently observed stability in personality maturity after young adulthood is by no means a fixed, natural law. We argue that gains in personality maturity are possible across adulthood given a special constellation of personal and contextual factors. Developmental goals must be considered first and foremost. Personality does not simply passively unfold as a consequence of the prewired maturational programs or the mechanistic reaction to environmental stimuli: The individual also plays an active role in shaping his or her own development (e.g., P. B. Baltes et al., 2006). Does the individual prioritize feeling good? Does the individual strive for growth? Such developmental goals will influence the kind of environments an individual seeks out (or avoids), how he or she reacts to the environment, and how he or she in turn contributes to that environment.

As for personal characteristics, a certain level of openness to new experience and internal control is necessary to achieve more complex forms of personality maturity. A person can only gain from his or her experiences given both a certain openness to receive and learn from contextual inputs and enough internal control to deny or delay immediate gratification to gain new insight. Even these internal factors should not be viewed as fixed qualities existing within the person. These qualities can only exist and develop when the individual is exposed to environmental contexts that elicit, support, and require such traits to be exercised. Moreover, individuals need continued access to environmental contexts that allow and ask for unexpected and challenging experience to achieve personality maturity. The importance of external, contextual resources for maintaining plasticity increases with age as the potential range of plasticity decreases (e.g., Greve & Staudinger, 2006; Staudinger et al., 1995). If and when individuals aspire to maintain previous levels of (personality) functioning as they age, culture-based resources (material, social, economic, psychological) are necessary to compensate for biological declines (P. B. Baltes, 1987). Indeed, there seem no new genetic contributions to differences in personality functioning over time but significant new environmental effects (Read, Vogler, Pedersen, & Johanson, 2006). We now turn our discussion to a more specific examination how contexts contribute to positive personality development—both personality adjustment as well as personality growth—across the life span. From a life-span perspective, developmental contexts are crucial to consider as they codetermine the degree to which developmental potential is exploited.

CONTEXTS FACILITATING POSITIVE PERSONALITY DEVELOPMENT: UNFOLDING PERSONALITY PLASTICITY

Together with a number of other authors (cf. Staudinger, 2005), we challenge the argument that the observed pattern of personality development (i.e., gains in adjustment, losses, or maintenance in growth after adolescence) predominantly reflects changes in genetic expression selected for by evolution (McCrae et al., 2000). Instead, we emphasize that the observed age-related patterns in personality as we have described in the previous section are at least in part the product of current historical and social *contexts* of aging (see also Kessler & Staudinger, 2006; Staudinger, 2005). Please note we do not dismiss the importance of evolutionary processes. Rather, we emphasize that although evolution may have selected for certain traits and abilities, their adaptive value depends on contextual demands. Potentialities will only be realized if the environmental demands favor their exercise. Furthermore, evolution may have selected for certain "tools" (e.g., the ability for perspective taking), evolution does not necessarily select to which end an individual uses a tool (e.g., for manipulating others or for building intimate relationships). In addition, modern molecular biology has taught us through the exploration of epigenetics that the genetic information that is handed down from evolution is not realized in an isomorphic fashion but rather depends on contextual features to be activated or suppressed. In short, we maintain that nature and nurture are not separable influences on human development. Rather, we emphasize that development is always the product of an ongoing, dynamic interaction between biology and context, as well as individual decisions. This applies as well to personality development.

Preliminary empirical evidence substantiates the potential for continuous personality development in as far as aging impairs personality functioning less so than other areas of functioning. The genetic component of personality measures is (a) between .4 and .6 and (b) stays relatively stable across the life span (see Bouchard & Loehlin, 2001, for a review). Indeed, personality is thought to maintain stable levels of functioning until at least the third age (cf. Staudinger et al., 1995). Furthermore, the importance of genetic influences on interindividual differences in personality seems to decrease slightly with increasing age (e.g., McGue, Bacon, & Lykken, 1993; Pedersen & Reynolds, 2002)—increasing the variability explained by contextual factors.

Indeed, developmental changes in personality traits can be related to environmental changes. For instance, the transition to partnership during early adulthood is accompanied by decreases in neuroticism and shyness and increases in conscientiousness (Neyer & Asendorpf, 2001). The experience of divorce has been associated with increased neuroticism and decreased extraversion in men, whereas women demonstrated the opposite pattern (Costa et al., 2000). Studies using latent growth modeling have revealed that individual differences in personality change increase with increasing age (Pedersen & Reynolds, 2002; Small et al., 2003). For instance, over a 12-year time period, older adults (60–64 years old at the first measurement time) became more heterogeneous with respect to openness to new experiences and conscientiousness (Allemand et al., 2008). As there is a decrease in the genetic effects on personality development, this increasing interindividual variability of change is most likely related to interindividual differences in life circumstances (Pedersen & Reynolds, 2002).

Intervention research has demonstrated that contextual resources can be used to not only compensate for age-related declines (e.g., memory, Li et al., 2008), but also to move the individual beyond the normal developmental trajectory toward more optimal levels of functioning. The very notion that contextual interventions could similarly stimulate *personality* change is such a radical idea, especially for older adults, that few empirical studies have even investigated this possibility. Still, some studies have indeed demonstrated that psychotherapy can actually change the personality traits of adults. For example, changes in neuroticism, agreeableness, and extraversion have been reported after 3 months of treatment (Bagby, Joffe, Parker, Kalemba, & Harkness, 1995; Trull et al., 1995).

Importantly, similar contextual effects have been reported for indicators of personality growth in adult samples. For instance, a 6-week treatment program led to significant increases in openness to experience (Piedmont, 2001). The experience of relocating to an independent-living setting (new and activating context) led to increases on Ryff's personal growth dimension 10 months after the move (Kling, Seltzer, & Ryff, 1997). In a quasi-experimental longitudinal study, older people (aged 55–80 years) with above-median internal control beliefs and who participated in a training program to facilitate competency in volunteering activities showed higher levels of Ryff's personal growth and openness compared with baseline assessment 3 months earlier and with a control group who were active as volunteers but had not participated in the training (Mühlig-Versen & Staudinger, 2010). For personal growth, this increase remained stable 1 year later; openness continued to increase even 1 year later. Importantly, this effect, which was specific to older adults with above median levels of internal control beliefs who had participated in a training program to facilitate competency in volunteering activities, demonstrates that facilitating personality growth depends on a number of personal and contextual circumstances. In this case, it was crucial that individuals first were empowered to take advantage of new contexts, and it was only individuals with above-median levels of internal control beliefs who were able to take advantage of the new circumstances in the sense of personality growth.

With regard to performance measures of personality growth, it was found that providing the possibility of reflecting on a life problem with a known person was shown to significantly increase the level of general wisdom-related knowledge and judgment given that there was time to individually consider the discussion before responding (Staudinger & Baltes, 1996). Similarly, receiving training on perspective taking increased the value relativism observed in responses to general wisdom-related tasks afterwards in younger and older adults (Böhmig-Krumhaar, Staudinger, & Baltes, 2002). A first intervention study on personal wisdom revealed, however, that discussing personal issues with a known person does not facilitate personal wisdom. However, receiving instruction on how to reflect upon oneself, in the sense of critical life reflection (Staudinger, 2000), turned out to improve personal wisdom-related performance in younger and older adults alike (Staudinger, Dörner, & Mickler, 2009). The authors interpreted this result such that established relationships are less useful when it comes to facilitating personal wisdom because ways to interact and taboo themes have been established. Most likely it is the interaction with a stranger that has the potential to be facilitative.

Recognizing the importance of contextual factors in personality development and the unfolding of personality plasticity leads one to consider the conditions that both promote and hinder the full actualization of human capabilities. This line of thinking has led to various typologies of environmental influences. Bronfenbrenner (1979) described four levels ("systems") of external contexts: (a) the microsystem, which is composed of immediate settings (including the person), such as social interactions; (b) the mesosystem, which contains the transactional relationship between two or more immediate settings containing the developing person at a particular point in life (e.g., the workplace); (c) the exosystem, which does not contain the developing person but impinges on or encompasses the immediate settings in which the person is found and thereby influences what goes on there (e.g., the job situation of older people's children); and (d) the macrosystem that comprises historical events (wars, famines, etc.) as well as cultural values and beliefs that may affect the other ecological systems. Contextual influences on all four levels have an effect on personality development.

We have chosen two specific contextual influences to illustrate how contextual characteristics can foster (or hinder) positive personality development: age stereotypes and the work context. We chose these two examples because of their relevance for personality adjustment and growth. *Age stereotypes* can be considered as contexts that are internalized quite early on in development. Some aspects of our age stereotypes are already absorbed in childhood (e.g., Filipp & Mayer, 1999). Because these stereotypes and attitudes towards aging become more and more self-relevant, they become an increasingly important influence on the kinds of positive personality development we have described. According to Bronfenbrenner's (1979) classification scheme, culturally prevalent age stereotypes reflect a macrocontext that affects personality development through its effects on the microcontexts (e.g., self-views and future expectations) of development.

The *work context* represents one of, if not the, major meso-contexts during adulthood. The overarching developmental task of youth is to prepare for the adult world. Central to this task is mastering the skills needed for contributing to society in the form of work; thus, the skills and traits demanded by the work context exert some influence on personality development even in youth. It is well known from work on self-concept development, for instance, that work experiences continue to their exert influence well into the period of retirement (e.g., Freund & Smith, 1999).

Old-Age Stereotypes: Important Contexts of Aging

Negative old-age stereotypes and globally negative old-age expectations are highly prevalent across various age groups, societies, and historical times (e.g., Ehmer & Höffe, 2009; Filipp & Mayer, 1999; Heckhausen, Dixon, & Baltes, 1989; Levy, 1999; Wentura & Rothermund, 2005). Evidence suggests that this process begins in childhood. School-age children categorize people by age; further, they also attach value to different age categorizations (Filipp & Mayer, 1999). For example, one third of a sample of school-age children falsely recalled a positive description of an older target as negative (e.g., an older person described as healthy was recalled as sick). This effect was not observed when the age of the target person was not given (Davidson, Cameron, & Jergovic, 1995). Another study found that among children aged 4 to 7, two thirds of the children did not want to become old (Burke, 1981). These negative stereotypes seem to translate into behavior toward older people: Six- and eight-year-olds interacted more cautiously and maintained greater interpersonal distance with an unknown 70-year-old relative to an unknown 35-year-old (Isaacs & Bearison, 1986). Interestingly, this pattern was not found for 4-year-olds, whose interpersonal behavior did not differ based on the target's age.

Studies of adults' old-age stereotypes have revealed similar results. Despite the complexity and multidimensionality of old-age stereotypes, researchers generally agree that, at least in Western countries, the negative stereotypes still prevail (Butler, 1980; Kite & Johnson, 1988; Kite, Stockdale, Whitley, & Johnsong, 2005). Aging tends to be more associated with losses than gains (Heckhausen et al., 1989). A recent meta-analysis of 232 effect sizes concluded that older adults were perceived as less competent, evaluated less favorably, and treated more negatively than younger adults, even when individuating information was available (Kite et al., 2005). Interestingly, adults' aging expectations generally correspond with our hypotheses about the age trajectories of personality adjustment and growth. In one study, adult participants anticipated that they would experience decreases (relative to past and present levels) in Ryff's personal growth as well as openness at age 65 to 70 (Fleeson & Heckhausen, 1997). In terms of our markers of personality adjustment, participants expected either gains or stability in late adulthood in agreeableness, positive relations with others, autonomy, and self-acceptance and decreases in emotional stability, purpose in life, and environmental mastery. Middle-aged participants (40–55 years) showed the same expectations, except that environmental mastery was not expected to differ in the future. Adult participants expected to grow in wisdom in later adulthood but also expected to decline on most other desirable characteristics in the same age period (Heckhausen & Krueger, 1993).

There are two major ways in which stereotypes about old age can influence personality development in adulthood and old age: (a) The social environment reinforces behaviors in older adults that conform with the stereotype and (b) the older person internalizes the old-age stereotype. We discuss these two forms of developmental influence exerted by old-age stereotypes in turn.

Social Expectations Reinforce Old-Age Stereotypes

Old-age stereotypes held by their social interaction partners seem to direct older adults' behavior in ways that lead to self-fulfilling prophecies. For instance, negative stereotypes about older workers' ability and motivation to participate in further training can affect the frequency with which older employees' actually participate in further training by influencing management decisions and treatment regarding training and developmental resources for older workers (e.g., Maurer, Andrews, & Weiss, 2003). In addition, employees' own age-related beliefs about their ability to learn may affect their willingness to participate in further training (Wrenn & Maurer, 2004). Because continued learning is considered ever more necessary for maintaining work performance and even one's job (e.g., Hall & Mirvis, 1995), negative stereotypes can affect an individual's personality adjustment. More fundamentally, it is a well-established fact that training can alleviate age-related cognitive decline (e.g., P. B. Baltes et al., 2006). As a further example, Margret Baltes and her colleagues (e.g., M. M. Baltes & Wahl, 1992) uncovered evidence that the old-age stereotypes held by caretakers led them to apply a dependency–support script in their interactions with the elderly. In laboratory and field studies in which elderly adults' social interactions in their living environments were observed, the researchers found that many aspects of older adults' dependent behaviors were reversible. Field observations revealed that many of the elderly adults' social interactions followed a "dependency–support" script and an "independence–ignore" script. In other words, social partners (i.e., caretakers) of older persons in the context of self-care exhibited a high frequency of behaviors that supported dependence rather than facilitated independence.

Younger people's negative old-age stereotype can affect the quantity and quality of intergenerational interactions and relationships in the sense that they avoid (or do not seek) contact with the older generation (e.g., McCann, Dailey, Giles, & Ota, 2005). It is known, however, that intergenerational interactions can potentially facilitate positive psychological functioning in both younger and older interaction partners. Older people's transmission of sociocultural knowledge to young people is thought to increase offsprings' survival rates (Mergler & Goldstein, 1983). For some older adults, in turn, fulfilling a respected role as a purveyor of wisdom and expecting to have such a role in the future may motivate individuals to pursue continued personality growth. Passing on advice to members of the younger generation also seems to increase older people's personality adjustment in terms of increasing positive affect, self-esteem, and life satisfaction (e.g., Kinnevy & Morrow-Howell, 1999). Prior intergenerational contact has also been shown to buffer older adults from the negative performance effects that occur when a negative stereotype about old age has been made salient (Abrams, Eller, & Bryant, 2006; Abrams et al., 2008). Typically, a salient negative old-age stereotype results in behavior consistent with the negative stereotype. Intergenerational contact appears to make the salience of age and age stereotypes less threatening.

Intergenerational interactions can also stimulate personality growth for both younger and older interaction partners. An experimental study recently supported the facilitative effects of intergenerational interaction: Intergenerational settings supportive of the generativity theme increased older adults' affective complexity, a key marker of personality maturity (Kessler & Staudinger, 2007). Likewise, the adolescent partners in this study reported more communion goals and demonstrated more prosocial behavior—motivation and behavior certainly conducive to adolescents' personality growth.

In sum, negative old-age stereotypes can create contexts that hamper older persons' personality adjustment and clearly constrain older adults' opportunities for further personality growth by limiting exposure to the kind of contexts necessary for personality growth to occur.

Old-Age Stereotypes are Internalized

The second way in which age stereotypes and attitudes toward aging affect positive personality development—both personality adjustment and personality growth—is through the expectations that we develop about our own old age as we internalize such beliefs. Contamination or infusion hypotheses (e.g., Kuypers & Bengtson, 1973; Levy, 1996; Rodin & Langer, 1980) posit that people tend to gradually incorporate stereotyped views of age and aging into the views on their own aging.

In line with cross-sectional studies (e.g., Heckhausen & Brim, 1997; Kearl, 1981; O'Gorman, 1980; Schulz & Fritz, 1987), longitudinal studies convincingly suggest that endorsement of negative age stereotypes has a causal effect on later self-views as one starts to self-define as old. For instance, in a cross-sequential study of older adults (initially aged 55–77 years; $N = 690$), stereotyped expectations of elderly people predicted self-appraisals 8 years later (Rothermund & Brandtstädter, 2003). Similarly, in a longitudinal study of older adults (initially aged 54–77, $N = 896$), initial views of the "typical old person" predicted subsequent changes in self-views 4 years later. Specifically, those who rated the "typical old person" more negatively at the first measurement occasion tended to see *themselves* less positively over time, whereas those who rated the "typical old person" more positively tended to see themselves more positively over time (Rothermund, 2005). Similarly, Levy (2008) found that endorsement of stereotypical statements regarding retirement at baseline predicted subsequent self-views on aging assessed at five time points over a 20-year time period.

Research has shown that negative beliefs about one's own aging become very powerful to the degree that the time of death is precipitated by seven years even after controlling for the usual predictors of survival such as health, socio-economic status or subjective well-being (cf. Levy, Slade, Kunkel, & Kasl, 2002). This effect on survival was partially mediated by the will to live that was much reduced in individuals who held negative views about their own aging. Similarly, it has been found that self-stereotypes about older people's sexuality (or, more accurately, the lack thereof) may lead an older adult to feel he or she is "too old" to invest resources into sexuality. Negative attitudes toward older people's sexuality are thought to influence how older people perceive their own sexuality and to be a key determinant of sexual behavior (DeLamater & Moorman, 2007). Changes in sexual functioning are a normal part of aging. However, an individual's belief about what is "age appropriate" as well as what is irreversible or inevitable influences how he or she will react to such changes.

Aging stereotypes and aging self-views shape the future expectations and possible selves of a person (cf. Ryff, 1991). The extent to which a person believes that aging is a process of progressive, inevitable, irreversible physical loss is presumed to correlate with the extent to one believes in his or her ability to influence the future. Such beliefs are assumed to be major regulators of current behavior (Bandura, 1986). In terms of health-related outcomes, age attitudes are expected to affect individual's control beliefs, which in turn affect how people manage their health: People with higher levels of perceived control take greater responsibility for their health (Rodin, 1986). In this vein, older people who attributed symptoms to their age instead of to an illness tended to have less beneficial health behaviors (e.g., Leventhal & Prohaska, 1986).

Negative aging-related beliefs might also have more direct effects on measures of personality adjustment by causing stress and anxiety, as the person feels pessimistic about the future and powerless to do anything about it (Wurm, Tesch-Römer, & Tomasik, 2007). Psychological stress is linked to immune down-regulation, particularly for older adults, which leads to health impairments (Kiecolt-Glaser, McGuire, Glaser, & Robles, 2002). In contrast, having a sense of control and an optimistic future outlook have direct positive effects on well-being indicators (e.g., Scheier & Carver, 1992; Taylor, Kemeny, Reed, Bower, & Grunewald, 2000), even for centenarians with a truly limited future time perspective (Jopp & Rott, 2006). Conversely, experimental studies have demonstrated that (subliminally) priming negative images of aging (e.g., dementia) led to stronger physiological stress responses in the face of a challenging cognitive task and consequently lowered levels of performance (Levy, Hausdorff, Henck, & Wei, 2000; Levy et al., 2008), variations in the shakiness and clarity of handwriting (Levy, 2000), variations in walking speed and balance (Hausdorff, Levy, & Wei, 1999), as well a reduced will to live (Levy, Ashman, & Dror, 1999–2000). Having negative attitudes toward old people predicted low self-esteem, even after controlling for self-reported health problems and other age-related changes (Ward, 1977). Adults' image of their own aging, their image of the "typical old person," and the interaction of these two factors were each independently associated with depressive tendencies. Negative age stereotypes about the "typical old person" *amplified* the negative impact of perceived self-deficits on depression, whereas relatively positive age stereotypes had a buffering effect (Rothermund, 2005).

Studies that have investigated attitudes toward old age and measures of health have found similar results. Self-views that characterized aging as a process of physical losses were significantly related to increases in physical illnesses 6 years later, whereas self-views of aging as a process of ongoing personal development led to lower increases or even decreases in the number of self-reported illnesses (Wurm et al., 2007). Aging attitudes had an impact on health more than the converse, and the predictive strength of aging attitudes remained significant even after controlling for hope. A recent study found that neuroticism influenced self-views of aging and also that the influence of neuroticism on self-rated health was mediated by self-views of aging (Moor, Zimprich, Schmitt, & Kliegel, 2006).

Ironically, in some situations, negative views on aging can lead to *enhanced* feelings of well-being (i.e., personality adjustment), at least for some older adults. Negative age stereotypes can in some instances serve as a reference standard for self-enhancing downward comparisons (e.g., Heckhausen & Krueger, 1993; Heidrich & Ryff, 1993; Pinquart, 2002b; Rickabaugh & Tomlinson-Keasey, 1997; Robinson-Whelen & Kiecolt-Glaser, 1997), leading to short-term increases in indicators of adjustment. Indeed, the outcome of comparison of the self with a generalized old person has been found to predict measures of well-being, such that viewing the self as "better off" leads to higher levels of subjective well-being (e.g., Heidrich & Ryff, 1993; Kwan, Love, Ryff, & Essex, 2003; Rickabaugh & Tomlinson-Keasey, 1997; Robinson-Whelen & Kiecolt-Glaser, 1997; Ryff & Essex, 1992). However, older adults normally do not seem to use their stereotypes about "typical old people" as sources for self-enhancing downward social comparisons (Rothermund, 2005). Results indicate that elderly people only rarely compare themselves with global views of old people when not explicitly instructed to do so (e.g., Rickabaugh & Tomlinson-Keasey, 1997). Furthermore, the overall adaptiveness of downward comparisons has to be considered relative to the particular outcome being considered. Downward comparisons are highly adaptive in situations of irreversible losses or unattainable gains, whereas upward social comparisons (i.e., role models) are functional whenever maintenance or improvement is at stake (P. B. Baltes et al., 2006). Although comparing oneself with others who are "worse off" may have short-term benefits in terms of personality adjustment, this might come at the expense of ignoring role models that may stimulate the individual to realize that gains could potentially be made. In particular, downward comparisons help to reinforce the personality status quo rather than motivate the individual toward further personality growth.

In sum, culturally pervasive one-sided negative age stereotypes represent a major risk factor for personality growth as well as adjustment, not only but especially in old age. Findings strongly support the assumption that in the long run, age stereotypes gradually become incorporated into adults' self-concepts and tend to contaminate both their current self-views and their future expectations. These self-views, in turn, affect indicators of adjustment such as well-being, cognitive functioning, health, and longevity.

It might be tempting to suppose that in turn stereotypes associating age with wisdom facilitate continued personality growth. Ironically, however, the belief in the positive association between age and personality maturity in fact may be *detrimental* to personality growth in that people might assume that such traits come *automatically* with age and do not require proactive resource investment.

Broadening the available images of aging might provide a better platform from which individuals can selectively and individually construct their own image of aging that may shield them from negative effects as they start to self-define as "old" (Rothermund, 2005; Rothermund et al., 1995; Wentura & Brandtstädter, 2003). However, we caution that one-sidedly positive images of aging, such as those generally found in the media (e.g., Kessler, Rakoczy, & Staudinger, 2004; Kessler, Schwender, & Bowen, 2010), are only half the story. Creating a fantasy world in which the losses associated with aging can be completely avoided may actually aggravate decreases in adjustment when losses are actually encountered by catching the individual mentally unprepared and by creating a sense of existential unfairness as the individual asks himself, "Why me?"

Greater access to complex images of aging that juxtapose and integrate the inevitable losses associated with aging alongside some of the more positive aspects should also promote personality growth for individuals of all ages. Furthermore, a greater emphasis on the opportunities for continued personality development and a greater cultural value placed on wisdom might stimulate more of an approach orientation to aging, in which the individual actively seeks out opportunities to develop himself or herself personally rather than adopting an avoidance orientation to aging in which the main focus is on avoiding and postponing the age-related losses (e.g., maintaining a youthful appearance). It would be interesting to observe whether and how such cultural change spill over into aging stereotypes.

The Work Context

The work context represents one of the major developmental contexts during adulthood and into old age. Experiences at work have a direct bearing on adult development as a source of stress, physical and intellectual activity, and social interaction, as well as potentially providing, a sense of purpose, identity, and self-respect (e.g., Jahoda, 1982). Middle-aged adults emphasize the importance of their jobs and careers (Ryff, 1989b) and report having more current and future goals in the work domain than in any other (e.g., family, personal development, leisure; Clark & Lachman, 1994; cited in Clark-Plaskie & Lachman, 1999). Adults are socialized to adjust to the norms, pressures, and demands associated with their work role (e.g., Hogan & Roberts, 2004; Roberts et al., 2005; Schooler, Mulatu, & Oates, 2004). People learn to act in certain ways within the work domain and develop attitudes that "spill over" into other domains of their lives. The degree to which work experiences influence personality development, however, at least to some extent depends on the centrality of the work context within the individual's self-concept (cf. Ryff & Essex, 1992).

Selection effects that draw certain people to certain (work) environments complicate the investigation of the causal role of contexts. However, the very characteristics that bring a person to an environment are also likely to be the characteristics demanded by the environment, and hence, it is precisely these characteristics that should change over time (e.g., Roberts, Caspi, & Moffitt, 2003). It has been hypothesized that the extent to which an individual's attributes match those demanded by the environment (i.e., the person–environment fit) is one determinant of the extent to which socialization effects occur. For instance, individuals immersed in an achievement-oriented, competitive, and unsupportive university context, over time also showed more of these characteristics (Roberts & Robins, 2004). High person–environment fit (i.e., high cognitive ability, low agreeableness, and low neuroticism) was associated with decreases in both agreeableness and neuroticism.

Work Experiences and Adjustment

According to the principle of social investment, individuals make commitments to important social institutions or roles such as work or marriage (Roberts et al., 2005). Successful fulfillment of these roles often demands certain behaviors and characteristics—for example, increased emotional stability, agreeableness, and conscientiousness. Over time these behaviors and characteristics become automatic as the person commits to and succeeds in these roles. Indeed, empirical studies have consistently revealed relationships between workforce participation and adjustment-related personality change. Working and succeeding in work robustly leads to increases in adjustment-related personality dimensions such as self-confidence, norm adherence, independence, and responsibility (e.g., Clausen & Gilens, 1990; Elder, 1969; Kohn & Schooler, 1978; Roberts, 1997).

Subjective experiences of the work context have also been associated with measures of adjustment. In particular, the relationship between job satisfaction and life satisfaction has been well studied. Researchers have generally concluded that job satisfaction is significantly related to life satisfaction, which is one aspect of subjective well-being (see Rain, Lane, & Steiner, 1991, and Tait, Padgett & Baldwin, 1989, for reviews). However, the relationship between job satisfaction and life satisfaction is clearly reciprocal; life satisfaction also affects job satisfaction (e.g., Judge & Watanabe, 1993). Some researchers have argued that the relationship between job satisfaction and life satisfaction is at least partly explained by a third variable that predicts both, such as income or certain personality characteristics (e.g., Rode, 2004). These results can be understood in terms of the selection–socialization hypothesis described earlier, such that characteristics that lead people to be satisfied with their lives (e.g., neuroticism–emotional stability) also lead them to be more satisfied with their jobs. In turn, being more satisfied with their jobs likely increases the personality traits associated with job and life satisfaction. This interpretation is supported by longitudinal findings that increased work satisfaction is associated with increases in measures of emotional stability (Roberts & Chapman, 2000; Roberts et al., 2003; Scollon & Diener, 2006).

Analyzing how work experiences affected adjustment-related personality change in young adulthood (age 18–26 years) while controlling for the participants' personality at baseline (age 18 years) demonstrated developmental patterns of decreased negative emotionality (cf. neuroticism) (Roberts et al., 2003). However, this decrease was faster for young adults in higher status jobs that were more satisfying and that provided more financial security. Increases in agentic positive emotionality (cf. environmental mastery) were observed for young adults in higher status, more satisfying jobs who earned sufficiently, had more resource power, and were more involved in their work. Young adults who gained power in their job became more confident and harder working. Finally, young adults increased in constraint (cf. conscientiousness; endorses social norms, security-oriented) if they were more involved in their jobs and financially secure. In contrast, young adults who invested less in their work role (as indicated by participating in a high number of counterproductive work behaviors such as being late for work or pretending to be sick to get time off) tended to *increase* in negative emotionality and maintain initial levels of constraint, contrary to typical developmental patterns in young adulthood (Roberts, Walton, Bogg, & Caspi, 2006).

Work Experiences and Personality Maturity

Significantly less work has investigated the relationship between the work context and indicators of personality growth. Uninterrupted, successful work experiences have been associated with women's ego development (Helson & Roberts, 1994). Intuitively, certain occupations facilitate personality growth more than others. Occupations that involve structured training, experience, and practice in thinking about the pragmatics of life should facilitate personality growth. Within a so-called age by experience paradigm (Charness, 1989; Salthouse, 1991), three contextual conditions have been specified as facilitating the development of general wisdom: (a) extensive exposure to and experience with a wide range of human conditions; (b) mentor-guided practice in dealing with difficult issues of life conduct and life interpretations, that is, social interaction with a more experienced person; and (c) a motivational drive to help endure extended periods of "practice" in fundamental matters of life (see also Staudinger, Kessler, & Dörner, 2006).

Occupations such as theologian, family doctor, judge, or social policy advisor, to name a few examples, would seem to meet such criteria. Clinical psychology is another example of an occupation that seems to meet these criteria: Clinical psychologists have an above-average amount of exposure to training and practice with dealing with the fundamental matters of life, as well as the experience of mentorship in how to interpret and deal with such life issues. Indeed, clinical psychologists displayed higher levels of wisdom-related performance than comparison groups from non–social service academic professions (Smith, Staudinger, & Baltes, 1994; Staudinger, Smith, & Baltes, 1992). Although this cross-sectional study cannot rule out selection effects, these results suggest that experiential features of the work context (including the necessary professional training) can facilitate personality growth. Furthermore, internal control beliefs have been found to be a necessary precursor for personality growth to arise from the exposure to work in the sense of volunteering activities (e.g., Mühlig-Versen & Staudinger, 2010; Staudinger & Kunzmann, 2005).

Features of the Work Context That Affect Personality Growth and Adjustment

Autonomy–Work Control. Job autonomy and work control (i.e., the degree of freedom to which an employee is allowed to self-determine his or her job and exercise his or her individual skills and interests) have important influences on more global control beliefs (Kohn & Schooler, 1973; Wickrama, Surjadi, Lorenz, & Elder, 2008). For instance, longitudinal analysis of middle-aged men indicated that changes in work control affected changes in personal control, which in turn predicted self-reported health 10 years later. This effect was independent from baseline levels of work control and global personal control (Wickrama et al., 2008). Job type and work experiences seem to predict internal control beliefs among middle-aged adults (e.g., Huyck, 1991; Kivett, Watschon, & Busch, 1977). In addition, low work control has been directly associated with adjustment indicators such as depression (Mausner-Dorsch & Eaton, 2000) as well as with physical health (Wickrama, Lorenz, Fang, Abraham, & Elder, 2005).

Jobs that offer a high degree of individual discretion allow employees to implement regulatory strategies such as selective optimization with compensation (Abraham & Hansson, 1995; B. Baltes & Dickson, 2001; Bajor & B. Baltes, 2003). In one study, older workers (aged 40–69 years) who reported using work-related SOC strategies likewise reported being better able to maintain their ability to do their jobs and achieve their goals (Abraham & Hansson, 1995). Supervisors rated the workers who reported using SOC strategies as better performers. Job type (i.e., managerial vs. clerical) and job autonomy moderated the relationship between SOC strategies and supervisor ratings. That is, the more autonomous the job, the more the person was able to apply SOC strategies successfully to achieve better job performance. As previously mentioned, workers who report using SOC strategies report being more satisfied with their jobs, having a better emotional balance at work, and being more successful (Wiese et al., 2002).

Workplace Diversity. The degree of workplace diversity would seem to be a proxy for this kind of challenging environment. Research on workplace diversity (i.e., the degree to which objective or subjective differences exist between group members, van Knippenberg & Schippers, 2007) has mainly focused on how workplace diversity affects group processes and performance as well as group member attitudes and subjective well-being. Reviews of the literature reveal two major arguments concerning how workplace diversity affects employees' well-being and performance. On one hand, higher group diversity is thought to challenge performance and well-being by creating group conflict. On the other hand, diverse groups are thought to possess a broader range of task-relevant knowledge, skills and abilities, and members with different opinions and perspectives, which can lead to better performance. Notably, empirical evidence does not consistently support either view: neither is diversity consistently conducive nor detrimental for performance, nor does diversity necessarily correlate with more social conflict (see van Knippenberg & Schippers, 2007, and Williams & O'Reilly, 1998, for reviews).

High levels of workplace diversity may challenge personality adjustment. If the challenges of workplace diversity can be managed, however, this might foster personality growth. Given the negative effects workplace diversity is likely to initially have, any positive effects, such as personality growth, are likely to take longer to emerge (cf. van Knippenberg & Schippers, 2007). Analogous to what we described for self-complexity and self-integration, high diversity and medium team cohesion may be most conducive to personality growth, whereas medium diversity and high cohesion may be supportive of personality adjustment. In light of recent experimental work, exposure to new contexts (such as those arising from workplace diversity) will most likely only result in increased personality growth when individuals are trained and empowered to master such new contexts (cf. Mühlig-Versen & Staudinger, 2010).

Age diversity is a particularly interesting example of how workplace diversity can potentially affect personality development. The work setting has the potential to be an important arena for intergenerational interactions. Such interactions are infrequent and are likely an important source of age bias (Hagestad & Uhlenberg, 2005). In their review of the literature, K. Y. Williams and O'Reilly (1998) found evidence that groups with higher variation in their age composition (independent of tenure diversity) have slightly lower levels of group efficiency than more age-homogenous groups, and advantage in performance. The literature also suggests that age diversity is associated with increased turnover and withdrawal, especially of those individuals who are the most different. This suggests that age diversity in the work context may pose a challenge to personality adjustment. In contrast, age diversity within work teams in which older employees act as mentors may promote adjustment and even personality growth (cf. Kessler & Staudinger, 2007).

Age Stereotypes in the Workplace. Finally, the presence or absence of negative age stereotypes represent an important characteristic of the workplace. Perceptions of the older worker within the work context influence supervisors' behaviors (e.g., providing access to promotions or training measures) and also seem to influence employees' self-views on aging, and hence personality adjustment and growth through the mechanisms described in the previous section. Initial work on age climate (Noack, B. B. Baltes, & Staudinger, 2010), or the extent to which employees perceive negative views on aging within their organization, suggests that companies differ in terms of the positivity of the age stereotypes they communicate. There is first evidence that management attitudes and company policies and practices (e.g., with regard to retirement, health management, and further training) contribute to how employees perceive the age climate (Noack & Staudinger, 2010). Age climate seems to be associated with job commitment and even job performance (Noack et al., 2010). Hence, there is first evidence that an organization's age climate can affect personality adjustment.

Negative stereotypes about older workers are also thought to bias hiring, firing, and other important work-related decisions. Such stereotypes, by hampering older adults' access to the financial, social, and cognitive rewards of working, training participation, and social integration, pose a threat to individual's ability to adjust to societal imperatives such as maintaining financial independence and well-being.

In sum, research on how work experiences affect personality development is gaining momentum. Research has demonstrated that experiences at work affect personality development, including indicators of adjustment and growth. Specifically, job autonomy can foster both personality growth and adjustment by facilitating self-regulation and internal control beliefs. Workplace diversity poses a challenge to adjustment but can also foster personality growth by challenging individuals with new perspectives. The workplace provides a setting where intergenerational interactions in the sense of mentoring relationships can take place and thereby support adjustment as well as growth for both. Finally, old-age stereotypes within the workplace need to be taken seriously in their effects on employees' satisfaction and performance.

CONCLUSION AND OUTLOOK

In this chapter, we have demonstrated the usefulness of taking a life-span approach to personality development in adulthood and old age. We have reviewed two forms of positive development occurring over the adult life span—namely, *adjustment*, aimed at mastering given life circumstances and thereby maintaining and increasing levels of well-being, and *growth*, aimed at transcending the self and given circumstances for the better of the community. We have provided evidence that personality adjustment and personality growth are distinct trajectories. Furthermore, we have argued that gains in personality adjustment across adulthood are (as of now) normative, whereas adulthood gains in personality maturity are (still) rare.

We have argued that gains in personality growth often times involve at least short-term losses in personality adjustment. In youth, biological maturation and exposure to a variety of social contexts serves the adaptive purpose of socializing new members into becoming successful adults. After this goal is achieved, it seems that few individuals are found to continue on a trajectory of personality growth. Adequate longitudinal studies that would allow clarification of some of the causal factors underlying this empirical pattern are still missing. In line with a contextual perspective (cf. Baltes et al., 1980), we have argued that neither personality adjustment nor personality growth are inherent processes of biological maturation. The quest for personality growth as well as the accomplishment of personality adjustment needs to be facilitated by the appropriate (social and cultural) contexts throughout adulthood and in particular in older age.

The flattening of the personality growth trajectory during young adulthood may have been less detrimental for the individual as well as society in the past, when average lives were shorter. However, given the rapid extension in average life expectancy over recent generations combined with a lowered fertility rate, new challenges to personality adjustment have emerged that at the same time may have increased the existential importance of personality growth to occur for individuals and society alike.

To ensure that individuals are able to lead happy, meaningful lives across a longer life span, we would like to suggest that societies rethink how they construct contexts for different age groups that are conducive to positive personality development with special focus on extending the normative personality growth trajectory. To date, there is too little systematic knowledge about which contextual characteristics have what effect on what type of individual. Future research on personality development should in particular focus on the investigation of the contextual conditions of positive personality plasticity.

We stress once more that people are active, not passive, composers of their own development. Failures to adjust are punished; failures to grow are not. Thus, in the current cultural context, growth depends even more on the individual's decisions. Consequently, we would recommend that societies reconsider such reinforcement systems. Finally, it may be necessary to support individuals in their effort to compose meaningful and satisfactory lives because many boundary conditions have changed in the recent past that make earlier learning channels such as family heritage and observation of role models obsolete. Findings from life-span psychology may provide a sound basis on which such "teachings" about the composition of longer lives can be grounded.

REFERENCES

Abraham, J. D., & Hansson, R. O. (1995). Successful aging at work: An applied study of selection, optimization, and compensation through impression management. *Journals of Gerontology Series B: Psychological Sciences, 50B,* 94–103.

Abrams, D., Crisp, R. J., Marques, S., Fagg, E., Bedford, L., & Provias, D. (2008). Threat inoculation: Experienced and imagined intergenerational contact prevents stereotype threat effects on older people's math performance. *Psychology and Aging, 23,* 934-939.

Abrams, D., Eller, A., & Bryant, J. (2006), An age apart: the effects of intergenerational contact and stereotype threat on performance and intergroup bias. *Psychology and Aging, 21,* 691–702.

Achenbaum, W., & Orwoll, L. (1991). Becoming wise: A psycho-gerontological interpretation of the Book of Job. *International Journal of Aging & Human Development, 32,* 21–39.

Aldwin, C. M. (1991). Does age affect the stress and coping process? Implications of age differences in perceived control. *Journal of Gerontology, 46,* 174–180.

Aldwin, C. M. (1994). *Stress, coping and development.* New York: Guilford Press.

Aldwin, C., & Stokols, D. (1988). The effects of environmental change on individuals and groups: Some neglected issues in stress research. *Journal of Environmental Psychology, 8,* 57–75.

Allemand, M., Zimprich, D., & Martin, M. (2008). Long-term correlated change in personality traits in old age. *Psychology and Aging, 23,* 545–557.

Allport, G. W. (1961). *Pattern and growth in personality.* New York: Holt, Rinehart and Winston.

Arnett, J. J. (2000). Emerging adulthood: A theory of development from the late teens through the twenties. *American Psychologist, 55,* 469–480.

Assagioli, R. (1989). Self-realization and psychological disturbance. In S. Grof & C. Grof (Eds.), *Spiritual emergency: When personal transformation becomes a crisis.* Los Angeles: Jeremy P. Tarcher. (Original work published 1978)

Bagby, R. M., Joffe, R. T., Parker, J. D. A., Kalemba, B., & Harkness, K. L. (1995). Major depression and the five-factor model of personality. *Journal of Personality Disorders, 9,* 224–234.

Bajor, J. K., & Baltes, B. B. (2003). Explicating the relationship between selection optimization with compensation, conscientiousness, motivation, and job performance. *Journal of Vocational Behavior, 63,* 347–367

Baltes, B. B., & Dickson, M. W. (2001). Using life-span models in industrial/organizational psychology: The theory of selective optimization with compensation. *Applied Developmental Science, 5,* 51–61.

Baltes, B. B., & Heydens-Gahir, H. A. (2003). Reduction of work-family conflict through the use of selection, optimization, and compensation behaviors. *Journal of Applied Psychology, 88,* 1005–1018.

Baltes, M. M., & Carstensen, L. L. (1996). The process of successful ageing. *Aging and Society, 16,* 397–422.

Baltes, M. M., & Lang, F. R. (1997). Everyday functioning and successful aging: The impact of resources. *Psychology and Aging, 12,* 433–443.

Baltes, M. M., & Wahl, H.-W. (1992). The dependency-support script in institutions: Generalization to community settings. *Psychology and Aging, 7,* 409–418.

Baltes, P. B. (1987). Theoretical propositions of life span developmental psychology: On the dynamics between growth and decline. *Developmental Psychology, 23,* 611–626.

Baltes, P. B., & Baltes, M. M. (1990). Psychological perspectives on successful aging: The model of selective optimization with compensation. In P. B. Baltes & M. M. Baltes (Eds.), *Successful aging: Perspectives from the behavioral sciences* (pp. 1–34). Cambridge, England: Cambridge University Press.

Baltes, P. B., & Freund, A. M. (2003). Human strengths as the orchestration of wisdom and selective optimization with compensation. In L. G. Aspinwall & U. M. Staudinger (Eds.), *A psychology of human strengths: Fundamental questions and future directions for a positive psychology* (pp. 23–35). Washington, DC: American Psychological Association.

Baltes, P. B., Lindenberger, U., & Staudinger, U. M. (2006). Lifespan theory in Developmental Psychology. In R. M. Lerner (Ed.), *Handbook of child psychology: Vol. 1. Theoretical models of Human Development* (6th ed., pp. 569–664). Hoboken, NJ: John Wiley & Sons.

Baltes, P. B., Reese, H. W., & Lipsitt, L. P. (1980). Life-span developmental psychology. *Annual Review of Psychology, 31,* 65–110.

Baltes, P. B., & Smith, J. (2003). New frontiers in the future of aging: From successful aging of the young old to the dilemmas of the Fourth Age. *Gerontology: Behavioural Science Section/Review, 49,* 123–135.

Baltes, P. B., Smith, J., & Staudinger, U. M. (1992). Wisdom and successful aging. In T. Sonderegger (Ed.), *Nebraska Symposium on Motivation* (Vol. 39, pp. 123–167). Lincoln: University of Nebraska Press.

Baltes, P. B., & Staudinger, U. M. (2000). Wisdom. A metaheuristic (pragmatic) to orchestrate mind and virtue toward excellence. *American Psychologist, 55,* 122–136.

Bandura, A. (1986). *Social foundations of thought and action: A social cognitive theory.* Englewood Cliffs, NJ: Prentice Hall.

Bauer, J. J., & McAdams, D. P. (2004). Growth goals, maturity, and well-being. *Developmental Psychology, 40,* 14–127.

Blanchard-Fields, F., Stein, R., & Watson, T. L. (2004). Age differences in emotion-regulation strategies in handling everyday problems. *Journals of Gerontology, 59B,* 261–269.

Block, J. (1961). Ego identity, role variability, and adjustment. *Journal of Consulting Psychology, 25,* 392–397.

Böhmig-Krumhaar, S., Staudinger, U. M., & Baltes, P. B. (2002). Mehr Toleranz tut Not: Läßt sich wert-relativierendes Denken und Urteilen verbessern? [In need of more tolerance: Is it possible to facilitate value relativism?]. *Zeitschrift für Entwicklungspsychologie und Pädagogische Psychologie [Journal of Developmental and Educational Psychology], 34,* 30–43.

Bouchard, T. J., Jr., & Loehlin, J. C. (2001). Genes, evolution, and personality. *Behavior Genetics, 31,* 243–273.

Brandtstädter, J., & Greve, W. (1994). The aging self: Stabilizing and protective processes. *Developmental Review,* 14, 52–80.

Brandtstädter, J., & Renner, G. (1990). Tenacious goal pursuit and flexible goal adjustment: Explication and age-related analysis of assimilative and accomodative strategies of coping. *Psychology and Aging, 5,* 58–67.

Brandtstädter, J., & Rothermund, K. (2002). The life-course dynamics of goal pursuit and goal adjustment: A two process framework. *Developmental Review, 22,* 117–150.

Brandtstädter, J., Rothermund, K., & Schmitz, U. (1997). Coping resources in later life. *European Review of Applied Psychology, 47,* 107–113.

Brandtstädter, J., & Wentura, D. (1995). Adjustment to shifting possibility frontiers in later life: Complementary adaptive modes. In R. A. Dixon & L. Bäckman (Eds.), *Compensating for psychological deficits and declines: Managing losses and promoting gains* (pp. 83–106). Hillsdale, NJ: Erlbaum.

Bronfenbrenner, U. (1979). *The ecology of human development.* Cambridge, MA: Harvard University Press.

Brown, G., & Rafaeli, E. (2007). Components of self-complexity as buffers for depressed mood. *Journal of Cognitive Psychotherapy, 21,* 308–331.

Brown, J. D., & Dutton, K. A. (1995). Truth and consequences: The costs and benefits of accurate self-knowledge. *Personality & Social Psychology Bulletin, 21,* 1288–1296.

Bühler, C. (1968). The general structure of the human life cycle. In C. Bühler & F. Massarik (Eds.), *The course of human life: A study of goals in the humanistic perspective* (pp. 12–26). New York: Springer.

Burke, J. L. (1981). Young children's attitudes and perceptions of older adults. *International Journal of Aging and Human Development, 14,* 205–222.

Butler, R. (1980). Ageism: A foreword. *Journal of Social Issues, 36,* 8–11.

Cacioppo, J. T., Gardner, W. L., & Berntson, G. G. (1999). The affect system has parallel and integrative processing components: Form follows function. *Journal of Personality and Social Psychology, 76,* 839–855.

Campbell, J. D., Assanand, S., & Di Paula, A. (2003). The structure of the self-concept and its relation to psychological adjustment. *Journal of Personality, 71,* 115–140.

Carrillo, J. M., Rojo, N., Sanchez-Bernardos, M. L., & Avia, M. D, (2001). Openness to experience and depression. *European Journal of Psychological Assessment, 17,* 130–136.

Carstensen, L. L. (1991). Selectivity theory: Social activity in life-span context. In K. W. Schaie (Ed.), *Annual review of gerontology and geriatrics* (pp. 195–217). New York: Springer.

Carstensen, L. L., Isaacowitz, D. M., & Charles, S. T. (1999). Taking time seriously: A theory of socioemotional selectivity. *American Psychologist, 54,* 165–181.

Carstensen, L. L., Pasupathi, M., Mayr, U., & Nesselroade, J. R. (2000). Emotional experience in everyday life across the adult life span. *Journal of Personality and Social Psychology, 79,* 644–655.

Cattell, R. B. (1982). *The inheritance of personality and ability: Research methods and findings.* New York: Academic Press.

Chan, R., & Joseph, S. (2000). Dimensions of personality, domains of aspiration, and subjective well-being. *Personality & Individual Differences, 28,* 347–354.

Chandler, M. J., & Holliday, S. (1990). Wisdom in a postapocalyptic age. In R. J. Sternberg (Ed.), *Wisdom: Its nature, origins, and development* (pp. 121–141). New York: Cambridge University Press.

Charles, S. T., & Carstensen, L. L. (1999). The role of time in the setting of social goals across the life-span. In F. Blanchard-Fields & T. Hess (Eds.), *Social cognition and aging* (pp. 319–342). New York: Academic Press.

Charles, S. T., Mather, M., & Carstensen, L. L. (2003). Aging and emotional memory: The forgettable nature of negative images for older adults. *Journal of Experimental Psychology, 132,* 310–324.

Charness, N. (1989). Expertise in chess and bridge. In D. Klahr & K. Kotovsky (Eds.), *Complex information processing: The impact of Herbert A. Simon* (pp. 183–289). Hillsdale, NJ: Erlbaum.

Chrouser Ahrens, C. J., & Ryff, C. D. (2006). Multiple roles and well-being: Sociodemographic and psychological moderators. *Sex Roles, 55(11–12),* 801–815.

Clark-Plaskie, M., & Lachman, M. E. (1999). The sense of control in midlife. In S. L. Willis & J. D. Reid (Eds.), *Life in the middle: Psychological and social development in middle age* (pp. 181–208). San Diego, CA: Academic Press.

Clausen, J. A., & Gilens, M. (1990). Personality and labor force participation across the life course: A longitudinal study of women's careers. *Sociological Forum, 5,* 595–618.

Cohn, L. D. (1998). Age trends in personality development: A quantitative review. In P. M. Westenberg, A. Blasi & L. D. Cohn (Eds.), *Personality development: Theoretical, empiricial, and clinical investigations of Loevinger's conception of ego development.* Mahwah, NJ: Erlbaum.

Cole, P. M., Michel, M. K., & Teti, L. O. D. (1994). The development of emotion regulation and dysregulation: A clinical perspective. *Monographs of the Society for Research in Child Development, 59(2–3),* 73–100, 250–283.

Coleman, L. M., Antonucci, T. C., & Adelmann, P. K. (1987). Role involvement, gender, and well-being. In F. J. Crosby (Ed.), *Spouse, parent, worker: On gender and multiple roles* (pp. 138–153). New Haven, CT: Yale University Press.

Compton, W. C. (2001). Toward a tripartite structure of mental health: Subjective well-being, personal growth, and religiosity. *The Journal of Psychology, 135,* 486–500.

Consedine, N. S., & Magai, C. (2006). Emotional development in adulthood: A developmental functionalist review and critique. In C. Hoare (Ed.), *Handbook of adult development and aging* (pp. 123–148). New York: Guilford Press.

Constantino, M. J., Wilson, K. R., Horowitz, L. M., & Pinel, E. C. (2006). Measures of self-organization and their association with psychological adjustment. *Journal of Social and Clinical Psychology, 25,* 333–360.

Costa, P. T., Herbst, J. H., McCrae, R. R., & Siegler, I. C. (2000). Personality at midlife: Stability, intrinsic maturation, and response to life events. *Assessment, 7,* 365–378.

Costa, P. T., & McCrae, R. R. (1980). Still stable after all these years: Personality as a key to some issues in adulthood and old age. In P. B. Baltes & O. G. Brim (Eds.), *Life-span development and behavior* (Vol. 3, pp. 66–102). New York: Academic Press.

Costa, P. T., & McCrae, R. R. (1994). Set like plaster? Evidence for the stability of adult personality. In T. F. Heatherton & J. L. Weinberger (Eds.), *Can personality change?* (pp. 21–40). Washington, DC: American Psychological Association.

Costa, P. T., Jr., & McCrae, R. R. (2006). Age changes in personality and their origins: Comment on Roberts, Walton, and Viechtbauer (2006). *Psychological Bulletin, 132,* 28–30.

Costa, P. T., Zonderman, A. B., & McCrae, R. R. (1991). Personality, defense, coping, and adaptation in older adulthood. In E. M. Cummings, A. L. Greene, & K. H. Karraker (Eds.), *Life-span developmental psychology: Perspectives on stress and coping* (pp. 277–293). Hillsdale, NJ: Erlbaum.

Cramer, P. (2004). Identity change in adulthood: The contribution of defense mechanisms and life experiences. *Journal of Research in Personality, 38,* 280–316.

Cummings, E. M., & Henry, W. E. (1961). *Growing old: The process of disengagement.* New York: Basic Books.

Davidson, D., Cameron, P., & Jergovic, D. (1995). The effects of children's stereotypes on their memory for elderly individuals. *Merrill-Palmer Quarterly, 41,* 70–90.

Deci, E. L., & Ryan, R. M. (2000). The "what" and "why" of goal pursuits: Human needs and the self-determination of behavior. *Psychological Inquiry, 11,* 227–268.

DeLamater, J., & Moorman, S. M., (2007). Sexual behavior in later life. *Journal of Aging and Health, 19,* 921–945.

Diehl, M., Coyle, N., & Labouvie-Vief, G. (1996). Age and sex differences in strategies of coping and defense across the life span. *Psychology and Aging, 11,* 127–139.

Diehl, M., Hastings, C. T., & Stanton, J. M. (2001). Self-concept differentiation across the adult life span. *Psychology and Aging, 16,* 643–654.

Diener, E. (1996). Traits can be powerful, but are not enough: Lessons from subjective well-being. *Journal of Research in Personality, 30,* 389–399.

Diener, E., & Fujita, F. (1995). Resources, personal strivings, and subjective well-being: A nomothetic and idiographic approach. *Journal of Personality and Social Psychology, 68,* 926–935.

Diener, E., Larsen, R. J., & Emmons, R. A. (1984). Person x situation interactions: Choice of situations and congruence response models. *Journal of Personality and Social Psychology, 47,* 580–592.

Dietz, B. E. (1996). The relationship of aging to self-esteem: The relative effects of maturation and role accumulation. *International Journal of Aging & Human Development, 43,* 249–266.

Digman, J. M. (1997). Higher-order factors of the Big Five. *Journal of Personality and Social Psychology, 73,*1246–1256.

Dixon, T. M., & Baumeister, R. F. (1991). Escaping the self: The moderating effect of self-complexity, *Personality and Social Psychology Bulletin, 17,* 363–368.

Dolge, K., Godde, B., Voelcker-Rehage, C., & Staudinger, U. M. (2010). *Linkages between emotional experiences and brain aging.* Manuscript in preparation. Bremen: Jacobs University.

Donahue, E. M., Robins, R. W., Roberts, B. W., & John, O. P. (1993). The divided self: Concurrent and longitudinal effects of psychological adjustment and social roles on self-concept differentiation. *Journal of Personality and Social Psychology, 64,* 834–846.

Donnellan, M. B., & Lucas, R. E. (2008). Age differences in the Big Five across the life span: Evidence from two national samples. *Psychology and Aging, 23,* 558–566.

Dörner, J., & Staudinger, U. M. (2010). *Self-concept maturity—A new measure of personality growth: Validation, age effects, and first processual explorations.* Unpublished manuscript. Bremen: Jacobs University.

Ehmer, J., & Höffe, O. (Eds.) (2009). Bilder des Alters im Wandel [Changing Images of Aging]: Vol. 1. *Altern in Deutschland [Aging in Germany],* J. Kocka & U. M. Staudinger (Editors). Stuttgart: Wissenschaftliche Verlagsgesellschaft.

Eid, M., Riemann, R., Angleitner, A., & Borkenau, P. (2003). Sociability and positive emotionality: Genetic and environmental contributions to the covariation between different facets of extraversion. *Journal of Personality, 71,* 319–346.

Elder, G. H. (1969). Occupational mobility: Life patterns, and personality. *Journal of Health and Social Behavior, 10,* 308–323.

Erikson, E. H. (1959). *Identity and the life cycle. Psychological issues monograph 1.* New York: International University Press.

Erikson, E. H. (1963). *Childhood and society* (2nd ed.). New York: Norton.

Erikson, E. H. (1968). *Identity. Youth and crisis.* New York, NY: Norton.

Evans, D. W. (1994). Self-complexity and its relation to development, symptomatology and self-perception during adolescence. *Child Psychiatry and Human Development, 24,* 173–182.

Evans, D. W., Brody, L., & Noam, G. G. (2001). Ego development, self-perception, and self-complexity in adolescence: A study of female psychiatric inpatients. *American Journal of Orthopsychiatry, 71,* 79–86.

Eysenck, H. J. (1967). *The biological basis of personality.* Springfield, IL: Charles C Thomas.

Filipp, S. H. (1999). A three-stage model of coping with loss and trauma: Lessons from patients suffering from severe and chronic disease. In A. Maercker, M. Schützwohl, & Z. Solomon (Eds.), *Posttraumatic stress disorder: A life span developmental perspective* (pp. 43–80). Seattle, WA: Hogrefe & Huber.

Filipp, S. H., & Mayer, A. K. (1999). *Bilder des alters-altersstereotype und die beziehungen zwischen den generationen [Images of aging: Age stereotypes and the relationships between generations].* Stuttgart: Kohlhammer.

Fleeson, W., & Heckhausen, J. (1997). More or less "me" in past, present and future: Perceived lifetime personality during adulthood. *Psychology and Aging, 12,* 125–136.

Forster, J. M., & Gallagher, D. (1986). An exploratory study comparing depressed and nondepressed elders' coping strategies. *Journal of Gerontology, 41,* 91-93.

Frazier, L. D., Newman, F. L., & Jaccard, J. (2007). Psychosocial outcomes in later life: A multivariate model. *Psychology and Aging, 22,* 676–689.

Fredrickson, B. L. (2000). Cultivating positive emotions to optimize health and well-being. *Prevention and Treatment, 3.*

Fredrickson, B. L. (2001). The role of positive emotions in positive psychology: The broaden-and-build theory of positive emotions. *American Psychologist, 56,* 218–226.

Freud, S. (1953). *The standard edition of the complete psychological works of Sigmund Freud.* London: Hogarth Press.

Freud, S. (1961). Inhibitions, symptoms, and anxiety. In J. Strachey (Ed.), *The standard edition of the complete psychological works of Sigmund Freud* (Vol. 20, pp. 77–175). London: Hogarth. (Original work published 1923)

Freud, S. (1993). *Vorlesungen zur Einführung in die Psychoanalyse [Introduction to Psycholanalysis]*. Frankfurt: Fischer. (Original work published 1917)

Freund, A. M. (1995). Wer bin ich? Die Selbstdefinition alter Menschen. [Who am I? The self-definition of older adults.] Berlin: Sigma.

Freund, A. M., & Baltes, P. B. (1998). Selection, optimization, and compensation as strategies of life management: Correlations with subjective indicators of successful aging. *Psychology and Aging, 13,* 531–543.

Freund, A. M., & Baltes, P. B. (2002). Life-management strategies of selection, optimization, and compensation: Measurement by self-report and construct validity. *Journal of Personality and Social Psychology, 82,* 642–662.

Freund, A. M., & Smith, J. (1999). Content and function of the self-definition in old and very old age. *Journals of Gerontology: Series B: Psychological Sciences and Social Sciences, 54B,* 55–67.

Fromm, E. (1941). *Escape from freedom.* New York: Avon.

Fromm, E. (1947). *Man for himself.* New York: Rinehart.

Funder, D. C. (2001). Personality. *Annual Review of Psychology, 52,* 197–221.

Gignac, M. A. M., Cott, C., & Badley, E. M. (2002). Adaptation to disability: Applying selective optimization with compensation to the behaviors of older adults with osteoarthritis. *Psychology and Aging, 17,* 520–524.

Glenn, N. D. (1980). Values, attitudes, and beliefs. In O. G. Brim & J. Kagan (Eds.), *Constancy and change in human development* (pp. 596–640). London: Harvard University Press.

Gough, H. G. (1957). *Manual for the California Psychological Inventory.* Palo Alto, CA: Consulting Psychologists Press.

Greve, W., & Staudinger, U. M. (2006). Resilience in later adulthood and old age: Resources and potentials for successful aging. In D. Cicchetti & D. J. Cohen (Eds.), *Developmental psychopathology: Vol. 3. Risk, disorder, and adaptation* (2nd ed., pp. 796–840). Hoboken, NJ: John Wiley & Sons.

Griffin, P. W., Mroczek, D. K., & Spiro, A. (2006). Variability in affective change among aging men: Longitudinal findings from the VA Normative Aging Study. *Journal of Research in Personality, 40,* 942–965.

Gross, J. J. (1998). Antecedent- and response-focused emotion regulation: Divergent consequences for experience, expression, and physiology. *Journal of Personality and Social Psychology, 74,* 224–237.

Gross, J. J., Carstensen, L. L., Pasupathi, M., Hsu, A. Y., Tsai, J., & Skorpen, C. G. (1997). Emotion and aging: Experience, expression, and control. *Psychology and Aging, 12,* 590–599.

Grühn, D., Smith, J., & Baltes, P. B. (2005). No aging bias favoring memory for positive material: Evidence from a homogeneity list paradigm using emotionally toned words. *Psychology and Aging, 20,* 579–588.

Haan, N. (1977). *Coping and defending: Processes of self-environment organization.* New York: Academic Press.

Habermas, T., & Bluck, S. (2000). Getting a life: The emergence of the life story in adolescence. *Psychological Bulletin, 126,* 748–769.

Hagestad, G. O., & Uhlenberg, P. (2005). The social separation of old and young: A root of ageism. *Journal of Social Issues, 61,* 343–360.

Hall, D. T., & Mirvis, P. H. (1995). The new career contract: Developing the whole person at midlife and beyond. *Journal of Vocational Behavior, 47,* 269–289.

Harter, S. (1999). *The construction of the self: A developmental perspective.* New York: Guilford.

Hausdorff, J. M., Levy, B. R., & Wei, J. Y. (1999). The power of ageism on physical function of older persons: Reversibility of age-related gait changes. *Journal of the American Geriatrics Society, 47,* 1346–1349.

Hauser, S. T., Jacobson, A. M., Noam, G., & Powers, S. (1983). Ego development and self-image complexity in early adolescence. Longitudinal studies of psychiatric and diabetic patients. *Archives of General Psychiatry, 40,* 325–332.

Heckhausen, J., & Brim, O. G. (1997). Perceived problems for self and others: Self-protection by social downgrading throughout adulthood. *Psychology and Aging*, 12, 610–619.

Heckhausen, J., Dixon, R. A., & Baltes, P. B. (1989). Gains and losses in development throughout adulthood as perceived by different adult age groups. *Developmental Psychology, 25,* 109–121.

Heckhausen, J., & Krueger, J. (1993). Developmental expectations for the self and most other people: Age grading in three functions of social comparison. *Developmental Psychology, 29,* 539–548.

Heckhausen, J., & Schulz, R. (1995). A life-span theory of control. *Psychological Review, 102,* 284–304.

Heidrich, S. M., & Ryff, C. D. (1993). The role of social comparisons processes in the psychological adaptation of elderly adults. *Journals of Gerontology: Psychological Sciences, 48,* 127–136.

Helson, R., Elliot, T., & Leigh, J. (1990). Number and quality of roles: A longitudinal personality view. *Psychology of Women Quarterly, 14,* 83–101.

Helson, R., Jones, C., & Kwan, V. S. Y. (2002). Personality change over 40 years of adulthood: Hierarchical linear modeling analyses of two longitudinal samples. *Journal of Personality and Social Psychology, 83,* 752–766.

Helson, R., & Kwan, V. S. Y. (2000). Personality change in adulthood: The broad picture and processes in one longitudinal study. In S. Hampson (Ed.), *Advances in personality psychology* (Vol. 1, pp. 77–106). Hove, England: Psychology Press.

Helson, R., Kwan, V. S. Y., John, O. P., & Jones, C. (2002). The growing evidence for personality change in adulthood: Findings from research with personality inventories. *Journal of Research in Personality, 36,* 287–306.

Helson, R., & Roberts, B. W. (1994). Ego development and personality change in adulthood. *Journal of Personality and Social Psychology, 66,* 911-920.

Helson, R., & Srivastava, S. (2001). Three paths of adult development; conservers, seekers and achievers. *Journal of Personality and Social Psychology, 80,* 90–1010.

Helson, R., & Wink, P. (1987). Two conceptions of maturity examined in the findings of a longitudinal study. *Journal of Personality and Social Psychology, 53,* 531–541.

Hogan, R., & Roberts, B. W. (2004). A socioanalytic model of maturity. *Journal of Career Assessment, 12,* 207–217.

Hogansen, J., & Lanning, K. (2001). Five factors in Sentence Completion Test categories: Towards rapprochement between trait and maturational approaches to personality, *Journal of Research in Personality, 35,* 449–462.

Holt, R. R. (1980). Loevinger's measure of ego development: Reliability and national norms for male and female short forms. *Journal of Personality and Social Psychology, 39,* 909-920.

Huyck, M. H. (1991). Predicates of personal control among middle-aged and young-old men and women in middle America. *International Journal of Human Development, 32,* 261–275.

Isaacs, L. W., & Bearison, D. J. (1986). The development of children's prejudice against the aged. *International Journal of Aging and Human Development, 23,* 175–194.

Isen, A. M. (2003). Positive affect as a source of human strength. In L. G. Aspinwall & U. M. Staudinger (Eds.), *A psychology of human strengths: Fundamental questions and future directions for a positive psychology* (pp. 211–225). Washington, DC: American Psychological Association.

Isen, A. M., Daubman, K. A., & Nowicki, G. P. (1987). Positive affect facilitates creative problem solving. *Journal of Personality and Social Psychology, 52,* 1122–1131.

Jahoda, M. (1982). *Employment and unemployment: A social psychological analysis.* Cambridge, England: Cambridge University Press.

James, W. (1948). *Psychology: Briefer course.* New York: Henry Holt. (Original work published 1890)

Jang, K. L., Livesley, W. J., Angleitner, A., Riemann, R., & Vernon, P. A. (2002). Genetic and environmental influences on the covariance of facets defining the domains of the five-factor model of personality. *Personality and Individual Differences, 33,* 83–101.

Joireman, J., & Duell, B. (2005). Mother Teresa vs. Ebenezer Scrooge: Mortality salience leads proselfs to endorse self-transcendent values (unless proselfs are reassured). *Personality and Social Psychology Bulletin, 31,* 307–320.

Jopp, D., & Rott, C. (2006). Adaptation in very old age: Exploring the role of resources, beliefs, and attitudes for centenarians' happiness. *Psychology and Aging, 21,* 266–280.

Jopp, D., & Smith, J. (2006). Resources and life-management strategies as determinants of successful aging: On the proactive effect of selection, optimization and compensation. *Psychology and Aging, 2,* 253–265.

Judge, T. A., & Watanabe, S. (1993). Another look at the job satisfaction-life satisfaction relationship. *Journal of Applied Psychology, 78,* 939-948.

Jung, C. G. (1934). *Modern man in search of a soul.* Oxford England: Harcourt, Brace.

Jung, C. G. (1969). *The symbolic life* (2nd ed., R. F. C. Hull, Trans.) Princeton: Princeton University Press.

Kang, S.-M., & Shaver, P. R. (2004). Individual differences in emotional complexity: Their psychological implications. *Journal of Personality, 72,* 687–726.

Kasser, T., & Ryan, R. M. (1996). Further examining the American dream: Differential correlates of intrinsic and extrinsic goals. *Personality and Social Psychology Bulletin, 22,* 280–287.

Kearl, M. C. (1981). An inquiry into the positive personal and social effects of old age stereotypes among the elderly. *International Journal of Aging and Human Development, 14,* 277–290.

Kennedy, Q., Mather, M., & Carstensen, L. L. (2004). The role of motivation in the age-related positivity effect in autobiographical memory. *Psychological Science, 15,* 208–214.

Kessler, E.-M., Rakoczy, K., & Staudinger, U. M. (2004). The portrayal of older people in prime time television series: The match with gerontological evidence. *Ageing & Society, 24,* 531–552.

Kessler, E.-M., Schwender, C., & Bowen, C. (2010). The portrayal of older people's social participation on German prime-time TV advertisements. *Journal of Gerontology: Social Sciences, 65B,* 97–106.

Kessler, E.-M., & Staudinger, U. M. (2006). Plasticity in old age: Micro and macro perspectives on social contexts. In H. W. Wahl, C. Tesch-Römer, & A. Hoff (Eds.), *Emergence of new person-environment dynamics in old age: A multidisciplinary exploration* (pp. 263–283). Amityville, NY: Baywood.

Kessler, E.-M., & Staudinger, U. M. (2007). Intergenerational potential: Effects of social interaction between older adults and adolescents. *Psychology and Aging, 22,* 690–704.

Kessler, E.-M., & Staudinger, U. M. (2009). Affective experience in adulthood and old age: The role of affective arousal and affect regulation. *Psychology and Aging, 24,* 349–362.

Kessler, E.-M., & Staudinger, U. M. (in press). Emotional resilience and beyond: A synthesis of findings from lifespan psychology and psychopathology. In P. S. Fry & C. L. M. Corey (Eds.), *Frontiers of resilient aging.* Cambridge, England: Cambridge University Press.

Keyes, C. L. M., Shmotkin, D., & Ryff, C. D. (2002). Optimizing well-being: The empirical encounter of two traditions. *Journal of Personality and Social Psychology, 82,* 1007–1022.

Kiecolt-Glaser, J. K., McGuire, L., Glaser, R., & Robles, T. F. (2002). Psychoneuroimmunology: Psychological influences on immune function and health. *Journal of Consulting and Clinical Psychology, 70,* 537–547.

Kiecolt-Glaser, J. K., McGuire, L., Robles, T., & Glaser, R. (2002). Emotions, morbidity, and mortality: New perspectives from psychoneuroimmunology. *Annual Review of Psychology, 53,* 83–107.

Kinnevy, S. C., & Morrow-Howell, N. (1999). The perceived benefits of participating in an intergenerational tutoring program, *Journal of Gerontology and Geriatrics Education, 20,* 3–17.

Kite, M. E., & Johnson, B. T. (1988). Attitudes towards younger and older adults: A meta-analysis. *Psychology and Aging, 3,* 233–244.

Kite, M. E., Stockdale, G. D., Whitley, B. E., & Johnson, B. T. (2005). Attitudes toward younger and older adults: An updated meta-analytic review. *Journal of Social Issues, 61,* 241—266.

Kivett, V. R., Watson, J. A., & Busch, J. C. (1977). The relative importance of physical psychological and social variables to locus of control orientation in middle age. *Journal of Gerontology, 32,* 203–210.

Kling, K. C., Seltzer, M. M., & Ryff, C. D. (1997). Distinctive late-life challenges: Implications for coping and well-being. *Psychology and Aging, 12,* 288–295.

Koch, E. J., & Shepperd, J. A. (2004). Is self-complexity linked to better coping? A review of the literature. *Journal of Personality, 72,* 727–760.

Kohlberg, L. (1963). The development of children's orientation toward a moral order. *Vita Humana, 6(1–2),* 11–33.

Kohn, M. L., & Schooler, C. (1973). Occupational experience and psychological functioning: An assessment of reciprocal effects. *American Sociological Review, 34,* 97–118.

Kohn, M. L., & Schooler, C. (1978). The reciprocal effects of the substantive complexity of work and intellectual flexibility: A longitudinal assessment. *American Journal of Sociology, 84,* 24–52.

Kunzmann, U., & Baltes, P. B. (2003). Wisdom-related knowledge: Affective, motivational, and interpersonal correlates. *Personality & Social Psychology Bulletin, 29,* 1104–1119.

Kunzmann, U., Kupperbusch, C. S., & Levenson, R. W. (2005). Behavioral inhibition and amplification during emotional arousal: A comparison of two age groups. *Psychology and Aging, 20,* 144–158.

Kunzmann, U., Little, T. D., & Smith, J. (2000). Is age-related stability of subjective well-being a paradox? Cross-sectional and longitudinal evidence from the Berlin aging study. *Psychology and Aging, 15,* 511–526.

Kurtz, J. E., & Tiegreen, S. B. (2005). Matters of conscience and conscientiousness: The place of ego development in the Five-Factor Model. *Journal of Personality Assessment, 85,* 312–317.

Kuypers, J. A., & Bengtson, V. L. (1973). Social breakdown and competence: A model of normal aging. *Human Development, 16,* 181–201.

Kwan, C. M. L., Love, G. D., Ryff, C. D., & Essex, M. J. (2003). The role of self-enhancing evaluations in a successful life transition. *Psychology and Aging, 18,* 3–12.

Labouvie-Vief, G. (1982). Dynamic development and mature autonomy: A theoretical prologue. *Human Development, 25,* 161–191.

Labouvie-Vief, G. (1990). Wisdom as integrated thought: Historical and developmental perspectives. In R. J. Sternberg (Ed.), *Wisdom: Its nature, origins, and development* (pp. 52–83). New York: Cambridge University Press.

Labouvie-Vief, G. (1999). Emotions in adulthood. In V. L. Bengtson & K. W. Schaie (Eds.), *Handbook of theories of aging* (pp. 253–267). New York: Springer.

Labouvie-Vief, G. (2003). Dynamic integration: Affect, cognition, and the self in adulthood. *Current Directions in Psychological Science, 12,* 201–206.

Labouvie-Vief, G. (2005). Self-with-other representations and the organization of the self. *Journal of Research in Personality, 39,* 185–205.

Labouvie-Vief, G. (2008) When differentiation and negative affect lead to integration and growth. *American Psychologist, 63,* 564–565.

Labouvie-Vief, G., Chiodo, L. M., Goguen, L. A., Diehl, M., & Orwoll, L. (1995). Representations of self across the life span. *Psychology and Aging, 10,* 404–415.

Labouvie-Vief, G., DeVoe, M., & Bulka, D. (1989). Speaking about feelings: Conceptions of emotion across the life span. *Psychology and Aging, 4,* 425–437.

Labouvie-Vief, G., & Medler, M. (2002). Affect optimization and affect complexity: Modes and styles of regulation in adulthood. *Psychology and Aging, 17,* 571–588.

Lachman, M. (2006). Perceived control over aging-related declines: Adaptive beliefs and behaviors. *Current Directions in Psychological Science, 15*, 282–286.

Larsen, J. T., Hemenover, S. H., Norris, C. J., & Cacioppo, J. T. (2003). Turning adversity to advantage: On the virtues of the coactivation of positive and negative emotions. In L. G. Aspinwall & U. M. Staudinger (Eds.), *A psychology of human strengths: Fundamental questions and future directions for a positive psychology* (pp. 211–225). Washington, DC: American Psychological Association.

Larsen, R. J., & Cutler, S. E. (1996). The complexity of individual emotional lives: A within-subject analysis of affect structure. *Journal of Social and Clinical Psychology, 15,* 206–230.

Lawton, M. P. (1996). Quality of life and affect in later life. In C. Magai & S. H. McFadden (Eds.), *Handbook of emotion, adult development and aging* (pp. 327–348). San Diego, CA: Academic Press.

Lawton, M. P., Kleban, M. H., & Dean, J. (1993). Affect and age: Cross-sectional comparisons of structure and prevalence. *Psychology and Aging, 8*, 165–175.

Lazarus, R. S. (1996). The role of coping in the emotions and how coping changes over the life course. In C. Magai & S. H. McFadden (Eds.), *Handbook of emotion, adult development, and aging* (pp. 284–306). San Diego, CA: Academic Press.

Lerner, R. M. (1984). *On the nature of human plasticity.* New York: Cambridge University Press.

Leventhal, E. A., & Prohaska, T. R. (1986). Age, symptom interpretation and health behavior. *Journal of American Geriatrics Society, 34,* 185–191.

Levy, B. R. (1996). Improving memory in old age through implicit self-stereotyping. *Journal of Personality and Social Psychology, 71,* 1092–1107.

Levy, B. R. (1999). The inner self of the Japanese elderly: A defense against negative stereotypes of aging. *International Journal of Aging and Human Development, 48,* 131–144.

Levy, B. R. (2000). Handwriting as a reflection of aging stereotypes. *Journal of Geriatric Psychiatry, 33,* 81–94.

Levy, B. R. (2008). Rigidity as a predictor of older persons' aging stereotypes and aging self-perceptions. *Social Behaviour and Personality, 36*, 559–570.

Levy, B. R., Ashman, O., & Dror, I. (1999–2000). To be or not to be: The effects of aging self-stereotypes on the well-to-live. *Omega: Journal of Death and Dying, 40,* 409–420.

Levy, B. R., Hausdorff, J. M., Hencke, R., & Wei, J. Y. (2000). Reducing cardiovascular stress with positive self-stereotypes of aging. *Journals of Gerontology: Series B: Psychological Sciences and Social Sciences, 55B,* 205–213.

Levy, B. R., & Myers, L. M. (2004). Preventive health behaviors influenced by self-perceptions of aging. *Preventive Medicine, 39,* 625–629.

Levy, B. R., Ryall, A. L., Pilver, C. E., Sheridan, P. L., Wei, J. Y., & Hausdorff, J. M. (2008). Influence of African American elders' age stereotypes on their cardiovascular response to stress. *Anxiety, Stress & Coping, 21,* 85-93.

Levy, B. R., Slade, M., Kunkel, S., & Kasl, S. (2002). Longitudinal benefit of positive self-perceptions of aging on functioning health. *Journal of Gerontology: Psychological Sciences, 57B,* 409–417.

Linville, P. W. (1985). Self-complexity and affective extremity: Don't put all of your eggs in one cognitive basket. *Social Cognition, 3,* 94–120.

Linville, P. W. (1987). Self-complexity as a cognitive buffer against stress-related depression and illness. *Journal of Personality and Social Psychology, 52,* 663–676.

Loevinger, J. (1976). *Ego development: Conception and theory.* San Francisco: Jossey-Bass.

Loevinger, J. (1997). Stages of personality development. In R. Hogan, J. Johnson, & S. Briggs (Eds.), *Handbook of personality psychology.* San Diego, CA: Academic Press.

Lutz, C. J., & Ross, S. R. (2003). Elaboration versus fragmentation: Distinguishing between self-complexity and self-concept differentiation. *Journal of Social & Clinical Psychology, 22,* 537–559.

Lyubomirsky, S. (2001). Why are some people happier than others? *American Psychologist, 56,* 239–249.

Magai, C. (2001). Emotions over the life span. In J. E. Birren & K. W. Shaie (Eds.), *Handbook of the psychology of aging* (pp. 399–426). San Diego, CA: Academic Press.

Magai, C., Consedine, N. S., Krivoshekova, Y. S., Kudadjie-Gyamfi, E., & McPherson, R. (2006). Emotion experience and expression across the adult life span: Insights from a multimodel assessment study. *Psychology and Aging*, 21, 303–317.

Maier, H., & Smith, J. (1999). Psychological predictors of mortality in old age. *Journals of Gerontology: Psychological Sciences, 54B,* 44–54.

Marcia, J. E. (1980). Identity in adolescence. In J. Adelson (Ed.), *Handbook of adolescent psychology* (pp. 159–187). New York: John Wiley & Sons.

Markus, H. R., & Herzog, A. R. (1991). The role of the self-concept in aging. In K. W. Schaie & M. P. Lawton (Eds.), *Annual review of gerontology and geriatrics* (Vol. 11, pp. 110–143). New York: Springer.

Marsiske, M., Lang, F. R., Baltes, M. M., & Baltes, P. B. (1995). Selective optimization with compensation: Life span perspectives on successful human development. In R. A. Dixon & L. Bäckman (Eds.), *Compensation for psychological defects and declines: Managing losses and promoting gains* (pp. 35–79). Hillsdale, NJ: Erlbaum.

Martire, L. M., Stephens, M. A. P., & Townsend, A. L. (2000). Centrality of women's multiple roles: Beneficial and detrimental consequences for psychological well-being. *Psychology and Aging, 15,* 148–156.

Maslow, A. H. (1962). *Toward a psychology of being.* Princeton, NJ: Van Nostrand.

Maslow, A. H. (1994). *Motivation und Persönlichkeit [Motivation and personality].* Hamburg: Rowohlt.

Mather, M., & Carstensen, L. L. (2003). Aging and attentional biases for emotional faces. *Psychological Science, 14,* 409–415.

Mather, M., & Knight, M. R. (2006). Angry faces get noticed quickly: Threat detection is not impaired among older adults. *Journals of Gerontology: Series B: Psychological Sciences and Social Sciences, 61B,* 54–57.

Maurer, T., Andrews, K., & Weiss, E. (2003). Toward understanding and managing stereotypical beliefs about older workers' ability and desire for learning and development. *Research in Personnel and Human Resources Management, 22,* 253–285.

Mausner-Dorsch, H., & Eaton, W. W. (2000). Psychosocial work environment and depression: Epidemiologic assessment of the demand-control model. *American Journal of Public Health, 90,* 1765–1770.

McAdams, D. P., & de St. Aubin, E. (1992). A theory of generativity and its assessment through self-report, behavioral acts, and narrative themes in autobiography. *Journal of Personality and Social Psychology, 62,* 1003–1015.

McAdams, D. P., de St. Aubin, E., & Logan, R. L. (1993). Generativity among young, midlife, and older adults. *Psychology and Aging, 8,* 221–230.

McCann, R. M., Dailey, R. M., Giles, H., & Ota, H. (2005). Beliefs about intergenerational communication across the lifespan: Middle age and the roles of age stereotyping and respect norms. *Communication Studies, 56,* 293–311.

McConnell, A. R., Renaud, J. M., Dean, K. K., Green, S. P., Lamoureaux, M. J., Hall, C. E., et al. (2005). Whose self is it anyway? Self-aspect control moderates the relation between self-complexity and well-being. *Journal of Experimental Social Psychology, 41,* 1–18.

McCrae, R. R. (1989). Age differences and changes in the use of coping mechanisms. *Journal of Gerontology, 44,* 919-928.

McCrae, R. R., & Costa, P. T. (1980). Openness to experience and ego level in Loevinger's Sentence Completion Test: Dispositional contributions to developmental models of personality. *Journal of Personality and Social Psychology, 39,* 1179–1190.

McCrae, R. R., & Costa, P. T. (1991). Adding Liebe und Arbeit: The full five-factor model and well-being. *Personality and Social Psychology Bulletin, 17,* 227–232.

McCrae, R. R., & Costa, P. T. (1997). Conceptions and correlates of openness to experience. In R. Hogan, F. Johnson, & S. Briggs (Eds.), *Handbook of personality psychology* (pp. 825–847). San Diego: Academic Press.

McCrae, R. R., Costa, P. T., Lima, M. P., Simoes, A., Ostendorf, F., Anglitner, A., et al. (1999). Age differences in personality across the adult lifespan: Parallels in five cultures. *Developmental Psychology, 35,* 466–477.

McCrae, R. R., Costa, P. T., Ostendorf, F., Angleitner, A., Hrebickova, M., Avia, M. D., et al. (2000). Nature over nurture: Temperament, personality, and life span development. *Journal of Personality and Social Psychology, 78,* 173–186.

McGue, M., Bacon, S., & Lykken, D. T. (1993). Personality stability and change in early adulthood: A behavioral genetic analysis. *Developmental Psychology, 29,* 96–109.

Mead, G. H. (1934). *Mind, self, and society.* Chicago: Chicago University Press.

Mergler, N. L., & Goldstein, M. D. (1983). Why are there old people? *Human Development, 35,* 172–177.

Mickler, C., & Staudinger, U. M. (2008). Personal wisdom: Validation and age-related differenes of a performance measure. *Psychology and Aging, 23,* 787–799.

Midlarsky, E., & Kahana, E. (1994). *Altruism in later life.* Thousand Oaks, CA: Sage.

Mischel, W., & Mendoza-Denton, R. (2003). Harnessing willpower and socio-emotional intelligence to enhance human agency and potential. In L. G. Aspinwall & U. M. Staudinger (Eds.), *A psychology of human strengths: Fundamental questions and future directions for a positive psychology* (pp. 245–256). Washington, DC: American Psychological Association.

Mischel, W., & Shoda, Y. (1999). The cognitive-affective personality system. Integrating dispositions and processing dynamics within a unified theory of personality. In L. A. Pervin & O. P. John (Eds.), *Handbook of personality: Theory and research* (pp. 197–218). New York: Guilford Press.

Moneta, G. B., Schneider, B., & Csikszentmihalyi, M. (2001). A longitudinal study of the self-concept and experiental components of self-worth and affect across adolescence. *Applied Developmental Science, 5,* 125–142.

Moor, C., Zimprich, D., Schmitt, M., & Kliegel, M. (2006). Neuroticism, aging self-perceptions, and subjective health: A mediation model. *International Journal of Aging and Human Development, 63,* 241–257.

Morling, B., & Evered, S. (2006). Secondary control reviewed and defined. *Psychological Bulletin, 132,* 269–296.

Mroczek, D. K., & Kolarz, C. M. (1998). The effect of age on positive and negative affect: A developmental perspective on happiness. *Journal of Personality and Social Psychology, 75,* 1333–1349.

Mroczek, D. K., & Spiro, A. I. (2005). Change in life satisfaction during adulthood: Findings From the Veterans Affairs Normative Aging Study. *Journal of Personality and Social Psychology, 88,* 189–202.

Mueller, J. H., Wonderlich, S., & Dugan, K. (1986). Self-referent processing of age-specific material. *Psychology and Aging, 1,* 293–299.

Mühlig-Versen, A., & Staudinger, U. M. (2010). *A quasi-experimental longitudinal study of personality plasticity in later adulthood: The sample case of openness to new experiences.* Manuscript submitted for publication. Bremen: Jacobs University.

Neugarten, B. L. (1968). The awareness of middle age. In B. L. Neugarten (Ed.), *Middle age and aging* (pp. 88–92). Chicago and London: University of Chicago Press.

Neugarten, B. L., Havighurst, R. J., & Tobin, S. S. (1961). The measurement of life satisfaction. *Journal of Gerontology, 16,* 134–143.

Neyer, F. J., & Asendorpf, J. B. (2001). Personality–relationship transaction in young adulthood. *Journal of Personality and Social Psychology, 81,* 1190–1204.

Noack, C. M. G., Baltes, B. B., & Staudinger, U. M. (2010). *Psychological age climate in organizations: Associations with work-related outcomes.* Manuscript submitted for publication. Bremen: Jacobs University.

Noack, C. M. G., & Staudinger, U. M. (2010). *Organizational age climate: Measurement and validation.* Manuscript submitted for publication. Bremen: Jacobs University.

O'Gorman, H. J. (1980). False consciousness of kind: Pluralistic ignorance among the aged. *Research on Aging, 2,* 105–128.

Ong, A. D., & Bergeman, C. S. (2004). The complexity of emotions in later life. *Journal of Gerontology: Psychological Sciences, 59,* 117–122.

Orwoll, L., & Perlmutter, M. (1990). The study of wise persons: Integrating a personality perspective. In R. J. Sternberg (Ed.), *Wisdom: Its nature, origins, and development* (pp. 160–177). New York: Cambridge University Press.

Parker, C. P., Baltes, B. B., Young, S. A., Huff, J. W., Altmann, R. A., Lacost, H. A., et al. (2003). Relationships between psychological climate perceptions and work outcomes: A meta-analytic review. *Journal of Organizational Behavior, 24,* 389–416.

Pasupathi, M., Staudinger, U. M., & Baltes, P. B. (2001). Seeds of wisdom: Adolescents' knowledge and judgment about difficult life problems. *Developmental Psychology, 37,* 351–361.

Pedersen, N. L., & Reynolds, C. A. (2002). Stability and change in adult personality: Genetic and environmental components. *European Journal of Personality, 16,* 77–78.

Peng, K., & Nisbett, R. E. (1999). Culture, dialectics, and reasoning about contradiction, *American Psychologist, 54,* 741–754.

Perlmutter, M. (1988). Cognitive potential throughout life. In J. E. Birren & V. L. Bengtson (Eds.), *Emergent theories of aging* (pp. 247–268). New York: Springer.

Piedmont, R. L. (2001). Cracking the plaster cast: Big Five personality change during intensive outpatient counseling. *Journal of Research in Personality 35*, 500–520.

Pinquart, M. (2001). Age differences in positive affect, negative affect, and affect balance in middle and old age. *Journal of Happiness Studies, 2,* 345–405.

Pinquart, M. (2002a). Creating and maintaining purpose in life in old age: A meta-analysis. *Ageing International, 27,* 90–114.

Pinquart, M. (2002b). Good news about the effects of bad old-age stereotypes. *Experimental Aging Research, 28,* 317–336.

Rafaeli-Mor, E., & Steinberg, J. (2002). Self-complexity and well-being: A review and research synthesis. *Personality and Social Psychology Review, 6,* 31–58.

Rain, J. S., Lane, I. M., & Steiner, D. D. (1991). A current look at the job satisfaction/life satisfaction relationship: Review and future considerations. *Human Relations, 44,* 287–307.

Read, S., Vogler, G. P., Pedersen, N. L., & Johansson, B. (2006): Stability and change in genetic and environmental components of personality in old age. *Personality and Individual Differences, 40,* 1637–1647.

Rickabaugh, C. A., & Tomlinson-Keasey, C. (1997). Social and temporal comparisons in adjustment to aging. *Basic and Applied Social Psychology, 19,* 307–328.

Riediger, M., Freund, A. M., & Baltes, M. M. (2005). Managing life through personal goals: Intergoal facilitation and intensity of goal pursuit in younger and older adulthood. *Journal of Gerontology: Psychological Sciences, 60B,* 84–91.

Roberts, B. W. (1997). Plaster or plasticity: Are adult work experiences associated with personality change in women? *Journal of Personality, 65,* 205–232.

Roberts, B. W., Caspi, A., & Moffitt, T. E. (2003). Work experiences and personality development in young adulthood. *Journal of Personality and Social Psychology*, *84,* 582–593.

Roberts, B. W., & Chapman, C. N. (2000). Change in dispositional well-being and its relationto role quality: A 30-year longitudinal study. *Journal of Research in Personality, 34,* 26–41.

Roberts, B. W., & Mroczek, D. (2008). Personality trait change in adulthood. *Current Directions in Psychological Science, 17,* 3135.

Roberts, B. W., & Robins, R. W. (2004). A longitudinal study of person–environment fit and personality development. *Journal of Personality, 72,* 89–110.

Roberts, B. W., Walton, K. E., Bogg, T., & Caspi, A. (2006). De-investment in work and non-normative personality trait change in young adulthood. *European Journal of Personality, 20,* 461–474.

Roberts, B. W., Walton, K. E., & Viechtbauer, W. (2006). Patterns of mean-level change in personality traits across the life course: A meta-analysis of longitudinal studies. *Psychological Bulletin, 132,* 1–25.

Roberts, B. W., Wood, D., & Smith, J. L. (2005). Examining five-factor theory and social investment perspectives on personality trait development. *Journal of Research in Personality, 39,* 166–184.

Robinson-Whelen, S., & Kiecolt-Glaser, J. (1997). The importance of social versus temporal comparison appraisals among older adults. *Journal of Applied Social Psychology, 27,* 959-966.

Roccas, S., Sagiv, L., Schwartz, S. H., & Knafo, A. (2002). The Big Five personality factors and personal values. *Journal of Personality and Social Psychology, 28,* 789–801.

Rode, J. C. (2004). Job satisfaction and life satisfaction revisited: A longitudinal test of an integrated model. *Human Relations, 57,* 1205–1230.

Rodin, J. (1986). Aging and health: Effects of the sense of control. *Science, 233,* 1271–1276.

Rodin, J., & Langer, E. J. (1980). Aging labels: The decline of control and the fall of self-esteem. *Journal of Social Issues, 36,* 12–29.

Rogers, C. R. (1961). *On becoming a person.* Boston: Houghton Mifflin.

Rokeach, M. (1973). *The nature of human values.* New York: Free Press.

Rothermund, K. (2005). Effects of age stereotypes on self-views and adaptation. In W. Greve, K. Rothermund, & D. Wentura (Eds.), *The adaptive self: Personal continuity and intentional self-development* (pp. 223–242). Göttingen: Hogrefe & Huber.

Rothermund, K., & Brandtstädter, J. (2003). Age stereotypes and self-views in later life: Evaluating rival assumptions. *International Journal of Behavioral Development, 27,* 549–554.

Rothermund, K., & Meiniger, C. (2004). Stress-buffering effects of self-complexity: Reduced affective spillover or self-regulatory processes? *Self & Identity, 3,* 263–281.

Ryff, C. D. (1989a). Happiness is everything, or is it? Explorations on the meaning of psychological well-being. *Journal of Personality and Social Psychology, 57,* 1069–1081.

Ryff, C. D. (1989b). In the eye of the beholder: Views of psychological well-being among middle-aged and older adults. *Psychology and Aging, 4,* 195–210.

Ryff, C. D. (1991). Possible selves in adulthood and old age: A tale of shifting horizons. *Psychology and Aging, 6,* 286–295.

Ryff, C. D., & Baltes, P. B. (1976). Values and transitions in adult development of women: The instrumentality-terminality sequence hypothesis. *Developmental Psychology, 12,* 567–568.

Ryff, C. D., & Essex, M. J. (1992). The interpretation of life experience and well-being: The sample case of relocation. *Psychology and Aging, 7,* 507–517.

Ryff, C. D., & Keyes, C. L. M. (1995). The structure of psychological well-being revisited. *Journal of Personality and Social Psychology, 69,* 719–727.

Ryff, C. D., Keyes, C. L. M., & Hughes, D. L. (2003). Status inequalities, perceived discrimination, and eudaimonic well-being: Do the challenges of minority life hone purpose and growth? *Journal of Health and Social Behavior, 44,* 275–291.

Ryff, C. D., & Singer, B. (1998). The contours of positive human health. *Psychological Inquiry, 9,* 1–28.

Sagiv, L., & Schwartz, S. H. (2000). Value priorities and subjective well-being: Direct relations and congruity effects. *European Journal of Social Psychology, 30,* 177–198.

Salthouse, T. A. (1991). *Theoretical perspectives on cognitive aging.* Hillsdale, NJ: Erlbaum.

Schaie, K. W., Willis, S. L., & Caskie, G. I. L. (2004). The Seattle Longitudinal Study: Relationship between personality and cognition. *Aging Neuropsychology and Cognition, 11,* 304–324.

Scheier, M. F., & Carver, C. S. (1992). Effects of optimism on psychological and physical well-being: Theoretical overview and empirical update. *Cognitive Therapy and Research, 16,* 201–228.

Schindler, I., & Staudinger, U. M. (2005). Lifespan perspectives on self and personality: The dynamics between the mechanics and pragmatics. In W. Greve, K. Rothermund, & D. Wentura (Eds.), *The adaptive self: Personal continuity and intentional self-development.* Göttingen: Hogrefe/Huber.

Schindler, I., & Staudinger, U. M. (2008). Obligatory and optional personal life investments in old and very old age: Validation and functional relations. *Motivation and Emotion, 32,* 23–36.

Schmuck, P., Kasser, T., & Ryan, R. M. (2000). Intrinsic and extrinsic goals: Their structure and relationship to well-being in German and U. S. college students. *Social Indicators Research, 50,* 225–241.

Schmutte, P. S., & Ryff, C. D. (1997). Personality and well-being: Reexamining methods and meanings. *Journal of Personality and Social Psychology, 73,* 549–559.

Schneider, B. (1990). The climate for service: An application of the climate construct. In B. Schneider (Ed.), *Organizational climate and culture* (pp. 383–412). San Francisco: Jossey-Bass.

Schooler, C., Mulatu, M. S., & Oates, G. (2004). Occupational self-direction, intellectual functioning, and self-directed orientation in older workers: Findings and implications for individuals and societies. *American Journal of Sociology, 110,* 161-197.

Schulz, R., & Fritz, S. (1987). Origins of stereotypes of the elderly: An experimental study of the self other discrepancy. *Experimental Aging Research, 13,* 189–195.

Schwartz, S. H. (1992). Universals in the content and structure of values: Theoretical advances and empirical tests in 20 countries. In M. P. Zanna (Ed.), *Advances in experimental social psychology* (Vol. 25, pp. 1–65). San Diego, CA: Academic Press.

Scollon, C. N., & Diener, E. (2006). Love, work, and changes in extraversion and neuroticism over time. *Journal of Personality and Social Psychology, 91,* 1152–1165.

Segal, D. L., Coolidge, F. L., & Mizuno, H. (2007). Defense mechanism differences in younger and older adults: A cross-sectional investigation. *Aging & Mental Health, 11,* 415–422.

Sheldon, K. M. (2005). Positive value change during college: Normative trends and individual differences. *Journal of Research in Personality, 39,* 209–223.

Sheldon, K. M., & Kasser, T. (2001). Getting older, getting better? Personal strivings and personality development across the life-course. *Developmental Psychology, 37,* 491–501.

Sheldon, K. M., Kasser, T., Houser-Marko, L., Jones, T., & Turban, D. (2005). Doing one's duty: Chronological age, felt autonomy, and subjective well-being. *European Journal of Personality, 19* , 97–115.

Sheldon, K. M., Ryan, R. M., Deci, E. L., & Kasser, T. (2004). The independent effects of goal contents and motives on well-being: It's both what you pursue and why you pursue it. *Personality & Social Psychology Bulletin, 30,* 475–486.

Showers, C. (1992). Evaluatively integrative thinking about characteristics of the self. *Personality and Social Psychology Bulletin, 18,* 719–729.

Showers, C. J., & Kevlyn, S. B. (1999). Organization of knowledge about a relationship partner: Implications for liking and loving. *Journal of Personality and Social Psychology, 76,* 958–971.

Showers, C. J., & Kling, K. C. (1996). Organization of self-knowledge: Implications for recovery from sad mood. *Journal of Personality and Social Psychology, 70,* 578–590.

Silvia, P. J., & Gendolla, G. H. E. (2001). On introspection and self-perception: Does self-focused attention enable accurate self-knowledge? *Review of General Psychology, 5,* 241–269.

Small, B. J., Hertzog, C., Hultsch, D. F., & Dixon, R. A. (2003). Stability and change in adult personality over 6 years: Findings from the Victoria Longitudinal Study. *Journals of Gerontology: Series B: Psychological Sciences and Social Sciences, 58B,* 166–176.

Smith, J., & Baltes, P. B. (1997). Profiles of psychological functioning in the old and oldest old. *Psychology and Aging, 12,* 458–472.

Smith, J., & Baltes, P. B. (1999). Trends and profiles of psychological functioning in very old age. In P. B. Baltes & K. U. Mayer (Eds.), *The Berlin Aging Study: Aging from 70 to 100* (pp. 197–226). New York: Cambridge University Press.

Smith, J., Staudinger, U. M., & Baltes, P. B. (1994). Occupational settings facilitating wisdom-related knowledge: The sample case of clinical psychologists. *Journal of Consulting and Clinical Psychology, 62,* 989–999.

Solomon, A., & Haaga, A. F. (2003). Reconsideration of self-complexity as a buffer against depression. *Cognitive Therapy and Research, 27,* 579–591.

Spiegel, D., Bloom, J. R., Kramer, H. C., & Gottheil, E. (1989). Effects of psychosocial treatment on survival of patients with metastatic breast cancer. *Lancet, 2,* 888–891.

Srivastava, S., John, O. P., Gosling, S. D., & Potter, J. (2003). Development of personality in early and middle adulthood: Set like plaster or persistent change? *Journal of Personality and Social Psychology, 84,* 1041–1053.

Staudinger, U. M. (1999). Older and wiser? Integrating results on the relationship between age and wisdom-related performance. *International Journal of Behavioral Development, 23*(3), 641–664.

Staudinger, U. M. (2001). Life reflection: A social–cognitive analyses of life review. *Review of General Psychology, 5,* 148–160.

Staudinger, U. M. (2005). Personality and aging. In M. Johnson, V. L. Bengtson, P. G. Coleman, & T. Kirkwood (Eds.), *Handbook of age and ageing* (pp. 237–244). Cambridge, England: Cambridge University Press.

Staudinger, U. M., & Baltes, P. B. (1996). Interactive minds: A facilitative setting for wisdom-related performance? *Journal of Personality and Social Psychology, 71,* 746–762.

Staudinger, U. M., & Dörner, J. (2006). Wisdom. In *Encyclopedia of Gerontology* (2nd ed., pp. 674–683). Oxford, England: Elsevier.

Staudinger, U. M., Dörner, J., & Mickler, C. (2005). Wisdom and personality. In R. Sternberg & J. Jordan (Eds.), *Handbook of wisdom* (pp. 191–219). New York: Cambridge University Press.

Staudinger, U. M., Dörner, J., & Mickler, C. (2010). *Facilitating personal wisdom: The sample case of a life-review intervention.* Manuscript in preparation. Bremen: Jacobs University.

Staudinger, U. M., & Fleeson, W. (1996). Self and personality in old and very old age: A sample case of resilience? *Development and Psychopathology, 8,* 867–885.

Staudinger, U. M., Freund, A., Linden, M., & Maas, I. (1999). Self, personality, and life regulation: Facets of psychological resilience in old age. In P. B. Baltes & K. U. Mayer (Eds.), *The Berlin Aging Study: Aging from 70 to 100* (pp. 302–328). New York: Cambridge University Press.

Staudinger, U. M. & Glück, J. (in press). Wisdom. *Annual Review of Psychology.*

Staudinger, U. M., & Kessler, E.-M. (2009). Adjustment and growth: Two trajectories of positive personality development across adulthood. In M. C. Smith & N. DeFrates-Densch (Eds.), *Handbook of research on adult learning and development* (pp. 241–268). New York and London: Routledge.

Staudinger, U. M., Marsiske, M., & Baltes, P. B. (1995). Resilience and reserve capacity in later adulthood: Potential and limits of development across the life span. In D. Cicchetti & D. J. Cohen (Eds.), *Developmental psychopathology: Vol. 2. Risk, disorder, and adaptation* (pp. 801–947). New York: John Wiley & Sons.

Staudinger, U. M., Kessler, E.-M., & Dörner, J. (2006). Wisdom in social context. In K. W. Schaie & L. Carstensen (Eds.), *Social structures, aging, and self-regulation in the elderly* (pp. 33–54). New York: Springer.

Staudinger, U. M., & Kunzmann, U. (2005). Positive adult personality development: Adjustment and/or growth? *European Psychologist, 10,* 320–329.

Staudinger, U. M., Lopez, D. F., & Baltes, P. B. (1997). The psychometric location of wisdom-related performance: Intelligence, personality, and more? *Personality and Social Psychology Bulletin, 25,* 1200–1214.

Staudinger, U. M., & Pasupathi, M. (2000). Life-span perspectives on self, personality, and social cognition. In T. A. Salthouse & F. I. M. Craik (Eds.), *The handbook of aging and cognition* (2nd ed., pp. 633–688). Mahwah, NJ: Erlbaum.

Staudinger, U. M., Smith, J., & Baltes, P. B. (1992). Wisdom-related knowledge in a life review task: Age differences and the role of professional specialization. *Psychology and Aging, 7,* 271–281.

Sternberg, R. J. (1998) A balance theory of wisdom. *Review of General Psychology, 2,* 347–365.

Stewart, A. J., & Ostrove, J. M. (1998). Women's personality in middle age. Gender, history, and midcourse corrections. *American Psychologist, 53,* 1185–1194.

Sullivan, H. S. (1972). *Personal psychopathology.* New York: Knopf.

Tait, M., Padgett, M. Y., & Baldwin, T. (1989). Job and life satisfaction: A revaluation of the strength of the relationship and gender effects as a function of the date of the study. *Journal of Applied Psychology, 74,* 502–507.

Taylor, S. E., Kemeny, M. E., Reed, G. M., Bower, J. E., & Gruenewald, T. L. (2000). Psychological resources, positive illusions, and health. *American Psychologist, 55,* 99–109.

Terracciano, A., McCrae, R. R., Brant, L. J., & Costa, P. T., Jr. (2005). Hierarchical linear modeling analyses of NEO-PI-R scales in the Baltimore Longitudinal Study of Aging. *Psychology and Aging, 20,* 493–506.

Thoits, P. A. (1986). Multiple identities: Examining gender and marital status differences in distress. *American Sociological Review, 51,* 259–271.

Tomkins, S. (1984). Affect theory. In K. R. Scherer & P. Ekman (Eds.), *Approaches to emotion* (pp. 163–195). Hillsdale, NJ: Erlbaum.

Trull, T. J., Useda, D. J., Costa, P. T. J., & McCrae, R. R. (1995). Comparison of the MMPI–2 Personality Psychopathology Five (PSY–5), the NEO-PI, and the NEO-PI-R. *Psychological Assessment, 7,* 508–516.

Vaillant, G. E. (2000). Adaptive mental mechanisms: Their role in a positive psychology. *American Psychologist, 55,* 89–98.

Vandewater, E. A., Ostrove, J. M., & Stewart, A. J. (1997). Predicting women's well-being in midlife: The importance of personality development and social role involvements. *Journal of Personality and Social Psychology, 72,* 1147–1160.

van Knippenberg, D., & Schippers, M. C. (2007). Work group diversity. *The Annual Review of Psychology, 58,* 15–41.

Ward, R. A. (1977). The impact of subjective age and stigma on older persons. *Journal of Gerontology, 32,* 227–232.

Waterman, A. S., & Archer, S. L. (1990). A life-span perspective on identity formation: Developments in form, function, and process. In P. B. Baltes, D. L. Featherman, & R. M. Lerner (Eds.), *Life-span development and behavior* (Vol. 10, pp. 29–57). Hillsdale, NJ: Erlbaum.

Watson, D., & Blanchard-Fields, F. (1998). Thinking with your head and your heart: Age differences in everyday problem solving strategy and preferences. *Aging, Neuropsychology, and Cognition, 5,* 225–240.

Watson, D., & Clark, L. A. (1992). On traits and temperament: General and specific factors of emotional experience and their relation to the Five-factor Model. *Journal of Personality, 60,* 441–476.

Wentura, D., & Brandtstädter, J. (2003). Age stereotypes in younger and older women: Analyses of accommodative shifts with a sentence-priming task. *Experimental Psychology, 50,* 16–26.

Wentura, D., & Rothermund, K. (2005). Alterssterotype und Altersbilder [Age stereotypes and images of old age]. In F. S.-H. & U. M. Staudinger (Eds.), *Entwicklungspsychologie des mittleren und höheren Erwachsenenalters [Developmental Psychology during middle and later adulthood]* (pp. 616–654). Göttingen: Horgrefe.

Westphal, M., & Bonnano, G. A. (2004). Emotion self-regulation. In M. Beauregard (Ed.), *Consciousness, emotional self-regulation and the brain* (pp. 1–33). Amsterdam: John Benjamins.

Whitbourne, S. K., & Waterman, A. S. (1979). Psychosocial development during the adult years: Age and cohort comparisons. *Developmental Psychology, 15,* 373–378.

Whitty, M. T. (2003). Coping and defending: Age differences in maturity of defense mechanisms and coping strategies. *Aging and Mental Health, 7,* 123–132.

Wicklund, R. A., & Eckert, M. (1992). *The self-knower: A hero under control.* New York: Plenum Press.

Wickrama, K. A. S., Lorenz, F. O., Fang, S. A., Abraham, W. T., & Elder, G. H., Jr. (2005). Gendered trajectories of work control and health outcomes in the middle years: A perspective from the rural Midwest. *Journal of Health and Social Behavior, 38,* 363–375.

Wickrama, K. A. S., Surjadi, F. F., Lorenz, F. O., & Elder, G. H., Jr. (2008). The influence of work control trajectories on men's mental and physical health during the middle years: Mediational role of personal control. *Journal of Gerontology: Social Sciences, 63B,* 135–145.

Wiese, B. S., Freund, A. M., & Baltes, P. B. (2002). Subjective career success and emotional well-being: Longitudinal predictive power of selection, optimization and compensation. *Journal of Vocational Behavior, 60,* 321–335.

Wiese, B. S., & Schmitz, B. (2002). Studienbezogenes Handeln im Kontext eines entwicklungspsychologischen Meta-Modells [Study-related action as predicted by developmental meta-models]. *Zeitschrift für Entwicklungspsychologie und Pädagogische Psychologie, 34,* 80–94.

Williams, K. Y., & O'Reilly, C. A., III. (1998). Demography and diversity in organizations: A review of 40 years of research. *Research in Organizational Behavior, 20,* 77–140.

Williams, L. M., Brown, K. J., Palmer, D., Liddell, B. J., Kemp, A. H., Olivieri, G., et al. (2006). The mellow years? Neural basis of improving emotional stability over age. *The Journal of Neuroscience, 26,* 6422–6430.

Wilson, T. D., & Dunn, E. W. (2004). Self-knowledge: Its limits, value and potential for improvement. *Annual Review of Psychology, 55,* 493–518.

Wolfenstein, M., & Trull, T. J. (1997). Depression and openness to experience. *Journal of Personality Assessment, 69,* 614–632.

Wood, S., & Kisley, M. A. (2006). The negativity bias is eliminated in older adults: Age-related reduction in event-related brain potentials associated with evaluative categorization. *Psychology and Aging, 21,* 815–820.

Woolfolk, R. L., Novalany, J., Gara, M. A., Allen, L. A., & Polino, M. (1995). Self-complexity, self-evaluation, and depression: An examination of form and content within the self-schema. *Journal of Personality and Social Psychology, 68,* 1108–1120.

Wrenn, E., & Maurer, T. (2004). Age discrimination in personnel decisions: A reexamination. *Journal of Applied Social Psychology, 34,* 1555–1562.

Wrosch, C., Heckhausen, J., & Lachman, M. E. (2000). Primary and secondary control strategies for managing health and financial stress across adulthood. *Psychology and Aging, 15,* 387–399.

Wrosch, C., Scheier, M. F., Carver, C. S., & Schulz, R. (2003). The importance of goal disengagement in adaptive self-regulation: When giving up is beneficial. *Self and Identity, 2,* 1–20.

Wurm, S., Tesch-Römer, C., & Tomasik, M. J. (2007). Longitudinal findings on aging-related cognitions, control beliefs, and health in later life. *Journal of Gerontology: Psychological Sciences, 62B,* 156–164.

CHAPTER 9

Coping across the Life Span[1]

CAROLYN M. ALDWIN, LORIENA A. YANCURA, and DARIA K. BOENINGER

Coping and development are inextricably intertwined (Skinner & Edge, 2006). The resources and abilities underlying the coping process depend heavily on developmental stages in both neurocognitive (Gunnar & Quevedo, 2007) and socioemotional domains (Eisenberg, Valiente, & Sulik, 2009). How individuals cope, in turn, affects development in a wide variety of domains. Differences in developmental history, including non-normative events, and socioenvironmetal and historical contexts also affect how individuals cope with stress (Elder & Shanahan, 2006; Skinner & Zimmer-Gebeck, 2009). Integrating information across these different areas, however, is complicated by the fact that the different fields that address coping and adaptation often utilize different terms for similar phenomena, or focus more heavily on one or another aspect of the process.

The purpose of this chapter is to bring together studies of how individuals cope with stress across the life span, from infancy through late life, with a view toward identifying common themes that provide scaffolding for a life-span theory of coping. In the first section of this chapter, we provide a brief primer or introduction to the field, discussing various definitions of and approaches to coping, and differentiating it from related constructs such as self-regulation and emotion regulation, as well as from everyday problem solving. We also provide a brief introduction to the biological, neurocognitive, psychological, and socioenvironmental foundations of coping.

The second section provides an in-depth examination of coping at different life stages, from infancy through late life. We examine the specific neurocognitive and psychosocial factors that underlie the types of coping strategies normatively observed for individuals in each section of the life span. In infancy, for example, much of the range of coping behavior is influenced by the development of the prefrontal cortex (PFC); deterioration of the PFC in dementias in late life may impair the cognitive abilities involved in coping (Sherod et al., 2009). We also examine how developmental histories, including non-normative events, and socioenvironmental contexts influence coping trajectories in each stage, as well as subsequent ones.

[1] Work on this chapter by the third author was supported by the National Institutes of Health grant T32 MH018387.

The third section identifies four themes that emerged from this review, including the contextual nature of coping; the social nature of coping; energy regulation, conceptualized in terms of engagement/disengagement; and self-development. While there are theories of coping from infancy through adolescence (Compas, 2009; Skinner & Zimmer-Gebeck, 2009), and several theories of developmental changes in general adaptation across the life span, to date no one has a theory that describes change in coping throughout the life course. Based on these four themes, we outline what such a theory might entail, as well as identify directions for future research.

COPING: A BRIEF PRIMER

In everyday use, the term *coping* refers to efforts to manage stress. More precise definitions are not as straightforward. Academic definitions of coping encompass many domains of study and there is little consensus among researchers on how to conceptualize central constructs in the field (Skinner, Edge, Altman, & Sherwood, 2003). Lazarus and Folkman (Folkman & Lazarus 1980; Lazarus & Folkman, 1984) focus on appraisal and cognitive aspects, defining it as "thoughts and behaviors that people use to manage the internal and external demands of situations that are appraised as stressful" (Folkman & Moskowitz, 2004, p. 746). Others define coping as "efforts to regulate emotion, cognition, behavior, physiology, and the environment in response to stressful events or circumstances" (Compas et al., 2001, p. 89). Yet others have called attention to the organization and coordination of efforts in multiple domains. For example, Skinner and Wellborn (1994) define coping as "how people mobilize, modulate, manage, and coordinate their behavior, emotion, and attention . . . under stress" (p.113). This difficulty in reaching a consensus on what constitutes coping and how these elements are integrated is further confounded by conceptual overlaps among coping and related constructs and notable self-regulation (Eisenberg, Valiente, & Sulik, 2009), which includes emotion regulation (Little & Geldhof, this volume). According to Eisenberg and Zhou (2000), emotion regulation is defined as the process of

> initiating, maintaining, modulating, or changing the occurrence, intensity, or duration of internal feeling states and emotion-related physiological processes, often in the service of accomplishing one's goals. . . . In our view, emotion regulation often is accomplished through effortful management of attention (e.g., attention shifting and focusing, cognitive distraction) and cognitions that affect the interpretation of situations (e.g., positive cognitive restructuring), as well as through neurophysiological processes. (p. 167)

In contrast, the National Research Council (NRC) (2000, p. 103) defines self-regulation as "learning to wait before acting, self-monitoring, and acquiring the ability to organize segments of behavior sequentially" (p. 103), while Eisenberg and Zhou (2000) also include issues in self-presentation in culturally acceptable ways. Thus, self-regulation is an overarching construct that includes emotion regulation.

Coping may be thought of as one aspect of self-regulation under stress. While coping processes generally focus on coping with particular stressful episodes, broader definitions encompass unconscious defense mechanisms and life management skills that may be routinized or used to forestall general stress, such as proactive and anticipatory coping (Aspinwall & Taylor, 1997; Schwarzer & Knoll, 2003). Anticipatory coping refers to strategies used to manage a stressful event that is likely to occur (such as studying for a mid-term), while proactive coping involves efforts carried out in advance of a potentially stressful event to prevent it from occurring or modifying its form (Aspinwall & Taylor, 1997) (such as saving for college).

The relation between coping and general self-regulation processes is also complex and a matter of some debate. While Gross (1998) subsumes self-regulation under coping, others consider coping to be a subcategory of self-regulation, an unfolding process directed toward attaining and maintaining personal goals (Maes & Karoly, 2005). This overarching construct includes both coping and emotion regulation, two closely related constructs. Coping has been described as emotion regulation in response to stress (Eisenberg, Fabes, & Guthrie, 1997). However, there are also aspects of coping that fall outside the realm of emotion regulation. For example, problem-focused coping efforts targeted toward changing the source of stress might be considered to be nonemotional actions (Gross, 1998). Other coping efforts, such as seeking social support, involve the regulation of emotion, attention, and behavior, but also involve exercising social skills (Eisenberg, Valiente, & Sulik, 2009). Folkman and Moskowitz (2004) note that coping may also be distinguished from emotion regulation in that coping lends itself more easily to cognitive-behavioral intervention (but see Jennings & Greenberg, 2009).

Thus, while coping involves some aspects of emotional regulation, the two constructs differ in scope and focus. In the domain of affect, emotion regulation has a much broader scope, including all affective processes, whereas coping includes only affective processes in the face of stress. Further, coping includes cognition and behaviors directed toward solving the problem.

Everyday problem solving is a related construct. Blanchard-Fields (2007) argued that effective everyday problem solving contains essential cognitive and emotional components. Because problems in everyday life are ill-structured and transpire in continually transforming socioemotional contexts, effective everyday problem solving calls on a greater or lesser degree of emotion regulation. For example, early measures of everyday problem solving ability in late life involved whether individuals can follow the directions for baking a microwave cake (Diehl, Willis, & Schaie, 1995), which presumably would not require a great deal of emotion regulation. However, the later work of Blanchard-Fields (2007) has begun to incorporate emotional elements. For example, decisions of what to do during a divorce contain instrumental elements, such as which attorney to hire and how large of a settlement to request, as well as emotional elements, may require a great deal of emotion regulation.

Expertise in the use of socioemotional strategies in everyday problem solving does not appear to be related to the level of one's cognitive skills. That is, an individual may have the cognitive ability to solve everyday problems, but not be effective because he or she is not capable of regulating emotional reactions to problems. Because solving everyday problems requires coordination of cognitive, emotional, and behavioral elements, Blanchard-Fields' (2007) conceptualization of everyday problem solving falls within Skinner and Wellborn's (2004) view of coping as involving coordination among cognitive, behavioral, and emotional domains.

Figure 9.1 demonstrates the overlap between the constructs of self-regulation, coping, and everyday problem solving. Self-regulation is an overarching construct that includes the regulation of behavior under both stressful and non-stressful conditions. In stressful circumstances, however, attempts at self-regulation become coping strategies. When anticipating the occurrence of a problem in the near future, self-regulation overlaps with anticipatory coping. Similarly, one can use everyday problem solving in non-stressful conditions, but under stressful conditions it falls into the domain of coping. Proactive coping can be seen as overlapping with everyday problem solving, such as when individuals store up resources in anticipation of a future need (e.g., "saving for a rainy day"). Thus, these three spheres—self-regulation, coping, and everyday problem solving—represent overlapping but nonetheless distinct sets of processes.

Like the construct of coping, the concept of stress also involves layers of complexity around a simple core. Mason

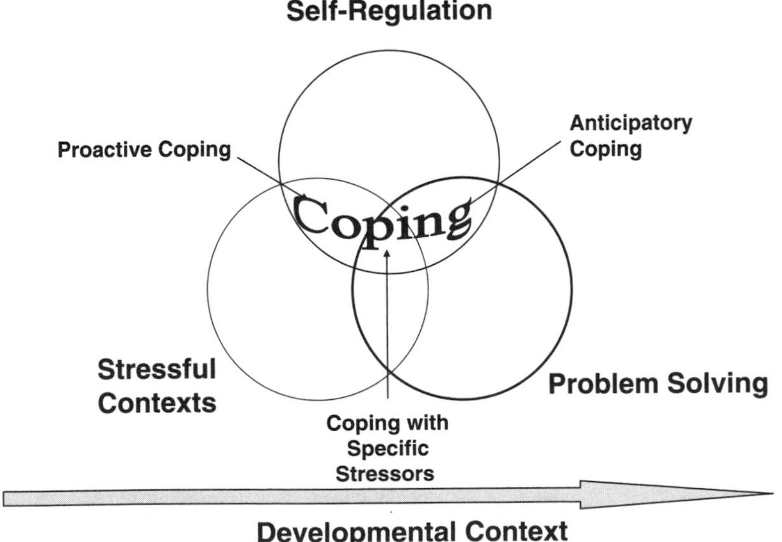

Figure 9.1 Coping as Self-Regulation and Problem Solving in Stressful Contexts

(1975) defined stress in three ways. First, it may refer to internal states of the organism. These may be physiological, such as heart palpitations or sweating, or emotional, such as anger, sadness, or guilt. It may also be defined as external situations, such as natural disasters, major life events, environmental characteristics, daily hassles, or chronic role strain. These external stressors may differ in duration, rapidity of onset, and linkage with other stressors. For example, job loss, an external stressor, may be accompanied by financial hassles and guilt. Stress may also be conceptualized as a combination of the above two approaches, or as a person–environment transaction (Lazarus & Folkman, 1984). Aldwin (2007) defines stress as "that quality of experience, produced through a person–environment transaction that, through either overarousal or underarousal, results in psychological or physiological distress" (p. 24). That is, the appraisal of stress occurs as a result of an individual's perception that external demands exceed his or her internal resources.

External stressors vary over the course of the life span and may be normative or non-normative. Understanding the heterogeneity of stressors within and across different phases in the life span is important to a developmental examination of coping, as changes in coping may reflect changes in environmental exigencies rather than developmental processes in coping *per se*.

THEORETICAL VIEWS OF COPING

Defense Mechanisms

The construct of coping has its conceptual roots in psychodynamic models of defense mechanisms (Aldwin, 2007), which are ways that the ego uses to evade anxiety and exercise control over threatening impulses and instincts. Defense mechanisms, such as denial, projection, obsessive-compulsive behaviors, and sublimation, are unconscious attempts to minimize anxiety by distorting reality. Because they occur outside of conscious awareness and do not represent reality, defense mechanisms are characterized by rigidity and manifest in psychopathological symptoms.

Despite the fact that a few definitions of coping include unconscious thoughts or behaviors, this inclusion of unconscious elements reflects theoretical origins, rather than current conceptualizations. However, Compas (1998) argues for inclusion of an involuntary aspect of coping that is somewhat analogous to defense mechanisms or emotional reactions. Most views of coping differentiate it from defense mechanisms by defining it as conscious thoughts, feelings, and behaviors. Folkman and Moskowitz (2004) believe that unconscious processes should not be included in the study of coping. Cramer (2000) differentiates between coping and defense mechanisms on several levels. In addition to being characterized by their unconscious nature, defense mechanisms are hierarchically organized and associated with pathology. In contrast, coping processes are conscious, situationally determined, and not associated with pathology. As a result of these differences, methodology used in the study of defense mechanisms differs greatly from that of coping and the two are quite separate in the academic literature. Researchers who study defense mechanisms typically rely on the use of qualitative data (but see Bond, 2004). Those who study coping generally approach it by conceptualizing coping as a style (trait) or as a process. These approaches rest on different assumptions and require different methodologies.

Coping Styles

Some views of coping rest on the assumption that individuals exhibit relatively stable types of styles of coping in response to a variety of situations. These views may be grouped into two broad categories, perceptual styles and trait typologies (Aldwin, 2007). The perceptual style approach has been most frequently used in the literature on coping with illness. It is based on the notion that people characteristically prefer different amounts of information. For example, one individual coping with a diagnosis of breast cancer may want to gather as much information about prognosis and treatment as possible, while another might not want to know anything, preferring to let health professionals or family members make decisions. Byrne (1964) proposed the earliest typology, repression-sensitization, which identified those who suppress or avoid information as repressors and those who seek information as sensitizers. Over the years, researchers have put forth variations on this approach, notably blunting-monitoring (Miller, 1980) and approach-avoidance (Moos, 1997).

Despite criticisms on a conceptual level, recent studies of coping styles have found that they may have interesting implications for health prevention and disease management. For example, Williams-Piehota and colleagues (2005) found that matching information about health risks matched to coping styles significantly increase the likelihood of seeking preventive care. Thus, coping style dichotomies may be useful in the health education context. However, generalizing people into simple categories may be useful in only a limited number of situations, because detailed information is lost when people are classified into overly broad categories (Aldwin, 2007). In addition to this, dichotomous approaches to the study of coping have been criticized because repressive types of coping tend to be highly correlated with anxiety, individuals demonstrate very little cross-situational consistency in coping styles, and there is little evidence that questionnaire measures of these coping styles predict coping behavior (Lazarus, Averill, & Opton, 1974).

Typologies of coping styles may avoid some of these problems because they generally include several styles. These typologies characterize people into categories according to how they differ in response to a particular type of stress. Coping styles may be similar to personality styles because they describe a person's characteristic response to stress, but these two constructs differ in that personality styles are purported to remain the same in a broad variety of situations, while coping styles occur in response to specific types of stress. For example, in a classic study of older women coping with bereavement, Wortman and Silver (1989) identified four descriptive categories of coping styles: no distress, chronic grief, acute grief, and delayed reaction. In contrast, a study of coping styles in older adults coping with age-related visual impairment identified four very different categories: maverick copers relied on self-perceived attributes, autonomous copers were independent yet sought help when needed, pragmatic copers relied on both instrumental and emotional support to optimize their sight, hermits used social avoidance, and "nonchalants" failed to report many coping strategies (Lee & Brennan, 2006). The discrepancies between the number and type of coping styles identified in these two studies illustrate a fundamental weakness in coping typology approaches: They appear to be situation-specific but do not clearly identify their range of generalizability. Despite this, they do allow for much more flexibility than dichotomous approaches.

Process Approaches

A process or cognitive approach to the study of coping is currently the most commonly used. This approach allows for the greatest amount of flexibility in response to situational or environmental demands because it considers intraindividual variability in the appraisal of stressors and use of coping strategies within and across situations. It considers coping to be an ongoing transactional process between the person and the situation that is responsive to both individual characteristics and environmental demands (Lazarus & Folkman, 1984). Aldwin (2007) noted that cognitive approaches are based on four main assumptions. First, coping is dependent on cognitive appraisals of the situation. That is, it involves conscious evaluation of the impact of situations, which may be benign, threatening, harmful, or resulting from loss. Second, individuals may modify their coping strategies in response to environmental demands. Someone might use an entirely different set of coping strategies in dealing with a rebellious child than in solving a problem with a co-worker. Third, coping includes strategies aimed at managing the situation or problem as well as those aimed at controlling one's internal reaction to it. Fourth, no coping strategies are considered to be inherently superior to others. According to these approaches, coping strategies are not hierarchical; their effectiveness depends on the situations in which they are used. For example, focusing on solving the problem might be the best course of action when one is faced with a major deadline at work, but might not be the most effective strategy when one is faced with a diagnosis of inoperable cancer or the death of a loved one.

The flexibility of these approaches allows for the study of coping across the great range of stressors that occur in everyday life and across the life span, from self-soothing *in utero* (Field, 1991) to meaning making in late life (Danhauer, Carlson, & Andrykowski, 2005). However, this situational heterogeneity has also been a source of weakness in developing theoretical cohesiveness in coping constructs. This is especially true in consideration of coping across the life span, given the various forms that coping may take. For example, the strategy of self-soothing by thumb sucking is often seen in infants who wake up in the middle of the night (Goodlin-Jones, Burnham, Gaylor, & Anders, 2001). Older adults are not likely to suck their thumbs to cope with insomnia, but they may try to return to sleep by attempts to reduce the anxiety keeping them awake (Morin, Rodrigue, & Ivers, 2003). It is also important to consider the different terminologies used by researchers. For example, one researcher might use the term *withdrawal* for the strategy of managing a problem by staying away from other people (Laux & Weber, 1991), while another might call it *social isolation* (Folkman & Lazarus, 1985).

A related problem stems from confusion in the structural organization of coping categories. Whether implicitly or explicitly, researchers generally conceptualize coping as organized by lower-order strategies and higher-order categories (Skinner, Edge, Altman, & Sherwood, 2003). For example, strategies such as "told myself the situation was my fault" or "criticized my handling of the situation" are strategies that might be contained in the higher-order category of *self-blame*. Specific categories of coping strategies have been derived from both theoretical and empirical (i.e., factor analyses) techniques, or a combination of both

(Folkman & Moskowitz, 2004), yet there is no generally accepted classification of coping strategies in the field of coping research (Skinner et al., 2003). This may be due in part to difficulties in the measurement of coping strategies (for reviews see Aldwin, 2007; Coyne & Raccioppo, 2000; Folkman & Moscowitz, 2004). It may also be due to the aforementioned difficulties in nomenclature of coping strategies (Folkman & Moskowitz, 2004), as well as difficulties arising from theoretical and methodological differences in the empirical analysis of coping (Skinner et al., 2003).

Historically, coping has been classified in many different ways. One of the most basic distinctions is between problem-focused and emotion-focused coping strategies. The former includes strategies to manage the stressor (e.g., took medicine to control the pain), while the latter includes strategies to manage one's emotional reaction to it (e.g., told myself that it wouldn't last much longer). However, these two categories represent just the tip of the iceberg. Other dimensions that have appeared in the literature include social support (Delongis & Holzman, 2005), meaning-making (Park, 2005), religious coping (Pargament, Koenig, & Perez, 2000), cognitive reframing (Lazarus & Folkman, 1984), and communal coping (Hobfoll, 2002), as well as proactive and anticipatory coping (Aspinwall & Taylor, 1997; Schwarzer & Knoll, 2003). In addition to these, there are literally hundreds of less commonly used categories, each composed of various numbers of coping strategies.

In order to minimize this confusion and unify the field, Skinner and colleagues (2003) examined more than 100 categorical assessments of coping strategies to lay the groundwork for developing a structural model of coping. Their proposed model included suggestions for organizing existing coping strategies into higher-order coping categories. The published assessments that they reviewed contained over 400 lower-order coping strategies previously classified into heterogeneous categories. They considered the number of appearances each category made in coping assessments (taking into account variations in nomenclature), whether the strategy appeared in general or specific coping inventories (i.e., measuring coping with general stress or a specific stressor, such as bereavement or illness), and whether the strategy appeared in measures designed for children, adolescent, or adult populations.

Based on this analysis, Skinner et al. (2003) concluded that five categories of coping are "central" to the field: *problem solving*, *support seeking*, *avoidance*, *distraction*, and *positive cognitive restructuring*. *Problem solving* includes strategies involving instrumental action, planning, and persistence. *Support seeking* includes strategies eliciting assistance and advice from other people, parents, peers, and professionals. The category of *avoidance*, sometimes termed *escapism*, includes strategies such as cognitive avoidance, avoidant actions, and denial. *Distraction* includes engaging in pleasurable strategies, such as watching TV or exercising, that minimize stress by focusing attention away from the stressor. Interestingly, Skinner, et al. (2003) found that distraction strategies were not statistically related to escape/avoidance strategies; rather, they emerged as a distinct category. *Positive cognitive restructuring* includes strategies that actively reinterpret stressors in a more positive light, such as focusing on the bright side of the problem.

Four additional categories were also included as "strong candidates" for general higher-order coping strategies: *rumination*, *helplessness*, *social withdrawal*, and *emotional regulation*. *Rumination* was defined as repetitive emphasis on the negative aspects of a situation and included strategies such as catastrophizing and self-blame. *Helplessness* involved relinquishing control over a situation with such strategies as passivity and dejection. *Social withdrawal* was distancing other people from knowing about a problem or its effects. It was composed of strategies such as social isolation and emotional withdrawal. *Emotional regulation* was defined as active attempts to manage emotional reactions to the stressor or to express emotion in appropriate situation. Strategies consisted of emotional expression, relaxation, and self-encouragement.

Skinner and colleagues' (2003) approach to making sense of the myriad of categories used in coping research is a promising attempt to reconcile one of the most-oft criticized aspects of the field, the situational variability and psychometric instability of measurements of coping (c.f., Coyne & Racioppo, 2000). Although the article by Skinner and colleagues (2003) appears to having some impact on the field (with 121 citations in the *Social Science Citation Index* as of this writing), the structure of coping is far from standardized. Thus, many of the studies to illustrate coping across the life span in this review will reflect overlaps of coping categories and process approaches to coping.

Recent Developments

Another relatively recent criticism of coping research concerns the ecological validity of the construct. Individuals might exhibit qualitatively different problem solving abilities in contrived settings (e.g., assessments, interviews, scenarios, or laboratories) than in contextually rich everyday settings (Denney & Palmer, 1981). The relatively new area of everyday problem solving examines older adults' abilities in multidimensional situations. Some aspects of the study of everyday problem solving are concerned with assessing cognitive performance in real-life settings (Diehl, et al., 2005; Marsiske & Margrett, 2006). However, approaches to studying everyday problem solving differ from traditional approaches to cognition because individuals are expected to generate alternative strategies to solving problems and decide among them (Thornton & Dumke, 2005). As mentioned earlier, Blanchard-Fields (2007) argued that effective everyday problem solving contains essential cognitive and emotional components.

Another emerging area of coping research rests on the assumption that coping is embedded in interpersonal contexts (Revenson & Pranikoff, 2005). This area studies the coping of dyads facing a single stressor and has been called *dyadic, interpersonal,* or *collaborative* coping (Berg et al., 2008). Many stressors, such as chronic illness, affect both the person diagnosed with them and those with whom they are connected, usually a spouse. Thus, partners' attempts to cope with such stressors are mutually influential. Dyadic coping may occur in several ways: partners' involvement in coping efforts, partners' instrumental or emotional support, partners' active collaboration in problem solving, and domination or control (Berg, Meegan, & Deviney, 1998). Dyadic coping strategies may have different implications for psychological and physical health outcomes of each partner.

The effect of dyadic coping depends, in part, on how it is measured. It may be measured by the patient's perception of the spouse's involvement or congruence between the partner's coping strategies. When dyadic coping is measured by patients' perceptions of partners' involvement; partners' coping with collaboration and support led to better outcomes than partners' attempts at control (Berg & Upchurch, 2007). When dyadic coping is measured by congruence between partners, the effect of coping appears to depend on which type of coping strategy partners are congruent. Berg et al. (2008) found that couples who were not congruent in their coping efforts experienced more distress than congruent couples. However, this study only covered coping over a two-week period, so it is possible that congruency in some types of coping strategies may be effective in the short run, but ineffective in the long run. For example, a couple that collectively copes with a threatening diagnosis with avoidant strategies, such as denial or substance abuse, might report little psychological distress in the short run, but a great deal of distress in the long run when they must face the inevitable.

Badr (2004) reported a positive relationship between couples' marital adjustment and use of active engagement coping strategies. Couples' marital adjustment was also positively related to their complementary use of protective buffering and avoidance coping strategies. Berg and Upchurch (2007) note that the study of dyadic coping is complex because it depends on sociocultural context, the context of the illness (stressor), the outcome assessed, and diversity in the developmental life course. Thus, as noted in the introduction, the study of coping necessitates a complex theoretical approach that is capable of taking these factors, and their interactions, into account. The next section of this review will discuss aspects of one such approach, the developmental systems approach, that are relevant to the study of coping across the life span.

A Developmental Systems Theory Approach to Coping Research

Coping is a complex construct, cutting across multiple domains of academic literature. Contemporary approaches to the study of coping consider mutually influential transactions across stress physiology (Gunnar & Quevedo, 2007), personality and temperament (Derryberry, Reed, & Pilkenton-Taylor, 2003; Suls & David, 1996), developmental history (Skinner & Zimmer-Gebeck, 2009; Stroebe, Schut, & Stroebe, 2005), motivation (Rothermund & Brandtstädter, 2003), and social contexts (Berg & Upchurch, 2007). This view is in line with a current paradigm shift in both the physical and social sciences, which are moving from reductionistic (cause and effect) and interactionist (multiply determined) views of the world to transactionist (reciprocally influential) views (Aldwin, 2007).

The perspective that coping involves transactions among biological, psychological, and sociocultural contexts is germane to the developmental study of coping in everyday contexts. For example, a middle-aged woman coping with a diagnosis of diabetes might choose to join a support group encouraging the behavioral coping strategies of exercising and eating properly to cope with this disease. These strategies might result in a reduction in diabetic symptoms. However, a teenager faced with a diagnosis of diabetes might initially cope by negative rumination, resulting in an increase in emotional distress, making it more difficult to regulate her blood sugar. Her friends may try to distract her with a pizza or other comfort food, also resulting in problems regulating her diabetes. Thus, physiology, coping, and social context, as well as developmental stage, all transact to create different trajectories of change over time (Aldwin, 2007; Skinner & Edge, 1998; Skinner & Zimmer-Gembeck, 2009).

Developmental biocultural co-constructivism (Baltes & Smith, 2004) acknowledges the influence of biological trajectories, which necessitate the direction of resources from growth through maintenance to the regulation of loss. Traditional approaches to the study of development over the life course have been concerned with contextual influences on development, including age-graded, history-graded, and non-normative influences (Elder & Shanahan, 2006). A more integrated view of developmental science views human development as occurring along mutually influential pathways involving multiple levels of organization (Lerner, Theokas, & Bobak, 2005). These multiple interacting levels include basic biological processes (e.g., neurons and neurotransmitters), individual-level variables (e.g., emotion, cognition, and motivation), social variables (e.g., family, school, and employment settings), and cultural settings (e.g., time and geographical place).

The following section of this review will provide background relevant to a developmental systems approach to the study of coping over the life span in three transacting domains. Our discussion is organized around biological aspects (e.g., neurocognitive development and stress physiology), psychological aspects (e.g., personality, motivation, cognition, and developmental history), and sociocultural contexts (e.g., culture and role transitions).

Biological Aspects of Coping

Coping and physiological processes are mutually influential. First, physiology underlies the development of coping abilities. Neurocognitive developments in the brain enable the regulation of emotion, behavior, and motivation essential to coping (LeDoux, 2002; Rueda & Rothbart, 2009). Second, changes in physiology processes can also be outcomes of coping. Coping moderates relationships between stress and physical and psychological health (Penley, Tomaka, & Weibe, 2002). This effect occurs via changes in the physiological systems most implicated in the stress response, the endocrine and immune systems. Dysregulation of these systems can lead to disease, which then becomes the context for subsequent coping efforts. If this dysregulation is extreme, as in cases of trauma, it may also influence the brain and central nervous system, which can influence further coping efforts by causing neurocognitive damage or altering an individual's threshold for future stressors (Gunnar & Fisher, 2006; Mroczek et al., 2006). Because each of these aspects of coping primarily involves different physiological systems, they will be discussed separately in the following sections.

Coping and neurocognitive development. Biological changes in the brain at each phase of the life span influence cognitive, emotional, and behavioral aspects of coping. Andersen (2003) described brain development as occurring in a series of broad phases. Life span development of the brain consists of a shift in focus beginning with enervation patterns and continuing through adaptive patterns and compensatory activity. The earliest phases of development are associated with the greatest vulnerability to environmental insults. The NRC (2000) also noted that the earliest phases of neurocognitive development are of critical importance because they provide the foundation for later development.

Neurological development, including the differentiation, maturation, and myelination of neurons, is both experience-expectant (i.e., common to all members of a species) and experience-dependent (i.e., dependent on specific physical and social environments) (Greenough, Black, & Wallace, 1987). The timing of neurogenesis, synaptogenesis, and myelination differs across regions of both cortical (Huttenlocher, 1999) and subcortical areas (Johnson, 2001). This variation in patterning of neurocognitive development parallels changes in cognition, emotion, behavior—the substrates of coping—over different phases of the life span. Regarding the development of coping, this means that cortical functions, such as planning and the integration of emotion and cognition, develop over time. The second section of this chapter discusses how each of these functions matures in various developmental periods.

Coping and health. Much of the literature on coping has focused on coping in the context of health outcomes. This research is typically done within the field of health psychology and examines pathways by which psychological stress influences physical health through specific changes in the endocrine and immune systems, as well as indirectly through changes in health behaviors. The psychological process of appraising a situation as stressful (Lazarus & Folkman, 1984) initiates the physiological stress response. The initial physiological reaction involves two systems within the sympathetic nervous system (SNS) (Gevirtz, 2000). The initial "fight" or "flight" response (Cannon, 1929) involves an immediate release of catecholamines, epinephrine (EPI), and norepinephrine (NE), which directly stimulates organs such as the heart and lungs, and is also released into the bloodstream. This is accompanied by increases in heart rate, respiratory rate, and releases of glucose and lipids into the blood to prepare the brain and the striated muscles for action. When the EPI and NE stored in nerve endings are depleted, the second system, the sympathetic-adrenal medulla (SAM) is activated, mediating sustained manufacture and release of EPI and NE. Long-term exposure to catecholamines can have toxic effects on the activated organs (Sapolsky, 1988).

More prolonged stress responses initiate activation of the hypothalamic-pituitary-adrenal (HPA) axis, which stimulates the release of glucocorticoids (including cortisol) from the adrenal cortex into the bloodstream. Glucocorticoids regulate carbohydrate metabolism and are anti-inflammatory, thus mitigating the toxic effects of catecholamines. Glucocorticoids also signal feedback mechanisms in the hypothalamus and pituitary gland, which decrease future glucocorticoid responses. However, prolonged exposure to cortisol this regulatory process also has a detrimental effect on many other systems, including the reproductive and immune systems, as well as levels of lipids in the bloodstream (Charmandari, Tsigos, & Chrousos, 2005).

Prolonged and profound stress can modify the HPA stress response (Hellhammer & Wade, 1993; Gunnar & Fisher, 2006; Sapolsky, 1996). The way in which this response is modified appears to depend on characteristics of the individual and the stressor (Miller, Chen, & Zhou, 2007). HPA activity is higher in individuals responding to stressors with high levels of subjective distress, and is dysregulated (e.g., either too high or too low) in individuals who had been exposed to extreme stressors, such as those associated with post-traumatic stress disorder (PTSD). Individuals who are able to cope by reducing levels of subjective stress or shortening the duration of chronic stressors might avoid alteration of the HPA response to stress.

The stress response also influences physical health and function through dysregulation of the immune system. Stress appears to enhance some elements of the immune system and suppress others (Robles, Glaser, & Kiecolt-Glaser, 2005), depending on its timing and duration. A meta-analytic study categorized the effects of stress on the immune system by stressor characteristic (Segerstrom & Miller, 2004). Chronic stress was associated with the most deleterious effect of global immunosuppression; other types of stress result in downregulation of some components of the immune system and upregulation of others. For example, acute time-limited stressors, such as public speaking tasks, appear to be associated with increases in immune factors that serve as the first line of defense against invaders (innate immunity. These relationships are moderated by individual characteristics, such as the ability to moderate the effects of stress through coping. The effect of stress on the immune system is important to the stress-health relationship because prolonged dysregulation of the immune system can lead to disease, one of the most common stressors people face as they enter late life.

A number of studies in adults have addressed the question of whether there are reliable associations between coping and physical and psychological health outcomes (Vitaliano, Zhang, & Scanlan, 2003). Penley, Tomaka, and Weibe (2002) reported reliable associations between coping and health outcomes for certain coping strategies. In general, problem-focused coping strategies were associated with positive health outcomes. Emotion-focused strategies such as *wishful thinking* and *distancing* were associated with more negative outcomes. The adaptiveness of any particular coping strategy appeared to depend strongly on contextual effects, such as type of stressor and health outcome (Aldwin, Yancura, & Boeninger, 2007).

Contextual Effects of Coping on Health

From a developmental consideration, the reciprocal effects of coping and health are important because both physical and mental health create a context and a resource for further coping efforts. For example, if a psychologically healthy individual experiences the death of a loved one, one might expect her or him to experience difficulties in adjusting to the situation and temporary depressive symptoms. However, if someone with a history of depression experiences the death of a loved one, a major depressive episode is much more likely. As discussed more fully below, this effect might be particularly strong in certain developmental periods, such as infancy, which may be a sensitive period for the development of certain types of coping.

Psychological Aspects of Coping

Psychological characteristics also influence the choice and effectiveness of coping strategies. Several characteristics have been examined in the research literature as potential influences on coping over the course of the life span, including personality/temperament, motivation, and developmental history. The following section discusses each of these psychological characteristics in turn.

Coping and temperament/personality. Temperament refers to inborn individual differences in physiological responses to environmental stimuli, characterized by reactivity—individual variation in arousability or thresholds of positive or negative responses—and temperamental regulation, which involves individual differences in ability to modulate reactivity via basic attentional, motor, and affective responses (Rothbart & Bates, 2006; Skinner & Zimmer-Gembeck, 2007). Unlike personality, temperament does not include behavior, thinking, emotion, and values (Rothbart & Bates, 2006). Temperament is relevant to infancy and early childhood, whereas personality becomes relevant in middle childhood and later (Caspi, Roberts, & Shiner, 2005). Temperament maps onto certain aspects of personality, with the personality traits of negative emotionality, extraversion, and agreeableness probably rooted in temperament (Rothbart & Bates, 2006). Temperament is believed to greatly influence emotional regulation in infancy and early childhood (Eisenberg et al., 1997; Rothbart, 2004), and is viewed as a core basis of the earliest patterns of coping (Rueda & Rothbart, 2009). Dual process models of coping describe coping in terms of two systems, a "cool" cognitive system and a "hot" emotional system (Metcalfe & Mischel, 1999). Skinner and Zimmer-Gembeck (2007) suggest that these two systems mature on different developmental time tables, with the hot system being linked to temperament during infancy and early childhood.

Research on personality and coping in adulthood has focused on the extent to which personality influences the choice of coping strategies. Much of the research on this issue has used the Big Five model of personality, which assumes that the structure of individual differences is represented by five basic personality dimensions: neuroticism, extraversion, openness to experience, agreeableness, and conscientiousness (McCrae & Costa, 1997). In an early study of personality and coping, McCrae and Costa (1986) reported that both self- and spouse-ratings of neuroticism were associated with the coping strategies of escape, self-blame, and wishful thinking, while ratings of extraversion were associated with rational action and positive thinking. Penley, Tomaka, and Wiebe (2002) linked Big Five personality dimensions with perceived coping ability and reported that perceived coping ability was negatively associated with neuroticism and positively associated with conscientiousness. David and Suls (1999) found that individuals scoring high on neuroticism were likely to use catharsis and relaxation coping strategies, while those scoring high on extraversion were likely to use redefinition and religion. A recent meta-analysis concluded that most of the relationship between personality and coping occurred with three traits. Neuroticism was related to emotion-focused strategies such as wishful thinking and withdrawal, while extraversion and conscientiousness were related to problem solving and cognitive restructuring (Connor-Smith & Flachsbert, 2007).

The influence of personality on coping may occur directly, although its effect on the choice of coping strategies, or indirectly through appraisals or perceptions of coping efficacy (Connor-Smith & Flachsbert, 2007). Bolger and Zuckerman (1995) suggested that people scoring high on neuroticism might tend to both choose ineffective coping strategies and implement these coping strategies less effectively (e.g., seek social support through whining, which might alienate those from whom they are seeking support). From a developmental perspective, these ineffective coping efforts might lead to further problems down the line and further ineffective coping efforts, or a "neurotic cascade" (Suls & Martin, 2005).

Despite these links between coping and personality, studies using the relatively new methodologies of experience sampling or daily diaries to collect data suggest that there is a very strong influence of situational factors on coping. For example, De Ridder and Kerssens (2003) compared the relative statistical contribution of personal characteristics (e.g., dispositional coping styles) and situational characteristics (e.g., social context) to the choice of coping responses and found that most of the variance in coping was explained by situational characteristics. Other daily process methods examine interactions among personality, coping resources, and stressor contexts to predict coping strategies (DeLongis & Holtzman, 2005). For example, Lee-Bagley, Preece, and DeLongis (2005) found several interactions between Big Five personality traits and the stressor context on use of coping strategies. Individuals scoring high on extraversion were more likely to report using confrontation and interpersonal withdrawal in response to marital conflict than when they were coping with a child's misbehavior. There were no interactions between neuroticism and stressor context, indicating that neuroticism may be more stable across a variety of contexts than other personality traits. Connor-Smith and Flachsbart's (2007) meta-analysis also concluded that relationships among personality traits and coping were influenced by stressor characteristics as well as the age and cultural composition of the sample. This consideration of both situational and dispositional factors is closely aligned with a developmental systems approach reflecting transactions among multiple influences of coping.

Coping and developmental history. Coping both depends on unique constellations of stressors and capacities at discrete developmental phases and contributes to resources for managing stressors in subsequent phases of the life span (Aldwin, 2007; Skinner & Edge, 1998; Skinner & Zimmer-Gembeck, 2009). However, in this section we will focus on the influence of coping on developmental history.

Skinner and Edge (1998) suggest many theoretical frameworks that map on the study developmental aspects of coping. They propose attachment theory as one potential framework, noting parallels between concepts in both areas. Stressors are represented as separation and novelty, personal and social resources are represented as the internal working model and secure base, and coping is represented as proximity seeking. This is particularly interesting from a developmental perspective because it specifies how developmental history influences coping processes. For example, adjustment to stressors such as job loss and the empty nest have been shown to vary by attachment style (Hobdy et al., 2007). Similarly, Stroebe, Schut, and Stroebe (2005) propose that the coping styles chosen by bereaved older adults reflect their attachment styles. For example, adults classified with a dismissing attachment style are likely to avoid necessary and complicated grief work. These same authors have argued that the benefits of emotional disclosure vary by attachment style, with securely attached individuals benefiting least because they are capable of healthy disclosure in their daily lives (Stroebe, Schut, & Stroebe, 2006).

Generalization of constructs across phases of the life span raises a number of problems for developmentalists, notably the comparability and construct validity of variables across the life span. Ryan, Deci, Grolnick, and La Guardia (2006) have argued that the concepts of autonomy, agency, self-efficacy, and mastery are essentially all the same core concepts labeled differently in various lifespan phases. Skinner and Zimmer-Gembeck (2009) suggest that different behaviors at different developmental levels might be established as conceptually analogous by considering how adaptive functions served by families of coping strategies might be fulfilled by capacities at each level. For example, the intent to avoid stressors might be operationalized as gaze aversion in infancy, running away in toddlerhood, social withdrawal in adolescence, and alcohol abuse in late adulthood. These seemingly diverse strategies may, or may not, represent a single underlying construct of avoidant coping.

Coping and motivation. Skinner and Edge (1998) argue that knowledge of how motivation and other organizational constructs function under stress is critical to understanding development across the life span because coping is essentially goal oriented. Coping strategies may serve to satisfy relatively simple goals such as stressor resolution, reduction of psychological distress, preservation of social functioning, or maintenance of self-esteem (Zeidner & Saklofske, 1996). They may also serve multiple goals or outcomes. Such goals may be proximal (e.g., decrease in negative emotions) or distal (e.g., mastery of new skills). A single coping strategy may have contradictory effects on different outcomes. For example, yelling at an annoying co-worker may satisfy the goal of decreasing her irritating behavior, but might negatively impact the simultaneous goal of maintaining a harmonious workplace. In addition, coping goals are relative to the context in which they occur. Stressor resolution is attainable when stressors are controllable, but may not be possible when stressors are not controllable, as in caregiving for a chronically ill loved one. In that case, the goals of coping might be mastery over caregiving skills or one's emotions rather than resolution of the stressor.

Carver and Scheier (1998) proposed that stress and coping processes subside once goals are achieved. However, many goals are incremental, especially the developmental goals that provide salient contexts for coping. Skinner and Zimmer-Gembeck (2009) described developmental shifts in means of coping from infancy through late adolescence. Goals of coping have different manifestations at each developmental stage. For example, coping during preschool age (from 2 to 5 years) is characterized by the use of voluntary direct actions. This type of coping corresponds to concurrent developmental goals of autonomy.

Theories of adult development also propose changes in goal structure over adulthood (Brandtstädter & Rothermund, 2003; Carstensen, Mikels, & Mather, 2006; Freund & Baltes, 2002). A sense of self is based on identity and chosen values, which change over the life span (McAdams, 2006) and are also closely intertwined with motivation (Little, 1999). Older adults are more likely than younger adults or adolescents to cope using impulse control and to react to conflict situations by transforming conflicts into lessons or by reinterpreting situations as positive (Diehl, Coyle, & LaBouvie-Vief, 1996).

Motivation may also influence the outcome of coping strategies. For example, one might solve the aforementioned problem of convincing a co-worker to reduce annoying behavior in several ways: hostile demands, polite requests, or offering something in return. Each of these solutions would be classified as taking direct action, a problem-focused coping strategy. Yet the decision of which one to use would be motivated by values of action or interpersonal harmony, which vary over the life span. Additional considerations, such as self-development or personal growth (Schwarzer & Knoll, 2003), may also influence the goals of coping strategies (which will be discussed next). As Shiraishi, Aldwin, and Widaman (under review) point out, factor structures are more stable in coping scales that include the underlying motivation in their items.

Thus, developmental goals at each phase of the life span influence the choice, use, and effectiveness of coping strategies. Coping in earlier phases of the life span serves developmentally appropriate goals such as autonomy and the establishment of identity. Coping in later phases of the life span appears to serve self-development.

Sociocultural Context of Coping

Each aspect of the coping process is also embedded in sociocultural contexts. Social and cultural norms define stressors, appropriate coping strategies, and successful outcomes. For example, in the 1950s and 1960s in the United States, women pursuing stereotypically male careers, such as medicine, law, or academia, faced many challenges. Many of these women coped with the stress of pioneering in male-dominated professions by excelling in them, sometimes at the expense of building their own families, and risked being labeled as "masculine" or "unfulfilled" by society. Today, women pursuing careers in these fields face a different set of challenges and have a greater repertoire of coping resources (e.g., female mentors, stay-at-home husbands) as well as a greater range of successful outcomes (e.g., possible jobs) available to them.

The following sections describe considerations relevant to the study of coping within multilayered and transactional sociocultural contexts (Bronfenbrenner, 1979). Social, cultural, and physical contexts influence the stress and coping process in two main ways—they can provide sources of stress and/or coping resources. In addition, roles and transitions at various phases of the life span also provide contexts for coping.

The importance of social contexts. Social contexts can be sources of stress. Aldwin (2007) cited literature in the fields of sociology, community psychology, and social epidemiology characterizing stressors as systematic contextual phenomena. There is a great deal of literature examining the influence of job stress on physical and mental health (Stansfeld & Candy, 2006). Jobs with high physical or psychological demands and low control are highly stressful, often leading to chronic illness (Chandola, Brunner, & Marmot, 2006). School environments are also characterized by high demands and low control and may be quite stressful for children and adolescents. Chronic role strains such as poverty (Berkman, 2009), caregiving for ill relatives (Pinquart & Sorensen, 2007), and social stigmas such as minority status (Gallagher-Thompson et al., 2006), socioeconomic status (Adler, Epel, Casetellazzo, & Ickovics, 2000), and obesity (Epel et al., 2000), are also sources of stress over the life span.

However, social contexts can also provide resources for coping. They allow for social and instrumental support from dyads (Berg, Meegan, & DeViney, 1998; Berg & Upchurch, 2007) as well as families (Conger & Donnellan, 2007; Zimmer-Gembeck & Locke, 2007). Neighborhoods can also provide resources for coping in various life phases, from crossing guards and librarians in childhood (Spilsbury, 2005) to service accessibility and residential stability in late adulthood (Subramanian et al., 2006). Even political environments can provide wherewithal for coping efforts in the forms of health-care resources and social service programs (Berkman, 2009; NRC, 2000).

The importance of role transitions and timing. A life-span perspective on coping must also acknowledge the importance of role transitions and the timing of stressful events. Life course theory (Elder & Shanahan, 2006) proposes that the life course is characterized by turning points (e.g., family restructuring, military service) that can instigate positive or negative adaptive spirals. These turning points are embedded in historical time, with different cohorts experiencing different economic, political, and social milieus. For example, a family's move to a neighborhood with better schools in the 1980s might have prompted a young adolescent to academic achievement, thus enabling her to attend college and have access to a greater variety of resources than if she had not attended college. However, this move might not have resulted in such favorable outcomes if it had occurred in the 1950s, when women's academic success was not normative. Life course theory also proposes that the timing of transitions is important. The family move described above might have had a different outcome if it had occurred during late rather than early adolescence. It might have disrupted established social networks and facilitated maladaptive patterns of coping, which could have resulted in her dropping out of high school.

Summary

Thus, there may be sensitive periods for the development of coping resources (Greenough, Black, & Wallace, 1987), as well as appropriate etiologic periods for coping interventions (Berkman, 2009). Evidence for these periods can clearly be seen in the neurobiology of stress development (Gunnar & Quevedo, 2007), which plays an important role in coping. Skinner & Zimmer-Gembeck's (2007, 2009) proposition of the existence of shifts in multiple systems underlying coping abilities that enable qualitatively different types of coping from infancy to late adolescence supports the notion of sensitive periods. The existence of sensitive periods also suggests that the development of coping may be hierarchical, with lower-order skills providing a foundation for higher-order skills.

GENERAL OVERVIEW OF COPING BY LIFE PHASE

Skinner and Zimmer-Gembeck (2009) have recommended that a discussion of the development of coping describe both age-graded shifts in coping and the developmental changes likely to underlie those shifts. This follows from the concept that "component developmental processes... eventually integrate and organize into a more holistic, dynamic, adaptive coping system" (Kopp, 2009, p. 36). This chapter section therefore will cover the probable biological and psychological bases for coping during each life phase and describe the typical developmental progression in these domains. For each developmental period, we then describe the kinds of coping behaviors and strategies typically observed, highlighting what is known about age differences in coping processes.

For infancy through middle childhood, adolescence through young adulthood, and middle through late adulthood, we present integrative summaries that delineate how developmental history and sociocultural context combine to create individual variability in the resources and trajectories related to stress and coping processes; and outline the normative progression of coping across those broad life epochs. This section includes empirical examples that demonstrate the four themes that we have identified as central to a life-span view of coping: engagement versus disengagement; the social nature of coping; the importance of self-development for adaptation to stress; and the role of developmental history and sociocultural context in shaping both individuals' stressors and coping resources.

Infancy

Discussion of coping during infancy and early childhood arises from research on self-regulation and emotion regulation (see, for example, Eisenberg, et al., 2009; Little & Geldhof, this volume; NRC, 2000). Investigation of how infants and very young children manage distressing or challenging situations highlights the interplay of the different domains of development, as well as the aspects of development that may limit or promote coping abilities (Kopp, 2009). The contrast between involuntary stress responses and voluntary coping strategies (Compas et al., 2001) is particularly salient in these life phases, as well. Coping strategies in infancy consist of largely automatic behaviors based on reflexes and subcortical neurological circuits involved with approach and withdrawal behaviors (for reviews, see Rueda & Rothbart, 2009; Skinner & Zimmer-Gembeck, 2009). The shift to more volitional coping efforts arguably emerges in late infancy after sufficient sensorimotor and perceptual-cognitive-motor development is in place.

Biopsychological Changes Underlying the Development of Coping during Infancy

Neurocognition. Neurocognitive development within the first year and a half of life pave the way for various types of coping throughout the life span. Emotion, cognition, and behavior are highly intertwined (Shonkoff, 2006), and emotional states of infants are largely dependent on physical needs such as hunger and thirst. The elements of what will later become coping exist as regulatory efforts that have been variously called self-regulation, attentional control, or emotional regulation (Kopp, 2009; Rueda & Rothbart, 2009).

Neuronal activity and myelination appear to follow predictable paths of development during infancy. They begin in the base of the brain (which serves basic homeostatic functions) and areas involved in basic motor coordination and balance (cerebellum), sensory and motor skills (sensorimotor cortex), and then areas involved in vision (occipital cortex), manipulation of objects (parietal cortex), and finally the frontal lobes (which serve executive functions) (Johnson, 2001; Paus et al., 2001). Cognitive and behavioral developments during this same time reflect these changes in the brain (Little & Geldhof, this volume). By late infancy (between 8 and 12 months of age), infants begin to exhibit fledgling language skills, as well as nascent executive attentional control and behavioral inhibition. Neurocognitive development during this time also underlie a growing capacity for social interaction and thus the ability to utilize social partners to cope with stressors. Even the earliest aspects of motor coordination and protoverbalization interconnect with the development of infants' social worlds, as they learn to nurse and develop the ability to produce different cries, for example (Thelen & Smith, 1998). By the end of infancy, perceptual-cognitive-motor development has progressed to the point where older infants can demonstrate joint attention (focusing on the same object as another person) and social referencing (looking at others' reactions to determine one's own actions; Goswami, 2006), which enables more active dyadic coping, as discussed below.

Temperament and personality. Self-regulation in infancy is strongly influenced by temperament, which involves individual differences in attentional processes, levels of arousal and ease of soothability, physiological rhythmicity, affective tone, activity level, aspects of sociability, and approach behavior (Rothabart & Bates, 2006; Little & Geldhof, this volume). Although one may readily observe individual differences in these characteristics among infants, intraindividual stability of these patterns remains very low, in large part due to the rapid shifts in neurophysiological development that change the parameters of the processes in question (e.g., attentional control remains very underdeveloped until late infancy, when frontal lobe development enables more control; Rothbart & Bates, 2006). Temperamental traits in infancy and toddlerhood are linked to differential biases toward activation of either neural circuits involved in inhibition and withdrawal, or those involved with approach and engagement (Kagan & Fox, 2006; Rothbart & Bates, 2006). These tendencies can translate directly into propensities to cope with stress via engagement or disengagement (Rueda & Rothbart, 2009). Further, although infant temperament is malleable and very likely to change across the first several years of life (Roberts & DelVecchio, 2000), temperamental traits such as sociability and irritability can influence important coping resources such as social support (e.g., Werner & Smith, 1992).

Sense of self and motivation. A sense of agency or selfhood begins developing at birth as infants experience environmental contingencies (Erikson, 1963; Harter, 1998; Ryan et al., 2006). While a sense of mastery appears to influence the choice of coping strategies in adulthood (Aldwin, Sutton, & Lachman, 1996), it is far less clear how a preverbal sense of agency would influence both involuntary and voluntary coping efforts. Infants could come to a place of inaction in the face of stress if their previous action in such circumstances had never yielded the desired (or necessary) outcome (see Henry, 1971). This may be thought of as an early (preverbal) experience of *expectancies* (i.e., optimism-pessimism; Carver & Scheier, 2001) and helplessness-hopelessness (Abramson, Alloy, & Metalsky, 1990). Skinner and Zimmer-Gembeck (2007) have proposed that a primary function or task of coping behaviors is to coordinate one's actions with environmental contingencies; a sense of self as efficacious versus helpless is therefore strongly implicated in this process.

The final aspect of psychological development is the conative domain, which includes goals, strivings, and motivation. Goals during infancy seem largely centered on physical needs, although emotional comfort is also a common goal, as when an infant cries to be held after being startled or left alone.

Coping Strategies Observed in Infancy

Although their preverbal, premobile, and dependent state presents challenges for active coping, infants use different kinds of cries, as well as somatic actions such as wriggling, arching, reaching and pointing, kicking, and (when older) crawling, to express their needs, influence their caregivers' behavior, and try to assert some control over their environment (Kopp, 2009; Murphy & Moriarty, 1976). As infants gain visual acuity and control over their visual processes, they can regulate incoming stimuli by engaging and disengaging their gaze (Rueda & Rothbart, 2009). For example, if social or visual stimuli become too overwhelming, infants can turn their attention away and then re-engage their gaze after coming to equilibrium (Murphy & Moriarty, 1976). A recent review concluded that this form of distraction is replaced by that of turning to other objects as means of distraction between the ages of 6 to 12 months as motor control and locomotion develop (Skinner & Zimmer-Gembeck, 2007).

In addition to practicing a balance of engagement and disengagement strategies, a second core aspect of learning to cope effectively with stress also begins during infancy. It involves using social partners to collaboratively define and solve a given problem or challenge (Berg & Upchurch, 2007; Skinner & Zimmer-Gembeck, 2009). Regulation during infancy is generally framed as co-regulation between infants and caregivers, in which caregivers respond to infants' needs (Skinner & Zimmer-Gembeck, 2009; Thompson, 1994). After about the first half year of life, infants are better at projecting their facial expressions in ways that elicit support or specific actions from those around them, and will also seek eye contact with their caregivers when desiring comfort (Skinner & Zimmer-Gembeck, 2007). Older infants' emerging use of social referencing, in particular, may be viewed as nascent instances of dyadic coping. As infants become more mobile and widen their experiential repertoire, they orient to and seek out their caregivers' reactions to a novel and potentially threatening situation or environment, to learn how to appraise and respond to the situation. If the caregiver responds with expressions of fear, for example, the infant is likely to appraise the situation as a threat and engage in behavioral avoidance (i.e., move away from the threat and toward the caregiver; Goswami, 2006). Thus, infants rely on their social network to help them identify and cope with threatening situations.

Toddlerhood

The first major shift in coping occurs between the toddler and preschool years (i.e., between 3 and 4 years of age), as children move from mostly automatic stress reactions in infancy to a greater ability to control their own behavior (Kopp, 2009; Skinner & Zimmer-Gembeck, 2009). As mentioned in the introductory section of this chapter, several major skills need to develop in order for young children to engage in problem-focused coping (NRC, 2000): attention skills, including selectively orienting to one's environment and anticipating events; means–ends behavior and representing the world symbolically; and self control (inhibition, initiation, and modulation of behavior; monitoring oneself). This complex of skills is part of executive function, and its developmental course and role in self-regulation is reviewed by Little and Geldhof in this volume. Executive function emerges rapidly across the toddler and early childhood years, creating significant change in coping strategies during these stages.

Biopsychological Changes Underlying the Development of Coping

Neurocognition. Research on biological development in toddlerhood has highlighted the importance of brain maturation, especially of the prefrontal cortex (PFC), in the ability to regulate emotion (Thompson, 1994) and behavior (Diamond, 2002) during toddlerhood. Major development of the PFC occurs by about the second year, and underlies the executive functions. The ability to inhibit an automatic, dominant response in the face of conflicting tasks or demands, as well as the capacity to inhibit disruptive emotional responses during upsetting circumstances represent critical aspects of executive function that develop across the second year of life (Rueda & Rothbart, 2009). Along with basic executive function, the development of language, a sense of self, an awareness and internalization of standards (related to the self-conscious emotions), and an awareness of the intentions and emotions of others emerge during the toddler years (Kopp, 2009; Kunzmann, this volume). These major neurocognitive advances shift regulation and coping, specifically, from the mostly external forms seen in infancy to more internal forms (Kopp, 2009; Skinner & Zimmer-Gembeck, 2009). For example, by the late toddler years, children begin to demonstrate a "conscious willingness to keep emotions in check" during conflicts with their parents (Kopp, 2009).

Temperament and personality. Temperament at this age appears to be quite malleable, and responsive to social experiences and coaching (Kagan & Fox, 2006). Certain aspects of temperament, however, do become moderately stable. For example, effortful control increases after the first year of life, and shows moderate stability and coherence during the toddler years, especially as the third year approaches (Rothbart & Bates, 2006). Once inhibitory control has emerged, reasonable stability also is observed in individual differences in approach versus inhibition, as well as in the tendency to disengage from distressing stimuli. These temperamental traits have clear conceptual links to coping (Eisenberg et al., 2009; Skinner & Zimmer-Gembeck, 2007). Temperamental traits of negative and positive affectivity and sociability during toddlerhood can begin to set in motion reinforcing cycles of support and involvement or coercive cycles of hostility and indulgence from caregivers (Caspi, Bem, & Elder, 1989), which may profoundly influence the kinds of attachment resources and dyadic coping opportunities that a child has as she or he grows older.

Sense of self and motivation. Although a rich theoretical tradition posits how a sense of agency develops, very little is actually known about the normative developmental progression of mastery or self-efficacy beliefs (Harter, 1998; Wigfield et al., 2006). With their increased mobility and ability to communicate, toddlers have far more opportunities than infants to experience their power to affect the environment and other people (Harter, 1998). Toddlers experience the emergence of their "me-self"—the awareness of self as an object of knowledge (Harter, 1998). This self-development involves the social emotions (see Kunzmann, this volume) and beginnings of "true" self-regulation, in that toddlers engage in rudimentary forms of monitoring themselves. This mostly occurs via more sophisticated social referencing, in which toddlers check with caregivers about the appropriateness or praiseworthiness of their actions (Harter, 1998). Motivation during toddlerhood more obviously includes social and emotional goals in addition to the satisfaction of physical needs, which alter the toddler's behavior in situations of conflict with their parents, for example (Kopp, 2009).

Coping Strategies Observed during Toddlerhood

Toddlers' newfound mobility enables them to exercise greater self-initiated, direct environmental control when coping with distressing situations (Skinner & Zimmer-Gembeck, 2009). Given their level of cognitive ability, toddlers still employ mostly behavioral coping strategies, even for managing emotions. For example, they are likely to use behavioral self-soothing strategies such as thumb-sucking. An additional source of self-soothing for toddlers versus infants involves the use of symbolic (or "transitional") objects, such as a favorite stuffed animal or blanket. The development of language also opens new possibilities for coping, as toddlers can learn how to express their emotions in upsetting circumstances; communication with parents about emotions generally emerges during late toddlerhood (Kopp, 2009).

Social support coping also changes during toddlerhood. Toddlers are able to more actively solicit caregivers' help in solving problems, and are able to articulate, even if in rudimentary form, what their needs and goals are. As described previously, toddlers also engage in more sophisticated and intentional social referencing, appraising their own behavior relative to external feedback. Coaching, modeling, and feedback from caregivers regarding how they are "supposed to" cope with stressors and with emotions (Kliewer, Sandler, & Wolchik, 1994) therefore take on relevance during the toddler years.

Early Childhood

Preschool-age children develop greater integration among regulatory subsystems, a better balance between their own goals and desires and those of their caregivers, and more differentiated emotional and behavioral responses compared to toddlers (Kopp, 2009; Skinner & Zimmer-Gembeck, 2009). These developmental changes likely underlie the second major transition in coping, which occurs during the age 5-to-7 shift between early childhood (or, the preschool years) and middle childhood.

Biopsychological Changes Underlying the Development of Coping during Early Childhood

Neurocognition. Synaptic density in the frontal cortex appears to reach a maximum by the end of the toddler years and then remain fairly stable until middle childhood; this density corresponds to great flexibility and ability to learn (Huttenlocher, 1999). Compared to toddlers, young children demonstrate longer periods of inhibitory control, especially when using strategic aids to delay or inhibit action. Concomitant with greater inhibitory control is more use of focused, or executive, attention, which may well help young children better appraise situations and their possible consequences (Kopp, 2009). Early childhood also ushers in improved memory, including working memory capacity, which enables young children to start developing a sense of means and ends behavior (Compas, Worsham, & Ey, 1992). In the social-cognitive domain, young children are rapidly developing a theory of mind, which generally includes perspective-taking skills, subsequent empathy, and a more sophisticated understanding of social interactions and self in relation to others, thereby altering the way in which young children approach actual or potential interpersonal stressors (Eisenberg & Fabes, 1998; Kopp, 2009).

Temperament and personality. It remains unclear whether significant, normative changes occur in the domain of temperament and personality during early childhood. Some have suggested that the early temperamental trait of orienting becomes effortful control in childhood, and that rhythmicity becomes agreeableness or adjustability (Rothbart & Bates, 2006). Overall, it seems unlikely that development in this domain directly underlies changes in coping during this life phase. However, as noted before, temperament influences interactional patterns between young children and their caregivers and peers, as well as their responses to socialization experiences (Kochanska, 1995). It therefore may indirectly influence young children's coping, based on their developmental history.

Sense of self and motivation. Although not much is known about young children's sense of mastery or efficacy, it does appear that they are not very accurate in their control beliefs, generally overestimating their level of control over outcomes (Little & Geldhof, this volume; Wigfield et al., 2006). Other aspects of self-awareness ensure improved self-regulation (and, by extension, coping): Young children are able to use others' views and reactions toward them as rudimentary "self-guides" (Higgins, 1989). Preschool-age children can begin to internalize standards and thereby regulate themselves even apart from caregiver's presence. For example, young children show their own reactions to success and failure, apart from first referencing the adults' responses (Wigfield et al., 2006). They also adopt behaviors and choose to comply with adults' requests in ways that follow from or reinforce their nascent self-identity and accepted (internalized) standards (e.g., Kochanska, 2002). These developments in the domain of self-development also reveal a greater integration between the goals of autonomy and cooperation (Kopp, 2009).

Coping Strategies Observed during Early Childhood

Young children possess an expanded repertoire of coping strategies compared to toddlers, because of their greater experience and physical and cognitive autonomy. Importantly, young children start to recognize that certain strategies work better in some contexts or with certain people than others (Davidson, Nurcombe, Kearney, & Davis, 1978). Because of their neurocognitive development, especially in working memory, they are able to generate a number of possible solutions to interpersonal problems, although such problem solving is still not very sophisticated as far as proper means–ends estimation (Compas et al., 1992). Although this life phase is characterized by increased differentiation of coping behaviors and more problem solving, under serious duress, children this age may regress to more automatic, infantile stress reactions (e.g., losing bladder control or sucking their thumb) (Murphy & Moriarty, 1976). Finally, young children differ considerably in their range of social experiences and available coping partners depending on exposure to contexts such as childcare and preschool. However, family members remain young children's primary sources for social support coping.

Middle Childhood

A major shift in children's social and cognitive worlds occurs in middle childhood as they enter formal, all-day schooling. Children's landscape of stressors, challenges, and supports changes dramatically as they face the daily demands in the school setting. Entirely new kinds of stressors, such as exams and other evaluations of achievement, emerge during this life phase. Meso-system stresses (Bronfenbrenner, 1979), such as parental disengagement from the school micro-system, also become relevant. This shift in sociocultural context opens many avenues for both positive and negative developmental processes, including children learning how to cope effectively with challenging, stressful situations.

Biopsychological Changes Underlying the Development of Coping

Neurocognition. Synaptic density, especially in the prefrontal cortex, decreases dramatically during middle childhood (Andersen, 2003; Huttenlocher, 1999). However, as discussed previously, this decrease in density actually reflects an increase in function as superfluous neuronal connections are pruned. There is an increase in white (myelinated) matter versus grey matter in the prefrontal cortex (Casey, Galvan, & Hare, 2005). The maturation of the prefrontal cortex is paralleled by changes in cognition. Between the ages of 6 and 12, children become increasingly capable of suppressing irrelevant thoughts and behavior and sustaining attention (Casey, Galvan, & Hare, 2005), even without using visible strategic aids, suggesting more internal, cognitive and attentional control (Kopp, 2009). The ability to filter out irrelevant elements also applies to emotions, thereby increasing the capacity for emotion regulation (Rueda & Rothbart, 2009).

Salient cognitive advances during middle childhood include the development of concrete operations (especially regarding means–ends relationships), increased perspective-taking skills, and greater ability to recognize and verbalize emotions (Compas et al., 1992; Eisenberg & Fabes, 1998; see also Kunzmann, this volume). These advances allow children to better differentiate between potential responses to stressors, as well as possible outcomes. Elementary-school–age children also possess a wider range of behavioral and emotional strategies.

Temperament and personality. Middle childhood is the first life phase during which researchers investigate personality traits in addition to or in place of temperamental traits (Shiner & Caspi, 2003). As children amass sufficient experience and strategies for navigating daily life tasks, their characteristic habits of thinking, feeling, and behaving (i.e., their personality traits) may influence the types of coping strategies they use. For example, children with pessimistic expectations likely use positive reinterpretation less frequently than optimistic children (Aldwin, 2007). Similarly, temperamental underpinnings such as low attentional control may influence how effective a child might be in using cognitive distraction. While personality differences may help explain variability in coping strategies among school-age children, personality traits do not appear to demonstrate much mean-level change across the middle childhood years (Roberts, Walton, & Viechtbauer, 2006). Given a lack of normative change in temperament/personality, it does not appear to underlie the significant normative shift in coping during this life phase.

Sense of self and motivation. Important changes occur in the development of self and motivation across middle childhood, which, in turn, influence coping. Although the sense of control declines, this appears to reflect a generally more accurate view of agency, ability, and cause-and-effect relationships (Wigfield et al., 2006). Children also start to use dispositional traits to describe themselves, evaluating themselves in general terms as a certain type of person (Harter, 1998). This involves using self-guides based on internalized standards and values (Higgins, 1989), as well as developing desired and feared "possible selves" (for review, see Harter, 1998).

Concomitant with their burgeoning cognitive skills and exposure to new social contexts, the range of motivations and goals also broadens during this developmental phase. In accord with Erikson's (1963) theory, children's goals pertinent to solving problems often center on themes of achievement or competence, compared to reported goals of adults (Berg et al., 1998; Sansone & Berg, 1993). This goal tendency appears driven at least in part by the contextual (i.e., school) demands during middle childhood: When asked to report goals around solving problems in specific (rather than unconstrained) domains, children this age, compared to adults, are very likely to report interpersonal goals. This latter development highlights the increase in interpersonal (rather than instrumental) goals around friendships; indeed children's friendship-related goals become more reciprocal, and longer-term as they enter middle childhood (Asher, Erdley, & Gabriel, 1994).

Children this age also may display a greater need for social approval, whether at home or in school, reflecting their growing self-awareness and ability to compare themselves to internal or external standards (Harter, 1998). Finally, Erikson (1963) proposed that formal schooling in middle childhood exposes children to the possibilities available to them in adulthood, giving them a sense of their potential "place," or role, in society, which then acts as a guide for their academic and vocational goals. As we will discuss next, children's emerging sense of identity and capability vis-à-vis academic success influences their level of engagement with academic tasks, and even their social relationships, setting up cycles that amplify either advantage or disadvantage as they enter adolescence.

Coping Strategies Observed during Middle Childhood

Given the cognitive advances, greater repertoire and settings of experiences, and wider range of goals during middle childhood, we see a greater differentiation of coping strategies used compared to early childhood (Spirito, Stark, Grace, & Stamoulis, 1991). Problem-focused coping increases, although children's action plans are usually still simple, short sequences (Welsh, Pennington, & Groisser, 1991). The increase in problem-focused coping abilities observed during this time is believed to be related to increases in problem-solving capacity, being able to tolerate distraction, and social coordination of efforts (Skinner & Zimmer-Gembeck, 2007). Children also use much more emotion-focused coping than in previous life phases (Compas et al., 1992), which in part appears linked to their greater ability to differentiate emotions. Cognitive advances also likely underlie change from employing mostly behavioral avoidance to more often using cognitive distraction coping strategies (Altschuler & Ruble, 1989). School-age children use cognitive coping strategies such as basic kinds of re-structuring or positive re-framing as well as self-reassuring statements and symbolic means of coping, including written forms of self reassurance or guidance and cognitive representations of absent caregivers (Compas et al., 2001; Wallerstein & Kelly, 1980). However, a problematic cognitively-based response that potentially emerges at this age is rumination—the perseverance of negative thoughts about situations and how individuals did (or should have) handled them (Nolen-Hoeksema, 2000). A child's likelihood of ruminating when dealing with stressful situations appears to be influenced by gender, with girls reporting more rumination (Nolen-Hoeksema, 2000). Overall, the increase in the number of coping strategies, and the ability to choose among them, is an important development of middle childhood.

Finally, it is common for children this age to seek social support outside of the family (Skinner & Zimmer-Gembeck, 2007), which certainly reflects the broader array of people in children's lives. There are also gender differences in the overall amount of reported social support coping, with girls reporting greater use (Wertlieb, Weigel, & Feldstein, 1987). Given the major role that school stress and performance plays in children's lives, parental and teacher coaching, involvement, and support around children's academic challenges represent common foci of dyadic coping during this life phase (see Pomerantz, Moorman, & Litwack, 2007; Skinner, Furrer, Marchand, & Kindermann, 2008).

Cross-Cutting Developmental Issues

As highlighted in the introduction, the normative processes described above are shaped by developmental history and socioenvironmental context (Aldwin, 2007; Kliewer et al., 1994; Skinner & Edge, 1998). The resources, demands, and constraints offered and created by interactions with the environment across time lead to individual variability in coping resources, processes, and trajectories. For example, the developing brain is exquisitely responsive to experience, and exposure to overwhelming stress, trauma, or emotional neglect during infancy and childhood can create pervasive and persistent decrements in brain development and function and physiological regulation, as can nutritional and sensorimotor deprivation or exposure to neurotoxins such as lead (Johnson, 2000; De Bellis, 2001; Gunnar & Quevedo, 2007; Pollitt et al., 1996). Because the development of coping in childhood depends heavily on neurocognitive development, neurocognitive deficits and malfunction pose challenges for effective coping.

Longitudinal studies of fetuses, infants, and toddlers who experienced serious deprivation or exposure to toxins indicate that even in the absence of outright disease, young children can demonstrate deficits in their ability to effectively regulate themselves physiologically, behaviorally, and emotionally, especially in the face of stress (Johnson, 2000; Pollitt et al., 1996). Child abuse, specifically, may create long-term vulnerability to the effects of stress, as indicated by studies revealing greater likelihood of cognitive-affective dysregulation (i.e., higher rates of depression and suicidality) in response to negative life events among adolescents and young adults who were abused when young (e.g., Caspi et al., 2003). Research on nonhuman and human populations is slowly delineating the mechanisms via which early adversity affects later capacity for regulation and coping (De Bellis, 2001; Gunnar & Fisher, 2006).

In addition to the neurotoxic effects of trauma and prolonged stress, more normatively varying experiences with caregivers induces alterations in the primary physiological stress response systems, especially the limbic-HPA system. The serotonin system is also altered by exposure to prolonged stress, and by changes in the limbic-HPA system (De Bellis, 2001; Gunnar & Quevedo, 2007). Because the serotonin and dopamine systems act in tandem to regulate the activity of the PFC (LeDoux, 2002), stress-induced alterations in the serotonin system likely influence the executive functions upon which the capacity for coping is based. Further, high levels of stress can overwhelm or essentially circumvent executive functions, such as planning (LeDoux, 2002); because children do not have as much practice and expertise in suppressing strong emotion, they are particularly likely to experience the disorganizing effects of stress. Temperamental differences in reactivity and genetic differences in monoamine regulation, in particular, are important modifiers of children's outcomes under stress (Collins et al., 2000).

Nonetheless, development early in life may be extremely plastic; many children can and do compensate for early injury. Experiences of nurturance, support, and environmental enrichment can create turning points in children's lives, diverting them from negative trajectories (Elder & Shanahan, 2006; Werner & Smith, 1992), and may reverse or ameliorate the neurophysiological and neuroendocrine dysregulation caused by earlier adversity (Gunnar & Fisher, 2006).

Parental coaching, modeling, and creation of the home environment help shape patterns of coping (Kliewer et al., 1994) via social-emotional domains of development, as well, as parental modeling and responses to the children begin to form the rules of behavior that the child then internalizes and uses for self-regulation (Higgins, 1989). As mentioned previously, secure attachment to caregivers during childhood provides various important resources for coping. A particularly salient pathway via which attachment influences subsequent coping early in life involves the development of the self (Siegel, 1999). Patterns of interaction with caregivers across the first several years of life are critical in the co-construction of the child's sense of self (Harter, 2006; Siegel, 1999), and, as we have indicated earlier, the development of the self enables young children to move from external forms of regulation to internal forms.

Finally, regarding extrafamilial social contexts, the transition into school creates new challenges and opportunities. Early differences in social and personal capital dependent on school performance and peer relations may carry into middle and high school, at which point the ramifications of social isolation or deviance versus social competence and support, as well as of academic failure or dropout versus success and completion, can be lifelong (Caspi et al., 1989).

From a life-span perspective, the emerging literature strongly suggests that adverse experiences early in life can exert far-reaching effects on physiological, behavioral, and cognitive-affective responses to stress into adulthood for some individuals (Caspi et al., 2003; see also Felitti et al., 1998), while others show patterns of resilience (Werner & Smith, 1992). Life course perspectives emphasizing the cumulative and reinforcing nature of advantage and disadvantage over years (Elder & Shanahan, 2006; Moen, 2001) delineate how events occurring during infancy and childhood may influence coping-related processes across the life span, although the notion of turning points during which individuals may change their developmental trajectories is also relevant. From both life-span and life-course perspectives, physical and emotional nurturance during infancy and childhood plays a foundational role in individuals' ability to effectively cope with stress. However, both perspectives emphasize the plasticity of development, and myriad shifts in biological and psychological development, as well as in the sociocultural context, provide ample opportunities for changes in stress and coping processes.

Summary of Childhood

When considering how developmental factors and processes play into stress and coping processes, the social nature of coping becomes immediately apparent. In infancy and toddlerhood, children rely primarily on behavioral strategies for gaining caregivers' attention in order to meet their basic physical needs. The concept of *dyadic coping* appears very relevant in consideration of the immense dependence infants and toddlers have on those around them for appraising and responding to challenges. In early and middle childhood, children gain greater autonomy and the ability to verbalize their needs (Berg et al., 1998).

From infancy onward, the dialectic between engagement and disengagement remains a central issue in coping processes. Infants use mostly behavioral coping strategies (Murphy & Moriarty, 1976). Children use social interactions, such as trying to enter a circle of peers (e.g., Schantz, 1987). While early patterns of engagement–disengagement appear strongly influenced by neurocognitive development and temperament (see Rothbart & Bates, 2006; Rueda & Rothbart, 2009), children's social environment take on increasing importance from toddlerhood through middle childhood.

Rapid neurocognitive development across these years can also alter the capacity for coping. Social-cognitive advances allows toddlers and young children to begin to more effectively solicit help in navigating stress, internalize rules around behavior and emotion and begin to monitor modulating their behavior accordingly (Compas et al., 2001). Elementary-school–age children engage in more varied, emotion-focused coping as well as more problem-focused coping, albeit with simple, short action sequences. Their sense of self transforms coping behavior from simple, reflexive approach and avoidance to more differentiated, deliberate action.

Developmental changes in the needs and abilities of the individual at every level (biological, psychological, and sociocultural) therefore help shape the parameters of these core elements of coping. Finally, developmental experiences within the family, school, and other settings have tremendous influence on both what kinds of stressors children likely face in a given developmental phase, and what kinds of physiological, psychological, and sociocultural resources they will have to cope effectively with the stress they encounter.

Adolescence

The third major shift in coping occurs at the onset of adolescence, between ages 10 and 12, with additional transitions during middle adolescence and between late adolescence and emerging adulthood (Skinner & Zimmer-Gembeck, 2007). Dramatic changes occur as adolescents begin to mature sexually and start taking on more adult roles. Some characterize this developmental period as a time of risk, in part because of potential mismatch between developmental domains, such as discrepancies between adolescents' status goals and what roles society allows them, or between their physical and emotional maturity (Moffitt, 1993; Spears, 2000). Nonetheless, advances in cognition, social skills, and personality and self-development mark this developmental phase as one of burgeoning opportunities and growth.

Biopsychological Changes Underlying the Development of Coping

Neurocognition. Neurocognitive development in adolescence is characterized by increasing maturation of many areas of the prefrontal cortex (Spears, 2000). This occurs via elimination of some synaptic pathways and enhanced connectivity of others and is supported by evidence from neuroimaging studies (Andersen, 2003; Paus et al., 2001). Changes in the brain are paralleled by increased capacity for self-evaluation and executive functions such as metacognition, long-term planning, and planning longer and more complex action sequences (seriation) (Spears, 2000). Compared to children, adolescents demonstrate a greater ability to use abstract reasoning (i.e., formal operations), anticipate the future, and reason through probable consequences of actions (Greene & Larson, 1991). Adolescents also possess a less egocentric frame, with greater perspective-taking skills than children.

Although adolescents have nearly mature planning and decision-making capacities, they often endanger their own safety and health by engaging in risky behaviors such as unprotected sex or smoking cigarettes. Steinberg (2005) suggests that this might be explained by considering both "hot" and "cold" cognition. Hot cognitions occur in the presence of strong affect and high arousal, while cold cognitions occur in conditions of neutral affect and low arousal. During early adolescence, puberty amplifies sensation seeking and arousability, thus creating heightened vulnerability to risk taking and problems in regulating affect in middle adolescence. However, by late adolescence, increased maturation in the frontal lobes and integration of cortical and limbic areas of the brain allow for reintegration of cognitive and affective processes.

Temperament and personality. Although substantial within-person change in personality traits occurs (Roberts & DelVecchio, 2000), evidence suggests mean-level change in only a few traits across these years (Roberts et al., 2006). Roberts and colleagues (2006) separated mean-level change in extraversion into the two primary facets of social vitality (sociability, gregariousness) and social dominance (social independence, dominance, and self-confidence), based on prior evidence that they may follow different developmental trajectories. Despite the expanded social opportunities of adolescence, their meta-analysis found no mean-level change in social vitality. Social dominance, however, did show increases during adolescence, perhaps reflecting the greater levels of experience in the social domain (Roberts, et al., 2006). Emotional stability also increases, compared to middle childhood—despite the proverbial emotional "ups and downs" of puberty. Perhaps this greater likelihood for reporting less negativity and reactivity in the face of stress is due in part to adolescents' greater ability to engage effectively in both problem- and emotion-focused coping, as described below.

Sense of self and motivation. Based on the scant literature examining age differences in a sense of environmental mastery, mean levels appear to remain fairly stable across adolescence (Shanahan & Bauer, 2004). Although there may be some increase in mastery in early adolescence dependent on the experience of positive interpersonal problem solving in the family (Conger et al., 2009). Attributions of control over school performance appear most likely to influence children's helpless versus persistent behavior starting around the onset of adolescence (Skinner, Wellborn, & Connell, 1990).

Identity development is particularly important during adolescence. Adolescents can hold abstract representations of self, which are compartmentalized in early adolescence (Harter, 1998). Social pressures arising from different social roles can lead to different "selves" in different settings, including different self-guides in different contexts (Higgins, 1989). As they mature, adolescents construct their own standards and identities integrating these disparate self-guides. These integrated self-guides are removed from their social origins, and help adolescents regulate themselves toward "ideal" and "ought" selves. Adolescence is therefore the first life phase during which deliberate self-development emerges as a potential motivation.

Coping Strategies Observed during Adolescence

A number of new coping strategies emerge during adolescence. Some changes reflect developmental advances initiated during middle childhood. For example, just as elementary-school–age children demonstrate greater ability to engage in problem-focused coping compared to younger children because of their neurocognitive development, adolescents appear to use more cognitive problem-solving strategies compared to children. However, recent reviews have noted the difficulty of assessing change in problem-focused coping given the variable manner of categorizing such strategies across studies, as well as the paucity of such comparison studies (Aldwin, 2007; Skinner & Zimmer-Gembeck, 2007). Given adolescents' growth in their ability to anticipate consequences, they also may begin engaging in anticipatory or preventive coping. However, envisioning possible problems may also lead to anxiety, and research suggests that rumination also increases during adolescence (Skinner & Zimmer-Gembeck, 2007).

Another addition to adolescents' coping repertoire is using humor as a means of dealing with stress (Führ, 2002). Boys may employ this strategy more often than girls (Plancherel & Bolognini, 1995). Adolescents use self-monitoring and positive self-talk and re-framing more often than do children (Skinner & Zimmer-Gembeck, 2007). Adolescent girls, however, apparently use more self-soothing strategies than do boys (Horton, 2002). Adolescent boys demonstrate a tendency toward using physical means of regulating distress, with younger boys often using sports, exercise, and other physical activity, and older adolescent boys turning more often to sexual activity as a distraction and release (Horton, 2002).

Other changes in coping strategies during the adolescent years are closely tied to the shifts that occur in social context. For example, the use of substances (i.e., drugs and alcohol) to cope with stress markedly increases during this life phase (Wills et al., 2001). Greater mobility and independence may allow more access to substances and opportunities for their use. Compared to school children, adolescents experience greater exposure to peer groups who may be using and distributing such substances in school, work, or other community settings (Mortimer, Harley, &

Staff, 2002). Aldwin (2007) notes that using substances to cope with stress may be an extension of earlier strategies for emotion regulation. If a child has not learned internal strategies for self-soothing, they may easily turn to substances as a means of self-soothing once exposed to them.

Finally, adolescents' choices for whom to tap for social support shift toward friends and siblings (Murphy & Moriarty, 1976), although parents continue to play an important role (Perosa & Perosa, 1993; Wolfradt, Hempel, & Miles, 2003). On average, adolescents are better than children at knowing from whom to solicit support for problems in a given domain (Skinner & Zimmer-Gembeck, 2007). Further, adolescents begin to form romantic relationships, which provide both new kinds of stressors and a new type of coping partner. It can take until mid to late adolescence before adolescents engage in effective, active (problem-focused) dyadic coping with romantic partners (Nieder & Seiffge-Krenke, 2001; Seiffge-Krenke, 2006).

Many studies of social influence have focused on the adolescent problem behavior, such as substance use and delinquency, support, modeling, and the values and goals of peers in shaping those behaviors (Costa, Jessor, & Turbin, 1999; Meeus, Branje, & Overbeek, 2004; Slomkowski et al., 2001); these processes can apply specifically to patterns of coping, as well. Being surrounded by siblings, friends, and peers who model ineffective or destructive responses to stressful situations can negatively influence an adolescent's ability to effectively navigate life stressors. For example, having friends and siblings who respond to negative life events or circumstances by planning or attempting suicide appears to increase an adolescents' own risk of suicidal thoughts and behavior (Lewinsohn, Rohde, & Seeley, 1994; Rueter & Kwon, 2005). Just as the coaching and modeling of parents and teachers either equips or hampers children's ability to effectively cope with challenges, so do adolescents' chosen sources of coaching and modeling in the form of peers, friends, and siblings.

Some negative types of social support coping also gain importance during this life phase. Adolescents have more opportunity to withdraw and socially isolate themselves than do younger children. Social withdrawal during times of stress may prevent an individual from receiving support and guidance, adversely affects relationships (i.e., creates conflict and dissatisfaction), or lead to social isolation. It is thus likely to create further stress, including mental and physical problems (Cacioppo et al., 2002; Thoits, 1984). Adolescents also are more likely than children to use aggression in response to stress, and to blame others for their problems (Skinner & Zimmer-Gembeck, 2007), both of which can alienate others and reduce social resources (Caspi et al., 1989). Adolescents' growth in kinds and sophistication of coping strategies therefore opens widely divergent paths of development as they enter the adult world.

Young Adulthood

The transition period from adolescence to adulthood is known as *emerging adulthood* (Arnett, 2000), although some extend *late adolescence* into the early 20s (Skinner & Zimmer-Gembeck, 2007). We include the years from the end of high school through the age of 30 in young adulthood. Although many transitions of young adulthood involve gains, such as earning degrees and starting families, young adults report more stressful events and hassles than older adults (Aldwin & Levenson, 2001). Changes in roles and societal expectations during this developmental phase create many new demands with which the young adult must learn to cope.

Biopsychological Changes Underlying the Development of Coping

Neurocognition. The prefrontal cortex continues to develop into young adulthood (Diamond, 2002). Although executive functions typically reach near-adult levels in mid-adolescence, they continue to marginally improve in early adulthood up until age 30 (Luna et al., 2004; see also Little & Geldhof, this volume). In some ways, young adults are at the peak of their cognitive powers—at least in terms of speed of cognitive processing. Salthouse and Davis (2006) examined age-related differentiation in a large sample of 3,400 individuals and found that fluid intelligence, which refers to speed of processing in identifying patterns, appears to peak in the 20s. Some executive functions, such as working memory and the ability to switch between tasks, continue to develop in young adulthood (Huizinga, Dolan, & van der Molen, 2006). This improvement in working memory and attentional control may underlie the emotional maturity that emerges in young adulthood (Roberts, Caspi, & Moffit, 2001), which in turn might underlie the improved ability to cope with the challenges of shifting from adolescence to young adulthood.

Temperament and personality. The social dominance facet of extraversion continues to increase from adolescence through emerging and young adulthood, until about age 40 (Roberts, Walton, & Viechtbauer, 2006), perhaps signaling less anxiety about one's "place" in one's social world, and a greater propensity to take direct action, including confrontation, when interpersonal problems arise (Seiffge-Krenke, 2006). Small mean-level increases in emotional stability also occur from the emerging adult (college) years through the 30s. Conscientiousness (constraint, order, industriousness) increases between ages 20 to 40 (Roberts et al., 2006), likely because of the experiences and demands of occupations and long-term romantic relationships (Roberts, Caspi, & Moffitt, 2002; Robins, Caspi, & Moffitt, 2003). Finally, openness to experience shows mean-level increases in the college years (Roberts, et al., 2006).

Sense of self and motivation. Environmental mastery demonstrates mean-level increases in young adulthood compared to adolescence (Parker & Aldwin, 1997). Emerging adulthood, in particular, is characterized by striving to secure an adult identity and typical "adult" achievements (Arnett, 2000). Young adults report high levels of interpersonal strivings (Sansone & Berg, 1993), and the motivation to expand their social networks and increase their knowledge base (Carstensen et al., 2006). Notably, young adults display an increased ability to self-generate goals, and engage in more goal-directed behavior (Arnett, 2000).

Coping Strategies Observed during Young Adulthood

Generally, development of coping during young adulthood appears to be a refinement of existing strategies. Compared to adults in mid and late life, young adults may, on average, still use immature defense mechanisms, such as passive aggression, fantasy, and hypochondriasis when faced with stressful circumstances (Vaillant, 1977). However, commensurate with final maturation of the PFC and attendant cognitive development, relative to adolescents, young adults demonstrate greater sophistication in problem-focused coping, especially anticipatory coping and planning, and self-reflection as a means of improving coping efficacy (Skinner & Zimmer-Gembeck, 2007). Increases in *openness to experience* may also link to more use of positive re-framing (see Connor-Smith & Flachsbart, 2007). Young adults are the most likely to use assimilative (problem-focused) and primary control (exerting control over the external environment) coping strategies (Skinner & Zimmer-Gembeck, 2007).They have the most options and flexibility for problem-focused coping, before taking on roles such as parenthood and facing chronic illnesses of late life. Given that they also have more energy to expend than adults in late life, their tendency to employ more confrontational coping strategies likewise fits their life phase. Coping with interpersonal stress appears to become more positive and mature, with possible mean-level decreases in negative coping strategies such as lying or expressing hostility (Shiraishi et al., under review).

Cross-Cutting Developmental Issues

As in earlier phases, developmental history and sociocultural context play a constitutive role in coping processes during adolescence and young adulthood. In the neurocognitive domain, brain maturation during adolescence is complicated by concurrent changes in other physiological systems, notably pubertal changes in the neuroendocrine system. Because of both independent and common biological processes involved with the maturation of various systems in the body and the reorganization of regulatory systems, adolescence is a particularly sensitive developmental transition for patterns of adjustment. For example, stress can affect the onset of puberty, which, in turn, carries implications for adjustment and behavioral health (Brooks-Gunn & Reiter, 1990; Ge, Conger, & Elder, 1996). The social ramifications of pubertal timing also depend on socioenvironmental factors such as socializing patterns of younger girls with older boys (Caspi, Lynam, Moffitt, & Silva, 1993). Off-time entrance into parenthood, or problems with serious delinquency or drug use during adolescence or young adulthood create negative turning points that can involve long-term trajectories of disadvantage.

Neurocognitive capacity and trajectories in adulthood depend on educational opportunities, daily intellectual habits, and health behaviors (Schaie, 1996). Young adult developmental settings of education, work, military service, and long-term romantic relationships may offer very different opportunities and stressors in the neurocognitive domain. They also influence personality development (Roberts et al., 2002; Robins et al., 2003), which, as discussed, appears to influence coping resources and strategies.

Aspects of self-development both guide and are influenced by interpersonal, academic, and occupational experiences. A sense of mastery or self-efficacy, for example, is associated with greater use of social support, but the experience of support also increases a sense of agency (Benight & Bandura, 2004). Similarly, self-efficacy increases the likelihood of employing problem-focused versus avoidant coping (Benight & Bandura, 2004), and the experience of effective problem solving can increase a sense of mastery (Conger et al., 2009). Judgments about one's academic ability determine one's engagement in school, which then elicits differential investment and support from teachers, reinforcing and amplifying the cycle (Skinner et al., 1990). The extent of self-reflection that an adolescent or young adult employs when coping with challenges may therefore influence whether her or his developmental course proceeds in relatively automatic fashion, or in a more self-directed (autonomous) and deliberate fashion (cf. Aldwin, 2007; Ryan et al., 2006).

Finally, parents still have a major, direct influence on how adolescents cope. Families with effective, positive problem-solving skills have teens who are less likely to use substances to cope with stress (McCubbin, Needle, & Wilson, 1985; Perosa & Perosa, 1993). Parental warmth supports adolescents' use of more active, problem-focused, and "integrated" coping strategies (Wolfradt et al., 2003). These adolescent coping resources and patterns influence young adult romantic relationship quality and dyadic coping (Seiffge-Krenke, 2006), highlighting the importance of fostering positive parent–adolescent relationships.

Summary of Adolescence through Young Adulthood

In most cases, coping processes in late adolescence have progressed from "diffuse to differentiated, from uncoordinated to integrated, from egocentric to cooperative, and from reactivity to proactive autonomous regulation" (Skinner & Zimmer-Gembeck, 2007, p. 136). Maturation of the PFC and environmental stimulation allows for the application of progressively more nuanced, complex coping strategies, including anticipatory or proactive coping. Normative developments in the domain of temperament and personality during young adulthood, especially conscientiousness, may also influence the use of coping strategies such as planning.

Increases in emotional stability (or, decreases in negative emotionality) across these years may underlie part of the shift away from negative interpersonal coping strategies. Important changes during adolescence that carry over into young adulthood involve choices of dyadic coping partners, with young people increasingly choosing friends and romantic partners over parents. Friends and partners likely influence coping both through attachment processes and through the values and modeling they provide (Berkman, Glass, Brissette, & Seeman, 2000).

Several newer forms of disengagement, such as social withdrawal, substance abuse, and suicidal behavior, become salient during adolescence and young adulthood, all of which carry potentially long-term negative consequences (Catanzaro, 2000). The serious nature of these means of disengagement in the face of stress highlights the importance of supporting healthy cognitive and psychosocial development and concomitant effective means of coping during childhood.

The development of integrated self-guides and abstract representations of identity open the possibility for mature adolescents and young adults to begin to cope with life stress in ways that are consistent with their values and goals. Identity also becomes linked to choices for social support coping, both in terms of who is chosen, and whether collaboration is sought. On the whole, young adults' greater ability to use self-reflection to improve the effectiveness of their coping may lead to more autonomous and even growth-oriented coping (cf. Aldwin, 2007).

Middle Adulthood

Midlife spans decades that involve potentially dramatic changes in social roles, such as moving from parenting young children to having the children leave home. Most adults enter this life phase with two living parents, but the vast majority experience the loss of both parents by the end of it (Winsborough, Bumpass, & Aquilino, 1991). Many women also experience the death of their husbands; up to half of all widows are in their 60s or younger (Smith & Tillipman, 2000). Middle adulthood also spans major transitions in the professional domain, moving from the peak of professional power, expertise, and recognition to retirement. Health and physical functioning also undergo transitions; women experience menopause, and health concerns become increasingly important to both sexes (Hooker & Kaus, 1994). Middle adulthood is a time of great change across life domains, all of which create specific demands on adults' coping efforts.

Biopsychological Changes Underlying the Development of Coping during Middle Adulthood

Neurocognition. With age comes increasing susceptibility to neuronal damage, including loss of neurons, dendrites, and myelinization. However, repair mechanisms maintain neural health (Alan, 2007). Further, there is strong evidence that some cognitive functions continue to develop in middle adulthood. For example, verbal memory tends to peak in the 40s and 50s (Salthouse & Davis, 2006), as does verbal IQ (Kaufman, 2001). Verbal meaning, inductive reasoning and spatial orientation also peak in midlife (Schaie, 1996).

Schaie (2000) has argued that adults in midlife are at the height of their cognitive powers. Middle-aged adults hold very responsible positions in careers and families. This responsibility requires a fair amount of cognitive complexity, as they must understand and monitor the structural dynamics of organizations, and integrate past, present, and future information. Often they must also balance the demands of both aging parents and adolescent children, which can require high levels of organization and emotional empathy. In other words, coping in mid-life requires a high level of cognitive-affective complexity and integration as individuals juggle multiple family and career demands (Labouvie-Vief & Diehl, 2000; Kunzmann, this volume).

Temperament and personality. As adults approach late life (age 65+), they demonstrate mean-level declines in social vitality and openness (Roberts et al., 2006). Mean levels of emotional stability may increase between ages 50 and 60, but the current literature on this may be affected by publication bias (Roberts et al.). Conscientiousness increases both between ages 40 and 50 and ages 60 to 70. The only decade during which demonstrable, reliable changes in agreeableness occur falls in midlife: On average, agreeableness increases between age 50 and 60 (Roberts et al.). Research suggests that emotional stability and agreeableness play an important role in adults' social resources, positively influencing marital quality and satisfaction for midlife couples, for example (e.g., Donnellan, Conger, & Bryant, 2004).

Sense of self and motivation. Middle-aged adults appear to have a greater sense of mastery than do young adults, and report greater autonomy compared to both younger and older adults (Ryff, 1991). Adults in midlife also have accumulated enough life experience to form a sense of "life-course mastery," which represents their "understanding of themselves as having directed and managed the trajectories that connect their past to their present" (Pearlin, Nguyen, Schieman, & Milkie, 2007, p. 166) and influences their framing of current problems.

Major shifts in motivation and goals begin during the middle adult years. As adults realize that the end of life is approaching, they focus increasingly on maximizing positive affect, minimizing negative affect and its disruptive effects, and maintaining meaningful social connections (Carstensen et al., 2006; Coats & Blanchard-Fields, 2008). Consistent with this, generativity appears to increase from young to middle adulthood (Erikson, 1963; McAdams, this volume). Compared to young adults, midlife adults report problem solving that contains a balance of competence and interpersonal goals (Berg et al., 1998).

Coping Strategies Observed during Middle Adulthood

Given their cognitive-affective complexity and integration, sense of mastery, growing focus on emotional equanimity, and life experience, middle-aged adults should arguably be at the height of their coping abilities. However, little research actually compares coping strategies between the different phases of adulthood, *per se*, as most research investigating age differences in coping uses age as a continuous predictor. What emerges from the literature, however, is that, on average, coping during middle adulthood becomes more effective than in young adulthood, especially with interpersonal stressors (Coats & Blanchard-Fields, 2008) and negative emotional states (Chapman & Hayslip, 2006). Middle-aged adults appear to respond to stress and trauma with more mature defense mechanisms (Vaillant, 1977) and less rumination, emotional numbing, escape, and wishful thinking (Wadsworth et al., 2004) than younger adults. They also use more optimistic mood regulation (e.g., imagining a positive outcome) (Chapman & Hayslip, 2006); positive reappraisal or re-framing (Wadsworth et al., 2004); employ more proactive coping strategies; and report fewer hassles (Chiriboga, 1997). Compared to adults in late life, they appear to engage in more problem-focused coping (Aldwin, Sutton, Chiara, & Spiro, 1996). On the whole, middle adulthood is a period of cognitive-affective maturity that translates into effective stress management in the face of multiple and potentially conflicting roles and responsibilities.

Late Adulthood

Developments in nutrition and medicine in the past century have altered late life in unprecedented ways. Compared to previous generations, many more individuals survive into late life. Given medical advances, people can live far longer with chronic diseases. Stressors such as illness and bereavement that once were defining features of midlife are now typical challenges in late life. Although late life is often described as a time of loss, it also holds the potential for growth. Stress and coping processes appear to shift toward increased insight and wisdom.

Biopsychological Changes Underlying the Development of Coping during Late Adulthood

Neurocognition. Studies in late life reveal a great deal of individual differences in cognitive functioning (Schaie, 1996). While some neuronal degradation and cell death occur, most older adults have enough cognitive reserve to maintain good functioning in everyday life. However, impaired aging can involve massive decreases in the number of neuronal cells and impaired ability to heal and maintain the ones that remain. This can be seen most obviously with Alzheimer's disease (AD) and other forms of dementia, which can severely impair older adults' ability to cope with stress.

In AD, neurofibrillary plaques and tangles invade the hippocampus, impairing short-term and working memory, and they also invade the prefrontal cortex, impairing other executive function (Sherod et al., 2009). Older adults suffering from dementia have impaired ability to concentrate and focus, organize and sequence information, and regulate emotions. Judgment is often impaired. All of these decreases in executive function severely degrade an older individual's ability to cope with stress, leading to poor problem- and emotion-focused coping.

In addition to neurological diseases, cardiovascular and metabolic diseases such as diabetes can also strongly influence cognitive functioning and thus the ability to cope. High levels of APO4 cholesterol impair both cardiovascular and neurological functioning (Luciano et al., 2009). Diabetes promotes hypertension, increasing the risk for stroke. This relationship between cognition and health may be widespread across a number of illnesses. Poor self-reported health is associated with a rapid rate of cognitive decline (Spiro & Brady, 2008). Cognitive function in early life is a fairly strong predictor of cognitive functioning in later life, but this relationship is moderated by the presence of disease (Schaie, 2000). Good physical health is important for maintaining neurological health, which in turn is important for the ability to cope with stress.

Temperament and personality. Although much individual variation exists in personality development across the years of late life (Aldwin & Levenson, 1994), the definitive meta-analysis to date assessing mean-level change (Roberts et al., 2006) found changes in a few traits only in the first part of the young-old stage, during the transition from mid to late life (between ages 60 and 70). There may be some decline in social vitality and openness, and some increase in conscientiousness as people enter late life. However, the minimal findings regarding personality change may be due to the fact that relatively few studies of personality change in late life exist.

Sense of self and motivation. Older adults (especially men) appear to report higher mastery than younger adults (Ryff, 1991), but not higher levels of autonomy. Some evidence suggests that older adults also feel less responsible for both the occurrence and management of problems, but maintain their sense of coping efficacy (Aldwin, 1991). In light of the normative increases in limitations of late life, such assessments likely represent an accurate reflection of what one can or cannot control. The motivational shift toward maintaining emotional equanimity and meaningful social relationships continues and intensifies in late life as individuals see their time left to live becoming shorter (Carstensen, et al., 2006). Specific goals for solving problems tend to be more diverse in late adulthood compared to previous phases (Berg et al., 1998).

Coping Strategies Observed during Late Adulthood

Adults in late life demonstrate a fundamental shift in processing potential stressors. Compared to younger adults, they are less likely to report problems, tend to appraise the problems they do report as less stressful and make fewer primary appraisals of their problems. They also process positive stimuli more rapidly than negative input, remember the positive more than the negative; and report less intense episodes of anger in response to stressors (Aldwin, Sutton, Chiara, & Spiro, 1996; Boeninger, Shiraishi, & Aldwin, 2009; Coats & Blanchard-Fields, 2008; Carstensen et al., 2006; Wentura, Rothermund, & Brandtstädter, 1995).

Findings regarding age differences in problem-focused coping strategies are mixed, with some studies finding decreases, but most finding no differences (Aldwin, 2007). However, this may be due to older adults' differential use of strategies in various problem domains. Compared to young adults, older adults used more problem-focused coping for financial problems, but more avoidant coping for interpersonal problems (Coats & Blanchard-Fields, 2008). This is consistent with other findings that older adults use less interpersonal confrontation (Aldwin, Sutton, Chiara, & Spiro, 1996), but not with those finding that older adults use less escapism and avoidance (McCrae, 1989). The picture that emerges suggests more nuances in these processes, which may speak to older adults' better sense of "what works" and "what is worth it" for problems in given domains.

Coping with health problems in late life perhaps has received the most research attention. Older adults frequently use downward social comparison as a coping strategy (Johnson & Barer, 1993). Adults in late life appear to increasingly use proactive coping and routinization to manage chronic health problems by preventing acute episodes (Aldwin & Brustrom, 1997). Dyadic coping around health problems includes the influential role of dyadic processes of appraisal and coping options (Berg & Upchurch, 2007). Dyadic coping strategies, with long-term spouses as one of the most common coping partners, become very important in late life as individual resources begin to decline somewhat. The presence of lower marital conflict and higher marital quality (Levenson, Carstensen, & Gottman, 1993) in long-term couples provides a positive context for increased collaboration in coping for these late-life adults.

Cross-Cutting Developmental Issues

Middle and late adulthood can be times of quite rapid change, both in terms of role transitions and, for some, psychological and physical health. Role transitions include the empty-nest transition, retirement, and grandparenthood. Losses in social networks through bereavement start increasing in midlife, including widowhood (Aldwin, 1990; Smith & Tillipman, 2000). Surprisingly, widowhood may be more closely associated with mortality in midlife than in late life (Johnson, Backlund, Sorlie, & Loveless, 2000), in part because it may be perceived as an off-time stressor. Non-normative events such as divorce may have particularly devastating impacts in middle and late life (Chiriboga, 1989). Many, if not most, older adults also assume the role of caregiver for their parents, spouse, and siblings (Vitaliano et al., 2003).

There are also normative changes in physical health status in midlife, such as menopause. Further, midlife is a time when chronic illnesses such as hypertension, diabetes, and cancers start manifesting. For example, most breast cancer cases occur between the ages of 50 and 65 (Bouchardy et al., 2006). The incidence of chronic and life-threatening illnesses increases dramatically in late life, and disability rates increase after age 80. Thus, it is remarkable that older adults typically report fewer stressors in late life (Boeninger et al., 2009), and may be a testament to their coping ability. However, dementias create particular difficulties for individuals trying to cope with stress.

Developmental trajectories start diverging more dramatically in midlife, reflecting lifelong processes of cumulative advantage and disadvantage (Moen, 2001). For example, children coming from supportive, financially stable backgrounds are more likely to have positive developmental trajectories, achieving educational goals, job and marital stability, and close relationships with family and friends, while those with more difficult childhoods may have more trouble achieving these developmental milestones in adulthood (Conger & Donnellan, 2007). However, childhood stress does not necessarily set off irrevocable trajectories of cumulative disadvantage; effects of childhood stress on outcomes in late life generally are mediated via adult circumstances, such as quality of relationships in the family of procreation (e.g., Labouvie-Vief & Diehl, 2000), adult socioeconomic status (Cupertino, 2001), and personal narratives such as life-course mastery (Pearlin et al., 2007).

The opening of new opportunities during adulthood in life domains such as work and close relationships can create turning points in individuals' trajectories (Elder & Shanahan, 2006). Turning points also can consist of stressors that force individuals to confront the realities of their life, and provide opportunities for stress-related growth, including the development of new coping resources, which can allow individuals to turn their developmental trajectories into more positive paths (Aldwin, Levenson, & Kelly, 2007). These turning points are sometimes embedded in sociohistorical events, such as the Great Depression or World War II, which alter developmental trajectories, for good or for ill, in large numbers of individuals in particular cohorts (Elder & Shanahan, 2006).

Figure 9.2 illustrates different developmental trajectories subsequent to childhood stress. Stressors such as parental loss or physical and emotional abuse in childhood can set up negative developmental trajectories (Felitti et al., 1998; Werner & Smith, 1992), accumulating risk factors leading to a greater likelihood of future stress (Rutter, 2002). Coping through substance abuse, including smoking, alcohol, and drugs, can increase the risk for morbidity and mortality in midlife, for example. In addition, difficult childhoods can lead adolescents to cut short their education, resulting in poorer outlooks for stable employment, often leading to financial struggles that can be exacerbated by the premature development of chronic illnesses (Elder & Shanahan, 2006). This pattern is also associated with less marital stability, often leading to estranged relationships with children. However, resilience factors such as having high intelligence, a "sunny" disposition, support from adults, and better coping strategies can set up positive trajectories (Werner & Smith, 1992) leading to better educational outcomes, marital histories, relationship with children, and financial stability, for example. These factors contribute to better health in middle and late life, and perhaps longevity, as well (Liang et al., 1999).

Finally, Schaie (1996) pointed out that aging has been hugely influenced by the sociohistorical context. Changes in sanitation, nutrition, education, and medical care have resulted in massive increases in longevity, as well as lower

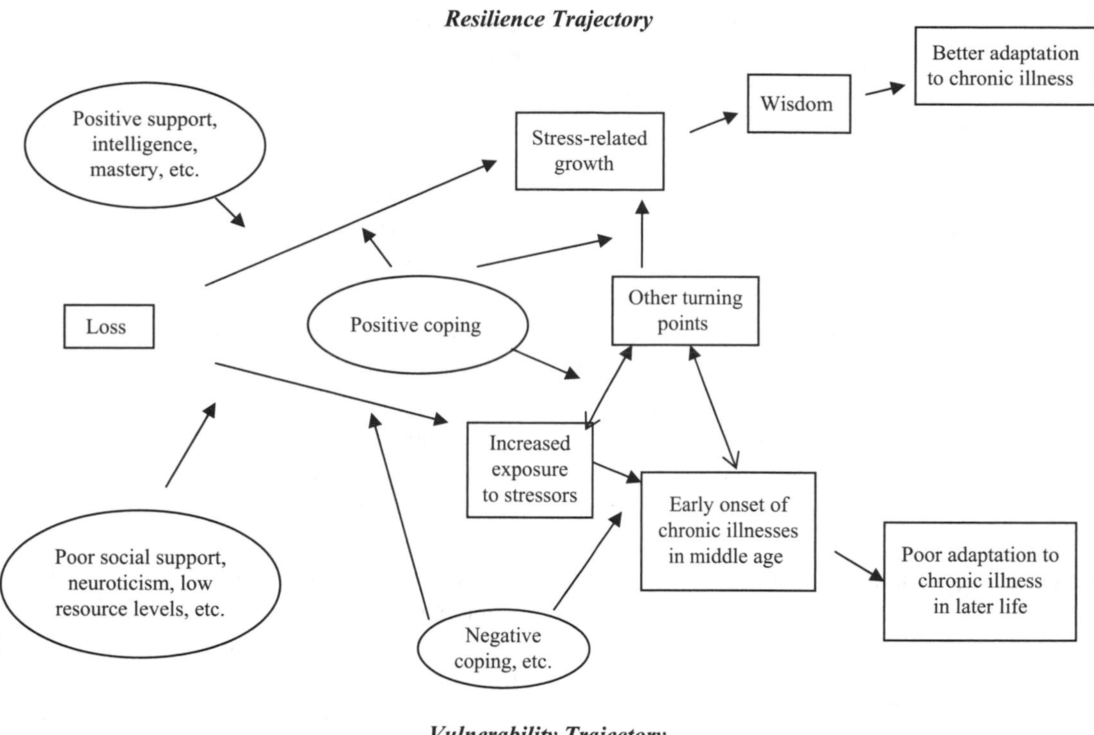

Figure 9.2 Resilience and vulnerability developmental trajectories.

From Aldwin, C. M., Levenson, M. R., & Kelly, L. L. (2009). Lifespan developmental perspectives on stress-related growth. In C. L. Park, S. Lechner, A. Stanton, & M. Antoni (Eds.), *Positive life changes in the context of medical illness* (pp. 87–104). Washington, DC: APA Press.

rates of morbidity and disability in later life (Aldwin & Gilmer, 2004). This has also resulted in better maintenance of cognitive facilities in later life (Schaie, 1996), which is a major resource for effective coping in later life.

Summary of Middle through Late Adulthood

In addition to major changes in social roles and health status, adults in mid and late life undergo significant shifts in cognitive-affective processes and sense of self and motivation. Striking differences emerge in how mature adults process and respond to stress compared to younger individuals. Older adults appear to make greater use of appraisal processes to downregulate stress (Boeninger et al., 2009). Generative concerns for others' well-being and a focus on sustaining and enjoying one's close relationships appears to increase across the mature adult years and influence problem-solving and coping strategies in the interpersonal domain, in particular. Older adults are less likely to use interpersonal confrontation and other more active strategies to resolve interpersonal problems than are younger adults (Aldwin, Sutton, Chiara, & Spiro, 1996; Berg et al., 1998; Coats & Blanchard-Fields, 2008), and may make greater use of dyadic coping to offset declines in physical and cognitive capacities decline (Berg & Upchurch, 2007; Dixon, 1999).

Older adults face more uncontrollable and chronic stressors, such as bereavement, the development of chronic illness, and providing caregiving for sick and dying relatives that requires them to more clearly differentiate between the controllable and uncontrollable facets of these situations, and fine tune their coping strategies appropriately by engaging controllable aspects and disengaging from the uncontrollable aspects (Johnson & Barer, 1993). Mature adults may use more acceptance and re-framing strategies that maximize controlling aspects of their own self, rather than of the external environment (Rothermund & Brandtstädter, 2003; Schulz & Heckhausen, 1998).

Our overall impression is that adults in mid and late life may use more reflective coping and self-monitoring to ensure that their coping efforts match their values and motivations. How deliberate, goal-directed coping may promote further self-development in late life is as yet poorly understood, although Jennings et al., (2006) found that the best predictors of wisdom in late life were coping and prior stress-related growth.

TOWARD A LIFE-SPAN DEVELOPMENTAL THEORY

In this section, we provide an overview of theories that discuss how coping changes across the life span. It is organized around the four themes we identified at the beginning of the chapter as important to the development of coping across the life span: the contextual nature of coping, energy management (engagement–disengagement), the social nature of coping, and the transactional nature of coping and self-development. Based on this synthesis of the literature, we will outline an agenda for future research.

Contextual Nature of Coping

The environmental contexts for coping change tremendously across the life span, requiring a great number of strategies tailored for diverse circumstances. In early childhood, infants and toddlers are primarily engaged in developing the basic building blocks for the physical, cognitive, and social skills necessary to function effectively in society. The immediate context is the family. Parents (and presumably other family members) affect the development of coping strategies by modeling, direct instruction, or by encouraging or discouraging particular strategies (Kliewer et al., 1994). In middle childhood, the developmental context broadens to include school situations. Children must learn a new set of adaptive strategies, and often become quite fluid in recognizing which strategies are appropriate for different contexts (Davidson, et al., 1978). In adolescence, peer contexts become more important in influencing the choice of coping strategies, pressures for academic performance may increase, and career environments become relevant. The developmental tasks and contexts involved in early adulthood include establishing autonomy in competence and values; young adults typically face many stressors in trying to establish careers and families (Arnett, 2000). Coping resources increase dramatically in young adulthood, individuals become more adept at self-regulation and develop adult coping repertoires, which may be more efficient and also more nuanced toward situational demands and goals (Aldwin, Sutton, Chiara, & Spiro, 1996; Blanchard-Fields, 2007).

Middle adulthood is a time of great responsibility, in both the family and work contexts (Schaie, 1996). As adults become more generative in midlife (McAdams, 2006), they learn to shape their coping efforts in a way that facilitates the ability of others to develop their own coping skills. In late adulthood, adults are likely to be coping with loss, including loss of parents, spouses, siblings, and friends. They also may face more chronic stressors such as long-term illnesses, including arthritis, heart disease, and diabetes (Aldwin, Sutton, Chiara, & Sutton, 1996), which necessitate greater routinization and management strategies (Aldwin & Brustrom, 1997).

A central theme in the study of the contexts of coping concerns the controllability of the stressors in any particular developmental context. While theories of coping emphasize agency—proactive ways of dealing with problems—the widespread (although seldom examined) assumption is that control follows an inverted U-curve, with relatively little control in early childhood and late life, and peak control in mid-life. For example, it is widely assumed that older adults face fewer controllable stressors and thus are less likely to be able to exercise control over their environments than at earlier points in the life span. Schulz and Heckhausen (1998) proposed a life-span theory of development which proposes that individuals engage in primary control early in adulthood and resort to secondary control in later life when they can no longer exert environmental control. Translating their theory into stress and coping terms, this suggests that older individuals switch from problem-focused, assimilative, and engaged coping to emotion-focused, accommodative, and disengaged coping in later life (see Brandtstädter, 1999).

Skaff (2007) has argued that control is a multidimensional construct, and there is good evidence that different types of control have different trajectories with age (Lachman, 1986). Further, there are individual differences in individuals' ability to and preference for exercising control. In addition, the evidence for simple changes in problem-focused coping with age is not strong. Studies sometimes find decreases in problem-focused coping, which would support Schulz and Heckhausen's (1998) position. However, other studies find stability (Folkman, Berstein, & Lazarus, 1987; Folkman & Moskowitz, 2004).

Further, just as control is a multidimensional process, so, too, are chronic stressors. Aldwin (1991) examined the issue of illness, perceived control, and coping efficacy in an adult community sample. Older individuals were more likely to be coping with health problems than were younger adults, but there was a direct and positive link between health problems and perceived coping efficacy. In other words, individuals did not feel helpless in the face of chronic illness. They used a number of management strategies such as medication adherence, dietary changes, and exercise regimens designed to minimize symptoms, increase cardiovascular functioning and regulate blood sugar levels. Thus, problem-focused coping may not be able to change whether a problem exists, such as a chronic illness or the loss of a loved one, but it may be able to mitigate the impact of the problem on other areas of individuals' lives.

Similarly, one could argue that children, even young children, may have more control than is usually assumed. We have known for some time that parenting is a dyadic process, with children influencing their parents (Bell & Harper, 1977). Similarly, adults are usually quite careful to match the demands of developmental context to the skill set of the children involved. Thus, we send children to kindergarten and elementary school, not to college. Young children may evince a sense of mastery within their developmental contexts, just as older adults may feel a sense of mastery through surmounting the effects of seemingly uncontrollable stressors (Pearlin et al., 2007). Clearly, more work is needed to understand the different types of control that can be exerted at different stages of the life span, and the coping strategies that are recruited to maintain a sense of control.

Social Nature of Coping

As Hobfoll (2001) pointed out, coping does not occur in a social vacuum. Rather, others in the situation influence how individuals appraise and cope with stressors, both directly through social sanctions and advice-giving, and indirectly through modeling (Berg & Upchurch, 1997; Kliewer et al., 1994; Thoits, 1986). Some of the most interesting changes in coping with age involve dyadic coping strategies. Skinner and Zimmer-Gembeck (2009) note that the dyadic relationship between parents and children changes across different stages. In infancy, parental contribution to the relationship is to divine and carry out coping actions based on the infant's expressed distress. During the preschool stage, parents are available for direct help and participate in children's coping efforts. During middle childhood, parents cooperate with and support children's coping efforts. Further, children begin to seek social support from their siblings and peers. In young adolescence, parents' contribution to the dyad consists of what Skinner and Zimmer-Gembeck termed "reminder" coping, while in middle adolescence parents are more likely to let their teens try to cope with most problems on their own, and provide mainly back-up coping. In late adolescence, parents are most likely to provide "mentoring" coping, that is, providing advice about general life strategies, as well as prepare to be of assistance during crises.

In adolescence, teens often are more likely to turn to peers for help in coping with problems, although parents still play a major role. They may also become more reliant on their romantic partners (Seiffge-Krenke, 2006). In young adulthood and midlife, the primary source of support becomes one's spouse or long-term partner. For those widowed, divorced, or single in late life, siblings may become primary sources of social support (Berg & Upchurch, 2007). In young adulthood and midlife, the primary source of support becomes one's spouse or long-term partner. For those widowed, divorced, or still single in late life, siblings may become primary sources of social support (Vitaliano et al., 2003).

With the exception of infants, long-term partners in late life are the most likely to engage in dyadic problem solving (Berg & Upchurch, 2007). Dixon (1999) noted the existence of dyadic memory, in which couples, especially those in long-term marital relationships, often assisted each other in memory tasks, providing prompts and corrections. In laboratory tests of dyadic memory, older adults working in pairs often had performance on memory tasks that were equal to that of younger individuals.

Berg and Upchurch (2007) argued that an increase in dyadic coping in general is a hallmark of change in adaptive strategies with age. Some problems, such as chronic illnesses, impact both individuals and their partners. Indeed, in later life, both members of a couple may have chronic illnesses necessitating mutual changes in how they cope. Indeed, such stressors may occasion mutual appraisals, coping, and resource management. Berg and Upchurch argued that the heightened marital satisfaction and intimacy and decreased conflict in older couples (Levenson, Carstensen, & Gottman, 1993; Carstensen, Gottman, & Levenson, 1995) may be due to an increase in the use of collaborative coping styles (as opposed, for example, to controlling ones). It is very likely that individuals in long-term marriages have learned to draw on each other's resources and become more accepting of each other's foibles.

Thus, the social nature of coping manifests itself throughout the life course, supporting Thoits's (1986) early observation. With age and maturity comes a more nuanced and collaborative mode of dyadic coping, which makes more efficient use of energy in later life, allowing individuals to share in tasks and compensate for limitations.

Engagement/Disengagement

The process of coping via engagement or disengagement is fundamental to self-regulation (Compas, 2009; Connor-Smith & Flaschsbart, 2007). Even infants are able to evince primitive forms of this strategy, for example, by using gaze aversion when external stimuli threaten to overwhelm them (Murphy & Moriarty, 1976). In traditional coping theory, engagement–disengagement strategies are referred to as approach–avoidant coping (Moos, 1997). Understanding how approach/avoidance change across the life span is an important component of any life-span theory. While some theorists have argued that repression increases with age (Johnson & Barer, 1993; McCrae, 1989), others suggest decreases in avoidance and escapism (Aldwin, Sutton, Chiara, & Spiro, 1996). Perhaps the repression may be better conceptualized as detachment, or a way of energy regulation, which will be discussed further in the last section.

For example, using TAT (Thematic Apperception Test) cards, Gutmann (1974) focused on a shift in mastery styles across the life span. Active mastery themes (approach coping) were more frequently found in TAT stories told by young adults. These themes consisted of active patterns that were directed toward confronting and resolving problems. In contrast, in middle-aged adults, the themes reflected what Gutmann termed "passive" mastery techniques characterized by acceptance and resignation. Finally, the stories told by older adults—often "fairy tales" or myths from local lore—were characterized by "magical mastery"—which could be seen as avoidance. In these stories, the problems seemed to resolve themselves. Sometimes these elders would draw on mythological themes, or they would focus on what Gutmann initially thought of as irrelevant aspects of the picture. Gutmann found these same themes in both Druze and American samples.

However, there is an alternative explanation of Gutmann's (1974) theory. Acceptance should not necessarily be confused with passivity. Rather than actively trying to manage all problems, with age and experience comes the recognition that that some problems are self-limiting and will resolve themselves, while others are not resolvable. This recognition allows one to be more selective about which problems to actively pursue. Gutmann's (1987) revision of his theory did recast this withdrawal into something closely resembling transcendence in late life. In other words, these elders were putting the problem into the larger context, integrating them into culturally meaningful themes.

Vaillant (1977) proposed a more positive model of aging and defensive styles using qualitative data from the Grant study, which followed male college students at an Ivy League college from their freshman year in the 1940s into late life (Vaillant, 2002). In early adulthood, defensive styles are characterized by neurotic mechanisms such as intellectualization, repression, reaction formation and displacement, and by immature adaptive mechanisms by fantasy, projection, hypochondriasis, passive–aggressive behavior, and acting out. With age, Vaillant observed a shift from these neurotic and immature defensive styles to more mature defensive styles among those in midlife. These mechanisms include sublimation, altruism, anticipation, and humor. Unfortunately, these intriguing age-related trends were not replicated in other longitudinal samples of inner city children (Vaillant, Bond, & Vaillant, 1986) and women (Vaillant, 1993).

However, others have found some corroboration for this shift in defense mechanisms using self-report inventories. Costa, Zonderman, and McCrae (1991) found that projection and other maladaptive patterns were negatively correlated with age. Whitty (2003) also found that younger adults were more likely than middle-aged or older adults to use immature defense mechanisms. In contrast, mature defense mechanisms were more likely to be reported by middle-aged and older adults.

Costa, Zonderman, and McCrae (1991) also found an increase in repressive defense mechanisms/denial with age, as did McCrae (1989). Folkman, Lazarus, Pimley, and Novacek (1987) also found more denial coping strategies with age. In a qualitative study of the very old in San Francisco, Johnson and Barer (1993) provided some very poignant examples of older adults repressing the seriousness of their health problems, including cardiovascular disease, mobility, or sensory problems. Another interpretation of these strategies would be that they were excellent examples of "downward comparisons" (Taylor, Lichtman, & Wood, 1984). Older adults could always point to others whose health problems were, in their opinions, worse than theirs. As Skinner and Edge (1998) point out, a little repression in the face of massive problems is probably a fairly adaptive strategy. In a similar vein, McCrae (1989) argued that the age differences in coping were more reflective of changes in contextual demands.

Both Aldwin (2007) and Skinner and Edge (1998) have suggested that decreases in problem-focused coping over the course of adulthood may not necessarily index passivity, but rather a more efficient use of energy. Baltes (1987) and Hobfoll (2001) have both proposed that energy resources decrease with age, and older individuals may need to cope in a way that conserves resources. Long experience may provide indications of what types of strategies are likely to work and which are not, and older adults may have learned to be more selective in their application of these strategies.

One major theory illustrating this type of selectivity has been proposed by Baltes and Baltes (1990; Freund & Baltes, 2002). This theory delineates the processes of selection, optimization, and compensation (SOC). Selection refers to strategic decisions on where to focus one's energy, and presumes that there a decrease in activity with age. Older individuals can also optimize their functioning for those areas that are selected. For example, concert pianists may include fewer pieces in their musical repertoire, but practice those more assiduously. Individuals may also compensate in various ways to mitigate barriers to adequate performance.

Simple examples of compensation are glasses and hearing aids to compensate for sensory deficits with age, canes and other assistive devices for mobility problems, and altering the environment to maximize competence (Lawton & Nahemow, 1973) by installing adequate lighting, grab bars, and the like. Individuals may compensate for cognitive deficits in some extremely interesting ways (Dixon, 1999). For example, a classic work by Salthouse (1988) has shown that older typists compensated for the generalized neuronal slowing that comes with age. By reading ahead further, they were able to maintain comparable typing speeds to younger typists. Individuals may also compensate for memory and other cognitive declines by using metamemory strategies, which can be seen as anticipatory and proactive coping strategies (Aspinwall & Taylor, 1997) designed to forestall the occurrence of a problem or to mitigate its severity once it occurs. Examples of metamemory strategies include actively using a calendar to maintain appointments, medication counters to keep track of complex medication regimes, and asking others to help in remembering anticipated events.

The focus on compensation is fully in accordance with Lawton and Nahemow's (1973) theory of environmental competence. This theory states that competence is an interaction between individual abilities and environmental demands. By designing environments that accommodate increasing disabilities, such as grab bars in bathrooms or better lighting, the competence of older individuals can be increased. This theory underlies the current movement in gerotechnology, which provides not only compensatory environmental change but also promotes unobtrusive monitoring to detect changes that may signal impending problems (Mahmood, Yamamoto, Lee, & Steggell, 2008).

There is widespread acceptance of the SOC theory, and there is a growing body of evidence supporting it. As reviewed in Baltes, Freund, and Li (2005), SOC surprisingly appears to peak in midlife. A study by Aldag (1997) may shed some light on this conundrum. She examined self-reported change in activities over five years in five domains among old-old residents in a public housing complex. Contrary to expectations, in most domains, individuals were just as likely to report increases in activities as they were to report decreases. Activities that were most likely to decrease were things such as housework. Further, individuals were very unlikely to attribute decreases to aging *per se*, but rather to life events. For example, decreases in housework were sometimes reported as widows downsized, moving from houses to apartments. At other times, decreases that an outside observer would perceive as stemming from aging, such as decreases in exercise, were also attributed to external causes, such as a lack of time. Respondents often reported substituting activities, for example, switching from running to bicycling. Again, the attribution would be to injury (e.g., bad knees), rather than aging. This is similar to Baltes, Freund, and Li's (2005) finding that elective selection increases in late life, while loss-related selection decreases. This may be due to older adults' use of appraisal and coping strategies to avoid defining everyday problems as stressors (Aldwin, Sutton, Chiara, & Spiro, 1996; Boeninger et al., 2009). Clearly, substitution of activities to accommodate age-related declines in abilities should be added as an example of compensation to the SOC theory.

With chronic stressors such as chronic illness, impaired mobility and sensory deficits, coping with individual stressful episodes may become less important than anticipatory and proactive coping strategies that seek to forestall anticipated problems. Thus, the decrease in reported problems and problem-focused coping strategies seen with age may be due to a shift in from coping to management strategies (Aldwin, Sutton, Chiara, & Spiro, 1996).

Facing chronic illnesses, especially life-threatening ones, also changes individuals' perspectives. Carstensen and colleagues (2006) have argued that age and/or life-threatening illness such as AIDS are accompanied by an increasing emphasis on deriving meaning from one's experiences and a decreased emphasis on seeking novel experiences. This change in perspective is brought about by the realization that the life span is finite and the perception of a decreasing amount of time left to live. According to this theory, young adults focus on expanding social networks, increasing their knowledge about the world and also their coping repertoires. They are interested in exploring new situations and experiences. In contrast, older adults are more interested in spending their time with close friends and loved ones, in meaningful occupations, and in environments that promote emotion regulation. Consequently, coping efforts will be increasingly focused on the regulation of both emotions and emotional responses in late life (or when the end of life is perceived as being near). Thus, rather than shifting from problem-focused to emotion-focused coping due to an inability to control their environment, the recognition that the life span is limited leads to a greater desire for emotion regulation and close relationships.

In summary, just as internal/external ideas of control may be too simplistic to capture the complexity of change across the life span, so, too, must notions of approach/avoidance become more nuanced. All organisms must learn how to regulate their activity levels, and use a dual processing mode of engagement versus disengagement. Both infants and older adults have limited amounts of energy, but they use very different means of regulating their attention. Infants and toddlers can resort to "melt-downs" when faced with overwhelming challenges, but with age comes more modulated approaches. Adolescents and young adults often utilize escapism, but that has been shown repeatedly to be an ineffective strategy (Aldwin, 2007). With age comes the ability to differentiate between what can be controlled and what must be accepted, and older adults are more likely to use repressive coping strategies to disengage. But older adults have learned to utilize appraisal to maintain emotional equilibrium, either by being less likely to appraise potentially problematic situations as stressors (Boeninger et al., 2009), or by disclaiming responsibility for the occurrence (and even management) of problems, but nonetheless using problem-focused strategies, where appropriate (Aldwin, 1991). Thus, one could argue that older adults are more likely to use nuanced approaches to the balance of engagement and disengagement coping strategies as a means of regulating and conserving energy resources.

Self-Development

Skinner and Zimmer-Gebeck (2009) presented an ambitious developmental theory of the change in coping strategies from infancy through adolescence. In infancy, coping strategies change from reflexes to coordinated action schema. Preschoolers start demonstrating coping strategies that utilize voluntary direct actions. In middle childhood, coping shifts to strategies that are more cognitive in nature, and early adolescents start using coping that relies on meta-cognition. In middle adolescence, coping becomes based on personal values, while in late adolescence becomes based on long-term goals. In this section, we will argue that coping in adulthood serves not only long-term goals but becomes an integral element of self-development.

For example, Brandtstädter and colleagues (Brandtstädter, 1999; Rothermund & Brandtstädter, 2003) have proposed a theory based on action plans stating that development in adulthood occurs because individuals, influenced by their personal histories and sociocultural contexts, choose long-term goals based on desirable personal selves, or who they wish to become (Hooker & Kaus, 1994). Pursuit of these goals requires both adequate self-regulatory skills and intentional action, and results in development of the requisite skills and characteristics. Borrowing from Piaget, Brandtstädter calls this the *assimilative mode*. However, situational, temporal, and other constraints may force individuals to change their goals, called the *accommodative mode*. According to this theory, individuals use a coping strategy called tenacious goal pursuit in the accommodative mode, and one called flexible goal adjustment in the accommodative mode. Examination of the individual items in this scale suggests that tenacious goal pursuit consists primarily of problem-focused items, while flexible goal adjustment consists of emotion-focused items. Throughout the life course, a sense of personal efficacy and positive well-being may depend on the dynamic interplay between these two modes.

Rothermund and Brandtstädter's (2003) found that the accommodative mode in coping with physical disabilities was associated with positive outcomes up until age 70, but negative outcomes after this age, at which point assimilative modes become associated with positive outcomes. Note that recognizing and adjusting to the limitations of old age does not necessarily entail passive strategies, but rather means adjusting one's goals, which, as Carstensen and her colleagues (2006) point out, may entail positive changes.

Dynamic developmental theories of adaptation in adulthood may also focus on integration across domains. For example, Labouvie-Vief (2003) has argued that there is an increase in emotional and cognitive complexity from young adulthood to midlife that may decrease in later life. Presumably, these adaptational changes both grew out of and promoted individuals' positive coping with stressful problems (Aldwin, Sutton, & Lachman, 1996; Pearlin et al., 2007; Skinner & Zimmer-Gembeck, 2009). However, in Labouvie-Vief's (2003) study, affective complexity was lower in older adults; although they had high positive affect, they had lower levels of negative affect. One possible explanation for this is that older adults cannot physically tolerate emotional distress, due to chronic illnesses such as hypertension, cardiovascular disease, and diabetes (Aldwin, Park, & Spiro, 2007). However, it is also possible that for some individuals, switching from efforts to regulate the environment to regulating one's own self may well entail a balance toward positive affect, and complexity is not necessarily more developed than simplicity (*pace* Heinz Werner). A developmental process may well involve increasing complexity in early stages, but then increasing simplicity at more advanced stages. For example, Vaillant (2002) found that, in late life, older men exhibited almost a "Zen-like" acceptance of problems. In the clarity of wisdom, the complex often becomes simple.

As mentioned earlier, life course mastery develops from individuals coping with seemingly insurmountable problems (Pearlin et al., 2007). Bluck and Glück (2004) have also presented convincing evidence that older adults report that wisdom develops from coping with difficult life trials (see also McAdams, 2006). Drawing on work by Curnow (1999), Levenson, Jennings, Aldwin, and Shiraishi (2005) argued that wisdom is a developmental process that consists of four iterative processes: self-knowledge, detachment or nonattachment, self-integration, and self-transcendence. Applying this perspective to a life-span theory of coping extends our understanding of how coping might develop in adulthood, in an admittedly speculative way.

For example, Levenson, Aldwin, and Cupertino (2001) have suggested that the process of coping with loss forms a context for the development of wisdom. Difficult life circumstances often force individuals to confront their own assumptions, not only about world schemata but also about their own beliefs, values, and actions. This self-reflection can result in greater self-knowledge. Coping with stress can also force individuals to develop self-regulatory processes that promote the development of the capacity to detach. Detachment does not mean noncaring, but rather the ability "to 'let go' of problems, obsessions, and perceived threats, thus freeing awareness to achieve integration" (Levenson, 2009, p. 47). As mentioned earlier, themes of engagement/disengagement are central to understanding change in coping across the life span. Detachment allows one to disengage emotionally from stressors, and focus one's attention more effectively on finding solutions to or managing difficult problems.

Self-integration refers to the coherence of self (Diehl, Hastings, & Stanton, 2001). One could argue that stress often result from internal conflicts, in which individuals have competing and incommensurate goals. This fragmentation of attention and thus coping strategies across conflicting goals is a hallmark of the fragmented self. To the extent that self-coherence increases with age (Diehl, et al.), one would expect that coping strategies also become more coherent and thus more efficient.

Finally, self-transcendence refers to the ability to decenter from the self, allowing one to more readily take the perspective of the other (Levenson, 2009). As mentioned earlier, in mid-life, generative concerns promote cognitive and emotional complexity, and also may provide new insights into coping in ways that promote not only one's own development but also promotes the development of others in the situation.

Aldwin (1991) argued that the goal of self-development in adulthood is wisdom, and that stressors form a context for self-development. More precisely, how individuals cope with stress may promote the development of wisdom through self-knowledge, learning to detach, integrate the self, and transcend one's own personal concerns. This iterative and reflective process requires subtle changes in coping strategies from an egocentric stance in early life to a self-transcendent one in later life (Levenson et al., 2001; Levenson et al., 2005).

Thus, coping is a highly complex phenomenon, encompassing emotional regulation, problem solving, dyadic efforts, and energy regulation, that both changes across contexts and reflect self-development. As such, it is at the heart of life-span development, and it is not surprising that so many current theories touch on coping modalities, even if different terminology is used. As such, it provides a window into developmental processes. Theories of life-span development would be greatly enhanced with explicit inclusion of coping research.

An Agenda for Future Research

The future of developmental coping research depends in large part on the development of better coping theory and better measures. We believe that the four dimensions outlined in this review—the contextual nature of coping, energy management (engagement–disengagement), the social nature of coping, and the transactional nature of coping and self-development—may intersect in some interesting ways to form a framework for explaining how coping develops across the life span.

First, we hypothesize that there is a dialectic between contextual influences on coping and the autonomy implied in theories of self-development. As indicated by Skinner and Zimmer-Gembeck (2009), coping changes from being largely determined by context (notably, the social contexts of parents and peers) to greater autonomy, implied in setting one's own goals (Arnett, 2000). As Levenson and Crumpler (1996) pointed out, development in adulthood in part entails transcending social determinism. This does not mean that coping becomes more rigid and less responsive to environmental contingencies, but rather that mature coping involves understanding that how one behaves in the immediate context can affect long-term goals. For example, Carrère and Gottman (1999) demonstrated that couples who go on to divorce are often stuck in escalating patterns, answering anger with more anger. Couples whose marriages survive, on the other hand, can be seen to defuse angry situations through the use of redirective strategies such as humor. One could argue that the long-term goal—preserving the marriage—takes precedence over short-term goals that are embedded in the immediate context (e.g., defending oneself against perceived unjust attacks). More attention must be paid to the goals underlying the use of coping strategies (Folkman & Moskowitz, 2004). Further, the outcomes of coping should not be restricted to physical and psychological symptoms, but rather should include development outcomes, such as the ability to detach from problematic situations (Ryan & Deci, 2006). Second, there is an additional dialectic between self-development and the social nature of coping. In an earlier study of emotional maturity in the military context, Aldwin and Levenson (2005) suggested that there was a dialectic between autonomy and the ability to work well in social settings. On the one hand, emotional maturity involves being able to autonomously set one's own goals and take responsibility for one's own actions (Arnett, 2000), while at the same time being able to subordinate one's personal goals in order to achieve group goals. Berg and Upchurch (2007) found that dyadic coping becomes more collaborative (as opposed to controlling) with age, suggesting that older adults become more skilled at working collaboratively. This increased collaborative ability might shift the choice of coping strategies from those that promote one's own well-being to those that promote the well-being of others, reflecting the generativity which is thought to increase in midlife (Erikson, 1963; McAdams, 2006). Compassion can be seen as underlying both generativity and moral development (Levenson, 2009), and the relationship between moral development and coping is a potentially interesting area of research.

This leads to the third hypothesis—that the ability to engage in dual-process coping (Stroebe & Schut, 1999), alternating between approach and avoidance, is a hallmark of self-regulatory ability. The earlier hypotheses assume that age is accompanied by increasing ability to regulate emotions and the self. Self-regulation underlies autonomy and the ability to pursue long-term goals, as well as the ability to work well in collaborative situations. Young adults may exhibit what Zuckerman and colleagues (1996) called unrealistic control expectations, leading them to waste energy trying to control uncontrollable situations, while older adults may become more adept at both accurately appraising the controllability of situations and in efficient coping strategies, which allows them to achieve goals while conserving resources and energy.

Coherence of coping strategies also provides a promising area for future research. An early study by Coyne, Aldwin, and Lazarus (1981) showed that individuals who were chronically depressed were more likely to use multiple coping strategies, which flies in the face of the widely held notion that larger coping repertoires are more adaptive. Coyne and colleagues argued that depressed individuals may be ineffective in their execution of coping strategies, and thus will try multiple strategies. Developing ways of examining whether the range of coping strategies used are mutually contradictory (e.g., reflect contradictory goals), or provide a coherent approach to problem solving, might be an interesting approach to understanding effective coping (Labouvie-Vief & Diehl, 2000; Ryan et al., 2006).

Finally, the role of coping in the development of wisdom is also a fruitful area for future research. In lay understandings of wisdom, the constructs of fairness and perspicacity are often central (Glück, Strasser, & Bluck, 2009), and indeed, discussions of wisdom often center on difficult moral decisions made in the face of overwhelming stress. Thus, the constructs of coping, self-development, moral development, and wisdom are intertwined, and further delineation of their inter-relationships may inform the next generation of theories of life-span development.

These hypothesized changes in coping are admittedly subtle, and it is unlikely that the coping scales currently available are able to test them. General inventories have been criticized for not including items that accurately reflect mature emotion regulation or dyadic coping, but unfortunately the tendency has been to develop specialty scales that better address these facets of coping but which unfortunately include only a narrow range of strategies (e.g., DeLongis & Preece, 2002; Stanton, Danoff-Burg, Cameron, & Ellis, 1994). Further, the lack of general inventories with a stable factor structure (Schwarzer & Schwarzer, 1996) is especially troubling for developmental research. Nonetheless, we have learned much about coping in the past 40 years of research, and this knowledge will hopefully inform the next generation of coping scales, allowing for the examination of more complex coping theories.

REFERENCES

Abramson, L. Y., Alloy, L. B., & Metalsky, G. I. (1990). The hopelessness theory of depression: Current status and future directions. In N. L. Stein, B. Leventhal, & T. Trabasso (Eds.), *Psychological and biological approaches to emotion* (pp. 333–358). Hillsdale, NJ: Erlbaum.

Adler, N. E., Epel, E. S., Castellazzo, G., & Ickovics, J. R. (2000). Relationship of subjective and objective social status with psychological and physiological functioning: Preliminary data in healthy white women. *Health Psychology, 19*, 586–592.

Aldag, L. D. (1997). *Is use of selective optimization with compensation associated with successful aging?* Unpublished doctoral dissertation, University of California, Davis.

Aldwin, C. (1990). The Elders Life Stress Inventory (ELSI): Egocentric and nonegocentric stress. In M. A. P. Stephens, S. E. Hobfoll, J. H. Crowther, & D. L. Tennenbaum (Eds.), *Stress and coping in late life families* (pp. 49–69). New York: Hemisphere.

Aldwin, C. (1991). Does age affect the stress and coping process? Implications of age differences in perceived control. *Journal of Gerontology, 46,* 174–180.

Aldwin, C. M. (2007). *Stress, coping, and development (2nd ed.).* New York: Guilford Press.

Aldwin, C. M., & Brustrom, J. (1997). Theories of coping with chronic stress: Illustrations from the health psychology and aging literatures. In B. Gottlieb (Ed.), *Coping with chronic stress* (pp. 75–103). New York: Plenum.

Aldwin, C. M., & Gilmer, D. F. (2004). *Health, illness, and optimal aging: Biological and psychosocial perspectives*. Thousand Oaks, CA: Sage.

Aldwin, C. M., & Levenson, M. R. (1994). Aging and personality assessment. In M. P. Lawton & J. Teresi (Eds.), *Annual Review of Gerontology/Geriatrics, Vol. 14* (pp. 182–209). New York: Springer.

Aldwin, C. M., & Levenson, M. R. (2001). Stress, coping, and health at mid-life: A developmental perspective. In M. E. Lachman (Ed.), *The Handbook of Midlife Development* (pp. 188–214). New York: John Wiley & Sons.

Aldwin, C. M., & Levenson, M. R. (2005). Military service and emotional maturation: The Chelsea Pensioners. In K. W. Warner & G. Elder, Jr. (Eds.), *Historical influences on lives and aging* (pp. 255–281). New York: Plenum.

Aldwin, C. M., Levenson, M. R., & Kelly, L. L. (2009). Lifespan developmental perspectives on stress-related growth. In C. L. Park, S. Lechner, A. Stanton, & M. Antoni (Eds.), *Positive life changes in the context of medical illness* (pp. 87–104). Washington, DC: APA Press.

Aldwin, C. M., Park, C. L., & Spiro, A., III. (2007). Health psychology and aging: Moving to the next generation of research. In In C. M. Aldwin, C. L. Park, & A. Spiro III (Eds.), *Handbook of Health Psychology & Aging* (pp. 413–426). New York: Guilford.

Aldwin, C. M., Sutton, K. J., Chiara, G., & Spiro, A., III. (1996). Age differences in stress, coping, and appraisal: Findings from the Normative Aging Study. *Journals of Gerontology: Psychological Sciences, 51B,* P179.

Aldwin, C. M., Sutton, K., & Lachman, M. (1996). The development of coping resources in adulthood. *Journal of Personality, 64,* 91–113.

Aldwin, C. M., Yancura, L. A., & Boeninger, D. K. (2007). Coping, health, and aging. In C. M. Aldwin, C. L. Park, & A. Spiro, III (Eds.), *Handbook of health psychology & aging* (pp. 210–226). New York: Guilford Press.

Altschuler, J. A., & Ruble, D. N. (1989). Developmental changes in children's awareness of strategies for coping with uncontrollable stress. *Child Development, 60,* 1337–1349.

Andersen, S. L. (2003). Trajectories of brain development: Point of vulnerability or window of opportunity? *Neuroscience and Biobehavioral Reviews*, *27*, 3–18.

Arnett, J. J. (2000). Emerging adulthood: A theory of development from the late teens through the twenties. *American Psychologist, 55,* 469–480.

Asher, S., Erdley, C. A., & Gabriel, S. W. (1994). Peer relations. In M. Rutter & D. F. Hay (Eds.), *Development through life: A handbook for clinicians* (pp. 456–487). Boston, MA: Blackwell.

Aspinwall, L., & Taylor, S. (1997). A stitch in time: Self-regulation and pro-active coping. *Psychological Bulletin, 121*, 417–436.

Badr, H. (2004). Coping in marital dyads: A contextual perspective on the role of gender and health. *Personal Relationships, 11*, 197–211.

Baltes, P. B. (1987). Theoretical propositions of life-span developmental psychology: On the dynamics between growth and decline. *Developmental Psychology, 24,* 611–626.

Baltes, P. B., & Baltes, M. M.. (1990). Psychological perspectives on successful aging: The model of selective optimization with compensation. In P. B. Baltes & M. M. Baltes (Eds.), *Successful aging: Perspectives from the behavioral sciences* (pp. 1–34). New York: Cambridge University Press.

Baltes, P. B., Freund, A., & Li, Shu-Chen. (2005). In M. L. Johnson, V. L. Bengtson, P. G. Coleman, & T. B. L. Kirkwood (Eds.), *The Cambridge handbook of age and ageing* (pp. 47–71). Cambridge: Cambridge University Press.

Baltes, P. B., & Smith, J. (2004). Lifespan psychology: From developmental contextualism to developmental biocultural co-constructivism. *Research in Human Development, 1*, 123–144.

Bell, R. Q., & Harper, L. V. (1977). *Child effects on adults.* Hillsdale, NJ: Erlbaum.

Benight, C. C., & Bandura, A. (2004). Social cognitive theory of post-traumatic recovery: The role of perceived self-efficacy. *Behaviour Research and Therapy, 42*, 1129–1148.

Berg, C. A., Meegan, S. P., & Deviney, F. P. (1998). A social-contextual model of coping with everyday problems across the lifespan. *International Journal of Behavioral Development, 22*, 239–261.

Berg, C. A., Strough, J., Calderone, K. S., Sansone, C., Weir, C. (1998). The role of problem definitions in understanding age and context effects on strategies for solving everyday problems. *Psychology and Aging, 13*, 29–44.

Berg, C. A., & Upchurch, R. (2007). A developmental-contextual model of couples coping with chronic illness across the adult life span. *Psychological Bulletin*, *133*, 920–954.

Berg, C. A., Wiebe, D. J., Butner, J., Bloor, L., Bradstreet, C., Upchurch, R., et al. (2008). Collaborative coping and daily mood in couples dealing with prostate cancer. *Psychology and Aging, 23*, 505–516.

Berkman, L. F. (2009). Social epidemiology: Social determinants of health in the United States: Are we losing ground? *Annual Review of Public Health*, 30, 27–41.

Berkman, L. F., Glass, T., Brissette, I., & Seeman, T. E. (2000). From social integration to health: Durkheim in the new millennium. *Social Science & Medicine, 51*, 843–857.

Blanchard-Fields, F. (2007). Everyday problem solving and emotion: An adult developmental perspective. *Current Directions in Psychological Science, 16*, 26–31.

Bluck, S., & Glück, J. (2004). Making things better and learning a lesson: Experiencing wisdom across the life span. *Journal of Personality, 72,* 543–572.

Boeninger, D. K., Shiraishi, R. W., Aldwin, C. M., & Spiro, A. III. (2009). Why do older men report low stress ratings? Findings from the Veterans Affairs Normative Aging Study. *International Journal of Aging & Human Development*, 68, 149–170.

Bolger, N., & Zuckerman, A. (1995). Personality processes and individual differences A Framework for studying personality in the stress process. *Journal of Personality and Social Psychology, 69*, 890–902.

Bond, M. (2004). Empirical studies of defense style: Relationships with psychopathology and change. *Harvard Review of Psychiatry, 12*, 263–278.

Bouchardy, C., Morabia, A, Verkooijen, H. M., Fioretta, G., Wespi, Y., & Schäfer, P. (2006). Remarkable change in age-specific breast cancer incidence in the Swiss canton of Geneva and its possible relation with the use of hormone replacement therapy. *BMC Cancer, 6*, 78.

Brandtstädter, J. (1999). The self in action and development: Cultural, biosocial and ontogenetic bases of intentional self-development. In J. Brandtstädter's & R. M. Lerner (Eds.), *Action and self-development: Theory and research through the life span* (pp. 37–66). Thousand Oaks, CA: Sage.

Bronfenbrenner, U. (1979). *The ecology of human development: Experiments by nature and design*: Harvard University Press.

Brooks-Gunn, J., & Reiter, E. O. (1990). The role of pubertal processes. In S. S. Feldman & G. R. Elliott (Eds.), *At threshold: The developing adolescent* (pp. 17–53). Cambridge, MA: Harvard University Press.

Byrne, D. (1964). Repression-sensitization as a dimension of personality. In B. A. Maher (Ed.), *Progress in experimental personality research*, Vol. 1 (pp. 169–220). New York: Academic Press.

Cacioppo, J. T., Hawkley, L. C., Crawford, L. E., Ernst, J. M., Burleson, M. H., Kowalewski, R. B., Malarkey, W. B., Van Cauter, E., & Berntson, G. G. (2002). Loneliness and health: Potential mechanisms. *Psychosomatic Medicine, 64*, 407–417.

Cannon, W. B. (1929). *Bodily changes in pain, hunger, fear and rage: An account of recent researches into the function of emotional excitement*, 2nd ed. New York: Appleton.

Carrère, S., & Gottman, J. (1999). Predicting divorce among newlyweds from the first three minutes of a marital conflict discussion. *Family Processes, 38*, 293–301.

Carstensen, L. L., Gottman, J. M., & Levenson, R. W. (1995). Emotional behavior in long-term marriage. *Psychology and Aging, 10,* 140–149.

Carstensen, L. L., Mikels, J. A., & Mather, M. (2006). Aging and the intersection of cognition, motivation and emotion. In J. Birren & K. W. Schaie (Eds.), *Handbook of the Psychology of Aging*, 6th ed. (pp. 343–362). San Diego: Academic Press.

Carver, C. S., & Scheier, M. F. (1998). *On the self-regulation of behavior*. New York: Cambridge University Press.

Carver, C. S., & Scheier, M. F. (2001). Optimism, pessimism, and self-regulation. In E. C. Chang (Ed.), *Optimism and pessimism: Implications for theory, research and practice* (pp. 31–51). Washington, DC: American Psychological Association.

Casey, B. J., Galvan, A., & Hare, T. A. (2005). Changes in cerebral functional organization during cognitive development. *Current Opinion in Neurobiology, 15*, 239–244.

Caspi, A., Bem, D. J., & Elder, G. H. (1989). Continuities and consequences of interactional styles across the life course. *Journal of Personality*, Special issue: Long-term stability and change in personality, *57*, 375–406.

Caspi, A., Lynam, D., Moffitt, T. E., & Silva, P. A. (1993). Unraveling girls' delinquency: Biological, dispositional, and contextual contributions to adolescent misbehavior. *Developmental Psychology, 29*, 19–30.

Caspi, A., Roberts, B. W., & Shiner, R. L. (2005). Personality development: Stability and change. *Annual Review of Psychology, 56*, 453–484.

Caspi, A., Sugden, K., Moffitt, T. E., Taylor, A., Craig, I. W., Harrington, H., McClay, J., Mill, J., Martin, J., Braithwaite, A., & Poulton, R. (2003). Influence of life stress on depression: Moderation by a polymorphism in the 5-Htt gene. *Science, 301*, 386–389.

Chandola, T., Brunner, E., & Marmot, M. (2006). Chronic stress at work and the metabolic syndrome: Prospective study. *British Medical Journal, 332*, 521–525.

Chapman, B. P., & Hayslip, B., Jr. (2006). Emotional intelligence in young and middle adulthood: Cross-sectional analysis of latent structure and means. *Psychology and Aging, 21*, 411–418.

Charmandari, E., Tsigos, C., & Chrousos, G. (2005). Endocrinology of the stress response. *Annual Review of Physiology, 67*, 259–284.

Chiriboga, D. A. (1989). Divorce at midlife. In R. A. Kalish (Ed.), *Midlife loss: Coping strategies* (pp. 42–88). Newbury Park, CA: Sage.

Chiriboga, D. A. (1997). Crisis, challenge, and stability in the middle years. In M. E. Lachman & J. B. James (Eds.), *Multiple paths of midlife development* (pp. 293–343). Chicago: University of Chicago.

Coats, A. H., & Blanchard-Fields, F. (2008). Emotion regulation in interpersonal problems: The role of cognitive-emotional complexity, emotion regulation goals, and expressivity. *Psychology and Aging, 23*, 39–51.

Collins, W. A., Maccoby, E. E., Steinberg, L., Hetherington, E. M., & Bornstein, M. H. (2000). Contemporary research on parenting: The case for nature and nurture. *American Psychologist, 55*, 218–232.

Compas, B. E. (1998). An agenda for coping research and theory: Basic and applied developmental issues. *International Journal of Behavioral Development, 22*, 231–237.

Compas, B. E. (2009). Coping, regulation, and development during childhood and adolescence. In E. A. Skinner & M. J. Zimmer-Gembeck (Eds.). *Coping and the development of regulation.* A volume for the series, R. W. Larson & L. A. Jensen (Eds.-in-Chief), *New Directions in Child and Adolescent Development* (pp. 87–100), San Francisco: Jossey-Bass.

Compas, B., O'Connor-Smith, J. K., Saltzman, S., Thomsen, A. H., & Wadsworth, M. E. (2001). Coping with stress during childhood and adolescence: Problems, progress, and potential in theory and research. *Psychological Bulletin, 127*, 87–127.

Compas, B. E., Worsham, N. L., & Ey, S. (1992). Conceptual and developmental issues in children's coping with stress. In A. M. La Greca, L. J. Siegel, J. L. Wallander, & C. E. Walker (Eds.), *Stress and coping in child health* (pp. 7–24). New York: Guilford Press.

Conger, J. K., Tierney Williams, S., Little, W. M., Masyn, K. E., & Shebloski, B. (2009). Development of mastery during adolescence: The role of family problem-solving. *Journal of Health and Social Behavior, 50*, 99–114.

Conger, R. D., & Donnellan, M. B. (2007). An interactionist perspective on the socioeconomic context of human development. *Annual Review of Psychology*, *58*, 175–199.

Connor-Smith, J. K., & Flachsbart, C. (2007). Relations between personality and coping: A meta-analysis. *Journal of Personality and Social Psychology, 93*, 1080–1107.

Costa, F. M., Jessor, R., & Turbin, M. S. (1999). Transition into adolescent problem drinking: The role of psychosocial risk and protective factors. *Journal of Studies on Alcohol, 60*, 480–490.

Costa, P. T., Zonderman, A. B., & McCrae, R. R. (1991). Personality, defense, coping, and adaptation in older adulthood. In E. M. Cummings, A. L. Greene, & K. H. Karraker (Eds.), *Life-span developmental psychology: Perspectives of stress and coping* (pp. 277–293). Hillsdale, NJ: Erlbaum.

Coyne, J., Aldwin, C., & Lazarus, R. (1981). Depression and coping in stressful episodes. *Journal of Abnormal Psychology, 90*, 439–447.

Coyne, J. C., & Racioppo, M. (2000). Never the twain shall meet? Closing the gap between coping research and clinical intervention research. *American Psychologist, 55*, 655–664.

Cramer, P. (2000). Defense mechanisms in psychology today: Further processes for adaptation. *American Psychologist, 55*, 637–646.

Cupertino, A. P. (2001). *The impact of life course socioeconomic status on cardiovascular disease and overall mortality.* Unpublished doctoral dissertation, University of California, Davis.

Curnow, T. (1999). *Wisdom, intuition, and ethics.* Aldershot, UK: Ashgate Publishing.

Danhauer, S. C., Carlson, C. R., & Andrykowski, M. A. (2005). Positive psychosocial functioning in later life: Use of meaning-based coping strategies by nursing home residents. *Journal of Applied Gerontology, 24*, 299–318.

David, J. P., & Suls, J. (1999). Coping efforts in daily life: Role of Big Five traits and problem appraisals. *Journal of Personality, 67*, 265–294.

Davidson, G. R., Nurcombe, B., Kearney, G. E., & Davis, K. (1978). Culture, conflict and coping in a group of Aboriginal adolescents. *Culture, Medicine and Psychiatry, 2*, 359–372.

De Bellis, M. D. (2001). Developmental traumatology: The psychobiological development of maltreated children and its implications for research, treatment, and policy. *Development and Psychopathology, 13*, 539–564.

DeLongis, A., & Holtzman, S. (2005). Coping in context: The role of stress, social support, and personality in coping. *Journal of Personality, 73*, 1633–1656.

DeLongis, A., & Preece, M. (2002). Emotional and relational consequences of coping in stepfamilies. *Marriage & Family Review, 34*, 115–138.

Denney, N. W., & Palmer, A. M. (1981). Adult age differences on traditional and practical problem-solving measures. *Journal of Gerontology, 36*, 323–328.

de Ridder, D., & Kerssens, J. (2003). Owing to the force of circumstances? The impact of situational features and personal characteristics on coping patterns across situations. *Psychology & Health, 18*, 217–236.

Derryberry, D., Reed, M. A., & Pilkenton-Taylor, C. (2003). Temperament and coping: Advantages of an individual differences perspective. *Development and Psychopathology, 15*, 1049–1066.

Diamond, A. (2002). Normal development of prefrontal cortex from birth to young adulthood: Cognitive functions, anatomy, and biochemistry. In D. T. Stuss & R. T. Knight (Eds.), *Principles of frontal lobe function* (pp. 466–503). New York: Oxford University Press.

Diehl, M., Coyle, N., & Labouvie-Vief, G. (1996). Age and sex differences in strategies of coping and defense across the life span. *Psychology and Aging, 11*, 127–139.

Diehl, M., Hastings, C. T., & Stanton, J. M. (2001). Self-concept differentiation across the adult life span. *Psychology and Aging, 16*, 643–654.

Diehl, M., Marsiske, M., Horgas, A. L., Rosenberg, A., Saczynski, J. S., & Willis, S. L. (2005). The revised observed tasks of daily living: A performance-based assessment of everyday problem solving in older adults. *Journal of Applied Gerontology, 24*(3), 211.

Diehl, M., Willis, S. L., & Schaie, K. W. (1995). Everyday problem solving in older adults: Observational assessment and cognitive correlates. *Psychology and Aging, 10*, 478–478.

Dixon, R. A. (1999). Exploring cognition in interactive situations: The aging of N + 1 minds. In T. M. Hess & F. Blanchard-Fields (Eds.), *Social cognition and aging* (pp. 267–290). San Diego, CA: Academic Press.

Donnellan, M. B., Conger, R. D., & Bryant, C. M. (2004). The Big Five and enduring marriages. *Journal of Research in Personality, 38*, 481–504.

Eisenberg, N., & Fabes, R. A. (1998). Prosocial development. In N. Eisenberg (Ed.), *Handbook of child psychology*. Vol. 3: *Social, emotional, and personality development* (5th ed., pp. 701–778). Editors in chief: W. Damon, R. M. Lerner. New York: John Wiley & Sons.

Eisenberg, N., Fabes, R. A., & Guthrie, I. K. (1997). Coping with stress: The roles of regulation and development. In S. A. Wolchik & I. N. Sandler (Eds.), *Handbook of children's coping: Linking theory and intervention* (pp. 41–72). New York: Plenum.

Eisenberg, N., Fabes, R. A., Shepard, S. A., Murphy, B. C., Guthrie, I. K., Jones, S., Friedman, J., Poulin, R., & Maszk, P. (1997). Contemporaneous and longitudinal prediction of children's social functioning from regulation and emotionality. *Child Development, 68*, 642–664.

Eisenberg, N., Valiente, C., & Sulik, M. J. (2009). How the study of regulation can inform the study of coping. *New Directions for the Study of Child and Adolescent Development, 124*, 75–86.

Eisenberg, N., & Zhou, Q. (2000). Regulation from a developmental perspective. *Psychological Inquiry, 11*, 166–171.

Elder, G. H., Jr., & Shanahan, M. J. (2006). The life course and human development. In R. M Lerner (Ed.), *Handbook of Child Psychology: Vol. 1. Theoretical Models of Human Development* (6th ed., pp. 665–715). Hoboken, NJ: John Wiley & Sons.

Epel, E. S., McEwen, B., Seeman, T., Matthews, K., Castellazzo, G., Brownell, K. D., et al. (2000). Stress and body shape: Stress-induced cortisol secretion is consistently greater among women with central fat. *Psychosomatic Medicine, 62*, 623–632.

Erikson, E. H. (1963). *Childhood and society*, 2nd ed. New York: Norton.

Felitti, V. J., Anda, R. F., Nordenberg, D., Williamson, D. F., Spitz, A. M., Edwards, V., Koss, M. P., & Marks, J. S. (1998). Relationship of childhood abuse and household dysfunction to many of the leading causes of death in adults. The Adverse Childhood Experiences (Ace) Study. *American Journal of Preventive Medicine, 14*, 245–258.

Field, T. (1991). Stress and coping from pregnancy through the postnatal period. In E. M. Cummings, A. L. Greene, & K. H. Karraker (Eds.), *Life-span developmental psychology: Perspectives on stress and coping* (pp. 45–59). Hillsdale, NJ: Erlbaum.

Folkman, S., Berstein, L., & Lazarus, R. S. (1987). Stress processes and the misuse of drugs in older adults. *Psychology and Aging, 2*, 366–374.

Folkman, S., & Lazarus, R. (1985). If it changes it must be a process: Study of emotion and coping during three stages of a college examination. *Journal of Personality and Social Psychology, 48*, 150–170.

Folkman, S., & Lazarus, R. S. (1980). An analysis of coping in a middle-aged community sample. *Journal of Health and Social Behavior, 21*, 219–239.

Folkman, S., Lazarus, R. S., Pimley, S., & Novacek, J. (1987). Age differences in stress and coping processes. *Psychology and Aging, 2*, 171–184.

Folkman, S., & Moskowitz, J. T. (2004). Coping: Pitfalls and promise. *Annual Review of Psychology, 55,* 745–774.

Freund, A. M., & Baltes, P. B. (2002). Life-management strategies of selection, optimization, and compensation: Measurement by self-report and construct validity. *Journal of Personality and Social Psychology, 82,* 642–662.

Führ, M. (2002). Coping humor in early adolescence. *Humor: International Journal of Humor Research, 15,* 283–304.

Gallagher-Thompson, D., Shurgot, G. R., Rider, K., Gray, H. L., McKibbin, C. L., Kraemer, H. C., et al. (2006). Ethnicity, stress, and cortisol function in Hispanic and non-Hispanic white women: A preliminary study of family dementia in caregivers and noncaregivers. *American Journal of Geriatric Psychiatry, 14,* 334.

Ge, X., Conger, R. D., & Elder, G. H., Jr. (1996). Coming of age too early: Pubertal influences on girls' vulnerability to psychological distress. *Child Development, 67,* 3386–400.

Gevirtz, R. (2000). The physiology of stress. In D. T. Kenny, J. G. Carson, F. J. McGuigan, & J. L. Sheppard (Eds.), *Stress and health: Research and clinical applications* (pp. 53–72). Amsterdam: Harwood.

Glück, J., Strasser, I., & Bluck, S. (2009). Gender differences in implicit theories of wisdom. *Research in Human Development, 6,* 27–44.

Goodlin-Jones, B. L., Burnham, M. M., Gaylor, E. E., & Anders, T. F. (2001). Night waking, sleep-wake organization, and self-soothing in the first year of life. *Journal of Developmental and Behavioral Pediatrics, 22,* 226–233.

Goswami, U. (2006). The foundations of psychological understanding. *Developmental Science, 9,* 545–550.

Greene, A. L., & Larson, R. W. (1991). Variation in stress reactivity during adolescence. In E. M. Cummings, A. L. Greene, & K. H. Karraker (Eds.), *Life-span developmental psychology: Perspectives on stress and coping* (pp. 195–209). Hillsdale, NJ: Erlbaum.

Greenough, W. T., Black, J. E., & Wallace, C. S. (1987). Experience and brain development. *Child Development, 58,* 539–559.

Gross, J. J. (1998). The emerging field of emotion regulation: An integrative review. *Review of General Psychology, 2,* 271–299.

Gunnar, M. R., & Fisher, P. A. (2006). Bringing basic research on early experience and stress neurobiology to bear on preventive interventions for neglected and maltreated children. *Development and Psychopathology, 18,* 651–677.

Gunnar, M., & Quevedo, K. (2007). The neurobiology of stress and development. *Annual Review of Psychology, 58,* 145–173.

Gutmann, D. L. (1974). Alternatives to disengagement: The old men of the Highland Druze. In R. A. LeVine (Ed.), *Culture and personality: Contemporary readings* (pp. 232–245). Chicago: Aldine.

Gutmann, D. L. (1987). *Reclaimed powers: Men and women in later life.* Evanston, IL: Northwestern University Press.

Harter, S. (1998). The development of self-representations. In N. Eisenberg (Ed.), *Handbook of Child Psychology: Vol. 3. Social, Emotional, and Personality Development* (5th ed., pp. 553–566). Editors in chief: W. Damon and R. M. Lerner. New York: John Wiley & Sons.

Harter, S. (2006). The development of self-representations. In N. Eisenberg (Vol. Ed.), *Handbook of Child Psychology: Vol. 3. Social, Emotional, and Personality Development* (6th ed., pp. 505–570). Editors in chief: W. Damon and R. M. Lerner. New York: Wiley.

Hellhammer, D. H., & Wade, S. (1993). Endocrine correlates of stress vulnerability. *Psychotherapy and Psychosomatics, 60,* 8–17.

Henry, J. (1971). *Pathways to madness.* New York: Random House.

Higgins, E. T. (1989). Continuities and discontinuities in self-regulatory and self-evaluative processes: A developmental theory relating self and affect. *Journal of Personality, 57,* 407–444.

Hobdy, J., Hayslip, B., Kaminski, P. L., Crowley, B. J., Riggs, S., & York, C. (2007). The role of attachment style in coping with job loss and the empty nest in adulthood. *International Journal of Aging and Human Development, 65,* 335–371.

Hobfoll, S. E. (2001). The influence of culture, community, and the nested-self in the stress process: Advancing conservation of resources theory. *Applied Psychology: An International Review, 50,* 337–370.

Hobfoll, S. E. (2002). Social and psychological resources and adaptation. *Review of General Psychology, 6,* 307–324.

Hooker, K., & Kaus, C. R. (1994). Health-related possible selves in young and middle adulthood. *Psychology and Aging, 9,* 126–133.

Horton, P. C. (2002). Self-comforting strategies used by adolescents. *Bulletin of the Menninger Clinic, 66,* 259–272.

Huizinga, M., Dolan, C. V., & van der Molen, M. W. (2006). Age-related change in executive function: Developmental trends and a latent variable analysis. *Neuropsychologia, 44,* 2017–2036.

Huttenlocher, P. R. (1999). Dendritic synaptic development in human cerebral cortex: Time course and critical periods. *Developmental Neuropsychology, 16*(3), 347–349.

Jennings, P. A., Aldwin, C. M., Levenson, M. R., Spiro, A., III, & Mroczek, D. (2006). Combat exposure, perceived benefits of military service, and wisdom in later life: Findings from the Normative Aging Study. *Research on Aging, 28,* 115–124.

Jennings, P. A., & Greenberg, M. (2009). The prosocial classroom: Teacher social and emotional competence in relation to student and classroom outcomes. *Review of Educational Research, 79,* 491–525.

Johnson, C. I., & Barer, B. M. (1993). Coping and a sense of control among the oldest old. *Journal of Aging Studies, 7,* 67–80.

Johnson, D. E. (2000). Medical and developmental sequelae of early childhood institutionalization in Eastern European adoptees. *Minnesota Symposia on Child Psychology, 31,* 113–161.

Johnson, M. H. (2001). Functional brain development in humans. *Nature Reviews Neuroscience, 2,* 475–483.

Johnson, N. J., Backlund, E., Sorlie, P. D., & Loveless, C. A. (2000). Marital status and mortality: The National Longitudinal Mortality Study. *Annals of Epidemiology, 10,* 224–238.

Kagan, J., & Fox, N. A. (2006). Biology, culture, and temperamental biases. In N. Eisenberg (Ed.), *Handbook of child psychology: Vol. 3. Social, emotional, and personality development,* (6th ed., pp. 167–225). Editors in chief: W. Damon and R. M. Lerner. Hoboken, NJ: John Wiley & Sons.

Kaufman, A. S. (2001). WAIS III, IQs, Horn's theory, and generational changes from young adulthood to old age. *Intelligence, 29,* 131–167.

Kliewer, W., Sandler, I. N., & Wolchik, S. (1994). Family socialization of threat appraisal and coping: Coaching, modeling, and family context. In K. Hurrelmann & F. Festmann (Eds.), *Social networks and social support in childhood and adolescence* (pp. 271–291). Berlin: Walter de Gruyter.

Kochanska, G. (1995). Children's temperament, mother's discipline, and security of attachment: Multiple pathways to emerging internalization. *Child Development, 66,* 597–615.

Kochanska, G. (2002). Committed compliance, moral self, and internalization: A mediational model. *Developmental Psychology, 38,* 339–351.

Kopp, C. B. (2009). Emotion-focused coping in young children: Self and self-regulatory processes. *New Directions for Child and Adolescent Development, 124,* 33–46.

Kunzmann, U. (this volume). Emotional development across the lifespan. In A. Freund & M. Lamb (Eds.), *Handbook of life-span development.* Hoboken, NJ: John Wiley & Sons.

Labouvie-Vief, G. (2003). Dynamic integration: Affect, cognition, and the self in adulthood. *Current Directions in Psychological Science, 12,* 201–206.

Labouvie-Vief, G., & Diehl, M. (2000). Cognitive complexity and cognitive-affective integration: Related or separate domains of adult development? *Psychology & Aging, 15*, 490–504

Lachman, M. E. (1986). Locus of control in aging research: A case for multidimensional and domain-specific assessment. *Psychology and Aging, 1*, 34–40.

Laux, L., & Weber, H. (1991). Presentation of self in coping with anger and anxiety: An intentional approach. *Anxiety, Stress & Coping, 3*, 233–255.

Lawton, M. P., & Nahemow, L. (1973). Ecology and the aging process. In C. Eisdorfer & M. P. Lawton (Eds.), *Psychology of adult development & aging* (pp. 660–676). Washington, DC: American Psychological Association.

Lazarus, R. S., Averill, J. R., & Opton, E. M., Jr. (1974). The psychology of coping: Issues of research and assessment. In G. V. Coelho, D. A. Hamburg, & J. E. Adams (Eds.), *Coping and adaptation* (pp. 249–315). New York: Basic Books.

Lazarus, R. S., & Folkman, S. (1984). *Stress, appraisal, and coping*. New York: Springer.

LeDoux, J. (2002). *Synaptic self: How our brains become who we are.* New York: Penguin.

Lee, E. K. O., & Brennan, M. (2006). Stress constellations and coping styles of older adults with age-related visual impairment. *Health and Social Work, 31*, 289–298.

Lee-Bagley, D., Preece, M., & DeLongis, A. (2005). Coping with interpersonal stress: Role of Big Five traits. *Journal of Personality, 73*, 1141–1180.

Lerner, R. M., Theokas, C., & Bobek, D. (2005). Concepts and theories of human development: Historical and contemporary dimensions. In M. H. Bornstein & M. E. Lamb (Eds.), *Developmental science: An advanced textbook* (5th ed., pp. 3–43). Mahwah, NJ: Erlbaum.

Levenson, M. R. (2009). Gender differences in moral development and wisdom: The importance of compassion. *Research in Human Development, 6*, 45–59.

Levenson, M. R., Aldwin, C. M., & Cupertino, A. P. (2001). Transcending the self: Towards a liberative model of adult development. In A. L. Neri (Ed.), *Maturidade & Velhice: Um enfoque multidisciplinar* (pp. 99–116). São Paulo, Brazil: Papirus.

Levenson, M. R., & Crumpler, C. A. (1996). Three models of adult psychological development. *Human Development, 39*, 135–194.

Levenson, M. R., Jennings, P. A., Aldwin, C. M., & Shiraishi, R. W. (2005). Self-transcendence, conceptualization and measurement. *International Journal of Aging & Human Development, 60*, 127–143.

Levenson, R. W., Carstensen, L. L., & Gottman, J. M. (1993). Long-term marriage: Age, gender, and satisfaction. *Psychology and Aging, 8*, 301–313.

Lewinsohn, P. M., Rohde, P., & Seeley, J. R. (1994). Psychosocial risk factors for future adolescent suicide attempts. *Journal of Consulting & Clinical Psychology, 62*, 297–305.

Liang J., Bennett, J. M., Krause, N. M., Chang, M. C., Lin, H. S., Chuang, Y. L., & Wu, S. C. Stress, social relations, and old age mortality in Taiwan. *Journal of Clinical Epidemiology, 52*, 983–995.

Little, B. R. (1999). Personality and motivation: Personal action and the conative revolution. In L. A. Pervin & O. P. John (Eds.), *Handbook of personality: Theory and research* (2nd ed., pp. 501–524). New York: Guilford Press.

Little, T., & Geldhof, J. (this volume). Self-control and self-regulation across the lifespan. In A. Freund & M. Lamb (Eds.), *Handbook of life-span development*. Hoboken, NJ: John Wiley & Sons.

Luciano, M., Gow, A. J., Harris, S. E., Hayward, C., Allerhand, M., Starr, J. M., Visscher, P. M., & Deary, I. J. (2009). Cognitive ability at age 11 and 70 years, information processing speed, and APOE variation: The Lothian Birth Cohort 1936 study. *Psychology and Aging, 24*, 129–38.

Luna, B., Garver, K. E., Urban, T. A., Lazar, N. A., & Sweeney, J. A. (2004). Maturation of cognitive processes from late childhood to adulthood. *Child Development, 75*, 1357–1372.

Maes, S., & P. Karoly (2005). Self-regulation assessment and intervention in physical health and illness: A review. *Applied Psychology: An International Review, 54*, 267–299.

Mahmood, A., Yamamoto, T., Lee, M., & Steggell, C. (2008). Use and perception of gerotechnology: Implications for "aging in place." *Journal of Housing for the Elderly, 21*, 104–126.

Marsiske, M., & Margrett, J. A. (2006). Everyday problem solving and decision making. In K. W. Schaie, J. E. Birren, R. P. Abeles, M. Gatz, & T. A. Salthouse (Eds.), *Handbook of the Psychology of Aging* (pp. 315–342). New York: Academic Press.

Mason, J. W. (1975). A historical view of the stress field. *Journal of Human Stress, 1*, 6–27.

McAdams, D. P. (2006). The redemptive self: Generativity and the stories Americans live by. *Research in Human Development, 3*, 81–100.

McAdams, R. R. (this volume). Self and identity across the life span. In A. Freund & M. Lamb (Eds.), *Handbook of life-span development.* Hoboken, NJ: John Wiley & Sons.

McCrae, R. R. (1989). Age differences and changes in the use of coping mechanisms. *Journal of Gerontology: Psychological Sciences, 44*, 161–169.

McCrae, R. R., & Costa, P. T. (1986). Personality, coping, and coping effectiveness in an adult sample. *Journal of Personality, 54*, 385–404.

McCrae, R. R., & Costa, P. T. (1997). Personality trait structure as a human universal. *American Psychologist, 52*, 509–516.

Meeus, W., Branje, S., & Overbeek, G. J. (2004). Parents and partners in crime: A six-year longitudinal study on changes in supportive relationships and delinquency in adolescence and young adulthood. *Journal of Child Psychology and Psychiatry, 45*, 1288–1298.

Metcalfe, J., & Mischel, W. (1999). A hot/cool-system analysis of delay of gratification: Dynamics of willpower. *Psychological Review, 106*, 3–19.

Miller, G. E., Chen, E., & Zhou, E. S. (2007). If it goes up, must it come down? Chronic stress and the hypothalamic-pituitary-adrenocortical axis in humans. *Psychological Bulletin, 133*, 25–45.

Miller, S. (1980). When is a little information a dangerous thing? Coping with stressful events by monitoring vs. blunting. In S. Levine & H. Ursin (Eds.), *Coping and health* (pp. 145–170). New York: Plenum.

Moen, P. (2001). The gendered life course. In R. H. Binstock & L. K. George (Eds.), *Handbook of aging and the social sciences* (5th ed., pp. 179–196). San Diego, CA: Academic Press.

Moffitt, T. E. (1993). Adolescent-limited and life-course-persistent antisocial behavior: A developmental taxonomy. *Psychological Bulletin, 100*, 674–701.

Moos, R. H. (1997). Coping Responses Inventory: A measure of approach and avoidance coping skills. In C. P. Zalaquett and R. J. Wood (Eds.), *Evaluating stress: A book of resources* (pp. 51–65). Lanham, MD: Scarecrow Education.

Morin, C. M., Rodrigue, S., & Ivers, H. (2003). Role of stress, arousal, and coping skills in primary insomnia. *Psychosomatic Medicine, 65*(2), 259–267.

Mortimer, J. T., Harley, C., & Staff, J. (2002). The quality of work and youth mental health. *Work and Occupations, 29*, 166–197.

Mroczek, D. K., Almeida, D. M., Spiro, A., & Pafford, C. (2006). Modeling intraindividual stability and change in personality. In D. K. Mroczek & T. D. Little (Eds.), *Handbook of Personality Development* (pp. 163–180). New York: Routledge.

Murphy, L. B., & Moriarty, A. E. (1976). *Vulnerability, coping and growth from infancy to adolescence.* New Haven, CT: Yale University Press.

National Research Council [NRC] (2000). *From neurons to neighborhoods.* J. P. Shonkoff & D. Phillips, Eds. Washington, DC: National Academies Press.

Nieder, T., & Seiffge-Krenke, I. (2001). Coping with stress in different phases of romantic development. *Journal of Adolescence, 24,* 297–311.

Nolen-Hoeksema, S. (2000). The role of rumination in depressive disorders and mixed anxiety/depressive symptoms. *Journal of Abnormal Psychology, 109,* 504–511.

Pargament, K. I., Koenig, H. G., & Perez, L. M. (2000). The many methods of religious coping: development and initial validation of the RCOPE. *Journal of Clinical Psychology, 56,* 519–543.

Park, C. L. (2005). Religion as a meaning-making framework in coping with life stress. *Journal of Social Issues, 61,* 707–729.

Parker, R., & Aldwin, C. M. (1997). Do aspects of gender identity change from early to middle adulthood? Disentangling age, cohort, and period effects. In M. Lachman & J. James (Eds.), *Multiple paths of mid-life development* (pp. 67–107). Chicago: University of Chicago Press.

Paus, T., Collins, D. L., Evans, A. C., Leonard, G., Pike, B., & Zijdenbos, A. (2001). Maturation of white matter in the human brain: A review of magnetic resonance studies. *Brain Research Bulletin, 54,* 255–266.

Pearlin, L. I., Nguyen, K. B., Schieman, S., & Milkie, M. A. (2007). The life-course origins of mastery among older people. *Journal of Health and Social Behavior, 48,* 164–179.

Penley, J. A., Tomaka, J., & Wiebe, J. S. (2002). The association of coping to physical and psychological health outcomes: A meta-analytic review. *Journal of Behavioral Medicine, 25,* 551–603.

Perosa, S. L., & Perosa, L. M. (1993). Relationships among Minuchin's Structural Family Model, identity achievement, and coping style. *Journal of Consulting Psychology, 40,* 479–489.

Pinquart, M., & Sorensen, S. (2007). Correlates of physical health of informal caregivers: A meta-analysis. *Journals of Gerontology Series B: Psychological Sciences and Social Sciences, 62,* P126–P137.

Plancherel, B., & Bolognini, M. (1995). Coping and mental health in early adolescence. *Journal of Adolescence*. Special Issue, Adolescent research: A European perspective, *18,* 459–474.

Pollitt, E., Golub, M., Gorman, K., Grantham-McGregor, S., Levitsky, D., Schurch, B., Strupp, B., & Wachs, T. (1996). A reconceptualization of the effects of undernutrition on children's biological, psychosocial, and behavioral development. *SRCD Policy Report, 10,* 1–21.

Pomerantz, E. M., Moorman, E. A., & Litwack, S. D. (2007). The how, whom, and why of parents' involvement in children's academic lives: More is not always better. *Review of Educational Research, 77,* 373–410.

Revenson, T. A., & Pranikoff, J. R. (2005). A contextual approach to treatment decision making among breast cancer survivors. *Health Psychology, 24,* S93–S98.

Roberts, B. W., Caspi, A., & Moffitt, T. E. (2001). The kids are alright: Growth and stability in personality development from adolescence to adulthood. *Journal of Personality and Social Psychology, 81,* 670–683.

Roberts, B. W., Caspi, A., & Moffitt, T. E. (2003). Work experiences and personality development in young adulthood. *Journal of Personality and Social Psychology, 84,* 582–593.

Roberts, B. W., & DelVecchio, W. F. (2000). The rank-order consistency of personality traits from childhood to old age: A quantitative review of longitudinal studies. *Psychological Bulletin, 126,* 3–25.

Roberts, B. W., Walton, K. E., & Viechtbauer, W. (2006). Patterns of mean-level change in personality traits across the life course: A meta-analysis of longitudinal studies. *Psychological Bulletin, 132,* 1–25.

Robins, R. W., Caspi, A., & Moffitt, T. E. (2002). It's not just who you're with, it's who you are: Personality and relationship experiences across multiple relationships. *Journal of Personality, 70,* 925–964.

Robles, T. F., Glaser, R., & Kiecolt-Glaser, J. K. (2005). Out of balance: A new look at chronic stress, depression, and immunity. *Current Directions in Psychological Science, 14,* 111–115.

Rothbart, M. K., & Bates, J. E. (2006). Temperament. In N. Eisenberg (Ed.), *Handbook of child psychology: Vol. 3. Social, emotional, and personality development* (6th ed., pp. 99–166). Editors in chief: W. Damon and R. M. Lerner. Hoboken, NJ: John Wiley & Sons.

Rothermund, K., & Brandtstädter, J. (2003). Coping with deficits and losses in later life: From compensatory action to accommodation. *Psychology and Aging, 18,* 896–905.

Rueda, M. R., & Rothbart, M. K. (2009). The influence of temperament on the development of coping: The role of maturation and experience. *New Directions for Child and Adolescent Development, 124,* 19–31.

Rueter, M. A., & Kwon, H.-K. (2005). Developmental trends in adolescent suicidal ideation. *Journal of Research on Adolescence, 15,* 205–222.

Rutter, M. (2002). Nature, nurture and development: From evangelism through science toward policy and practice. *Child Development, 73,* 1–21.

Ryan, R. M., & Deci, E. L. (2006). Self-regulation and the problem of human autonomy: Does psychology need choice, self-determination, and will? *Journal of Personality, 74,* 1557–1585.

Ryan, R. M., Deci, E. L., Grolnick, W. S., & La Guardia, J. G. (2006). The significance of autonomy and autonomy support in psychological development and psychopathology. In D. Cicchetti & D. J. Cohen (Eds.), *Developmental Psychopathology: Vol 1. Theory and Method* (2nd ed., pp. 795–849). Hoboken, NJ: John Wiley & Sons.

Ryff, C. D. (1991). Possible selves in adulthood and old age: A tale of shifting horizons. *Psychology and Aging, 6,* 286–295.

Salthouse, T. A. (1988). Cognitive aspects of motor functioning. *Annals of the New York Academy of Sciences, 515,* 33–41.

Salthouse, T. A., & Davis, H. P. (2006). Organization of cognitive abilities and neuropsychological variables across the lifespan. *Developmental Review, 26,* 31–54.

Sansone, C., & Berg, C. (1993). Adapting to the environment across the life span: Different process or different inputs? *International Journal of Behavioral Development, 16,* 215–241.

Sapolsky, R. M. (1996). Why stress is bad for your brain. *Science, 273,* 749–750.

Sapolsky, R. M. (1998). *Why zebras don't get ulcers: An updated guide to stress, stress-related diseases, and coping.* New York: W. H. Freeman.

Schaie, K. W. (1996). *Intellectual development in adulthood: The Seattle Longitudinal Study.* New York: Cambridge University Press.

Schaie, K. W. (2000). The impact of longitudinal studies on understanding development from young adulthood to old age. *International Journal of Behavioral Development 24,* 257–266.

Schantz, C. U. (1987). Conflicts between children. *Child Development, 58,* 283–305.

Schulz, R., & Heckhausen, J. (1998). Emotion and control: A life-span perspective. In K. W. Schaie & M. P. Lawton (Eds.), *Annual review of gerontology and geriatrics: Vol. 17. Focus on emotion and adult development* (pp. 185–205). New York: Springer.

Schwarzer, R., & Knoll, N. (2003). Positive coping: Mastering demands and searching for meaning. In S. J. Lopez & C. R. Snyder (Eds.), *Positive psychological assessment: A handbook of models and measures* (pp. 393–409). Washington, DC: American Psychological Association.

Segerstrom, S. C., & Miller, G. E. (2004). Psychological stress and the human immune system: A meta-analytic study of 30 years of inquiry. *Psychological Bulletin, 130*, 601–630.

Seiffge-Krenke, I. (2006). Coping with relationship stressors: The impact of different working models of attachment and links to adaptation. *Journal of Youth and Adolescence, 35*, 25–39.

Shanahan, M. J., & Bauer, D. J. (2004). Developmental properties of transactional models: The case of life events and mastery from adolescence to young adulthood. *Development and Psychopathology*. Special Issue: Transition from Adolescence to Adulthood, *16*, 1095–1117.

Sherod, M. G., Griffith, H. R., Copeland, J., Belue, K., Krzywanski, S., Zamrini, E. Y., Harrell, L. E., Clark, D. G., Brockington, J. C., Powers, R. E., Marson, D. C. (2009). Neurocognitive predictors of financial capacity across the dementia spectrum: Normal aging, mild cognitive impairment, and Alzheimer's disease. *Journal of the International Neuropsychological Society*, *15*, 258–67.

Shiner, R., & Caspi, A. (2003). Personality differences in childhood and adolescence: Measurement, development, and consequences. *Journal of Child Psychology and Psychiatry, 44*, 2–32.

Shiraishi, R. W., Aldwin, C. M., & Widaman, K. F. (under review). Change and stability in the factor structure of coping in young adulthood and midlife: Longitudinal findings from the Davis Longitudinal Study.

Shonkoff, J. P. (2006). A promising opportunity for developmental and behavioral pediatrics at the interface of neuroscience, psychology, and social policy: Remarks on receiving the 2005 C. Anderson Aldrich Award. *Pediatrics, 118*, 2187.

Siegel, D. (1999). *The developing mind: Toward a neurobiology of interpersonal experience.* New York: Guilford Press.

Skaff, M. (2007). Sense of control and health: A dynamic duo in the aging process. In C. M. Aldwin, C. L. Park, & A. Spiro, III (Eds.), *Handbook of Health Psychology and Aging* (pp. 186–209). New York: Guilford Press.

Skinner, E., & Edge, K. (1998). Reflections on coping and development across the lifespan. *International Journal of Behavioral Development, 22*, 357–366.

Skinner, E. A., Edge, K., Altman, J., & Sherwood, H. (2003). Searching for the structure of coping: A review and critique of category systems for classifying ways of coping. *Psychological Bulletin, 129*, 216–269.

Skinner, E., Furrer, C., Marchand, G., & Kindermann, T. (2008). Engagement and disaffection in the classroom: Part of a larger motivational dynamic? *Journal of Educational Psychology, 100*, 765–781.

Skinner, E. A., & Wellborn, J. G. (1994). Coping during childhood and adolescence: A motivational perspective. In R. M. Lerner, D. Featherman, & M. Perlmuter (Eds.), *Life-span development and behavior: Vol. 12* (pp. 91–123). Hillsdale, NJ: Erlbaum.

Skinner, E. A., Wellborn, J. G., & Connell, J. P. (1990). What it takes to do well in school and whether I've got it: A process model of perceived control and children's engagement and achievement in school. *Journal of Educational Psychology, 82*, 22–32.

Skinner, E. A., & Zimmer-Gembeck, M. J. (2007). The development of coping. *Annual Review of Psychology, 58*, 119–144.

Skinner, E. A., & Zimmer-Gembeck, M. J. (2009). Challenges to the developmental study of coping. *New Directions in child and adolescent development*, *124*, 5–17.

Slomkowski, C., Rende, R., Conger, K. J., Simons, R. L., & Conger, R. D. (2001). Sisters, brothers, and delinquency: Evaluating social influence during early and middle adolescence. *Child Development, 72*, 271–283.

Smith, D., & Tillipman, H. (2000). *The older population in the United States* (U.S. Census Bureau, P250–P532). Washington, DC: U.S. Department of Commerce, Economics and Statistics Administration.

Spears, L. P. (2000). The adolescent brain and age-related behavioral manifestations. *Neuroscience and Biobehavioral Review,* 24, 417–463.

Spilsbury, J. C. (2005). Children's perceptions of the social support of neighborhood institutions and establishments. *Human Organization, 64*, 126–134.

Spirito, A., Stark, L. J., Grace, N., & Stamoulis, D. (1991). Common problems and coping strategies reported in childhood and early adolescence. *Journal of Youth and Adolescence, 20,* 531–544.

Spiro, A., III, & Brady, C. (2008). Integrating health into cognitive aging research and theory: Quo vadis? In S. Hofer & D. Alwin (Eds.), *Handbook of cognitive aging: Interdisciplinary perspectives* (pp. 260–283). Los Angeles: Sage.

Stansfeld, S., & Candy, B. (2006). Psychosocial work environment and mental health: A meta-analytic review. *Scandinavian Journal of Work, Environment & Health, 32*, 443–462.

Stanton, A. L., Danoff-Burg, S., Cameron, C. L., & Ellis, A. P. (1994). Coping through emotional approach: Problems of conceptualization and confounding. *Journal of Personality & Social Psychology*, *66*, 350–362.

Steinberg, L. (2005). Cognitive and affective development in adolescence. *Trends in Cognitive Sciences*, *9*, 69–74.

Stroebe, M., & Schut, H. (1999). The dual process model of coping with bereavement: Rationale and description. *Death Studies, 23*, 197–224.

Stroebe, M., Schut, H., & Stroebe, W. (2005). Attachment in coping with bereavement: A theoretical integration. *Review of General Psychology, 9*, 48–66.

Stroebe, M., Schut, H., & Stroebe, W. (2006). Who benefits from disclosure? Exploration of attachment style differences in the effects of expressing emotions. *Clinical Psychology Review, 26*, 66–85.

Subramanian, S. V., Kubzansky, L., Berkman, L., Fay, M., & Kawachi, I. (2006). Neighborhood effects on the self-rated health of elders: Uncovering the relative importance of structural and service-related neighborhood environments. *Journals of Gerontology Series B: Psychological Sciences and Social Sciences, 61*, 153–160.

Suls, J., & David, J. P. (1996). Coping and personality: Third time's the charm? *Journal of Personality*, *64*, 993–1005.

Suls, J., & Martin, R. M. (2005). The daily life of the garden variety neurotic: Reactivity, stressor exposure, mood spillover, and maladaptive coping. *Journal of Personality 73*, 1–25.

Taylor, S. E., Lichtman, R. R., & Wood, J. V. (1984). Attributions, beliefs about control, and adjustment to breast cancer. *Journal of Personality and Social Psychology, 46,* 489–502.

Thelen, E., & Smith, L. B. (1998). Dynamic systems theories. In R. M. Lerner (Ed.), *Handbook of child psychology: Vol. 1. Theoretical models of human development* (5th ed., pp. 563–634). Editor in chief: W. Damon. New York: John Wiley & Sons.

Thoits, P. A. (1984). Coping, social support, and psychological outcomes: The central role of emotion. *Review of Personality & Social Psychology, 5*, 219–238.

Thoits, P. A. (1986). Social support as coping assistance. *Journal of Consulting and Clinical Psychology, 54,* 416–423.

Thompson, R. A. (1994). Emotion regulation: A theme in search of definition. *Monographs of the Society for Child Development, 59,* 25–52.

Thornton, W. J., & Dumke, H. A. (2005). Age differences in everyday problem-solving and decision-making effectiveness: A meta-analytic review. *Psychology and Aging, 20*, 85–99.

Vaillant, G. (1977). *Adaptation to life: How the best and the brightest came of age.* Boston: Little Brown.

Vaillant, G. (2002). *Aging well: Surprising guideposts to a happier life from the landmark Harvard Study of Adult Development.* Boston: Little, Brown.

Vaillant, G. E. (1993). *The wisdom of the ego.* Cambridge, MA: Harvard University Press.

Vaillant, G. E., Bond, M., & Vaillant, C. O. (1986). An empirically validated hierarchy of defense mechanisms. *Archives of General Psychiatry, 43,* 786–794.

Vitaliano, P. P., Zhang, J., & Scanlan, J. M. (2003). Is caregiving hazardous to one's physical health? A meta-analysis. *Psychological Bulletin, 129*, 946–972.

Wadsworth, M. E., Gudmundsen, G. R., Raviv, T., Ahlkvist, J. A., McIntosh, D. N., Kline, G. H., et al. (2004). Coping with terrorism: Age and gender differences in effortful and involuntary responses to September 11th. *Applied Developmental Science, 8*, 143–157.

Wallerstein, J. S., & Kelly, J. B. (1980). *Surviving the breakup: How children and parents cope with divorce.* New York: Basic Books.

Welsh, M. C., Pennington, B. F., & Groisser, D. B. (1991). A normative-developmental study of executive function: A window on prefontal function in children. *Developmental Neuropsychology, 7*, 131–149.

Wentura, D., Rothermund, K., & Brandtstädter, J. (1995). Experimental studies on the processing of negative information: Differential and age-related aspects/ Experimentelle Analysen zur Verarbeitung belastender Informationen: differential- und alternspsychologische Aspekte. *Zeitschrift Fur Experimentelle Psychologie, 42,* 152–175.

Werner, E. E., & Smith, R. S. (1992). *Overcoming the odds.* Ithaca, NY: Cornell University Press.

Wertlieb, D., Weigel, C., & Feldstein, M. (1987). Measuring children's coping. *Journal of Orthopsychiatry, 57,* 548–560.

Whitty, M. T. (2003). Coping and defending: Age differences in maturity of defense mechanisms and coping strategies. *Aging & Mental Health, 7*, 123–132.

Wigfield, A., Eccles, J. S., Schiefele, U., Roeser, R. W., & Davis-Kean, P. (2006). Development of achievement motivation. In N. Eisenberg (Ed.), *Handbook of child psychology: Vol. 3. Social, emotional, and personality development* (6th ed., pp. 933–1002). Editors in chief: W. Damon and R. M. Lerner. Hoboken, NJ: John Wiley & Sons.

Williams-Piehota, P., Pizarro, J., Schneider, T. R., Mowad, L., & Salovey, P. (2005). Matching health messages to monitor-blunter coping styles to motivate screening mammography. *Health Psychology, 24*, 58–67.

Wills, T. A., Sandy, J. M., Yaeger, A. M., Cleary, S. D., & Shinar, O. (2001). Coping dimensions, life stress, and adolescent substance use: A latent growth analysis. *Journal of Abnormal Psychology, 110*, 309–323.

Winsborough, H. H., Bumpass, L. L., & Aquilino, W. S. (1991). *The death of parents and the transition to old age*. National Survey of Families and Households Working Paper No. 39. Madison: University of Wisconsin, Center for Demography and Ecology.

Wolfradt, U., Hempel, S., & Miles, J. N. V. (2003). Perceived parenting styles, depersonalisation, anxiety and coping behavior in adolescents. *Personality & Individual Differences, 34*, 521–532.

Wortman, C. B., & Silver, R. C. (1989). The myths of coping with loss. *Journal of Consulting and Clinical Psychology, 57*, 349–357.

Zeidner, M., & Saklofske, D. (1996). Adaptive and maladaptive coping. In M. Zeidner & N. S. Endler (Eds.), *Handbook of coping: Theory, research, applications* (pp. 505–531). Oxford, UK: John Wiley & Sons.

Zimmer-Gembeck, M. J., & Locke, E. M. (2007). The socialization of adolescent coping behaviours: Relationships with families and teachers. *Journal of Adolescence, 30*, 1–16.

Zuckerman, M., Knee, C. R., Kieffer, S. C., Rawsthorne, L., & Bruce, L. M. (1996). Beliefs in realistic and unrealistic control: Assessment and implications. *Journal of Personality*, *64*, 435–464.

CHAPTER 10

Gendered Behavior across the Life Span

MELISSA HINES

Sex is an important social category, and, both socially and physiologically, the sexing of a baby begins before birth. Socially, expectant parents often prepare differently for a child based on its anticipated sex. Possible names are selected from largely separate pools (girls' names or boys' names), and clothes and nursery furnishings with different characteristics are selected based on the child's anticipated gender. Physiologically, sex determination begins even earlier, at conception, when the ovum is fertilized by a sperm carrying either an X or a Y chromosome. Hormones from the gonads, particularly the male testes, also play a role in neural and behavioral sexual differentiation. These hormones direct physical development, producing not only the differing genitalia that define the baby's sex at birth, but also influencing some aspects of neural architecture and function. The sexing process continues postnatally as well, again both socially and physiologically. This chapter will begin at conception, and describe the prenatal processes that lead to physical development in a male-typical or female-typical direction, and the prenatal and postnatal processes that lead to male-typical and female-typical behavior. The aim will be to elucidate not only the causes of differences between the sexes, but also the causes of differences within each sex. The chapter will thus address questions regarding differences between males and females, as well as questions as to why some males and some females are more sex-typical than others.

GENDER DEVELOPMENT BEFORE BIRTH: EARLY HORMONAL INFLUENCES

Much of physical sexual differentiation is accomplished by gonadal hormones, particularly testosterone. The male gonads, the testes, produce large amounts of testosterone and other androgens beginning at about the eighth week of gestation, whereas the fetal ovaries do not appear to produce large amounts of hormones before birth. As a consequence, male fetuses are exposed to higher levels of testosterone than are female fetuses (Wilson, George, & Griffin, 1981). Testosterone, and another androgen produced from it, called dihydrotestosterone (DHT), stimulate androgen receptors on the external genital structures and cause their masculinization, resulting in an infant with a penis and scrotum. In the absence of androgens, androgen receptors are not activated and the same structures differentiate in the female pattern, producing an infant with a clitoris and labia. Internally too, testicular hormones are responsible for male-typical development. Both male and female fetuses begin with two sets of structures, Mullerian ducts and Wolffian ducts. A substance from the testes, called Mullerian inhibiting factor, causes the Mullerian ducts to regress, while testosterone causes the Wolffian ducts to differentiate in the male pattern, as epidydimus, vas deferens, seminal vesicles, and ejaculatory ducts. In the absence of testicular hormones, the Wolffian ducts regress, and the Mullerian ducts differentiate in the female pattern, as oviducts, uterus, and upper vagina.

Receptors for testosterone and other gonadal hormones are located in some brain regions, as well as in the genitalia, and experimental research with rodents and non-human primates shows that gonadal hormones play an important role in the development of these brain regions, and therefore exert permanent influences on behavior across the life span (Goy & McEwen, 1980). For instance, female rodents exposed to testosterone during early development show male-typical sexual behavior, but not female-typical sexual behavior, in adulthood. Similarly, castration of male animals early in life produces adults who can show female-typical, but not male-typical, sexual behavior. Early hormone manipulations also produce permanent changes in brain structure. Perhaps the best-known example involves a group of cells in the anterior hypothalamus, called the sexually dimorphic nucleus of the pre-optic area (SDN-POA). This nucleus is several times larger in male than in female rats (Gorski, Gordon, Shryne, & Southam, 1978; Gorski et al., 1980), and treating females with testicular hormones during early development enlarges the nucleus, while withdrawing these hormones from developing males reduces its volume (Gorski, Gordon, Shryne, & Southam, 1978; Jacobson et al., 1981).

In contrast to the dramatic effects produced by manipulating testicular hormones, removal of the ovaries at comparable early stages of development generally has little or no impact on male-typical or female-typical behavior or on the SDN-POA (Goy & McEwen, 1980; Jacobson et al., 1981). In addition, treating genetically female (XX) rodents with estrogens during early development can have similar influences to treatment with testosterone, promoting male-typical behavioral and brain development, including development of the SDN-POA, and impairing female-typical behavior (Goy & McEwen, 1980; MacLusky & Naftolin, 1981). These outcomes originally were considered to be paradoxical, because in adult animals estrogens are produced by the female gonads, the ovaries, and have feminizing effects. During early development, however, testosterone is converted within the brain to estrogen before interacting with receptors to produce male-typical development, at least in regard to many brain regions and behaviors in rodents.

Much of the research showing influences of testosterone and other gonadal hormones on brain development and behavior has involved rodents, but similar evidence has come from dogs, sheep, and non-human primates. In rhesus monkeys, for example, treating pregnant animals with testosterone produces female offspring who resemble males behaviorally. As juveniles, they show increased male-typical, rough-and-tumble play, and reduced female-typical grooming of their mothers; as adults, they show increased male-typical, and reduced female-typical, sexual behavior (Goy, 1978; Goy & McEwen, 1980; Goy, Bercovitch, & McBrair, 1988).

In general, these early programming influences of testicular hormones occur during critical or sensitive periods of prenatal or neonatal development, meaning that the hormone must be present at a specific time to have its permanent effect. The timing of these critical periods varies somewhat across species, but they appear to correspond to times when testosterone concentrations are higher in developing males than females. In the rat, such periods extend from about the 17th to the 19th day of an approximately 21-day gestation and from about the first to the 10th day postnatally. In addition, within this overall critical period, there are sub-periods when specific characteristics are most sensitive to hormonal influences. For instance, in rhesus monkeys, testosterone influences juvenile mounting and rough-and-tumble play at different times. Exposure only early in gestation (days 40 to 64) produces females who resemble males in showing low levels of maternal grooming, but not in showing high levels of rough-and-tumble play. In contrast, exposure only late in gestation (days 115 to 139) produces females who show increased male-typical rough-and-tumble play, but also high levels of female-typical maternal grooming (Goy, Bercovitch, & McBrair, 1988). Similarly, in rats, hormone exposure on the second postnatal day has maximal influence on female-typical sexual behavior, whereas exposure on the fifth postnatal day has maximal influence on male-typical sexual behavior (Christensen & Gorski, 1978). One implication of this difference in the timing of influences is that brief perturbations in hormones could affect development of particular brain regions and behaviors without influencing others (Collaer & Hines, 1995).

Hormonal influences are graded, and so when more hormone is administered there is a more dramatic effect (Collaer & Hines, 1995). Also, hormones influence not only behavioral differences between the sexes, but also differences within each sex, with naturally occurring variation in hormones relating to naturally occurring variation in behavior. For example, some female rats show male-typical sexual behavior whereas others do not. Females who were exposed prenatally to blood that has contacted male littermates (because of their position relative to these males in utero) are more likely to show male-typical behavior as adults than those who were not so positioned (Meisel & Ward, 1981). Studies in other rodents, including mice and gerbils, show similar outcomes (Clark & Galef, Jr., 1998). In support of testosterone as the responsible agent, gerbil fetuses positioned between two males have higher levels of testosterone than those positioned between two females (Clark, Crews, & Galef, 1991).

Summary for Early Hormonal Influences on Sex-Related Neural and Behavioral Development in Mammals

Research on gonadal hormones and sexual differentiation of brain and behavior in non-human mammals leads to several general conclusions (Hines, 2004). First, exposure to testosterone during early critical periods promotes male-typical development of brain and behavior. Second, estrogen is not needed to produce female-typical development during these early periods. Instead, exposure to high levels of estrogen at these times can promote male-typical development. Third, the effects of exposure to testosterone and its metabolites are linear and graded—the more hormone, the larger the effect. Fourth, naturally occurring variations in hormones during early development can influence sex-related behavior within each sex, helping to explain why some individuals are more or less sex-typical than others. Fifth, the behaviors influenced by the early hormone environment are those that show sex differences, and the brain regions influenced are those that have receptors for testosterone and hormones produced from it. Many of these brain regions also show sex differences. Therefore, testosterone and hormones produced from it are thought to exert permanent influences on behavior by influencing the development of these brain structures during early critical periods of life. Sixth, because different brain regions develop at different times, and different behaviors have different specific neural underpinnings, sexual differentiation is a multidimensional process, and individuals can show inconsistent combinations of male-typical and female-typical characteristics.

Early Hormones and Human Development

When are the critical periods when hormones could influence human brain development and behavior? As noted above, these periods are likely to correspond to times when testosterone is higher in developing males than females. For humans, one such period begins at about week 8 of gestation, when the fetal testes begin to produce testosterone. Testosterone production appears to taper off later in gestation. Information on testosterone levels in human fetuses is hard to obtain, but the available data from fetal blood samples suggests that the period of maximum difference between males and females extends from about week 8 to week 24 of gestation (Reyes, Winter, & Faiman, 1973; Smail, Reyes, Winter, & Faiman, 1981). Data from amniotic fluid samples also show higher testosterone in males at weeks 15 to 21 of gestation than at weeks 36 to 40, producing a sex difference at the earlier, but not the later, time (Carson et al., 1982).

If hormones work in humans as they do in other mammals, infants may be born with different proclivities toward male-typical and female-typical behavior, depending on their hormone environment prenatally. It is difficult to evaluate this possibility experimentally in human beings, because ethical considerations generally preclude the kinds of manipulations conducted in other species. However, researchers have found several sources of information. These include studies of individuals with genetic disorders that cause unusual hormone environments during early development, and individuals whose mothers were prescribed hormones during pregnancy, as well as studies relating normal variability in hormones during early development to normal variability in subsequent behavior. Such studies suggest that the early hormone environment contributes to sex differences, as well as to individual differences within each sex, in several areas. Androgenic influences on the toy, playmate, and activity preferences associated with girls or boys are well established, and provide a good example of how prenatal dispositions, as well as postnatal socialization and cognitive development, combine to produce behavioral differences between girls and boys, as well as between individual children within each sex. Because these sex differences also occur early in the life span, this chapter begins by discussing these childhood sex differences and the factors that influence them and then moves on to discuss other gender-related behaviors.

SEX DIFFERENCES IN HUMAN BEHAVIOR

Before beginning a detailed discussion of factors influencing gendered behavior across the life span it is useful to define what is meant by gendered behavior. For the purposes of this chapter, gendered behavior is behavior that differs on the average for males and females, and saying that a behavior is gendered is equivalent to saying that is shows a sex, or gender, difference. Meta-analyses, reviews that combine the results of many studies to get an idea of the size of group differences, have led to the conclusion that men and women are largely similar behaviorally and psychologically (Hyde, 2005). At the same time, there are some average differences between the sexes (Hines, 2004; Hyde, 2005; Maccoby & Jacklin, 1974). This chapter will detail these differences, and summarize and critically evaluate the evidence regarding their causes. Some material in this chapter is also covered in Hines (2004, 2009a, in press).

When behavioral scientists say that a characteristic shows a sex or gender difference they mean that men and women, or girls and boys, differ on the average. On the average implies that there is overlap between the sexes. This is the case for all behavioral sex differences, although the overlap is more dramatic for some characteristics than for others. In the following sections, the size of each sex difference will be highlighted at the beginning of its discussion, using the metric of standard deviation units ("d" where d = the mean for males minus the mean for females divided by the pooled or average standard deviation) (Cohen, 1988). The sex difference in height provides a familiar comparison for the size of psychological sex differences. The sex difference in height is about 2.0 d both in the United Kingdom and the United States (International Committee on Radiological Protection, 1975; Tanner, Whitehouse, & Takaishi, 1966). Most psychological or behavioral sex differences are smaller than the sex difference in height. In general, behavioral sex differences are viewed as large if they are 0.8 d or greater, moderate if they are in the range of 0.5 d, small if they are about 0.2 d and negligible below 0.2 d (Cohen, 1988).

GENDERED BEHAVIOR IN CHILDHOOD

Girls and boys differ on the average in their preferences for particular toys, in their preferences for girls versus boys as playmates and in their interest in certain activities, such as rough-and-tumble play (Hines, 2004). In the case of toys, boys prefer vehicles and weapons, whereas girls prefer dolls and tea sets (Maccoby & Jacklin, 1974; Pasterski et al., 2005; Sutton-Smith, Rosenberg, & Morgan, 1963). Sex differences in toy preferences appear early in life, by the age of 12 months (Snow, Jacklin, & Maccoby, 1983), and grow larger as childhood progresses (Golombok & Hines, 2002). In addition to changing with age, the size of the sex differences can differ with the mode of assessment (e.g., questionnaire vs. direct observation) and the specific toys compared. However, sex differences in toy preferences can be large (d > 0.80) (Alexander & Hines, 1994; Berenbaum & Hines, 1992; Pasterski et al., 2005; Sutton-Smith, Rosenberg, & Morgan, 1963). In regard to playmate preferences, children tend to sex segregate with approximately 80 to 90% of play partners being of the same sex (Hines & Kaufman, 1994; Maccoby, 1988). As for toy preferences, this sex difference becomes larger as childhood progresses. At age 4.5 years, children spend about three times as much time with peers of the same than the other sex, whereas by age 6.5 years they spend about 10 times as much time with the same-sex peers (Maccoby & Jacklin, 1987). Regarding other interests, boys are more physically active than girls and engage in more rough, active play, including rough-and-tumble interactions that involve playful aggression and overall body contact. Meta-analytic findings suggest that the sex difference in activity level begins prenatally and is of moderate size (d = about 0.5) (Eaton & Enns, 1986). Individual studies suggest that the sex difference in rough-and-tumble play also is of moderate size (DiPietro, 1981; Hines & Kaufman, 1994; Maccoby, 1988). Composite measures that include toy, activity, and playmate preferences, along with personality dimensions that differ by sex, can show large sex differences (d > 2.5) (Hines et al., 2002a; Hines et al., 2002b). To put this difference in a familiar context, it is larger than the sex difference in height (d = 2.0).

There is evidence that many different factors, including the early hormone environment, socialization by parents, peers and others, and the child's own increasing cognitive understanding of gender contribute to these sex-linked childhood behaviors, and the following section of this chapter summarizes this evidence.

Hormones and Gendered Behavior in Childhood

Evidence of hormonal influence comes from studies of children with genetic disorders that cause abnormal hormone environments during gestation and children whose mothers took prescription hormones during pregnancy, as well as from studies relating normal variability in hormones prenatally to normal variability in behavior postnatally. Evidence for inborn influences on sex-typical toy preferences also comes from studies of non-human primates.

Classical congenital adrenal hyperplasia (CAH) is the genetic condition that has been studied most extensively in the attempt to determine if gonadal hormones influence sexual differentiation of human behavior. Classical CAH is an autosomal recessive disorder of sexual development (DSD) that causes overproduction of testosterone and other androgens beginning early in gestation. It involves an enzymatic deficiency, typically of 21-hydroxylase (21-OH), causing an inability to produce cortisol and the consequent overproduction of adrenal androgens. The incidence of classical CAH caused by 21-OH deficiency in Europe and the United States is estimated at 1 in 5,000 to 1 in 15,000 births (New, 1998). Androgen levels in female fetuses with classical CAH are markedly elevated (Pang et al., 1980; Wudy et al., 1999a), and girls with the disorder typically are born with some degree of genital virilization (e.g., clitoral hypertrophy, labial fusion), caused by the prenatal androgen exposure. In rare cases the virilization is so severe that the girls are mistaken for, and assigned and reared as, boys (Money & Daléry, 1976). Generally, however, affected girls are born with partial labial fusion and clitoral hypertrophy, leading to diagnosis near the time of birth, and female sex assignment. They then are treated with hormones to regulate cortisol, androgens, and other hormones postnatally, and their genitalia often are feminized surgically. There are different forms of CAH, and the different forms are associated with differences in the degree of androgen abnormality. The most severe form is classical, salt-losing CAH, followed by classical, simple-virilizing CAH, and then late-onset CAH. Late-onset CAH is thought to involve only postnatal androgen elevation, whereas both classical forms involve prenatal hormone perturbation.

Girls, rather than boys, with CAH have been the main focus of psychological research, because they are exposed to high levels of hormones hypothesized to increase male-typical behavior. Male fetuses with CAH appear to experience elevated levels of a weak androgen, androstenedione, but their testosterone levels appear to be within the normal male range, at least at mid-gestation when they have been studied (Pang et al., 1980; Wudy et al., 1999a). Assumedly, adrenal androgens are elevated initially, with feedback mechanisms reducing subsequent testicular androgen production, resulting in the near normal levels observed in mid-pregnancy. Boys with CAH are born with normal-appearing male genitalia and, in areas without universal screening at birth, CAH is usually detected in boys because of salt-losing crises caused by aldosterone deficiency. Diagnosis typically occurs within a few weeks of birth, but in some cases affected boys are not identified until elevated adrenal androgens induce precocious puberty in early childhood. Because girls with CAH are usually diagnosed based on their virilized genitalia at birth, they are less likely to experience salt-losing crises or precocious puberty. Improved screening at birth is also decreasing salt-losing crises and precocious puberty in boys with CAH.

Several independent research groups have found that girls with CAH show increased interest in male-typical toys, activities, and playmates, and reduced interest in female-typical toys, activities, and playmates. These findings have been reported based on interview and questionnaire assessments, as well as direct observation of toy choices in playroom settings (Berenbaum & Hines, 1992; Nordenstrom et al., 2002; Pasterski et al., 2005; Dittmann et al., 1990; Ehrhardt, Epstein, & Money, 1968; Ehrhardt & Baker, 1974). Consistent findings have been reported in the United States, Canada, Germany, the Netherlands, and Sweden, and girls with CAH have been found to differ from matched controls as well as from female relatives (sisters and cousins) who do not have CAH (Hines, 2004). The amount of male-typical behavior shown by girls with CAH correlates with the severity of their disorder (Nordenstrom et al., 2002), and with the degree of genital virilization at birth (Hall et al., 2004), strengthening the argument that androgens are the responsible agents. Convergent evidence that the effect is caused by androgen exposure, rather than other aspects of CAH, comes from studies of girls whose mothers were prescribed hormones during pregnancy for medical reasons. Girls whose mothers took androgenic progestins during pregnancy resemble girls with CAH in showing high levels of male-typical play behavior (Ehrhardt & Money, 1967), and girls whose mothers took the anti-androgen, medroxyprogesterone acetate (MPA), show the opposite outcome, reduced male-typical and increased female-typical play (Ehrhardt, Grisanti, & Meyer-Bahlburg, 1977). These findings of behavioral change in healthy offspring following hormone treatment during pregnancy argue against the possibility that the behavioral changes in girls with CAH result from non-hormonal consequences of the genetic disorder or from postnatal androgen abnormality.

Although research on rodents shows that some masculinizing influences of androgen are exerted following its conversion to estrogen, this does not seem to be the case for hormonal influences on sex-typical play in children. Interviews and questionnaires have been used to assess childhood activities retrospectively in women whose mothers took a synthetic estrogen, diethylstilbestrol (DES), during pregnancy, and in a variety of control groups, with no consistent group differences seen (Ehrhardt et al., 1989; Lish et al., 1991; Lish et al., 1992). Thus, hormonal influences on the development of childhood play behavior in humans appear to be exerted directly by androgens, rather than following conversion to estrogen.

It has been suggested that the genital virilization at birth in girls with CAH explains their increased male-typical behavior, for example, by altering self perceptions or parental encouragement of sex-typical play (Fausto-Sterling, 1992). However, the impact of MPA taken by the mother during pregnancy on sex-typical play in female offspring argues against this suggestion, since MPA, unlike the CAH disorder, does not noticeably alter the external genitalia of females. In addition, parents are instructed by medical personnel to treat their daughters with CAH as they would any other girl, and their responses to interview and questionnaire items (Berenbaum & Hines, 1992; Ehrhardt & Baker, 1974), as well as observation of parent–child interactions in the playroom (Pasterski et al., 2005) suggest that they do so. In fact, Pasterski et al. (2005) found that parents encouraged female-typical play more, rather than less, in their daughters with CAH than in their unaffected daughters, but that, despite this encouragement, the girls with CAH showed reduced interest in female-typical toys.

CAH in boys generally has not been found to increase male-typical childhood behavior, consistent with the evidence that their prenatal androgen levels are largely normal. For instance, their toy and playmate preferences do not differ from those of male relatives of similar age (Berenbaum & Hines, 1992; Hines & Kaufman, 1994; Pasterski et al., 2005). However, one study found reduced rough-and-tumble play in boys with CAH (Hines & Kaufman, 1994), despite finding no alterations in playmate preferences or toy choices (Berenbaum & Hines, 1992; Hines & Kaufman, 1994). The boys with CAH came from areas without screening at birth and they had experienced frequent hospitalizations in infancy. The number of hospitalizations correlated negatively with rough-and-tumble behavior, suggesting that illness aspects of CAH, rather than androgens, might be responsible. One study of 10 boys with CAH reported no differences in toy or playmate preferences from unaffected brothers, but increased high-intensity energy expenditure in outdoor play and sports (Ehrhardt & Baker, 1974). A subsequent larger study, however, found no difference in activity level between boys with and without CAH (Pasterski et al., 2007).

Exposure to the anti-androgen, MPA, during gestation has been reported to reduce male-typical play in boys (Meyer-Bahlburg, Grisanti, & Ehrhardt, 1977), although a study of boys exposed to 17-alpha-hydroxyprogesterone caproate, a different anti-androgenic progestin, found no evidence of reduced male-typical childhood behavior (Kester, Green, Finch, & Williams, 1984). Regarding effects of prenatal estrogen exposure, a study of boys exposed to estrogen plus progestins reported reduced athleticism at age 6 years, but no alterations in other aspects of sex-typical play and no reduction in athleticism at age 16 (Yalom, Green, & Fisk, 1973); given the large number of comparisons, the finding could have resulted from chance. Studies of males exposed to DES also report no consistent alterations in sex-typical childhood behavior (Kester, Green, Finch, & Williams, 1980). These findings of no demasculinizing effects of estrogen are consistent with predictions from experimental work in other species.

Another DSD that has provided information on androgen and human behavior is androgen insensitivity syndrome (AIS). People with AIS have a deficiency in androgen receptor response (Grumbach et al., 2003). The insensitivity can be complete (CAIS) or partial (PAIS). Both forms are transmitted as X-linked, recessive traits, and so occur almost exclusively in XY individuals. Children with CAIS appear female at birth, and typically are raised as girls with no suspicion of the underlying disorder or the Y chromosome. At puberty, estrogen derived from testicular androgens feminizes breast development, and CAIS typically is not detected until menstruation fails to occur, because of the lack of female internal reproductive structures. Physical appearance in PAIS varies, and can be similar to that of CAIS, or involve various degrees of genital ambiguity, or even other manifestations, such as hypospadias, infertility, or gynecomastia. Estimates of the incidence of CAIS vary widely, although it is far rarer than CAH. The incidence of PAIS is unknown, perhaps partly because its milder forms often are undetected (Hines, Ahmed, & Hughes, 2003a).

Retrospective assessments suggest female-typical childhood play in XY girls with CAIS (Hines, Ahmed, & Hughes, 2003a; Wisniewski et al., 2000), suggesting that the Y chromosome does not influence the development of children's sex-typical behavior in the absence of an ability to respond to androgen. If it did, XY females with CAIS would show more male-typical behavior than other females do.

Childhood sex-typed behavior also relates to normal variability in the early hormone environment. In a population sample of 3.5-year-old children and their mothers, the mothers of girls whose behavior was extremely masculine were found to have higher levels of testosterone during pregnancy than the mothers of girls whose behavior was extremely feminine, and mothers of a random sample of girls, who showed normative female behavior, had testosterone levels intermediate to those of the mothers of the extremely masculine and feminine girls (Hines et al., 2002b). In the same study, maternal testosterone did not relate to childhood behavior in boys. One possible explanation of these findings is that maternal testosterone has more impact on girls than on boys, because boys already have high levels of testosterone. It is generally thought, however, that maternal testosterone does not affect fetuses of either sex, because the placenta protects the fetus from maternal hormones. An alternative explanation involves genetic similarity between mothers and daughters. Studies of twins and of parents and offspring suggest 40 to 60% heritability for testosterone (Harris, Vernon, & Boomsma, 1998). In addition, testosterone is correlated in mothers and daughters, but not in mothers and sons (Harris, Vernon, & Boomsma, 1998), perhaps because the sources of testosterone in both mothers and daughters are ovarian and adrenal, whereas, in sons, testosterone comes mainly from the testes. Thus, the relationship between maternal hormones and daughters' behavior may result from genetic similarity. Mothers with relatively high testosterone may have daughters with relatively high testosterone, including during the fetal period (Hines et al., 2002b). Indeed, a study using blood samples from fetuses, as well as their pregnant mothers, found a moderate to large correlation between testosterone from these two sources ($r = .414$) (Gitau, Adams, Fisk, & Glover, 2005).

Testosterone measured in amniotic fluid also has been related to subsequent play behavior. Testosterone enters human amniotic fluid by diffusion through the fetal skin, and through fetal urination (Robinson et al., 1977), and so is thought to reflect testosterone levels in the fetus. One study found that amniotic fluid testosterone related positively to male-typical childhood behavior within a sample of girls and within a sample of boys (Auyeung et al., 2009). Two prior studies had reported insignificant relationships between amniotic fluid testosterone and sex-typical behavior in both boys and girls (Knickmeyer et al., 2005; van de Beek et al., 2008), but these negative results probably resulted from small samples or insufficiently sensitive behavioral measures. The study finding positive effects used a larger sample and a measure that had been shown to be sensitive to effects of prenatal androgen in prior studies (Hines, Brook, & Conway, 2004; Hines et al., 2002b).

Studies of twins do not support the hypothesis that girls with male co-twins are masculinized in their childhood play behavior by sharing the uterus with them and their testosterone (Henderson & Berenbaum, 1997; Iervolino, 2003). No differences have been found between girls with male vs. female twins, even in a study of over 6000 twins (Iervolino, 2003). In contrast, the sex of older siblings relates to sex-typed play in both twins and non-twins (Iervolino, 2003; Rust et al., 2000). Children's behavior is more male-typical if they have an older brother and more female-typical if they have an older sister. These findings illustrate the difficulty of interpreting data from studies of same- and other-sex twins, unless the problem of separating social from hormonal factors is addressed, for example, by looking at the impact of siblings as well as co-twins, or by looking at twins who were raised without their co-twin.

Evidence that children with an older brother show increased male-typical behavior, whereas those with an older sister show increased female-typical behavior (Rust et al., 2000), suggests that socialization influences, as well as hormones, play a role in the development of children's sex-typed behavior. Specifically, these findings suggest that interacting with an older sibling leads to engagement with the behaviors that are associated with that older sibling's sex. This could come about through modeling the behavior of the sibling, through learning to enjoy the behaviors the sibling engages in by playing with the older sibling, or simply by engaging in those behaviors when with the sibling.

Social/Cognitive Perspectives on Gendered Behavior in Childhood

Gender is an important social category, and the first question addressed to new parents typically concerns the gender of their baby. One study found that 80% of the first questions asked of new parents had to do with whether the baby was a girl or a boy. Far fewer first questions (18%) had to do with the health of the mother or child (Intons-Peterson & Reddel, 1984). Names for girls and boys also are chosen from largely different sets of possibilities, suggesting that it is important to signal whether a child is a girl or a boy. Similarly, male and female infants are dressed differently, again suggesting the importance of communicating their sex to strangers.

The major mechanism by which sex-typed behavior is thought to be instilled in children by society is learning, both learning with reinforcement and learning without obvious reinforcement (Mischel, 1966). As in less gendered realms, reinforcement is a powerful shaper of behavior, and a positive response makes it more likely that a behavior will be repeated. From this perspective, children engage in sex-typical behavior in part because they get positive responses for doing so. Observational learning, without obvious reinforcement, is also thought to influence the development of sex-typical behavior. Men and women and boys and girls are portrayed differently in society. Think, for instance, of advertisements on children's television, where girls wear pink and play with dolls, and boys wear darker colors and play with vehicles. It is thought that children model these portrayals of individuals of their own sex, and respond to labels regarding what is "for girls" and what is "for boys" by adopting the sex-appropriate behaviors.

Cognitive developmental theorists explain the motivation for observational learning in children, and social cognitive theories posit that cognitive processes play an important role in the acquisition of sex-typed behavior (Bussey & Bandura, 1984). Cognitive developmental theorists propose that children's gradual acquisition of the gender concept, from initial identity as male or female through to an understanding that this identity will not change with time or with changes in appearance or activities, underpins the adoption of gender-appropriate behaviors (Kohlberg, 1966; Ruble & Martin, 1998). Cognitive theorists also posit that children are active agents in their own gender development, and that gender schemas, or systems of knowledge related to gender (similar to stereotypes), are involved in the acquisition of sex-typical behavior (Martin, Ruble, & Szkrybalo, 2002).

Children are more likely to model the behavior of people of the same sex than the other sex, and this is particularly true for boys. After seeing videotapes of men and women consistently choosing one or the other of a pair of neutral items (e.g., an apple vs. a banana), children subsequently express more interest in the items that they have seen people of their own than the other sex choose, and the impact of the models is greater for boys than for girls (Perry & Bussey, 1979). Gender labels, which also tell children what items or activities are for their own versus the other sex, also influence children's choices. If told, for instance, that brown xylophones are for boys and yellow xylophones are for girls (or vice versa), children tend to prefer the xylophone of the color they were told is for their sex (Masters et al., 1979). Television and other media are another source of information about gender-related behaviors, and the portrayal of males and females on television is highly sex stereotypical (Ruble, Martin, & Berenbaum, 2006). Television viewing also relates positively to sex stereotypic beliefs (Huston et al., 1992; Morgan & Shanahan, 1997). Although it is not possible to separate cause and effect in these studies of television and sex stereotypes (e.g., watching television may increase sex-stereotypic beliefs or people with stronger stereotypes to begin with may watch more television), the findings are consistent with predictions based on laboratory studies of the effects of modeling and labeling, lending some credence to the first interpretation.

Girls and boys also experience different patterns of reinforcement for sex-typical toy play. Parents encourage sex-typical play and discourage cross-sex play (Fagot, 1978; Langlois & Downs, 1980; Pasterski et al., 2005), and the amount of sex-typed reinforcement by parents correlates positively with the amount of sex-typed behavior in their offspring, at least among healthy children (Pasterski et al., 2005). Measures of sex-typed parental behavior (e.g., who takes out the trash, who cooks dinner) also correlate positively with sex-typed behavior in offspring (Hines et al., 2002a). In addition, mothers who are highly educated and who work outside the home have children who show reduced sex-typical behavior (Hines et al., 2002a; Ruble & Martin, 1998).

Teachers and peers, like parents, encourage sex-typical and discourage sex-atypical play (Fagot & Patterson, 1969). Children's tendencies to sex-segregate also provide additional opportunities for the socialization of sex-typical behaviors. By interacting largely with children of the same sex as themselves, children may experience extended observation, practice, and encouragement of sex-typical behavior (Leaper, 1994; Maccoby & Jacklin, 1987). Consistent with this suggestion, children who show high levels of same-sex play early in the school year show a greater increase in gender-typical play by the end of the year than children who show low levels of same-sex play at the start of the year (Martin & Fabes, 2001). Similarly, children who are strongly gender-typical or atypical at age 2.5 years become progressively more extreme as they progress to age 8 years (Golombok et al., 2008).

Cognitive developmental theorists describe three levels of gender understanding: gender identity, or basic awareness of being a girl or a boy; gender stability, or awareness that gender does not change over time; and gender consistency, or awareness that gender does not change with changes in appearance or activities. They view these progressive stages of gender awareness as important factors in children's acquisition and consolidation of gender-typical behavior. The first two levels in particular relate to gender-typed beliefs and preferences. For instance, awareness of gender stability relates to increased stereotype knowledge and rigidity about gender-related behavior (Ruble, Martin, & Berenbaum, 2006). There is evidence linking the third level of understanding, gender consistency, to reduced rigidity about gender, perhaps because children now understand that their sex will not change if they engage in cross-gender behavior (Huston, 1983; Ruble et al., 2007).

Gender schemas are active, dynamic constructions that organize knowledge about gender, and they are thought to influence perceptions, thoughts, and behaviors related to gender (Martin, Ruble, & Szkrybalo, 2002). In a sense, they are scientific formulations of gender-related stereotypes. Some children are more strongly gender schematized than others, and those who are strongly schematized have more information about gender stereotypes than do those who are weakly schematized; they also tend to remember less counter-stereotypic information (Levy and Carter, 1989).

How does cognitive information about gender translate into behavior? Bussey and Bandura (1992) investigated this question by having children ages 2 to 4 years rate how they would feel (good, bad) after playing with a gender-appropriate toy or with a gender-inappropriate toy. They also asked the children to predict how other children would feel in the same situations, and they observed the children playing in a room with the same toys. Boys and girls showed the expected sex differences in toy play at all ages. In addition, both boys and girls at all ages said other children would feel good after playing with gender-appropriate toys and bad after playing with inappropriate toys. Only older children, however, said that they themselves would have these feelings. Bussey and Bandura (1992) also found that the differential between feeling good for playing with a same-sex toy and bad for playing with a cross-sex toy predicted actual sex-typical toy play. They interpreted these data to suggest that children begin to choose sex-typed toys because they are reinforced for doing so, and then, with time and age, children incorporate social expectations and values and come to value gender-appropriate behavior and attach emotions to complying with gender expectations. These are thought to become self-evaluations that further contribute to sex-typed behavior. Of course, the initial tendencies to play with sex-typical toys could relate to prenatal hormone exposure, as well as to reinforcement, although Bussey and Bandura did not include the possibility of innate contributions to sex-typed toy choices in their formulation.

Combining Nature and Nurture

A different source of evidence regarding the role of inborn factors and postnatal socialization in children's toy and activity preferences has been the study of the behavior of other species, particularly non-human primates. For instance, rhesus monkeys show sex differences in rough-and-tumble play similar to those seen in children, and these sex differences are influenced by prenatal androgen exposure (Goy & McEwen, 1980). Perhaps more surprisingly, both vervet monkeys and rhesus monkeys show sex differences in toy preferences that resemble those of children (Alexander & Hines, 2002; Hassett et al., 2008). The study of vervet monkeys found that, like children, male animals spent more time than female animals contacting boys' toys and female animals spent more time than male animals contacting girls' toys. Unlike boys, however, male vervets did not avoid feminine toys (i.e., they did not spend more time with boys' toys than with girls' toys). This result was interpreted to suggest that although some aspects of sex-typed toy preferences are part of our evolutionary heritage, the male avoidance of feminine toys may be a socialized phenomenon (Alexander & Hines, 2002). This interpretation is consistent with evidence of stronger discouragement of cross-gendered behavior in boys than in girls (Langlois & Downs, 1980; Pasterski et al., 2005).

Summary for Gendered Behavior in Childhood

Androgen exposure prenatally influences sex-typed childhood behaviors, including toy, playmate, and activity preferences. Several studies from a number of independent research groups have found that girls with CAH show more male-typical preferences for toys, playmates, and activities than various female control groups. In addition, these effects are graded; girls with more severe forms of CAH, involving the most dramatic androgen elevation, show the most male-typical play, as do girls with more severe genital virilization. Skeptics have suggested that these outcomes might relate to the non-hormonal aspects of the CAH disorder, to awareness of genital virilization at birth, to postnatal hormone exposure, or to parental encouragement of male-typical play. However, these alternative explanations are unlikely. For instance, girls without a genetic disorder, but exposed prenatally to androgenic progestins because these hormones were prescribed to their mothers during pregnancy, also show increased male-typical play, and healthy girls and boys exposed to anti-androgenic progestins prenatally for similar reasons show reduced male-typical play. Also, normal variability in testosterone prenatally, measured either from maternal blood or from amniotic fluid, predicts normal variability in male-typical childhood behavior. Finally, self-report data from parents and direct observation of their behavior toward their children with CAH provide no evidence that they are encouraging the male-typical play shown by their daughters. Thus, several approaches all point to the same conclusion—the amount of androgen exposure prenatally influences the amount of male-typical behavior in childhood.

In addition to hormones producing sex-typed predispositions, the postnatal social environment further encourages sex-typical behavior. Boys and girls are encouraged to engage in sex-typical behavior by parents, peers, teachers, and others, and boys, in particular, are discouraged from engaging in cross-sex behavior. Children also learn that they are male or female and that this will not change. Based on this understanding that they are male or female, they respond to models of the same sex, and to information that objects or activities are for their sex, with appropriate behavior. Thus, inborn predispositions as well as postnatal socialization and cognitive understanding of gender, contribute to children's sex-typical behavior, producing average differences between the sexes, as well as variability within each sex.

CORE GENDER IDENTITY

Core gender identity, or the sense of self as male or female, shows the largest sex difference of any human psychological characteristic. The vast majority of men have a sense of themselves as male, whereas the vast majority of women have a sense of themselves as female. Even in regard to this striking sex difference, however, there is overlap between men and women. Some people who have the physical characteristics of men (Y chromosome, masculine secondary sexual characteristics) have a sense of themselves as female and some people who have the physical characteristics of women (two X chromosomes, feminine secondary sexual characteristics) have a sense of themselves as male. These people are sometimes referred to as gender dysphoric or transsexual and may choose to undergo hormonal and surgical treatment to change their physical sex, making their body match their psychological sense of themselves. Such sex change is very rare, however. It is estimated that about 1 in 20,000 to 30,000 genetic males and 1 in 50,000 to 100,000 genetic females change their sex (American Psychiatric Association, 2000). The sex difference in core gender identity is not typically represented quantitatively, but findings from small data sets where quantification has been attempted suggest a very large magnitude (d = about 11.0) (Hines, Ahmed, & Hughes, 2003a; Hines, Brook, & Conway, 2004).

What causes variability in core gender identity? Gender dysphoric individuals often recall cross-gendered interests in childhood (Green, 1987), and among women with CAH, those who recall the most cross-gendered interests in childhood are the least identified with the female sex as adults (Hines, Brook, & Conway, 2004). Hence, factors that influence children's toy, playmate, and activity preferences might contribute to gender identity as well. Evidence supporting a contribution from the early hormone environment comes from studies of females exposed to high levels of androgen prenatally, because of CAH. Although the great majority of women with CAH have a female gender identity, 3 to 5% choose to live as males in adulthood, despite having been assigned and reared as girls (Zucker et al., 1996; Meyer-Bahlburg et al., 1996; Cohen-Kettenis, 2005). This number (3 to 5%) may seem low, but it is extremely high compared to the likelihood of choosing to live as a man in the female population at large (1 in 50,000 to 100,000, or 0.001 to 0.002%) (American Psychiatric Association, 2000). So, the likelihood of wishing to change sex is increased by about 3,000% in women with CAH. Also, among women with CAH who do not wish to live as men, identification with the female gender is somewhat reduced (Hines, Brook, & Conway, 2004). As children, girls with CAH also indicate lower satisfaction with being a girl compared to controls (Ehrhardt, Epstein, & Money, 1968), and 10 to 20% of girls with CAH or other DSDs involving prenatal exposure to high levels of androgen have been reported to be gender dysphoric in childhood (Slijper, Drop, Molenaar, & Muinck Keizer-Schrama, 1998).

XY females with CAIS appear to be uniformly happy with the female sex of assignment (Hines, Ahmed, & Hughes, 2003a; Masica, Money, & Ehrhardt, 1971; Mazur et al., 2004; Wisniewski et al., 2000), suggesting that the lack of stimulation by androgen, at least in combination with an unambiguously female sex of rearing, produces a female core gender identity. A second X chromosome is apparently not needed, nor are ovaries, and the presence of a Y chromosome does not prevent a female core gender identity.

Additional information regarding hormonal influences on core gender identity has come from individuals with DSDs involving deficiencies in enzymes needed to produce the full range of androgens. These individuals have slightly ambiguous or female-appearing genitalia at birth, and are typically assigned and reared as girls. If detected in childhood, they may have their testes removed, but if undetected and untreated, they virilize physically at puberty. Many who experience this pubertal virilization then choose to live as men (Cohen-Kettenis, 2005; Wilson, 2001; Zucker, 2002). Others with the same disorders remain women, particularly if their testes are removed prior to puberty, or shortly after virilization, as is done in most Western countries. This could suggest a role of physical virilization in gender identity, since those who change to look like men, and do not have the opportunity of surgical treatment to reverse physical virilization, live as men. However, cultural influences are confounded with physical virilization and the availability of surgical reversal in these cases. The cultures where virilization is not prevented or reversed also tend to be cultures where male and female social roles are very different and particularly disadvantageous for infertile women, and it has been suggested that individuals who change to live as men in these cultures may do so because it is extremely undesirable to be an infertile female in their cultural setting (Ghabrial & Girgis, 1962; Rosler & Kohn, 1983). The differing outcomes in different cultural contexts, and with versus without physical virilization, suggest that sexual orientation, if influenced by the early hormonal environment, is not determined by it, and may be influenced by social and cultural factors, or by changes in physical appearance that accompany virilization at puberty.

Other rare DSDs also sometimes result in female sex assignment of XY infants. This can occur in cases of penile agenesis or aphallia, where no phallus is present at birth, or in cloacal exstrophy, where the phallus is poorly formed and bifid. One research group has reported that these children often experience serious gender-identity problems, despite female sex assignment and surgical feminization in infancy (Reiner, Gearhart, & Jeffs, 1999; Reiner & Gearhart, 2004). However, other researchers find fewer such problems in individuals with the same diagnosis and history (Meyer-Bahlburg, 2005; Schober, Carmichael, Hines, & Ransley, 2002).

In very rare instances, healthy boys have been reassigned to the female sex, because of early damage to their penis. Two such cases have been documented in terms of outcomes for core gender identity, and these outcomes have differed. In one case, a boy had his penis accidentally ablated during a surgical procedure at the age of 8 months, and was reassigned as a girl by the age of 17 months. Although initial reports suggested that the sex reassignment was successful, he ultimately chose to live as a man and reportedly had been unhappy as a female for many years (Diamond & Sigmundson, 1997). This outcome has been interpreted to suggest inborn determination of gender identity, but for at least the first 8 months of life, and probably somewhat longer, this child's sex of rearing was male. Also, there is little information on the rearing environment after the child was reassigned to the female sex. A similar case of penile damage at the age of 2 months and, in this case, reassignment as female sometime before the age of 7 months, produced a different outcome. Psychosexual evaluation at the ages of 16 and 26 years showed a female core gender identity with no evidence of gender dysphoria (Bradley, Oliver, Chernick, & Zucker, 1998). This outcome of a female gender identity, despite a Y chromosome and a male-typical early hormonal environment, suggests powerful influences of sex of rearing or of physical appearance on core gender identity.

Imprinted genes also may be involved in at least some instances of gender dysphoria. A study of 417 male-to-female (M-to-F) transsexuals found that they had an excess of maternal aunts compared to uncles (Green & Keverne, 2000). The authors proposed an explanation involving imprinted X chromosome genes that escape inactivation, and retention of the epigenotype of the grandparent on the X chromosome. This would cause a first generation characterized by failure to erase the imprint on the paternal X, with sons who inherit this paternal X from their mothers in the following generation failing to survive, and those in the generation after that inheriting a feminizing paternal imprinted X after a second passage through the female germline. This feminizing X would predispose the individual to gender dysphoria.

Genes associated with the production of sex steroids also have been linked to gender dysphoria in men. One study reported that the repeat length of the estrogen receptor beta gene was greater in a group of 29 M-to-F transsexual individuals compared to 229 healthy male controls (Henningsson et al., 2005). A subsequent study failed to replicate this finding in a group of 112 similar individuals compared to 258 male controls, but instead found significantly longer mean repeat lengths in the androgen receptor gene in the M-to-F group than in controls (Hare et al., 2009). This finding was interpreted as consistent with an influence of androgen on gender identity development, because the longer repeat in the androgen receptor gene is associated with reduced testosterone signaling (Kazemi-Esfarjani, Trifiro, & Pinsky, 1995). Both the longer repeat for the estrogen receptor beta gene and the androgen receptor gene are common, however, whereas the desire to change sex is uncommon. Therefore, these genetic differences, if replicable, are likely to be predisposing factors, rather than genetic factors that cause gender dysphoria on their own (Henningsson et al., 2005).

Prenatal hormones are thought to exert permanent influences on behavior by acting through neural receptors to alter basic processes of brain development, and, in rodents, early manipulations of androgen change the structure of several steroid-sensitive brain regions. Thus, hormonal contributions to gender dysphoria might involve discernible changes in the human brain in comparable steroid-sensitive regions.

Two neural regions that show volumetric sex differences in the human brain have been reported to relate to core gender identity. These are the third interstitial nucleus of the anterior hypothalamus (INAH-3) and the central region of the bed nucleus of the stria terminalis (BSTc). INAH-3 is thought to be the human equivalent of the rodent SDN-POA, which is larger in male than in female animals and is influenced by early hormone manipulations. A hormonally influenced structural sex difference in the rodent BST, also has been described (Hines, Davis, Coquelin, Goy, & Gorski, 1985; Hines, Allen, & Gorski, 1992), but in the posterodorsal, not the central, region. Nevertheless, all of the BST, like the anterior hypothalamus, has receptors for androgens and estrogens, and BSTc could also be hormone responsive during early development.

An initial report found that six M-to-F transsexuals had smaller (i.e., more female-typical) BSTcs than either heterosexual or homosexual males (Zhou, Hofman, Gooren, & Swaab, 1995). The same research group also found that BSTc contained fewer neurons expressing the neurohormone somatostatin in the M-to-F group, and female controls, than in the male controls (Kruijver et al., 2000). In addition, the brain of one female-to male (F-to-M) transsexual showed a similar number of somatostatin-expressing neurons to the male controls. A subsequent study of healthy individuals found that the sex difference in BSTc was not present in children, only in adults (Chung, De Vries, & Swaab, 2002). This last finding is surprising, because transsexuals typically recall feeling cross-gendered beginning very early in life. Thus, it is possible that the difference in BSTc in transsexuals results from cross-gender identification or experiences associated with it, rather than being an underlying causal factor. Alternatively, the structural difference could be a delayed expression of early influences, such as early hormone exposure. The same research group also has reported that a separate brain region, INAH-3, previously linked to sexual orientation, is smaller in volume and contains fewer cells in both 11 control females and 11 M-to-F transsexuals than in 14 control males (Garcia-Falgueras & Swaab, 2008).

Summary for Core Gender Identity

Data on clinical syndromes involving androgen abnormality and on sex reassignment following surgical accidents suggest that androgen exposure during early development influences core gender identity, but does not completely determine it. Gender dysphoria in individuals reared as females is markedly increased in those exposed to high levels of androgens during early life, but is still far from universal. Most individuals assigned and reared as female are content with that identity regardless of their exposure to high levels of androgens during early development. XY individuals who are unable to respond to androgen because of CAIS are reared as girls and have a female gender identity, suggesting that the Y chromosome, on its own, does not determine core gender identity. Males with enzymatic disorders that impair production of certain androgens often choose to live as men after virilizing puberty, despite having been reared as girls, whereas others appear content to live as women, particularly if virilizing puberty is prevented or reversed. These findings argue that factors other than the prenatal hormone environment and the Y chromosome can have powerful influences on gender identity. Outcomes for XY individuals reared as girls, because of cloacal exstrophy or other causes of severely undervirilized external genitalia, are variable. Additionally, outcomes differ for two well-documented cases of XY individuals with male-typical hormone levels prenatally who were reassigned as girls after a period of postnatal socialization as boys. In one case, the sex reassignment was successful in terms of gender identity and in the other, it was not. More information is needed before strong conclusions can be made about the likelihood of successful sex change in these difficult cases where severe penile damage occurs, or where the external genitalia are markedly undervirilized at birth. However, the ability of a genetically male (XY) infant, exposed to normal levels of testicular hormones prenatally and in early infancy, and reared as a boy for at least the first 2 months of life, to be reassigned as a girl and develop a female gender identity is remarkable. It provides additional evidence that human gender identity is not determined by the sex chromosomes or the early hormone environment but, instead, can be determined by socialization. In fact, the most obvious conclusion based on data from these two reassigned infants, as well as on individuals with other hormonal abnormalities, is that, given the right social environment, it is possible for an XY individual to develop a female gender identity, despite a functional Y chromosome and exposure to male-typical levels of androgens during critical periods of brain development. The specific aspects of postnatal socialization and experience that contribute to variability in gender identity have yet to be identified, however. Two neural regions have been observed to covary with gender. In one case, the neural sex difference does not appear until after puberty, raising interesting questions about cause and effect. Another intriguing possibility is that genomic imprinting may be involved in cases where gender identity does not accord with gender appearance, gender socialization, or the sex chromosomes.

SEXUAL ORIENTATION

Sexual orientation shows a very large difference between the sexes. The great majority of men are sexually attracted to women, whereas the great majority of women are sexually attracted to men. Kinsey reported that about 10% of men and about 5% of women expressed bisexual or homosexual interests (Kinsey, Pomeroy, & Martin, 1948; Kinsey, Pomeroy, Martin, & Gebhard, 1953). More recent studies suggest lower estimates among men for homosexual experience, ranging from 2 to 6% in the United States, France, and Great Britain (Billy, Tanfer, Grady, & Klepinger, 1993; Johnson et al., 1992; Spira et al., 1992), but estimates that include homosexual attractions as well as behavior are higher, ranging from 16 to 21% for males, and 17 to 19% for females in the same three countries (Sell, Wells, & Wypij, 1995). Sell and colleagues also found homosexual behavior during the most recent 5-year period to be more common than suggested by other recent studies (6.2, 4.5, and 10.7% for males and 3.6, 2.1, and 3.3% for females in the United States, United Kingdom, and France, respectively). When assessed quantitatively, the sex difference in interest in females as sexual partners in fantasy and behavior appears to be very large (d = about 6.0 to 7.0) (Hines, Ahmed, & Hughes, 2003a; Hines, Brook, & Conway, 2004; Meyer-Bahlburg et al., 2008).

Homosexual men and women tend to recall more cross-gendered activities in childhood than do heterosexual men and women (Bailey & Zucker, 1995) and this has been observed cross-culturally (Whitam, 1980; Whitam & Mathy, 1986; Whitam & Mathy, 1991). Longitudinal evidence also supports a link between strongly cross-gendered behavior and subsequent homosexuality in adolescence or adulthood, at least for men (Green, 1985; Zucker & Bradley, 1995; Zuger, 1978). In one study, three-quarters of 44 boys who were identified in childhood as being extremely feminine in their interests and activities matured into homosexual or bisexual adolescents or adults (Green, 1985). In contrast, 34 of 35 controls, who were conventionally masculine in childhood, were heterosexual. Although these findings could suggest that extremely cross-gendered childhood activities cause atypical sexual orientation (Bem, 1996), a third factor or factors could be involved causally. That is, factors that cause extremely cross-gendered childhood interests could also influence sexual orientation.

A prime candidate for such a factor is the early hormone environment. For women in particular, prenatal exposure to high concentrations of androgens is associated with atypical sexual orientation. Several independent research groups have found that women with CAH are more likely to be non-heterosexual (bisexual or lesbian) than are women without CAH (Dittmann, Kappes, & Kappes, 1992; Hines, Brook, & Conway, 2004; Meyer-Bahlburg et al., 2008; Money, Schwartz, & Lewis, 1984; Mulaikal, Migeon, & Rock, 1987). In addition, among women with CAH, heterosexual interest correlates negatively with recollections of male-typical behavior in childhood (Hines, Brook, & Conway, 2004). In a particularly comprehensive study (Meyer-Bahlburg et al., 2008), lifetime sexual orientation was not exclusively or almost exclusively heterosexual in 47% of women with salt-wasting CAH, and in 33% of those with the less severe, simple virilizing form of CAH. Comparable figures for individuals with non-classical CAH, and for female relative controls were 24 and 5%, respectively. The figures for bisexual or lesbian orientation in classical CAH, either salt-wasting or simple virilizing, are similar to those reported by others. Two studies have reported no differences in sexual orientation between women with and without CAH (Bullinger, 1997; Lev-Ran, 1974), but methodological weaknesses could explain the negative findings. These weaknesses include focus on patients with the less severe, and later onset, non-classical, form of CAH, assessment of sexual orientation based solely on participants' current relationships, and cultural factors that would make participants reluctant to report an atypical sexual orientation (Hines, 2004). Several studies have found that women with the more severe, salt-losing form of CAH are more likely than those with the less severe, simple virilizing form to show atypical sexual orientation (Dittmann, Kappes, & Kappes, 1992; Meyer-Bahlburg et al., 2008; Mulaikal, Migeon, & Rock, 1987), as are women with more dramatically virilized genitalia, suggesting more androgen exposure prenatally (Gastaud et al., 2007). These findings, linking the amount of androgen exposure with the amount of behavioral change, strengthen the argument that women with CAH show altered sexual orientation because of their prenatal androgen exposure.

As for childhood play behavior, it has been suggested that aspects of CAH, other than elevated androgen prenatally, could influence sexual orientation. As noted earlier, girls with CAH are born with varying degrees of genital virilization, and their external genitalia typically are surgically feminized. However, surgical procedures do not necessarily produce genitalia identical to those of healthy females, and some women with CAH report pain with intercourse (Schober, 1999). Knowledge of virilization at birth, and experience with genital surgery, also have been suggested as possible influences on sexual behavior (Fausto-Sterling, 1992; Quadagno, Briscoe, & Quadagno, 1977). These concerns make data on women exposed to hormones, such as DES, that would not virilize the external genitalia, but would be hypothesized to promote male-typical brain development, of interest. DES-exposed women have been found to show reduced heterosexual orientation in three samples, totaling 97 women, studied by one research group (Ehrhardt et al., 1985; Meyer-Bahlburg et al., 1995). The incidence of lifelong homosexual or bisexual orientation was higher in the DES-exposed women than in their respective controls (24 vs. 0% in the first sample, 35 vs. 13% in the second, and 16 vs. 5% in the third). For 20 sister pairs in the studies, the DES-exposed sister also was more likely than her unexposed sibling to be bisexual or homosexual (40 vs. 10%). The only other study of sexual orientation in women exposed prenatally to DES looked at 3,946 exposed women and 1,740 unexposed women and found no differences in their replies to a question as to whether their sexual partners had been only the opposite sex, mostly the opposite sex, mostly the same sex, only the same sex, or they had had no sexual contact (Titus-Ernstoff et al., 2003). Although the large sample in this study is impressive, the assessment of sexual orientation may not have been sufficiently sensitive, particularly given social constraints on atypical sexual behavior itself, as well as reporting atypical behavior to others. In contrast, the earlier studies of DES-exposed women used extensive interview assessments of sexual orientation in a variety of contexts, including fantasy and desire, as well as actual behavior.

Sexual orientation in XY women with CAIS appears to be female-typical (i.e., they are sexually interested in men). Women with CAIS do not differ in sexual orientation from female population norms (Wisniewski et al., 2000), or from age-matched female controls (Hines, Ahmed, & Hughes, 2003a). In fact, these XY females who lack functional androgen receptors are more female-typical in their sexual orientation than are XX females with CAH (Money, Schwartz, & Lewis, 1984). XY women with CAIS are socialized as girls, making it impossible to know if as yet unidentified socialization influences, rather than their lack of effective androgen exposure, are responsible for their female-typical sexual orientation. Nevertheless, the female-typical sexual orientation shown by XY women with CAIS shows that the Y chromosome alone does not produce male-typical sexual orientation.

The two boys who were reassigned as girls following serious surgical damage to their external genitalia also have been studied in regard to sexual orientation. One child, in whom the damage occurred at the age of 8 months and who was reassigned to the female sex by the age of 18 months, had erotic interest exclusively in women as an adult (Diamond & Sigmundson, 1997). The second child, for whom the damage occurred at the age of 2 months and reassignment as a girl by the age of 7 months, was later bisexual (Bradley, Oliver, Chernick, & Zucker, 1998). Although the two outcomes differ in that one individual was bisexual and the other interested only in female partners, both cases suggest that early exposure to male-typical levels of testicular hormones, in combination with a Y chromosome and early rearing as a male, influences sexual orientation away from the primary erotic interest in men that is typical of females.

Another source of information regarding sexual orientation in men is individuals with DSDs involving deficiencies in enzymes needed to produce the full range of androgens. As described before, these individuals have slightly ambiguous or female appearing genitalia at birth, and are typically reared as females. If detected in childhood they may have their testes removed, but if undetected and untreated, they virilize physically at puberty. Many who experience this pubertal virilization then choose to live as men and assumedly interact sexually with women (Cohen-Kettenis, 2005; Wilson, 2001; Zucker, 2002). Others with the same disorders remain as females, and, in these cases, sexual orientation appears to remain that of a typical female.

Sexual orientation has not been studied systematically in individuals with these DSDs, however.

Men exposed to the synthetic estrogen, DES, or to progestins prenatally do not appear to differ from other men in their sexual orientation. One study (Kester, Green, Finch, & Williams, 1980) found no differences in sexual orientation in fantasy or behavior between men exposed to DES alone, DES plus progesterone, progesterone alone, or progestins alone, from control groups of men matched for demographic background. A second study compared two groups of DES-exposed men to matched controls, with similar results (Meyer-Bahlburg et al., 1987). Interviewer assessments of sexual orientation in fantasy and behavior were similar in the DES-exposed men to unexposed men identified from the same clinics. A large-scale study of DES-treated offspring also found no differences in self-report of same-sex sexual partners in 1,342 DES-exposed, versus 1,342 unexposed men (Titus-Ernstoff et al., 2003), although, as noted above, the assessment procedure in this last study may have lacked sensitivity.

A final approach to assessing early hormone influences on sexual orientation has investigated finger ratios that differ for men and women and are thought to be determined by prenatal androgen exposure (Manning, 2002). The ratio used most frequently is calculated by measuring the length of the second finger and the fourth finger and dividing the first value by the second (2D/4D). This ratio is greater on average in women than in men. Studies finding that individuals with CAH show more male-typical 2D/4D ratios (Brown, Hines, Fane, & Breedlove, 2002; Okten, Kalyonku, & Yaris, 2002), support the link to prenatal androgen exposure (but see Buck, Williams, Hughes, & Acerini, 2003).

Finger ratios are easy to obtain and numerous studies have related sexual orientation to 2D/4D, particularly in men. An early study reported that homosexual men had more male-typical ratios than heterosexual men (Williams et al., 2000), a surprising finding, given that androgen would be hypothesized to increase, not decrease, male-typical behavior. Subsequent studies have not produced similar results, instead finding more female-typical ratios in homosexual than in heterosexual men, or no differences between these groups (McFadden et al., 2005). The inconsistent results may reflect the ease with which these studies can be conducted on relatively small samples and a consequent proliferation of spurious findings. A study commissioned by the British Broadcasting Corporation (BBC), involving participants who completed procedures online, found that 2D/4D ratios were more male-typical in 102,499 heterosexual men than in 11,060 homosexual or bisexual men (Collaer, Reimers, & Manning, 2007). These findings are consistent with the typical pattern of androgenic influences on behavior. The 2D/4D ratio did not differ for 84,417 heterosexual, compared to 9,153 homosexual or bisexual, women, however.

Twin studies have investigated possible genetic contributions to sexual orientation. This approach compares the similarities among monozygotic twins and dizygotic twins to estimate the heritability of a trait, and suggest some degree of heritability for sexual orientation in both males (Bailey & Pillard, 1991; Whitam, Diamond, & Martin, 1993) and females (Bailey, Pillard, Neale, & Agyei, 1993). The heritability estimates appear to be larger when twins are recruited by advertisement or word of mouth, than when recruited from an Australian twin register (Bailey et al., 2000), or a national probability sample in the United States (Kendler et al., 2000).

Monozygotic twins may be treated more similarly than dizygotic twins, thus inflating heritability estimates, and so it is useful to look at monozygotic twins reared apart. Finding twins reared apart where one of the pair is homosexual is difficult, but eight such pairs, four male and four female, have been studied. Among the male twins, two of the four pairs were concordant for sexual orientation (Eckert, Bouchard, Bohlen, & Heston, 1986; Whitam, Diamond, & Martin, 1993); among the female twins, none of the four were (Eckert, Bouchard, Bohlen, & Heston, 1986). Overall, data from twin studies suggest some heritability for sexual orientation, at least among males. However, the genes involved are not known. It also is possible that genetic and hormonal contributions to sexual orientation overlap. That is, any genes that are found to be involved could act by influencing hormone production or sensitivity.

The search for specific genes associated with variability in sexual orientation has investigated candidate genes, genes on the X chromosome, and genes on the entire genome. In regard to candidate genes, neither the androgen receptor gene (Macke et al., 1993), nor aromatase cytochrome (DuPree et al., 2004), which is needed to convert androgen to estrogen, appear to vary with sexual orientation, at least for men. Evidence of maternal transmission of male homosexuality led to examination of genes on the X chromosome and linkage to markers on Xq28 (Hamer et al., 1993), a finding replicated by the same research group for a second sample of men (Hu et al., 1995), but not by a second research group (Rice, Anderson, Risch, & Ebers, 1999), although differences between the studies could be involved in the failure to replicate. A genomewide scan also failed to replicate the linkage (Mustanski et al., 2005), but, again, methodological differences, particularly reduced resolution of markers in the Xq28 region, could account for the different results. The genomewide scan suggested possible involvement of D7S798 in 7q36, D8S505 in 8p12, and D10S217 in 10q26, but the authors suggest that these findings would benefit from replication using denser linkage maps in these regions, as well as the Xq28 region.

Another genetic approach, pedigree analysis, found that homosexual men have fewer maternal uncles than aunts (132 vs. 209 in one sample of over 100 families, and 241vs. 367 in a second sample of similar size) (Turner, 1995). Numbers of maternal uncles and aunts were approximately equal for homosexual women. The result for men was interpreted to indicate more fetal death among maternal brothers than sisters, and the author suggested that a semi-lethal genetic trait carried by the mother is a cause of male homosexuality. Others have interpreted the excess of maternal aunts to suggest involvement of genomic imprinting (Green & Keverne, 2000), similar to that suggested above in the section on core gender identity.

Older brothers also have been linked to sexual orientation in men. Several studies have found that the likelihood of being homosexual increases with the number of older brothers, at least for right-handed men (Blanchard & Bogaert, 1996). A similar effect has not been seen for older sisters, or for younger siblings of either sex, nor has a similar finding been seen in women or in left-handed men (Blanchard & Bogaert, 1996). The magnitude of the increase has been described as each older brother increasing the odds of homosexuality by 33%. Thus, the likelihood of being non-heterosexual for men is about 2% with no older brothers, 2.6% with one older brother, 3.5% with two older brothers, 4.6% with three older brothers, 6% with four older brothers, and 7.8% with more than four older brothers (Blanchard, 2001). One study found the effect for biological older brothers only, not for non-biological older brothers, and that the existence of older brothers was effective, regardless of the amount of time reared together, suggesting that intrauterine factors are responsible (Bogaert, 2006). The specific mechanism involved is unknown, but one speculation is that the mother's immune system produces antibodies to male fetuses that increase with successive pregnancies and that somehow influence sexual orientation (Blanchard, 2004). A confusing aspect of the effect is that it applies only to right-handed men. In addition, men and women who are not heterosexual are also less likely to be right-handed than those who are heterosexual (Blanchard & Lippa, 2007; Lalumiere, Blanchard, & Zucker, 2000). However, non–right-handed homosexual men have fewer, rather than more, older brothers. There is no obvious explanation for the interaction of number of older brothers with hand preferences in influencing sexual orientation (Blanchard, 2008).

No social/cognitive aspects of development have been linked convincingly to variation in sexual orientation. Psychoanalytic formulations suggested that parent variables influence sexual orientation, with weak or absent fathers and strong or overly close mothers, among other parental issues, leading to male homosexuality (see Green, 1987, for a review). However, retrospective assessments of hundreds of heterosexual and homosexual men and women who were not psychoanalytic patients, and a longitudinal study following boys into adulthood, have not supported these suggestions (Bell, Weinberg, & Hammersmith, 1981; Green, 1987). There also is no evidence that homosexual men or women experienced different learning histories related to gender, or were reinforced in unusual ways in terms of sexual behavior. Similarly, there are no reports of alterations in the cognitive understanding of gender or in gender schemas among non-heterosexual men or women. One suggestion is that for men, exotic individuals become erotic (i.e., boys who avoid boys and boys' activities in childhood then find males erotic after puberty) (Bem, 1996). However, this proposal would predict that other exotic individuals (e.g., people of other races) would be more erotic than more familiar individuals as well, which does not seem to be the case. Studies of children who are strongly cross-gendered in childhood and who are non-heterosexual males in adulthood suggest links to illness in infancy, being a beautiful baby, parental desire for a girl baby, and parental tolerance of cross-gendered behavior (Green, 1987). If replicable, these findings might apply only to non-heterosexual men who were strongly cross-gendered in childhood, rather than non-heterosexual men in general. Also, some factors (e.g., being a beautiful baby) could be manifestations of a different underlying cause, such as hormones prenatally.

Factors influencing sexual orientation may differ for men and women. For instance, as noted above, there is stronger evidence of genetic contributions for men than for women, and the number of older brothers relates to sexual orientation in right-handed men, but not women. For women, but not men, sexual orientation has been suggested to be a part of an erotic career, so that a person might choose to engage in sexual activity or sexual relationships with individuals of the same sex for practical reasons (Peplau, Spalding, Conley, & Veneigas, 1999). Neural mechanisms underlying attachment relationships and erotic relationships also may overlap more in women than in men, providing different pathways to variability in sexual orientation for the two sexes (Diamond, 2003; Diamond, 2004).

What neural regions have been linked to sexual orientation? INAH-3, which is thought to be the human counterpart of the rodent SDN-POA, is smaller (i.e., more female-typical) in men who are homosexual or bisexual than in those who are heterosexual (Byne et al., 2001; LeVay, 1991). In the study by LeVay, a subgroup of heterosexual men had died of AIDS, as had most of the non-heterosexual men, and the volume of INAH-3 in this subgroup was similar to that in other heterosexual men, suggesting that AIDS or its consequences were not responsible for the difference between heterosexual and homosexual men. The other three INAH did not show sex differences in this study and did not differ for heterosexual versus non-heterosexual men, providing additional evidence that the difference in INAH-3 does not reflect general neural changes related to AIDS. The Byne et al. (2001) study replicated the finding of a larger INAH-3 in heterosexual than in homosexual or bisexual men. In addition, this study counted the number of neurons in INAH-3. Like the volume of the nucleus, the number of neurons was smaller in females than in males, but the two groups of men did not differ in this respect.

The anterior commissure, a fiber tract connecting the left and right cerebral hemispheres, has been reported to be larger in women and non-heterosexual men than in heterosexual men (Allen & Gorski, 1992). A second study, however, found no sex difference in the anterior commissure and no difference between heterosexual and non-heterosexual men (Lasco et al., 2002).

The size of the isthmus region of the corpus callosum has been linked to sexual orientation as well, with 12 right-handed homosexual men having larger mid-sagittal isthmal areas than 10 right-handed heterosexual men (Witelson et al., 2008). Other callosal regions, including the anterior half, posterior mid-body, total callosum, and splenium also showed group differences of moderate size ($d = 0.41 - 0.66$), but only the difference in the isthmus ($d = 0.83$) was statistically significant.

Summary for Sexual Orientation

The early hormone environment appears to influence sexual orientation. Women exposed to high levels of androgens prenatally, because of CAH, show reduced erotic interest in men. Also, XY individuals who are insensitive to androgen, and reared as females, show primary erotic interest in men, and genetic males exposed to the complete male hormonal cascade, but sex reassigned in infancy and reared as females, because of penile damage early in life, develop either bisexual interest or erotic interest in women. Finger ratios, thought to reflect androgen levels prenatally, also suggest a hormonal contribution to sexual orientation, at least in men. Prenatal exposure to estrogen does not appear to alter sexual orientation in men, nor does exposure to progesterone or synthetic progestins. Evidence regarding prenatal exposure to estrogen in females is equivocal. Individuals with enzymatic deficiencies that impair androgen production appear capable of developing erotic interest in women following spontaneous virilization at puberty. However, when the testes are removed prior to or during puberty, and virilization does not occur or is quickly reversed, erotic interest appears to be similar to that of women in general. Whether these different outcomes relate to cultural influences, influences of hormones at puberty, or other factors is not known. Regardless, it appears that, although the early hormonal environment contributes to sexual orientation, it is not the only factor determining it. Twin studies suggest the involvement of genetic factors, although specific genes have yet to be identified, and the responsible genes could act by coding for hormone production or sensitivity. For right-handed men, having older brothers increases the likelihood of being non-heterosexual, although this association is small and the mechanism underlying it unknown. In addition, among males, sexual orientation has been related to the volume of INAH-3, a brain region that appears to correspond to the SDN-POA or rodents. In rodents, the volume of the SDN-POA is closely linked the hormone environment during early development, again consistent with a role for gonadal hormones in the development of sexual orientation. There may be other neural differences between those who are heterosexual and those who are not, but for other neural differences, there is as yet no replication.

COGNITION

Sex differences in general intelligence are negligible (see, e.g., Collaer & Hines, 1995; and Hines, 2004). The lack of a sex difference in intelligence may seem unsurprising, given that intelligence tests are designed to avoid sex differences. However, even before an effort was made to avoid sex differences, intelligence tests were largely gender neutral (Loehlin, 2000). It also has been suggested that males are more variable than females in intellectual ability, at least at some ages (Arden & Plomin, 2006; Deary et al., 2003), although these sex differences also are of negligible size. In addition, the evidence regarding the existence of greater male variability is mixed, with some studies finding no sex difference in variability, or more variability in girls than in boys at some ages (Arden & Plomin, 2006; Harnqvist, 1997; Reynolds et al., 2008). Despite the lack of an appreciable sex difference in general intelligence, males and females differ in performance on measures of some specific cognitive abilities, including aspects of spatial, mathematical, and verbal abilities, as well as perceptual speed.

Spatial Abilities

Spatial abilities have been conceptualized as including three constructs: mental rotations, spatial perception, and spatial visualization, and the sizes of sex differences appear to differ for these constructs. Males outperform females on speeded tests of mental rotations ability (i.e., the ability to rotate two- or three-dimensional stimuli in the mind). The sex difference is present in children (Linn & Petersen, 1985) and adults (Voyer, Voyer, & Bryden, 1995), and may increase with age, but the use of different tasks with different age groups could produce the apparent age effect. Meta-analyses suggest that sex differences are larger on three-dimensional tasks (d = 0.92) than on two-dimensional tasks (d = 0.26) (Linn & Petersen, 1985; Voyer, Boyer, & Bryden, 1995), although the sex difference may be attenuated on two-dimensional tests because they are easier. Men also outperform women on tests of spatial perception. These tasks require accurate positioning of a stimulus (e.g., a line) within a distracting array (e.g., a tilted frame). As was the case for mental rotations tests, the sex difference in spatial perception appears to be larger in adults than in children (d = 0.56 vs. 0.38, respectively) (Voyer, Voyer, & Bryden, 1995). The sex difference also may be larger in adults on more difficult tasks. A spatial perception task, adapted from the Benton Judgment of Line Orientation task to increase its difficulty, appears to show a sex difference as large as that seen for three-dimensional mental rotations (Collaer, Reimers, & Manning, 2007). The third type of visuospatial ability, spatial visualization, shows a negligible sex difference (d < 0.20) (Linn & Petersen, 1985; Voyer, Voyer, & Bryden, 1995). Spatial visualization tasks require complex, sequential manipulations of spatial information and typically have more than one solution strategy. Measures include tests that require identification of simple figures within complex designs (e.g., embedded figures, hidden patterns), construction of specified shapes from three-dimensional blocks (e.g., block design), and imagining what unfolded shapes would look like when folded to form three-dimensional-objects (e.g., paper folding, surface development).

Another area of spatial performance where males outperform females is on the motor task, targeting (e.g., throwing darts or balls at bull's eyes). This type of task shows large sex differences, in both children and adults (d > 1.0) (Hines et al., 2003b; Jardine & Martin, 1983; Watson & Kimura, 1991).

Mathematical Abilities

Meta-analytic results (Hyde, Fennema, & Lamon, 1990) suggest that the overall sex difference in mathematical abilities is negligible, and favors females (d = –.05), but that measures of problem solving show small sex differences favoring males, particularly among older, highly selected samples, such as college students (d = 0.32). Some standardized tests, again used with highly selected samples, also favor males, including the mathematics subtests of the Scholastic Aptitude Tests (SAT math: d = 0.38) and the Graduate Record Exam (GRE math: d = 0.77), which are used in the United States to select students for bachelor and doctoral degree programs, respectively. In contrast, in childhood, tests of computational skills show small sex differences favoring females (d = –0.21), and there are no sex differences in computational skills in adults (d = 0.00) or in understanding of mathematical concepts at any age (d = –0.06). Achievement test scores for mathematics performance in grades 4 and 8 in the United States show a negligible male advantage (d = 0.06) (The Nations Report Card, Mathematics 2007, and NAEDP data explorer).

Verbal Abilities

Meta-analytic results (Hyde & Linn, 1988) suggest a negligible female advantage for general verbal ability (d = –0.11) in children as well as adults, but somewhat larger sex differences on other types of verbal tasks. Males show a negligible advantage on analogies (d = 0.16), and females show a small advantage on speech production (d = –0.33). Females also show a moderate advantage on verbal fluency (e.g., the ability to generate words that begin with specified letters [d = –0.53]) (Kolb & Whishaw, 1985; Spreen & Strauss, 1991). Female infants begin to talk earlier than males do, and from 16 to 24 months of age girls have a larger vocabulary than boys (Halpern, 2000). However, this vocabulary advantage appears to be gone later in life; meta-analyses suggest that most tests of vocabulary and other verbal abilities, aside from verbal fluency, show essentially no sex difference in adults (d = –0.02 for vocabulary, d = –0.03 for reading comprehension, and d = 0.03 for the verbal subtest of the SAT) (Hyde & Linn, 1988). Other aspects of verbal performance that were not included in the Hyde and Linn meta-analyses may show sex differences (Halpern, 2000). For instance, data from the U.S. Department of Education show girls outperforming boys on writing proficiency in grades 4 through 12 from 1998 until 2007. This sex difference is moderate in size (d = 0.53 to 0.63 depending on the grade and year of assessment) (The Nations Report Card, Writing 2007, and NAEDP data explorer).

Perceptual Speed

Among high school students, the sex difference in perceptual speed favors females and ranges in size from d = 0.29 to 0.66 (mean d = 0.48), at least as assessed using the clerical speed and accuracy subtest of the Differential Aptitudes Test (DAT) (Feingold, 1988). Moderate sex differences also have been observed for similar tests from the Educational Testing Service (d = 0.49) (Ekstrom, French, & Harman, 1976). The magnitude of the sex difference on the DAT appears to have declined somewhat over the years, from a mean of 0.62 in 1947 to 0.34 in 1980 (Feingold, 1988).

Sex differences in some other cognitive abilities also seem to have declined over time. Feingold (1988) found that sex differences on almost all abilities declined linearly from the 1940s to the 1980s. Because the changes were linear, rather than stepwise, he concluded that they were unlikely to reflect changes in the tests, instead suggesting that social and educational changes were responsible. Measures of algebraic problem solving, such as the SAT math, were an exception to the general pattern in Feingold's study, continuing to favor males, especially at the upper end of the distribution. Subsequent research, however, suggests that even the sex difference in performance on the SAT math at the upper extreme has declined since 1982. At that time, the sex ratio for scoring over 700 at age 13 years was 13 boys to 1 girl, as opposed to the more recent sex ratio of 2.8 boys to 1 girl (Halpern et al., 2007). The sex difference on three-dimensional mental rotations tasks appears to have remained stable from the 1970s to the 1990s (Sanders, Soares, & D'Aquila, 1982; Voyer, Voyer, & Bryden, 1995).

Hormones and Cognitive Sex Differences

Infants show a sex difference in the perception of mentally rotated stimuli as early as 3 to 5 months of age (Moore & Johnson, 2008; Quinn & Liben, 2008), suggesting that inborn factors could contribute to subsequent performance differences, such as those seen later in life on three-dimensional mental rotations tasks. Androgen exposure during early life is a likely candidate for such an innate factor, but an early hormone influence on mental rotations performance has been surprisingly hard to document, and, if it exists, may be small.

Studies of individuals with DSDs have not produced clear findings. Men exposed to reduced androgens prenatally, because of idiopathic hypogonadotrophic hypogonadism, which causes reduced androgen production from early in life, show reduced performance on a range of spatial tasks, including mental rotations and spatial perception tasks (Buchsbaum & Henkin, 1980; Cappa et al., 1988; Hier & Crowley, 1982). Similar outcomes have been found for women exposed to reduced estrogen and androgen during early life, because of Turner Syndrome (Collaer et al., 2002; Ross & Zinn, 1999; Rovet, 1990; Waber, 1979). In both of these DSDs, however, other abilities, including some that do not show sex differences, also are impaired (Collaer et al., 2002; Ross & Zinn, 1999; Rovet, 1990; Waber, 1979), suggesting that non-hormonal factors associated with the disorders could contribute to the deficits.

Four studies of mental rotations performance in females with CAH have found only a negligible average difference in performance (d = 0.11) compared to female controls (Hines, 2009a). A meta-analysis of seven studies, including all measures of spatial abilities, not just mental rotations, concluded that females with CAH differed substantially from controls and estimated an effect size of d = 0.34 to 0.47 (Puts, McDaniel, Jordan, & Breedlove, 2008), but this meta-analysis included tasks that are not known to show sex differences. In addition, for unexplained reasons, the meta-analysis did not include either all the subjects or all the tasks in the seven studies, and both of these omissions increased the apparent effect sizes (Hines, 2009a). If the conceptualization of spatial abilities is extended to include targeting performance, women with CAH show enhanced performance (Hines et al., 2003b). They also have enhanced gross motor strength, but this motor enhancement does not explain the enhanced targeting ability (Collaer et al., 2009).

Initial studies relating finger ratios (2D/4D) to spatial performance produced variable, and generally non-significant, results (Puts, McDaniel, Jordan, & Breedlove, 2008). In contrast, the large-scale, online study conducted by the BBC found the predicted negative relationship between 2D/4D and both mental rotations (Peters, Manning, & Reimers, 2007) and spatial perception (Collaer et al., 2007) performance, and the relationship was significant for both tasks within men and within women. The amount of variance accounted for by the 2D/4D ratio was extremely small (less than 0.01% for mental rotations), but this could reflect the imprecise methodology necessitated by the online assessment (e.g., participants measured their own finger lengths using a ruler, rather than having the ratios measured by a trained assessor using calipers).

There is little to no evidence linking the enhanced performance of females on cognitive measures, such as verbal fluency, perceptual speed, or writing proficiency, to the early hormone environment. Indeed, the origins of these abilities at which females excel have not been studied as extensively in relationship to inborn factors as have mental rotations and other spatial abilities at which males excel. No information is available on writing proficiency in relationship to early hormone exposure, for instance. In regard to perceptual speed, verbal fluency, and other verbal abilities, several studies have found no differences in females with CAH compared to controls (Baker & Ehrhardt, 1974; Helleday, Bartfai, Ritzen, & Forsman, 1994; McGuire, Ryan, & Omenn, 1975; Resnick, Berenbaum, Gottesman, & Bouchard, 1986), or in combined groups of males and females with CAH compared to controls (Sinforiani et al., 1994). A single study reported impaired performance on a measure of perceptual speed in girls with CAH (Hampson, Rovet, & Altmann, 1998). Given the small sample (seven girls with CAH and six without), and the lack of similar findings in other studies, however, this could be a chance finding. Because sex differences on tasks at which females excel tend to be smaller than those on mental rotations tasks, larger sample sizes might be needed to detect any hormonal influences.

Boys with CAH generally do not differ from unaffected relatives or matched controls on measures of spatial abilities, verbal abilities, or perceptual speed (Baker & Ehrhardt, 1974; McGuire, Ryan, & Omenn, 1975; Perlman, 1973; Resnick, Berenbaum, Gottesman, & Bouchard, 1986). However, two studies found reduced spatial abilities in males with CAH, one in a sample of five boys with CAH and four without, and not using a mental rotations task (Hampson, Rovet, & Altmann, 1998), and one using two different mental rotations tasks in a sample of 29 males with CAH and 30 unaffected, male relative controls (Hines et al., 2003b). Testosterone levels appear to be largely normal prenatally in males with CAH (Pang et al., 1980; Wudy et al., 1999b), but reduced shortly after birth (Pang et al., 1979), perhaps because of feedback-related reduction in testicular androgen production coupled with postnatal treatment with corticosteroids that reduces adrenal androgen production. Thus, spatial abilities may be reduced in boys with CAH because they are affected by steroid-dependent cortical development in the early neonatal period, when boys with CAH have reduced androgen (Hines et al., 2003b). The spatial deficits also could result from salt-losing crises in infancy, as these are more common in males than females with CAH (Hines et al., 2003b).

Some studies have found impaired mathematical abilities, particularly computational ability, in children with CAH. One study reported impairment in girls with CAH but not boys (Perlman, 1973), one in girls with CAH and in boys with CAH (Baker & Ehrhardt, 1974), and one in a combined group of boys and girls with CAH (Sinforiani et al., 1994), although one study saw no difference between women with and without CAH (Helleday, Bartfai, Ritzen, & Forsman, 1994). Computational ability shows a small sex difference favoring females, but only in children (Hyde, Fennema, & Lamon, 1990). No studies have reported enhanced mathematical performance in males or females exposed to excess androgen prenatally.

Studies of DES-exposed women have not found any alterations in cognitive performance. One research group found no differences between 25 sister pairs, one in each pair exposed to DES for at least 20 weeks prenatally and one not exposed at all, on a two-dimensional mental rotations task or on a measure of verbal fluency (Hines & Shipley, 1984), and no differences between a second sample of 42 DES-exposed women and their 26 unexposed sisters on a three-dimensional mental rotations task, or on measures of spatial perception, perceptual speed, verbal fluency, vocabulary, or Raven's Progressive Matrices (Hines & Sandberg, 1996). A third study, from a different research group, found no differences between

175 DES-exposed and 150 placebo-exposed women in a double-blind, placebo-controlled study for any of four subtests of the American College Testing (ACT) battery, even though some of the subtests showed sex differences (Wilcox, Maxey, & Herbst, 1992). Males exposed to DES (n = 172) scored higher than males exposed to placebo (n = 175) on the social sciences subtest, a test on which males excelled, but the authors attributed this single, unpredicted finding to chance. Another study, of 10 boys exposed prenatally to DES, found impaired performance compared to 10 unexposed brothers on a composite of the Picture Completion, Object Assembly, and Block Design subtests of the Wechsler scales. These tests show small-to-negligible sex differences, and, given the small sample, the differences may have been spurious. The 10 pairs of brothers did not differ on composites of verbal or sequencing tasks (Reinisch and Sanders, 1992).

Normal variability in hormones also has been related to cognitive development. One study related testosterone in amniotic fluid, obtained during the second trimester of pregnancy, to cognitive performance in 28 female and 30 male offspring at the age of 4 years (Finegan, Nichols, & Sitarenios, 1992). Among girls, testosterone related negatively to counting and sorting, number questions, and block building, and it showed an inverted-U–shaped relationship to language comprehension and conceptual grouping. None of these relationships was predicted. Among boys, testosterone did not relate significantly to any of 11 abilities measured. The children were followed up at age 7 years, at which time amniotic fluid testosterone in girls related positively to the speed of mental rotations, but not to accuracy, the measure that typically shows a sex difference (Grimshaw, Sitarenios, & Finegan, 1995). Amniotic fluid testosterone also has been related to vocabulary size in infants at age 18 and 24 months, when girls have a larger vocabulary than boys (Lutchmaya, Baron-Cohen, & Raggatt, 2002). However, a significant correlation was seen only when data were analyzed for both sexes combined, not for each sex individually, suggesting that it reflected the existence of sex differences in both amniotic fluid testosterone and vocabulary size, rather than a causal relationship between these two variables. Another study related hormones in umbilical cord blood to cognitive performance at age 6.5 years (Jacklin, Wilcox, & Maccoby, 1988). For 53 boys, there were no significant relationships between any hormone and cognitive performance. For 43 girls, both testosterone and a weaker androgen, androstenedione, related negatively to spatial ability, a result opposite to that predicted. Most of the cognitive measures used in both studies did not show substantial sex differences, limiting their power to detect relationships to sex hormones.

Social/Cognitive Perspectives on Cognitive Sex Differences

Sex differences in children's play behavior may contribute to subsequent differences in cognitive performance, with activities typical of girls promoting verbal communication and those typical of boys promoting spatial abilities (Maccoby, 1966; Sherman, 1967). Childhood activities have been linked to concurrent abilities, with girls who engage in boys' activities, either by choice or by experimental manipulation, showing better spatial performance than those who do not (Sprafkin, Serbin, Denier, & Connor, 1983). Longitudinal data suggest a similar link over a 10-year period. Girls from a normal population sample, who were identified as gender-atypical in their interests at age 3.5 years, show similar mental rotations performance to boys at age 13 years, whereas girls who were sex-typical or extremely feminine in early childhood show reduced mental rotations performance at age 13 years compared to both boys and gender-atypical girls (Hines, Golombok, Rust, Croudace, Hall, D'Arcy, & Golding, submitted).

Meta-analytic results suggest that training improves performance on a range of spatial tasks (Baenninger & Newcombe, 1989), and computer and videogame usage have been found to mediate the sex difference in mental rotations performance (Terlecki & Newcombe, 2005). Experimental participation in videogaming also improves mental rotations performance (Feng, Spence, & Pratt, 2007; Terlecki & Newcombe, 2005), an improvement that generalizes to other spatial tasks (Terlecki & Newcombe, 2005), and, in one study, was found to eliminate the sex difference in performance (Feng, Spence, & Pratt, 2007). Although not all studies find that training eliminates the sex difference on mental rotation tasks, it has been suggested that it would do so with continued training to maximal performance (Terlecki & Newcombe, 2005).

Cultural differences on measures of mathematical abilities are much larger than differences between the sexes. For instance, a 2007 survey of mathematics performance in 36 nations at grade 4, and 49 nations at grade 8, found that students in Hong Kong and Singapore significantly outperformed all other countries at grade 4, while students in Chinese Tapei, Korea, and Singapore significantly outperformed all other countries at grade 8 (Mullis, Martin, & Foy, 2008). At grade 4, there was no significant sex difference in performance in Hong Kong, but in Singapore girls scored 7 points higher than boys, a significant difference in the opposite direction to that seen in the United States where boys scored 6 points higher than girls. Of the three leading countries at grade 8, only Singapore showed a significant sex difference, with girls outperforming boys by 14 points. Also, across all nations at grade 8, girls outperformed boys by 7 points, a significant difference. Most tellingly, boys and girls in Hong Kong outperformed boys and girls in the United States by 72 points and 79 points, respectively, at grade 4, and boys and girls in Chinese Tapei outperformed boys and girls in the United States by 88 points and 92 points, respectively, at grade 8 (Mullis, Martin, & Foy, 2008). At grade 8, the difference between children in Singapore versus the United States was 15 times as large as the difference between boys and girls in the United States.

Similar data have been collected for science performance (Martin, Mullis, & Foy, 2008). In this realm too, differences between nations are far larger than differences between the sexes. Overall, girls scored higher than boys by 3 points at grade 4 and by 6 points at grade 8. Singapore scored higher than any other country at grade 4, and Singapore and Chinese Tapei similarly led the world at grade 8. Neither country showed a significant sex difference in performance. Compared to the United States, boys in Singapore at grade 4 scored 46 points higher and girls in Singapore scored 51 points higher. At grade 8 these numbers were 37 and 57, respectively. In comparison, the difference between girls and boys in the United States at grade 8 was 12 points, about one-quarter the size of the difference between the United States and Singapore.

The cross-national variability in performance might be interpreted to reflect genetic rather than cultural differences. The science survey included two individual states, Massachusetts and Minnesota, however, and data from Massachusetts argue against this interpretation. Students in Massachusetts scored better than those in the United States as a whole, and were second to only Singapore at grade 4, and similar to the top four countries (Singapore, Chinese Taipei, Korea, and Japan) at grade 8. Unlike Singapore, however, where there were no sex differences in performance at either grade, in Massachusetts, boys significantly outperformed girls at both grade levels (by 10 points at each age). These findings suggest that the educational or cultural environment in Massachusetts promotes a male performance advantage, even when these factors foster high performance overall, whereas similar overall high performance in other cultures is not accompanied by a male advantage.

Other findings also suggest that culture is more important than sex, at least for mathematics performance. A study of math and reading scores in 15-year-old students across 40 countries found that overall boys averaged better scores than girls on math (10.5 points), and girls averaged better scores than boys on reading (32.7 points) (Guiso, Monte, Sapienza, & Zingales, 2008). The authors also looked at scores for each country on measures of gender equality and found that gender inequality positively predicted the male advantage in mathematics performance. In addition, this relationship was seen not only for average scores, but also for scores within the upper 1% of the distribution, suggesting that culture influences not only mean differences in math performance, but also the tendency for more males than females to be very high performers in some countries. In contrast, the size of the female reading advantage relates positively to gender equality; it is larger in countries that are more gender equitable. Finally, data analyses limited to two subgroups of nations with high genetic similarity produced the same results as the analyses for all 40 nations, suggesting that genetic factors do not explain the differences in the sizes of the sex differences in mathematics performance among cultural groups that differ in gender equity.

Socialization influences on gender differences in mathematics performance also come from within the family. Girls in the United States appear to perform more poorly in mathematics in part because their parents and they themselves expect them to do so (Eccles & Jacobs, 1986; Eccles, Jacobs, & Harold, 1990; Eccles & Jacobs, 1992; Eccles, 1994). The influences of expectations could relate to stereotype threat. Stereotype threat comes into play when negative stereotypes about a group's performance, such as the stereotype in the United States that women are not good at mathematics, are activated. It is thought that activation of the stereotype has psychological consequences, such as heightened anxiety, that impair performance. Stereotypes are already present, but can be made even more salient, by reminding research participants that one group performs better on the test they are about to take than another group does. Typically, girls or women perform worse than boys or men on measures of mathematics when the stereotype that males are better than females at mathematics is activated, but perform similarly when it is not, particularly if they are told that there is no sex difference in performance on a particular task (Cadinu, Maass, Rosabianca, & Kiesner, 2005; Good, Aronson, & Harder,

2008; Spencer, Steele, & Quinn, 1999). Stereotype threat also can be made salient, and women's performance reduced, by having women take a mathematics test in a room with a large number of men (Inzlicht & Ben-Zeev, 2000). Stereotype threat has been found to impair women's performance in other areas as well, including performance on spatial tasks, such as mental rotations (Moe & Pazzaglia, 2006; Moe, 2009; Wraga, Helt, Jacobs, & Sullivan, 2007) and success in chess matches (Maass, D'Ettole, & Cadinu, 2008).

Mechanisms involved in the negative effects of stereotype threat are thought to include stress and anxiety activation, effort to suppress negative thought processes, and performance monitoring, all of which reduce resources available to perform tasks (Schmader, Johns, & Forbes, 2008). Effective procedures for counteracting the effects of stereotype threat include training that focuses on the ability to increase performance and that helps individuals to attribute difficulties to situational factors (e.g., moving to a new school, assignment of more challenging material), rather than personal factors (e.g., lack of ability) (Good, Aronson, & Inzlicht, 2003).

Cognitive Sex Differences and the Brain

Both brain structure and brain function have been examined in relation to sex differences in cognitive performance. Unlike studies linking subcortical brain regions to sexual orientation and core gender identity, studies looking for the neural underpinnings of cognition have focused on the cerebral cortex.

A 1982 study reported a sex difference in the human corpus callosum, finding that the splenium of the corpus callosum (defined as the posterior fifth viewed in mid-sagittal section) was larger and "more bulbous" in a sample of female brains obtained at autopsy than in a similar sample of male brains (de Lacoste-Utamsing and Holloway, 1982). Maximum splenial width, splenial area and total callosal area were also larger (relative to total brain weight) in the female than the male brains. Similar findings were reported for a second sample of adult brains (Holloway & de Lacoste, 1986), and the sex difference in maximum splenial width adjusted for brain weight was observed in a sample of fetal brains (de Lacoste et al., 1986).

Reports of sex differences in the human corpus callosum were controversial. One review suggested that over 20 subsequent studies failed to replicate the sex difference in the splenium (Byne & Parsons, 1993), and a second, based on a meta-analysis of 49 studies, concluded that there was no sex difference (Bishop & Wahlsten, 1997). The validity of such reviews depends on the quality of the studies included and their use of methodology similar to that used in the original report. However, studies of the corpus callosum have used varied methodologies. For instance, some have defined the splenium as the posterior fourth, rather than the posterior fifth, of the callosum, have not adjusted values to reflect the overall sex difference in brain size, or have marked off fourths or fifths of the callosum along a straight line from front to back, rather than on a curved line bisecting it. (The curved-line procedure was used in the original reports of sex differences to adjust for individual differences in curvature of the callosum.) Many studies also used clinical images, obtained using magnetic resonance (MR) imaging, instead of autopsy material. Although both autopsy material and MR images could produce reliable results, images obtained for clinical purposes are not necessarily designed to produce precise midline images of the callosum. Because the fibers of the callosum fan out dramatically after passing the midline, an image that is not precisely positioned in the midline could add substantial error variability, making it difficult to detect group differences. (These and other methodological issues are discussed more extensively by Allen et al., 1991; Elster et al., 1990; and Hines & Collaer, 1993.)

Studies using procedures similar to those used in the original reports have found sex differences in the callosum (Allen et al., 1991; Clarke et al., 1989; Elster et al., 1990), although they are not as dramatic as they originally appeared, and the appropriateness of adjusting for overall callosal size or brain size is debated (Jancke et al., 1997). One relatively recent approach has been template deformation morphometry (TDM), which attempts to address this concern. TDM registers each subject to a template callosum, avoiding the problem of using overall brain size, while still adjusting for size differences. Using TDM analysis of MR images, the splenium has been found to be larger in the female, than the male, brain (Dubb et al., 2003).

The most anterior portion of the callosum also appears to show a sex difference. One report found that the genu of the callosum, defined as the anterior fourth as viewed in mid-sagittal section, was larger in males than in females (Reinarz et al., 1988), while a second, defining a smaller area of the callosum as the genu, also found the region to be larger in males than in females (Witelson, 1989). A similar difference was found using TDM (Dubb et al., 2003).

The isthmus of the callosum, lying just anterior to the splenium, and defined as the posterior third minus the posterior fifth, also has been reported to vary with sex

(Witelson, 1985; Witelson, 1989), although in this case, hand preferences must also be considered. The isthmus is smaller in individuals who consistently use their right hand for motor tasks than in those who do not. In addition, in consistent right-handers, the isthmus is larger in females than in males, whereas there is no sex difference in those who are not consistent right-handers. These reports, like those of sex differences in the splenium, were controversial and there were reported failures to replicate the initial findings (e.g., Kertesz et al., 1987;). Methodological differences similar to those described for studies of the splenium are also relevant here. In addition, some studies used different procedures to classify hand-preference groups, or based classifications only on the hand used for writing, rather than on preferences across a range of motor tasks.

Despite controversy over the existence of sex differences, the size and shape of the corpus callosum have been related to sex-linked cognitive functions. For instance, the mid-sagittal surface area of posterior regions of the callosum, particularly the splenial region, have been found to relate positively to verbal fluency in women (Hines et al., 1992), reflecting a positive correlation, within women, between female-typical brain structure and female-typical cognitive function.

Sex differences in the size of callosal subregions, similar to those seen in humans, have not been reported in rodents. However, under certain rearing conditions, numbers of some types of fibers in posterior regions of the callosum have been found to vary with sex (Juraska & Kopcik, 1988; Juraska, 1991). When rats are reared after weaning in complex environments (large group cages containing objects that are changed daily), females have more myelinated axons in the posterior callosum than males do. When animals are reared in isolation (single cages with no objects other than those needed to provide food and water), however, this sex difference is not seen. Other studies have shown that similar environmental manipulations influence dendritic growth in various regions of the cerebral cortex, and can produce, enhance, reduce, or even reverse sex differences in these neural characteristics (Juraska, 1991).

These findings illustrate the complexity of studying and interpreting findings about sex differences in brain structure, given their apparent dependence on postnatal experience. A sex difference in brain structure is sometimes interpreted to indicate an inborn or irreversible state. However, new neurons can be born under certain conditions in some regions of the adult cerebral cortex, and neuronal growth and survival can depend on adult experience (Kempermann et al., 1997 Kempermann et al., 1998). In addition, for subcortical regions with dense concentrations of steroid receptors, including the SDN-POA, and the anteroventral periventricular nucleus of the hypothalamus (AVPV), a structure that is larger in females than in males, gonadectomy just prior to puberty can alter subsequent neuron numbers (Ahmed et al., 2008). Specifically, prepubertal gonadectomy reduces the number of new cells born in the female, but not the male, AVPV, and the number of new cells born in the male, but not the female, SDN-POA, and reduces volumetric sex differences in both regions. Hence, structural sex differences in the brains of males and females cannot be assumed to reflect an inborn state, or even to be the result of experience during very early, as opposed to later, life.

Studies of sex differences in the human brain are not limited to investigations of structure. Technologies such as functional MR imaging and positron emission tomography (PET) allow investigation of the function of the living brain as well. These technologies continue to be refined, and research on sex differences in human brain function has not yet reached a stage where firm conclusions are possible. However, it appears that, to a large extent, male and female brains function similarly (Frost et al., 1999; Mansour, Haier, & Buchsbaum, 1996), even during performance on tasks, such as mental rotations and verbal fluency, that show sex differences (Halari et al., 2005).

The question of sex differences in the functioning brain is far more complex than it might appear at first. Many factors influence results and could be invoked to explain inconsistencies across studies. These include, for example, the age of subjects, their hand preferences, whether they are resting or conducting a task, the specific task being conducted, its difficulty level, the skill of the individual being tested or their prior experience with the task, the response modality, the specific imaging technique used, and the statistical procedures used to quantify neural function and evaluate group differences.

There also is evidence that male and female brains may sometimes use different mechanisms to achieve the same outcome. For instance, one study using PET found that scores on the SAT math subtest correlated with activation in the temporal lobes in men, whereas in women, who had been matched to the men for math ability, there was no correlation between performance and activation in this region or any other brain region identified (Haier & Benbow, 1995). Similarly, men and women show different patterns of activational asymmetry when engaged in a certain type of language task, even though the task does not show a sex difference in performance (Shaywitz et al., 1995). Performance on standard tests of intelligence also appears to correlate with the volume of different neural structures in men and women as assessed using MR imaging. In women, performance relates to the amount of gray and white matter in frontal regions, whereas in men, the relationship is to parietal regions (Haier et al., 2005).

Other studies suggest different patterns or amounts of neural activation in males and females while performing verbal and spatial tasks (for a review, see Halpern et al., 2007). However, many of these reports involved tasks that do not show sex differences. Even when the tasks do show sex differences, it is not clear that the different patterns of cognitive performance result from the different patterns or amounts of neural activation. In addition, the existence of neural sex differences that relate to sex differences in cognitive performance does not necessarily elucidate the developmental origins of the cognitive differences. Although evidence of brain differences is often assumed to suggest immutability, any performance difference, whether inborn or acquired, will be reflected in brain structure or function. Thus, differences in brain structure or function in males and females, even if causally related to differences in behavior, could result from differences in experience and learning, as well as from inborn influences.

Summary for Cognition

Gonadal hormones may contribute to sex differences in performance on measures of mental rotations and spatial perception. However, the evidence is not consistent, and any effect appears to be small. Postnatal experience, including playing videogames and other activities that are more characteristic of boys, also appears to influence spatial performance, and there are large cultural influences on performance, at least for mathematics and scientific understanding. These cultural differences are many times as large as the differences between girls and boys in any given culture. In addition, not all cultures show sex differences in mathematical abilities, and those that do not tend to be those with more gender equity. One mechanism that maintains the male advantage on measures of mathematics and spatial abilities in our culture is stereotype threat, which involves reduced cognitive capability in response to an expectation of poor performance. The widespread belief that males are better on these types of tasks may in fact cause females to fulfill the expectation that they will perform less well. The causes of the female advantage on measures of writing, verbal fluency, and perceptual speed have received relatively little research attention.

EMOTION

Other behaviors that show sex differences might be viewed as relating to emotional systems and responses. These include aggression and empathy, which are often measured with paper and pencil questionnaires, or personality inventories, as well as characteristics, such as interest in infants and in parenting. The size of these sex differences can vary depending on the assessment instrument, but they can be large ($d > 1.0$, for instance, on some measures of aggression) (Pasterski et al., 2007).

Tendencies to behave in a physically aggressive manner have been linked to the early hormone environment. Females with CAH show more physically aggressive behavior, such as fighting, in comparison to unaffected female relatives (Mathews et al., 2009; Pasterski et al., 2007). Similarly, both girls and boys exposed to androgenic progestins prenatally have been found to show higher propensities toward physical aggression (Reinisch, 1981). Although some studies have not found consistent differences in physical aggression in females with and without CAH (Berenbaum & Resnick, 1997; Ehrhardt et al., 1968; Ehrhardt & Baker, 1974), inconsistent findings probably reflect the use of small samples and relatively insensitive measures.

There is a broad cultural assumption that circulating levels of androgens, particularly testosterone, cause human aggression. This assumption may derive from substantial evidence that androgen treatment in other adult mammals increases aggression, and that androgen removal decreases it (Simon, 2002). Similar studies of androgen treatment effects in men have produced largely negative results, however (Alexander et al., 1997; O'Connor et al., 2002; Tricker et al., 1996). In addition, meta-analyses estimating the size of correlations between androgen and aggression in men find small to negligible relationships ($d = .14$ to $.28$) (Archer et al., 1998; Book, Starzyk, & Quinsey, 2001). Even this small correlation could be caused by behavior influencing testosterone levels, given evidence that a number of behaviors that relate to aggression, such as competition, stress, and dominance interactions, can influence testosterone levels (Bernstein, Rose, & Gordon, 1974; Bernstein, Gordon, & Rose, 1983; Booth, Shelley, Mazur, & Tharp, 1989; Elias, 1981).

Other perspectives on the causes of aggressive behavior stress cognitive and social influences. These perspectives do not focus specifically on sex differences in aggression, but provide evidence of powerful influences of the social environment, social history, and the individual's cognitive capacity and style on aggressive behavior. Indeed, even in rodents—thought to be more influenced by nature and less by nurture than humans—the rearing environment can have dramatic influences on aggression. For instance, a series of studies found that animals reared with their mothers, as well as another adult female animal who was not lactating so could not feed them, but who provided other aspects of care, such as grooming, showed 90% less aggressive behavior than animals reared with only their mother (Denenberg, 1970).

In humans, parenting behaviors, such as harsh discipline, low warmth, and child neglect predict aggression in offspring (Sameroff, Peck, & Eccles, 2004; Serbin & Karp, 2004), and, at least in some cases, these associations are mediated by changes in cognitive biases, such as tendencies to hostile thoughts and attributions, and by social learning, such as modeling of parental aggression (Chang, Schwartz, Dodge, & McBride-Chang, 2003; Serbin & Karp, 2004). In later childhood, negative peers and poor school outcomes also can increase aggressive behavior, whereas positive peers and good school outcomes can reduce it (Sameroff, Peck, & Eccles, 2004). Some activities that boys engage in more than girls do, such as playing with boys, involvement with aggressive computer games or other media, and drug use, also contribute to sex differences in aggression.

Individual differences in empathy have been related to the early hormone environment as well. Females with CAH score higher on a personality measure of empathy than do their healthy female relatives (Mathews et al., 2009). There also is some evidence linking testosterone measured in amniotic fluid to empathy in childhood (Chapman et al., 2006; Knickmeyer et al., 2006). Sometimes, however, the correlations between amniotic fluid testosterone and measures of empathy were not significant within each sex (Knickmeyer et al., 2006), making it impossible to know if the significant relationship is caused only by the sex differences in both empathy and testosterone, or by a more meaningful relationship between the two variables. The power of studies using amniotic fluid samples to measure the early hormone environment is limited, because only individuals referred for clinical amniocentesis can participate and only a single sample of fluid is available to reflect the fetal hormone environment over many months. Larger samples than have been studied to date in regard to empathy may be needed to produce robust results.

Other perspectives on the development of empathy include applications of social and cognitive theory. Empathy is seen as a feminine characteristic and, as such, girls and women are likely to report higher empathy than boys and men. They also might be expected to engage in more empathic behavior, because they have received more positive reinforcement for doing so in the past and they may adopt more empathic behavior based on knowing that they are female and that empathy is a feminine trait.

Parenting is generally viewed as more the realm of females than males. Indeed in many countries more parental leave is provided for mothers than for fathers when a baby is born. Is there any evidence that women are better parents than men? In other species, parenting behaviors, such as retrieving offspring and returning them to the nest and crouching over them, although seen in both male and female adults, appear more rapidly in females. In addition, in rodents, these behaviors relate partly to perinatal programming by androgen, but also to the effects of hormones that accompany birth and parturition (Bridges, Zarrow, & Denenberg, 1973; Bridges, 1990). Human beings appear to be emancipated, at least to some extent, from this immediate hormonal control of parenting behaviors, and parents who adopt children, and so have not recently experienced the hormone changes that accompany birth and parturition, can show excellent parenting. Similarly, there is no evidence that single male parents, or two male parents, produce children with more social, emotional, or educational difficulties than do their female single-parent or dual-parent counterparts, although this is a subject that is difficult to study rigorously (Golombok, 2000). Nevertheless, there is some evidence of vestigial hormonal influence on human parenting behavior. Girls exposed to high levels of androgen prenatally, because of CAH, show more interest in infants than do unaffected girls (Leveroni & Berenbaum, 1998; Mathews et al., 2009).

Life stage also influences interest in infants (Feldman & Nash, 1978; Feldman & Nash, 1979; Nash & Feldman, 1981). For instance, women who are mothers of infants respond more to unrelated infants than do pregnant women, single women, married women without children, or mothers of older children. Grandmothers of infants also respond more to babies than do women whose children are adolescent or older, but who are not yet grandmothers. Men also are influenced by anticipated or current involvement with children. Expectant fathers and grandfathers show more interest in pictures of babies than do men at other life stages. Interest in infants also responds to demand characteristics in situations, perhaps because it is thought to be such a prototypically female province. For example, men and women, as well as girls and boys, show similar psychophysiological responses, such as blood pressure, skin conductance, and heart rate changes, to babies crying or smiling (Frodi, Lamb, Leavitt, & Donovan, 1978; Frodi & Lamb, 1978), but girls show more overt behavioral responsiveness than boys, a result interpreted to indicate that the greater female behavioral responsiveness results from societal pressure, rather than innate factors (Frodi & Lamb, 1978). Similarly, self-report of interest in infants yields larger differences between males and females when in same-sexed groups, than when in private or in groups of mixed sex (Berman, 1976). Other situational variables also are important. Behavioral observation of interactions with infants suggest that sex differences are not clear in all situations, and are most obvious when the infant is a relative or there has been an instruction to care for the infant (Berman, 1980).

THE LIFE SPAN AFTER CHILDHOOD

Much of the psychological research on gender development has focused on children, and indeed some of the behaviors covered in this review, particularly childhood toy and playmate preferences, lose their relevance after puberty. Others, such as core gender identity and sexual orientation, once established in childhood or adolescence, appear to show little or no subsequent age-related changes.

Interest in infants is one of the gendered behaviors that has been studied to some extent in adults, but, even in this case, evidence is not extensive. One reason for the relative lack of information about adults may be the difficulty or cost associated with accessing large samples of adults willing to participate. Children and young adults can be accessed through schools until they finish formal education. In addition, children are not accustomed to being paid for their time, and so may be more willing volunteers. Whatever the reason, from a life-span perspective, there is clearly a need for more information. A life-span account of gender development would require, at a minimum, normative information on trajectories of cognitive and emotional functioning from young adulthood to old age, as well as information on how life stages and life changes influence gendered behavior. For instance, what impact does career choice or specific work involvement in various settings have on cognitive and emotional functioning? And how do life events, such as parenthood, parental leave, return to work, or retirement influence gendered psychological characteristics?

The relatively small body of information that exists suggests that cognitive function generally declines after middle age, and that this is true both for men and for women. Nevertheless, sex differences in cognitive performance appear to persist, at least among men and women in the United States. Although both sexes decline in performance, men maintain their advantage over women on mental rotations tasks, and women maintain their advantage over men on verbal recall tasks (Maitland et al., 2000). Women's advantage on perceptual speed may not persist into the oldest decades, however (Maitland et al., 2000). Also, even in older groups, training may be effective; one study trained elderly participants on mental rotations tasks and found that women benefited from the training more than men did, eliminating the sex difference in performance (Willis & Schaie, 1988).

One later life event that has been studied fairly extensively is menopause, and the effect of hormone replacement, especially replacement of estrogen, on cognitive function in postmenopausal women. Some such studies have produced encouraging findings, suggesting that estrogen treatment could improve cognitive function in aging women (Kimura, 1995; Wolf et al., 1999), but other studies did not find these effects (Barrett-Connor & Kritz-Silverstein, 1993; Wolf et al., 2005). In addition, the effects of estrogen were not limited to aspects of cognitive functioning that show sex differences (Cholerton, Gleason, Baker, & Asthana, 2002; Zec & Trivedi, 2002), suggesting that selection biases could explain the results (Zec & Trivedi, 2002). Women who are more cognitively capable, more educated, or who have healthier lifestyles might be more likely to take estrogen, and this could produce an association between estrogen use and enhanced performance on cognitive tasks. Consistent with the possibility of selection biases, postmenopausal women who have ever taken estrogen, even if no longer taking it, have been found to perform better cognitively than women who have never taken estrogen (Jacobs et al., 1998; Matthews, Cauley, Yaffe, & Zmuda, 1999). Also, double-blind, placebo-controlled research found that estrogen treatment did not preserve cognitive function in postmenopausal women and could instead impair it (Espeland et al., 2004; Shumaker et al., 2003; Shumaker et al., 2004). It has been suggested that these negative findings could reflect the age of the women in the study, who were over age 65, and so had gone through menopause many years before the estrogen treatment was initiated (Sherwin, 2005).

The possibility that estrogen treatment of younger women could maintain or improve cognitive function has not been examined rigorously.

In addition to the effects of hormones on cognition that have been hypothesized to exist late in the life span, some hormonal events that occur early in life and could also influence gendered behavior are areas of emerging interest. Although the gonads are quiescent during much of early childhood, there are two times in addition to the prenatal period when they are active and could exert programming effects on the brain. One is shortly after birth, when there is a surge of testosterone in males (Smail, Reyes, Winter, & Faiman, 1981), and of estrogen in females (Bidlingmaier, Versmold, & Knorr, 1974; Bidlingmaier et al., 1987). The testosterone surge has been linked to development of the external genitalia (Quigley, 2002), and either surge could relate to neural and behavioral development as well. The second time is puberty. Just as prenatal hormones influence genital differentiation as male or female, pubertal hormones have irreversible influences on other sexual characteristics in humans. For instance, estrogens promote breast development and androgens cause penile growth. It is possible that there are major, irreversible influences on the brain during this period too, and, as noted above, pubertal hormones appear to influence the birth of neurons in some brain regions in rodents. In this context, the relative lack of information on effects of pubertal hormones on human neurobehavioral development is striking.

There is some evidence, however, of changes in the human brain at puberty, and these changes differ somewhat for girls and boys. Total cerebral volume, assessed using MR imaging, has been found to peak at about age 10.5 years in girls, but at about age 14.5 years in boys (Lenroot et al., 2007). Males also show a steeper rate of increase in white matter than do females during adolescence, and both cortical and subcortical gray matter show an inverted-U–shape pattern of change that peaks 1 to 2 years earlier in girls than in boys (Lenroot et al., 2007). In addition, girls and boys differ in the growth of specific brain regions between the ages of 4 and 18 years. For instance, the volume of the amygdala increases in males, but not females, whereas the volume of the hippocampus increases in females, but not males, across this age span (Lenroot & Giedd, 2006). It will be challenging to determine whether these changes, or any behavioral changes coinciding with puberty, relate to gonadal hormones acting on brain receptors to alter neural structure and function, or from the consequences of the changing environments and experiences that accompany the physical and social changes of puberty.

Gendered behavior may also change at other life stages because of social and cognitive factors. For instance, the abovementioned increased interest in infants that is seen in expectant grandparents may be caused by their increased exposure to stimuli associated with babies and their cognitive focus on their impending identity as grandparents. This speculation too has yet to receive systematic empirical investigation, however. As mentioned above, for many gendered behaviors, few data are available for men and women beyond young adulthood.

CONCLUSIONS

Many types of factors influence the development of gendered behavior across the life span. Genes, hormones present during early development, socialization, and cognitive development all play a role, although the extent to which each type of factor is influential may vary from behavior to behavior, as well as from individual to individual. The behaviors that are best understood in terms of the processes that produce sex differences are those seen in childhood. Although no direct genetic influences on gendered play have been identified, genes on the Y chromosome cause the primordial gonads to differentiate as testes. Beginning prenatally, hormones produced by the testes, particularly the androgen, testosterone, then exert influences on sex-linked behavior across the life span. The earliest well-established manifestation of these influences involves childhood play behavior. Girls exposed to high levels of androgen prenatally show elevated male-typical play and reduced female-typical play; similarly, testosterone measured in amniotic fluid or in maternal blood samples during pregnancy predicts the amount of male-typical play in offspring. Postnatal socialization by parents, peers, teachers, and strangers encourages sex-typical behavior through reinforcement of gender-typical behavior and discouragement of gendered-atypical behavior. Children who are markedly sex-typical or atypical in early childhood become even more so by late childhood, perhaps because they seek out environments that intensify their early dispositions. Cognitive understanding of gender also further promotes engagement in sex-typical behavior. Children come to understand that they are male or female and then attach importance to behaving in ways that are consistent with this gender label, and to modeling others of their own sex.

Sex-typical, or atypical, behavior in childhood predicts sex-typical behavior in other areas in adolescence and adulthood. For instance, girls who are strongly cross-gendered in childhood are better at mental rotations tasks that usually favor males in early adolescence, and boys who are strongly cross-gendered in childhood are more likely to be non-heterosexual as adults. Hormonal influences also appear to be important with regard to sexual orientation and core gender identity. Females exposed to high levels of androgens prenatally show reduced heterosexual interest and increased likelihood of gender dysphoria in adulthood. Although social and cognitive factors appear to influence sexual orientation and core gender identity as well, the precise social and cognitive factors involved have yet to be identified. Sex differences in cognitive abilities, such as mathematical and mental rotations performance and verbal fluency and perceptual speed, also may relate in part to the early hormone environment, but influences of early androgen exposure on cognitive function have been surprisingly hard to demonstrate. In regard to mathematics performance, there also are large differences across cultures, and these cultural differences in performance are many times larger than the sex difference seen in some settings. Also, some cultures show no sex difference or even a reversed sex difference, and the size of the male advantage in mathematics relates negatively to how gender egalitarian the culture is. Stereotype threat and social expectations also seem to play a role in the male advantage seen on measures of mathematical ability, at least in the United States.

It is tempting to ask which type of influence, nature or nurture, is the most important in determining human gendered behavior. The answer to this question depends, however, on which behavior, which person, and in which setting. Imagine, for instance, a world where nurture was identical for girls and boys. In this world, differences in the behavior of males and females would be caused by nature. Similarly, if all factors subsumed under the term, nature, were identical, all behavioral differences would arise from other factors, that is, nurture. Another problem with assessing the role of nature and nurture involves defining these terms. For example, would ingestion of substances that cause hormone changes in the fetus during early development be nature or nurture? Similarly, if antenatal or neonatal experiences cause hormone changes in the fetus or infant and these influence brain development and subsequent behavior, is that nature or nurture? A more useful approach is to try to identify the numerous factors that contribute to the development of gendered behavior, and, if intervention is desired, intervene where intervention is possible.

The factors influencing gendered behavior across the life span are far from completely understood. For instance, we have some information on how prenatal hormones predispose individuals to different behaviors, and a fair understanding of how social and cognitive processes further contribute to the development of gender-typical or gender-atypical play behavior in children. Little is known, however, about how gendered predispositions at birth interact with parental behavior and other environmental influences during early life. The human brain, particularly the cerebral cortex, undergoes extensive development and remodeling during the first 2 postnatal years, and is responsive to environmental influence. It is possible, for instance, that infants with different temperaments elicit different caretaking responses and that these then influence the child's experience and the subsequent architecture of the brain across the life span. Empirical investigation in this area is limited or non-existent, however. Pubertal influences, both of the hormonal and social environment, also are relatively unexplored, and are a current focus of attention. The causes of variability in sexual orientation and core gender identity appear to be numerous, but largely unknown. In addition, very little is known about gender development beyond early adulthood. There are many important opportunities for additional research on gender development across the life span.

REFERENCES

Ahmed, E. I., Zehr, J. L., Schulz, K. M., Lorenz, B. H., DonCarlos, L. L., & Sisk, C. L. (2008). Pubertal hormones modulate the addition of new cells to sexually dimorphic brain regions. *Nature Neuroscience, 11,* 995–997.

Alexander, G. M., & Hines, M. (1994). Gender labels and play styles: Their relative contribution to children's selection of playmates. *Child Development, 65,* 869–879.

Alexander, G. M., & Hines, M. (2002). Sex differences in response to children's toys in nonhuman primates (cercopithecus aethiops sabaeus). *Evolution and Human Behavior, 23,* 467–479.

Alexander, G. M., Swerdloff, R. S., Wang, C., Davidson, T., McDonald, V., Steiner, B., et al. (1997). Androgen–behavior correlations in hypogonadal men and eugonadal men. I. Mood and response to auditory sexual stimuli. *Hormones and Behavior, 31,* 110–119.

Allen, L. S., & Gorski, R. A. (1992). Sexual orientation and the size of the anterior commissure in the human brain. *Proceedings of the National Academy of Sciences USA, 89,* 7199–7202.

Allen, L. S., Richey, M. F., Chai, Y. M., & Gorski, R. A. (1991). Sex differences in the corpus callosum of the living human being. *Journal of Neurosciences, 11,* 933–942.

American Psychiatric Association. (2000). *Diagnostic and Statistical Manual of Mental Disorders: DSM-IV-TR: Fourth Edition Text Revision.* Washington, DC: American Psychiatric Publishing.

Archer, J., Birring, S. S., & Wu, F. C. W. (1998). The association between testosterone and aggression among young men: Empirical findings and a meta-analysis. *Aggressive Behavior, 24,* 411–420.

Arden, R., & Plomin, R. (2006). Sex differences in variance of intelligence across childhood. *Personality and Individual Differences, 41,* 39–48.

Auyeung, B., Baron-Cohen, S., Chapman, E., Knickmeyer, R., Taylor, K., Hackett, G., et al. (2009). Fetal testosterone predicts sexually differentiated childhood behavior in girls and in boys. *Psychological Science, 20,* 144–148.

Baenninger, M., & Newcombe, N. (1989). The role of experience in spatial test performance: A meta-analysis. *Sex Roles, 20,* 327–344.

Bailey, J. M., Dunne, M. P., & Martin, N. G. (2000). Genetic and environmental influences on sexual orientation and its correlates in an Australian twin sample. *Journal of Personality & Social Psychology, 78,* 524–536.

Bailey, J. M., & Pillard, R. C. (1991). A genetic study of male sexual orientation. *Archives of General Psychiatry, 48,* 1089–1096.

Bailey, J. M., Pillard, R. C., Neale, M. C., & Agyei, Y. (1993). Heritable factors influence sexual orientation in women. *Archives of General Psychiatry, 50,* 217–223.

Bailey, J. M., & Zucker, K. J. (1995). Childhood sex-typed behavior and sexual orientation: A conceptual analysis and quantitative review. *Developmental Psychology, 31,* 43–55.

Baker, S. W., & Ehrhardt, A. A. (1974). Prenatal androgen, intelligence and cognitive sex differences. In R. C. Friedman, R. N. Richart, & R. L. Vande Wiele (Eds.), *Sex differences in behavior* (pp. 53–76). New York: John Wiley & Sons.

Barrett-Connor, E., & Kritz-Silverstein, D. (1993). Estrogen replacement therapy and cognitive function in older women. *JAMA, 269,* 2637–2641.

Bell, A., Weinberg, M., & Hammersmith, S. (1981). *Sexual Preference: Its Development in Men and Women*. Bloomington: Indiana University Press.

Bem, D. J. (1996). Exotic becomes erotic: A developmental theory of sexual orientation. *Psychological Review, 103,* 320–335.

Berenbaum, S. A., & Hines, M. (1992). Early androgens are related to childhood sex-typed toy preferences. *Psychological Science, 3,* 203–206.

Berenbaum, S. A., & Resnick, S. M. (1997). Early androgen effects on aggression in children and adults with congenital adrenal hyperplasia. *Psychoneuroendocrinology, 22,* 505–515.

Berman, P. A. (1980). Are women more responsive than men to the young? A review of developmental and situational variables. *Psychological Bulletin, 88,* 668–695.

Berman, P. W. (1976). Social context as a determinant of sex difference in adults' attraction to infants. *Developmental Psychology, 12,* 365–366.

Bernstein, I. S., Gordon, T. P., & Rose, R. M. (1983). The interaction of hormones, behavior, and social context in nonhuman primates. In B. B. Svare (Ed.), *Hormones and aggressive behavior* (pp. 535–561). New York: Plenum Press.

Bernstein, I. S., Rose, R. M., & Gordon, T. P. (1974). Behavioral and environmental events influencing primate testosterone levels. *Journal of Human Evolution, 3,* 517–525.

Bidlingmaier, F., Strom, T. M., Dörr, G., Eisenmenger, W., & Knorr, D. (1987). Estrone and estradiol concentrations in human ovaries, testes, and adrenals during the first two years of life. *Journal of Clinical Endocrinology and Metabolism, 65,* 862–867.

Bidlingmaier, F., Versmold, H., & Knorr, D. (1974). Plasma estrogens in newborns and infants. In M. Forest & J. Bertrand (Eds.), *Sexual endocrinology of the perinatal period* (pp. 299–314). Paris: Inserm.

Billy, J. O. G., Tanfer, K., Grady, W. R., & Klepinger, D. H. (1993). The sexual behavior of men in the United States. *Family Planning Perspectives, 25,* 52–60.

Bishop, K. M. & Wahlsten, D. (1997) Sex differences in the human corpus callosum: Myth or reality? *Neuroscience and Biobehavioral Reviews, 21,* 581–601.

Blanchard, R. (2001). Fraternal birth order and the maternal immune hypothesis of male homosexuality. *Hormones and Behavior, 40,* 105–114.

Blanchard, R. (2004). Quantitative and theoretical analyses of the relation between older brothers and homosexuality in men. *Journal of Theoretical Biology, 230,* 173–187.

Blanchard, R. (2008). Sex ratio of older siblings in heterosexual and homosexual, right-handed and non-right-handed men. *Archives of Sexual Behavior, 37,* 977–981.

Blanchard, R., & Bogaert, A. F. (1996). Homosexuality in men and number of older brothers. *American Journal of Psychiatry, 153,* 27–31.

Blanchard, R., & Lippa, R. A. (2007). Birth order, sibling sex ratio, handedness, and sexual orientation of male and female participants in a BBC Internet research project. *Archives of Sexual Behavior, 36,* 176.

Bogaert, A. F. (2006). Biological versus nonbiological older brothers and men's sexual orientation. *Proceedings of the National Academy of Sciences, USA, 103,* 10771–10774.

Book, A. S., Starzyk, K. B., & Quinsey, V. L. (2001). The relationship between testosterone and aggression: A meta-analysis. *Aggression and Violent Behavior, 6,* 579–599.

Booth, A., Shelley, G., Mazur, A., & Tharp, G. (1989). Testosterone, and winning and losing in human competition. *Hormones and Behavior, 23,* 556–571.

Bradley, S. J., Oliver, G. D., Chernick, A. B., & Zucker, K. J. (1998). Experiment of nurture: Ablatio penis at 2 months, sex reasignment at 7 months and a psychosexual follow-up in young adulthood. *Pediatrics, 102,* 102–101.

Bridges, R. S. (1990). Endocrine regulation of parental behavior in rodents. In N. Krasnegor & R. S. Bridges (Eds.), *Mammalian parenting: Biochemical, neurobiological, and behavioral determinants* (pp. 93–117). New York : Oxford University Press.

Bridges, R. S., Zarrow, M. K., & Denenberg, V. H. (1973). The role of neonatal androgen in the expression of hormonally induced maternal responsiveness in the adult rat. *Hormones and Behavior, 4,* 315–322.

Brown, W. M., Hines, M., Fane, B. A., & Breedlove, S. M. (2002). Masculinized finger length patterns in human males and females with congenital adrenal hyperplasia. *Hormones and Behavior, 42,* 380–386.

Buchsbaum, M. S., & Henkin, R. I. (1980). Perceptual abnormalities in patients with chromatin negative gonadal dysgenesis and hypogonadotropic hypogonadism. *International Journal of Neurosciences, 11,* 201–209.

Buck, J. J., Williams, R. M., Hughes, I. A., & Acerini, C. L. (2003). In-utero androgen exposure and 2nd to 4th digit length ratio—comparisons between healthy controls and females with classical congenital adrenal hyperplasia. *Human Reproduction, 18,* 976–979.

Bussey, K., & Bandura, A. (1984). Social cognitive theory of gender development and differentiation. *Journal of Personality and Social Psychology, 106,* 676–713.

Byne, W., & Parsons, B. (1993). Human sexual orientation: The biological theories reappraised. *Archives of General Psychiatry, 50,* 228–239.

Byne, W., Tobet, S. A., Mattiace, L. A., Lasco, M. S., Kemether, E., Edgar, M. A., et al. (2001). The interstitial nuclei of the human anterior hypothalamus: An investigation of variation with sex, sexual orientation, and HIV status. *Hormones and Behavior, 40,* 86–92.

Cadinu, M., Maass, A., Rosabianca, A., & Kiesner, J. (2005). Why do women underperform under stereotype threat? Evidence for the role of negative thinking. *Psychological Science, 16,* 572–578.

Cappa, S. F., Guariglia, C., Papagno, C., Pizzamiglio, L., Vallar, G., Zoccolotti, P., et al. (1988). Patterns of lateralization and performance levels for verbal and spatial tasks in congenital androgen deficiency. *Behavioural Brain Research, 31,* 177–183.

Carson, D. J., Okuno, A., Lee, P. A., Stetten, G., Didolkar, S. M., & Migeon, C. J. (1982). Amniotic fluid steroid levels: Fetuses with adrenal hyperplasia, 46,XXY fetuses, and normal fetuses. *American Journal of Diseases of Children, 136,* 218–222.

Chang, L., Schwartz, D., Dodge, K. A., & McBride-Chang, C. (2003). Harsh parenting in relation to child emotion regulation and aggression. *Journal of Family Psychology, 17,* 598–606.

Chapman, E., Baron-Cohen, S., Auyeung, B., Knickmeyer, R., Taylor, K., & Hackett, G. (2006). Fetal testosterone and empathy: Evidence from the Empathy Quotient (EQ) and the "Reading the mind in the eyes" Test. *Social Neuroscience, 1,* 135–148.

Cholerton, B., Gleason, C. E., Baker, L. D., & Asthana, S. (2002). Estrogen and Alzheimer's disease—The story so far. *Drugs & Aging, 19,* 405–427.

Christensen, L. W., & Gorski, R. A. (1978). Independent masculinization of neuroendocrine systems by intracerebral implants of testosterone or estradiol in the neonatal female rat. *Brain Research, 146,* 325–340.

Chung, W. C. J., De Vries, G. J., & Swaab, D. (2002). Sexual differentation of the bed nucleus of the stria terminalis in humans may extend into adulhood. *Journal of Neuroscience, 22,* 1027–1033.

Clark, M. M., Crews, D., & Galef, B. G., Jr. (1991). Concentrations of sex steroid hormones in pregnant and fetal mongolian gerbils. *Physiology and Behavior, 49,* 239–243.

Clark, M. M., & Galef, B. G., Jr. (1998). Effects of intrauterine position on the behavior and genital morphology of litter-bearing rodents. *Developmental Neuropsychology, 14,* 197–211.

Clarke, S., Kraftsik, R., van der Loos, H., & Innocenti, G. M. (1989) Forms and measures of adult and developing human corpus callosum: Is there sexual dimorphism? *The Journal of Comparative Neurology, 280,* 213–220.

Cohen, J. (1988). *Statistical power analysis for the behavioral sciences.* 2nd ed. Hillsdale, NJ: Erlbaum.

Cohen-Kettenis, P. T. (2005). Gender change in 46, XY persons with 5alpha-reductase-2 deficiency and 17beta-hydroxysteroid dehydrogenase-3 deficiency. *Archives of Sexual Behavior, 34,* 399–410.

Collaer, M. L., Brook, C. D. G., Conway, G. S., Hindmarsh, P. C., & Hines, M. (2009). Motor development in individuals with congenital adrenal hyperplasia: Strength, targeting, and fine motor skill. *Psychoneuroendocrinology, 34,* 249–258.

Collaer, M. L., Geffner, M., Kaufman, F. R., Buckingham, B., & Hines, M. (2002). Cognitive and behavioral characteristics of Turner syndrome: Exploring a role for ovarian hormones in female sexual differentiation. *Hormones and Behavior, 41,* 139–155.

Collaer, M. L., & Hines, M. (1995). Human behavioral sex differences: A role for gonadal hormones during early development? *Psychological Bulletin, 118,* 55–107.

Collaer, M. L., Reimers, S., & Manning, J. (2007). Visuospatial performance on an Internet line judgment task and potential hormonal markers: Sex, sexual orientation, and 2D:4D. *Archives of Sexual Behavior, 36,* 177–192.

Deary, I. J., Thorpe, G., Wilson, V., Starr, J. M., & Whalley, L. J. (2003). Population sex differences in IQ at age 11: The Scottish mental survey 1932. *Intelligence, 31,* 533–542.

de Lacoste-Utamsing, C., & Holloway, R. L. (1982). Sexual dimorphism in the human corpus callosum. *Science, 216,* 1431–1432.

de Lacoste, M. C., Holloway, R. L., & Woodward, D. J. (1986). Sex differences in the fetal human corpus callosum. *Human Neurobiology, 5,* 93–96.

Denenberg, V. H. (1970). The mother as a motivator. In W. J. Arnold & M. M. Page (Eds.), *Nebraska Symposium on Motivation* (pp. 69–93). Lincoln: University of Nebraska Press.

Diamond, L. M. (2003). What does sexual orientation orient? A biobehavioral model distinguishing romantic love and sexual desire. *Psychological Review, 110,* 173–192.

Diamond, L. M. (2004). Emerging perspectives on distinctions between romantic love and sexual desire. *Current Directions in Psychological Science, 13,* 116–119.

Diamond, M., & Sigmundson, H. K. (1997). Sex reassignment at birth: Long-term review and clinical implications. *Archives of Pediatric and Adolescent Medicine, 151,* 298–304.

DiPietro, J. A. (1981). Rough and tumble play: A function of gender. *Developmental Psychology, 17,* 50–58.

Dittmann, R. W., Kappes, M. E., & Kappes, M. H. (1992). Sexual behavior in adolescent and adult females with congenital adrenal hyperplasia. *Psychoneuroendocrinology, 17,* 153–170.

Dittmann, R. W., Kappes, M. H., Kappes, M. E., Börger, D., Stegner, H., Willig, R. H., et al. (1990). Congenital adrenal hyperplasia I: Gender-related behavior and attitudes in female patients and sisters. *Psychoneuroendocrinology, 15,* 401–420.

Dubb, A., Gur, R. C., Avants, G., & Gee, J. (2003) Characterization of sexual dimorphism in the human corpus callosum. *Neuroimage, 20,* 512–519.

DuPree, M. G., Mustanski, B. S., Bocklandt, S., Nievergelt, C., & Hamer, D. H. (2004). A candidate gene study of CYP19 (aromoatase) and male sexual orientation. *Behavior Genetics, 34,* 243–250.

Eaton, W. O., & Enns, L. R. (1986). Sex differences in human motor activity level. *Psychological Bulletin, 100,* 19–28.

Eccles, J. S. (1994). Understanding women's educational and occupational choices: Applying the Eccles et al. model of achievement related choices. *Psychology of Women Quarterly, 18,* 585–609.

Eccles, J. S., & Jacobs, J. E. (1986). Social forces shape math attitudes and performance. *Signs, 11,* 367–389.

Eccles, J. S., & Jacobs, J. E. (1992). The impact of mothers'gender-role sterotypic beliefs on mothers' and children's ability perceptions. *Journal of Personality and Social Psychology, 63,* 932–944.

Eccles, J. S., Jacobs, J. E., & Harold, R. D. (1990). Gender role stereotypes, expectancy effects and parents'socialization of gender differences. *Journal of Social Issues, 46,* 183–201.

Eckert, E. D., Bouchard, T. J., Bohlen, J., & Heston, L. L. (1986). Homosexuality in monozygotic twins reared apart. *British Journal of Psychiatry, 148,* 421–425.

Ehrhardt, A. A., & Baker, S. W. (1974). Fetal androgens, human central nervous system differentiation, and behavior sex differences. In R. C. Friedman, R. M. Richart, & R. L. van de Wiele (Eds.), *Sex differences in behavior* (pp. 33–52). New York: John Wiley & Sons.

Ehrhardt, A. A., Epstein, R., & Money, J. (1968). Fetal androgens and female gender identity in the early-treated adrenogenital syndrome. *Johns Hopkins Medical Journal, 122,* 165–167.

Ehrhardt, A. A., Grisanti, G. C., & Meyer-Bahlburg, H. F. L. (1977). Prenatal exposure to medroxyprogesterone acetate (MPA) in girls. *Psychoneuroendocrinology, 2,* 391–398.

Ehrhardt, A. A., Meyer-Bahlburg, H. F. L., Rosen, L. R., Feldman, J. F., Veridiano, N. P., Elkin, E. J., et al. (1989). The development of gender-related behavior in females following prenatal exposure to diethylstilbestrol (DES). *Hormones and Behavior, 23,* 526–541.

Ehrhardt, A. A., Meyer-Bahlburg, H. F. L., Rosen, L. R., Feldman, J. F., Veridiano, N. P., Zimmerman, I., et al. (1985). Sexual orientation after prenatal exposure to exogenous estrogen. *Archives of Sexual Behavior, 14,* 57–77.

Ehrhardt, A. A., & Money, J. (1967). Progestin-induced hermaphroditism: IQ and psychosexual identity in a study of ten girls. *The Journal of Sex Research, 3,* 83–100.

Ekstrom, R. B., French, J. W., & Harman, H. H. (1976). *Manual for Kit of Factor-Referenced Cognitive Tests*. Princeton, NJ: Educational Testing Service.

Elias, M. (1981). Serum cortisol, testosterone, and testosterone-binding globulin responses to competitive fighting in human males. *Aggressive Behavior, 7,* 215–224.

Elster, A. D., DiPersio, D. A., & Moody, D. M. (1990). Sexual dimorphism of the human corpus callosum studied by magnetic resonance imaging: Fact, fallacy and statistical confidence. *Brain Development, 12,* 321–325.

Espeland, M. A., Rapp, S. R., Shumaker, S. A., Brunner, R. L., Manson, J. E., Sherwin, B. B., et al. (2004). Conjugated equine estrogens and global cognitive function in postmenopausal women: The Women's Health Initiative Memory Study. *The Journal of the American Medical Association, 291,* 2959–2968.

Fagot, B. I. (1978). The influence of sex of child on parental reactions to toddler children. *Child Development, 49,* 459–465.

Fagot, B. I., & Patterson, G. R. (1969). An in vivo analysis of reinforcing contingencies for sex-role behaviors in the preschool child. *Developmental Psychology, 5,* 563–568.

Fausto-Sterling, A. (1992). *Myths of Gender*. New York: Basic Books.

Feingold, A. (1988). Cognitive gender differences are disappearing. *American Psychologist, 43,* 95–103.

Feldman, S. S., & Nash, S. C. (1978). Interest in babies during young adulthood. *Child Development, 49,* 617–622.

Feldman, S. S., & Nash, S. C. (1979). Sex differences in responsiveness to babies among mature adults. *Developmental Psychology, 15,* 430–436.

Feng, J., Spence, I., & Pratt, J. (2007). Playing an action video games reduces gender differences in spatial cognition. *Psychological Science, 18,* 850–855.

Finegan, J. K., Niccols, G. A., & Sitarenios, G. (1992). Relations between prenatal testosterone levels and cognitive abilities at 4 years. *Developmental Psychology, 28,* 1075–1089.

Frodi, A. M., & Lamb, M. E. (1978). Sex differences in responsiveness to infants: A developmental study of psychophysiological and behavioral responses. *Child Development, 49,* 1182–1188.

Frodi, A. M., Lamb, M. E., Leavitt, L. A., & Donovan, W. L. (1978). Fathers' and mothers' responses to infant smiles and cries. *Infant Behavior and Development, 1,* 187–198.

Frost, J. A., Binder, J. R., Springer, J. A., Hammeke, T. A., Bellgowan, S. F., Rao, S. M., et al. (1999). Language processing is strongly left lateralized in both sexes—Evidence from functional MRI. *Brain, 122,* 199–208.

Garcia-Falgueras, A., & Swaab, D. F. (2008). A sex difference in the hypothalamic uncinate nucleus: Relationship to gender identity. *Brain, 131,* 3132–3146.

Ghabrial, F., & Girgis, S. M. (1962). Reorientation of sex: Report of two cases. *International Journal of Fertility, 7,* 249–258.

Gitau, R., Adams, D., Fisk, N. M., & Glover, V. (2005). Fetal plasma testosterone correlates positively with cortisol. *Archives of Disease in Childhood Fetal and Neonatal Edition, 90,* F166–F169.

Golombok, S. (2000). *Parenting: What really counts?* London and New York: Routledge.

Golombok, S., & Hines, M. (2002). Sex differences in social behavior. In P. K. Smith & C. H. Hart (Eds.), *Blackwell Handbook of Childhood Social Development* (pp. 117–136). Cambridge, MA: Blackwell.

Golombok, S., Rust, J., Zervoulis, K., Croudace, T., Golding, J., & Hines, M. (2008). Developmental trajectories of sex-typed behavior in boys and girls: A longitudinal general population study of children aged 2.5–8 years. *Child Development, 79,* 1583–1593.

Good, C., Aronson, J., & Harder, J. A. (2008). Problems in the pipeline: Stereotype threat and women's achievement in high-level math courses. *Journal of Applied Developmental Psychology, 29,* 17–28.

Good, C., Aronson, J., & Inzlicht, M. (2003). Improving adolescents' standardized test performance: An intervention to reduce the effects of stereotype threat. *Applied Developmental Psychology, 24,* 645–662.

Gorski, R. A., Gordon, J. H., Shryne, J. E., & Southam, A. M. (1978). Evidence for a morphological sex difference within the medial preoptic area of the rat brain. *Brain Research, 148,* 333–346.

Gorski, R. A., Harlan, R. E., Jacobson, C. D., Shryne, J. E., & Southam, A. M. (1980). Evidence for the existence of a sexually dimorphic nucleus in the preoptic area of the rat. *Journal of Comparative Neurology, 193,* 529–539.

Goy, R. W. (1978). Development of play and mounting behaviour in female rhesus virilized prenatally with esters of testosterone or dihydrotestosterone. In D. J. Chivers & J. Herbert (Eds.), *Recent Advances in Primatology* (pp. 449–462). New York: Academic Press.

Goy, R. W., Bercovitch, F. B., & McBrair, M. C. (1988). Behavioral masculinization is independent of genital masculinization in prenatally androgenized female rhesus macaques. *Hormones and Behavior, 22,* 552–571.

Goy, R. W., & McEwen, B. S. (1980). *Sexual differentiation of the brain*. Cambridge, MA: MIT Press.

Green, R. (1985). Gender identity in childhood and later sexual orientation. *American Journal of Psychiatry, 142,* 339–341.

Green, R. (1987). *The "Sissy Boy Syndrome" and the Development of Homosexuality*. New Haven, CT: Yale University Press.

Green, R., & Keverne, E. B. (2000). The disparate maternal aunt–uncle ratio in male transsexuals: An explanation invoking genomic imprinting. *Journal of Theoretical Biology, 202,* 55–63.

Grimshaw, G. M., Sitarenios, G., & Finegan, J. K. (1995). Mental rotation at 7 years: Relations with prenatal testosterone levels and spatial play experiences. *Brain and Cognition, 29,* 85–100.

Guiso, L., Monte, F., Sapienza, P., & Zingales, L. (2008). Culture, gender and math. *Science, 320,* 1164–1165.

Haier, R. J., & Benbow, C. P. (1995). Sex differences and lateralization in temporal lobe glucose metabolism during mathematical reasoning. *Developmental Neuropsychology, 11,* 405–414.

Haier, R. J., Jung, R. E., Yeo, R. A., Head, K., & Alkire, M. T. (2005). The neuroanatomy of general intelligence: Sex matters. *Neuroimage, 25,* 320–327.

Halari, R., Sharma, T., Hines, M., Andrew, C., Simmons, A., & Kumari, V. (2005). Comparable fMRI activity with differential behavioural performance on mental rotation and overt verbal fluency tasks in healthy men and women. *Experimental Brain Research, 169,* 1–14.

Hall, C. M., Jones, J. A., Meyer-Bahlburg, H. F. L., Dolezal, C., Coleman, M., Foster, P., et al. (2004). Behavioral and physical masculinization are related to genotype in girls with congenital adrenal hyperplasia. *The Journal of Clinical Endocrinology and Metabolism, 89,* 419–424.

Halpern, D. F. (2000). *Sex differences in cognitive abilities*. 3rd ed. Mahwah, NJ: Erlbaum.

Halpern, D. F., Benbow, C. P., Geary, D. C., Gur, R. C., Hyde, J. S., & Gernsbacher, M. A. (2007). The science of sex differences in science and mathematics. *Psychological Science in the Public Interest, 8,* 1–51.

Hamer, D. H., Hu, S., Magnuson, V. L., Hu, N., & Pattatucci, A. M. L. (1993). A linkage between DNA markers on the X chromosome and male sexual orientation. *Science, 261,* 321–327.

Hampson, E., Rovet, J., & Altmann, D. (1998). Spatial reasoning in children with congenital adrenal hyperplasia due to 21-hydroxylase deficiency. *Developmental Neuropsychology, 14,* 299–320.

Hare, L., Bernard, P., Sánchez, F. J., Baird, P. N., Vilain, E., Kennedy, T., et al. (2009). Androgen receptor repeat length polymorphism associated with male-to-female transsexualism. *Biological Psychiatry, 65,* 93–96.

Harnqvist, K. (1997). Gender and grade differences in latent ability variables. *Scandinavian Journal of Psychology, 38,* 55–62.

Harris, J. A., Vernon, P. A., & Boomsma, D. I. (1998). The heritability if testosterone: A study of Dutch adolescent twins and their parents. *Behavior Genetics, 28,* 165–171.

Helleday, J., Bartfai, A., Ritzen, E. M., & Forsman, M. (1994). General intelligence and cognitive profile in women with congenital adrenal hyperplasia (CAH). *Psychoneuroendocrinology, 19,* 343–356.

Henderson, B. A., & Berenbaum, S. A. (1997). Sex-typed play in opposite-sex twins. *Developmental Psychobiology, 31,* 115–123.

Henningsson, S., Westberg, L., Nilsson, S., Lundstrom, B., Ekselius, L., Bodlund, O., et al. (2005). Sex steroid-related genes and male-to-female transsexualism. *Psychoneuroendocrinology, 30,* 657–664.

Hier, D. B., & Crowley, W. F. (1982). Spatial ability in androgen-deficient men. *New England Journal of Medicine, 306,* 1202–1205.

Hines, M. (2004). *Brain gender.* New York: Oxford University Press.

Hines, M. (2009a). Gonadal hormones and sexual differentiation of human brain and behavior. In D. W. Pfaff (Ed.), *Hormones, brain and behavior.* 2nd ed. Boston: Elsevier.

Hines, M. (in press). Sex and sex differences. In P. D. Zelazo (Ed.), *Oxford Handbook of Developmental Psychology.* New York: Oxford University Press.

Hines, M., Ahmed, S. F., & Hughes, I. (2003a). Psychological outcomes and gender-related development in complete androgen insensitivity syndrome. *Archives of Sexual Behavior, 32,* 93–101.

Hines, M., Allen, L. S., & Gorski, R. A. (1992). Sex differences in subregions of the bed nucleus of the stria terminalis and the medial nucleus of the amygdala of the rat. *Brain Research, 579,* 321–326.

Hines, M., Brook, C., & Conway, G. S. (2004). Androgen and psychosexual development: Core gender identity, sexual orientation and recalled childhood gender role behavior in women and men with congenital adrenal hyperplasia (CAH). *Journal of Sex Research, 41,* 1–7.

Hines, M., Chiu, L., McAdams, L. A., Bentler, P. M., & Lipcamon, J. (1992). Cognition and the corpus callosum: Verbal fluency, visuospatial ability and language lateralization related to midsagittal surface areas of callosal subregions. *Behavioral Neuroscience, 106,* 3–14.

Hines, M., & Collaer, M. L. (1993). Gonadal hormones and sexual differentiation of human behavior: Developments from research on endocrine syndromes and studies of brain structure. *Annual Review of Sex Research, 4,* 1–48.

Hines, M., Davis, F. C., Coquelin, A., Goy, R. W., & Gorski, R. A. (1985). Sexually dimorphic regions in the medial preoptic area and the bed nucleus of the stria terminalis of the guinea pig brain: A description and an investigation of their relationship to gonadal steroids in adulthood. *Journal of Neuroscience, 5,* 40–47.

Hines, M., Fane, B. A., Pasterski, V. L., Mathews, G. A., Conway, G. S., & Brook, C. (2003b). Spatial abilities following prenatal androgen abnormality: Targeting and mental rotations performance in individuals with congenital adrenal hyperplasia (CAH). *Psychoneuroendocrinology, 28,* 1010–1026.

Hines, M., Golombok, S., Croudace, T., Rust, J., Hall, A., D'Arcy, J., & Golding, J. (submitted). Male-typical interests at age 3.5 years positively predict mental rotations ability at age 13 years.

Hines, M., Golombok, S., Rust, J., Johnston, K., Golding, J., & the ALSPAC Study Team (2002b). Testosterone during pregnancy and childhood gender role behavior: A longitudinal population study. *Child Development, 73,* 1678–1687.

Hines, M., Johnston, K., Golombok, S., Rust, J., Stevens, M., Golding, J., et al. (2002a). Prenatal stress and gender role behavior in girls and boys: A longitudinal, population study. *Hormones and Behavior, 42,* 126–134.

Hines, M., & Kaufman, F. R. (1994). Androgen and the development of human sex-typical behavior: Rough-and-tumble play and sex of preferred playmates in children with congenital adrenal hyperplasia (CAH). *Child Development, 65,* 1042–1053.

Hines, M., & Sandberg, E. C. (1996). Sexual differentiation of cognitive abilities in women exposed to diethylstilbestrol (DES) prenatally. *Hormones and Behavior, 30,* 354–363.

Hines, M., & Shipley, C. (1984). Prenatal exposure to diethylstilbestrol (DES) and the development of sexually dimorphic cognitive abilities and cerebral lateralization. *Developmental Psychology, 20,* 81–94.

Holloway, R. L., & de Lacoste, M. C. (1986) Sexual dimorphism in the human corpus callosum: An extension and replication study. *Human Neurobiology, 5,* 87–91.

Hu, S., Pattatucci, A. M. L., Patterson, C., Li, L., Fulker, D. W., Cherny, S. S., et al. (1995). Linkage between sexual orientation and chromosome Xq28 in males but not in females. *Nature Genetics, 11,* 248–256.

Huston, A. C. (1983). Sex-typing. In P. H. Mussen (Ed.), *Handbook of child psychology: Vol. 4. Socialization, personality and social development* (pp. 387–467). New York: John wiley & Sons.

Huston, A. C., Dunnerstein, E., Fairchild, H., Feshbach, N. D., Katz, P. A., Murray, J. P., et al. (1992). *Big world, small screen: The role of television in American society.* Lincoln: University of Nebraska Press.

Hyde, J. S. (2005). The gender similarities hypothesis. *American Psychologist, 60,* 581–592.

Hyde, J. S., Fennema, E., & Lamon, S. J. (1990). Gender differences in mathematics performance: A meta-analysis. *Psychological Bulletin, 107,* 139–155.

Hyde, J. S., & Linn, M. C. (1988). Gender differences in verbal ability: A meta-analysis. *Psychological Bulletin, 104,* 53–69.

Iervolino, A. C. (2003). *Genetic and environmental influences on gender-role behaviour during the preschool years: A study of 3- and 4-year-old twins.* Unpublished doctoral dissertation. University of London, London.

International Committee on Radiological Protection. (1975). Report of the task group on reference man (Vol. 23). New York: Pergamon Press.

Intons-Peterson, M. J., & Reddel, M. (1984). What do people ask about a neonate? *Developmental Psychology, 20,* 358–359.

Inzlicht, M., & Ben-Zeev, T. (2000). A threatening intellectual environment: Why females are susceptible to experiencing problem-solving deficits in the presence of males. *Psychological Science, 11,* 365–371.

Jacklin, C. N., Wilcox, K. T., & Maccoby, E. E. (1988). Neonatal sex-steroid hormones and cognitive abilities at six years. *Developmental Psychobiology, 21,* 567–574.

Jacobs, D. M., Tang, M. X., Stern, Y., Sano, M., Marder, K., Bell, K. L., et al. (1998). Cognitive function in nondemented older women who took estrogen after menopause. *Neurology, 50,* 373.

Jacobson, C. D., Csernus, V. J., Shryne, J. E., & Gorski, R. A. (1981). The influence of gonadectomy, androgen exposure, or a gonadal graft in the neonatal rat on the volume of the sexually dimorphic nucleus of the preoptic area. *Journal of Neuroscience, 1,* 1142–1147.

Jancke, L., Staiger, J. F., Schlaug, G., Huang, Y. X., & Steinmetz, H. (1997). The relationship between corpus callosum size and forebrain volume. *Cerebral Cortex, 7,* 48–56.

Jardine, R., & Martin, N. G. (1983). Spatial ability and throwing accuracy. *Behavior Genetics, 13,* 331–340.

Johnson, A. M., Wadsworth, J., Wellings, K., Bradshaw, S., & Field, J. (1992). Sexual lifestyles and HIV risk. *Nature, 360,* 410–412.

Juraska, J. M., (1991). Sex differences in "cognitive" regions of the rat brain. *Psychoneuroendocrinology, 16,* 105–119.

Juraska, J. M., & Kopcik, J. R. (1988). Sex and environmental influences on the size and ultrastructure of the rat corpus callosum. *Brain Research, 450,* 1–8.

Kazemi-Esfarjani, P., Trifiro, M., & Pinsky, L. (1995). Evidence for a repressive function of the long polyglutamine tract in the human androgen receptor: Possible pathogenetic relevance for the (CAG) n-expanded neuronopathies. *Human Molecular Genetics, 4,* 523–527.

Kempermann, G., Brandon, E. P., & Gage, F. H. (1998). Environmental stimulation of 129 SvJ mice causes increased cell proliferation and neurogenesis in the adult dentate gyrus. *Current Biology, 8,* 939–942.

Kempermann, G., Kuhn, H. G., & Gage, F. H. (1997). More hippocampal neurons in adult mice living in an enriched environment. *Nature, 386,* 493–495.

Kendler, K. S., Thornton, L. M., Gilman, S. E., & Kessler, R. C. (2000). Sexual orientation in a US national sample of twin and nontwin sibling pairs. *American Journal of Psychiatry, 157,* 1843–1846.

Kertesz, A., Polk, M., Howell, J., & Black, S. E. (1987). Cerebral dominance, sex, and callosal size in MRI. *Neurology, 37,* 1385–1388.

Kester, P. A. (1984). Effects of prenatally administered 17 alpha hydroxyprogesterone caproate on adolescent males. *Archives of Sexual Behavior, 13,* 441–455.

Kester, P. A., Green, R., Finch, S. J., & Williams, K. (1980). Prenatal "female hormone" administration and psychosexual development in human males. *Psychoneuroendocrinology, 5,* 269–285.

Kimura, D. (1995). Estrogen replacement therapy may protect against intellectual decline in postmenopausal women. *Hormones and Behavior, 29,* 312–321.

Kinsey, A., Pomeroy, W., & Martin, C. (1948). *Sexual behavior in the human male*. Philadelphia: Saunders.

Kinsey, A., Pomeroy, W., Martin, C., & Gebhard, P. H. (1953). *Sexual behavior in the human female*. Philadelphia: Saunders.

Knickmeyer, R., Baron-Cohen, S., Raggatt, P., Taylor, K., & Hackett, G. (2006). Fetal testosterone and empathy. *Hormones and Behavior, 49,* 282–292.

Knickmeyer, R., Wheelwright, S., Hackett, G., Taylor, K., Raggatt, P., & Baron-Cohen, S. (2005). Gender-typed play and amniotic testosterone. *Developmental Psychobiology, 41,* 517–528.

Kohlberg, L. (1966). A cognitive-developmental analysis of children's sex-role concepts and attitudes. In E. E. Maccoby (Ed.), *The development of sex differences* (pp. 82–173). Stanford, CA: Stanford University Press.

Kolb, B., & Whishaw, I. Q. (1985). *Fundamentals of human neuropsychology*. 2nd ed. New York: W. H. Freeman.

Kruijver, F. P. M., Zhou, J., Pool, C. W., Hofman, M. A., Gooren, L. J. G., & Swaa, D. F. (2000). Male to female transsexuals have female neuron numbers in a limbic nucleus. *The Journal of Clinical Endocrinology and Metabolism, 85,* 2034–2041.

Lalumiere, M. L., Blanchard, R., & Zucker, K. J. (2000). Sexual orientation and handedness in men and women: A meta-analysis. *Psychological Bulletin, 126,* 575–592.

Langlois, J. H., & Downs, A. C. (1980). Mothers, fathers and peers as socialization agents of sex-typed play behaviors in young children. *Child Development, 51,* 1237–1247.

Lasco, M. S., Jordan, T. J., Edgar, M. A., Petito, C. K., & Byne, W. (2002). A lack of dimorphism of sex or sexual orientation in the human anterior commissure. *Brain Research, 936,* 95–98.

Leaper, C. (1994). Exploring the consequences of gender segregation on social relationships. In C. Leaper (Ed.), *Childhood gender segregation: Causes and consequences* (pp. 67–86). San Francisco: Jossey-Bass.

Lenroot, R. K., & Giedd, J. N. (2006). Brain development in children and adolescents: Insights from anatomical magnetic resonance imaging. *Neuroscience and Biobehavioral Reviews, 30,* 718–729.

Lenroot, R. K., Gogtay, N., Greenstein, D. K., Wells, E. M., Wallace, G. L., Clasen, L. S., et al. (2007). Sexual dimorphism of brain developmental trajectories during childhood and adolescence. *Neuroimage, 36,* 1065–1073.

LeVay, S. (1991). A difference in hypothalamic structure between heterosexual and homosexual men. *Science, 253,* 1034–1037.

Leveroni, C. L., & Berenbaum, S. A. (1998). Early androgen effects on interest in infants: Evidence from children with congenital adrenal hyperplasia. *Developmental Neuropsychology, 14,* 321–340.

Linn, M. C., & Petersen, A. C. (1985). Emergence and characterization of sex differences in spatial ability: A meta-analysis. *Child Development, 56,* 1479–1498.

Lish, J. D., Ehrhardt, A. A., Meyer-Bahlburg, H. F. L., Rosen, L. R., Gruen, R. S., & Veridiano, N. P. (1991). Gender-related behavior development in females exposed to diethylstilbestrol (DES) in utero: An attempted replication. *Journal of the American Academy of Child and Adolescent Psychiatry, 30,* 29–37.

Lish, J. D., Meyer-Bahlburg, H. F. L., Ehrhardt, A. A., Travis, B. G., & Veridiano, N. P. (1992). Prenatal exposure to diethylstilbestrol (DES): Childhood play behavior and adult gender-role behavior in women. *Archives of Sexual Behavior, 21,* 423–441.

Loehlin, J. C. (2000). Group differences in intelligence. In R. J. Sternberg (Ed.), *Handbook of intelligence* (pp. 176–193). Cambridge: Cambridge University Press.

Lutchmaya, S., Baron-Cohen, S., & Raggatt, P. (2002). Foetal testosterone and vocabulary size in 18- and 24-month-old infants. *Infant Behavior and Development, 24,* 418–442.

Maass, A., D'Ettole, C., & Cadinu, M. (2008). Checkmate? The role of gender stereotypes in the ultimate intellectual sport. *European Journal of Social Psychology, 38,* 231–245.

Maccoby, E. E. (1966). Sex differences in intellectual functioning. In E. E. Maccoby (Ed.), *The development of sex differences* (pp. 25–55). Stanford, CA: Stanford University Press.

Maccoby, E. E. (1988). Gender as a social category. *Developmental Psychology, 24,* 755–765.

Maccoby, E. E., & Jacklin, C. N. (1974). *The psychology of sex differences*. Stanford, CA: Stanford University Press.

Maccoby, E. E., & Jacklin, C. N. (1987). Gender segregation in children. In H. W. Reece (Ed.), *Advances in child development and behavior* (pp. 239–287). New York: Academic Press.

Macke, J. P., Hu, N., Bailey, M., King, V. L., Brown, T., Hamer, D., et al. (1993). Sequence variation in the androgen receptor gene is not a common determinant of male sexual orientation. *American Journal of Human Genetics, 53,* 844–852.

MacLusky, N. J., & Naftolin, F. (1981). Sexual differentiation of the central nervous system. *Science, 211,* 1294–1303.

Maitland, S. B., Intrieri, R. C., Schaie, K. W., & Willis, S. L. (2000). Gender differences and changes in cognitive abilities across the adult life span. *Aging, Neuropsychology and Cognition, 7,* 32–53.

Manning, J. T. (2002). *Digit ratio: A pointer to fertility, behavior, and health.* New Brunswick, NJ: Rutgers University Press.

Mansour, C. S., Haier, R. J., & Buchsbaum, M. S. (1996). Gender comparisons of cerebral glucose metabolic rate in healthy adults during a cognitive task. *Personality and Individual Differences, 20,* 183–191.

Martin, C. L., & Fabes, R. A. (2001). The stability and consequences of young children's same-sex peer interactions. *Developmental Psychology, 37,* 431–446.

Martin, C. L., Ruble, D. N., & Szkrybalo, J. (2002). Cognitive theories of early gender development. *Psychological Bulletin, 128,* 903–933.

Martin, M. O., Mullis, I. V. S., & Foy, P. (2008). *TIMSS 2007 International Science Report.* Boston: International Association ofor the Evaluation of Educational Achievement.

Masica, D. N., Money, J., & Ehrhardt, A. (1971). Fetal feminization and female gender identity in the testicular feminizing syndrome of androgen insensitivity. *Archives of Sexual Behavior, 1,* 131–142.

Masters, J. C., Ford, M. E., Arend, R., Grotevant, H. D., & Clark, L. V. (1979). Modeling and labelling as integrated determinants of children's sex-typed imitative behavior. *Child Development, 50,* 364–371.

Mathews, G. A., Fane, B. A., Conway, G. S., Brook, C., & Hines, M. (2009). Personality and congenital adrenal hyperplasia: Possible effects of prenatal androgen exposure. *Hormones and Behavior, 55,* 285–291.

Matthews, K., Cauley, J., Yaffe, K., & Zmuda, J. M. (1999). Estrogen replacement therapy and cognitive decline in older community women. *JAGS, 47,* 518–523.

Mazur, T., Sandberg, D. E., Perrin, M. A., Gallagher, J. A., & MacGillivray, M. H. (2004). Male pseudohermaphroditism: Long-term quality of life outcome in five 46,XY individuals reared female. *Journal of Pediatric Endocrinology and Metabolism, 17,* 809–823.

McFadden, D., Loehlin, J. C., Breedlove, S. M., Lippa, R. A., Manning, J. T., & Rahman, Q. (2005). A reanalysis of five studies on sexual orientation and the relative length of the 2nd and 4th fingers (the 2D:4D ratio). *Archives of Sexual Behavior, 34,* 341–356.

McGuire, L. S., Ryan, K. O., & Omenn, G. S. (1975). Congenital adrenal hyperplasia II: Cognitive and behavioral studies. *Behavior Genetics, 5,* 175–188.

Meisel, R. L., & Ward, I. L. (1981). Fetal female rats are masculinized by littermates located caudally in the uterus. *Science, 213,* 239–242.

Meyer-Bahlburg, H. F. L. (2005). Gender identity outcome in female-raised 46, XY persons with penile agenesis, cloacal exstrophy of the bladder, or penile ablation. *Archives of Sexual Behavior,* 423–438.

Meyer-Bahlburg, H. F. L., Dolezal, C., Baker, S. W., & New, M. I. (2008). Sexual orientation in women with classical or non-classical congenital adrenal hyperplasia as a function of degree of prenatal androgen excess. *Archives of Sexual Behavior, 37,* 85–99.

Meyer-Bahlburg, H. F. L., Ehrhardt, A. A., Rosen, L. R., Gruen, R. S., Veridiano, N. P., Vann, F. H., et al. (1995). Prenatal estrogens and the development of homosexual orientation. *Developmental Psychology, 31,* 12–21.

Meyer-Bahlburg, H. F. L., Ehrhardt, A. A., Whitehead, E. D., & Vann, F. H. (1987). Sexuality in males with a history of prenatal exposure to diethylstilbestrol (DES). In *Proceedings of the Workshop on Psychosexual and Reproductive Issues Affecting Patients with Cancer* (pp. 79–82). New York: American Cancer Society.

Meyer-Bahlburg, H. F. L., Grisanti, G. C., & Ehrhardt, A. A. (1977). Prenatal effects of sex hormones on human male behavior: Medroxyprogesterone acetate (MPA). *Psychoneuroendocrinology, 2,* 383–390.

Mischel, W. (1966). A social learning view of sex differences in behavior. In E. E. Maccoby (Ed.), *The development of sex differences.* Stanford, CA.: Stanford University Press.

Moe, A. (2009). Are males always better than females in mental rotation? Exploring a gender belief explanation. *Learning and Individual Differences, 19,* 21–27.

Moe, A., & Pazzaglia, F. (2006). Following the instructions! Effects of gender beliefs in mental rotation. *Learning and Individual Differences, 16,* 369–377.

Money, J., & Dalẽry, J. (1976). Iatrogenic homosexuality: gender identity in seven 46, XX chromosomal females with hyperadrenocortical hermaphroditism born with a penis, three reared as boys, four reared as girls. *Journal of Homosexuality, 1,* 357–371.

Money, J., Schwartz, M., & Lewis, V. (1984). Adult erotosexual status and fetal hormonal masculinization and demasculinization: 46 XX congenital virilizing adrenal hyperplasia and 46 XY androgen-insensitivity syndrome compared. *Psychoneuroendocrinology, 9,* 405–414.

Moore, D. S., & Johnson, S. P. (2008). Mental rotation in human infants: A sex difference. *Psychological Science, 19,* 1063–1066.

Morgan, M., & Shanahan, J. (1997). Two decades of cultivation research: An appraisal and meta-analysis. In B. R. Burleson (Ed.), *Communication Yearbook,* Vol. 20 (pp. 1–46). Thousand Oaks, CA: Sage.

Mulaikal, R. M., Migeon, C. J., & Rock, J. A. (1987). Fertility rates in female patients with congenital adrenal hyperplasia due to 21-hydroxylase deficiency. *New England Journal of Medicine, 316,* 178–182.

Mullis, I. V. S., Martin, M. O., & Foy, P. (2008). *TIMSS 2007 international maths report.* Boston: International Association for the Evaluation of Educational Achievement.

Mustanski, B. S., DuPree, M. G., Nievergelt, C. M., Bocklandt, S., Schork, N. J., & Hamer, D. H. (2005). A genomewide scan of male sexual orientation. *Human Genetics, 116,* 272–278.

Nash, S. C., & Feldman, S. S. (1981). Responsiveness to babies: Life-situation specific sex differences in adulthood. *Sex Roles, 7,* 1035–1042.

New, M. (1998). Diagnosis and management of congenital adrenal hyperplasia. *Annual Review of Medicine, 49,* 311–328.

Nordenstrom, A., Servin, A., Bohlin, G., Larsson, A., & Wedell, A. (2002). Sex-typed toy play behavior correlates with the degree of prenatal androgen exposure assessed by CYP21 genotype in girls with congenital adrenal hyperplasia. *Journal of Clinical Endocrinology and Metabolism, 87,* 5119–5124.

O'Connor, D. B., Archer, J., Hair, W. M., & Wu, F. C. W. (2002). Exogenous testosterone, aggression, and mood in eugonadal and hypogonadal men. *Physiology & Behavior, 75,* 557–566.

Okten, A., Kalyonku, M., & Yaris, N. (2002). The ratio of second- and fourth-digit lengths and congenital adrenal hyperplasia due to 21-hydroxylase deficiency. *Early Human Development, 70,* 47–54.

Pang, S., Levine, L. S., Cederqvist, L. L., Fuentes, M., Riccardi, V. M., Holcombe, J. H., et al. (1980). Amniotic fluid concentrations of delta 5 and delta 4 steroids in fetuses with congenital adrenal hyperplasia due to 21-hydroxylase deficiency and in anencephalic fetuses. *Journal of Clinical Endocrinology and Metabolism, 51,* 223–229.

Pang, S., Levine, L. S., Chow, D. M., Faiman, C., & New, M. I. (1979). Serum androgen concentrations in neonates and young infants with congenital adrenal hyperplasia due to 21-hydroxylase deficiency. *Clinical Endocrinology, 11,* 575–584.

Pasterski, V. L., Geffner, M. E., Brain, C., Hindmarsh, P., Brook, C., & Hines, M. (2005). Prenatal hormones and postnatal socialization by parents as determinants of male-typical toy play in girls with congenital adrenal hyperplasia. *Child Development, 76,* 264–278.

Pasterski, V. L., Hindmarsh, P., Geffner, M., Brook, C., Brain, C., & Hines, M. (2007). Increased aggression and activity level in 3- to 11-year-old girls with congenital adrenal hyperplasia (CAH). *Hormones and Behavior, 52,* 368–374.

Peplau, L. A., Spalding, L. R., Conley, T. D., & Veneigas, R. C. (1999). The development of sexual orientation in women. *Annual Review of Sex Research, 10,* 70–99.

Perlman, S. M. (1973). Cognitive abilities of children with hormone abnormalities: Screening by psychoeducational tests. *Journal of Learning Disabilities, 6,* 21–29.

Perry, D. G., & Bussey, K. (1979). The social learning theory of sex difference: Imitation is alive and well. *Journal of Personality & Social Psychology, 37,* 1699–1712.

Peters, M., Manning, J., & Reimers, S. (2007). The effects of sex, sexual orientation, and digit ratio (2D:4D) on mental rotation performance. *Archives of Sexual Behavior, 36,* 251–260.

Puts, D. A., McDaniel, M. A., Jordan, C. L., & Breedlove, S. M. (2008). Spatial ability and prenatal androgens: Meta-analyses of congenital adrenal hyperplasia and digit ratio (2D:4D) studies. *Archives of Sexual Behavior, 37,* 85–99.

Quadagno, D. M., Briscoe, R., & Quadagno, J. S. (1977). Effects of perinatal gonadal hormones on selected nonsexual behavior patterns: A critical assessment of the nonhuman and human literature. *Psychological Bulletin, 84,* 62–80.

Quigley, C. A. (2002). The postnatal gonadotrophin and sex steroid surge—Insights from the androgen insensitivity syndrome. *Clinical Endocrinology and Metabolism, 87,* 24–28.

Quinn, P. C., & Liben, L. S. (2008). A sex difference in mental rotation in young infants. *Psychological Science, 19,* 1067–1070.

Reinarz, S. J., Coffman, C. E., Smoker, W. R. K., & Godersky, F. C. (1988) MR imaging of the corpus callosum: Normal and pathologic findings and correlation with CT. *American Journal of Radiology, 151,* 791–798.

Reiner, W. G., & Gearhart, J. P. (2004). Discordant sexual identity in some genetic males with cloacal exstrophy assigned to female sex at birth. *New England Journal of Medicine, 350,* 333–341.

Reiner, W. G., Gearhart, J. P., & Jeffs, R. (1999). Psychosexual dysfunction in males with genital anomalies: Late adolescence, Tanner Stages IV to VI. *Journal of the American Academy of Child and Adolescent Psychiatry, 38,* 865–872.

Reinisch, J. M. (1981). Prenatal exposure to synthetic progestins increases potential for aggression in humans. *Science, 211,* 1171–1173.

Resnick, S. M., Berenbaum, S. A., Gottesman, I. I., & Bouchard, T. (1986). Early hormonal influences on cognitive functioning in congenital adrenal hyperplasia. *Developmental Psychology, 22,* 191–198.

Reyes, F. I., Winter, J. S. D., & Faiman, C. (1973). Studies on human sexual development. I. Fetal gonadal and adrenal sex steroids. *Journal of Clinical Endocrinology and Metabolism, 37,* 74–78.

Reynolds, M. R., Keith, T. Z., Ridley, K. P., & Patel, P. G. (2008). Sex differences in latent general and broad cognitive abilities for children and youth: Evidence from higher-order MG-MACS and MIMIC models. *Intelligence, 36,* 236–260.

Rice, G., Anderson, C. A., Risch, N., & Ebers, G. (1999). Male homosexuality: Absence of linkage to microsatellite markers at Xq28. *Science, 284,* 665–667.

Robinson, J., Judd, H., Young, P., Jones, D., & Yen, S. (1977). Amniotic fluid androgens and estrogens in midgestation. *Journal of Clinical Endocrinology and Metabolism, 45,* 755–761.

Rosler, A., & Kohn, G. (1983). Male pseudohermaphroditism due to 17 beta-hydroxysteroid dehydrogenase deficiency: studies on the natural history of the defect and effect of androgens on gender role. *Journal of Steroid Biochemistry, 19,* 663–674.

Ross, J. L., & Zinn, A. R. (1999). Turner syndrome: Potential hormonal and genetic influences on the neurocognitive profile. In Tager-Flusberg (Ed.), *Neurodevelopmental disorders* (pp. 251–267). Cambridge, MA: MIT Press.

Rovet, J. F. (1990). The cognitive and neuropsychological characteristics of females with Turner syndrome. In D. B. Berch & B. G. Bender (Eds.), *Sex chromosome abnormalities and human behavior* (pp. 38–77). Boulder, CO: Westview Press.

Ruble, D. N., & Martin, C. L. (1998). Gender development. In N. Eisenberg (Ed.), *Handbook of child psychology: Vol. 3. Personality and social development* (5th ed., pp. 933–1016). New York: John Wiley & Sons.

Ruble, D. N., Martin, C. L., & Berenbaum, S. A. (2006). Gender development. In W. Damon, R. M. Lerner, & N. Eisenberg (Eds.), *Handbook of child psychology: Vol. 3. Social, emotional and personality development* (6th ed., pp. 858–932). Hoboken, NJ: John Wiley & Sons.

Ruble, D. N., Taylor, L. J., Cyphers, L., Greulich, F. K., Lurye, L. E., & Shrout, P. E. (2007). The role of gender constancy in early gender development. *Child Development, 78,* 1121–1136.

Rust, J., Golombok, S., Hines, M., Johnston, K., Golding, J., & The ALSPAC Study Team (2000). The role of brothers and sisters in the gender development of preschool children. *Journal of Experimental Child Psychology, 77,* 292–303.

Sameroff, A. J., Peck, S. C., & Eccles, J. S. (2004). Changing ecological determinants of conduct problems from early adolescence to early adulthood. *Development and Psychopathology, 16,* 873–896.

Sanders, B., Soares, M. P., & D'Aquila, J. M. (1982). The sex difference on one test of spatial visualization: A nontrivial difference. *Child Development, 53,* 1106–1110.

Schmader, T., Johns, M., & Forbes, C. (2008). An integrated processing model of stereotype threat effects on performance. *Psychological Review, 115,* 336–356.

Schober, J. M. (1999). Quality-of-life studies in patients with ambiguous genitalia. *World Journal of Urology, 17,* 249.

Schober, J. M., Carmichael, P. A., Hines, M., & Ransley, P. G. (2002). The ultimate challenge of cloacal exstrophy. *Journal of Urology, 167,* 300–304.

Sell, R. L., Wells, J. A., & Wypij, D. (1995). The prevalence of homosexual behavior and attraction in the United States, the United Kingdom and France: Results of national population-based samples. *Archives of Sexual Behavior, 24,* 235–248.

Serbin, L. A., & Karp, J. (2004). The intergenerational transfer of psychosocial risk: Mediators of vulnerability and resilience. *Annual Review of Psychology, 55,* 333–363.

Shaywitz, B. A., Shaywitz, S. E., Pugh, K. R., Constable, R. T., Skudlarski, P., Fulbright, R. K., et al. (1995). Sex differences in the functional organization of the brain for language. *Nature, 373,* 607–609.

Sherman, J. A. (1967). Problem of sex differences in space perception and aspects of intellectual functioning. *Psychological Review, 74,* 290–299.

Sherwin, B. B. (2005). Estrogen and memory in women: How can we reconcile the findings? *Hormones and Behavior, 47,* 371–375.

Shumaker, S. A., Legault, C., Kuller, L., Rapp, S. R., Thal, L., Lane, D. S., et al. (2004). Conjugated equine estrogens and incidence of probable dementia and mild cognitive impairment in postmenopausal women. *Journal of the American Medical Association, 291,* 2947–2958.

Shumaker, S. A., Legault, C., Rapp, S. R., Thal, L., Wallace, R. B., Ockene, J. K., et al. (2003). Estrogen plus progestin and the incidence of dementia and mild cognitive impairment in postmenopausal women. *JAMA, 289,* 2651–2661.

Simon, N. G. (2002). Hormonal processes in the development and expression of aggressive behavior. In D. W. Pfaff, A. P. Arnold, A. M. Etgen, S. E. Fahrbach, & R. T. Rubin (Eds.), *Hormones, brain and behavior* (pp. 339–392). San Diego, CA: Academic Press.

Sinforiani, E., Livieri, C., Mauri, M., Bisio, P., Sibilla, L., Chiesa, L., et al. (1994). Cognitive and neuroradiological findings in congenital adrenal hyperplasia. *Psychoneuroendocrinology, 19,* 55 64.

Slijper, F. M. E., Drop, S. L. S., Molenaar, J. C., & de Muinck Keizer-Schrama, S. M. P. F. (1998). Long-term psychological evaluation of intersex children. *Archives of Sexual Behavior, 27,* 125–144.

Smail, P. J., Reyes, F. I., Winter, J. S. D., & Faiman, C. (1981). The fetal hormone environment and its effect on the morphogenesis of the genital system. In S. J. Kogan & E. S. E. Hafez (Eds.), *Pediatric Andrology* (pp. 9–20). The Hague: Martinus Nijhoff.

Snow, M. E., Jacklin, C. N., & Maccoby, E. E. (1983). Sex of child differences in father-child interaction at one year of age. *Child Development, 54,* 227–232.

Spencer, S. J., Steele, C. M., & Quinn, D. M. (1999). Stereotype threat and women's math performance. *Journal of Experimental Social Psychology, 35,* 4–28.

Spira, A., Bajos, N., Bejin, A., Beltzer, N., Bozon, M., Ducot, B., et al. (1992). AIDS and sexual behavior in France. *Nature, 360,* 407–409.

Sprafkin, C., Serbin, L. A., Denier, C., & Connor, J. M. (1983). Sex-differentiated play: Cognitive consequences and early interventions. In M. B. Liss (Ed.), *Social and cognitive skills* (pp. 167–192). New York: Academic Press.

Spreen, O., & Strauss, E. (1991). *A compendium of neuropsychological tests.* New York: Oxford University Press.

Sutton-Smith, B., Rosenberg, B. G., & Morgan, E. F., Jr. (1963). Development of sex differences in play choices during preadolescence. *Child Development, 34,* 119–126.

Tanner, J. M., Whitehouse, R. H., & Takaishi, M. (1966). Standards from birth to maturity for height, weight, height velocity and weight velocity: British children, 1965. *Archives of Disease in Childhood, 41,* 454–471.

Terlecki, M. S., & Newcombe, N. S. (2005). How important is the digital divide? The relation of computer and videogame usage to gender differences in mental rotation ability. *Sex Roles, 53,* 433–441.

Titus-Ernstoff, L., Perez, K., Hatch, E., Troisi, R., Palmer, J. R., Hartge, P., et al. (2003). Psychosexual characteristics of men and women exposed prenatally to diethylstilbestrol. *Epidemiology, 14,* 155.

Tricker, R., Casaburi, R., Storer, T. W., Clevenger, B., Berman, N., Shirazi, A., et al. (1996). The effects of supraphysiological doses of testosterone on anger behavior in healthy eugonadal men—A clinical reasearch center study. *Journal of Clinical Endocrinology and Metabolism, 81,* 3754–3758.

Turner, W. J. (1995). Homosexuality, type 1: an Xq28 phenomenon. *Archives of Sexual Behavior, 24,* 109–134.

van de Beek, C., Van Goozen, S. H. M., Buitelaar, J. K., & Cohen-Kettenis, P. T. (2009). Prenatal sex hormones (maternal and amniotic fluid) and gender-related play behavior in 13-month-old infants. *Archives of Sexual Behavior, 38,* 6–15.

Voyer, D., Voyer, S., & Bryden, M. P. (1995). Magnitude of sex differences in spatial abilities: A meta-analysis and consideration of critical variables. *Psychological Bulletin, 117,* 250–270.

Waber, D. P. (1979). Neuropsychological aspects of Turner's syndrome. *Developmental Neurology, 1979,* 58–70.

Watson, N. V., & Kimura, D. (1991). Nontrivial sex differences in throwing and intercepting: Relation to psychometrically-defined spatial functions. *Personality and Individual Differences, 12,* 375–385.

Whitam, F. L. (1980). Childhood predictors of adult homosexuality. *Journal of Sex Education and Therapy, 6,* 11–16.

Whitam, F. L., Diamond, M., & Martin, J. (1993). Homosexual orientation in twins: A report on 61 pairs and three triplet sets. *Archives of Sexual Behavior, 22,* 187–206.

Whitam, F. L., & Mathy, R. M. (1986). *Male Homosexuality in Four Societies: Brazil, Guatemala, the Phillipines, and the United States.* New York: Praeger.

Whitam, F. L., & Mathy, R. M. (1991). Childhood cross-gender behavior of homosexual females in Brazil, Peru, the Phillipines, and the United States. *Archives of Sexual Behavior, 20,* 151–170.

Wilcox, A. J., Maxey, J., & Herbst, A. L. (1992). Prenatal hormone exposure and performance on college entrance examinations. *Hormones and Behavior, 24,* 433–439.

Williams, T. J., Pepitone, M. E., Christensen, B. M., Cooke, B. M., Huberman, A. D., Breedlove, N. J., et al. (2000). Finger length patterns indicate an influence of fetal androgens on human sexual orientation. *Nature, 30,* 455–456.

Willis, S. L., & Schaie, K. W. (1988). Gender differences in spatial ability in old age: longitudinal and intervention findings. *Sex Roles, 18,* 189–203.

Wilson, J. D. (2001). Androgens, androgen receptors and male gender role behavior. *Hormones and Behavior, 40,* 358–366.

Wilson, J. D., George, F. W., & Griffin, J. E. (1981). The hormonal control of sexual development. *Science, 211,* 1278–1284.

Wisniewski, A. B., Migeon, C. J., Meyer-Bahlburg, H. F. L., Gearhart, J. P., Berkovitz, B., Brown, T. J., et al. (2000). Complete androgen insensitivity syndrome. Long-term medical, surgical, and psychosexual outcome. *Journal of Clinical Endocrinology and Metabolism, 85,* 2664–2669.

Witelson, S. F. (1985). The brain connection: The corpus callosum is larger in left-handers. *Science, 229,* 665–668.

Witelson, S. F. (1989). Hand and sex differences in the isthmus and genu of the human corpus callosum: A postmortem morphological study. *Brain, 112,* 799–835.

Witelson, S. F., Kigar, D. L., Scamvougeras, A., Kideckel, D. M., Buck, B., Stanchev, P. L., et al. (2008). Corpus callosum anatomy in right-handed homosexual and heterosexual men. *Archives of Sexual Behavior, 37,* 857–863.

Wolf, O. T., Heinrich, A. B., Hanstein, B., & Kirschbaum, C. (2005). Estradiol or estradiol/progesterone treatment in older women: No strong effects on cognition. *Neurobiology of Aging, 26,* 1029–1033.

Wolf, O. T., Kudielka, B. M., Hellhammer, D. H., Torber, S., McEwen, B. S., & Kirschbaum, C. (1999). Two weeks of transdermal estradiol treatment and its effect on memory and mood: Verbal memory changes are associated with the treatment induced estradiol levels. *Psychoneuroendocrinology, 24,* 727–741.

Wraga, M., Helt, M., Jacobs, E., & Sullivan, K. (2007). Neural basis of stereotype-induced shifts in women's mental rotation performance. *Social Cognitive and Affective Neuroscience, 2,* 12–19.

Wudy, S., Dorr, H. G., Solleder, C., Djalali, M., & Homoki, J. (1999a). Profiling steroid hormones in amniotic fluid of midpregnancy by routine stable isotope dilution/gas chromatography-mass spectrometry: Reference values and concentrations in fetuses at risk for 21-hydroxylase deficiency. *Journal of Clinical Endocrinology and Metabolism, 84,* 2724–2728.

Wudy, S. A., Dörr, H. G., Solleder, C., Djalali, M., & Homoki, J. (1999b). Profiling steroid hormones in amniotic fluid of midpregnancy by routine stable isotope dilution/gas chromatography-mass spectrometry: Reference values and concentrations in fetuses at risk for 21-hydroxylase deficiency. *Journal of Clinical Endocrinology and Metabolism, 84,* 2724–2728.

Yalom, I. D., Green, R., & Fisk, N. (1973). Prenatal exposure to female hormones: Effect on psychosexual development in boys. *Archives of General Psychiatry, 28,* 554–561.

Zec, R. F., & Trivedi, M. A. (2002). The effects of estrogen replacement therapy on neuropsychological functioning in postmenopausal women with and without dementia: A critical and theoretical review. *Neuropsychology Review, 12,* 65–109.

Zhou, J., Hofman, M. A., Gooren, L. J. G., & Swaab, D. F. (1995). A sex difference in the human brain and its relation to transsexuality. *Nature, 378,* 68–70.

Zucker, K. J. (2002). Intersexuality and gender identity differentiation. *Journal of Pediatric Adolescent Gynecology, 15,* 3–13.

Zucker, K. J., & Bradley, S. J. (1995). *Gender identity disorder and psychosexual problems in children and adolescents.* New York: Guilford.

Zuger, B. (1978). Effeminate behavior present in boys from childhood: Ten additional years of follow-up. *Comprehensive Psychiatry, 19,* 363–369.

CHAPTER 11

Intimate Relationships across the Life Span

LISA M. DIAMOND, CHRISTOPHER P. FAGUNDES, and MOLLY R. BUTTERWORTH

In 1975, Senator Henry Proxmire took the floor of the Senate to denounce publicly the awarding of a research grant to Ellen Berscheid and Elaine Hatfield by the National Science Foundation for the study of passionate and companionate love. Proxmire denounced the project as a waste of time and money, arguing that there was no hope that the methods and tools of science could be fruitfully applied to the understanding of romantic relationships. Furthermore, he argued, there were some questions that Americans simply did not want the answers to, and among those were the mysteries of love (Hatfield, 2001).

Nearly 50 years later, it is clear that nothing could be further from the truth. The explosion of scientific research on romantic relationships since that time, along with the proliferation of popular advice books on the topic, demonstrates that there are few subjects in which the average American is *more* interested than the science of intimate relationships. For a relatively young field, relationship science has made remarkable progress in documenting the fundamental cognitive, affective, behavioral, and biological bases of intimate relationships. Yet although researchers have devoted increasing attention to the distinctive dynamics of romantic relationships during adolescence versus adulthood versus late life, few have adopted a life-span theoretical approach to intimate relationships. By this we mean an approach that seeks to understand trajectories of romantic relationship experience from adolescence to late life, emphasizing the developmental antecedents and implications of different types of relationship experiences at different stages of life. In this chapter, we provide a comprehensive overview of current state-of-the-art research on intimate relationships, attempting to synthesize research findings within a broader life-span/developmental framework.

Toward this end, we begin by emphasizing three key premises, which we revisit throughout the review. First, *the individual's developmental status shapes the quality and functioning of his or her intimate relationships.* Through adolescence, emerging adulthood, middle adulthood, and late life, the individual's changing socioemotional capacities, goals, and motives influence the types of intimate relationships he or she desires (for example, serious vs. casual) as well as the functional properties of those relationships (for example, levels of intimacy, empathy, support, negotiation). Second, *intimate relationships shape social and psychological development.* Just as infant–caregiver relationships provide the foundation for the child's developing self-concept and interpersonal skills, intimate relationships from adolescence to late life promote continued maturation by eliciting a changing repertoire of developmentally specific tasks and abilities. As individuals strive, from relationship to relationship, to meet their own needs and those of their partners, they become increasingly adept at balancing a complex interplay of motives, goals, and skills. Hence, each successive experience is influenced by the individual's *current* developmental status (reflecting his or her cumulative developmental history up to that point) but also feeds forward to shape *future* development across multiple domains of psychological functioning.

Our third premise follows directly from the first two: Because intimate relationships represent both the "output" of prior psychosocial development and the "input" for the next stage of development, they necessarily exert *cumulative and dynamic* influences on mental and physical functioning over the life span. In essence, this amounts to a cascade model of relationships and development in which each of an individual's successive relationships exerts a lasting press on his or her entire trajectory of psychosocial development (although, of course, some relationships will prove more influential than others). In the ensuing review, we repeatedly reconsider whether certain types of romantic experiences—both positive and negative—have notably different implications depending on where they occur within an individual's entire relationship trajectory and the processes through which these trajectories change and stabilize over time. Our consideration of such questions is necessarily constrained by the lack of longitudinal data on sequential relationship experiences. Although a number of studies have charted the long-term course of single relationships (typically first-time marriages), researchers do not typically follow individuals as they move from relationship to relationship over long stretches of time, building skills, strengths, fears, and expectations along the way. Hence, at the moment a couple is captured within a "newlywed" sample or a study of marital conflict dynamics, we typically have little understanding of how each partner arrived at that point, and the distinctive developmental histories underlying his or her respective behaviors and cognitions. Given these gaps in the empirical literature, many of the developmental issues we address throughout this chapter take the form of questions rather than answers. By raising such questions, we hope to focus attention on some of the most important and productive avenues for future life-span/developmental research on intimate relationships.

BASIC QUESTIONS: LOVE AND PAIRBONDING

First, however, some conceptual clarifications are in order. Unlike studies of parent–child relationships or friendships, investigations of "intimate relationships" inevitably raise definitional quandaries. What exactly qualifies as an intimate relationship? Many researchers use this phrase to denote any and all romantic or sexual relationships, from one-night stands to 30-year marriages. In this framework, "intimate" simply refers to the element of sexual desire or behavior in the relationship. More commonly, however, intimate relationships are defined as relationships involving both emotional and physical intimacy, and these are the types of relationships which form the topic of this chapter. Although the ensuing review will focus on *social-psychological* investigations of intimate relationships, it bears noting that the past several decades have also seen increased attention to the *evolutionary* bases of these relationships—or *pairbonds*, as they are typically called—and to questions regarding the nature and origin of romantic love. Hence, a brief overview of this area provides a useful foundation for the review to follow.

Romantic love, as opposed to more general forms of love experienced for friends and family, has been defined in numerous ways by psychologists, but perhaps the most serviceable definition is that provided by Aron and Aron (1991): "the constellation of behaviors, cognitions, and emotions associated with a desire to enter or maintain a close relationship with a specific other person" (p. 26).

Notable in this definition is the *multifactorial* nature of love, involving "behaviors, cognitions, emotions," the *motivational* force of love (i.e., *desire* to enter or maintain a relationship), its focus on a *single target*, and, lastly, the absence of any mention of sexual desire. Historically, it was often assumed that sexual desire provided the motivational force behind love, but contemporary research clearly demonstrates that romantic love and sexual desire are governed by functionally independent social-behavioral systems that evolved for different reasons and that involve different neurochemical substrates (reviewed in Diamond, 2003).

The popular impression that romantic love necessarily involves sexual desire may be attributable to the fact that most individuals associate the notion of romantic love with a particular type of romantic love—*passionate love* (Hatfield, 1987; Hatfield, Schmitz, Cornelius, & Rapson, 1988). This form of love (or, more accurately, infatuation) typically characterizes the earliest stages of a developing romantic relationship and tends to be associated with extremely high levels of sexual desire, sexual activity, or both. In contrast, the form of love that endures long beyond this initial burst of passion, and that is characterized by deep feelings of mutual care and affection, has been denoted *companionate love.*

Among the most important revolutions in research on intimate relationships since the late 1980s has been the notion that adults' experiences of companionate love are governed by the same evolved social-behavioral system that governs infants' bonds to their caregivers: the attachment system. Accordingly, attachment theory (Bowlby, 1958, 1973a, 1973b, 1980, 1982), which began as a theory of infant–caregiver bonding, is now arguably the preeminent theoretical model of adult romantic pairbonding. We therefore take a brief digression into its core premises regarding the evolved biobehavioral dynamics of romantic love.

Attachment and Pairbonding

Evolutionary theorists have argued that in the environment in which humans evolved, highly vulnerable offspring were far more likely to survive if they had the care of both parents in the early years of life, introducing the evolutionary problem of how to keep reproductive partners together long enough to rear their offspring past the initial, most dangerous stage of development (Mellen, 1982). The social-behavioral system of *pairbonding*—in which reproductive partners are emotionally motivated to maintain an enduring close relationship with one another even after mating has occurred—is thought to have provided the solution.

Yet as Gould and Vrba (1982) argued, evolution does not generally result in the production of brand-new mechanisms when existing ones will suffice, and mammals already possessed a potent social-behavioral system for social bonding: *infant–caregiver attachment.* John Bowlby (1958, 1982) conceptualized attachment as an evolved behavioral system designed to regulate infants' proximity to caregivers and thereby maximize chances for survival. When an infant experiences distress, he or she immediately attempts to gain proximity to the attachment figure (by crying, clinging, etc.). In normative cases, this proximity reassures and soothes the infant, in which case he or she comes to associate the presence of the attachment figure with emotional security and distress alleviation. Even when the attachment figure is not consistently effective at alleviating distress, infants typically develop a unique, exclusive, emotionally primary relationship with the attachment figure, such that he or she becomes the preferred target for proximity and security seeking.

Although Bowlby developed attachment theory on the basis of observations of infant–caregiver behavior, he argued that the attachment system is operative across the entire life span (1988). Similarly, other evolutionary theorists have argued that once the "problem" of keeping human reproductive partners together emerged, the infant–caregiver attachment system was coopted for this purpose (Panksepp, 1998). Hence, adult pairbonding has been posited as an *exaptation*—a system that originally evolved for one reason but comes to serve another (Gould & Vrba, 1982). Support for the notion that adult romantic love is an adult version of infant–caregiver attachment comes from extensive research documenting that infant–caregiver attachment and adult pairbonding share the same core emotional and behavioral dynamics: heightened proximity maintenance, resistance to separation, and utilization of the partner as a preferred target for comfort and security seeking (Hazan & Zeifman, 1999). Of course, a key difference between infant–caregiver attachment and adult romantic pairbonding concerns the presence of sexual desire and behavior in the latter (Shaver, Hazan, & Bradshaw, 1988). Although the specific mechanisms through which sexuality becomes integrated into the adult attachment system has never been directly investigated, Hazan and Zeifman (1994) posited a critical role for physical intimacy in this regard. They observed that the same types of intimate physical contact which are reserved—among children—for their parents (nuzzling, kissing, stroking, and sustained chest-to-chest cuddling) are reserved among adults for their romantic partners. Hence, one possibility is that as adolescents increasingly reappraise such forms of physical intimacy as reflecting erotic rather than caregiving motives (due to the hormonally triggered postpubertal surges in their own sexual motivation), this may provide a gateway through which sexual thoughts and feelings become progressively intertwined with the adult attachment system. It bears noting, however, that although pairbonds usually involve the integration of love and desire, this is not a necessary condition for their formation or maintenance (Diamond, 2003), reflecting the fact that the mechanisms underlying pairbonding evolved in the context of infant–caregiver attachment (for which sexual desire is irrelevant).

Even more powerful evidence for the links between attachment and pairbonding, and the distinctions between pairbonding and sexual desire, is provided by the growing body of research on the neurobiological substrates of these systems. Because most work in this area has been conducted with animals, we remain in the hypothesis-generation rather than hypothesis-testing stage with respect to humans; nonetheless, converging lines of evidence (reviewed by Diamond, 2003; Fisher, 1998) suggest that the marked experiential differences among sexual desire, infatuation, and attachment may be partially attributable to their distinct neurochemical signatures. Sexual desire, for example, is directly mediated by gonadal estrogens and androgens (reviewed in Wallen, 1995). Yet these hormones do not mediate the formation of affectional bonds. Rather, animal research indicates that the intense proximity maintenance and separation distress associated with attachment formation (from its passionate onset to its quieter, enduring fruition) are mediated by an array of interacting neurochemicals that undergird the fundamental reward circuitry of the mammalian brain, such as endogenous opioids, dopamine, corticosterone, oxytocin, and vasopressin (reviewed in Carter, 1998; Carter & Keverne, 2002; Curtis & Wang, 2003; Panksepp, 1998; Panksepp, Nelson, & Bekkedal, 1997).

One of the most important contributions of this growing body of evolutionary, biobehavioral research on adult attachment formation is that it demonstrates the value of a thoroughgoing life-span/developmental approach to studying intimate relationships. In connecting the dynamics of adult romantic love to the dynamics of our earliest emotional bonds to caregivers, attachment-based perspectives on intimate relationships provide a uniquely generative framework for modeling the normative development of these bonds over the life span. Attachment theory also provides a powerful life-span/developmental framework for understanding the emergence and expression of individual differences in the quality of intimate relationships, and this is the topic to which we turn next.

Individual Differences in Attachment Style

When Hazan and Shaver argued in their seminal 1987 article that adult romantic relationships were, in essence, adult versions of infant–caregiver attachments, they maintained that the basic developmental continuity in the functioning of the attachment system extended to the question of individual differences in attachment. Mary Ainsworth, a student of Bowlby's, had demonstrated that children develop stable, traitlike *patterns of attachment* (eventually denoted *attachment styles*) based on the quality of their relationship with the caregiver (Ainsworth, Blehar, Waters, & Wall, 1978). In Ainsworth's framework, *secure* infants are those with sensitive and responsive caregivers, who consistently experienced proximity to these caregivers as distress alleviating. As a result, they come to view themselves as competent and worthy of love and to view others as willing and able to provide comfort and support. Infants with an *anxious* attachment style experienced inconsistent caregiving and consequently seek repeated reassurance of the availability of their attachment figures. Infants with an *avoidant* attachment style tended to be rebuffed by their attachment figures and therefore learned not to seek contact with them when distressed.

Hazan and Shaver argued that if adult romantic relationships are functionally analogous to infant–caregiver attachments, then the same individual differences that characterize children's orientations toward their attachment figures should also characterize adults' orientations toward romantic partners (Hazan & Shaver, 1987; Shaver, Hazan, & Bradshaw, 1988). They presented preliminary data in support of this claim, based on a brief community survey, and it was not long before numerous researchers were testing—and confirming—their basic claims using more rigorous research designs and increasingly diverse samples. Just as avoidant infants had been observed to resist contact with caregivers when distressed, avoidantly attached adults resisted contact with romantic partners when distressed; just as anxious infants were found to be hypervigilant for cues of the caregiver's attention and responsiveness, so, too, were anxiously attached adults with respect to their romantic partners.

Since that time, thousands of studies have documented associations between attachment styles and romantic relationship functioning (Shaver & Brennan, 1992). For example, anxiously and avoidantly attached individuals have less trust in their romantic partners than do secure individuals (Brennan & Shaver, 1995; Simpson, 1990); they adopt negative and suspicious interpretations of their partners' motives (Collins, 1996; Simpson, Rholes, & Phillips, 1996), and they respond with greater anger, hostility, and resentment to a partner's negative behavior (Collins, 1996; Mikulincer, 1998b; Rholes, Simpson, & Orina, 1999). They are less likely to seek and provide support and reassurance to partners (Carnelley, Pietromonaco, & Jaffe, 1996; Cobb, Davila, & Bradbury, 2001; Collins & Feeney, 2000; Ognibene & Collins, 1998; Simpson, Rholes, & Nelligan, 1992) and are more likely to pursue destructive patterns of escalation or withdrawal in response to conflict (Cohn, Silver, Cowan, Cowan, & Pearson, 1992; Crowell et al., 2002; Feeney, 1994; Fitzpatrick, Fey, Segrin, & Schiff, 1993; Gaines et al., 1997; Senchak & Leonard, 1992). Overall, anxiously and avoidantly attached individuals report lower levels of relationship satisfaction, stability, intimacy, cohesion, and commitment (Cobb et al., 2001; Hazan & Shaver, 1987; Meyers & Landsberger, 2002; Rholes, Paetzold, & Friedman, 2008; Shaver & Brennan, 1992; Simpson, 1990; Stackert & Bursik, 2003; Tucker & Anders, 1999).

Yet the implications of adult attachment styles extend beyond straightforward thoughts and behaviors regarding romantic partners; attachment styles are theorized to function as cognitive–affective frameworks that organize the encoding, storage, retrieval, and manipulation of information related to affective states and, in particular, experiences of stress versus security. Supporting this view, studies have demonstrated associations between attachment style and individuals' cognitive processing of interpersonal phenomena as well as capacities and strategies for regulating positive and negative emotions. For example, anxiously and avoidantly attached adults make less positive and benign interpretations of others' facial expressions (Magai, Hunziker, Mesias, & Culver, 2000), they endorse more negative interpretations of both hypothetical and actual relationship events (Collins, 1996; Lakey, McCabe, Fisicaro, & Drew, 1996; Mikulincer & Florian, 1998; Simpson, Ickes, & Grich, 1999; Simpson et al., 1996), and they make more hostile attributions of others' motives (Mikulincer, 1998a). These biased cognitive appraisals have direct implications for emotional experience. Anxiously and avoidantly attached individuals tend to report more frequent and intense negative emotions (Feeney, 1995, 1999; Feeney & Ryan, 1994; Mikulincer & Orbach, 1995), both in response to everyday events and interactions (Pietromonaco & Feldman-Barrett, 1997; Tidwell, Reis, & Shaver, 1996) as well as in response to naturally occurring (Magai & Cohen, 1998; Mikulincer, 1998a; Mikulincer, Florian, & Weller, 1993; Mikulincer, Horesh, Levy Shiff, Manovich, & Shalev, 1998) or laboratory-induced stressors (Mikulincer, 1998a; Rholes et al., 1999).

Attachment in a Life-Span/Developmental Context

One of the most compelling aspects of attachment theory is its life-span perspective. Bowlby famously argued that attachment processes remain central to mental and physical well-being "from the cradle to the grave" (Bowlby, 1988, p. 62). Accordingly, the extension of attachment theory to adult love relationships (Hazan & Shaver, 1987; Shaver et al., 1988) has created opportunities for building comprehensive developmental models that use the same core principles to explain the nature, dynamics, and effects of intimate human relationships at all stages of life.

Yet the promise of such sweeping life-span models has largely gone unfulfilled. Rather, contemporary attachment research remains largely bifurcated between developmental investigations of infant–caregiver bonds and social-psychological investigations of adult romantic bonds. Researchers within each tradition emphasize different aspects of attachment and use different methods to capture and evaluate attachment phenomena (reviewed in Allen & Land, 1999; Crowell, Fraley, & Shaver, 1999; Jacobvitz, Curran, & Moller, 2002). Furthermore, the social-psychological literature on adult romantic attachment yields a particularly static picture of attachment phenomena, given that many studies have focused on documenting associations between attachment style and relationship functioning at a single point in time rather than investigating change in both domains and how such change might synergistically interact across different time scales to shape life-span trajectories of relationship experiences and expectations.

To some degree, this is because attachment researchers continue to be somewhat divided over the nature and extent of associations between childhood and adult patterns of attachment security (see, for example, Lewis, Feiring, & Rosenthal, 2000; Waters, Hamilton, & Weinfield, 2000). Bowlby's (1973b) *prototype hypothesis*, which specified that early attachment security lays the foundation for adult romantic security by fundamentally shaping individuals' expectations and beliefs about love relationships, has been called the "boldest assertion of attachment theory," serving as "a lightning rod of controversy" among developmental psychologists (Roisman, Collins, Sroufe, & Egeland, 2005, p. 105). The strictest, most "traitlike" version of the prototype hypothesis maintains that infant–caregiver attachment style is laid down in the first year of life and largely "grows up" into adult romantic attachment style, establishing robust working models of adult love dynamics before the individual has even had his or her first relationship. From this perspective, subsequent romantic experiences usually end up strengthening and confirming the individual's initial attachment style because working models function as self-fulfilling prophecies, reliably altering individuals' selection of romantic partners and their ongoing appraisals of the partner's responsiveness and availability.

The evidence for this "strong trait" perspective is mixed. First, longitudinal studies have detected varying degrees of continuity in attachment style from childhood to adulthood (Hamilton, 2000; Lewis et al., 2000; Roisman et al., 2005; Waters, Merrick, Treboux, Crowell, & Albersheim, 2000; Weinfield, Sroufe, & Egeland, 2000) and over adulthood, from relationship to relationship (Baldwin & Fehr, 1995; Davila, Burge, & Hammen, 1997; Davila, Karney, & Bradbury, 1999; Fraley, 2007; Klohnen & Bera, 1998; Lopez & Gormley, 2002; Mitchell, 2007; Scharfe & Bartholomew, 1995; Zhang & Labouvie-Vief, 2004). One of the difficulties in drawing robust conclusions from this body of research concerns the wide diversity of measures used to assess adult attachment experiences. Whereas infant patterns of attachment are consistently assessed using the famous Strange Situation, adult attachment is usually evaluated through (a) adult *representations* of attachment to the caregiver (Grossmann, Grossmann, & Kindler, 2005; Sroufe, Egeland, Carlson, & Collins, 2005; Steele & Steele, 2005), using the Adult Attachment Interview (Main, Kaplan, & Cassidy, 1985); or (b) the coherence of adult *narratives* regarding the quality of current romantic relationships (Crowell & Waters, 2005; Grossmann et al., 2005; Sroufe et al., 2005), assessed in the Current Relationship Inventory (Crowell et al., 2002); (c) concrete qualities of the individual's current relationship, such as commitment, satisfaction, emotional tone, closeness, and constructive approaches to conflict (Crowell & Waters, 2005; Roisman et al., 2005, p. 105; Roisman, Madsen, Hennighausen, Sroufe, & Collins, 2001; Sroufe, Egeland, Carlson, & Collins, 2005); or a combination of these. Notably absent from the majority of long-term prospective studies (with some exceptions, such as Crowell & Waters, 2005) is the Experiences in Close Relationships Inventory (ECR; Fraley, Waller, & Brennan, 2000), the current self-report method of choice for assessing adult romantic anxiety and avoidance. Hence the degree to which romantic attachment styles (as represented by the ECR) can, in fact, be interpreted as "adult versions" of infant patterns of preoccupation and avoidance (as assessed by the Strange Situation or, later, by the Adult Attachment Interview) remains an open question.

Many researchers have sidestepped this debate by gravitating toward a "two-pronged" conceptualization of adult attachment style, in which individuals maintain both a global working model (carried forward from childhood) which provides a general, traitlike template for an individual's relationship expectations, and also a "relationship-specific" model based on specific attachment figures, such as current or recent romantic partners (Baldwin & Fehr, 1995; Baldwin, Keelan, Fehr, Enns, & Koh-Rangarajoo, 1996; Collins & Read, 1994; Klohnen, Weller, Luo, & Choe, 2005; La Guardia, Ryan, Couchman, & Deci, 2000). According to this view, individuals' multiple attachment representations are arranged hierarchically according to their centrality and cognitive accessibility. The appearance of instability in attachment style, then, can be attributed to the fact that current relationships may activate different representational components within the overall hierarchy.

This perspective takes more seriously the phenomenon of reciprocal influence between prior and current attachment expectations and experiences and hence holds more promise for the development of life-span models of attachment that take into account an individual's entire cumulative trajectory of attachment-relevant experiences. In fact, some of the most promising new approaches in this vein use information about the patterning, sequencing, and variability of attachment experiences over time to understand the conditions under which stability is either maintained or disrupted. Fraley and his colleagues, for example, have explored connectionist and dynamical systems models of attachment style over the life span (Fraley, 2007; Fraley & Brumbaugh, 2004), seeking to explain which types of relationship trajectories are likely to produce stability versus change in attachment representations and the *mechanisms* underlying these dynamic processes. Using a series of computer simulations, for example, Fraley has demonstrated that when an individual's history of attachment experiences changes gradually—but consistently—over the entire course of development so that it becomes increasingly differentiated from the prototypical infant–caregiver pattern, then by the time the individual reaches adulthood, the early pattern may be entirely "rewritten" by more recent and salient experiences. In such a case, infant–caregiver attachment style ceases to behave like a trait altogether, and its potential influence on future psychosocial development is superseded by current attachment experiences. However, using the same simulation strategy, Fraley also demonstrated that if the original, prototypical pattern is periodically *reexperienced* with enough frequency (for example, if an adult becomes involved with several romantic partners who are "just like my mother"), then the stability of the original pattern is notably reinforced and enhanced, magnifying its influence as an ongoing engine for developmental change over the life span.

What is important and generative about this approach is not only its emphasis on interindividual variation in the relative influence of developmental history (also emphasized by the seminal work of Davila and colleagues, Davila, Burge, & Hammen, 1997; Davila & Sargent, 2003), but its focus on identifying the underlying cognitive mechanisms through which different sequential histories of attachment experiences potentiate stability versus change. This dynamic, connectionist approach poses important correctives to the notion that one's "original" attachment style is always lying dormant, "underneath it all," ready to be reactivated at any time (see Sroufe, Egeland, & Kreutzer, 1990). At the same time, this approach also argues that the individual's attachment history is unlikely to be completely superseded by present experiences (i.e., Kagan, 1980). Rather, the relative influence of the past versus the present depends on the specific sequence of attachment experiences that the individual has encountered over time, a notion that harkens back to Bowlby's initial contention that development always represents an integration of developmental history and current circumstances (Bowlby, 1973b, 1980). From this perspective, questions regarding the "stability" and "change" of attachment patterns can never be answered globally. Rather, they depend fundamentally on individuals' specific sequencing of close relationships over the entire course of life-span development, as well as the sequencing of attachment-relevant experiences within an individual's most important and longstanding current relationships.

We have taken the time to spell out this dynamic, interactionist perspective on longitudinal trajectories of attachment because we think that this approach provides a powerful framework for understanding life-span/developmental trajectories of *all* romantic relationship phenomena. Each of the domains reviewed in this chapter—from relationship satisfaction to commitment to violence—can be conceptualized as having its own developmental history within an individual's life span, pushed and pulled by distinctive sequences of "person–situation," "trait–state" interactions at different stages of development. Hence, as with attachment style, we make no presumptions about the relative stability of certain cognitive, emotional, or behavioral phenomena enacted within intimate relationships. Rather, we consider all of these phenomena to show varying degrees of stability and change over the life span as a function of long-range sequences of intimate relationship experiences.

From this perspective, individuals' earliest romantic ties take on heightened significance. Bowlby (1973) argued, and dynamical systems theorists echo (reviewed in Fraley & Brumbaugh, 2004), that although early-developing prototypes do not have deterministic influences on later experiences, they nonetheless have enduring influences. In essence, then, the seeds of an individual's eventual pattern of romantic relationship experience can be discerned within the nascent relationships formed during adolescence and emerging adulthood. With this in mind, we now turn to the burgeoning research on adolescent romantic relationships and to the experiences and dynamics that provide the launching pad for their future romantic trajectories.

ADOLESCENT ROMANTIC RELATIONSHIPS

Although the vast majority of research on intimate relationships is conducted with adults between 20 and 40 years of age, clearly individuals begin participating in romantic ties much earlier. Men's and women's first substantive romantic ties are usually formed during their adolescent years, as they gradually shift their emotional investments to peers over parents (reviewed in Florsheim, 2003; Furman, Feiring, & Brown, 1999). In the National Longitudinal Study of Adolescent Health (Add Health), roughly a quarter of participants reported that they had been involved in a romantic relationship by age 12 and that percentage increased to nearly three quarters by age 18 (Carver, Joyner, & Udry, 2003). Yet historically, adolescent romantic relationships have received scant empirical attention. It has primarily been since the mid-1990s that their potential significance for adolescent social, psychological, and sexual development has been rigorously investigated (Crouter & Booth, 2006; Davila, Stroud, Miller, & Steinberg, 2007; Florsheim, 2003; Furman et al., 1999). Recent studies have consistently found that adolescent participation in romantic relationships poses both risks and benefits. On the positive side, youths' budding romantic ties provide opportunities to master strong emotions, regulate impulses, practice interpersonal skills, and make decisions about healthy behavior. On the negative side, they pose risks for sexually transmitted infections, unintended pregnancies, emotional distress, relationship violence, and physical health problems related to chronic stress. This, of course, is consistent with the developmental premises that we articulated earlier: Intimate relationships are driven by developmentally specific psychosocial capacities and simultaneously drive future psychosocial development. The critical issue, then, is to determine which developmentally specific skills and capacities provide the necessary foundations for youths' first intimate relationships and which types of relationships have adaptive or maladaptive effects on youths' subsequent development.

Pathways through Risk and Well-Being

Supporting the notion that successful intimate relationships require a certain degree of developmental maturity, research has found that the *timing and context* of youths' romantic involvements is associated with their adjustment and development. For example, negative consequences for adolescent psychological well-being and sexual risk behaviors appear to be greatest among adolescents who begin to date very early (i.e., 14 or younger) or who report a large number of concurrent or successive dating partners. Several studies have shown that higher levels of romantic involvement in early and middle adolescence are linked with earlier and more frequent sexual activity (Phinney, Jensen, Olsen, & Cundick, 1990; Scott-Jones & White, 1990), increased substance use and delinquency (Davies & Windle, 2000; Neemann, Hubbard, & Masten, 1995), lower educational aspirations and achievement (Neemann et al., 1995; Parks & Eggert, 1993), greater depression (Parks & Eggert, 1993; Quatman, Sampson, Robinson, & Watson, 2001), lower self-esteem (McDonald & McKinney, 1994), and negative trajectories of psychosocial adjustment (Zimmer-Gembeck, Siebenbruner, & Collins, 2001). In addition, romantic breakups during adolescence are frequent triggers for depression and suicidality (Monroe, Rohde, Seeley, & Lewinsohn, 1999).

Yet little is known about the specific psychological mechanisms through which these associations operate. Studies suggest a range of possibilities, including general unconventionality, preexisting adjustment and self-regulatory problems; involvement with older (and more delinquent) peers, cascading effects of premature social transitions, and disconnection from social institutions such as school, church, and family (Bearman & Bruckner, 2002; Bingham & Crockett, 1996; Crockett, Raffaelli, & Shen, 2006; Halpern, Waller, Spriggs, & Hallfors, 2006; Manlove et al., 2001; B. C. Miller et al., 1997; Resnick et al., 1997). It is likely that different factors prove significant for different youths, but at the present time, we lack the necessary longitudinal, process-oriented data to elucidate these potential pathways.

Alternative Relationship Forms

We also know little about the developmental implications of "alternative" forms of romantic relationships, which appear to be increasingly common. Historically, most youths pursued their first sexual experiences within established romantic relationships (Abma, Chandra, Mosher, Peterson, & Piccinino, 1997; Giordano, Longmore, & Manning, 2006; Manning, Longmore, & Giordano, 2000). Yet recent studies suggest that growing numbers of youths are pursuing intimate ties that deviate from a conventional "couple" model (i.e., relatively exclusive, mutually acknowledged romantic and sexual involvement), such as "friends with benefits" (Grello, Welsh, & Harper, 2006; Manning et al., 2000; Paul & Hayes, 2002; Paul, McManus, & Hayes, 2000). In these arrangements, the two partners start out as friends, and they decide to periodically engage in sexual behavior but not to become a "couple." The relationship is not expected to be exclusive and may or may not be disclosed to peers. The level of mutual intimacy, support, and closeness is not expected to change (if the partners started out as close friends, these dimensions might already be high), and there is no expectation of becoming a conventional couple in the future.

The overall prevalence of such relationships is unknown, but some researchers have questioned whether they introduce risks for youths' sexual and mental well-being, particularly women. Given that sexual behavior pursued outside the context of a romantic relationship remains less acceptable for girls than boys (Baumeister & Twenge, 2002; Crawford & Popp, 2003), it is likely that the immediate and long-term implications of "alternative" sexual-romantic experiences are gender-specific. Support for this view comes from research demonstrating that among women, alternative relationships are frequently associated with shame, disappointment, regret, and sometimes sexual coercion (Caruthers, 2006; M. Hughes, Morrison, & Asada, 2005; Paul & Hayes, 2002; Stepp, 2007). Other researchers have challenged these pessimistic accounts, arguing that alternative romantic arrangements may allow young women to break free of gender-stereotypical relationship roles and express their own interpersonal agency (Caruthers, 2006).

For example, Giordano and colleagues (2006) found that young adults who pursued "friends with benefits" relationships described these relationships as positive contexts for sexual experimentation and release, given that the underlying friendship was described as creating a context of stability and familiarity without the potential volatility and role constraints associated with conventional dating. Studies of college students suggest that when individuals feel that they know and understand a friend's intentions and feelings regarding casual sexual activity, it can be appraised as positive and beneficial (Afifi & Faulkner, 2000). In the end, then, alternative romantic relationships have the potential to be either maladaptive or adaptive, depending on the characteristics and expectations of the participants, their age and level of psychological maturity, the circumstances under which these relationships occur (for example, whether both partners chose the arrangement or whether one partner would prefer to have "something more"), and their positioning in a youth's overall trajectory of romantic-sexual experiences.

Before leaving adolescence, the question of gender differences deserves attention. Previous research suggests that close relationships play a particularly central role for girls' development (L. M. Brown & Gilligan, 1992; Gilligan, 1982) and that the negotiation of changing relationships is a primary struggle for girls during the adolescent years (Gilligan, 1990). A particular risk is for girls to subsume their own desires and needs for the sake of preserving their relationships (Impett, Schooler, & Tolman, 2006), which can have serious detrimental implications for their willingness and capacity to express their sexual and emotional needs; to walk away from partners who denigrate, harm, or threaten them; and to protect themselves from risky sexual practices (Impett et al., 2006; Tolman, 2002). In contrast, research indicates that adolescent boys' socialization toward stoicism and competition leads them to place less emphasis on emotional connection to romantic partners and to place a greater emphasis on sexuality within their romantic ties (Eder, Evans, & Parker, 1995). Others have argued that boys' seeming resistance to intimacy has been overemphasized (Giordano et al., 2006), and have used qualitative methodologies to elucidate the conflicts boys experience between cultural dictates regarding stoic masculinity and their own desires for emotional intimacy (Tolman, Spencer, Harmon, Rosen-Reynoso, & Striepe, 2004; Way, 1996).

Clearly, one of the most important areas for future research on adolescent romantic relationships concerns the differential developmental trajectories of girls versus boys and the ways in which these trajectories are influenced by youths' own histories of gender-based socialization, as well as the rigidity of their parents', peers', and communities' ideologies regarding gender.

THE RELEVANCE OF EMERGING ADULTHOOD

Romantic relationship researchers have increasingly emphasized *emerging adulthood* as a distinct stage of life (Arnett, 2000, 2001) with distinct developmental challenges in the domain of romantic relationship functioning (Crouter & Booth, 2006). Although most individuals begin dating during adolescence, it is usually not until emerging adulthood that their romantic relationships take on the depth and complexity of mature adult relations and during which stable patterns of interpersonal functioning become readily observable (Conger, Cui, Bryant, & Elder, 2000; Donnellan, Larsen-Rife, & Conger, 2005).

The relevance of emerging adulthood as a distinct developmental stage stems from historical and social-structural factors. Because of significant demographic changes in industrialized countries since the 1960s, individuals no longer transition into full-blown adult roles by their late teens and early 20s. Protracted postsecondary education, delayed marriage, and delayed childbearing create an extended period of transition between adolescence and adulthood (Arnett, 2006a, 2006b). Note, for example, that from 1950 to 1970, the median age for first marriage in the United States was between 20 and 21 for women and around 23 for men; these ages have been rising steadily and are now at an all-time high: 26 for women and 28 for men (U.S. Census Bureau, 2007). Presently, most 18- to 25-year-olds feel they have undoubtedly matured past adolescence yet do not consider themselves full adults (Arnett, 2000, 2001) and have not accepted the responsibilities associated with long-term interpersonal and occupational commitments (Arnett, 2001; Carroll et al., 2007).

Many emerging adults view this period of life as a time to explore and experiment with a wide range of possibilities regarding both work and love (Arnett, 2000), ideally with the goal of creating a life plan that will guide them through the ensuing years (Levinson, Darrow, Klein, Levinson, & McKee, 1978; Tanner, 2006). During this self-focused, exploratory, and uncertain life phase, emerging adults typically retain strong ties to parents. Studies of college-aged adults have found that around 60% continue to view their mother or their father as their primary source of emotional support and security. Hence, whereas friends and romantic partners typically rival parents as primary support providers by late adolescence (Doherty & Feeney, 2004), for many emerging adults, this process of "transferring attachment" from parents to peers (Hazan & Zeifman, 1994) is somewhat protracted. This fits with Carroll and colleagues' (2007) view of emerging adulthood as "a transitional period between a person's family of origin and his or her family of formation" (p. 223). Indeed, Arnett (2000) suggested that while the guiding relationship question for adolescents may be "Who would I enjoy being with, here and now?" that of emerging adults is "Given the kind of person I am, what kind of person do I wish to have as a partner through life?" (p. 473).

Does this shift in emphasis influence the quality and dynamics of emerging adults' romantic ties, relative to the ties they pursued during adolescence? Arnett (2000) has argued that the romantic relationships of emerging adulthood differ notably from those of adolescence, characterized by less emphasis on companionship and greater emphasis on the potential for deeper emotional intimacy. Commitment, too, tends to increase; emerging adults' relationships tend to last longer than those of adolescents and are more likely to involve cohabitation (Laumann, Gagnon, Michael, & Michaels, 1994; Martin, Martin, & Martin, 2001). Physical intimacy also becomes more important and more common, and emerging adults' romantic relationships are more likely than those of adolescents to include sexual intercourse (Laumann et al., 1994). Of note, sexual intimacy during emerging adulthood is another area in which we see a historical shift. In part because of the invention of the birth control pill, it is now normative and widely accepted for emerging adults to be sexually active before marriage (Arnett, 2006b).

The tendency for individuals in their early 20s to pursue protracted developmental transitions between adolescence and adulthood may be here to stay, and yet there has been relatively little research on the distinctive attributes *and* long-term implications of emerging adults' romantic ties. This is likely to be an area of increased investigation in the coming years and provides a fascinating domain in which to explore the interaction among individual-level, dyadic, familial, and cultural factors in shaping young men's and women's relationship trajectories.

SETTLING INTO ADULTHOOD: SATISFACTION AND STABILITY

Perhaps the two most intensively researched questions when it comes to mature romantic relationships during the adult years are "What keeps relationships together?" and "What keeps relationships happy?" Empirically based attempts to understand and predict the twin outcomes of relationship *stability* and *satisfaction* stretch back to the 1930s (Terman & Buttenweiser, 1935) and continue unabated to this day. Of course, from a life-span/developmental perspective, stability and satisfaction are not really outcomes at all but dynamic states constantly made and remade by the unfolding interaction between each partner's cognitions, emotions, and behaviors. We therefore prefer to think of *trajectories* of stability and satisfaction than fixed levels. At any point in time, we can take a snapshot of these moving targets and analyze their developmental history (across multiple prior relationships as well as within any one relationship), their immediate dynamics, and their future implications for individual and couple functioning.

To be sure, studies that attempt to move beyond isolated snapshots and strive to capture long-range trajectories of stability and satisfaction often yield pessimistic conclusions. For example, longitudinal studies have found that after an initial "newlywed peak," adults' marital satisfaction tends to decline progressively over time (Karney & Bradbury, 1997; Kurdek, 1998a), especially among couples with children (Belsky & Kelly, 1994; Cowan & Cowan, 1992), although there is notable variability among couples regarding the magnitude and rate of change (Carrère, Buehlman, Gottman, Coan, & Ruckstuhl, 2000; Cohan & Bradbury, 1997; Gottman, Coan, Carrère, & Swanson, 1998; Karney & Bradbury, 1997; Kurdek, 1998a; P. J. E. Miller, Niehuis, & Huston, 2006). Approximately 30% of U.S. couples divorce within 10 years of marriage. For people under age 45, 50% of first marriages will end in divorce for men and 45% to 50% for women. Rates of overall dissolution (taking into account unmarried, cohabiting couples) are undoubtedly much higher (Kitson, 2006). Clearly, staying together and staying happy are life-long, context-dependent, developmentally specific challenges. In this section, we review key findings from research on these challenges and consider their implications for understanding lifespan trajectories of intimate relationship functioning.

Conceptualization and Assessment of Relationship Satisfaction

Reliable assessment of relationship satisfaction is more difficult than it might at first appear. One problem is that the construct itself is notoriously vague (Gottman, 1998), making its operationalization problematic. Another hurdle is the lack of rigorous theory—and especially developmental theory—about the determinants of satisfaction across the life course. Accordingly, attempts to develop measures of satisfaction have been largely atheoretical (Fincham & Beach, 2006; Glenn, 1990). Existing measures of relationship satisfaction emphasize a wide array of domains, and there is no consensus on which remain the most central and important. Some domains are explicitly behavioral, focusing on objective events such as verbal disagreements or specific attempts to accommodate the others' needs. Others emphasize subjective feelings and attitudes, such as regrets about getting married or the degree to which one feels loved and admired. Reis, Clark, and Holmes (2004) argued that *perceived partner responsiveness* lies at the heart of relationship satisfaction and encompasses global beliefs (originating in childhood attachment relationships but constantly "updated" through day-to-day couple functioning) that one's partner affirms, supports, and values central features of one's self.

Because most measures contain a mix of objective and subjective elements, summary indices of "satisfaction" often prove difficult to interpret. One question which has received increasing attention is whether relationship satisfaction is categorical or continuous (Beach, Fincham, Amir, & Leonard, 2005; Fincham & Beach, 2006). Although many studies have detected linear correlations between *degrees* of relationship satisfaction and a variety of individual and couple-level processes, other studies suggest that when dissatisfaction is high and stable enough, it creates pervasive perceptual and behavioral biases which feed forward to escalate conflict and distress, making it increasingly difficult for couples to change the direction of their unraveling trajectories. In such cases, it may be more meaningful to characterize a couple as categorically "unhappy" than to try and pin down their specific *degree* of unhappiness.

Another issue for assessment is whether satisfaction reflects concrete, objective features of the relationship (for example, frequency of conflict) versus each partner's subjective *beliefs and feelings* regarding the relationship. Given that nearly all measures of relationship satisfaction are based on self-report, objective and subjective features of a relationship tend to be conflated. This is perhaps best demonstrated by the fact that two partners in a relationship often provide markedly divergent reports about the concrete behaviors and interactions supposedly occurring on a day-to-day basis (Bolger, Zuckerman, & Kessler, 2000; Christensen & Nies, 1980; S. L. Gable, Reis, & Downey, 2003; D. A. Smith & Peterson, 2008). Importantly, many researchers argue that identifying the objective "truth" of day-to-day behavior in a couple is not nearly as important as establishing partners' global evaluations of the relationship (Fincham & Bradbury, 1987a; Norton, 1983), particularly because these global evaluations shape the way that partners interpret, remember, and respond to each and every relationship experience (Gottman, 1990). Extensive research, for example, has documented the phenomenon of "sentiment override" in relationships, in which partners respond *non-contingently* to particular relationship events and partner behaviors (as well as to researchers' inquiries about the relationship) because they are guided by their dominant sentiment regarding the relationship, rather than the specific facts or experiences at hand. Hence, sentiment override represents one of the processes through which global views of one's current relationship may actually exert a stronger press on future interpersonal development than the "concrete facts" of day-to-day relationship behavior.

Finally, there is the dimension of time. The majority of relationship quality measures ask individuals to report on *current* feelings and behaviors. Yet of course, relationships evolve and change over time, and studies have reliably demonstrated that although newlyweds often report high levels of satisfaction, they also frequently report precipitous declines in satisfaction soon after the wedding (Karney & Bradbury, 1997; Kurdek, 1998a). Hence, *maintaining* satisfaction over broad stretches of time, especially in the face of each partner's changing life tasks, stressors, skills, and developmental challenges, might be viewed as the true marker of relationship success (Bradbury & Karney, 2004; Canary & Stafford, 1992, 1994). However, few assessment approaches adopt a broad-based, lifespan perspective on satisfaction. As a result, although we have ably documented the numerous cognitive, emotional, and behavioral components of satisfying versus dissatisfying relationships, we know little about how each component changes over the lifespan, and whether there are adaptive shifts in the relative importance of different components at different stages of life course. These are important questions for future developmental research on satisfaction.

Negative Behavior

One of the most widely assessed correlates of relationship satisfaction and stability concerns negative behaviors such as hostility, criticism, and disengagement. Studies using objective, laboratory–based observations of couple behavior have yielded similar conclusions as have studies relying on self-report measures: negative behaviors are associated with lower satisfaction and increased chances of dissolution (Creasey & Jarvis, 2008; Fincham & Beach, 2006; Gottman & Notarius, 2000, 2002; Weiss & Heyman, 1997). In fact, Gottman's well-known program of longitudinal, multimethod research found that divorce could be reliably predicted by the presence of four behaviors in particular, assessed during a videotaped laboratory session: stonewalling, criticism, contempt, and defensiveness (Gottman, 1991, 1994; Gottman et al., 1998; Gottman & Levenson, 1992). Gottman's research suggests that the most dangerous and detrimental pattern is one in which couples' negative behaviors—and perhaps more importantly, their associated negative affect—progressively escalate in intensity, making it increasingly difficult to terminate aversive interchanges (Gottman, 1998). For some partners, this is when they resort to "*stonewalling*," or disengaging from the interaction and ceasing to respond to the partner at all (Gottman, 1994; Gottman et al., 1998).

Another particularly common and aversive type of couple behavior is the "demand-withdrawal" pattern (Caughlin & Huston, 2002; Caughlin & Vangelisti, 2000; Christensen & Heavey, 1990; Eldridge & Christensen, 2002; Eldridge, Sevier, Jones, Atkins, & Christensen, 2007; Vogel & Karney, 2002), in which one partner (usually the female) makes a series of escalating demands and criticisms which are met by increased stonewalling, passivity, and unresponsiveness from the other partner (usually the male). Although there are reliable gender differences in demand-withdrawal behavior, studies have also found that demand-withdrawal behavior is structured by the power dynamics of the conflict, such that the partner who is criticizing or trying to change the other takes the "demand" role (Klinetob & Smith, 1996). However the roles are distributed, demand-withdrawal behavior is associated with decreased satisfaction in both partners, and a number of psychophysiological studies have also found it to be associated with heightened autonomic nervous system activity indicative of psychological stress and perceptions of threat (Heffner et al., 2006; Kiecolt-Glaser, Newton, Cacioppo, & MacCallum, 1996).

Not surprisingly, the negative behaviors just discussed occur most frequently in the context of conflict, and there is an extensive literature examining the predictors, topics, typologies, and implications of couple conflict over the life span (reviewed in Booth & Crouter, 2001; Kline, Pleasant, Whitton, & Markman, 2006). One of the obstacles in studying conflict dynamics in romantic couples is the unavoidable ambiguity regarding definitions of conflict. Technically, any interaction in which partners have opposing goals and interests can be defined as a conflict (Bell & Blakeney, 1977; Bradbury, Rogge, & Lawrence, 2001), yet this broad definition lumps together screaming matches with quietly seething "discussions." Hence, over the years, researchers investigating the nature and determinants of marital satisfaction and stability have moved away from studying discrete episodes of conflict in favor of understanding broad-based distinctions between functional versus dysfunctional conflict management. This body of research suggests that conflict patterns characterized by negative escalation, invalidation, withdrawal, and violence are particularly destructive, gradually and progressively eroding couples' bonds to one another (Gill, Christensen, & Fincham, 1999; Gottman et al., 1998; Gottman & Notarius, 2000, 2002; Markman & Notarius, 1987; Stanley, Blumberg, & Markman, 1999).

Notably, this body of research has found that destructive conflict-management patterns can be observed in couples long before their marriage began to develop signs of strain and that the detrimental effects of these patterns are not moderated by the presence of positive interchanges (Markman & Notarius, 1987; Notarius & Markman, 1993). This is not to suggest that positive interchanges are irrelevant; in sufficient amounts, positive interchanges can successfully prevent negative escalation and ameliorate some of the immediate affective consequences of conflict. However, relatively high and sustained levels of positivity are necessary to confer these benefits (Gottman & Levenson, 1992). The fact that negative behaviors are so predictive of relationship satisfaction might seem to offer some hope to distressed couples—after all, it would seem that negative behaviors such as excessive criticism can be easily curtailed with a little willpower. Yet studies have also found that dysfunctional behavioral patterns are observable early in a relationship and that they tend to remain stable over time (Bradbury & Karney, 1993; Gottman et al., 1998; Karney & Bradbury, 1995).

This, of course, raises again the central question of developmental change and whether there are discernible factors that differentiate between couples who successfully redirect and repair dysfunctional trajectories of conflict resolution and those who do not. Some researchers have argued that the stability of maladaptive interpersonal behaviors is partly attributable to the fact that these behaviors are strongly influenced by stable, early-developing temperament and personality factors (Caspi, 1987; Karney &

Bradbury, 1995; Newman, Caspi, Moffitt, & Silva, 1997). From this perspective, it would appear that certain individuals will repeatedly—and even increasingly—resort to maladaptive behaviors in their intimate relationships as their negative relationship experiences and expectations mutually reinforce one another again and again over the life span. Nonetheless, clinical psychologists such as Gottman have attempted to break these cycles, designing educational interventions aimed at pulling distressed couples back from the brink and teaching positive conflict management strategies to newlyweds *before* negative patterns have had a chance to become entrenched (Gottman, 2002; Notarius & Markman, 1993). Yet the question of how *much* lasting change is possible—among *which* couples—remains unknown, given the relatively short timeframe of most follow-up studies. On the basis of our developmental assumption that relationships tend to have "cascading" patterns of influence on psychosocial and interpersonal functioning over the life span, one might expect that certain key changes in negative behavior (for example, a reduction in demand–withdrawal interactions during conflict) might appear to be relatively trivial when first established but might have progressively larger positive effects on both relationship development and individual psychosocial functioning over the long-term course of development. A fascinating question for future research concerns whether there are reliable factors that maximize a couple's likelihood of experiencing *escalating* benefits, over the life span, of early reparative interventions.

Positive Behavior

Although positive behaviors have the potential to "counteract" the potentially detrimental effects of negative behaviors in a relationship, it takes a fairly large number of positive behaviors to do so. Gottman, for example, found that highly satisfied couples tended to report at least five positive behaviors for every negative behavior (Gottman, 1994). In such couples, a high and stable ratio of positive to negative behaviors may create a climate of warmth, support, and solidarity that facilitates adaptive responses to everyday relationship stressors, making it easier to "ride out" periods of strain and also feeding forward to promote continued positive interpersonal and overall psychosocial development. This may account for the fact that in couples with high levels of affectionate expression, negative behavior on the part of one's spouse is less strongly related to one's own marital satisfaction (Caughlin & Huston, 2002; Huston & Chorost, 1994).

Notably, Gottman, Coan, Carrère, and Swanson (1998) found that in a sample of newly married couples, exchanges of positive affect *during* conflict proved to be the only reliable predictor of marital satisfaction and stability 6 years later. Similarly, a study by Driver and Gottman (2004) found that even in the context of relatively trivial, mundane interactions, humor, playfulness, and affection proved adaptive. Couples with high levels of these behaviors in the course of everyday life were better able to mobilize such behaviors to maintain a constructive dialogue with their partner during conflict.

Rusbult, Verette, Whitney, Slovik, and Lipkus (1991) have described this phenomenon as *accommodation*, in which one partner responds constructively to the other partner's negative or potentially destructive behavior, rather than responding with defensiveness, criticism, or anger. Accommodation might take the form of apologizing to a partner, forgiving him or her for a transgression, introducing humor or affection into a potentially difficult interaction, or simply "letting go" of a complaint or a perceived slight. Accommodation is important because it can interrupt potentially negative chains of interaction, ensuring that periodic transgressions remain periodic (Arriaga & Rusbult, 1998; Gottman, 1993; Gottman & Levenson, 1992; Rusbult, Bissonnette, Arriaga, Cox, & Bradbury, 1998). Along these lines, we would further argue that accommodation is also likely to confer long-term benefits because it fundamentally changes the basic interpersonal foundation on which each partner's own ensuing interpersonal and individual development is based. Just as infant–caregiver attachment security is theorized to establish an enduring sense that the world is a safe place in which transgressions are be forgiven and in which mistakes do not result in the loss of love, accommodative processes may serve the same function, reinforcing both partners' sense of security and allowing them to "recover" from stressful and dysfunctional episodes in their relationship without incurring lasting shifts toward maladaptive trajectories of relationship development.

Accommodation, of course, is not easy. Most individuals' immediate responses to negative interpersonal behavior tend to be self-centered, self-protective, and potentially destructive (Thibaut & Kelley, 1978). To override these automatic tendencies, accommodation requires two key ingredients: the *motive* to respond constructively, which is strongly associated with one's commitment to and investment in the relationship (Rusbult et al., 1991), and *self-regulatory capacity*, which allows individuals to resist destructive, self-centered impulses and replace them with prosocial behaviors (Finkel & Campbell, 2001; see also Robins, Caspi, & Moffitt, 2000). Perunovic and Holmes (2008) argued that because the personality trait of agreeableness has been found to be associated with prosocial motivation (Graziano & Eisenberg, 1997) as well as strong capacities for self-regulation in the context of relationships (Ahadi & Rothbart, 1994), highly agreeable individuals should be more likely to adopt accommodative approaches to negative partner behavior and should do so relatively automatically, requiring relatively little effortful control or consideration. This was exactly what they found. In fact, highly agreeable individuals were actually more accommodating to their partners in experimental scenarios that did not permit them the time to consider rationally or weigh their behavior. Hence, this research helps to explain why agreeable individuals tend to report higher relationship satisfaction and stability: Not only do they tend to perceive their partners in a more positive light (making them less likely to react with extreme negative affect to problematic or ambiguous relationship events), but when they do take note of partner transgressions, their robust interpersonal self-regulation allows them to respond constructively and avoid negative escalation.

Although positive behaviors such as accommodation obviously carry immediate benefits, longitudinal research has found that day-to-day positive feelings and behaviors are also critically important for *long-term* relationship satisfaction and stability over the life span. Gottman and Levenson (2000) found that over a 14-year period, partners' negative affectivity during conflict reliably predicted early—but not later—divorcing. In direct contrast, low levels of positive affectivity during routine, nonconflictual discussions predicted later—but not early—divorcing. These findings demonstrate that to achieve long-term success with establishing and maintaining a satisfying romantic relationship, couples must work toward building a foundation of mutual enjoyment, pleasure, and playfulness with one another. Over the long term, such a climate can potentially buffer partners against "low points" in their relationship by creating a climate of positivity and security.

Social Support

Another form of positive behavior that has received extensive attention is social support. Yet contrary to the findings regarding accommodation, displays of social support have more complicated patterns of association with relationship satisfaction and well-being. Although individuals in satisfying relationships generally describe their partners as supportive and responsive (Collins & Feeney, 2000; Reis et al., 2004; Srivastava, McGonigal, Richards, Butler, & Gross, 2006), studies have found that *specific, observable* displays of support do not have beneficial effects on emotional well-being, a finding that has been attributed to the possibility that such observable displays simple reinforce the recipient's feelings of stress or weakness, implicitly suggesting that one's partner views him or her as incompetent (Bolger & Amarel, 2007; Bolger et al., 2000; Gleason, Iida, Shrout, & Bolger, 2008; Shrout, Herman, & Bolger, 2006).

Hence the most adaptive situation, according to these studies, is created when partners are confident of one another's overall supportiveness but remain unaware of *specific* supportive acts undertaken to assist them. Such "invisible support" (Bolger et al., 2000) provides all the benefits of social support with none of the downsides. It is also notable that this model of effective support provision shares many similarities with research findings reviewed earlier demonstrating the importance of an overall climate of positivity, playfulness, and responsiveness. Collectively, these findings indicate that positive behaviors between partners—even those that are transacted with such subtlety that they fail to be detected—provide the "bricks and mortar" of a well-functioning relationship. The beneficial effects of any one of these behaviors might not be immediately observable, but over the course of a long relationship, they weave a fabric of connectedness, trust, mutual support, and enjoyment between partners that fuels adaptive relationship processes over the long term.

Changes in Positive and Negative Behaviors over the Life Span

Research on the relative importance of positive and negative behaviors for relationship satisfaction helps to clarify some of the intriguing findings that have emerged from research on romantic relationships in late life. Contrary to the common stereotype that relationship satisfaction progressively declines across middle adulthood (Pineo, 1961), longitudinal studies have found evidence for a curvilinear pattern, in which the midlife dip in relationship satisfaction (relative to the early, giddy years) is followed by an *increase* in late life (Rollins, 1989). The explanation for this pattern may involve the all-important balance of positive to negative relationship experiences and dimensions: Younger couples tend report high levels of both positive and negative relationship qualities. Middle-aged couples—who report the lowest levels of satisfaction relative to other points in the life span—tend to report lower levels of positive qualities coupled with high levels of negative qualities. Yet intriguingly, older couples are *most* likely to exemplify a state of happy marriage, combining high amounts of positive qualities with low levels of negatives (Gilford & Bengtson, 1979).

Why are older couples more successful than younger couples in "accentuating the positive?" Carstensen's socioemotional selectivity theory (Carstensen, Isaacowitz, & Charles, 1999) provides one potential explanation. Carstensen and colleagues argued that individuals maintain an unconscious awareness of the passage of time in the context of their own life span, such that old age brings an inevitable awareness of the limited time horizon ahead. Carstensen et al. argued that this awareness of limited future time fundamentally shapes the social and psychological goals of older people, motivating them to realign their priorities to emphasize and maximize positive and emotionally meaningful experiences and to deemphasize trivial and negative experiences (Carstensen, 2006; Carstensen, Fung, & Charles, 2003; Carstensen, Pasupathi, Mayr, & Nesselroade, 2000). This shift in priority has direct implications for the quality of older adults' romantic ties (Carstensen, Gottman, & Levenson, 2004). Whereas younger couples are highly motivated to resolve ongoing conflicts for the sake of the long-term prospects of their relationship (inevitably heightening their awareness and experience of negative interactions), this goal becomes less pressing in late life, at which point couples have obviously succeeded in sustaining their relationship despite a certain number of irresolvable conflicts and ongoing tensions. Hence, as individuals' time horizons become shortened, they shift their focus from resolving relationship problems to deemphasizing them relative to the positive dimensions of their relationship.

Commitment

We have already extensively discussed the many factors that predict relationship satisfaction, and because satisfaction and commitment are highly correlated (reviewed in Rusbult, Coolsen, Kirchner, & Clarke, 2006), many of these factors also promote relationship commitment. Not always, however: Commitment also has its own psychological architecture, and understanding how it differs from satisfaction—and may thrive in the absence of satisfaction—provides important insights into the basic dynamics underlying long-term romantic bonds over the life span.

Much of the present interest in relationship commitment can be traced to the 1960s and 1970s, when sharp increases in the U.S. divorce rate sparked interest in understanding how and why some couples stayed together in the face of adversity, whereas others did not (reviewed in Adams & Jones, 1999; Levinger, 1966). Early research focused on identifying demographic predictors of marital stability, including partners' ages, levels of education, and socioeconomic status (Bentler & Newcomb, 1978). Yet researchers soon gravitated to an emphasis on the cognitive, affective, and interpersonal *processes* shaping individuals' decisions to enter—and capacities to maintain—committed relationships. It bears noting that although the majority of this research was initially conducted with married couples, studies of commitment have increasingly included unmarried, cohabiting, and same-sex couples, and many of the findings appear to generalize quite reliably to these ties. Perhaps the broadest and more serviceable definition of commitment is *the intention to maintain a relationship*. Despite its seeming simplicity, this straightforward intention appears to be the most powerful proximate predictor of relationship stability (reviewed in Rusbult et al., 2006). Why, then, do some individuals develop and maintain this powerful intention, whereas others do not? A number of theoretical models have been advanced over the years to answer this question. These models are not mutually exclusive, but they adopt somewhat different emphases and perspectives.

Levinger's pioneering work (1965) examined commitment—or "cohesiveness"—as a function of three fundamental interpersonal "forces": *present attractions*, *alternative attractions*, and *barriers*. Present attractions included the psychological and material benefits associated with one's current relationship, whereas alternative attractions included the benefits that could be gained by leaving the relationship (potentially—although not necessarily—for another partner). Barriers include obstacles to leaving the relationship, which include everything from inconvenience to financial hardship to social stigmatization to love. M. P. Johnson (1973, 1999) similarly emphasized the multifaceted nature of commitment, distinguishing motives such as love from those such as social disapproval. In his model, however, he used these motives to conceptualize three distinct types of commitment: Personal commitment (maintaining a relationship because one finds it enjoyable and satisfying), moral commitment (maintaining a relationship because of perceived moral or ethical obligations), and structural or "constraint" commitment (maintaining a relationship because it is too costly or too difficult to leave). Although Johnson's tripartite model might at first appear simplistic, he actually perceived each type of commitment as multidimensional and multifaceted. Moral commitment, for example, incorporated not only an individual's potential religious beliefs about the sanctity of marriage vows but also a sense of ethical obligation to one's partner, especially if the partner was perceived to have made notable sacrifices for the relationship over the years. Structural commitment included concrete barriers to dissolution (inability to support oneself financially without the partner, complex or expensive divorce proceedings) as well as perceived obstacles (fears of social ostracization). Another important facet of Johnson's model was its flexibility: He noted that any particular relationship might involve different "mixes" of the three types of commitment, potentially yielding quite different subjective experiences.

Of course, each of the aforementioned forces governing commitment—present attractions, alternative attractions, moral constraints, structural barriers—takes different forms and exerts different levels of influence at different stages of development, although little research has systematically examined such changes. For example, the balance of present versus alternative attractions may play a greater role in motivating commitment at earlier stages of the life course, and also at earlier stages of relationship development, whereas structural barriers to dissolution such as children, property, and economic dependence are likely to play more important roles at later stages of relationship development and later stages of the life course.

Investment, Satisfaction, and Alternatives

Arguably the most influential model of commitment is that of Rusbult (1983), who conceptualized individuals' needs and desires for maintaining a relationship as a function of their *satisfaction* with the relationship, the *quality of alternatives* available, and individuals' current and prior *investments* in the relationship (i.e., resources associated with the relationship which would be lost upon dissolution, such as time, money, mutual friends, intimacy). Importantly, Rusbult's model takes account of the fact that the links among satisfaction, commitment, investment, and attention to alternatives are mutually reinforcing. Not only are satisfied couples more likely to make commitments to one another, but high levels of commitment feed back to influence partners' experiences of satisfaction, motivating them to make continued investments in the relationship and to engage in positive behaviors toward one another. This makes Rusbult's model particularly applicable to a life-span/developmental approach to commitment, in which commitment is conceptualized as both the "output" and the "input" of a developing relationship, continually shaping and being shaped by relationship processes over time.

Rusbult's model has received widespread empirical support. As Le and Agnew reported (2003) in a meta-analysis of more than 50 studies including over 11,000 participants in all, there is strong support for the unique contributions of satisfaction, alternatives, and investments to relationship commitment. Furthermore, these distinct components—and commitment level overall—have been found to successfully predict relationship longevity (Arriaga & Agnew, 2001; Attridge, Berscheid, & Simpson, 1995), satisfaction (Davis & Strube, 1993), accommodation (Arriaga & Rusbult, 1998; Etcheverry & Le, 2005), willingness to sacrifice (Etcheverry & Le, 2005; Powell & Van Vugt, 2003; Van Lange et al., 1997), psychological attachment (Arriaga & Agnew, 2001), relationship violence (Gaertner & Foshee, 1999; Truman-Schram, Cann, Calhoun, & Vanwallendael, 2000), fidelity (Drigotas & Rusbult, 1992; Drigotas, Safstrom, & Gentilia, 1999), and forgiveness (Cann & Baucom, 2004; Finkel, Rusbult, Kumashiro, & Hannon, 2002). Furthermore, Rusbult's model has been shown to apply equally well to heterosexual and same-sex couples (Bui, Peplau, & Hill, 1996; Kurdek, 1992).

Some of the newer directions in research on commitment involve greater attention to patterns of linear and nonlinear change in levels of commitment (Kurdek, 2003; Rusbult et al., 2006). Commitment does not increase uniformly from the beginning of a relationship onward but may ebb and flow over the course of a relationship—for example, as a function of fluctuations in satisfaction, increased availability of alternatives, slackened efforts at relational maintenance, ruptures in trust, or changes in individual's basic needs for companionship, security, or identity (Arriaga, 2001; Drigotas & Rusbult, 1992; Rusbult et al., 2006). Researchers are increasingly investigating these changes within the context of the multiple perceptual, cognitive, and affective processes through which commitment is manifested over the life span (Agnew, Van Lange, Rusbult, & Langston, 1998; Etcheverry & Le, 2005). Importantly, both partners in a long-term relationship are likely to undergo gradual developmental changes in their socioemotional needs, life priorities, and the perceived importance of various relationship investments and structural constraints. Yet each partner's developmental changes may occur at drastically different rates or might take them in notably different directions. Hence, a particularly important topic for future research concerns the *dyadic* regulation of commitment over the life span, in the face of each partner's individual developmental trajectory.

The Role of Social Cognition in Relationship Satisfaction

One of the most interesting lines of research that has developed in research on romantic relationships since the 1990shas concerned the many ways in which our cognitions, perceptions, and interpretive "biases" shape the quality and functioning of our intimate relationships. There is a long history of research documenting that individuals generally seek consistency between their cognitions, attitudes, and behaviors (Festinger, 1957; Heider, 1958; Newcomb, 1961), and when applied to the realm of romantic relationships, this body of work raises fascinating questions about how subtle biases in our perceptions and interpretations of day-to-day relationship events can alter the everyday reality of relationship functioning, influencing not only our present experiences but also the long-term developmental course of the relationship.

To put it simply, one might posit that there are actually three relationships taking place at any time between two people: One representing the perceptions and biases of Partner 1, one representing the perceptions and biases of Partner 2, and something approximating "the truth." Much initial work on romantic relationship quality, functioning, and satisfaction strived to develop assessments of relationship functioning that most closely represented "the truth," judiciously weeding out the perceptual biases of each partner. Examples of this approach include observational investigations of couple behavior that use independent raters to code objectively partners' facial expressions, language use, and overall behavior (Driver et al., 2003; Gottman & Levenson, 1992; Hawkins, Carrère, & Gottman, 2002; Klinetob & Smith, 1996; Welsh, Galliher, Kawaguchi, & Rostosky, 1999). This research has reliably demonstrated that individuals' *perceptions* of their partner's motives, emotions, thoughts, and behaviors often diverge markedly from the *partner's* perceptions (Bolger et al., 2000; Gable et al., 2003) and from objective indices of behavior (Hawkins et al., 2002; Welsh & Dickson, 2005; Welsh et al., 1999). Most important, however, *perception is as important as reality* in predicting couple well-being.

Quite simply, individuals are inevitably biased judges of our own social worlds, and these biases take a range of forms in different individuals: One person perceives relationship threats where there are none; another overlooks his or her partners' obvious signs of dissatisfaction; one person maintains negative, uncharitable views of his or her partner's character, whereas another idealizes his or her partner and the relationship as a whole. Researchers have described these processes as "motivated construals" (Ickes, Simpson, & Ickes, 1997; Murray, 1999), and they help to explain how and why intimate relationships function as both "outputs" and "inputs" of psychosocial development over the life span. Specifically, motivated construals (such as pessimistic expectations of romantic abandonment) are largely derived from our own romantic histories, typically in concert with our histories of parent–child attachment. Hence, these biased perceptions and expectations can be conceptualized as a cognitive synthesis of one's relationship trajectory thus far, inevitably influencing the way in which one feels and behaves toward the current romantic partner. Yet the current partner's behavior is, of course, unpredictable—will he or she "live up" to one's abandonment fears or gradually dismantle them? This will determine whether such fears strengthen or weaken over the course of development, and hence the future shape of one's trajectory of intimate ties. All of the social–cognitive mechanisms in the ensuing discussion play analogous roles in the dynamic, circular linkages between intimate relationship experiences and psychosocial development over the life span.

Attributions

Perhaps the most widely researched form of cognitive "bias" in the context of romantic relationships takes the form of *attributions*, or the explanations that individuals adopt for relationship events and for partner behavior. For example, when a partner says something hurtful, it may be perceived as intentional (*he is really out to get me*) or unintentional (*he obviously didn't realize how touchy I am about my weight*). Loving gestures may be interpreted as genuine expressions of affection (*Flowers! So thoughtful!*) or attempts at manipulation (*What are you trying to cover up*?). Decades of research have shown that individuals in happy, stable relationships tend to attribute positive partner behaviors to stable, enduring characteristics of their partners, whereas negative behaviors are attributed to external, situational influences. In making such attributions, individuals create a perceptual reality in which (a) my partner has my best interests at heart; (b) when good things happen, they are likely to continue; and (c) when bad things happen, they are due to transient, situational factors that can be avoided in the future. These types of attributions are typically described as *relationship enhancing*.

Unhappy individuals make the opposite set of assumptions. The partner's motives are presumed to be selfish or malicious; positive partner behaviors are viewed as unpredictable "flukes," whereas negative behaviors are attributed to stable, enduring features of the partner's basic character. In this version of reality, there is little hope for alleviating current distress or preventing future distress, which is why this set of attributions is typically described as *distress maintaining*.

The influence of attributions on the ongoing development of intimate relationships has received extensive attention, given that distress-maintaining attributions not only predict lower current satisfaction (Bradbury, Beach, Fincham, & Nelson, 1996; Bradbury & Fincham, 1990; Fincham, 2004; Fincham & Bradbury, 1989; Fincham, Bradbury, Arias, Byrne, & Karney, 1997) but also longitudinal declines in satisfaction (Fincham, Harold, & Gano-Phillips, 2000; Finchman & Bradbury, 2004; M. D. Johnson, Karney, Rogge, & Bradbury, 2001). Of course, a key question concerns the direction of causation. Do relationship-enhancing attributions actually enhance the relationship, or do they *result* from an already well-functioning bond? Similarly, do distress-maintaining attributions actually impede the healthy development of a relationship, or do they simply provide a reliable marker of an individual's current distress? These questions have been widely debated over the years (M. D. Johnson et al., 2001), and research findings have not provided definitive answers. For example, Bradbury and colleagues (Bradbury et al., 1996) found in an experimental study of couples' problem-solving behavior that wives who initially made distress-maintaining attributions regarding their husbands tended to behave less positively and more negatively toward them in subsequent interactions. Yet this does not necessarily prove that the negative behavior was caused by the attribution—it might equally suggest that wives who tend to behave poorly toward their husbands adopt maladaptive relationship attributions to justify their behavior or that *both* phenomena spring from global dissatisfaction.

A number of longitudinal studies have attempted to resolve the question of causality and have established that although current levels of satisfaction do predict subsequent attributions, attributions also have unique predictive effect on future satisfaction, independent of prior satisfaction (Karney & Bradbury, 2000). Further evidence for the developmental significance of attributions has come from research demonstrating that when individuals succeed in changing their patterns of attributions, they typically experience corresponding improvements in relationship satisfaction (Karney & Bradbury, 2000). Hence, consistent with the developmental framework we emphasize throughout this chapter, attributions are both developmental "outputs" and "inputs," reflecting a dyad's prior *and* future trajectory of intimacy, security, and satisfaction.

Positive Illusions

Similar conclusions have emerged from research on "positive illusions," which represent extremely generous, optimistic beliefs about the partner's traits and motives that paint the partner in an overly positive light. Research on positive illusions was pioneered by Sandra Murray and John Holmes (Murray, Holmes, & Griffin, 1996, 2004), who demonstrated that individuals' biased perceptions of themselves and their partners had profound effects on both partners' behavior and satisfaction. Contrary to the notion that individuals maintaining positive illusions are living in a "fantasy land," doomed to disappointment when their idealized image of the partner eventually breaks down, they found that individuals maintaining overly positive—although still realistic (Neff & Karney, 2003)—perceptions of the partner, and whose partners maintained overly positive perceptions of *them*, were happier and more satisfied with their relationships. These results initially proved surprising because they ran counter to long-established thinking on the importance of *self-verification* in close relationships. Self-verification theory (Swann, 1983) maintains that individuals want to feel authentically known and understood by other individuals, and hence they are motivated to obtain information and evaluations from social partners which verify their own self-views. Self-verification motives were thought to be particularly strong within committed romantic relationships (Swann, De La Ronde, & Hixon, 1994). Whereas individuals usually want to convey an unduly positive impression of themselves in the early stages of dating and courtship, as a relationship becomes more established and committed, partners increasingly turn to one another for loving feedback on "who they are and who they should become" (Swann et al., 1994, p. 857) and are reassured that their partner loves and accepts their authentic self.

Research on positive illusions suggests that in the context of intimate relationships, motives for self-enhancement often win out over motives for self-verification (see Swann, 1990). Perhaps most intriguing, however, is that positive illusions also subtly influence the partner's behavior over time. Through progressive feedback mechanisms, it appears that partners gradually adjust their own behaviors—and, over the long term, their own self-concepts—in line with their partner's beneficent expectations and perceptions, essentially "living up" to the positive illusion over time (Murray et al., 1996). This process is similar to that observed by Drigotas, Rusbult, Wieselquist, and Whitton's (1999) and denoted the *Michelangelo phenomenon*: Both individual well-being and couple functioning appear to be enhanced when our partners respond to us as if we were, in fact, our own "ideal selves." One of the intriguing aspects of this finding, from a developmental perspective, is the degree to which it resembles some of the fundamental dynamics thought to characterize secure infant–caregiver attachment bonds. Attachment security is thought to shape the child's developing sense of *self* as well his or her developing sense of the attachment figure. The responsiveness, sensitivity, affection, and positive regard of the attachment figure theoretically demonstrates to the child that he or she is worthy of love and affection and also instills trust in, and positive regard for, social partners. The same dynamics are directly relevant to the beneficial effects of positive illusions. The consistent, generous regard of one's romantic partner might function to solidify an individuals' positive sense of self and to enhance positive regard for one's partner, providing a powerful and enduring motive for relationship-enhancing behavior.

Altogether, the provocative body of research on motivated cognition suggests that some of the most developmentally significant aspects of intimate relationships—those that are most strongly influenced by prior interpersonal and psychosocial development and most influential on subsequent development—are not actual interpersonal experiences but rather our *reconstructed interpretations* of these experiences. Does this mean that relationship satisfaction itself—and for that matter, developmental change in satisfaction—is all in our heads?

Not quite: Although individuals' biased perceptions of relational experiences clearly have enduring influences on subsequent relationship satisfaction and functioning (similar, in many ways, to the influence of attachment style), it is the *interaction* between "reality" and "interpretation" that proves most influential (Cook, 2000; Lakey et al., 1996; Matthews, Wickrama, & Conger, 1996). As Reis, Clark, and Holmes (2004) argued, phenomena such as positive illusions or distress-maintaining attributions involve "a kernel of truth and a shell of motivated elaboration" (p. 214). Hence, our biased interpretations of relationship experience are not fanciful imaginings but rather represent the distillation of day-to-day experience into schematic frameworks that allow us to make reasonable predictions about the future, based on the accumulating knowledge that we carry with us from our own pasts (Carrère et al., 2000; Hawkins et al., 2002; Matthews et al., 1996).

Individual Differences and Relationship Functioning

"Knowledge of the past" is not the only factor shaping our motivated cognitions and perceptual biases. An extensive body of social-personality research suggests that temperament and personality also play critical roles (reviewed in Cooper & Sheldon, 2002). Yet the overall pattern of associations between relationship experiences and personality dimensions is somewhat mixed (reviewed in Simpson, Winterheld, & Chen, 2006), largely because of the diversity of methods and conceptual approaches that have been adopted in investigating these linkages (Cooper & Sheldon, 2002; Simpson et al., 2006). It is also likely that these linkages take different forms, with different strengths, at different stages of the life course, although such developmental changes have not received previous systematic study.

Without question, the personality trait that has been most consistently and strongly related to relationship functioning is neuroticism or trait negative affectivity (Bouchard, Lussier, & Sabourin, 1999; Caspi, 1987; Caughlin, Huston, & Houts, 2000; Donnellan, Assad, Robins, & Conger, 2007; Donnellan, Conger, & Bryant, 2004; Karney & Bradbury, 1995, 1997; Robins et al., 2000; Robins, Caspi, & Moffitt, 2002; Watson, Hubbard, & Wiese, 2000). The prevailing explanation for this association is that neurotic individuals' low threshold for experiencing distress, hostility, anger, and anxiety has enduring implications for their interpersonal functioning at all stages of the life course (Asendorpf, 2002; Newman et al., 1997; B. W. Roberts, Kuncel, Shiner, Caspi, & Goldberg, 2007), specifically rendering them more reactive to day-to-day interpersonal stressors so that they tend to evaluate their relationships more negatively and to behave less constructively (Caughlin et al., 2000; Donnellan et al., 2007; White, Hendrick, & Hendrick, 2004). Hence, trait negative affectivity constitutes an "enduring vulnerability" that makes it more difficult for individuals to maintain adaptive relationship functioning, particularly in the face of both major and minor stressors (Karney & Bradbury, 1995). An alternative perspective is that negative affectivity does not necessarily precipitate relationship distress but instead results from it (see Amato & Booth, 2001). From this perspective, associations between neuroticism and relationship functioning are partly due to the fact that individuals in dysfunctional relationships end up "looking" more neurotic on conventional personality measures.

Of course, these two models are not mutually exclusive, and evidence certainly suggests the existence of reciprocal links between neuroticism and relationship dysfunction that tend to exacerbate both domains (T. L. Huston, 2000; Robins et al., 2002; Sturaro, Denissen, van Aken, & Asendorpf, 2008). Overall, however, longitudinal studies reliably indicate that personality traits appear to exert a stronger influence on relationship functioning than vice versa (Neyer & Asendorpf, 2001; B. W. Roberts & Mroczek, 2008) and that neuroticism in particular is a potent predictor of *future* relationship functioning and development (Caughlin et al., 2000; Karney & Bradbury, 1997; Kelly & Conley, 1987).

This model is bolstered by behavioral genetic research demonstrating that both marital distress and divorce have significant heritability (McGue & Lykken, 1992; Spotts et al., 2005) and that this heritability appears to be mediated by genetically influenced personality traits such as negative affectivity (Jocklin, McGue, & Lykken, 1996; Spotts et al., 2005; Spotts et al., 2004). Importantly, recent research demonstrates that genetically influenced personality traits influence marital quality not only by shaping the individual's own experience of their relationship but also that of their partner (Spotts et al., 2005). In essence, the negative perceptions and behaviors of highly neurotic individuals make them difficult to live with, gradually eroding their own satisfaction and that of their partners.

Positive personality traits such as agreeableness, constraint, and general positive affectivity have also been linked to romantic relationships, although with less consistency than negative emotionality (Bouchard et al., 1999; Karney & Bradbury, 1997; Robins et al., 2002; Watson et al., 2000). Some have argued that the effects of these positive traits might be attributable to the fact that such traits index an individual's general motivation to approach and pursue social rewards, which may lead him or her to interpret and approach close relationships with a more positive attitude (Simpson et al., 2006) and to become actively involved in maintaining and strengthening relationships through constructive behaviors such as accommodation (see especially the longitudinal research by Robins et al., 2000).

Dispositional optimism, too, appears to have beneficial effects. Several longitudinal studies have found associations between optimism and future marital quality, whereas current marital quality does not appear to make individuals more optimistic (Fincham, Beach, Harold, & Osborne, 1997; Fincham & Bradbury, 1987b; Fincham, Bradbury et al., 1997). The beneficial effects of optimism appear to be mediated by the fact that optimism facilitates positive, relationship-enhancing attributions of (and sometimes "positive illusions" about) the partner's behavior (Bradbury et al., 1996; Fincham & Bradbury, 1988). For example, one longitudinal study (Srivastava et al., 2006) found that during conflict interactions, optimists perceived their partners as behaving more constructively during the conflict and consequently felt that the conflict was successfully resolved. One year later, optimists reported perceiving more support from their partner and, in turn, greater relationship satisfaction. In line with our "cascade" model of relationships and development over the life span, we might expect that over time, such processes should have progressively greater cumulative effects on both partners' interpersonal and psychological development, progressively enhancing their interpersonal skills (such as support provision and conflict negotiation), their confidence in one another's positive regard and motives, and their mutual commitment to, and security within, the relationship.

Self-Esteem

Individual differences in self-esteem have been shown to relate to individuals' expectations, attributions, and perceptions regarding their intimate relationships (Murray, Holmes, MacDonald, & Ellsworth, 1998). Individuals with low self-esteem tend to be particularly sensitive to the risks of social rejection (Leary, Cottrell, & Phillips, 2001; Leary, Haupt, Strausser, & Chokel, 1998), and hence to protect themselves from this risk, they tend to be hypervigilant to cues of a partner's negative affect or dissatisfaction (Bellavia & Murray, 2003) and quicker to anticipate impending rejection on this basis (Murray, Rose, Bellavia, Holmes, & Kusche, 2002). Also, individuals with low self-esteem allow global self-doubts to "bleed over" into relational doubts. Studies that have experimentally manipulated low-self-esteem individuals' doubts about their own intelligence found that they subsequently express greater concerns about rejection from their romantic partner (Murray et al., 1998). Perhaps most distressing is the fact that the relational doubts experienced by individuals with low self-esteem tend to become "self-fulfilling prophecies" by virtue of the maladaptive ways that these individuals respond to such doubts (Murray et al., 1998).

This was elegantly demonstrated by Murray and colleagues (Murray, Bellavia, Rose, & Griffin, 2003) in a daily diary study of married couples. Individuals who felt less valued by their partners were disproportionately sensitive to any signs of negativity in their partner (even a partner's bad feelings about himself or herself), responding to these cues with heightened feelings of hurt and rejection. They subsequently displayed more cold, critical, and hurtful behaviors toward their partner (according to their own reports as well as the perceptions of their partner), which Murray and colleagues interpreted as a defensive attempt at "devaluing what they fear they might lose" (p. 137). The irony, of course, is that such behavior undermines the relationship itself, effectively *creating* the very rejection that individuals with low self-esteem so deeply fear. Similar dynamics have been observed among individuals with high levels of *rejection sensitivity* (Downey & Feldman, 1996; Downey, Freitas, Michaelis, & Khouri, 1998), defined as a predisposition to fear social rejection, to be hypervigilant to signs of such potential rejection, and to be hyperreactive to the experience of rejection. Rejection-sensitive individuals—like those with low self-esteem—tend to behave toward romantic partners in ways that actually make rejection more likely, such as displaying heightened hostility and defensiveness upon perceiving the slightest cue of disapproval.

Although these pernicious self-fulfilling prophecies may prove most evident among individuals with low self-esteem or high rejection sensitivity, Murray and colleagues have argued that they pose a potential risk for *all* individuals, because close relationships always entail some risk of anxiety-provoking rejection (Murray, 2008; Murray, Derrick, Leder, & Holmes, 2008). For this reason, they have argued that romantic relationships necessarily create a self-regulatory paradox: The more one seeks closeness, connection, and mutual dependence with a romantic partner, the more one stands to lose if the partner leaves. Every individual, therefore, faces a choice: pursuing intimacy and mutual dependence despite the risks of rejection or minimizing those risks by keeping the partner at a distance and reminding oneself of his or her shortcomings. Of course, the "catch" is that the latter approach might achieve the short-term aim of self-protection, but at the expense of undermining the relationship and making true intimacy impossible. They therefore posit that a sense of *felt security* in intimate relationships, representing an abiding certainty of the partner's positive regard—functions as a risk-regulation system, allowing individuals to set aside their fears of rejection and make the "leap of faith" that is necessary to pursue relationship-enhancing behaviors such as sacrifice, accommodation, trust, and mutual dependence (Murray, Holmes, & Griffin, 2000).

One intriguing but uninvestigated possibility is that individuals' willingness to make this leap of faith undergoes striking change over the life span, corresponding to developmental changes in individuals' needs and desires for supportive partners, their willingness to make themselves vulnerable, and their own sense of comfort in their shortcomings. For example, in late adolescence and early adulthood, individuals might tend to err on the side of self-protection, pursuing shorter term relationships that involve low levels of mutual dependence rather than taking the risk of deeper vulnerability and commitment. Yet as individuals move into adulthood, the trade-offs necessitated by self-protection are likely to become increasingly evident, and individuals may become more willing to risk rejection to achieve greater closeness and intimacy with a potential long-term partner. Similar developmental changes might occur and reoccur at multiple points over the life span (for example, after major life transitions such as having a child, divorce, or the death of a family member), whenever the perceived trade-offs between vulnerability and safety, loneliness versus companionship, and support versus self-reliance undergo change. Charting such developmental transitions, and how they interact with personality predispositions and relationship histories to shape individuals' ongoing approach to risk regulation over the life span, is a fascinating direction for future research.

Before leaving the topic of individual differences, it bears noting that the unique relationship dynamics observed among individuals with relatively extreme versions of a trait—chronically low self-esteem, high neuroticism, high rejection sensitivity—are not unique to such individuals. Rather, as shown by Murray and colleagues, they represent "extreme cases" of dynamics that are operative for all individuals. For example, even individuals with high self-esteem must keep fears of rejection at bay to achieve closeness and intimacy with their partners; they are simply more adept at this process than individuals with low self-esteem because of their higher threshold for perceived rejection. In a similar vein, the relationship hurdles faced by neurotic individuals provide a window into the potentially toxic repercussions of chronic negative affect among all individuals. In essence, the relationships of individuals who are particularly high or low on certain affective or motivational dimensions provide "natural experiments" that allow relationship researchers to understand the role of these various dimensions in current relationship satisfaction. Perhaps more important (albeit less often investigated), they allow researchers to understand how the effects of certain predispositions play out over life-span development, either magnifying over time as individuals choose the same types of partners and engage in the same behaviors and cognitions again and again or dissipating if they find themselves in a relationship that breaks the old pattern and establishes a new trajectory for subsequent interpersonal and psychosocial development.

RELATIONSHIP THREATS

Jealousy

At all stages of the life course, individuals must contend with a variety of direct and indirect threats to the quality and stability of their intimate relationships. Jealousy is one of the most consistent and pernicious of these threats. Researchers have outlined two types of jealousy: *reactive* and *suspicious*. Both types are associated with feelings of hurt, anger, and fear (Bringle, 1995; Bringle & Buunk, 1991), but they have different antecedents and implications. Reactive jealousy occurs in response to a legitimate threat to the relationship, such as reliable evidence of a partner's infidelity. Suspicious jealousy, in contrast, occurs when one member of the dyad is worried about the partner's fidelity without any reasonable basis for this fear. The distinction is important, given that reactive jealousy is considered an adaptive response to a legitimate relationship threat, serving to motivate individuals to protect and preserve their relationship (Rydell & Bringle, 2007). In contrast, suspicious jealousy is considered maladaptive, serving only to undermine one's relationship by creating a climate of mistrust and paranoia. Of course, differentiating between these types of jealousy requires that one determines what "counts" as reasonable evidence of infidelity, and much research on jealousy treats both types somewhat generically.

Are there individual differences in propensities for jealousy? Overall, studies have found that individuals who feel unable to attract alternative partners report greater jealousy compared with people who feel they can attract many alternative partners (Knobloch, Solomon, & Cruz, 2001). Similarly, individuals who feel inadequate as a relationship partner and who have low self-worth in general tend to report more jealousy (DeSteno, Valdesolo, & Bartlett, 2006). Not surprisingly, attachment anxiety has also been shown to be associated with excessive jealousy (Guerrero, 1998), consistent with the fact that one of the fundamental characteristics of attachment anxiety is heightened concern over the availability and responsiveness of the partner and heightened fears of abandonment (Buunk, 1997).

Evolutionary theorists have focused particular attention on gender differences in jealousy, arguing that such differences arise from the fact that females and males faced different reproductive challenges in the environment of evolutionary adaptedness. According to sexual strategies theory (Buss & Schmitt, 1993), a man should be primarily distressed by sexual jealousy, because his reproductive success is maximized by inseminating many women and is directly threatened if a female partner engages in sexual contact with another man (casting doubt on whether he is the father of her offspring). A woman, in contrast, should be primarily distressed by *emotional* jealousy, because her reproductive success is maximized by investing heavily in the survival of each of her children (unlike men, women do not have the option of producing large numbers of offspring, making it critical for them to ensure the survival of each one). According to this model, a woman's reproductive success is maximized if she can secure the resources and investment of her male partner but threatened if her partner withdraws these precious resources and invests them in someone else. Harris (2000, 2003) has referred to this set of predictions as the *JSIM* or "jealousy as a specific innate module" effect, because it purports an evolved, genetically based, sex-specific psychological "module" for the detection of threats to one's reproductive success.

Numerous social-psychological studies have been conducted to test the existence, magnitude, and context of these predicted gender differences in sexual versus emotional jealousy. In early studies that simply asked men and women which type of infidelity they found most troubling, the results confirmed the predictions of sexual strategies theory (Buss, Larsen, Westen, & Semmelroth, 1992; Buss et al., 1999; Buunk, Angleitner, Oubaid, & Buss, 1996). Yet studies using different methodologies and samples (particularly samples that do not comprise undergraduate students) often fail to replicate the effect (reviewed in DeSteno, Bartlett, Braverman, & Salovey, 2002; Harris, 2000; Sabini & Green, 2004) One well-known critique of the JSIM effect is the *double-shot hypothesis* (DeSteno & Salovey, 1996; Harris & Christenfeld, 1996), which maintains that women are more distressed by emotional jealousy because they presume that if a man became emotionally involved with another woman, he would almost certainly become sexually involved with her as well (thereby providing a "double shot" of infidelity), whereas men are more distressed by sexual jealousy because they presume that if a woman became sexually involved with another man, she would probably become emotionally involved with him as well (also thereby providing a double shot). Additionally, recent work by Sabini and Green (2004) has failed to confirm a key tenet of the JSIM hypothesis—namely, that women have a greater fear of resource withdrawal from men who are emotionally involved with another woman than from men who are sexually involved with another woman. Sabini and Green concluded that the JSIM effect is "replicable but not robust" (p. 1385). Also, variation in the findings regarding the JSIM effect across diverse samples has been interpreted to suggest that in some cases, the JSIM may reflect local norms rather than an innate evolved and universal "jealousy module."

Of course, a notable shortcoming of this body of research is the utter lack of a developmental perspective. Even if we set aside a strict evolutionary perspective and side with the double-shot hypothesis, it bears noting that this framework assumes that everyone "knows" what men and women tend to want and to do in intimate relationships (i.e., that men are unlikely to engage in "purely emotional" infidelity and that women are unlikely to pursue "purely sexual" infidelity). Yet where does this knowledge come from? The unstated assumption is that it develops through men's and women's direct experiences as participants in—and observers of—intimate relationships. However, this process ought to take a significant amount of time and progressive experience, in which case gender differences in sexual versus emotional jealousy should become progressively more pronounced over the life course and might not even be discernible at the very beginning of adolescents' romantic trajectories. Such developmental differences would provide strong evidence that social learning plays a stronger role in these gender differences than evolved jealousy modules, yet at the present time, such developmentally oriented investigations have not been undertaken.

Infidelity

The prevalence of infidelity at different stages of the life course and different points in the development of a single relationship has generated considerable scientific and popular interest over the years. Although it is difficult to gather accurate data on this question because of the social unacceptability of infidelity, certain reliable patterns have emerged: Infidelity appears substantially more common in young adults' dating relationships than in older couples' married relationships. For example, in a study of American college students, two thirds of males and half of females reported they had kissed and fondled someone other than their current romantic partner, and half of men and one third of women reported having had intercourse with someone other than their partner (Widmer, Treas, & Newcomb, 1998). Such statistics decrease dramatically among adult married couples. The vast majority of husbands and wives never have sex with someone other than their spouse after they marry; among those who have, males report higher rates of infidelity than females, at an average rate of 25% among men and 15% among women (Laumann et al., 1994). In addition to gender differences in the prevalence of infidelity, men's and women's motives for infidelity differ, with men more likely to report that sexual variety was their primary motive and women more likely to report that emotional connectedness was their primary motive (Blow & Hartnett, 2005).

Numerous studies have attempted to determine whether there are stable individual differences that characterize individuals "at risk" for infidelity. The findings suggest that individuals who have engaged in infidelity tend to have lower levels of mental well-being, greater attachment insecurity, greater narcissism, and more permissive attitudes regarding casual sex (Buss & Shackelford, 1997; Buunk, 1997; Gangestad & Thornhill, 2003; Sheppard, Nelson, & Andreoli-Mathie, 1995; Simpson & Gangestad, 1991; Treas & Giesen, 2000). As for relationship characteristics, individuals with low levels of commitment to their current partner have higher rates of infidelity as well as greater reported willingness to engage in infidelity (Buunk & Bakker, 1997; Drigotas, Safstrom, et al., 1999; Treas & Giesen, 2000). Particularly among women, emotional dissatisfaction with the primary relationship is associated with greater infidelity (Buss & Shackelford, 1997; Prins, Buunk, & VanYperen, 1993). The detrimental effects of infidelity appear to cut across gender: Around the world, infidelity is a primary cause of divorce (Betzig, 1989; Buss, 1994) particularly when dissatisfaction with their primary relationship is one of the triggers or justifications for the extramarital affair (Buunk, 1987; Spanier & Margolis, 1983).

Of course, the very notion of infidelity depends on the assumption that a successful committed relationship must be monogamous. Since the sexual revolution of the 1970s, many individuals and groups have challenged this notion and attempted to maintain "open" or "polyamorous" relationships (Bettinger, 2006; Rust, 1996; Sheff, 2005). Polyamory has increasingly garnered the attention of social scientists, yet its prevalence is impossible to estimate given that all studies of polyamorous individuals have involved nonrandom samples. Individuals who practice polyamory are diverse in their sexual orientations, including heterosexuals, bisexuals, lesbians, and gay men

(Weitzman, 2006), but there is some indication that among nonheterosexual individuals, bisexuals are more likely to practice polyamory than lesbians or gay men (Rust, 1996), perhaps because the process of questioning restrictive cultural standards regarding the authenticity of bisexual attractions prompts such individuals to question cultural standards regarding the supposed moral and psychological preeminence of monogamy.

Labriola (1999) identified three models for polyamorous relationships: the primary–secondary model, the multiple primary partners model, and the multiple nonprimary relationships model. Research to date indicates that the *primary–secondary model*, also known as hierarchical polyamory, is the most prevalent, at least among bisexuals and lesbians (Labriola, 1999; Rust, 1996; Weitzman, 2006). In this model, a couple views their relationship with each other as their "primary" bond and devote the majority of their time, energy, and loyalty to this bond but remain open to additional lovers (Weitzman, 2006). In the *multiple primary partners model*, an individual might have two partners, each of which is considered to be of equal importance. In some cases, the two partners will also be involved with one another, thereby establishing a triadic relationship (Rust, 1996). Some of these arrangements are "open," meaning that all of the participants are free to enter into other relationships, and some are closed.

Polyamorous relationships clearly pose fundamental challenges to many of our established notions about the nature and functioning of romantic relationships, all of which are based on an assumption of monogamy (Ritchie & Barker, 2006). They also require different models and terminologies regarding relational commitment and relational maintenance. For example, although "attention to attractive alternatives" is considered a key factor potentially undermining commitment in the context of a conventional monogamous couple, within polyamorous arrangements the "attractive alternative" of the secondary partner poses no such threat (at least not in theory). The degree to which it is necessary to modify existing models of relationship functioning to accommodate polyamorous relationships versus jettisoning monogamous models altogether and developing new frameworks for understanding polyamorous arrangements is not yet clear and is an important question for future research. Additionally, given that polyamory remains highly stigmatized, invisible, and misunderstood, the strategies through which polyamorous individuals preserve a sense of identity, community, and well-being is a critical area for research (Barker, 2005). Investigating the cognitive, affective, psychological, and behavioral processes through which individuals maintain these unconventional arrangements and whether polyamory poses different challenges at different stages of the life span can address a arrange of fascinating, fundamental questions about the nature of adult sexual-romantic bonding.

INTIMATE PARTNER VIOLENCE

Intimate partner violence has been increasingly acknowledged as a major public health concern threatening the well-being of women and men over the life span (Black & Breiding, 2008; Lamberg, 2000). A study of more than 16,000 men and women conducted by the Centers for Disease Control and Prevention found that 22% of women and 7% of men reported having experienced a violent physical assault by an intimate partner (Tjaden & Thoennes, 2000), and other surveys have reported that one in every six couples experience some form of physical violence in their relationship (Williams & Frieze, 2005). Rates of nonphysical forms of aggression, such as screaming at or ridiculing one's partners, are substantially more common (Fergusson, Horwood, & Ridder, 2005), although typically viewed as less serious than physical violence (Capezza & Arriaga, 2008). Notably, however, studies have found that verbal aggression shows the same patterns of association with individual-level mental health problems and couple-level power dynamics as does physical violence (Sagrestano, Heavey, & Christensen, 1999; South, Turkheimer, & Oltmanns, 2008), suggesting the importance of systematically assessing both physical and nonphysical violence. Nonetheless, the majority of research on intimate partner violence focuses on physical violence, and our review necessarily reflects this orientation in the literature. Hence, the generic term *violence* should be interpreted to denote physical violence unless noted otherwise.

The most common forms of physical violence appear to be mild manifestations of violence (pushing, grabbing, shoving) perpetrated by both partners against one another (Williams & Frieze, 2005). The high prevalence of *mutual* physical violence runs counter to longstanding stereotypes portraying men as the exclusive perpetrators of violence against their female partners. It is now well documented that women and men participate in comparable levels of relationship violence (Archer, 2000), although the context, correlates, and consequences of their violence remain distinct. For example, women engage in less severe forms of physical violence than do men (kicking and punching vs.

choking and strangling) and are less likely to inflict serious injury on their partner (Archer, 2000).

Also, some research suggests that women are less likely than men to *initiate* violence and that they tend to aggress against their partners in defense and retaliation for violence directed at them, a pattern called *violent resistance* (M. P. Johnson, 2006). Others, however, have argued that women initiate violence just as frequently as men (Hettrich & O'Leary, 2007). There is insufficient empirical data to determine which view is more accurate, given that few studies (or police officers, or social workers) take pains to establish which partner initiated an episode of mutual violence. Furthermore, both partners are often motivated by self-presentation concerns to portray their partner as the instigator. Johnson (2006) argued that the defining characteristic of violent resistance is that the resisting partner is violent but not controlling, whereas the initiating partner is both violent and controlling. Hence, accurately assessing gender differences in violent resistance requires more than simply finding out "who started it" but understanding the entire psychological and dyadic context of the violence.

This emphasis on the larger psychological and dyadic context of partner violence arguably represents one of the most substantive recent changes in research on intimate partner violence. As Johnson summarized, "personal relationship violence *arises out of and shapes* the dynamics of an ongoing relationship" (2006, p. 557, emphasis added). This perspective represents a departure from much of the early research on intimate partner violence, which was based primarily on couples sampled from clinics, courts, and domestic violence agencies (M. P. Johnson, 2006; Williams & Frieze, 2005) and which inadvertently bolstered a stereotype portraying partner violence as attributable to domineering, pathological husbands exerting dictatorial control over their wives. To be sure, such couples do exist, but they represent only one potential form of partner violence. Researchers now distinguish between *intimate terrorism*, in which the perpetrator uses violence to assert systematic control over his or her partner (Kirkwood, 1993; Pence & Paymar, 1993), and *situational couple violence*, in which high levels of anger, tension, and emotion in a particular interaction escalate into violence, often unexpectedly.

Because situational couple violence is often milder, less frequent, and less regularized than intimate terrorism, couples who experience these forms of violence are rarely represented in the court, clinic, and agency samples on which so much early work on intimate partner violence was based (M. P. Johnson, 2006). As researchers have increasingly conducted research using broad-based community samples and representative national surveys, it has become clear that minor and major forms of situational couple violence are extremely common across a wide range of relationships, including short-term dating relationships and even the fledgling romances of adolescents (Burcky, Reuterman, & Kopsky, 1988; Foshee, Benefield, Ennett, Bauman, & Suchindran, 2004; Jasinski & Williams, 1998; M. P. Johnson & Ferraro, 2000; Silverman, Raj, Mucci, & Hathaway, 2001; Sugarman & Hotaling, 1989; Wekerle & Wolfe, 1999; Wolf & Foshee, 2003). Data collected as a part of the Massachusetts Youth Risk Behavior Surveys paint an alarming picture of adolescent violence: Approximately 20% of girls between the ages of 14 and 18 reported being physically or sexually abused by a dating partner, and these girls were more likely to report substance use, sexual risk behaviors, pregnancy, and suicidality (Silverman et al., 2001).

Such studies demonstrate that partner violence is not the purview of a small group of pathological, domineering men but a potential outcome in any relationship, at any stage in its development. All individuals experience the angry and aggressive impulses that provide the potential trigger for a violent outburst, demonstrated by the frequency with which individuals report threatening and screaming at their partners during conflicts (Fergusson et al., 2005). The basic emotions that motivate someone to publicly humiliate their partner in a fit of anger appear to be exactly the same as those that motivate physical aggression: The question, then, is not which types of *people* aggress against their partner but what *constellations* of individual, interpersonal and situational factors give rise to different forms and degrees of violence in intimate relationships?

Understanding Partner Violence

Toward this end, Finkel (2007, 2008) proposed an organizing framework to understand the antecedents of situational couple violence. He modeled such violence as the function of three interacting influences: *instigating triggers, impelling influences*, and *inhibiting influences*. Instigating triggers represent circumstances or conditions that give rise to anger and frustration, such as a bad mood or a particularly difficult conflict. Once the instigating trigger has been activated, the balance between impelling and inhibiting influences moderates the risk for actual violence. These influences include distal factors such as cultural and community norms regarding gender and power and family histories of violence (Archer, 2006; Arriaga & Foshee, 2004; F. M. Hughes, Stuart, Gordon, & Moore, 2007); dispositional factors such as neuroticism, hostility, anger expression style, and self-regulation (Hellmuth & McNulty, 2008; Jensen-Campbell, Knack, Waldrip, & Campbell, 2007; Wolf & Foshee, 2003); relational factors such as present relationship distress, degree of commitment, and conflict resolution strategies (Gottman, 1993; M. P. Johnson & Ferraro, 2000; Simpson, Collins, Tran, & Haydon, 2007); and situational factors such as whether the couples is alone and whether weapons are available. One of the key strengths of this approach is that it provides a way to organize and interpret systematically the voluminous data on predictors of partner violence, which include everything from alcohol use to job loss to childhood sexual abuse (Flett & Hewett, 2002; Gelles & Loseke, 1993; Jasinski & Williams, 1998; M. P. Johnson, 2006; Stith et al., 2000; Straus & Gelles, 1990; Sugarman, Aldarondo, & Boney-McCoy, 1996), and to make sense of the fact that the key predictors may vary markedly between intimate terrorism and situational couple violence (M. P. Johnson, 2006).

Now that researchers have adopted a broader and more comprehensive approach to investigating partner violence, new and intriguing questions have emerged regarding the potentially distinct developmental pathways through which men and women come to violent relationships, the differential impacts of certain forms of violence on men and women (Anderson, 2002; Katz, Kuffel, & Coblentz, 2002; Stith et al., 2000; Sugarman et al., 1996), and the factors that differentiate mutual violence from one-sided violence, regarding both its antecedents and its consequences (Swan & Snow, 2003). For example, in data collected from more than 3,500 respondents to the National Comorbidity Survey, Williams and Frieze (2005) found that more than half of the reported violence was mutual, and women were actually more likely to admit perpetrating violence than men. Among both men and women, the most common pattern of partner violence—mild mutual violence—was significantly associated with high levels of distress and low levels of relationship satisfaction in both men and women. Yet when all forms of violence were taken into account (mild and severe; mutual and nonmutual), violence was more strongly related to women's psychosocial outcomes then men's, consistent with much prior research (reviewed in Williams & Frieze, 2005). As Johnson (2006) argued, to interpret such patterns we must understand violence *as a property of an ongoing relationship* and seek to understand the specific dynamics between a couple that shape the antecedents, manifestations, and consequences of violence at different stages of the relationship and the life course.

Reconsidering Gender: Violence in Same-Sex Relationships

Researchers have increasingly investigated partner violence in same-sex couples to better understand the specific role played by gender in shaping violent couple dynamics. Contrary to the notion that partner violence is unique to the patriarchal dynamics of male–female pairings, studies have documented a wide range of violence and abuse within same-sex relationships, ranging from physical behaviors such as hitting, slapping, scratching, and attacking with a weapon, to nonphysical behaviors such as threats, denigration, and sexual coercion (Burke & Follingstad, 1999; Regan, Bartholomew, Oram, & Landolt, 2002; Walder-Haugrud, 1999; West, 1998, 2002). Although accurate prevalence estimates are difficult to obtain, prior studies have found incidence rates ranging from 25% to 50% (Alexander, 2002; West, 2002). Notably, sexual-minority adolescents are not immune from these problems: Elze (2002) found that one-third of female sexual-minority youths in northern England had experienced verbal or physical abuse in their dating relationships in the previous 12 months, including 28% of the girls who had *only* dated other girls.

Thus far, studies have found that the triggers for relationship violence in same-sex couples parallel those found in heterosexual couples, such as conflicts over dependency, jealousy, money, power, and substance abuse (McClennen, Summers, & Vaughan, 2002). Some unique patterns, however, have emerged. For example, one study of gay male couples (Regan et al., 2002) found that some forms of violence that typically occupy the upper end of the severity continuum for heterosexual couples, such as punching and hitting, tended to cluster with lower severity violent behaviors among gay male couples. Alternatively, some behaviors that are lower in severity for heterosexual couples, such as twisting arms, pulling hair, and scratching, cluster with higher severity violent behaviors among gay men. The authors suggested that men might resort to punching and hitting earlier in a male–male conflict than in a male–female conflict, given that this behavior has more serious consequences when directed toward a weaker and smaller woman (and also potentially because some boys become accustomed to hitting and punching other boys in the context of childhood fights). With regard to hair pulling and scratching, they argued that these behaviors in gay male couples might index the escalation of a fight to a prolonged, close-proximity struggle. Unique dynamics have also been observed in lesbian couples. For example, one recent study (D. H. Miller, Greene, Causby, White, & Lockhart, 2001) found that physical aggression was more common than outright violence in lesbian relationships and that it was best predicted by relationship fusion, whereas physical violence was best predicted by measures of control. Such findings raise important questions about how male and female socialization, as well as males' and females' different developmental histories of physically aggressive conflicts, relates to the patterns of violence and abuse observed in male–female, male–male, and female–female couples.

Understanding such dynamics is critically important for the design and implementation of effective antiviolence interventions. For example, given that the majority of domestic violence in heterosexual relationships is conducted by males, the training of clinicians and social workers may be inadequate to address the factors underlying female relationship violence. Additionally, it is important to consider whether sexual-minority relationships might be particularly vulnerable to relationship violence as a function of the stress and pressure of social stigmatization or maladaptive patterns of social functioning derived from histories of parental or peer rejection or victimization. Such information might prove to be particularly important in preventing sexual-minority youths from developing stable, maladaptive patterns of dealing with social stigma and with relationship problems (Lie, Schilit, Bush, Montagne, & Reyes, 1991).

WHEN ALL EFFORTS FAIL: DIVORCE

In the 1960s, approximately 30% of U.S. marriages ended in divorce. This figure increased to a little over 50% by the mid-1970s and has stayed relatively stable ever since (Bramlet & Mosher, 2002). Divorce has been consistently rated as one of life's most stressful events (Kendler, Karkowski, & Prescott, 1999), and studies have found that divorced individuals have higher risks for a variety of mental and physical health problems over the life span (Booth & Amato, 1991; Braver, Shapiro, & Goodman, 2006; Coombs, 1991; Mastekaasa, 1994; Ross, 1995; Waite, 1995). The reasons for this robust association, however, remain widely debated. On one hand, the short- and long-term stress that people typically experience as a result of getting divorced is thought to confer mental health risks (Booth & Amato, 1991; Ross, 1995); on the other hand, people who end up getting divorced might have always been different "types" of people, with personality traits (such as neuroticism) and interpersonal skill deficits that predispose them to troublesome relationships as well as longstanding adjustment problems (Aseltine & Kessler, 1993; Avison, 1999; Ceglian & Gardner, 1999; Jocklin, McGue, & Lykken, 1996; D. R. Johnson & Wu, 2002; Lucas, 2005; B. W. Roberts et al., 2007). These two models have notably different implications for life-span development: If the negative mental health correlates of divorce are attributable to divorce-related stress, then they should dissipate over time as the acute stress of the transition gradually dissipates. If, on the other hand, they are attributable to the individual's own long-standing psychosocial problems, then they should persist long after the divorce and should have similarly negative effects on the individual's subsequent relationships.

Studies suggest that both perspectives are partly true; certain temperamental traits and family backgrounds do, in fact, appear to predispose certain individuals for troublesome relationships and, by extension, divorce (Jocklin et al., 1996; Karney & Bradbury, 1995). Longitudinal studies have found that individuals who eventually divorce typically begin to show elevations in generalized distress long before the divorce itself, often due to longstanding relationship dysfunction (Hope, Rodgers, & Power, 1999; D. R. Johnson & Booth, 1998). For these individuals, the stress of divorce may have added to their difficulties but did not create them.

Yet the majority of studies also show that the stress of divorce poses considerable adjustment challenges that have equal (and often greater) influences on adjustment than individuals' preexisting vulnerabilities (D. R. Johnson & Wu, 2002). Although many individuals do, in fact, end up better off by leaving a distressing marriage, the trajectory of adjustment is a long one, and some individuals never attain predivorce levels of happiness and well-being (Lucas, 2005). This overall pattern of results strongly supports the first two developmental premises that we have emphasized throughout this chapter: that relationships simultaneously function as "outputs" of longstanding developmental processes and "inputs" for subsequent development. We might therefore view divorce as a likely outcome for individuals with long-standing developmental deficits in psychosocial and interpersonal functioning, including emotion regulation, empathy, and communication. At the same time, divorce also represents the failure of an intimate relationship to provide a safe context for the repair of these developmental deficits, the retraining of social cognitions and behaviors, and finally a redirection of the individual's long-term trajectory of psychological and interpersonal development.

Why is it, however, that some couples manage to achieve this repair and retraining, whereas others do not? In trying to answer this question, many researchers have followed Karney and Bradbury's lead (1995) in focusing on the complex interactions among individual-level risk factors for divorce, the interpersonal processes in which these risks are made manifest (Carrère et al., 2000; Driver et al., 2003; Gottman & Levenson, 1992, 2000, 2002), and the contexts in which maladaptive processes are most likely to take root and to eventually erode the marital bond (Karney & Bradbury, 1995; Mastekaasa, 1995; Neff & Karney, 2004).

Vulnerability, Stress, and Adaptation

Karney and Bradbury (1995) called their model a *vulnerability–stress–adaptation* model, and it highlights three sets of factors that coordinate to influence a couples' risk for divorce: partners' *enduring vulnerabilities* (ranging from neuroticism to a familial history of divorce to attachment insecurity), *adaptive and maladaptive processes* (including behavioral factors such as communication and conflict resolution as well as cognitive factors such as attributions), and *stressful events* (such as income loss, job transitions, new parenthood, or any stressor that potentially places a burden on a couple's coping resources). This model is best conceived as a model of general marital functioning, rather than divorce specifically, yet one of its strengths when applied specifically to divorce is that it helps to reconcile the fact that there is such extensive agreement among researchers on the key predictors of divorce, albeit disagreement regarding the relative importance of different types of predictors. From the perspective of Karney and Bradbury's model, this is to be expected. Because vulnerabilities, adaptational processes, and stressors interact with one another dynamically over time to influence marital outcomes, it is impossible to designate one domain as causally prior or central.

Additional Sociodemographic Predictors of Divorce

Given that Karney and Bradbury's model highlights the importance of contextual factors that create potential sources of stress for couples, it is useful to review some of the most reliable sociodemographic predictors of divorce from the vulnerability–stress–adaptation perspective. For example, couples with lower household incomes have higher rates of divorce (e.g., see Kurdek, 1993b). This makes perfect sense when considering the stress introduced by economic problems, but notably, recent research has suggested that the link between economic strain and divorce is moderated by the economic dependency of the female partner. Specifically, couples in which the female partner is economically dependent on the male partner have lower risks for divorce (Rogers, 2004), which has been attributed to the fact that women may "settle" for a dissatisfying marriage if they perceive that divorce would place them (and potentially their children) in financial jeopardy. In contrast, women with independent financial resources are better able to make decisions about divorce that are based exclusively on psychological rather than material concerns. The material concerns can be quite significant, given that women's standard of living typically declines precipitously after divorcing, whereas men's typically improves (Sayer, 2006). Another important moderator of the link between household income and divorce is the couple's overall financial state. Although all couples tend to argue about money (Kirchler, Rodler, Hölzl, & Meier, 2001; Sayer, 2006; Solomon, Rothblum, & Balsam, 2005), the stakes of these arguments are obviously higher among low-income couples than high-income couples, necessarily changing the relative importance of financial stress in the constellation of factors predicting relationship dissolution. Accordingly, couples from lower socioeconomic groups are more likely to blame their marital difficulties on money problems than on interpersonal factors, whereas couples from higher socioeconomic groups show the opposite pattern (Amato & Previti, 2003; Rodrigues, Hall, & Fincham, 2006).

Educational level is also inversely related to the probability of divorce (Kurdek, 1993b; Orbuch, Veroff, Hassan, & Horrocks, 2002). To some extent, this association is attributable to the link between educational level and socioeconomic status (Orbuch, Verloff, Hassan, & Horrocks, 2002; Rodrigues et al., 2006). However, researchers have noted that low educational attainment may also be associated with divorce through its association with a range of other individual-level characteristics, such as problem behavior, jealousy, and infidelity (Amato & Rogers, 1997). Also, similar to the findings noted earlier regarding the female partner's economic dependence on her husband, women with higher levels of education than their husbands are more likely to divorce (Heaton, 2002), likely reflecting their greater range of postdivorce economic and social options.

Another intriguing sociodemographic predictor of divorce is age. Couples who marry at younger ages—especially under age 25—have higher risks for divorce (Heaton, 2002). Interpreting this association requires attention to all three dimensions in Karney and Bradbury's model. First, given that the age of first marriage has been increasing over the past several decades (Popenoe & Whitehead, 2005), men and women who currently marry young can be viewed as "self-selecting" themselves into early marriage, potentially as a function of vulnerabilities such as impulsivity, emotional problems, low educational attainment, jealousy, substance use, and parental history of divorce—all of these factors also make such individuals more susceptible to marital problems (Amato & Rogers, 1997; Wallerstein, Corbin, Lewis, Hetherington, & Arasteh, 1988). Young couples are also likely to face greater financial strain than older couples, given that the contemporary economy requires more protracted education and job training to secure a secure, high-paying job (Booth, Crouter, & Shanahan, 1999; Furstenberg, Kennedy, Mcloyd, Rumbaut, & Settersten, 2004). Hence, the combination of individual-level vulnerabilities and contextual stressors may markedly increase young couples' risks for marital dysfunction and dissolution, especially if they also tend to develop maladaptive patterns of communication and conflict resolution early on in their relationship (Carrère et al., 2000; Gottman, 1993, 1994).

Cohabitation: Why Does It Confer Risk?

Another widely investigated predictor of divorce is premarital cohabitation. Rates of cohabitation have increased dramatically over the past several decades. In 1960, there were approximately 400,000 heterosexual cohabiting couples in the United States, compared with nearly 5 million currently (Seltzer, 2004). The specific pattern of cohabiting before marriage has also increased: Between 1965 and 1974, approximately 10% of couples cohabited before marriage, compared with more than 50% among those marrying between 1990 and 1994 (Bumpass & Lu, 2000; Bumpass & Sweet, 1989). Contrary to the popular belief that cohabitation gives couples the chance to "prepare" for married life (Bachman, Johnston, & O'Malley, 2001), studies have consistently found that couples who cohabitate before marriage have higher divorce rates after marriage, with the exception of couples who enter into cohabitation with the distinct intention to marry (Kline et al., 2004; Stafford, Kline, & Rankin, 2004). In explaining this seemingly counterintuitive finding, researchers have proposed that a couple's choice to cohabit rather than marry may reflect one or both partners' ambivalence about committing to the relationship, a generalized acceptance of untraditional relationships, and a greater psychological tolerance for divorce (Bennett, Blanc, & Bloom, 1988; Stanley, Whitton, & Markman, 2004). From this perspective, cohabitation does not necessarily lead to divorce; rather, couples who elect to cohabit have higher probabilities of divorce to begin with (reviewed in Dush, Cohan, & Amato, 2003).

Research suggests that selection effects do, in fact, account for some of the association between cohabitation and divorce (Lillard, Brian, & Waite, 1995; Thomson & Colella, 1992), but not entirely. Some research suggests that the experience of cohabitation might confer additional risk to such couples, potentially by undermining their attitudes toward marriage and their determination to make a relationship work (Axinn & Thornton, 1992; Dush et al., 2003; McGinnis, 2003). This notion is consistent with research demonstrating that cohabiting couples become progressively less likely to marry (but no less likely to break up) the longer that they cohabit, whereas married couples become progressively less likely to break up the longer that they have been married (Wolfinger, 2005). Also, if selection effects were entirely attributable for the link between cohabitation and divorce, then this association should become progressively weaker over time, as overall rates of cohabitation increase and cohabitation becomes a more normative component of young adults' relationship trajectories. To test this hypothesis, Dush and colleagues (2003) compared two U.S. marriage cohorts: those married between 1964 and 1980 and those married between 1981 and 1997. They found that after controlling for self-selection factors such as income, education, history of parental divorce, and whether a marriage was a first or second marriage, couples who cohabited before marriage had significantly poorer marital functioning and lower marital happiness in both cohorts, and these associations did not significantly vary across cohorts.

This surprising finding highlights how little is known about the subjective meaning and phenomenology of marriage versus cohabitation within the long-range developmental trajectory of an established couple and the conditions under which that subjective meaning might change over time as couples traverse different stages in their own respective life spans and also the life span of their relationship. Clearly, this is an area in which we need longitudinal, qualitative research to investigate the potentially nonconscious processes through which cohabiting couples' intentions regarding marriage and other major relationship decisions gradually change over time.

RELATIONSHIPS, HEALTH, AND PSYCHOBIOLOGY

One of the most robust findings to emerge from health psychology since the 1980s is that individuals in enduring, committed romantic relationships have longer, healthier, and happier lives than unmarried individuals (Cheung, 1998; Horwitz, McLaughlin, & White, 1998; Mastekaasa, 1994; Murphy, Glaser, & Grundy, 1997; Ross, 1995; Ryff, Singer, Wing, & Love, 2001; Stack, 1998; Stack & Eshleman, 1998). This effect cannot be attributed to overall social integration, given that individuals' most intimate relationships appear to promote health and well-being above and beyond generalized social support (Ross, 1995; Ryff et al., 2001). Rather, the key variable appears to be the long-term maintenance of an enduring, emotionally intimate affectional bond (Ross, 1995). For example, simply knowing whether an individual "feels loved" significantly predicts his or her future cardiovascular disease risk (Seeman & Syme, 1987).

The task now is to determine how these linkages develop, the conditions under which they are established and maintained, the specific psychological and physiological processes involved, and their long-term implications for health and well-being. Much of the existing psychobiological research on these questions implicitly or explicitly draws on models of cumulative biopsychosocial adversity and advantage (for example, Repetti, Taylor, & Seeman, 2002; Ryff et al., 2001; Seeman, 2001). Such models explain the long-term health consequences of interpersonal relationships as a function of the cumulative impact of positive and negative relationship experiences on physiological processes related to stress regulation. This theoretical framework is based on the extensive body of research demonstrating that the positive and negative emotions elicited within intimate relationships are primary pathways through which day-to-day relationship experiences influence health-related physiological processes over the life span, such as cardiovascular and neuroendocrine functioning (Cacioppo et al., 2003; Kiecolt-Glaser, McGuire, Robles, & Glaser, 2002; Ryff et al., 2001).

Many studies testing this model have focused on identifying the immediate effects of discrete relationship events (such as conflict, problem solving, provision of support) on physiological functioning, most commonly activity in the autonomic nervous system (assessed through heart rate, blood pressure, electrodermal activity, respiratory sinus arrhythmia), the immune system (assessed through immune lymphocytes and pro-inflammatory cytokines), and the hypothalamic-pituitary-adrenocortical (HPA) axis of the endocrine system (assessed via salivary cortisol). By understanding how an individual's body responds to a single hostile interaction with their partner, we can make inferences about how long-term participation in a hostile marriage might expose an individual to chronic psychophysiological stress that takes a progressively greater toll on their health over the life span. In addition, models of cumulative adversity also take into account the possibility that for some individuals, the state of being exposed to aversive marital interactions on a day-to-day basis might give rise to "habits" of physiological reactivity that come to characterizes individuals' responses to stress more generally and place them at risk for the gradual accumulation of detrimental "wear and tear" on stress-regulatory systems or the course of many years (Lupien et al., 2006; Marin, Martin, Blackwell, Stetler, & Miller, 2007; G. E. Miller, Chen, & Zhou, 2007; Seeman & Gruenewald, 2006; Seeman, Singer, Ryff, Dienberg Love, & Levy-Storms, 2002).

Importantly, such patterns are known to be moderated by individual differences in physiological functioning that have been found to be linked to individual differences in emotion regulation (reviewed in Diamond & Hicks, 2004). For example, individuals who are already predisposed to heightened cardiovascular reactivity in response to stress might be especially reactive to marital conflict, exposing them to heightened physical risks over the long-term course of a lasting marriage. Alternatively, such individuals may not benefit as much as low-reactive individuals from the potentially stress-buffering effects of support and nurturance. Understanding such complex links between person-level and situation-level factors in explaining the links between relationships and health is a priority for life-span/developmental research in this area. In reviewing some of the major findings here, space precludes us from providing a comprehensive introduction and review of each of the physiological systems discussed; we refer the reader to the excellent reviews of these systems, and of methodologies for measuring them, that can be found elsewhere (Cacioppo, Tassinary, & Berntson, 2000; Diamond & Otter-Henderson, 2007; Loving, Heffner, & Kiecolt-Glaser, 2006).

Reactivity to Marital Interactions

Direct evidence for associations between marital interactions and physiological processes has been found in a variety of experimental studies. In some cases, the primary effects concern global properties of the relationship, and in others, the primary effects concern characteristics of the immediate interaction. Examples of the latter include research by Ewart, Taylor, Kraemer, and Agras (1991), which found that hostile behavior during a 10-minute spousal discussion was associated with significant elevations in women's blood pressure. Similarly, Kiecolt-Glaser and colleagues found that wives with a pattern of negative escalation during conflict showed concurrent changes in cortisol, adrenocorticotropic hormone, and norepinephrine (Kiecolt-Glaser et al., 1997), Notably, women also appear particularly reactive to their partners' behavior, showing heightened endocrine and immunological reactivity to male withdrawal during conflict discussions (Heffner et al., 2006; Kiecolt-Glaser et al., 1996). The tendency for women to show greater physiological reactivity than their male partners to conflict discussions—especially in response to a partner's negative behavior—has emerged across numerous studies (Dopp, Miller, Myers, & Fahey, 2000; Kiecolt-Glaser & Newton, 2001; Mayne, O'Leary, McCrady, & Contrada, 1997) and stands in notable contrast to the fact that men tend to show greater physiological reactivity to general laboratory stressors (Earle, Linden, & Weinberg, 1999; Kirschbaum, Wust, & Hellhammer, 1992). Such patterns suggest intriguing gender differences in the ways that men and women approach marital conflict and have important implications for understanding why men and women show different patterns of association between relationship status and physical health over the life span, a topic addressed in greater detail later.

Other studies have investigated associations between physiological reactivity and partners' *global* assessments of relationship functioning. For example, Broadwell and Light (1999) investigated spouses' blood pressure during conflictual and nonconflictual interactions. They found lower levels of vascular resistance during both types of interactions (as well as during the resting baseline) among spouses who reported high levels of overall family support. Similarly, Heffner, Kiecolt-Glaser, Loving, Glaser, and Malarkey (2004) found lower levels of cortisol reactivity in response to marital conflict among spouses who were generally satisfied with the type of support they received from their partners. Kiecolt-Glaser and colleagues (1997) found that spouses who described their marital disagreements as highly negative (and who displayed more negative conflict behavior in the laboratory) showed poor immunological responses, suggesting increased risk for suppressed immune functioning in response to chronic strain and stress. One particularly intriguing study (Kiecolt-Glaser, Bane, Glaser, & Malarkey, 2003) examined whether the patterns of physiological response that wives and husbands showed during a laboratory problem-solving interaction were predictive of relationship dissolution 10 years later. They found that couples who eventually divorced, as well as couples who stayed together but reported notable dissatisfaction, had shown significantly higher rates of epinephrine and norepinephrine during both the laboratory problem-solving discussion as well as during the ensuing day and night, at home. The authors suggested that their results provide insight into the types of physiological and emotional responses that might accompany maladaptive forms of conflict on a day-to-day level, even outside of conscious awareness, and that exert powerful cumulative effects on each partner's health over the life span.

It is important to note that most of the research on associations between romantic relationship dimensions and physiological reactivity has focused on negative rather than positive behaviors and emotions (with some exceptions, such as Ewart et al., 1991; Kiecolt-Glaser et al., 1996; Robles, Shaffer, Malarkey, & Kiecolt-Glaser, 2006). This may appear to be out of balance, given the extensive evidence for the independent importance of positive behaviors and emotions for marital functioning (Carstensen et al., 2004; Heyman, Weiss, & Eddy, 1995). Yet overall, negative behaviors appear to show stronger patterns of association with physiological reactivity than positive behaviors (Ewart, 1993). Of course, positive and negative behaviors often occur in dynamic interaction with one another over the course of a single interaction, or the long-term course of a well-established relationship, and in many cases it may be the sequence, coordination, and mutual regulation of partners' positive and negative moods and behaviors that proves significant for couple functioning and individual health (for example, Butner, Diamond, & Hicks, 2007). Understanding the role that such complex affective processes play in the psychobiology of intimate relationships and how these processes may change over the life span is an important direction for future research.

Gender, Health, and Development

As noted earlier, laboratory studies have reliably found that women exhibit greater physiological reactivity to negative interpersonal interactions with their partners than do men, and this finding corresponds to the fact that marital status overall appears to have a more health-protective effect on men than on women over the life span (see the comprehensive review by Kiecolt-Glaser & Newton, 2001). Women, it seems, appear especially sensitive to the cumulative "downsides" of long-term marriages (conflict, hostility, etc.), whereas men appear especially sensitive to the cumulative benefits (support, companionship, etc.). Numerous factors may contribute to this pattern of results. As reviewed by Kiecolt-Glaser and colleagues (2001), women are typically socialized to maintain a relational, interdependent sense of self that prioritizes the maintenance of close social ties (Acitelli & Young, 1996). Accordingly, women may be more vigilant in monitoring their relationships for conflicts and problems and may interpret such conflicts and problems as more threatening. Women also tend to be more empathic than men (reviewed in Eisenberg & Lennon, 1983), particularly with respect to decoding nonverbal cues, which may render them particularly sensitive to signs of negative affectivity in their partners. This is consistent with the fact that distressed wives tend to be more accurate in interpreting their husbands' negative messages than vice versa (Notarius, Benson, Sloane, & Vanzetti, 1989) and also that wives' negative emotions are better predicted by their husbands' negative emotions than vice versa (Larson & Almeida, 1999; L. J. Roberts & Krokoff, 1990). In addition to these psychological factors, women may also experience greater day-to-day stress than their husbands because of their disproportionate responsibility for child care and household labor (Hochschild & Machung, 2003), and these stressors often accumulate over the course of many years. Given the ongoing changes in the social roles afforded to men and women, as well as evolving standards and expectations for men's and women's interpersonal behavior within their intimate relationships, a critical question for future research concerns whether gender differences regarding the life-span health implications of intimate relationships will gradually decline.

Another important question for future research concerns the developmental antecedents of such differences. The vast majority of research on physiological reactivity within the context of couple interaction has focused on adult married couples. However, consistent with the developmental premises we have repeatedly emphasized, any observed pattern of emotional and physiological reactivity must be conceptualized as the product of a long chain of interactions that each partner has had with prior partners, family members, and so on, which fundamentally shape his or her particular pattern of stress appraisals and reactivity. Furthermore, as noted earlier, individuals' pattern of reactivity is potentially moderated by both their own and their partner's individual differences regarding hostility, anxiety, attachment style, and other affective and interpersonal dimensions (Carpenter & Kirkpatrick, 1996; Denton, Burleson, Hobbs, Von Stein, & Rodriguez, 2001; Diamond, 2001; Diamond & Hicks, 2004, 2005; Diamond, Hicks, & Otter-Henderson, 2006; Powers, Pietromonaco, Gunlicks, & Sayer, 2006; T. W. Smith & Brown, 1991).

Hence, links between relationship experiences and patterns of physiological reactivity are likely to be progressive and bidirectional, potentially increasing over the course of the life span. Tracing these linkages back to childhood and adolescence, we might imagine that individuals with predispositions for heightened stress reactivity might struggle early on with regulating the negative emotions triggered by day-to-day interpersonal interactions and may therefore develop maladaptive approaches to conflict resolution. This, in turn, might lead to difficulties establishing and sustaining secure and supportive relationships. When these individuals succeed in forming long-term ties, their heightened reactivity and maladaptive interpersonal processes might provoke frequent conflict and exacerbate its negative emotional repercussions, creating increased opportunities for episodes of heightened cardiovascular reactivity. Researchers investigating such potential patterns have emphasized *cascade* models of cumulative adversity and advantage (Repetti et al., 2002; Seeman, 2001; Seeman & Gruenewald, 2006; Singer & Ryff, 1999) in which initial risks for maladaptive patterns of patterns of physiological functioning become magnified over time as a result of behavioral and selection factors which increase individuals' exposure to negative relationships. One key question for future research concerns *when* such pathways become established and the specific individual difference dimensions—including gender as well as personality—that prove most influential in shaping individuals' social-psychological-biological trajectories and their long-term health.

Relationships and Health in Late Life

If the links between relationship experiences and health-related physiological processes are progressive and bidirectional, as just argued, then we should expect to observe particularly strong associations between relationship factors and health status among older couples, who may have spent decades reinforcing such connections through their day-to-day interactions. In fact, evidence suggests this to be the case, and an increasing body of research has found that some of the most distinctive features of late-life intimate relationships (as opposed to those in early or middle adulthood) concern the multiple processes through which mental and physical health become fundamentally interbraided with relationship functioning.

Much research has focused on the simple fact that simply having an intimate relationship in late life appears to be health-protective. A recent comprehensive meta-analysis found that elderly married individuals have, on average, a 12% reduction in the risk of death compared with never-married, divorced, and widowed adults (Manzoli, Villari, Pirone, & Boccia, 2007). Other studies have pinpointed a range of more specific associations between relationship status and mental and physical well-being among the elderly. For example, divorced older adults show greater risk factors for chronic health conditions such as diabetes, and they also have fewer financial resources available to manage their escalating health care costs (Ellis, 2008). Research by Prigerson, Maciejewski, and Rosenheck (2000) pinpointed these costs even more specifically and found interactive effects of marital status and marital quality. They found that older adults who placed the lowest financial "burden" on the health care system (in terms of average usage and cost) were those with intact, well-functioning marriages. The next most "costly" older adults were those with intact but discordant marriages. Individuals who were widowed after having enjoyed a harmonious marriage placed the greatest burden on the health care system, with costs that were more than twice as high as those of individuals in intact, well-functioning marriages (and that were greater than the costs associated with being widowed after a discordant marriage). Notably, other studies have found that the benefits of relationship involvement in late life extend even to basic cognitive functioning. One longitudinal study found that older men who lost a partner or lived alone during a 5-year period had twice as much cognitive decline over a subsequent 10-year period than did men who were married or who lived with someone in those years (van Gelder et al., 2006). Clearly, even when day-to-day interactions between older couples involve periodic conflict and strain, the overall social support and stimulating interpersonal exchange afforded by day-to-day contact with an intimate partner has undoubtedly salubrious effect on older adults' physical and mental well-being.

With respect to basic interpersonal processes, in many respects older couples strongly resemble younger couples, with similar relationship hurdles, such as disagreements over leisure, intimacy, money, housework, in-laws, and basic concerns over fairness and equity (Henry, Miller, & Giarrusso, 2005). They also show similar linkages between positive day-to-day relationship qualities and overall well-being. For example, a daily-diary study found greater levels of life satisfaction among older individuals who reported enjoying their day-to-day spousal interactions, who felt a sense of control and self-assurance in these interactions, and who felt that their partners were responding to their needs (Nezlek, Richardson, Green, & Schatten-Jones, 2002). These findings echo the results of other daily-diary studies showing that feelings of autonomy, social connectedness, and clear demonstrations of partners' positive responsiveness make important contributions to adults' psychological well-being (Gable, Gonzaga, & Strachman, 2006; Reis, Sheldon, Gable, Roscoe, & Ryan, 2000). Although such studies suggest that many of the core components of positive relationship functioning have the same antecedents and correlates in older couples as among younger couples, older couples nonetheless have a number of distinguishing characteristics that confer unique sources of resiliency *and* stress. On the positive side, their children are typically grown and have long since left home, which reduces the burdens of child rearing that are known to introduce stress and dissatisfaction among couples (Belsky & Kelly, 1994; Cowan & Cowan, 1992). Older adults who have retired from their careers no longer need face the demands of work life, reducing the potent "spill over" of work stress into home life that often impairs marital functioning (Bolger, DeLongis, Kessler, & Wethington, 1989; Matjasko & Feldman, 2006). These late-life changes can provide couples with an opportunity to reinvest in their relationship and experience a renewal of intimacy and support. Yet of course, this is not always the case. Some older individuals find themselves lonely and restless without the demands of child rearing and work life, which might introduce new sources of marital strain, and health problems—one's own and those of one's friends and relatives—introduce new emotional and financial stressors (Henry, Miller, & Giarrusso, 2005).

Studies have found that the patterns of association among older couples' relationship satisfaction and their overall well-being are complex and differentiated by gender. For example, in a study of older couples married approximately 50 years, Cohen and colleagues (Cohen, Geron, & Farchi, 2009) found that for men, marital quality appears to be compartmentalized from other aspects of their lives. Hence, even men facing multiple problems and low global well-being were capable of sustaining positive and satisfying marriages. By the same token, marital strain did not necessarily impair older men's overall well-being. However, the results for women were notably different: Older wives' marital satisfaction was strongly linked to multiple factors outside the marriage, most notably the ongoing quality of their relationships with their children. Importantly, the authors noted that there are potential benefits and drawbacks to both patterns. Older men's compartmentalization might "protect" them from suffering broad-based problems as a result of a troubled marriage, but it might also prevent them from drawing on a well-functioning marriage as a buffer against general psychological and social stressors. The permeability between older women's global well-being and their marital quality means that positive and negative features of each domain will spill over to influence the other.

Other studies have demonstrated complex patterns of bidirectional association among husbands' and wives' mental and physical health in late life. For example, Sandberg and Harper (2000) focused specifically on depression in older adult couples and found that both partners' depressive symptoms were strongly related to their joint marital quality. Furthermore, marital quality was found to mediate associations between each partner's health and daily stressors and the other partner's depression levels. Hence, as an older adult's physical and mental health problems spill over into day-to-day marital functioning, they can quickly become *joint* problems, potentially reducing both partners' ability to provide supportive resources for the other. For example, one recent study of older couples found that if one partner was depressed, the couples' overall affective communication and problem solving showed impairments. These impairments were even greater if both partners were depressed (Harper & Sandberg, 2009). Pruchno and colleagues detected important cross-partner effects on physical and mental health in a longitudinal study of older couples in which one partner had end-stage renal disease (Pruchno, Wilson-Genderson, & Cartwright, 2009). Not only did they find a positive association between partners' respective depressive symptoms, they also found notable cross-partner effects linking the ailing partner's health to the healthy partner's depressive symptoms. Strikingly, they found that for the healthy spouse, depressive symptoms were more strongly associated with longitudinal declines in the ailing partner's physical health than with declines in the healthy spouse's own physical health. Such findings clearly demonstrate that clinical interventions aimed at promoting both physical and mental well-being among older adults will be ineffective unless they take into account transactional marital processes through which stressors, symptoms, and strengths become shared within the dyad, especially for couples facing the types of chronic health problems that become practically inevitable with advanced age. For these reasons, it is encouraging to see that many clinicians have devoted particular attention to developing therapeutic approaches specifically designed for older couples aimed at addressing their unique needs and challenges (Wolinsky, 1990).

EMERGING PERSPECTIVES ON A UNIQUE POPULATION: SAME-SEX COUPLES

Up until now we have focused almost exclusively on heterosexual couples, yet one of the most notable developments in psychological research on intimate relationships since the 1990s has been the explosion of inquiry into the relationships of lesbian, gay, and bisexual (collectively denoted *sexual-minority*) individuals. Research indicates that between 40% and 60% of gay men and 50% and 80% of lesbians are partnered (reviewed in Peplau & Spalding, 2000), and their relationships are a significant part of the American interpersonal landscape. The 2000 census found that one in nine cohabitating, unmarried couples in the United States was a same-sex couple (Simons & O'Connell, 2003). A central question addressed by this line of research is the degree to which the relationships of sexual minorities are distinct from those of heterosexuals. Although there is no unified body of psychological theory purporting to explain the specific degree and extent of differences between same-sex and heterosexual couples, much research has been implicitly guided by two explanatory frameworks. The first emphasizes the impact of *social stigmatization and homophobia* on sexual-minority couples, and the second focuses on the influence of *gender-related dynamics* (i.e., combining two males or two females in the same relationship).

Social Stigmatization

Although attitudes toward same-sex sexuality have grown more tolerant in recent years (reviewed in Loftus, 2001), considerable stigma and intolerance remain pervasive. One large survey of American lesbian-gay-bisexual adults found that three fourths had experienced some form of discrimination as a result of their sexual orientation, and almost one-third had suffered violence against themselves or their property (Kaiser Foundation, 2001). Same-sex couples are also frequently disparaged or denied legitimacy by their families of origin and the culture at large (Caron & Ulin, 1997; Gillis, 1998; LaSala, 2000; Oswald, 2002; Patterson, 2000). Even couples who do not face stark and explicit rejection must typically contend with everyday stressors such as poor service and rude treatment when shopping together (Walters & Curran, 1996), difficulty making hotel reservations as a couple (Jones, 1996), and discomfort when attending family functions together (Caron & Ulin, 1997; Oswald, 2002).

These challenges exemplify the many ways in which same-sex couples are exposed to "minority stress"—the unique strain experienced as a direct result of occupying a socially marginalized category. Minority stress has been advanced as an explanation for the finding that although same-sex sexuality is not a mental disorder, sexual minorities do exhibit higher rates of anxiety and mood disorders over the life span, and these problems are amplified among subsets of sexual minorities who report greater prejudice and stigmatization (Meyer, 2003).

Also, whereas family members typically serve as buffers against stress for heterosexuals, among sexual minorities, family members can pose additional sources of minority stress. Gay men and lesbians typically report receiving less support from their biological families than do heterosexuals (Harkless & Fowers, 2005), with approximately one third of gay men and one half of lesbians reporting that a friend or family member refused to accept them because of their sexual orientation (Kaiser Foundation, 2001). In some cases, parents may quietly tolerate the situation (L. Brown, 1989; D'Augelli, Grossman, & Starks, 2005; Herdt & Beeler, 1998) while still conveying disapproval by refusing to acknowledge or validate the sexual-minority individual's romantic relationships. Such behavior has important consequences, given that the degree of explicit community support a couple perceives for their relationship influences their well-being (Kurdek, 1998b, 2004).

Legal Status

Such findings are obviously notable in light of the ongoing debates over formal recognition for same-sex relationships (for reviews, see Brewer & Wilcox, 2005; Herek, 2006). As of 2009, same-sex marriages were only available in Vermont, Connecticut, Iowa, Maine, New Hampshire, Massachusetts, Canada, Spain, Belgium, South Africa, and the Netherlands. In contrast, 40 American states have explicitly *banned* same-sex marriage, either through state laws or constitutional amendments. Yet a number of American states and other countries allow same-sex couples to enter into legally recognized civil unions or domestic partnerships, (including California, New Jersey, England, and New Zealand), and survey data consistently suggest greater public support for "nonmarital" forms of legal recognition than for same-sex marriage. One relatively recent national survey (Pew Research Center for the People and the Press, 2006) suggests that the majority of Americans (55%) oppose same-sex marriage, yet research by Brewer (2005), has found that many of these individuals support the notion of same-sex civil unions or domestic partnerships, and in fact the proportion of Americans who would support some form of legal recognition for same-sex relationships consistently exceeds the proportion favoring no recognition whatsoever. Thus, despite consistent opposition to same-sex marriage, most Americans view longstanding, committed same-sex partnerships as deserving of some form of legal recognition.

As noted earlier in the section on commitment, studies have consistently found that legal marriage and other structural "ties" between individuals, such as joint property and the presence of children, function to promote relationship stability by instantiating couples' commitment to one another and providing robust barriers to dissolution (reviewed in Rusbult et al., 2006). Accordingly, the fact that same-sex couples lack formal recognition for their relationships has been posited as a key factor explaining why they have higher breakup rates than married (but not unmarried cohabiting) heterosexual couples (Kurdek, 1992, 1998b, 2000). A 12-year longitudinal study found breakup rates of 19% among gay male couples and 24% among lesbian couples. Notably, after controlling for demographic factors such as length of cohabitation, these rates were not statistically higher than the breakup rate (14%) among unmarried cohabiting heterosexuals (Kurdek, 2004). We might therefore expect that same-sex couples with the opportunity and inclination to marry or enter civil unions (which provide the same rights as marriage at the state level) would show greater stability than their unmarried counterparts. Recent findings from a 3-year follow-up of same-sex couples who had civil unions in Vermont are consistent with this expectation. Balsam and colleagues (2008) found same-sex couples who had formalized their relationship with a civil union were less likely to have ended their relationships than same-sex couples without civil unions. Of course, longer term longitudinal data are necessary to understand whether the stabilizing influence of civil unions and domestic partnerships operates equivalently over the long-term course of a relationship, and at different stages of each partner's life span.

Another fascinating question concerns the mechanisms through which different forms of formal recognition for same-sex relationships have short- and long-term stabilizing effects. Even couples who have not pursued a civil union might develop numerous other structural ties to one another, such as having a child, naming one another as insurance beneficiaries or legal heirs, purchasing property together, giving one another power of attorney, designating one another as medical proxies, legally taking the same last name, or merging finances (Badgett, 1998; Beals, Impett, & Peplau, 2002; Suter & Oswald, 2003). Comparing breakup rates across couples with different degrees of legal, logistical, bureaucratic, and religious formalization would provide a unique opportunity to examine the relative stabilizing effects of structural versus personal–moral dimensions of relationship commitment over the long-term course of same-sex relationships (M. P. Johnson, 1999).

Gender-Related Dynamics in Couple Functioning

Overall, the similarities between same-sex and heterosexual relationships appear to outweigh the differences. The happiest same-sex couples, like the happiest heterosexual couples, are those who perceive that their relationships provide more benefits than downsides (Beals et al., 2002), and in which partners have similar attitudes (Kurdek & Schmitt, 1987; Kurdek & Schnopp-Wyatt, 1997), similar social and economic backgrounds (Hall & Greene, 2002), similar expectations and perceptions regarding fairness and equity (Kurdek, 1995, 1998b; Schreurs & Buunk, 1996), and similar views and priorities regarding things such as shared activities, commitment, and sexual exclusivity (Deenen, Gijs, & van Naerssen, 1994).

Other predictors of relationship quality that have been found to function equivalently for same-sex and other-sex couples include partners' personality characteristics; their communication and conflict resolution skills; appraisals of intimacy, autonomy, equality, and mutual trust; and the degree of support the couple perceives for their relationship from their local community (Kurdek, 1998b, 2004). Same-sex and other-sex couples also use the same basic strategies to maintain their relationships, such as sharing tasks, communicating about the relationship, and sharing time together (Dainton & Stafford, 1993; Solomon et al., 2005). They have even been found to fight about the same core issues: finances, affection, sex, criticism, and household tasks (Kurdek, 2004; Solomon et al., 2005). Also, as with heterosexual couples, same-sex couples with higher levels of overall relationship satisfaction report higher levels of sexual satisfaction (Bryant & Demian, 1994; Deenen et al., 1994; Peplau, Cochran, & Mays, 1997).

Yet notably, the most consistent differences that have been observed between same-sex and heterosexual couples concern gender-based dynamics. Contrary to stereotypes positing that same-sex couples implicitly designate one partner to take the classically "female" role and one partner to take the "male" role, studies of interpersonal attitudes, behaviors, and cognitions have generally found that lesbian-gay-bisexual men and women show largely the same gender-related patterns that have been observed among heterosexuals (e.g., Bailey, Gaulin, Agyei, & Gladue, 1994; Kenrick, Keefe, Bryan, & Barr, 1995). Hence, *combining* two women or two men in the same relationship often magnifies gender-specific patterns, providing a "double dose" of female-typical behavior in female–female relationships and of male-typical behavior in male–male relationships.

For example, gender differences are salient in lesbian and gay men's contrasting approaches to relationship formation. Women's greater relational orientation in comparison to men (reviewed in Cross & Madson, 1997) is reflected in the fact that lesbians have often been found to follow a "friendship script" in developing new romantic relationships, in which emotional compatibility and communication are more important than explicit sexual interest or interaction, whereas gay men's relationship scripts more often involve the establishment of sexual intimacy before the development of emotional intimacy (Rose, Zand, & Cimi, 1993).

Although noticeable from the earliest stages of relationship formation, such differences are also readily observed in established relationships. Kurdek (1998b) found that female–female couples tend to report greater intimacy (manifested in shared time together and the degree to which partners maintained a "couple" identity) than male–male or male–female couples. Similarly, Zacks, Green, and Marrow (1988) found that compared with heterosexual couples, female–female couples reported higher levels of cohesion, adaptability, and satisfaction in their relationships, a result that the authors attributed to women's gender role socialization. Some clinicians have expressed concern that female–female couples' heightened intimacy can sometimes border on detrimental tendencies toward "fusion" or "merger" (Biaggio, Coan, & Adams, 2002), whereas tendencies toward interpersonal distance have been raised as a unique challenge facing gay male couples (Tunnell & Greenan, 2004).

Gender-magnification effects are also evident with regard to sexual exclusivity. Numerous studies have found that male–male couples are more likely than either male–female or female–female couples to report engaging in extradyadic sexual activity, often with the explicit knowledge of their partner (Bryant & Demian, 1994; Peplau et al., 1997; Solomon, Rothblum, & Balsam, 2004). This is commonly attributed to the fact that men's socialization allows them to separate sex from love more easily than do women, making it possible for two men in a committed, enduring bond to understand mutually and agree that extradyadic sexual activity does not threaten their primary tie to one another. In such arrangements, extradyadic sex may have few negative repercussions for relationship satisfaction or stability and might actually foster some benefits (Deenen et al., 1994; Hickson et al., 1992).

Gender dynamics also play a role in issues of power and equality, manifested in decision making and division of household labor. Overall, same-sex couples show more equitable distributions of household labor than do heterosexual couples (Kurdek, 1993a; Patterson, 1995; Solomon et al., 2004), although male–male and female–female couples appear to operationalize equity in different ways, with male couples dividing up responsibility for specific tasks and female couples sharing the performance of each task (Kurdek, 1993a). It is not uncommon for same-sex partners to mix and match "female-typed" and "male-typed" tasks and roles according to their respective skills and interests (M. Huston & Schwartz, 2002). Also, same-sex couples appear to place a higher value on equity between partners and are less likely to take for granted a lopsided distribution of labor, decision making, and influence. For such reasons, same-sex couples provide a fascinating model for contemporary couples seeking creative relationship and household practices that serve the unique needs of their families more effectively than rigid, traditional, gender-based relationship roles (Steil, 2000).

Overall, then, the factors that make same-sex romantic relationships different from other-sex romantic relationships appear to have far more to do with gender than with sexual orientation. Sexual-minority and heterosexual individuals do not go about the processes of forming and maintaining romantic ties all that differently from one another, but men and women do, and such differences are echoed and magnified in same-sex couples.

PROMISING NEW DIRECTIONS IN RELATIONSHIP RESEARCH

Relationship Development

In the 1960s and 1970s, during the heyday of early research on romantic relationships, the focus was almost entirely on initial romantic attraction (primarily coming from an evolutionary perspective). As the field of relationship research developed and expanded, researchers gradually shifted their attention away from initial relationship processes and toward the examination of intact relationship dynamics (Eastwick & Finkel, 2008a). As a result, our field now boasts a comprehensive understanding of existing relationships but understands little about how these relationships got started. Although some studies have used retrospective reports to assess partners' perceptions of why they first became attracted to one another and how the early stages of pairbonding progressed, such data are of limited use given the unavoidable retrospective bias that comes into play. Individuals who have already committed to a romantic partner are likely to perceive the early days of their relationship in an overly positive light, as if it had always been "meant to be." Even more important, retrospective approaches fail to capture unsuccessful relationships. If a couple does not make it to the 4- to 6-month point, they are unlikely to end up in a research study on romantic relationships, thereby hampering our attempts to understand whether there are certain interpersonal dynamics, or certain combinations of personalities, that presage early relationship failure. The only solution to this quandary, of course, is longitudinal research. One approach would be to follow the same individual as he or she starts and progresses through a variety of relationships; another approach would be to sample brand-new couples and follow them through the entire course of their relationship. Both approaches, of course, are logistically demanding and, in some cases, unfeasible. In particular, individuals who have just formed brand-new relationships may be too self-conscious—and too concerned about "scaring off" their new partner—to participate in a study that will ask them and their partner detailed, intimate questions about their fledgling romance.

Yet in recent years, a creative new solution to the problem of studying relationship formation has emerged. Eli Finkel and his colleagues (Finkel, Eastwick, & Matthews, 2007) have pioneered the investigation of "speed dating" as a naturalistic context in which to study early relationship processes. Speed-dating events were initally organized as an alternative to conventional dating (in which "trying out" each potential partner took an entire evening) and online dating (in which there were many potential partners to choose from but no opportunity to interact with them face-to-face). At speed-dating events, multiple singles gather together in the same place, and over the course of the evening, every individual has the chance to interact one-on-one with every other individual there for a short amount of time. Afterward, participants have the opportunity to indicate which individuals they liked the most, and the organizers put individuals in contact with one another if they show reciprocal liking.

To adapt speed dating for research purposes, Finkel and his team simply asked participants to fill out a variety of self-report measures before the speed-dating session, including assessments of personality, attachment style, expectations, and so on. They then tracked the "matches" established after the event, following their development into full-blown relationships or their early demise. Given the amount of initial data available on each partner, they were able to analyze factors that predicted partners' liking for one another as well as the success of the relationship. The findings have the potential to reveal early relationship dynamics that, up until now, have never been prospectively assessed. For example, a recent speed-dating study conducted by Eastwick and Finkel (2008b) has called into question the well replicated finding that men prefer physical attractiveness in a mate more than women do and that women prefer good earning prospects in a mate more than men do. Eastwick and Finkel's study showed a discrepancy between stated preferences (before the speed-dating session) and individuals' eventual "flesh-and-blood" choices. In another speed-dating study, Eastwick and Finkel (2008a) demonstrated strong effects of attachment anxiety on initial relationship formation, thereby proving that a full-blown attachment bond need not be in place for an individual's attachment anxiety to begin shaping the course and dynamics of the relationship.

Innovative research paradigms such as speed dating greatly increase researchers' capacity to investigate the entire developmental course of an intimate relationship, which continues to be among the largest and most important gaps in our attempt to understand intimate relationships from a life-span/developmental perspective. Such new methodological approaches have the potential to challenge many long-standing notions about romantic relationship development and to generate and answer important new questions about the factors that initially draw individuals to one another, keep them together, or push them apart.

Modeling Dynamic Change: New Approaches

By now, it may be clear that our "cascade" model of the cumulative, bidirectional influences between intimate relationships and developmental processes over the life span raises intractable "chicken-and-egg" problems when trying to determine why certain individuals end up in certain types of relationships with certain types of outcomes. As reviewed in this chapter, individuals bring a range of individual characteristics into their relationships, including their gender, ethnicity, personality, attachment style, family history, religious background, and so on, as well as their developmental status with regard to a range of different social and psychological skills and capacities. All of these characteristics interact dynamically with the characteristics of the other partner to shape the behavioral, cognitive, and affective features of the relationship (good vs. poor communication, warm accommodation vs. hostile criticism, frequent support vs. neglect). Over time, as we have emphasized, partners' experiences in their relationships feed forward to shape the continued development of their skills and capacities, either reinforcing or redirecting the long-range developmental trajectories of multiple psychosocial characteristics. An initially optimistic and secure person saddled with a unremittingly critical and negative partner might, over time, become more pessimistic and avoidant. Alternatively, an anxious and rejection-sensitive individual who spends 20 years with a warm, reliable, and responsive partner might eventually become secure and confident.

The existence of such complex, bidirectional influences between individuals and their relationship experiences has long been acknowledged, yet in recent years, there has been growing interest in capturing and modeling the ongoing, dynamic processes through which these mutual influences shape the course of relationship development over different time scales and at different stages of each partner's life span. Although long-term follow-up studies of established relationships are capable of detecting change after it has occurred, they are usually unable to identify how the change took place, whether there were certain turning points that proved significant (and why), and the specific combinations of traits and processes which drove the process of change. Follow-up studies are also unable to capture dynamic *discontinuities* during the course of a relationship, when longstanding stable processes suddenly produce unexpected transformations through which relationships shift into qualitatively different states (Gottman, Swanson, & Swanson, 2002). Understanding and capturing such processes is critical for understanding how and why couples progress—sometimes slowly, sometimes rapidly—from states of satisfaction to distress, from betrayal to forgiveness, and from despair to renewal.

Such "transformative processes" and their underlying parameters have garnered increasing research attention in recent years (Amato, 2007; Fincham, Stanley, & Beach, 2007; Hill, 2007). Researchers such as Fincham (2007) have argued that conventional, linear approaches to modeling relationship development, many of which overemphasize the predictive influence of specific negative traits or behaviors, are ill equipped to model such transformations appropriately. He noted that a sizable proportion of couples—contrary to all reasonable expectations—have been observed to recover spontaneously from pernicious marital discord over time, without undergoing any sort of intervention. To understand such cases, Fincham called for greater attention to *self-regulatory repair mechanisms* in couples—attributable to potent interactions between each partner's traits and characteristics and their own developing chains of adaptive interaction—which may prove critical for understanding why some relationships succeed over time, against all odds, whereas others inexplicably erode.

Close attention to the potent bidirectional interactions between individuals and relationship processes is critical for understanding these phenomena. Accordingly, a number of researchers have begun to explore *dynamical systems theory* as a conceptual and analytical framework for modeling transformation and adaptation in relationships over time (Gottman, Murray, Swanson, Tyson, & Swanson, 2002; Gottman, Swanson, & Swanson, 2002). Dynamical systems models seek to explain how complex patterns *emerge, stabilize, change, and restabilize* over time. Although originally developed by mathematicians and physicists to model complex physical phenomena in the natural world, they have increasingly been applied to social-behavioral phenomena ranging from motor development to cognition to language (for early, seminal examples, see Fogel & Thelen, 1987; Thelen, Kelso, & Fogel, 1987) in order to better represent how dynamic interchanges between endogenous factors (such as genes, hormones, skills, capacities, thoughts, and feelings) and exogenous factors (such as relationships, experiences, cultural norms, family history, etc.) give rise to novel forms of thought and behavior that are substantively more than the "sum of their parts." As noted earlier in our review of attachment style, some of the most provocative and generative new approaches to understanding continuity and change in attachment style over the life span are based in dynamical systems theory (Fraley & Brumbaugh, 2004).

According to dynamical systems theory, novel forms of thought and behavior arise as a function of *self-organization*, defined as the spontaneous development of order within a complex system (Kelso, 1997). A closely related concept is *emergence*, defined as the coming-into-being of altogether original behaviors or experiences through dynamic, unpredictable interactions between different elements in the system. As reviewed by Fogel (2006), researchers and theorists have increasingly come to view emergence and transformation as fundamental processes of psychological change, encompassing not only qualitative shifts in subjective experience but also processes of cognitive discovery and creativity (e.g., Gottlieb, 1992; Tronick et al., 1998).

The value of this approach for studies of relationship development and transformation over the life span is obvious. The more we have learned about the multidetermined, multidimensional nature of relationship functioning, the more evident it becomes that there are no single, determinative predictors. The questions we must ask are not "which marriages will fail?" but "which dynamic processes are most likely to provide couples—and individuals—with the resiliency they need to adapt to an unknowable future? How do such processes become established among couples with vastly different prior trajectories of interpersonal functioning?" Capturing such processes is, of course, logistically difficult. Dynamical systems approaches require longitudinal observation over both short and long stretches of time, aimed at capturing change as it takes place, rather than simply comparing specific outcomes before and after a presumed shift (Fogel, 2006). Many relationship researchers have already gravitated toward the use of daily diaries to capture everyday relationship processes (Bolger, Davis, & Rafaeli, 2003; Brandstatter, 2007; Laurenceau &

Bolger, 2005), and such methods offer great promise for applications of dynamical systems perspectives. The difficulty, however, comes with selecting the right period of observation (The very beginning of the relationship? Somewhere in the middle?) and the right time scale (Daily experiences? Weekly? Multiple interactions within the course of a single day?). Many of these decisions are driven more by logistical than theoretical concerns, but the inconvenient truth is that life-span/developmental models of intimate relationships necessitate much broader time scales. The next generation of developmentally oriented research on intimate relationships will likely bring an increasingly diverse range of methodological approaches to bear on the study of intimate relationships at multiple stages of development. By revealing the fundamental dynamics of such relationships "in action," unfolding over real time, such research will undoubtedly make critical contributions to our understanding of the nature and developmental significance of intimate relationships over the life span.

CONCLUSION

Presently, relationship research might well represent one of the fastest developing and influential branches of psychological theory and research, with enormous potential to directly affect human health and happiness. As psychologists, sociologists, anthropologists, and physicians increasingly document the wide-ranging effects of intimate relationships on psychological and physical well-being, it becomes increasingly important to understand the basic processes through which individuals form, maintain, change, and dissolve these relationships and the diverse and interacting mechanisms through which they shape our thoughts, feelings, behaviors, and physiological functioning over the life course. The field of relationship science has already yielded an enormous body of knowledge regarding these topics, and it is likely that we will continue to observe dramatic developments and transformations in our understanding of intimate relationships in the years to come.

REFERENCES

Abma, J., Chandra, A., Mosher, W., Peterson, L., & Piccinino, L. (1997). Fertility, family planning, and women's health: New data from the 1995 National Survey of Family Growth. In *Vital Health Statistics* (Vol. 23, pp. 1–114). Hyattsville, MD: National Center for Health Statistics.

Acitelli, L. K., & Young, A. M. (1996). Gender and thought in relationships. In G. J. O. Fletcher & J. Fitness (Eds.), *Knowledge structures in close relationships: A social psychological approach.* (pp. 147–168): Mahwah, NJ: Erlbaum.

Adams, J. M., & Jones, W. H. (1999). *Handbook of interpersonal commitment and relationship stability*. Dordrecht, The Netherlands: Kluwer Academic.

Afifi, W. A., & Faulkner, S. L. (2000). On being "just friends": The frequency and impact of sexual activity in cross-sex friendships. *Journal of Social and Personal Relationships, 17,* 205–222.

Agnew, C. R., Van Lange, P. A. M., Rusbult, C. E., & Langston, C. A. (1998). Cognitive interdependence: Commitment and the mental representation of close relationships. *Journal of Personality and Social Psychology, 74,* 939–954.

Ahadi, S. A., & Rothbart, M. K. (1994). Temperament, development, and the Big Five. In C. F. J. Halverson, G. A. Kohnstamm, & R. P. Martin (Eds.), *The developing structure of temperament and personality from infancy to adulthood* (pp. 189–207). Hillsdale, NJ: Erlbaum.

Ainsworth, M. D. S., Blehar, M. C., Waters, E., & Wall, S. (1978). *Patterns of attachment: A psychological study of the Strange Situation*. Hillsdale, NJ: Erlbaum.

Alexander, C. J. (2002). Violence in gay and lesbian relationships. *Journal of Gay and Lesbian Social Services: Issues in Practice, Policy and Research, 14,* 95–98.

Allen, J. P., & Land, D. (1999). Attachment in adolescence. In J. Cassidy & P. R. Shaver (Eds.), *Handbook of attachment: Theory, research, and clinical applications* (pp. 319–335). New York: Guilford Press.

Amato, P. R. (2007). Transformative processes in marriage: Some thoughts from a sociologist. *Journal of Marriage and Family, 69,* 305–309.

Amato, P. R., & Booth, A. (2001). The legacy of parents' marital discord: Consequences for children's marital quality. *Journal of Personality and Social Psychology, 81,* 627–638.

Amato, P. R., & Previti, D. (2003). People's reasons for divorcing: Gender, social class, the life course, and adjustment. *Journal of Family Issues, 24,* 602–626.

Amato, P. R., & Rogers, S. J. (1997). A longitudinal study of marital problems and subsequent divorce. *Journal of Marriage & the Family, 59,* 612–624.

Anderson, K. L. (2002). Perpetrator or victim? Relationships between intimate partner violence and well-being. *Journal of Marriage and Family, 64,* 851–863.

Archer, J. (2000). Sex differences in aggression between heterosexual partners: A meta-analytic review. *Psychological Bulletin, 126,* 651–680.

Archer, J. (2006). Cross-cultural differences in physical aggression between partners: A social-role analysis. *Personality and Social Psychology Review, 10,* 133–153.

Arnett, J. J. (2000). Emerging adulthood: A theory of development from the late teens through the twenties. *American Psychologist, 55,* 469–480.

Arnett, J. J. (2001). Conceptions of the transition to adulthood: Perspectives from adolescence through midlife. *Journal of Adult Development, 8,* 133–143.

Arnett, J. J. (2006a). Emerging adulthood: Understanding the new way of coming of age. In J. J. Arnett & J. L. Tanner (Eds.), *Emerging adults in America: Coming of age in the 21st-century* (pp. 3–19). Washington, DC: American Psychological Association Press.

Arnett, J. J. (2006b). The psychology of emerging adulthood: What is known, and what remains to be known? In J. J. Arnett & J. L. Tanner (Eds.), *Emerging adult in America: Coming of age in the 21st-century* (pp. 303–330). Washington, DC: American Psychological Association Press.

Aron, A. P., & Aron, E. N. (1991). Love and sexuality. In K. McKinney & S. Sprecher (Eds.), *Sexuality in close relationships* (pp. 25–48). Hillsdale, NJ: Erlbaum.

Arriaga, X. B. (2001). The ups and downs of dating: Fluctuations in satisfaction in newly formed romantic relationships. *Journal of Personality and Social Psychology, 80,* 754–765.

Arriaga, X. B., & Agnew, C. R. (2001). Being committed: Affective, cognitive, and conative components of relationship commitment. *Personality and Social Psychology Bulletin, 27,* 1190–1203.

Arriaga, X. B., & Foshee, V. A. (2004). Adolescent dating violence: Do adolescents follow in their friends', or their parents', footsteps? *Journal of Interpersonal Violence, 19,* 162–184.

Arriaga, X. B., & Rusbult, C. E. (1998). Standing in my partner's shoes: Partner perspective taking and reactions to accommodative dilemmas. *Personality and Social Psychology Bulletin, 24,* 927–948.

Aseltine, R. H., & Kessler, R. C. (1993). Marital disruption and depression in a community sample. *Journal of Health and Social Behavior, 34,* 237–251.

Asendorpf, J. B. (2002). Personality effects on personal relationships over the life span. In A. L. Vangelisti, H. T. Reis, & M. A. Fitzpatrick (Eds.), *Stability and change in relationships.* (pp. 35–56). New York: Cambridge University Press.

Attridge, M., Berscheid, E., & Simpson, J. A. (1995). Predicting relationship stability from both partners versus one. *Journal of Personality and Social Psychology, 69,* 254–268.

Avison, W. R. (1999). Family structure and processes. In A. V. Horvitz & T. L. Scheid (Eds.), *A handbook for the study of mental health: Social contexts, theories, and the systems* (pp. 228–240). New York: Cambridge University Press.

Axinn, W. G., & Thornton, A. (1992). The relationship between cohabitation and divorce: Selectivity or causal influence. *Demography, 29,* 357–374.

Bachman, J. G., Johnston, L. D., & O'Malley, P. M. (2001). *Monitoring the future: Questionnaire responses from the nation's high school seniors, 2000.* Ann Arbor, MI: Institute for Social Research.

Badgett, M. V. L. (1998). The economic well-being of lesbian, gay, and bisexual adults' families. In C. Patterson & A. R. D'Augelli (Eds.), *Lesbian, gay, and bisexual identities in families: Psychological Perspectives* (pp. 231–248). New York: Oxford University Press.

Bailey, J. M., Gaulin, S., Agyei, Y., & Gladue, B. (1994). Effects of gender and sexual orientation on evolutionarily relevant aspects of human mating psychology. *Journal of Personality and Social Psychology, 66,* 1081–1093.

Baldwin, M. W., & Fehr, B. (1995). On the instability of attachment style ratings. *Personal Relationships, 2,* 247–261.

Baldwin, M. W., Keelan, J. P. R., Fehr, B., Enns, V., & Koh-Rangarajoo, E. (1996). Social-cognitive conceptualization of attachment working models: Availability and accessibility effects. *Journal of Personality and Social Psychology, 71,* 94–109.

Balsam, K. F., Beauchaine, T. P., Rothblum, E. D., & Solomon, S. E. (2008). Three-year follow-up of same-sex couples who had civil unions in Vermont, same-sex couples not in civil unions, and heterosexual married couples. *Developmental Psychology, 44,* 102–116.

Barker, M. (2005). This is my partner, and this is my… partner's partner: Constructing a polyamorous identity in a monogamous world. *Journal of Constructivist Psychology, 18,* 75–88.

Baumeister, R. F., & Twenge, J. M. (2002). Cultural suppression of female sexuality. *Review of General Psychology, 6,* 166–203.

Beach, S. R. H., Fincham, F. D., Amir, N., & Leonard, K. E. (2005). The taxometrics of marriage: Is marital discord categorical? *Journal of Family Psychology, 19,* 276–285.

Beals, K. P., Impett, E. A., & Peplau, L. A. (2002). Lesbians in love: Why some relationships endure and others end. *Journal of Lesbian Studies, 6,* 53–63.

Bearman, P. S., & Bruckner, H. (2002). Opposite-sex twins and adolescent same-sex attraction. *American Journal of Sociology, 107,* 1179–1205.

Bell, E. C., & Blakeney, R. N. (1977). Personality correlates of conflict resolution modes. *Human Relations, 30,* 849–857.

Bellavia, G., & Murray, S. L. (2003). Did I do that? Self esteem-related differences in reactions to romantic partner's mood. *Personal Relationships, 10,* 77–95.

Belsky, J., & Kelly, J. (1994). *The transition to parenthood: How a first child changes a marriage. Why some couples grow closer and others apart.* New York: Dell.

Bennett, N. G., Blanc, A. K., & Bloom, D. E. (1988). Commitment and the modern union: Assessing the link between premarital cohabitation and subsequent marital stability. *American Sociological Review, 53,* 127–138.

Bentler, P. M., & Newcomb, M. D. (1978). Longitudinal study of marital success and failure. *Journal of Consulting and Clinical Psychology, 46,* 1053–1070.

Bettinger, M. (2006). Polyamory and gay men: A family systems approach. In J. J. Bigner (Ed.), *An introduction to GLBT family studies* (pp. 161–181). New York: Haworth Press.

Betzig, L. (1989). Causes of conjugal dissolution: A cross-cultural study. *Current Anthropology, 30,* 654–676.

Biaggio, M., Coan, S., & Adams, W. (2002). Couples therapy for lesbians: Understanding merger and the impact of homophobia. *Journal of Lesbian Studies, 6,* 129–138.

Bingham, C. R., & Crockett, L. J. (1996). Longitudinal adjustment patterns of boys and girls experiencing early, middle, and late sexual intercourse. *Developmental Psychology, 32,* 647–658.

Black, M. C., & Breiding, M. J. (2008). Adverse health conditions and health risk behaviors associated with intimate partner violence—United States, 2005. *Journal of the American Medical Association, 300,* 646–649.

Blow, A. J., & Hartnett, K. (2005). Infidelity in committed relationships II: A substantive review. *Journal of Marital & Family Therapy, 31,* 217–233.

Bolger, N., & Amarel, D. (2007). Effects of social support visibility on adjustment to stress: Experimental evidence. *Journal of Personality and Social Psychology, 92,* 458–475.

Bolger, N., Davis, A., & Rafaeli, E. (2003). Diary methods: Capturing life as it is lived. *Annual Review of Psychology, 54,* 579–616.

Bolger, N., DeLongis, A., Kessler, R. C., & Wethington, E. (1989). The contagion of stress across multiple roles. *Journal of Marriage & the Family, 51,* 175–183.

Bolger, N., Zuckerman, A., & Kessler, R. C. (2000). Invisible support and adjustment to stress. *Journal of Personality and Social Psychology, 79,* 953–961.

Booth, A., & Amato, P. (1991). Divorce and psychological stress. *Journal of Health and Social Behavior, 32,* 396–407.

Booth, A., & Crouter, A. C. (Eds.). (2001). *Couples in conflict.* Mahwah, NJ: Erlbaum.

Booth, A., Crouter, A., & Shanahan. (1999). *Transitions to adulthood in a changing economy: no work, no family, no future?* Westport, CT: Praeger.

Bouchard, G. V., Lussier, Y., & Sabourin, S. P. (1999). Personality and marital adjustment: Utility of the five-factor model of personality. *Journal of Marriage & the Family, 61,* 651–660.

Bowlby, J. (1958). The nature of the child's tie to his mother. *International Journal of Psychoanalysis, 39,* 350–373.

Bowlby, J. (1973a). Affectional bonds: Their nature and origin. In R. W. Weiss (Ed.), *Loneliness: The experience of emotional and social isolation* (pp. 38–52). Cambridge, MA: MIT press.

Bowlby, J. (1973b). *Attachment and loss: Vol. 2. Separation: Anxiety and anger*. New York: Basic Books.

Bowlby, J. (1980). *Attachment and loss: Vol. 3. Loss: Sadness and depression*. New York: Basic Books.

Bowlby, J. (1982). *Attachment and loss: Vol. 1. Attachment* (2nd ed.). New York: Basic Books.

Bowlby, J. (1988). *A secure base: Parent–child attachment and healthy human development*. New York: Basic Books.

Bradbury, T. N., Beach, S. R. H., Fincham, F. D., & Nelson, G. M. (1996). Attributions and behavior in functional and dysfunctional marriages. *Journal of Consulting and Clinical Psychology, 64,* 569–576.

Bradbury, T. N., & Fincham, F. D. (1990). Attributions in marriage: Review and critique. *Psychological Bulletin, 107,* 3–33.

Bradbury, T. N., & Karney, B. R. (1993). Longitudinal study of marital interaction and dysfunction: Review and analysis. *Clinical Psychology Review, 13,* 15–27.

Bradbury, T. N., & Karney, B. R. (2004). Understanding and altering the longitudinal course of marriage. *Journal of Marriage & Family, 66,* 862–879.

Bradbury, T. N., Rogge, R., & Lawrence, E. (2001). Reconsidering the role of conflict in marriage. In A. Booth, A. C. Crouter, & M. Clements (Eds.), *Couples in conflict* (pp. 59–81). Mahwah, NJ: Erlbaum.

Bramlet, M. D., & Mosher, W. D. (2002). Cohabitation, marriage, divorce, and remarriage in the United States. In *Vital and Health Statistics* (Series 23, No. 22, pp. 1–93). Hyattsville, MD: National Center for Health Statistics.

Brandstatter, H. (2007). The time sampling diary (TSD) of emotional experience in everyday life situations. In J. A. Coan & J. J. B. Allen (Eds.), *Handbook of emotion elicitation and assessment* (pp. 318–331). New York: Oxford University Press.

Braver, S. L., Shapiro, J. R., & Goodman, M. R. (2006). Consequences of divorce for parents. In M. A. Fine & J. H. Harvey (Eds.), *Handbook of divorce and relationship dissolution* (pp. 313–337). Mahwah, NJ: Erlbaum.

Brennan, K. A., & Shaver, P. R. (1995). Dimensions of adult attachment, affect regulation, and romantic relationship functioning. *Personality and Social Psychology Bulletin, 21,* 267–283.

Brewer, P. R., & Wilcox, C. (2005). The polls-trends: Same-sex marriage and civil unions. *Public Opinion Quarterly, 69,* 599–616.

Bringle, R. G. (1995). Sexual jealousy in the relationships of homosexual and heterosexual men: 1980 and 1992. *Personal Relationships, 2,* 313–325.

Bringle, R. G., & Buunk, B. P. (1991). Extradyadic relationships and sexual jealousy. In K. McKinney & S. Sprecher (Eds.), *Sexuality in close relationships* (pp. 135–153). Hillsdale, NJ: Erlbaum.

Broadwell, S. D., & Light, K. C. (1999). Family support and cardiovascular responses in married couples during conflict and other interactions. *International Journal of Behavioral Medicine, 6,* 40–63.

Brown, L. (1989). Lesbians, gay men, and their families: Common clinical issues. *Journal of Gay and Lesbian Psychotherapy, 1,* 65–77.

Brown, L. M., & Gilligan, C. (1992). *Meeting at the crossroads: Women's psychology and girls' development*. Cambridge, MA: Harvard University Press.

Bryant, A. S., & Demian. (1994). Relationship characteristics of American gay and lesbian couples: Findings from a national survey. *Journal of Gay and Lesbian Social Services, 1,* 101–117.

Bui, K. T., Peplau, L. A., & Hill, C. T. (1996). Testing the Rusbult model of relationship commitment and stability in a 15-year study of heterosexual couples. *Personality and Social Psychology Bulletin, 22,* 1244–1257.

Bumpass, L. L., & Lu, H. (2000). Trends in cohabitation and implications for children's family contexts in the US. *Population Studies, 54,* 29–41.

Bumpass, L. L., & Sweet, J. A. (1989). National estimates of cohabitation. *Demography, 26,* 615–625.

Burcky, W., Reuterman, N., & Kopsky, S. (1988). Dating violence among high school students. *The School Counselor, 35,* 353–358.

Burke, L. K., & Follingstad, D. R. (1999). Violence in lesbian and gay relationships: Theory, prevalence, and correlational factors. *Clinical Psychology Review, 19,* 487–512.

Buss, D. M. (1994). *The evolution of desire: Strategies of human mating*. New York: Basic Books.

Buss, D. M., Larsen, R. J., Westen, D., & Semmelroth, J. (1992). Sex differences in jealousy: Evolution, physiology, and psychology. *Psychological Science, 3,* 251–255.

Buss, D. M., & Schmitt, D. P. (1993). Sexual strategies theory: A contextual evolutionary analysis of human mating. *Psychological Review, 100,* 204–232.

Buss, D. M., & Shackelford, T. K. (1997). Susceptibility to infidelity in the first year of marriage. *Journal of Research in Personality, 31,* 193–221.

Buss, D. M., Shackelford, T. K., Kirkpatrick, L. A., Choe, J. C., Lim, H. K., Hasegawa, M., et al. (1999). Jealousy and beliefs about infidelity: Tests of competing hypotheses in the United States, Korea, and Japan. *Personal Relationships, 6,* 125–150.

Butner, J., Diamond, L. M., & Hicks, A. M. (2007). Attachment style and two forms of affect coregulation between romantic partners. *Personal Relationships, 14,* 431–455.

Buunk, B. P. (1987). Conditions that promote breakups as a consequence of extradyadic involvements. *Journal of Social & Clinical Psychology, 5,* 271–284.

Buunk, B. P. (1997). Personality, birth order and attachment styles as related to various types of jealousy. *Personality and Individual Differences, 23,* 997–1006.

Buunk, B. P., Angleitner, A., Oubaid, V., & Buss, D. M. (1996). Sex differences in jealousy in evolutionary and cultural perspective: Tests from the Netherlands, Germany, and the United States. *Psychological Science, 7,* 359–363.

Buunk, B. P., & Bakker, A. B. (1997). Commitment to the relationship, extradyadic sex, and AIDS prevention behavior. *Journal of Applied Social Psychology, 27,* 1241–1257.

Cacioppo, J. T., Giese Davis, J., Spiegel, D., Ryff, C. D., Singer, B. H., Berntson, G. G., et al. (2003). Emotion and health. In R. J. Davidson & K. R. Scherer (Eds.), *Handbook of affective sciences* (pp. 1047–1137). London: Sage.

Cacioppo, J. T., Tassinary, L. G., & Berntson, G. G. (Eds.). (2000). *Handbook of psychophysiology, Second edition*. New York: Cambridge University Press.

Canary, D. J., & Stafford, L. (1992). Relational maintenance strategies and equity in marriage. *Communication Monographs, 59,* 243–267.

Canary, D. J., & Stafford, L. (1994). *Maintaining relationships through strategic and routine interaction*. San Diego, CA: Academic Press.

Cann, A., & Baucom, T. R. (2004). Former partners and new rivals as threats to a relationship: Infidelity type, gender, and commitment as factors related to distress and forgiveness. *Personal Relationships, 11,* 305–318.

Capezza, N. M., & Arriaga, X. B. (2008). You can degrade but you can't hit: Differences in perceptions of psychological versus physical aggression. *Journal of Social and Personal Relationships, 25,* 225–245.

Carnelley, K. B., Pietromonaco, P. R., & Jaffe, K. (1996). Attachment, caregiving, and relationship functioning in couples: Effects of self and partner. *Personal Relationships, 3,* 257–278.

Caron, S. L., & Ulin, M. (1997). Closeting and the quality of lesbian relationships. *Families in Society, 78,* 413–419.

Carpenter, E. M., & Kirkpatrick, L. A. (1996). Attachment style and presence of a romantic partner as moderators of psychophysiological responses to a stressful laboratory situation. *Personal Relationships, 3,* 351–367.

Carrère, S., Buehlman, K. T., Gottman, J. M., Coan, J. A., & Ruckstuhl, L. (2000). Predicting marital stability and divorce in newlywed couples. *Journal of Family Psychology, 14,* 42–58.

Carroll, J. S., Willoughby, B., Badger, S., Nelson, L. J., Barry, C. M., & Madsen, S. D. (2007). So close, yet so far away: The impact of varying marital horizons on emerging adulthood. *Journal of Adolescent Research, 22,* 219–247.

Carstensen, L. L. (2006). The influence of a sense of time on human development. *Science, 312,* 1913–1915.

Carstensen, L. L., Fung, H. H., & Charles, S. T. (2003). Socioemotional selectivity theory and emotion regulation in the second half of life. *Motivation and Emotion, 27,* 103–123.

Carstensen, L. L., Gottman, J. M., & Levenson, R. W. (2004). Emotional behavior in long-term marriage. In H. T. Reis & C. E. Rusbult (Eds.), *Close relationships: Key readings* (pp. 457–470). New York: Taylor & Francis.

Carstensen, L. L., Isaacowitz, D. M., & Charles, S. T. (1999). Taking time seriously: A theory of socioemotional selectivity. *American Psychologist, 54,* 165–181.

Carstensen, L. L., Pasupathi, M., Mayr, U., & Nesselroade, J. R. (2000). Emotional experience in everyday life across the adult life span. *Journal of Personality and Social Psychology, 79,* 644–655.

Carter, C. S. (1998). Neuroendocrine perspectives on social attachment and love. *Psychoneuroendocrinology, 23,* 779–818.

Carter, C. S., & Keverne, E. B. (2002). The neurobiology of social affiliation and pair bonding. In J. Pfaff, A. P. Arnold, A. E. Etgen, & S. E. Fahrbach (Eds.), *Hormones, brain and behavior* (Vol. 1, pp. 299–377). New York: Academic Press.

Caruthers, A. S. (2006). *"Hookups" and "friends with benefits": Nonrelational sexual encounters as contexts of women's normative sexual development.* Unpublished doctoral dissertation, University of Michigan, Ann Arbor.

Carver, K., Joyner, K., & Udry, J. R. (2003). *National estimates of adolescent romantic relationships.* Mahwah, NJ: Erlbaum.

Caspi, A. (1987). Personality in the life course. *Journal of Personality and Social Psychology, 53,* 1203–1213.

Caughlin, J. P., & Huston, T. L. (2002). A contextual analysis of the association between demand/withdraw and marital satisfaction. *Personal Relationships, 9,* 95–119.

Caughlin, J. P., Huston, T. L., & Houts, R. M. (2000). How does personality matter in marriage? An examination of trait anxiety, interpersonal negativity, and marital satisfaction. *Journal of Personality and Social Psychology, 78,* 326–336.

Caughlin, J. P., & Vangelisti, A. L. (2000). An individual difference explanation of why married couples engage in the demand/withdraw pattern of conflict. *Journal of Social and Personal Relationships, 17,* 523–551.

Ceglian, C. P., & Gardner, S. (1999). Attachment style: A risk for multiple marriages? *Journal of Divorce and Remarriage, 31,* 125–139.

Cheung, Y. B. (1998). Accidents, assaults, and marital status. *Social Science & Medicine, 47,* 1325–1329.

Christensen, A., & Heavey, C. L. (1990). Gender and social structure in the demand/withdraw pattern of marital conflict. *Journal of Personality and Social Psychology, 59,* 73–81.

Christensen, A., & Nies, D. C. (1980). The spouse observation checklist: Empirical analysis and critique. *American Journal of Family Therapy, 8,* 69–79.

Cobb, R. J., Davila, J., & Bradbury, T. N. (2001). Attachment security and marital satisfaction: The role of positive perceptions and social support. *Personality and Social Psychology Bulletin, 27,* 1131–1143.

Cohan, C. L., & Bradbury, T. N. (1997). Negative life events, marital interaction, and the longitudinal course of newlywed marriage. *Journal of Personality & Social Psychology, 73,* 114–128.

Cohen, O., Geron, Y., & Farchi, A. (2009). Marital quality and global well-being among older adult Israeli couples in enduring marriages. *American Journal of Family Therapy, 37,* 299–317.

Cohn, D. A., Silver, D. H., Cowan, C. P., Cowan, P. A., & Pearson, J. (1992). Working models of childhood attachment and couple relationships. In Intergenerational relationships [Special Issue]. *Journal of Family Issues, 13,* 432–449.

Collins, N. L. (1996). Working models of attachment: Implications for explanation, emotion, and behavior. *Journal of Personality and Social Psychology, 71,* 810–832.

Collins, N. L., & Feeney, B. C. (2000). A safe haven: An attachment theory perspective on support seeking and caregiving in intimate relationships. *Journal of Personality and Social Psychology, 78,* 1053–1073.

Collins, N. L., & Read, S. J. (1994). Cognitive representations of attachment: The structure and function of working models. In K. Bartholomew & D. Perlman (Eds.), *Advances in personal relationships: A research annual* (Vol. 5, pp. 53–90). London: Kingsley.

Conger, R. D., Cui, M., Bryant, C. M., & Elder, G. H., Jr. (2000). Competence in early adult romantic relationships: A developmental perspective on family influences. *Journal of Personality and Social Psychology, 79,* 224–237.

Cook, W. L. (2000). Understanding attachment security in family context. *Journal of Personality and Social Psychology, 78,* 285–294.

Coombs, R. H. (1991). Marital status and personal well-being: A literature review. *Family Relations, 40,* 97–102.

Cooper, M. L., & Sheldon, M. S. (2002). Seventy years of research on personality and close relationships: Substantive and methodological trends over time. *Journal of Personality, 70,* 783–812.

Cowan, C. P., & Cowan, P. A. (1992). *When partners become parents.* New York: Basic Books.

Crawford, M., & Popp, D. (2003). Sexual double standards: A review and methodological critique of two decades of research. *Journal of Sex Research, 40,* 13–26.

Creasey, G., & Jarvis, P. (2008). Attachment and marriage. In M. C. Smith & T. G. Reio (Eds.), *Handbook of research on adult development and learning* (pp. 269–304). Mahway, NJ: Erlbaum.

Crockett, L. J., Raffaelli, M., & Shen, Y.-L. (2006). Linking self-regulation and risk proneness to risky sexual behavior: Pathways through peer pressure and early substance use. *Journal of Research on Adolescence, 16,* 503–525.

Cross, S. E., & Madson, L. (1997). Models of the self: Self-construals and gender. *Psychological Bulletin, 122,* 5–37.

Crouter, A. C., & Booth, A. (2006). *Romance and sex in adolescence and emerging adulthood: Risks and opportunities.* Mahwah, NJ: Erlbaum.

Crowell, J. A., Fraley, R. C., & Shaver, P. R. (1999). Measurement of individual differences in adolescent and adult attachment. In J. Cassidy & P. R. Shaver (Eds.), *Handbook of attachment: Theory, research, and clinical applications* (pp. 434–465). New York: Guilford Press.

Crowell, J. A., Treboux, D., Gao, Y., Fyffe, C., Pan, H., & Waters, E. (2002). Assessing secure base behavior in adulthood: Development of a measure, links to adult attachment representations and relations to couples' communication and reports of relationships. *Developmental Psychology, 38,* 679–693.

Crowell, J. A., & Waters, E. (2005). Attachment representations, secure-based behavior, and the evolution of adult relationships. In K. E. Grossmann, K. Grossmann, & E. Waters (Eds.), *Attachment from infancy to adulthood: The major longitudinal studies* (pp. 223–244). New York: Guilford Press.

Curtis, T. J., & Wang, Z. (2003). The neurochemistry of pair bonding. *Current Directions in Psychological Science, 12,* 49–53.

Dainton, M., & Stafford, L. (1993). Routine maintenance behaviors: A comparison of relationship type, partner similarity, and sex differences. *Journal of Social and Personal Relationships, 10,* 255–272.

D'Augelli, A. R., Grossman, A. H., & Starks, M. T. (2005). Parents' awareness of lesbian, gay, and bisexual youths' sexual orientation. *Journal of Marriage & Family, 67,* 474–482.

Davies, P. T., & Windle, M. (2000). Middle adolescents' dating pathways and psychosocial adjustment. *Merrill-Palmer Quarterly, 46,* 90–118.

Davila, J., Burge, D., & Hammen, C. (1997). Why does attachment style change? *Journal of Personality and Social Psychology, 73,* 826–838.

Davila, J., Karney, B. R., & Bradbury, T. N. (1999). Attachment change processes in the early years of marriage. *Journal of Personality and Social Psychology, 76,* 783–802.

Davila, J., & Sargent, E. (2003). The meaning of life (events) predicts changes in attachment security. *Personality & Social Psychology Bulletin, 29,* 1383–1395.

Davila, J., Stroud, C. B., Miller, M. R., & Steinberg, S. J. (2007). Commentary: Defining and understanding adolescent romantic competence: Progress, challenges, and implications. *Journal of Clinical Child and Adolescent Psychology, 36,* 534–540.

Davis, L. E., & Strube, M. J. (1993). An assessment of romantic commitment among Black and White dating couples. *Journal of Applied Social Psychology, 23,* 212–225.

Deenen, A. A., Gijs, L., & van Naerssen, A. X. (1994). Intimacy and sexuality in gay male couples. *Archives of Sexual Behavior, 23,* 421–431.

Denton, W. H., Burleson, B. R., Hobbs, B. V., Von Stein, M., & Rodriguez, C. P. (2001). Cardiovascular reactivity and initiate/avoid patterns of marital communication: A test of Gottman's psychophysiologic model of marital interaction. *Journal of Behavioral Medicine, 24,* 401–421.

DeSteno, D., Bartlett, M. Y., Braverman, J., & Salovey, P. (2002). Sex differences in jealousy: Evolutionary mechanism or artifact of measurement? *Journal of Personality and Social Psychology, 83,* 1103–1116.

DeSteno, D., & Salovey, P. (1996). Evolutionary origins of sex differences in jealousy? Questioning the "fitness" of the model. *Psychological Science, 7,* 367–372.

DeSteno, D., Valdesolo, P., & Bartlett, M. Y. (2006). Jealousy and the threatened self: Getting to the heart of the green-eyed monster. *Journal of Personality and Social Psychology, 91,* 626–641.

Diamond, L. M. (2001). Contributions of psychophysiology to research on adult attachment: Review and recommendations. *Personality and Social Psychology Review, 5,* 276–295.

Diamond, L. M. (2003). What does sexual orientation orient? A biobehavioral model distinguishing romantic love and sexual desire. *Psychological Review, 110,* 173–192.

Diamond, L. M., & Hicks, A. M. (2004). Psychobiological perspectives on attachment: Implications for health over the lifespan. In J. A. Simpson & W. S. Rholes (Eds.), *Adult attachment: New directions and emerging issues* (pp. 240–263). New York: Guilford Press.

Diamond, L. M., & Hicks, A. M. (2005). Attachment style, current relationship security, and negative emotions: The mediating role of physiological regulation. *Journal of Social and Personal Relationships, 22,* 499–518.

Diamond, L. M., Hicks, A. M., & Otter-Henderson, K. A. (2006). Physiological evidence for repressive coping among avoidantly attached adults. *Journal of Social and Personal Relationships, 23,* 205–229.

Diamond, L. M., & Otter-Henderson, K. A. (2007). Physiological measures. In R. W. Robins, R. C. Fraley, & R. R. Krueger (Eds.), *Handbook of research methods in personality psychology* (pp. 370–388). New York: Guilford Press.

Doherty, N. A., & Feeney, J. A. (2004). The composition of attachment networks throughout the adult years. *Personal Relationships, 11,* 469–488.

Donnellan, M. B., Assad, K. K., Robins, R. W., & Conger, R. D. (2007). Do negative interactions mediate the effects of negative emotionality, communal positive emotionality, and constraint on relationship satisfaction? *Journal of Social and Personal Relationships, 24,* 557–573.

Donnellan, M. B., Conger, R. D., & Bryant, C. M. (2004). The Big Five and enduring marriages. *Journal of Research in Personality, 38,* 481–504.

Donnellan, M. B., Larsen-Rife, D., & Conger, R. D. (2005). Personality, family history, and competence and early adult romantic relationships. *Journal of Personality and Social Psychology, 88,* 562–576.

Dopp, J. M., Miller, G. E., Myers, H. F., & Fahey, J. L. (2000). Increased natural killer-cell mobilization and cytotoxicity during marital conflict. *Brain, Behavior, and Immunity, 14,* 10–26.

Downey, G., & Feldman, S. I. (1996). Implications of rejection sensitivity for intimate relationships. *Journal of Personality and Social Psychology, 70,* 1327–1343.

Downey, G., Freitas, A. L., Michaelis, B., & Khouri, H. (1998). The self-fulfilling prophecy in close relationships: Rejection sensitivity and rejection by romantic partners. *Journal of Personality and Social Psychology, 75,* 545–560.

Drigotas, S. M., & Rusbult, C. E. (1992). Should I stay or should I go? A dependence model of breakups. *Journal of Personality and Social Psychology, 62,* 62–87.

Drigotas, S. M., Rusbult, C. E., Wieselquist, J., & Whitton, S. W. (1999). Close partner as sculptor of the ideal self: Behavioral affirmation and the Michelangelo phenomenon. *Journal of Personality and Social Psychology, 77,* 293–323.

Drigotas, S. M., Safstrom, C. A., & Gentilia, T. (1999). An investment model prediction of dating infidelity. *Journal of Personality and Social Psychology, 77,* 509–524.

Driver, J. L., & Gottman, J. M. (2004). Daily marital interactions and positive affect during marital conflict among newlywed couples. *Family Process, 43,* 301–314.

Driver, J. L., Tabares, A., Shapiro, A. F., Nahm, E. Y., Gottman, J. M., & Walsh, F. (2003). Interactional patterns in marital success and failure: Gottman laboratory studies. In F. Walsh (Ed.), *Normal family processes: Growing diversity and complexity* (3rd ed., pp. 493–513). New York: Guilford Press.

Dush, C. M. K., Cohan, C. L., & Amato, P. R. (2003). The relationship between cohabitation and marital quality and stability: Change across cohorts? *Journal of Marriage and Family, 65,* 539–549.

Earle, T. L., Linden, W., & Weinberg, J. (1999). Differential effects of harassment on cardiovascular and salivary cortisol stress reactivity and recovery in women and men. *Journal of Psychosomatic Research, 46,* 125–141.

Eastwick, P. W., & Finkel, E. J. (2008a). The attachment system in fledgling relationships: An activating role for attachment anxiety. *Journal of Personality and Social Psychology, 95,* 628–647.

Eastwick, P. W., & Finkel, E. J. (2008b). Sex differences in mate preferences revisited: Do people know what they initially desire in a romantic partner? *Journal of Personality and Social Psychology, 94,* 245–264.

Eder, D., Evans, C., & Parker, S. (1995). *School talk: Gender and adolescent culture.* New Brunswick, NJ: Rutgers University Press.

Eisenberg, N., & Lennon, R. (1983). Sex differences in empathy and related capacities. *Psychological Bulletin, 94,* 100–131.

Eldridge, K. A., & Christensen, A. (2002). Demand–withdraw communication during couple conflict: A review and analysis. In P. Noller & J. A. Feeney (Eds.), *Understanding marriage: Developments in the study of couple interaction* (pp. 289–322). New York: Cambridge University Press.

Eldridge, K. A., Sevier, M., Jones, J., Atkins, D. C., & Christensen, A. (2007). Demand-withdraw communication in severely distressed, moderately distressed, and nondistressed couples: Rigidity and polarity during relationship and personal problem discussions. *Journal of Family Psychology, 21,* 218–226.

Ellis, W. L. (2008). Well-being of marital groups in later life: Are divorced elders disadvantaged? *Marriage & Family Review, 44,* 125–139.

Elze, D. E. (2002). Against all odds: The dating experiences of adolescent lesbian and bisexual women. *Journal of Lesbian Studies, 6,* 17–29.

Etcheverry, P. E., & Le, B. (2005). Thinking about commitment: Accessibility of commitment and prediction of relationship persistence, accommodation, and willingness to sacrifice. *Personal Relationships, 12,* 103–123.

Ewart, C. K. (1993). Marital interaction: The context for psychosomatic research. *Psychosomatic Medicine, 55,* 410–412.

Ewart, C. K., Taylor, C. B., Kraemer, H. C., & Agras, W. S. (1991). High blood pressure and marital discord: Not being nasty matters more than being nice. *Health Psychology, 10,* 155–163.

Feeney, J. A. (1994). Attachment style, communication patterns and satisfaction across the life cycle of marriage. *Personal Relationships, 1,* 333–348.

Feeney, J. A. (1995). Adult attachment and emotional control. *Personal Relationships, 2,* 143–159.

Feeney, J. A. (1999). Adult romantic attachment and couple relationships. In J. Cassidy & P. R. Shaver (Eds.), *Handbook of attachment: Theory, research, and clinical applications* (pp. 355–377). New York: Guilford Press.

Feeney, J. A., & Ryan, S. M. (1994). Attachment style and affect regulation: Relationships with health behavior and family experiences of illness in a student sample. *Health Psychology, 13,* 334–345.

Fergusson, D. M., Horwood, L. J., & Ridder, E. M. (2005). Partner violence and mental health outcomes in a New Zealand birth cohort. *Journal of Marriage and Family, 67,* 1103–1119.

Festinger, L. (1957). *A theory of cognitive dissonance.* Stanford, CA: Stanford University Press.

Fincham, F. D. (2004). Attributions in close relationships: From Balkanization to integration. In M. B. Brewer & M. Hewstone (Eds.), *Social cognition* (pp. 165–193). Malden, MA: Blackwell.

Fincham, F. D., & Beach, S. R. H. (2006). Relationship satisfaction. In A. L. Vangelisti & D. Perlman (Eds.), *The Cambridge handbook of personal relationships* (pp. 579–594). New York: Cambridge University Press.

Fincham, F. D., Beach, S. R. H., Harold, G. T., & Osborne, L. N. (1997). Marital satisfaction and depression: Different causal relationships for men and women? *Psychological Science, 8,* 351–357.

Fincham, F. D., & Bradbury, T. N. (1987a). The assessment of marital quality: A reevaluation. *Journal of Marriage & the Family, 49,* 797–809.

Fincham, F. D., & Bradbury, T. N. (1987b). The impact of attributions in marriage: A longitudinal analysis. *Journal of Personality and Social Psychology, 53,* 510–517.

Fincham, F. D., & Bradbury, T. N. (1988). The impact of attributions in marriage: An experimental analysis. *Journal of Social & Clinical Psychology, 7,* 147–162.

Fincham, F. D., & Bradbury, T. N. (1989). The impact of attributions in marriage: An individual difference analysis. *Journal of Social and Personal Relationships, 6,* 69–85.

Finchman, F. D., & Bradbury, T. N. (2004). Marital satisfaction, depression, and attributions: A longitudinal analysis. In R. M. Kowalski & M. R. Leary (Eds.), *The interface of social and clinical psychology: Key readings.* (pp. 129–146). New York: Psychology Press.

Fincham, F. D., Bradbury, T. N., Arias, I., Byrne, C. A., & Karney, B. R. (1997). Marital violence, marital distress, and attributions. *Journal of Family Psychology, 11,* 367–372.

Fincham, F. D., Harold, G. T., & Gano-Phillips, S. (2000). The longitudinal association between attributions and marital satisfaction: Direction of effects and role of efficacy expectations. *Journal of Family Psychology, 14,* 267–285.

Fincham, F. D., Stanley, S. M., & Beach, S. R. H. (2007). Transformative processes in marriage: An analysis of emerging trends. *Journal of Marriage and Family, 69,* 275–292.

Finkel, E. J. (2007). Impelling and inhibiting forces in the perpetration of intimate partner violence. *Review of General Psychology, 11,* 193–207.

Finkel, E. J. (2008). Intimate partner violence perpetration: Insights from the science of self-regulation. In J. P. Forgas & J. Fitness (Eds.), *Social relationships: Cognitive, affective, and motivational processes* (pp. 271–288). New York: Psychology Press.

Finkel, E. J., & Campbell, W. K. (2001). Self-control and accommodation in close relationships: An interdependence analysis. *Journal of Personality and Social Psychology, 81,* 263–277.

Finkel, E. J., Eastwick, P. W., & Matthews, J. (2007). Speed-dating as an invaluable tool for studying romantic attraction: A methodological primer. *Personal Relationships, 14,* 149–166.

Finkel, E. J., Rusbult, C. E., Kumashiro, M., & Hannon, P. A. (2002). Dealing with betrayal in close relationships: Does commitment promote forgiveness? *Journal of Personality and Social Psychology, 82,* 956–974.

Fisher, H. E. (1998). Lust, attraction, and attachment in mammalian reproduction. *Human Nature, 9,* 23–52.

Fitzpatrick, M. A., Fey, J., Segrin, C., & Schiff, J. L. (1993). Internal working models of relationships and marital communication. *Journal of Language and Social Psychology, 12,* 103–131.

Flett, G. L., & Hewett, P. L. (2002). Personality factors and substance abuse in relationship violence and child abuse: A review and theoretical analysis. In C. Wekerle & A. M. Wall (Eds.), *The violence and addiction equation: Theoretical and clinical issues in substance abuse and relationship violence* (pp. 64–97). New York: Brunner Routledge.

Florsheim, P. (Ed.). (2003). *Adolescent romantic relations and sexual behavior: Theory, research, and practical implications.* Mahweh, NJ: Erlbaum.

Fogel, A. (2006). Dynamic systems research on interindividual communication: The transformation of meaning-making. *Journal of Developmental Processes, 1,* 7–30.

Fogel, A., & Thelen, E. (1987). Development of early expressive and communicative action: Reinterpreting the evidence from a dynamic systems perspective. *Developmental Psychology, 23,* 747–761.

Foshee, V. A., Benefield, T., Ennett, S. T., Bauman, K. E., & Suchindran, C. (2004). Longitudinal predictors of serious physical and sexual dating violence victimization during adolescence. *Preventive Medicine, 19,* 220–227.

Fraley, R. C. (2007). A connectionist approach to the organization and continuity of working models of attachment. *Journal of Personality, 75,* 1157–1180.

Fraley, R. C., & Brumbaugh, C. C. (2004). A dynamical systems approach to conceptualizing and studying stability and change in attachment security. In J. A. Simpson & W. S. Rholes (Eds.), *Adult attachment: New directions and emerging issues* (pp. 86–132). New York: Guilford Press.

Fraley, R. C., Waller, N. G., & Brennan, K. A. (2000). An item response theory analysis of self-report measures of adult attachment. *Journal of Personality and Social Psychology, 78,* 350–365.

Furman, W., Feiring, C., & Brown, B. B. (Eds.). (1999). *Contemporary perspectives on adolescent romantic relationships.* New York: Cambridge University Press.

Furstenberg, F. F., Kennedy, S., Mcloyd, V., Rumbaut R. G., & Settersten, R. J. (2004). Growing up is harder to do. *Caliber, Journal of the University of California Press, 3,* 33–41.

Gable, S. L., Gonzaga, G. C., & Strachman, A. (2006). Will you be there for me when things go right? Supportive responses to positive event disclosures. *Journal of Personality and Social Psychology, 91,* 904–917.

Gable, S. L., Reis, H. T., & Downey, G. (2003). He said, she said: A quasi-signal detection analysis of daily interactions between close relationship partners. *Psychological Science, 14,* 100–105.

Gaertner, L., & Foshee, V. (1999). Commitment and the perpetration of relationship violence. *Personal Relationships, 6,* 227–239.

Gaines, S. O., Jr., Reis, H. T., Summers, S., Rusbult, C. E., Cox, C. L., Wexler, M. O., et al. (1997). Impact of attachment style on reactions to accommodative dilemmas in close relationships. *Personal Relationships, 4,* 93–113.

Gangestad, S. W., & Thornhill, R. (2003). Facial masculinity and fluctuating asymmetry. *Evolution and Human Behavior, 24,* 231–241.

Gelles, R. J., & Loseke, D. R. (Eds.). (1993). *Current controversies on family violence.* Thousand Oaks, CA: Sage.

Gilford, R., & Bengtson, V. (1979). Measuring marital satisfaction in three generations: Positive and negative dimensions. *Journal of Marriage & the Family, 41,* 387–398.

Gill, D. S., Christensen, A., & Fincham, F. D. (1999). Predicting marital satisfaction from behavior: Do all roads really lead to Rome? *Personal Relationships, 6,* 369–387.

Gilligan, C. (1982). *In a different voice: Psychological theory and women's development.* Cambridge, MA: Harvard University Press.

Gilligan, C. (1990). Remapping the moral domain: New images of the self in relationship. In C. Zanardi (Ed.), *Essential papers on the psychology of women* (pp. 480–495). New York: New York University Press.

Gillis, J. R. (1998). Cultural heterosexism and the family. In C. Patterson & A. R. D'Augelli (Eds.), *Lesbian, gay, and bisexual identities in families: Psychological Perspectives* (pp. 249–269). New York: Oxford University Press.

Giordano, P. C., Longmore, M. A., & Manning, W. D. (2006). Gender and the meanings of adolescent romantic relationships: A focus on boys. *American Sociological Review, 71,* 260–287.

Gleason, M. E. J., Iida, M., Shrout, P. E., & Bolger, N. (2008). Receiving support as a mixed blessing: Evidence for dual effects of support on psychological outcomes. *Journal of Personality and Social Psychology, 94,* 824–838.

Glenn, N. D. (1990). Quantitative research on marital quality in the 1980s: A critical review. *Journal of Marriage and the Family, 52,* 818–831.

Gottlieb, G. (1992). *Individual development and evolution: The genesis of novel behavior.* New York: Oxford University Press.

Gottman, J. M. (1990). How marriages change. In G. R. Patterson (Ed.), *Depression and aggression in family interaction* (pp. 75–102). Hillsdale, NJ: Erlbaum.

Gottman, J. M. (1991). Predicting the longitudinal course of marriages. *Journal of Marital and Family Therapy, 17,* 3–7.

Gottman, J. M. (1993). The roles of conflict engagement, escalation, and avoidance in marital interaction: A longitudinal view of 5 types of couples. *Journal of Consulting and Clinical Psychology, 61,* 6–15.

Gottman, J. M. (1994). *What predicts divorce?* Hillsdale, NJ: Erlbaum.

Gottman, J. M. (1998). Psychology and the study of marital processes. *Annual Review of Psychology, 49,* 169–197.

Gottman, J. M. (2002). A multidimensional approach to couples. In F. W. Kaslow & T. Patterson (Eds.), *Comprehensive handbook of psychotherapy: Cognitive–behavioral approaches* (Vol. 2, pp. 355–372). Hoboken, NJ: John Wiley & Sons.

Gottman, J. M., Coan, J., Carrère, S., & Swanson, C. (1998). Predicting marital happiness and stability from newlywed interactions. *Journal of Marriage & the Family, 60,* 5–22.

Gottman, J. M., & Levenson, R. W. (1992). Marital processes predictive of later dissolution: Behavior, physiology, and health. *Journal of Personality and Social Psychology, 63,* 221–233.

Gottman, J. M., & Levenson, R. W. (2000). The timing of divorce: Predicting when a couple will divorce over a 14-year period. *Journal of Marriage & the Family, 62,* 737–745.

Gottman, J. M., & Levenson, R. W. (2002). A two-factor model for predicting when a couple will divorce: Exploratory analyses using 14-year longitudinal data. *Family Process, 41,* 83–96.

Gottman, J. M., Murray, J. D., Swanson, C. C., Tyson, R., & Swanson, K. R. (2002). *The mathematics of marriage: Dynamic nonlinear models.*: MIT Press.

Gottman, J. M., & Notarius, C. I. (2000). Decade review: Observing marital interaction. *Journal of Marriage & the Family, 62,* 927–947.

Gottman, J. M., & Notarius, C. I. (2002). Marital research in the 20th century and a research agenda for the 21st century. *Family Process, 41,* 159–197.

Gottman, J. M., Swanson, C., & Swanson, K. (2002). A general systems theory of marriage: Nonlinear difference equation modeling of marital interaction. *Personality & Social Psychology Review, 6,* 326–340.

Gould, S. J., & Vrba, E. S. (1982). Exaptation: A missing term in the science of form. *Paleobiology, 8,* 4–15.

Graziano, W. G., & Eisenberg, N. (1997). Agreeableness: A dimension of personality. In R. Hogan, J. A. Johnson, & S. R. Briggs (Eds.), *Handbook of personality psychology* (pp. 795–824). San Diego, CA: Academic Press.

Grello, C. M., Welsh, D. P., & Harper, M. S. (2006). No strings attached: The nature of casual sex in college students. *Journal of Sex Research, 43,* 255–267.

Grossmann, K., Grossmann, K. E., & Kindler, H. (2005). Early care and the roots of attachment and partnership representations. In K. E. Grossmann, K. Grossmann, & E. Waters (Eds.), *Attachment from infancy to adulthood: The major longitudinal studies* (pp. 98–136). New York: Guilford Press.

Guerrero, L. K. (1998). Attachment-style differences in the experience and expression of romantic jealousy. *Personal Relationships, 5,* 273–291.

Hall, R. L., & Greene, B. (2002). Not any one thing: The complex legacy of social class on African American lesbian relationships. *Journal of Lesbian Studies, 6,* 65–74.

Halpern, C. T., Waller, M. W., Spriggs, A., & Hallfors, D. D. (2006). Adolescent predictors of emerging adult sexual patterns. *Journal of Adolescent Health, 39,* e1–e10.

Hamilton, C. E. (2000). Continuity and discontinuity of attachment from infancy through adolescence. *Child Development, 71,* 690–694.

Harkless, L. E., & Fowers, B. J. (2005). Similarities and differences in relational boundaries among heterosexuals, gay men, and lesbians. *Psychology of Women Quarterly, 29,* 167–176.

Harper, J. M., & Sandberg, J. G. (2009). Depression and communication processes in later life marriages. *Aging & Mental Health, 13,* 546–556.

Harris, C. R. (2000). Psychophysiological responses to imagined infidelity: The specific innate modular view of jealousy reconsidered. *Journal of Personality and Social Psychology, 78,* 1082–1091.

Harris, C. R. (2003). A review of sex differences in sexual jealousy, including self-report data, psychophysiological responses, interpersonal violence, and morbid jealousy. *Personality and Social Psychology Review, 7,* 102–128.

Harris, C. R., & Christenfeld, N. (1996). Gender, jealousy, and reason. *Psychological Science, 7,* 364–366.

Hatfield, E. (1987). Passionate and companionate love. In R. J. Sternberg & M. L. Barnes (Eds.), *The psychology of love* (pp. 191–217). New Haven, CT: Yale University Press.

Hatfield, E. (2001). Elaine Hatfield. In A. N. O'Connell (Ed.), *Models of achievement: Reflections of eminent women in psychology* (Vol. 3, pp. 136–147). New York: Columbia University Press.

Hatfield, E., Schmitz, E., Cornelius, J., & Rapson, R. L. (1988). Passionate love: How early does it begin? *Journal of Psychology and Human Sexuality, 1,* 35–52.

Hawkins, M. W., Carrère, S., & Gottman, J. M. (2002). Marital sentiment override: Does it influence couples' perceptions? *Journal of Marriage and Family, 64,* 193–201.

Hazan, C., & Shaver, P. R. (1987). Romantic love conceptualized as an attachment process. *Journal of Personality and Social Psychology, 52,* 511–524.

Hazan, C., & Zeifman, D. (1994). Sex and the psychological tether. In D. Perlman & K. Bartholomew (Eds.), *Advances in personal relationships: A research annual* (Vol. 5, pp. 151–177). London: Kingsley.

Hazan, C., & Zeifman, D. (1999). Pair-bonds as attachments: Evaluating the evidence. In J. Cassidy & P. R. Shaver (Eds.), *Handbook of attachment theory and research* (pp. 336–354). New York: Guilford Press.

Heaton, T. B. (2002). Factors contributing to increasing marital stability in the US. *Journal of Family Issues, 23,* 392–409.

Heffner, K. L., Kiecolt-Glaser, J. K., Loving, T. J., Glaser, R., & Malarkey, W. B. (2004). Spousal support satisfaction as a modifier of physiological responses to marital conflict in younger and older couples. *Journal of Behavioral Medicine, 27,* 233–254.

Heffner, K. L., Loving, T. J., Kiecolt-Glaser, J. K., Himawan, L. K., Glaser, R., & Malarkey, W. B. (2006). Older spouses' cortisol responses to marital conflict: Associations with demand/withdraw communication patterns. *Journal of Behavioral Medicine, 29,* 317–325.

Heider, F. (1958). *The psychology of interpersonal relations.* New York: John Wiley & Sons.

Hellmuth, J. C., & McNulty, J. K. (2008). Neuroticism, marital violence, and the moderating role of stress and behavioral skills. *Journal of Personality and Social Psychology, 95,* 166–180.

Henry, R. G., Miller, R. B., & Giarrusso, R. (2005). Difficulties, disagreements, and disappointments in late-life marriages. *International Journal of Aging & Human Development, 61,* 243–264.

Herdt, G., & Beeler, J. (1998). Older gay men and lesbians in families. In C. Patterson & A. R. D'Augelli (Eds.), *Lesbian, gay, and bisexual identities in families: Psychological Perspectives* (pp. 177–196). New York: Oxford University Press.

Herek, G. M. (2006). Legal recognition of same-sex relationships in the United States: A social science perspective. *American Psychologist, 61,* 607–621.

Hettrich, E. L., & O'Leary, K. D. (2007). Females' reasons for their physical aggression in dating relationships. *Journal of Interpersonal Violence, 22,* 1131–1143.

Heyman, R. E., Weiss, R. L., & Eddy, J. M. (1995). Marital Interaction Coding System: Revision and empirical evaluation. *Behaviour Research and Therapy, 33,* 737–746.

Hickson, F. C. I., Davies, P. M., Hunt, A. J., Weatherburn, P., McManus, T. J., & Coxon, A. P. M. (1992). Maintenance of open gay relationships: Strategies for protection against HIV. *AIDS Care, 4,* 409–419.

Hill, S. A. (2007). Transformative processes: Some sociological questions. *Journal of Marriage and Family, 69,* 293–298.

Hochschild, A., & Machung, A. (2003). *The second shift.* New York: Penguin.

Hope, S., Rodgers, B., & Power, C. (1999). Marital status transitions and psychological distress: Longitudinal evidence from a national population sample. *Psychological Medicine, 29,* 381–389.

Horwitz, A. V., McLaughlin, J., & White, H. R. (1998). How the negative and positive aspects of partner relationships affect the mental health of young married people. *Journal of Health and Social Behavior, 39,* 124–136.

Hughes, F. M., Stuart, G. L., Gordon, K. C., & Moore, T. M. (2007). Predicting the use of aggressive conflict tactics in a sample of women arrested for domestic violence. *Journal of Social and Personal Relationships, 24,* 155–176.

Hughes, M., Morrison, K., & Asada, K. J. K. (2005). What's love got to do with it? Exploring the impact of maintenance roles, love attitudes, and network support on friends with benefits relationships. *Western Journal of Communication, 69,* 49–66.

Huston, M., & Schwartz, P. (2002). Gendered dynamics in the romantic relationships of lesbians and gay men. In A. E. Hunter (Ed.), *Readings in the psychology of gender: Exploring our differences and commonalities* (pp. 167–178). Needham Heights, MA: Allyn & Bacon.

Huston, T. L. (2000). The social ecology of marriage and other intimate unions. *Journal of Marriage & the Family, 62,* 298–319.

Huston, T. L., & Chorost, A. F. (1994). Behavioral buffers on the effect of negativity on marital satisfaction: A longitudinal study. *Personal Relationships, 1,* 223–239.

Ickes, W., Simpson, J. A., & Ickes, W. J. (1997). Managing empathic accuracy in close relationships. In H. T. Reis & C. E. Rusbult (Eds.), *Empathic accuracy* (pp. 218–250). New York: Guilford Press.

Impett, E. A., Schooler, D., & Tolman, D. L. (2006). To be seen and not heard: Femininity ideology and adolescent girls' sexual health. *Archives of Sexual Behavior, 35,* 131–144.

Jacobvitz, D., Curran, M., & Moller, N. (2002). Measurement of adult attachment: The place of self-report and interview methodologies. *Attachment & Human Development, 4,* 207–215.

Jasinski, J. L., & Williams, L. M. (Eds.). (1998). *Partner violence: A comprehensive review of 20 years of research.* Thousand Oaks, CA: Sage.

Jensen-Campbell, L. A., Knack, J. M., Waldrip, A. M., & Campbell, S. D. (2007). Do Big Five personality traits associated with self-control influence the regulation of anger and aggression? *Journal of Research in Personality, 41,* 403–424.

Jocklin, V., McGue, M., & Lykken, D. T. (1996). Personality and divorce: A genetic analysis. *Journal of Personality and Social Psychology, 71,* 288–299.

Johnson, D. R., & Booth, A. (1998). Marital quality: A product of the dyadic environment or individual factors? *Social Forces, 76,* 883–904.

Johnson, D. R., & Wu, J. (2002). An empirical test of crisis, social selection, and role explanations of the relationship between marital disruption and psychological distress: A pooled time-series analysis of four-wave panel data. *Journal of Marriage and Family, 64,* 211–224.

Johnson, M. D., Karney, B. R., Rogge, R., & Bradbury, T. N. (2001). The role of marital behavior in the longitudinal association between attributions and marital quality. In V. Manusov & J. H. Harvey (Eds.), *Attribution, communication behavior, and close relationships* (pp. 173–192). New York: Cambridge University Press.

Johnson, M. P. (1973). Commitment: A conceptual structure and empirical application. *Sociological Quarterly, 14,* 395–406.

Johnson, M. P. (1999). Personal, moral, and structural commitment to relationships: Experiences of choice and constraint. In J. M. Adams & W. H. Jones (Eds.), *Handbook of interpersonal commitment and relationship stability* (pp. 73–87). Dordrecht, the Netherlands: Kluwer Academic.

Johnson, M. P. (2006). Violence and abuse in personal relationships: Conflict, terror, and resistance in intimate partnerships. In A. L. Vangelisti & D. Perlman (Eds.), *The Cambridge handbook of personal relationships* (pp. 557–576). New York: Cambridge University Press.

Johnson, M. P., & Ferraro, K. J. (2000). Research on domestic violence in the 1990s: Making distinctions. *Journal of Marriage & the Family, 62,* 948–963.

Jones, D. A. (1996). Discrimination against same-sex couples in hotel reservation policies. *Journal of Homosexuality, 31,* 153–159.

Kagan, J. (1980). Four questions in psychological development. *International Journal of Behavioral Development, 3,* 231–241.

Kaiser Foundation. (2001). *Inside-out: Report on the experiences of lesbians, gays and bisexuals in America and the public's view on issues and policies related to sexual orientation.* Menlo Park, CA: Author.

Karney, B. R., & Bradbury, T. N. (1995). The longitudinal course of marital quality and stability: A review of theory, methods, and research. *Psychological Bulletin, 118,* 3–34.

Karney, B. R., & Bradbury, T. N. (1997). Neuroticism, marital interaction, and the trajectory of marital satisfaction. *Journal of Personality and Social Psychology, 72,* 1075–1092.

Karney, B. R., & Bradbury, T. N. (2000). Attributions in marriage: State or trait? A growth curve analysis. *Journal of Personality and Social Psychology, 78,* 295–309.

Katz, J., Kuffel, S. W., & Coblentz, A. (2002). Are there gender differences in sustaining dating violence?: An examination of frequency, severity, and relationship satisfaction. *Journal of Family Violence, 17,* 247–271.

Kelly, E. L., & Conley, J. J. (1987). Personality and compatibility: A prospective analysis of marital stability and marital satisfaction. *Journal of Personality and Social Psychology, 52,* 27–40.

Kelso, J. A. S. (1997). *Dynamic patterns: The self-organization of brain and behavior.* The MIT Press.

Kendler, K. S., Karkowski, L. M., & Prescott, C. A. (1999). Causal relationship between stressful life events and the onset of major depression. *American Journal of Psychiatry, 156,* 837–848.

Kenrick, D. T., Keefe, R. C., Bryan, A., & Barr, A. (1995). Age preferences and mate choice among homosexuals and heterosexuals: A case for modular psychological mechanisms. *Journal of Personality and Social Psychology, 69,* 1166–1172.

Kiecolt-Glaser, J. K., Bane, C., Glaser, R., & Malarkey, W. B. (2003). Love, marriage, and divorce: Newlyweds' stress hormones foreshadow relationship changes. *Journal of Consulting and Clinical Psychology, 71,* 176–188.

Kiecolt-Glaser, J. K., Glaser, R., Cacioppo, J. T., MacCallum, R. C., Snydersmith, M., Kim, C., et al. (1997). Marital conflict in older adults: Endocrinological and immunological correlates. *Psychosomatic Medicine, 59,* 339–349.

Kiecolt-Glaser, J. K., McGuire, L., Robles, T. F., & Glaser, R. (2002). Emotions, morbidity, and mortality: New perspectives from psychoneuroimmunology. *Annual Review of Psychology, 53,* 83–107.

Kiecolt-Glaser, J. K., & Newton, T. L. (2001). Marriage and health: His and hers. *Psychological Bulletin, 127,* 472–503.

Kiecolt-Glaser, J. K., Newton, T., Cacioppo, J. T., & MacCallum, R. C. (1996). Marital conflict and endocrine function: Are men really more physiologically affected than women? *Journal of Consulting and Clinical Psychology, 64,* 324–332.

Kirchler, E., Rodler, C., Hölzl, E., & Meier, K. (2001). *Conflict and decision-making in close relationships: Love, money, and daily routines.* New York: Psychology Press.

Kirkwood, C. (1993). *Leaving abusive partners: From the scars of survival to the wisdom for change.* Thousand Oaks, CA: Sage.

Kirschbaum, C., Wust, S., & Hellhammer, D. (1992). Consistent sex differences in cortisol responses to psychological stress. *Psychosomatic Medicine, 54,* 648–657.

Kitson, G. C. (2006). Divorce and relationship dissolution research: Then and now. In M. A. Fine & J. H. Harvey (Eds.), *Handbook of divorce and relationship dissolution* (pp. 15–40). Mahwah, NJ: Erlbaum.

Kline, G. H., Pleasant, N. D., Whitton, S. W., & Markman, H. J. (2006). Understanding couple conflict. In A. L. Vangelisti & D. Perlman (Eds.), *The Cambridge handbook of personal relationships* (pp. 445–462). New York: Cambridge University Press.

Kline, G. H., Stanley, S. M., Markman, H. J., Olmos-Gallo, P. A., St. Peters, M., Whitton, S. W., et al. (2004). Timing is everything: Pre-engagement cohabitation and increased risk for poor marital outcomes. *Journal of Family Psychology, 18,* 311–318.

Klinetob, N. A., & Smith, D. A. (1996). Demand–withdraw communication in marital interaction: Tests of interpersonal contingency and gender role hypotheses. *Journal of Marriage & the Family, 58,* 945–957.

Klohnen, E. C., & Bera, S. (1998). Behavioral and experiential patterns of avoidantly and securely attached women across adulthood: A 31-year longitudinal perspective. *Journal of Personality & Social Psychology, 74,* 211–223.

Klohnen, E. C., Weller, J. A., Luo, S., & Choe, M. (2005). Organization and predictive power of general and relationship-specific attachment models: One for all, and all for one? *Personality and Social Psychology Bulletin, 31,* 1665–1682.

Knobloch, L. K., Solomon, D. H., & Cruz, M. G. (2001). The role of relationship development and attachment in the experience of romantic jealousy. *Personal Relationships, 8,* 205–224.

Kurdek, L. A. (1992). Relationship stability and relationship satisfaction in cohabiting gay and lesbian couples: A prospective longitudinal test of the contextual and interdependence models. *Journal of Social and Personal Relationships, 9,* 125–142.

Kurdek, L. A. (1993a). The allocation of household labor in gay, lesbian, and heterosexual married couples. *Journal of Social Issues, 49,* 127–139.

Kurdek, L. A. (1993b). Predicting marital dissolution: A 5-year prospective longitudinal study of newlywed couples. *Journal of Personality and Social Psychology, 64,* 221–242.

Kurdek, L. A. (1995). Developmental changes in relationship quality in gay and lesbian cohabiting couples. *Developmental Psychology, 31,* 86–94.

Kurdek, L. A. (1998a). The nature and predictors of the trajectory of change in marital quality over the first 4 years of marriage for first-married husbands and wives. *Journal of Family Psychology, 12,* 494–510.

Kurdek, L. A. (1998b). Relationship outcomes and their predictors: Longitudinal evidence from heterosexual married, gay cohabiting, and lesbian cohabiting couples. *Journal of Marriage and the Family, 60,* 553–568.

Kurdek, L. A. (2000). Attractions and constraints as determinants of relationship commitment: Longitudinal evidence from gay, lesbain, and heterosexual couples. *Personal Relationships, 7,* 245–262.

Kurdek, L. A. (2003). Methodological issues in growth-curve analyses with married couples. *Personal Relationships, 10,* 235–266.

Kurdek, L. A. (2004). Are gay and lesbian cohabiting couples really different from heterosexual married couples? *Journal of Marriage & Family, 66,* 880–900.

Kurdek, L. A., & Schmitt, J. P. (1987). Partner homogamy in married, heterosexual cohabiting, gay, and lesbian couples. *Journal of Sex Research, 23,* 212–232.

Kurdek, L. A., & Schnopp-Wyatt, D. (1997). Predicting relationship commitment and relationship stability from both partners' relationship values: Evidence from heterosexual dating couples. *Personality and Social Psychology Bulletin, 23,* 1111–1119.

Labriola, K. (1999). Models of open relationships. *Journal of Lesbian Studies, 3,* 217–225.

La Guardia, J. G., Ryan, R. M., Couchman, C. E., & Deci, E. L. (2000). Within-person variation in security of attachment: A self-determination theory perspective on attachment, need fulfillment, and well-being. *Journal of Personality and Social Psychology, 79,* 367–384.

Lakey, B., McCabe, K. M., Fisicaro, S. A., & Drew, J. B. (1996). Environmental and personal determinants of support perceptions: Three generalizability studies. *Journal of Personality and Social Psychology, 70,* 1270–1280.

Lamberg, L. (2000). Domestic violence: what to ask, what to do. *The Journal of the American Medical Association, 284,* 554–556.

Larson, R. W., & Almeida, D. M. (1999). Emotional transmission in the daily lives of families: A new paradigm for studying family process. *Journal of Marriage & the Family, 61,* 5–20.

LaSala, M. C. (2000). Gay male couples: The importance of coming out and being out to parents. *Journal of Homosexuality, 39,* 47–71.

Laumann, E. O., Gagnon, J. H., Michael, R. T., & Michaels, F. (1994). *The social organization of sexuality: Sexual practices in the United States*. Chicago: University of Chicago Press.

Laurenceau, J.-P., & Bolger, N. (2005). Using diary methods to study marital and family processes. *Journal of Family Psychology, 19,* 86–97.

Le, B., & Agnew, C. R. (2003). Commitment and its theorized determinants: A meta-analysis of the investment model. *Personal Relationships, 10,* 37–57.

Leary, M. R., Cottrell, C. A., & Phillips, M. (2001). Deconfounding the effects of dominance and social acceptance on self-esteem. *Journal of Personality and Social Psychology, 81,* 898–909.

Leary, M. R., Haupt, A. L., Strausser, K. S., & Chokel, J. T. (1998). Calibrating the sociometer: The relationship between interpersonal appraisals and the state self-esteem. *Journal of Personality and Social Psychology, 74,* 1290–1299.

Levinger, G. (1965). Marital cohesiveness and dissolution: An integrative review. *Journal of Marriage & the Family, 27,* 19–28.

Levinger, G. (1966). Sources of marital dissatisfaction among applicants for divorce. *American Journal of Orthopsychiatry, 36,* 803–807.

Levinson, D., Darrow, C., Klein, E., Levinson, M., & McKee, B. (1978). *The seasons of a man's life*. New York: Knopf.

Lewis, M., Feiring, C., & Rosenthal, S. (2000). Attachment over time. *Child Development, 71,* 707–720.

Lie, G.-Y., Schilit, R., Bush, J., Montagne, M., & Reyes, L. (1991). Lesbians in currently aggressive relationships: How frequently do they report aggressive past relationships? *Violence and Victims, 6,* 121–135.

Lillard, L. A., Brian, M. J., & Waite, L. J. (1995). Premarital cohabitation and subsequent marital dissolution: A matter of self-selection? *Demography, 32,* 437–457.

Loftus, J. (2001). America's liberalization in attitudes toward homosexuality. *American Sociological Review, 66,* 762–782.

Lopez, F. G., & Gormley, B. (2002). Stability and change in adult attachment style over the first-year college transition: Relations to self-confidence, coping, and distress patterns. *Journal of Counseling Psychology, 49,* 355–364.

Loving, T. J., Heffner, K. L., & Kiecolt-Glaser, J. K. (2006). Physiology and interpersonal relationships. In A. L. Vangelisti & D. Perlman (Eds.), *The Cambridge handbook of personal relationships* (pp. 385–405). New York: Cambridge University Press.

Lucas, R. E. (2005). Time does not heal all wounds: A longitudinal study of reaction and adaptation to divorce. *Psychological Science, 16,* 145–950.

Lupien, S. J., Ouellet-Morin, I., Hupbach, A., Tu, M. T., Buss, C., Walker, D., et al. (2006). Beyond the stress concept: Allostatic load—a developmental biological and cognitive perspective. In D. Cicchetti & D. J. Cohen (Eds.), *Developmental psychopathology: Vol. 2. Developmental neuroscience* (2nd ed., pp. 578–628). Hoboken, NJ: John Wiley & Sons.

Magai, C., & Cohen, C. I. (1998). Attachment style and emotion regulation in dementia patients and their relation to caregiver burden. *Journals of Gerontology. Series B, Psychological Sciences and Social Sciences, 53,* P147–P154.

Magai, C., Hunziker, J., Mesias, W., & Culver, L. C. (2000). Adult attachment styles and emotional biases. *International Journal of Behavioral Development, 24,* 301–309.

Main, M., Kaplan, N., & Cassidy, J. (1985). Security in infancy, childhood, and adulthood: A move to the level of representation. *Monographs of the Society for Research in Child Development, 50,* 66–104.

Manlove, J. S., Terry-Humen, E., Papillo, A. R., Franzetta, K., Williams, S., & Ryan, S. (2001). *Background for community-level work on positive reproductive health in adolescence: Reviewing the literature on contributing factors*. Washington, DC: Child Trends.

Manning, W. D., Longmore, M. A., & Giordano, P. C. (2000). The relationship context of contraceptive use at first intercourse. *Family Planning Perspectives, 32,* 104–110.

Manzoli, L., Villari, P., Pirone, G. M., & Boccia, A. (2007). Marital status and mortality in the elderly: A systematic review and meta-analysis. *Social Science & Medicine, 64,* 77–94.

Marin, T. J., Martin, T. M., Blackwell, E., Stetler, C., & Miller, G. E. (2007). Differentiating the impact of episodic and chronic stressors on hypothalamic-pituitary-adrenocortical axis regulation in young women. *Health Psychology, 26,* 447–455.

Markman, H. J., & Notarius, C. I. (1987). Coding marital and family interaction: Current status. In T. Jacob (Ed.), *Family interaction and psychopathology: Theories, methods, and findings* (pp. 329–390). New York: Plenum Press.

Martin, P. D., Martin, D., & Martin, M. (2001). Adolescent premarital sexual activity, cohabitation, and attitudes toward marriage. *Adolescence, 36,* 601–609.

Mastekaasa, A. (1994). Marital-status, distress, and well-being: An international comparison. *Journal of Comparative Family Studies, 25,* 183–205.

Mastekaasa, A. (1995). Marital dissolution and subjective distress: Panel evidence. *European Sociological Review, 11,* 173–185.

Matjasko, J. L., & Feldman, A. F. (2006). Bringing work home: The emotional experiences of mothers and fathers. *Journal of Family Psychology, 20,* 47–55.

Matthews, L. S., Wickrama, K. A. S., & Conger, R. D. (1996). Predicting marital instability from spouse and observer reports of marital interaction. *Journal of Marriage & the Family, 58,* 641–655.

Mayne, T. J., O'Leary, A., McCrady, B., & Contrada, R. (1997). The differential effects of acute marital distress on emotional, physiological and immune functions in maritally distressed men and women. *Psychology & Health, 12,* 277–288.

McClennen, J. C., Summers, A. B., & Vaughan, C. (2002). Gay men's domestic violence: Dynamics, help-seeking behaviors, and correlates. *Journal of Gay and Lesbian Social Services: Issues in Practice, Policy and Research, 14,* 23–49.

McDonald, D. L., & McKinney, J. P. (1994). Steady dating and self-esteem in high school students. *Journal of Adolescence, 17,* 557–564.

McGinnis, S. L. (2003). Cohabitating, dating, and perceived costs of marriage: A model of marriage entry. *Journal of Marriage and Family, 65,* 105–116.

McGue, M., & Lykken, D. T. (1992). Genetic influence on risk of divorce. *Psychological Science, 3,* 368–373.

Mellen, S. L. W. (1982). *The evolution of love*. San Francisco: Freeman.

Meyer, I. H. (2003). Prejudice, social stress, and mental health in lesbian, gay, and bisexual populations: Conceptual issues and research evidence. *Psychological Bulletin, 129,* 674–697.

Meyers, S. A., & Landsberger, S. A. (2002). Direct and indirect pathways between adult attachment style and marital satisfaction. *Personal Relationships, 9,* 159–172.

Mikulincer, M. (1998a). Adult attachment style and individual differences in functional versus dysfunctional experiences of anger. *Journal of Personality and Social Psychology, 74,* 513–524.

Mikulincer, M. (1998b). Attachment working models and the sense of trust: An exploration of interaction goals and affect regulation. *Journal of Personality and Social Psychology, 74,* 1209–1224.

Mikulincer, M., & Florian, V. (1998). The relationship between adult attachment styles and emotional and cognitive reactions to stressful events. In J. A. Simpson & W. S. Rholes (Eds.), *Attachment theory and close relationships* (pp. 143–165). New York: Guilford Press.

Mikulincer, M., Florian, V., & Weller, A. (1993). Attachment styles, coping strategies, and posttraumatic psychological distress: The impact of the Gulf War in Israel. *Journal of Personality and Social Psychology, 64,* 817–826.

Mikulincer, M., Horesh, N., Levy Shiff, R., Manovich, R., & Shalev, J. (1998). The contribution of adult attachment style to the adjustment to infertility. *The British Journal of Medical Psychology, 71,* 265–280.

Mikulincer, M., & Orbach, I. (1995). Attachment styles and repressive defensiveness: The accessibility and architecture of affective memories. *Journal of Personality and Social Psychology, 68,* 917–925.

Miller, B. C., Norton, M. C., Curtis, T., Hill, E. J., Schvaneveldt, P., & Young, M. H. (1997). The timing of sexual intercourse among adolescents—family, peer and other antecedents. *Youth & Society, 29,* 54–83.

Miller, D. H., Greene, K., Causby, V., White, B. W., & Lockhart, L. L. (2001). Domestic violence in lesbian relationships. *Women and Therapy, 23,* 107–127.

Miller, G. E., Chen, E., & Zhou, E. S. (2007). If it goes up, must it come down? Chronic stress and the hypothalamic-pituitary-adrenocortical axis in humans. *Psychological Bulletin, 133,* 25–45.

Miller, P. J. E., Niehuis, S., & Huston, T. L. (2006). Positive illusions in marital relationships: A 13-year longitudinal study. *Personality and Social Psychology Bulletin, 32,* 1579–1594.

Mitchell, V. (2007). Earning a secure attachment style: A narrative of personality change in adulthood. In R. Josselson, A. Lieblich & D. P. McAdams (Eds.), *The meaning of others: Narrative studies of relationships* (pp. 93–116). Washington, DC: American Psychological Association.

Monroe, S. M., Rohde, P., Seeley, J. R., & Lewinsohn, P. M. (1999). Life events and depression in adolescence: Relationship loss as a prospective risk factor for first onset of major depressive disorder. *Journal of Abnormal Psychology, 108,* 606–614.

Murphy, M., Glaser, K., & Grundy, E. (1997). Marital status and long-term illness in Great Britain. *Journal of Marriage and the Family, 59,* 156–164.

Murray, S. L. (1999). The quest for conviction: Motivated cognition in romantic relationships. *Psychological Inquiry, 10,* 23–34.

Murray, S. L. (2008). Risk regulation in relationships: Self-esteem and the if–then contingencies of interdependent life. In J. V. Wood, A. Tesser, & J. G. Holmes (Eds.), *The self and social relationships* (pp. 3–25). New York: Psychology Press.

Murray, S. L., Bellavia, G. M., Rose, P., & Griffin, D. W. (2003). Once hurt, twice hurtful: How perceived regard regulates daily marital interactions. *Journal of Personality and Social Psychology, 84,* 126–147.

Murray, S. L., Derrick, J. L., Leder, S., & Holmes, J. G. (2008). Balancing connectedness and self-protection goals in close relationships: A levels-of-processing perspective on risk regulation. *Journal of Personality and Social Psychology, 94,* 429–459.

Murray, S. L., Holmes, J. G., & Griffin, D. W. (1996). The self-fulfilling nature of positive illusions in romantic relationships: Love is not blind, but prescient. *Journal of Personality and Social Psychology, 71,* 1155–1180.

Murray, S. L., Holmes, J. G., & Griffin, D. W. (2000). Self-esteem and the quest for felt security: How perceived regard regulates attachment processes. *Journal of Personality and Social Psychology, 78,* 478–498.

Murray, S. L., Holmes, J. G., & Griffin, D. W. (2004). The benefits of positive illusions: Idealization and the construction of satisfaction in close relationships. In H. T. Reis & C. E. Rusbult (Eds.), *Close relationships: Key readings* (pp. 317–338). Philadelphia: Taylor & Francis.

Murray, S. L., Holmes, J. G., MacDonald, G., & Ellsworth, P. C. (1998). Through the looking glass darkly? When self-doubts turn into relationship insecurities. *Journal of Personality and Social Psychology, 75,* 1459–1480.

Murray, S. L., Rose, P., Bellavia, G. M., Holmes, J. G., & Kusche, A. G. (2002). When rejection stings: How self-esteem constrains relationship-enhancement processes. *Journal of Personality and Social Psychology, 83,* 556–573.

Neemann, J., Hubbard, J., & Masten, A. S. (1995). The changing importance of romantic relationship involvement to competence from late childhood to late adolescence. *Development and Psychopathology, 7,* 727–750.

Neff, L. A., & Karney, B. R. (2003). The dynamic structure of relationship perceptions: Differential importance as a strategy of relationship maintenance. *Personality and Social Psychology Bulletin, 29,* 1433–1446.

Neff, L. A., & Karney, B. R. (2004). How does context affect intimate relationships? Linking external stress and cognitive processes within marriage. *Personality & Social Psychology Bulletin, 30,* 134–148.

Newcomb, T. M. (1961). *The acquaintance process.* New York: Holt, Rinehart & Winston.

Newman, D. L., Caspi, A., Moffitt, T. E., & Silva, P. A. (1997). Antecedents of adult interpersonal functioning: Effects of individual differences in age 3 temperament. *Developmental Psychology, 33,* 206–217.

Neyer, F. J., & Asendorpf, J. B. (2001). Personality–relationship transaction in young adulthood. *Journal of Personality and Social Psychology, 81,* 1190–1204.

Nezlek, J. B., Richardson, D. S., Green, L. R., & Schatten-Jones, E. C. (2002). Psychological well-being and day-to-day social interaction among older adults. *Personal Relationships, 9,* 57–71.

Norton, R. (1983). Measuring marital quality: A critical look at the dependent variable. *Journal of Marriage & the Family, 45,* 141–151.

Notarius, C. I., Benson, P. R., Sloane, D., & Vanzetti, N. A. (1989). Exploring the interface between perception and behavior: An analysis of marital interaction in distressed and nondistressed couples. *Behavioral Assessment, 11,* 39–64.

Notarius, C. I., & Markman, H. J. (1993). *We can work it out: Making sense of marital conflict.* New York: Putnam.

Ognibene, T. C., & Collins, N. L. (1998). Adult attachment styles, perceived social support and coping strategies. *Journal of Social and Personal Relationships, 15,* 323–345.

Orbuch, T. L., Veroff, J., Hassan, H., & Horrocks, J. (2002). Who will divorce: A 14-year longitudinal study of Black couples and White couples. *Journal of Social and Personal Relationships, 19,* 179–202.

Oswald, R. F. (2002). Inclusion and belonging in the family rituals of gay and lesbian people. *Journal of Family Psychology, 16,* 428–436.

Panksepp, J. (1998). *Affective neuroscience: The foundations of human and animal emotions.* New York: Cambridge University Press.

Panksepp, J., Nelson, E., & Bekkedal, M. (1997). Brain systems for the mediation of social separation-distress and social-reward: Evolutionary antecedents and neuropeptide intermediaries. *Annals of the New York Academy of Sciences, 807,* 78–100.

Parks, M. R., & Eggert, L. L. (1993). The role of social context in the dynamics of personal relationships. *Advances in Personal Relationships, 2,* 1–34.

Patterson, C. J. (1995). Families of the baby boom: Parents' division of labor and children's adjustment. *Developmental Psychology, 31,* 115–123.

Patterson, C. J. (2000). Family relationships of lesbians and gay men. *Journal of Marriage and the Family, 62,* 1052–1069.

Paul, E. L., & Hayes, K. A. (2002). The causalities of "casual" sex: A qualitative exploration of the phenomenology of college students' hookups. *Journal of Social and Personal Relationships, 19,* 639–661.

Paul, E. L., McManus, B., & Hayes, K. A. (2000). "Hookups": Characteristics and correlates of college students' spontaneous and anonymous sexual experiences. *Journal of Sex Research, 37,* 76–88.

Pence, E., & Paymar, M. (1993). *Education groups for men who batter: The Duluth model.* New York: Springer.

Peplau, L. A., Cochran, S. D., & Mays, V. M. (1997). A national survey of the intimate relationships of African American lesbians and gay men: A look at commitment, satisfaction, sexual behavior, and HIV disease. In B. Green (Ed.), *Ethnic and cultural diversity among lesbians and gay men. Psychological perspectives on lesbian and gay issues* (pp. 11–38). Thousand Oaks, CA: Sage.

Peplau, L. A., & Spalding, L. R. (2000). The close relationships of lesbians, gay man, and bisexuals. In C. Hendrick & S. S. Hendrick (Eds.), *Close relationships: A sourcebook* (pp. 111–123). Thousand Oaks, CA: Sage.

Perunovic, M., & Holmes, J. G. (2008). Automatic accommodation: The role of personality. *Personal Relationships, 15,* 57–70.

Pew Research Center for the People and the Press. (2006). *Gay marriage, inheritance tax among the lowest public priorities.* Washington, DC: Author.

Phinney, V. G., Jensen, L. C., Olsen, J. A., & Cundick, B. (1990). The relationship between early development and psychosexual behaviors in adolescent females. *Adolescence, 25,* 321–332.

Pietromonaco, P. R., & Feldman-Barrett, L. (1997). Working models of attachment and daily social interactions. *Journal of Personality and Social Psychology, 73,* 1409–1423.

Pineo, P. C. (1961). Disenchantment in the later years of marriage. *Marriage & Family Living, 23,* 3–11.

Popenoe, D., & Whitehead, B. D. (2005). *The state of our unions, 2007: The social health of marriage in America.* Piscataway, NJ: The National Marriage Project.

Powell, C., & Van Vugt, M. (2003). Genuine giving or selfish sacrifice? The role of commitment and cost level upon willingness to sacrifice. *European Journal of Social Psychology, 33,* 403–412.

Powers, S. I., Pietromonaco, P. R., Gunlicks, M., & Sayer, A. (2006). Dating couples' attachment styles and patterns of cortisol reactivity and recovery in response to a relationship conflict. *Journal of Personality and Social Psychology, 90,* 613–628.

Prigerson, H. G., Maciejewski, P. K., & Rosenheck, R. A. (2000). Preliminary explorations of the harmful interactive effects of widowhood and marital harmony on health, health service use, and health care costs. *The Gerontologist, 40,* 349–357.

Prins, K. S., Buunk, B. P., & VanYperen, N. W. (1993). Equity, normative disapproval and extramarital relationships. *Journal of Social and Personal Relationships, 10,* 39–53.

Pruchno, R., Wilson-Genderson, M., & Cartwright, F. (2009). Self-rated health and depressive symptoms in patients with end-stage renal disease and their spouses: A longitudinal dyadic analysis of late-life marriages. *The Journals of Gerontology: Series B: Psychological Sciences and Social Sciences, 64,* 212–221.

Quatman, T., Sampson, K., Robinson, C., & Watson, C. M. (2001). Academic, motivational, and emotional correlates of adolescent dating. *Genetic, Social, and General Psychology Monographs, 127,* 211–234.

Regan, K. V., Bartholomew, K., Oram, D., & Landolt, M. A. (2002). Measuring physical violence in male same-sex relationships: An item response theory and analysis of the conflict tactics scales. *Journal of Interpersonal Violence, 17.*

Reis, H. T., Clark, M. S., & Holmes, J. G. (2004). Perceived partner responsiveness as an organizing construct in the study of intimacy and closeness. In D. J. Mashek & A. P. Aron (Eds.), *Handbook of closeness and intimacy* (pp. 201–225). Mahwah, NJ: Erlbaum.

Reis, H. T., Sheldon, K. M., Gable, S. L., Roscoe, J., & Ryan, R. M. (2000). Daily well-being: The role of autonomy, competence, and relatedness. *Personality and Social Psychology Bulletin, 26,* 419–435.

Repetti, R. L., Taylor, S. E., & Seeman, T. E. (2002). Risky families: Family social environments and the mental and physical health of offspring. *Psychological Bulletin, 128,* 330–366.

Resnick, M. D., Bearman, P. S., Blum, R. W., Bauman, K. E., Harris, K. M., Jones, J., et al. (1997). Protecting adolescents from harm: Findings from the National Longitudinal Study on Adolescent Health. *Journal of the American Medical Association, 278,* 823–832.

Rholes, W. S., Paetzold, R. L., & Friedman, M. (2008). Ties that bind: Linking personality to interpersonal behavior through the study of adult attachment style and relationship satisfaction. In F. Rhodewalt (Ed.), *Personality and social behavior* (pp. 117–148). New York: Psychology Press.

Rholes, W. S., Simpson, J. A., & Orina, M. M. (1999). Attachment and anger in an anxiety-provoking situation. *Journal of Personality and Social Psychology, 76,* 940–957.

Ritchie, A., & Barker, M. (2006). "There aren't words for what we do or how we feel so we have to make them up": Constructing polyamorous languages in a culture of compulsory monogamy. *Sexualities, 9,* 584–601.

Roberts, B. W., Kuncel, N. R., Shiner, R., Caspi, A., & Goldberg, L. R. (2007). The power of personality: The comparative validity of personality traits, socioeconomic status, and cognitive ability for predicting important life outcomes. *Perspectives on Psychological Science, 2,* 313–345.

Roberts, B. W., & Mroczek, D. (2008). Personality trait change in adulthood. *Current Directions in Psychological Science, 17,* 31–35.

Roberts, L. J., & Krokoff, L. J. (1990). A time-series analysis of withdrawal, hostility, and displeasure in satisfied and dissatisfied marriages. *Journal of Marriage & the Family, 52,* 95–105.

Robins, R. W., Caspi, A., & Moffitt, T. E. (2000). Two personalities, one relationship: Both partners' personality traits shape the quality of their relationship. *Journal of Personality and Social Psychology, 79,* 251–259.

Robins, R. W., Caspi, A., & Moffitt, T. E. (2002). It's not just who you're with, it's who you are: Personality and relationship experiences across multiple relationships. *Journal of Personality, 70,* 925–964.

Robles, T. F., Shaffer, V. A., Malarkey, W. B., & Kiecolt-Glaser, J. K. (2006). Positive behaviors during marital conflict: Influences on stress hormones. *Journal of Social and Personal Relationships, 23,* 305–325.

Rodrigues, A. E., Hall, J. H., & Fincham, F. D. (2006). What predicts divorce and relationship dissolution? In M. A. Fine & J. H. Harvey (Eds.), *Handbook of divorce and relationship dissolution* (pp. 85–112). Mahwah, NJ: Erlbaum.

Rogers, S. J. (2004). Dollars, dependency, and divorce: Four perspectives on the role of wives' income. *Journal of Marriage and Family, 66,* 59–74.

Roisman, G. I., Collins, W. A., Sroufe, L. A., & Egeland, B. (2005). Predictors of young adults' representations of and behavior in their current romantic relationship: Prospective tests of the prototype hypothesis. *Attachment & Human Development, 7,* 105–121.

Roisman, G. I., Madsen, S. D., Hennighausen, K. H., Sroufe, L. A., & Collins, W. A. (2001). The coherence of dyadic behavior across parent–child and romantic relationships as mediated by the internalized representation of experience. *Attachment & Human Development, 3,* 156–172.

Rollins, B. C. (1989). Marital quality at midlife. In S. Hunter & M. Sundel (Eds.), *Midlife myths: Issues, findings, and practice implications* (pp. 184–194). Thousand Oaks, CA: Sage.

Rose, S., Zand, D., & Cimi, M. A. (1993). Lesbian courtship scripts. In E. D. Rothblum & K. A. Brehony (Eds.), *Boston marriages* (pp. 70–85). Amherst: University of Massachusetts Press.

Ross, C. E. (1995). Reconceptualizing marital-status as a continuum of social attachment. *Journal of Marriage and the Family, 57,* 129–140.

Rusbult, C. E. (1983). A longitudinal test of the investment model: The development (and deterioration) of satisfaction and commitment in heterosexual involvements. *Journal of Personality and Social Psychology, 45,* 101–117.

Rusbult, C. E., Bissonnette, V. L., Arriaga, X. B., Cox, C. L., & Bradbury, T. N. (1998). Accommodation processes during the early years of marriage. In T. N. Bradbury (Ed.), *The developmental course of marital dysfunction* (pp. 74–113). New York: Cambridge University Press.

Rusbult, C. E., Coolsen, M. K., Kirchner, J. L., & Clarke, J. A. (2006). Commitment. In A. L. Vangelisti & D. Perlman (Eds.), *The Cambridge handbook of personal relationships.* (pp. 615–635). New York: Cambridge University Press.

Rusbult, C. E., Verette, J., Whitney, G. A., Slovik, L. F., & Lipkus, I. (1991). Accommodation processes in close relationships: Theory and preliminary empirical evidence. *Journal of Personality and Social Psychology, 60,* 53–78.

Rust, P. C. R. (1996). Monogamy and polyamory: Relationship issues for bisexuals. In B. A. Firestein (Ed.), *Bisexuality: The psychology and politics of an invisible minority* (pp. 127–148). Thousand Oaks, CA: Sage.

Rydell, R. J., & Bringle, R. G. (2007). Differentiating reactive and suspicious jealousy. *Social Behavior and Personality, 35,* 1099–1114.

Ryff, C. D., Singer, B. H., Wing, E., & Love, G. D. (2001). Elective affinities and uninvited agonies: Mapping emotion with significant others onto health. In C. D. Ryff & B. H. Singer (Eds.), *Emotions, social relationships, and health* (pp. 133–174). New York: Oxford University Press.

Sabini, J., & Green, M. C. (2004). Emotional responses to sexual and emotional infidelity: Constants and differences across genders, samples, and methods. *Personality and Social Psychology Bulletin, 30,* 1375–1388.

Sagrestano, L. M., Heavey, C. L., & Christensen, A. (1999). Perceived power and physical violence in marital conflict. *Journal of Social Issues, 55,* 65–79.

Sandberg, J. G., & Harper, J. M. (2000). In search of a marital distress model of depression in older marriages. *Aging & Mental Health, 4,* 210–222.

Sayer, L. C. (2006). Economic aspects of divorce and relationship dissolution. In M. A. Fine & J. H. Harvey (Eds.), *Handbook of divorce and relationship dissolution* (pp. 385–406). Mahwah, NJ: Erlbaum.

Scharfe, E., & Bartholomew, K. (1995). Accommodation and attachment representations in young couples. *Journal of Social and Personal Relationships, 12,* 389–401.

Schreurs, K. M. G., & Buunk, B. P. (1996). Closeness, autonomy, equity, and relationship satisfaction in lesbian couples. *Psychology of Women Quarterly, 20,* 577–592.

Scott-Jones, D., & White, A. B. (1990). Correlates of sexual activity in early adolescence. *Journal of Early Adolescence, 10,* 221–238.

Seeman, T. E. (2001). How do others get under our skin? Social relationships and health. In C. D. Ryff & B. H. Singer (Eds.), *Emotion, social relationships, and health* (pp. 189–209). New York: Oxford University Press.

Seeman, T. E., & Gruenewald, T. L. (2006). Allostasis and allostatic load over the life course. In W. W. Eaton (Ed.), *Medical and psychiatric comorbidity over the course of life* (pp. 179–196). Washington, DC: American Psychiatric Publishing.

Seeman, T. E., Singer, B. H., Ryff, C. D., Dienberg Love, G., & Levy-Storms, L. (2002). Social relationships, gender, and allostatic load across two age cohorts. *Psychosomatic Medicine, 64,* 395–406.

Seeman, T. E., & Syme, S. L. (1987). Social networks and coronary artery disease: A comparison of the structure and function of social relations as predictors of disease. *Psychosomatic Medicine, 49,* 341–354.

Seltzer, J. A. (2004). Cohabitation in the United States and Britain: Demography, kinship, and the future. *Journal of Marriage and Family, 66,* 921–928.

Senchak, M., & Leonard, K. E. (1992). Attachment styles and marital adjustment among newlywed couples. *Journal of Social and Personal Relationships, 9,* 51–64.

Shaver, P. R., & Brennan, K. A. (1992). Attachment styles and the "Big Five" personality traits: Their connections with each other and with romantic relationship outcomes. *Personality and Social Psychology Bulletin, 18,* 536–545.

Shaver, P. R., Hazan, C., & Bradshaw, D. (1988). Love as attachment: The integration of three behavioral systems. In J. Sternberg & M. L. Barnes (Eds.), *The psychology of love* (pp. 193–219). New Haven, CT: Yale University Press.

Sheff, E. (2005). Polyamorous women, sexual subjectivity, and power. *Journal of Contemporary Ethnography, 34,* 251–283.

Sheppard, V. J., Nelson, E. S., & Andreoli-Mathie, V. (1995). Dating relationships and infidelity: Attitudes and behaviors. *Journal of Sex & Marital Therapy, 21,* 202–212.

Shrout, P. E., Herman, C. M., & Bolger, N. (2006). The costs and benefits of practical and emotional support on adjustment: A daily diary study of couples experiencing acute stress. *Personal Relationships, 13,* 115–134.

Silverman, J. G., Raj, A., Mucci, L. A., & Hathaway, J. E. (2001). Dating violence against adolescent girls and associated substance use, unhealthy weight control, sexual risk behavior, pregnancy, and suicidality. *Journal of the American Medical Association, 286,* 572–579.

Simons, T., & O'Connell, M. (2003). *Married-couple and unmarried-partner households: 2000.* Retrieved May 23, 2006, from http://www.census.gov/prod/2003pubs/censr-5.pdf.

Simpson, J. A. (1990). Influence of attachment styles on romantic relationships. *Journal of Personality and Social Psychology, 59,* 971–980.

Simpson, J. A., Collins, W. A., Tran, S., & Haydon, K. C. (2007). Attachment and the experience and expression of emotions in romantic relationships: A developmental perspective. *Journal of Personality and Social Psychology, 92,* 355–367.

Simpson, J. A., & Gangestad, S. W. (1991). Individual differences in sociosexuality: Evidence for convergent and discriminant validity. *Journal of Personality and Social Psychology, 60,* 870–883.

Simpson, J. A., Ickes, W., & Grich, J. (1999). When accuracy hurts: Reactions of anxious-ambivalent dating partners to a relationship-threatening situation. *Journal of Personality and Social Psychology, 76,* 754–769.

Simpson, J. A., Rholes, W. S., & Nelligan, J. S. (1992). Support seeking and support giving within couples in an anxiety-provoking situation: The role of attachment styles. *Journal of Personality and Social Psychology, 62,* 434–446.

Simpson, J. A., Rholes, W. S., & Phillips, D. (1996). Conflict in close relationships: An attachment perspective. *Journal of Personality and Social Psychology, 71,* 899–914.

Simpson, J. A., Winterheld, H. A., & Chen, J. Y. (2006). Personality and relationships: A temperament perspective. In A. L. Vangelisti & D. Perlman (Eds.), *The Cambridge handbook of personal relationships* (pp. 231–250). New York: Cambridge University Press.

Singer, B. H., & Ryff, C. D. (1999). Hierarchies of life histories and associated health risks. In N. E. Adler, M. Marmot, B. S. McEwen, & J. Stewart (Eds.), *Socioeconomic status and health in industrial nations: Social, psychological, and biological pathways* (pp. 96–115). New York: New York Academy of Sciences.

Smith, D. A., & Peterson, K. M. (2008). Overperception of spousal criticism in dysphoria and marital discord. *Behavior Therapy, 39,* 300–312.

Smith, T. W., & Brown, P. C. (1991). Cynical hostility, attempts to exert social control, and cardiovascular reactivity in married couples. *Journal of Behavioral Medicine, 14,* 581–592.

Solomon, S. E., Rothblum, E. D., & Balsam, K. F. (2004). Pioneers in partnership: Lesbian and gay male couples in civil unions compared with those not in civil unions and married heterosexual siblings. *Journal of Family Psychology, 18,* 275–286.

Solomon, S. E., Rothblum, E. D., & Balsam, K. F. (2005). Money, housework, sex, and conflict: Same-sex couples in civil unions, those not in civil unions, and heterosexual married siblings. *Sex Roles, 52,* 561–575.

South, S. C., Turkheimer, E., & Oltmanns, T. F. (2008). Personality disorder symptoms and marital functioning. *Journal of Consulting and Clinical Psychology, 76,* 769–780.

Spanier, G. B., & Margolis, R. L. (1983). Marital separation and extramarital sexual behavior. *Journal of Sex Research, 19,* 23–48.

Spotts, E. L., Lichtenstein, P., Pedersen, N., Neiderhiser, J. M., Hansson, K., Cederblad, M., et al. (2005). Personality and marital satisfaction: A behavioural genetic analysis. *European Journal of Personality, 19,* 205–227.

Spotts, E. L., Neiderhiser, J. M., Towers, H., Hansson, K., Lichtenstein, P., Cederblad, M., et al. (2004). Genetic and environmental influences on marital relationships. *Journal of Family Psychology, 18,* 107–119.

Srivastava, S., McGonigal, K. M., Richards, J. M., Butler, E. A., & Gross, J. J. (2006). Optimism in close relationships: How seeing things in a positive light makes them so. *Journal of Personality and Social Psychology, 91,* 143–153.

Sroufe, L. A., Egeland, B., Carlson, E., & Collins, W. A. (2005). Placing early attachment experiences in developmental context: The Minnesota longitudinal study. In K. E. Grossmann, K. Grossmann, & E. Waters (Eds.), *Attachment from infancy to adulthood: The major longitudinal studies* (pp. 48–70). New York: Guilford Press.

Sroufe, L. A., Egeland, B., & Kreutzer, T. (1990). The fate of early experience following developmental change: Longitudinal approaches to individual adaptation in childhood. *Child Development, 61,* 1363–1373.

Stack, S. (1998). Marriage, family and loneliness: A cross-national study. *Sociological Perspectives, 41,* 415–432.

Stack, S., & Eshleman, J. R. (1998). Marital status and happiness: A 17-nation study. *Journal of Marriage and the Family, 60,* 527–536.

Stackert, R. A., & Bursik, K. (2003). Why am I unsatisfied? Adult attachment style, gendered irrational relationship beliefs, and young adult romantic relationship satisfaction. *Personality and Individual Differences, 34,* 1419–1429.

Stafford, L., Kline, S. L., & Rankin, C. T. (2004). Married individuals, cohabiters, and cohabiters who marry: A longitudinal study of relational and individual well-being. *Journal of Social and Personal Relationships, 21,* 231–248.

Stanley, S. M., Blumberg, S. L., & Markman, H. J. (1999). Helping couples fight for their marriages: The PREP approach. In R. Berger & M. T. Hannah (Eds.), *Preventive approaches in couples therapy* (pp. 279–303). Philadelphia: Brunner/Mazel.

Stanley, S. M., Whitton, S. W., & Markman, H. J. (2004). Maybe I do: Interpersonal commitment and premarital or nonmarital cohabitation. *Journal of Family Issues, 25,* 496–519.

Steele, H., & Steele, M. (2005). Understanding and resolving emotional conflict: The London parent-child project. In K. E. Grossmann, K. Grossmann, & E. Waters (Eds.), *Attachment from infancy to adulthood: The major longitudinal studies* (pp. 137–164). New York: Guilford Press.

Steil, J. M. (2000). Contemporary marriage: Still an unequal partnership. In C. Hendrick & S. S. Hendrick (Eds.), *Close relationships: A sourcebook* (pp. 125–136). Thousand Oaks, CA: Sage.

Stepp, L. S. (2007). *Unhooked: How young women pursue sex, delay love and lose at both.* New York: Riverhead Books.

Stith, S. M., Rosen, K. H., Middleton, K. A., Busch, A. L., Lundeberg, K., & Carlton, R. P. (2000). The intergenerational transmission of spouse abuse: A meta-analysis. *Journal of Marriage & the Family, 62,* 640–654.

Straus, M. A., & Gelles, R. J. (Eds.). (1990). *Physical violence in American families: Risk factors and adaptations to violence in 8,145 families*. New Brunswick, NJ: Transaction Press.

Sturaro, C., Denissen, J. J. A., van Aken, M. A. G., & Asendorpf, J. B. (2008). Person-environment transactions during emerging adulthood: The interplay between personality characteristics and social relationships. *European Psychologist, 13,* 1–11.

Sugarman, D. B., Aldarondo, E., & Boney-McCoy, S. (1996). Risk marker analysis of husband-to-wife violence: A continuum of aggression. *Journal of Applied Social Psychology, 26,* 313–337.

Sugarman, D. B., & Hotaling, G. T. (1989). Dating violence: Prevalence, context, and risk markers. In M. A. Pirog-Good & J. E. Stets (Eds.), *Violence in dating relationships: Emerging social issues* (pp. 3–32). New York: Praeger.

Suter, E. A., & Oswald, R. F. (2003). Do lesbians change their last names in the context of a committed relationship? *Journal of Lesbian Studies, 7,* 71–83.

Swan, S. C., & Snow, D. L. (2003). Behavioral and psychological differences among abused women who use violence in intimate relationships. *Violence Against Women, 9,* 75–109.

Swann, W. B. (1983). Self-verification: Bringing social reality into harmony with the self. In J. M. Suls & A. G. Greenwald (Eds.), *Psychological perspectives on the self* (Vol. 2, pp. 33–66). Hillsdale, NJ: Erlbaum.

Swann, W. B. (1990). To be adored or to be known: The interplay of self-enhancement and self-verification. In R. M. Sorrentino & E. T. Higgins (Eds.), *Foundations of social behavior* (Vol. 2, pp. 408–448). New York: Guilford Press.

Swann, W. B., De La Ronde, C., & Hixon, G. J. (1994). Authenticity and positivity strivings in marriage and courtship. *Journal of Personality and Social Psychology, 66,* 857–869.

Tanner, J. L. (2006). Recentering during emerging adulthood: A critical turning point in lifespan human development. In J. J. Arnett & J. L. Tanner (Eds.), *Emerging adults in America: Coming of age in the 21st century* (pp. 21–55). Washington DC: American Psychological Association Press.

Terman, L. M., & Buttenweiser, P. (1935). Personality factors in marital compatibility. *Journal of Social Psychology, 6,* 143–171.

Thelen, E., Kelso, J. A. S., & Fogel, A. (1987). Self-organizing systems and infant motor development. *Developmental Review, 7,* 39–65.

Thibaut, J. W., & Kelley, H. H. (1978). *Interpersonal relations: A theory of interdependence*. New York: John Wiley & Sons.

Thomson, E., & Colella, U. (1992). Cohabitation and marital stability: Quality or commitment? *Journal of Marriage & the Family, 54,* 259–267.

Tidwell, M. O., Reis, H. T., & Shaver, P. R. (1996). Attachment, attractiveness, and social interaction: A diary study. *Journal of Personality and Social Psychology, 71,* 729–745.

Tjaden, P., & Thoennes, N. (2000). *Extent, nature, and consequences of intimate partner violence: Findings from the National Violence Against Women Survey*. Washington, DC: National Institute of Justice.

Tolman, D. L. (2002). *Dilemma of desire: Teenage girls and sexuality*. Cambridge, MA: Harvard University Press.

Tolman, D. L., Spencer, R., Harmon, T., Rosen-Reynoso, M., & Striepe, M. (2004). Getting close, staying cool: Early adolescent boys' experiences with romantic relationships. In N. Way & J. Y. Chu (Eds.), *Adolescent boys: Exploring diverse cultures of boyhood* (pp. 235–255). New York: New York University Press.

Treas, J., & Giesen, D. (2000). Sexual infidelity among married and cohabiting Americans. *Journal of Marriage & the Family, 62,* 48–60.

Tronick, E. Z., Brushweiller-Stern, N., Harrison, A. M., Lyons-Ruth, K., Morgan, A. C., Nahum, J. P., et al. (1998). Dyadically expanded states of consciousness and the process of therapeutic change. *Infant Mental Health Journal, 19,* 290–299.

Truman-Schram, D. M., Cann, A., Calhoun, L., & Vanwallendael, L. (2000). Leaving an abusive dating relationship: An investment model comparison of women who stay versus women who leave. *Journal of Social & Clinical Psychology, 19,* 161–183.

Tucker, J. S., & Anders, S. L. (1999). Attachment style, interpersonal perception accuracy, and relationship satisfaction in dating couples. *Personality and Social Psychology Bulletin, 25,* 403–412.

Tunnell, G., & Greenan, D. E. (2004). Clinical issues with gay male couples. In J. J. Bigner & J. L. Wetchler (Eds.), *Relationship therapy with same-sex couples* (pp. 13–26). Binghamton, NY: Haworth Press.

U.S. Census Bureau. (2007). *Statistical abstract of the United States, 2007*. Washington, DC: U.S. Census Bureau.

van Gelder, B. M., Tijhuis, M., Kalmijn, S., Giampaoli, S., Nissinen, A., & Kromhout, D. (2006). Marital status and living situation during a 5-year period are associated with a subsequent 10-year cognitive decline in older men The FINE Study. *The Journals of Gerontology: Series B: Psychological Sciences and Social Sciences, 61,* P213–P219.

Van Lange, P. A. M., Rusbult, C. E., Drigotas, S. M., Arriaga, X. B., Witcher, B. S., & Cox, C. L. (1997). Willingness to sacrifice in close relationships. *Journal of Personality and Social Psychology, 72,* 1373–1395.

Vogel, D. L., & Karney, B. R. (2002). Demands and withdrawal in newlyweds: Elaborating on the social structure hypothesis. *Journal of Social and Personal Relationships, 19,* 685–701.

Waite, L. J. (1995). Does marriage matter? *Demography, 32,* 483–507.

Walder-Haugrud, L. K. (1999). Sexual coercion in lesbian and gay relationships: A review and critique. *Aggression and Violent Behavior, 6,* 139–149.

Wallen, K. (1995). The evolution of female sexual desire. In P. R. Abramson & S. D. Pinkerton (Eds.), *Sexual nature/sexual culture* (pp. 57–79). Chicago: University of Chicago Press.

Wallerstein, J. S., Corbin, S. B., Lewis, J. M., Hetherington, E. M., & Arasteh, J. D. (1988). Children of divorce: A 10-year study. In *Impact of divorce, single parenting, and stepparenting on children* (pp. 197–214). Hillsdale, NJ: Erlbaum.

Walters, A. S., & Curran, M. C. (1996). "Excuse me, sir? May I help you and your boyfriend?": Salespersons' differential treatment of homosexual and straight customers. *Journal of Homosexuality, 31,* 135–152.

Waters, E., Hamilton, C. E., & Weinfield, N. S. (2000). The stability of attachment security from infancy to adolescence and early adulthood: General introduction. *Child Development, 71,* 690–694.

Waters, E., Merrick, S., Treboux, D., Crowell, J., & Albersheim, L. (2000). Attachment security in infancy and early adulthood: A twenty-year longitudinal study. *Child Development, 71,* 678–683.

Watson, D., Hubbard, B., & Wiese, D. (2000). General traits of personality and affectivity as predictors of satisfaction in intimate relationships: Evidence from self- and partner-ratings. *Journal of Personality, 68,* 413–449.

Way, N. (1996). Between experiences of betrayal and desire: Close friendships among urban adolescents. In B. J. R. Leadbeater & N. Way (Eds.), *Urban girls: Resisting stereotypes, creating identities* (pp. 173–192). New York: New York University Press.

Weinfield, N. S., Sroufe, L. A., & Egeland, B. (2000). Attachment from infancy to early adulthood in a high-risk sample: Continuity, discontinuity, and their correlates. *Child Development, 71,* 695–702.

Weiss, R. L., & Heyman, R. E. (1997). A clinical-research overview of couples interactions. In W. K. Halford & H. J. Markman (Eds.), *Clinical handbook of marriage and couples interventions* (pp. 13–41). New York: John Wiley & Sons.

Weitzman, G. (2006). Therapy with clients who are bisexual and polyamorous. *Journal of Bisexuality, 6,* 137–164.

Wekerle, C., & Wolfe, D. A. (1999). Dating violence in mid-adolescence: Theory, significance, and emerging prevention initiatives. *Clinical Psychology Review, 19,* 435–456.

Welsh, D. P., & Dickson, J. W. (2005). Video-recall procedures for examining subjective understanding in observational data. *Journal of Family Psychology, 19,* 62–71.

Welsh, D. P., Galliher, R. V., Kawaguchi, M. C., & Rostosky, S. S. (1999). Discrepancies in adolescent romantic couples' and observers' perceptions of couple interaction and their relationship to depressive symptoms. *Journal of Youth and Adolescence, 28,* 645–666.

West, C. M. (1998). Leaving a second closet: Outing partner violence in same-sex couples. In J. L. Jasinski & L. M. Williams (Eds.), *Partner violence: A comprehensive review of 20 years of research* (pp. 163–183). Thousand Oaks, CA: Sage.

West, C. M. (2002). Lesbian intimate partner violence: Prevalence and dynamics. *Journal of Lesbian Studies, 6,* 121–127.

White, J. K., Hendrick, S. S., & Hendrick, C. (2004). Big Five personality variables and relationship constructs. *Personality and Individual Differences, 37,* 1519–1530.

Widmer, E. D., Treas, J., & Newcomb, R. N. (1998). Attitudes toward nonmarital sex in 24 countries. *Journal of Sex Research, 35,* 349–358.

Williams, S. L., & Frieze, I. H. (2005). Patterns of violent relationships, psychological distress, and marital satisfaction in a national sample of men and women. *Sex Roles, 52,* 771–784.

Wolf, K. A., & Foshee, V. A. (2003). Family violence, anger expression styles, and adolescent dating violence. *Journal of Family Violence, 18,* 309–316.

Wolfinger, N. H. (2005). *Understanding the divorce cycle: The children of divorce in their own marriages.* New York: Cambridge University Press.

Wolinsky, M. A. (1990). *A heart of wisdom: Marital counseling with older and elderly couples.* Philadelphia: Brunner/Mazel.

Zacks, E., Green, R.-J., & Marrow, J. (1988). Comparing lesbian and heterosexual couples on the Circumplex Model: An initial investigation. *Family Process, 27,* 471–484.

Zhang, F., & Labouvie-Vief, G. (2004). Stability and fluctuation in adult attachment style over a 6-year period. *Attachment & Human Development, 6,* 419–437.

Zimmer-Gembeck, M. J., Siebenbruner, J., & Collins, W. A. (2001). Diverse aspects of dating: Associations with psychosocial functioning from early to middle adolescence. *Journal of Adolescence, 24,* 313–336.

CHAPTER 12

Convoys of Social Relations: Integrating Life-Span and Life-Course Perspectives

TONI C. ANTONUCCI, KATHERINE L. FIORI, KIRA BIRDITT, and LISA M. H. JACKEY

This chapter examines the convoy model of social relations. To begin, a brief summary of the original model is presented. The different components of social relations—that is, their structure, function, and quality— are outlined, as are their antecedents and consequences. Empirical studies of the convoy model are presented, offering insight into how relationships themselves may be different across the life span (e.g., in childhood and adulthood) and in different contexts (e.g., in families, at work). These data demonstrate that each component of the convoy model develops and changes over time. It is noted that social relations are both developmental and contextual in nature. Thus, this chapter advances both the life-span and life-course perspectives as critical to understanding the processes and mechanisms through which social relations develop and social support is exchanged. We illustrate the life-span and life-course dynamics of the convoy model by highlighting the convoy model's four basic tenets: (a) social relationships are multifaceted involving objective and subjective characteristics, (b) social relationships and networks change over time because of developmental and contextual processes, (c) social relationships vary by personal and situational factors, and (d) social relationships and networks influence well-being. Recent findings are presented, focusing especially on the unique perspective offered by a pattern-centered approach to relationships. The chapter ends with a summary and call for future research to address the specific issues raised by current evidence.

SOCIAL RELATIONS: THE CONVOY MODEL

The study of social relations is the study of interpersonal interactions—that is, how individuals interact with each other. Previous work in this area took a nondevelopmental or stagnant approach to social relations, examining each individual interaction as though it occurred in a vacuum, not acknowledging the influence of previous interactions on present and future ones. The convoy model, developed in 1980 and modified over the years, sought to incorporate the developmental and dynamic aspects of relationships into a single model. It builds on the traditionally developmental perspective of attachment theory, the contextual basis of role theory, as well as the fields of social networks and social support (Antonucci, 2001; Antonucci & Akiyama, 1995; Antonucci, Birditt, & Akiyama, 2009; Kahn & Antonucci, 1980).

Convoys focus on the life-span nature of close social relations. Attachment theory is perhaps the most well-known and heavily researched theory of very close social relations. First introduced by John Bowlby (1969) and later articulated by Mary Ainsworth and colleagues (1978), attachment theory states that infants initially become attached to their primary caregiver, usually their mother. This relationship is based on responsive caregiving and allows the infant to develop internal working models of social relationships. Under optimal conditions, the child develops the belief that others are trustworthy and that the world is predictable. The result is a secure attachment that leads to higher levels of competence in children and more successful relationships among adults (Antonucci, 2001; Levitt, 2005).

Convoys also incorporate aspects of role theory, associated with the work of Mead (1934) and Merton (1957), to include life-course elements of social relations. Roles refer to the common socially ascribed positions in society, including norms and expectations of behavior. Whereas attachment theory focuses on individuals, role theory refers to intergroup or societal expectations. Roles might be personal or professional, for example, parent, child, spouse, or factory worker, business executive, politician. According to this perspective, multiple roles (e.g., worker, spouse, churchgoer, friend, club member, neighbor) promote greater social connectedness and integration (Moen, 2001). Importantly, role positions may change over time, highlighting the life-course nature of convoys (e.g., one may acquire the role of spouse but then lose that role due to divorce or death). Roles may be ascribed, developed, and achieved through social interaction.

The metaphor of the convoy was chosen to recognize social relations not as simple singular events but rather as linked interactions that accumulate and develop over time. According to the convoy model, individuals are surrounded by close social relationships at various stages of the life span and over the life course. Social relationships vary in terms of objective characteristics (e.g., the number, age, gender) as well as the support they provide. Social relationships differ by personal and situational characteristics, the combination of which influences the individual's health and well-being. The convoy is meant to protect and to socialize the individual by providing help and guidance with life's challenges. As noted earlier, the first and most significant relationship is usually with the mother in her capacity as the primary caregiver, but then extends to other close and significant "attachment" relationships. These relationships expand as the individual's world expands and are influenced by individual and situational characteristics. With growth and maturation (individual life-span characteristics) and changing roles and responsibilities (situational life-course characteristics), the convoy itself changes. We outline the four basic tenets of the convoy model next.

First, social relationships are multifaceted. A convoy of relationships refers to an individual's identified close and important social ties. These ties vary in terms of the characteristics of the network overall, the support they provide, and the quality of those ties. Social networks can be defined as the structural or objective characteristics of network members. If network members are defined as those with whom the individual has close and important relations, network structure details their objective characteristics. These might include the number of network members as well as their age, race, and relationship to the target person. Other network characteristics include contact frequency, geographic proximity, and density (i.e., the degree to which network members know each other). Recent work by Smith and Christakis (2003) has particularly exploited this last factor as a means of understanding the influence of networks on health.

Social support refers to the function or exchange of social support, that is, what precisely is given or received. Kahn and Antonucci (1980) identified three main categories of social support exchange: aid, affect and affirmation. Aid refers to the instrumental support that one might receive from others such as help with housework, money, or sick care. Affect refers to the emotional exchanges common in close social relations including love, affection, sympathy, and compassion. Finally, affirmation refers to a much less tangible aspect of social relations that implies an acceptance, agreement, or affirmation of one's values. In such cases, neither tangible aid nor emotion are necessarily involved, but individuals benefit from knowing that others share their values or perspective on life. This combination of aid, affect, and affirmation is meant to encompass the multiple types of support that individuals provide each other.

Support adequacy or satisfaction is a psychological dimension of the convoy model. It is recognized that different individuals experiencing the same network and support exchanges might evaluate them differently. One might find the support received or provided completely adequate, to be of high quality and, therefore, be satisfied with their relationships, whereas another might see the same relationship as inadequate, of poor quality, and be completely dissatisfied. It should be noted that relationship quality includes both positive and negative dimensions. Positive aspects of relationships include feeling loved, cared for, and understood, whereas negative aspects of relationships include feeling criticized and irritated. These qualities can also be combined to examine ambivalent feelings, which involve the simultaneous feelings of positive and negative quality. Research shows that the closest network ties are often the most ambivalent (Fingerman, Hay & Birditt, 2004).

A second critical tenet is the convoy's malleability, its reflection of the individual and circumstances within which that person lives over time. The term *convoy* is meant to reflect this flexibility. Theoretically, it is meant to recognize that intraindividual development is usually a sign of certain general phenomena such as physical growth and maturity but that these phenomena do vary by circumstance, thus highlighting its life-span and life-course foundations. Infants become children and later adults, but even physical development can vary, for example, in circumstances of poverty or plenty, or in different historical periods, for example, from the 1800s to the 2000s. Similarly, situational circumstances vary, creating different roles, expectations, and demands. The adolescent girl in a conservative Indian family may be expected to marry whomever her family chooses, whereas the adolescent girl in the United States is more likely to seek her parents' guidance as she chooses her high school classes. Certain aspects of the convoys are likely to remain stable under changing circumstances. The child is likely to include a parent as a convoy member whether the child is 5 or 50 years old. However, the nature of the relationship and the associated role expectations and demands are likely to change considerably over time. Nevertheless, some convoy membership will change. With adulthood, a spouse and children are often added, as are coworkers and friends. Whereas the former are expected to be stable additions, the latter may not be.

The third tenet of the convoy model indicates that social relations are shaped by both personal and situational characteristics of the individual. Personal characteristics will shape the types of social relations the individual is likely to seek, need, and develop. However, personal characteristics alone cannot completely account for the development of social relations. The situational characteristics within which an individual lives also play an important part. Thus, role or normative expectations and demands can also influence an individual's social relations. Neither personal nor situational characteristics influence social relations alone. Personal and situational characteristics also interact with each other, grow and develop over time, and exist within an interactive loop with other aspects of the model—that is, specific aspects of social relations as well as the health and well-being of the individual.

Finally, the fourth tenet is that social relationships influence both health and well-being. Outcome variables that are influenced by one's convoy of social relations include physical and mental health as well as mortality. An abundant amount of research either implicitly or explicitly using the convoy model has documented these associations (see recent reviews, e.g., Antonucci, 2001; Berkman, Glass, Brissette, & Seeman, 2000; Uchino, 2004). Importantly, one interpretation or evaluation is no less valid than the other but must be understood and appreciated because of its significant impact on how social relations affect health and well-being. One of the most interesting findings concerning social relations is that whereas social networks and social support both influence health, support quality has the most significant effect (Antonucci, Fuhrer, & Dartigues, 1997; Blazer, 1982) on both physical and mental health. Hence, although objective characteristics of relationships are important, it is the individual's evaluation of those characteristics that is most influential.

Overall the convoy is dynamic, and none of the influences outlined here are either static or stable. Each aspect of the model can interact with other aspects of the model, thereby influencing change and development over time. Convoys develop and evolve: The past influences but does not determine the present and future. The convoy is conceived of as an important socializing agent that under optimal conditions both teaches and protects, as well as influences and shapes, the developing individual. Life-course experiences, for example, normative or nonnormative group or societal changes, are also likely to influence social relations. With life-span and life-course experiences, one's convoy moves with the individual through time either to promote and protect or to increase the risk and vulnerability of the individual's well-being (i.e., both physical and mental health).

CONVOY MODEL: UPDATE

Since the convoy model was first introduced, a number of researchers have successfully used this model as an organizing framework. Much of the variable-centered research has been reviewed elsewhere (cf. Antonucci, 2001; Antonucci et al., 2009; Levitt, 2005) and will not be reiterated here. In this section, we briefly outline theoretical modifications that have been added to or reemphasized from the original convoy model. In particular, we highlight the specific inclusion of the association between social relations and stress and the importance of recognizing the longitudinal and dynamic nature of social relations.

It is a logical assumption that a positive and supportive convoy would help an individual cope with stressful experiences. However, this point was not made explicitly in early iterations of the model. More recently, we have specifically incorporated stress into the model, arguing that an individual can be protected from the most negative effects of stress by various aspects of their convoy. Of course, personal and situational characteristics will influence the kind and amount of stress that an individual experiences. However, the convoy model suggests that each of the specific aspects of social relations—that is, social networks (the structure of the network), social support (the exchange of aid, affect, and affirmation), and the quality of social relations (the evaluation or satisfaction with their social network and social support)—influence both how much stress the person will experience and how negatively or positively they will be affected by that stress.

In keeping with the theme of this volume, it is important to highlight the longitudinal and dynamic aspects of this association. Convoys exist over one's lifetime, and each of the characteristics that contribute to the convoy can also change. These changes can be positive or negative; consequently, one must note that convoys can either positively or negatively influence how a person experiences stress. It is an interesting but also logical observation that past experiences can influence the degree to which one assumes that support will be provided in times of stress. For example, anticipated support might have as positive an effect as received support and, under some circumstances, actually prevent the common negative effects of stress on health and well-being (Krause, 2001).

Identifying convoys as longitudinal and dynamic theoretically is one thing; exploring these concepts empirically is quite another and represents both theoretical and methodological challenges. Appropriate measures of social relations are likely to vary by age, circumstance, and experience. In addition, our work in other cultures has made us aware that although there are similarities in social relations, there are also important cultural differences (Antonucci, Akiyama, & Takahashi, 2004; Antonucci et al., 2001; Takahashi, Ohara, Antonucci, & Akiyama, 2002). As we began to conduct convoy research among different age groups, in different cultures, and longitudinally, we became increasingly sensitive to these issues. It was important, therefore, that the measurement of convoys be relatively culture- and expectation-free. The measure often used involves showing people a diagram of three concentric circles and asking them to name the individuals to whom they feel closest, closer, and close (see Antonucci, 1986, for details). This simple assessment procedure, with relatively little adaptation, has proved surprisingly easy to use for individuals of all ages, from preschoolers to the oldest-old, as well as in cultures as varied as the United States, Japan, Europe, and South America.

In the sections that follow, we review the life-span and life-course perspectives and then highlight social relations at different points in the life span, considering people in different life-course roles and in different cultures using a pattern-centered approach. This provides a unique perspective on convoys that is appropriate for use among different ages and across cultures both cross-sectionally and longitudinally. We turn next to a consideration of the life-span and life-course perspectives, in particular, detailing their incorporation into the convoy model.

LIFE-SPAN AND LIFE-COURSE PERSPECTIVES

The past fifty years have seen a tremendous increase in the acceptance of both the life-span and life-course perspectives. The combination of these approaches serves to articulate more completely the critical factors affecting social relationships and development. Indeed, as stated previously, an important tenet of the convoy model is that relationships change over time due to life-span and life-course factors.

Life-span development had its early roots in the stage theories of Freud, Erikson, and Piaget and the more recent work of Baltes (1987, 1997, 2003) in which he articulated the "incomplete architecture of human ontogeny." Inherent in each of the theories is the conception that the individual develops over time from a relatively simplistic level to a more complex one. Critical to this view is the understanding that each stage or period develops from and is based on the previous one. Although there has been some controversy about whether this development is universally singular, monotonic, and positive, all agree that development is generally cumulative and usually progressive. A popular term for this among developmental scientists is *intraindividual development*.

Of critical importance to the study of social relations is the life-span perspective, which offers an organized account of the structure and sequence of development over the life span and hence of social relations over the life span. The life-span perspective is critical because it identifies the interconnections between earlier and later developmental events and processes. As is quite clear in the case of social relations, there are important and undeniable interconnections. The infant's early relationships are known to influence how the child and even the adult view later relationships. It is also known that these are rarely rigidly fixed and can change on the basis of later life experiences. Of similar importance is the life span delineation of factors and mechanisms that are the foundation of development.

Whereas the life-span perspective examines individual development over time, the life-course perspective considers the organizations, subgroups, or contexts within which individuals develop. Of special interest to the life-course perspective is the differentiation that occurs across subgroups and, in particular, how membership in these subgroups influence the social pathways that are available to individuals. These social pathways are defined by sequences of events and transitions, as well as the roles and experiences of individuals (Alwin & Wray, 2005; Settersen, 2003, 2007).

Family and work roles have changed in fundamental ways. For example, whereas traditionally families in the early 1900s often included 10 or 12 children, families in the 1950s included 4 or 5 people. Families during this latter period of postwar prosperity usually included a father who worked outside the home, a mother who was a full-time homemaker, and two or three children. Now families are more likely to consist of two adults, both of whom work outside the home, and no, one, or two children. Most people expect to change jobs or that the jobs themselves will change. Gender roles, although still existent, are blurring, mostly in that women do many of the things that only men once did, although men are increasingly likely to be found in what were once female-dominated roles, such as nursing, and to play a more active role in parenting. Other changes in the family are evident. People are marrying later, if at all. They are having children later, and more children are born out of wedlock with parents feeling little pressure to marry either before or after the child is born. Divorce and remarriage is common, as are blended families which include children from various previous relationships. These changing societal structures influence the nature of social relations at every level.

As noted previously, and in the tenets of the convoy model, convoys are presumed to be dynamic over time. Although each individual's convoy is unique and influenced by personal and situational factors, some characteristics of convoys or social networks are typical of different developmental periods, and, on average, networks can be expected to change in predictable ways throughout development.

Childhood

Although relatively little research has been conducted specifically examining changes in children's social networks over time, descriptions of children's networks at different ages can present a first glimpse at how these networks may evolve developmentally. Children's early social networks tend to be dominated by close family members, such as parents, siblings, and grandparents (Levitt, Guacci-Franco, & Levitt, 1993). These same individuals, especially parents, provide the majority of support during middle childhood (Furman & Buhrmester, 1992; Levitt et al., 1993; Reid, Landesman, Treder, & Jacard, 1989). However, over the course of childhood, children's networks tend to increase in size, particularly adding kin, nonkin adults, and friends (Feiring & Lewis, 1991a, 1991b; Levitt et al., 1993). Corresponding to the increasing size of the social network, children also report more overall support from network members at age 10 than they do at age 7 (Levitt et al., 1993).

Adolescence

As children move into adolescence, friends take on increased prominence in the social network, whereas the number of extended family members and the support received from them may wane (Feiring & Lewis, 1991b; Levitt et al., 1993; Levitt et al., 2005; Reid et al., 1989). In addition, romantic partners may be added to the social networks of many adolescents (e.g., Furman & Buhrmester, 1992). Unlike children, adolescents tend to report friends as their top supporters (Demaray & Malecki, 2002). Parents and other family members, nevertheless, both remain in the social network and continue to function as important sources of social support for most adolescents. However, some evidence indicates that adolescents perceive lower levels of social support than do children from parents, teachers, friends, and classmates (Demaray & Malecki, 2002).

Adulthood

Adults, on average, continue to maintain social ties with and receive support from both family and friends; romantic partners often become the primary supporters for many adults (Takahashi, 2005). Takahashi and her colleagues (Takahashi et al., 2002) also found that most Americans feel supported by a variety of sources, rather than relying primarily on one individual. Networks continue to evolve throughout adulthood. By the time young adults are in college, romantic partners are the primary supporters of young men, whereas romantic partners, mothers, friends, and siblings are all important sources of support for young women (Furman & Buhrmester, 1992). Among young adults, relationships with friends are described in more positive terms than are relationships with parents (O'Connor, 1995), but young adults' reliance on friends also differs based on their marital and parental status (Carbery & Buhrmester, 1998). Among older adults, in contrast, relationships with children are described as equally or more positive and interactions with children as more intrinsically motivating than those with friends (O'Connor, 1995).

Older Adulthood

Older adults tend to have fewer social partners than do younger adults (Johnson & Barer, 1997; Lang, 2001; Lang & Carstensen, 1994; Troll, 1988), and at least in Europe, older adults have half as many social partners as do individuals in their 20s and 30s (cf. Lang, 2001). However, according to Antonucci (1985), *among* older adults (i.e., aged 50–95), there are few age differences in network size. In general however, people report providing fewer supports to their network members as they get older. Older adults may also have less frequent contact with network members and have fewer confidants. In late life (that is, 85+), according to Johnson and Troll (1994), individuals may change their criteria for or definition of "friendship" due to various constraints to friendship maintenance that accompany old age. For instance, very old individuals may include acquaintances or even hired help as friends and may not require face-to-face contact or a lot of expressive content to maintain "friendships." Interestingly, however, older adults actually seem to be more satisfied with their social networks than are younger adults (Antonucci, 1985) and often report having less demanding networks (Crohan & Antonucci, 1989).

Relationships appear to improve with age. A great deal of evidence suggests that older adults experience fewer problems in their relationships (Fingerman & Birditt, 2003), less anger (Birditt & Fingerman, 2003), and less stress in response to conflict (Birditt, Fingerman, & Almeida, 2005). They are also less likely to use overtly negative strategies and more likely to use avoidant strategies (Birditt & Fingerman, 2005; Blanchard-Fields, Jahnke, & Camp, 1995; Blanchard-Fields, Stein, & Watson, 2004). Furthermore, with the exception of the spousal tie, relationships with children and friends become less negative over time (Birditt, Jackey, & Antonucci, 2009).

Although age-associated losses increase the risk for loneliness in old age, only about 10% of older adults report frequent loneliness, and the correlation between loneliness and age is fairly weak until very old age (Dykstra, van Tilburg, & de Jong-Gierveld, 2005; Pinquart & Sörensen, 2003). In a study of a national sample of 718 American adults aged 50 to 95, Crohan and Antonucci (1989) found that among older adults, only quality of social relations, as opposed to quantity of social relations (e.g., network size), were predictive of life satisfaction. Furthermore, only for older respondents was the presence of a spouse in the network positively associated with the perception of the network as demanding. According to Matt and Dean (1993), friend support frequently becomes more important as people age because of aging-related changes in social networks (e.g., reduced availability of spouse support due to divorce or widowhood).

Across Developmental Periods

Research examining individuals across developmental periods reveals change as well as stability in relationships. Antonucci, Fuller-Iglesias, and Birditt (2007) found that although network size during childhood was not predictive of network size in adulthood, the proportion of family in the child's network did predict the proportion of family in his/her network as an adult. The number of close social relationships and the amount of emotional support received from network members remains relatively stable across the life span until very old age (Antonucci, 2001; Wagner, Schütze, & Lang, 1999). Longitudinal research indicates that perceived support is more likely than received support to be stable over time (Krause, 1999), and whereas receipt of emotional support tends to be relatively stable with increasing age (Gurung, Taylor, & Seeman, 2003), the receipt of instrumental support may increase as health declines (Aartsen, van Tilburg, Smits, & Knipscheer, 2004). Importantly, there is significant individual variation in the way that social support changes as people move across the life span (Krause, 1999; van Tilburg, de Jong-Gierveld Lecchini, & Marsiglia, 1998) thus, examining change from a person-centered perspective may be key. However, the majority of person-centered studies have been cross-sectional and conducted among only older adults. Little attention has been given to changes across the life span and the health effects of moving into and out of certain network types (Litwin, 1995). Later in the chapter, we address existing person-centered studies and discuss some important transitions occurring across the life span that may influence longitudinal changes in network types but that have not been extensively studied in such a context.

First, we turn to several key theories of social relations that have attempted to explain developmental changes in social relations from either a life-span or life-course perspective. In addition to the convoy model, these theories help guide our expectations for changes in social relations across the life span from a theoretical perspective. It should be noted that many of these theories were developed with older adults in mind (because life-span research on social relations has typically focused on older adults) but are considered here because many of them apply equally well to other points of the life span.

DISENGAGEMENT THEORY AND ACTIVITY THEORY

In the 1960s, researchers attempted to explain the reduction in social partners among older adults with several somewhat controversial theories. The disengagement theory and the activity theory both take a life-course perspective in explaining changes in social networks. In their disengagement theory, Cumming and Henry (1960) claimed that the aging individual and society mutually disengage from each other, beginning in late midlife. First, the individual experiences a narrowing of his or her social sphere, which he or she must then accept or to which he or she must adapt. Then, the individual changes her or his lifestyle by becoming more passive and less active until eventually disengaging by giving up social roles.

As part of a backlash against this theory of older adults as willingly passive individuals, Havighurst (1961) proposed the activity theory. According to this theory, older adults both need and want to involve themselves in activities within the social realm, especially to replace losses (e.g., deaths, loss of roles). However, due to a lack of resources (e.g., money) and other social and physical barriers to interaction, such activities become impossible and older adults appear passive and quiet. More recent research over the past few decades has made it clear that these seminal theories of aging are outdated (or perhaps cohort-specific) and do not provide a complete framework for studying social relations among today's elderly. Neither of these theories portrays older individuals as actively shaping their ongoing development as proposed by Baltes (1987) and other life-span psychologists (e.g., Heckhausen & Schulz, 1995).

SOCIOEMOTIONAL SELECTIVITY THEORY

Rather than interpreting the attenuation of older individuals' social spheres as "disengagement" or as due to a lack of resources, researchers have more recently begun to attribute this reduction to more agentic factors, such as selection, optimization, and compensation (e.g., Baltes, 1987; Carstensen, 1992; Lang, 2001). In her theory of socioemotional selectivity, Carstensen (1992) argued that the goal hierarchies that organize social motives change across the life span. Specifically, she posits that social interactions become increasingly motivated by the regulation of emotion and less by the acquisition of information or the development and maintenance of self-concept, which are goals that are more likely to motivate younger adults. Thus, Carstensen theorized that older adults take an active role in narrowing their social environments. The dynamics of personal relationships can be viewed as a motivational process, whereby individuals' developmental resources and goals interact in the formation, maintenance, and changes of individuals' social networks (Lang, 2004). Interestingly, Carstensen and her colleagues (Carstensen, 1992; Carstensen, Isaacowitz, & Charles,

1999) have shown that it is not chronological age per se but rather limited time that is responsible for a goal shift toward emotion regulation; thus, even younger adults can demonstrate such a shift in goal hierarchies given a situation in which their "time" becomes limited (e.g., before a major relocation or in the face of a terminal illness).

Several studies have found support for SST theory. Lansford, Sherman, and Antonucci (1998) found support for socioemotional selectivity theory across several large cohorts of representative older Americans. They found that, in general, older adults were more satisfied with their current number of friends than were younger adults, even though the younger adults had more frequent contact with their network members. Furthermore, age, above and beyond other sociodemographic factors, consistently predicted satisfaction with network size. Lang and Carstensen (1994) found that the positive effects of socioemotional selectivity on well-being are not as marked for older adults with a spouse and a child as for childless and unmarried older adults. Interestingly, childless, unmarried older adults, if they have a larger number of very close emotional ties in their networks, have similar levels of well-being as those with a spouse and a child (Lang, Staudinger, & Carstensen, 1998). This finding implies that one way in which older adults may adapt to losses or absences in the social domain is through compensation. The compensatory aspect of social relations, in particular, has implications for the use of person-centered approaches in an examination of older adults' social networks. It may be that certain combinations of social network characteristics are more or less adaptive for older adults, highlighting the importance of examining individuals' networks from a holistic, pattern-centered perspective.

SOCIAL INPUT MODEL

According to the social input model, age-related improvements in the quality of relationships and emotional experiences in later life are due to reciprocal processes (Fingerman & Pitzer, 2007). The improvements are not only due to changes that occur among older adults but are also a reflection of the people with whom they interact. Older people tend to interact with older social partners. Older adults also tend to receive more positive input from their social network members than do younger individuals. For example, in a study of greeting cards, Fingerman and Griffiths (1999) found that older adults were more likely to receive sentimental greeting cards than were younger individuals.

Fingerman and her colleagues tested this model in an experiment in which they had younger and older individuals respond to vignettes involving young and older adults (Fingerman, Miller, & Charles, 2008). Young and older participants were more likely to use avoidant strategies and less likely to use confrontational strategies in response to negative vignettes involving an older person. In addition, young and older individuals were more likely to choose sentimental cards for older individuals than younger individuals. These studies reveal that developmental or age-related changes in social relationships and experiences are due to the developmental stages of both social partners as well as the social context.

EXCHANGE AND RECIPROCITY MODEL

According to exchange theorists, developed by and reflecting researchers with a Western perspective, it is detrimental to psychological well-being to underbenefit in relationships; rather, individuals attempt to maintain reciprocal or overbenefitting relationships (Antonucci, 1990). However, as individuals age and experience physical decline and other resource deficits that will result in increases in dependency, it may become more difficult to maintain strict reciprocity in relationships. According to Antonucci (1990), individuals "bank" resources gained from interactions with others in earlier points of the life course and summon these resources in later periods when failing health and other losses in resources may not allow the individuals to act in a strict reciprocal manner. The notion of a "support bank" helps to explain how older individuals' relationships can continue to be adaptive in the absence of reciprocity. According to Troll (1994), reciprocity may be more essential for the formation of bonds than for their maintenance, particularly among older women. Thus, attachments to individuals may remain (for example, into very old age) despite any lack of reciprocity in the relationship.

SUBSTITUTION MODELS

To help explain individual differences in support networks and what happens when certain key elements from these networks are missing, Cantor (1979) proposed the hierarchical-compensatory model in which there exists an order of preference in the choice of one's source of support (e.g., kin, then nonkin, and then formal organizations). This model is closely related to the idea of compensation in social relationships mentioned above. Relatedly, according to Shanas (1979), the "principle of substitution" operates within kin, such that members of the family are available in serial order ranging from the spouse and child to more distant relatives.

Empirical work, however, shows that the hierarchical-compensatory model and the principle of substitution may not operate in such a simple, straightforward manner. Johnson and Troll (1994), for instance, found that attenuated families (those with few family resources) received no more formal supports than did those with more family resources. In particular, among childless older adults or those with distant, inactive children, the principle of substitution did not seem to operate effectively. Again, it does not seem that adaptive compensation works in a simple substitutive manner; rather, a more complex mechanism may be at work. For example, it may be that no single relationship can always substitute for another relationship but that different combinations of several aspects of social relationships (e.g., the quantity and quality of social relationships) may compensate for other deficits in one's social network (e.g., Lang et al., 1998). A person-centered methodology could shed light on this more complex mechanism by identifying those combinations of social network characteristics that are more or less typical, and by understanding which combinations are most functional.

FUNCTIONAL MODELS

Related to these substitution models are functional or task-specific models of social relations. According to Litwak's (1985) model, informal support systems tend to be task-specific. So, for example, whereas kin fulfill tasks involving long-term commitment and intimacy, neighbors perform tasks requiring speed of response, knowledge of resource, and geographical proximity, and friends deal with problems involving peer group status and parallel experience and history. Similarly, according to Weiss's (1969, 1974) theory of the functional specificity of relationships, different relationships perform different functions for individuals. These functions include attachment (normally provided by parents, spouses, and close friends), social integration (provided by social activity groups), reliable alliance (provided by kin), guidance, reassurance of worth (e.g., from work colleagues), and opportunity for nurturance (e.g., to children). According to Weiss (1974), although the salience of these provisions may vary both inter- and intraindividually (e.g., across the life span), all are essential for adequate personal adjustment.

ROLE THEORY

Some researchers believe that it is multiple roles (e.g., worker, spouse, churchgoer, friend, club member, neighbor) that promote greater social connectedness and integration (Moen, 2001). This social integration, in turn, can improve psychological and physical health directly, by reducing isolation, or more indirectly, by elevating self-esteem, affecting preventative health behavior, enhancing health-related resources and choices, or providing social support. Researchers using role theory generally come from one of three theoretical perspectives: the role enhancement perspective, in which there is basically a positive and linear relationship between number of roles and health; the role strain perspective, in which roles and health are negatively related; or the role context perspective, in which it is actually the particular contingencies and role combinations that promote or hamper health (Moen, 2001). From the role context perspective, for instance, it is hypothesized that those roles that provide social support, rather than the total number of roles, are important facilitators of health. This perspective is most closely related to the assumptions made in the pattern-centered approach discussed in this chapter—namely, that it is important to look at various combinations of social integration variables to understand which patterns are most adaptive in terms of health outcomes.

To achieve a fuller picture of social relations and human development, one must consider the intersection of life-span development, that is, of the developing individual at the micro level such as the brain, as well as the broader life course or macro context of the groups, for example, the family, within which the social relations develop. The study of social relations generally and of convoys of social relations more specifically has achieved a new level in which we now seek not only to describe social relations but also to understand and even predict them and their effects. We propose that only by integrating a life-span and life-course perspective can this be achieved.

THE UNIQUE CONTRIBUTION OF THE PATTERN-CENTERED APPROACH WITH LIFE-SPAN SOCIAL RELATIONS RESEARCH

We outline the benefits of the pattern-centered approach and how it allows for a more comprehensive examination of the four tenets of the convoy model. Research has established that social relations can improve or buffer health and increase longevity, although specific findings have sometimes been inconsistent (e.g., Berkman & Syme, 1979; Blazer, 1982; Lin & Peek, 1999; Ryff & Singer, 2000; Sabin, 1993; Seeman, 2000; Sugisawa, Liang, & Liu, 1994). For example, whereas some researchers have found positive associations between particular types of social support (e.g., instrumental support, contact frequency) and survival (Blazer, 1982; Yasuda et al., 1997), others have found either no association (Hanson, Isacsson, Janzon, & Lindell, 1989) or negative associations (Lund, Modvig, Due, & Holstein, 2000). In their 1999 review of social network and mental health studies, Lin and Peek (1999) reported conflicting findings; for example, in terms of social network size, they found 12 studies showing positive effects on various mental health outcomes, 6 studies with nonsignificant results, and 2 studies showing negative effects. Similarly, frequency of contact with network members had positive effects on mental health in 6 studies, nonsignificant effects in 6 studies, and negative effects in one study.

Such a variable-centered approach is valuable and informative, but in reality, individuals, as highlighted in the convoy model (Antonucci, 2001; Antonucci et al., 2009), are embedded in social networks with arrays of attributes (e.g., small network size, frequent contact with family, significant amounts of emotional support; Antonucci & Akiyama, 1987; Antonucci, Akiyama, & Birditt, 2004; Bosworth & Schaie, 1997; Magai, Consedine, King, & Gillespie, 2003). Relationships are multifaceted. For example, a large network size may only be beneficial if all, or at least the majority, of the relationships in the network are of relatively high quality. Thus, it may be more informative to examine social network types, including the quality of social networks and their mental and physical health implications (Bosworth & Schaie, 1997; Fiori, Antonucci, & Cortina, 2006; Magai et al., 2003). Social network types, or typologies, can be defined as sets of social relations variables (for example, network size, emotional support) that, when considered together, distinguish among major groups in a population.

In addition, as stated previously, a crucial source of variation in network types stems from changes across the life course (e.g., childhood, adolescence, adulthood) and the transitions embedded within these different life-course stages (e.g., school, work, marriage, divorce, retirement). The social compositions in one's network may change over the life course (Antonucci & Akiyama, 1995; Lin & Peek, 1999). For example, siblings may be important in the lives of children and adolescents; lose importance, or at least salience, as individuals marry and have children; then become important again as individuals age, their children become less demanding, or they become widowed or retire from full-time employment. However, recent findings (Fuller-Iglesais, 2009) suggest that there are both cultural and demographic influences on sibling relationships. Families with 5 to 10 children, as is more common in some cultures today and was common in the United States in the past, may provide important close relationships that would otherwise be filled by friendships among individuals with only one or two siblings. Similarly, and perhaps related to these demographic differences, in cultures where families are large, it may be expected that close relationships would be confined to family rather than extended to friends. The old proverb "blood is thicker than water" reflects this perspective, indicating that family bonds are assumed to be stronger than friendships and thus should take primacy over nonfamily bonds.

The number of types of networks that exist might actually increase across the life span, as individual and subgroup differences in family histories and social convoy gains and losses accumulate (Antonucci, 2001; Antonucci et al., 2009; Kahn & Antonucci, 1980) and individuals diverge in terms of within-network dynamics of dependency and interdependency, closeness, and exchange of support over time (Antonucci, Akiyama, & Takahashi, 2004; Carstensen, 1992). The convoy model (Antonucci, Langfahl, & Akiyama, 2004; Kahn & Antonucci, 1980) suggests that a particularly wide range of network types might be found among certain cultures or age groups. Variations in expectations, gains, and losses among different social, religious, or economic groups or among certain samples or groups of older adults (e.g., widowhood) with particular family histories (e.g., marital status, number of children), the specific historical context (e.g., World War II, Vietnam, Iranian, and Afghanistan Wars), and within-network dynamics of structure, function, and quality, constitute important factors that shape network types. For example, whereas the network of an older married individual may focus on family (e.g., children, grandchildren), a never-married/never-partnered individual may either have a smaller or more structurally restricted network as a result of fewer available contacts or lifelong preferences, or a diverse network built on kin and nonkin relationships. Cultures may contribute to variations as well; for example, a sex-segregated society would suggest that some convoys would consist of only same-sex relations with perhaps a few exceptions of spouse, siblings, and children. Furthermore, the within-network dynamics of structure, function, and quality are complex; for instance, networks with similar structures or levels of support may vary in perceived quality. Bosworth and Schaie (1997) pointed out that

> typologies of support patterns may be particularly useful for gerontological research because of the increased differentiation among older adults, and because nonlinear analytical approaches allow researchers to examine heterogeneity of their samples. (p. 204)

We propose that this may be equally true of all ages. However, it is known that for the majority of individuals, social networks tend to focus on close family and friends and that structure (i.e., network composition) and function (i.e., support exchanged) are often interrelated in specific ways (R. G. Adams & Blieszner, 1995; Antonucci, 2001; Johnson & Barer, 1997). Thus, friend-focused networks tend to be high on emotional support, because friends are generally age-peers (R. G. Adams & Blieszner, 1995; Crohan & Antonucci, 1989), but low on instrumental support possibly because peers tend to have the same resources (Antonucci & Akiyama, 1995; Johnson & Barer, 1997). In contrast, diverse networks are thought to fulfill a variety of functions (Weiss, 1974).

The advantages of certain social compositions or networks may change over the life-course depending on life stage and transitions. Some research shows that "dense" networks (networks in which members are highly interconnected, i.e., know each other), which are generally beneficial, may not be good under certain circumstances, for example, going through a divorce with a dense network means that everyone knows everything about the ongoing divorce (Wilson, 1981b, in Lin & Peek, 1999; Smith & Christakis, 2003). Similarly, in some nonnormative circumstances such as being a young widow, a dense network may mean that no one you know has had a similar nonnormative experience or has the kind of distal connections that might help you cope with this nonnormative event.

Different aspects of the network may also be more or less advantageous (e.g., for survival) at different stages of the life course. Seeman, Kaplan, Knudsen, Cohen, and Guralnik (1987), in a cross-sequential study of those aged 38 to 70+, found that being unmarried is a predictor of increased mortality risk 17 years later only in the younger age groups (38–49 and 50–59), whereas greater social isolation from family or friends is a predictor of increased mortality risk only for those aged 60 or older. The authors concluded that there may be a shift in the relative importance of marital status and contacts with friends or relatives in the older age groups. Lund et al. (2000) found that whereas women aged 70 to 74 who maintained low contact frequency over time increased their risk of mortality, there was no increased risk for those aged 75 to 79, and there was actually a decreased risk of mortality among those women aged 85 and older who maintained low contact frequency. This may speak to the fact that a small but emotionally close network can be more health protective than a large and perhaps less emotionally close (or even emotionally draining) network among older women.

According to R. G. Adams and Blieszner (1995) "no one constellation of characteristics of personal relationships is optimal for people as they age" (p. 211). For instance, although a homogenous network provides intimacy, a heterogeneous network offers more variety for support. In this sense, it may be best to consider the adaptiveness of social networks in terms of a person–network fit (R. G. Adams & Blieszner, 1995), and that person–network fit is by definition idiosyncratic and may change dramatically across the life span. As noted earlier, the convoy model argues that personal and situational characteristics combine to shape the social networks and social relations needed to optimally meet the ongoing challenges of life. These are likely to change over time. The pattern-centered approach to research on social relations across the life span described in this chapter may therefore be particularly appropriate.

OVERVIEW OF PATTERN-CENTERED APPROACH

The pattern- (or person-) centered approach, as opposed to the variable-centered approach, allows for an examination of several variables at the same time, thus permitting the identification or description of network types rather than the consideration of specific variables individually. According to Magnusson (2003), in the person-centered approach the emphasis is on the individual as part of an integrated, dynamic person–environment system. An important aspect of such a system is the fact that no single variable alone can determine how the system functions. Furthermore, any single variable cannot "be understood by studying it in isolation, out of its context with other, simultaneously operating components of the individual" (Magnusson, 2003, p. 11). We note and agree with Magnusson (2003) and Bergman and El-Khouri (2003) that the person-centered approach is no "better" or "worse" than the variable-centered approach; it is simply an alternative perspective. Therefore, of primary importance when deciding between the variable- and person-centered approaches is the match between the scientific question and the method used to address it. However, in the case of convoys of social relations, the pattern-centered approach offers a particularly unique and relevant perspective on social relationships. Before discussing the evidence, we briefly consider the analytic strategies used to assess network typologies.

Network typology researchers have employed a variety of analytical techniques to determine network types, but the most popular is cluster analysis. Cluster analysis is used as a statistical strategy to extract information about the existence of subgroups with social relations profiles that resemble each other more than they resemble other subgroups within each sample and captures the "complex interactions that exist between social relationships and health" (Bosworth & Schaie, 1997, p. 204). More recently, some researchers have begun using latent class analysis to determine network types (e.g., Agneessens, Waege, & Lievens, 2006; Doeven-Eggens, De Fruyt, Hendriks, Bosker, & Van der Werf, 2008), a similar approach that is more advanced in the sense that it allows for model testing of different numbers of "classes" or clusters. Other researchers have used still other approaches, such as qualitative analysis (e.g., Wenger, 1997b). We turn next a summary of the empirical evidence examining structural network typologies, organized by age from childhood through old age.

Structural Network Typology Studies

Several researchers have specifically applied the pattern-centered approach to the study of typologies of social networks to better understand the "combination and interaction of disparate network characteristics" (Litwin, 1995, p. 155). The large majority of these studies have focused solely on the structural aspects of individuals' social networks. In addition, much of this research has been conducted among older adults, who (as mentioned earlier) tend to be particularly heterogeneous. However, using the limited existing research on network type approaches to social relations, the following discussion has been organized by age, beginning with childhood and adolescence and ending with late life. A comprehensive summary of all of the social network type studies mentioned in this chapter, along with the major characteristics of the studies, can be found in Table 12.1. We also organize the following

Table 12.1 Summary of social network type studies

Authors	Country	*N*	Age Range	Type of Analysis	Variables Included	Nature of Variables	Profiles
Agnesessens, Waege, & Lievens (2006)	Netherlands	623	23–75	Latent class analysis	Emotional support (talk, comfort), instrumental support (sick, money), companionship (trip) from 6 role relations (partner, immediate kin, extended kin, close friends, colleagues, and acquaintances/ mates)	Functional Only	Six separate LCAs for 6 role relations (2–4 of the following classes for each LCA): None, All Types, Emotional, Emotional/Instrumental, Emotional/Companionship, and Companionship
Auslander (1996)	Israel	200	60–95	Factor analysis	Social support (affective, affirmational, and instrumental), average frequency and duration of contact, network membership, attendance at religious services, network reduction	Structural and Functional	Supportive Replacement Traditional

(continued)

Table 12.1 ***Continued***

Authors	Country	*N*	Age Range	Type of Analysis	Variables Included	Nature of Variables	Profiles
Bosworth & Schaie (1997)	U.S.	387	36–82	Cluster analysis	Structural Social Network: number of friends and confidants, time at church/synagogue, meeting attendance, number of visits, number of social activities, number of neighbors	Structural Only	4 clusters
Doeven-Eggens et al. (2008)	Netherlands	1,835	*M* = 23.8 (*SD* = 0.68)	Latent class analysis	Top three role relationships (e.g., friend, parent, etc.)	Structural Only	Mixed family/friend oriented (46%) Peer-oriented (32%) Family oriented (22%)
Fiori, Antonucci, & Akiyama (2008)	U.S./Japan	514/ 491	US: 60–93 Japan: 60–92	Cluster analysis	Marital status, network size, proportion nearby, frequency contact with family, friends, proportion close others, instrumental support, emotional support, negative relations	Structural and Functional	US: Diverse/extensive (32%) Friend focused/supported (22%) Structurally restricted (17%) Friend-focused/unsupported (11%) Family focused/negative (10%) Functionally restricted (8%) Japan: Family focused/close (29%) Married and distal (24%) Friend-focused (20%) Diverse/supported (17%) Restricted/unsupported (10%)
Fiori, Antonucci, & Cortina (2006)	U.S.	1,669	60–96	Cluster analysis	Marital status, number of children, frequency of contact with children and friends, frequency of attendance at religious services, frequency of attendance at meetings	Structural Only	Diverse (32%) Friends (24%) Non-family/restricted (16%) Non-friends (16%) Family (12%)
Fiori, Smith, & Antonucci (2007)	Germany	516	70–103	Cluster analysis	Marital status, network size, proportion nearby, frequency of contact with family, friends, number of activities, proportion of close others, instrumental support, emotional support, satisfaction with family/friends	Structural and Functional	Friend-focused/supported (29%) Family focused (19%) Restricted-nonfriends-unsatisfied (16%) Friend-focused/unsupported (15%) Diverse-supported (13%) Restricted-nonfamily/ unsupported (9%)

(continued)

Table 12.1 ***Continued***

Authors	Country	*N*	Age Range	Type of Analysis	Variables Included	Nature of Variables	Profiles
Jackey (2009)	U.S.	205	8–12	Cluster analysis	Network size, proximity of network, frequency of contact with network, proportion female, proportion adult, the number of immediate family, number of extended family, number of friends, includes mother, includes father, includes sibling, includes grandparent, includes aunt/uncle, includes cousin, includes friend	Structural Only	Small family networks (21%) Large family networks (36%) Friend networks (13%) Diverse networks (30%)
Jackey (2009)	U.S.	205	8–12	Cluster anslysis	Number of positive (of 18) and negative (of 2) support functions filled by their mothers, fathers, siblings, friends, and extended family members	Functional Only	Friend-supported (42%) Little friend support (48%)
Litwin (1995)	Israel (Russian Jewish immigrants)	259	62–92	Cluster analysis	Network size, network composition, frequency of contact, percentage of intimates, duration of ties, residential proximity, supportive content	Structural Only	Kin (40%) Family intensive (<25%) Diffuse-ties (20%) Friend-focused (16%)
Litwin (2001)	Israel	2,079	60+	Cluster analysis	Marital status, number of adult children in vicinity, frequency of contact with children, friends, and neighbors, frequency of attendance at synagogue, frequency of attendance at a social club	Structural Only	Diverse (30%) Friends (<24%) Restricted (20%) Neighbors (17%) Family (9%)
Litwin (2004)	Israel	3,403	60+	Cluster analysis	Marital status, number of adult children in proximity, frequency of contact with children, friends, and neighbors, frequency of attendance at a place of worship, frequency of attendance at a social club	Structural Only	Diverse (30%) Friend-focused (~20%) Restricted (~20%) Neighbor-focused (17%) Family focused (9%) Community-clan (7%)
Litwin & Landau (2000)	Israel	194	75+	Cluster analysis	Network size, proportion of ties considered intimate, network composition (percentage of network composed of spouse, adult children, relatives, friends, and all others)	Structural Only	Diffuse-ties (42%) Friend-focused (28%) Kin (22%) Family intensive (8%)
Litwin & Shiovitz-Ezra (2006)	Israel	5,055	60+	Cluster analysis	Marital status, number of adult children in proximity, frequency of contact with children, friends, and neighbors, frequency of attendance at a place of worship, frequency of attendance at a social club	Structural Only	Diverse Friend-focused Restricted Neighbor-focused Family focused Community-clan

(*continued*)

Table 12.1 ***Continued***

Authors	Country	*N*	Age Range	Type of Analysis	Variables Included	Nature of Variables	Profiles
Meeuwesen, Hortulanus, & Machielse (2001)	Netherlands	2400	18–65+	Cut-off scores	Network size, loneliness	Structural and Functional	Socially competent (64%) Lonely (22%) Socially inhibited (8%) Socially isolated (6%)
Melkas & Jylhä (1996)	Finland	1,655	60+	Cluster analysis	Number of friends, having a confidant, frequency of contact with network members, exchange of practical help	Structural and Functional	Defective (35%) Family intensive (26%) Agentic (15%) Endowed (12%) Perceived (11%)
Rosenfeld, Richman, & Bowen, (2000)	U.S.	2,099	6th–12th grade	Cut-off scores	Support from parents, teachers, friends	Functional Only	Low Support (19.6% in middle school) (14.4% in high school) Support from Parents Only (7.4% in middle school) (5.5% in high school) Support from Friends Only (11.5% in middle school) (14.5% in high school) Support from Teachers Only (6.5% in middle school) (6.9% in high school) Support from Parents and Friends (9.8% in middle school) (12.4% in high school) Support from Parents and Teachers (6.4% in middle school) (7.6% in high school) Support from Friends and Teachers (10.3% in middle school) (13.2% in high school) High Support (26.5% in middle school) (25.6% in high school)
Stone & Rosenthal (1996)	Canada	3,186	Elderly	Cluster analysis	Network size, network composition (proportion of network composed of children, siblings, friends, parents, and spouse), presence of spouse or partner, living arrangement, frequency of seeing and telephoning children, siblings, friends, and parents	Structural Only	Small: Child-focused (19% men, 33% women) Medium: Balanced (19% men, 24% women) Small: Friendship-poor and socially isolated (19% men, 18% women) Small: Extended-family and friend-focused (17% men, 10% women) Large: Balanced (19% men, 11% women) Very Large: Balanced (8% men, 4% women)

(*continued*)

Table 12.1 ***Continued***

Authors	Country	*N*	Age Range	Type of Analysis	Variables Included	Nature of Variables	Profiles
Takahashi, Tamura, & Tokoro (1997)	Japan	148	60+	Self-report (Picture Affective Relationships Test)	Seeking proximity, receiving encouragement and help, receiving emotional support, receiving reassurance for behavior and/or being, sharing information and experience, giving nurture	Functional Only	Spouse-dominant (38%) Friend-dominant (18%) Child-dominant (16%) "Lone-wolf" (14%) Relatives-dominant (5%) Daughter-in-law-dominant (5%) Unclassifiable (4%)
Wenger	England, Wales		Elderly	Qualitative analysis	Availability of local close kin, level of involvement with family, friends, and neighbors, and level of interaction with community groups	Structural Only	Locally integrated (most common and robust) Wider-community-focused Local self-contained Local family dependent Private restricted

sections by the types of social relationship variables included in the analyses. We first describe network studies that only include structural characteristics (e.g., number of ties, types of relationships), followed by network studies that only include quality variables, and end with network studies that include both types of variables.

Using the pattern-centered approach allows for a test of the four tenets of the convoy model simultaneously. In particular, the pattern-centered approach allows for the examination of how multifaceted social networks change over time, vary by personal and situational characteristics, and predict well-being and health.

Structural Network Types in Childhood and Adolescence

Little research has examined patterns of network structure among children and adolescents. Although most studies used a variable- rather than pattern-centered approach, several important studies have documented the importance of social relations for children. For example, in their landmark, longitudinal studies of the social networks of parents and children, Cochran, Larner, Riley, Gunnarsson, and Henderson (1990) used Brofrenbrenner's ecological model of development to examine how networks evolve across macro and mirco levels and how parents use these networks to optimize their child's development. Similarly, focusing on school performance and well-being, Rosenfeld, Richman, and Bowen (2000) showed that children who were supported by others had better attendance, studied more, had better grades, and reported higher levels of self-efficacy. Interestingly, students reporting support from teachers, parents, and peers did better than students who reported support from none, one, or two of the same sources.

Only recently have studies using a pattern-centered approach to children's networks emerged. Jackey (2009) identified four main patterns of network structure among 8- to 12-year-old children (N = 204) with regards to the relationship types included in their networks: immediate family, extended family, and friends. Most children (57%) exhibited family-centered patterns. Some (21%) exhibited the "small family networks" pattern, including almost exclusively immediate family in their networks. All of these children included a mother in their networks, but fewer than average included a sibling, grandparent, aunt or uncle, or cousin. Other children (36%) exhibited the "large family networks" pattern, including both immediate and extended family members in their social networks. Their networks consisted of a larger than average proportion of adults and more extended family than children in any other clusters, but fewer friends than average.

A small group of children (13%) were identified as belonging to "friend networks." Their networks consisted of a low proportion of adults and included fewer immediate and extended family members than average. These children were also least likely to include parents in their social networks, with under half including a mother and fewer than 10% including a father.

Finally, 30% of children were identified as exhibiting a "diverse networks" pattern, based on their inclusion of both family and friends in their social networks. They had a lower than average proportion of adults in their networks, as well as fewer extended family members. However, they had more immediate family members and friends in their networks than average. All of these children included both a mother and a father in their networks, and they were more likely than average to include a sibling and a friend. Children exhibiting this pattern were the most likely to be White and to have married mothers.

These patterns of social relations, when considered alone, were not predictive of children's well-being, their orientation toward educational pursuits, or their educational attainment 12 years later. However, interesting interactions emerged between the network type and children's personal and situational characteristics. For boys, but not girls, belonging to the diverse or the friend network pattern at age 8 to 12 predicted more depression by early adulthood (age 20–27). Similarly, for children who were not White (95% Black), exhibiting the diverse network type was associated with better educational attainment by early adulthood, but among White children, there was no association. For children, then, the effects of network structure type may vary by race, gender, and the outcome examined.

In addition, childhood patterns of social relations seemed to affect children's later (12 years) response to life stress. Only children with diverse or large family network types at age 8 to 12 showed a negative association between stressful life events and well-being (subjective well-being and feelings about the self) 12 years later, whereas children in the other social networks did not show this buffering effect. Taken as a whole, the results of these studies suggest that, at least among children and adolescents, structural network types can be importantly related to health and well-being both immediately and at later points in the life span.

Structural Network Types in Adulthood

Adulthood covers a large portion of the life span which often includes a series of transitions that likely have substantial effects on individuals' social networks and their associations with well-being. Common transitions of adulthood include marriage, the birth of children, retirement, divorce, widowhood, institutionalization, and end of life. Unfortunately, most network typology research has either focused solely on the later part of the life span (60+) or has assessed individuals spanning a large age range (e.g., 23–75) with only superficial considerations of age differences in the network types. Research more closely examining shifts in network types stemming from life transitions is lacking. However, there is a great deal of empirical evidence to indicate that network types would change as a result of these transitions (i.e., research on changes in individual aspects of the social network stemming from these transitions).

Although research on adult structural social network types has focused primarily on older adults, there are a few exceptions. Doeven-Eggens and colleagues (2008) examined the association between personality and personal network types in college-aged students in the Netherlands. To determine the network types, these researchers used a latent class analysis to examine role relationships with three focal figures of the participants. Paralleling Jackey's (2009) findings with children and adolescents, they identified three types of personal networks: family-oriented, peer-oriented, and mixed family and peer-oriented. Interestingly, and reflecting the Convoy Model's prediction that personal characteristics influence the structure of social networks, Doeven-Eggens and colleagues found that individual differences in personality predicted network type membership. Thus, for example, extraverted students were more likely to have a primarily peer-oriented network.

Bosworth and Schaie (1997) examined a subsample of 387 adults ranging in age from 36 to 82 from the stratified random community-dwelling sample of the Seattle Longitudinal Study. These researchers conducted a cluster analysis with the following variables: number of friends, rank of confidants and neighbors, amount of time at church/synagogue, meetings attended, number of visits received, number of neighbors, and number of social activities per week. They found four (unnamed) clusters with different implications for health. The "oldest" cluster (mean age, 60.09 years) consisted of individuals below the sample mean for six of the seven measures but with more church visits than any other group, and the "youngest" cluster (mean age, 56.73 years) consisted of individuals with the most neighbors and who participated in more meetings relative to other groups, but had the fewest confidants or friends. A third cluster (mean age, 59.57) reported relatively high levels on all of the structural social variables, and a fourth cluster (mean age, 59.08) reported high levels on five of the seven measures, in particular number of visits received and number of hours spent participating in social activities.

Bosworth and Schaie (1997) demonstrated an important link between social relations and health by indicating that individuals who lacked social networks were more likely to have severe health problems, whether or not they were involved with a church. Furthermore, they found that married persons tended to have fewer physical health problems than unmarried persons. Nevertheless, it should be noted that not all social relationships are supportive, thus more extensive social networks did not always have cumulative positive and beneficial influences (see Antonucci, Akiyama, & Lansford, 1998; Antonucci, Lansford, & Akiyama, 2001). If Bosworth and Schaie had taken a variable-centered approach to the analyses of social relations, it is unlikely that they would have been able to identify the specific nuances of the social relations–health associations just described.

We next turn to the research focused primarily on older adults. Using a longitudinal, qualitative approach, Wenger (1997b) created a social network typology of a small sample ($N = 25$) of older adults in Wales. Based on the availability of local close kin, the level of involvement of family, friends, and neighbors, and the level of interaction with the community and volunteer groups, she developed five support network "types." These types included: (a) locally integrated, (b) wider-community focused, (c) local self-contained, (d) local family dependent, and (e) private restricted. These network types have been replicated in several countries, including Germany and the Netherlands (Wenger, 1996).

Wenger (1997b) argued that individuals in "locally integrated" support networks, characterized by informal help to and from local family, friends, and neighbors and involvement in community groups, are least at risk for mental health problems such as isolation, loneliness, and depression. In contrast, elderly individuals in the "private restricted support" support network, characterized by an absence of local kin and no local source of informal support, are most at risk.

The quality of support received from various network members was not assessed, limiting the conclusions that can be drawn from this series of studies. For example, it may be that there are some individuals in the "locally integrated" support network who have highly negative relations and others whose relationships are highly positive. Such possibilities highlight the need to consider both network structure and relationship quality to obtain a fuller representation of the individual's convoy of social relations. This broader conceptualization of social relations increases the probability of identifying potential causal pathways to health and well-being.

In a study using a representative sample of elderly immigrants from the former Soviet Union who arrived in Israel between 1989 and 1992 ($N = 259$), Litwin (1995) conducted a cluster analysis using the variables network size, network composition, frequency of contact, percentage of intimates, duration of ties, and residential proximity. He identified four network types: (a) kin networks, with an average composition and extended family emphasis; (b) family-intensive networks, with a close family composition; (c) friend-focused networks, with a composition of primarily friends; and (d) diffuse-tie networks, with an even distribution of all types of social relations. Litwin examined the availability of social support as an outcome variable and found that the "family-intensive" network type was the most supportive, whereas the "diffuse-ties" network type was the least supportive. It may be that individuals within each of these network types vary widely in their perceived availability of social support. Thus, once again the importance of including assessments of the quality of relationships including factors such as emotional support exchanged should be noted. Such a more detailed examination within the derivation of network types is likely to provide additional insight into how and why social relations influence other aspects of an individual's life.

This issue of variation in support within network types is highlighted in a similar cluster analytic study of a different random sample of Israeli adults aged 75 and older ($N = 194$), in which Litwin and Landau (2000) found identical clusters but found that the "diffuse-ties" network had the *highest* average support, whereas the "family-intensive" network type had the *lowest* average support. These findings are in direct contrast to Litwin's (1995) previous findings. Again, this discrepancy is likely due to the fact that the authors used measures of relationship function (specifically, emotional support) as outcome measures rather than including them in the cluster analyses; clearly, not all family-intensive networks are either supportive or not supportive.

In a substantively similar study, Stone and Rosenthal (1996) conducted a cluster analysis of a representative sample of elderly Canadians ($N = 3{,}186$) using the following variables: network size, an index of network composition assessing the relative numbers of network members (e.g., children, siblings, etc.), the presence of a spouse or a partner, living arrangement, and an index of frequency of seeing and telephoning each of children, siblings, friends, and parents. They identified six network profiles: (a) small: friendship-poor and socially isolated, which was a small family-dominated network; (b) small: child-focused; (c) small: extended-family- and friend-focused, characterized by the relative absence of children; (d) medium: balanced, which tended to be at least twice as large as any of the other networks; (e) large: balanced, which was bigger than the medium balanced network and had a greater presence of friends and higher rates of interaction with friends; and (f) very large: balanced, characterized by high rates of contact of each kind. Again, this study is limited in that an assessment of the quality of relations was not included in the network type derivation; furthermore, the authors did not examine well-being outcomes for the different network types.

In his examination of a representative national sample of community-dwelling older (60+) Jewish persons residing in Israel, Litwin (2001) used the following variables to determine types of social networks: current marital status, number of proximate children, frequency of contact with children, frequency of contact with friends, frequency of contact with neighbors, frequency of attendance at a synagogue, and frequency of attendance at a social club. Litwin identified a typology of five networks: (a) diverse, (b) friends, (c) neighbors, (d) family, and (e) restricted. He found that individuals in the restricted and family networks had the lowest average morale (a measure of psychological well-being similar to happiness), whereas those in the diverse and friends networks had the highest morale. These findings are consistent with previous research indicating that interactions with friends may be more self-esteem enhancing than interactions with kin (R. G. Adams & Blieszner, 1995; Antonucci & Akiyama, 1995). Furthermore, Litwin's findings concerning diverse and restricted networks are consistent with Wenger's findings regarding locally integrated and private-restricted networks. Specifically, it seems that having a variety of people in one's network is better for psychological health than is having a restricted network. An interesting point is the degree to which this finding is consistent across ages and cultures. As noted in Jackey's (2009) research, a diverse network is not always beneficial for children. Furthermore, some cultures are more restrictive in terms of who is considered an appropriate convoy or network member. In some sex-segregated and family-focused societies, it may be that having opposite-sex network members would be considered unacceptable and having nonfamily members would be seen as an indication that one either does not have sufficient family to meet his or her needs or is not a loyal family member.

Fiori and colleagues' (2006) U.S. study revealed networks similar to those found in the Litwin (2001) study. Fiori et al. conducted a cluster analysis in a stratified, multistage probability sample of 1,669 American adults aged 60 and over (the Americans' Changing Lives study) using variables parallel to those used in Litwin's (2001) study. They found Diverse, Family, and Friends network types, consistent with Litwin (2001). However, they found two types of restricted networks rather than just one: a nonfamily network and a nonfriends network. It could be that these two types of restricted networks (nonfamily and nonfriends) are unique to the American culture, given that most previous network typology studies have been conducted in Europe and Israel. Depressive symptomatology was highest for the nonfriends network and lowest for the diverse network, which is also consistent with past adult network typology research (e.g., Litwin, 2001).

With a larger and more ethnically diverse sample drawn from a national survey of Israelis, Litwin (2004) replicated the network types found in his previous study (2001; diverse, friend-focused, neighbor-focused, family-focused, and restricted), and identified a sixth: the "community-clan" network type. Interestingly, this network type, which reflects a traditional and unified "micro-societal structure" (p. 929), was made up primarily of Arab-Israelis, an ethnic group not included in his original 2001 study. Litwin (2004) found that the individuals in the community-clan network type were the least likely to use formal care services, regardless of functional health status, whereas the neighbor-focused and restricted networks were the most likely to use public home-care. Given the ethnic differences among the network types, these results have two implications. First, culture influences network types perhaps directly through expectations or indirectly, for example, through discrimination; and second, within specific cultures, behaviors appear to be associated with or are customary within certain social network types. Community-clan network types may be less likely to use formal services because their needs are addressed informally or because they fear discrimination in formal agencies. Contrarily, the restricted and neighbor-focused types may be more likely to use formal services, because they have fewer informal sources to rely on and they have less fear of discrimination.

In 2006, Litwin and Shiovitz-Ezra (2006) conducted a study of network types and mortality risk in a similar (but larger) sample. They found that of the six network types identified (diverse, friend-focused, neighbor-focused, family-focused, community-clan, and restricted), the diverse and friend-focused types (and to a lesser degree the community-clan type) had lower risk of mortality compared with those in restricted networks. These studies highlight the importance of examining cultural differences in social network types, an issue we return to later.

The convoy model of social relations recognizes the importance of each element of social relations, that is, the structure, function, and quality of social relations. Pattern-centered studies of social networks offer a unique perspective on structural aspects of social relations. Although relatively objective, because the term *social networks* represents a description of objective, observable aspects of social relations, these findings suggest that even these objective characteristics are influenced by other elements of the convoy. Personal characteristics such as age and situational characteristics such as culture influence structural characteristics. Furthermore, as predicted by the convoy model, social networks have been shown to influence health and well-being.

The social network type research discussed thus far has focused solely on the structural aspects of social networks, such as network size and frequency of contact (e.g., Litwin, 1995; Wenger, 1997b). However, it is clear from the literature that various aspects of social relations, such as the structural and functional characteristics of social convoys, have different implications for physical and psychological health (e.g., Antonucci, 2001; Rook, 1984; Russell & Cutrona, 1991; Seeman, 1996). Some researchers argue that functional aspects of the network (such as the actual support exchanged or the quality of relationships) may, in fact, be more important than structural indicators such as network size. In the following section, we summarize those network type studies using solely functional or qualitative aspects of social networks in the network type derivation.

Function and Quality Network Typology Studies

Prominent models and theories of social relations, such as the theory of functional specificity (Cantor, 1979; Litwak, Silverstein, Bengtson, & Hirst, 2003; Weiss, 1974) and the convoy model of social relations (Antonucci, 2001; Antonucci et al., 2009; Kahn & Antonucci, 1980) emphasize the importance of the structure and function of social networks. For instance, according to functional specificity theory, relationships tend to become specialized in terms of the functions they serve, so that individuals require a number of different relationships to maintain well-being. According to the convoy model, in addition to the structure and function of social relations, the qualitative evaluations of individuals' social relations are also fundamental to understanding the effects of social relations on mental and physical health. As with structural network type studies, research on functional and qualitative network characteristics has focused primarily on adults and has used a variety of methods, such as latent class analysis and cluster analysis, to determine the network types. However, some studies have examined social relationship quality in childhood and adolescence. The following sections include a discussion of studies examining relationship quality profiles, as well as how those profiles vary by individual differences and their association with well-being among people in four stages of the life span: childhood, adolescence, adulthood, and old age.

Childhood and Adolescence

Several studies have examined profiles of relationship quality in childhood and adolescence (Harvey & Bray, 1991; Levitt et al., 2005; Mandara & Murray, 2002; Takahashi, 2005; Takahashi et al., 2002). Stocker (1994) examined children's relationships with siblings, friends, and mothers. She found that relationships seemed to follow patterns in that children with good quality relationships with one member of their network tended to have good relationships with others. In her study of second graders, she found that children with warm relationships with their mothers also reported good relationships with siblings and friends. At the same time, conflict with siblings and friends was negatively related to positive mother–child relations.

In a series of studies, Takahashi and her colleagues (for example, Takahashi, 2005; Takahashi, & Majima, 1994; Takahashi et al., 2002) grouped Japanese children according to the relationship that provided them with the most support. They identified three clusters: family-focused, friend-focused, and the lone-wolf type. Takahashi (2005) reports that junior high and high school adolescents most commonly report a same-sex friend as the focal figure. Takahashi and colleagues (2002) found that lone-wolf types have poorer adjustment than those who report receiving support from either family or friends. In the United States, Levitt and her colleagues examined profiles of relationships among children ages 9 to 13. They examined children's reports of the relationships that provided them with different types of support. Levitt et al. (2005) found that children fit into three clusters: close family and friend, close family, and close and extended family. Among children, receiving support from multiple sources (close family and friends or extended family) rather than from only close family is associated with higher self-concept and less loneliness (Levitt et al., 2005). Other studies, for example among adolescents, found that family profiles characterized by high quality and low conflict are associated with higher self-esteem compared with profiles characterized by conflict or neglect (Mandara & Murray, 2002).

Teachers appear to play an especially important role during the adolescent years, with middle and high school students who received support from their teachers plus at least one other source (parents, friends, or both) showing more successful adaptation to adolescence and school success as indicated by such constructs as school attendance, hours spent studying, avoiding problem behavior, school satisfaction, school engagement, self-efficacy, and grades (Rosenfeld et al., 2000). These results suggest that a supportive teacher may be a necessary but not sufficient source of support for adolescents. Furthermore, considering overall network types as well as the provision of social support from multiple sources, may be more informative than considering any one type of relationship.

Examining patterns based on school-age children's sources of social support, Jackey (2009) found that children fit into two main network types, based on the number of positive (of 18) and negative (of 2) support functions filled by their mothers, fathers, siblings, friends, and extended family members. Fewer than half of the participants (42%) exhibited a pattern of social support referred to as "friend-supported." These children were characterized by high positive and negative support from friends, as well as high negative support from both father and extended family, little positive or negative support from siblings, and little negative support from mother. In contrast, more of the participants (58%) exhibited the opposite pattern of social support. These children were characterized as reporting little positive or negative support from friends, as well as high negative support from mother and siblings and no negative support from father or extended family. Overall, the extent of support from friends and the predominant source of negativity were the distinguishing features of these patterns.

Adulthood and Old Age

Studies of functional and quality profiles among adults have often focused exclusively on family or marital relations (Fincham & Linfield, 1997; Fisher & Ransom, 1995). For example, Fisher and Ransom (1995) examined typologies of families with a husband, wife, and child using measures including family worldview (e.g., locus of control, optimism), emotion management (e.g., affiliative tone, emotional expression, conflict strategies), structure (e.g., roles, rules), and problem solving. Using cluster analyses they found four types of families including balanced (average levels of the variables), traditional, disconnected, and strained families. Balanced and traditional families were healthier than disconnected and strained families, indicating that there are multiple ways families can be functional or dysfunctional.

Researchers have also used cluster analyses to identify types of marital couples. For example, Lavee and Olson (1993) used cluster analyses to group couples across several dimensions including personality, communication, conflict, finances, leisure, parenting, sex, family and friends, and religion. Couples fit into seven clusters, which were labeled as follows: devitalized, financially focused, conflicted, traditional, balanced, harmonious, and vitalized. Devitalized couples (with low-quality marriages, i.e., couples who were dissatisfied with every dimension of the marriage) were the least satisfied followed by financially focused and conflicted. Vitalized couples were the most satisfied, that is, they had the highest quality marriages. Devitalized couples were married for a shorter period of time, had lower income, were younger, and included a greater proportion of minorities.

Birditt and Antonucci (2007) investigated a more extensive set of relationships that, in addition to assessing family and spousal relations, also included friendships. Their study examined family and friend relationship profiles among married people aged 22 to 79. Birditt and Antonucci used cluster analyses to identify profiles of positive and negative quality relations with spouse, friend, and other family (child, parent). Profiles of relationship quality included high-quality (high positive, low negative across relationships) and low-quality (low positive, high negative across relationships) network profiles. More than half of the participants belonged to profiles with some combination of high-quality relationships, in which they rated at least one or all of their relationships (friend, family, and spouse) as positive and lacking in negativity.

Adults with friends may have different profiles than those without friends. Birditt and Antonucci (2007) therefore examined the profiles separately. Both groups had a high-quality family profile and low-quality spouse and family profiles. In addition, three unique profiles emerged among people without best friends including a moderate quality network profile and profiles that had exclusively low spouse or family quality. The findings may be due to variations in the demographics of each group, that is, age, gender, education, and differences between people with and without friends. For example, people without best friends were older, which may explain the moderate quality network because older people report less intense emotional experiences in relationships (Birditt & Fingerman, 2003).

Consistent with the convoy model, there were demographic differences in profile membership (Antonucci, 2001; Kahn & Antonucci, 1980). Older adults were less likely to report low-quality networks (low positive, high negative) and more likely to report networks that included high-quality relationships. Similarly, socioemotional selectivity theory, suggests that as people age, they are more motivated to maintain emotionally meaningful relations and better able to regulate their reactions to problems (Carstensen et al., 1999). Emotion regulation may occur across relationships (e.g., spouse, family, friends) among older adults rather than only in certain relationships (e.g., spouse).

Women were more likely to belong to low-quality networks, whereas men were more likely to belong to high-quality networks. Although women often have more positive and emotionally close relations, they also feel more burdened by the problems of others and report more negativity in their relationships than do men (Almeida & Kessler, 1998; Antonucci, 2001; Antonucci, Lansford, & Akiyama, 2002).

In addition, profile membership varied by race. Individuals in the low quality network cluster (among individuals without best friends) were more likely to be African American than were participants in the high-quality family group. It is possible that as a minority group, African Americans may experience more relationship strain than do others, perhaps because they have access to fewer economic resources (Connidis & McMullin, 2002; Jackson, 1991). African Americans may also be less likely to report high-quality family networks because they tend to have smaller networks with more family members who have fewer resources and are in need of more support (Ajrouch, Antonucci, & Janevic, 2001; Lee, Peek, & Coward, 1998; Jackson, 1991). These differences in social networks have implications for interventions. Rather than consistently nominating a particular family member (for example, spouse, child) for support in times of need, interventions should consider individual characteristics and relationship quality.

As a result of their in-depth comparison of individuals with and without best friends, Birditt and Antonucci (2007) found that the link between relationship profiles and well-being varied depending on the presence of a best friend. Among people with best friends, having at least two high-quality relations (not necessarily with one's spouse) is associated with better well-being. There were few variations in well-being between people who had high-quality relationships with three sources (spouse, family, and friend) and high quality relationships with two sources (e.g., family, spouse). This finding parallels research with children indicating that receiving support from a variety of relationship types predicts greater well-being than receiving support from fewer relationship types (Levitt et al., 2005). In addition, these results support the functional specificity theory, which suggests that receiving support from diverse sources is beneficial for well-being (Litwak et al., 2003; Weiss, 1969).

The findings just summarized suggest that among people with best friends, having three high-quality types of relationships is no more beneficial for well-being than having two. Individuals may reach a point of diminishing returns at which having a greater number of high-quality relationships is not necessarily better for well-being, as has been suggested by previous research (e.g., Berkman & Syme, 1979). Furthermore, unlike studies in which aggregate assessments of relationships are associated with well-being (e.g., Antonucci et al., 1998; Ingersoll-Dayton, Morgan, & Antonucci, 1997; Pagel, Erdly, & Becker, 1987), this research demonstrates that links between relationship quality and well-being depend on the number, type, and context of relationships. Having a high-quality friend relationship, however, did not appear to reduce the negative effects on well-being of having low-quality spouse or family relationships. Indeed, this group had lower well-being than people who had low-quality relations across network members. These findings are consistent with research indicating that although friends are important for daily well-being, family relations are important for maintaining overall well-being (Larson, Mannell, & Zuzanek, 1986).

Interestingly, among individuals without best friends, the spousal relationship appeared particularly important for well-being. Having high- or low-quality family relations did not differentiate people by well-being. The absence of spousal support may be particularly detrimental to the well-being among individuals without best friends because they rely more on their spouse for needed support. Indeed, they may view their spouse as a best friend. Thus, interventions should consider the availability and meaning of relationships.

These findings suggest that for people with a best friend, having a high-quality relationship with spouse is not necessary for psychological well-being. People with high-quality family and best friend relations had high levels of well-being despite their moderate quality spousal relations. In contrast, previous literature has suggested the spousal relationship is more highly associated with well-being than all other relationships (Walen & Lachman, 2000). Thus, Birditt and Antonucci's (2007) findings suggest that clinicians and policy makers should take note of the multiple relationships in which people are engaged and consider ways to improve quality across at least two types of relationships. In particular, this finding offers promise to those who have only moderate-quality relations with their spouse. Maintaining high-quality family and friend relationships may improve well-being. Changing cohorts and cultural norms may lead to variations in marital expectations that in some cases will lead the spousal relationship to be pervasively important, whereas in other cases this will be less true.

Research regarding profiles of relationship quality has also been conducted in Europe and Japan, lending additional support to the notion that there are cultural differences in expectations about relationships. Agneessens, Waege, and Lievens (2006) explored whether a large sample of adults living in the Netherlands (N = 623, ranging in age from 23 to 75) could be categorized into typologies depending on the types of support they expect from specific relationships. Agneessens et al. (2006) conducted six separate latent class analyses for each type of relationship examined (partner, immediate kin, extended kin, friends, colleagues, and acquaintances/mates) using three major types of support (emotional, instrumental, and companionship). They found three typologies of support for the partner relationship: a typology of individuals who receive "All types" of support from their partner (emotional, instrumental, and companionship), which was the largest typology for this relationship, as well as an "Emotional" typology (consisting of individuals who receive primarily emotional support from their partner), and a typology of individuals who receive no support from their partner (most likely because they do not have a partner). For both relationships with friends and relationships with acquaintances/mates, individuals were most likely to fall into the "Emotional–Companionship" typology, whereas for relationships with colleagues the largest typology was "Companionship." Individuals were most likely to receive all types of support from both immediate kin and extended kin. Although this approach allowed the researchers to determine if specific role relationships tend to provide specific types of support, it did not give a clear picture as to how individuals' networks vary in terms of what role relationships they actually have, nor what the consequences of these network types are for health and well-being.

Takahashi, Tamura, and Tokoro (1997) categorized people on the basis of the social partner they identified as providing the most support using a volunteer sample (N = 148) of elderly community- and institution-dwelling Japanese. They found three groups of individuals: family-dominant, friend-dominant, and "lone wolves" (no dominant source of support). Takahashi et al. report that although there were no differences in psychological well-being among people with friend and family support, lone wolves had significantly lower self-esteem and life satisfaction than individuals in networks with any dominant affective figure. Creating social relations patterns based only on dominant affective figures is limited, however, because it does not address other aspects of the social network, such as frequency of contact or quality of relationships. Takahashi (2004) agrees that focal figures do not always necessarily provide a complete picture of an individual's social relations.

Conclusions

Although it is often thought that good relationships lead to better well-being and bad relationships lead to poor well-being, the relationship quality profiles reviewed in this section suggest that the associations among these variables are considerably more complex. There are many ways to have functional or dysfunctional relationships. In addition, profiles that include family and nonfamily relations appear to challenge the common conclusion in the literature that the spousal relation is the most important relationship for well-being. However, rather than contradict existing variable-centered research, these pattern-centered studies simply stress the importance of considering the multiple relationships within which people are involved. Also important may be culture, cohort, and individual specificity. All these factors may need to be considered more completely for the association between social networks and well-being to be fully understood.

Furthermore, the health advantages of having a diverse network over a very restricted network are consistent with the role context and role enhancement perspective of role theory (Moen, 2001), which claim that multiple roles (especially those providing social support) promote greater social connectedness or integration, which in turn relates positively to physical and psychological well-being. It seems especially critical to consider the quality of these restricted social environments; having only a few network members may be adaptive if the relationships are positive but may clearly not be adaptive if the relationships are negative.

Network Typology Studies Including Structure and Function and Quality

Most studies of network typologies have focused heavily or solely on morphological or structural criteria, such as number of friends and contact frequency (Litwin, 1996). Litwin (1996) points out, however, that larger networks do not necessarily translate into getting more support; in other words, the function of the network and the quality of support may be independent of the extent of available assistance. Here we discuss those social network type studies that have included both structure and function or quality in their derivations of network types.

In addition to examining patterns based on network structure and support separately (as described earlier), Jackey (2009) also examined children's patterns on the basis of structure and support together. This examination revealed that among children, patterns were primarily driven by structural characteristics, at least given the social support indicators available for that analysis. The three clusters identified were distinguished from one another by network size; time known network; proximity of the network; contact frequency with the network; the proportion of adults in the network; the number of immediate family, extended family, and friends included in the network; the inclusion of at least one mother, father, sibling, grandparent, aunt or uncle, and cousin in the network; positive support from father; negative support from sibling; and positive and negative support from extended family members. However, clusters were not distinguished from one another on the basis of the proportion of females in the network, the inclusion of a friend in the network, positive or negative support from mother, negative support from father, positive support from sibling, or positive or negative support from friends. Thus, whereas 88% of the structural variables distinguished significantly among the clusters, only 40% of the support variables did so. This may be an indication that among children, the structure and composition of one's social network is a more important determinant of one's pattern of social relations—that is, similarity with others on social relations—than are the sources from whom one receives these types of social support.

Alternatively, these findings may be artifactual, reflecting the specific properties of the measures used to examine social support, in that only one source could be named for each support function. The results may, therefore, be less sensitive or inclusive indicators of the social support available from each partner than would be required to identify clear patterns. The three clusters that were identified were labeled as the "low family presence and support" (23%), "immediate-family centered" (34%), and "extended family included" (43%).

Related work considered the structure and function of adults' social relations. Melkas and Jylhä (1996) examined social network types in a stratified random sample of noninstitutionalized older adults (60+) living in Finland (N = 1,655). They included the following variables in a cluster analysis to determine network types: number of friends, whether respondents had at least one confidant, frequency of meetings with members of the network, help received, and help provided. They identified five network types: (a) the endowed network, characterized by a large number of friends, the presence of a confidant, frequent meetings with nonkin, and active exchange of practical help; (b) the perceived network, characterized by many network resources but very infrequent contact with people outside the family; (c) the agentic network, characterized by an average number of friends and proportion with a confidant but very frequent contact with people outside the household; (d) the family-intensive network, which consisted of individuals who were particularly active in maintaining ties between parents and their children; and (e) the defective network, which was characterized by a small number of friends, a low proportion of individuals with a confidant, and a small total and kin network. Interestingly, some of these network types were distinguished by sociodemographic variables, whereas others seemed to represent special types of individual lifestyles. For example, although the agentic network consisted of mostly older widowed women and the perceived network was dominated by relatively healthy young-old married individuals, the endowed network was sociodemographically diverse.

Melkas and Jylhä (1996) also examined the impact of these different network types on feelings of loneliness, life satisfaction, and satisfaction with emotional support. They found that those in the endowed network had the highest functioning, with little loneliness, high life satisfaction, and high satisfaction with emotional support. Although individuals in the perceived network were not lonely, they had only average satisfaction with emotional support. Individuals in the agentic network, although lonelier, had a higher level of satisfaction. Individuals in the family-oriented network had average levels of loneliness and satisfaction, and those in the defective network were the most dissatisfied and lonely. These findings are consistent with those reported by Litwin concerning diverse and restricted networks as well as Wenger's findings regarding her locally integrated and private restricted network. In general, it seems that having a variety of people in one's network is better for psychological health than is having a very restricted network.

Auslander (1996) and Meeuwesen, Hortulanus, and Machielse (2001) are among the few researchers who have included measures of support quality in a network typology derivation, although neither of these researchers employed cluster analysis. In her study of 200 Israeli older adults aged 60 to 95 obtained through quota and random sampling, Auslander (1996) used factor analysis (a variable-centered approach) rather than a more pattern-centered approach, such as cluster analysis, in the derivation of her network types. She used 13 variables (3 social support measures, average frequency and duration of contact, 6 components of network membership, attendance at religious services, and 2 indicators of network reduction) in the factor analysis. They identified 3 factors or network types: (a) the supportive network, which included affirmational, affective, and instrumental supportiveness variables as well as frequency of contact; (b) the replacement network, which included the loss of a network member during the last year, amount of support lost, and number of friends; and (c) the traditional network, which included the presence of a spouse, number of children, and synagogue attendance.

Meeuwesen and colleagues (2001) took a very unique approach to the examination of network types. On the basis of evidence of low correlations between network size and feelings of loneliness, these researchers argue, as we do, that it is important to look at both quantity and quality of social relations. They interviewed 2,400 Dutch individuals (18+) drawn from all individuals 18 and over in four communities in the Netherlands and measured network size, loneliness, support given and received, satisfaction with social contacts, life events, personal competencies, social responsibility, and demographic variables. On the basis of a theoretically driven division of the respondents into two network size categories (small: 0–4 individuals in the network; large: 5–24) and two loneliness categories (not or slightly lonely: 0, 1, or 2 on an 11-item scale; and moderate or very strong feelings of loneliness: 3+), the researchers determined which individuals belonged in each of the following four social network types: (a) socially competent (large network and not lonely), (b) socially inhibited (small network and not lonely), (c) lonely (large network and lonely), and (d) socially isolated (small network and lonely). This division is also consistent with Johnson and Barer's (1997) distinction between loners (those individuals who have never been active socializers and who have little desire to make friends late in their lives) and the lonely (those who are "victims of circumstances," e.g., death of network members). Similarly, Wagner, Schütze, and Lang (1999) distinguished between objective isolation (in which individuals have few or no social relationships) and subjective isolation (in which individuals feel lonely and isolated).

Meeuwesen et al. (2001) discovered that 64% of their sample was socially competent, 22% was lonely, 8% was socially inhibited, and 6% was socially isolated. They found that socially competent individuals received and gave the most support, followed by the lonely, the socially inhibited, and finally, the socially isolated, who received and gave the least support. Furthermore, whereas the socially competent individuals gave more support than they received, the socially isolated individuals received more support than they gave. The percentage of socially isolated individuals was 6 times higher among respondents with low socioeconomic status, and the lonely and socially isolated groups mentioned twice as many negative events as the other groups. Finally, on a measure of personal competence (self-confidence, coping behavior, and social skills), the socially competent group scored higher than all other groups. This study highlights the importance of including both quantitative and qualitative measures in a network typology analysis.

In a study of 516 older German adults (*M* age = 85 years), Fiori, Smith, and Antonucci (2007) used structural, functional, and qualitative variables in a cluster analysis to derive multidimensional network types. They included the following measures of social relations in their analysis: marital status, total network size, proportion of network living nearby (in Berlin), frequency of contact with family, frequency of contact with friends, number of activities, proportion of close others, instrumental support, emotional support, and satisfaction with family and friends. Fiori et al. (2007) derived six network types: diverse-supported, family focused, friend focused-supported, friend focused-unsupported, restricted-nonfriends-unsatisfied, and restricted-nonfamily-unsupported. By considering not just the structure but also the function and quality of the network, they identified six network types, as opposed to the four most commonly found in research focused on structure only.

Although certain structures are generally associated with certain functions, as the convoy model suggests (Antonucci, 2001; Kahn & Antonucci, 1980), structure and function are not always correlated. For example, Fiori and colleagues (2007) found both supported and unsupported friend-focused network types. This distinction seems to be due at least in part to age; whereas 77% of those in the unsupported type were young-old individuals, the majority of those in the supported type (72%) consisted of oldest-old individuals, whose increasing levels of dysfunction (Baltes & Smith, 2003) may make them less active and more reliant on their networks for instrumental aid. Fiori and colleagues also found two types of restricted networks—one restricted in terms of support (but with relatively high satisfaction), the other in terms of support and satisfaction. From a life-span perspective, it may be that individuals in the former (the restricted-nonfamily-unsupported) network type have always preferred such a network, and that those in the latter (the restricted-nonfriends-unsatisfied) network type are disappointed by failed attempts to maximize emotional support from close relationships (Carstensen, 1992). Carstensen's socioemotional selectivity theory may best apply to the former rather than the latter group.

In terms of age differences, Fiori and colleagues (2007) found that the restricted network types were more common among the oldest-old individuals (85+) than among the young-old individuals (70–84 years of age). This finding is consistent with increasing constraints experienced by the oldest-old, due at least in part to losses of close partners and age-peers (Baltes & Smith, 2003). In terms of well-being differences, individuals in the diverse-supported network type had relatively high well-being and those in the restricted types had relatively low well-being, consistent with previous research on structural social network types (e.g., Litwin, 2001; Wenger, 1996, 1997b). However, those individuals with the highest levels of depressive symptomatology, lowest levels of subjective well-being, and highest morbidity were in the friend-focused-supported network type. It is likely that the poor physical health of these individuals actually led to a greater need for instrumental support and possibly higher depressive symptoms and lower well-being. Alternatively, it may be that the receipt of instrumental support from friends contributes to negative affect stemming from dependency (Penninx et al., 1998).

In a similar study of two cultures, Fiori, Antonucci, and Akiyama (2008) conducted cluster analyses in the United States and Japan, using samples of approximately 500 adults aged 60 or older. They conducted separate cluster analyses for each country using structural measures of social relations (proportion married, total network size, proportion in proximity, frequency of contact with family, frequency of contact with friends), functional measures of social relations (proportion of close others, instrumental support, emotional support) and evaluative (i.e., quality) measures of social relations (negative relations). Although they uncovered four common or shared network types (diverse, restricted, friend-focused, and family-focused), in the United States, the researchers found two types of friend-focused networks (supported and unsupported) and two types of restricted networks (structurally and functionally restricted). In addition, in Japan a unique network type was uncovered, which the researchers called the "married and distal" network type. As in Fiori et al.'s (2007) study, it seems that although certain structures are often associated with certain functions, structure and function are not always correlated (e.g., the two U.S. friend-focused network types and the two types of restricted network types). Furthermore, the findings suggest that there are common network types across cultures but also that there are some culturally specific network types.

In terms of age, the youngest individuals tended to be in the most diverse networks, and the oldest tended to be in the most restricted. This is consistent with previous research (e.g., Fiori et al., 2006; Litwin, 2001). Interestingly, individuals in the functionally restricted network type had the worst physical and mental health in the United States, whereas those in the structurally restricted network type had the lowest survival rates at a 12-year follow-up. It appears that having unsupportive and negative relationships is better for longevity than having no relationships at all. In contrast, in Japan there were no well-being differences by network type. This implies that social network types hold different meanings across different cultures. The authors suggest that because relationships in Japan are more likely to be viewed as obligatory rather than voluntary, the Japanese may simply learn to accept, or at least to say they accept, whatever network they have—hence the lack of an association of network types with well-being in this country.

Summary

Earlier in the chapter, Table 12.1 provided a summary of all known network typology studies, with network types arranged in descending order of frequency when available. Across studies, and in particular those using cluster analysis or latent class analysis and those including structural social relations variables, several relatively robust network types can be identified that are associated with well-being: specifically, a diverse or diffuse network type, a restricted or socially-isolated network type, a friend- or community-focused (or both) network type, and a family-focused network type (Bosworth & Schaie, 1997; Doeven-Eggens et al., 2008; Fiori et al., 2006; Litwin, 1995, 2001; Litwin & Landau, 2000; Stone & Rosenthal, 1996). Studies using more qualitative methodological approaches have identified similar structural social network types (e.g., Takahashi et al., 1997; Wenger, 1996, 1997b). The diverse network type tends to be the most common, whereas the family-focused and restricted network types tend to be the least common (although there are cultural differences; see Fiori et al., 2008).

Many of those studies that have included functional measures of social relations in the derivation of network types were inconclusive either because of the non-pattern-centered statistical approach used (factor analysis, Auslander, 1996;

cutoff scores, Meeuwesen et al., 2001) or because of the deficiency of other social relations variables in the analysis (Agnessessens et al., 2006; Meeuwesen et al., 2001; Takahashi et al., 1997). Those studies that included both structural and functional social relations variables (e.g., Fiori et al., 2007; Fiori et al, 2008) indicate that although structure and function are often correlated, some network types that are similar in structure can vary in function, quality, or both. In sum, it appears that heterotypy in social networks is constrained to some extent (Consedine, Magai, & Conway, 2004); in other words, we see evidence of "bounded diversity" (Agneessens et al., 2006, p. 432).

In terms of well-being, it seems that in general having a variety of people in one's network is better for psychological health than is having a very restricted network (e.g., Fiori et al., 2006; Litwin, 2001; Melkas & Jylhä, 1996; Wenger, 1997b). As mentioned earlier, this is consistent with the role context perspective and role enhancement perspective of role theory (Moen, 2001), as well as with functional specificity theory (Weiss, 1974). Furthermore, Litwin's (2001) and Fiori et al.'s (2006) findings indicate that individuals in friend-focused networks tend to have better mental health outcomes than those in family-focused networks. These findings are consistent with previous research indicating that interactions with friends may be more self-esteem enhancing than interactions with kin (R. G. Adams & Blieszner, 1995). However, it is also clear that not all friend-focused networks are beneficial for health; it clearly depends on the type of support provided by those friends (e.g., instrumental support provided by friends may be less beneficial than that provided by family) and the age of the individual (e.g., Fiori et al., 2007). Fiori et al.'s (2007) study shows that friend-focused networks may actually become less adaptive with old age. Furthermore, some restricted networks are better for health than others (e.g., Fiori et al., 2007; Fiori et al., 2008). Clearly, it is important when considering outcomes to understand how the structure and function of an individual's network interact; they cannot be understood in isolation.

TRANSITIONS DURING CHILDHOOD AND THEIR EFFECT ON SOCIAL NETWORK TYPES

In addition to the typical developmental changes in social networks discussed earlier that occur throughout childhood and adolescence, specific transitions that occur within these periods are also likely to affect children's social networks. During childhood and adolescence, the most commonly studied transitions are those involving families and school. Within the family, many children experience the transition to siblinghood, and some children will experience transitions surrounding the divorce and subsequent remarriage of their parents. Within the school realm, nearly all children will experience at least two major transitions, the first at their initial entry into formal schooling, followed by the transition to middle school or junior high school. With respect to the two family transitions, network changes including the addition of network members, changes in contact with network members, and changes in relationship quality with network members are common during the transition to siblinghood and to parental divorce or remarriage. Although little research has focused specifically on how social networks change during school transitions, an examination of the relevant research clearly indicates that changes in social networks are expected as children enter school and again as they move from elementary or primary school to middle or junior high school. Theoretical predictions and indirect evidence regarding network changes over each of these transitions is presented in the following sections, although more direct empirical evidence on these matters is clearly needed.

Transition to Siblinghood

Within the family, one transition experienced by many children that affects the social network is the transition to siblinghood. With the addition of a new baby to a family, the older sibling's social network may change most notably by the addition of the new sibling, who will likely become one of his or her longest lasting network members. In addition, relationships with other network members, including parents and extended family, may change as the family dynamics adapt to the addition of a new member. For instance, if the mother has been the child's primary caregiver, the child's relationships with both parents may shift as the mother becomes heavily involved in day-to-day care of the newborn and the father takes over a greater proportion of the older sibling's care (Volling, 2005). Parent–child relationships may also be affected by the stress on both parents of caring for a newborn or by accompanying changes in the parents' relationship with one another (Volling, 2005). In addition, the birth of a younger sibling may make it less likely that the child's mother will work outside the home over the next few years (e.g., Baydar, Greek, & Brooks-Gunn, 1997). The older child will therefore be less likely to be in out-of-home childcare, making his or her social networks more focused on the family and family friends, rather than on child-care peers and caregivers.

Divorce and Remarriage

For those children who experience the divorce of their parents and/or the remarriage of one or both parents, these events typically initiate significant transitions in the child's life. Inherent in these transitions are a variety of changes to the child's social network, from decreased contact with the noncustodial parent to potentially increased influence of peers and adults outside the family. As Hetherington (2003) noted in her extensive review of the literature on social support and children's adjustment following divorce and remarriage, however, the experience of parental divorce and remarriage for children varies tremendously from one family to the next.

Perhaps the most obvious network change following parental divorce is the decreased contact, or in some cases, complete cessation of contact, with the noncustodial parent, typically the father. By extension, this distancing may also result in decreased contact with kin of the noncustodial parent, including grandparents or other extended family. This decreased contact may have differential effects on children depending on the quality of their relationship with the noncustodial parent before the divorce. Relationships with the custodial parent (typically the mother) may also change following a divorce or remarriage, but the nature of the change varies a great deal between children. For instance, many girls develop close, intimate relationships with their mothers following a divorce, whereas boys are more likely to experience conflict with their divorced mothers. Changes in the parent–child relationship also depend on individual characteristics of the parent and child, parenting style, and the amount of stress caused by the divorce (Hetherington, 2003).

Following a parent's remarriage, children's networks adjust to incorporate relationships with a new stepparent and in some cases, new step-siblings. These new network members may be sources of social support as well as conflict, particularly during the initial adjustment period. In addition, remarriage can alter the relationship between the child and his or her custodial parent as more of the parent's attention is directed toward the new spouse and as the parent adjusts to his or her own altered circumstances (Hetherington, 2003).

In her review, Hetherington (2003) reported that following a divorce or remarriage, children's relationships with parents, siblings, and peers also tend to increase in negativity, conflict, aggression, and coercion. These network difficulties tend to diminish over time as families adjust to their new situations, but some indirect effects on children's interactions with their social networks may persist into adulthood. For example, young adults from divorced and remarried families tend to report difficulty in their relationships with family members, colleagues, and romantic partners, including a higher divorce rate than young adults from nondivorced families. However, if the divorce decreases conflict between the mother and father, the child may actually benefit. Social support and positive relationships both within and outside the family can help children cope with the challenges of parental divorce and remarriage. In some cases, peer relationships, both positive and negative, may be more influential on children of divorced parents than on children whose parents remain married (Hetherington, 2003).

Transition into School

As young children enter formal schooling for the first time, their social networks are widely presumed to expand because of the addition of school-related social contacts such as classmates and teachers. For those children who have not previously been involved in preschool or group child care, this expansion may be especially pronounced.

Perhaps one of the most notable changes to the social network upon the commencement of formal schooling is the wealth of new peers available to the child for companionship and friendship formation. When considering that most children beginning school will spend 6 or more hours per day, 5 days per week with this group of classmates, the potential for integration of these peers into the child's social network is clear. Despite the availability of a multitude of new social partners, however, Dunn, Cutting, and Fisher (2002) found that the majority of children who had a close friend in preschool (75%) retained these friendships through the first year of school. Some children did not remain friends with their preschool friends due to different schools or classrooms, or one member of the pair having moved to a different neighborhood (Dunn et al, 2002). Thus, it appears that children's existing friendships are frequently maintained over the transition to school when circumstances allow.

Some evidence suggests that aspects of the social network, including stability of certain network members, may be beneficial for children's adjustment to the new setting. A series of studies of friendship across the transition to school has shown that both starting school with an established friend and the formation of friendships during the first year of school are influential for children's attitudes toward school and academic performance (Ladd, 1990,

1999; Ladd & Kochenderfer, 1996). In another line of research, Entwisle and Alexander (1998) found that children with coresident grandmothers tended to perform better in first grade than other children. In addition to the authors' explanation that grandmothers provided an additional supervisory adult at home, the stability in support from a grandmother during a time of many other changes may have been a source of strength.

Transition to Middle School

In United States school systems, between about fifth and seventh grade, children typically transition from a relatively small, neighborhood-based elementary or primary school setting in which they remain with one teacher and 20 to 30 classmates for the majority of the school day, to a middle school or junior high school, which is typically much larger, may be more diverse, and in which they likely do not remain with the same teacher and classmates during the school day. Thus, as in the transition into formal schooling, the transition to middle school is likely to introduce the child to a wide range of new social contacts, thereby potentially expanding the social network.

This expansion of the social network by exposure to new peers typically comes at a time (entry into adolescence) when the importance of peers in the social network is sharply increasing, as discussed earlier, making successful navigation of this expanded peer group potentially quite an important developmental task. Indeed, integration into the peer group has been conceptualized as one marker of a successful transition to middle school (McDougall & Hymel, 1998). Such integration may also promote adaptive functioning in other domains during this transition. In one study, students' sense of belonging at school and their goals with respect to relationships with classmates were associated with nearly all indicators of their academic goals and performance (Anderman & Anderman, 1999), indicating that as in the initial transition into school, success in the transition to middle school is influenced by social network factors.

TRANSITIONS IN ADULTHOOD AND THEIR EFFECT ON SOCIAL NETWORK TYPES

As mentioned above, the adult portion of the life span consists of a variety of transitions that likely have substantial effects on individuals' social networks and their associations with well-being, such as marriage, the birth of children, retirement, divorce, widowhood, institutionalization, and end-of-life issues. In addition, research examining shifts in network types stemming from life transitions is lacking. However, a great deal of empirical evidence indicates that network types *would* change as a result of these transitions. Let us turn now to a consideration of this evidence.

Marriage

Marriage is likely to increase an individual's network size, both through the addition of kin (i.e., in-laws) and the addition of the spouse's friends. Being married has a dramatic influence on the people with whom individuals spend their time (Larson et al., 1986). Research does indeed show that married individuals have larger networks than do separated, divorced, widowed, or never married individuals (Antonucci, 1985). However, Dykstra (1990) found that having a partner does not necessarily serve a socially integrating function. After marriage, one's partner may begin to fill an increasing number of functions generally provided by one's social network as a whole (e.g., attachment, social integration, reliable alliance, guidance, reassurance of worth, and opportunity for nurturance; Weiss, 1969, 1974) and individuals may become less dependent on other social network members to fulfill these functions.

Married people tend to have better psychological and physical well-being than unmarried individuals (e.g., Berkman & Syme, 1979; Kiecolt-Glaser & Newton, 2001). This finding is thought to be due in part to the receipt of more social support (Kessler & Essex, 1982). According to Johnson and Barer (1997), being married is the single most significant factor preventing institutionalization of the oldest-old (85+). Furthermore, although being with one's spouse may not have much to do with moment-to-moment current feelings due to a lifetime of companionship, time spent with one's spouse may still relate to one's longer term morale (Larson et al., 1986). Lee (1978) found that morale is positively related to marital satisfaction and that the effect of marital satisfaction on morale varies by gender, with the effect being stronger for wives. Thus, the quality of a marriage seems to be as important (if not more important) than the simple fact of being married for psychological well-being, which speaks directly to the nature of the differences among relationship structure, function, and quality.

Divorce

Divorce may result in the loss of social network members (as individuals have less contact with in-laws and friends who have decided to "take sides") but may also result in an increase in support from family or friends. These alternatives are sometimes referred to as the *isolation hypothesis*, which predicts a decrease in social integration, and the *liberation hypothesis*, which predicts an increase in integration (Kalmijn & van Groenou, 2005). According to Milardo (1987) who reviewed research examining changes in social networks of women and men following divorce, individuals' networks tend to shrink after a divorce, and network members are less likely to know one another (i.e., network density also shrinks). According to Milardo, the effects of divorce are different for men and women; whereas the "kinkeeping" responsibility of women both before and after marriage encourages continued contact with kin and discourages bonds with friends, for men the post-divorce environment tends to encourage the formation of personal friendships.

A recent study conducted in the Netherlands (Kalmijn & van Groenou, 2005) however, showed that both divorced men and women are more involved with friends than married men and women, whereas divorce has a negative direct effect on neighborhood contacts for both men and women. The authors concluded that the isolation hypothesis may hold for certain dimensions of social integration, such as those strongly connected to the spouse, whereas the liberation hypothesis may hold for social contacts more loosely connected to the spouse. Kalmijn and van Groenou (2005) also found that long-term single divorced women are often less integrated because they have fewer resources (e.g., financial, time) after divorce. Importantly, according to Daniels-Mohring and Berger (1984), network changes stemming from a divorce tend to decrease the quality of the individual's adjustment to this life crisis. The more stable the network, the more positive the postdivorce adjustment.

Children

The birth of children may also dramatically change the shape and functionality of individuals' social networks. Ishii-Kuntz and Seccombe (1989) found that after the birth of a child and throughout the child's school-age years, parents report increasing support from neighbors and confidants. However, they also found that the presence of children often weakens marital support. In terms of well-being, mothers benefit from a "sense of community," close relationships, and individuals in the network who assist with child care, provide emotional support, or both (Balaji et al., 2007). In addition, frequent contact with kin and nonkin can help allay feelings of loneliness in new mothers (Cutrona, 1986). However, consistent with the convoy model (Antonucci et al., 2009; Kahn & Antonucci, 1980), it is always important to consider the context in which the new mother is embedded. Zarling, Hirsch, and Landry (1988) found that having a tightly knit network (i.e., many ties between family and friends) can be very supportive for a new mother of a full-term infant (leading to higher maternal sensitivity) but can actually make mothers of preterm infants less effective parents by reducing maternal sensitivity. The authors speculate that fewer ties may actually decrease the likelihood of ambiguous or stressful interactions. Ishii-Kuntz and Seccombe (1989) found that after the last child leaves home, the structure and functions of the network may again shift as "empty nest" adults strengthen ties with the spouse, neighbors, and friends.

Individuals who never have children (either voluntarily or not) tend to be less integrated into their kin networks and to develop a greater need for mutually dependent relationships with spouse and friends (Ishii-Kuntz & Seccombe, 1989). In her review of European empirical findings, Wenger (1997a) found that never married or childless individuals, or individuals who live alone or only with a spouse, tend to have more friends and neighbors and to be more integrated in the community than those who live with others. Those childless individuals who never married have greater involvement with siblings, other relatives, friends, and neighbors than other childless people.

In terms of well-being, childlessness has a minimal effect on the well-being of married individuals (Zhang & Hayward, 2001). The childless are usually less involved socially but are no more likely than parents to be depressed or impaired (Johnson & Barer, 1997). With advancing age, however, as friends die or become incapacitated, the potential for friendship involvement declines and the advantages of having children increases (Johnson & Barer, 1997). Childless widows may be at a particular risk for experiencing negative effects (Zhang & Hayward, 2001) due to "family deprivation" (Johnson & Barer, 1997; Wagner et al., 1999).

Retirement and Widowhood

Other major life changes, such as retirement and widowhood, may also influence social network characteristics. For instance, retirement may trigger increases in social activities (Antonucci, 1985; Antonucci, Ajrouch, & Birditt, 2006). Van Tilburg (1992) found that retirees experience a dramatic change in the composition of their networks. In particular, many relationships (especially those with colleagues) are terminated, and the function of the network tends to change as well. Namely, retirees tend to give more support and experience less reciprocity in their relationships than individuals who are not retired. The author speculated that retirees may be getting less and giving more support to reinforce their self-reliance as they try to compensate for the loss of employment. Individuals who experience the death of a spouse also tend to experience changes in their social networks. Although widowhood may lead to an initial decrease in social contacts (Johnson & Troll, 1994), widows and widowers tend to see friends much more regularly than their married, divorced, or single counterparts (Wagner et al., 1999). They may also receive more support from children and friends, at least in the initial period after the loss of spouse.

Assisted Living Facilities

Moving to a specialized residential community or assisted living facility can also present unique opportunities and challenges to an individual's social network. According to Antonucci (1985), having a higher proportion of older people in one's immediate residence (e.g., within retirement communities) increases the amount of social interchange among the elderly. Relocation, in contrast, may dissipate friendships, and migration may also affect the availability of close kin (Wenger, 1996). Potts (1997) found that higher levels of social support from friends living outside the retirement community rather than those within the retirement community were associated with lower levels of depression in a small sample of older adults. Thus, although specialized residential communities may increase some types of social interaction and peer interdependency, the friendships formed may be superficial, and individuals may feel isolated from the larger community, including their friends and family. Often, moves to assisted living facilities or specialized residential communities are associated with other disruptions to the social support network, such as retirement, an acute health event, or death of a spouse, that pose additional risks to individuals' social networks and ability to adjust.

End of Life

As older individuals near the end of life, they may face even more challenges to their social networks. According to Carstensen's (1992) theory of socioemotional selectivity, because of a limited time perspective, these individuals are likely to focus their energy on maximizing emotionally meaningful interactions with their closest social relationships. However, although close friendships might be highly significant for such individuals (especially never married or widowed childless individuals), the potentially exclusive boundaries established around different role relationships may threaten those friendships (Young, Seale, & Bury, 1998). In fact, close friends may even be excluded by health professionals because they are not family members. However, a dying individual may bring family and friends closer together as they try to support the individual together.

In sum, transitions across the adult life span clearly influence the composition, function, and quality of individuals' networks. Future research needs to examine more closely shifts in network types across various life transitions and how those shifts affect well-being. One of the coauthors of this chapter (Fiori) is currently examining changes in network types across the transition into retirement and how these might affect physical and psychological well-being, whereas others (Antonucci, Birditt) are examining how the financial crisis of 2009 is affecting the social relations, stress reactivity, and health of community-dwelling adults.

CULTURAL DIFFERENCES IN NETWORK TYPES

As Jackson, Antonucci, and Brown (2004) have suggested, it is important to recognize that people experience all aspects of their lives through a cultural lens. Consistent with the convoy model, which emphasizes the importance of personal and situational characteristics, there are cultural differences in social networks and the impact of social networks on well-being, highlighting the importance of studying social network types in different cultural contexts. According to Höllinger and Haller (1990), levels of economic development and sociocultural patterns are crucial to explaining cultural differences in social networks. For example, Höllinger and Haller (1990) found that sociocultural differences in the prevailing type of housing could explain differences in the frequency of face-to-face contacts with kin among seven nations: Italy, Hungary, Austria, West Germany, Britain, the United States, and Australia. Specifically, the popularity of single-family houses in Britain, the United States, and Australia, leading to larger distances between different parts of the family, could explain the much lower frequency of kin contact for individuals in those countries as compared with those living in Italy and Hungary. According to van Tilburg, de Jong-Gierveld, Lecchini, and Marsiglia (1998), in southern Europe and other family-oriented societies (e.g., Japan), living alone may provoke loneliness and other negative feelings, but in societies with more of an individualistic orientation (e.g., northern Europe or the United States), living with family may actually result in higher levels of loneliness. Relatedly, in the United States daughters often provide the most support to older parents, whereas in Japan daughter-in-laws provide the most support. This cultural difference may be due to traditional living arrangements in Japan in which the daughter-in-law lives with her husband in his parents' home (Antonucci, 2001, 2008).

Some cultural differences (e.g., Israeli social networks tend to be smaller and have fewer family members than American networks) could be due to histories of immigration or war (Antonucci, 1990). Other differences may be more closely linked with differing sociocultural values and concepts of relationships. For example, in North America, friends are made easily but are not always intimate, whereas in Europe (e.g., Germany), people are slower to confide and disclose, but friendships tend to be intimate and long-lasting (Rokach, Bacanli, & Ramberan, 2000). According to Höllinger and Haller (1990), the fact that Americans tend to have many more friends than Germans could be due to these different sociocultural concepts of friendship (i.e., Americans tend to define the concept in a wider and more casual manner than do people in other nations). Thus, friend-focused networks may have different implications for well-being in the United States and Germany.

Gender differences in social relations may also be significantly influenced by culture. Antonucci, Ajrouch, and Janevic (2002), using large representative samples from France, Germany, Japan, and the United States, found that gender differences in social relations, resource deficits, and depressive symptomatology varied by culture. For example, they found that associations among these variables were similar for American men and women, whereas they were different for Japanese men and women. Some researchers have proposed that observed "cultural differences" may really be differences between men only and that women are actually more similar across cultures (Bell et al., 2004).

There may also be cultural differences in the association between social relations and well-being (Antonucci, 1994). In a comparison of network characteristics in France, Germany, Japan, and the United States using large national samples, Antonucci, Lansford, Schaberg, et al. (2001) identified cultural differences in the effects of resource deficits (specifically, having an illness or being widowed) on social networks. The social networks of older adults with resource deficits were smaller than the networks of those without deficits only in France and Germany. In addition, only the social interactions of older people with resource deficits in Germany were more likely to be limited to a higher proportion of very close, inner-circle members. Eriksson et al. (1999) found that social networks were associated with a decreased mortality risk for both older Swedes and older Americans but that the form of the protective network was culturally determined; specifically, contact with children was positively associated with survival among Swedes but not Americans.

As mentioned earlier in this chapter, Fiori and colleagues (2008) found that in contrast to a sample of older adults from the United States, a similar sample of Japanese individuals evidenced no well-being differences by network type. The authors use cross-cultural literature stressing the differences between "West" and "East" to explain this finding. The traditional distinction made between "West" (i.e., the United States) and "East" (i.e., Japan) is that of individualism (in the United States) and collectivism (in Japan; Markus & Kitayama, 1991), although more recent research has brought into question this somewhat simplistic dichotomy (e.g., Takahashi et al., 2002; Triandis, 2001). In any case, according to the distinction, in individualist cultures, such as the United States, people are autonomous and independent, give priority to personal goals, and behave primarily on the basis of attitudes rather than norms (Triandis, 2001). In collectivist cultures such as Japan, people are interdependent, give priority to the goals of in-groups, and behave in a communal way primarily on the basis of in-group norms rather than personal attitudes (Triandis, 2001). Although researchers have examined the impact of individualism and collectivism on a wide array of factors, for example, cognition, emotion, motivation, personality, cultural practices, close relationships, life satisfaction, and well-being (e.g., Morline, Kitayama, & Miyamoto, 2002; Rothbaum, Pott, Azuma, Mikaye, & Weisz, 2000; Triandis, 2001), the discussion that follows focuses on the impact of these norms specifically on social relations.

According to G. Adams et al. (2004), affective individualism in Europe and North America (e.g., Germany and the United States) may be an historical product of social changes from the 1800s. These researchers suggest that such affective individualism, compared with the collectivism of other settings or earlier time periods, reflects different conceptions of closeness and intimacy. Specifically, in independent cultures such as the present-day United States, relationships may be seen as voluntary creations, whereas in interdependent cultures such as Japan, relationships are viewed as inherent connections. The major cultural task for the Japanese is to fit in and adjust to relationships while constraining personal desires; connectivity is normative in Japan, and relationships are considered focal and objective (Kitayama, Markus, & Kurokawa, 2000; Markus & Kitayama, 1991). In the United States, group ties are governed less by group norms, and Americans may have to rely instead on trust of unfamiliar others (Rothbaum et al., 2000). As such, relationship goals may differ between individuals in the United States and those in Japan. In the United States, the goal of self-disclosure may be key, because connection is not readily afforded and trust is paramount, whereas in Japan, relationship goals may focus on the mutual fulfillment of complementary obligations (G. Adams et al., 2004). Fiori and colleagues (2008) explain the lack of an association of network types with well-being in Japan in their study by suggesting that because the Japanese tend to view relationships as obligatory, they are more likely to accept and learn to live with the networks within which they find themselves.

Recently, researchers have begun to recognize that the collectivism–individualism distinction may be too simplistic. According to Triandis (2001), independent of collectivism and individualism, there also exists a distinction between "vertical" and "horizontal" societies often used to describe Japan and the United States, respectively. Whereas vertical societies emphasize hierarchy, horizontal societies emphasize equality. The high respect that is afforded to elderly Japanese individuals by their society likely stems from the lasting historical influence of Confucian filial piety, and from the fact that social relations are largely governed by vertical relationships (Rothbaum et al., 2000; Sugisawa, Shibata, Hougham, Sugihara, & Liang, 2002). In contrast, social relations in the United States are governed primarily by horizontal relationships. These theoretical distinctions may lead to concrete differences in social networks (G. Adams et al., 2004). For example, Japanese elders express a stronger preference for living with their children than do U.S. elders (Sugisawa et al., 2002). The "stem-family-structure" (i.e., elders living together with their oldest son, his wife, and their grandchildren, as mentioned earlier) is also much more common in Japan. Nevertheless, it should be noted that this has been changing in recent years, with at least one third of Japanese elders living alone.

Because intimacy with one's spouse has deeper cultural roots in horizontal societies like the United States than in vertical societies like Japan (Palmore & Maeda, 1985), it may be that the spouse plays a more important role in the lives of United States elders compared with Japanese elders. According to Sugimoto (1997), Japanese husbands and wives tend to have separate spheres of life and communication gaps are accepted realities. This situation often leads to "mother–child adhesion" (p. 161), in which full-time housewives direct all of their attention and energy to their children to "obtain the psychological gratification that they cannot get from their spouse" (p. 161). This mother–child adhesion is more common in urban Japanese environments, compared with rural ones in which individuals generally have a wider range of interactions with more relatives and neighbors. Relatedly, social support systems among Japanese elderly tend to be centered around the family (Koyano, Hashimoto, Fukawa, Shibata, & Gunji, 1994). Takahashi et al. (2002) found that when rating the top figures in their networks, Americans tended to make nonfamily members at least one of the top three figures (e.g., closest same-gender friend), whereas for the Japanese, a larger majority of individuals rated only family members in the top three (e.g., children, spouse). This may relate to the Japanese custom of being more concerned with biological and ascribed relationships than other relationships.

Cultural differences between the United States and Japan may lead not only to differences in the types of social networks formed but also in the links among various aspects of those social networks. How relationships influence one another may depend on the cultural context in which the relationships are embedded. For instance, given that the United States and Japan are often used as prototypical examples of individualistic versus collectivistic societies, respectively, Lansford (2004) hypothesized that she would find stronger links between family relationships and friendships in Japan compared with the United States using large nationally representative samples of American and Japanese individuals from the *Social Relations and Mental Health Over the Life Course Study*. Lansford did, in fact, find that the association between family relationship quality and friendship quality was stronger in Japan than in the United States.

Takahashi et al. (2002), in their examination of commonalities and differences in the close relationships of American and Japanese people using the same cross-national data, found only partial support for the individualism–collectivism concept. Specifically, they did not find that individuals in the United States (a so-called individualistic culture) were more independent in social relationships than individuals in Japan (a so-called collectivistic culture) as assessed by interrelations among aspects of these relationships, nor did they find that more people in the United States than in Japan were willing to state which person meant the most to them affectively, as might be predicted by the individualism–collectivism concept. These researchers concluded that although the individualism–collectivism concept may be a useful heuristic framework, it should not be treated as a universally applicable theory. They stress the necessity of making multidimensional comparisons across cultures, such as the use of a pattern-centered approach.

There might also be differences across countries in the impact of various social networks on well-being. For example, although links between having a spouse and psychological and physical well-being have consistently been found in the United States (e.g., Berkman & Syme, 1979; Kiecolt-Glaser & Newton, 2001), findings have been more inconsistent in Japan (Sugisawa et al., 2002). Furthermore, unlike in the United States, it appears that in Japan contact with friends does not always lead to reduced depressive symptoms (Sugisawa et al., 2002). Unfortunately, few studies have included more than one country in their analyses of social relations and health, so it is difficult to draw conclusions from these results. Fiori and colleagues' (2008) study is one exception. Another is Sugisawa et al.'s (2002) study, in which direct and conditional effects of key social ties (spousal presence; living with children; contact with friends, neighbors, and relatives; participation in community groups) on depressive symptoms were examined in U.S. and Japanese individuals aged 60 and older.

In an illustrative example of cultural differences in networks, Sugisawa and colleagues (2002) found that having a spouse had a stronger impact on depressive symptom reduction in the United States than in Japan, although spousal presence in both samples contributed to a decline in depressive symptoms. In addition, they found that the presence of children among unmarried Japanese elderly was associated with reductions in depressive symptom levels, whereas there was no evidence for this spousal presence substitution in the United States. These findings imply that the functional specificity of relationships (Weiss, 1974) may operate differently in different cultures. Inconsistent with Sugisawa and colleagues' (2002) hypotheses, children living together and apart had the same effect on depressive symptoms among Japanese elderly. This could be because relationships between elderly parents and adult children in Japan are moving away from the norm of filial piety to include more affection-based relationships or to the fact that children living apart lived close enough to be seen daily, thereby meeting their filial obligations.

In any discussion of cultural differences, it is important to recognize that there may be greater variation within cultures than between. According to Wenger's (1997a) review of empirical studies conducted in Western Europe, gender, marital status, and parenthood were all significant for network outcomes regardless of the culture studied. It may be that some cultural differences lie not in network structure (e.g., distance from children) but rather in network function (e.g., satisfaction with distance from children), as evidenced by van Tilburg et al.'s (1998) study of loneliness and living arrangements in southern and northern Europeans mentioned earlier. Or, conversely, it may be that other cultural differences lie in the structure of networks (e.g., reduced face-to-face kin contacts) but not in their function (importance of kin support in times of need; Höllinger & Haller, 1990). It may also be that there are more cultural differences in the association of support with well-being than there are straightforward structural or functional differences in networks (Antonucci, 1994; Janevic, Ajrouch, Merline, Akiyama, & Antonucci, 2000).

FUTURE RESEARCH, SUMMARY, AND CONCLUSIONS

We think these complex findings suggest many interesting directions for future work. In particular, we believe that this work should be expanded to include biological indicators of well-being. Social networks may be linked to patterns of biological indicators of health as well as self-reported health. By including biological indicators, we may uncover the processes by which social networks are associated with health. In addition, we are interested in linking social network patterns to daily interactions and daily well-being. We know that individuals fit into different network types, but we do not know how those overall network types influence daily interaction patterns. For example, are individuals in diverse networks better able to cope with interpersonal tensions on a daily basis? Do embedded individuals report less daily stress? Another area of interest is in linking these social network patterns to the subjective feelings of loneliness. A burgeoning literature suggests that although individuals may be highly socially embedded, they often still feel disconnected from others. Indeed, a recent study found that up to 25% of spouses feel lonely in later life (Gierveld, van Groenou, Hoogendoorn, & Smit, 2009). We believe this work should be further explored by examining links among social network patterns, emotional loneliness, and social loneliness.

In sum, the convoy model suggests that individuals are usually surrounded by supportive others across the life span. These supportive others are multifaceted and vary in their structural, functional, and affective characteristics. In addition, the convoy model incorporates the life-span and life-course theories by hypothesizing that convoys vary by developmental period, social roles, societal changes, and norms. The convoys vary by personal and situational characteristics and have important implications for health and well-being. Although variable-centered approaches have typically been used to examine social relationships and health, we propose that the pattern-centered approach is a useful alternative for examining convoys of relationships across the life span. By using pattern-centered approaches, a more holistic and realistic depiction of the social networks in which people are embedded is achieved. In addition, the pattern-centered approach provides a way to examine how these social network types vary by important societal and individual factors. Similar types of networks are found in numerous societies and age groups, but the specific types of networks in which people belong and the impact of those networks on health and well-being vary by the individual and the context. In sum, this chapter outlines the usefulness of the convoy model of social relations, highlights insights garnered from multiple research perspectives, and identifies potentially productive directions for future research.

REFERENCES

Aartsen, M. J., van Tilburg, T., Smits, C. H. M., Knipscheer, K. C. P. M. (2004). A longitudinal study of the impact of physical and cognitive decline on the personal network in old age. *Journal of Social and Personal Relationships, 21,* 249–266.

Adams, G., Anderson, S. L., & Adonu, J. K. (2004). The cultural grounding of closeness and intimacy. In D. J. Mashek & A. Aron (Eds.), *Handbook of closeness and intimacy* (pp. 321–339), Mahwah, NJ: Erlbaum.

Adams, R. G., & Blieszner, R. (1995). Aging well with friends and family. *The American Behavioral Scientist, 39,* 209–224.

Agneessens, F., Waege, H., & Lievens, J. (2006). Diversity in social support by role relations: A typology. *Social Networks, 28,* 427–441.

Ainsworth, M. S., Blehar, M. C., Waters, E., & Wall, S. (1978). *Patterns of attachment: A psychological study of a strange situation.* Oxford, England: Erlbaum.

Ajrouch, K. J., Antonucci, T. C., & Janevic, M. R. (2001). Social networks among Blacks and Whites: The interaction between race and age. *Journals of Gerontology, 56B,* S112–S118.

Almeida, D. M., & Kessler, R. C. (1998). Everyday stressors and gender differences in daily distress. *Journal of Personality and Social Psychology, 75,* 670–680.

Alwin, D. F., & Wray, L. A. (2005). A life-span developmental perspective on social status and health. *Journals of Gerontology Series B—Psychological Sciences and Social Sciences, 60,* 7–14.

Anderman, L. H., & Anderman, E. M. (1999). Social predictors of changes in students' achievement goal orientations. *Contemporary Educational Psychology, 25,* 21–37.

Antonucci, T. C. (1985). Personal characteristics, social networks and social behavior. In R. H. Binstock & E. Shanas (Eds.), *Handbook of aging and the social sciences* (pp. 94–128). New York: Van Nostrand Reinhold.

Antonucci, T. C. (1986). Social support networks: A hierarchical mapping technique. *Generations, X*(4), 10–12.

Antonucci, T. C. (1990). Social supports and social relationships. In R. H. Binstock & L. K. George (Eds.), *The handbook of aging and the social sciences* (3rd ed., pp. 205–226). San Diego, CA: Academic Press.

Antonucci, T. C. (1994). A life-span view of women's social relations. In B. F. Turner & L. E. Troll (Eds.), *Women growing older: Psychological perspectives* (pp. 239–269). Thousand Oaks, CA: Sage.

Antonucci, T. C. (2001). Social relations: An examination of social networks, social support, and sense of control. In J. E. Birren (Ed.), *Handbook of the psychology of aging* (5th ed., pp. 427–453). San Diego, CA: University of California; Center on Aging.

Antonucci, T. C. (2008). Aging families in global context. *Research in Human Development, 5,* 60–63.

Antonucci, T. C., Ajrouch, K. J., & Birditt, K. S. (2006). Social relations in the third age: Assessing strengths and challenges using the Convoy Model. In J. B. James & P. Wink (Eds.), *Annual review of gerontology and geriatrics: Vol. 26. The crown of life dynamics of the early postretirement period* (pp. 193–209). Editor in Chief: K. W. Schaie. New York: Springer.

Antonucci, T. C., Ajrouch, K. J., & Janevic, M. R. (2002). The effect of social relations with children on the education-health link in men and women aged 40 and over. *Social Science and Medicine, 56,* 949–960.

Antonucci, T. C., & Akiyama, H. (1987). Social networks in adult life and a preliminary examination of the convoy model. *Journal of Gerontology, 42,* 519–527.

Antonucci, T. C., & Akiyama, H. (1995). Convoys of social relations: Family and friendships within a life span context. In R. Blieszner & V. H. Bedford (Eds.), *Handbook of aging and the family* (pp. 355–372). Westport, CT: Greenwood Press.

Antonucci, T. C., Akiyama, H., & Birditt, K. (2004). Intergenerational exchange in the United States and Japan. In M. Silverstein, R. Giarrusso, & V. L. Bengtson (Eds.), *Intergenerational relations across time and place. Springer Annual Review of Gerontology and Geriatrics* (Vol. 24, pp. 224–248). New York: Springer.

Antonucci, T. C., Akiyama, H., & Lansford, J. (1998). Negative effects of close relations. *Family Relations, 47,* 379–384.

Antonucci, T. C., Akiyama, H., & Takahashi, K. (2004). Attachment and close relationships across the life span. *Attachment and Human Development, 6,* 353–370.

Antonucci, T. C., Birditt, K. S., & Akiyama, H. (2009). Convoys of social relations: An interdisciplinary approach. In V. Bengston, M. Silverstein, N. Putney, & D. Gans (Eds.), *Handbook of theories of aging* (pp. 247-260). New York: Springer.

Antonucci, T. C., Fuhrer, R., & Dartigues, J. (1997). Social relations and depressive symptomatology in a sample of community-dwelling French older adults. *Psychology and Aging, 12,* 189–195.

Antonucci, T. C., Fuller-Iglesias, H., & Birditt, K. S. (2007, August). Are socially connected children happy in young adulthood?

Poster presented at the Convention of the American Psychological Association, San Francisco, CA.

Antonucci, T. C., Langfahl, E. S., & Akiyama, H. (2004). Relationships as contexts and outcomes. In F. R. Lang & K. L. Fingerman (Eds.), *Growing together: Personal relationships across the lifespan* (pp. 24–44). Cambridge, England: Cambridge University Press.

Antonucci, T. C., Lansford, J. E., & Akiyama, H. (2001). The impact of positive and negative aspects of marital relationships and friendships on well-being of older adults. *Applied Developmental Science, 5,* 68–75.

Antonucci, T. C., Lansford, J. E., & Akiyama, H. (2002). Differences between men and women in social relations, resource deficits and depressive symptomotology during later life in four nations. *Journal of Social Issues, 58,* 767–783.

Antonucci, T. C., Lansford, J. E., Schaberg, L., Smith, J., Akiyama, H., Takahashi, K., Fuhrer, R., & Dartigues, J. F. (2001). Widowhood and illness: A comparison of social network characteristics in France, Germany, Japan, and the United States. *Psychology and Aging, 16*(4), 655–665.

Auslander, G. K. (1996). The interpersonal milieu of elderly people in Jerusalem. In H. Litwin (Ed.), *The social networks of older people: A cross-national analysis* (pp. 183–204). Westport, CT: Praeger.

Balaji, A. B., Claussen, A. H., Smith, D. C., Morales, M. J., Perou, R., & Visser, S. N. (2007). Social support networks and maternal mental health and well-being. *Journal of Women's Health, 16,* 1386–1396.

Baltes, P. B. (1987). Theoretical propositions of life-span developmental psychology: On the dynamics between growth and decline. *Developmental Psychology, 23,* 611–626.

Baltes, P. B. (1997). On the incomplete architecture of human ontogeny: Selection, optimization, and compensation as foundation of developmental theory. *American Psychologist, 52,* 366–380.

Baltes, P. B. (2003). On the incomplete architecture of human ontogeny: Selection, optimization, and compensation as foundation of developmental theory. In U. M. Staudinger & U. Lindenberger (Eds.), *Understanding human development: Dialogues with lifespan psychology* (pp. 17–43). Dordrecht, The Netherlands: Kluwer Academic.

Baltes, P. B., & Smith, J. (2003). New frontiers in the future of aging: From successful aging of the young old to the dilemmas of the Fourth Age. *Gerontology: Behavioural Science Section/Review, 49,* 123–135.

Baydar, N., Greek, A., & Brooks-Gunn, J. (1997). A longitudinal study of the effects of the birth of a sibling during the first 6 years of life. *Journal of Marriage and the Family, 59,* 939–956.

Bell, L. G., Dendo, H., Nakata, Y., Bell, D. C., Munakata, T., & Nakamura, S. (2004). The experience of family in Japan and the United States: Working with the constraints inherent in cross-cultural research. *Journal of Comparative Family Studies, 35,* 351–372.

Bergman, L. R., & El-Khouri, B. M. (2003). A person-oriented approach: Methods for today and methods for tomorrow. *New Directions for Child and Adolescent Development, 101,* 25–38.

Berkman, L. F., Glass, T., Brissette, I., & Seeman, T. E.(2000). From social integration to health: Durkheim in the new millennium. *Social Science and Medicine, 51,* 843–857

Berkman, L. F., & Syme, S. L. (1979). Social networks, host resistance, and mortality: A nine year follow up of Alameda county residents. *American Journal of Epidemiology, 109,* 186–204.

Birditt, K., & Antonucci, T. (2007). Relationship quality profiles and well-being among married adults. *Journal of Family Psychology, 21,* 595–604.

Birditt, K. S., & Fingerman, K. L. (2003). Age and gender differences in adults' descriptions of emotional reactions to interpersonal problems. *Journals of Gerontology: Psychological Sciences, 58,* P237–P245.

Birditt, K. S., & Fingerman, K. L. (2005). Do we get better at picking our battles? Age differences in descriptions of behavioral reactions to interpersonal tensions. *Journals of Gerontology: Psychological Sciences, 60B,* P121–P128.

Birditt, K. S., Fingerman, K. L., & Almeida, D. (2005). Age differences in exposure and reactions to interpersonal tensions: A daily diary study. *Psychology and Aging, 20,* 330–340.

Birditt, K. S., Jackey, L. M. H., & Antonucci, T. C. (2009). Longitudinal patterns of negative relationship quality across adulthood. *Journals of Gerontology: Psychological Sciences, 64B,* 55–64.

Blanchard-Fields, F., Jahnke, H. C., & Camp, C. (1995). Age differences in problem-solving style: The role of emotional salience. *Psychology and Aging, 10,* 173–180.

Blanchard-Fields, F., Stein, R., & Watson, T. L. (2004). Age differences in emotion-regulation strategies in handling everyday problems. *Journal of Gerontology: Psychological Sciences, 59B,* 261–269,

Blazer, D. G. (1982). Social support and mortality in an elderly community population. *American Journal of Epidemiology, 115,* 684–693.

Bosworth, H. B., & Schaie, K. W. (1997). The relationship of social environment, social networks, and health outcomes in the Seattle Longitudinal Study: Two analytical approaches. *Journals of Gerontology: Psychological Sciences, 52B,* P197–P205.

Bowlby, J. (1969). *Attachment and loss: Volume 1. Attachment.* London: Hogarth.

Cantor, M. H. (1979). Neighbors and friends: An overlooked resource in the informal support system. *Research on Aging, 1,* 434–463.

Carbery, J., & Buhrmester, D. (1998). Friendship and need fulfillment during three phases of young adulthood. *Journal of Social and Personal Relationships, 15,* 393–409.

Carstensen, L. L. (1992). Motivation for social contact across the life span: A theory of socioemotional selectivity. In J. E. Jacobs (Ed.), *Nebraska Symposium on Motivation: Developmental perspectives on motivation* (pp. 209–254). Lincoln: University of Nebraska Press.

Carstensen, L. L., Isaacowitz, D. M., & Charles, S. T. (1999). Taking time seriously: A theory of socioemotional selectivity. *American Psychologist, 54,* 165–181.

Cochran, M., Larner, M., Riley, D., Gunnarsson, L., & Henderson, C. R. (1990). *Extending families: The social networks of parents and their children.* Cambridge: Cambridge University Press.

Connidis, I. A., & McMullin, J. A. (2002). Sociological ambivalence and family ties: A critical perspective. *Journal of Marriage and Family, 64,* 558–567.

Consedine, N., Magai, C., & Conway, F. (2004). Predicting ethnic variation in adaptation to later life: Styles of socioemotional functioning and constrained heterotypy. *Journal of Cross Cultural Gerontology, 19,* 97–131.

Crohan, S. E., & Antonucci, T. C. (1989). Friends as a source of social support in old age. In R. G. Adams & R. Blieszner (Eds.), *Older adult friendship: Structure and process* (pp. 129–146). Newbury Park, CA: Sage.

Cumming, E., & Henry, W. (1960). Growing old. New York: Basic Books.

Cutrona, C. E. (1986). Objective determinants of perceived social support. *Journal of Personality and Social Psychology, 50,* 349–355.

Daniels-Mohring, D., & Berger, M. (1984). Social network changes and the adjustment to divorce. *Journal of Divorce, 8,* 17–32.

Demaray, M. K., & Malecki, C. K. (2002). Critical levels of perceived social support associated with student adjustment. *School Psychology Quarterly, 17,* 213–241.

Doeven-Eggens, L., De Fruyt, F., Hendriks, A. A. J., Bosker, R. J., & Van der Werf, M. P. C. (2008). Personality and personal network type. *Personality and Individual Differences, 45,* 689–693.

Dunn, J., Cutting, A. L., & Fisher, N. (2002). Old friends, new friends: Predictors of children's perspective on their friends at school. *Child Development, 73,* 621–635.

Dykstra, P. A. (1990). Next of (non)kin: The importance of primary relationships for older adults' well-being. Lisse, The Netherlands: Swets & Zeitlinger.

Dykstra, P. A., van Tilburg, T. G., & de Jong-Gierveld J. (2005). Changes in older adult loneliness: Results from a seven-year longitudinal study. *Research on Aging, 27,* 725–747.

Entwistle, D. R., & Alexander, K. L. (1998). Facilitating the transition to first grade: The nature of transition and research on factors affecting it. *Elementary School Journal, 4,* 351–364.

Eriksson, B. G., Hessler, R. M., Sundh, V., & Steen, B. (1999). Cross-cultural analysis of longevity among Swedish and American elders: The role of social networks in the Gothernburg and Missouri longitudinal studies compared. *Archives of Gerontology and Geriatrics, 28,* 131–148.

Feiring, C., & Lewis, M. (1991a). The development of social networks from early to middle childhood: Gender differences and the relation to school competence. *Sex Roles, 25,* 237–252.

Feiring, C., & Lewis, M. (1991b). The transition from middle childhood to early adolescence: Sex differences in the social network and perceived self-competence. *Sex Roles, 24,* 489–509.

Fincham, F. D., & Linfield, K. J. (1997). A new look at marital quality: Can spouses feel positive and negative about their marriage? *Journal of Family Psychology, 4,* 489–502.

Fingerman, K. L., & Birditt, K. S. (2003). Does variation in close and problematic family ties reflect the pool of living relatives? *Journals of Gerontology: Psychological Sciences, 58,* P80–P87.

Fingerman, K. L., & Griffiths, P. C. (1999). Season's greetings: Adults' social contact at the holiday season. *Psychology and Aging, 14,* 192–205.

Fingerman, K. L., Hay, E. L., & Birditt, K. S. (2004). The best of ties, the worst of ties: Close, problematic, and ambivalent social relationships. *Journal of Marriage and Family, 66,* 792–808.

Fingerman, K. L., Miller, L., & Charles, S. T. (2008). Saving the best for last: How adults treat social partners of different ages. *Psychology and Aging, 23,* 399–409.

Fingerman, K. L., & Pitzer, L. M. (2007). Socialization in old age. In P. D. Hastings & J. E. Grusec (Eds.), *Handbook of socialization* (pp. 232–255). New York: Guilford Press.

Fiori, K. L., Antonucci, T. C., & Akiyama, H. (2008). Profiles of social relations among older adults: A cross-cultural approach. *Ageing & Society, 28,* 203–231.

Fiori, K. L., Antonucci, T. C., & Cortina, K. S. (2006). Social network typologies and mental health among older adults. *Journals of Gerontology: Psychological Sciences, 61B,* P25–P32.

Fiori, K. L., Smith, J., & Antonucci, T. C. (2007). Social network types among older adults: A multidimensional approach. *The Journals of Gerontology: Psychological Sciences, 62B,* 322–330.

Fisher, L., & Ransom, D. C. (1995). An empirically derived typology of families: I. Relationships with adult health. *Family Process, 34,* 161–182.

Fuller-Iglesias, H. (2009). *Social relations and well-being in Mexico: The impact of emigration.* Unpublished doctoral dissertation, University of Michigan, Ann Arbor.

Furman, W., & Buhrmester, D. (1992). Age and sex differences in perceptions of networks of personal relationships. *Child Development, 63,* 103–115.

Gierveld, J. D., van Groenou, M. B., Hoogendoorn, A. W., & Smit, J. H. (2009). Quality of marriages in later life and emotional and social loneliness. *Journals of Gerontology: Psychological Sciences and Social Sciences, 64B*(4), 497-506.

Gurung, R. A. R., Taylor, S. E., & Seeman, T. E. (2003). Accounting for changes in social support among married older adults: Insights from the MacArthur studies of successful aging. *Psychology and Aging, 18,* 487–496.

Hanson, B. S., Isaacsson, S-O., Janzon, L., & Lindell, S-E. (1989). Social network and social support influence mortality in elderly men. *American Journal of Epidemiology, 130,* 100–111.

Harvey, D. M., & Bray, J. H. (1991). Evaluation of an intergenerational theory of personal development: Family process determinants of psychological and health distress. *Journal of Family Psychology, 4,* 298–325.

Havighurst, R. J. (1961). Successful aging. *The Gerontologist, 1,* 8–13.

Heckhausen, J., & Schulz, R. (1995). A life-span theory of control. *Psychological Review, 102,* 284–304.

Hetherington, E. M. (2003). Social support and the adjustment of children in divorced and remarried families. *Childhood, 10,* 217–236.

Höllinger, F., & Haller, M. (1990). Kinship and social networks in modern societies: A cross-cultural comparison among seven nations. *European Sociological Review, 6,* 103–124.

Ingersoll-Dayton, B., Morgan, D., & Antonucci, T. (1997). The effects of positive and negative social exchanges on aging adults. *Journals of Gerontology: Social Sciences, 52B,* S190–S199.

Ishii-Kuntz, M., & Seccombe, K. (1989). The impact of children upon social support networks throughout the life course. *Journal of Marriage & the Family, 51,* 777–790.

Jackey, L. H. (2009). *The long-term implications of childhood social relations.* Unpublished doctoral dissertation, University of Michigan, Ann Arbor.

Jackson, J. S. (1991). *Life in Black America.* Thousand Oaks, CA: Sage.

Jackson, J. S., Brown, E., & Antonucci, T. C. (2004). A cultural lens on biopsychosocial models of aging. In P. Costa & I. Siegler (Eds.), *Advances in cell aging and gerontology: Vol. 15* (pp. 221–241). New York: Elsevier.

Janevic, M. R., Ajrouch, K. J., Merline, A., Akiyama, H., & Antonucci, T. C. (2000). The social relations-physical health connection: A comparison of elderly samples from the United States and Japan. *Journal of Health Psychology, 5,* 413–429.

Johnson, C. L., & Barer, B. M. (1997). Life beyond 85 years: The aura of survivorship. New York: Springer.

Johnson, C., L., & Troll, L. (1992). Family functioning in late late life. *Journals of Gerontology: Social Sciences, 47,* S66-S72.

Johnson, C. L., & Troll, L. E. (1994). Constraints and facilitators to friendships in late late life. *The Gerontologist, 34,* 79–87.

Kahn, R. L., & Antonucci, T. C. (1980). Convoys over the life course: Attachment, roles, and social support. In P. B. Baltes & O. C. Brim (Eds.), *Life-span, development, and behavior* (pp. 254–283). New York: Academic Press.

Kalmijn, M., & van Groenou, M. B. (2005). Differential effects of divorce on social integration. *Journal of Social and Personal Relationships, 22,* 455–476.

Kessler, R. C., & Essex, M. (1982). Marital status and depression: The importance of coping resources. *Social Forces, 16,* 484–507.

Kiecolt-Glaser, J. K., & Newton, T. L. (2001). Marriage and health: His and hers. *Psychological Bulletin, 127,* 472–503.

Kitayama, S., Markus, H. R., & Kurokawa, M. (2000). Culture, emotion, and well-being: Good feelings in Japan and the United States. *Cognition and Emotion, 14,* 93–124.

Koyano, W., Hashimoto, M., Fukawa, T., Shibata, H., & Gunji, A. (1994). The social support system of the Japanese elderly. *Journal of Cross-Cultural Gerontology, 9,* 323–333.

Krause, N. (1999). Assessing change in social support during late life. *Research on Aging, 21,* 539–569.

Krause, N. (2001). Social support. In R. H. Binstock (Ed.), *Handbook of aging and the social sciences* (5th ed., pp. 272–294). San Diego, CA: Academic Press.

Ladd, G. W. (1990). Having friends, keeping friends, making friends, and being liked by peers in the classroom: Predictors of children's early school adjustment? *Child Development, 61,* 1081–1100.

Ladd, G. W. (1999). Peer relationships and social competence during early and middle childhood. *Annual Review of Psychology, 50,* 333–359.

Ladd, G. W., & Kochenderfer, B. (1996). Linkages between friendship and adjustment during early school transitions. In W. M. Bukowski, A. F. Newcomb, & W. W. Hartup (Eds.), *The company they keep* (pp. 322—345). Cambridge, England: Cambridge University Press.

Lang, F. R. (2001). Regulation of social relationships in later adulthood. *Journals of Gerontology: Psychological Sciences, 56B,* P321–P326.

Lang, F. R. (2004). Social motivation across the life span. In F. R. Lang & K. L. Fingerman (Eds.), *Growing together: Personal relationships across the lifespan* (pp. 341–362). New York: Cambridge University Press.

Lang, F. R., & Carstensen, L. L. (1994). Close emotional relationships in late life: Further support for proactive aging in the social domain. *Psychology and Aging, 9,* 315–324.

Lang, F. R., Staudinger, U. M., & Carstensen, L. L. (1998). Perspectives on socioemotional selectivity in late life: How personality and social context do (and do not) make a difference. *Journals of Gerontology: Psychological Sciences, 53B,* P21–P30.

Lansford, J. E. (2004). Links between family relationships and best friendships in the United States and Japan. *International Journal of Aging & Human Development, 59,* 287–304.

Lansford, J. E., Sherman, A. M., & Antonucci, T. C. (1998). Satisfaction with social networks: An examination of socioemotional selectivity theory across cohorts. *Psychology and Aging, 13,* 544–552.

Larson, R., Mannell, R., & Zuzanek, J. (1986). Daily well-being of older adults with friends and family. *Psychology and Aging, 1,* 117–126.

Lavee, Y., & Olson, D. (1993). Seven types of marriage: Empirical typology based on ENRICH. *Journal of Marital & Family Therapy, 19,* 325–340.

Lee, G. R. (1978). Marriage and morale in later life. *Journal of Marriage and the Family, 40,* 131–139.

Lee, G. R., Peek, C. W., & Coward, R. T. (1998). Race differences in filial responsibility expectations among older parents. *Journal of Marriage and the Family, 60,* 404–412.

Levitt, M. J. (2005). Social relations in childhood and adolescence: The convoy model perspective. *Human Development, 48,* 28–47.

Levitt, M. J., Guacci-Franco, N., & Levitt, J. L. (1993). Convoys of social support in childhood and early adolescence: Structure and function. *Developmental Psychology, 29,* 811–818.

Levitt, M., Levitt, J., Bustos, G. L., Crooks, N. A., Santos, J. D., Telan, P., Hodgetts, J., & Milevsky, A. (2005). Patterns of social support in the middle childhood to early adolescent transition: Implications for adjustment. *Social Development, 14,* 398–420.

Lin, N., & Peek, M. K. (1999). Social networks and mental health. In A. V. Horwitz & T. L. Scheid (Eds.), *A handbook for the study of mental health: Social contexts, theories, and systems* (pp. 241–258). New York: Cambridge University Press.

Litwak, E. (1985). Complementary roles for formal and informal support groups: A study of nursing homes and mortality rates. *Journal of Applied Behavioral Science, 21,* 407–425.

Litwak, E., Silverstein, M., Bengtson, V., & Hirst, Y. W. (2003). Theories about families, organizations and social support. In V. L. Bengtson & A. Lowenstein (Eds.), *Global aging and challenges to families* (pp. 27–53). Hawthorne, NY: Aldine de Gruyter.

Litwin, H. (1995). The social networks of elderly immigrants: An analytic typology. *Journal of Aging Studies, 9,* 155–174.

Litwin, H. (1996). *The social networks of older people: A cross-national analysis.* Westport, CT: Praeger.

Litwin, H. (2001). Social network type and morale in old age. *The Gerontologist, 41,* 516–524.

Litwin, H. (2004). Social networks, ethnicity and public home-care utilization. *Aging and Society, 24,* 921–939.

Litwin, H., & Landau, R. (2000). Social network type and social support among the old-old. *Journal of Aging Studies, 14,* 213–228.

Litwin, H., & Shiovitz-Ezra, S. (2006). The association between activity and wellbeing in later life: What really matters? *Ageing and Society, 26*(2), 225–242.

Lund, R., Modvig, J., Due, P., & Holstein, B. E. (2000). Stability and change in structural social relations as predictor of mortality among elderly women and men. *European Journal of Epidemiology, 16,* 1087–1097.

Magai, C., Consedine, N. S., King, A. R., & Gillespie, M. (2003). Physical hardiness and styles of socioemotional functioning in later life. *Journals of Gerontology: Psychological Sciences, 58B,* P269–P279.

Magnusson, D. (2003). The person approach: Concepts, measurement models, and research strategy. *New Directions for Child and Adolescent Development, 101,* 3–23.

Mandara, J., & Murray, C. B. (2002). Development of an empirical typology of African American family functioning. *Journal of Family Psychology, 16,* 318–337.

Markus, H. R. & Kitayama, S. (1991). Culture and the self: Implications for cognition, emotion, and motivation. *Psychological Review, 98,* 224–253.

Matt, G. E., & Dean, A. (1993). Social support from friends and psychological distress among elderly persons: Moderator effects of age. *Journal of Health and Social Behavior, 34,* 187–200.

McDougall, P., & Hymel, S., (1998). Moving into middle school: Individual differences in the transition experience. *Canadian Journal of Behavioral Science, 30,* 108–120.

Mead, G. H. (1934). *Mind, self, and society, from the standpoint of a social behaviorist.* Chicago: University of Chicago Press.

Meeuwesen, L., Hortulanus, R., & Machielse, A. (2001). Social contacts and social isolation: A typology. *The Netherlands' Journal of Social Sciences, 37,* 132–154.

Melkas, T., & Jylhä, M. (1996). Social network characteristics and social network types among elderly people in Finland. In H. Litwin (Ed.), *The social networks of older people: A cross-national analysis* (pp. 99-116). Westport, CT: Praeger.

Merton, R. K. (1957). Social theory and social structure (rev. ed.). New York: Free Press.

Milardo, R. M. (1987). Changes in social networks of women and men following divorce: A review. *Journal of Family Issues, 8,* 78–96.

Moen, P. (2001). The gendered life course. In R. H. Binstock & L. K. George (Eds.), *Handbook of Aging and the Social Sciences* (5th ed.). San Diego, CA: Academic Press.

Morline, B., Kitayama, S., & Miyamoto, Y. (2002). Cultural practices emphasize influence in the United State and adjustment in Japan. *Personality and Social Psychology Bulletin, 28,* 311–323.

O'Connor, B. P. (1995). Family and friend relationships among older and younger adults: interaction motivation mood, and quality. *International Journal of Aging and Human Development, 40,* 9–29.

Pagel, M. D., Erdly, W. W., & Becker, J. (1987). Social networks: We get by with (and in spite of) a little help from our friends. *Journal of Personality & Social Psychology, 53,* 793–804.

Palmore, E., & Maeda D. (1985). *The honorable elders revisited.* Durham, NC: Duke University Press.

Penninx, B. W. J. H., van Tilburg, T., Boeke, A. J. P., Deeg, D. J. H., Kriegsman, D. M. W., & van Eijk, J. Th. M. (1998). Effects of social support and personal coping resources on depressive symptoms: Different for various chronic diseases? *Health Psychology, 17,* 551–558.

Pinquart, M., & Sörensen, S. (2003). Risk factors for loneliness in adulthood and old age: A meta-analysis. In S. P. Shohov (Ed.), *Advances in psychology research* (Vol. 19, pp. 111–143). Hauppauge, NY: Nova Science.

Potts, M. K. (1997). Social support and depression among older adults living alone: The importance of friends within and outside of a retirement community. *Social Work, 42,* 348–362.

Reid, M., Landesman, S., Treder, R., & Jaccard, J. (1989). "My family and friends": Six to twelve-year-old children's perceptions of social support. *Child Development, 60,* 896–910.

Rokach, A., Bacanli, H., & Ramberan, G. (2000). Coping with loneliness: A cross-cultural comparison. *European Psychologist, 5,* 302–311.

Rook, K. (1984). The negative side of social interaction: Impact on psychological well being. *Journal of Personality and Social Psychology, 46,* 1097–1108.

Rosenfeld, L. B., Richman, J. M., & Bowen, G. L. (2000). Social support networks and school outcomes: The centrality of the teacher child and adolescent. *Social Work Journal, 17,* 205–226.

Rothbaum, F., Pott, M., Azuma, H., Miyake, K., & Weisz, J. (2000). The development of close relationships in Japan and the United States: Paths of symbiotic harmony and generative tension. *Child Development, 71,* 1121–1142.

Russell, D. W., & Cutrona, C. E. (1991). Social support, stress, and depressive symptoms among the elderly: Test of a process model. *Psychology and Aging, 6,* 190–201.

Ryff, C. D., & Singer, B. (2000). Interpersonal flourishing: A positive health agenda for the new millennium. *Personality and Social Psychology Review, 4,* 30–44.

Sabin, E. P. (1993). Social relationships and mortality among the elderly. *Journal of Applied Gerontology, 12,* 44–60.

Seeman, T. E. (1996). Social ties and health: The benefits of social integration. *Annals of Epidemiology, 6,* 442–451.

Seeman, T. E. (2000). Health promoting effects of friends and family on health outcomes in older adults. *The American Journal of Health Promotion, 39,* 472–480.

Seeman, T. E., Kaplan, G. A., Knudsen, L., Cohen, R., & Guralnik, J. (1987). Social network ties and mortality among the elderly in the Alameda County Study. *American Journal of Epidemiology, 126,* 714–723.

Settersten, R. A., Jr. (2003). Age structuring and the rhythm of the life course. In J. T. Mortimer & M. J. Shanahan (Eds.), *Handbook of the life course* (pp. 81–102). New York: Kluwer Academic/Plenum.

Settersten, R. A., Jr. (2007). The new landscape of adult life: Roadmaps, signposts, and speedlines. *Research in Human Development, 4,* 239–252.

Shanas, E. (1979). Social myth as hypothesis: The case of the family relations of old people. *The Gerontologist, 19,* 3–9.

Smith, K. P., & Christakis, N. A. (2003). Social networks and health. *Annual Review of Sociology, 34,* 405–429.

Stocker, C. M. (1994). Children's perceptions of relationships with siblings, friends, and mothers: Compensatory processes and links with adjustment. *Journal of Child Psychology and Psychiatry, 35,* 75–84.

Stone, L., & Rosenthal, C. (1996). Profiles of the social networks of Canada's elderly: An analysis of 1990 General Social Survey data. In H. Litwin (Ed.), *The social networks of older people: A cross-national analysis* (pp. 77–97). Westport, CT: Praeger.

Sugimoto, Y. (1997). Gender stratification and the family system. In *An introduction to Japanese society* (pp. 136–168). Cambridge, United Kingdom: Cambridge University Press.

Sugisawa, H., Liang, J., & Liu, X. (1994). Social networks, social support, and mortality among older people in Japan. *Journal of Gerontology, 49,* S3–S13.

Sugisawa, H., Shibata, H., Hougham, G. W., Liang, J., & Sugihara, Y. (2002). The impact of social ties on depressive symptoms in U.S. and Japanese elderly. *Journal of Social Issues, 58,* 785–804.

Takahashi, K. (2004). Close relationships across the life span: Toward a theory of relationship types. In F. R. Lang & K. L. Fingerman (Eds.), *Growing together: Personal relationships across the lifespan* (pp. 130–158). New York: Cambridge University Press.

Takahashi, K. (2005). Toward a lifespan theory of close relationships: The affective relationships model. *Human Development, 48,* 48–66.

Takahashi, K., & Majima, N. (1994). Transition from home to college dormitory: The role of preestablished affective relationships in adjustment to a new life. *Journal of Research on Adolescence, 4,* 367–384.

Takahashi, K., Ohara, N., Antonucci, T. C., & Akiyama, H. (2002). Commonalities and differences in close relationships among the Americans and Japanese: A comparison by the individualism/collectivism concept. *International Journal of Behavioral Development, 26,* 453–465.

Takahashi, K., Tamura, J., & Tokoro, M. (1997). Patterns of social relationships and psychological well-being among the elderly. *International Journal of Behavioral Development, 21,* 417–430.

Triandis, H. C. (2001). Individualism-collectivism and personality. *Journal of Personality, 69,* 907–924.

Troll, L. E. (1988). New thoughts on old families. *The Gerontologist, 28,* 586–591.

Troll, L. E. (1994). Family connectedness of older women: Attachments in later life. In B. F. Troll & L. E. Troll (Eds.), *Women growing older: Psychological perspectives* (pp. 169–201). Thousand Oaks, CA: Sage.

Uchino, B. N. (2004). Social support and physical health: Understanding the health consequences of relationships. New Haven, CT: Yale University Press.

Van Tilburg, T. (1992). Support networks before and after retirement. *Journal of Social and Personal Relationships, 9,* 433–445.

Van Tilburg, T. (1998). Losing and gaining in old age: Changes in personal network size and social support in a four-year longitudinal study. *Journals of Gerontology: Social Sciences, 53B*(6), S313–S323.

Van Tilburg, T., de Jong-Gierveld J., Lecchini, L., & Marsiglia, D. (1998). Social integration and loneliness: A comparative study among older adults in the Netherlands and Tuscany, Italy. *Journal of Social and Personal Relationships, 15,* 740–754.

Volling, B. L. (2005). The transition to siblinghood: A developmental ecological systems perspective and directions for future research. *Journal of Family Psychology, 19,* 542–549.

Wagner, M., Schütze, Y., & Lang, F. R. (1999). Social relationships in old age. In P. B. Baltes & K. Ulrich (Eds.), *The Berlin aging study: Aging from 70 to 100.* New York: Cambridge University Press.

Walen, H. R., & Lachman, M. E. (2000). Social support and strain from partner, family, and friends: Costs and benefits for men and women in adulthood. *Journal of Social & Personal Relationships, 17,* 5–30.

Weiss, R. S. (1969). The fund of sociability. *Transaction, 6,* 36–43.

Weiss, R. S. (1974). The provisions of social relationships. In Z. Rubin (Ed.), *Doing unto others* (pp. 17–26). Englewood Cliffs, NJ: Prentice-Hall.

Wenger, G. C. (1996). Social networks and gerontology. *Reviews in Clinical Gerontology, 6,* 285–293.

Wenger, G. C. (1997a). Review of findings on support networks of older Europeans. *Journal of Cross-Cultural Gerontology, 12,* 1–21.

Wenger, G. C. (1997b). Social networks and the prediction of elderly people at risk. *Aging and Mental Health, 1,* 311–320.

Yasuda, N., Zimmerman, S. I., Hawkes, W., Fredman, L., Hebel, J. R., & Magaziner, J. (1997). Relation of social network characteristics to 5-year mortality among young-old versus old-old white women in an urban community. *American Journal of Epidemiology, 145,* 516–523.

Young, E., Seale, C., & Bury, M. (1998). "It's not like family going is it?": Negotiating friendship boundaries towards the end of life. *Mortality, 3,* 27–42.

Zarling, C. L., Hirsch, B. J., & Landry, S. (1988). Maternal social networks and mother–infant interactions in full-term and very low birthweight, preterm infants. *Child Development, 59,* 178–185.

Zhang, Z., & Hayward, M. (2001). Childlessness and the psychological well-being of older persons. *The Journals of Gerontology: Social Sciences, 56B,* S311–S320.

CHAPTER 13

Achievement Motives and Goals: A Developmental Analysis

ANDREW J. ELLIOT, DAVID E. CONROY, KENNETH E. BARRON, and KOU MURAYAMA

Achievement motivation represents the energization and direction of competence-based behavior. Despite the ubiquity and importance of achievement motivation across the life span, developmental research in this area is quite sparse. In this chapter, we discuss developmental considerations and provide an overview of the developmentally relevant research that has been conducted on achievement motivation. Our review focuses specifically on the two most prominent constructs that have emerged in the achievement motivation literature in the past century: Motive dispositions (the need for achievement and fear of failure) and goals (mastery-approach, performance-approach, mastery-avoidance, and performance-avoidance achievement goals).

In infancy, children manifest behavior that seems to be motivated by a desire to have an effect on their immediate environment. Throughout childhood, these early, nascent achievement-oriented behaviors become more precise and intentional and appear in school, sports, music, art, and other avocational pursuits. In adolescence and early adulthood, achievement strivings extend to the domain of work and become increasingly complex and elaborate. Throughout the adult working years, individuals display the full breadth of vocational and avocational achievement behavior in multiple variations and in a diversity of contexts. Retirement may bring the cessation of official occupational toiling, but life in advanced adulthood commonly remains rife with a variety of voluntary vocational pursuits and engagement in avocational interests of many types.

Given the clear presence of motivated achievement behavior across the life course, one might expect a vast and detailed scholarly literature on the development of achievement motivation. This is not so. Despite the ubiquity and importance of achievement motivation from "womb to tomb," developmental research in this area is sparse, and at present, we know surprisingly little about this critical domain of striving. In this chapter, we discuss developmental considerations and overview the developmentally relevant research that has been conducted in this area. In doing so, we focus on the two most prominent constructs that have emerged in the achievement motivation literature in the past century of scholarly inquiry: motive dispositions and goals (for reviews of other achievement motivation constructs from a developmental perspective, see Linnenbrink-Garcia & Fredericks, 2008; Wigfield, Eccles, Schiefele, Roeser, & Davis-Kean, 2006). Our starting place, however, must be a consideration of how achievement motivation itself is conceptualized, because this lays the foundation for all subsequent discourse.

COMPETENCE AND MOTIVATION: THE CONCEPTUAL FOUNDATION OF ACHIEVEMENT MOTIVATION

For most of the history of the achievement motivation literature, no precise definition of *achievement* was proffered. Accordingly, researchers and theorists tended to rely on a variety of colloquial and, typically, externally focused meanings of the term (e.g., "an accomplishment valued and recognized by society") in their work. Unfortunately, this lack of a clearly articulated conceptual definition of achievement produced a literature that lacked consistency, coherence, and a firm set of structural parameters to guide theoretical and empirical efforts (see Elliot & Thrash, 2001; Rawsthorne & Elliot, 1999, for details). Elliot and colleagues (Elliot, 1997; Elliot & Dweck, 2005; Elliot & McGregor, 2001; Elliot, McGregor, & Thrash, 2002) recognized this problem and responded by proposing that competence be considered the conceptual core of the achievement motivation literature. Competence was selected for this prominent place because it can be precisely defined and because competence-based motivation would appear to play a central role in human functioning. That is, competence motivation is ubiquitous in daily life, has a substantial impact on emotion and well-being, is evident in all individuals across cultures, and is clearly operative across the life span (see Elliot et al., 2002).

Drawing on *Webster's Revised Unabridged Dictionary* and the *Oxford English Dictionary*, competence may be defined as a condition or quality of effectiveness, ability, or success. Competence may be evaluated or determined in several ways: Individuals may use an absolute standard inherent in a task, they may use an intrapersonal standard, or they may use an interpersonal standard. The way that competence is evaluated influences the psychological meaning that competence has and the form that competence pursuits take in any given situation. Competence is relevant across a broad range of levels, from concrete actions (e.g., putting a puzzle piece where it belongs) to specific outcomes (e.g., winning or losing a sporting event) to identifiable patterns of skill and ability (e.g., playing the cello) to overarching characteristics (e.g., being intelligent) to omnibus compilations (e.g., living a good life).

Although no consensual definition of motivation exists, nearly all definitions that are offered include reference to both the energization and direction of behavior (see, for example, Arkes & Garske, 1977; Bindra, 1959; Cofer & Appley, 1964; Ford, 1992; Franken, 1988; Heckhausen, 1991; Jones, 1955; McClelland, 1985; Mook, 1987; Petri, 1996; Pintrich & Schunk, 1996; Reeve, 1996; Steers & Porter, 1987; Young, 1961). Energization represents the instigation or activation of behavior, whereas direction represents the focus or aim of behavior. Thus, achievement motivation may be conceptualized as the energization and direction of competence-based behavior.

Importantly, competence-based behavior is motivated not only by the positive, appetitive possibility of competence, but also by the negative, aversive possibility of incompetence. We view this distinction between approach (appetitive) and avoidance (aversive) motivation to be integral to a motivational analysis of competence (Elliot, 1999). Using a dictionary alone, competence may be defined in purely appetitive fashion in terms of effectiveness, ability, and success; but from a motivational standpoint, the study of competence must entail consideration of ineffectiveness, inability, and failure as well. In other words, a motivational analysis of competence must account for why and how people strive toward competence and away from incompetence.

Theoretical models of achievement motivation rely on a variety of constructs to seek to explain and predict competence-based behavior and its implications. The first construct to receive significant research attention in the literature was the motive disposition construct. A motive disposition is an affectively based tendency that orients individuals toward domain-specific positive or negative stimuli (McClelland, 1985). Motive dispositions account for the energization and general orienting of behavior. The other construct that has received a considerable amount of research attention is the goal construct. A goal is a cognitive representation of a future object that the organism is committed to approach or avoid (Elliot & Fryer, 2008). Goals account for the specific direction of behavior. This chapter addresses developmental questions in the achievement motivation literature through the lens of the achievement motive and achievement goal constructs, thereby attending to both the energization and the direction of competence-based behavior. Throughout, the distinction between approach and avoidance forms of motivation are applied because this distinction is basic to any and all forms of motivated behavior (Elliot, 2006, 2008). We begin with achievement motives, starting with the seminal work of Robert White.

ACHIEVEMENT MOTIVES

Undifferentiated Competence Motivation: A Developmental Progression Toward Differentiated Motives

White (1959) proposed that some of the earliest infant behaviors could not be adequately explained by the prevailing drive theories of the day. These behaviors—"visual exploration, grasping, crawling and walking, attention and perception, language and thinking, exploring novel objects and places, manipulating the surroundings, and producing effective changes in the environment" (p. 329)—are incompletely developed and, therefore, unlikely to satisfy any primary drives. Assuming that such behavior is not randomly produced by excess energy, the behavior must be motivated, and the most likely incentive is the satisfaction of an "intrinsic need to deal (effectively) with the environment" (p. 318). Relational transactions and the psychological situations in which we find ourselves are dynamic, so this motivation is inherently dynamic. One moment's behavioral intentions quickly give way to the next moment's behavioral intentions in an unending rhythm that precludes the "consummatory climax" (p. 322) required by drive theories.

White (1959) went on to state that progress toward effective ongoing behaviors produces pleasant feelings of *efficacy* rather than clear-cut satisfaction of the intention. The quest for these feelings of efficacy is characterized by "behavior that shows a lasting focalization and that has the characteristics of exploration and experimentation" (p. 323); White labeled this *effectance motivation*. Others have conceived of similarly undifferentiated purposeful behavior in infants and toddlers using the term *mastery motivation* (Barrett & Morgan, 1995; Kagan, 1994). In this line of work, mastery motivation is typically inferred from task engagement and persistence toward an attainable but moderately challenging goal (MacTurk, Morgan, & Jennings, 1995; McCall, 1995). Such mastery motivation requires that children be able to differentiate means from ends, so it is thought to emerge between 8 and 12 months of age (McCall, 1995).

This conceptualization of undifferentiated competence motivation is extremely broad and casts competence-seeking behavior as an inherent end in and of itself. From this perspective, the seeds of competence-motivated behavior are sown by nature, and the first shoots can be seen in infancy as the child begins to interact with the environment. Despite these key early developments, most scientific attention has focused on the blossoming of competence motivation as evidenced by the child's increasing mastery of and autonomy within her or his environment.

The increasing complexity of competence strivings suggests that the undifferentiated competence motivation in infancy branches out into more complex forms with age. White (1959) focused on undifferentiated competence motivation in childhood, but he explicitly noted that "the motives of later childhood and of adult life are no longer simple and can almost never be referred to a single root" (p. 323). In other words, differentiated competence motives may emerge over the life span and may be influenced by multiple processes. This notion of a differentiated competence motive paralleled the pioneering theorizing by Henry Murray, as well as the work of David McClelland, John Atkinson, and their contemporaries.

Differentiated Competence Motives

In a landmark study of motivation and personality, Murray (1938) attempted to classify the needs that organized behavior among college-age males. Needs were conceptualized quite flexibly as being either "a temporary happening … [or] a more or less consistent trait of personality" (Murray, 1938, p. 61). This distinction is important because it speaks to the potential for both intraindividual (i.e., situational) variability as well as interindividual (i.e., dispositional) variability in competence motivation. The distinction between intraindividual and interindividual motivational variability is revisited later in our discussion of achievement goals. At this point, our review of the literature on achievement motives focuses on dispositional variation that distinguishes people from each other over time and across their competence pursuits.[1]

[1] A terminological note may prove useful at this point. Needs and motives have been defined in a variety of ways in the literature. Our focus at this point of the chapter is on phenotypic individual differences in motivational dispositions, rather than on universal motivational incentives, the satisfaction of which regulates well-being.

According to Murray (1938), competence-based needs tend to persist and energize competence striving until (temporarily) satisfied. Each need is "characteristically accompanied by a particular feeling or emotion" (Murray, 1938, p. 124), and he specifically identified achievement and infavoidance as the competence-based needs that motivate human behavior.[2]

The *need for achievement* was posited to motivate individuals to strive for excellence, mastery, efficiency, and superiority over others. Individuals high in this need seek "to increase self-regard by the successful exercise of talent" (p. 164). "Need for achievement was also linked to feelings of zest and ambition. In contrast, the *need for infavoidance* was posited to motivate individuals to avoid humiliation[,] to quit embarrassing situations,...[and] to refrain from action because of the fear of failure" (p. 192). Infavoidance was linked to embarrassment, anxiety, and nervousness preceding an event and shame following the event. From these definitions, it is clearly evident that self-evaluation and emotion were central to the earliest conceptualizations of differentiated achievement motivation dispositions.

The theoretical link between self-evaluative emotions and competence striving was strengthened and made more explicit with the conceptualization of achievement motives proffered by David McClelland and John Atkinson (e.g., Atkinson, 1957; McClelland, 1958; McClelland, Atkinson, Clark, & Lowell, 1953). McClelland (1958) grounded motives in anticipated affective associations with environmental cues (p. 466). Atkinson (1957) proposed that the salient affective associations for understanding achievement motivation are "pride in accomplishment" and "experiencing shame and humiliation as a consequence of failure" (p. 360). These speculations about the emotional roots of achievement motives converge nicely with Murray's (1938) description of the needs for achievement and infavoidance. They also seem on target in light of subsequent theorizing and research that has established pride and shame as products of competence and incompetence or, more specifically, internally attributed successes and failures at meeting internalized rules, standards, or goals (Lewis & Sullivan, 2005; Tracy & Robins, 2004; Weiner, 1985).

Thus, achievement motives may be distinguished according to the nature of the anticipated affective response to success or failure that energizes achievement strivings. The tendency to experience pride in anticipation of success provides an approach-based motive disposition conventionally referred to as the need for achievement (nAch; McClelland et al., 1953; Murray, 1938), motive to approach success (Atkinson, 1957), or the hope for success (Heckhausen, 1963). The tendency to experience shame in anticipation of failing underlies an avoidance-based motive disposition typically referred to as the need for infavoidance (Murray, 1938), the motive to avoid failure (Atkinson, 1957), or the fear of failure (FF; Birney, Burdick, & Teevan, 1969). For consistency within this chapter, we refer to these motives as nAch and FF.

Assessment of Achievement Motives

Two broad classes of techniques have been used to assess achievement motives. Some researchers have used *fantasy-based, projective measures* (e.g., McClelland et al., 1953; Murray, 1938), whereas other researchers have incorporated *self-report questionnaires* into their assessment repertoire for achievement motives (e.g., deCharms, Morrison, Reitman, & McClelland, 1955). These approaches were initially viewed as operational differences, but it later became evident that greater differences existed between these measures.

Fantasy-Based Measures

The fantasy-based assessment technique was derived from the Thematic Apperception Test (Murray, 1943) and is generally referred to as the Picture Story Exercise (McClelland, Koestner, & Weinberger, 1989). In the Picture Story Exercise, participants are typically presented with a set of pictures for approximately 15 seconds each and asked to construct a narrative about each image. They are typically given four questions to stimulate their narrative: "(1) What is happening? Who are the persons?, (2) What has led up to this situation? That is, what has happened in the past?, (3) What is being thought? What is wanted? By whom?, (4) What will happen? What will be done?" (p. 98, McClelland et al., 1953). Schultheiss and Pang (2007) recommended using no fewer than four pictures to generate valid and reliable motive scores. Specialized scoring systems are then applied to code narratives for imagery that reflects the nAch (Heckhausen,

[2] For a period of time, there was a trend to focus research on a resultant achievement motivation score that represented the difference between the approach and avoidance achievement motives. Research using that approach is excluded from our review because of the volume of research establishing unique consequences for approach and avoidance motives and the difficulties inherent in interpreting the meaning of resultant motive scores.

Table 13.1 Summary of Thematic Categories in Implicit Need for Achievement Coding Systems

McClelland, Atkinson, Clark, & Lowell (1953)	Heckhausen (1963), English translation by Schultheiss (2001)
Achievement imagery[a]	Need for achievement and success
Stated need for achievement	Instrumental activity to achieve success
Instrumental activity (successful, doubtful, or unsuccessful)	Expectation of success
Anticipatory goal states (positive or negative)	Praise
Obstacles or blocks (personal or environmental)	Positive affect
Nurturant press	Success thema
Affective states (positive or negative)	
Achievement thema	

[a] Stories in which achievement imagery is altogether absent receive a negative achievement motivation score. Those in which achievement imagery is doubtful receive a zero score.

1963; McClelland et al., 1953) or FF (Birney et al., 1969; Heckhausen, 1963).

To illustrate some of the thematic content differences between these coding systems, Tables 13.1 and 13.2 present a summary of the major coding categories used to infer the presence of nAch and FF, respectively. Some of these early coding systems included categories of questionable theoretical relevance (e.g., obstacles or blocks for nAch, successful instrumental activity for FF). Nevertheless, these coding systems have helped generate a large volume of empirical research on achievement motivation, including many of the most well-known studies in the literature. For future research, we recommend using the coding system developed by Heckhausen (1963; English translation by Schultheiss, 2001), and we fully concur with the practical recommendations recently offered by Schultheiss and Pang (2007).

A complementary coding system was developed by Winter (1994) to identify achievement imagery in running text (i.e., text that was not stimulated by standardized images and is at least partially imaginative). This technique is especially valuable for analyzing real-world or archival data when it is not possible to conduct standardized assessments. For example, it has been applied profitably to assess motivational imagery in presidential speeches and news conferences (for a fascinating review, see Winter, 2005). Achievement motives are inferred from the presence of adjectives that (a) positively evaluate performance, (b) goals or performances described in ways that suggest positive evaluation, (c) mention of winning or competing with others, (d) failure (or lack of excellence), and (e) unique accomplishments (Winter, 1994). One drawback of this running text approach is that the present system does not differentiate between imagery motivated by approach and avoidance motives. Nevertheless, it has proved to be a powerful tool when standardized assessments are not possible, and it may certainly be revised and extended to differentiate between the need for achievement and fear of failure.

Self-Report Measures

The second class of techniques for assessing achievement motives involves self-reports on structured questionnaires. This approach was also used in early research (e.g., deCharms et al., 1955) and became especially common in research on FF in which researchers frequently operationalized the motive in terms of test anxiety (e.g., Atkinson & Litwin, 1960; Feather, 1965). The logic behind this

Table 13.2 Summary of Thematic Categories in Implicit Fear of Failure Coding Systems

Heckhausen (1963), English translation by Schultheiss (2001)	Birney, Burdick, & Teevan (1969)
Need to avoid failure	Hostile press imagery
Instrumental activity to avoid failure	Need press relief
Expectation of failure	Successful/unsuccessful instrumental activity
Criticism	Goal anticipation
Negative affect	Affective reactions to press
Failure	Blocks
Failure thema	Press thema

approach was that individuals who fear failing will exhibit anxiety during tests and, due to defensive processes, anxiety may be the dominant characteristic of their subjective experience when their competence is being evaluated (McClelland, 1985). This argument has some empirical support in the contemporary literature (e.g., Elliot & McGregor, 1999); however, it is limited to applications that study FF in formal testing environments. In general, it seems preferable to employ measures that assess the FF motive more broadly and directly. Research on nAch has followed this route of using general measures, with the most popular being the Achievement subscale of the Personality Research Form (Jackson, 1999) and the Work, Mastery, and Competitiveness subscales of the Work and Family Orientation Questionnaire (Spence & Helmreich, 1983).

Comparing Methods

Proponents of the fantasy-based and self-report approaches to assessing motives have laid out strong critiques of the alternative method and the psychometric properties of the scores derived therein. Fantasy-based approaches have been criticized for yielding scores with poor reliability and limited predictive validity (Entwisle, 1972; Fineman, 1977; Klinger, 1966; Scott & Johnson, 1972; Spangler, 1992; Weinstein, 1969). Self-report measures, in contrast, are thought to be limited because individuals do not have adequate insight into what motivates their competence pursuits, and therefore may not be able to report on their motives accurately (McClelland et al., 1953); self-report measures are also more vulnerable to self-presentation biases (McClelland, 1985). Although these critiques certainly have some degree of merit, over time researchers have come to see them as overstated. Fantasy-based approaches, when carried out in careful, controlled fashion, lead to motive scores with respectable psychometric properties and impressive predictive utility (McClelland, 1985; Schultheiss, 2007). Likewise, individuals are able to report on consciously endorsed aspects of their motive dispositions in reasonably accurate fashion, and carefully devised measures can effectively counteract the self-presentation biases that pose problems for all self-report measures (Podsakoff, MacKenzie, Lee, & Podsakoff, 2003).

In research using both fantasy-based and self-report measures, small and inconsistent correlations tend to emerge between the scores derived from these two assessment methods (McClelland et al., 1989; Spangler, 1992). This finding of poor convergence among scores from different methods stimulated an important theoretical insight—namely, that these methods may tap into separate motivational systems rather than merely representing a methodological nuisance. That is, the fantasy-based measures appear to assess *implicit achievement motives*, and the self-report measures appear to assess *explicit (or self-attributed) achievement motives*. Several differences exist between these two types of achievement motivation.

First, they appear to be based in different memory systems. McClelland et al. (1989) proposed that implicit and explicit motives were grounded in semantic and episodic memory, respectively; however, Schultheiss (2007) proposed that these motives were grounded in nondeclarative and declarative memory systems, respectively. This difference is significant because declarative memory systems include both episodic and semantic memory, whereas nondeclarative memory relies on much more primitive learning processes (e.g., classical conditioning). This difference implies that different socialization mechanisms may be involved in the development of implicit and explicit motives (McClelland, Koestner, & Weinberger, 1989).

A second difference between implicit and explicit motives involves differential responsiveness to situational cues. McClelland et al. (1989) argued that implicit motives are most responsive to task incentives (e.g., challenge), whereas explicit motives are most responsive to social incentives (e.g., demands, rewards, expectations; McClelland et al., 1989). Schultheiss and Pang (2007) suggested that implicit motives are more likely to predict responses to nonverbal cues, whereas explicit motives are more likely to predict responses to verbal cues.

Finally, explicit and implicit motives have been found to predict different achievement outcomes that correspond to their respective memory systems. McClelland et al. (1989) framed the difference as one between "spontaneous behavioral trends" versus "immediate specific responses to specific situations or choice behavior" (p. 691). Schultheiss and Pang (2007) proposed that implicit motives predict nondeclarative outcomes—behaviors and processes not controlled by conscious intentions or the self-concept—whereas explicit motives predict declarative outcomes. For example, implicit nAch is well suited to predict entrepreneurial activity (McClelland, 1965, 1987), whereas explicit nAch is well suited to predict self-regulation strategies such as achievement goal adoption and short-term performance outcomes (Elliot & Church, 1997). Findings that explicit nAch predicts nondeclarative outcomes such as salaries of business professionals and scientists' citation counts (Spence & Helmreich, 1983) and peer-reported interpersonal problems (Conroy, Elliot, & Pincus, 2009) suggest that this distinction between the classes of outcomes differentially predicted by implicit and explicit motives indeed requires additional research attention.

A lingering question regarding implicit and explicit achievement motives is whether they are best conceptualized as completely separate motivational systems or as separate components of a single system. Thrash and Elliot (2002) proposed the latter, arguing that it is more conceptually parsimonious to retain a singular motive construct with explicit and implicit facets than it is to declare implicit and explicit motives entirely independent constructs. In addition, in a set of studies, Thrash and Elliot (2002) and Thrash, Elliot, and Schultheiss (2007) demonstrated that the statistical independence of implicit and explicit motives at the grand mean level (i.e., across all participants) is partially due to methodological factors and masks considerable implicit–explicit concordance among subsets of the sample in question (e.g., those with a high need for consistency, those with a high level of awareness of their bodily states). This research does not call into question the fact that important differences exist between implicit and explicit motives, but it does raise questions about how to represent such differences theoretically and stands as a caution against equating statistical independence and developmental independence (for further discussion, see Thrash, Cassidy, Maruskin, & Elliot, in press).

In the following sections, we review existing empirical work on the socialization of implicit and explicit achievement motives and age-related differences in the achievement motives over time. As will soon be evident, the existing research on these issues is quite sparse.

Implicit Competence Motive Development

McClelland (1958) argued strongly that childhood experiences were critical in the socialization of motives. His rationale for this statement was based on four claims: primacy, undeveloped symbolic processes, repetition, and the conditions for forgetting. Children's early experiences establish a template for interpreting later experiences. Contemporary research has developed this concept of primacy by using concepts such as representational models of early experience (e.g., Blatt, Auerbach, & Levy, 1997; Bowlby, 1969/1982; Dweck & London, 2004). Furthermore, children's earliest learning experiences were thought to predate the development of verbal symbolism in particular and, therefore, to be more resistant to change. Early learning also provides opportunities for tremendous repetition over time. McClelland (1958) identified feeding and toilet training as specific competence-based experiences that are repeated thousands of times in the early years of life and are thus likely to play an important role in shaping motives. With respect to achievement motives, it seems that any experience in which the child receives feedback on his or her effectiveness in interacting with the environment would be relevant for shaping motive development. Finally, early experience was thought to be instrumental in the development of motives due to the difficulty of forgetting formative affective experiences.

Two landmark studies on the socialization of implicit nAch were published in the late 1950s. Rosen and D'Andrade (1959) studied parents and their 9- to 11-year-old sons using observational methods during a series of controlled competence pursuits. Forty families were represented in the study. The results indicated that parents of high nAch boys expected higher levels of performance from their children, selected harder tasks for their children to perform, were quicker to assist their children, and responded to their sons' competence pursuits with warmth. Fathers and mothers of high nAch children differed in that fathers provided more autonomy for their children, whereas mothers were somewhat more dominating. Fathers of high nAch children were also relatively less rejecting than mothers of those same children, pushed their boys less, and provided more general as opposed to specific instructions. In essence, high nAch boys appeared to have warm and supportive parents, but their fathers' behaviors were more psychologically differentiated, whereas their mothers' behaviors were more psychologically enmeshed. As Rosen and D'Andrade (1959) succinctly concluded, fathers "tend to beckon from ahead rather than push from behind," whereas mothers focus on "achievement training rather than independence training" (p. 216).

Winterbottom (1958) conducted a similar study on a sample of 29 mother–son dyads in which the boys were aged 8 years. The results showed that mothers of high nAch boys expressed greater demands before age 8 for independence and mastery on tasks such as knowing his way around town, going outside to play when wanting to be noisy or boisterous, trying hard things for himself, making his own decisions about clothes or how to spend his money, and doing well in competition with other children (for the complete list of demands, see Winterbottom, 1958). These mothers were also more positive in evaluating and rewarding their children's competence pursuits but expected children to learn which behaviors were prohibited at an earlier age. Combined with the Rosen and D'Andrade (1959) results, these findings point to warm and affectionate, albeit somewhat demanding, parenting for high nAch boys. Mothers appear to be more demanding in the socialization process than fathers, whose contributions seem to involve supporting their sons' burgeoning autonomy.

A third major investigation of implicit nAch socialization processes was a prospective study in which parents' attitudes toward various child-rearing practices were assessed when children were aged 5 years, and the children's implicit nAch was assessed 26 to 27 years later at age 31 or 32 years (McClelland & Pilon, 1983). Whereas the findings of the previous studies highlighted the importance of early demands for mastery and independence, such early childhood demands were not associated with adult nAch levels in this study. In fact, McClelland and Pilon (1983) suggested that premature or inappropriate demands for mastery and independence may be antithetical to the development of nAch. In white-collar families, parental values for their child's academic achievement were positively associated with the children's level of nAch in adulthood; however, this relation was not significant among blue-collar families. Two specific child-rearing attitudes assessed at age 5 were consistently associated with adult nAch: scheduled feeding and severity of toilet training.[3] The more parents emphasized a regular schedule for feeding or were strict in the toilet training of their child, the greater the level of nAch that the child developed in adulthood. Thus, it appears that parental values for effective self-control at age 5 contribute to long-term nAch.

Research on the development of implicit FF did not appear until over a decade after the classic Rosen and D'Andrade (1959) and Winterbottom (1958) studies were published. Teevan and McGhee (1972) extended Winterbottom's (1958) research to implicit FF with a sample of 41 high school juniors and seniors (approximately age 17). The results indicated that mothers of high FF high school students reported that they expected earlier independence and mastery than did mothers of low FF children. Schmalt (1982) used a semiprojective measure of FF and found that a form of FF focused on the emotional and social costs of failure was associated with early maternal demands for independence and mastery. A second form of FF based more on low perceived competence was not associated with these demands (Schmalt, 1982). Parents of high implicit FF children also reported that they responded to their children's successes more neutrally than did parents of low implicit FF children (Teevan & McGhee, 1972). Teevan (1983) subsequently replicated this finding with college students and their perceptions of their mothers' behavior. He also found that parents of high implicit FF children recalled their mothers' being more punitive when they failed at independence or mastery tasks.

Implicit FF also appears to have roots in affectional deprivation. Greenfeld and Teevan (1986) reported that college students whose father was absent from their home while growing up had higher implicit FF than peers who grew up in two-parent homes. Singh (1992) found that children (mean age of 12.8 years) in India who scored high in implicit FF had mothers who reported more marital conflict, irritability, avoidance of communication, inconsideration of their husbands, and suppression of sexuality than did mothers of low implicit FF children.

In sum, the factors that appear to be involved in socializing high implicit nAch children include a generally warm and affectionate relationship, age-appropriate demands for effective self-control, age-appropriate demands for independence and mastery, and a balance between dominance and autonomy that serves to direct children while allowing them to identify with their competence pursuits. All of the extant studies focused on samples of boys; there is a clear need for research on the socialization processes underlying implicit nAch development in girls. Moreover, there have been no studies of parenting before age 5, despite some of the critical developments that occur in the early childhood years (reviewed later in this chapter).

The socialization of implicit FF appears to involve an affectionally deprived home environment that does not adequately satisfy children's affiliative needs, early expectations for independence and mastery, and punishment for failing to meet those expectations. Children may come to view incompetence as aversive because it heightens the affectional deprivation that they already experience in their home environments. As in the study of implicit nAch, there are major gaps in our understanding of early childhood developmental processes for implicit FF. These gaps are striking given the critical theoretical importance of early learning for the development of achievement motives.

Explicit Competence Motive Development

Much like research on the development of implicit achievement motives, empirical work on how explicit achievement motives are socialized is quite sparse. Hermans, Ter Laak, and Maes (1972) selected 20 fourth- and fifth-grade boys and girls based on the extremity of their explicit nAch

[3] A third child-rearing variable, emphasis on neatness, was also significantly associated with adult levels of nAch; however, its reliability was low, and McClelland and Pilon (1983) did not attempt to interpret the finding.

and FF scores and observed how their parents interacted with them during competence tasks. The results showed that parents of high-nAch children had the highest expectations for their children's performance but only when the child was concomitantly low in FF. Parents of high-nAch kids also provided less specific help, more nonspecific help, and were quicker to assist their children than parents of low-nAch kids. Interestingly, high-nAch children refused parental help more frequently than did low-nAch children. It is not entirely clear whether these parental efforts to help were the source of high nAch or the product of their refusals. Following children's successes, the parents of high-nAch children gave the most positive task-oriented reinforcement. These parents were also less responsive to their high-nAch children's expressions of insecurity. This finding contrasts somewhat with findings that high-nAch college students report greater attachment security (Elliot & Reis, 2003). In general, it seems that parents of high-nAch children are available to their children, but perhaps task-focused and not interested in off-task expressions of insecurity.

In the Hermans et al. (1972) study, parents of high-FF children had lower expectations for their children's performance and more frequently withheld reinforcement for success relative to parents of low-FF children. High-FF girls received less nonspecific help and less frequent task-oriented reinforcement from their parents than did low-FF girls. The parents of high-FF girls also displayed more negative and less positive affect during the parent–child interaction than did parents of low-FF children. They were also less responsive to their high-FF children's expressions of insecurity, especially when their child was also low in nAch.

Elliot and Thrash (2004) reported evidence of concordance between the explicit FF of parents and that of their college-age children. Furthermore, they found that children of high-FF mothers described their mothers as using love withdrawal more frequently as a disciplinary strategy; children did not perceive high-FF fathers as being any more likely to use love withdrawal as a disciplinary strategy. Children's perceptions of their mothers' or fathers' use of love withdrawal was positively associated with their own FF. Relations between maternal (but not paternal) FF and children's FF were partially mediated by the children's perceptions of maternal love withdrawal. This result is consistent with other findings indicating that FF in college students is associated with insecure (anxious and avoidant) attachment styles (Elliot & Reis, 2003). The findings also support early proposals that FF is grounded in shame (Atkinson, 1957; see also findings from McGregor & Elliot, 2005) because love withdrawal is thought to be central to the socialization of shame (Lewis, 1995).

Mental representations of parental behaviors were also the focus of Conroy (2003), who studied a sample of high school and college-age students. The students described their parents as using more hostile and fewer affiliative behaviors when the students were 5 to 10 years old. This pattern paralleled how the children described treating themselves when they were failing (Conroy, 2003; Conroy & Metzler, 2004). Other studies have found that children's descriptions of how they treat themselves while failing are significantly similar to their descriptions of how they recalled their parents treating them as children (Conroy & Pincus, 2006). Collectively, these findings suggest that children internalize their parents' more hostile, less affiliative, and more love-withdrawing behavior and treat themselves in a similar fashion when they fail.

Clearly, more empirical work is needed on the socialization of explicit achievement motives. The data on hand are so minimal as to preclude any clear summary statement or conclusion regarding nAch. As for FF, it appears that children's FF is grounded in nonoptimal parental practices, particularly those that establish a contingency between competence and acceptance–affiliation.

Age-Related Differences in Competence Motives

Achievement motives presumably change, albeit slowly, throughout the life span as a function of continued socialization and experience over time in competence-relevant settings (see Conroy & Coatsworth, 2007; McClelland, 1985; McClelland et al., 1989). However, longitudinal data concerning the rate or shape of implicit or explicit achievement motive score change over the life span are sparse. Cross-sectional data on age-related differences in achievement motives are more common, albeit still limited. Some of the most informative findings have been reported by Veroff and colleagues, who contrasted implicit nAch scores from two national surveys in 1957 and 1976 (Veroff, Depner, Kulka, & Douvan, 1980). This time period was characterized by major social changes—including the civil rights and women's right movements—and one might expect to see a corresponding increase in achievement motivation, particularly among women. The study focused on the proportion of females and males of different ages who had nAch scores above the median of the combined distribution in each of those surveys. In 1957, there was a clear trend for nAch to be negatively associated with age from early adulthood into the adult years among both females and males. Also, more men were consistently above the median at all ages at that time. Twenty years later, the number of women above the median for nAch had increased substantially, whereas the proportion of men was approximately the same as it was in 1957. Similar to 1957, women's nAch scores were negatively associated with age in the 1976 survey. In contrast, men's nAch scores were quite variable across age groups, defying any clear age-related trend. These cross-sectional data suggest that, beginning in early adulthood, nAch decreases as age increases. It bears repeating that these findings are based on cross-sectional data and may not be appropriate for drawing conclusions about intraindividual developmental processes.

In the lone longitudinal study of which we are aware, Jenkins (1987) reported that implicit nAch increased in the 14 years following college (d = 0.59) and that nAch increased the most for women who became college professors and entrepreneurs during that time. There are several plausible explanations for the divergent results from the Veroff et al. and Jenkins studies, with the most obvious involving a selection threat. The Veroff et al. (1980) findings were based on national survey data, whereas the Jenkins (1987) data drew from a narrowly defined sample of Midwestern college-educated women in early- to middle-adulthood. Cleary, educational, occupational, and geographic factors should be considered before drawing conclusions about the developmental course of implicit nAch over the life span. To the best of our knowledge, comparable data on implicit fear of failure do not exist.

The data on age-related differences in explicit motive scores are equally limited. The manual for the Personality Research Form (Jackson, 1999) reported norms for nAch scores from eighth grade to college. These mean scores are relatively stable for both males and females during the adolescent and early adult years. Moreover, it appears that considerably more variability can be attributed to individual differences other than age.

Perhaps the next best available source of evidence on age-related differences in achievement motives may be derived from data on self-reports of imaginal processes (i.e., daydreams). Daydream content is relevant for the present purposes because there are documented links between imaginal processes and competence motivation (Oettingen & Hagenah, 2005). Nevertheless, conclusions about explicit motive trajectories must be drawn cautiously. Giambra (1974) administered the Inventory of Imaginal Processes to assess the frequency of various daydream contents. Data on younger participants' imaginal content was obtained from a university population (which was overrepresented in the data set), whereas data on older participants were drawn from the Baltimore Longitudinal Study conducted by the National Institute of Child Health and Human Development. The results indicated that achievement-oriented daydreams declined in frequency from late adolescence until the beginnings of old age, at which time the daydreams increased dramatically, returning to a level last seen around age 30. Fear of failure daydreams declined immediately following the college years but remained relatively stable until the retirement years, at which time they decreased again. The frequency of both types of daydreams were negatively correlated with age ($r_{\text{Ach}} = -.29$, $r_{\text{Fail}} = -.33$), and this finding was robust when the overall frequency of daydreaming was controlled. Although explicit achievement motives are not commonly assessed using this measure, and daydreams may not fully capture variance in the core self-evaluative and affective processes represented by motives, these findings are suggestive and provide the closest available empirical evidence suggesting how explicit achievement motives may change over the life span.

Several issues limit our ability to draw strong conclusions about change in achievement motives over the life span. The biggest limitations involve the sparse data that are available, the lack of data on achievement motive trajectories before the end of adolescence–beginning of adulthood, and concerns about the validity of scores in available studies. Notably, FF data are nearly completely absent from the literature. It bears reiterating that the studies reviewed in this section are almost entirely cross-sectional in nature. There is no guarantee that the functional form of individual growth trajectories will match the patterns seen in aggregated data. For example, it is possible that critical developmental periods exist or that certain experiences can accelerate or delay changes in achievement motives. Likewise, adults' contemporary experiences with their families or careers might stimulate differential change trajectories (e.g., Jenkins, 1987). Research that examines intraindividual growth trajectories for both implicit and explicit achievement motives would be an extremely valuable addition to the literature.

Self-Evaluative Emotions as a Mechanism of Implicit and Explicit Competence Motive Development

Since the earliest conceptions of achievement motives, the emotions of pride and shame (or related concepts) have been placed at the core of these motives (McClelland et al., 1953; Murray, 1938). To enrich theorizing about how approach- and avoidance-valenced achievement motives develop, it may help to consider how pride and shame develop. Pride and shame have been described variously as social, self-conscious, and self-evaluative emotions (e.g., Barrett & Campos, 1987; Lewis & Sullivan, 2005; Tracy & Robins, 2004). The earliest displays of these emotions in response to (in)competence have been documented at approximately 3 years of age from facial, postural, and gestural displays (Heckhausen, 1984; Lewis, Alessandri, & Sullivan, 1992; Lewis, Sullivan, Stanger, & Weiss, 1989; Stipek, Recchia, & McClintic, 1992), although it is possible that pride and shame are experienced earlier without being displayed by these commonly accepted social signals (Barrett & Campos, 1987; see e.g., Jennings, 2004). Several perspectives have been advanced to explain the nature, origins, and consequences of these emotions. Cognitive-attributional and functionalist theories are the most relevant for understanding their influence on the development of achievement motives in early childhood (for other perspectives, see Mills, 2005; Nathanson, 1992).

From a *cognitive-attributional* perspective, self-evaluative emotions belong to a broader class of self-conscious emotions that require self-awareness (Lewis & Sullivan, 2005). Self-awareness refers to the emergence of a cognitive meta-representation of the self as an explicit conscious entity and emerges between ages 15 and 24 months (Lewis, 1995). Between 24 and 41 months, children are thought to internalize the rules, standards, and goals (RSG) conveyed by their parents' interpersonal behavior and attributions (e.g., evaluative feedback, praise, control). After children develop the ability to compare their actions against internalized RSG, self-evaluative emotions such as pride and shame are possible, although factors such as task difficulty and gender are known to moderate these self-evaluative processes (Alessandri & Lewis, 1993, 1996; Lewis et al., 1992). Pride represents appraisals that a desirable outcome (relative to the internalized RSG) occurred because of the individual's behavior or action (i.e., a specific internal, unstable attribution, Lazarus, 1991; Lewis & Sullivan, 2005). This emotion corresponds to authentic or achievement-oriented pride (as opposed to hubristic pride, Tracy & Robins, 2004, 2007). In contrast, shame represents appraisals that an undesirable outcome (relative to the internalized RSG) occurred because an individual's self is deficient (i.e., a global, internal, stable attribution, Lazarus, 1991; Lewis & Sullivan, 2005).

From a *functionalist* perspective, self-evaluative emotions reflect the organization of the individual's behavior, goals, and progress toward those goals (Barrett & Campos, 1987). These theories make no assumptions about the necessity of self-awareness and view the overt expression of the emotion (e.g., posture, gestures, facial expressions) as serving adaptive functions. Functionalist theories also propose that self-evaluative emotions reflect the status of the self-in-relationships (Barrett, 2000; Barrett & Campos, 1987). Children who believe they are satisfying important RSG feel proud because of their perceived high status with their parents (or their mental representations of their parents; see Dweck & London, 2004). Likewise, children who realize that they are not satisfying important RSG feel shame because of their perceived low status with their parents (or their mental representations thereof).

Emergence of Pride and Shame During Early Childhood

There are no longitudinal studies of children's pride responses and only one longitudinal study that has focused explicitly on shame responses in early childhood (Mills, 2003). Other longitudinal studies have assessed related constructs such as shame–guilt composites (e.g., Kochanska, Gross, Lin, & Nichols, 2002); however, the majority of the available evidence is cross-sectional in nature. One major complication in comparing different studies is that they often use different emotion-elicitation procedures and coding systems. These design differences complicate the task of comparing results across studies so we have used the available results to estimate effect sizes (standardized mean differences when possible, odds ratios otherwise) for age-related differences in children's pride–shame displays. Table 13.3 summarizes these effect sizes for age-related differences in pride- and shame-like responses to success and failure (note that not all studies provided sufficient information to estimate effect sizes, so this table is not exhaustive).

With regard to children's pride, this analysis revealed that substantial individual differences in pride responses have emerged by age 30 months, and that young children are much more likely than toddlers to display pride for succeeding (Jennings, 2004; Stipek et al., 1992). This section of the table also reveals how limited the research base is in this area, and highlights the need for longitudinal studies to establish the intraindividual trajectories that chart the development of pride-proneness for succeeding.

TABLE 13.3 Age-Related Differences in Pride and Shame During Early Childhood: Effect Sizes

Study	Design	Age Range	Outcome	*d*	OR
Pride					
Jennings (2004)	CS	18 vs. 30 months	Pride (O)	1.93	n/a
Stipek et al. (1992, Study 1)	CS	13–21 vs. 30–39 months	Pride (O)	n/a	10.6
Stipek et al. (1992, Study 3)	CS	33–41 vs. 51–60 months	Saying "I did it" (O)	n/a	158.9
Shame					
Mills (2003)	L	3–5 years	Shame (O)	0.20	n/a
Kochanska et al. (2002)	L	33 vs. 45 months	Gaze avoidance (O)	0.16	n/a
			General distress (O)	0.09	n/a
			Negative affect (O)	0.06	n/a
Bennett et al. (2005)	CS	3–7 years	Shame (O)	0.43	n/a
Alessandri & Lewis (1996)	CS	4–5 years	Shame (O)	0	n/a
Stipek et al. (1992, Study 3)	CS	24–32 vs. 51–60 months	Gaze aversion after failing (O)	n/a	43.9
			Avoidant posture after failing (O)	n/a	12.5
Kochanska et al. (1994)	CS	21–33 vs. 47–70 months	Concern over good feelings with parent (PR)	0.25	n/a
			Affective discomfort (PR)	0.51	n/a

Note: d = standardized mean difference between groups; OR = odds ratio; CS = cross-sectional design; L = longitudinal design; O = observed; PR = parent reported. For Stipek et al. (2002), the OR was calculated by converting proportions into logits and taking the antilog of the difference between logits for two groups. Several notable studies were excluded from this table because the age ranges sampled were less than 12 months (e.g., Alessandri & Lewis, 1993; Belsky et al., 1997; Kelley et al., 2000; Lewis & Ramsay, 2002; Lewis, Alessandri, & Sullivan, 1992).

The bottom half of Table 13.3 presents effect sizes for studies on age-related differences in shame (Alessandri & Lewis, 1996; Bennett, Sullivan, & Lewis, 2005; Kochanska, DeVet, Goldman, Murray, & Putnam, 1994; Kochanska et al., Mills, 2003; Stipek et al., 1992). These effect sizes were consistently positive, but there was substantial variability in their magnitude. Figure 13.1 presents a scatterplot of the age-related differences in shame responses as a function of the interval between the age groups used to estimate the effect sizes. This figure reveals that the magnitude of effect sizes is a strong linear function of the time between assessments (R^2 = .73). In practical terms, this finding indicates that differences in shame propensities for failing change over time, with the amount of time required to observe medium-sized increases in shame is approximately three years. It is important to note that these findings are based largely on cross-sectional studies, and, similar to pride, few longitudinal studies have examined changes in shame during the early childhood years. Without longitudinal data, it is not clear whether these mean differences accurately characterize how these individual differences emerge. It is worth highlighting at this point that pride and shame displays are not isomorphic with appetitive and aversive achievement motives (i.e., nAch, FF) and that these results are presented to suggest one pathway that we believe to be particularly relevant to the development of those motives. Research on the early development of achievement motives themselves is needed to fill the major gap in this literature. Pending that evidence, it may be valuable to examine a contemporary theoretical account for how pride and shame propensities develop.

The Socialization of Pride and Shame Propensities

In light of the central role of pride and shame in competence motivation, it is important to understand how these self-evaluative emotion propensities develop. Children's temperament, parent behaviors, and their interaction are likely to explain substantial variance in emerging self-evaluative emotion propensities.

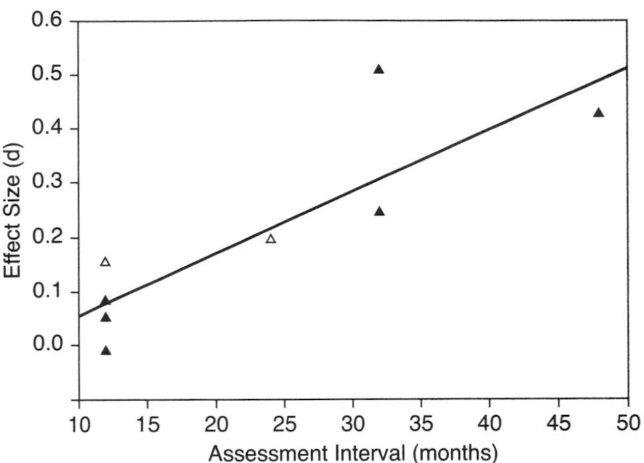

Figure 13.1 Effect sizes for age-related changes in early childhood shame propensities as a function of the assessment interval.

Temperament Assumptions that infants begin life as tabula rasae are ill founded and can distort interpretations of social influences (Pinker, 2002). Temperament refers to biologically based behavioral tendencies, expressed from birth onward in characteristics such as positive emotionality, negative emotionality, activity level, and attention regulation (to name a few dimensions; Bates, 1989; Rothbart & Bates, 1998; Rothbart & Hwang, 2005; Wachs, 2006). Since the emergence of findings that individual differences in fearfulness are heritable and consistent from infancy into young adulthood (Kagan, 1994; Kagan & Moss, 1962), individual differences in approach and avoidance–inhibition tendencies have been a centerpiece of temperament research and theorizing (Elliot & Thrash, 2002; Eysenck, 1976; Gray, 1970; Rothbart & Bates, 1998). Recent work using observer ratings of positive affect, negative affect, and behavioral approach–inhibition in 2-year-old children has revealed a slightly more complex model with three temperament clusters (Fox, Henderson, Rubin, Calkins, & Schmidt, 2001; Putnam & Stifter, 2005). Children with an *exuberant temperament* (~38%) have high levels of positive affect and behavioral approach with low levels of negative affect. Children with an *inhibited temperament* (~26%) have high levels of negative affect and low levels of both positive affect and behavioral approach to high- and low-intensity stimuli. Children with a *low reactive temperament* (~36%) exhibit low levels of positive and negative affect and moderate behavioral approach to high- and low-intensity stimuli.

In general, temperamental characteristics of exuberance and positive affectivity are associated with greater reward sensitivity and responsiveness (Carver & White, 1994; Cohen, Young, Baek, Kessler, & Ranganath, 2005; Gray, 1987, 1990; Lucas, Diener, Grob, Suh, & Shao, 2000). This reward sensitivity should orient children to appetitive aspects of achievement strivings and create associations between competence and self-evaluative rewards, thereby promoting an enduring propensity for pride following success. Belsky, Domitrovich, and Crnic (1997) found no relation between parent-reported positive temperament among 1-year-old boys and the boys' pride for succeeding at age 3. To our knowledge, no studies have examined whether temperament influences pride responses after age 3. This gap in the literature requires attention, because preschool-age children are increasingly self-evaluative, sensitive to RSG, and agentic in their pursuits—factors that should facilitate pride among exuberant children.

In contrast, inhibition and negative affectivity involve sensitivity to punishment and signals of nonreward (Carver & White, 1994; Gable, Reis, & Elliot, 2000; Gray, 1987, 1990; Watson, Wiese, Vaidya, & Tellegen, 1999). These sensitivities should focus inhibited children on the aversive possibility of incompetence and punitive self-evaluations. The high stress reactivity associated with an inhibited temperament is thought to increase self-focus and the potential for self-evaluative emotions (Lewis & Sullivan, 2005). The distressful nature of failure may contribute to inhibited children experiencing more shame (Lewis & Ramsay, 2002; Mills, Walling, Imm, & Weiler, 2007). Research testing this proposition has yielded mixed results. Studies using parent reports of temperament at 2 years have found no relations with 3- or 5-year-old children's observed pride–shame responses to success–failure (Belsky et al., 1997; Mills, 2003). In contrast, parents' ratings of children's effortful control and negative affect positively predicted parents' ratings of 6- to 7-year-old children's guilt–shame (Rothbart, Ahadi, & Hershey, 1994). Reactivity, a temperamental dimension akin to inhibition, positively predicted parent ratings of girls' affective discomfort but not boys' affective discomfort (a shame–guilt composite; Kochanska et al., 1994). This sex difference may reflect basic biological differences between the sexes or may be a consequence of gender-typed socialization practices that interact with inhibition.

Collectively, these findings suggest that an inhibited temperament creates a vulnerability to shame for some, but not all, children. Inhibition also appears to be insufficient by itself for creating individual differences in self-evaluative emotions or achievement motivation. It is possible that individual differences in shame propensities require more than a temperamental disposition alone. Inhibition may create a vulnerability for shame, but a particular social context may be essential to transform that vulnerability into a propensity for shame. Unfortunately, this possibility has not received much empirical attention. Research on guilt, a social emotion often compared (and entangled) with shame, demonstrates that fearful (inhibited) children not only exhibit more guilt following transgressions but also exhibit an increase in guilt during early childhood compared with nonfearful children (Kochanska et al., 2002). This is thought to occur because children with a fearful (inhibited) temperament are more likely to internalize parental RSG because of the distress they associate with parental criticism (Kagan, 1998; Kochanska, 1998; Kochanska et al., 2002; Rothbart & Bates, 1998). When combined with critical–rejecting parenting, the inhibited child's sensitivity to punishment should focus them on the aversive nature of incompetence and increase punitive self-evaluations, thereby creating an enduring propensity for shame following failure. In sum, parenting and temperament may interact in the development of shame-inhibited children, with children of critical–rejecting mothers displaying significantly more shame for failing than either inhibited children without critical–rejecting mothers or noninhibited children.

Both in interaction with temperament and by itself, parenting may influence the development of self-evaluative emotion propensities. Three theoretically derived pathways of parenting influence are proposed: (a) the mutually responsive orientation of the parent–child relationship, (b) parents' use of critical–rejecting behaviors with their children, and (c) parents' use of generic versus nongeneric praise while working on a competence task with their children.

Socialization via Mutually Responsive Parenting Orientations Research on conscience sheds light on processes that promote the internalization of RSG—a necessary condition for self-evaluative emotions in cognitive-attributional theories. Children's development of conscience has been linked to having mutually responsive orientations in parent–child interactions (Kochanska, 1997, 2002; Kochanska & Murray, 2000). Conceptually, these relationships are "positive, close, mutually binding, and cooperative" (Kochanska, 2002, p. 192). Operationally, mutually responsive orientations are exemplified by high-quality parental responses to children's needs (e.g., distress signals, bids for attention, influence attempts, and requests for help), overall levels of sensitivity, acceptance, and cooperation, shared positive affect, and children's committed compliance to parental instructions (e.g., requests to put away toys, prohibitions from touching attractive toys). Mutually responsive orientations in parent–child dyads increase children's internalization of parents' RSG for their behavior because they (a) create a positive mood that promotes prosocial behavior and (b) engender a responsive stance to parenting among children (Forman & Kochanska, 2001; Kochanska, 1997, 2002; Kochanska & Murray, 2000).

The internalization of RSG should enhance self-evaluative emotional responses to behaviors involving those RSG (see Lewis & Sullivan, 2005). Because mutually responsive orientations involve shared positive affect, this type of relationship orientation is more likely to promote a propensity for pride than shame. Nevertheless, mutually responsive orientations may promote a propensity for shame if parents also use disciplinary strategies that convey contingencies for children's worth (e.g., love withdrawal, criticism, rejection; see Grusec & Goodnow, 1994; Lewis, 1995).

It is worth highlighting that links between mutually-responsive orientations and children's pride–shame have never been documented directly (Tangney & Dearing, 2002). Nevertheless, we would expect that (a) mutually responsive orientations in mother–child dyads will promote the development of pride responses to success and (b) mutually responsive orientations will promote the development of shame responses to failure only if mothers also convey competence-based contingencies for their child's worth (i.e., critical–rejecting parenting).

Socialization via Critical–Rejecting Parenting Parental criticism, rejection, and love withdrawal for failing are part of a constellation of parenting practices (referred to hereafter as critical–rejecting parenting) thought to heighten children's risk for developing maladaptive self-evaluative emotion propensities (Lewis, 1995). Parent behaviors shape the mental representations that children develop about others and their attributions for personal achievements; they also provide a basis for children's inferences about themselves. In effect, these mental representations serve as "carriers of socialization and experience" (Dweck & London, 2004, p. 433) that connect children's early experiences with parents to later affect, behavior, and cognition. In achievement settings, critical–rejecting parenting contributes to a sense of contingent self-worth and a pattern of global internal attributions for failure because the self is wholly rejected following failure. These self-beliefs and attributions are the cognitive-attributional foundation of shame.

Consistent with the logic just outlined, maltreated children (who presumably experienced more critical–rejecting parenting) exhibit greater shame than nonmaltreated children (Alessandri & Lewis, 1996; Sullivan, Bennett, & Lewis, 2003). Parents of children who are more shame-prone after failure describe themselves as being more authoritarian and as using more harsh and rejecting parenting strategies (Mills, 2003; Stuewig & McCloskey, 2005). Observational research also indicates that the parents of children who are more shame-prone following failure exhibit more negative behaviors during an achievement task and offer more negative evaluative comments (Alessandri & Lewis, 1993, 1996; Kelley, Brownell, & Campbell, 2000).

Although the available evidence generally supports the hypothesis that critical–rejecting parenting promotes children's shame regarding failure, one discrepant finding warrants attention. Mothers of children who were more shameful after failing in laboratory tasks have been observed to be less intrusive at home (Belsky et al., 1997). These mothers were observed in a naturalistic environment around mealtimes and not specifically while interacting with their child on an achievement task. Borrowing from recent theorizing in the personality literature, parent behaviors are unlikely to influence children's self-evaluative processes unless they reflect parents' "behavioral signatures" following their child's successes and failures (i.e., *if* child succeeds, *then* X; *if* child fails, *then* Y; see Mischel & Shoda, 1995). With this caveat in mind, critical–rejecting parenting associated with internalized RSG (e.g., during achievement tasks) is hypothesized to lead children to develop a tendency to exhibit more shame after failing, especially when the mother–child dyad is otherwise mutually responsive.

It is possible that critical–rejecting parenting may inhibit the development of the tendency to experience pride for succeeding, but the evidence concerning such effects is more limited. Maltreated preschoolers exhibit less pride following success than nonmaltreated children, and this effect is larger for girls than boys (Alessandri & Lewis, 1996; Sullivan et al., 2003). Intrusive maternal control during a teaching task with their 24-month-old failed to predict children's pride when succeeding at 36 months (Kelley et al., 2000). In a sample of 4- and 5-year-olds, pride following success was associated with fewer observations of maternal "statement[s] or physical demonstration[s] that indicate dislike, disapproval, or lack of support of the child's actions" during a dyadic problem-solving activity (Alessandri & Lewis, 1996, p. 1860). Given the limited theoretical grounds for linking critical–rejecting parenting with pride, formal hypotheses about such relations will not be made. To summarize, critical–rejecting parenting during children's achievement strivings is thought to promote the development of shame for failing, both on its own and in interaction with either an inhibited temperament or a mutually responsive parent–child orientation.

Praise and Attributions A third line of work that informs our understanding of how parenting influences the development of self-evaluative emotion propensities is research on the effects of different forms of praise on behavior. Pride- and shame-prone children would be expected to exhibit mastery and helpless responses to incompetence, respectively (e.g., Diener & Dweck, 1978, 1980; Dweck, 1975). The *mastery pattern* involves responding to failure with low-effort attributions, persistence, increased competence expectancies, selecting challenging tasks, and improving performance. In contrast, the *helpless pattern* involves responding to failure with poor-ability attributions, unpleasant affect, decreased competence expectancies, selection of easy tasks, and reduced performance. Helplessness has been documented in early childhood (Burhans & Dweck, 1995; Heyman, Dweck, & Cain, 1992; Smiley & Dweck, 1994) and has been linked to contingent self-worth (Burhans & Dweck, 1995), entity theories of intelligence (Cain & Dweck, 1995; Dweck & Leggett, 1988; Heyman et al., 1992), and generic, person-focused praise (Cimpian, Arce, Markman, & Dweck, 2007; Kamins & Dweck, 1999). Mastery responses, in contrast, have been associated with nongeneric, process-focused praise for competence (Cimpian et al., 2007; Kamins & Dweck, 1999).

Of particular interest here is the distinction between *generic praise*, focused on stable traits of the child (e.g., "You are a great block stacker"), and *nongeneric praise*, focused on episodic behavior (e.g., "You did a great job stacking those blocks," Cimpian et al., 2007). The former engenders internal attributions to global, stable, and uncontrollable sources (e.g., the child's self), whereas the latter fosters internal attributions to specific, unstable, and controllable sources (e.g., the child's effort or actions). These attributions influence how children construct meaning about their achievement behavior, the feedback they receive, and their relationship to the RSG that guide their behavior. Nongeneric praise should orient children toward specific, unstable, and controllable attributions for achievement outcomes and thus promote pride. In contrast, generic praise may foster a sense of contingent self-worth and increase children's likelihood of experiencing shame for failing.

Some evidence is available to evaluate the proposed links between praise and self-evaluative emotions in children. In an experimental study that manipulated whether an experimenter provided nongeneric praise, children displayed more pride for succeeding when they were praised than when they were not praised (Stipek et al., 1992); however, this finding has not been replicated in subsequent studies that assessed the frequency of parental praise and the presence of children's pride (Alessandri & Lewis, 1993, 1996; Kelley et al., 2000). However, shame for failing has been consistently linked with observations of mothers using fewer positive behaviors and making fewer positive evaluative statements while working on an achievement task with their children (Alessandri & Lewis, 1993, 1996).

Studies that failed to support the differential roles of generic and nongeneric praise have contained minimal generic praise and employed tasks that implicitly provided clear competence-based feedback. In contrast, Dweck's work has drawn on more subtle achievement tasks in which children's competence at the end of the task remains somewhat ambiguous and dependent on external evaluation (e.g., drawing a picture, role-playing scenarios, Cimpian et al., 2007; Kamins & Dweck, 1999). In such situations, the subtle differences in praise may be especially influential, because children are seeking evidence to use in a self-evaluation. Stated differently, when tasks are manipulated to provide unambiguous success feedback, the intrinsic competence cues from the task may overpower any attributional cues. In sum, we propose that mothers' nongeneric praise during play will promote a propensity to experience pride upon succeeding, and their generic praise will promote a propensity to experience shame upon failing.

Summary

In sum, we propose that the development of self-evaluative emotion propensities serves as a primary mechanism through which achievement motives develop. Temperament and parenting are likely to interact in this socialization process. We have outlined our best understanding of the parenting practices that are putatively involved in this process, as well as how they might interact with temperament. Of course, this mechanism requires empirical validation in future research, and we believe should be a priority for developmental research on achievement motivation. Such research will require a shift of attention to the early childhood years that have received insufficient attention in the achievement motivation literature to date.

It is unclear at present whether this process differs qualitatively for the development of implicit and explicit achievement motives. The available research suggests more consistency in the developmental antecedents of these types of motives than has typically been assumed; however, far too little evidence is available to draw strong conclusions on this point. Given previous proposals that these motive systems are based on different learning and memory systems, the timing of socialization practices may be a key factor in determining whether parenting affects the development of implicit motives, explicit motives, or both. For example, early exposure to achievement demands may promote stronger implicit motives, whereas later exposure may promote stronger explicit motives. Cognitive developments, such as the emergence of anticipatory ability and future-oriented thinking, may also have an influence on when emerging self-evaluative propensities transform into the motive dispositions nAch and FF (cf. Atance, 2008; Haith, 1997).

A final factor that warrants attention in this developmental process is gender. Most studies examining gender differences in early childhood shame have found that girls are more shame-prone than boys (Kochanska et al., 1994; Lewis et al., 1992; Mills et al., 2007; for exceptions, see Kelley, Brownell, & Campbell, 2000; Stipek et al., 1992). Fewer studies have examined gender differences in pride during early childhood but there is no evidence of such a difference (Kelley et al., 2000; Lewis et al., 1992; Stipek et al., 1992). The shame difference may reflect the consequences of different parenting practices or more fundamental differences between the sexes. In general, these differences suggest that there is little reason to anticipate gender differences in the development of nAch, but girls may be more prone than boys to developing a strong FF motive.

MOVING FROM ACHIEVEMENT MOTIVES TO ACHIEVEMENT GOALS

The achievement motive construct is important in models of competence-based behavior, because achievement motives explain the way such behavior is energized and instigated. These dispositional proclivities represent competence-emotion associations that are deeply embedded in personality and are evoked by any situation in which competence evaluation is relevant (Atkinson, 1957; McGregor & Elliot, 2005). However, a full account of competence-based behavior needs to explain how such behavior is guided toward specific possibilities in specific situations, and it is here that the achievement goal construct makes its contribution (Elliot, 1997; Elliot & Thrash, 2001).

Achievement goals are the concrete, cognitive aims through which individuals pursue their more general desires and concerns. Achievement motives provide a general orienting of attention toward emotion-laden desires or concerns, but they do not provide specific guidelines for how one may attend to these concerns. As such, individuals commonly adopt more concrete aims or goals that help guide and direct their behavior toward more specific competence-based possibilities. In this sense, achievement goals are the proximal predictors of competence-relevant processes and outcomes, and these goals serve their underlying motives, which may be viewed as the distal predictors of competence-relevant processes and outcomes. That is, the motive that is activated in the achievement setting prompts the adoption of achievement goals, which serve as the direct regulators of achievement behavior.

Achievement motives sometimes lead to the strategic channeling of achievement behavior in a more concrete direction, but they do not always do so. Achievement motives can and sometimes do lead directly to behavior, but such regulation often appears rigid or unfocused (Elliot et al., 2002). Goals provide precise direction that can lead to more effective and efficient regulation. Thus, achievement motives can influence behavior in two ways: They can impel competence-based behavior directly, or they can lead to competence-based behavior indirectly by prompting the adoption of competence goals that proximally regulate behavior.

When achievement goals are viewed as conceptually separate from, but hierarchically linked to, achievement motives, the flexibility of competence-based self-regulation comes into bold relief. That is, it becomes easy to see that the same goal can be used in the service of different underlying motives, and the same motive can be channeled through many types of goals (Elliot & Church, 1997; Elliot & Thrash, 2001; Thrash & Elliot, 2001).

Achievement motives represent dispositional tendencies that are presumed to remain relatively stable over the life course. Change in achievement motives can occur throughout the life span as individuals encounter different age-related developmental tasks, enter and exit various formal and informal achievement settings, and experience shifts in their internal and external resources. However, this change is thought to be rather constrained and slow to emerge over time, given the firm foundation of these motives in early, emotion-laden, competence-relevant socialization. Achievement goals, in contrast, are viewed as highly malleable self-regulatory tools that can be used in flexible, strategic fashion across time and situation.

The achievement goal construct emerged in the literature quite a bit later than the achievement motive construct, but research in this area has burgeoned to the point that it now exceeds that on achievement motives (Brophy, 2004; Elliot, 2005; Schunk, Pintrich, & Meece, 2007). Nevertheless, as will become evident in the following section, developmental questions in this literature, like that on achievement motives, have not received sufficient empirical attention.

ACHIEVEMENT GOALS

The Achievement Goal Construct

The achievement goal construct was introduced to the achievement motivation literature in the late 1970s and early 1980s through the work of Carole Ames (1984), Carol Dweck (Dweck & Elliott, 1983), Marty Maehr (1984), and John Nicholls (1984; see also Maehr & Nicholls, 1980). These theorists recognized the limitations of focusing on achievement motives alone to account for competence-based behavior and sought to develop a more cognitive and situation-specific construct to complement the achievement motive construct. They did not explicitly cast their work in terms of energization and direction as we have herein but seemed to be attending to this distinction in an implicit way nonetheless. Moreover, the impetus for this work was also highly practical in nature. Specifically, these theorists sought to understand why some individuals, particularly children, display adaptive behavior in achievement settings, whereas others manifest maladaptive behavior.

Ames, Dweck, Maehr, and Nicholls converged in characterizing achievement goals as the purpose of achievement-relevant behavior. The type of achievement goal that an individual adopts was proposed to create a framework or cognitive schema for how an individual approaches, experiences, and reacts to a given achievement situation.

In empirical research, achievement goals may be straightforwardly measured by asking individuals the degree to which they have adopted a particular type of goal (e.g., Nicholls, Cheung, Lauer, & Patashnick 1989) or by asking individuals to indicate the primary type of goal they are pursuing in an achievement situation (e.g., Van Yperen, 2006). Achievement goals may also be experimentally manipulated by asking participants to pursue a particular type of goal (e.g., Harackiewicz & Elliot, 1993) or by establishing a context that highlights a particular type of goal (E. S. Elliott & Dweck, 1988).

The definition of achievement goal, and its purported function in achievement motivation, has remained relatively consistent in the literature across the years. The main exception is that Elliot and colleagues (Elliot, 1997; Elliot & Thrash, 2001) have argued for a more precise definition of achievement goal focused on competence-based aims alone, in contrast to the more inclusive definition implied by the term *purpose* (see, especially, Elliot & Thrash, 2001; Thrash & Elliot, 2001). Several models of achievement goals have emerged since the 1980s, and it is to an overview of these models that we now turn (for a more in-depth overview, see Elliot, 2005; Kaplan & Maehr, 2007).

The Dichotomous Achievement Goal Model

During the 1980s and early 1990s, achievement goal theorists proposed two types of achievement goal to capture the different foci that an individual could bring to a given achievement activity (Dweck & Elliott, 1983; Nicholls, 1984). First, theorists identified an achievement goal that reflected an overarching aim to develop one's competence in the achievement activity (e.g., My goal is to learn as much as possible). With this aim, an individual is motivated by a goal to improve and develop his or her competence, and success is gauged in reference to the task or self. Different theorists proposed a variety of labels for this first goal, such as *learning goal* (Dweck & Leggett, 1988), *task goal* (Nicholls, 1984), *intrinsic goal* (Pintrich & Garcia, 1991), and *mastery goal* (Ames & Archer, 1988). Second, theorists identified an achievement goal that reflected an overarching aim to demonstrate one's competence in the achievement activity relative to others (e.g., My goal is to show that I'm better than others). In this case, an individual's aim is to prove his or her competence relative to others, and success is gauged through normative comparison. Again different theorists proposed different labels to capture this second goal, such as *ability goal* (Midgley et al., 1998), *ego goal* (Nicholls, 1984), *extrinsic goal* (Pintrich & Garcia, 1991), and *performance goal* (Ames & Archer, 1988; Dweck & Leggett, 1988). Ames (1992) called for integrating the various conceptualizations and terminologies used by achievement goal researchers, and the field responded by generally coalescing around the terms mastery goal and performance goal since the mid-1990s.

Thus, initial theorizing and research on achievement goals used a mastery–performance goal dichotomy that centered on being motivated to improve one's competence or to prove one's competence. As a result, this first model is commonly referred to as the *dichotomous achievement goal model*. This use of the term *dichotomous* is not meant to imply that individuals adopt a mastery *or* performance goal in a given achievement context or that mastery goal and performance goal pursuits are negatively correlated. Rather, achievement goal theorists have recognized that individuals can endorse one, both, or neither achievement goal in a given achievement setting, and empirical studies measuring mastery and performance goal endorsement have found that correlations between the goals are commonly null or positive (see Harackiewicz, Barron, & Elliot, 1998, for a review).

Theorists working on the dichotomous achievement goal model paid considerable attention to one particular developmental issue—namely, the age at which children have the capacity to evaluate competence according to various standards. The assumption was that children's initial motivational focus is on task mastery and that that ability to make intrapersonal and, more important, normative evaluations emerged later, during the elementary school years (Dweck & Elliott, 1983; Maehr, 1983; Nicholls & Miller, 1984). This assumption has been borne out by the data in part, although two unexpected findings must be highlighted. First, the research showed that normative judgments of competence emerged earlier than intrapersonal judgments of competence, rather than vice versa as anticipated (Butler, 1998; Ruble, Eisenberg, & Higgins, 1994). Second, the age at which children are capable of engaging in normative comparison (Heckhausen, 1991; Jennings, 1993; Stipek et al., 1992) and exercise this capacity (Levine, 1983) is much earlier than initially anticipated (see Butler, 2005, for a review of the literature).

The empirical yield from early achievement goal research using the dichotomous model linked mastery goal constructs to a wide range of adaptive learning processes and achievement outcomes and performance goals to maladaptive learning processes and outcomes (for one of the earliest and most comprehensive reviews of initial work done on the dichotomous model, see Ames, 1992). For example, when pursuing mastery goals, individuals were said to be more likely to experience more positive affect, use higher level cognitive strategies, select more difficult tasks, and persist in the face of difficulty than when pursuing performance goals (Ames & Archer, 1988; Elliott & Dweck, 1988; Meece, Blumenfeld, & Hoyle, 1988; Nolen, 1988). This prompted a call by achievement goal researchers to maximize the promotion of mastery goals and minimize the promotion of performance goals in achievement contexts (Ames, 1992; Maehr & Midgley, 1991, 1996).

However, shortly after Ames's (1992) article was published, it became evident that the empirical pattern for performance goals was much less consistent than the empirical pattern for mastery goals. Some researchers found that performance goals were linked to maladaptive processes and outcomes, whereas others found that performance goals often yielded null or even positive effects (for reviews, see Elliot & Harackiewicz, 1996; Rawsthorne & Elliot, 1999). One explanation for the mixed pattern of performance goal effects centered on the possibility that performance goals could have beneficial effects in certain situations and for certain types of individuals (Elliot & Harackiewicz, 1994; Harackiewicz & Elliot, 1993, 1998). A second explanation centered on reevaluating how performance goals were conceptualized and operationalized in the dichotomous model. Specifically, some definitions and (especially) operationalizations of the performance goal construct included both approach motivation (demonstrating competence) and avoidance motivation (avoiding the demonstration of incompetence). Approach and avoidance manifestations of performance goals could have different, even opposite, implications for processes and outcomes, leading to the mixed empirical yield. This prompted Elliot and colleagues (Elliot, 1997; Elliot & Church, 1997; Elliot & Harackiewicz, 1996) to incorporate the approach-avoidance distinction into the achievement goal literature.

The Trichotomous Achievement Goal Model

Initially, the approach-avoidance distinction was only applied to performance-based goals, resulting in a trichotomous achievement goal model comprising mastery, performance-approach, and performance-avoidance goals (Elliot & Harackiewicz, 1996). When pursuing performance-approach goals, individuals aim to attain competence relative to others (e.g., My goal is to perform better than others), whereas individuals pursuing performance-avoidance goals aim to avoid incompetence compared with others (e.g., My goal is to avoid doing poorly comparing to others). The mastery goal construct was virtually the same in the dichotomous and trichotomous models.

Distinguishing between performance-approach goals and performance-avoidance goals helped elucidate when performance-based goals were most likely to have adaptive or maladaptive consequences. Reanalyses of extant data (Rawsthorne & Elliot, 1999), as well as newly emerging data told the same story (Elliot & Church, 1997; Elliot, McGregor, & Gable, 1999; Middleton & Midgley, 1997; Skaalvik, 1997; VandeWalle, 1997): Performance-avoidance goals were clearly linked to maladaptive learning behaviors and outcomes (e.g., disorganized study strategies, lower grades, lower intrinsic motivation), whereas performance-approach goals tended to be linked to a number of positive behaviors and outcomes (e.g., effort, persistence, higher grades; see Elliot, 1999, for a review). These patterns led several theorists to rethink (a) whether optimal motivation is represented by mastery goal pursuit alone or a combination of mastery and performance-approach goals (see Barron & Harackiewicz, 2000, 2001; Harackiewicz, Barron, Pintrich, Elliot, & Thrash, 2002; Pintrich, 2000) and (b) when performance-approach goals are likely to lead to adaptive consequences versus maladaptive consequences (Elliot & Moller, 2003; Midgley, Kaplan, & Middleton, 2001).

The 2 × 2 Achievement Goal Model

At the turn of the century, Elliot and colleagues (Elliot, 1999; Elliot & McGregor, 2001; see also Pintrich, 2000) extended the approach-avoidance distinction to mastery-based goals as well as performance-based goals. The result was a 2 × 2 achievement goal model in which two components of competence were identified: definition and valence. As noted at the outset of our chapter, competence can be defined in terms of absolute (i.e., task), intrapersonal (i.e., self), or interpersonal (i.e., normative) standards. When absolute standards are used, competence is evaluated on the basis of one's ability to complete a particular task. When intrapersonal standards are used, competence is evaluated on the basis of one's own performance trajectory. When interpersonal standards are used, competence is evaluated on the basis of normative comparison. The original mastery-performance goal distinction fits within this definition component of competence, with mastery-based goals using an absolute or intrapersonal standard of competence and performance-based goals using a normative standard of competence. Competence can also be valenced in that it can represent a positive possibility (competence) or a negative possibility (incompetence). The approach-avoidance distinction was seen as nicely capturing this valence component of competence, with approach goals focusing on the positive possibility of competence and avoidance goals focusing on the negative possibility of incompetence. When the definition and valence components are crossed, four goals are represented: mastery-approach (striving to attain task-/self-based competence, e.g., My goal is to do better than I have done before), mastery-avoidance (striving to avoid task- and self-based incompetence, e.g., My goal is to avoid doing worse than I have done before), performance-approach (striving to attain normative competence, e.g., My goal is to do better than others), and performance-avoidance goals (striving to avoid normative incompetence, e.g., My goal is to avoid doing worse than others; see Figure 13.2).

Empirical research on the 2 × 2 model has revealed patterns for mastery-approach, performance-approach, and performance-avoidance goals that are directly in line with the patterns seen in research on the trichotomous achievement model. Mastery-avoidance goals have been linked to fewer adaptive processes and outcomes than mastery-approach goals but also to fewer maladaptive processes and outcomes than performance-avoidance goals (Conroy, Elliot, & Hofer, 2003; Cury, da Fonseca, Elliot, & Moller, 2006; Elliot & McGregor, 2001; Elliot & Murayama, 2008; Elliot & Reis, 2003; for reviews, see Elliot & Moller, 2003; Roberts, Treasure, & Conroy, 2007). Research on mastery-avoidance goals remains at a very early stage, and it is difficult at present to clearly identify the empirical profile that will ultimately be associated with this form of goal. In addition, it is likely that task- and self-based goals produced somewhat different affect, cognition, and behavior in certain instances, meaning that the final instantiation of the 2 × 2 model will actually be a 3 × 2 model that fully crosses absolute, intrapersonal, and interpersonal definitions of competence by approach and avoidance valence (see Elliot, 1999, 2005). Finally, other achievement goal candidates have been proposed in the literature, such as work-avoidance goals (Nicholls, 1989) and social goals (Wentzel, 1994). However, these goals either represent the absence of an achievement goal (work-avoidance) or a goal that an individual may have in an achievement setting, as distinct from a goal focused on competence; thus we do not consider them achievement goals per se.

Valence Strivings	Definition of Competence: Mastery (task/self)	Definition of Competence: Performance (other)
Approach (strive toward competence)	Mastery-Approach Goal	Performance-Approach Goal
Avoidance (strive away from incompetence)	Mastery-Avoidance Goal	Performance-Avoidance Goal

Figure 13.2 The 2 × 2 model of achievement goals.

In the following sections, we review the longitudinal and cross-sectional research that has been conducted on change in achievement goal adoption over time. The main focus of our review is on empirical work conducted on the trichotomous and 2 × 2 achievement goal models; therefore, our review is on work conducted from 1996 (the date the trichotomous model was proffered) to the present (for a review focused primarily, although not exclusively, on the dichotomous achievement goal model, see E. Anderman, Austin, & Johnson, 2002). Furthermore, our review focuses on personal achievement goal adoption, rather than achievement goal structures (i.e., the achievement goal climate promoted in a particular setting), although achievement goal structures will be addressed in the studies that have examined them as predictors of change in personal achievement goal adoption. Similar to developmentally based research on achievement motives, research considering change in personal achievement goals across transitions, grades levels, and achievement events is quite sparse.

Change in Achievement Goal Adoption

Longitudinal Studies

Although longitudinal studies investigating achievement goal constructs are limited, a number do exist. We begin with the pioneering work of Carol Midgley and her colleagues (see Midgley, 2002, and Midgley et al., 2000, for reviews) that tracked students' progression from elementary school to middle school. This research focused primarily on the transition from elementary to middle school, because it was considered a crucial period given the important physical changes (e.g., onset of puberty) and school context changes (e.g., larger and more impersonal classes) encountered by children at this time. Initially, this work was grounded in the dichotomous model of achievement goals, assessing both students' personal goals for their academic work and the achievement goals that students perceived being promoted in their classrooms and schools (E. Anderman & Midgley, 1997; E. Anderman, Maehr, & Midgley, 1999; L. Anderman & E. Anderman, 1999). Later Midgley and colleagues incorporated the trichotomous model of achievement goals into their research, and it is this work that we focus on here.

Urdan and Midgley (2003) evaluated personal achievement goal adoption in students across fifth, sixth, and seventh grades. In the initial, fifth-grade assessment, a measure of achievement goals that bifurcated performance-based goals was not available, but performance-approach and performance-avoidance goals were assessed in sixth and seventh grade. Using a novel approach to the data analysis, the researchers formed three groups to compare students who perceived an increase, a decrease, or no change in their classroom achievement goal climate over a given year. As in prior studies by Midgley and her colleagues (on the dichotomous achievement goal model), Urdan and Midgley were interested in how perceived classroom goal climate changes were linked to changes in students' personal goal adoption, and their subsequent patterns of adaptive or maladaptive learning. They created one set of groups to look at change in perceived mastery goal climate and another set of groups to look at change in perceived performance goal climate.

From fifth to sixth grade, students who perceived a decrease in mastery goal climate exhibited a decrease in mastery goal adoption. However, students who perceived no change in mastery goal climate also showed a decrease in mastery goal adoption (rather than no change), and students who perceived an increase in mastery goal climate showed no change in mastery goal adoption (rather than an increase). Thus, a link between change in perceived mastery goal climate and change in mastery goal adoption was established for only one of the three groups. In contrast, change in perceived performance goal climate was more clearly associated with change in performance goal adoption. Students who reported an increase in performance goal climate reported an increase in performance goal adoption, students who reported no change in performance goal climate did not change their performance goal adoption, and students who reported a decrease in performance goal climate tended to report lower performance goal adoption (although this difference did not attain statistical significance).

From sixth to seventh grade, perceived change in mastery goal climate was more clearly linked to change in mastery goal adoption. Students who perceived a decrease in mastery goal climate showed a decrease in mastery goal adoption, those who perceived no change in mastery climate did not change their mastery goal adoption, and those who perceived an increase in mastery climate showed an increase in mastery goal adoption. Perceived change in performance goal climate, however, was less clearly linked to change in performance-approach and performance-avoidance goal adoption. Only a decrease in perceived performance goal climate was linked to a decrease in both performance-approach and performance-avoidance goal adoption. However, students who exhibited no change in perceived performance goal climate also showed a decrease in both performance-approach and performance-avoidance goal adoption (rather than no change), and students who exhibited an increase in perceived performance goal climate showed no change in either performance-approach or performance-avoidance goal adoption (rather than an increase). Thus, other factors besides change in the perceived environment appear to be at play in accounting for change in achievement goal adoption. Finally, Urdan and Midgley (2003) noted that change in perceived mastery goal climate was more strongly related to subsequent cognition, affect, and performance attainment than change in perceived performance goal climate, with the most maladaptive pattern occurring when a decrease in mastery goal climate was perceived. When students perceived an increase in mastery goal climate in middle school, they did not exhibit a decline in motivation-relevant processes and outcomes during the transition period.[4]

[4] It is important to note that the three categories used by the researchers in their grouping of students indicated that the majority of students did not perceive a change in mastery goal climate from fifth to sixth grades (n = 283, compared with 123 who saw a decrease and 146 who saw an increase). Similarly, the majority of students did not perceive a change in performance goal climate from fifth to sixth grade (n = 280, compared with 148 who saw a decrease and 127 who saw an increase). The pattern was similar for the sixth- to seventh-grade groupings. Thus, Urdan and Midgley's work highlights the oft overlooked point that there is considerable interstudent variability in perceptions of goal climate change across grade levels.

Middleton, Kaplan, and Midgley (2004) examined the trichotomous model of achievement goals for students making the transition from sixth to seventh grade with a particular emphasis on student self-efficacy. Middleton and colleagues were interested in determining what factors contribute to a shift from a performance-approach goal to a performance-avoidance goal. It is important to note that the schools being evaluated in this study incorporated a number of mastery goal interventions targeted at the sixth-grade students (such as no ability grouping and no formal tracking of students) that were not included for seventh-grade students. Although no formal significance tests were reported to determine whether the adoption of different achievement goals increased, decreased, or remained constant over time, descriptively, all three goals were lower in seventh grade than in sixth grade. The main focus of this study was on predicting students' seventh-grade achievement goals for math from students' sixth-grade achievement goals for math, as well as student self-efficacy in math. The results indicated that each sixth-grade goal positively predicted its corresponding goal in seventh grade, and one additional relationship was revealed: sixth-grade performance-approach goals also predicted seventh-grade performance-avoidance goals. Additional analyses revealed an interaction between performance-approach goals and self-efficacy, whereby students who reported higher levels of both were at risk of adopting performance-avoidance goals when they transitioned to the seventh grade. That is, counterintuitively, it was not students high in performance-approach goals and low in self-efficacy who were susceptible; rather it was students high in both goal variables who were likely to experience a problematic shift in motivational focus. Middleton et al. (2004) concluded that performance-approach goals may be linked to some adaptive outcomes but may also make students vulnerable over time. They also speculated that students high in self-efficacy may be particularly vulnerable when making a shift to more performance-oriented environments if they also focus on trying to do well compared with others.

Husman, Brem, and Duggan (2005) evaluated the trichotomous achievement goal model with regard to reading for students in third through sixth grade. In addition to looking at within year variation, the design of the study afforded the opportunity to compare across different elementary school grade cohorts. Another key feature of the study is that it was designed to evaluate the impact of a new schoolwide reading program on the basis of continuous formative assessment. The investigators were interested in whether the feedback provided via formative assessment would promote a performance goal classroom climate, given the additional testing and grade information that would now be available for social comparison, or a mastery goal climate by providing students timely feedback that would enable them to better track their self-referential progress and development. In addition to students' own goals, Husman et al. (2005) collected students' perceptions of their teacher's achievement goals for reading; this served as another method to capture the type of achievement goal climate being promoted in the classroom. The results indicated that students' performance-approach and performance-avoidance goals for reading dropped across all grade levels, while their mastery goals remained consistent. They also found that personal performance-approach and performance-avoidance goals were positively associated with the perception that teachers held performance-based goals, whereas personal mastery goals were positively associated with the perception that teachers held mastery goals. Surprisingly, students' performance-approach and performance-avoidance goals were also positively correlated with perceptions that their teacher was mastery focused. Thus, the results point to two environmental influences on students' goal adoption: The schoolwide formative assessment program appeared to reinforce mastery goals and downplay performance-approach and avoidance goals for reading, and variation in the perceived achievement goals of teachers was linked to students' own pattern of achievement goal pursuit.

Bong (2005) evaluated the stability of achievement goals for Korean high school girls over an academic year. In the first semester, she used the dichotomous model of achievement goals to assess students' personal goals and perceptions of the classroom goal climate; in the second semester, she used the trichotomous achievement goal model to assess students' personal goals. In addition, students' achievement goals were measured for academics in general, as well as for three specific subject domains (English, math, and Korean). The results indicated that students perceived an increase in performance goal climate from the first to the second semester for general academics and all three specific subjects and that students perceived a decrease in mastery goal climate during this same period for general academics and English. These findings were anticipated, given the heavy emphasis on competition and testing in the Korean high school system. Despite the change in perceived goal climates, Bong did not find that an increase in students' performance-based goals or a decrease in their mastery-based goals occurred.

Surprisingly, the only change observed in personal goals across semesters was an increase in students' mastery goals for general academics. Interestingly, when simultaneously modeling first and second semester classroom climate perceptions, personal achievement goals, and self-efficacy, Bong found that an increase in second semester perceptions of the mastery goal classroom climate (both in general and for all three specific domains) was linked to an increase in personal mastery goals and self-efficacy and was also positively linked to performance-approach and performance-avoidance goal adoption in the second semester for specific domains. Like Urdan and Midgley (2003), Bong (2005) concluded that it is change in the mastery goal classroom climate rather than change in the performance goal classroom climate that best accounts for students' ongoing motivation.

Moving to an athletic achievement context, Conroy, Kaye, and Coatsworth (2006) conducted a longitudinal investigation of youth swimmers ranging in age from 7 to 18. Specifically, they tracked swimmers' 2 × 2 achievement goals over the course of a 6-week season to see whether the swimmers' perception of the coaches' achievement goals led to subsequent changes in achievement goal adoption or situational motivation over the course of the season. Situational motivation was assessed by asking participants about their reasons for participating in swimming (ranging from self-determined reasons to amotivated reasons; see Guay, Vallerand, & Blanchard, 2000). At the end of the season, swimmers' perceptions of their coaches' achievement goals for them were associated with change in their personal avoidance-based goals. That is, perceived coach mastery-avoidance goals were associated with an increase in personal mastery-avoidance goal adoption, and perceived coach performance-avoidance goals were associated with an increase in personal performance-avoidance goal adoption (relative to the beginning of the season). However, no links between perceived coaches' approach-based goals and swimmers' own approach-based goals were observed. These changes were consequential because increases in swimmers' mastery-avoidance goals over this time period were linked to changes situational motivation—the swimmers who increased their focus on mastery-avoidance goals becoming less self-determined and more amotivated over the course of the season. Thus, once again, a situational perception—perception of the coaching climate—affected swimmers' personal goals and their underlying motivation across a short longitudinal time frame.

Moving to longitudinal studies using a university-age population, Senko and Harackiewicz (2005) evaluated achievement goal stability at two points (10 weeks apart) during an introductory psychology course and evaluated how early performance feedback alters subsequent achievement goal endorsement. Using the trichotomous achievement goal model, they found that mastery goals and performance-approach goals decreased over the two time points, whereas performance-avoidance goals increased. Then, in a series of hierarchical regression analyses predicting Time 2 achievement goals from Time 1 achievement goals and early exam performance, they found considerable goal stability, in that Time 1 goals were all positively linked to their respective Time 2 goals (e.g., Time 1 mastery goals predicted Time 2 mastery goals). However, early exam performance was also a systematic predictor of each T2 goal, suggesting that students did alter their goals as a function of initial performance feedback. Specifically, early exam performance was a positive predictor of Time 2 mastery and performance-approach goals and was a negative predictor of Time 2 performance-avoidance goals.

Fryer and Elliot (2007) also evaluated stability and change in achievement goal adoption over the course of an undergraduate semester-long period. First, they offered a number of reasons why achievement goals might display stability over time: (a) their grounding in stable personality dispositions (see Conroy & Elliot, 2004; Elliot, 1999), (b) the stability of achievement contexts (e.g., class formats and environments tend to remain fixed), and (c) achievement goals establish a "biased" framework for how to approach, experience, and react to an achievement context that may end up reinforcing the initial goal choice. Second, they also noted a number of reasons to expect change, even over the short term, specifically: (a) goals represent a form of self-regulation, which entails monitoring goal progress and the need for goal revision; (b) the initial goal may be based on incomplete information; (c) individuals receive additional information about the task (e.g., its difficulty) and the environment in which the task is completed (e.g., the degree to which it reflects competitiveness); and (d) other life events may alter commitment to competence or resources to accomplish the task. They argued that goal pursuit might best be seen as a continuous process involving both goal intensification and goal switching (see Senko & Harackiewicz, 2005).

Fryer and Elliot (2007) also proposed and evaluated four ways in which goal stability and change could be manifested. The first is differential continuity, which represents an index of the level of rank order consistency in a construct over time. This is simply evaluated by looking at the correlation coefficient of the same construct at different times and is the most common form of stability assessed in the literature. Indeed, past achievement goal studies have shown moderate to high positive correlations between the same goals across time (e.g., Bong, 2005; Senko & Harackiewicz, 2005). Nevertheless, even if differential continuity is present, it is still possible for other types of change to occur. A second method is to evaluate mean-level change, which indexes the average amount of change in a goal over time within the same sample. This approach to testing change was also used in several of the aforementioned longitudinal studies (e.g., Bong, 2005; Senko & Harackiewicz, 2005; Husman et al., 2005). A third method is to evaluate individual-level change, which indexes the amount of change in a goal over time exhibited by an individual. In other words, the analysis is now shifted from the group or sample level to the individual level. This type of change is often assessed through the creation of a reliable change index (RCI) that involves transforming the data, and grouping individuals into categories showing an increase, decrease, or no change on the basis of their individual responses (e.g., see the methodology used by Urdan & Midgley, 2003, described earlier). The fourth and final method is ipsative continuity, which indexes the amount of stability or change in an individual's configuration of constructs over time. This last method is also referred to as either profile consistency or profile dispersion, depending on the pattern that is found. Ipsative continuity is indexed by a within-person correlation, known as the Q-correlation, which again focuses on individual level change and on the configuration of goals rather than single goal constructs. High positive correlations reflect stability, and low positive or negative correlations suggest that change has occurred.

A series of three studies were conducted by Fryer and Elliot (2007) to examine these four forms of change and stability using both the trichotomous and 2 × 2 achievement goal models. Achievement goals were assessed at three time points (approximately every 5 weeks) over a 15-week term in undergraduate psychology courses. In Study 1, the investigators found evidence for differential continuity for each of the trichotomous achievement goals, and they also found mean-level change, whereby students became less mastery-approach focused and more performance-avoidance focused from Exam 1 to Exam 2. Individual-level change was also found, corresponding to the mean-level change for mastery-approach and performance-avoidance goals. Interestingly, similar amounts of increase and decrease occurred for performance-approach goals, which masked performance-approach goal change in mean-level tests. Finally, the ipsative continuity analysis showed profile consistency. In Study 2, Fryer and Elliot (2007) replicated the Study 1 findings and also showed that students' fear of failure positively predicted their degree of ipsative change. In Study 3, they replicated the goal change results from the first two studies and the fear of failure finding from Study 2 but also examined the fourth goal of the 2 × 2 achievement goal model. The results for mastery-avoidance goals were similar to those for performance-approach goals in that stability was supported in differential continuity and mean-level change, but change was supported in individual-level change (with equal numbers of students increasing and decreasing over time on mastery-avoidance goals, thus masking any overall mean-level change for these goals).

In an instructional physical activity context, Conroy, Elliot, and Hofer (2003) examined three forms of temporal stability in achievement goals: factorial invariance over time, differential stability (i.e., test–retest reliability at the latent variable level), and latent mean stability. Achievement goal assessments took place 2, 7, and 21 days after a baseline assessment, which permitted estimation of stability coefficients over 2-, 5-, 7-, 14-, 19-, and 21-day intervals. Factorial invariance was shown to be strong for all achievement goals across the assessments. For mastery-approach goals, these stability coefficients ranged from .51 to .77. For mastery-avoidance goals, the stability coefficients ranged from .54 to .77. For performance-approach goals, the stability coefficients ranged from .71 to .87. For performance-avoidance goals, the stability coefficients ranged from .69 to .85. The mean level of performance-avoidance goals remained stable over the 3-week period, but a very small reduction was observed in the mean levels of mastery-approach, mastery-avoidance, and performance-approach goals during that time. Conroy and Elliot (2004) extended these analyses to examine whether the explicit FF motive predicted changes in any of the 2 × 2 goals in this study. Results indicated that FF predicted residualized change in both mastery-avoidance and performance-avoidance goals but did not predict changes in either of their approach goal counterparts. As expected, all four goal scores were less stable over time than explicit FF scores in this study, thereby reinforcing the dynamic nature of goals relative to motive dispositions.

In sum, although the empirical yield from longitudinal studies is clearly limited, the following tentative conclusions may be drawn. First, mastery-approach goals appear to remain stable across the elementary school years (Husman et al., 2005) but decline across middle school (Middleton et al., 2004). Within a given academic year, mastery-approach goals seem to remain stable in elementary school (Husman et al., 2005) and high school (Bong, 2005), but evidence a decline over the course of the college semester (Fryer & Elliot, 2007; Senko & Harackiewicz, 2005). Within a physical activity context, mastery-approach goals seem quite stable over time.

Second, performance-approach goals appear to decline across both elementary school (Husman et al., 2005) and middle school (Middleton et al., 2004). Within a given academic year, performance-approach goals seem to decline over the year in elementary school (Husman et al., 2005), exhibit no change over the year in high school (Bong, 2005), and decline or show no change over the course of the college semester (Fryer & Elliot, 2007; Senko & Harackiewicz, 2005). Within a physical activity context, performance-approach goals appear to be quite stable over time.

Third, the data for avoidance-based achievement goals are even more limited than those for approach-based achievement goals. Performance-avoidance goals appear to decline across grades during the middle school years (Middleton et al., 2004). Within a given academic year, performance-avoidance goals seem to decline over the year in elementary school (Husman et al., 2005) but increase over the collegiate semester (Fryer & Elliot, 2007; Senko & Harackiewicz, 2005); mastery-avoidance goals show no change over the course of the semester in college (Fryer & Elliot, 2007). Within a physical activity context, both types of avoidance goal seem quite stable over time.

Fourth, the existing data link achievement goal change to a number of environmentally based variables. These variables include perceptions of teachers' achievement goals (Husman et al., 2005), perceptions of coaches' achievement goals (Conroy et al., 2006), and externally provided performance feedback (Senko & Harackiewicz, 2005).

Fifth, the existing longitudinal studies provide an illustration of the designs and data-analytic approaches that can be used to study achievement goal change systematically. In addition, the field could also benefit from the reanalysis of results from existing studies using new data-analytic approaches (e.g., see Fryer & Elliot, 2007). Furthermore, examples of the types of longitudinal research that achievement goal theorists would, optimally, begin to pursue in the future are available in the work of other motivational researchers examining other motivational constructs (see, for example, Fredericks & Eccles, 2002; Jacobs, Lanza, Osgood, Eccles, & Wigfield, 2002; Otis, Grouzet, & Pelletier, 2005; Skinner, Zimmer-Gembeck, & Connell, 1998).

Finally, Middleton et al. (2004) asserted that "future research should pay attention to the development of goals within and across learning environments, to their interaction with other motivational processes, and to their longitudinal relations with a variety of outcomes" (p. 307). We wholeheartedly agree and would add that our review of the literature reveals a number of additional gaps in need of research attention. First and foremost, studies have yet to evaluate fully achievement goal change among older populations or to evaluate achievement goals longitudinally in other competence-relevant contexts beyond academics. Although achievement goal research per se has yet to be conducted with older adults, some recent research by Freund and colleagues is relevant in this regard. Freund (2006) had older adult participants perform a sensorimotor task and focused them on either doing as well as possible on the task (akin to a mastery-approach goal) or on not doing worse than a previous level of performance (akin to a mastery-avoidance goal). Results across several studies indicated that older participants persisted longer on the task when it was framed in terms of not doing worse than before. In other research, Freund and colleagues (see Ebner, Freund, & Baltes, 2006; Freund, & Ebner, 2005) have found that avoidance-based goals seem to be adaptive in terms of subjective well-being for older adults. This work suggests that avoidance goals may be more prevalent later in the life course and may be more effective at this time because they appropriately reflect the developmental opportunities and constrains facing individuals in daily life (for related ideas, see Baranik et al., 2007; Elliot & McGregor, 2001).

Second, the studies that do exist are in need of replication before clear patterns of achievement goal change and stability can be established with certainty. Third, most longitudinal research on goal change has yet to incorporate fully the avoidance goals of the trichotomous and, especially, the 2×2 achievement goal models. Our examination of the literature revealed a few longitudinal studies, beyond those reviewed herein that focused on variants of the trichotomous model, but the data from these studies were analyzed in a way that make clear statements regarding goal change over time difficult to discern (e.g., Braten & Stromso, 2004, 2006; Veermans & Tapola, 2004). In addition, it should be noted that other longitudinal studies of achievement goals were conducted during the dates under consideration for our review that focused on the dichotomous rather than the trichotomous or 2×2 achievement goal models (Chouinard & Roy, 2008; Gutman, 2006; Meece & Miller, 2001; Obach, 2003;

Pintrich, 2000; Todorovich & Curtner-Smith, 2003; Wolters, Yu, & Pintrich, 1996; see also the studies by Midgley and colleagues that were referred to at the beginning of this section).

Cross-Sectional Studies

Studies that compare and contrast different age cohorts using a cross-sectional design provide a second methodology with which to explore developmental differences in achievement goal adoption. Again, our review focuses on empirical investigations using the trichotomous and 2 × 2 models of achievement goals, organized (roughly) by the age of cohorts being compared.

Liu (2003) used the trichotomous achievement goal model to compare Chinese student cohorts in their last year of elementary school (fifth grade) and their first year of middle school (sixth grade). Only one difference was found: Students in the middle school cohort reported being more performance-approach focused than those in the elementary school cohort. No differences were observed between the cohorts, however, in perceived mastery and performance goal climates. Liu noted that the Chinese classroom practices may not be substantially different between the two grades considered. Education is compulsory for all children until the ninth grade and then is highly selective regarding who continues into high school and college. As a result, the general context is highly competitive and grounded in social comparison, but students may still feel more press to adopt performance-approach goals as they get closer to taking exams that will dictate who can continue beyond ninth grade.

Leondari and Gialamas (2002) also used the trichotomous achievement goal model to compare Greek student cohorts in elementary school and middle school. Differences emerged for all three achievement goals, with students in middle school reporting lower levels for all three goals than students in elementary school. The largest difference was found for mastery goals. In a subsequent study, Leondari and Gonida (2007) extended their investigation of trichotomous achievement goals to compare Greek student cohorts in elementary, middle, and high school. Another novel feature of this study involved the level of specificity of the achievement goals evaluated. In Leondari and Gialamas (2002), achievement goals for school in general were evaluated, but in Leondari and Gonida (2007), achievement goals in the specific domain of math were the focus. One goal difference was found: Mastery goals decreased across all cohorts as students progressed from elementary to middle to high school.

An additional component of the study was to look at differences in self-handicapping in the different age cohorts, as well as the link between achievement goals and self-handicapping. In elementary school, performance-approach and performance-avoidance goals both positively predicted self-handicapping. In middle school, performance-avoidance goals positively predicted self-handicapping and mastery goals negatively predicted self-handicapping. Finally, in high school, mastery goals negatively predicted self-handicapping. Thus, not only were changes in mastery goals over time noted across the different cohorts, but the role of mastery goals in negatively predicting other maladaptive achievement behavior became more important as students progressed through the school system.

Pajares, Britner, and Valiante (2000) evaluated the trichotomous model of achievement goals with cohorts of sixth-, seventh-, and eighth-grade students progressing through middle school. Initially, the study did not analyze the data by grade cohort, so the degree of mean level goal change over time was not reported. However, analyses with outcome variables involving writing were conducted within each grade. For writing self-concept, the pattern of achievement goal predictors was the same across grade levels: Mastery goals positively predicted and performance-avoidance goals negatively predicted writing self-concept. For writing apprehension, the results were similar across grade levels: Mastery goals negatively predicted writing apprehension (except in seventh grade) and performance-avoidance goals positively predicted writing apprehension. For writing self-regulation, mastery goals were a positive predictor in sixth, seventh, and eighth grade, with the addition of performance-approach goals as a positive predictor and performance-avoidance goals as a negative predictor in eighth grade. Finally, the most differences were found for writing self-efficacy. In sixth grade, mastery goals were a positive predictor and performance-avoidance goals were a negative predictor; in seventh grade, mastery goals and performance-approach goals were a positive predictor and performance-avoidance goals were a negative predictor; and in eighth grade, mastery goals were a positive predictor and null relations were observed for performance-based goals. In comparing their results to other research, Pajares et al. (2000) noted that they found more benefits in middle school for performance-approach goals than other studies (e.g., Middleton & Midgley, 1997), and they hypothesized that performance-approach goals may not be adaptive early on but may become more so as students get older.

Nelson and DeBacker (2008) investigated the trichotomous model of achievement goals in science classes with cohorts of middle school and high school students to evaluate the transition from middle school to high school. Students in middle school were drawn from the sixth and seventh grades, and students in high school were in the ninth grade. Two differences in achievement goal adoption were noted, with students in the high school cohort endorsing less mastery and performance-approach goals than middle school students. Another unique aspect of this study was evaluation of the influence of best friends and classmates in goal endorsement. The investigators found that mastery goals were positively linked to social intimacy and responsibility goals, class belongingness, classmates' involvement, and best friend's academic valuing, and they were negatively linked to social approval goals and best friend's resistance to school norms. Performance-approach goals were positively related to social intimacy, approval, and responsibility goals, classmates' resistance to school norms, class belongingness, and best friend's academic valuing. Performance-avoidance goals, in contrast, were positively linked to social intimacy and approval goals and classmates' resistance to school norms.

Gonida, Kiosseoglou, and Voulala (2007) used the trichotomous achievement goal model with Greek student cohorts in seventh, ninth, and eleventh grades (which reflect three levels of schooling in the Greek system, better known as junior high, middle high, and senior high school, respectively). In addition to students' personal goals, Gonida et al. (2007) examined students' perceptions of their parents' goals to investigate how both personal and perceived parental goals affected student engagement in the classroom. Student cohorts reported lower levels of achievement goal endorsement as they progressed through school, and they reported lower perceptions of their parents' achievement goals for them. That is, personal achievement goal adoption for eleventh-grade students was significantly lower than seventh-grade students for each goal variable examined, and ninth-grade students' goal adoption was significantly lower than that of the seventh-grade students for performance-approach goals and perceived parent performance goals. Only one difference was observed between the ninth- and eleventh-grade cohorts, with eleventh-grade students endorsing less performance-avoidance goals than their ninth-grade counterparts.

In terms of predicting classroom engagement variables, personal mastery goals positively predicted emotional and behavioral engagement in all cohorts and personal performance-approach goals were unrelated to engagement in all cohorts. Personal performance-avoidance goals, in contrast, were found to negatively predict both emotional and behavioral engagement in seventh grade, to be unrelated to engagement in ninth grade, and to only predict behavioral engagement in eleventh grade. Interestingly, perceived parent mastery goals positively predicted students' mastery and performance-approach goal adoption in seventh grade, but only predicted students' mastery goal adoption in ninth and eleventh grades. Also in seventh grade, perceived parent mastery goals were a positive predictor of both emotional and behavioral engagement but were unrelated to engagement in later cohorts. Finally, perceived parent performance goals positively predicted students' performance-approach and performance-avoidance goals in all three cohorts.

Skaalvik and Skaalvik (2004) examined the trichotomous achievement goal model across three levels of school settings to compare cohorts of students in elementary school, middle school, and high school. Norwegian students were selected from the sixth-, ninth-, and eleventh-grade years for the study. Interestingly, the investigators also added a fourth cohort of returning adult students ranging in age from 18 to 52 ($M = 27.7$) to compare achievement goals of an older adult population to those of the younger cohorts. Students' goals were collected in both the math and verbal domains, with the primary purpose being an investigation of gender differences in math and verbal self-concept, performance expectations, and intrinsic motivation. In the sixth-grade cohort, boys had higher performance-approach and performance-avoidance goals for math than in the verbal domain, whereas girls had higher performance-avoidance goals in the verbal than in the math domain. In both the ninth- and eleventh-grade cohorts, boys had higher mastery and performance-avoidance goals in the math domain than in verbal domain, and no achievement goal differences were observed for girls across domains. For the returning adult cohort, men had higher performance-avoidance goals for the math domain than the verbal domain, and women had higher mastery goals in the verbal domain than the math domain. Unfortunately, no formal tests of achievement goal differences by year were made, and no additional tests were conducted to link goals to other variables collected within each cohort. However, comparison of the descriptive statistics that were reported suggest a number of general trends. In the math domain, mastery goal endorsement decreased slightly between the sixth and ninth grades, increased slightly in the eleventh-grade cohort, and then increased more dramatically to reach the highest level in the adult cohort. Performance-approach goals in math also dropped slightly between the sixth- and ninth-grade cohorts, increased again in the eleventh-grade cohort, and dropped to reach the lowest level for the adult cohort. Performance-avoidance goals showed a steady decline across the sixth-, ninth-, and eleventh-grade cohorts, followed by slight increase for the adult cohort. In the verbal domain, the pattern of mastery goal endorsement was similar to the math domain in that it dropped slightly from the sixth to the ninth grade, increased slightly in the eleventh-grade cohort, and increased more dramatically to reach the highest level in the adult cohort. Performance-approach goals in the verbal domain were similar for the sixth and ninth grade cohorts, but then increased in the eleventh grade cohort, and decreased in the adult cohort. Finally, performance-avoidance goals in the verbal domain decreased steadily between the sixth, ninth, and eleventh grade cohorts, and then remained the same for the adult cohort.

Ross, Shannon, Salisbury-Glennon, and Guarino (2002) examined the trichotomous achievement goal model with a more radical difference in age cohorts. Midgley et al.'s (1998) Pattern of Adaptive Learning Survey (PALS) was originally validated to assess the trichotomous goal model for middle school students, and Ross et al. were interested in evaluating the PALS survey in both fourth-grade students and college students. First, the investigators showed that the proposed trichotomous factor structure held for both cohorts. Second, in terms of mean level differences in goal adoption, both cohorts had the same mastery goal scores, but the elementary school group evidenced slightly higher performance-approach and performance-avoidance goal adoption. The authors concluded that their results challenged the assumption made by other researchers that younger students are more mastery-goal-focused and older students are more performance-goal-focused (e.g., E. Anderman & Midgley, 1997). However it should be noted that the cohorts of college students in this study were upper-level juniors and seniors involved in teacher education training who were also being taught using nontraditional methods that entailed learner-centered and project-based approaches to teaching rather than more traditional methods. Thus, the college student achievement goal profile may not be representative of other college-aged populations. Nevertheless, the findings do highlight the potential role of environmental factors in maintaining and shaping the type of achievement goals endorsed by students.

In a study focused on athletic activities, Agbuga and Xiang (2008) the trichotomous achievement goal model was used in a physical education context with Turkish students in middle school and high school. Middle school students in the eighth grade were found to have higher levels of performance-approach goals for physical education than high school students in the eleventh grade. No differences emerged for mastery or performance-avoidance goals. Both cohorts displayed a similar pattern of relationships when the achievement goals were linked to effort and persistence. Mastery and performance-approach goals were positive predictors of effort and persistence, whereas performance-avoidance goals were unrelated. However, the researchers did note that the observed relations were stronger for the younger cohort.

In sum, as with longitudinal studies, the number of existing cross-sectional studies on achievement goals is limited. However, a number of conclusions and suggestions for future research can be drawn from the current yield of investigations. First, mastery-approach goal adoption is lower in middle school relative to elementary school cohorts (Leondari & Gialamas, 2007; Leondari & Gonida, 2002; Skaalvik & Skaalvik, 2004) or shows no difference (Liu, 2003); these goals continue to decline in cohorts between middle school and high school (Gonida et al., 2007; Leondari & Gonida, 2007; Nelson & DeBacker, 2008), although some data indicate that they may remain constant (Agbuga & Xiang, 2008) or even increase (Skaalvik & Skaalvik, 2004).

Second, cohort comparisons for performance-approach goals evidenced a rather variable pattern across the cross-sectional studies. Performance-approach goals were found to decline between elementary school and middle school (Leondari & Gialamas, 2002; Skaalvik & Skaalvik, 2004), show no change (Leondari & Gonida, 2007; Skaalvik & Skaalvik, 2004), or increase (Liu, 2003). In similar fashion, performance-approach goals were found to decline between middle school and high school (Gonida et al., 2007; Nelson & DeBacker, 2008), show no change (Leondari & Gonida, 2007), or increase (Skaalvik & Skaalvik, 2004).

Third, performance-avoidance goals were found to decline in comparisons between elementary school and middle school (Leondari & Gialamas, 2002; Skaalvik & Skaalvik, 2004) or show no change (Leondari & Gonida, 2007; Liu, 2003), and performance-avoidance goals continued to decline between middle school and high school (Gonida et al., 2007; Skaalvik & Skaalvik, 2004) or show no change (Leondari & Gonida, 2007; Nelson & DeBacker, 2008).

Fourth, comparison of the samples used in the studies reviewed herein highlights another factor that needs to be considered by researchers, as well as those seeking to interpret the empirical yield. The extant cross-sectional studies have focused on a wide array of international student samples (including participants from China, Greece,

Norway, and Turkey), and only three of the nine cross-sectional studies to date have focused on samples from North America. Achievement goal research is often reviewed and discussed by scholars from North America who may be unfamiliar with the cultural emphases present in China, Greece, and other societies. Culture undoubtedly plays a role in achievement goal endorsement (Murayama, Zhou, & Nesbit, 2009), and this role may differ as individuals progress throughout the life span. As such, given the considerable cultural diversity present in the research conducted to date, it seems best to be cautious in deriving firm or general conclusions from the data at hand.

Fifth, another factor in need of consideration when interpreting the existing studies is highlighted by juxtaposing the two studies conducted by Leondari and colleagues. Leondari and Gialamas (2002) evaluated Greek students' general academic achievement goals, whereas Leondari and Gonida (2007) evaluated Greek students' specific achievement goals for math. In the study focused on general achievement goals, all of the goals declined between elementary school and middle school, suggesting a general decline in achievement motivation during this time. However, in the study focused on math-specific achievement goals, mastery-approach goals declined, whereas performance-approach and performance-avoidance goals remained unchanged between elementary school and middle school. Thus, the specificity of achievement goals may also contribute to whether change is observed, and this, too, must be borne in mind when seeking to derive summary statements from the literature (see Finney, Pieper, & Barron, 2004).

Sixth, achievement goals may be assessed and examined at varying degrees of temporal resolution, from the goals that one typically adopts in achievement situations in general, to the goals that one adopts over several months of engagement in specific domains of activity, to the goals that one adopts for a specific task in a specific achievement setting, to the goals that one uses at any given moment during the dynamic process of task engagement (i.e., a continuum ranging from disposition-like goal orientations to dynamic states of involvement). Researchers to date have favored the middle range of this spectrum, with few studies focusing on dynamic goal states in particular (for exceptions, see Gernigon, d'Arippe-Longueville, Delignières, & Ninot, 2004; Schantz & Conroy, 2009). Goal change is more likely to be observed as one moves toward the dynamic end of this continuum, and this issue clearly deserves more careful consideration in the literature than it has received. Moreover, explicit attention to the time scale of goals and comparisons of their consequences at different time scales will reveal processes that are masked in static models of motivation. Illuminating these processes through careful research design, operational measurement, and data analysis will likely uncover causal relations that may be obscured in the existing literature. As these short-term causal processes unfold and accumulate, they develop into the foundation on which long-term differences in competence motivation are built. Understanding those differences is the penultimate aim of achievement motivation research.

Finally, our review of the cross-sectional literature, like our review of the longitudinal literature, has revealed several empirical lacunae in need of attention. First, nearly all studies have focused on late elementary school to high school students in academic contexts. Clearly, investigations focused on a wider age range and a more diverse array of achievement contexts are welcomed. Second, empirical work has yet to be conducted using the 2×2 achievement goal model, meaning we have no data at present on mastery-avoidance goal adoption. Third, our review uncovered a few cross-sectional studies, beyond those discussed herein, that contained achievement goal data across cohorts but that neglected to report analyses testing for cohort differences (Beghetto, 2006; Chouinard, Karsenti, & Roy, 2007; Wang, Biddle, & Elliot, 2007). We urge researchers to attend to the cohort question in any and all data in which it is relevant. Finally, it should be noted that a few other cross-sectional studies of achievement goals were conducted during the dates under consideration that focused on the dichotomous rather than trichotomous or 2×2 achievement goal models (Steinberg, Greive, & Glass, 2001; Xiang, Lee, & Shen, 2001).

CONCLUDING STATEMENTS

As we noted at the beginning of this chapter, research on the development of achievement motivation is far less common than one would expect given the critical importance of the competence construct for understanding physical and psychological growth and well-being. This is the case with regard to the achievement motivation literature in general and, as documented herein, the achievement motive and goal literatures specifically. In part this underdevelopment of the developmental component of the achievement motivation literature may be due to ambiguity in conceptualizing achievement motivation itself. This ambiguity has certainly retarded conceptual progress in other aspects of research on achievement motives and goals, and it is natural that it should influence progress on the developmental front as well. Our hope is that by clearly and emphatically establishing competence as the conceptual core of the achievement motivation literature (Elliot & Dweck, 2005), the foundation is in place for rapid progress in all areas of inquiry, and especially areas involving developmental questions that have received such limited attention to date.

In addition to lacking quantity, one could argue that research on the development of achievement motivation lacks quality as well. This, of course, is not meant as a global indictment of the literature; a number of excellent, informative studies have been conducted on both achievement motives and achievement goals. However, we would be remiss if we did not point out that there has been noteworthy methodological and data analytic advances in scholarship on developmental change since the 1990s (Boker & Wenger, 2007; Collins & Sayer, 2001; Raudenbush & Bryk, 2002; Singer & Willett, 2003), and suffice it to say that research on achievement motives and goals has not kept pace with such advances. Perhaps most noteworthy is the general absence of longitudinal research at present focusing on intraindividual change processes over time, such as links between growth trajectories of achievement motives or goals and growth trajectories of important processes and outcomes in achievement settings (for exceptions, see Conroy, Coatsworth, & Fifer, 2005; Schantz & Conroy, 2009). Cutting-edge research of this nature would be welcomed because it holds great promise to clarify the ways in which competence desires and strivings emerge and function across the life course.

We close by noting several developmentally relevant issues that we think are in particular need of immediate and sustained empirical attention. We present these issues in question form. When does FF develop, and does it emerge directly from nAch or does it emerge in independent fashion? Through what developmental processes do explicit achievement motives emerge from implicit achievement motives, and what traits and socialization experiences give rise to implicit–explicit concordance in these motives? Is there a critical period for implicit and/or explicit achievement motive development, and even if there is such a critical period, how substantial is change in achievement motives throughout the life span? When do individuals begin to regulate their dispositional achievement motivation tendencies with the strategic adoption of situation-specific achievement goals, and what person-based and environmentally based factors prompt such self-regulation? To what degree can avoidance-based achievement goal adoption be changed by features of evaluative environments, what are the strongest and most robust predictors of such change, and are such predictors invariant across age and domain of achievement activity? At what age, in what contexts, and for what types of tasks is performance-approach goal adoption adaptive? At what age and under what circumstances are performance-approach goals susceptible to becoming performance-avoidance goals? At what age, in what contexts, and for which types of tasks is mastery-avoidance goal adoption adaptive?

In addition to these specific questions, we would like to highlight two broad issues that we think are in particular need of consideration in developmental research on achievement motives and goals. First, adulthood has been largely ignored in achievement motive and goal research, and this is particularly so with regard to advanced adulthood. Competence is a core motivational need that is operative throughout the entire life course (Elliot et al., 2002; White, 1963), and achievement strivings may take place in avocational pursuits (e.g., gardening, stamp collecting) as well as more prototypic achievement settings (i.e., the classroom, the sport field, the workplace). Nevertheless, we do believe that achievement motives may decline to some degree as individuals move into old age. Specifically, we suspect that the nAch declines somewhat, most likely due to a reduction in competitiveness, whereas FF likely decreases more substantially. Regarding achievement goal pursuit, we would anticipate stability in mastery-approach goals, a decline in performance-approach and performance-avoidance goals, and an increase in mastery-avoidance goals (Elliot, 1999; Elliot & McGregor, 2001; see also Ebner et al., 2006). Beyond these most basic of questions, we suspect that there are many surprises and insights awaiting researchers who delve further into the exploration of intraindividual change processes in this overlooked age cohort.

Second, the issue of culture has not received sufficient consideration in the conducting of empirical work on achievement motives and goals nor in the interpretation of findings that have been obtained. It is clear from existing research on culture and motivation that different cultural emphases produce different motivational tendencies. For example, the collectivist emphasis present in the East (e.g., China, Japan, South Korea) relative to the West (e.g., North America) appears to foster more fear of failure (Eaton & Dembo, 1997) and more avoidance goal adoption (Elliot, Chirkov, Sheldon, & Kim, 2001).

Furthermore, it seems that achievement motives and goals may have a somewhat different influence on processes and outcome in achievement settings in the East relative to the West (see Tanaka & Yamauchi, 2001; Zusho, Pintrich, & Cortina, 2005). In reviewing and interpreting developmental research, this cultural variation must be systematically taken into consideration (for an excellent example, see Ng, Pomerantz, & Lam, 2007), as such variation at minimum adds noise to the signal emerging from the literature and at worst can lead to mistaking cultural differences for age differences.

In short, and simply stated, we are disappointed to report that the developmental study of achievement motivation remains at a nascent stage of development. It is our hope that theoretical advancement in the achievement motivation literature will serve as a launching point for more and more cutting-edge research in this vitally important area of inquiry.

REFERENCES

Agbuga, B., & Xiang, P. (2008). Achievement goals and their relations to self-reported persistence/effort in secondary physical education: A trichotomous achievement goal framework. *Journal of Teaching in Physical Education, 27,* 179–191.

Alessandri, S. M., & Lewis, M. (1993). Parental evaluation and its relation to shame and pride in young children. *Sex Roles, 29,* 335–343.

Alessandri, S. M., & Lewis, M. (1996). Differences in pride and shame in maltreated and nonmaltreated preschoolers. *Child Development, 67,* 1857–1869.

Ames, C. (1984). Competitive, cooperative, and individualistic goal structures: A cognitive–motivational analysis. In C. Ames & R. Ames (Eds.), *Research on motivation in education* (Vol. 3, pp. 177–207). New York: Academic Press.

Ames, C. (1992). Classrooms: Goals, structures, and student motivation. *Journal of Educational Psychology, 84,* 261–271.

Ames, C., & Archer, J. (1988). Achievement goals in the classroom: Students' learning strategies and motivation processes. *Journal of Educational Psychology, 80,* 260–267.

Anderman, E. M., Austin, C., & Johnson, D. (2002). The development of goal orientation. In A. Wigfield & J. Eccles (Eds.), *Development of achievement motivation* (pp. 197–220). San Diego, CA: Academic Press.

Anderman, E. M., Maehr, M. L., & Midgley, C. (1999). Declining motivation after the transition to middle school: Schools can make a difference. *Journal of Research and Development in Education, 32,* 131–147.

Anderman, E. M., & Midgley, C. (1997). Changes in achievement goal orientations, perceived academic competence, and grades across the transition to middle-level schools. *Contemporary Educational Psychology, 22,* 269–298.

Anderman, L. H., & Anderman, E. M. (1999). Social predictors of changes in students' achievement goal orientations. *Contemporary Educational Psychology, 24,* 21–37.

Arkes, H., & Garske, J. (1977). *Psychological theories of motivation.* Monterry, CA: Brooks/Cole.

Atance, C. M. (2008). Future thinking in young children. *Psychological Science, 17,* 295–298.

Atkinson, J. W. (1957). Motivational determinants of risk-taking behavior. *Psychological Review, 64,* 359–372.

Atkinson, J. W., & Litwin, G. H. (1960). Achievement motive and test anxiety conceived as motive to approach success and motive to avoid failure. *Journal of Abnormal and Social Psychology, 60,* 52–63.

Baranik, L. E., Barron, K. E., Finney, S. J. (2007). Measuring goal orientation in a work domain: Construct validity evidence for the 2 × 2 framework. *Educational and Psychological Measurement, 67,* 697–718.

Barrett, K. C. (2000). The development of the self-in-relationships. In R. S. L. Mills & S. Duck (Eds.), *The developmental psychology of personal relationships* (pp. 91–107). Chichester, England: John Wiley & Sons.

Barrett, K. C., & Campos, J. J. (1987). Perspectives on emotional development II: A functionalist approach to emotions. In J. D. Osofsky (Ed.), *Handbook of infant development* (2nd ed., pp. 555–578). Oxford, England: John Wiley & Sons.

Barrett, K. C., & Morgan, G. A. (1995). Continuities and discontinuities in mastery motivation during infancy and toddlerhood: A conceptualization and review. In R. H. MacTurk & G. A. Morgan (Eds.), *Mastery motivation: Origins, conceptualizations, and applications* (Vol. 12, pp. 57–93). Westport, CT: Ablex.

Barron, K. E., & Harackiewicz, J. M. (2000). Achievement goals and optimal motivation: A multiple goals approach. In C. Sansone & J. Harackiewicz (Eds.), *Intrinsic and extrinsic motivation: In search of optimal motivation.* San Diego, CA: Academic Press.

Barron, K. E., & Harackiewicz, J. M. (2001). Achievement goals and optimal motivation: Testing multiple goal models. *Journal of Personality and Social Psychology, 80,* 706–722.

Bates, J. E. (1989). Concepts and measures of temperament. In G. A. Kohnstamm, J. E. Bates, & M. K. Rothbart (Eds.), *Temperament in childhood* (pp. 3–26). Oxford, England: John Wiley & Sons.

Beghetto, R. A. (2006). Creative self-efficacy: Correlates in middle and secondary students. *Creativity Research Journal, 18,* 447–457.

Belsky, J., Domitrovich, C., & Crnic, K. (1997). Temperament and parenting antecedents of individual differences in three-year old boys' pride and shame reactions. *Child Development, 68,* 456–466.

Bennett, D. S., Sullivan, M. W., & Lewis, M. (2005). Young children's adjustment as a function of maltreatment, shame, and anger. *Child Maltreatment, 10,* 311–323.

Bindra, D. (1959). *Motivation: A systematic reinterpretation.* New York: Roland Press.

Birney, R. C., Burdick, H., & Teevan, R. C. (1969). *Fear of failure.* New York: Van Nostrand-Reinhold.

Blatt, S. J., Auerbach, J. S., & Levy, K. N. (1997). Mental representations in personality development, psychopathology, and the therapeutic process. *Review of General Psychology, 1,* 351–374.

Boker, S. M., & Wenger, M. J. (2007). *Data analytic techniques for dynamical systems.* Mahwah, NJ: Erlbaum.

Bong, M. (2005). Within-grade changes in Korean girls' motivation and perceptions of the learning environment across domains and achievement levels. *Journal of Educational Psychology, 97,* 656–672.

Bowlby, J. (1969/1982). *Attachment and loss: Vol. 1. Attachment.* New York: Basic Books.

Braten, I., & Stromso, H. I. (2004). Epistemological beliefs and implicit theories of intelligence as predictors of achievement goals. *Contemporary Educational Psychology, 29,* 371–388.

Braten, I., & Stromso, H. I. (2006). Predicting achievement goals in two different academic contexts: A longitudinal study. *Scandinavian Journal of Educational Research, 50,* 127–148.

Brophy, J. (2004). *Motivating students to learn.* New York: Taylor & Francis.

Burhans, K. K., & Dweck, C. S. (1995). Helplessness in early childhood: The role of contingent worth. *Child Development, 66,* 1719–1738.

Butler, R. (1998). Age trends in the use of social and temporal comparison for self-evaluation: Examination of a novel developmental hypothesis. *Child Development, 69,* 1054–1073.

Butler, R. (2005). Competence-assessment, competence and motivation between early and middle childhood. In A. Elliot & C. Dweck (Eds.), *Handbook of competence and motivation.* New York: Guilford Press.

Cain, K. M., & Dweck, C. S. (1995). The relation between motivational patterns and achievement cognitions through the elementary school years. *Merrill-Palmer Quarterly, 41,* 25–52.

Carver, C. S., & White, T. L. (1994). Behavioral inhibition, behavioral activation, and affective responses to impending reward and punishment: The BIS/BAS Scales. *Journal of Personality and Social Psychology, 67,* 319–333.

Chouinard, R., Karsenti, T., & Roy, N. (2007). Relations among competence beliefs, utility value, achievement goals, and effort in mathematics. *British Journal of Educational Psychology, 77,* 501–517.

Chouinard, R., & Roy, N. (2008). Changes in high-school students' competence beliefs, utility value and achievement goals in mathematics. *British Journal of Educational Psychology, 78,* 31–50.

Cimpian, A., Arce, H.-M. C., Markman, E. M., & Dweck, C. S. (2007). Subtle linguistic cues affect children's motivation. *Psychological Science, 18,* 314–316.

Cofer, C. N., & Appley, M. H. (1964). *Motivation: Theory and research.* New York: John Wiley & Sons.

Cohen, M. X., Young, J., Baek, J., Kessler, C., & Ranganath, C. (2005). Individual differences in extraversion and dopamine genetics predict neural reward responses. *Cognitive Brain Research, 25,* 851–861.

Collins, L. M., & Sayer, A. G. (2001). *New methods for the analysis of change.* Washington, DC: American Psychological Association.

Conroy, D. E. (2003). Representational models associated with fear of failure in adolescents and young adults. *Journal of Personality, 71,* 757–783.

Conroy, D. E., & Coatsworth, J. D. (2007). Coaching behaviors associated with changes in fear of failure: Changes in self-talk and need satisfaction as potential mechanisms. *Journal of Personality, 75,* 383–419.

Conroy, D. E., Coatsworth, J. D., & Fifer, A. M. (2005). Testing dynamic relations between perceived competence and fear of failure in young athletes. *European Review of Applied Psychology, 26,* 99–110.

Conroy, D. E., & Elliot, A. J. (2004). Fear of failure and achievement goals in sport: Addressing the issue of the chicken and the egg. *Anxiety, Stress, and Coping: An International Journal, 17,* 271–285.

Conroy, D. E., Elliot, A. J., & Hofer, S. M. (2003). A 2 × 2 achievement goals questionnaire for sport: Evidence for factorial invariance, temporal stability, and external validity. *Journal of Sport and Exercise Psychology, 25,* 456–476.

Conroy, D. E., Elliot, A. J., & Pincus, A. L. (2009). The expression of achievement motives in interpersonal problems. *Journal of Personality, 77,* 495-526.

Conroy, D. E., Kaye, M. P., & Coatsworth, J. D. (2006). Coaching climates and the destructive effects of mastery–avoidance achievement goals on situational motivation. *Journal of Sport and Exercise Psychology, 28,* 69–92.

Conroy, D. E., & Metzler, J. N. (2004). Patterns of self-talk associated with different forms of competitive anxiety. *Journal of Sport & Exercise Psychology, 26,* 69–89.

Conroy, D. E., & Pincus, A. L. (2006). A comparison of mean partialing and dual-hypothesis testing to evaluate stereotype effects when assessing profile similarity. *Journal of Personality Assessment, 86,* 142–149.

Cury, F., da Fonseca, D., Elliot, A. J., & Moller, A. (2006). The social-model of achievement motivation and the 2 × 2 achievement goal framework. *Journal of Personality and Social Psychology, 90,* 666–679.

deCharms, R., Morrison, H. W., Reitman, W., & McClelland, D. C. (1955). Behavioral correlates of directly and indirectly measured achievement motivation. In D. C. McClelland (Ed.), *Studies in motivation* (pp. 414–423). New York: Appleton-Century-Crofts.

Diener, C. I., & Dweck, C. S. (1978). An analysis of learned helplessness: Continuous changes in performance, strategy, and achievement cognitions following failure. *Journal of Personality and Social Psychology, 36,* 451–462.

Diener, C. I., & Dweck, C. S. (1980). An analysis of learned helplessness: II. The processing of success. *Journal of Personality and Social Psychology, 39,* 940–952.

Dweck, C. S., (1975). The role of expectations and attributions in the alleviation of learned helplessness. *Journal of Personality and Social Psychology, 80,* 706–722.

Dweck, C. S., & Elliott, E. (1983). Achievement motivation. In E. M. Hetherington (Ed.), *Handbook of child psychology: Vol. 4. Socialization, personality, and development* (4th ed., pp. 643–691). Editor in chief: P. H. Mussen. New York: John Wiley & Sons.

Dweck, C. S., & Leggett, E. L. (1988). A social–cognitive approach to motivation and personality. *Psychological Review, 95,* 256–273.

Dweck, C. S., & London, B. (2004). The role of mental representation in social development. *Merrill-Palmer Quarterly, 50,* 428–444.

Eaton, M., & Dembo, M. (1997). Differences in the motivational beliefs of Asian American and non-Asian students. *Journal of Educational Psychology, 89,* 433–440.

Ebner, N. C., Freund, A. M., & Baltes, P. B. (2006). Developmental changes in personal goal orientation from young to late adulthood: From striving for gains to maintenance and prevention of losses. *Psychology and Aging, 21,* 664–678.

Elliot, A. J. (1997). Integrating "classic" and "contemporary" approaches to achievement motivation: A hierarchical model of approach and avoidance achievement motivation. In P. Pintrich & M. Maehr (Eds.), *Advances in motivation and achievement* (Vol. 10, pp. 143–179). Greenwich, CT: JAI Press.

Elliot, A. J. (1999). Approach and avoidance motivation and achievement goals. *Educational Psychologist, 34,* 149–169.

Elliot, A. J. (2005). A conceptual history of the achievement goal construct. In A. J. Elliot & C. S. Dweck (Eds.), *Handbook of competence and motivation* (pp. 52–72). New York: Guilford Press.

Elliot, A. J. (2006). The hierarchical model of approach-avoidance motivation. *Motivation and Emotion, 30,* 111–116.

Elliot, A. J. (2008). Approach and avoidance motivation. In A. Elliot (Ed.), *Handbook of approach and avoidance motivation* (pp. 3–14). New York: Taylor & Francis.

Elliot, A. J., Chirkov, V. I., Sheldon, K. M., & Kim, Y. (2001). A cross-cultural analysis of avoidance (relative to approach) personal goals. *Psychological Science, 12,* 505–510.

Elliot, A. J., & Church, M. A. (1997). A hierarchical model of approach and avoidance achievement motivation. *Journal of Personality and Social Psychology, 72,* 218–232.

Elliot, A. J., & Dweck, C. S. (2005). Competence as the core of achievement motivation. In A. Elliot & C. Dweck (Eds.), *Handbook of competence and motivation* (pp. 3–12). New York: Guilford Press.

Elliot, A., & Fryer, J. (2008). The goal construct in psychology. In J. Y. Shah & W. L. Gardner (Eds.), *Handbook of motivation science* (pp. 235–250). New York: Guilford Press.

Elliot, A. J., & Harackiewicz, J. M. (1994). Goal setting, achievement orientation, and intrinsic motivation: A mediational analysis. *Journal of Personality and Social Psychology, 66*, 968–980.

Elliot, A. J., & Harackiewicz, J. M. (1996). Approach and avoidance achievement goals and intrinsic motivation: A mediational analysis. *Journal of Personality and Social Psychology, 70*, 461–475.

Elliot, A. J., & McGregor, H. A. (1999). Test anxiety and the hierarchical model of approach and avoidance achievement motivation. *Journal of Personality and Social Psychology, 76*, 628–644.

Elliot, A. J., & McGregor, H. A. (2001). A 2 × 2 achievement goal framework. *Journal of Personality and Social Psychology, 80*, 501–519.

Elliot, A. J., McGregor, H. A., & Gable, S. L. (1999). Achievement goals, study strategies, and exam performance: A mediational analysis. *Journal of Educational Psychology, 91*, 549–563.

Elliot, A. J., McGregor, H. A., & Thrash, T. M. (2002). The need for competence. In E. Deci & R. Ryan (Eds.), *Handbook of self-determination research* (pp. 361–387). Rochester, NY: University of Rochester Press.

Elliot, A. J., & Moller, A. C. (2003). Performance-approach goals: Good or bad forms of regulation? *International Journal of Educational Research, 39*, 339–356.

Elliot, A. J., & Murayama, K. (2008). On the measurement of achievement goals: Critique, illustration, and application. *Journal of Educational Psychology, 100*, 613–628.

Elliot, A. J., & Reis, H. T. (2003). Attachment and exploration in adulthood. *Journal of Personality and Social Psychology, 85*, 317–331.

Elliot, A. J., & Thrash, T. M. (2001). Achievement goals and the hierarchical model of achievement motivation. *Educational Psychology Review, 12*, 139–156.

Elliot, A. J., & Thrash, T. M. (2002). Approach-avoidance motivation in personality: Approach and avoidance temperaments and goals. *Journal of Personality and Social Psychology, 82*, 804–818.

Elliot, A. J., & Thrash, T. M. (2004). The intergenerational transmission of fear of failure. *Personality and Social Psychology Bulletin, 30*, 957–971.

Elliott, E. S., & Dweck, C. S. (1988). Goals: An approach to motivation and achievement. *Journal of Personality and Social Psychology, 54*, 5–12.

Entwisle, D. R. (1972). To dispel fantasies about fantasy-based measures of achievement motivation. *Psychological Bulletin, 77*, 377–391.

Eysenck, H. J. (1976). *The measurement of personality.* Baltimore, MD: University Park Press.

Feather, N. T. (1965). The relationship of expectation of success to need achievement and test anxiety. *Journal of Personality and Social Psychology, 1*, 118–126.

Fineman, S. (1977). The achievement motive and its measurement: Where are we now? *British Journal of Psychology, 68*, 1–22.

Finney, S. J., Pieper, S., & Barron, K. E. (2004). Examining the psychometric properties of the Achievement Goal Questionnaire in a general academic context. *Educational and Psychological Measurement, 64*, 365–382.

Ford, M. E. (1992). *Motivating humans: Goals, emotions, and personal agency beliefs.* Newbury Park, CA: Sage.

Forman, D. R., & Kochanska, G. (2001). Viewing imitation as child responsiveness: A link between teaching and discipline domains of socialization. *Developmental Psychology, 37*, 198–206.

Fox, N. A., Henderson, H. A., Rubin, K. H., Calkins, S. D., & Schmidt, L. A. (2001). Continuity and discontinuity of behavioral inhibition and exuberance: Psychophysiological and behavioral influences across the first four years of life. *Child Development, 72*,1–21.

Franken, R. E. (1988). *Human motivation.* Pacific Grove, CA: Brooks/Cole.

Fredricks, J. A., & Eccles, J. S. (2002). Children's competence and value beliefs from childhood through adolescence: Growth trajectories in two male-sex typed domains. *Developmental Psychology, 38*, 519–533.

Freund, A. M. (2006). Age-differential motivational consequences of optimization versus compensation focus in younger and older adults. *Psychology and Aging, 21*, 240–252.

Freund, A. M., & Ebner, N. C. (2005). The aging self: Shifting from promoting gains to balancing losses. In W. Greve, K. Rothermund, & D. Wentura (Eds.), *The adaptive self: personal continuity and intentional self-development* (pp. 185–202). Ashland, OH: Hogrefe & Huber.

Fryer, J. W., & Elliot, A. J. (2007). Stability and change in achievement goals. *Journal of Educational Psychology, 99*, 700–714.

Gable, S. L., Reis, H. T., & Elliot, A. J. (2000). Behavioral activation and inhibition in everyday life. *Journal of Personality and Social Psychology, 78*, 1135–1149.

Gernigon, C., d'Arippe-Longueville, F., Delignières, D., & Ninot, G. (2004). A dynamical systems perspective on goal involvement states in sport. *Journal of Sport & Exercise Psychology, 26*, 572–596.

Giambra, L. M. (1974). Daydreaming across the lifespan: Late adolescent to senior citizen. *International Journal of Aging and Human Development, 5*, 115–140.

Gonida, E. N., Kiosseoglou, G., & Voulala, K. (2007). Perceptions of parent goals and their contribution to student achievement goal orientation and engagement in the classroom: Grade-level differences across adolescence. *European Journal of Psychology of Education, 22*, 23–39.

Gray, J. A. (1970). The psychophysiological basis of introversion-extroversion. *Behavior Research & Therapy, 8*, 249–266.

Gray, J. A. (1987). *The psychology of fear and stress* (2nd ed.). Cambridge, England: Cambridge University Press.

Gray, J. A. (1990). Brain systems that mediate both emotion and cognition. *Cognition & Emotion, 4*, 269–288.

Greenfeld, N., & Teevan, R. C. (1986). Fear of failure in families without fathers. *Psychological Reports, 59*, 571–574.

Grusec, J. E., & Goodnow, J. J. (1994). Impact of parental discipline methods on the child's internalization of values: A reconceptualization of current points of view. *Developmental Psychology, 30*, 4–19.

Guay, F., Vallerand, R., & Blanchard, C. (2000). On the assessment of situational intrinsic and extrinsic motivation: The Situational Motivation Scale (SIMS). *Motivation and Emotion, 24*, 175–213.

Gutman, L. M. (2006). How student and parent goal orientations and classroom goal structures influence the math achievement of African Americans during the high school transition. *Contemporary Educational Psychology, 31*, 44–63.

Haith, M. M. (1997). The development of future thinking as essential for the emergence of skill in planning. In S. L. Friedman & E. K. Scholnick (Eds.), *The developmental psychology of planning: Why, how, and when do we plan?* (pp. 25–42). Mahwah, NJ: Erlbaum.

Harackiewicz, J. M., Barron, K. E., & Elliot, A. J., (1998). Rethinking achievement goals: When are they adaptive for college students and why? *Educational Psychologist, 33*, 1–21.

Harackiewicz, J. M., Barron, K. E., Pintrich, P. R., Elliot, A. J., & Thrash, T. M. (2002). Revision of achievement goal theory: Necessary and illuminating. *Journal of Educational Psychology, 94*, 562–575.

Harackiewicz, J. M., & Elliot, A. J. (1993). Achievement goals and intrinsic motivation. *Journal of Personality and Social Psychology, 65*, 904–915.

Harackiewicz, J. M., & Elliot, A. J. (1998). The joint effect of target and purpose goals on intrinsic motivation. *Personality and Social Psychology Bulletin, 65*, 904–915.

Heckhausen, H. (1963). *Hoffnung und Furcht in der Leistungsmotivation [Hope and fear components of achievement motivation]*. Meisenheim am Glan, Germany: Anton Hain.

Heckhausen, H. (1984). Emergent achievement behavior: Some early developments. In J. Nicholls (Ed.), *Advances in motivation and achievement: The development of achievement motivation* (Vol. 3, pp. 1–32). Greenwich, CT: JAI Press.

Heckhausen, H. (1991). *Motivation and action* (P. Leppman, Trans.). New York: Springer-Verlag.

Hermans, H. J. M., Ter Laak, J. J. F., & Maes, P. C. J. M. (1972). Achievement motivation and fear of failure in family and school. *Developmental Psychology, 6*, 520–528.

Heyman, G. D., Dweck, C. S., & Cain, K. M. (1992). Young children's vulnerability to self-blame and helplessness: Relationship to beliefs about goodness. *Child Development, 63,* 401–415.

Husman, J., Brem, S., & Duggan, M.A. (2005). Student goal orientation and formative assessment. *Academic Exchange Quarterly, 9*, 355–359.

Jackson, D. N. (1999). *Personality Research Form manual* (3rd ed.). Port Huron, MI: Sigma Assessment Systems.

Jacobs, J. E., Lanza, S., Osgood, D. W., Eccles, J. S., & Wigfield, A. (2002). Ontogeny of children's self-beliefs: Gender and domain differences across grades one through twelve. *Child Development, 73*, 509–527.

Jenkins, S. R. (1987). Need for achievement and women's careers over 14 years: Evidence for occupational structure effects. *Journal of Personality and Social Psychology, 53,* 922–932.

Jennings, K. D. (1993). Mastery motivation and the formation of self-concept from infancy through early adulthood. In D. Messer (Ed.), *Mastery Motivation in Early Childhood* (pp. 36–54). London: Routledge.

Jennings, K. D. (2004). Development of goal-directed behavior and related self-processes in toddlers. *International Journal of Behavioral Development, 28*, 319–327.

Jones, M. R. (Ed.). (1955). *Nebraska symposium on motivation.* Lincoln: University of Nebraska Press.

Kagan, J. (1994). *Galen's prophecy: Temperament in human nature.* New York: Basic Books.

Kagan, J. (1998). Biology and the child. In N. Eisenberg (Ed.), *Handbook of child psychology: Vol. 3. Social, emotional, and personality development* (pp. 177–235). New York: John Wiley & Sons.

Kagan, J., & Moss, H. A. (1962). *Birth to maturity: A study of psychological development.* New York: John Wiley & Sons.

Kamins, M. L., & Dweck, C. S. (1999). Person versus process praise and criticism: Implications for contingent self-worth and coping. *Developmental Psychology, 35,* 835–847.

Kaplan, A., & Maehr, M. L. (2007). The contributions and prospects of goal orientation theory. *Educational Psychology Review, 19*, 141–184.

Kelley, S. A., Brownell, C. A., & Campbell, S. B. (2000). Mastery motivation and self-evaluative affect in toddlers: Longitudinal relations with maternal behavior. *Child Development, 71*, 1061–1071.

Klinger, E. (1966). Fantasy need achievement. *Psychological Bulletin, 66,* 291–306.

Kochanska, G. (1997). Mutually responsive orientation between mothers and their young children: Implications for early socialization. *Child Development, 68,* 94–112.

Kochanska, G. (1998). Mother–child relationship, child fearfulness, and emerging attachment: A short-term longitudinal study. *Developmental Psychology, 34*, 480–490.

Kochanska, G. (2002). Mutually responsive orientation between mothers and their young children: A context for the early development of conscience. *Current Directions in Psychological Science, 11,* 191–195.

Kochanska, G., DeVet, L., Goldman, M., Murray, K., & Putnam, S. P. (1994). Maternal reports of conscience development and temperament in young children. *Child Development, 65,* 852–868.

Kochanska, G., Gross, J. N., Lin, M.-H., & Nichols, K. E. (2002). Guilt in young children: Development, determinants, and relations with a broader system of standards. *Child Development, 73,* 461–482.

Kochanska, G., & Murray, K. T. (2000). Mother–child mutually responsive orientation and conscience development: From toddler to early school age. *Child Development, 71,* 471–431.

Lazarus, R. C. (1991). *Emotion and adaptation.* New York: Oxford University Press.

Leondari, A., & Gialamas, V. (2002). Implicit theories, goal orientations, and perceived competence: Impact on students' achievement behavior. *Psychology in the Schools, 39,* 279–291.

Leondari, A., & Gonida, E. (2007). Predicting academic self-handicapping in different age groups: The role of personal achievement goals and social goals. *British Journal of Educational Psychology, 77,* 595–611.

Levine, J. M. (1983). Social comparison and education. In J. Levine & M. Wang (Eds.), *Teacher and student perceptions: Implications for learning* (pp. 29–55). Hillsdale, NJ: Erlbaum.

Lewis, M. (1995). *Shame: The exposed self.* New York: Free Press.

Lewis, M., Alessandri, S. M., & Sullivan, M. W. (1992). Differences in shame and pride as a function of children's gender and task difficulty. *Child Development, 63,* 630–638.

Lewis, M., & Ramsay, D. (2002). Cortisol response to embarrassment and shame. *Child Development, 73,* 1034–1045.

Lewis, M., & Sullivan, M. W. (2005). The development of self-conscious emotions. In A. J. Elliot & C. S. Dweck (Eds.), *Handbook of competence and motivation* (pp. 185–201). New York: Guilford Press.

Lewis, M., Sullivan, M. W., Stanger, C., & Weiss, M. (1989). Self development and self-conscious emotions. *Child Development, 60,* 146–156.

Linnenbrink-Garcia, E. A., & Fredericks, J. A. (2008). Developmental perspectives on achievement motivation: Personal and contextual influences. In J. Shah & W. Gardner (Eds.), *Handbook of motivation science* (pp. 448–464). New York: Guilford Press.

Liu, P. (2003). Transition from elementary to middle school and change in motivation: An examination of Chinese students. *Journal of Research in Childhood Education, 18*, 71–83.

Lucas, R. E., Diener, E., Grob, A., Suh, E. M., & Shao, L. (2000). Cross-cultural evidence for the fundamental features of extraversion. *Journal of Personality and Social Psychology, 79,* 452–268.

MacTurk, R. H., Morgan, G. A., & Jennings, K. D. (1995). The assessment of mastery motivation in infants and young children. In R. H. MacTurk & G. A. Morgan (Eds.), *Mastery motivation: Origins, conceptualizations, and applications* (Vol. 12, pp. 19–56). Westport, CT: Ablex.

Maehr, M. L. (1983). On doing well in science: Why Johnny no longer excels, why Sarah never did. In S. Paris, G. Olson, & H. Stevenson (Eds.), *Learning and motivation in the classroom* (pp. 179–210). Hillsdale, NJ: Erlbaum.

Maehr, M. L. (1984). Meaning and motivation. In R. Ames & C. Ames (Eds.), *Research on motivation in education: Student motivation.* (Vol. 1, pp. 115–144). New York: Academic

Maehr, M. L., & Midgley, C. (1991). Enhancing student motivation: A schoolwide approach. *Educational Psychologist, 26,* 399–427.

Maehr, M. L., & Midgley, C. (1996). *Transforming school cultures.* Boulder, CO: Westview.

Maehr, M. L., & Nicholls, J. G. (1980). Culture and achievement motivation: A second look. In N. Warren (Ed.), *Studies on cross-cultural psychology* (Vol. 2, pp. 221– 267). New York: Academic.

McCall, R. B. (1995). On definitions and measures of mastery motivation. In R. H. MacTurk & G. A. Morgan (Eds.), *Mastery motivation: Origins, conceptualizations, and applications* (Vol. 12, pp. 273–292). Westport, CT: Ablex.

McClelland, D. C. (1958). Methods of measuring human motivation. In J. W. Atkinson (Ed.), *Motives in fantasy, action, and society* (pp. 7–42). Princeton, NJ: Van Nostrand.

McClelland, D. C. (1965). Achievement and entrepreneurship: A longitudinal study. *Journal of Personality and Social Psychology, 1,* 389–392.

McClelland, D. C. (1985). *Human motivation* (2nd ed.). Glenview, IL: Scott Foresman Press.

McClelland, D. C. (1987). Characteristics of successful entrepreneurs. *Journal of Creative Behavior, 3,* 219–233.

McClelland, D. C., Atkinson, J. W., Clark, R. A., & Lowell, E. L. (1953). *The achievement motive.* East Norwalk, CT: Appleton Century Crofts.

McClelland, D.C., Koestner, R., & Weinberger, J. (1989). How do self-attributed and implicit motives differ? *Psychological Review, 96,* 690–702.

McClelland, D. C., & Pilon, D. A. (1983). Sources of adult motive sin patterns of parent behavior in early childhood. *Journal of Personality and Social Psychology, 44,* 564–474.

McGregor, H. A., & Elliot, A. J. (2005). The shame of failure: Examining the link between fear of failure and shame. *Personality and Social Psychology Bulletin, 31,* 218–231.

Meece, J. L., Blumenfeld, P. C., & Hoyle, R. H. (1988). Students' goal orientations and cognitive engagement in classroom activities. *Journal of Educational Psychology, 80,* 514–523.

Meece, J. L., & Miller, S. D. (2001). A longitudinal analysis of elementary school students' achievement goals in literacy activities. *Contemporary Educational Psychology, 26,* 454–480.

Middleton, M. J., Kaplan, A., & Midgley, C. (2004). The change in middle school students' achievement goals in math over time. *Social Psychology of Education, 7,* 289–311.

Middleton, M. J., & Midgley, C. (1997). Avoiding the demonstration of lack of ability: An underexplored aspect of goal theory. *Journal of Educational Psychology, 89,* 710–718.

Midgley, C. (2002). *Goals, goal structures, and patterns of adaptive learning.* Mahwah, NJ: Erlbaum.

Midgley, C., Kaplan, A., & Middleton, M. (2001). Performance approach goals: Good for what, for whom, under what circumstances, and at what cost? *Journal of Educational Psychology, 93,* 77–86.

Midgley, C., Kaplan, A., Middleton, M., Maehr, M., Urdan, T., Anderman, L., et al. (1998). The development and validation of scales assessing students' achievement goal orientations. *Contemporary Educational Psychology, 23,* 113–131.

Midgley, C., Maehr, M. L., Hruda, L. Z., Anderman, E., Anderman, L., Freeman, K. E., et al. (2000). *Manual for the Patterns of Adaptive Learning Scales (PALS).* Ann Arbor: University of Michigan.

Mills, R. S. L. (2003). Possible antecedents and developmental implications of shame in young girls. *Infant and Child Development, 12,* 329–349.

Mills, R. S. L. (2005). Taking stock of the developmental literature on shame. *Developmental Review, 25,* 26–63.

Mills, R. S. L., Walling, B. R., Imm, G. P., & Weiler, H. A. (2007, November). Shame and cortisol in early childhood. Paper presented at the annual meeting of the Canadian Psychological Association.

Mischel, W., & Shoda, Y. (1995). A cognitive-affective system theory of personality: Reconceptualizing situations, dispositions, dynamics, and invariance in personality structure. *Psychological Review, 102,* 246–268.

Mook, D. (1987). *Motivation: The organization of action.* New York: Norton.

Murayama, K., Zhou, M., & Nesbit, J. C. (2009). A cross-cultural examination of the Psychometric properties of the achievement goal questionnaire. *Educational and Psychological Measurement, 69,* 432–447.

Murray, H. A. (1938). *Explorations in personality.* Oxford, England: Oxford University Press.

Murray, H. A. (1943). *Thematic Apperception Test.* Cambridge, MA: Harvard University Press.

Nathanson, D. L. (1992). *Shame and pride: Affect, sex, and the birth of the self.* New York: Norton.

Nelson, R. M., & DeBacker, T. K. (2008). Achievement motivation in adolescents: The role of peer climate and best friends. *Journal of Experimental Education, 76,* 170–189.

Ng, F., Pomerantz, E. M., & Lam, S. (2007). European American and Chinese parents' responses to children's success and failure: Implications for children's responses. *Developmental Psychology,* 43, 1239–1255.

Nicholls, J. G. (1984). Achievement motivation: Conceptions of ability, subjective experience, task choice, and performance. *Psychological Review, 91,* 328–346.

Nicholls, J. G. (1989). *The competitive ethos and democratic education.* Cambridge, MA: Harvard University Press.

Nicholls, J. G., Cheung, P., Lauer, J., & Patashnick, M. (1989). Individual differences in Academic motivation: Perceived ability, goals, beliefs, and values. *Learning and Individual Differences, 1,* 63–84.

Nicholls, J. G., & Miller, R. (1994). Cooperative learning and student motivation. *Contemporary Educational Psychology, 19,* 167–178.

Nolen, S. B. (1988). Reasons for studying: Motivational orientations and study strategies. *Cognition and Instruction, 5,* 269–287.

Obach, M. (2003). A longitudinal-sequential study of perceived academic competence and motivational beliefs for learning among children in middle school. *Educational Psychology, 23,* 323–338.

Oettingen, G., & Hagenah, M. (2005). Fantasies and the self-regulation of competence. In A. J. Elliot & C. S. Dweck (Eds.), *Handbook of competence and motivation* (pp. 647–665). New York: Guilford Press.

Otis, N., Grouzet, F. M. E., & Pelletier, L. G. (2005). Latent motivational change in an academic setting: A 3-year longitudinal study. *Journal of Educational Psychology, 97,* 170–183.

Pajares, F., Britner, S., & Valiante, G. (2000). Relation between achievement goals and self-beliefs of middle school students in writing and science. *Contemporary Educational Psychology, 25,* 406–422.

Petri, H. (1996). *Motivation.* Pacific Grove, CA: Brooks/Cole Publishing Company.

Pinker, S. (2002). *The blank slate: The modern denial of human nature.* New York: Penguin.

Pintrich, P. R. (2000). Multiple goals, multiple pathways: The role of goal orientation in learning and achievement. *Journal of Educational Psychology, 92,* 544–555.

Pintrich, P. R., & Garcia, T. (1991). Student goal orientation and self-regulation in the college classroom. In M. L. Maehr & P. R. Pintrich

(Eds.), *Advances in motivation and achievement* (Vol. 7, pp. 371–402). Greenwich, CT: JAI Press.

Pintrich P. R., & Schunk, D. H. (1996). *Motivation in education: Theory, research, and applications*. Englewood Cliffs, NJ: Prentice Hall.

Podsakoff, P. M., MacKenzie, S. B., Lee, J. Y., & Podsakoff, N. P. (2003). Common method biases in behavioral research: A critical review of the literature and recommended remedies. *Journal of Applied Psychology, 88,* 879–903.

Putnam, S. P., & Stifter, C. A. (2005). Behavioral approach-inhibition in toddlers: Prediction from infancy, positive and negative affective components, and relations with behavior problems. *Child Development, 76,* 212–226.

Raudenbush, S. W., & Bryk, A. S. (2002). *Hierarchical linear models: Applications and data analysis methods* (Vol. 2). Thousand Oaks, CA: Sage.

Rawsthorne, L. J., & Elliot, A. J. (1999). Achievement goals and intrinsic motivation: A meta-analytic review. *Personality and Social Psychology Review, 3,* 326–344.

Reeve, J. (1996). *Understanding motivation and emotion*. Fort Worth, TX: Harcourt Brace Jovanovich College.

Roberts, G. C., Treasure, D. C., & Conroy, D. E. (2007). The dynamics of motivation in sport: The influence of achievement goals on motivation processes. In G. Tenenbaum & R. C. Eklund (Eds.), *Handbook of sport psychology* (3rd ed., pp. 3–30.). Hoboken, NJ: John Wiley & Sons.

Rosen, B. C., & D'Andrade, R. (1959). The psychosocial origins of achievement motivation. *Sociometry, 22,* 185–218.

Ross, M., Shannon, D., Salisbury-Glennon, J., & Guarino, A. (2002). The Patterns of Adaptive Learning Survey: A comparison across grade levels. *Educational and Psychological Measurement, 62,* 483–497.

Rothbart, M. K., Ahadi, S. A., & Hershey, K. L. (1994). Temperament and social behavior in childhood. *Merrill-Palmer Quarterly, 40,* 21–39.

Rothbart, M. K., & Bates, J. E. (1998). Temperament. In W. Damon & N. Eisenberg (Eds.), *Handbook of child psychology: Social, emotional, and personality development* (Vol. 3, pp. 105–176). New York: John Wiley & Sons.

Rothbart, M. K., & Hwang, J. (2005). Temperament and the development of competence and motivation. In A. J. Elliot & C. S. Dweck (Eds.), *Handbook of competence and motivation* (pp. 167–184). New York: Guilford Press.

Ruble, D. N., Eisenberg, R., Higgins, E. (1994). Developmental changes in achievement evaluation: Motivational implications of self-other differences. *Child Development, 65,* 1095–1110.

Schantz, L. H., & Conroy, D. E. (2009). Achievement motivation and intraindividual affective variability during competence pursuits: A round of golf as a multilevel data structure. *Journal of Research in Personality, 43,* 472–481.

Schmalt, H. D. (1982). Two concepts of fear of failure motivation. In R. Schwarzer, H. M. van der Ploeg, & C. D. Spielberger (Eds.), *Advances in test anxiety research* (Vol. 1, pp. 45–52). Lisse, The Netherlands: Swets & Zeitlinger.

Schultheiss, O. C. (2001). *Manual for the assessment of hope of success and fear of failure* [English translation of Heckhausen's need achievement measure]. Ann Arbor, MI: University of Michigan.

Schultheiss, O. C. (2007). A memory-systems approach to the classification of personality tests: Comment on Meyer and Kurtz (2006). *Journal of Personality Assessment, 89,* 197–202.

Schultheiss, O. C., & Pang, J. S. (2007). Measuring implicit motives. In R. W. Robins, R. C. Fraley, & R. Krueger (Eds.), *Handbook of research methods in personality psychology* (pp. 322–344). New York: Guilford Press.

Schunk, D. H., Pintrich, P. R., & Meece, J. (2007). *Motivation in education: Theory, research, and applications* (3rd ed.). Upper Saddle River, NJ: Pearson/Merrill Prentice Hall.

Scott, W. A., & Johnson, R. C. (1972). Comparative validities of direct and indirect personality tests. *Journal of Consulting and Clinical Psychology, 38,* 301–318.

Senko, C., & Harackiewicz, J. (2005). Regulation of achievement goals: The role of competence feedback. *Journal of Educational Psychology, 97,* 320–336.

Singer, J. D., & Willet, J. B. (2003). *Applied longitudinal data analysis: Modeling change and event occurrence.* Oxford: Oxford University Press.

Singh, S. (1992). Hostile Press measure of fear of failure and its relation to child-rearing attitudes and behavior problems. *Journal of Social Psychology, 132,* 397–399.

Skaalvik, E. M. (1997). Self-enhancing and self-defeating ego orientation: Relations with task and avoidance orientation, achievement, self-perceptions, and anxiety. *Journal of Educational Psychology, 89,* 71–81.

Skaalvik, S., & Skaalvik, E. (2004). Gender differences in math and verbal self-concept, performance expectations, and motivation. *Sex Roles, 50,* 241–252.

Skinner, E., Zimmer-Gembeck, M., & Connell, J. (1998). Individual differences and the development of perceived control. *Monographs of the Society for Research in Child Development, 63,* v–220.

Smiley, P. A., & Dweck, C. S. (1994). Individual differences in achievement goals among young children. *Child Development, 65,* 1723–1743.

Spangler, W. D. (1992). Validity of questionnaire and TAT measures of need for achievement: Two meta-analyses. *Psychological Bulletin, 112,* 140–154.

Spence, J. T., & Helmreich, R. L. (1983). Achievement-related motives and behaviors. In J. T. Spence (Ed.), *Achievement and achievement motives: Psychological and sociological approaches* (pp. 7–74). San Francisco: Freeman.

Steers. R. M., & Porter, L. W. (1987). *Motivation and work behavior* (4th ed.). New York: McGraw-Hill.

Steinberg, G., Grieve, F. G., & Glass, B. (2001). Achievement goals across the lifespan. *Journal of Sport Behavior, 24,* 1–7.

Stipek, D., Recchia, S., & McClintic, S. (1992). Self-evaluation in young children. *Monographs of the Society for Research in Child Development, 57,* 1–83.

Stuewig, J., & McCloskey, L. A. (2005). The relation of child maltreatment to shame and guilt among adolescents: Psychological routes to depression and delinquency. *Child Maltreatment, 10,* 324–336.

Sullivan, M. W., Bennett, D. S., & Lewis, M. (2003). Darwin's view: Self-evaluative emotions as context-specific emotions. *Annals of the New York Academy of Sciences, 1000,* 304–308.

Tanaka, A., & Yamauchi, H. (2001). A model for achievement motives, goal orientations, intrinsic interest, and academic achievement. *Psychological Reports, 88,* 123–135

Tangney, J. P., & Dearing, R. L. (2002). *Shame and guilt.* New York: Guilford Press.

Teevan, R. C. (1983). Childhood development of fear of failure motivation: A replication. *Psychological Reports, 53,* 506.

Teevan, R. C., & McGhee, P. E. (1972). Childhood development of fear of failure motivation. *Journal of Personality and Social Psychology, 21,* 345–348.

Thrash, T. M., Cassidy, S. E., Maruskin, L. A., & Elliot, A. J. (in press). Factors that influence the relation between implicit and explicit motives: A general implicit-explicit congruence framework. Chapter to appear in O. Schultheiss & J. Brunstein (Eds.), *Implicit motives.* New York: Cambridge University Press.

Thrash, T. M., & Elliot, A. J. (2001). Delimiting and integrating the goal and motive constructs in achievement motivation. In A. Efklides,

J. Kuhl, & R. Sorrentino (Eds.), *Trends and prospects in motivation research* (pp. 3–21). Amsterdam: Kluwer Academic.

Thrash, T. M., & Elliot, A. J. (2002). Implicit and self-attributed achievement motives: Concordance and predictive validity. *Journal of Personality, 70,* 729–755.

Thrash, T. M., Elliot, A. J., & Schultheiss, O. C. (2007). Methodological and dispositional predictors of congruence between implicit and explicit need for achievement. *Personality and Social Psychology Bulletin, 33,* 961–974.

Todorovich, J., & Curtner-Smith, M. (2003). Influence of the motivational climate in physical education on third grade students' task and ego orientations. *Journal of Classroom Interaction, 38,* 36–46.

Tracy, J. L., & Robins, R. W. (2004). Putting the self into self-conscious emotions: A theoretical model. *Psychological Inquiry, 15,* 103–125.

Tracy, J. L., & Robins, R. W. (2007). The psychological structure of pride: A tale of two facets. *Journal of Personality and Social Psychology, 92,* 506–525.

Urdan, T., & Midgley, C. (2003). Changes in the perceived classroom goal structure and pattern of adaptive learning during early adolescence. *Contemporary Educational Psychology, 28,* 524–551.

VandeWalle, D. (1997). Development and validation of a work domain goal orientation instrument. *Educational and Psychological Measurement, 57,* 995–1015.

Van Yperen, N. W. (2006). A novel approach to assessing achievement goals in the context of the 2 × 2 framework: Identifying distinct profiles of individuals with different dominant achievement goals. *Personality and Social Psychology Bulletin, 32,* 1432–1445.

Veermans, M., & Tapola, A. (2004). Primary school students' motivational profiles in longitudinal settings. *Scandinavian Journal of Educational Research, 48,* 373–395.

Veroff, J., Depner, C., Kulka, R., & Douvan, E. (1980). Comparison of American motives: 1957 versus 1976. *Journal of Personality and Social Psychology, 39,* 1249–1262.

Wachs, T. D. (2006). The nature, etiology, and consequences of individual differences in temperament. In L. Balter & C. S. Tamis-LeMonda (Eds.), *Child psychology: A handbook of contemporary issues* (pp. 27–52). New York: Psychology Press.

Wang, C., Biddle, S., & Elliot, A. (2007). The 2 × 2 achievement goal framework in a physical education context. *Psychology of Sport and Exercise, 8,* 147–168.

Watson, D., Wiese, D., Vaidya, J., & Tellegen, A. (1999). The two general activation systems of affect: Structural findings, evolutionary considerations, and psychobiological evidence. *Journal of Personality and Social Psychology, 76,* 820–838.

Weiner, B. (1985). An attributional theory toward achievement motivation and emotion. *Psychological Review, 92,* 548–573.

Weinstein, M. S. (1969). Achievement motivation and risk preference. *Journal of Personality and Social Psychology, 13,* 153–172.

Wentzel, K. R. (1994). Relations of social goal pursuit to social acceptance, classroom behavior, and perceived social support. *Journal of Educational Psychology, 86,* 173–182.

White, R. W. (1959). Motivation reconsidered: The concept of competence. *Psychological Review, 66,* 297–333.

White, R. W. (1963). *Ego and reality in psychoanalytic theory* (Psychological Issues Series, Monograph No. 11). New York: International Universities Press.

Wigfield, A., Eccles, J. S., Schiefele, U., Roeser, R., & Davis-Kean, P. (2006). Development of achievement motivation. In W. Damon & N. Eisenberg (Eds.), *Handbook of child psychology* (6th ed., Vol. 3, pp. 933–1002). Hoboken, NJ: John Wiley & Sons.

Winter, D. G. (1994). *Manual for scoring motive imagery in running text* (4th ed.). Unpublished manuscript, Department of Psychology, University of Michigan, Ann Arbor.

Winter, D. G. (2005). Things I've learned about personality from studying political leaders at a distance. *Journal of Personality, 73,* 557–584.

Winterbottom, M. R. (1958). The relation of need for achievement to learning experiences in independence and mastery. In J. W. Atkinson (Ed.), *Motives in fantasy, action, and society* (pp. 453–478). Princeton, NJ: Van Nostrand.

Wolters, C. A., Yu, S. L., & Pintrich, P. R. (1996). The relation between goal orientation and students' motivational beliefs and self-regulated learning. *Learning and Individual Differences, 8,* 211– 238.

Xiang, P., Lee, A., & Shen, J. (2001). Conceptions of ability and achievement goals in physical education: Comparisons of American and Chinese students. *Contemporary Educational Psychology, 26,* 348–365.

Young, P. T. (1961). *Motivation and emotion.* New York: John Wiley & Sons.

Zusho, A., Pintrich, P. R., & Cortina, K. S. (2005). Motives, goals, and adaptive patterns of performance in Asian American and Anglo American students. *Learning and Individual Differences, 15,* 141–158.

CHAPTER 14

Developmental Psychopathology

DANTE CICCHETTI

Over the course of the past 4 decades, the field of developmental psychopathology has emerged as an influential interdisciplinary science (Cicchetti, 1984a, 1984b, 1989, 2006; Cicchetti & Sroufe, 2000; Masten, 2006; Rutter & Garmezy, 1983; Rutter & Sroufe, 2000). Although there exists definitional divergence in the literature (Institute of Medicine [IOM], 1989; Masten, 2006; Rutter, 2005; Sroufe & Rutter, 1984), developmental psychopathology can be conceptualized as an evolving interdisciplinary scientific field that strives to elucidate the interplay among the biological, psychological, and social-contextual aspects of normal and abnormal development across the lifespan (Cicchetti, 1993; Cicchetti & Sroufe, 2000; Greve & Staudinger, 2006; Rutter & Sroufe, 2000; Staudinger, Marsiske, & Baltes, 1995; Zigler & Glick, 1986). Because psychopathology unfolds over time in a dynamically developing organism, the adoption of a developmental perspective is critical to comprehending the processes underlying individual pathways to adaptive and maladaptive outcomes (Cicchetti, 1993; Sroufe, 1989). A *developmental analysis* presupposes change and novelty, highlights the critical role of timing in the organization of behavior, underscores multiple determinants, and cautions against expecting invariant relations between causes and outcomes. Moreover, a developmental analysis is as applicable to the study of the gene or cell as it is to the individual, family, or society (Cicchetti & Pogge-Hesse, 1982; Gottlieb, 1992; Kaplan, 1967; Werner, 1948). Whereas in the not so remote past few psychologists and psychiatrists investigating adult mental disorders would have considered a developmental perspective as appropriate, let alone necessary, this is currently not the case. A developmental approach to psychopathology has become much more mainstream (Rutter, Kim-Cohen, & Maughan, 2006).

In this chapter, a developmental psychopathology approach to high-risk conditions and psychiatric disorders is presented. Following a brief account of its historical underpinnings, the interdisciplinary field of developmental psychopathology is described. In the next section, the definitional parameters and principles of developmental psychopathology are discussed, and illustrations of these tenets are provided through examples from a number of high-risk conditions and psychiatric disorders across the life span. In the penultimate section, research on the genetic, neurobiological, and psychological correlates and sequelae of child maltreatment is used as an exemplar of a multilevel developmental psychopathology approach. Finally, autism, depression, substance abuse, and schizophrenia are presented as illustrations of a developmental perspective on mental disorder. For a more elaborate, in-depth treatment of a developmental psychopathology approach to high-risk conditions and mental disorders, the reader is referred to Cicchetti and Cohen (1995a, 1995b, 2006a, 2006b, 2006c).

HISTORICAL UNDERPINNINGS OF DEVELOPMENTAL PSYCHOPATHOLOGY

Despite its relatively recent crystallization as a coherent framework for investigating the relation between normality and psychopathology, the field of developmental psychopathology owes its emergence and coalescence to a number of historically based endeavors in a variety of disciplines, including embryology; epidemiology; genetics; the neurosciences; philosophy; psychoanalysis; clinical, developmental, and experimental psychology; and sociology (Cicchetti, 1990; Costello & Angold, 2006; Kaplan, 1967; Masten, 2006). Many of the great theorists in these influential disciplines have reasoned that we can learn more about the normal functioning of an organism by studying its pathology and, likewise, more about its pathology by investigating its normal condition (Cicchetti, 1984). A number of these integrative thinkers conceived of psychopathology as a magnifying mirror in which normal biological and psychological processes could better be observed. Because these systematizers conceptualized psychopathology as a distortion or exaggeration of the normal condition, the study of pathological phenomena was thought to throw into sharper relief one's understanding of normal processes.

For example, Heinz Werner (1948) asserted that "the results of psychopathology ... become valuable in many ways for the general picture of mental development, just as psychopathology is itself enriched and its methods facilitated by the adoption of the (organismic developmental) approach" (p. 34). Likewise, the embryologist Paul Weiss, whose work greatly influenced the field of developmental psychology (Sameroff, 1983), defined development as a hierarchic systems operation and demonstrated that the experimental study of pathological embryos could enhance the understanding of normal embryogenesis. In a seminal work titled "Deformities as Cues to Understanding Development of Form," Weiss (1961) enunciated his viewpoint on the nature of the interrelation between normality and pathology: "Pathology and developmental biology must be reintegrated so that our understanding of the 'abnormal' will become but an extension of our insight into the 'normal,' while ... the study of the 'abnormal' will contribute to the deepening of that very insight" (p. 50).

A basic theme that appears in the writings of these earlier thinkers is that because all psychopathology can be conceived as a distortion, disturbance, or degeneration of normal functioning, it thus follows that, if one wishes to understand pathology more fully, then one must understand the normal functioning against which psychopathology is compared (Cicchetti, 1984b). Not only is knowledge of normal biological, psychological, and social processes extremely helpful for understanding, preventing, and treating psychopathology but also the deviations and distortions of normal development that are seen in pathological processes indicate in exciting ways how normal ontogenesis may be better investigated and understood. Indeed, for many thinkers the very essence and uniqueness of a developmental psychopathology approach lies in its focus on both normal and abnormal, adaptive and maladaptive, ontogenetic processes (Cicchetti, 1984b, 1993; Rutter, 1986; Sroufe, 1989, 1990).

The field of developmental psychopathology first came into ascendance during the 1970s (see, e.g., Achenbach, 1974), predominantly through being highlighted as an important perspective by researchers conducting prospective longitudinal studies of children at risk for becoming schizophrenic (Garmezy & Streitman, 1974; Watt, Anthony, Wynne, & Rolf, 1984). Also instrumental in the field's emergence were epidemiological investigations of families exhibiting discord, disharmony, and disruption but where there was no parental mental disorder (Rutter & Quinton, 1984) and studies of the links between cumulative risk factors and developmental outcome (Sameroff, Seifer, Barocas, Zax, & Greenspan, 1987). Likewise, research on the causes, correlates, and consequences of secure and insecure attachment (Ainsworth, Blehar, Waters, & Wall, 1978; Main, Kaplan, & Cassidy, 1985; Sroufe, 1983), investigations of children with a variety of handicapping conditions (Cicchetti & Pogge-Hesse, 1982; Cicchetti & Sroufe, 1976, 1978; O'Connor & Hermelin, 1978; Zigler, 1969), and studies in life-span developmental psychology (Baltes, Reese, & Lipsitt, 1980) were influential in furthering interest in developmental psychopathology. These investigations generated important knowledge about basic processes in a variety of developmental domains that provided a solid empirical basis against which developmental psychopathologists could discover new truths (Cicchetti, 1990).

Before the emergence of developmental psychopathology as an integrative discipline with its own integrity, the efforts of those working in these areas had been separate and distinct (Cicchetti, 1984b). Some of the lack of integration stemmed from long-standing tensions between the philosophical traditions underlying clinical practice and academic training and between basic experimental versus applied research (Cahan & White, 1992; Cicchetti, 1984b; Gunnar & Cicchetti, 2009; Santostefano, 1978; Santostefano & Baker, 1972).

Rather than competing with existing theories and facts, the developmental psychopathology perspective represents a broad, integrative framework within which the contributions of separate disciplines can be realized in the larger context of understanding individual development and functioning. The principles of developmental psychopathology can provide the conceptual scaffolding for facilitating this multidisciplinary integration. Through the organizing principles of the concept of development and of systems theory, the discipline of developmental psychopathology has brought together fields of study and investigators that were once disparate to examine complex questions of the etiology, course, and sequelae of psychopathology and resilience (Masten, 2006).

Throughout its matriculation as an increasingly mature scientific discipline, an ongoing goal of developmental psychopathology has been to become a science that not only bridges fields of study and aids in the discovery of important new truths about the processes underlying adaptation and maladaptation across the life span but also provides the best means of preventing and ameliorating maladaptive and pathological outcomes (Cicchetti, 1990; Cicchetti & Hinshaw, 2002; Cicchetti & Toth, 2006; Ialongo et al., 2006; Sroufe & Rutter, 1984). Moreover, the field of developmental psychopathology has continuously sought to reduce the dualisms that exist between empirical research and the clinical study and treatment of childhood and adult high-risk conditions and disorders, between the behavioral and biological sciences and between basic and applied research (see Cicchetti & Cohen, 2006a, 2006b, 2006c).

WHAT IS DEVELOPMENTAL PSYCHOPATHOLOGY?

Alan Sroufe and Michael Rutter (1984) originally defined developmental psychopathology as "*the study of the origins and course of individual patterns of behavioral maladaptation*, whatever the age of onset, whatever the causes, whatever the transformations in behavioral manifestation, and however complex the course of the developmental pattern may be" (p. 18, italics theirs). An IOM (1989) report devoted to mental and behavioral disorders of childhood and adolescence asserted that a developmental perspective on psychopathology should entail an examination of "the emerging behavioral repertoire, cognitive and language functions, social and emotional processes, and changes occurring in anatomical structures and physiological processes of the brain" (p. 14). Theory and research conducted within the discipline of developmental psychopathology seek to unify within a life-span framework the many contributions to the study of high-risk and disordered individuals emanating from multiple fields of inquiry (Cicchetti, 1990; Cicchetti & Cohen, 1995a, 1995b; Cicchetti & Cohen, 2006a, 2006b, 2006c).

The central focus of developmental psychopathology involves the elucidation of developmental processes and how they function as indicated and elaborated by the examination of extremes in developmental outcome. In addition to studying extremes in the distribution (i.e., individuals with disorders), developmental psychopathologists also direct attention toward variations in the continuum between the mean and the extremes. These variations may represent individuals who are currently not divergent enough to be considered disordered but who may progress to further extremes as development continues. Such individuals may be vulnerable to developing future disordered outcomes, or, viewed within Wakefield's (1992, 1997) concept of harmful dysfunction, developmental deviations may, for some individuals, reflect either the earliest signs of an emerging dysfunction or an already existing dysfunction that is partially compensated for by other processes within or outside the individual.

Developmental psychopathologists strive to integrate knowledge across scientific disciplines at multiple levels of analysis and within and between developmental domains (Cicchetti & Dawson, 2002; Cicchetti & Posner, 2005; Masten, 2007a). From the perspective of developmental psychopathology, it is critical to engage in a comprehensive evaluation of these biological, psychological, and social factors and to ascertain how these multiple levels of analysis may influence individual differences, the continuity of adaptive or maladaptive behavioral patterns, and the pathways by which the same developmental outcomes may be achieved (Cicchetti & Rogosch, 1996a, 1996b; Cicchetti & Schneider-Rosen, 1986; Kim-Cohen et al., 2003; Kohlberg, LaCrosse, & Ricks, 1972; Moffitt, 1993, 2006; L. Robins & Rutter, 1990; Rutter, 1995; Rutter & Garmezy, 1983, Rutter et al., 2006; Sroufe, 1989, 1997).

In practice, this entails comprehension of and appreciation for the developmental transformations and reorganizations that occur over time; an analysis of the risk and protective factors and mechanisms operating within and outside the individual and his or her environment over the course of life-span development; the investigation of how emergent function, competencies, and developmental tasks modify the expression of a disorder or lead to new symptoms and difficulties; and the recognition that a particular stressor or set of stressful circumstances may eventuate in different biological and psychological difficulties, depending on when in the developmental period the stress occurs (Cicchetti, Rogosch, Gunnar, & Toth, 2010; Fox & Rutter, 2010; Masten, Burt, & Coatsworth, 2006; Masten & Coatsworth, 1998; Rutter, 2009; Sroufe, 2007). Moreover, various problems will constitute different meanings for an individual depending on cultural considerations (Garcia-Coll, Akerman, & Cicchetti, 2000; Serafica & Vargas, 2006). The interpretation of the experience, in turn, will affect the adaptation or maladaptation that ensues.

Importantly, the increasing diversity among populations within and outside of the United States demands that developmental psychopathology must similarly evolve to conduct culturally appropriate and sensitive empirical investigations and preventive interventions with racially and ethnically diverse groups (Whaley & Davis, 2007). For example, because individuals in Puerto Rican and Hispanic cultures operate in the context of familism, which is defined as a strong identification to the family group, it may be more adaptive for adolescents in these cultures to remain dependent on parents for longer periods and to strive less for autonomy than adolescents from Eurocentric cultures (Rossello & Bernal, 1999). Therefore, considerations of cultural context must be prominent when determining whether an individual has diverted onto a maladaptive pathway and then deciding whether, or how best, to intervene.

Consequently, the field of developmental psychopathology transcends traditional disciplinary boundaries and provides fertile ground for moving beyond descriptive facts to a process level understanding of normal and abnormal developmental trajectories. Research conducted within a developmental psychopathology framework may challenge assumptions about what constitutes health or pathology and may redefine the manner in which the mental health community operationalizes, assesses, classifies, communicates about, and treats the adjustment problems and functioning impairments of infants, children, adolescents, and adults. Thus, its own potential contribution lies in the heuristic power it holds for translating facts into knowledge, understanding, and practical application.

A focus on the boundary between normal and abnormal development also is central to a developmental psychopathology analysis (Cicchetti, 1984b, 1990, 1993; Cicchetti & Toth, 1991; Masten, 2006; Rutter, 1986; Rutter & Garmezy, 1983; Sroufe, 1990). Such a perspective emphasizes not only how knowledge from the study of normal development can inform the study of high-risk conditions and psychopathology but also how the investigation of risk and pathology can enhance our comprehension of normal development. Even before a psychopathological disorder emerges, certain pathways signify adaptational failures in normal development that probabilistically forebode subsequent pathology (Cicchetti & Rogosch, 1996b; Sroufe, 1989). Because of the interrelations between the investigation of normality and psychopathology, developmental psychopathologists must be aware of normal pathways of development within a given cultural context, uncover deviations from these pathways, articulate the developmental transformations that occur as individuals progress through these deviant courses, and identify the processes and mechanisms that may divert an individual from a particular pathway and onto a more or less adaptive course (Sroufe, 1989).

The dynamic interplay between risk and protective factors is conceived as influencing the developmental course through the impact it has on the quality of the organization of biological and psychological systems as the individual develops (Cicchetti & Schneider-Rosen, 1986; Cicchetti & Toth, 1995). Developmental psychopathology research emphasizes probabilistic, rather than deterministic, models of dysfunction (Gottlieb & Willoughby, 2006; Rutter & Sroufe, 2000). However, various risk factors have been shown to be especially harmful to competent functioning, thereby promoting the development of psychopathology (Cicchetti & Sroufe, 2000; Sameroff, 1989). In addition, as risk factors become multiplicative, their influence on development becomes increasingly pernicious (Sameroff et al., 1987). Thus, for example, being a teen parent in and of itself may not significantly increase the risk of developmental maladaptation in offspring; however, if the young mother resides within an impoverished community with frequent intra- and extra-familial violence present, then the likelihood of negative offspring adaptation increases exponentially. It is important to note that the establishment of a process or condition as a risk factor is not a simple matter and that, even when the predictive status of a risk factor has been confirmed, this represents the starting point of a developmental psychopathology analysis. For example, although negative attributional biases that are associated with depression have been established for both children and adults (e.g., Abramson, Seligman, & Teasdale, 1978; Garber, Quiggle, Panak, & Dodge, 1991), a developmental psychopathology perspective requires an understanding of how these biases originate and develop (Cicchetti & Sroufe, 2000).

Furthermore, attention to the protective factors that individuals possess and experience throughout development is critical, especially because these intra- and extra-organismic sources of protection may promote adaptation and resilience in their own right (Luthar, 2006; Masten, 2001). Indeed, some protective factors may be influential in preserving competent functioning in the context of specific risk factors. Research on both biological and psychological protective factors is vitally important for identifying processes that contribute to the development of either the recovery of adaptive function or the achievement of resilient adaptation in the face of adversity (Charney, 2004; Curtis & Cicchetti, 2003). In addition, understanding the dynamic transactions between risk and protective factors plays a central role in building developmentally informed models of prevention (Cicchetti & Toth, 1998; Ialongo et al., 2006). Through increasing the relative balance of protective processes over risk factors, the potential for reducing the emergence of psychopathology may be achieved.

Developmental psychopathologists stress that disordered individuals may move between pathological and nonpathological forms of functioning. In addition, even in the midst of psychopathology, individuals may display adaptive and maladaptive processes so that it becomes possible to delimit the presence, nature, and boundaries of the underlying psychopathology. Developmental psychopathology is a perspective that is especially applicable to the investigation of transitional turning points in development across the life span (Rutter, 1990; Schulenberg, Sameroff, & Cicchetti, 2004; Toth & Cicchetti, 1999). This is because of its acknowledgment that disorders may appear for the first time in later life and because of its advocacy for the examination of the course of disorders once manifest, including their phases and sequelae (Goodwin & Jamison, 2007; Moffitt, 2006; Post, Weiss, & Leverich, 1994; Zigler & Glick, 1986).

Development extends throughout the entire course of life, and adaptive and maladaptive processes emerge over the life span. It is only by examining a range of conditions and populations from infancy through adulthood and into old age that developmental continuities and discontinuities can be elucidated fully. Studies on the emergence of conduct disorders serve to illustrate this point. For example, Moffitt (1993, 2006) has distinguished between childhood-onset (*life-course-persistent*) and adolescent-onset (*adolescence-limited*) conduct disorders and has found that individuals with adolescent-onset behavior problems are less likely to engage in adult criminality than are those with life-course-persistent conduct disorders. In a similar developmental analysis of the continuity–discontinuity of early externalizing behavior problems, Campbell, Shaw, and Gilliom (2000) found that a number of intra- and extra-organismic factors affect continuity of behavior problems. For example, multiple risk factors, including high levels of early hyperactivity and aggression, in combination with high levels of negative parenting and family stress, have been associated with problems at school entry for boys. Likewise, Zigler and Glick (1986) have conceptualized premorbid social competence as a developmental attainment achieved through success in adaptive tasks and shown that it contributes to individual differences in functioning among persons with schizophrenic disorders (i.e., in terms of course of disorder, recovery, relapse, and treatment effectiveness).

These examples highlight that all periods of life usher in new biological and psychological challenges, strengths, and vulnerabilities. From infancy through senescence, each period of life has its own developmental agenda and contributes in a unique manner to the past, present, and future organization of individual development (Masten & Coatsworth, 1998). Rutter has conjectured that key life turning points may be times when the presence of protective mechanisms could help individuals redirect themselves from a risk trajectory onto a more adaptive developmental pathway (cf. Elder, 1974; Quinton & Rutter, 1988). Likewise, Toth and Cicchetti (1999) suggested that these periods of developmental transition may also constitute times when individuals may be most amenable to profiting from therapeutic interventions.

Whereas change in functioning remains possible at each transitional turning point in development, prior adaptation does place constraints on subsequent adaptation. In particular, the longer an individual continues along a maladaptive ontogenic pathway, the more difficult it is to reclaim an adaptive developmental trajectory (Sroufe, 1989). Furthermore, recovery of function to an adaptive level of biological and psychological organization is more likely to occur following a period of psychopathology if the level of biological and psychological organization before the breakdown was a competent and adaptive one (Cicchetti & Tucker, 1994; Sroufe, Egeland, & Kreutzer, 1990).

Because adaptation at any point is the product of current circumstances as well as prior experiences and adaptations, maladaptation and mental disorder may best be understood in terms of present potentiating and compensatory risk and protective factors within the context of prior developmental experiences that have been carried forward into the individual's present organization of biological and behavioral systems. When psychopathology is conceptualized in this manner, it becomes crucial to identify the specific developmental arrests or failures and the unsuccessfully resolved developmental tasks implicated in an episode of mental illness, the environmental stressors involved, and the biological and psychological circumstances that may have interfered with the resolution of the developmental issues. Furthermore, it is essential to characterize each mental disorder in terms of its specific form of nonintegration, or its own integration of pathological structures, to distinguish it from other forms of mental disorder, each of which leaves its own fingerprint of incompetence by leading to peculiar patterns of maladaptation.

With respect to the emergence of psychopathology, all stages of life are consequential in that the developmental processes may undertake a pernicious turn toward mental disorder at any phase (Cicchetti & Cannon, 1999; Cicchetti & Rogosch, 2002; Cicchetti & Walker, 2003; Gottesman & Shields, 1972; Miklowitz & Cicchetti, 2010; Romer & Walker, 2007; Zigler & Glick, 1986). Moreover, the factors that are associated with the onset of a disorder may be different from those that are associated with the cessation of a disorder or with its repeated occurrence (Courchesne, Townsend, & Chase, 1995; Post et al., 1996). For example, although genetic factors frequently are associated with the onset of a major depressive disorder (MDD), relapse has been linked with aspects of the family climate, such as negative expressed emotion (Hooley & Teasdale, 1989). In contrast to the dichotomous world of mental disorder–nondisorder adhered to by many mental health providers, a developmental psychopathology perspective recognizes that normality often fades into abnormality, that adaptive and maladaptive may assume differing definitions depending on whether one's time referent is immediate circumstances or long-term development, and that processes within the individual can be characterized as having shades or degrees of psychopathology (Cicchetti, 1993; Zigler & Glick, 1986).

Developmental psychopathologists are as interested in individuals at high risk for the development of pathology who do not manifest it over time as they are in individuals who develop an actual disorder (Sroufe & Rutter, 1984). Relatedly, developmental psychopathologists also are committed to understanding pathways to competent adaptation despite exposure to conditions of adversity (Cicchetti & Garmezy, 1993; Masten, Best, & Garmezy, 1990; Luthar, 2006; Rutter, 1990). In addition, developmental psychopathologists emphasize the need to understand the functioning of individuals who, after having diverged onto deviant developmental pathways, resume more positive functioning and achieve adequate adaptation (Cicchetti & Rogosch, 1997; Kim, Cicchetti, Rogosch, & Manly, 2009).

Theoretical and empirical work in developmental psychopathology has contributed to the emergence of dramatic knowledge gains in the multiple domains of child and adult development (Cicchetti & Cohen, 1995a, 1995b, 2006a, 2006b, 2006c). Notably, there has been an emphasis on increasingly specific process-level models of normal and abnormal development, a growing acknowledgment that multiple pathways exist to the same outcome and that the effects of one component's value may vary in different systems, and an intensification of interest in genetic and neurobiological factors, as well as in social and contextual factors, related to the development of maladaptation, psychopathology, and resilience (Caspi et al., 2002; Caspi et al. 2003; Cicchetti & Aber, 1998; Cicchetti & Cohen, 2006b; Gottesman & Hanson, 2005; Rutter, 2006; Sameroff, 2000).

In addition, there is increasing recognition of the dynamic interplay of influences over developmental time (Cicchetti & Dawson, 2002; Masten, 2007a; Moffitt, Caspi, & Rutter, 2006). One of the most dramatic examples of this has been the work conducted on experience-dependent brain development (J. Black, Jones, Nelson, & Greenough, 1998; Cicchetti & Tucker, 1994; Greenough, Black, & Wallace, 1987). The viewpoint that neurobiological development and experience are mutually influential is now widely accepted in the field (Cicchetti & Tucker, 1994; Eisenberg, 1995; E. R. Kandel, 1998; Nelson & Bloom, 1997). Brain development exerts impacts on behavior; reciprocally, experience exerts impacts on the development of the brain itself.

For example, research with nonhuman animals demonstrates that social and psychological experiences can modify gene expression and brain structure, functioning, and organization (Boyce et al., 1998; E. R. Kandel, 1998, 1999; Meaney & Szyf, 2005). Alterations in gene expression influenced by social and psychological experiences produce changes in patterns of neuronal and synaptic connections (E. R. Kandel, 1998, 1999). These changes not only contribute to the biological bases of individuality but also play a prominent role in initiating and maintaining the behavioral aberrations that are induced by social and psychological experiences (E. R. Kandel, 1998).

Multiple theoretical perspectives and diverse research strategies have contributed to the emergence of the field of developmental psychopathology (Cicchetti & Cohen, 2006a; Cicchetti & Rogosch, 1999; Rutter & Sroufe, 2000). A wide array of content areas, scientific disciplines, and methodologies have been germane. Risk and protective factors have been identified and validated at multiple levels of analysis and in multiple domains. In keeping with its integrative focus, contributions to developmental psychopathology have come from many areas of the natural and social sciences.

DEFINITIONAL PARAMETERS AND PRINCIPLES OF DEVELOPMENTAL PSYCHOPATHOLOGY

The Mutual Interplay between the Study of Normality and Psychopathology

As described earlier in this chapter, a developmental psychopathology perspective emphasizes not only how knowledge from the investigation of normal development can inform the study of high-risk conditions and psychopathology but also how the study of risk and pathology can enhance our comprehension of normal development. The examination of individuals with high-risk conditions and mental disorders can provide a natural entrée into the study of system organization, disorganization, and reorganization that is otherwise not possible because of the constraints associated with conducting studies on the determinants of adaptation and maladaptation in human participants. Because there are limitations to the experimental manipulations that can be conducted with humans, it may be that the best, and perhaps the only, way to investigate developmental processes in their fullest complexity is to study individuals who already are experiencing difficulties. Therefore, the direction of our attention toward conducting research on so-called experiments of nature may help to elucidate our understanding of normal and abnormal developmental processes and mechanisms (Cicchetti, 1996, 2003; Rutter, 1994, 2007). In particular, these "natural experiments" are especially important for the purpose of dissociating possible mechanisms that offer alternative explanations (Rutter, 1994).

Often, the investigation of a system in its smoothly operating, normal or healthy state does not afford the opportunity to comprehend the interrelations among its component subsystems. Noam Chomsky (1968) reflected on this state of affairs when he asserted: "One difficulty in the psychological sciences lies in the familiarity of the phenomena with which they deal....One is inclined to take them for granted as necessary or somehow 'natural'" (p. 21). Furthermore, Chomsky (1968) lamented, "We also lose sight of the need for explanation when phenomena are too familiar and 'obvious.' We tend too easily to assume that explanations must be transparent and close to the surface" (p. 22).

Because pathological conditions such as brain damage, mental disorder, and growing up in a malignant environment enable scientists to isolate the components of the integrated system, their investigation sheds light on the normal structure of the system and prevents us from falling prey to the problems identified by Chomsky. Consequently, examinations of developmental extremes and imperfections must be conducted.

If we choose simply to ignore or bypass the study of these atypical phenomena, then the eventual result is likely to be the construction of theories that are contradicted by the revelation of critical facts in risk and psychopathology (cf. Lenneberg, 1967). Similar to genetic research on pathological embryos and to molecular genetic and neurobiological studies on psychopathology, investigations of the ecological, biological, and psychological factors that cause development to go awry can help to inform our understanding of more normative ontogenetic processes.

For example, children with Down syndrome are a particularly interesting population to study from a developmental viewpoint. An examination of the postnatal development of individuals with an extra autosomal chromosome may provide a clear test of the hypothesis that abnormal chromosomal material may be used as an independent variable to study biological and behavioral similarities and differences. Whereas few autosomal trisomies are viable, nor do they occur frequently enough to be tested for behavioral phenotypes, Down syndrome is a notable exception. Down syndrome is etiologically homogeneous and is detectable at birth so that it can be charted developmentally. It possesses a suitable complexity and intactness of phenotypic expression and occurs with sufficient frequency to allow for meaningful developmental analysis. It results in diverse outcomes varying from severe retardation to near normal development (Cicchetti & Beeghly, 1990).

The slower cognitive development of infants with Down syndrome allows a separation of the early prototypes of what will later be affective expression from genuine emotional reactions that are dependent on psychological processes (Cicchetti & Sroufe, 1978). Their developmental heterogeneity allows specification of the interdependence between affect and cognition. In fact, these developmentally delayed infants provide an important test of the relationship between emotional and cognitive development. Unlike the case with the rapidly developing normal infant, in whom the simultaneous emergence of behaviors may be viewed as coincidental, the slower advance of infants with Down syndrome through the same stages of affect and cognition enables us to demonstrate true convergences and divergences in development.

Research on autism, a pervasive developmental disorder with its origins in infancy that is characterized by impairments in social communication and interaction (e.g., joint attention; theory of mind), cognitive and executive functioning deficits, and behavioral stereotypes (American Psychiatric Association, 1994; Baron-Cohen, Leslie, & Frith, 1985; Dawson & Toth, 2006; Mundy, 2009), also provides an illustration of the relation between the investigation of normal and abnormal development. Many neurobiological theories concerning autism have tended to focus on possible abnormalities of individual brain structures as underlying the observed behavioral and neuropsychological symptoms. A range of investigations have focused on dysfunction of the brain and have implicated abnormalities in virtually every brain system examined. More recently, influenced by a developmental psychopathology perspective, investigators have begun to take into account the impact that autism has on diverse developmental processes and the interconnected nature of multiple brain systems involved in normal neurobiological development and in autism (see, e.g., Dawson & Toth, 2006). Advances in our understanding of autism have come as a result of close collaborations between behavioral and biological scientists working across multiple levels of analysis (e.g., Akshoomoff, Pierce, & Courchesne, 2002; Baron-Cohen et al., 1985; Mundy, 2009; Mundy & Sigman, 1989a, 1989b; Rodier, 2002).

When extrapolating from nontypical populations with the goal of informing developmental theory, it is critical to investigate a range of high-risk and mentally disordered individuals. The study of a single pathological or risk process may result in spurious conclusions if generalizations are made solely on the basis of that condition or disorder. However, if a given biological or behavioral pattern is viewed in the light of an entire spectrum of disordered modifications, then it may be possible to attain significant insight into the processes of development not generally achieved through sole reliance on studies of relatively nondisordered populations (cf. Lenneberg. 1967).

Continuity—and Discontinuity

The nature of the developmental process elucidates a clear perspective on how to conceptualize empirical research on the origins and course of later psychopathology. Researchers conducting investigations aimed at identifying early precursors of later emerging psychopathology face numerous conceptual and methodological challenges (for examples from schizophrenia, see Bearden, Meyer, Loewy, Niendam, & Cannon, 2006; Keshavan & Hogarty, 1999). Because of developmental changes in neurobiological and physiological systems, as well as parallel developments in cognitive, social cognitive, socioemotional, and representational systems, investigators cannot presume phenotypic similarity between early precursors and later impairments (G. A. Carlson & Meyer, 2006; Cicchetti & Schneider-Rosen, 1986; Kagan, 1981, 2008; Youngstrom, Meyers, Youngstrom, Calabrese, & Findling, 2006). Consequently, studies of the early precursors of later psychopathology should conceptualize and measure features of early development that are theoretically related, but not necessarily behaviorally identical, to the emergence of subsequent disorder.

Given the importance of a life-span view of developmental processes and an interest in delineating how prior development influences later development, a major issue in developmental psychopathology involves how to determine continuity in the quality of adaptation across developmental time (Kohlberg et al., 1972; Sroufe, 1979, 1997). Sroufe (1979) has articulated the concept of coherence in the organization of behaviors in successive developmental periods as a means of identifying continuity in adaptation despite changing behavioral presentations of the developing individual. Crucial to this concept is a recognition that the same behaviors in different developmental periods may represent quite different levels of adaptation. Behaviors indicating competence within a developmental period may indicate incompetence when evidenced within subsequent developmental periods. Normative behaviors early in development may indicate maladaptation when exhibited later in development. Thus, the manifestation of competence in different developmental periods is rarely indicated by isomorphism in behavioral presentation (i.e., *homotypic continuity*; cf. Kagan, 1981).

Additionally, it must be recognized that the same function in an organized behavioral system can be fulfilled by two dissimilar behaviors, whereas the same kind of behavior may serve two different functions (Werner & Kaplan, 1963), and the same behavior also may play different roles in different systems. As a result, it is especially important to distinguish between similarities and differences in higher order organization of symptomatology *(molar level)* and component behavioral manifestations of symptomatology *(molecular level)* during different developmental periods. The reorganization of biological and psychological systems that takes place at each new level of development means researchers could not expect to see, for any symptom, isomorphism at the molecular level, even if there is isomorphism at the molar level. For example, children who experience recurrent depressions as part of their bipolar disorder that span the transition from preoperational to concrete-operational thought may display excessive and inappropriate guilt, a loss of self-esteem, and a decrease in activity throughout the episode. Consequently, at a molar level, the depressive symptoms at the latter concrete operational period will be isomorphic to those of the earlier preoperational period. Nonetheless, the particular manifestation of the guilt feelings, loss of self-esteem, and psychomotor retardation may change and develop during the transition, when the child's cognitive, representational, socioemotional, and behavioral competencies undergo a rather radical development across these developmental periods. In this way, there may be noteworthy differences at the molecular level.

For example, because development typically involves the organization through integration of previously differentiated behaviors, the expression of bipolar illness may indeed be characterized by molar continuities but additionally by molecular discontinuities and changes. At the molar level, continuity will be preserved by an orderly development in the organization of behaviors; however, at the molecular level, the behaviors that are present at different periods may vary, but the underlying meaning may remain coherent (i.e., heterotypic continuity; cf. Kagan, 1981). Thus, a child who exhibits symptoms of attention-deficit/hyperactivity disorder (ADHD) at age 7 and a bipolar mixed episode at age 13 may have the same molar organization but different molecular behaviors at different phases of development. The study of the development of the mood disorders over the life course is likely to be most fruitful, and to reveal the relationship between pathological processes and normal development, only if the behavior of individuals with an affective disorder is examined simultaneously at the molar and molecular levels.

Furthermore, examining the course of adaptation after an episode of bipolar disorder has remitted would benefit from the use of a developmental perspective. For example, the examination of the functioning characteristics of individuals previously diagnosed with bipolar disorder who have returned to a nondisordered condition would provide additional valuable information about bipolar disorder. It may be possible to identify core characteristics of functioning that remain stable but that no longer give rise to bipolar disorder because of compensatory factors in the environment, within the individual, or through gene × environment (G×E) interactions that promote resilient adaptations (Cicchetti & Curtis, 2006, 2007). It is conceivable that research such as this might reveal that certain functioning characteristics that were causally relevant to bipolar disorder in an earlier environment have become positively adaptive in a new context. They may not only not detract from but actually facilitate successful adaptation. An example might be the personality trait of *novelty seeking* or *exuberance*, which before the onset of bipolar disorder might be associated with abusing drugs, keeping chaotic sleep–wake schedules, or conflict in family relationships. After multiple episodes, a person high in novelty seeking might be more willing to try innovative treatments, to use his or her high energy states in artistic and other creative endeavors, or to experiment with new social contexts that might provide protection against recurrences.

It also may be erroneous to assume that normalized behavior necessarily reflects improvements in processes that were once causal to the development of bipolar disorder. Accordingly, a developmental psychopathology perspective encourages us to remain open to the possibility that at least some of the characteristics we typically view as functioning deficits in fact may be neutral or even advantageous. Stated differently, they may translate into assets or deficits depending on other characteristics of the individual, the environment, or both. For example, in some contexts, acting on impulse may lead individuals with bipolar disorder to noteworthy and creative achievements, whereas in other contexts, impulsive acts may result in persons with bipolar disorder behaving in a dangerous fashion, resulting in self-destructive outcomes.

Developmental Pathways

Since the emergence of developmental psychopathology as an interdisciplinary science, diversity in process and outcome has been conceived as one of the hallmarks of the approach. Developmental psychopathologists have shown that there are multiple contributors to adaptive and maladaptive outcomes in any individual, that these factors and their relative contributions vary among individuals, and that there are myriad paths to any particular manifestation of adaptive and disordered behavior (Cicchetti, 1993; Moffitt, 1993, 2006; L. Robins, 1966; L. Robins & Rutter, 1990; Sroufe & Jacobvitz, 1989; Zucker, 2006). Additionally, heterogeneity is thought to exist among individuals who develop a specific disorder with respect to the features of their disturbance, as well as among individuals who evidence maladaptation but do not develop a disorder. Congruent with this viewpoint, the principles of equifinality and multifinality, derived from general systems theory (von Bertalanffy, 1968), are germane.

Equifinality refers to the observation that in any open system (cf. Mayr, 1964, 1988), a diversity of pathways, including chance events or what biologists refer to as nonlinear epigenesis, may lead to the same outcome. Stated differently, in an open system (i.e., one in which there is maintenance in change and dynamic order in processes, organization, and self-regulation), the same end state may be reached from a variety of initial conditions and through different processes. In contrast, in a closed system, the end state is inextricably linked to and determined by the initial conditions. If the conditions change or the processes are modified, then the end state will also be modified (von Bertalanffy, 1968).

Early descriptions of equifinality emanated from work in embryology. For example, the development of a normal organism was shown to occur from a whole ovum, a divided ovum, or two fused ova. Further, it was demonstrated that different initial sizes and different courses of growth could eventuate in the same ultimate size of an organism (von Bertalanffy, 1968; Waddington, 1957). Within the discipline of developmental psychopathology, equifinality has been invoked to explain why a variety of developmental pathways may eventuate in a given outcome rather than expecting a singular primary pathway to the adaptive or maladaptive outcome.

For example, some individuals who develop a major depressive episode in adolescence may have a genetic predisposition for the disorder, whereas others may have grown up in a home with substance-abusing parents or experienced child maltreatment (Cicchetti & Toth, 2009). Parental loss through death early in development may have occurred for others; still other adolescents may have had more benign early experiences but may have struggled with the physical changes of puberty occurring as they entered junior high school (Ge, Brody, Conger, & Simons, 2006; Nolen-Hoeksema & Hilt, 2009). Thus, the common outcome of depression in adolescence is likely to result from diverse processes across different individuals rather than from all adolescents following the same progression to depression.

Relatedly, Duggal, Carlson, Sroufe, and Egeland (2001) reported that there appear to be different predictors of childhood-onset depression compared with adolescent-onset depression, suggesting variation in processes promoting depression in different developmental periods. Maternal depression during childhood was related to both childhood and adolescent onset of depression (Duggal et al., 2001). In contrast, childhood-onset depression was also strongly influenced by additional factors related to pervasive deficits in the overall family context, including poor early supportive care of the child, abuse, and early maternal stress. Among adolescents, gender differences emerged for the predictors of depression. For girls, maternal depression during childhood was strongly associated with high depressive symptomatology during adolescence, whereas for boys, high depressive symptomatology was linked to deficits in the early supportive care they received. Thus, different processes appear to be prominent in promoting a common depressive outcome for boys versus girls during adolescence.

The identification of diverse pathways through which neurodevelopmental anomalies may result in schizophrenia provides further insight into how specificity and differentiation into a syndrome may result from a commonality of initiating circumstances (Bearden et al., 2006). These multiple pathways embrace a number of possible contributors that may potentiate or mediate the links between early neurodevelopmental anomalies and the later development of schizophrenia in genetically vulnerable individuals. These include prenatal and perinatal complications and the normal developmental changes that take place during late adolescence and early adulthood, such as (a) synaptic pruning of the prefrontal cortex, (b) pubertal increases in gonadal hormones during adolescence, (c) developmental transformations in prefrontal cortex and limbic brain regions, (d) continued myelination of intracortical connections, (d) alterations in the balance between mesocortical and mesolimbic dopamine systems, (e) the stress that arises during postnatal social development, (f) the transformations that occur in cognitive and social–cognitive development, and (g) the growing importance of the peer group (Bearden et al., 2006). Such an integrative, interdisciplinary approach is necessary to capture the full complexity of schizophrenic illness, including the multiple pathways to, and the diverse outcomes associated with, the disorder (Cicchetti & Cannon, 1999). Furthermore, such a perspective suggests that specific treatments should be developed and implemented for use at particular developmental stages, before, after, and during illness episodes.

The principle of multifinality (Wilden, 1980) suggests that any one component may function differently depending on the organization of the system in which it operates. Multifinality states that the effect on functioning of any one component's value may vary in different systems. Actual effects will depend on the conditions set by the values of additional components with which it is structurally linked. Consequently, the pathology or health of a system must be identified in terms of how adequately its essential functions are maintained. Stated differently, a particular adverse event should not necessarily be seen as leading to the same psychopathological or nonpsychopathological outcome in every individual. Likewise, individuals may begin on the same major pathway and, as a function of their subsequent "choices," exhibit very different patterns of adaptation or maladaptation (Cicchetti & Tucker, 1994; Rutter, 1989; Sroufe, 1989; Sroufe et al., 1990). Multifinality specifies that diverse outcomes are likely to evolve from any original starting point. Thus, individuals who share characteristics at a particular point in time will not necessarily exhibit the same pattern of later developmental outcomes. Rather, the ongoing dynamic transaction of risk and protective processes experienced uniquely by individuals will eventuate in different outcomes unfolding over the course of development.

An illustration of multifinality is provided in Lee Robins's (1966) classic work, *Deviant Children Grow Up.* Children with conduct disorder were found to manifest differential outcomes in adulthood. Some displayed adult antisocial personality disorder, whereas others developed schizophrenia, and yet others exhibited normal adaptation.

Likewise, not all maltreated children are equally affected by their traumatic experiences. An array of biological and psychological deviations are displayed by individuals who have experienced sexual and physical abuse, neglect, and emotional abuse (see, e.g., Cicchetti & Rogosch, 2001a; Cicchetti, Rogosch, Gunnar, & Toth, in press; Cicchetti & Valentino, 2007; DeBellis, Baum, et al., 1999; DeBellis, Keshavan, et al., 1999; DeBellis, 2005; Pollak, 2008; Pollak, Cicchetti, Klorman, & Brumaghim, 1997).

A pathways approach builds on knowledge gained from studies that focus on variables (i.e., variable-centered research); however, the emphasis of pathways research shifts to exploring the common and the uncommon outcomes, as well as alternative routes by which outcomes are achieved by different individuals (i.e., person-centered research; von Eye & Bergman, 2003). Thus, what might be considered error variance at the group level must be critically examined for understanding diversity in process and outcome. The emphasis on person-centered observation highlights a transition from a focus on variables to a focus on individuals, and this transition is essential for demonstrating equifinality and multifinality in the developmental course. The examination of patterns of commonality within relatively homogeneous subgroups of individuals and concomitant similarity in profiles of contributory processes becomes an important data-analytic strategy (Muthen & Muthen, 2004;

Nagin, 2005; von Eye & Bergman, 2003). Moreover, the need to examine the totality of attributes, psychopathological conditions, and risk and protective processes in the context of each other rather than in isolation is seen as crucial for understanding the course of development taken by individuals across the life course.

For example, the presence of a childhood depressive disorder has different developmental implications depending on whether it occurs alone or in conjunction with conduct disorder, with comorbid depression and conduct disorder resulting in more deleterious sequelae (Cicchetti & Toth, 1995). Similarly, the nature of alcoholism varies considerably depending on differences in the life course of antisociality (Zucker, 2006). Zucker differentiated three types of alcoholism, including antisocial, developmentally limited, and negative affect. The antisocial and developmentally limited types have considerable similarity to the life-course-persistent and adolescence-limited types of conduct disorder that Moffitt identified (1993). Specifically, life-course-persistent antisocial development emerges from early neurodevelopmental, genetic, and family adversity risk factors. Individuals with life-course-persistent conduct disorder embark on this pathway early in life, manifest these behaviors across settings, possess aggressive personality traits, and are characterized by more genetic influence than the adolescence-limited pattern of the disorder (Moffitt, 2006). The negative affect type of alcoholism does not emerge until young adulthood. The developmental precursors to these three types of alcoholism are substantially different, underscoring the importance of identifying multiple developmental patterns that may eventuate in disorder rather than assuming a common set of etiological factors operates for all. Likewise, Schulenberg, Wadsworth, O'Malley, Bachman, and Johnston (1996), in studying different patterns of binge drinking across the transition from adolescence to young adulthood, demonstrated that a person-centered approach provided a more differentiated understanding of etiological processes operating within distinct subgroups of individuals than that which was achieved through a variable-oriented level of analysis.

Attention to the distinct causal processes that operate in different subgroups through the use of person-centered approaches provides a more complex view of the varied developmental trajectories of substance use disorders and their impact on long-term risk for disorder as well as recovery. Thus, a pathways approach highlights the importance of an organizational view of development (cf. Cicchetti, 1993; Cicchetti & Sroufe, 1978; Sroufe, 1979). The meaning of any one attribute, process, or psychopathological condition needs to be considered in light of the complex matrix of individual characteristics, experiences, and social-contextual influences involved, the timing of events and experiences, and the developmental history of the individual.

This attention to diversity in origins, processes, and outcomes in understanding developmental pathways does not suggest that prediction is futile as a result of the many potential individual patterns of adaptation (Sroufe, 1989). There are constraints on how much diversity is possible, and not all outcomes are equally likely (Cicchetti & Tucker, 1994; Sroufe et al., 1990). Nonetheless, the appreciation of equifinality and multifinality in development encourages theorists and researchers to entertain more complex and varied approaches to how they conceptualize and investigate development and psychopathology. Researchers should increasingly strive to demonstrate the multiplicity of processes and outcomes that may be articulated at the individual, person-oriented level within existing longitudinal data sets. Ultimately, future endeavors must conceptualize and design research at the outset with these differential pathways concepts as a foundation. In so doing, progress toward achieving the unique goal of developmental psychopathology—to explain the development of individual patterns of adaptation and maladaptation—will be realized (Sroufe & Rutter, 1984).

Developmental Cascades

Developmental theory and empirical findings have long suggested that there are regular cascades or indirect influences in the course of development in which function at one level or in one domain or generation come to influence other levels or domains or generations in significant ways (Masten & Cicchetti, 2010). These effects have gone by different names, including chain reactions, snowballing effects, dual failure models, and progressive effects, as well as developmental cascades (Burt, Obradović, Long, & Masten, 2008; Cicchetti & Tucker, 1994; Dodge & Pettit, 2003; Hinshaw & Anderson, 1996; Masten & Coatsworth, 1998; Masten et al., 2005; Patterson, Reid, & Dishion, 1992; Rutter, 1999; Rutter & Sroufe, 2000). Theoretically, these effects explain a wide range of developmental phenomena resulting from the transactional interactions of a complex living system as it develops (Ford & Lerner, 1992; Gottlieb, 1992; Sameroff, 2000; Thelen & Smith, 1998) and the sometimes unexpected effects of changes in one aspect of function for future development.

Developmental cascades are important for the field of developmental psychopathology in multiple ways (Masten & Cicchetti, 2010). Cascade effects could explain the widely observed consequences of antisocial behavior or academic achievement in childhood for many other outcomes in adulthood, as well as some cases of comorbidity that emerge over time for a variety of disorders. Cascade models also can account for the pathways by which gene–environment interplay unfolds over time to shape development, linking genes to neural levels of function to behavior to social experience, as in the multilevel dynamics suggested by Gottlieb's (2007) model of development. Developmental theories about competence (see Masten et al., 2006) also invoke cascades in the fundamental assertion that effectiveness in one domain of competence in one period of life becomes the scaffold on which later competence in newly emerging domains develop. Others have described these as positive chain reactions (e.g., Rutter, 1999). Developmental scientists have delineated cascades in cognitive development in which an early advantage or disadvantage in one cognitive domain influences another, later developing and high-order domain; indirect connections linking early infant behaviors to later intellectual function also have been observed (e.g., Bornstein et al., 2006; Colombo, Shaddy, Richman, Maikranz, & Blaga, 2004). Similarly, executive function in a child may in part mediate the influence of positive parenting on lower risk for externalizing problems (see Eisenberg et al., 2005). In each case in various ways, such progressions appear to be central to models of normal development, the development of psychopathology, and resilience.

Intergenerational transmission of behavior (mediated by genes, experience, and their interplay) or risk can also be viewed as cascade effects that link multiple generations and multiple behaviors or levels of analysis. The intergenerational transmission of parenting (e.g., Conger, Neppi, Kim, & Scaramella, 2003) or psychosocial risk (Serbin & Karp, 2004) offer examples.

Masten et al. (2005), among others, have argued that the most convincing evidence of cascade effects are those empirical studies that are longitudinal, include at least three assessment points, and measure all relevant variables at each point in time. In effect, the role of within-time correlation and also across-time continuity are controlled in the most informative designs.

Cascade models have important implications for prevention and intervention as well as the etiology of competence or problems (Masten et al., 2006). Well-delineated cascade effects have implications for the timing and targets of strategic intervention. The high return on investment of early interventions (Heckman, 2006) may be due in part to the timely interruption of negative cascades. Intervention designs that target mediating processes for change are cascade models.

Multiple Levels of Analysis

Since its inception, developmental psychopathology has been conceived as a multidisciplinary and an interdisciplinary science (Cicchetti, 1984, 1990; Cicchetti & Toth, 1991). A number of influential theoretical perspectives, including the organizational perspective (Cicchetti & Schneider-Rosen, 1986; Cicchetti & Sroufe, 1978; Sroufe, 1979) and Gottlieb's notions of probabilistic epigenesis (Gottlieb, 1992; Gottlieb & Halpern, 2002), have long advocated the importance of multidomain, interdisciplinary research. For example, Gottlieb (1991) depicted individual development as "an increase of complexity of organization…at all levels of analysis…as a consequence of horizontal and vertical coactions among the organisms' parts, including organism-environment coactions" (p. 7). Horizontal coactions are thought to take place at the same level of analysis, whereas vertical coactions occur at a different level of analysis and are reciprocal. Accordingly, vertical coactions are capable of influencing developmental organization from either lower-to-higher (i.e., bottom-up) or higher-to-lower (i.e., top-down) levels of the developing system (Cicchetti & Tucker, 1994; Gottlieb, 1992). Thus, from this framework, not only can biological factors exert impact on psychological processes but psychosocial experiences can also modify the structure, function, and organization of the brain, as well as affect gene expression (Eisenberg, 1995; E. R. Kandel, 1998, 1999). Thus, epigenesis is viewed as probabilistic rather than predetermined or preformational, with the bidirectional and transactional nature of genetic, neural, behavioral, and environmental influences over the life course, capturing the essence of probabilistic epigenesis. As is apparent, systems views of brain–behavior relations are multidimensional. Therefore, no component, subsystem, or level of organization possesses causal privilege in the developmental system (Cicchetti & Cannon, 1999; Thelen & Smith, 1998).

As the history of science attests, there certainly are problems that are best examined using the conceptual and methodological tools of a single disciplinary perspective. However, because many of the issues associated with understanding mental illnesses and resilient adaptation in their full complexity are not as effectively approached by a single investigator or through a single disciplinary model, there are other scientific questions that can be best addressed through an integrative, multidisciplinary framework (Pellmar & Eisenberg, 2000). Because one of the major goals of a developmental psychopathology approach is to understand individual patterns of adaptation and maladaptation and to comprehend the "whole organism" (Cicchetti & Sroufe, 1976; Goldstein, 1939; Zigler, 1973), calls for an interdisciplinary approach have been gaining momentum. Successful interdisciplinary scientific research has the potential to transform the field of developmental psychopathology given the increased likelihood that such investigations will lead to innovative scientific discoveries and generate findings that will influence multiple disciplines (Cacioppo et al., 2007).

To date, much of what is known about the correlates, causes, pathways, and sequelae of mental disorders has been gleaned from investigations that focused on relatively narrow domains of variables. It is apparent from the questions addressed by developmental psychopathologists that progress toward a process-level understanding of mental disorders will require research designs and strategies that call for the simultaneous assessment of multiple domains of variables both within and outside of the developing person (Cicchetti & Dawson, 2002). In some instances, reference to variables measured in other domains is essential to clarify the role(s) of variables of interest; for other questions, it is necessary to consider variables from other domains as competing explanations for postulated causal paths. To understand psychopathology and resilience fully, all levels of analysis must be examined and integrated. Each level both informs and constrains all other levels of analysis. Moreover, the influence of levels on one another is almost always bidirectional (Cicchetti & Cannon, 1999; Cicchetti & Tucker, 1994).

Because different levels of analysis constrain other levels, as scientists learn more about multiple levels of analysis, researchers conducting their work at each level will need to develop theories that are consistent across all levels. When disciplines function in isolation, they run the risk of creating theories that ultimately will be incorrect because vital information from other disciplines has either been ignored or is unknown. Just as is the case in systems neuroscience, it is critical that there be an integrative framework that incorporates all levels of analysis about complex systems in the development of psychopathology.

Over the course of the past several decades, there has been a growing acknowledgment that the investigation of developmental processes, both normal and abnormal, necessitates that scientists use different methods and levels of analysis depending on the questions addressed in their research. Rather than adhering to a unidimensional belief in the deterministic role that unfolding biology exerts on behavior, it is now widely believed that brain function and its subsequent influence on behavior possesses self-organizing functions that can, in fact, be altered by experiences incurred during sensitive periods of development (Cicchetti & Tucker, 1994; Eisenberg, 1995; Nelson & Bloom, 1997).

Moreover, the mechanisms of neural plasticity are integral to the anatomical structure of cortical tissue and cause the formation of the brain to involve an extended malleable process that presents developmental psychopathologists with new avenues for understanding the vulnerability of the brain as a basis for the emergence of mental disorder. Perturbations that take place in the developing brain can trigger a cascade of growth and function changes that lead the neural system down a path that deviates from that usually taken in normal neurobiological development, leading to the development of aberrant neural circuitry that contributes to these early developmental abnormalities eventuating in relatively enduring forms of psychopathology (J. Black et al., 1998; Cicchetti & Cannon, 1999; Courchesne, Chisum, & Townsend, 1994; Nowakowski & Hayes, 1999).

One of the major challenges confronting scientific progress in research using a multiple-levels-of-analysis perspective involves establishing communication systems among disciplines (Gunnar & Cicchetti, 2009; Pellmar & Eisenberg, 2000). For example, despite tremendous technological advances in neuroimaging and molecular genetics, great knowledge gaps remain between scientists who possess competence with the technologies and methods of brain imaging and genetics and those who are comfortable with the complex issues inherent in the investigation of development and psychopathology. Consequently, the field has not yet made optimal use of the advances in technology that have taken place (Cicchetti & Posner, 2005; Posner, Rothbart, Farah, & Bruer, 2001; Thomas & Cicchetti, 2008).

Resilience

Resilience has been operationalized as the individual's capacity for adapting successfully and functioning competently despite experiencing chronic adversity or following exposure to prolonged or severe trauma (Masten et al., 1990). Resilience is a dynamic developmental process; it is multidimensional in nature, exemplified by findings that individuals who are at high-risk for, or who have, a mental disorder may manifest competence in some domains and contexts, whereas they may exhibit problems in others (Egeland, Carlson, & Sroufe, 1993; Luthar, Cicchetti, & Becker, 2000).

Research on the determinants of resilience also highlights the need to examine functioning across multiple domains of development and through multiple levels of analysis. Research in the area of resilience has begun to follow this interdisciplinary, multiple-levels-of-analysis perspective (Cicchetti & Blender, 2006; Cicchetti & Rogosch, 2007; Curtis & Cicchetti, 2007; also see articles in Cicchetti & Curtis, 2007).

Furthermore, the ability to function in a resilient fashion in the presence of biological, psychological, environmental, and sociocultural disadvantage may be achieved through the use of developmental pathways that are less typical than those negotiated in usual circumstance. Thus, an important question for researchers to address is whether the employment of alternative pathways to attaining competence renders individuals more vulnerable to manifesting delays or deviations in development. Although only prospective longitudinal investigations can fully address this issue, it is critical to ascertain whether these individuals are more prone to developing maladaptation or psychopathology in later life. Given the nonstatic nature of the construct, we do not expect children identified as resilient to be immune to declines in functioning at each subsequent developmental period.

Investigations aimed at discovering the processes leading to resilient outcomes and on the processes underlying recovery of adaptive function offer great promise as an avenue for facilitating the development of prevention and intervention strategies (Luthar et al., 2000; Toth & Cicchetti, 1999). Through the examination of the proximal and distal processes and mechanisms that contribute to positive adaptation in situations that more typically eventuate in maladaptation, researchers, and clinicians will be better prepared to devise ways to promote competent outcomes in individuals at high risk for developing psychopathology (Luthar & Cicchetti, 2000).

Despite the attention paid to discovering the processes through which individuals at high risk do not develop maladaptively, the empirical study of resilience has focused primarily on detecting the psychosocial determinants of the phenomenon (Charney, 2004; Curtis & Cicchetti, 2003). For research on resilience to grow in ways that are commensurate with the complexity inherent to the construct, efforts to understand underlying processes will be facilitated by the increased implementation of multidisciplinary investigations designed within a developmental psychopathology framework. Research of this nature would entail a consideration of biological, psychological, and environmental–contextual processes from which varied pathways to resilience (equifinality) might eventuate, as well as those that result in diverse outcomes among individuals who have achieved resilient functioning (multifinality; see Cicchetti & Curtis, 2007).

The role of biological factors in resilience is suggested by evidence on neurobiological and neuroendocrine function in relation to stress regulation and reactivity (Cicchetti et al., 2010; Gunnar & Vazquez, 2006), by behavior-genetics research on nonshared environment effects (Rende & Waldman, 2006), and by molecular genetics research that may reveal the genetic elements that serve a protective function for individuals experiencing significant adversity (Cicchetti & Blender, 2006). Along these lines, the investigation of multiple aspects of the processes underlying resilience can shed light on the nature of the interrelation among various developmental domains in individuals at high risk for, or who already have, one or more psychiatric disorders. For example, how do cognition, affect, and neurobiological growth relate with one another at various developmental periods? When an advance or a lag occurs in one biological or psychological system, what are the consequences for other systems?

It is important that these issues receive focused attention from researchers, because the presence of capacities of one of these systems may be a necessary condition for the development or exercise of capacities of another system. For example, certain cognitive skills may be necessary for the development of particular affective expressions and experiences (Hesse & Cicchetti, 1982). Lags in these systems may then result in compensatory development, which may leave the child vulnerable to psychopathology in some instances. Over time, difficulty in the organization of one biological or psychological system may tend to promote difficulty in the way in which other systems are organized as hierarchical integration between the separate systems occurs. The organization of the individual may then appear to consist of poorly integrated component systems. As the converse of the effects of early competence, early incompetence will tend to promote later incompetence because the individual arrives at successive developmental stages with less than optimal resources available for responding to the challenges of that period. Again, however, this progression is not inevitable but probabilistic. Changes in the internal and external environment may lead to improvements in the ability to grapple with developmental challenges, resulting in a redirection in the developmental course.

Children who develop in a resilient fashion despite having experienced significant adversity play an active role in constructing, seeking, and receiving the experiences that are developmentally appropriate for them. To date, research investigations that search for mechanisms of G×E interaction have yet to address the role that genetic factors may play in influencing how children who are developing in a resilient fashion have actively transformed their social environment (known as evocative gene–environment correlation; Rende & Waldman, 2006; Scarr & McCartney, 1983). At the neurobiological level, different areas of the brain may attempt to compensate; on another level, individuals may seek out new experiences in areas in which they have strength (J. Black et al., 1998; Cicchetti & Tucker, 1994). The effects of social experiences, such as child abuse and neglect or institutional upbringing, on brain biochemistry and microstructure may be either pathological or adaptive. With respect to the experience of child maltreatment, depending on how the individual interprets and responds to the abuse, as well as the genetic elements that are expressed, the effects may be either pathological (i.e., the typical outcome) or may not preclude normative development (i.e., a resilient outcome; Cicchetti & Rogosch, 2009; Cicchetti & Valentino, 2007). Thus, neither early neurobiological anomalies nor aberrant experiences should be considered as determining the ultimate fate of individuals at high risk for maladaptation and psychopathology (the notion of probabilistic epigenesis).

A multilevel approach to resilience also affords an additional avenue for examining the biological and social constraints that may operate on aspects of the developmental process throughout the life course. Moreover, by investigating the multiple determinants of resilient adaptation, we are in a position to discover the range and variability in individuals' attempts to respond adaptively to challenge and ill fortune.

Translational Research

The principles of developmental psychopathology lend themselves to fostering research with applications for practice and implications for society, policy makers, and individuals with mental disorders and their families. The subject matter of the field, which encompasses risk, psychopathology, and resilience, the elucidation of precipitants of mental disorder, the mediating and moderating processes that contribute to or mitigate against the emergence and maintenance of psychopathology, prevention and intervention, and the incorporation of knowledge of normal development into the conduct of empirical investigations, necessitates that researchers think clearly about the practical implication of their work.

The translation of basic research into practice was at the heart of the child development movement in the United States (Senn, 1975). Stokes (1997) labeled this *use-inspired basic research* and asserted the criticality of grounding research in practice to meet the needs of society. Further, he believed that the relationship between research and practice should be bidirectional, with each contributing to the knowledge base of the other. Historically, many examples can be found regarding the interplay among research, practice, and policy (see Zigler, 1998, for a review). In fact, the first White House Conference on Children, held in 1909, united researchers and social reformers with the goal of enhancing the quality of children's lives.

Although the field of developmental psychology has made a number of important contributions to improving the lives of children and families, we now are immersed in a new era in which heightened emphasis is being paid to the translation of basic research into practical application and treatments. The translational *push* is designed to speed up the translation of basic scientific findings into practical applications. Indeed, more than 4 decades ago Martin and Lois Hoffman (1964) advocated greater communication between researchers and social service providers toward the goal of having behavioral science contribute to the social good.

Consistent with the prevailing viewpoint that it is essential to apply findings from basic research to the context of practice, the past two editions of the *Handbook of Child Psychology* have included volumes devoted to *Child Psychology in Practice* (Sigel, 2006; Sigel & Renninger, 1998). Unlike chapters in prior editions that "served as a standard of dispassionate, scientific rigor," contributors were asked to write reviews that bridged research and practice (Sigel & Renninger, 1998, p. xxii).

In the closing paragraphs to the *Child Psychology in Practice* volume of the *Handbook of Child Psychology*, Sigel (2006) posed the following question: "Should not developmental research offer useful and meaningful explanations for the course of development and where needed provide approaches for the prevention and amelioration of conditions that may hinder the optimization of the developmental trajectory?" (p. 1022). I echo this question and strongly agree with Sigel that the application of research to practice "requires stretching and/or adapting the root metaphors in which we have been trained so that collaborations between researchers and practitioners are the basis of research and of any application of research to practice" (Sigel, 2006, p. 1022).

The new era of translational research not only is exerting impact on developmental psychology it is also affecting all fields of research in the medical, physical, social, and clinical sciences. Furthermore, the push for translational research is closely tied to funding priorities at the major federal agencies that provide financial support for university research. The impetus to conduct translational research in the behavioral sciences has emanated largely from the National Institute of Mental Health (Insel, 2005; Insel & Scolnick, 2006) and was spurred by the recognition of the tremendous individual, social, and economic burden associated with mental illness (Insel, 2009; National Advisory Mental Health Council, 2000). Hence, the emphasis on translational research at the funding agencies is quickly translating itself into priorities within the academy.

Despite the current emphasis on translational research, there is little consensus on what constitutes a translational research program. National meetings organized around discussions highlighting the importance of translational research (National Institute of Mental Health, 2005) have involved long discussions of the definition without reaching a clear consensus. Program announcements from various funding agencies tend to emphasize the translation of basic ideas, insights, and discoveries into the treatment or prevention of human disease (National Institute of Neurological Disorders and Stroke, 2005). Likewise, statements from the National Institute of Mental Health emphasize the translation of basic research into improvements in diagnosis, prevention, treatment, and delivery of services for mental illness (Pellmar & Eisenberg, 2000).

In a report of the National Advisory Mental Health Council on Behavioral Sciences (2000) titled *Translating Behavioral Science into Action*, strategies for enhancing contributions of behavioral science to society more broadly were proposed. In this report, translational research is defined as "research designed to address how basic behavioral processes inform the diagnosis, prevention, treatment, and delivery of services for mental illness, and, conversely, how knowledge of mental illness increases our understanding of basic behavioral processes" (p. iii). Research examining basic biological processes, as in genetic and neuroscience investigations on mental illness, also can be translated into preventive interventions and treatment initiatives (Cicchetti & Gunnar, 2008, 2009; Cicchetti & Thomas, 2008). The formulation of translational research in the behavioral and biological sciences is in direct accord with three of the key tenets of a developmental psychopathology perspective—namely, the reciprocal interplay between basic and applied research, the interplace between normal and abnormal development, and a multiple-levels of analysis approach (Cicchetti & Toth, 2006).

Why, then, we may rightly ask, have there been roadblocks erected between basic research and its application to the development of interventions and to the formulation and enactment of policies of social import? Shonkoff (2000) proffered an enlightening perspective on this issue. In commenting on the formidable obstacles involved with the translation of academic knowledge to the social policy and practice arenas, Shonkoff (2000) described the "cultural" differences that accompany each of these domains. He argued that scientists are trained to pose questions and to be guided by fact, whereas policy makers are governed by political and economic forces that emanate from society. Service providers are more akin to policy makers in needing to "act" before all of the data are in, so to speak. In reflecting on the tension among these groups, Shonkoff (2000) stated: "Science is focused on what we do not know. Social policy and the delivery of health and human services are focused on what we should do." (p. 182). Shonkoff concluded that a commitment to "cross-cultural" translation among these three groups provides a mechanism for reconciling these differences and increasing the utilization of knowledge to improve the lives of children and families.

To reduce the gap between basic and applied research, researchers who are receptive to approaches that may go beyond the boundaries and "comfort zones" of their areas of expertise are needed. Clearly, translational research is necessary to impart more scientific knowledge of genetic, neurobiological, cognitive, social–cognitive, and socioemotional processes to the understanding and treatment of mental disorders. Similarly, it is important that basic research be guided by recognition that, ultimately, such research must have a clear and demonstrable impact on clinical problems that emerge across the life span. Rather than advocating an all-or-none approach, the conduct of translational research involves a process with various steps taken along the way. There must be a recognition and agreement that basic research needs to be conceived within a conceptual framework that understands the goal of informing future application. Such a perspective does not dictate that only research directed at treatment is appropriate (Gunnar & Cicchetti, 2009). Rather, sciences have exerted, and will continue to exert, major impacts on clinical practice. Before appropriate interventions can be developed and evaluated, there must be a clear understanding of the mechanisms and processes that initiate and maintain the developmental pathways to disease. Moreover, the discovery of the processes that contribute to high-risk populations averting mental disorder can be informative in guiding translational research and treatment development (Luthar & Cicchetti, 2000). If basic research conducted on individuals who are at high risk for, or who possess one or more, mental disorders is designed with clinical and policy questions at the forefront, rather than as a post hoc afterthought, then a true research informed practice and policy agenda would be achieved that could benefit the welfare of persons suffering from mental disorders and their families.

Prevention and Intervention

The preeminent objective of the field of prevention science is to intervene in the course of development to reduce or eliminate the emergence of maladaptation and mental disorder, as well as to promote resilient adaptation in individuals at high risk for psychopathology (Cicchetti & Hinshaw, 2002; Ialongo et al., 2006; Luthar & Cicchetti, 2000). To attain this important goal, it is critical that prevention scientists possess a complex, multilevel understanding of the course of normality to formulate an in-depth portrayal of how deviations in normal developmental processes can eventuate in maladaptation and mental disorder. Because of its focus on the interplay between the study of normal and abnormal development, the discipline of developmental psychopathology is well poised to provide the theoretical foundation for prevention and intervention initiatives (IOM, 1994).

From a developmental psychopathology perspective, maladaptation and mental disorder are viewed as evolving from progressive liabilities in the organization of biological and psychological systems, resulting in the undermining of the individual's efforts to adapt effectively to stressful and adverse experience (Cicchetti & Tucker, 1994; Gunnar, 2003; Gunnar & Vazquez, 2006). Developmentally informed prevention scientists are cognizant that there are multiple pathways to mental disorder and dysfunction and that diverse causal processes are likely operative for different individuals. Moreover, prevention researchers understand that a variety of maladaptive and adaptive outcomes will occur despite a common early liability or risk condition (Cicchetti & Rogosch, 1996b).

Developmental psychopathologists believe that efforts to prevent the emergence of psychopathology or to ameliorate its effects also can be informative for understanding processes involved in psychopathological development (Cicchetti & Hinshaw, 2002; Hinshaw, 2002; Kellam & Rebok, 1992). For example, if the course of development is altered as a result of the implementation of randomized control prevention trials (RCTs) and the risk for negative outcomes is reduced, then prevention research helps to specify processes that may be involved in the emergence of psychopathology or other maladaptive developmental outcomes. As a consequence, RCTs can be conceptualized as true experiments in modifying the developmental course, thereby providing insight into the etiology and pathogenesis of disordered outcomes (Cicchetti & Hinshaw, 2002; Howe, Reiss, & Yuh, 2002). Thus, prevention research not only leads to support or lack of support for theoretical formulations accounting for the development of psychopathology but can also contribute to the knowledge base of strategies that can be implemented to reduce psychopathology and promote positive adaptation.

One example of such a preventive strategy involved an RCT that was directed toward the offspring of mothers with MDD (Toth, Rogosch, Manly, & Cicchetti, 2006). The development of insecure attachment relationships in the offspring of mothers with MDD may initiate a negative trajectory that leads to future psychopathology (Cicchetti & Toth, 1995, 1998; Toth, Rogosch, Sturge-Apple, & Cicchetti, 2009). Therefore, the provision of theoretically guided interventions designed to promote secure attachment is of paramount importance and may ultimately prevent the emergence of future depression. In an intervention designed to promote secure attachment and to prevent insecure attachment relationships in toddlers of mothers with MDD, dyads were randomized to toddler–parent psychotherapy (i.e., depressed intervention [DI] group) or to a treatment-as-usual (i.e., depressed control [DC]) group.

At baseline (age 18 months), higher rates of insecure attachment were present in toddlers in both the DI and DC groups than in a normal comparison group (NC) of toddlers whose parents had no history of present or past Axis I (American Psychiatric Association, 1994) mental disorder. At postintervention at age 36 months, insecure attachment continued to predominate in the DC group. In contrast, the rate of secure attachment had increased substantially in the DI group and was significantly higher than that for the DC group. There were no differences between the DI and the NC group in attachment security at the conclusion of the intervention (Toth et al., 2006). These results demonstrate the efficacy of toddler–parent psychotherapy in fostering secure attachment relationships in offspring of clinically depressed mothers and highlight how preventive strategies that are implemented in at-risk groups of children during the early years of life may ultimately prevent or reduce the emergence of depression during childhood or adolescence.

Comparisons of treated individuals to normative groups on diverse aspects of functioning provide a stringent test of treatment efficacy beyond symptom remission, and knowledge of normal variation on various indicators of adaptation is vital for informing such evaluations (Cicchetti, Rogosch, & Toth, 2006; Toth et al., 2006). Knowledge of developmental norms, appreciation of how developmental level may vary within the same age group, sensitivity to the changing meaning that problems have at different developmental levels, attention to the effects of developmental transitions and reorganizations, and understanding of the factors that are essential features to incorporate into the design and implementation of preventive interventions all may serve to enhance the potential for optimal intervention efficacy (Cicchetti & Toth, 1992; Coie et al., 1993; IOM, 1994; Noam, 1992; Toth & Cicchetti, 1999; Weisz & Hawley, 2002).

At present, the theories, experimental designs, and measurement batteries that undergird most randomized preventive trial interventions, especially those conducted with children and adolescents, have been dominated by the assessment of processes at the psychosocial and behavioral levels of analysis (Cicchetti & Gunnar, 2008; Ialongo et al., 2006). Although predominantly nondevelopmental in nature, a number of preventive interventions conducted with adult patients who have mental disorders have begun to incorporate biological measurements into their evaluation of treatment efficacy (see, e.g., Baxter et al., 1992; Brody et al., 2001; Felmingham et al., 2007; Goldapple et al., 2004; Martin, Martin, Rai, Richardson, Royall, & Eng, 2001; Paquette et al., 2003; Schwartz, Stoessel, Baxter, Martin, & Phelps, 1996). In contrast, preventive interventions conducted with children and adolescents have paid minimal attention to neurobiological and physiological systems in their evaluations of treatment efficacy (Cicchetti & Gunnar, 2008; for exceptions, see Bakermans-Kranenberg, van IJzendoorn, Pijlman, Mesman, & Juffer, 2007; Dozier, Albus, Fisher, & Sepulveda, 2002; Fisher, Gunnar, Dozier, Bruce, & Pears, 2006).

The dearth of attention to biological processes in the evaluation of preventive interventions with children and adolescents may partly stem from a tradition in developmental psychology of measuring biological processes as indices of heritable, constitutional individual differences reflecting the neurobiological bases of temperament (e.g., Kagan, Reznick, & Snidman, 1988; Schmidt & Fox, 1998). This tradition encourages beliefs that biological processes are not malleable or are more refractory to positive change as a result of experience. Because there are bidirectional relations between different levels of psychological and biological organization, it is essential to recognize that experience also influences biology (Cicchetti & Tucker, 1994; Eisenberg, 1995; Gunnar, 2003; Gunnar & Quevedo, 2007). Evidence for neurobiological reorganization in response to alterations in the environment may be less apparent in normative populations in which there likely is greater stability in supportive milieus, although even here there is increasing evidence that variations in the range of typical caregiving are associated over time with variations in neurobiological activity (e.g., Hane & Fox, 2006). Nonetheless, investigations of individuals reared in extreme environments, such as those who have been maltreated or who have resided in an institution, as well as examinations of persons with mental disorder, should enable us to isolate more clearly the components of these diverse systems, thereby shedding light on the bidirectional effects of experience and neurobiology.

Although adversity and trauma are believed to exert deleterious effects on biological systems (Cicchetti, 2002; Cicchetti & Tucker, 1994; DeBellis, 2001; Gunnar & Vazquez, 2006), one of the major challenges in identifying biological targets for intervention is the nonexperimental nature of nearly all of our data on the biological impact of trauma and adversity in human development. Although we may observe differences in neurobiological activity between children who have and have not been exposed to traumatic events, we can neither randomly assign children to trauma nor do we have preexposure data that would allow assessment of trauma impact. Thus, we are left with correlates of trauma exposure that, instead of reflecting the impact of exposure to adversity or trauma, may potentially reflect preexisting differences that predispose children to heightened risk of exposure to adverse conditions or vulnerability in the face of such conditions. We face a different but related problem in isolating neurobiological targets in studies of mental disorder in children and adolescents. Specifically, although we may identify neurobiological correlates of different disorders, we do not know whether these reflect processes that affect core features of the disorder. Thus, it is not always clear whether changes in these biological correlates of the disorder over the course of an intervention will improve functions core to the disorder.

However, although these challenges may seem daunting, they provide a strong impetus for including biological measures in preventive interventions. Although random assignment to adversity and trauma are not possible, random assignment to intervention is. If biological systems recover in response to the intervention, then this provides support for arguments that the systems under study are sensitive to environmental input during development (Cicchetti & Curtis, 2006). Furthermore, if randomized interventions alter neurobiological systems associated with disorders and it can be shown that they mediate changes in psychosocial and behavioral functioning, then this fosters a better understanding of the neurobiological bases of the disorder (Cicchetti, 2002). Moreover, preventive interventions may contribute to recovery or repair of biological sequelae in ways that have only begun to be understood. Improved comprehension of the neurobiological processes that increase risk of maladaptive development may also suggest novel targets for preventive intervention. Thus, it is important for prevention scientists to investigate the means by which changes in experience and psychological functioning resulting from preventive interventions may modify biological processes. Nevertheless, in the absence of theories about the nature of the effects that would be expected in a multilevel intervention, a multisystems approach to the design and evaluation of a RCT is not likely to provide clear answers (Gunnar, Fisher, & The Early Experience, Stress, and Prevention Science Network, 2006).

The incorporation of biological measures into the design and evaluation of these RCT preventive interventions will enable prevention scientists to examine the development of maladaptation, psychopathology, and resilience in their full complexity. Methodologically sound prevention science that incorporates a theoretically informed and guided multiple levels of analysis perspective will provide a unique lens through which the processes responsible for the development, maintenance, and modification of both typical and atypical functional outcomes can be discerned (Cicchetti & Hinshaw, 2002).

Translational research and multiple-levels-of-analysis approaches have been increasingly implemented in the field of developmental psychopathology (Cicchetti & Toth, 2006; Gunnar & Cicchetti, 2009; Masten, 2007). Collaborative interdisciplinary preventive interventions between researchers and clinicians that take into account multiple levels of influence will also help to reduce the schisms that have long existed between science and practice. The incorporation of an interdisciplinary, multiple-level perspective will enable prevention scientists to derive a more precise and comprehensive understanding of the mediators and moderators underlying successful and unsuccessful intervention outcomes.

Now that it has been demonstrated in animal studies that experience can exert impacts on the microstructure and biochemistry of the brain (e.g., Meaney & Szyf, 2005), a vital role for continuing neural plasticity throughout epigenesis in contributing to the recovery from various forms of maladaptation and mental disorder may be suggested (Cicchetti & Curtis, 2006). Thus, the time has come increasingly to conduct interventions that not only assess behavioral changes but that also investigate whether abnormal neurobiological structures, functions, and organizations are modifiable or are refractory to therapeutic alteration. There is growing evidence in the animal literature that efficacious interventions modify not only maladaptive behavior but also the cellular and physiological correlates of behavior (D. Kandel, 1979; 1999; Nelson, 2000; Nowakowski & Bates, 1999). Successful preventive interventions may alter behavior and physiology by producing alterations in gene expression that create a new structural reorganization in the brain (E. R. Kandel, 1999). These data provide biologically plausible hypotheses about how effective interventions in children, adolescents, and adults function to affect development. Indeed, it seems highly likely that the efficacy of any preventive intervention ultimately depends on the ability of the nervous system, at the cellular, metabolic, or anatomical level, to be modified by experience.

Neural plasticity has predominantly been thought of as reorganization within systems of the central nervous system (CNS), evidenced by changes in anatomy, neurochemistry, or metabolism. The neuroplastic changes that occur are often dramatic, and can include observable changes in the neural substrate that are translated into changes at the behavioral level. Such changes that are the hallmarks of plasticity can take place on one or more levels of analysis, including molecular, cellular, neurochemical, and neuroanatomical, as well as at the level of brain systems (Cicchetti & Curtis, 2006). The assumption underlying the concept of neural plasticity is that such modification is adaptive for the ongoing survival and optimal functioning of the organism (Hebb, 1949; Huttenlocher, 2002; Kempermann, 2005). Plasticity is an inherent property of the central nervous system (CNS; Kempermann, van Praag, & Gage, 2000), and it is thought that plasticity is one of the defining mechanisms of the evolutionary success of the human species (Hyman & Nestler, 1993).

However, plasticity cuts both ways (Nelson & Carver, 1998). Neuroplastic adaptations that improve survival in some contexts may impair functioning in others or may come at a cost to the organism (McEwen, 2001). Plasticity is also the hallmark of the developing nervous system. Critical or sensitive periods exist during which plasticity is heightened in particular neural systems and following which these systems become less open to change. One important goal of preventive intervention work is to identify periods of development when a specific intervention may be more efficacious so that the intervention can be targeted to that period. One hope of preventive intervention work that includes measures of neural activity is to better identify sensitive periods for intervention (Zeanah et al., 2003).

In implementing studies of neurobiological functioning into work on preventive interventions, it is likely that researchers will need to grapple with many of the same challenges faced by researchers studying brain–behavior and physiology–behavior relations in typically developing children. One of the most challenging issues for the prevention researcher will be dealing with the low correlation, at times, between physiological and behavioral assessments. For measures of autonomic activity and hormones, low correlations with behavior may reflect, in part, the fact that the measure is biologically distant from the neurobiology of interest. That is, brain activity may be what the researcher is most interested in assessing, and the biological measure is a reflection, albeit dim, of activity in the CNS. However, the problem of low association is also seen when the researcher collects more proximal measures of brain activity (e.g., event-related potentials [ERPs], electroencephalograms [EEGs], and functional magnetic resonance imaging [fMRI]). Here the assumption is that the brain measures may be more sensitive than the behavioral measures or the behavioral measure reflects the operation of multiple systems, of which the neural activity under study composes only a part. In some instances, however, it may be that the biological measure may precede changes on the behavioral level (see, e.g., Fox, Henderson, Rubin, Calkins, & Schmidt, 2001), or the neurobiological assessment may be more sensitive than the behavioral assessment (see, e.g., Bauer, Wiebe, Carver, Waters, & Nelson, 2003).

Given these challenges, we may need to be circumspect in heralding the clarity of insight that adding physiological and neurobiological measures into preventive intervention will provide. As in other studies of brain–behavior and physiology–behavior relations, we can anticipate a period of decreased clarity before we come to understand what these measures are telling us. In addition, in instances in which the neurobiological changes may be sensitive to changes that contribute to processes supporting reorganization of behavior, we may find that preventive intervention studies with multiple assessments and longer time windows will be more informative than interventions that assess physiological and behavioral changes concurrently. The prevention of maladaptation and mental disorder requires an in-depth knowledge of the dynamic relations among risk and protective factors and typical and atypical developmental processes. Clearly, the results of randomized prevention trials will be informative to practitioners. Nonetheless, it is essential that prevention scientists conceptualize, design, and evaluate prevention trials in such a way that also enables their results to enhance the understanding of development and the pathways contributing to intervention efficacy at multiple levels of influence.

Determining the multiple levels at which change is engendered through randomized prevention trials will provide more insight into the mechanisms of change, the extent to which neural plasticity may be promoted, and the interrelations between biological and psychological processes in maladaptation, psychopathology, and resilience (Cicchetti & Curtis, 2006; Nelson, 2000). Furthermore, preventive interventions with the most in-depth empirical support, based on integrative multilevel theories of normality, psychopathology, and resilience, can be implemented in effectiveness trials in community or real-world settings to reach the broadest number of people and prevent, or alleviate, suffering from mental disorders (Toth, Manly, & Nilsen, in 2008).

CHILD MALTREATMENT: A MULTILEVEL PERSPECTIVE

This section focuses on child maltreatment as an illustration of how theory and research in the area of normal development can contribute to elucidating knowledge of the etiology, course, sequelae, and treatment of high-risk conditions and mental disorders. Moreover, research on child maltreatment can reciprocally inform normal developmental theory. Maltreatment represents perhaps the most studied high-risk condition to date from a classic developmental psychopathology perspective. Consequently, because much research on maltreatment is paradigmatic of a developmental psychopathology perspective, it is presented in some detail herein. This section on child maltreatment addresses many of the principles of developmental psychopathology delineated earlier in this chapter. Because research on the developmental sequelae of child maltreatment has focused predominantly on children and to a lesser degree on adolescents, future research on abuse and neglect must continue to follow-up participants longitudinally into adulthood to be fully congruent with the goal of developmental psychopathology to be a life-span science.

The notion of an average expectable environment for promoting normal development proposes that there are species-specific ranges of environmental conditions that elicit normative developmental processes (Hartman, 1958). Humans, like all other species, develop within a "normal range" when presented with such an average expectable environment (Dobzhansky, 1972; Gottesman, 1963). For infants, the expectable environment includes protective, nurturant caregivers and a larger social group to which the child will be socialized, whereas for older children, the normative environment includes a supportive family, a peer group, and continued opportunities for exploration and mastery of the environment. Variations within this range of environments afford opportunities for individuals to dynamically engage in the construction of their own experiences (Scarr & McCartney, 1983). When environments fall outside the expectable range, normal development is impeded.

Since the late 1990s, our understanding of the role of the environment and its interaction with genes has been further clarified, whereby reciprocal coactions between the environment and the individual have resulted in differential expression of genetic material (Cicchetti, 2002; Eisenberg, 1995; E. R. Kandel, 1998, 1999). Environmental conditions may interact with an individual's genetic makeup to alter processes such as the timing of the initiation of transcription and translation for a specific gene, the duration for which it does so, or whether the gene will ultimately be expressed.

In typical development, the component developmental systems may be so well integrated that it is difficult to determine how normal functioning is dependent on this integration (Cicchetti & Sroufe, 1976). From a systems perspective, the environment also exists as a component of the developmental system. Thus, when the conditions of an average expectable environment are available, the manner in which its components interact is also challenging to identify.

Child maltreatment represents a severe dysfunction in parenting, as well as a substantial disturbance in parent–child relationships, that may result in serious child maladaptation and aberrant development across the life span. Child maltreatment may represent the greatest failure of the caregiving environment to provide opportunities for normal development. By definition, maltreating parents are at best an aberration of the supportive, nurturant adults that are expected by the organism in the evolutionary contexts of species-typical development. Moreover, from the perspective of a systems view of development, maltreatment experiences may provide serious challenges to the species-typical organism–environment "coactions" that play important roles in the emergence and timing of normal developmental change.

In contrast to what is anticipated in response to an average expectable environment, the social, biological, and psychological conditions that are associated with maltreatment set in motion a probabilistic path of epigenesis for maltreated children that is characterized by an increased likelihood of failure and disruption in the successful resolution of major stage-salient issues of development, resulting in grave implications for functioning across the life span. These repeated developmental disruptions create a profile of relatively enduring vulnerability factors that increase the probability of the emergence of maladaptation and psychopathology as negative transactions between the child and the environment continue over developmental time.

Research on child maltreatment has an urgency characteristic of all problems of great social concern. Writing over a quarter of a century ago, Aber and Cicchetti (1984) emphasized the criticality of conducting studies on the developmental sequelae of maltreatment and asserted that such investigations could serve to enhance the quality of clinical, legal, and policy-making decisions for abused and neglected children. Aber and Cicchetti (1984) further stated that child welfare issues, such as the effect of removing a child coercively from the home, the development of specific services to meet the psychological needs of maltreated children, and the evaluation of these services would benefit from a more solid and sophisticated database on the developmental consequences of child abuse and neglect. Aber and Cicchetti (1984) cautioned that "without rigor in design and method…myth will be put forward in place of knowledge as a guide to social action" (pp. 196–197).

Issues of Definition

Despite widespread agreement that child maltreatment is a serious societal problem, placing children's welfare and normal development in jeopardy, there has been a long history of discordance among researchers, lawmakers, and clinicians on what constitutes maltreatment and how it should be defined (Aber & Zigler, 1981; Barnett, Manly, & Cicchetti, 1993; Besharov, 1981; Cicchetti & Manly, 2001; Cicchetti & Rizley, 1981; Emery, 1989; Juvenile Justice Standards Project, 1977). Contributing to the lack of consensus is a debate regarding whether it is realistic to expect professionals from various domains to agree on a single definitional approach given the widespread differences between fields in the purpose and utilization of such a definition. For example, the medical-diagnostic definition of maltreatment revolves around the individual abuse (Aber & Zigler, 1981) and focuses on overt signs of maltreatment. This approach tends to highlight physical abuse while minimizing emotional maltreatment. The legal definition focuses on demonstrable physical and emotional harm to children, particularly that which would be useful as evidence for prosecution (Juvenile Justice Standards Project, 1977). In contrast, parental acts and society's role in perpetuating maltreatment are important for the sociological definition and evidence of environmental and familial contributors to the occurrence of maltreatment are necessary elements of the ecological approach (Cicchetti & Lynch, 1993; Cicchetti, Toth, & Maughan, 2000). Many researchers have asserted that the definition of maltreatment should focus on specific acts that endanger the child in some way (Barnett, Manly, & Cicchetti, 1991; Barnett et al., 1993; Cicchetti & Barnett, 1991; Zuravin, 1991). This type of definition would allow researchers to concentrate on the identifiable behaviors that compromise the child's maladaptive caretaking environment.

Even within the domain of research, however, a number of complexities contribute to the lack of consensus regarding the definition of maltreatment employed by various investigators, making comparability across studies difficult to achieve (Barnett et al., 1993). First, maltreatment is largely influenced by legal matters because it is identified and defined by social service systems rather than by researchers or mental health professionals. Furthermore, there is not a clear standard regarding the distinction between acceptable parental disciplinary practices and maltreatment (M. H. Black & Dubowitz, 1999; Cicchetti & Lynch, 1995); there is a lack of agreement on whether child maltreatment should be defined on the basis of the actions of the perpetrator, the effects on the child, or a combination of the two (Barnett et al., 1991, 1993); and there is debate as to whether parental intent should be considered. These issues raise additional methodological concerns because it is a greater challenge to measure parental intent than parental behavior. Moreover, linking maltreatment to child outcome leads to difficulty in separating child maltreatment from its subsequent sequelae (Barnett et al., 1991; Cicchetti & Manly, 2001; McGee & Wolfe, 1991a, 1991b).

On the basis of the wide range of challenges faced by maltreatment researchers, one clearly cannot expect all who study maltreatment to use the same methodology for operationalizing child abuse and neglect. However, all approaches must be derived from clear operational definitions of maltreatment such that replication may be possible across investigations (Cicchetti & Manly, 2001; Manly, 2005). Despite the challenges facing maltreatment researchers, four general categories of child maltreatment have been distinguished from one another and are widely accepted:

1. *Sexual abuse* refers to sexual contact or attempted sexual contact between a caregiver or other responsible adult and a child, for the purposes of the caregiver's sexual gratification or financial benefit.
2. *Physical abuse* refers to injuries that have been inflicted on a child by nonaccidental means.
3. *Neglect* refers to failure to provide minimum standards of care as well as adequate supervision.
4. *Emotional maltreatment* refers to persistent and extreme thwarting of a child's basic emotional needs.

Additionally, McGee and Wolfe (1991b) offered a slightly different conceptualization for emotional maltreatment, which they called psychological maltreatment and encompasses both psychologically abusive and psychologically neglectful experiences. Although each of these subtypes represents distinct deviations from the average expectable caregiving environment, it is well documented that they rarely occur in isolation from each other (Cicchetti & Manly, 2001). In actuality, the majority of maltreated children experience more than one subtype of maltreatment, presenting significant challenges for clinicians and researchers who strive to understand the unique effects of each type of maltreatment experience on development.

Responding to the need for a detailed classification system for maltreatment, Cicchetti and Barnett (1991b; see also Barnett et al., 1993) developed a multidimensional nosological system for categorizing children's maltreatment histories. In recognition of the need to include developmental considerations in assessing maltreatment, the Maltreatment Classification System (Barnett et al., 1993) not only provides operational definitions of maltreatment subtypes, with inclusion and exclusion criteria and exemplars of each of the five levels of severity for each subtype, but also includes measurement of the onset, frequency, and chronicity of each subtype, the developmental period(s) during which each subtype occurred, the severity of each subtype, and the perpetrator(s) of each subtype. This comprehensive assessment across and within dimensions of maltreatment has allowed for a more detailed understanding of the maladaptive developmental pathways associated with children's maltreatment experiences (Cicchetti & Manly, 2001; Cicchetti et al., 2010; Manly, Cicchetti, & Barnett, 1994; Manly, Kim, Rogosch, & Cicchetti, 2001).

Etiology

Cicchetti and Lynch (1993) proposed an ecological–transactional model of child maltreatment. By incorporating the ideas of the average expectable environment and probabilistic epigenesis into a broad integrative framework, this model explains how processes at each level of the ecology exert reciprocal influences on each other and shape the course of child development (Cicchetti & Lynch, 1993). As such, potentiating and compensatory risk factors associated with maltreatment are present at each level of the ecology and can influence processes in the surrounding environmental levels. These dynamic transactions, which operate both horizontally and vertically throughout the levels of ecology, determine the amount of risk for maltreatment that an individual faces at any given time (see Figure 14.1). The levels of ecology most proximal to the child have the most direct impact on child development relative to the more distally located macrosystem. Although characterized by an overall pattern in which risk factors outweigh protective factors, there are infinite permutations of these risk variables across and within each level of the ecology, providing multiple pathways to the occurrence of maltreatment and its developmental sequelae.

Ultimately, it is the child's own ontogenic processes, as manifested by the particular developmental pathway that individuals engage in, that culminate in eventual adaptation or maladaptation. The challenges or supports presented to children by the family (i.e., microsystem), community (i.e., exosystem), society (i.e., macrosystem), and cross-system interactions (i.e., mesosystem) contribute to these ontogenic processes; however, children also play an active role in their own development as they respond to these influences and engage in the resolution of stage-salient developmental issues.

The ecological–transactional model possesses significant implications for how maltreatment affects development. An increased presence of risk factors associated with the occurrence of maltreatment at any or at all ecological levels represents a deviation from the conditions that promote normal development. As such, children who have been maltreated have a greater likelihood of manifesting negative developmental outcomes and psychopathology (Cicchetti & Lynch, 1995). Conversely, an ecological–transactional model also can explain the fact that not all children who have been maltreated are similarly affected and, in fact, that despite

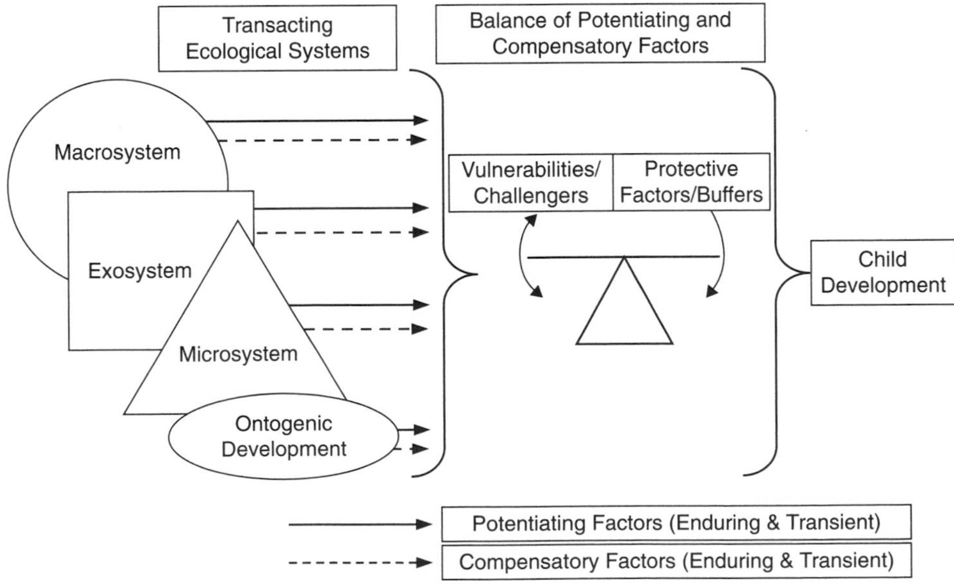

Figure 14.1 An ecological-transactional model of the effects of child maltreatment

maltreatment some children do not succumb to negative developmental consequences. The most critical contributor to eventual competence or incompetence is the negotiation of the central tasks of each developmental period.

An ecological–transactional perspective views child development as a progressive sequence of age- and stage-appropriate tasks in which successful resolution of tasks at each developmental level must be coordinated and integrated with the environment, as well as with subsequently emerging issues across the life span (Cicchetti & Lynch, 1993). These tasks include the development of emotion regulation, the formation of attachment relationships, the development of an autonomous self, representational development, the formation of peer relationships, adaptation to school, psychological autonomy, forming close relationships within and across gender, and deriving a cohesive sense of self-identity (Cicchetti & Rogosch, 2002; Masten & Coatsworth, 1998). Stage-salient tasks are hierarchically organized; each new task builds on and is influenced by the resolution of previous developmental tasks. Poor resolution of stage-salient issues may contribute to maladaptation over time because prior history influences the selection, engagement, and interpretation of subsequent experience; however, the current context is in constant transaction with environmental supports (Sroufe, Carlson, Levy, & Egeland, 1999). Thus, ontogenic development is a lifelong dynamic task, and consistent with Gottlieb's (1991, 1992) notions of probabilistic epigenesis, individuals are continually affected by new biological and psychological experiences, leaving developmental pathways susceptible to modification throughout the life span (Cicchetti & Lynch, 1995; Cicchetti & Tucker, 1994).

The ecological–transactional model of child maltreatment (Cicchetti & Lynch, 1993) has remained the predominant etiological model in the field, albeit with some modifications as we have come to a better understanding of ontogenic development in neurobiological as well as psychological realms. This model is used in this section as a heuristic for reviewing the literature on the consequences of child maltreatment for individual developmental and for addressing the question of how aberrant experiences exert have an impact on biological and psychological processes.

How Early Adverse Experiences Affect Brain Development and Function: Illustration from the Study of Child Maltreatment

Although brain development is guided and controlled to some extent by genetic information (Rakic, 1988a, 1988b), a not insignificant portion of brain structuration and neural patterning is thought to occur through interaction with the environment (Greenough et al., 1987; O'Leary, 1989). Changes in the internal and external environment may lead to improvements in the ability of the individual to grapple with developmental challenges, including the experience of significant adversity. Consequently, neural plasticity may be possible throughout the life span as a result of adaptive self-organization (Cicchetti & Tucker, 1994). Moreover, because the mechanisms of plasticity cause the brain's anatomical differentiation to be dependent on stimulation from the environment, it is now clear that the cytoarchitecture of the cerebral cortex is shaped by input from the social environment. Because the human cerebral cortex is only diffusely structured by the genetic plan, and because the eventual differentiation of the cortex is highly reactive to the individual's active coping and "meaning making" in a particular environment, it is likely that both abnormal and resilient outcomes following the experience of significant adversity would encompass a diverse range of cortical network anatomies and personalities (cf. Cicchetti & Tucker, 1994). As Luu and Tucker (1996) articulated: "To understand neuropsychological development is to confront the fact that the brain is mutable, such that its structural organization reflects the history of the organism. Moreover, this structure reflects both what is most important to the organism and what the organism is capable of at that particular time" (p. 297). Cortical development and organization should no longer be viewed as passive processes that depend solely on genetics and environmental input. Development—psychological and biological—is more than nature–nurture interaction. Thus, corticogenesis should be conceived as processes of self-organization guided by self-regulatory mechanisms (Cicchetti & Tucker, 1994).

J. Black and colleagues (1998) described brain development as a complex scaffolding of three types of neural processes: gene-driven, experience-expectant, and experience-dependent. *Gene-driven processes*, thought to be relatively impervious or insensitive to experience to protect the development of the brain, guide the migration of neurons, target many of their synaptic connections, and determine their differentiated function (Rakic, 1988a, 1988b; Sidman & Rakic, 1973).

Experience-expectant processes occur during periods when the brain is primed to receive particular classes of information from the environment and correspond roughly to critical or "sensitive" periods (Greenough et al., 1987). During experience-expectant periods, which take place in early age-locked sensory-system development, the brain builds an overabundance of synapses, and this is followed by a pruning process that appears to be initiated by competitive interactions between neuronal connections (Bruer, 1999; Courchesne et al., 1994; Edelman, 1987). Specifically, inactive neural connections are eliminated, and synapses that are most actively mediated by experience are selectively maintained (Courchesne et al., 1994; Edelman, 1987; Greenough et al., 1987). Experience-expectant brain plasticity is usually embedded in a developmental program, and it requires appropriate timing and quality of the information stored for brain development to be normal. Abnormal experience or deprivation during experience-expectant development may exert enduring deleterious effects on neurobiological and behavioral epigenesis (J. Black et al., 1998).

In later development, synaptogenesis seems to be generated in response to events that provide information to be encoded in the nervous system. This *experience-dependent* synapse formation involves the brain's adaptation to information that is unique to the individual (Greenough et al., 1987). Because all individuals encounter distinctive environments, each brain is modified in a singular fashion. Experience-dependent synaptogenesis is localized to the brain regions involved in processing information arising from the event experienced by the individual. Unlike experience-expectant processes, experience-dependent processes do not take place within a stringent temporal interval because the timing or nature of experience that the individual engages or chooses cannot be entirely and dependably envisioned. An important central mechanism for experience-dependent development is the formation of new neural connections in contrast to the overproduction and pruning back of synapses often associated with experience-expectant processes (Greenough et al., 1987). Because experience-dependent processes can occur throughout the life span, social interactions, psychotherapy, and pharmacotherapy, in conjunction with individuals' self-righting tendencies, have the capacity to repair brains that are afflicted with disorders (J. Black et al., 1998; Cicchetti, 1996).

The normal brain develops from a network of few elements, infrequent interactions among elements, less stability, and less structural and functional differentiation to one of additional elements, more intricate interactions among elements, greater stability, and increased structural and functional parcellation and specialization (e.g., J. W. Brown, 1994; Cicchetti & Tucker, 1994; Courchesne et al., 1994). In this view of normal brain development, one can clearly see parallels with organismic, holistic developmental systems theory views of behavioral development. For example, Wapner and Demick (1998) conceptualize optimal development as a differentiated and hierarchically integrated person-in-environment system that possesses the characteristics of flexibility, self-mastery, and the ability to shift from one mode of person-in-environment relationship to another as required by the contextual demands of the situation, the individual's goals, and so on.

Abnormal brain development is also a dynamic, self-organizing process. Unlike the case for normal neurobiological development, the final product of abnormal brain development includes a substantial measure of misorganization. Perturbations that occur during brain development can potentiate a cascade of maturational and structural changes that eventuate in the neural system proceeding along a trajectory that deviates from that generally taken in normal neurobiological development (Cicchetti & Tucker, 1994; Courchesne et al., 1994; Nowakowski & Hayes, 1999). Early stresses, either physiological or emotional, may condition young neural networks to produce cascading effects through later development, possibly constraining the child's flexibility to adapt to challenging situations with new strategies rather that with old conceptual and behavioral prototypes. Thus, early psychological trauma may eventuate not only in emotional sensitization (A. Maughan & Cicchetti, 2002; Pollak, 2008), but also in pathological sensitization of neurophysiological reactivity (Pollak, Cicchetti, & Klorman, 1998).

Accordingly, abnormal perturbations at one stage of brain development hinder the creation of some new structures and functions, distort the form of later-emerging ones, make possible the construction of ones that normally never become manifest, or limit the elaboration and usage of structures and functions that had appeared earlier (Courchesne et al., 1994; Steingard & Coyle, 1998). Eventually, successively more complex, specialized, and stable abnormal neural network configurations and operations develop that differ greatly from antecedent ones (Courchesne et al., 1994). Abnormal competition between, and abnormal correlated activity within, undamaged as well as damaged neural networks can drive the abnormal elimination of some connections and neural elements (e.g., remote loss) and the abnormal selective stabilization of others (e.g., aberrant connections are retained or created; Courchesne et al., 1994).

Children whose gene-driven processes construct a disordered brain are likely to experience the world in a vastly different fashion than children who do not have such a genetic predisposition (J. Black et al., 1998). Genes often exert different functional roles in divergent cell types at varying developmental periods (Alberts et al., 1994; J. D. Watson, Hopkins, Roberts, Steitz, & Weiner, 1987). Accordingly, defects in such genes may trigger a cascade of changes that are not confined to a particular neural structure, functional system, or behavioral domain. Even if the subsequent experience-expectant and experience-dependent processes are unimpaired, the experience distorted by the neuropathology is not likely to be appropriately utilized (J. Black et al., 1998). Thus, children with genetically constructed abnormal brains must have their environments tailored to their specific deficits. If such environmental modifications are not introduced, then these children's subsequent experience-expectant and experience-dependent processes will manifest additional aberrations, and development will proceed on an even more maladaptive pathway.

Likewise, children endowed with normal brains may encounter a number of experiences (e.g., extreme poverty, community violence, physical abuse, sexual abuse, emotional maltreatment, and neglect) that can negatively affect developing brain structure, function, and organization and contribute to distorting these children's experiences of the world (e.g., DeBellis et al., 1999a, 1999b; Pollak et al., 1998). Children may be especially vulnerable to the effects of pathological experiences during periods of rapid creation or modification of neuronal connections (J. Black et al., 1998). Pathological experience may become part of a vicious cycle: The pathology induced in brain structure may distort the child's experience, with subsequent alterations in cognition or social interactions causing additional pathological experience and added brain pathology (Cicchetti & Tucker, 1994). Because experience-expectant and experience-dependent processes may continue to operate during psychopathological states, children who incorporate pathological experience during these processes may add neuropathological connections into their developing brains instead of functional neuronal connections (J. Black et al., 1998).

Children may be especially vulnerable to the effects of pathological experiences during periods of rapid creation or modification of neuronal connections (synapses; Black et al., 1998). Pathological experiences may become part of a reinforcing cycle because alterations in brain structure distort the child's processing of experience, with subsequent alterations in cognitive or social interactions causing additional pathological experience and added brain pathology (J. Black et al., 1998; Cicchetti & Tucker, 1994).

Adverse life experiences, exemplified by the experience of child maltreatment, are thought to affect neurobiological and psychological processes. Physiological and behavioral responses to maltreatment are expected to be interrelated and to contribute to children's making choices and responding to experiences in ways that generally produce pathological development. Because maltreated children experience the extremes of "caretaking causality" (Sameroff & Chandler, 1975), they provide one of the clearest opportunities for scientists to discover the multiple ways in which social and psychological stressors can affect biological systems. Numerous interconnected neurobiological systems are affected by the various stressors associated with child maltreatment (Cicchetti, 2002; DeBellis, 2001). Moreover, each of these neurobiological systems influences and is influenced by multiple domains of psychological and biological development. Furthermore, in keeping with the principle of multifinality, the neurobiological development of maltreated children is not affected in the same way in all individuals. Not all maltreated children exhibit anomalies in their brain structure or functioning.

Until the past several decades, scientific research conducted on child maltreatment focused almost exclusively on psychological processes and outcomes. The examination of neurobiological correlates and sequelae of child maltreatment and G×E interactions have begun to receive more emphasis from researchers.

Neuroimaging and Child Maltreatment

Magnetic resonance imaging (MRI) technology provides a noninvasive and safe methodology for examining brain morphology, physiology, and function in individuals who have experienced child maltreatment. Several MRI investigations have found reduced hippocampal volume in victims of psychological trauma with posttraumatic stress disorder (PTSD). Bremner, Krystal, Southwick, and Charney (1995) discovered that male combat veterans with PTSD evidenced decreased MRI-derived right-side hippocampal volume and that aspects of the memory deficits exhibited by the combat veterans with PTSD correlated with hippocampal volume. Gurvits and colleagues (1996) replicated the finding of reduced hippocampal volume in an MRI study of male combat veterans. In contrast to Bremner et al., they found hippocampal reduction bilaterally. In a heterogeneous sample of men and women who experienced abuse in their childhood, Bremner et al. (1997) discovered a reduction in left-side hippocampal volume compared with nonabused participants. Relatedly, M. B. Stein, Yehuda, Koverola, and Hanna (1997) found that women who reported being sexually abused in childhood showed a reduced left-side hippocampal volume compared to nonsexually traumatized women. Vythilingam and colleagues (2002) conducted an MRI investigation of a group of adult females who had a current diagnosis of MDD. Two thirds of the women with MDD had a history of child physical or sexual abuse; the other depressed women had no abuse histories. The two groups of women with MDD were compared with a group of healthy women. Depressed women who had experienced abuse in their childhood had a significantly smaller hippocampal volume than the nonabused depressed women and the women in the healthy comparison group.

In another investigation, Bremner and colleagues (2003) conducted an MRI and a positron emission tomography (PET) study with a group of women who experienced sexual abuse and PTSD in their childhood, another group of women who had experienced sexual abuse but who did not have PTSD, and a comparison group of women without sexual abuses or PTSD. Using MRI, Bremner et al. found that women who had been sexually abused had significantly smaller hippocampi than either women who had been sexually abused without PTSD or women who were without sexual abuse histories or PTSD. Additionally, the women with sexual abuse and PTSD showed a failure of left hippocampal activation during a verbal memory task that was measured by PET. This finding remained significant after adjusting for hippocampal atrophy.

In an fMRI study, Anderson, Teicher, Polcari, and Renshaw (2002) performed steady-state fMRI (T2 relaxometry) to assess resting blood flow in the cerebellar vermis. Adults who had been sexually abused in childhood manifested higher T2 relaxation times (T2-RT) than controls. Elevated T2-RT measures have been shown to be associated with decreased blood volume and neuronal activity. Anderson et al. interpreted the elevated T2-RT found in the cerebellar vermis of these adults who had experienced sexual abuse as indicative of a possible pathway from early abuse → functional deficits in the cerebellar vermis → reduced neuronal activity → decreased blood volume.

Over the course of the past two decades, neuroimaging studies have been conducted with maltreated children and adolescents. DeBellis, Keshavan, and colleagues (1999) conducted an in-depth whole-brain volumetric analysis of a group of hospitalized maltreated children and adolescents with PTSD and a group of medically and psychiatrically well nonmaltreated comparison subjects. In keeping with the literature on child maltreatment, most of the participants had experienced multiple types of maltreatment. Moreover, in addition to PTSD, most of the children and adolescents who were maltreated had comorbid mental disorders. These included MDD, dysthymia, oppositional defiant disorder, and ADHD. Of particular importance, given that the hippocampus is susceptible to the harmful effects of chronic alcohol abuse, substance and alcohol abuse were rare in the DeBellis, Keshavan, et al. (1999) study.

In contrast to the findings of the investigations of adults who had childhood histories of abuse reviewed above, DeBellis, Keshavan, et al. (1999) did not find a decrease in hippocampal volume in the group of maltreated children and adolescents with PTSD. Moreover, DeBellis, Hall, Boring, Frustaci, and Moritz (2001) examined hippocampal volumes longitudinally to determine whether a history of childhood maltreatment and PTSD alter the growth of the hippocampus during puberty. DeBellis and colleagues (2001) used MRI to scan the brains of maltreated children with PTSD and healthy nonmaltreated comparison children matched on socioeconomic status (SES) on two occasions, once when they were prepubertal and then again 2 to 3 years later during the later stages of puberty (i.e., Tanner stages IV and V). MRI was used to measure the temporal lobes, amygdala, or hippocampal volume between the group of maltreated children with PTSD and the matched group of nonmaltreated children, either at baseline or across longitudinal follow-up.

These apparent discrepant findings may be a function of the increase in volume that normatively occurs in neurobiological development during adolescence (Spear, 2000, 2003). Specifically, subcortical gray matter structures that include the hippocampus continue to develop, and these normative adolescent increases (i.e., the normal processes of brain development) may mask any effects that maltreatment and PTSD exert on the developing limbic system (e.g., amygdala, hippocampus). It is conceivable that the stress-induced hippocampal damage may not become apparent until postpubertal development has been initiated. Alternatively, because the maltreated children with PTSD in the DeBellis et al. (2001) sample were in ongoing individual or group treatment, it may be the case that these interventions may have eventuated in increased hippocampal neurogenesis, thereby contributing to the lack of statistically significant differences.

After controlling for intracranial volume and SES, DeBellis and colleagues (DeBellis, Keshavan, et al., 1999) discovered a number of other MRI-based brain structural anomalies in their sample of maltreated children and adolescents with PTSD. These included smaller intracranial volumes, cerebral volumes, and midsagittal corpus callosum areas and larger lateral ventricles than in the group of nonmaltreated comparison children and adolescents. In additional, DeBellis, Keshavan, et al. found a positive correlation of intracranial volumes with age of onset of PTSD trauma and a negative correlation with the duration of maltreatment that led to a PTSD diagnosis, suggesting that there may be sensitive periods and dose effects for stress-related alterations in brain development. Furthermore, DeBellis, Keshavan, et al. interpreted their finding that enlarged lateral ventricles in maltreated children and adolescents were correlated positively with the duration of the maltreatment experienced as suggesting that there may have been neuronal loss associated with severe stress (cf. Sapolsky, 1992).

In another investigation, DeBellis, Keshavan, Spencer, and Hall (2000) used magnetic resonance spectroscopy (MRS), a safe and novel neuroimaging methodology, to investigate the in vivo neurochemistry of neurobiological alterations in the brains of living children. DeBellis and colleagues used MRS to measure the relative concentration of N-acetylaspartate (NAA) and creatine in the anterior cingulate cortex of a small group ($n = 11$) of maltreated children and adolescents who also had PTSD and a healthy nonmaltreated comparison group ($n = 11$) matched on SES. NAA is considered to be a marker of neural integrity; moreover, decreased concentrations of NAA are associated with increased metabolism and loss of neurons (Prichard, 1996). DeBellis et al. found that maltreated children and adolescents with PTSD had lower NAA-to-creatine ratios, which are suggestive of neuronal loss in the anterior cingulate region of the medial prefrontal cortex compared to the nonmaltreated, SES-matched comparisons. The reduction of NAA to creatine, in addition to DeBellis, Keshavan, et al.'s (1999) finding of enlargement in the lateral ventricles, buttress the hypothesis that maltreatment in childhood may alter the development of cortical neurons.

Teicher and colleagues (2004) investigated the corpus callosum in children who had been abused or neglected to ascertain whether there were structural abnormalities in its regional anatomy. The corpus callosum connects the left and right hemispheres and is the major myelinated tract in the brain. Regional corpus callosum area was measured by MRI in three groups of children: abused and neglected children, children admitted for psychiatric evaluation, and healthy comparisons. Teicher et al. found that the total area of the corpus callosum of the children who had experienced abuse and neglect was smaller than that of the children evaluated for psychiatric problems and the healthy comparisons. The latter two groups of children did not differ from each other. Child neglect was associated with 15% to 18% reduction in corpus callosum regions; in contrast, reduced corpus callosum size in girls was most strongly associated with sexual abuse. These findings are congruent with the earlier assertion that negative early experiences can adversely affect neurobiological development.

In summary, the neuroimaging studies reviewed attest to the harmful impact that child maltreatment can exert on brain development and function. As important, not all maltreated children evidence the same neurobiological structural and functional anomalies. Moreover, some maltreated children appear to have normal neurobiological development despite experiencing great adversity. We do not know whether the neurobiological structural and/or functional difficulties displayed by some maltreated children are permanent or irreversible, or, if reversible, when and to what degree. Additionally, we do not possess the knowledge regarding whether some neural systems may be more plastic than other neural systems that may be more refractory to change or have a more time-limited window when neural plasticity can occur. Thus, a personal-oriented approach (Bergman & Magnusson, 1997; von Eye & Bergman, 2003), in which multiple neurobiological systems are studied within individuals over developmental time, should also be implemented in future research on the effects of maltreatment on biological, genetic, and psychological processes. In this manner, we can acquire vital information on how the neurobiological systems of maltreated children develop at different periods, as well as when such developing neural systems may be most vulnerable in different profiles of individuals who share similar aspects of neurobiological and psychological functioning and who may range from none or minimal damage to major neurobiological and psychological dysfunction.

Even in instances of long-term damage, the neurobiological and psychological consequences of maltreatment may not prove to be irreversible. Because postnatal brain structuration and neural patterning are thought to occur, in part, through interactions and transactions of the person with his or her environment, changes in the internal and external environment may lead to improvement in the ability of the individual to grapple with developmental challenges. Thus, although genetic and historical developmental factors canalize and constrain the adaptive process to some degree, it is conceivable that behavioral and neural plasticity are possible throughout the life course as a result of adaptive neural and psychological self-organization (Cicchetti, 2002; Cicchetti & Tucker, 1994; Curtis & Cicchetti, 2003). Additionally, pharmacological and behavioral–psychological interventions can be implemented to modify the structure and function of the brain and to ascertain how the structural and functional changes that are produced will change the ability of the brain to process the information it confronts during stressful situations.

Much of the scientific literature published to date on the neurobiology of child maltreatment has focused on hospitalized samples. Many of these maltreated individuals also have comorbid mental disorders, use or abuse substances and alcohol, or both (cf. DeBellis, Keshavan, et al., 1999). Moreover, maltreated children in hospitalized samples also are receiving pharmacological or psychotherapeutic interventions, or both. Although one can attempt to control for these factors statistically, their presence makes it difficult to disentangle the effects of maltreatment on brain structure and function from other competing conditions (e.g., mental illness, drug abuse, intervention) on the neurodevelopmental anomalies (or lack thereof) found in hospitalized maltreated children. It also will be essential for future research using neuroimaging technologies to examine brain structure and function in community samples of maltreated children. Neuroscientists using neuroimaging techniques to examine neurobiological structures in maltreated children must move beyond the descriptive anatomical level of the structural MRI and begin to incorporate functional MRI technology into their research armamentaria. Because the brain is a dynamic, self-organizing system that is mutable, future neuroimaging research should ascertain whether the brain structures and brain functioning of the maltreated children designated as resilient through psychological criteria (see, e.g., Cicchetti & Rogosch, 1997) differ from those of nonresilient maltreated children.

Neurobiological Functioning I: Acoustic Startle

Startle expression in humans and laboratory animals is affected by emotional factors, a connection that may be grounded in the evolutionary value of startle for immediate protection. The disturbances of anxiety and traumatization observed in childhood maltreatment (Cicchetti & Lynch, 1995), as well as the sensitivity of the startle reflex to these conditions, suggest a utility of examining startle patterns in maltreated children toward possible identification of an objective physiological marker of traumatization severity. Klorman, Cicchetti, Thatcher, and Ison (2003) investigated acoustic startle to a range of auditory intensities to identify possible abnormalities in response magnitude, onset latency, and habituation.

The acoustic startle reflex is an obligatory response to a sudden and unexpected stimulus that is marked by the cessation of ongoing behaviors and by a particular series of protective behaviors (Davis, 1984). The eyeblink is the most sensitive and consistent startle response across individuals, and this is the response that is most often measured in studies of this reflex. The startle eyeblink in humans is measured by electromyographic activity by electrodes overlying the orbicularis oculi muscle, located below each eye.

Klorman et al. (2003) examined acoustic startle to 24 randomly ordered 50-millisecond binaural white noise burst probes of 70, 85, 100, and 115 decibels while children were watching silent cartoons. Participants were maltreated and nonmaltreated children matched for age, sex, and SES (see Klorman et al., 2003). Maltreated boys' startle blinks had smaller amplitude and slower onset latency and were less affected by increasing probe loudness than were those of comparison boys. Among maltreatment subtypes, this pattern was most salient for physically abused boys. There were not enough physically abused girls to detect any potential differences from comparison children. The results for maltreated boys are consistent with those of Ornitz and Pynoos (1989) for diminished startle responses among children with PTSD. These investigators suggested that startle diminution in traumatized children may reflect cortically mediated attentional dysfunction, which affects brainstem mechanisms for startle responses.

Findings obtained from physically abused boys are consistent with those of Cicchetti and Rogosch (2001a). These investigators discovered that children who experienced physical abuse displayed a greater suppression of cortisol and significantly less variation in hypothalamic-pituitary-adrenal (HPA) axis functioning than did maltreated children who were sexually abused, emotionally abused, or neglected (cf. Susman, 2006). Although startle responsiveness and cortisol regulation are linked to separate but interconnected neurobiological systems, in both the Klorman et al. (2003) and the Cicchetti and Rogosch (2001a) investigations, physically abused children exhibited diminished physiological responses. Physically abused children are often exposed to threat and danger, so their smaller responses to startle and their suppression of cortisol may reflect allostatic load, the cumulative long-term effect of physiologic responses to stress (Davies, Sturge-Apple, Cicchetti, & Cummings, 2007; Lupien et al., 2006; McEwen & Stellar, 1993). Repetitive social challenges in a children's environment, such as those engendered by physical abuse, can cause disruptions in basic homeostatic and regulatory processes that are essential to the maintenance of optimal physical and mental health (Repetti, Taylor, & Seeman, 2002).

Neurobiological Functioning II: Neuroendocrine Regulation

Incidents of child maltreatment, such as sexual, physical, and emotional abuse, as well as neglect, may engender massive stress in vulnerable children. Acute threat and emotional distress, as is found in instances of child maltreatment, may activate the locus coeruleus, the major noradrengergic-containing nucleus in the brain, and the sympathetic nervous system (SNS), eventuating in the biological changes accompanying the "fight-or-flight" reaction (Gunnar & Vazquez, 2006; Kaufman & Charney, 2001). Stressful experiences such as child maltreatment may potentiate the increased production of corticotrophin releasing hormone (CRH) in the central amygdala and in the hypothalamus. CRH from the amygdala causes increased SNS activity, thereby promoting heightened behavioral and attentional arousal (Kaufman & Charney, 2001). CRH from the paraventricular nucleus of the hypothalamus, in concert with other hormones such as vasopressin, stimulate the production of adrenocorticotropic hormone (ACTH) in the anterior pituitary. The ACTH that is secreted into circulation selectively stimulates cells of the adrenal cortex to produce and release cortisol, a potent steroid hormone that affects nearly all organs and tissues of the body (Gunnar & Vazquez, 2006; Lopez, Akil, & Watson, 1999). Cortisol, through negative feedback inhibition on the hypothalamus, pituitary, and additional brain structures such as the hippocampus, suppresses the HPA axis, thereby bringing about restoration of basal levels of cortisol. Among its many influences, cortisol affects the central neural processes that are implicated in cognition, memory, and emotion.

The capacity to elevate cortisol in response to acute trauma is critical for survival. Brief elevations in corticosteroids following acute stressors appear to enhance the individual's ability to manage stressful experiences competently, both physiologically and behaviorally. However, chronic hyperactivity of the HPA axis (hypercortisolism) may eventuate in the accelerated loss or metabolism of hippocampal neurons, the inhibition of neurogenesis, lags in the development of myelination, abnormalities in synaptic pruning, and impaired affective and cognitive abilities (Gould et al., 1998; Sapolsky, 1992). Moreover, the elimination of glucocorticoids also can damage neurons (Gunnar & Vazquez, 2001; Heim, Ehlert, & Hellhammer, 2000). Hypocortisolism, in which individuals who are experiencing chronic stressors such as ongoing maltreatment, manifests in reduced adrenocortical secretion, reduced adrenocortical reactivity, and enhanced negative feedback inhibition of the HPA axis (Gunnar & Vazquez, 2001; Heim et al., 2000). Consequently, it is in an organism's best interests to avoid both chronic glucocorticoid hypersecretion and hyposecretion (Sapolsky, 1996).

A number of investigations have been conducted that reveal atypical physiological processes in maltreated children. Noradrenergic, dopaminergic, serotonergic, and glucocorticoid systems, which are all activated by stress, are affected by child maltreatment. For example, abnormal noradrenergic activity, as evidenced by lower urinary norepinephrine (NE), has been found in children who have been abused and neglected (Rogeness, 1991). Additionally, neglected children often exhibit lower levels of dopamine-beta-hydroxylase (DBH), an enzyme involved in the synthesis of NE, than do abused children or normal comparison participants (Rogeness & McClure, 1996). Neglected children also have lower systolic and diastolic blood pressure, both of which are functions mediated in part by the NE system.

Furthermore, several investigations have shown that girls who have experienced sexual abuse display augmented morning cortisol levels, implicating altered glucocorticoid functioning in the HPA axis. Moreover, sexually abused girls excrete significantly more of the dopamine metabolite homovanillic acid (DeBellis et al., 1994; Putnam et al., 1991). These findings, along with other in the literature, suggest that sexual abuse is associated with enduring alterations of biological stress systems.

In another study, Cicchetti and Rogosch (2001a) found substantial elevations in the morning cortisol levels of maltreated children who had been both physically and sexually abused, as well as neglected or emotionally maltreated. Moreover, many of the children in this multiple-abuse group also had cortisol levels that were elevated in both the morning and the afternoon. In contrast to the findings of the multiple-abuse group, a subgroup of children who had been physically abused showed only a marginally significant linkage with lower morning cortisol, relative to nonmaltreated children. In addition, this physically abused subgroup of children displayed a significantly smaller decrease in cortisol from morning to afternoon. This pattern suggests less diurnal variation for the physically abused group of children. Finally, no differences in patterns of cortisol regulation were obtained between the neglected and the emotionally maltreated groups of children and the comparison group of nonmaltreated children.

The divergent patterns of cortisol regulation for the varying subgroup configurations of maltreated children suggest that it is highly unlikely the brains of all children are uniformly affected by the experience of maltreatment. Not all maltreated children display dysregulation of the HPA axis. The group of children who experienced sexual and physical abuse, in combination with neglect or emotional maltreatment, exhibited patterns akin to hypercortisolism. In addition, the pattern of HPA axis functioning in children in the physically abused subgroup is suggestive of hypocortisolism (Gunnar & Vazquez, 2001).

The children in the multiple-abuse group had experienced chronic maltreatment across a range of developmental periods. This multifaceted assault on cognitive, social, emotional, and biological systems is likely to contribute to these children's expectations of continued adversity. In essence, the pervasiveness of negative experiences results in these children's construction of their worlds as marked by fear and hypersensitivity to future maltreatment.

The development of behavior problems and psychopathology that often accompany stress-induced hyper- and hypocortisolism are partially a consequence of hormonal effects on gene expression (Cicchetti & Rogosch, 2001b; Cicchetti & Walker, 2001). Investigations have documented the role of stress hormones, such as cortisol, in the expression of genes (C. Watson & Gametchu, 1999). When stress hormones bind to nuclear receptors, these hormones can trigger DNA transcription and protein synthesis of particular genes. In turn, the resulting proteins influence neuronal structure and function, including neuronal growth, neurotransmitter synthesis, receptor density and sensitivity, and neurotransmitter reuptake.

Early Experience, Maltreatment, and HPA Axis Regulation

Among the array of difficulties exhibited by maltreated children, one of the most prevalent and widely documented is an increased risk for internalizing problems and depression in childhood and MDD in adulthood (DuMont, Widom, & Czaja, 2007; Gibb, Wheeler, Alloy, & Abramson, 2001; Kaplow & Widom, 2007; Keiley, Howe, Dodge, Bates, & Pettit, 2001; Manly, Kim, Rogosch, & Cicchetti, 2001; Toth, Manly, & Cicchetti, 1992). A variety of factors have been posited to mediate the impact of child maltreatment on depression. These include subtype of maltreatment, genetic vulnerability, the quality of children's relationships with their mothers, social support, stressful life events, attributional styles, social competence, self-esteem, and stress hormone activity (Tarullo & Gunnar, 2006). Regarding stress hormones, it has been argued that for those at genetic risk of affective disorder, elevations in stress hormones during episodes of abuse may shape the development of more reactive fear and neuroendocrine systems, and hence increase the risk of developing internalizing disorders (Heim & Nemeroff, 2001).

The animal literature provides support for this hypothesis (Heim, Owen, Plotsky, & Nemeroff, 1997). Chronic elevations in glucocorticoids (cortisol in humans and other primates), produced by the HPA axis, increase the production of fear-mediating neurochemicals in the central nucleus of the amygdala (Makino, Gold, & Schulkin, 1994). In nonhuman primates, individuals carrying gene variants associated with risk for depression in abused children (e.g., Caspi et al., 2003), exhibit larger cortisol responses to psychosocial stressors (Barr et al., 2004; Sánchez et al., 2005). Furthermore, a large body of animal studies shows that adverse parental care during early development increases fearful–anxious behavior and shapes increased reactivity in neurobiological systems involved in defensive behaviors and physiological stress reactions (see Gunnar & Quevedo, 2007, and Gunnar & Vazquez, 2006, for reviews). In rodents and nonhuman primates, this has been demonstrated through studies of fear behavior and activity of the HPA axis (Levine, 2005; Maestripieri, 1999; Meaney & Szyf, 2005; Sánchez, McCormack, & Maestripieri, in press).

The neurobiological signature of adverse early care has been shown to be highly consistent at the systems and molecular levels to neurobiological findings in the study of adult mood disorder (see Heim, Newport, Mletzko, Miller, & Nemeroff, 2008; Heim, Plotsky, & Nemeroff, 2004). It has been argued that these early effects reflect both the dependence of the very young on maternal care for survival and the rapid development of the brain during the early period of life (Gunnar, 2003; Gunnar & Vazquez, 2006; Heim & Nemeroff, 2001). Thus, these animal studies suggest that inadequate or abusive parenting early in life persistently sensitizes the neurocircuits that are involved in the regulation of stress and emotion and also suggests that individuals at genetic risk for depression may be the most susceptible to these early experience effects (Heim & Nemeroff, 2001).

Models of the impact of early caregiving adversity typically have focused on *increased* reactivity of the HPA axis as a likely outcome. However, particularly as the research has been extended to human and nonhuman primates, it has become clear that a more accurate prediction is that the HPA axis will likely exhibit evidence of *dysregulation* and that this dysregulation may involve both hyper- and hypofunctioning (Heim et al., 2004, 2008; McEwen, 2000). Although not yet fully understood, a number of factors have been shown to affect whether elevated or suppressed activity is noted. The HPA axis tends to down-regulate in response to prolonged hyperactivation; thus, in response to chronic stressors first hyper- and later hypoactivity of the axis may be noted (for review, see Miller, Chen, & Zhou, 2007). With regard to basal cortisol, chronic stress and negative emotionality tend to be associated with slight elevations in the late afternoon and evening but often lower than typical levels in the early morning (e.g., DeSantis et al., 2007; Gunnar & Quevedo, 2007). Thus, whether elevations or suppressions in baseline levels are reported may depend on time of measurement, both in terms of time of day and time since the onset of a chronic stressor. Furthermore, in part because of counterregulation within the axis, cortisol measures (baseline or reactivity) may appear normal, even when assessments higher up in the axis (e.g., ACTH response to CRH challenge or pharmacological probes of feedback sensitivity) may reveal dysfunction (see, for example, Heim et al., 2008). Finally, there is some speculation that individuals at genetic risk for antisocial personality disorder will exhibit attenuation or down-regulation of cortisol activity (Susman, 2006), whereas individuals at risk for depression will exhibit elevations or hyperactivity of the HPA axis following adverse early life conditions (Heim & Nemeroff, 2001; Heim et al., 2004). Overall, predicting that the measures of the HPA system will reflect dysregulation of the axis, rather than predicting that any given measure will be elevated or suppressed, reflects the current status of knowledge in the field. This is especially true in research on young children from vulnerable populations, where researchers are often limited to assessing basal measures of cortisol at only one or a few times during the day.

Evidence of dysregulation extends to studies of pharmacological challenge. Specifically, Kaufman et al. (1997) administered a CRH challenge test to a sample of depressed abused, depressed nonabused, and normal control group children. Compared with the depressed nonabused and the normal control group children, the depressed abused children exhibited significantly greater peak, total, and net ACTH secretion post-CRH infusion. Finally, Cicchetti and Rogosch (2001b) found that compared with symptomatic nonmaltreated children, maltreated children with clinical-level internalizing problems were distinguished by higher morning, afternoon, and average daily cortisol levels across a 5-day period, suggestive of HPA axis dysregulation.

Although dysregulation of the HPA axis appears to be associated with maltreatment for children who are high in internalizing problems or who are clinically depressed, it remains unclear whether this is related to the type, severity, or developmental timing of the maltreatment. To date, the relevant published studies have either focused on physical or sexual abuse (or both; DeBellis, Baum, et al., 1999; Heim & Nemeroff, 2001; Kaufman et al., 1997) or have not examined a specific subtype of maltreatment. However, most maltreated children experience multiple types of maltreatment, and the previous studies have not attempted to differentiate among them. In particular, abuse and neglect frequently co-occur. Moreover, these maltreatment subtypes have different onsets, occur with varying severities, and can recur (Bolger, Patterson, & Kupersmidt, 1998; English et al., 2005; Manly et al., 2001). In addition, children experience maltreatment during different developmental periods. Thus, maltreatment is a heterogeneous phenomenon, and researchers and clinicians must consider the diversity in the type(s), perpetrator(s), onset, frequency, chronicity, and timing of maltreatment experiences. Even more striking, few such investigations also include a measure of timing, a critical variable in neuroendocrinology (Tarullo & Gunnar, 2006). In particular, inclusion of the temporal dimension is especially important because animal studies have revealed that timing is a crucial factor. Indeed the empirical evidence gleaned from rodent and nonhuman primate investigation indicates that adverse or maltreating (i.e., neglectful and abusive) care early in an animal's life has long-lasting effects. Attempts to translate the animal research on the criticality of timing have used a range of time periods (i.e., infancy through adolescence) to specify what constitutes early adverse care. Thus, although there is some evidence that HPA axis dysregulation is associated with maltreatment in the context of depression, little is known about whether the type, timing, or duration of maltreatment is relevant to these findings.

Studies conducted to date suggest that early occurring maltreatment may be particularly important in the experience of later depression and anxiety. However, limitations in the range of subtypes examined within these investigations or the extent to which specific subtypes were adequately represented in the sample preclude definitive conclusion. In a recent investigation of school-age maltreated and nonmaltreated children between the ages of 7 and 10 who attended a week-long summer day camp, Cicchetti et al. (2010) operationalized early maltreatment as any incident of physical abuse, sexual abuse, neglect, or emotional maltreatment occurring with the first 5 years of life. Cicchetti and colleagues (in press) chose the infancy, toddler, and preschool periods as their index of early maltreatment for two primary reasons. First, national epidemiological studies of child maltreatment highlight this period as a critical time for the emergence of neglect and abuse (Hussey, Chang, & Kotch, 2006; U.S. Department of Health and Human Services, Administration on Children, Youth, and Families, 2000). Second, despite the fact that the neural systems underlying stress reactivity–regulation and internalizing problems undergo a prolonged period of development, components of the limbic system such as the hippocampus, amygdala, and the pathways to the prefrontal cortex from these structures develop rapidly over the first years of life (Thompson & Nelson, 2001).

Cicchetti and colleagues (2010) also chose to focus on physical–sexual abuse experienced early in the child's life (in the first 5 years). To extend the work of Heim (see, e.g., Heim et al., 2008), Cicchetti et al. (in press) used prospective reporting of abuse, an earlier age of abuse onset, and evidence of depressive–internalizing symptomatology and cortisol dysregulation occurring earlier in development during the school-age years. They hypothesized that children who were physically or sexually abused (or both) before age 5 (early physical abuse–sexual abuse; EPA/SA) and who expressed high depressive and internalizing symptoms would exhibit a more dysregulated pattern of diurnal cortisol activity (less decline; flatter slope) than would other maltreated children (no early physical and/or sexual abuse; NEPA/SA) or nonmaltreated comparison (NC) children.

The results of Cicchetti and colleagues (2010) supported their predictions. Children experiencing abuse in the first 5 years of life exhibited more internalizing symptoms than maltreated children without early abuse and nonmaltreated children of the same low SES. Second, children experiencing early abuse who had high internalizing symptoms exhibited an atypical flattening of cortisol production over the daytime hours. Further analyses indicated that even among children high on internalizing symptoms, other parameters of maltreatment, including developmental period of onset, recency, chronicity, diversity, and type of perpetrator, did not provide a better explanation of the phenomena than did the experience of early physical–sexual abuse.

The pattern of cortisol production noted for the children who were early abused and high internalizing provided consistent evidence of HPA axis dysregulation as noted in adults and children under chronic stress (Gunnar & Vazquez, 2001; Heim et al., 2000, 2008; Miller et al., 2007). That is, Cicchetti and colleagues (in press) obtained evidence of a less marked decline in cortisol over the daytime due to a slight lowering of a.m. and slight increase in p.m. levels. Given the times they were able to sample saliva (i.e., 9 a.m. and 4 p.m. daily over the course of the camp week), it is somewhat remarkable that Cicchetti and colleagues (2010) were able to detect this pattern of dysregulation. Cortisol is at its daily peak approximately 30 minutes after morning awakening, drops steeply for the next 30 minutes to an hour, and then declines gradually over the day, until it reaches almost a zero nadir soon after the onset of nighttime sleep (cf. Susman et al., 2007). Most studies that have identified this stress-related pattern of daytime cortisol dysregulation have sampled at morning wake up and at bedtime. In contrast, children in the Cicchetti et al. (2010) study were sampled at 9 a.m. It is thus very likely that the children had been awake long enough so that these investigators missed the early morning cortisol peak. Although 4 p.m. is late in the afternoon, levels at this time are not as low as the nadir that they will reach later in the evening. Accordingly, it is possible that the pattern noted by Cicchetti and colleagues (2010) would have been even more marked had they been able to sample earlier and later in the day.

Although the pattern noted is not the same as that seen among adults with clinical depression, the findings are consistent with those described in two other reports on depressed, maltreated children studied in a day-camp setting (J. Hart, Gunnar, & Cicchetti, 1996; Kaufman, 1991). Hart and colleagues found that maltreated children who were also depressed showed a less marked diurnal decrease in cortisol from 9 a.m. to 4 p.m., although no attempt was made in that study to differentiate patterns on the basis of subtype of maltreatment. Kaufman (1991) noted that maltreated and depressed children in her sample were less likely than nondepressed maltreated children to show a decrease in cortisol from 9 a.m. to 4 p.m. Notably similar to the Cicchetti et al. (2010) investigation, she also observed that the depressed maltreated children were more likely to have suffered abuse in addition to neglect, rather than solely neglect. Neither the Hart et al. study nor the Kaufman et al. study examined the influence of the developmental timing of maltreatment subtypes.

Early abuse may be more damaging to developing emotion and stress systems because it occurs during periods of rapid neurodevelopment (Cicchetti & Walker, 2001; Gunnar & Vazquez, 2006). Very young children also may be less able than older children to discern the cues predictive of an abusive attack, and this lack of predictability may engender chronic stress and hypervigilance to aggression in these youngsters, even when abusive events are not occurring (Rieder & Cicchetti, 1989; Teisl & Cicchetti, 2008). School-age physically abused children, in contrast, have been shown to be highly sensitive to even very degraded signals of threat, which although potentially maladaptive in some contexts, may provide some relief from constant vigilance in the abusive home (Pollak et al., 1998; Pollak & Sinha, 2002; Shackman, Shackman, & Pollak, 2007). In addition, the impact of early physical–sexual abuse on developing brain systems may be especially pernicious because it occurs during a period when the child is nearly wholly dependent on parents for survival. For the abused infant, toddler, or preschooler, a hypervigilant state of mind and chronic stress with respect to unpredictable parental attacks may shift neurobiological development onto pathways leading to depression and neuroendocrine dysregulation (Cicchetti & Rogosch, 2001a; Tarullo & Gunnar, 2006).

Another question pertains to why early neglect in the absence of physical–sexual abuse did not have a significant impact on either internalizing–depressive symptoms or HPA axis activity. Even though early neglect has been shown to have marked effects on young children's social and cognitive competence (Pears & Fisher, 2005), neglect experiences may not be as fear–threat arousing as are the experiences of being physically attacked and hurt. Although it is not uncommon to find early neglect in the absence of abuse, it is rare to find early abuse in the absence of neglect, especially in low-income samples such as the one studied by Cicchetti and colleagues (2010). Nearly three fourths of their early physical–sexual abuse sample was also neglected and emotionally maltreated. It is not possible to ascertain whether their neglect and emotional maltreatment contributed to their increased internalizing symptomatology and HPA dysregulation; however, it is possible that neglect made these children even more vulnerable to the fear and stress engendered by early abuse.

There are many parallels between the neurobiological effects of early abuse and those of MDD (Heim et al., 2004, 2008). It is likely that prior investigations of individuals with MDD have included persons who had experienced early abuse (Bemporad & Romano, 1992; Heim et al., 2008). As such, many of the established neurobiological findings in depression may be due to the undetected presence of early physical–sexual abuse (Heim et al., 2004). In the absence of early abuse, depression may not be related to changes in the HPA system. Thus, there may be different neurobiological subtypes of depression. Accordingly, a history of early abuse, as well as the clinical presentation, onset, and course of depression, should be incorporated into the formulation of potential etiological models of mood disorder (Heim et al., 2004, 2008). For example, because cortisol dysregulation rarely occurs in depressed children who did not experience abuse early in life (Feder et al., 2004), childhood depression without early physical–sexual abuse may be caused by different processes and have different neurobiological features than childhood depression with early abuse. The findings of Cicchetti and colleagues (2010) that nonmaltreated children with high levels of depressive–internalizing symptomatology did not exhibit atypical cortisol regulation attest to this divergence. There may be biologically distinct subtypes of depression as a function of the presence or absence of abuse early in life (cf. Heim et al., 2004, 2008). Thus, not all individuals with depression exhibited cortisol dysregulation; Cicchetti et al. (2010) found it only for the early physically–sexually abused children with high internalizing and depressive symptomatology—a group that is more likely to have dysfunctions in early neurobiological development through the high allostatic load caused by abuse.

Neurobiological Functioning, III: Brain Event-Related Potentials and Emotion Processing

Attachment systems have been theorized to be constructed to (a) permit flexible responses to environmental circumstances, (b) influence emotion regulation, and (c) function through mental representations (*internal working models*) that children hold of themselves and of their relationships with others. Cicchetti and Tucker (1994) proffered the hypothesis that these representations may be reflected through physiological activity as well as behavior. Research investigations have focused on one type of physiological reaction, the event-related potential (ERP). The ERP is an index of CNS functioning thought to reflect the underlying neurological processing of discrete stimuli. ERPs enable researchers to monitor neural activity associated with cognitive processing in real time.

Pollak, Cicchetti, Klorman, and Curtis have conducted several experiments in which they examined ERPs of maltreated and nonmaltreated children in response to a variety of emotion-eliciting stimuli that were presented as facial displays. The stimuli used in the experiments were photographs of prototypic facial expressions (e.g., happy, sad, fear, anger, neutral). The maltreated and nonmaltreated children were of comparable cognitive maturity and low SES backgrounds.

Two experiments investigated school-age maltreated and nonmaltreated children (Pollak et al., 1997; Pollak et al., 2001), and a third experiment studied toddlers who had experienced maltreatment in the first year of life plus a comparable group of nonmaltreated toddlers (Cicchetti & Curtis, 2005). In each of these three studies, the ERPs of maltreated youngsters showed an increased amplitude to facial displays of anger compared with other facial displays, whereas the ERPs of the nonmaltreated youngsters were comparable across all emotion conditions. The results of these ERP experiments suggest that the experiences that maltreated children encountered during their development caused particular stimuli to become personally meaningful, based in part on the stored mental representations that had been associated with that particular stimulus over time. Accordingly, prior experiences of maltreated children are reflected in their psychophysiological responses.

Maltreatment also appears to affect children's interpretations and comprehension of particular emotional displays. Specifically, neglected children, who often suffer from an extremely limited emotional environment, have more difficulty discriminating among emotional expressions than do nonmaltreated children or non–physically abused children (Pollak, Cicchetti, Hornung, & Reed, 2000). Furthermore, physically abused children, who are often exposed to impending threat, display a response bias for angry facial expressions (Pollak et al., 2000; Pollak & Sinha, 2002) and are more likely than other maltreated children to impute negative intentions to ambiguous situations (Teisl & Cicchetti, 2008). This pattern is known in the literature as the *hostile attribution bias* (see Dodge, Pettit, & Bates, 1997). Such selectivity in responding may allow maltreated children to use behavioral responses that are adaptive to address the challenges presented by their environments; however, responding in this fashion may provide maladaptive solutions when employed outside of the maltreating situation and may contribute to their social-cognitive difficulties and increased risk for behavior problems and psychopathology (Pollak et al., 1998).

Gene × Environment Interaction

Influenced by the upsurge of interest in molecular genetics within the social and neurosciences, developmental psychopathologists have begun to investigate how the interdependence between an identified variation in the DNA sequence of a particular gene and a well-defined and appropriately measured environmental pathogen can exert impact on behavioral outcomes (Moffitt et al., 2006; Plomin & Crabbe, 2000; Plomin & Rutter, 1998; Rende & Waldman, 2006; Rutter, 2006). Before the advent of molecular genetics approaches, most research in the area of genetics and psychopathology was conducted within the field of behavior genetics, with its assumption that genetic and environmental influences operate in an additive fashion. An additional supposition of behavior genetics was that G×E effects are so infrequent and trivial that their presence could be ignored in quantitative behavior–genetic analyses (Moffitt et al., 2006). Such core assumptions from quantitative behavior genetics were carried over into the much newer field of psychiatric molecular genetics.

The perpetuation of the belief that additive effects predominate in the relation between genes and mental illnesses contributed to a scientific strategy wherein single genes were examined in relation to specific mental disorders but without consideration of the impact of different environmental circumstances on different forms of the same gene. Thus, the investigation of the interaction between measured genes and environments is a relatively recent empirical phenomenon (Moffitt et al., 2006; Rutter, 2006).

The assumptions of behavioral genetics have been challenged and researchers in the field of developmental psychopathology have been exhorted to examine G×E effects (Moffitt et al., 2006; Rutter, 2006). A number of cogent arguments support the position that G×E effects occur more frequently than heretofore assumed. As such, G×E effects play an important role in comprehending the development of mental health and disorder.

One of the most compelling reasons for encouraging increased research on G×E interactions in the field of developmental psychopathology is gleaned from the human and animal literature on behavioral responses to environment challenges. Consistent with a developmental psychopathology perspective (Cicchetti & Rogosch, 1996a, 1996b), heterogeneity (multifinality) is characteristic of the response to even the most pernicious and hazardous traumas, including the array of environmental risk factors for mental disorder (Moffitt et al., 2006; Rutter, 2006). In other words, even in the face of extreme stress, individuals differ markedly with respect to their ultimate outcomes.

In empirical research guided by diathesis-stress models of psychopathology (Gottesman & Shields, 1972), as well as investigations of the determinants of resilient functioning in the face of serious adversity, it has been shown that individual differences in response to environmental risks are associated with preexisting individual variations that are under genetic influence (Cicchetti & Blender, 2006; Curtis & Cicchetti, 2003; Moffitt et al., 2006; Plomin, DeFries, McClern, & McGuffin, 2001; Rutter, 2006). Accordingly, in instances in which there is individual variation among the psychological responses of humans to environmental risk factors for psychopathology, it is highly likely that G×E may be operating in some fashion.

Emerging Empirical Evidence of G×E and Psychopathology

Caspi et al. (2002) examined how genetic factors contribute to why some maltreated children grow up to develop antisocial personality characteristics, whereas other maltreated children do not. In this longitudinal investigation of males who were studied from birth to adulthood, it was discovered that a functional polymorphism in the promoter region of the gene encoding the neurotransmitter metabolizing enzyme monoamine oxidase A (MAOA) moderated the effect of maltreatment, which was defined broadly to include physical abuse and other serious and stressful experiences at home. MAOA degrades several biogenic amines including dopamine, norepinephrine, and serotonin. The link between child maltreatment and antisocial behavior was far less pronounced among males with high MAOA activity than among those with low MAOA activity. In other words, the functional polymorphism (high vs. low activity) regulated the extent to which the MAOA gene was expressed.

Maltreated children grow up in extremely stressful environments. The results of the Caspi et al. (2002) investigation were the first to demonstrate that a G×E interaction helps to explain why some maltreated children, but not others, develop antisocial behavior through the effect that stressful experiences such as child abuse and neglect exert on neurotransmitter system development. Specifically, the probability that child maltreatment eventuated in adult's antisocial behavior was greatly increased at low levels of MAOA expression. Because maltreatment was a clearly but broadly defined and well-measured environmental pathogen, the ability of Caspi and colleagues (2002) to detect a G×E interaction in the development of psychopathology was strengthened.

Foley and colleagues (2004) investigated the link among the MAOA polymorphism, adverse childhood environments, and resulting conduct disorder in adolescents. Consistent with the findings of Caspi et al. (2002), Foley et al. (2004) also found that the alleles resulting in low MAOA activity increased risk for conduct disorder only in the presence of an adverse childhood environment. Likewise, Kim-Cohen et al. (2006) replicated and extended the results of Caspi et al. (2002) through their demonstration that the MAOA polymorphism moderated the development of mental health problems after exposure to physical abuse in children.

To date, not all attempts at replicating the findings of Caspi et al. (2002) have reached similar conclusions. For example, Beitchman, Mik, Ehtesham, Douglas, and Kennedy (2004) found that persistent, pervasive, child-onset aggression was influenced by the MAOA polymorphism, but in an opposite way than obtained in the aforementioned studies. Specifically, clinically aggressive boys were more likely to have the allele that results in high MAOA activity; however, these boys had not been identified as maltreated.

Two meta-analyses of existing published studies addressing the moderating effects of MAOA on relations between child maltreatment and psychopathology conducted by Kim-Cohen and colleagues (2006; Taylor & Kim-Cohen, 2007) demonstrated that across all studies, males who had the genotype conferring low as opposed to high MAOA activity were significantly more likely to develop mental health difficulties in the context of stressful environments. The results of these meta-analyses provide strong support for the hypothesis that the MAOA gene confers vulnerability to environmental stressors such as child abuse and neglect and that this biological process begins to unfold during early childhood (cf. Kim-Cohen et al., 2006).

In another seminal G×E investigation, Caspi et al. (2003) discovered that a functional polymorphism in the promoter region of the serotonin transporter (5-HTT) gene moderated the influence of stressful life events on the development of depression by early adulthood. Those with one or two copies of the short (s) allele of the 5-HTT promoter polymorphism exhibited more depressive symptoms, depressive disorders, and suicidality than individuals homozygous for the long (l) allele, but only when confronted with high life stress during adolescence.

This study, a large-scale prospective investigation of a representative birth cohort, provides additional evidence of a G×E interaction in which an individual's response to environmental insults is moderated by his or her genetic makeup. In addition, consistent with a G×E hypothesis, adult depression was predicted by the interaction between the s allele in the 5-HTT gene-linked-polymorphic region (5-HTTLPR) and child maltreatment that occurred during the first decade of life (Caspi et al., 2003). Child maltreatment predicted adult depression only among individuals carrying an s allele (i.e., s/s or s/l) but not among l/l homozygotes.

Cicchetti, Rogosch, and Sturge-Apple (2007) also examined G×E interaction by contrasting adolescents who had high versus low MAOA activity gentoypes and who varied in terms of the extensiveness of their maltreatment experiences. Cicchetti and colleagues (2007) also measured adolescents' reports of their coping strategies for managing stress. Among the adolescents who experienced extensive maltreatment (i.e., sexual abuse, physical abuse, neglect, emotional maltreatment, or a combination thereof), the MAOA genotype influenced the level of adolescents' depressive symptoms; only adolescents with the low MAOA activity genotype evidence high depressive symptoms, whereas their peers with high MAOA activity and extensive maltreatment had comparable levels of depressive symptoms to other youth in the sample. Cicchetti and colleagues (2007) then sought to determine whether the extensively maltreated adolescents varied in their coping strategies depending on their MAOA genotype. Interestingly, self-related coping processes contributed to lower depressive symptoms among high MAOA, extensively maltreated youth, whereas help seeking and avoidant coping did not. In contrast, not one of these coping processes contributed to individual differences in depressive symptoms among adolescents with extensive maltreatment and the low MAOA activity genotype. Thus, self-related coping appeared to confer further protection from depressive symptoms among the youth with extensive maltreatment and the protective variant of the MAOA gene.

The multiple-levels-of-analysis perspective that characterizes molecular G×E research on psychopathology has moved beyond the behavior–genetics focus on heritability coefficients and additive models and has begun to address complex dynamic developmental questions such as, "how do genetic and environmental factors transact throughout development in the course of disorder *X*?" and "what factors cause which genes to turn on and off during specific phases of the epigenetic course?" In contrast to findings emanating from quantitative behavior–genetic research in which mental illnesses are thought to originate from many genes, each accounting for a small amount of variance, G×E research suggests that at least for some multifactorial mental disorders, a small number of genes with effects that are contingent on exposure to specific environmental pathogens (such as child maltreatment) may be sufficient for increasing the risk for development of some forms of psychopathology.

Future G×E investigations should examine brain endophenotypes that may be intermediate between the MAOA gene and antisocial behavior and the 5-HTT gene and depression. Endophenotypes are constructs beneath the observable surface, such as psychophysiological parameters, posited to underlie mental disorders or psychopathological symptoms (Gottesman & Gould, 2003). Endophenotypes are thought to be more directly influenced by the genes relevant to the disorder than are the manifest symptoms (Hanson & Gottesman, 2007). For example, the incorporation of assessments of HPA axis functioning into research on G×E interactions could further enhance the predictive efficiency of such investigations. Maltreated children who demonstrate stress-induced neuroendocrine dysregulation (i.e., hyper- or hypocortisolism), have a paucity of social supports, and possess the s/s genotype for the 5-HTT gene may be even more likely to develop depressive disorder than has been the case in previous studies. Delineation of stress-sensitive neural processes may pave the way for the formulation of pharmacological and behavioral prevention and intervention efforts to ameliorate the harmful impact that early stressful experiences exert on neurobiological development.

Although we currently possess rudimentary knowledge about molecular genetics and child maltreatment, because social experiences affect gene expression and brain structure and function, and vice versa, it is likely that maltreatment affects the expression of genes that have an impact on brain structure and function as well as basic regulatory processes. Molecular genetic methods now exist that enable researchers to investigate the expression of particular genes or of large numbers of genes simultaneously (i.e., *gene profiles*). Through the use of DNA microarrays, researchers can determine the type and quantity of messenger RNA being produced by a given cell, thereby indicating which genes are "turned on" (i.e., activated; Mirnics, Middleton, Lewis, & Levitt, 2001). DNA microarrays can be used to index changes in the expression of genes that are essential for brain function (Greenberg, 2001). By examining concurrent environmental, psychological, neurobiological, hormonal, and gene expression changes longitudinally, researchers may be in a stronger position to elucidate the development of resilient adaptation. Such multilevel investigations may reveal the mechanisms responsible for inhibiting the expression of genes that are probabilistically associated with maladaptive developmental outcomes and psychopathology. Likewise, these interdisciplinary approaches may proffer insights into the mechanisms that "turn on" genes that may serve a protective function for individuals experiencing adversity.

Psychological Sequelae of Child Maltreatment

Comprehending the developmental pathways between successive prior adaptations and current functioning is central to a developmental psychopathology approach (Cicchetti, 1993). At each period of development, specific issues confront individuals for the first time and require them to garner and expand available resources in attempts to master new challenges. Adaptation at a particular developmental level implies the successful resolution of the developmental task or tasks most salient for that period. Rather than construing development as a series of unfolding tasks that need to be accomplished and then decrease in importance, development is conceived as consisting of a number of important age and stage-appropriate tasks that, on emergence, remain critical to other newly emerging developmental tasks (Cicchetti & Schneider-Rosen, 1986; Sroufe, 1979).

For example, the development of a secure attachment is not viewed as a developmental issue of the later part of the first year of life alone; rather, once an attachment relationship develops, it continues to undergo transformations and reintegrations with subsequent accomplishments such as emerging autonomy and entrance into the peer world. As a result, throughout the life span, from infancy to old age, individuals are continually renegotiating the balance between being connected to others and being independent and autonomous as they encounter each new developmental issue (cf. Erikson, 1950; Sroufe, 1979). Consequently, each of the issues represents life-span/developmental tasks that require continual coordination and integration in the individual's adaptation to the environment. Each stage-salient issue, thematically, becomes a lifelong feature of importance for adaptation.

Affect Regulation

An early stage-salient developmental issue of infancy involves the ability to regulate and differentiate affective experience. Affect regulation is defined as the intra- and extra-organismic factors by which emotional arousal is redirected, controlled, modulated, and modified so that an individual can function adaptively in emotionally challenging situations (Cicchetti, Ganiban, & Barnett, 1991). Child maltreatment represents a significant threat to the optimal development of affective processing abilities. Maltreated children evidence numerous deficits in the recognition, expression, and understanding of emotions (for a review, see Camras, Sachs-Alter, & Ribordy, 1996). In the early months of life, distortions in affect differentiation have been noted (Gaensbauer & Hiatt, 1984). Specifically, either excessive amounts of negative affect or blunted patterns of affect have been observed long before they occur in normal development.

The early maladaptive processing of stimuli that contributes to affective regulatory problems may lay the foundation for future difficulties in modulating affect. For example, physically abused preschool boys who witnessed an angry simulated interaction directed at their mothers evinced greater aggressiveness and more coping directed toward the alleviation of maternal distress than did nonabused boys (Cummings, Hennessy, Rabideau, & Cicchetti, 1994). In a related inquiry, abused boys who viewed videotaped vignettes of angry and friendly interactions reported experiencing more distress than did nonabused boys in response to interadult hostility. Physically abused boys also reported more fear in response to angry interaction between adults especially when the interactions were unresolved (Hennessy, Rabideau, Cicchetti, & Cummings, 1994). Finally, in an investigation of 4- to 6-year-old children, approximately 80% of maltreated preschoolers exhibited patterns of emotion dysregulation in response to witnessing interadult anger. Undercontrolled–ambivalent emotion regulation patterns were associated with maternal reports of child behavior problems and were found to mediate the link between maltreatment and children's symptoms of anxiety or depression (A. Maughan & Cicchetti, 2002). Findings such as these support a sensitization model whereby repeated exposure to anger and familial violence results in greater emotional reactivity.

Difficulties in mentally representing and processing social information also have been noted in children with histories of maltreatment. Children with histories of neglect have difficulty discriminating emotional expressions, whereas physically abused children demonstrate a response bias to angry emotional expressions (Pollak et al., 2000). Pollak and Sinha (2002) demonstrated that physically abused children required less sensory input than did comparison children to identify facial displays of anger accurately. Pollak and Sinha used a gradual evolution of images depicting facial expressions of various emotions. Physically abused children detected angry emotions at lower steps of the sequence but did not exhibit increased sensitivity for the other facial displays. The authors concluded that physically abused children have facilitated access to representations of anger. Similarly, in a task in which pairs of photographs of emotional expressions were morphed into each other (Pollak & Kistler, 2002), physically abused children detected anger with lower signal strength than did control participants. In combination, these studies suggest that physically abused children can detect facial expressions of anger more accurately and at lower levels of perceptual intensity compared with other emotions.

In an investigation of the attentional mechanisms underlying the finding that physically abused children overattend to angry experiences, Pollak and Tolley-Schell (2003) found that children who had experienced physical abuse demonstrated delayed disengagement when angry faces served as invalid cues and exhibited increased attention on valid angry trials. These results suggest that early adverse experiences influence maltreated children's selective attention to threat-related signals.

For the physically abused child, displays of anger may be the strongest predictor of threat; however, increased sensitivity to anger could result in decreased attention to other emotional cues. Conversely, the neglected child may suffer from an extremely limited emotional learning environment. A solution to the problem created for maltreated children by aberrant emotional signals from parents may be general constraints imposed on children in the form of immature or limited resources, which require young children to filter or select some environmental cues over others (Bjorklund, 1997). This developmentally normal aspect of selective attention suggests that irrespective of the initial state of the organism, emotional development is contingent on the nature of the input or experiences made available to the child.

Perlman, Kalish, and Pollak (2008) conducted an investigation of emotion understanding in maltreated and nonmaltreated children. To assess how well children understood the antecedents of emotional reactions in others, children were presented with a variety of emotional situations that varied in outcome and equivocality. Children were told the emotional outcomes and asked to rate whether a situation was a likely cause of such an outcome. The investigators tested the effects of maltreatment experience on children's ability to map emotions to their eliciting events and their understanding of emotion–situation pairings. The findings suggest that typically developing children are able to distinguish between common elicitors of negative and positive events. In contrast, children who develop within maltreating contexts, in which emotions are extreme and inconsistent, interpret positive, equivocal, and negative events as being equally plausible causes of sadness and anger. This difference in maltreated children's reasoning about emotions suggests a critical role of experience in aiding children's mastery of the structure of interpersonal discourse.

Deviations in understanding negative affect and in affective processing have also been identified in maltreated children, and these difficulties have been shown to relate to undercontrolled and aggressive behavior in the school setting (Rogosch et al., 1995). Affective processing also was found to partially mediate the effect of maltreatment on later social effectiveness. In an investigation of attributional processes, Toth, Cicchetti, and Kim (2002) found that attributional style moderated externalizing behavior problems and perceptions of mothers mediate both internalizing and externalizing symptoms. In a prospective longitudinal study, Bolger and Patterson (2001) reported that higher levels of perceived external control mediated the associations between specific subtypes of maltreatment and children's internalizing behavior problems. Moreover, moderator analyses revealed that among maltreated children, greater perceived internal control predicted fewer internalizing problems, suggesting that perceive internal control acts as a protective factor. Findings such as these have advanced our knowledge of how cognitive processes contribute to behavior problems, as well as to the avoidance of such problems, in maltreated children.

Drawing on previously developed models of social information processing, Dodge and his colleagues (Dodge, Pettit, Bates, & Valente, 1995) hypothesized that children who had experienced harsh discipline or who had been physically abused in their first 5 years of life would develop deviant patterns of information processing in the school-age years. Specifically, abused children were found to be defensively hypervigilant to hostile cues and to fail to adequately attend to relevant nonhostile cures. In essence, maltreated children were found to attribute hostility to others in situations in which most people would not make such an attribution (see also Teisl & Cicchetti, 2008). In addition, physically abused children were found to acquire large repertoires of highly accessible aggressive responses to interpersonal problems so that, when provoked, aggressive retaliatory responses were likely. Finally, physically abused children appear to learn that aggressive behavior can have positive consequences for the aggressor.

Evidence from cross-sectional investigations suggests specific developmental trajectories from affect-regulatory problems to behavioral dysregulation among maltreated children. Maltreated preschool- and school-age children exhibit a range of dysregulated behaviors that are often characterized by disruptive and aggressive actions. Maltreated toddlers also have been shown to react to peer distress with poorly regulated and situationally inappropriate affect and behavior, including anger, fear, and aggression, as opposed to the more normatively expected response of empathy and concern (Klimes-Dougan & Kistner, 1990). Shields and Cicchetti (1998) found that maltreated children also evidenced attention deficits, and subclinical or nonpathological dissociation was more likely among children with histories of physical or sexual abuse. A history of abuse also predicted emotion dysregulation, affective lability–negativity, and socially inappropriate emotion expressions. The emotion dysregulation was a mechanism through which maltreatment resulted in reactive aggression.

In another relevant investigation, Murray-Close, Han, Cicchetti, Crick, and Rogosch (2008) examined the association between circadian rhythms of cortisol and physical and relational aggression. Morning arrival, prelunch, and afternoon predeparture salivary cortisol were assessed among maltreated and nonmaltreated children attending a summer day camp. Counselors and peers rated participants' involvement in physically and relationally aggressive behaviors. Results indicated that physical aggression was associated with heightened cortisol following morning arrival and relatively steep declines in cortisol over the day (cf. Susman, 2006), whereas relational aggression was associated with low cortisol following morning arrival and blunted diurnal change in cortisol. Moreover, maltreatment was a significant moderator of this relationship such that aggression was related to greater cortisol dysregulation among nonmaltreated than among maltreated children. These findings suggest that physiological correlates of aggression may differ for physical and relational forms of aggression and among maltreated versus nonmaltreated populations.

Development of Attachment Relationships

The establishment of a secure attachment relationship between an infant and his or her caregiver represents a primary task during the first year of life. As development proceeds, attachment theorists have posited that a secure attachment relationship provides a base from which to explore and ultimately contributes to the integration of cognitive, affective, and behavioral capacities that influence ongoing and future relationships, as well as the understanding of the self (Bowlby, 1969/1982; Sroufe, 1979). Not surprisingly, maltreated children are at considerable risk for the development of insecure attachment relationships. In fact, investigations have found that maltreated infants evidence insecure attachment rates as high as 95% (V. Carlson, Cicchetti, Barnett, & Braunwald, 1989; Cicchetti, Rogosch, & Toth, 2006; Crittenden, 1988; Lyons-Ruth, Connell, Zoll, & Stahl, 1987). In a longitudinal investigation of 12-, 18-, and 24-month-old maltreated and nonmaltreated comparison infants, Barnett, Ganiban, and Cicchetti (1999) found that maltreated infants were significantly less likely than are nonmaltreated infants to be securely attached (86%, 61%, and 75%, at 12, 18, and 24 months, respectively) and to have disorganized–disoriented types of attachments to their caregivers.

Children construct *internal working models* of their attachment figures out of their interactions with their caregivers, their own actions, and the feedback they receive from these interactions. Once organized, these internal working models tend to operate outside of conscious awareness and to be relatively resistant to change. Children formulate their conceptions of how acceptable or unacceptable they are in the eyes of their attachment figures (i.e., their self-image) on the basis of their interactional history with their primary caregiver.

Although particularly salient during infancy and toddlerhood, attachment continues to be important beyond the early years of life as internal working models are carried forward. Consistent with attachment patterns identified in infancy, maltreated children are more likely than nonmaltreated children to exhibit insecure attachments throughout the preschool years (Cicchetti & Barnett, 1991; Crittenden, 1988). Moreover, insecure attachment has been found to be present in school-age children when self-report measures have been used. For example, Lynch and Cicchetti (1991) found a preponderance of insecure patterns of relatedness among maltreated children. Such insecure patterns of relatedness also have been linked with the presence of depressive symptoms (Toth & Cicchetti, 1996a).

The Development of Self-System Processes

Following the consolidation of the attachment relationship, the succeeding stage-salient issue for children involves the establishment of a sense of self as separate from the caregiver and as capable of autonomous functioning (Sroufe, 1979). Increasingly during this period, responsibility for self-regulation and the regulation of affect is transferred from the caregiver–child dyad to the child alone. To make this transition successfully, caregiver sensitivity to and tolerance of toddler strivings for autonomy are needed.

As self-capacities emerge, children raised in maltreating environments are at heightened risk for maladaptive self-development. Investigations on visual self-recognition in maltreated children provide information on their emerging self-system processes. Although maltreated and nonmaltreated toddlers do not differ with respect to their capacities to recognize themselves (Schneider-Rosen & Cicchetti, 1991), differences have been observed with respect to affective responsivity. Specifically, maltreated toddlers are more likely than comparison children to display either neutral or negative affect upon seeing their rouge-marked images in a mirror, possibly suggesting an early precursor of low self-esteem.

Similar delays in the self-system of maltreated toddlers have been noted with respect to their ability to talk about the internal states and feelings of self and other. Because socialization exerts a significant role in a child's expression of affect, caregivers can influence a child's ability to express various emotions. Maltreated toddlers, although not differing from nonmaltreated children in receptive vocabulary, have been found to exhibit proportionally fewer internal-state words, to show less differentiation in their attributional focus, and to be more context-bound in their use of internal-state language than were their nonmaltreated peers (Beeghly & Cicchetti, 1994). Specifically, maltreated toddlers produced fewer utterances about physiological states and fewer utterances about negative affect, which suggests that the use of negative emotion words, or references to the self and the self's desires, may provoke negative responses in the caregiver and, ultimately, contribute to modification in the use of such verbalizations. Further evidence about the effect of communication styles in maltreating homes emerges with respect to the development of theory-of-mind abilities. Delays in theory of mind, considered an index of the ability to attribute beliefs, desires, emotions, and intentions to others, have been found in maltreated children. Maltreatment during the toddler period and a history of physical abuse both were related to delays in the development of theory of mind (Cicchetti, Rogosch, Maughan, Toth, & Bruce, 2003). Thus, it appears that aberrations in internal state language may be an early precursor of theory of mind. Within a maltreating environment, children may learn that it is unacceptable, threatening, or even dangerous to discuss feelings and emotions, particularly negative ones. As such, the internal state language deficits of maltreated children may reflect inhibited development in understanding the experience of self and other, thereby contributing to difficulty in acquiring theory-of-mind abilities (Cicchetti et al., 2003).

Aberrations in the self-systems of maltreated children continue to be evident during the preschool period. Alessandri and Lewis (1996) found differences between maltreated and nonmaltreated preschoolers in the expression of pride and shame. Maltreated girls evidence less pride and more shame as compared to both maltreated and comparison boys. A considerable body of work using story-stem narratives has also revealed self-system deficits in maltreated preschoolers. For example, maltreated preschoolers tell stories that contain more negative self-representations than do the stories told by nonmaltreated preschoolers (Toth, Cicchetti, Macfie, & Emde, 1997; Toth et al., 2000). Negative representations of caregivers have also been associated with emotion dysregulation, aggression, and peer rejection, whereas positive representations have been related to prosocial behavior and peer preferences (Shields, Ryan, & Cicchetti, 2001). These negative representations mediate maltreatment's effects on peer rejection, in part by undermining emotion regulation. The narratives of these preschoolers also contain more negative representations of caregivers, suggesting a trajectory from negative caregiving experiences and resultant negative representations of caregivers to negative self-representations. Moreover, evidence shows that preschool-age maltreated children, especially those with histories of physical and sexual abuse, demonstrate more dissociation during a storytelling task than do nonmaltreated children (Macfie, Cicchetti, & Toth, 2001a). These findings suggest that as early as the preschool years, fragmentation in the self-system of maltreated youngsters may be present.

Importantly, aberrations in the self-systems of young maltreated children may also be reflected in their moral judgment and reasoning. Although research has shown that maltreated children do not differ from nonmaltreated children in their moral judgment or reasoning (Smetana, Daddis, Toth, Cicchetti, Bruce, & Kane, 1999), evidence does support the presence of behavioral and affective differences in domains related to moral reasoning. Deficits also have been found in areas involving the internalization of moral standards and socialization. In an observational study, physically abused children engaged in more stealing behaviors and neglected children exhibited more cheating behaviors and less rule-compatible behavior than did nonmaltreated children (Koenig, Cicchetti, & Rogosch, 2004). Furthermore, maltreated children exhibit less empathy (Macfie et al., 1999), fewer prosocial and more aggressive behaviors (Shields, Cicchetti, & Ryan, 1994), less internalization of compliance (Koenig, Cicchetti, & Rogosch, 2000), and higher rates of delinquency (Smith & Thornberry, 1995; Widom, 1989) than do their nonmaltreated peers.

Abnormalities in the self-systems of maltreated children continue to be seen in their self-concepts. However, different patterns of findings emerge for children of varying ages. Young maltreated children overrate their level of competence and peer acceptance, whereas by the age of 8 or 9 years, maltreated children evidence lower rates of self-esteem and perceive themselves as being less competent than do nonmaltreated children (Vondra, Barnett, & Cicchetti, 1989). Fragmentations in self-organization also have been found in sexually abused adolescent girls, who demonstrate deviant splitting between both positive and negative self-references (Calverley, Fischer, & Ayoub, 1994).

Peer Relations

Derived from the early attachment relationship, children's mental representations of their caregivers should consolidate and generalize to form an organizing schema through which subsequent relationships may be interpreted. Therefore, in theory, children's mental representations of caregivers will influence their ability to engage in peer relationships. To assess the relationship between such mental representations and children's peer relationships, Shields et al. (2001) assessed maltreated and nonmaltreated children's narrative representations of caregivers and emotion regulation as predictors of later rejection by peers. Consistent with an organizational perspective of development, positive and coherent representations of caregivers were related to prosocial behavior and peer preference, whereas maladaptive representations were associated with emotion dysregulation, aggression, and peer rejection. Furthermore, mental representations mediated maltreatment's effects on peer rejection in part by undermining the ability for competent emotion regulation. Thus, mental representations of caregivers serve an important function in the development of peer relationships of at-risk children, in addition to the development of emotion regulation.

Given the preponderance of difficulties evidenced by maltreated children on the early stage-salient issues of development, difficulties in the peer arena are not unexpected. In general, maltreated youngsters evidence elevated aggression toward or withdrawal from peers. Among the most salient findings are the following: (a) Maltreated children evidence more antisocial behaviors, including aggressiveness, meanness, and disruptiveness, and fewer prosocial behaviors such as leadership and sharing (Salzinger, Feldman, Hammer, & Rosario, 1993) and (b) maltreated preschoolers are more likely to cause distress in their peers than are nonabused children (Klimes-Dougan & Kistner, 1990). Dodge and his colleagues (Dodge, Pettit, & Bates, 1994) found that maltreated children were rated by peers, teachers, and mothers as more disliked, less popular, and more socially withdrawn than were nonmaltreated children. Additionally, rejection of maltreated children by their peers was found to increase over a 5-year period.

In some maltreated children, a combination of aggressive and withdrawn behavior has been rated by peers, and, when such behavior is present, such children evidence much lower social effectiveness (Rogosch & Cicchetti, 1994). Finally, difficulties in developing and maintaining friendships have been noted in physically abused children (Parker & Herrera, 1996). Preadolescent and adolescent physically abused children display less intimacy in their friendships than do abused children. Moreover, the friendships of physically abused children are marked by more conflict, especially during competitive activities in which emotion-regulation skills are particularly stressed.

Maltreated children also are more likely than nonmaltreated children to bully others. Shields and Cicchetti (2001) found that bullying behaviors were particularly prevalent among children with histories of physical or sexual abuse. Histories of maltreatment also place children at risk for victimization by peers. Both bullies and victims evidenced problems with emotion regulation, and emotion dysregulation made a unique contribution toward the differentiation of bullies and victims from those without such problems. In addition, emotion dysregulation mediated maltreatment's effects on children's risk for bullying and victimization.

Recently, Cullerton-Sen et al. (2008) examined the associations between maltreatment and aggression using a gender-informed approach. Maltreatment was found to be associated with aggressive conduct; however, these effects were qualified by gender, subtype of maltreatment, and the form of aggression under investigation. Physical abuse was associated with physically aggressive behavior for boys only, whereas sexual abuse predicted relational aggression for girls only (cf. Crick & Grotpeter, 1995, 1996). This study adds to existing research by demonstrating that violent and relationally toxic maltreating family systems (often characterized by ambivalence, avoidance, enmeshment, and disorganization; Cerezo, 1997; Howes & Cicchetti, 1993; Howes, Cicchetti, Toth, & Rogosch, 2000; Rogosch et al., 1995) affect not only the extent to which children exhibit physical aggression but also the extent to which they relationally manipulate their peers.

Adaptation to School

Adaptation to school represents the major extrafamilial environment in which children are exposed to a novel group of unfamiliar peers and adults. As such, it presents both a challenge to functioning and an opportunity to break free of patterns that have been established within a maltreating home. However, because an organizational perspective suggests that children's experiences in the home provide a foundation on which future transitions are built, probabilistically children who have been maltreated are at risk for failure in the school environment.

Abused and neglected children are at considerable risk for academic failure (Eckenrode, Laird, & Doris, 1993). In efforts to identify those factors that might mitigate against the impact of abuse on school performance, Trickett, McBride-Chang, and Putnam (1994) conducted an investigation with adolescent girls who had been sexually abused. Previous abuse was found to predict poorer social competence, impaired competence in learning, and lower overall academic performance. Higher levels of anxious depression, bizarre destructiveness, and dissociation also were present in victims of sexual abuse. Importantly, cognitive ability and perceived competence emerged as mediators of overall academic performance and achievement, whereas dissociative and destructive behaviors exacerbated the child's level of school success. Okun and colleagues (1994) also sought to examine the independent and interactive effects of physical abuse, recent exposure to additional life events such as death or illness, and social disadvantage on children's social, cognitive, and affective adjustment during middle childhood. Abused children were found to evidence difficulties in three areas: peer adjustment, self-perception, and depression. Further analyses identified unique effects of negative events and socioeconomic disadvantage on children's adjustment. Additive contributions of abuse status and socioeconomic disadvantage also predicted behavior problems at school and in the home.

In yet another investigation of links between relationship patterns and school adaptation, Toth and Cicchetti (1996b) found that the security a child experienced in relation to his or her mother, in interaction with maltreatment status, significantly affected school functioning. Nonmaltreated children who reported secure patterns of relatedness to their mothers exhibited less externalizing behavior problems, more ego resilience, and fewer school risk factors (e.g., poor attendance, poor achievement test performance, suspensions, failure in 50% of courses, and grade retention) than did maltreated children who reported insecure patterns of relatedness. Moreover, nonmaltreated children with secure patterns of relatedness to their mothers exhibited more positive school adaptation than did nonmaltreated children who reported insecure patterns of relatedness.

Finally, in an investigation of more than 200 low-income children, impairments in academic engagement, social skills, and ego resiliency were found to be present in children with histories of maltreatment (Shonk & Cicchetti, 2001). Maltreated children manifested multiple forms of academic risk and exhibited more externalizing and internalizing behavior problems. The effects of maltreatment on academic adjustment were partially mediated by academic engagement, and maltreatment's effects on behavior problems were fully mediated by social competencies and ego resiliency.

Personality Organization and Psychopathology

The extent of variation in personality characteristics and personality organization among maltreated children represents an area of investigation that has recently gained attention in the maltreatment literature. Given the vast array of developmental sequelae evidenced by maltreated children, this domain of development is likely to contribute to our understanding of differential vulnerability and resilience processes among maltreated youth (Rogosch & Cicchetti, 2004).

The application of temperament models has been prominent in characterizing individual differences among infants and young children (Kagan, 1994; Rothbart, Posner, & Hershey, 1995). These models emphasized variation in behavioral characteristics that are presumed to be biologically based (Rothbart & Bates, 1998). As children proceed through development, the features of these temperamental systems are elaborated and consolidated into an individual's personality as they are modified by environmental experiences (Kagan, 1994). Given the extreme failure of the average expectable environment that is associated with child maltreatment, one might expect maltreated children to manifest maladaptive personality organization.

Rogosch and Cicchetti (2004) used the five factor model (FFM) to study the emergent personality organization of maltreated children. The FFM approach is well established as a synthesizing descriptive system of personality that involves five primary personality dimensions: extraversion, agreeableness, conscientiousness, neuroticism, and openness to experience (McCrae & John, 1992). Research on children using the FFM has taken a personality-centered approach to identify individuals exhibiting patterns of organization among the FFM dimensions. For example, by applying a factor-analytic strategy, R. W. Robins, John, Caspi, Moffitt, and Stouthamer-Loeber (1996) identified three personality configurations emerging from the FFM, which they named resilients, overcontrollers, and undercontrollers.

In their longitudinal assessment, Rogosch and Cicchetti (2004) examined the personality organization of 6-year-old maltreated and nonmaltreated children who were then followed up at 7, 8, and 9 years of age. Results indicated that the 6-year-old maltreated children exhibited lower agreeableness, conscientiousness, and openness to experience and higher neuroticism than nonmaltreated children. Using a similar analytic approach to that of Robins and colleagues, five personality clusters emerged: overcontroller, undercontroller, reserved, dysphoric, and gregarious. Taken together, the gregarious and reserved clusters closely resemble the resilient organization noted in previous studies (both are adaptive personality organizations). Maltreated children, however, were more frequently represented in the less adaptive personality clusters (overcontroller, undercontroller, and dysphoric). One particular vulnerable profile, dysphoric, emerged predominantly among maltreated children who had been both abused and neglected; this organization, which represents a newly identified personality cluster, was characterized by low conscientiousness, agreeableness, and openness to experience, with high neuroticism. The dysphoric cluster was rarely observed among nonmaltreated children, which may explain why it had not been previously identified (D. Hart, Hofmann, Edelstein, & Keller, 1997; R. W. Robins et al., 1996).

Overall, maltreatment and personality clusters were related to individual differences that were perceived by peers. Furthermore, continuity and stability of children's personality organization and personality liabilities were found such that personality clusters at age 9 were maintained from age 6. Thus, there is substantial vulnerability in the personality features of maltreated children, highlighting the need for interventions to promote competence and prevent the consolidation of maladaptive personality organization.

Behavior Problems and Psychopathology

Maltreated children are at risk for developing a profile of relatively enduring vulnerability factors that places them at high risk for future psychopathology. Several long-term consequences to child maltreatment have been identified in adulthood (see Arnow, 2004, for review). However, the majority of research regarding the adverse outcomes of child maltreatment is limited by its reliance on retrospective reports (Brewin, Andrews, & Gotlib, 1993; Horwitz, Widom, McLaughlin, & White, 2001). For example, a retrospective study of homeless women found that childhood abuse has significant indirect effects on depression, chronic homelessness, and drug and alcohol problems, which are mediated through later physical abuse and self-esteem (J. A. Stein, Leslie, & Nyamathi, 2002). However, because of the use of retrospective methodology, it is difficult to determine causal links between abuse and later outcomes in adulthood. Given evidence that recollections of past abusive experience may change over time in light of later events and changing definitions of abuse (Loftus, 1993), the reliability of findings of the long-term mental health effects of childhood abuse based on retrospective data has been subject to serious critique (Widom & Morris, 1997; Widom & Shepard, 1996). Furthermore, this technique is often applied to adult populations who have been identified as expressing a specific problem, thus bringing the generalizability of such findings into question.

Keeping in mind the limitations of retrospective analysis within specific pathological populations, the link between abuse and aggressive and violent behavior in adolescents and adults has been consistently documented in the literature. For example, higher rates of physical abuse are reported among adolescents who have specified problems with violence and aggression (Lewis, Mallouh, & Webb, 1989; Moffitt, 1993, 2006), among adults who are convicted of violent offenses or who are institutionalized and have violent tendencies (Rosenbaum & Bennett, 1986; Sack & Mason, 1980), and among adults who engage in partner violence (Ehrensaft et al., 2003), as well as among those who experience revictimization in adulthood (Lang, Stein, Kennedy, & Foy, 2004).

A history of physical abuse also has been linked to other forms of psychological disturbance. For example, depressed inpatients who had been physically abused have demonstrated higher levels of impulsivity, aggression, and lifetime suicide attempts in comparison to nonabused depressed inpatients (Brodsky et al., 2001). Children who have been physically abused are at risk for suicidal ideation (Finzi et al. 2001; Thompson et al., 2005), and this risk may extend into adulthood (Dube et al., 2001). Research on suicidality among maltreated children suggests that profound interpersonal difficulties during middle adolescence may mediate the associations between child maltreatment and suicide attempts during late adolescence and early adulthood (Johnson et al., 2002). Providing further support for the centrality of proximal stressors in predicting maltreated children's risk for suicide, a study with maltreated adolescents suggested that the link between maltreatment and suicidality could be largely accounted for by risk factors such as family functioning and parent or child psychopathology (Kaplan et al., 1999). Among younger (age 8) maltreated children, witnessed violence and child maltreatment, as well as child psychological distress, substance use, and poor social problem solving, have each been associated with suicide. The effects of maltreatment and witnessed violence on suicidal ideation, however, were mediated by child functioning (Thompson et al., 2005). Consistent with an organizational developmental perspective, prior experiences of maltreatment leave children with fewer resources to master new developmental tasks and to protect themselves against subsequent challenges, thereby increasing their vulnerability for suicide in the face of proximal stress.

Although the aforementioned investigations have identified a number of maladaptive long-term sequelae of child maltreatment, studies that are prospective and longitudinal in design are much more informative with regard to identifying individual developmental pathways to adaptation or maladaptation. For example, a prospective longitudinal study by Horwitz and colleagues (2001) indicated that men and women who were physically abused and neglected as children had higher rates of dysthymia and antisocial personality disorder as adults than did matched control subjects. Women who had experienced abuse and neglect as children additionally endorsed more problems with alcohol abuse than did control subjects. Moreover, the abused and neglected groups reported not only more symptoms of psychopathology as adults but also a greater number of lifetime stressors; these stressors accounted for much of the relationship between childhood abuse and adult mental health outcomes (Horwitz et al., 2001).

Among children, a longitudinal study conducted by Kim and Cicchetti (2004) demonstrated that maltreatment and mother–child relationship quality independently contributed to the development of children's internalizing and externalizing problems over time, both directly and indirectly through self-esteem and social competence. Specifically, maltreated children showed less socially adaptive behaviors with peers than the nonmaltreated children. Furthermore, maltreatment was related to internalizing and externalizing symptomatology, directly as well as indirectly through deficits in social competencies. Self-esteem mediated the impact of mother–child relationship quality on child adjustment outcomes for both maltreated and nonmaltreated children, such that secure attachment was negatively related to internalizing and externalizing at Time 2 (1 year later) through its influence on self-esteem at Time 1. Elevated internalizing and externalizing symptomatology is consistent with several additional studies showing that maltreated school-age children and adolescents manifest higher levels of depressed symptomatology, behavior problems at home and at school, and juvenile delinquency than do nonmaltreated children (Crittenden, Claussen, & Sugarman, 1994; Okun et al., 1994; Zingraff, Leiter, Myers, & Johnsen, 1993). Moreover, the maladaptive trajectories of maltreated children diverge from those of nonmaltreated children over time such that maltreated children's problems become more severe as children get older, especially in the domains of peer relationships and behavior problems such as aggression (Crittenden at al., 1994; Dodge et al., 1994).

Beyond general adjustment problems, maltreatment is associated with a higher prevalence of clinical-level psychiatric symptomatology and diagnoses than is observed among nonmaltreated children. For example, a significantly higher incidence of ADHD, oppositional defiant disorder, and PTSD was found among maltreated children than nonmaltreated children, according to both the parent and child administrations of the Diagnostic Interview for Children and Adults (Famularo, Kinscherff, & Fenton, 1992). The child interviews revealed higher incidence of psychotic symptoms as well as personality and adjustment disorders, and the parent interviews indicated a greater incidence of conduct and mood disorders among maltreated children (Famularo et al., 1992). Physical and sexual abuse in particular have been related to a number of psychiatric disorders in childhood and adulthood, including panic disorders, anxiety disorders, depression, eating disorders, somatic complaints, dissociation and hysterical symptoms, sexual dysfunction, and borderline personality disorder (BPD; Browne & Finklehor, 1986; Kessler, Davis, & Kendler, 1997; Merry & Andrews, 1994; Putnam, 2003; Weaver & Clum, 1993; Wolfe & Jaffe, 1991).

In general, research has focused largely on the role of maltreatment in the development of depression, PTSD, dissociative disorders, and personality disorders. Elevated rates of depressive symptomatology are consistently found among maltreated children in comparison to nonmaltreated children (Kim & Cicchetti, 2004; Sternberg et al., 1993; Toth & Cicchetti, 1996b; Toth et al., 1992). Additionally, many maltreated children meet diagnostic criteria for dysthymia (Kaufman, 1991). A variety of factors have been posited to mediate the impact of maltreatment on depression: subtype of maltreatment, children's patterns of relatedness to their mother, social support and stressful life events, attributional styles, social competence and self-esteem, and psychophysiology (Kaufman, 1991; Kim

& Cicchetti, 2004; Koverla, Pound, Heger, & Lytle, 1993; Toth & Cicchetti, 1996a; Toth et al., 1992; Toth, Maughan, Manly, Spagnola, & Cicchetti, 2002). For example, the relationship between cognitive style and subtype of maltreatment has been associated with the development of both nonendogenous depression and hopelessness depression in adulthood (Gibb et al., 2001). Specifically, levels of child emotional maltreatment, but not physical or sexual abuse, have been related to levels of hopelessness and episodes of nonendogenous major depression and hopelessness depression (Gibb et al., 2001).

In an investigation of the relationship between child maltreatment, cognitive style, and depression, Toth, Cicchetti, and Kim (2002) concurrently assessed cognitive styles and behavioral internalizing and externalizing symptomatology among maltreated and nonmaltreated school-age children. Children's attributional style emerged as a significant moderator of the relationship between maltreatment and externalizing symptoms, suggesting that attributional style may exert a protective effect against the negative consequences of maltreatment. Moreover, results indicated that children's perceptions of their mother functions as a mediator between maltreatment and the development of internalizing and externalizing symptomatology. Specifically, the findings support that maltreatment is related both directly and indirectly to behavioral maladjustment. The indirect pathway suggests that maltreatment contributes to children's forming less positive perceptions of their mother, which then exacerbates internalizing and externalizing psychopathology (Toth, Cicchetti, & Kim, 2002).

Alternatively, the experience of sexual abuse has been associated with an increased likelihood of impairments in a number of interrelated areas of development, including the development of self-esteem and self concepts; beliefs about personal power, control, and self-efficacy; the development of cognitive and social competencies; and emotional and behavioral self-regulation (Putnam & Trickett, 1993). A review of all published literature between 1989 and 2003 containing empirical data relevant to childhood sexual abuse found that depression in adulthood and sexualized behaviors in children are the best-documented outcomes of child sexual abuse (Putnam, 2003). In an investigation among a sample of depressed women, those with and without a history of sexual abuse were comparable regarding the severity of depression; however, the women with child sexual abuse history were more likely to have attempted suicide or engaged in deliberate self-harm (Gladstone et al., 2004). Thus, depressed women with a history of sexual abuse may constitute a subgroup of patients who may require tailored interventions to battle depression recurrence and harmful and self-defeating coping strategies.

Kendler, Kuhn, and Prescott (2004) examined whether childhood sexual abuse (CSA) in women altered sensitivity in adulthood to the depressogenic effects of stressful life events (SLEs). Using a population-based sample of 1,404 female adult twins, Kendler and colleagues found that previously assessed neuroticism and CSA and past-year SLEs predicted MDD. Moreover, women with severe CSA had an increased risk for major depression and an increased sensitivity to the depressogenic effects of SLEs. These findings illustrate that early environmental risk factors, just as is the case with genetic factors, can produce long-term increased in the sensitivity of women to depressogenic life experiences.

PTSD develops in response to the occurrence of a major stressor and is characterized by frequent reexperiencing of the traumatic event through flashbacks, nightmares, or intrusive thoughts; a numbing of general responsiveness to current events; and persistent symptoms of increased arousal (American Psychiatric Association, 1987, 1994). The experience of childhood sexual abuse has been related to the development of immediate as well as long-term PTSD symptoms (Briere & Runtz, 1993; McLeer, Callaghan, Henry, & Wallen, 1994). Furthermore, children who have been sexually abused experience PTSD at rates higher than children who have experienced other subtypes of maltreatment (Deblinger, McLeer, Atkins, Ralphe, & Foa, 1989; Kendall-Tackett, Williams, & Finkelhor, 1993; Kiser, Heston, Millsap, & Pruitt, 1991; Merry & Andrews, 1994).

Dissociation refers to a psychological phenomenon manifest by a disruption in the normally self-integrative processes of memory, identity, and consciousness (American Psychological Association, 1987, 1994). Dissociation states range on a continuum from normal minor occurrences of everyday life, such as daydreaming, to pathological manifestations such as that seen in multiple personality disorder and fugue states (Fischer & Ayoub, 1994; Putnam & Trickett, 1993; Westen, 1994). Given the severe disruptions in self system development, including dissociative symptoms, that have been observed among maltreated children (Macfie et al., 2001a, 2001b), it follows that these children would be at risk for later emergence of dissociative psychopathology.

Sexual abuse in particular has been associated with dissociation, conceptualized clinically as a defensive process against overwhelming trauma (Nash, Hulsey, Sexton, Harralson, & Lambert, 1993). Higher rates of dissociation and splitting are seen among sexually abused children than in any other comparison group (Calverley et al., 1994; Kirby, Chu, & Dill, 1993; Nash et al., 1993). Further, there seems to be a unique relationship between sexual abuse and dissociation that is not present for physical abuse such that dissociation has been shown to have an important mediating role between sexual abuse and psychiatric disturbance (Kisiel & Lyons, 2001).

In another investigation, childhood interpersonal trauma as a whole was highly predictive of a diagnosis of depersonalization disorder and of scores denoting dissociation, pathological dissociation, and depersonalization (Simeon, Guralnik, Schmeidler, Sirof, & Knutelska, 2001). When analyzing the effects of specific subtypes of trauma, emotional abuse alone emerged as the most significant predictor of both depersonalization disorder diagnosis and severity; it did not, however, predict general scores denoting dissociation. General dissociation scores were best predicted by the combined severity of emotional and sexual abuse. This suggests that a unique relationship may exist between emotional abuse and depersonalization disorder, whereas other subtypes or combinations of abuse may contribute to more severe dissociative symptoms.

Personality disorders are conceptualized as rather enduring, character-based patterns of pathology that emerge in adolescence or early adulthood. Etiological accounts often point to childhood experiences as central to the development of personality disorder (Battle et al., 2004; Johnson et al., 1999; Laporte & Guttman, 1996). Evidence supports that personality disorders are more prevalent among those who have a history of child abuse (Pribor & Dinwiddie, 1992; Silverman, Reinherz, & Giaconia, 1996), suggesting that child abuse and neglect may play a role in their etiology.

Of the personality disorders, BPD has been best investigated with regard to adverse child experiences (for a review, see Zanarini, 2000). In general, research with BPD patients indicates higher reporting of childhood abuse (Herman, Perry, & van der Kolk, 1989; Ogata et al., 1990; Soloff, Lynch, & Kelly, 2002; Zanarini, Gunderson, Marino, Schwartz, & Frankenburg, 1989; Zanarini et al., 1997) and child neglect (Johnson et al., 2000; Zanarini et al., 1989, 1997) than among patients with other personality disorders (Zanarini et al., 1989) or other Axis I psychiatric disorders (Ogata et al., 1990); however, these reports should have been interpreted with caution given that they are retrospective in nature.

The impact of the subtypes of maltreatment on the development of BPD is somewhat less clear. Childhood sexual abuse has been identified as a factor that discriminated patients with BPD from those with other personality disorders (Weaver & Clum, 1993); however, it has been noted that when childhood sexual abuse history has been identified among BPD patients, multiple forms of abuse and neglect are additionally present (Ogata et al., 1990; Zanarini et al., 1997, 2000).

The majority of research on maltreatment and personality disorders has compared BPD with an "other personality disorder" category, with limited research into specific disorders (for a review, see Battle et al., 2004). Although there seems to be some empirical support that in addition to BPD, other personality disorder groups report a high prevalence of childhood maltreatment histories (Gibb et al., 2001), much of this evidence is again based on retrospective reports by psychiatric patients (B. Maughan & Rutter, 1997; Paris, 1997) and should be interpreted with caution (Widom & Morris, 1997; Widom & Shepard, 1996).

To address the limitation of retrospective data, a small body of longitudinal evidence is emerging in the field to support the hypothesis that childhood maltreatment increased risk for personality disorders in adulthood (Drake, Adler, & Vaillant, 1988; Johnson et al., 1999; Luntz & Widom, 1994). Such investigations have revealed that maltreatment is associated with the development of antisocial personality disorder. Further, family instability and lack of parental affection and supervision during adolescence were associated with dependent and passive-aggressive personality disorder among men. An additional community-based, longitudinal study showed that persons with documented child abuse were more than 4 times as likely as those who were not abused or neglected to be diagnosed with personality disorder, after age, parental education, and parental psychiatric disorders were controlled statistically (Johnson et al., 1999). Specifically, physical abuse, sexual abuse, and neglect were each uniquely associated with elevated personality disorder symptom levels during early adulthood. Physical abuse was associated with antisocial and depressive personality disorder symptoms, sexual abuse was associated with elevated BPD symptoms, and neglect was associated with antisocial, avoidant, borderline, narcissistic, and passive-aggressive personality disorders. This investigation highlights the particular impact of neglect on personality disorder development (Johnson et al., 1999).

Finally, child maltreatment has been associated with maladaptive trajectories in the development of sexuality (i.e., J. Brown, Cohen, Chen, Smailes, & Johnson, 2004; Noll, Trickett, & Putnam, 2003). A prospective longitudinal study revealed that a history of two or more incidents of sexual abuse was associated with early puberty and early pregnancy, after gender, race, class, paternal absence, and mother's age at the birth of the study child were controlled statistically (J. Brown et al., 2004). In addition to heightened sexual activity and preoccupation, a subset of women with sexual abuse histories has been identified who exhibit sexual ambivalence or a heightened sexual preoccupation coupled with greater sexual aversion (Trickett & Putnam, 2003). In particular, pathological dissociation and biological father abuse may be associated with greater sexual aversion and sexual ambivalence. These investigations highlight the risk for premature sexual behavior among maltreated adolescents; efforts to prevent teenage pregnancy should pay particular attention to sexually abused children as they enter puberty.

Resilience

Consistent with a developmental psychopathology perspective, there is multifinality in developmental processes such that the manner in which the individual responds to and interacts with vulnerability and protective factors at each level of ecology allows for diversity of outcomes. Just as deviations from the average expectable environment potentiate some children toward the development of maladaptation, others evidence adaptation in the face of the same challenges. Thus, it is equally informative to understand the mechanisms that promote resilient functioning among maltreated children as it is to investigate developmental trajectories toward psychopathology. Maltreatment undisputedly represents an extremely adverse and stressful experience, yet not all maltreated children demonstrate maladaptive outcomes. Thus, the study of resilience among maltreated children seeks to understand the dynamic processes that influence how the various aspects of children's ecologies eventuate in multiplicity in child developmental outcome, adaptive or maladaptive.

Resilience research may elucidate the mechanisms through which individuals are able to initiate or maintain their self-righting tendencies when confronted with adversity (cf. Cicchetti & Rizley, 1981; Waddington, 1957). Understanding resilience will contribute to our understanding of how ontogenic processes play a critical role in determining whether adaptation or maladaptation will manifest at each stage of development (Cicchetti & Tucker, 1994).

Initial resilience research sought to identify correlates of resilient outcomes in maltreated children; however, given the nature of resilience as a dynamic process, longitudinal research most adequately can address its development. Unfortunately, there are few longitudinal studies that track subsequent adaptive functioning among maltreated children.

In perhaps the most comprehensive assessments of resilient functioning among maltreated school-age children, Cicchetti and Rogosch (1997) improved on their prior cross-sectional investigation of predictors and correlates of resilience (Cicchetti, Rogosch, Lynch, & Holt, 1993) by assessing the longitudinal adaptation of more than 200 children over a 3-year period. For both studies, resilient adaptation among multiple areas of functioning was evaluated within a heterogeneous sample of economically disadvantaged maltreated children and nonmaltreated comparison children. In their earlier investigation, maltreated children evinced lower overall competence across multiple indices of functioning than the nonmaltreated children. Moreover, maltreated children were rated as more withdrawn, with significantly greater levels of internalizing symptomatology, more disruptive, and more aggressive. Nonetheless, ego resiliency, ego overcontrol, and self-esteem emerged as predictors of resilient adaptation for maltreated children. In contrast, only ego resilience and positive self-esteem were associated with resilient functioning among nonmaltreated children (Cicchetti, Rogosch, et al., 1993).

Similarly, the longitudinal investigation revealed that a higher percentage of nonmaltreated children evidenced resilient functioning than did maltreated children; furthermore, a high percentage of maltreated children were functioning in the low-adaptive range (Cicchetti & Rogosch, 1997). Notably, different predictors of resilience emerged for the maltreated and nonmaltreated children such that for maltreated children, positive self-esteem, ego resilience, and ego overcontrol predicted resilient functioning, whereas relationship features were more influential for nonmaltreated children. These findings suggest that perhaps, in the face of unfulfilling relationships, the maltreated children who demonstrate resilient functioning have developed an adaptive coping mechanism toward less reliance on relatedness in their everyday functioning. Considering that personality resources and self-confidence were major predictors of resilient adaptation in maltreated children, Cicchetti and Rogosch posit that interventions that focus on the enhancement of self system processes such as autonomy, mastery, and self-determination may be effective (Ryan, Deci, & Grolnick, 1995).

Highlighting additional pathways to resilient functioning, Flores, Cicchetti, and Rogosch (2005) conducted a similar assessment of multiple domains of functioning with a sample of high-risk Latino maltreated and nonmaltreated children. Although prior research had identified predictors of resilient adaptation in maltreated children, there was a lack of knowledge regarding whether these same factors would be applicable to Latino children. Considering evidence that relationship are very highly valued in Latino cultures (Harrison, Wilson, Pine, Chan, & Buriel, 1990), Flores and colleagues sought to determine whether relationship features would serve as predictors of resilient adaptation for both maltreated and nonmaltreated Latino children. Consistent with prior investigations of resilience, which have been composed of mainly African American and Caucasian American children (Cicchetti & Rogosch, 1997; Cicchetti, Rogosch, et al., 1993; McGloin & Widom, 2001), maltreated Latino children demonstrated a lower level of resilient functioning than did equally disadvantaged nonmaltreated Latino children. For both maltreated and nonmaltreated Latino children, higher ego resiliency and moderate ego overcontrol were associated with higher resilient functioning. Thus, in contrast to prior investigations (Cicchetti & Rogosch, 1997), the effects of ego resiliency and ego overcontrol did not differentially predict resilience for maltreated and nonmaltreated Latino children. In accord with previous findings, however, the predictive impact of relationship variables on resilience was more significant for nonmaltreated than maltreated Latino children (Flores et al., 2005).

Multilevel Influences on Resilience

Stress has been conceptualized as a perceived threat to an individual's homeostasis and as a situation that brings about increases in the reactivity of the autonomic nervous system through hormone secretion (McEwen, 1994). Stressful experiences engender both biological and psychological responses. The biological response to stress includes the activation of specific neural circuits and neuroendocrine systems (Cicchetti & Walker, 2001). Furthermore, psychological factors such as the anticipation of stress and perceived lack of control can serve as the initial link in a chain of events that can trigger a biological stress response (Cicchetti & Walker, 2001).

The experience of chronic stress is typically associated with deleterious outcomes such as neurobiological dysfunction, immunological difficulties, neuroendocrine dysregulation, and increases in autonomic activity, as well as with maladaptation and mental disorder (Gunnar & Vazquez, 2006). Yet not all individuals who are exposed to stressful experiences are affected in a uniform fashion at either the biological or psychological level. There are multiple converging processes that determine such variability in the responses to stressors. These include the neural circuits that are activated by physiological and psychological stressors, as well as the influences of genetics, prior experience, and ongoing life events (Sapolsky, 1994).

Despite the growing attention paid to discovering how individuals avoid maladaptation after experiencing great risks and adversity, the empirical study of resilience has predominantly focused on detecting the psychosocial determinants of the phenomenon and largely eschewed the inclusion of genetic and biological measures (Curtis & Cicchetti, 2003). This artificial distinction among genetics, neurobiology, and behavior in research on resilience contradicts years of research indicating coactions between all levels of analysis, from the environment broadly construed to the molecular. The pathways to either psychopathology or resilience are influenced, in part, by a complex matrix of the individual's level of biological and psychological organization, experience, social context, timing of adverse events and experiences, and developmental history. In recent years, scientists have argued that efforts to understand the underlying processes of resilient adaptation would be facilitated by more interdisciplinary research (Charney, 2004; Cicchetti & Curtis, 2007; Curtis & Cicchetti, 2003).

Two recent studies have examined psychological and biological contributors to resilience in maltreated children. In a sample of nearly 700 maltreated and nonmaltreated children from stressful low-SES backgrounds, Cicchetti and Rogosch (2007) focused on the contribution that the personality features of ego-resiliency and ego-control could make to resilience and coping under adversity. This investigation also examined the regulation of two stress-responsive adrenal steroid hormones, cortisol and dehydroepiandrosterone (DHEA), primary products of secretory activity occurring in the HPA axis (Cicchetti & Rogosch, 2007), to the development of resilient functioning. DHEA is a precursor of androstenedione, testosterone, and estradiol and exerts an impact on diverse biologic systems, as well as emotionality, cognitive functioning, and health. Although operating at different levels of analysis, behavioral–psychological and biological factors each made unique contributions to resilience in this study.

Consistent with their earlier studies, Cicchetti and Rogosch (2007) found that ego resiliency and ego overcontrol were significant predictors of resilience. Moreover, they operated as mediators of the relation between maltreatment and resilient functioning. In contrast to the findings obtained in our prior investigations, ego overcontrol did not operate differentially in the maltreatment and comparison groups of children. For both maltreated and nonmaltreated children, resilient overcontrol personality organizations, a more reserved, controlled, and rational style of interacting with peers and adults, likely contributed to these children being more attuned to behave in ways that were critical for adapting successfully to their stress-laden environments.

At the biological level, the adrenal steroid hormones cortisol and DHEA were associated with resilience. Prolonged stress, as is often the case in child maltreatment, can lead to allostatic load, characterized by cumulative physiological dysregulation across multiple biological systems through a cascade of causes and sequelae that can damage the brain, organ systems, and the neurochemical balance that undergirds cognition, emotion, mood, personality, and behavior (Davies et al., 2007). Interacting genetic, developmental, and experiential factors, including child maltreatment, play prominent roles in the wide array of individual differences among individuals in coping with stressful challenges throughout their lives.

For the nonmaltreated comparison children, higher morning cortisol levels were related to lower levels of resilient strivings, whereas, for the maltreated children, morning levels of cortisol were not found to be related to increasing levels of resilience. Among nonmaltreated children, high basal cortisol may be indicative of children who are undergoing greater stress exposure and as a consequence are constrained in their capacity to adapt competently. A closer examination of the maltreated children revealed differences according to the subtype of maltreatment experienced. Cicchetti and Rogosch (2007) found that physically abused children with high morning cortisol had higher resilient functioning than children with lower levels of morning cortisol. The positive role of increased cortisol for physically abused children is divergent from the more general pattern of higher cortisol being related to lower resilient functioning as was discovered in the nonmaltreated and sexually abused children.

Prior research on neuroendocrine regulation has indicated that physically abused children generally exhibit lower levels of morning cortisol secretion (Cicchetti & Rogosch, 2001a). It may be that the subgroup of physically abused children who were able to elevate cortisol to cope with the stressors in their lives was demonstrating a greater striving for resilient adaptation. In contrast, the larger subgroup of physically abused children with lower levels of morning cortisol may have developed hypocortisolism over time in response to chronic stress exposure. As a result, for the larger subgroup of physically abused children, there may be a diminished capacity to mobilize the HPA axis to promote positive adaptation under conditions of ongoing stress. Additionally, the findings of a very low level of resilience among sexually abused children with high basal cortisol may be a product of their different traumatic experiences and the consequences of chronic excessive vigilance and preoccupation, with commensurate HPA axis hyperarousal.

Another noteworthy discovery was the unique, atypical pattern of a relative diurnal increase in DHEA exhibited in maltreated children with high resilient functioning. It may be that maltreated children who possess the capacity to increase DHEA over the course of the day are better equipped to cope with the demands of high chronic exposure to stress in their lives and to adapt competently. The nonmaltreated children who functioned in a resilient fashion did not demonstrate the pattern of diurnal DHEA increase; rather, they exhibited the lowest levels of DHEA across the day.

Importantly, when considered jointly, independent main effects of both personality features and adrenal steroid hormones on resilient functioning were observed. Thus, steroid hormones and personality features were not reducible to each other; both levels of analysis, behavior and stress neurobiology, made important contributions to the ability of maltreated children to cope successfully with the major stresses they encountered in their daily lives.

In an extension of the multilevel perspective on resilient coping in maltreated children experiencing significant adversity, Curtis and Cicchetti (2007) conducted a study investigating the association between an index of neural function, EEG asymmetry, and resilience. Relative activation of the left versus right hemisphere of the cerebral cortex has been related to differential emotion experience. More specifically, the right hemisphere is associated with negative emotion and withdrawal, whereas the left hemisphere is linked to positive emotion and approach behavior (Davidson, 2000). Curtis and Cicchetti (2007) sought to determine at the neural level whether a greater propensity for positive emotion would contribute to resilience. In addition, at the behavioral level, they incorporated an observational assessment of emotion regulation to examine how differences in emotion regulatory capacities might promote resilient functioning.

Emotion regulation contributed to resilience in both maltreated and nonmaltreated children. For all children striving to cope with adversity, a greater capacity to modulate the expression of negative emotions fostered resilience. In contrast, EEG asymmetry contributed to resilience only in the maltreated group of children. Specifically, maltreated children who exhibited greater relative EEG activation in the left hemisphere were found to be more likely to function in a resilient fashion. However, children with restricted capacity to cope with maltreatment and adversity exhibited relatively greater right hemisphere activation.

Within the explanatory framework of the emotion theory of differential hemispheric lateralization (Davidson, 2000), the observed left hemisphere asymmetry in resilient maltreated children may reflect a bias in the recognition and representation of emotion. In conjunction with better emotion regulation abilities, the increased left hemisphere asymmetry in the group of resilient maltreated children may be associated with greater social competence with peers and adults. For example, in peer interactions, the bias toward perceiving emotion positively and the presence of emotion regulatory ability would be highly adaptive in the context of adversity. Investigations have shown the devastating consequences that a hostile attributional bias exerts on the peer relations of physically abused children (Dodge et al., 1997). The left hemisphere EEG asymmetry observed in resilient maltreated children may reflect a positive attribution bias and hence contribute to these children being better prepared to navigate peer relations successfully. Parallel to the previous findings of Cicchetti and Rogosch (2007), there were no interactions observed between EEG asymmetry and emotion regulation. Thus, each level, neural and behavioral, uniquely contributed to resilient adaptation in maltreated children.

Studies of resilience in maltreated children reveal the possibility of coping processes and resources on multiple levels as children strive to adapt under conditions of high stress. Aspects of self-organization, including self-esteem, self-reliance, emotion regulation, and adaptable yet reserved personalities likely contribute to more competent coping. Moreover, individual differences in biological processes ranging from genes to the HPA axis to brain organization related to emotion also are likely to influence the coping capacities of maltreated youth. At this stage, multilevel research on resilience has shown the relative independence of these varied domains of influence, highlighting the multifaceted contributions to successful coping. Further work will be invaluable to begin to decipher coactions across these multiple levels of analysis during the course of development for a more integrated appreciation of the varied ways in which coping with stress may be achieved.

Prevention and Intervention

Research on the psychological and biological sequelae of child maltreatment is particularly important for enhancing the quality of clinical services that can be directed toward this serious social problem. By conducting research that elucidates the developmental processes through which maltreatment exerts its deleterious impact on children, theoretically and empirically informed interventions for maltreated children and their families can be developed, provided, and evaluated for effectiveness. Although not all children who have been maltreated develop maladaptively, the extant literature conveys the negative and often lifelong effects of child abuse and neglect. Therefore, the provision of services designed to prevent the occurrence of maltreatment and to treat its sequelae must be a priority. In recognition of the criticality of preventing child maltreatment, in 2001 the Children's Bureau initiated the Emerging Practices in the Prevention of Child Abuse and Neglect project (Administration for Children & Families, 2003). The goal of this project was to develop information on programs and initiatives throughout the United States and to disseminate findings to the professional community. Current child maltreatment prevention services typically fall within a number of broad areas, including public awareness campaigns, skill-based curricula designed to teach children safe practices, parent education programs and support groups, home visitation programs, respite and crisis care programs, and family resource centers.

With respect to information on the effectiveness of prevention services, research has generally focused on home visitation programs, parent education programs, and school-based programs for the prevention of sexual abuse. However, the most compelling research that has demonstrated success at preventing child maltreatment has been conducted in the area of home visitation services. Although not all models of home visitation have been shown to be effective in preventing child abuse and neglect (cf. Duggan, McFarlane, Fuddy, Burrell, Higman, et al., 2004), the work of David Olds and his colleagues emerges as an exemplary home visitation model (Olds, Henderson, Chamberlin, & Tatelbaum, 1986; Olds & Kitzman, 1990). Home visitation was initially provided to 400 pregnant women and continued through the first 2 years of their child's life. Improvement on a number of maternal and child health outcomes was found as a result of the prevention program.

Moreover, women considered to be at high risk for child maltreatment evidenced a 75% reduction in state-verified cases of child abuse and neglect during the first 2 years of a child's life. Follow-up data on these children continue to reveal lower rates of child maltreatment through age 15 (Olds, Henderson, Kitzman, Eckenrode, Cole, et al., 1998). Unfortunately, the majority of home-visitation programs has not yielded such long-term effects, most likely because they are less intensive and do not use theoretically guided models or highly trained staff.

Clearly, the prevention of child maltreatment emerges as an important strategy. However, despite efforts in this arena, far too many youngsters continue to be victimized by child maltreatment (Reynolds, Mathieson, & Topitzes (2009). Therefore, it also is clear that treatment initiatives need to be brought to bear when a child has been maltreated. Despite calls for the use of treatments based on our knowledge regarding the consequences of maltreatment (Toth & Cicchetti 1993, 1999), a theoretically derived approach to therapy for this population has been slow to emerge. Although writings on considerations in the conduct of child therapy with maltreated children have become more visible (Toth & Cicchetti 1993), developmentally based and empirically validated approaches to addressing the sequelae of maltreatment are infrequent. Diverse methods of evidence-based treatments might be applied successfully to maltreated children; however, modifications are most likely to be needed based on the maltreatment experiences of a given child.

One area in which research-based and theoretically informed treatments for maltreated children have begun to emerge relates to the attachment relationship. In an RCT, 12-month-old infants and their maltreating mothers were assigned to one of three intervention groups: (a) a home-visitation psychoeducational parenting intervention (PPI) that focused on improving parenting, reducing maternal stress, increasing maternal social supports, and enhancing maternal knowledge of child development; (b) an attachment-theory-informed intervention, infant–parent psychotherapy (IPP), that focused on improving the mother–child attachment relationship; and (c) the community standard (CS), consisting of treatment typically available in the community for maltreating families. A fourth group of nonmaltreated comparison (NC) infants was matched to the intervention groups on sociodemographic indices. At the conclusion of the intervention approximately 1 year later, the maltreated infants in the PPI and IPP interventions demonstrated a statistically significant change in their attachment security from baseline and did not differ in the percentages of attachment security from the babies in the NC group (Cicchetti, Rogosch, & Toth, 2006). In contrast, infants in the CS group manifested no improvements in their attachment security with their mothers, suggesting that traditional services designed to ensure child safety do little to foster positive developmental attainments. The fact that both the PPI and IPP interventions were effective highlights the plasticity of development during infancy and suggests that early interventions do not necessarily need to target attachment during infancy to improve this developmental domain.

Using a similar treatment design, Toth, Maughan, et al. (2002) compared the relative efficacy of two interventions in altering maltreated preschool children's representational models. Maltreating families were assigned to either child–parent psychotherapy (CPP), psychoeducational parenting visitation intervention (PPI), or a CS condition, and an NC group served as an additional control condition. Children in the CPP intervention evidenced more of a decline in maladaptive maternal representations over time, as assessed through story-stem narratives, than did children in the PPI and CS conditions. In addition, CPP children displayed a greater decrease in negative self-representations than did children in the CS, PPI, and NC groups. Mother–child relationship expectations of CPP children became more positive over the course of intervention compared to NC and PPI. In contrast to interventions that target maltreated children in infancy (Cicchetti et al., 2006), the results of this study suggest that an attachment theory-informed model of intervention (CPP) is more effective at improving representations of the self and of caregivers than is a didactic model of intervention (PPI) directed at parenting skills. The major limitation of this study, however, was its exclusive focus on representations and not other outcomes such as parental knowledge about developmentally appropriate expectations, which may have had more substantial gains in the PHV group. Additional outcome measures would greatly inform our understanding of advantages and disadvantages of each approach to intervention.

Preventive programs in the community are also important for promoting competent parenting and reducing maltreatment. These programs typically strive to promote competence and sensitivity in parents and to improve their coping strategies with regard to stressful living conditions (Wolfe, 1993) by enhancing their social support system. For example, self-help groups, crisis intervention, and in-home services that are run community agencies may reduce the incidence of problematic parenting and maltreatment, thereby reducing the need for more intensive intervention services when maltreatment does emerge (Wolfe & Wekerle, 1993).

Reduction in the rate of maltreatment has also been associated with participation in early school-based interventions, such as child–parent centers in the Chicago Longitudinal Study (Reynolds & Robertson, 2003). The child–parent centers provided child education and family support services in high-poverty areas. Participation in the program for 4 to 6 years was associated with significantly lower rates of maltreatment than participation in alternative kindergarten interventions.

Finally, knowledge gained from research on resilience among maltreated children is especially relevant to the development of intervention and prevention efforts (Luthar & Cicchetti, 2000). As resilience research identifies mechanisms that contribute to positive adaptation in the face of adversity, prevention and intervention programs may be tailored to capitalize on and enhance these processes in at-risk children. Consistent with an ecological–transactional model, these adaptive processes may derive from multiple levels of the ecology, including family, community, and cultural features, in additional to individual characteristics (Cicchetti & Rogosch, 2002). Moreover, Luthar and Cicchetti (2000) argued that because resilience is an ongoing dynamic process, preventions that are designed to promote resilience are likely to be most effective as long-term programs that support children through successive periods of development.

Undeniably, there is a need for sufficient breadth in intervention and prevention programs that can address the complex developmental consequences of maltreated children as well as the parenting practices, relationship disturbances, and extensive needs of these families (Cicchetti & Toth, 1993, 2000). The wide variety of techniques that have been applied to intervention efforts, ranging from nondirective play therapy to behavior modification, speaks to the multifinality of experience of maltreated children (Cicchetti & Rogosch, 1996a, 1996b) and to the notion that no one treatment paradigm will be equally appropriate for all maltreated children.

ILLUSTRATIVE DISORDERS FROM A DEVELOPMENTAL PSYCHOPATHOLOGY PERSPECTIVE

Autism

Nearly seven decades ago, Leo Kanner (1943), who originally coined the term *autism*, suggested that the disorder represented a biological dysfunction that reduced the capacity of children to form emotional contact with people. A short time later, however, Kanner modified his position on the etiology of autism and, along with many others, came to view it as environmentally caused. The prevailing belief of these thinkers was that autism was the result of emotionally distant, rejecting, "refrigerator parents" (Bettelheim, 1967). In recent decades, etiological formulations have emphasized the neurobiological and genetic bases of this pervasive developmental disorder that has its symptomatic origins in infancy (Courchesne, 1987; Dawson & Toth, 2006; Rodier, 2002).

Some theories have been based on animal models of medial temporal lobe dysfunction (Bachevalier & Loveland, 2003), whereas others have underscored abnormalities in brain structures, such as the amygdala, hippocampus, and cerebellum (Baron-Cohen, Hoekstra, Knickmeyer, & Wheelright, 2006; Courchesne, 1997; Damasio & Maurer, 1978), as well as other cortical and subcortical regions as fundamental to the etiology of autism. Increasingly, these etiological formulations of autism have begun to take into account the impact of developmental processes and the interconnected nature of multiple brain systems at multiple levels of analysis.

Neuropsychological assessments have revealed deficits in attentional functioning, wherein speed of orienting to and processing novel stimuli is reduced in persons with autism, as is the ability to shift attention (Dawson & Toth, 2006; Townsend, Courchesne, & Egaas, 1997). Individuals with autism have widespread executive functioning impairments that are perhaps a result of the more fundamental attentional deficits found with this disorder. Detailed analyses of executive functioning in persons with autism have revealed that they exhibit impairments in cognitive flexibility but do not exhibit deficits in inhibiting responses or in working memory functioning (Ozonoff, 2001).

One interesting neuroanatomical finding in individuals with autism is abnormal developmental changes in overall brain volume. Courchesne and colleagues have shown that the brain volume of children later diagnosed with autism appeared to be normal at birth; however, by age 2 to 4 years, volumetric MRI data indicated that 90% of the children with autism had a larger than average brain volume compared with nonautistic children (Courchesne et al., 2001). The observed excessive brain size was primarily due to the presence of increased white matter volume in the cerebellum and cerebrum.

In another study, Courchesne et al. (2003) found that although head circumference (HC) was similar in all infants enrolled in their study during the first few months of life, those who later developed autism exhibited a marked accelerated rate of increase in HC beginning several months after birth. On average, between birth and 6 to 14 months of age, HC increased from the 25th to the 84th percentile. This increase in HC was associated with greater cerebral and cerebellar volume in these children by 2 to 5 years of age. It is striking that brain size in young children with autism reaches its maximum by age 4 to 5 years (Courchesne et al., 2001). Average overall maximum brain size in children with autism is statistically equivalent to that achieved by health children (approximately 1,350 mL) but is achieved, on average, 8 years sooner than in normally developing, healthy children (Courchesne et al., 2001). However, in adolescence and adulthood, brain size of those with autism does not differ from that of nonautistic individuals (Aylward, Minshew, Field, Sparks, & Singh, 2002).

Although the increases in brain volume are marked, the specific underlying cellular components of increased brain volumes are unknown to date. The increased volume found in children with autism may potentially reflect abnormalities in any number of microstructural features, including excessive numbers of neurons or glial cells (or both), excessive dendritic arborization, or atypically large numbers of axonal connections (Courchesne at al., 2003). In addition, the cause of the increase in brain volume is not completely understood but clearly reflects some type of dysregulation in one or more stages of brain developmental processes; however, it appears that the early transient period of brain overgrowth occurs during an important period of brain development when normative experience-dependent processes of neural plasticity are potentially at a maximum. This extended period of gradual axonal and dendritic growth and synapse refinement and elimination appears to occur well into the first decade of postnatal life. In children with autism, however, it appears that the physical growth of the brain is compressed into a relatively short period of time that may in turn result in aberrantly rapid and disordered growth (Courchesne et al., 2003). Such a rapid pace of growth would not allow the normal process of experience-dependent neural plasticity to take place.

Observations of disturbances in normal neurodevelopmental processes in autism have helped to refine theory and guide research concerning the underlying biological mechanisms of this pervasive developmental disorder. The accumulated knowledge on normal brain development has enabled investigators of autism to differentiate the abnormal neurodevelopmental processes that appear to underlie this disorder. Ultimately, it appears that the key etiological feature of autism is abnormality of the neurodevelopmental process across a wide spectrum of brain regions and networks. The emerging evidence increasingly points to abnormal regulation of brain growth in autism, with pathological deviation from normative mechanisms underlying the typical progression through neurogenesis and synaptogenesis, followed by axon pruning and synapse elimination.

Despite the wide range of theoretical formulations and the relative paucity of consistent data pointing to a common underlying neurobiological "cause" of autism, the study of this disorder provides an excellent example of the increasingly important role played by neuroscience in examining the potential biological contributors to a developmental disorder. Examining the evolution of theory and research in autism also provides useful information concerning the developmental trajectory of this disorder and perhaps could provide insight into how the study of the development of the neural substrate underlying this disorder could inform the study of other disorders, as well as normal development. As we noted earlier, one of the fundamental tenets of developmental psychopathology is that the study of the development of disordered outcomes can be informed by an understanding of normal development (Cicchetti, 1984b, 1990, 1993, 2003). Ideally, the study of normal and abnormal developmental sequelae can work in tandem to inform each other (Cicchetti, 1984a, 1984b, 1993; Sroufe, 1990). Autism is an excellent example of this principle at work.

Depression

Mood disorders are of particular interest to developmental psychopathologists because of the complex interplay of psychological (e.g., affective, cognitive, interpersonal) and biological (e.g., genetic, neurophysiological, neurobiological) components that are involved (Cicchetti & Toth, 1995; Nolen-Hoeksema & Hilt, 2009). Furthermore, depressive conditions may be conceived as forming a spectrum of severity from transient dysphoria that is universally experienced, to elevated levels of depressive symptoms that do not meet the diagnostic criteria for disorder, to long term periods of dysthymia and episodes of MDD (American Psychiatric Association, 1994). Even within more narrowly defined disorders such as MDD, there are likely to be heterogeneous conditions with phenotypic similarity, despite differences in etiology. Although there are diverse pathways leading to depressive disorders, potential risk factors for depression may result in a multitude of outcomes, of which depression may be one. Moreover, depressive phenomena and disorders are present throughout the life span, from early childhood through senescence (Cicchetti & Toth, 1995; Costello & Angold, 1995). Because of the continuities and divergences from normal functioning manifested in depressive disorders across the life course, the study of depression holds promise for understanding the interface of normal and abnormal adaptation. Knowledge of normal development and functioning assist in characterizing the deviations evident among those with depression, and understanding the aberrations in functioning among depressed persons also elucidates how normal adaptation may be achieved.

Individuals with depressive disorders, as well as their offspring, are at increased risk for the development of emotion regulatory difficulties, insecure attachment relationships, impaired representational and self-system development, social information processing deficits, and problems in peer and marital relationships. A variety of genetic and neurobiological anomalies also are characteristic of depressive illness (Cicchetti & Toth, 1995, 2009). Additionally, comorbid conduct disorder and alcohol and substance use disorders exacerbate the developmental course of depressed individuals, resulting in even worse outcomes for these multiply-affected persons. Moreover, many individuals with depression experience maltreatment (i.e., sexual and physical abuse) in their childhoods, and the co-occurrence of maltreatment and depression results in a dysregulated stress neurobiology signature (Cicchetti & Rogosch, 2001b; Cicchetti et al., 2010; Heim et al., 2008; see Cicchetti & Toth, 1995; Dahl & Ryan, 1996; Downey & Coyne, 1990; and Nolen-Hoeksema & Hilt, 2009, for detailed accounts of the multilevel precursors and pathways to depression and its developmental sequelae).

The developmental psychopathology perspective also provides important insights useful for intervention after depression has occurred as well as to prevent the emergence of depressive disorders. Understanding the organization of developmental competencies among depressed persons is invaluable for conceptualizing the meaning of symptom expression and the capacities of different depressed persons to benefit from different types of treatment. For example, understanding the attachment organization of adults and the manner in which that attachment organization is involved in symptom expression have important implications for how treatment will succeed and for choosing what types of treatment are likely to be efficacious. Dozier (1990), in studying adults with severe psychopathology, found that patients with affective disorders were more likely to have greater security in their adult attachment organizations than were patients with thought disorders. Greater security was associated with more effective treatment compliance, whereas increased rejection of therapists, less self-disclosure, and poorer treatment involvement occurred with patients having avoidant attachment organization. Additionally, in another study involving dysthymic patients, Patrick, Hobson, Castle, Howard, and Maughan (1994) found that 83% were insecurely attached, with 50% exhibiting dismissing and 33% exhibiting preoccupied adult attachment organizations. These different attachment orientations suggest different approaches may be needed to address how affect, cognition, and interpersonal behaviors are organized within individual patients' depressive presentations. Similarly, the differentiation of dependent and self-critical personality styles among depressed individuals (Blatt & Luyten, 2009) implies that different domains of developmental deficit are involved for the two types of depressed individuals, and, as a result, alternative foci of treatment are required.

Treatment for depression also may need to vary depending on the history of prior depressive episodes. In studying the developmental progression of episodes among mood-disordered patients, Post (1992) notes that the more automatic triggering of episodes later in the course of these disorders likely requires different treatments. For first episodes of depressive disorder, interpersonal psychotherapies may have greater utility in reorganizing the affective, cognitive, and interpersonal difficulties depressed patients exhibit. However, as later episodes may become increasingly primed biologically, psychopharmacological intervention with more directive cognitive-behavioral techniques is likely to be more essential. Additionally, alternative drug treatments may become necessary, as the progression of episodes and concomitant biological alterations may make previously effective drugs no longer effective (see also Post et al., 1996).

For younger depressed patients, interventions must always be mindful of the varying capacities children at different development levels have to make use of various child therapy approaches (Shirk, 1988; Toth & Cicchetti, 1999). Moreover, children continue to develop in an ongoing matrix of risk and protective factors that influences the course of their adaptation. Interventions to alter parental, familial, and social–contextual sources of risk are necessary to alleviate ongoing contributors to the difficulty depressed children have in resolving stage-salient issues of development. Because depressed children are likely to have experienced maladaptive resolutions of prior stage-salient issues (e.g., homeostatic and physiological regulation, affect differentiation and regulation, attachment organization, self-system processes), attention to reorganizing these critical domains through therapeutic interventions is crucial. Moreover, helping children to attain adaptive functioning in current stage-salient domains (e.g., peer relations, school achievement) is likely to be beneficial in beginning to reorganize and rework prior developmental incompetencies.

Given that the roots of depressotypic developmental organizations may extend down to infancy, prevention efforts that focus on early intervention in high-risk conditions are likely to be important for promoting competent early developmental attainments on the sequence of stage-salient developmental issues (Cicchetti, Rogosch, & Toth, 1999, 2000; Toth et al., 2006). Although parental depression is a risk condition that may impair developmental functioning in offspring, numerous disadvantageous familial and societal circumstances (e.g., parental psychopathology, parental substance abuse, marital violence, child maltreatment, poverty) constitute situations that may detract from children competently resolving developmental challenges, thereby contributing to risk for depressive outcomes. Broad-based community programs to promote children's competence and to support adaptive family relationships are likely to be important for preventing developmental failures associated with depressotypic organizations, thereby reducing the prevalence of depression on a population level.

Because of the potential for increased genetic as well as psychological risk with which offspring of depressed parents are faced, preventive interventions for such families may be particularly important. Such prevention strategies, beginning at an early age, should incorporate multiple foci and strategies, including attention to alleviating the parental depression, enhancing parent–child adaptive communication and interaction, and reducing larger family stresses, such as marital discord. In so doing, the likelihood of promoting competence as these children confront the universal challenges of development will be enhanced, and depressive outcomes may be prevented. The need for and provision of preventive services for offspring of depressed parents will likely require changes in social and health care policy. All too often services are designated restrictively for the individual with the "disorder," and the larger needs of family systems, offspring, and the functioning of depressed adults as parents are neglected.

Despite the fact that depression is a treatable illness, considerable social stigma continues to be associated with seeking treatment for depression, and large numbers of individuals who are clinically depressed remain untreated (IOM, 1985, 1989). Increased awareness of the availability and utility of treatments for depression, both for children and adults, and reducing the negative public attitudes toward treatment necessitates social and health policies that educate the public regarding depression, its effects, and the importance of intervention, as well as increase the availability and accessibility of treatment.

Substance Abuse

Despite Denise Kandel's (1978) assertion that "drug use and related behaviors...cannot be properly studied apart from concurrent developmental processes" (p. 34), until the past several decades, classic disease models of addiction were the predominant viewpoint espoused in the drug abuse literature. In 1996, the IOM published the results of its examination on pathways to drug addiction. The IOM (1996) report made explicit recommendations for the kinds of research needed to expand the understanding of the etiology of drug use disorders, including the following points, each of which is consistent with a developmental psychopathology approach: (a) multidisciplinary research to investigate the combined effects of biological, psychosocial, and contextual factors as they relate to the development of drug use, abuse, and dependence; (b) studies of sufficient duration to enable follow-up of participants in determining the role of risk and protective factors related to the transition from drug use to abuse to dependence; (c) research investigating the role of family factors in the etiology of drug use and abuse; (d) examination of psychopathology as a precursor to drug use and abuse in adolescents and adults; (e) studies of risk and protective factors related to drug use and abuse, especially during discrete developmental stages; and (f) investigation of childhood risk and protective factors that are associated with adult drug abuse and dependence.

It has now become increasingly common for research on substance use and abuse to adopt a developmental perspective. The growing movement to a developmental approach to drug abuse requires that the present status of an individual's functioning be examined within the broader context of how that status was attained across the earlier course of development. Consequently, the life-span perspective strives to move beyond the proximal causes of current outcomes to examining the developmental progression of distal sources of influence that have eventuated in present functioning (Cicchetti & Tucker, 1994; Sroufe et al., 1990). For example, the social, genetic, biological, and psychological factors that are connected with initiating a pattern of drug use are not necessarily isomorphic with those factors that influence the persistence of the pattern and subsequent abuse. Individuals exhibit variability in neuronal circuitry and neurochemistry that affect their likelihood of becoming compulsive drug users. Likewise, drugs alter numerous biological processes, including neurotransmitter formation, reuptake, and receptor function and brain neuroregulators (Bloom, 1993; Hyman & Nestler, 1996; IOM, 1985). Furthermore, individual differences exist in how persons react to the pharmacological effects of drugs, including their differential sensitivity to the reinforcing effects of drugs, the varying expectancies associated with drug use, and variability in the likelihood of developing sensitization tolerance and addiction to drugs (IOM, 1996). Finally, there is heterogeneity in the motivational processes underlying individual's inclinations to engage in drug use, including factors such as varying predispositions to experiencing negative affect and, therefore, to seek out altered states of consciousness; heightened life stress; and adequacy of coping skills (Sher, 1994). Thus, given that a confluence of influences contribute to the use and abuse of drugs at different developmental periods (i.e., equifinality) and that entry into or out of a problem drug-consumption pathway may occur at any point in the life course, it is critical that researchers not view the initiation, cessation, or maintenance of drug abuse as the sole or primary phenomenon of interest (Zucker, Fitzgerald, & Moses, 1995). It should not be surprising that no biological or psychological characteristic has been discovered that antedates initiation into drug abuse in all individuals or that there is no common predisposing factor, other than drug use, that is shared by all individuals who develop into substance abusers.

The concept of multifinality described earlier in this chapter specifies that diverse outcomes are likely to emanate from any original starting point. The ongoing transaction of risk and protective processes, which vary across individuals, will eventuate in different outcome emerging over the course of development. For example, being the offspring of a parent with a drug addiction may contribute to an individual developing a subsequent drug use problem. However, all such individuals will not inevitably become substance abusers. Other psychopathological outcomes (e.g., antisocial personality disorder, major depression), as well as normal, adaptive functioning, may occur.

In addition to proximal influences at the period when drug use and problem use emerges, the research lens must be extended to include the progression of developmental organization in the context of transacting risk and protective processes from early in development. The meanings of many of the proximal influences on drug use and abuse are likely to be clarified when knowledge on how these influences have been derived developmentally is obtained. Moreover, although studying the onset of drug abuse and dependence in adolescence is important in its own right for understanding processes leading to succumbing to an early onset of drug problems, the longitudinal window on development also must be extended into adulthood because there are inevitably many individuals who are vulnerable to substance use problems who have not yet developed these problems in adolescence. In particular, further pathways involving different developmental organizations, in addition to the frequent conduct disorder–antisocial prototype, may become more prominent beyond the adolescent years.

During the course of development, there may be prototypic organizations of biological and psychological systems that have the potential for transformation into a spectrum of drug-abusing presentations. The relation among components of each system rather than the individual components of each system per se generates patterns or levels of drug-abusing organization (cf. Zucker et al., 1995). Aberrations in the organization of the cognitive, emotional, interpersonal, representational, and genetic–biological domains most likely exist to different degrees among drug-abusing individuals and their offspring. Notably, these varied developmental systems do not exist in isolation. Rather, they are complexly interrelated and mutually interdependent. In adaptively functioning individuals, there is a coherent organization among these psychological and biological domains (Cicchetti & Schneider-Rosen, 1986; Sroufe, 1979). In contrast, in drug-abusing individuals, there is likely to be an incoherent organization among these systems or an organization of pathological structures—that is, a prototypic drug-abusing organization. Such problematic organizations evolve developmentally and may eventuate in substance abuse disorders at different points in the life span. Consequently, comprehending the interrelations among these psychological and biological domains is vital to delineate the nature and course of these drug-abusing disorders, as well as to elucidate how these domains also promote adaptive functioning.

There may be numerous forms of such incoherent organizations that, depending on the nature of subsequent experiences in development, may eventuate in drug abuse or other psychopathological outcomes. For example, in a longitudinal investigation of drug abuse and other problems behaviors, Jessor and Jessor (1977) examined three classes of variables: personality, perceived environment, and behavior. These investigators theorized that each system comprised structures of variables that were organized and interrelated so as to generate a resultant dynamic state, which they designated a "problem behavior proneness" (Jessor & Jessor, 1977, p. 26) that had implications for greater or lesser likelihood of engaging in problematic behaviors, including drug abuse.

Early forms of maladaptive prototypic organizations of biological and psychological systems may not resemble later drug abuse phenotypically, even though coherence in molar organization between a prior prototype and later drug abuse may be discerned. For example, difficulties modulating emotional impulses may be an early prototypic feature with linkages to later drug abuse and perhaps to subsequent conduct disorder and antisocial personality disorder. These difficulties with emotion regulation throughout development may also become integrated with other changes in psychological (e.g., cognitive, interpersonal, social–cognitive, and representational) and biological development that may eventually result in a drug-abusing presentation. Alternatively, difficulties modulating and regulating emotion, given disparate developmental processes and experiences, including social, biological, and psychological, might eventuate in different forms of disorder or comorbidity of disorders (Sroufe, 1997). For some individuals, however, there may be continuity between early difficulties in emotion regulation and later drug abuse, although the phenotypic presentation in later life might appear discontinuous with its early-life predecessor.

In summary, the possibility of a prototypical drug-abusing organization suggests an integration of maladaptive features across the various psychological and biological systems. Difficulties may arise in one component system and subsequently, through hierarchic integration, affect other psychological or biological systems. Such a prototypic drug-abusing organization might have high potential for transforming into later drug abuse, depending on subsequent biological, social, and psychological transactions in development. The recognition of prototypic organizations that predate actual clinical levels of drug abuse can be factored into prevention programs, to deflect a person from a maladaptive pathway.

Additionally, increased attention to the pathways and trajectories followed by individuals who avoid developing drug abuse despite the presence of significant enduring vulnerability and transient challenging factors may be helpful to informing prevention and intervention efforts. For example, what mechanisms protect a child who lives in an environment permeated by intrafamilial, community, and sociocultural risk factors from becoming involved in drug-abusing behavior? In high-risk environmental contexts, a child may be placed at risk for drug abuse through the presence of factors such as family history (e.g., the presence of drug abuse or antisocial personality disorder in one or both parents), learning (e.g., modeling drug-using behaviors), and the pursuit of concrete needs (e.g., food, clothing) because of pervasive poverty conditions. Despite this aggregation of risk factors, however, many children experiencing these circumstances avoid developing drug abuse. To address questions such as these, prospective longitudinal investigations of individuals at risk for the development of disorders of drug abuse must be initiated.

Finally, it is essential that etiologic research on pathways to addiction increasingly begins to use prevention research as a means to uncover the causal risk mechanisms and processes for substance use disorders. The emerging discipline of prevention science (IOM, 1994) has provided examples of how prevention research, informed by developmental principles, can make major contributions to the understanding of mechanisms that have gone awry in the development of maladaptive or psychopathological outcomes. The discovery of such mechanisms has the potential to suggest prevention and intervention strategies for improving the lives of substance-abusing individuals.

Schizophrenia

Congruent with the theoretical principles of a developmental systems approach on brain development, it is expected that a de-differentiation and disintegration would characterize the neurobiological and psychological development and functioning of individuals with mental disorders. Much of the contemporary research in the area of neurodevelopment and schizophrenia owes a significant portion of its historical roots to the formulations of Emil Kraepelin (1919), who conceived of schizophrenia as a deteriorating brain disease in its natural history, albeit with an onset in early adult life. Since the 1980s, when a resurgence of interest in initiating neurobiological studies in schizophrenia took place, Kraepelin's viewpoint has been challenged and radically altered by advances from several levels of inquiry that point to a prenatal–perinatal origin of at least some of the brain abnormalities found in individuals with schizophrenia. During the early 1980s, a number of investigations converged, and all found evidence for increased ventricle size in persons with schizophrenic illness (Shenton et al., 2001). These enlarged ventricles were present at the onset of the illness and did not protract in size as the illness proceeded over time, even in prospective longitudinal studies. This finding suggested that a neurodegenerative process was not responsible for causing the illness.

The retrospective observations of Laura Bender (1947) and Barbara Fish (1957), as well as the follow-back study by Norman Watt (1971), in which a pattern of abnormalities in neurological and behavioral parameters dating back to childhood were found in adults with schizophrenia, laid the seeds of the neurodevelopmental hypothesis of schizophrenia (Marenco & Weinberger, 2000). Moreover, a number of longitudinal studies demonstrated that some degree of recovery was possible in some cases of schizophrenia (Garmezy, 1970; Tsuang, Wollson, & Fleming, 1979; Zigler & Glick, 1986), thereby casting further doubt on the Kraepelinian viewpoint that schizophrenia is a degenerative disease of early adulthood ("dementia praecox").

Similarly, prospective longitudinal high-risk offspring studies have revealed that behavioral antecedents of schizophrenia occurred before the disease. Fish (1977) demonstrated that neurobiologic disorder exists in infants and children before the onset of more chronic forms of schizophrenia. Fish's (1977) discovery of pan-developmental retardation was considered an early marker of the inherited neurointegrative defect (i.e., schizotaxia) postulated by Paul Meehl (1962, 1989) to exist in schizophrenia. Importantly, Fish noted that the phenotypic manifestations of the neurointegrative defect change over epigenesis and that the signs of dysregulation of maturation are found in many developing systems. Specifically, Fish reported that the neurointegrative disorder present from infancy disrupted the normal timing, sequence, and overall organization of development. Moreover, in a landmark prospective longitudinal investigation, Fish, Marcus, Hans, Auerbach, and Perdue (1992) discovered that the infant offspring of schizophrenic mothers displayed greater lags in their motor development during infancy and that a number of these infants themselves went on to develop schizophrenia or schizotypal personality disorders (see also the seminal work of Walker, Davis, & Gottlieb, 1991, in this regard).

Relatedly, Cannon, Rosso, Bearden, Sanchez, and Hadley (1999), in their epidemiological investigation of the Philadelphia cohort of the National Collaborative Perinatal Project, provided compelling evidence that adverse experiences during gestation and birth, as well as deviant cognitive, motor, and behavioral functioning during early childhood, are associated with an increased risk for schizophrenia. In particular, these investigators demonstrated that the risk for schizophrenia increases linearly with the severity of fetal oxygen deprivation. In prior neuroimaging studies of high-risk samples (Cannon, Mednick, Parnas, & Schulsinger, 1993; Cannon et al., 2002), a history of perinatal hypoxia was found to be associated with increased severity of a neuropathological indicator of schizophrenia (i.e., ventricular enlargement) among individuals with an elevated genetic risk for the disorder but not among control subjects at low genetic risk. Together, this evidence suggests that a genetic factor in schizophrenia may render the fetal brain particularly susceptible to the effects of oxygen deprivation and encourages search for molecular mechanisms underlying this heightened neural vulnerability.

Cannon et al. (1999) also discovered that preschizophrenic individuals show evidence of cognitive, motor, and behavioral dysfunction during the first 7 years of life (cf. Walker et al., 1991). Because there was not evidence of significant intraindividual decline during this period within any domain of functioning, the results argue against the view that a deteriorative neural process underlies these early phenotypic expressions of liability to schizophrenia. Rather, the findings suggest that an increasing number of diverse phenotypic signs emerge with age as the various brain systems required for their expression reach fundamental maturity. Finally, because similar functional disturbances were observed in the unaffected siblings of the preschizophrenic cases, it would appear that these cognitive, motor, and behavioral disturbances are indicators of an inherited neural diathesis to schizophrenia (cf. Walker & Diforio, 1997).

In addition to the early and more recent work with preschizophrenic infants and children that served as an impetus for modifying the Kraepelinian (1919) view of schizophrenia, contemporary findings have contributed to the belief that the neurobiological foundations of schizophrenia are established, at least in part, during the development of the brain. These include the following:

1. A number of prospective longitudinal investigations have discovered an association between prenatal and perinatal complications (e.g., fetal hypoxia) and an increased risk for the later development of schizophrenia. As Rakic (1988a, 1998b, 1996; Sidman & Rakic, 1982) and Nowakowski (1987; Nowakowski & Hayes, 1999) have concluded, during periods of rapid brain development in which neuronal migration is occurring and synaptic connections are formed, the fetal brain is especially vulnerable. Exogenous teratogens, such as maternal influenza (J. Brown et al., 2004; Mednick, Machon, Huttunen, & Bonett, 1988) and maternal exposure to toxoplasmosis (A. S. Brown et al., 2005), along with

obstetric complications, such as perinatal hypoxia (Cannon, 1998), in concert with the genetic predisposition to schizophrenia, may exert dramatic effects on the regions of the brain experiencing the most rapid growth. Introducing birth complications and teratogens may also place the cortical connections being established and refined at increased risk for aberrant development.

2. A number of postmortem neuropathology studies have found evidence of heterotopic displacement of neurons in various regions of the brain, including the hippocampus and the frontal and temporal cortices. These findings suggest that there are disturbances of brain development in utero in many individuals with schizophrenia.
3. Disturbances in neurogenesis, neuronal migration and differentiation, synaptogenesis, neuronal and synaptic pruning (perhaps results in reduced synaptic connectivity; cf. McGlashan & Hoffman, 2000), and myelination, occurring at the cellular and molecular levels, suggest that schizophrenia is a disorder that is instantiated in brain development (Arnold, 1999; Breslin & Weinberger, 1990; Weinberger, 1987).

   For example, the laminar distribution of cortical neurons is displaced inward in schizophrenia, indicating a defect in cortical organization, suggesting that the normal process of "inside-out" neuronal migration (cf. Rakic, 1988a, 1988b) during the second trimester of gestation also is likely to be anomalous, as should the neuronal connectivity and circuitry (Arnold, 1999; Weinberger, 1995). In addition, Lewis, Hashimoto, and Volk (2005) concluded that there are atypicalities in cortical inhibitory neurons (i.e., gamma-aminobutyric acid neurons) in schizophrenia and that these abnormalities play a role in the impairments of working memory function that are a core feature of clinical schizophrenia. Moreover, alterations in dopamine and glutamate neurotransmission in the dorsolateral prefrontal cortex (DLPFC) also are involved in the working memory dysfunction in schizophrenia. Relatedly, Meyer-Lindenberg et al. (2005) have discovered that hippocampal dysfunction may manifest in schizophrenia because of an inappropriate bidirectional modulatory relation with the DLPFC.
4. A growing body of neuroimaging studies has identified gross structural neuroanatomical changes in young, untreated patients in their first psychotic episode. Further, and in contrast to a Kaepelinian (1919) neurodegenerative viewpoint, these investigations also have failed to discover evidence of deterioration in these neuropathological markers with increasing length of illness (Marenco & Weinberg, 2000).
5. A number of the unaffected first-degree relatives of patients with schizophrenia manifest the structural and functional brain abnormalities observed in the disorder, implying that such abnormalities may be mediated, in part, by genetic predisposition to the disorder. Homeobox genes, which serve as transcription factors regulating gene expression, represent potential candidate genes in disorders in which a disruption of cortical neurogenesis has been implicated, such as in schizophrenia (Steingard & Coyle, 1998).

The extant models linking neurodevelopment and schizophrenia point to a nonlinearity of relations (Bearden et al., 2006). Specifically, a significant amount of time elapses between the gestational events hypothesized to create a predisposition to schizophrenia and the onset of the symptoms of the disorder later in life. Longitudinal follow-up of individuals who have experienced traumatic insults to the brain at early stages of development, such as is likely the case in many instances of schizophrenia, enables investigators to chart and observe the changing expression of these early lesions as development modifies behavior in general.

Alternatively, for some individuals it also is conceivable that the lesion directly affects later developmental processes through cascade, propagation, and expansion (Cicchetti & Tucker, 1994; Courchesne et al., 1994; Post et al., 1994; Steingard & Coyle, 1998). These options all provide an opportunity to discover how brain and behavior reorganize following the experience of insults at different points in the developmental course.

Because not all persons who experience the gestational disturbances noted in the literature go on to develop clinical schizophrenia, Gottlieb's (1992) concept of probabilistic epigenesis is evoked. Furthermore, the existing research reveals that there are a number of pathways through which the early neurodevelopmental anomalies may result in schizophrenia. The identification of these diverse pathways to schizophrenia provides insight into how specificity and differentiation into a syndrome may result from a commonality of initiating circumstances (i.e., equifinality). Accordingly, it appears that the processes underlying the normal development and maturation of cortical circuitry and connectivity may have gone awry in schizophrenia (Arnold, 1999; Benes, 1995; McGlashan

& Hoffman, 2000; Weinberger, 1987). Unraveling these misorganizations in brain development should contribute greatly to understanding the genesis and epigenesis of schizophrenic disorders. Advances in molecular genetics and in the identification of endophenotypes that are associated genetically with neurobiological development hold much promise for enhancing the understanding of the origins and course of schizophrenia (Gottesman & Gould, 2003; see also Gottesman, 1991, and Gottesman & Shields, 1972).

The incorporation of a developmental psychopathology perspective is well suited to schizophrenic disorder. The ontogenesis and epigenesis of schizophrenia is a long-term process that involves multiple phases, risk factors, and mechanisms (Bearden et al., 2006). Moreover, not all persons at risk for schizophrenia develop the psychosis (Garmezy & Streitman, 1974; Meehl, 1989). As longitudinal, multidomain, and multiple-levels-of-analysis investigations increase, it is likely that our comprehension of the developmental trajectories of neurobiological processes to schizophrenic disorder will enhance our ability to intervene earlier in the disorder. These multidisciplinary research programs may provide insight into the stages of schizophrenic illness that offer the best windows of time within which intervention can occur.

CONCLUSION

In a relatively brief period, research in developmental psychopathology has contributed significantly to our understanding of risk, disorder, and adaptation across the life course (see Cicchetti & Cohen, 1995a, 1995b, 2006a, 2006b, 2006c, and Special Issues of *Development and Psychopathology*). Much of the momentum of developmental psychopathology has stemmed from an openness to preexisting knowledge in combination with a willingness to question established beliefs, thereby continuing to promote disciplinary growth. The integration of concepts and methods derived from areas of endeavor that are too often isolated from each other has resulted in knowledge advances that might have been missed in the absence of cross-disciplinary dialogue (Cicchetti & Sroufe, 2000; Gunnar & Cicchetti, 2009).

Numerous challenges lie ahead, and we must continue to examine critically the implicit as well as the explicit conceptual and scientific assumptions that exist in the field of developmental psychopathology to sustain our momentum and to foster new advances (Cicchetti & Richters, 1997). Future investigations must strive to attain enhanced fidelity between the elegance and complexity of the theoretical models and definitional parameters inherent to a developmental psychopathology perspective and the design, measurement, and data analytic strategies employed in our investigations (Granic & Hollenstein, 2003; Richters, 1997). Moreover, the continuation and elaboration of the mutually enriching interchanges that have occurred within and across disciplines interested in normal and abnormal development will enhance not only the science of developmental psychopathology but also the benefits to be derived for society as a whole.

The impressive array of findings in the psychological developmental literature, in concert with the concomitant progress made in the neurosciences, molecular genetics, and related disciplines, has led to increasing acknowledgment of the need to conduct collaborative, multidisciplinary, multidomain studies on normal, high-risk, and psychopathological populations. It has now become more widely accepted that research into pathological conditions must proceed hand in hand with so-called basic research into human functioning. As progress in knowledge in the various subdisciplines of developmental psychopathology continues, the common theoretical and empirical threads running through this work will coalesce to establish a foundation on which an increasingly sophisticated developmental psychopathology discipline can grow. The power embodied by cross-disciplinary collaborations that use multiple-levels-of-analysis methodologies promise to strengthen significantly our capacity to decrease the burden of mental illness for individuals, families, and society (cf. Insel, 2009; Insel & Scolnick, 2006).

In contrast to the viewpoint that mental disorders are "brain disorders" or "brain diseases," developmental psychopathologists conceptualize mental disorders in a more complex, systems fashion (Cicchetti & Cannon, 1999; Cicchetti & Tucker, 1994; Sroufe, 1997). Although the brain is clearly involved in all mental disorders, many other systems contribute and transact with the brain in dynamic fashion over the life course to bring about experience-dependent brain development (e.g., Greenough et al., 1987). The motivation underlying the promotion of the viewpoint that mental disorders are "brain diseases" may, in part, be to help reduce personal and familial blame for aberrant behavior and emotion. Nonetheless, it is essential that researchers convey scientific truth to the lay public regarding the complex, multilevel, and dynamic processes that undergird the development of psychopathology. Although there are clearly strong psychobiologic predispositions to many forms of mental disorder, the concept of "brain disorder" may connote primacy or exclusivity for the biology and fail to underscore transactional developmental processes. The increased emphasis on a multilevel, dynamic systems approach to psychopathology and resilience (Cicchetti & Blender, 2006; Cicchetti & Curtis, 2007; Cicchetti & Dawson, 2002; Masten, 2007b), the growing attention paid to G×E interactions in the development of psychopathology and resilience (Cicchetti, 2007; Moffitt et al., 2006; Rutter, 2006), and the application of a multilevel developmental psychopathology perspective to mental illnesses that have traditionally been empirically investigated in a nondevelopmental fashion (e.g., bipolar disorder and the personality disorders—Cicchetti & Crick, in 2009a, 2009b; Lenzenweger & Cicchetti, 2005; Miklowitz & Cicchetti, 2006, 2010) will contribute to educating the public about the causes and consequences of mental disorder.

REFERENCES

Aber, J. L., & Cicchetti, D. (1984). Socioemotional development in maltreated children: An empirical and theoretical analysis. In H. Fitzgerald, B. Lester, & M. Yogman (Eds.), *Theory and research in behavioral pediatrics* (Vol. 2, pp. 147–205). New York: Plenum Press.

Aber, J. L., & Zigler, E. (1981). Developmental considerations in the definition of child maltreatment. *New Directions for Child Development, 11,* 1–29.

Abramson, L. Y., Seligman, M. E. P., & Teasdale, J. D. (1978). Learned helplessness in humans: Critique and reformulation. *Journal of Abnormal Psychology, 87,* 49–74.

Achenbach, T. M. (1974). *Developmental psychopathology*. New York: Ronald Press.

Administration for Children and Families. (2003). *Prevention pays: The costs of not preventing child abuse and neglect*. Washington, DC: National Clearinghouse on Child Abuse and Neglect Information.

Ainsworth, M. D. S., Blehar, M. C., Waters, E., & Wall, S. (1978). *Patterns of attachment: A psychological study of the Strange Situation*. Hillsdale, NJ: Erlbaum.

Akshoomoff, N., Pierce, K., & Courchesne, E. (2002). The neurobiological basis of autism from a developmental perspective. *Development and Psychopathology, 14,* 613–634.

Alberts, B., Bray, D., Lewis, J., Raff, M., Roberts, K., & Watson, J. D. (1994). *Molecular biology of the cell* (3rd ed.). New York: Guilford Press.

Alessandri, S. M., & Lewis, M. (1996). Differences in pride and shame in maltreated and non-maltreated preschoolers. *Child Development, 67,* 1857–1869.

American Psychiatric Association. (1987). *Diagnostic and statistical manual of mental disorders* (3rd ed.). Washington, DC: Author.

American Psychiatric Association. (1994). *Diagnostic and statistical manual of mental disorders* (4th ed.). Washington, DC: Author.

Anderson, C. M., Teicher, M. H., Polcari, A., & Renshaw, P. F. (2002). Abnormal T2 relaxation time in the cerebellar vermis of adults sexually abused in childhood: Potential role of the vermis in stress-enhanced risk for drug abuse. *Psychoneuroendocrinology, 27,* 231–244.

Arnold, S. E. (1999). Neurodevelopment abnormalities in schizophrenia: Insights from neuropathology. *Development and Psychopathology, 11,* 439–456.

Arnow, B. A. (2004). Relationships between childhood maltreatment, adult health and psychiatric outcomes, and medical utilization. *Journal of Clinical Psychiatry, 65,* 10.

Aylward, E. H., Minshew, N. J., Field, K., Sparks, B. F., & Singh, N. (2002). Effects of age on brain volume and head circumference in autism. *Neurology, 59,* 175–183.

Bachevalier, J., & Loveland, K. A. (2003). Early orbitofrontal-limbic dysfunction and autism. In D. Cicchetti & E. Walker (Eds.), *Neurodevelopmental mechanisms in psychopathology* (pp. 215–236). New York: Cambridge University Press.

Bakermans-Kranenberg, M. J., Van IJzendoorn, M. H., Pijlman, F. T. A., Mesman, J., & Juffer, F. (2007). Experimental evidence for differential susceptibility: Dopamine D4 receptor polymorphism (DRD4 VNTR) moderates intervention effects on toddlers' externalizing behavior in randomized controlled trial. *Developmental Psychology, 44*, 293–300.

Baltes, P. B., Reese, H. W., & Lipsitt, L. P. (1980). Life-span developmental psychology. *Annual Review of Psychology, 32,* 65–110.

Barnett, D., Ganiban, J., & Cicchetti, D. (1999). Maltreatment, negative expressivity, and the development of Type D attachments from 12- to 24-months of age. *Society for Research in Child Development Monograph, 64,* 97–118.

Barnett, D., Manly, J. T., & Cicchetti, D. (1991). Continuing toward an operational definition of psychological maltreatment. *Development and Psychopathology, 3,* 19–30.

Barnett, D., Manly, J. T., & Cicchetti, D. (1993). Defining child maltreatment: The interface between policy and research. In D. Cicchetti & S. L. Toth (Eds.), *Child abuse, child development, and social policy* (pp. 7–73). Norwood, NJ: Ablex.

Baron-Cohen, S., Hoekstra, R. A., Knickmeyer, R., & Wheelwright, S. (2006). The Autism-Spectrum Quotient (AQ)—adolescent version. *Journal of Autism and Developmental Disorders, 36*(3), 343–350.

Baron-Cohen, S., Leslie, A. M., & Frith, U. (1985). Does the autistic child have a "theory of mind"? *Cognition, 21,* 37–46.

Barr, C. S., Newman, T. K., Shannon, C., Parker, C., Dvoskin, R. L., Becker, M. L., et al. (2004). Rearing condition and rh5-HTTLPR interact to influence limbic-hypothalamic-pituitary adrenal axis response to stress in infant macaques. *Biological Psychiatry, 55,* 733–738.

Battle, C. L., Shea, M. T., Johnson, D. M., Yen, S., Zlotnick, C., Zanarini, M. C., et al. (2004). Childhood maltreatment associated with adult personality disorders: Findings from the collaborative longitudinal personality disorders study. *Journal of Personality Disorders, 18,* 193–211.

Bauer, P. J., Wiebe, S. A., Carver, L. J., Waters, J. M., & Nelson, C. A. (2003). Developments in long-term explicit memory late in the first year of life. *Psychological Science, 14,* 629– 635.

Baxter, L. R., Jr., Schwartz, J. M., Bergman, K. S., Szuba, M. P., Guze, B. H., Mazzi-Otta, J. C., et al. (1992). Caudate glucose metabolic rate changes with both drug and behavior therapy for obsessive-compulsive disorder. *Archives of General Psychiatry, 49,* 681–689.

Bearden, C. E., Meyer, S. E., Loewy, R. L., Niendam, T. A., & Cannon, T. D. (2006). The neurodevelopmental model of schizophrenia: Updated. In D. Cicchetti & D. Cohen (Eds.), *Developmental psychopathology, Vol. 3: Risk, disorder, and adaptation* (2nd ed., pp. 542–569). Hoboken, NJ: John Wiley & Sons.

Beeghly, M., & Cicchetti, D. (1994). Child maltreatment, attachment, and the self system: Emergence of an internal state lexicon in toddlers at high social risk. *Development and Psychopathology, 6*, 5–30.

Beitchman, J. H., Mik, H. M, Ehtesham, S., Douglas, L., & Kennedy, J. L. (2004). MAOA and persistent, pervasive childhood aggression *Molecular Psychiatry, 9*, 546–547.

Bemporad, J. R., & Romano, S. J. (1992). Childhood maltreatment and adult depression: A review of research. In D. Cicchetti & S. L. Toth (Eds.), *Rochester Symposium on Developmental Psychopathology: Vol. 4. Developmental perspectives on depression* (pp. 351–376). Rochester, NY: University of Rochester Press.

Bender, L. (1947). Childhood schizophrenia: Clinical study of 100 schizophrenic children. *American Journal of Orthopsychiatry, 17*, 40–56.

Benes, F. M. (1995). A neurodevelopmental approach to the understanding of schizophrenia and other mental disorders. In D. Cicchetti & D. J. Cohen (Eds.), *Developmental psychopathology: Vol. 1. Theory and methods* (pp. 227–253). New York: John Wiley & Sons.

Bergman, L. R., & Magnusson, D. (1997). A person-oriented approach in research on developmental psychopathology. *Development and Psychopathology, 9*, 291–319.

Besharov, D. (1981). Toward better research on child abuse and neglect: Making definitional issues an explicit methodological concern. *Child Abuse and Neglect, 5*, 383–389.

Bettelheim, B. (1967). *The empty fortress*. New York: The Free Press.

Bjorklund, D. F. (1997). The role of immaturity in human development. *Psychological Bulletin, 122*, 153–169.

Black, J., Jones, T. A., Nelson, C. A., & Greenough, W. T. (1998). Neuronal plasticity and the developing brain. In N. E. Alessi, J. T. Coyle, S. I. Harrison, & S. Eth (Eds.), *Handbook of child and adolescent psychiatry* (pp. 31–53). New York: John Wiley & Sons.

Black, M. H., & Dubowitz, H. (1999). Child neglect: Research recommendations and future directions. In H. Dubowitz (Ed.), *Neglected children: Research, practice, and policy*. Thousand Oaks, CA: Sage.

Blatt, S. J., & Luyten, P. (2009). A structural-developmental psychodynamic approach to psychopathology: Two polarities of experience across the life span. *Development and Psychopathology, 21*, 793–814.

Bloom, F. (1993). The neurobiology of addiction: An integrative view. In S. Korenman & J. Barchas (Eds.), *Biological basis of substance abuse* (pp. 3–16). New York: Oxford University Press.

Bolger, K. E., & Patterson, C. J. (2001). Pathways from child maltreatment to internalizing problems: Perceptions of control as mediators and moderators. *Development and Psychopathology, 13*, 913–940.

Bolger, K. E., Patterson, C. J., & Kupersmidt, J. B. (1998). Peer relationships and self-esteem among children who have been maltreated. *Child Development, 69*, 1171–1197.

Bornstein, M. H., Hahn, C. S., Bell, C., Haynes, O. M., Slater, A., Golding, J., et al. (2006). Stability in cognition across early childhood: A developmental cascade. *Psychological Science, 17*, 151–158.

Bowlby, J. (1982). *Attachment and loss: Vol. 1. Attachment.* New York: Basic Books. (Original work published 1969)

Boyce, W. T., Frank, E., Jensen, P. S., Kessler, R. C., Nelson, C. A., Steinberg, L., et al. (1998). Social context in developmental psychopathology: Recommendations for future research from the MacArthur Network on Psychopathology and Development. *Development and Psychopathology, 10*, 143–164.

Bremner, J. D., Krystal, J. H., Southwick, S. M., & Charney, D. S. (1995). Functional neuroanatomical correlates of the effects of stress on memory. *Journal of Traumatic Stress, 8*, 527–553.

Bremner, J. D., Randall, P., Vermetten, E., Staib, L., Bronen, R. A., Mazure, C. J., et al. (1997). Magnetic resonance imaging-based measurement of hippocampal volume in posttraumatic stress disorder related to childhood physical and sexual abuse-a preliminary report. *Biological Psychiatry, 41*, 23–32.

Bremner, J. D., Vythilingam, M., Vermetten, E., Southwick, S. M., McGlashan, T., Nazeer, A., et al. (2003). MRI and PET study of deficits in hippocampal structure and function in women with childhood sexual abuse and posttraumatic stress disorder. *American Journal of Psychiatry, 160*, 924–932.

Breslin, N. A., & Weinberger, D. R. (1990). Schizophrenia and the normal functional development of the prefrontal cortex. *Development and Psychopathology, 2*, 409–424.

Brewin, C., Andrews, B., & Gotlib, I. H. (1993). Psychopathology and early experience: A reappraisal of retrospective reports. *Psychological Bulletin, 113*, 82–98.

Briere, J., & Runtz, M. (1993). Childhood sexual abuse: Long-term sequelae and implications for psychological assessment. *Journal of Interpersonal Violence, 8*, 312–330.

Brodsky, B. S., Oquendo, M., Ellis, S. P., Haas, G. L., Malone, K. M., & Mann, J. J. (2001). The relationship of childhood abuse to impulsivity and suicidal behavior in adults with major depression. *American Journal of Psychiatry, 158*, 1871–1877.

Brody, A. L., Saxena, S., Stoessel, P., Gillies, L. A., Fairbanks, L. A., Alborzian, S., et al. (2001). Regional brain metabolic changes in patients with major depression treated with either paroxetine or interpersonal therapy: Preliminary findings. *Archives of General Psychiatry, 58*, 631–640.

Brown, A. S., Schaefer, C. A., Quesenberry, C. P., Liu, L., Babulas, V. P., & Susser, E. S. (2005). Maternal exposure to toxoplasmosis and risk of schizophrenia in adult offspring. *American Journal of Psychiatry, 162*(4), 767–773.

Brown, J., Cohen, P., Chen, H., Smailes, E., & Johnson, J. G. (2004). Sexual trajectories of abused and neglected youths. *Journal of Developmental & Behavioral Pediatrics, 25*, 77–82.

Brown, J. W. (1994). Morphogenesis and mental process. *Development and Psychopathology, 6*, 551–563.

Browne, A., & Finkelhor, D. (1986). Impact of child sexual abuse: A review of the literature. *Psychological Bulletin, 99*, 66–77.

Bruer, J. (1999). *The myth of the first three years: A new understanding of early brain development and lifelong learning*. New York: Free Press.

Burt, K. B., Obradović, J., Long, J. D., & Masten, A. S. (2008). The interplay of social competence and psychopathology over 20 years: testing transactional and cascade models. *Child Development, 79*, 359–374.

Cacioppo, J. T., Amaral, D. G., Blanchard, J. J., Cameron, J. L., Carter, C. S., Crews, D., et al. (2007). Social neuroscience: Progress and implications for mental health. *Perspectives on Psychological Science, 2*, 99–123.

Cahan, E., & White, S. (1992). Proposals for a second psychology. *American Psychologist, 47*, 224–235.

Calverley, R. M., Fischer, K. W., & Ayoub, C. (1994). Complex splitting of self representations in sexually abused adolescent girls. *Development and Psychopathology, 6*, 195–213.

Campbell, S. B., Shaw, D. S., & Gilliom, M. (2000). Early externalizing behavior problems: Toddlers and preschoolers at risk for later maladjustment. *Development and Psychopathology, 12*, 467–488.

Camras, L. A., Sachs-Alter, E., & Ribordy, S. (1996). Emotion understanding in maltreated children: Recognition of facial expressions and integration with other emotion cues. In M. Lewis & M. W. Sullivan (Eds.), *Emotional development in atypical children* (pp. 203–225). Hillsdale, NJ: Erlbaum.

Cannon, T. D. (1998). Neurodevelopmental influences in the genesis and epigenesis of schizophrenia: An overview. *Applied and Preventive Psychology, 1*, 47–62.

Cannon, T. D., Mednick, S. A., Parnas, J., & Schulsinger, F. (1993). Developmental brain abnormalities in the offspring of schizophrenic mothers: I. Contributions of genetic and perinatal factors. *Archives of General Psychiatry, 50*, 551–564.

Cannon, T. D., Rosso, I. M., Bearden, C. E., Sanchez, L. E., & Hadley, T. (1999). A prospective cohort study of neurodevelopmental processes in the genesis and epigenesis of schizophrenia. *Development and Psychopathology, 11*, 467–485.

Cannon T. D., Thompson, P. M., van Erp, T. G., Toga, A. W., Poutanen, V. P., et al. (2002). Cortex mapping reveals regionally specific patterns of genetic and disease-specific gray-matter deficits in twins discordant for schizophrenia. *Proceedings of the National Academy of Sciences, 99*, 3228–33.

Carlson, G. A., & Meyer, S. E. (2006). Phenomenology and diagnosis of bipolar disorder in children, adolescents, and adults: Complexities and development issues. *Development and Psychopathology, 18*, 939–969.

Carlson, V., Cicchetti, D., Barnett, D., & Braunwald, K. (1989). Disorganized/disoriented attachment relationships in maltreated infants. *Developmental Psychology, 25*, 525–531.

Caspi, A., McClay, J., Moffitt, T., Mill, J., Martin, J., Craig, I. W., et al. (2002). Role of genotype in the cycle of violence in maltreated children. *Science, 297*, 851–854.

Caspi, A., Sugden, K., Moffitt, T. E., Taylor, A., Craig, I. W., Harrington, H. L., et al. (2003). Influence of life stress on depression: Moderation by a polymorphism in the 5-HTT gene. *Science, 301*, 386–389.

Cerezo, M. A. (1997). Abusive family interaction: A review. *Aggression and Violent Behavior, 2*, 215–240.

Charney, D. (2004). Psychobiological mechanisms of resilience and vulnerability: Implications for successful adaptation to extreme stress. *American Journal of Psychiatry, 161*, 195–216.

Chomsky, N. (1968). *Language and mind.* New York: Harcourt, Brace & World.

Cicchetti, D. (Ed.). (1984a). *Developmental psychopathology*. Chicago: University of Chicago Press.

Cicchetti, D. (1984b). The emergence of developmental psychopathology. *Child Development, 55*, 1–7.

Cicchetti, D. (Ed.). (1989). *Rochester symposium on developmental psychopathology: The emergence of a discipline* (Vol. 1). Hillsdale, NJ: Erlbaum.

Cicchetti, D. (1990). A historical perspective on the discipline of developmental psychopathology. In J. Rolf, A. Masten, D. Cicchetti, K. Nuechterlein, & S. Weintraub (Eds.), *Risk and protective factors in the development of psychopathology* (pp. 2–28). New York: Cambridge University Press.

Cicchetti, D. (1993). Developmental psychopathology: Reactions, reflections, projections. *Developmental Review, 13*, 471–502.

Cicchetti, D. (1996). Child maltreatment: Implications for developmental theory. *Human Development, 39*, 18–39.

Cicchetti, D. (2002). The impact of social experience on neurobiological systems: Illustration from a constructivist view of child maltreatment. *Cognitive Development, 17*, 1407–1428.

Cicchetti, D. (2003). Experiments of nature: Contributions to developmental theory. *Development and Psychopathology, 15*, 833–835.

Cicchetti, D. (2006). Development and psychopathology. In D. Cicchetti & D. Cohen (Eds.), *Developmental Psychopathology: Vol. 1. Theory and method* (2nd ed., pp. 1–23). Hoboken, NJ: John Wiley & Sons.

Cicchetti, D. (Ed.). (2007). G×E interactions and developmental psychopathology [Special issue]. *Development and Psychopathology, 19*(4), 957–1208.

Cicchetti, D., & Aber, J. L. (1998). Editorial: Contextualism and developmental psychopathology. *Development and Psychopathology, 10*, 137–141.

Cicchetti, D., & Barnett, D. (1991a). Attachment organization in pre-school-aged maltreated children. *Development and Psychopathology, 3*, 397–411.

Cicchetti, D., & Barnett, D. (1991b). Toward the development of a scientific nosology of child maltreatment. In W. Grove & D. Cicchetti (Eds.), *Thinking clearly about psychology: Essays in honor of Paul E. Meehl: Personality and psychopathology* (Vol. 2, pp. 346–377). Minneapolis, MN: University of Minnesota Press.

Cicchetti, D., & Beeghly, M. (Eds.). (1990). *Children with Down syndrome: A developmental perspective*. New York: Cambridge University Press.

Cicchetti, D., & Blender, J. A. (2006). A multiple-levels-of-analysis perspective on resilience: Implications for the developing brain, neural plasticity, and preventive interventions. *Annals New York Academy of Science, 1094*, 248–258.

Cicchetti, D., & Cannon, T. D. (1999). Neurodevelopmental processes in the ontogenesis and epigenesis of psychopathology. *Development and Psychopathology, 11*, 375–393.

Cicchetti, D., & Cohen, D. J. (Eds.). (1995a). *Developmental psychopathology: Vol. 1. Theory and method.* New York: John Wiley & Sons.

Cicchetti, D., & Cohen, D. J. (Eds.). (1995b). *Developmental psychopathology: Vol. 2. Risk, disorder, and adaptation.* New York: John Wiley & Sons.

Cicchetti, D., & Cohen, D. (Eds.). (2006a). *Developmental psychopathology: Vol. 1. Theory and method* (2nd ed.). Hoboken, NJ: John Wiley & Sons.

Cicchetti, D., & Cohen, D. (Eds.). (2006b). *Developmental psychopathology: Vol. 2. Developmental neuroscience* (2nd ed.). Hoboken, NJ: John Wiley & Sons.

Cicchetti, D., & Cohen, D. (Eds.). (2006c). *Developmental psychopathology: Vol. 3. Risk, disorder, and adaptation* (2nd ed.). Hoboken, NJ: John Wiley & Sons.

Cicchetti, D., & Crick, N. R. (Eds.). (2009a). Precursors of and diverse pathways to personality disorder in children and adolescents: Part I [Special issue]. *Development and Psychopathology, 21*(3).

Cicchetti, D., & Crick, N. R. (Eds.). (2009b). Precursors of and diverse pathways to personality disorder in children and adolescents: Part II [Special issue]. *Development and Psychopathology, 21*(4).

Cicchetti, D., & Curtis, W. J. (2005). An event-related potential study of the processing of affective facial expressions in young children who experienced maltreatment during the first year of life. *Development and Psychopathology, 17*, 641–677.

Cicchetti, D., & Curtis, W. J. (2006). The developing brain and neural plasticity: Implications for normality, psychopathology, and resilience. In D. Cicchetti & D. Cohen (Eds.), *Developmental Psychopathology: Vol. 2. Developmental Neuroscience* (2nd ed., pp. 1–64). Hoboken, NJ: John Wiley & Sons.

Cicchetti, D., & Curtis, W. J. (Eds.). (2007). A multi-level approach to resilience [Special issue]. *Development and Psychopathology, 19*(3).

Cicchetti, D., & Dawson, G. (Eds.). (2002). Multiple levels of analysis [Special issue]. *Development and Psychopathology, 14*(3).

Cicchetti, D., Ganiban, J., & Barnett, D. (1991). Contributions from the study of high risk populations to understanding the development of emotion regulation. In J. Garber & K. A. Dodge (Eds.), *The development of emotion regulation and dysregulation* (pp. 15–48). New York: Cambridge University Press.

Cicchetti, D., & Garmezy, N. (1993). Prospects and promises in the study of resilience. *Development and Psychopathology, 5*, 497–502.

Cicchetti, D., & Gunnar, M. R. (2008). Integrating biological processes into the design and evaluation of preventive interventions. *Development and Psychopathology, 20,* 737–743.

Cicchetti, D., & Gunnar, M. R. (Eds.). (2009). *Meeting the challenge of translational research in child psychology: Minnesota Symposia on Child Psychology* (Vol. 35). Hoboken, NJ: John Wiley & Sons.

Cicchetti, D., & Hinshaw, S. P. (2002). Prevention and intervention science: Contributions for developmental theory. *Development and Psychopathology, 14,* 667–671.

Cicchetti, D., & Lynch, M. (1993). Toward an ecological/transactional model of community violence and child maltreatment: Consequences for children's development. *Psychiatry, 56,* 96–118.

Cicchetti, D., & Lynch, M. (1995). Failures in the expectable environment and their impact on individual development: The case of child maltreatment. In D. Cicchetti & D. J. Cohen (Eds.), *Developmental psychopathology: Vol. 2. Risk, disorder, and adaptation* (pp. 32–71). New York: John Wiley & Sons.

Cicchetti, D., & Manly, J. T. (Eds.). (2001). Operationalizing child maltreatment: Developmental processes and outcomes [Special issue]. *Development and Psychopathology, 13*(4).

Cicchetti, D., & Pogge-Hesse, P. (1982). Possible contributions of the study of organically retarded persons to developmental theory. In E. Zigler & D. Balla (Eds.), *Mental retardation: The developmental difference controversy* (pp. 277–318). Hillsdale, NJ: Erlbaum.

Cicchetti, D., & Posner, M. I. (2005). Cognitive and affective neuroscience and developmental psychopathology. *Development and Psychopathology, 17,* 569–575.

Cicchetti, D., & Richters, J. E. (Eds.). (1997). Conceptual and scientific underpinnings of research in developmental psychopathology [Special issue]. *Development and Psychopathology, 9*(2).

Cicchetti, D., & Rizley, R. (1981). Developmental perspectives on the etiology, intergenerational transmission, and sequelae of child maltreatment. *New Directions for Child Development, 11,* 32–59.

Cicchetti, D., & Rogosch, F. A. (1996a). Developmental pathways: Diversity in process and outcome [Special issue]. *Development and Psychopathology, 8,* 597–896.

Cicchetti, D., & Rogosch, F. A. (1996b). Equifinality and multifinality in developmental psychopathology. *Development and Psychopathology, 8,* 597–600.

Cicchetti, D., & Rogosch, F. A. (1997). The role of self-organization in the promotion of resilience in maltreated children. *Development and Psychopathology, 9,* 799–817.

Cicchetti, D., & Rogosch, F. A. (1999). Conceptual and methodological issues in developmental psychopathology research. In P. C. Kendall, J. N. Butcher, & G. N. Holmbeck (Eds.), *Handbook of research methods in clinical psychology* (pp. 433–465). New York: John Wiley & Sons.

Cicchetti, D., & Rogosch, F. A. (2001a). Diverse patterns of neuroendocrine activity in maltreated children. *Development and Psychopathology, 13,* 677–694.

Cicchetti, D., & Rogosch, F. A. (2001b). The impact of child maltreatment and psychopathology upon neuroendocrine functioning. *Development and Psychopathology, 13,* 783–804.

Cicchetti, D., & Rogosch, F. A. (2002). A developmental psychopathology perspective on adolescence. *Journal of Consulting and Clinical Psychology, 70,* 6–20.

Cicchetti, D., & Rogosch, F. A. (2007). Personality, adrenal steroid hormones, and resilience in maltreated children: A multilevel perspective. *Development and Psychopathology, 19,* 787–809.

Cicchetti, D. & Rogosch, F. A. (2009). Adaptive coping under conditions of extreme stress: Multi-level influences on the determinants of resilience in maltreated children. In E. A. Skinner & M. J. Zimmer-Gembeck (Eds.). *Coping and the Development of Regulation*, a volume for the series, *New directions in child and adolescent development,* R. W. Larson & L. A. Jensenn (Editors in chief) (pp. 47–59). San Francisco: Jossey-Bass.

Cicchetti, D., Rogosch, F. A., Gunnar, M. R., & Toth, S. L. (2010). The differential impacts of early abuse on internalizing problems and diurnal cortisol activity in school-aged children. *Child Development, 25,* 252–269.

Cicchetti, D., Rogosch, F. A., Lynch, M., & Holt, K. (1993). Resilience in maltreated children: Processes leading to adaptive outcome. *Development and Psychopathology, 5,* 629–647.

Cicchetti, D., Rogosch, F. A., Maughan, A., Toth, S. L., & Bruce, J. (2003). False belief understanding in maltreated children. *Development and Psychopathology, 15,* 1067–1091.

Cicchetti, D., Rogosch, F. A., & Sturge-Apple, M. L. (2007). Interactions of child maltreatment and serotonin transporter and monoamine oxidase A polymorphisms: Depressive symptomatology among adolescents from low socioeconomic backgrounds. *Development and Psychopathology, 19,* 1161–1180.

Cicchetti, D., Rogosch, F. A., & Toth, S. L. (2000). The efficacy of toddler-parent psychotherapy for fostering cognitive development in offspring of depressed mothers. *Journal of Abnormal Child Psychology, 28,* 135–148.

Cicchetti, D., Rogosch, F. A., & Toth, S. L. (2006). Fostering secure attachment in infants in maltreating families through preventive interventions. *Development and Psychopathology, 18,* 623–650.

Cicchetti, D., & Schneider-Rosen, K. (1986). An organizational approach to childhood depression. In M. Rutter, C. Izard, & P. Read (Eds.), *Depression in young people, clinical and developmental perspectives* (pp. 71–134). New York: Guilford Press.

Cicchetti, D., & Sroufe, L. A. (1976). The relationship between affective and cognitive development in Down's syndrome infants. *Child Development, 47,* 920–929.

Cicchetti, D., & Sroufe, L. A. (1978). An organizational view of affect: Illustration from the study of Down's syndrome infants. In M. Lewis & L. Rosenblum (Eds.), *The development of affect* (pp. 309–350). New York: Plenum Press.

Cicchetti, D., & Sroufe, L. A. (2000). The past as prologue to the future: The times they've been a changin'. *Development and Psychopathology, 12,* 255–264.

Cicchetti, D., & Thomas, K. M. (2008). Imaging brain systems in normality and psychopathology. *Development and Psychopathology, 20,* 1023–1027.

Cicchetti, D., & Toth, S. L. (1991). The making of a developmental psychopathologist. In J. Cantor, C. Spiker, & L. Lipsitt (Eds.), *Child behavior and development: Training for diversity* (pp. 34–72). Norwood, NJ: Ablex.

Cicchetti, D., & Toth, S. L. (1992). The role of developmental theory in prevention and intervention. *Development and Psychopathology, 4,* 489–493.

Cicchetti, D., & Toth, S. L. (Eds.). (1993). *Child abuse, child development, and social policy*. Norwood, NJ: Ablex.

Cicchetti, D., & Toth, S. L. (1995). Developmental psychopathology and disorders of affect. In D. Cicchetti & D. J. Cohen (Eds.), *Developmental psychopathology: Vol. 2. Risk, disorder, and adaptation* (pp. 369–420). New York: John Wiley & Sons.

Cicchetti, D., & Toth, S. L. (1998). Perspectives on research and practice in developmental psychopathology. In W. Damon (Ed.), *Handbook of child psychology* (5th ed., Vol. 4, pp. 479–583). New York: John Wiley & Sons.

Cicchetti, D., & Toth, S. L. (Eds.). (2000). Social policy implications of research in developmental psychopathology [Special issue]. *Development and Psychopathology, 12*(4).

Cicchetti, D., & Toth, S. L. (2005). Child maltreatment. *Annual Review of Clinical Psychology, 1,* 409–438.

Cicchetti, D., & Toth, S. L. (Eds.). (2006). Translational research and developmental psychopathology [Special issue]. *Development and Psychopathology, 18*(3).

Cicchetti, D., & Toth, S. L. (2009). A developmental psychopathology perspective on adolescent depression. In S. Nolen-Hoeksema & L. Hilt (Eds.), *Handbook of adolescent depression* (pp. 3–31). New York: Taylor & Francis.

Cicchetti, D., Toth, S. L., & Maughan, A. (2000). An ecological–transactional model of child maltreatment. In A. Sameroff, M. Lewis, & S. Miller (Eds.), *Handbook of developmental psychopathology* (2nd ed., pp. 689–722). New York: Kluwer Academic/Plenum Press.

Cicchetti, D., Toth, S. L., & Rogosch, F. A. (1999). The efficacy of toddler–parent psychotherapy to increase attachment security in offspring of depressed mothers. *Attachment and Human Development, 1*, 34–66.

Cicchetti, D., & Tucker, D. (1994). Development and self-regulatory structures of the mind. *Development and Psychopathology, 6*, 533–549.

Cicchetti, D., & Valentino, K. (2007). Toward the application of a multiple-levels-of-analysis perspective to research in development and psychopathology. In A. S. Masten (Ed.), *Minnesota Symposia on Child Psychology* (Vol. 34, pp. 243–284). Mahwah, NJ: Erlbaum.

Cicchetti, D., & Walker, E. F. (2001). Editorial: Stress and development: Biological and psychological consequences. *Development and Psychopathology, 13*, 413–418.

Cicchetti, D., & Walker, E. F. (Eds.). (2003). *Neurodevelopmental mechanisms in psychopathology*. New York: Cambridge University Press.

Coie, J. D., Watt, N. F., West, S. G., Hawkins, D., Asarnow, J. R., Markman, H. J., et al. (1993). The science of prevention: A conceptual framework and some directions for a National Research Program. *American Psychologist, 48*, 1013–1022.

Colombo, J., Shaddy, D. J., Richman, W. A., Maikranz, J. M., & Blaga, O. M. (2004). The developmental course of habituation in infancy and preschool outcome. *Infancy, 5*, 1–38.

Conger, R. D., Neppi, T., Kim, K. J., & Scaramella, L. (2003). Angry and aggressive behavior across three generations: A prospective, longitudinal study of parents and children. *Journal of Abnormal Child Psychology, 31,* 143–160.

Costello, E. J., & Angold, A. (1995). Developmental epidemiology. In D. Cicchetti & D. J. Cohen (Eds.), *Developmental psychopathology: Vol. 1. Theory and method* (pp. 23–56). New York: John Wiley & Sons.

Costello, E. J., & Angold, A. (2006). Developmental epidemiology. In D. Cicchetti & D. Cohen (Eds.), *Developmental psychopathology: Vol. 1. Theory and method* (2nd ed., pp. 41–75). Hoboken, NJ: John Wiley & Sons.

Courchesne, E. (1987). A neurophysiological view of autism. In E. Schopler & G. B. Mesibov (Eds.), *Neurobiological issues in autism* (pp. 285–324). New York: Plenum Press.

Courchesne, E. (1997). Brainstem, cerebellar, and limbic neuroanatomical abnormalities in autism. *Current Opinion in Neurobiology, 7*, 269–278.

Courchesne, E., Carper, R., & Akshoomoff, N. (2003). Evidence of brain overgrowth in the first year of life in autism. *Journal of the American Medical Association, 290*, 337–344.

Courchesne, E., Chisum, H., & Townsend, J. (1994). Neural activity-dependent brain changes in development: Implications for psychopathology. *Development and Psychopathology, 6*, 697–722.

Courchesne, E., Karns, C., Davis, H. R., Ziccardi, R., Carper, R., Tigue, Z., et al. (2001). Unusual brain growth patterns in early life in patients with autistic disorder: An MRI study. *Neurology, 57*, 245–254.

Courchesne, E., Townsend, J., & Chase, C. (1995). Neurodevelopmental principles guide research on developmental psychopathologies. In D. Cicchetti & D. J. Cohen (Eds.), *Developmental psychopathology: Vol. 1. Theory and methods* (pp. 195–226). New York: John Wiley & Sons.

Crick, N. R., & Grotpeter, J. K. (1995). Relational aggression, gender, and social-psychological adjustment. *Child Development, 66*, 710–722.

Crick, N. R., & Grotpeter, J. K. (1996). Children's treatment by peers: Victims of relational and overt aggression. *Development and Psychopathology, 8,* 367–380.

Crittenden, P. M. (1988). Relationships at risk. In J. Belsky & T. Nezworski (Eds.), *Clinical implications of attachment theory* (pp. 136–174). Hillsdale, NJ: Erlbaum.

Crittenden, P. M., Claussen, A. H., & Sugarman, D. B. (1994). Physical and psychological maltreatment in middle childhood and adolescence. *Development and Psychopathology, 6*, 145–164.

Cullerton-Sen, C., Cassidy, A. R., Murray-Close, D., Cicchetti, D., Crick, N. R. et al. (2008). Childhood maltreatment and development of relational and physical aggression: The importance of a gender-informed approach. *Child Development, 79,* 1736–1751.

Cummings, E. M., Hennessy, K. D., Rabideau, G. J., & Cicchetti, D. (1994). Responses of physically abused boys to interadult anger involving their mothers. *Development and Psychopathology, 6*, 31–41.

Curtis, W. J., & Cicchetti, D. (2003). Moving research on resilience into the 21st century: Theoretical and methodological considerations in examining the biological contributors to resilience. *Development and Psychopathology, 15*, 773–810.

Curtis, W. J., & Cicchetti, D. (2007). Emotion and resilience: A multilevel investigation of hemispheric electroencephalogram asymmetry and emotion regulation in maltreated and nonmaltreated children. *Development and Psychopathology, 19*, 811–840.

Dahl, R., & Ryan, N. (1996). The psychobiology of adolescent depression. In D. Cicchetti & S. L. Toth (Eds.), *Rochester symposium on developmental psychopathology: Adolescence: Opportunities and challenges* (Vol. 7, pp. 197–232). Rochester, NY: University of Rochester Press.

Damasio, A. R., & Maurer, R. G. (1978). A neurological model for childhood autism. *Archives of Neurology, 35*, 777–786.

Davidson, R. J. (2000). Affective style, psychopathology, and resilience: Brain mechanisms and plasticity. *American Psychologist, 55*, 1196–1214.

Davies, P. T., Sturge-Apple, M. L., Cicchetti, D., & Cummings, E. M. (2007). The role of child adrenocortical functioning in pathways between interparental conflict and child maltreatment. *Developmental Psychology, 43*, 918–930.

Davis, M. (1984). The mammalian startle response. In R. C. Eaton (Ed.), *Neural mechanisms of startle behavior* (pp. 287–351). New York: Plenum Press.

Dawson, G., & Toth, K. (2006). Autism spectrum disorders. In D. Cicchetti & D. Cohen (Eds.), *Developmental psychopathology: Vol. 3. Risk, disorder, and adaptation* (2nd ed., pp. 317–357). Hoboken, NJ: John Wiley & Sons.

DeBellis, M. D. (2001). Developmental traumatology: The psychobiological development of maltreated children and its implications for research, treatment, and policy. *Development and Psychopathology, 13*, 539–564.

DeBellis, M. D. (2005). The psychobiology of neglect. *Child Maltreatment, 10*, 150–172.

DeBellis, M. D., Baum, A. S., Birmaher, B., Keshavan, M. S., Eccard, C. H., Boring, A. M., et al. (1999). Developmental traumatology

Part I: Biological stress systems. *Biological Psychiatry, 45*, 1259–1270.

DeBellis, M. D., Chrousos, G. P., Dorn, L. D., Burke, L., Helmers, K., Kling, M. A., et al. (1994). Adrenal axis dysregulation in sexually abused girls. *Journal of Clinical Endocrinology and Metabolism, 78*, 249–255.

DeBellis, M. D., Hall, J., Boring, A. M., Frustaci, K., & Moritz, G. (2001). A pilot longitudinal study of hippocampal volumes in pediatric maltreatment related posttraumatic stress disorder. *Society of Biological Psychiatry, 50*, 305–309.

DeBellis, M. D., Keshavan, M. S., Casey, B. J., Clark, D. B., Giedd, J., Boring, A. M., et al. (1999). Developmental traumatology: Biological stress systems and brain development in maltreated children with PTSD. Part II: The relationship between characteristics of trauma and psychiatric symptoms and adverse brain development in maltreated children and adolescents with PTSD. *Biological Psychiatry, 45*, 1271–1284.

DeBellis, M. D., Keshavan, M. S., Spencer, S., & Hall, J. (2000). N-acetylaspartate concentration in the anterior cingulated in maltreated children and adolescents with PTSD. *American Journal of Psychiatry, 33*, 320–327.

Deblinger, E., McLeer, S. V., Atkins, M. S., Ralphe, D., & Foa, E. (1989). Post-traumatic stress in sexually abused physically abused and nonabused children. *Child Abuse and Neglect, 13*, 403–408.

DeSantis, A. S., Adam, E. K., Doane, L. D., Mineka, S., Zinbarg, R. E., & Craske, M. G. (2007). Racial/ethnic differences in cortisol diurnal rhythms in a community sample of adolescents. *Journal of Adolescent Health, 41*, 3–13.

Dobzhansky, T. (1972). Genetics and the diversity of behavior. *American Psychologist, 27*, 523–530.

Dodge, K. A., & Pettit, G. S. (2003). A biopsychosocial model of the development of chronic conduct problems in adolescence. *Developmental Psychology, 39*, 349–371.

Dodge, K. A., Pettit, G. S., & Bates, J. E. (1994). Effects of physical maltreatment on the development of peer relations. *Development and Psychopathology, 6*, 43–55.

Dodge, K. A., Pettit, G. S., & Bates, J. E. (1997). How the experience of early physical abuse leads children to become chronically aggressive. In D. Cicchetti & S. L. Toth (Eds.), *Rochester Symposium on Developmental psychopathology: Vol. 8. Trauma: Perspectives on theory, research, and intervention* (pp. 263–288). Rochester, NY: University of Rochester Press.

Dodge, K. A., Pettit, G. S., Bates, J. E., & Valente, E. (1995). Social information-processing patterns partially mediate the effect of early physical abuse on later conduct problems. *Journal of Abnormal Psychology, 104*, 632–643.

Downey, G., & Coyne, J. C. (1990). Children of depressed parents: An integrative review. *Psychological Bulletin, 108*, 50–76.

Dozier, M. (1990). Attachment organization and treatment use for adults with serious psychopathological disorders. *Development and Psychopathology, 2*, 47–60.

Dozier, M., Albus, K., Fisher, P. A., & Sepulveda, S. (2002). Intervention for foster parents: Implications for developmental theory. *Development and Psychopathology, 14*, 843–860.

Drake, R. E., Adler, D. A., & Vaillant, G. E. (1988). Antecedents of personality disorders in a community sample of men. *Journal of Personality Disorders, 2*, 60–68.

Dube, S. R., Anda, R. F., Felitti, V. J., Chapman, D. P., Williamson, D. F., & Giles, W. H. (2001). Childhood abuse, household dysfunction, and the risk of attempted suicide throughout the life span: Findings from the Adverse Childhood Experiences Study. *Journal of the American Medical Association, 286*, 3089–3096.

Duggal, S., Carlson, E. A., Sroufe, L. A., & Egeland, B. (2001). Depressive symptomatology in childhood and adolescence. *Development and Psychopathology, 13*, 143–164.

Duggan, A., McFarlane, E., Fuddy, L., Burrell, L., Higman, S. M., Windham, A., et al. (2004). Randomized trial of a statewide home visiting program: impact in preventing child abuse and neglect. *Child Abuse and Neglect, 28*, 597–622.

DuMont, K. A., Widom, C. S., & Czaja, S. J. (2007). Predictors of resilience in abused and neglected children grown-up: The role of individual and neighborhood characteristics. *Child Abuse and Neglect, 31*, 255–274.

Eckenrode, J., Laird, M., & Doris, J. (1993). School performance and disciplinary problems among abused and neglected children. *Developmental Psychology, 29*, 53–62.

Edelman, G. M. (1987). *Neural Darwinism: The theory of neuronal group selection*. New York: Basic Books.

Egeland, B., Carlson, E. A., & Sroufe, L. A. (1993). Resilience as process. *Development and Psychopathology, 5*, 517–528.

Ehrensaft, M. K., Cohen, P., Brown, J., Smailes, E., Chen, H., & Johnson, J. G. (2003). Intergenerational Transmission of Partner Violence: A 20-Year Prospective Study. *Journal of Consulting and Clinical Psychology, 71*, 741–753.

Eisenberg, L. (1995). The social construction of the human brain. *American Journal of Psychiatry, 152*, 1563–1575.

Eisenberg, N., Sadovsky, A., Spinrad, T. L., Fabes, R. A., Losoya, S. H., Valiente, C., et al. (2005). The relations of problem behavior status to children's negative emotionality, effortful control, and impulsivity: Concurrent relations and prediction of change. *Developmental Psychology, 41*, 193–211.

Elder, G. H. (1974). *Children of the great depression*. Chicago: University of Chicago Press.

Emery, R. E. (1989). Family violence. *American Psychologist, 44*, 321–328.

English, D. J., Upadhyaya, M. P., Litrownik, A. J., Marshall, J. M., Runyan, D. K., Graham, J. C., et al. (2005). Maltreatment's wake: The relationship of maltreatment dimensions to child outcomes. *Child Abuse & Neglect, 29*, 597–619.

Erikson, E. H. (1950). *Childhood and society*. New York: Norton.

Famularo, R., Kinscherff, R., & Fenton, T. (1992). Psychiatric diagnoses of maltreated children: Preliminary findings. *Journal of the American Academy of Child and Adolescent Psychiatry, 31*, 863–867.

Feder, A., Coplan, J. D., Goetz, R. R., Mathew, S. J., Pine, D. S., Dahl, R. E., et al (2004). Twenty-four-hour cortisol secretion patterns in prepubertal children with anxiety of depressive disorders. *Biological Psychiatry, 56*, 198–204.

Felmingham, K., Kemp, A., Williams, L., Das, P., Hughes, G., Peduto, A., et al. (2007). Changes in anterior cingulated and amygdala after cognitive behavior therapy of posttraumatic stress disorder. *Psychological Science, 18*, 127–129.

Finzi, R., Ram, A., Har-Even, D., Shnit, D., & Weizman, A. (2001). Attachment styles in physically abused and neglected children. *Journal of Youth and Adolescence, 30*, 769–786

Fischer, K. W., & Ayoub, C. (1994). Affective splitting and dissociation in normal and maltreated children: Developmental pathways for self in relationships. In D. Cicchetti & S. L. Toth (Eds.), *Rochester Symposium on Developmental Psychopathology: Vol. 5. Disorders and dysfunction of the self* (pp. 149–222). Rochester, NY: University of Rochester Press.

Fish, B. (1957). The detection of schizophrenia in infancy. *Journal of Nervous and Mental Disorders, 125*, 1–24.

Fish, B. (1977). Neurologic antecedents of schizophrenia in children: Evidence for an inherited, congenital neurointegrative deficit. *Archives of General Psychiatry, 34*, 1297–1313.

Fish, B., Marcus, J., Hans, S., Auerbach, J., & Perdue, S. (1992). Infants at risk for schizophrenia: Sequelae of genetic neurointegrative defect. *Archives of General Psychiatry, 49*, 221–235.

Fisher, P. A., Gunnar, M. R., Dozier, M., Bruce, J., & Pears, K. C. (2006). Effects of therapeutic interventions for foster children on behavioral problems, caregiver attachment, and stress regulatory neural systems. *Annals of the New York Academy of Sciences, 1094*, 215–225.

Flores, E., Cicchetti, D., & Rogosch, F. A. (2005). Predictors of resilience in maltreated and nonmaltreated Latino children. *Developmental Psychology, 41*, 338–351.

Foley, D. L., Eaves, L. J., Wormley, B., Silberg, J. L., Maes, H. H., Kuhn, J., et al. (2004). Childhood adversity, monoamine oxidase: A genotype, and risk for conduct disorder. *Archives of General Psychiatry, 61*(7), 738–744.

Ford, D. H., & Lerner, R. M. (1992). *Developmental systems theory: An integrated approach.* Newbury Park, CA: Sage.

Fox, N. A., Henderson, H. A., Rubin, K. H., Calkins, S. D., & Schmidt, L. A. (2001). Continuity and discontinuity of behavioral inhibition and exuberance: Psychophysiological and behavioral influences across the first four years of life. *Child Development*, *72*, 1–21.

Fox, N. A., & Rutter, M. (Eds.) (2010). Special Section: The effects of early experience on cognitive and/or sociodevelopment. *Child Development, 81(1).*

Gaensbauer, T., & Hiatt, S. (1984). Facial communication of emotion in early infancy. In N. A. Fox & R. J. Davidson (Eds.), *The psychobiology of affective development* (pp. 207–230). Hillsdale, NJ: Erlbaum.

Garber, J., Quiggle, N., Panak, W., & Dodge, K. (1991). Aggression and depression in children: Comorbidity, specificity, and social cognitive processing. In D. Cicchetti & S. L. Toth (Eds.), *Rochester Symposium on Developmental Psychopathology: Vol. 2. Internalizing and externalizing expressions of dysfunction* (pp. 225–264). Hillsdale, NJ: Erlbaum.

Garcia-Coll, C., Akerman, A., & Cicchetti, D. (2000). Cultural influences on developmental processes and outcomes: Implications for the study of development and psychopathology. *Development and Psychopathology, 12*, 333–356.

Garmezy, N. (1970). Process and reactive schizophrenia: Some conceptions and issues. *Schizophrenia Bulletin, 2*, 30–74.

Garmezy, N., & Streitman, S. (1974). Children at risk: Conceptual models and research methods. *Schizophrenia bulletin, 9*, 55–125.

Ge, X., Brody, G. H., Conger, R. D., & Simons, R. L. (2006). Pubertal maturation and African American children's internalizing and externalizing symptoms. *Journal of Youth and Adolescence, 35*, 528–537.

Gibb, B. E., Wheeler, R., Alloy, L. B., & Abramson, L. Y. (2001). Emotional, physical, and sexual maltreatment in childhood versus adolescence and personality dysfunction in young adulthood. *Journal of Personality Disorders, 15*, 505–511.

Gladstone, G. L., Parker, G. B., Mitchell, P. B., Malhi, G. S., Wilhelm, K., & Austin, M. P. (2004). Implications of childhood trauma for depressed women: An analysis of pathways from childhood sexual abuse to deliberate self-harm and revictimization. *American Journal of Psychiatry, 161*, 1417–1425.

Goldapple, K., Segal, Z., Garson, C., Lau, M., Bieling, P., Kennedy, S., et al. (2004). Modulation of cortical-limbic pathways in major depression. *Archives of General Psychiatry, 61*, 34–41.

Goldstein, K. (1939). *The organism.* New York: American Book Company.

Goodwin, F. K., & Jamison, K. R (Ed.). (2007). *Manic-depressive illness: Bipolar disorders and recurrent depression* (2nd ed.). Oxford, England: Oxford University Press.

Gottesman, I. I. (1963). Genetic aspects of intelligent behavior. In N. R. Ellis (Ed.), *Handbook of mental deficiency: Psychological theory and research* (pp. 253–296). New York: McGraw-Hill.

Gottesman, I. I. (1991). *Schizophrenia genesis.* San Francisco: Freeman.

Gottesman, I. I., & Gould, T. D. (2003). The endophenotype concept in psychiatry: Etymology and strategic intentions. *American Journal of Psychiatry, 160*, 636–645.

Gottesman, I. I., & Hanson, D. R. (2005). Human development: Biological and genetic processes. *Annual Review of Psychology, 56*, 263–286.

Gottesman, I. I., & Shields, J. (1972). *Schizophrenia and genetics: A twin study vantage point.* New York: Academic Press.

Gottlieb, G. (1991). Experiential canalization of behavioral development: Theory. *Developmental Psychology, 27*, 4–13.

Gottlieb, G. (1992). *Individual development and evolution: The genesis of novel behavior.* New York: Oxford University Press.

Gottlieb, G. (2007). Probabilistic epigenesis. Developmental Science, 10, 1–11.

Gottlieb, G., & Halpern, C. T. (2002). A relational view of causality in normal and abnormal development. *Development and Psychopathology, 14*, 421–436.

Gottlieb, G., & Willoughby, M. T. (2006). Probabilistic epigenesis of psychopathology. In D. Cicchetti & D. Cohen (Eds.), *Developmental psychopathology: Vol. 1. Theory and method* (2nd ed., pp. 673–700). Hoboken, NJ: John Wiley & Sons.

Gould, E., Tanapat, P., McEwen, B. S., Flugge, G., & Fuchs, E. (1998). Proliferation of granule cell precursors in the dentale gyrus of adult monkeys is diminished by stress. *Proceedings of the National Academy of Sciences, 95*, 3168–3171.

Granic, I., & Hollenstein, T. (2003). Dynamic systems methods for models of developmental psychopathology. *Development and Psychopathology, 15*, 641–670.

Greenberg, S. A. (2001). DNA microarray gene expression analysis technology and its application to neurological disorders. *Neurology, 57*, 755–761.

Greenough, W., Black, J., & Wallace, C. (1987). Experience and brain development. *Child Development, 58*, 539–559.

Greve, W., & Staudinger, U. M. (2006). Resilience in later adulthood and old age: Resources and potentials for successful aging. In D. Cicchetti & D. Cohen (Eds.), *Developmental Psychopathology: Vol. 3. Risk, disorder, and adaptation* (2nd ed., pp. 796–840). Hoboken, NJ: John Wiley & Sons.

Gunnar, M. R. (2003). Integrating neuroscience and psychological approaches in the study of early experiences. *Annals of the New York Academy of Sciences, 1008*, 238–247.

Gunnar, M. R., & Cicchetti, D. (2009). Meeting the challenge of translational research in child psychology. In M. R. Gunnar & D. Cicchetti (Eds.). *Minnesota Symposia on Child Psychology: Vol. 35. Meeting the Challenge of Translational Research in Child Psychology* (pp. 1–27). Hoboken, NJ: John Wiley & Sons.

Gunnar, M. R., Fisher, P. A., & The Early Experience and Prevention Network. (2006). Bringing basic research on early experience and stress neurobiology to bear on preventive interventions for neglected and maltreated children. *Development and Psychopathology, 18*, 651–678.

Gunnar, M. R., & Quevedo, K. (2007). The neurobiology of stress and development. *Annual Review of Psychology, 58*, 145–173.

Gunnar, M. R., & Vazquez, D. M. (2001). Low cortisol and a flattening of expected daytime rhythm: Potential indices of risk in human development. *Development and Psychopathology, 13*, 515–538.

Gunnar, M. R., & Vazquez, D. (2006). Stress neurobiology and developmental psychopathology. In D. Cicchetti & D. Cohen (Eds.), *Developmental Psychopathology: Vol. 2. Developmental Neuroscience* (2nd ed., pp. 533–577). Hoboken, NJ: John Wiley & Sons.

Gurvits, T. V., Shenton, M. E., Hokama, H., Ohta, H., Lasko, N. B., Gilbertson, M. W., et al. (1996). Magnetic resonance imaging study of hippocampal volume in chronic, combat-related posttraumatic stress disorder. *Biological Psychiatry, 40*, 1091–1099.

Hane, A., & Fox, N. (2006). Ordinary variations in maternal caregiving influence human infants' stress reactivity. *Psychological Science, 17*, 550–556.

Hanson, D. R., & Gottesman, I. I. (2007). Choreographing genetic, epigenetic, and stochastic steps in the dances of developmental psychopathology. In A. S. Masten (Ed.), *Multilevel dynamics in developmental psychopathology: Pathways to the future* (pp. 27–43). Mahwah, NJ: Erlbaum.

Harrison, A. O., Wilson, M. N., Pine, C. J., Chan, S. Q., & Buriel, R. (1990). Family ecologies of ethnic minority children. *Child Development, 61*, 346–362.

Hart, D., Hofmann, V., Edelstein, W., & Keller, M. (1997). The relation of childhood personality types to adolescent behavior and development: A longitudinal study of Icelandic children. *Developmental Psychology, 33*, 195–205.

Hart, J., Gunnar, M. R., & Cicchetti, D. (1996). Altered neuroendocrine activity in maltreated children related to depression. *Development and Psychopathology, 8*, 201–214.

Hartmann, H. (1958). *Ego psychology and the problem of adaptation.* New York: International Universities Press.

Hebb, D. O. (1949). *Organization of behavior: A neuropsychological theory.* New York: John Wiley & Sons.

Heckman, J. J. (2006). Skill formation and the economics of investing in disadvantaged children. *Science*, 312, 1900–1902.

Heim, C., Ehlert, U., & Hellhammer, D. (2000). The potential role of hypocortisolism in the pathophysiology of stress-related bodily disorders. *Psychoneuroendocrinology, 25*, 1–35.

Heim, C., & Nemeroff, C. B. (2001). The role of childhood trauma in the neurobiology of mood and anxiety disorders: preclinical and clinical studies. *Biological Psychiatry, 49*, 1023–1039.

Heim, C., Newport, J. D., Mletzko, T., Miller, A. H., & Nemeroff, C. B. (2008). The link between childhood trauma and depression: Insights from HPA axis studies in humans. *Psychoneuroendocrinology, 33*, 693–710.

Heim, C., Owen, M. J., Plotsky, P. M., & Nemeroff, C. B. (1997). The role of early life adverse events in the etiology of depression and posttraumatic stress disorder. *Annals of the New York Academy of Sciences, 821*, 194–207.

Heim, C., Plotsky, P., & Nemeroff, C. B. (2004). The importance of studying the contributions of early adverse experiences to the neurobiological findings in depression. *Neuropsychopharmacology, 29*, 641–648.

Hennessy, K. D., Rabideau, G. J., Cicchetti, D., & Cummings, E. M. (1994). Responses of physically abused and nonabused children to different forms of interadult anger. *Child Development, 65*, 815–828.

Herman, J. L., Perry, J. C., & van der Kolk, B. A. (1989). Childhood trauma in borderline personality disorder. *American Journal of Psychiatry, 146*, 490–495.

Hesse, P., & Cicchetti, D. (1982). Perspectives on an integrative theory of emotional development. *New Directions for Child Development, 16*, 3–48.

Hinshaw, S. P. (2002). Intervention research, theoretical mechanisms, and causal processes related to externalizing behavior problems. *Development and Psychopathology, 14*, 789–818.

Hinshaw, S. P., & Anderson, C. A. (1996). Conduct and oppositional defiant disorders. In E. J. Mash & R. A. Barkley (Eds.), *Child psychopathology* (pp. 113–149). New York: Guilford Press.

Hoffman, M., & Hoffman, L. (1964). *Review of child development research* (Vol.1). New York: Russell Sage Foundation.

Hooley, J., & Teasdale, J. D. (1989). Predictors of relapse in unipolar depressives: Expressed emotion, marital distress, and perceived criticism. *Journal of Abnormal Psychology, 98*, 229–235.

Horwitz, A. V., Widom, C. S., McLaughlin, J., & White, H. R. (2001). The impact of childhood abuse and neglect on adult mental health: a prospective study. *Journal of Health and Social Behavior, 42*, 184–201.

Howe, G. W., Reiss, D., & Yuh, J. (2002). Can prevention trials test theories of etiology? *Development and Psychopathology, 14*, 673–694.

Howes, P. W., & Cicchetti, D. (1993). A family/relational perspective on maltreating families: Parallel processes across systems and social policy implications. In D. Cicchetti & S. L. Toth (Eds.), *Child abuse, child development, and social policy* (pp. 249–300). Norwood, NJ: Ablex.

Howes, P. W., Cicchetti, D., Toth, S. L., & Rogosch, F. A. (2000). Affective, structural, and relational characteristics of maltreating families: A systems perspective. *Journal of Family Psychology, 14*, 95–110.

Hussey, J. M., Chang, J. J., & Kotch, J. B. (2006). Child maltreatment in the United States: Prevalence, risk factors, and adolescent health consequences. *Pediatrics, 118*, 933–942.

Huttenlocher, P. (2002). *Neural plasticity: The effects of environment on the development of the cerebral cortex.* Cambridge, MA: Harvard University Press.

Hyman, S. E., & Nestler, E. J. (1993). *The molecular foundations of psychiatry.* Washington, DC: American Psychiatric Press.

Hyman, S. E., & Nestler, E. J. (1996). Initiation and adaptation: a paradigm for understanding psychotropic drug action. *American Journal of Psychiatry, 153*, 151–162.

Ialongo, N., Rogosch, F. A., Cicchetti, D., Toth, S. L., Buckley, J., Petras, H., et al. (2006). A developmental psychopathology approach to the prevention of mental health disorders. In D. C. Cicchetti, (Ed.), *Developmental psychopathology: Vol. 1. Theory and method* (2nd ed., pp. 968–1018). Hoboken, NJ: John Wiley & Sons.

Insel, T. R. (2005). Developmental psychobiology for public health: A bridge for translational research. *Developmental Psychobiology, 47*, 209–216.

Insel, T. R. (2009). Translating scientific opportunity into public health impact. *Archives of General Psychiatry, 66*, 128–133.

Insel, T. R., & Scolnick, E. M. (2006). Cure therapeutics and strategic prevention: Raising the bar for mental health research. *Molecular Psychiatry, 11*, 11–17.

Institute of Medicine. (1985). Research on mental illness and addictive disorders: Progress and prospects. *The American Journal of Psychiatry, 1142*, 1–41.

Institute of Medicine. (1989). *Research on children and adolescents with mental, behavioral, and developmental disorders.* Washington, DC: National Academy Press.

Institute of Medicine. (1994). *Reducing risks for mental disorders: Frontiers for preventive intervention research.* Washington, DC: National Academy Press.

Institute of Medicine. (1996). *Pathways of addiction. Opportunities in drug abuse research.* Washington, DC: National Academy Press.

Jessor, R., & Jessor, S. L. (1977). *Problem behavior and psychosocial development: A longitudinal study of youth.* New York: Academic Press.

Johnson, J. G., Cohen, P., Gould, M. S., Kasen, S., Brown, J., & Brook, J. S. (2002). Childhood adversities, interpersonal difficulties, and risk for suicide attempts during late adolescence and early adulthood. *Archives of General Psychiatry, 59*, 741–749.

Johnson, J. G., Cohen, P., Skodol, A. E., Oldham, J. M., Kasen, S., & Brook, J. S. (1999). Personality disorders in adolescence and risk of major mental disorders and suicidality during adulthood. *Archives of General Psychiatry, 56*, 805–811.

Johnson, J. G., Smailes, E. M., Phil, M., Cohen, P., Brown, J., & Bernstein, D. P. (2000). Associations between four types of childhood neglect and personality disorder symptoms during adolescence and early adulthood: Findings from a community-based longitudinal study. *Journal of Personality Disorders, 14*, 171–187.

Juvenile Justice Standards Project. (1977). *Standards for juvenile justice: A summary and analysis.* Cambridge, MA: Ballinger.

Kagan, J. (1981). *The second year: The emergence of self-awareness.* Cambridge, MA: Harvard University Press.

Kagan, J. (1994). *Galen's prophecy: Temperament in human nature.* New York: Basic Books.

Kagan, J. (2008). In defense of qualitative changes in development. *Child Development, 79,* 1606–1624.

Kagan, J., Reznick, J. S., & Snidman, N. (1988). The physiology and psychology of behavioral inhibition in children. *Child Development, 58,* 1459–1473.

Kandel, D. (1978). Convergences in prospective longitudinal surveys of drug use in normal populations. In D. Kandel (Ed.), *Longitudinal research on drug use* (pp. 3–38). Washington, DC: Hemisphere.

Kandel, E. R. (1979). Psychotherapy and the single synapse. *The New England Journal of Medicine, 301*, 1028–1037.

Kandel, E. R. (1998). A new intellectual framework for psychiatry. *American Journal of Psychiatry, 155*, 475–469.

Kandel, E. R. (1999). Biology and the future of psychoanalysis: A new intellectual framework for psychiatry revisited. *American Journal of Psychiatry, 156*, 505–524.

Kanner, L. (1943). Autistic disturbances of affective content. *Nervous Child, 2*, 217–250.

Kaplan, B. (1967). Meditations on genesis. *Human Development, 10*, 65–87.

Kaplan, P. S., Bachorowski, J., & Zarlengo-Strouse, P. (1999). Child-directed speech produced by mothers with symptoms of depression fails to promote associative learning in 4-month-old infants. *Child Development, 70*, 560–570.

Kaplan, S. J., Pelcovitz, D., & Labruna, V. (1999). Child and adolescent abuse and neglect research: A review of the past 10 years. Part I: Physical and emotional abuse and neglect. *Journal of the American Academy of Child & Adolescent Psychiatry, 38,* 1214–1222.

Kaplow, J. B., & Widom, C. S. (2007). Age of onset of maltreatment predicts long-term mental health outcomes. *Journal of Abnormal Psychology, 116*, 176–187.

Kaufman, J. (1991). Depressive disorders in maltreated children. *Journal of the American Academy of Child and Adolescent Psychiatry, 30*, 257–265.

Kaufman, J., Birmaher, B., Perel, J., Dahl, R. E., Moreci, P., Nelson, B., et al. (1997). The corticotropic-releasing hormone challenge in depressed abused, depressed nonabused, and normal control children. *Biological Psychiatry, 42*, 669–679.

Kaufman, J., & Charney, D. (2001). Effects of early stress on brain structure and function: Implications for understanding the relationship between child maltreatment and depression. *Development and Psychopathology, 13*, 451–471.

Keiley, M. K., Howe, T., Dodge, K., Bates, J., & Pettit, G. (2001). Timing of abuse: Group differences and developmental trajectories. *Development and Psychopathology*, *13,* 891–912.

Kellam, S. G., & Rebok, G. W. (1992). Building developmental and etiological theory through epidemiologically based preventive intervention trials. In J. McCord & R. E. Tremblay (Eds.), *Preventing antisocial behavior: Interventions from birth through adolescence* (pp. 162–195). New York: Guilford Press.

Kempermann, G. (2005). *Adult neurogenesis: Stem cells and neuronal development in the adult brain.* Oxford, England: Oxford University Press.

Kempermann, G., van Pragg, H., & Gage, F. H. (2000). Activity-dependent regulation of neuronal plasticity and self-repair. *Progress in Brain Research, 127*, 35–48.

Kendall-Tackett, K. A., Williams, L. M., & Finkelhor, D. (1993). Impact of sexual abuse on children: A review and synthesis of recent empirical studies. *Psychological Bulletin, 113*, 164–180.

Kendler, K. S., Kuhn, J. W., & Prescott, C. A. (2004). Childhood sexual abuse, stressful life events and risk for major depression in women. *Psychological Medicine, 34*(8), 1475–1482.

Keshavan, M. S., & Hogarty, G. E. (1999). Brain maturational processes and delayed onset in schizophrenia. *Development and Psychopathology, 11,* 525–543.

Kessler, R. C., Davis, C. G., & Kender, K. S. (1997). Childhood adversity and adult psychiatric disorder in the U.S. National Comorbidity Study. *Psychological Medicine, 27*, 1079–1089.

Kim, J., & Cicchetti, D. (2004). A process model of mother-child relatedness and psychological adjustment among maltreated and nonmaltreated children: The role of self-esteem and social competence. *Journal of Abnormal Child Psychology, 32*, 341–354.

Kim, J., Cicchetti, D., & Rogosch, F. A., & Manly, J. T. (2009). Child maltreatment and trajectories of personality and behavioral functioning: Implications for the development of personality disorder. *Development and Psychopathology, 21*(3), 889–912.

Kim-Cohen, J., Caspi, A., Moffitt, T. E., Harrington, H., Milne, B. J., & Poulton, R. (2003). Prior juvenile diagnoses in adults with mental disorder: Developmental follow-back of a prospective longitudinal cohort. *Archives of General Psychiatry, 60,* 709–717.

Kim-Cohen, J., Caspi, A., Taylor, A., Williams, B., Newcombe, R., Craig, I. W., et al. (2006). MAOA, maltreatment, and gene-environment interaction predicting children's mental health: New evidence and a meta-analysis. *Molecular Psychiatry, 11*, 903–913.

Kirby, J. S., Chu, J. A., & Dill, D. L. (1993). Correlates of dissociative symptomatology in sexually abused and nonabused children. *Behavioral Assessment, 13,* 341–357.

Kiser, L. J., Heston, J., Millsap, P. A., & Pruitt, D. B. (1991). Physical and sexual abuse in childhood: Relationship with post-traumatic stress disorder. *Journal of the American Academy of Child and Adolescent Psychiatry, 30*, 776–783.

Kisiel, C. L., Lyons, J. S. (2001). Dissociation as a mediator of psychopathology among sexually abused children and adolescents. *American Journal of Psychiatry, 158,* 1034–1039.

Klimes-Dougan, B., & Kistner, J. A. (1990). Physically abused preschoolers' responses to peer distress. *Developmental Psychology, 26*, 599–602.

Klorman, R., Cicchetti, D., Thatcher, J. E., & Ison, J. R. (2003). Acoustic startle in maltreated children. *Journal of Abnormal Child Psychology, 31*, 359–370.

Koenig, A. L., Cicchetti, D., & Rogosch, F. A. (2000). Child compliance/noncompliance and maternal contributors to internalization in maltreating and nonmaltreating dyads. *Child Development, 71*, 1018–1032.

Koenig, A. L., Cicchetti, D., & Rogosch, F. A. (2004). Moral development: The association between maltreatment and young children's prosocial behaviors and moral transgressions. *Social Development, 13*, 87–106.

Kohlberg, L., LaCrosse, J., & Ricks, D. (1972). The predictability of adult mental health from child behavior. In B. Wolman (Ed.), *Manual of child psychopathology* (pp. 1217–1284). New York: John Wiley & Sons.

Korvela, C., Pound, J., Heger, A., & Lytle C. (1993). Relationship of child sexual abuse to depression. *Child Abuses and Neglect, 17,* 393–400.

Kraepelin, E. (1919). *Dementia praecox and paraphrenia*. Edinburgh, Scotland: Livingston.

Lang, A. J., Stein, M. B., Kennedy, C. M., & Foy, D. W. (2004). Adult psychopathology and intimate partner violence among survivors of childhood maltreatment. *Journal of Interpersonal Violence, 19,* 1102–1118.

Laporte, L., & Guttman, H. (1996). Traumatic childhood experiences as risk factors for borderline and other personality disorders. *Journal of Personality Disorders, 10*, 247–259.

Lenneberg, E. (1967). *Biological foundations of language*. New York: Wiley.

Lenzenweger, M. F., & Cicchetti, D. (2005). Toward a developmental psychopathology approach to Borderline Personality Disorder. *Development and Psychopathology, 17*, 893–898.

Levine, S. (2005). Developmental determinants of sensitivity and resistance to stress. *Psychoneuroendocrinology, 30,* 939–946.

Lewis, D. A., Hashimoto, T., & Volk, D. W. (2005). Cortical inhibitory neurons and schizophrenia. *Nature, 6*, 312–324.

Lewis, D. O., Mallouh, C., & Webb, V. (1989). Child abuse, delinquency, and violent criminality. In D. Cicchetti & V. Carlson (Eds.), *Child maltreatment: Theory and research on the causes and consequences of child abuse and neglect* (pp. 707–721). New York: Cambridge University Press.

Loftus, E. E., (1993). The reality of repressed memories. *American Psychologist, 48,* 518–537.

Lopez, J. F., Akil, H., & Watson, S. J. (1999). Neural circuits mediating stress. *Biological Psychiatry, 46*, 1461–1471.

Lopez, J. F., Akil, H., & Watson, S. J. (1999). Neural circuits mediating stress. *Biological Psychiatry, 46*, 1461–1471.

Luntz, B., & Widom, C. S. (1994). Antisocial personality disorder in abused and neglected children grown up. *American Journal of Psychiatry, 151*, 670–674.

Lupien, S. J., Ouellet-Morin, I., Hupbach, A., Tu, M. T., Buss, C., Walker, D., et al. (2006). Beyond the stress concept: Allostatic load — a developmental biological and cognitive perspective. In D. Cicchetti & D. Cohen (Eds.), *Developmental psychopathology (2nd ed.), Vol. 2: Developmental neuroscience* (pp. 578-628). Hoboken, NJ: John Wiley & Sons. Wiley.

Luthar, S. S. (2006). Resilience in development: A synthesis of research across five decades. In D. Cicchetti & D. Cohen (Eds.), *Developmental psychopathology: Vol. 3. Risk, disorder, and adaptation* (2nd ed., pp. 739–795). Hoboken, NJ: John Wiley & Sons. Wiley.

Luthar, S. S., & Cicchetti, D. (2000). The construct of resilience: Implications for intervention and social policy. *Development and Psychopathology, 12*, 857–885.

Luthar, S. S., Cicchetti, D., & Becker, B. (2000). The construct of resilience: A critical evaluation and guidelines for future work. *Child Development, 71*, 543–562.

Luu, P., & Tucker, D. (1996). Self-regulation and cortical development: Implications for functional studies of the brain. In R. W. Thatcher, G. R. Lyon, J. Rumsey, & N. A. Krasnegor (Eds.), *Developmental neuroimaging; Mapping the development of brain behavior* (pp. 298–305). San Diego, CA: Academic Press.

Lynch, M., & Cicchetti, D. (1991). Patterns of relatedness in maltreated and nonmaltreated children: Connections among multiple representational models. *Development and Psychopathology, 3*, 207–226.

Lyons-Ruth, K., Connell, D., Zoll, D., & Stahl, J. (1987). Infants at social risk: Relationships among infant maltreatment, maternal behavior, and infant attachment behavior. *Developmental Psychology, 23*, 223–232.

Macfie, J., Cicchetti, D., & Toth, S. L. (2001a). The development of dissociation in maltreated preschool-aged children. *Development and Psychopathology, 13*, 233–254.

Macfie, J., Cicchetti, D., & Toth, S. L. (2001b). Dissociation in maltreated versus nonmaltreated preschool-aged children. *Child Abuse and Neglect, 25*, 1253–1267.

Macfie, J., Toth, S. L., Rogosch, F. A., Robinson, J., Emde, R. N., & Cicchetti, D. (1999). Effect of maltreatment on preschoolers' narrative representations of responses to relieve distress and of role reversal. *Developmental Psychology, 35*, 460–465.

Maestripieri, D. 1999. The biology of human parenting: Insights from nonhuman primates. *Neuroscience and Biobehavioral Reviews, 23,* 411–22.

Main, M., Kaplan, N., & Cassidy, J. C. (1985). Security in infancy, childhood and adulthood: A move to the level of representation. In I. Bretherton & E. Waters (Eds.), *Growing points of attachment theory and research* (Vol. 209, pp. 66–104). Ann Arbor, MI: Society for Research in Child Development Monograph.

Makino, S., Gold, P. W., & Schulkin, J. (1994). Corticosterone effects on corticotropin-releasing hormone mRNA in the central nucleus of the amygdala and the parvocellular region of the paraventricular nucleus of the hypothalamus. *Brain Research, 640,* 105–112.

Manly, J. T. (2005). Advances in research definitions of child maltreatment. *Child Abuse and Neglect, 29,* 425–439.

Manly, J. T., Cicchetti, D., & Barnett, D. (1994). The impact of subtype, frequency, chronicity, and severity of child maltreatment on social competence and behavior problems. *Development and Psychopathology, 6*, 121–143.

Manly, J. T., Kim, J. E., Rogosch, F. A., & Cicchetti, D. (2001). Dimensions of child maltreatment and children's adjustment: Contributions of developmental timing and subtype. *Development and Psychopathology, 13*, 759–782.

Marenco, S., & Weinberger, D. R. (2000). The neurodevelopmental hypothesis of schizophrenia: Following a trail of evidence from cradle to grave. *Development and Psychopathology, 12*, 501–528.

Martin, S. D., Martin, R. M. N., Rai, S. S., Richardson, M. A., Royall, R., & Eng, I. E. E. (2001). Brain blood flow changes in depressed patients treated with interpersonal psychotherapy or venlafaxine hydrochloride: preliminary findings. *Archives of General Psychiatry, 58,* 641–648.

Masten, A. S. (2001). Ordinary magic: Resilience processes in development. *American Psychologist, 56*, 227–238.

Masten, A. S. (2006). Developmental psychopathology: Pathways to the future. *International Journal of Behavioral Development, 31*, 47–54.

Masten, A. S. (Ed.). (2007a). *Multilevel dynamics in developmental psychopathology: The Minnesota symposia on child psychology* (Vol. 34). Mahwah, NJ: Erlbaum.

Masten, A. S. (2007b). Resilience in developing systems: Progress and promise as the fourth wave rises. *Development and Psychopathology, 19*, 921–930.

Masten, A. S., Best, K., & Garmezy, N. (1990). Resilience and development: Contributions from the study of children who overcome adversity. *Development and Psychopathology, 2*, 425–444.

Masten, A. S., Burt, K. B., & Coatsworth, J. D. (2006). Competence and psychopathology in development. In D. Cicchetti & D. Cohen (Eds.), *Developmental psychopathology (2nd ed.): Vol. 3. Risk, disorder, and adaptation* (pp. 696–738). Hoboken, NJ: John Wiley & Sons.

Masten, A. S., Cicchetti, D. (Eds.) (2010). Developmental cascades. *Development and Psychopathology, 22,* 491–715.

Masten, A. S., & Coatsworth, J. D. (1998). The development of competence in favorable and unfavorable environments: Lessons from research on successful children. *American Psychologist, 53*, 205–220.

Masten, A. S., Roisman, G. I., Long, J. D., Burt, K. B., Obradovi, J., Riley, J. R., et al. (2005). Developmental cascades: Linking academic achievement, externalizing, and internalizing symptoms over 20 years. *Developmental Psychology, 41*, 733–746.

Maughan, A., & Cicchetti, D. (2002). The impact of child maltreatment and interadult violence on children's emotion regulation abilities. *Child Development, 73*, 1525–1542.

Maughan, B., & Rutter, M. (1997). Retrospective reporting of childhood adversity: Issues in assessing long-term recall. *Journal of Personality Disorders, 11*, 19–33.

Mayr, E. (1964). The evolution of living systems. *Proceedings of the National Academy of Sciences, 51*, 934–941.

Mayr, E. (1988). *Toward a new philosophy of biology*. Cambridge, MA: Harvard University Press.

McCrae, R. R., & John, O. P. (1992). An introduction to the five-factor model and its applications. *Journal of Personality, 60*, 175–215.

McEwen, B. S. (1994). Steroid hormone actions on the brain: When is the genome involved? *Hormones and Behavior, 28*, 396–405.

McEwen, B. S. (2000). Effects of adverse experiences for brain structure and function. *Biological Psychiatry, 48*, 721–731.

McEwen, B. S. (2001). Plasticity of the hippocampus: Adaptation to chronic stress and allostatic load. *Annals of the New York Academy of Science, 933*, 265–277.

McEwen, B. S., & Stellar, E. (1993). Stress and the individual mechanisms leading to disease. *Archives of Internal Medicine, 153*, 2093–2101.

McGee, R. A., & Wolfe, D. A. (1991a). Between a rock and a hard place: Where do we go from here in defining psychological maltreatment? *Development and Psychopathology, 3*, 119–124.

McGee, R. A., & Wolfe, D. A. (1991b). Target Article: Psychological maltreatment: Toward an operational definition. *Development and Psychopathology, 3*, 3–18.

McGlashan, T. H., & Hoffman, R. E. (2000). Schizophrenia as a disorder of developmentally reduced synaptic connectivity. *Archives of General Psychiatry, 57*, 637–648.

McGloin, J. M., & Widom, C. S. (2001). Resilience among abused and neglected children grown up. *Development and Psychopathology, 13*, 1021–1038.

McLeer, S. V., Callaghan, M., Henry, D., & Wallen, J. (1994). Psychiatric disorders in sexually abused children. *Journal of the American Academy of Child and Adolescent Psychiatry, 33*, 313–319.

Meaney, M. J., & Szyf, M. (2005). Environmental programming of stress responses through DNA methylation: Life at the interface between a dynamic environment and a fixed genome. *Dialogues in Clinical Neuroscience, 7*, 103–123.

Mednick, S. A., Machon, R. A., Huttunen, M. O., & Bonett, D. (1988). Adult schizophrenia following prenatal exposure to an influenza epidemic. *Archives of General Psychiatry, 45*, 189–192.

Meehl, P. E. (1962). Schizotaxia, schizotypy, schizophrenia. *American Psychologist, 17*, 827–838.

Meehl, P. E. (1989). Schizotaxia revisited. *Archives of General Psychiatry, 46*, 935–944.

Merry, S. N., Andrews, L. K. (1994). Psychiatric status of sexually abused children 12 months after disclosure of abuse. *Journal of the American Academy of Child and Adolescent Psychiatry, 33*, 939–944.

Meyer-Lindenberg, A. S., Olsen, R. K., Kohn, P. D., Brown, T., Egan, M. F., Weinberger, D. R., et al. (2005). Regionally specific disturbance of dorsolateral prefrontal-hipposcampal functional connectivity in schizophrenia. *Archives of General Psychiatry, 62*, 379–386.

Miklowitz, D. J., & Cicchetti, D. (Eds.). (2006). A developmental perspective on bipolar disorder [Special issue]. *Development and Psychopathology, 18*, 935–1317.

Miklowitz, D. J., & Cicchetti, D. (Eds.). (2010). *Bipolar disorder: A developmental psychopathology approach.* New York: Guilford Press.

Miller, G. E., Chen, E., & Zhou, E. S. (2007). If it goes up, must it come down? Chronic stress and the hypothalamic-pituitary-adrenocortical axis in humans. *Psychological Bulletin, 133*, 25–45.

Mirnics, K., Middleton, F. A., Lewis, D. A., & Levitt, P. (2001). Analysis of complex brain disorders with gene expression microarrays: Schizophrenia as a disease of the synapse. *Trends in Neurosciences, 24*, 479–486.

Moffitt, T. E. (1993). Adolescence-limited and life-course-persistent anti-social behavior: A developmental taxonomy. *Psychological Review, 100*, 674–701.

Moffitt, T. E. (2006). Life-course-persistent versus adolescence-limited antisocial behavior. In D. Cicchetti & D. Cohen (Eds.), *Developmental psychopathology: Vol. 3. Risk, disorder, and adaptation* (2nd ed., pp. 570–598). Hoboken, NJ: John Wiley & Sons.

Moffitt, T. E., Caspi, A., & Rutter, M. (2006). Measured gene–environment interactions in psychopathology: Concepts, research strategies, and implications for research, intervention, and public understanding of genetics. *Perspectives on Psychological Science, 1*, 5–27.

Mundy, P. (2009). Lessons learned from Autism: An information-processing model of joint attention and social-cognition. In D. Cicchetti & M. R. Gunnar (Eds.), *The Minnesota Symposium on Child Psychology: Vol. 35. Meeting the challenge of translational research in child psychology* (pp. 59–113). Hoboken, NJ: John Wiley & Sons.

Mundy, P., & Sigman, M. (1989a). Specifying the nature of the social impairment in autism. In G. Dawson (Ed.), *Autism: Nature, diagnosis, and treatment* (pp. 3–21). New York: Guilford Press.

Mundy, P., & Sigman, M. (1989b). The theoretical implications of joint-attention deficits in autism. *Development and Psychopathology, 1*, 173–183.

Murray-Close, D., Han, G., Cicchetti, D., Crick, N. R., & Rogosch, F. A. (2008). Neuroendocrine regulation and aggression: The moderating roles of physical and relational aggression and child maltreatment. *Developmental Psychology*, 1160–1176.

Muthen, L. K., & Muthen, B. O. (1998–2004). M*plus* (Version 3.11) [Computer software]. Los Angeles: Authors.

Nagin, D. S. (2005). *Group-based modeling of development.* Boston: Harvard University Press.

Nash, M. R., Hulsey, T. L., Sexton, M. C., Harralson, T. L., & Lambert, W. (1993). Long-term sequelae of childhood sexual abuse: Perceived family environment, psychopathology, and dissociation. *Journal of Consulting and Clinical Psychology, 61*, 276–283.

National Advisory Mental Health Council. (2000). *Translating behavioral science into action: Report of the National Advisory Mental Health Counsel's behavioral science workgroup* (No. 00–4699). Bethesda, MD: National Institute of Mental Health.

National Institutes of Mental Health: National Center for Research Resources. (2005, May). *National Meeting on Enhancing the Discipline of Clinical and Translational Sciences*, Doubletree Crystal City National Airport Hotel, Arlington, VA.

National Institute of Neurological Disorders and Stroke. (2005). *NINDS Cooperative Program in Translational Research* (PA-05-158). Bethesda, MD: National Institutes of Health.

Nelson, C. A. (2000). The neurobiological bases of early intervention. In J. Shonkoff & S. Meisels (Eds.), *Handbook of early childhood intervention* (2nd ed., pp. 204–227). New York: Cambridge University Press.

Nelson, C. A., & Bloom, F. E. (1997). Child development and neuroscience. *Child Development, 68*, 970–987.

Nelson, C. A., & Carver, L. J. (1998). The effects of stress and trauma on brain and memory: A view from developmental cognitive neuroscience. *Development and Psychopathology, 10*, 793–809.

Noam, G. (1992). Development as the aim of clinical intervention. *Development and Psychopathology, 4*, 679–696.

Nolen-Hoeksema, S., & Hilt, L. M. (Eds.). (2009). *Handbook of Adolescent Depression*. New York: Taylor & Francis.

Noll, J. G., Trickett, P. K., & Putnam, F. W. (2003). A prospective investigation of the impact of childhood sexual abuse on the development of sexuality. *Journal of Consulting and Clinical Psychology, 71*, 575–586.

Nowakowski, R. S. (1987). Basic concepts of CNS development. *Child Development, 58*, 568–595.

Nowakowski, R. S., & Hayes, N. L. (1999). CNS development: An overview. *Development and Psychopathology, 11*, 395–418.

O'Connor, N., & Hermelin, B. (1978). *Seeing and hearing and space and time*. London: Academic Press.

Ogata, S. N., Silk, K. R., Goodrich, S., Lohr, N. E., Westen, D., & Hill, E. M. (1990). Childhood sexual and physical abuse in adult patients with borderline personality disorder. *American Journal of Psychiatry, 147*, 1008–1013.

Okun, A., Parker, J. G., & Levendosky, A. A. (1994). Distinct and interactive contributions of physical abuse, socioeconomic disadvantage, and negative life events to children's social, cognitive, and affective adjustment. *Development and Psychopathology, 6*, 77–98.

Olds, D., Henderson, C. R., Chamberlin, R., & Tatelbaum, R. (1986). Preventing child abuse and neglect: A randomized trial of nurse home visitation. *Pediatrics, 78*, 65–78.

Olds, D., Henderson, C., Kitzman, H., Eckenrode, J., Cole, R., & Tatelbaum, R. (1998). The promise of home visitation: Results of two randomized trials. *Journal of Community Psychology, 26*, 5–21.

Olds, D. L., & Kitzman, H. (1990). Can home visitation improve the health of women and children at environmental risk? *Pediatrics, 86*, 108–116.

O'Leary, D. (1989). Do cortical areas emerge from a protocortex? *Trends in Neurosciences, 12*, 400–406.

Ornitz, E. M., & Pynoos, R. S. (1989). Startle modulation in children with posttraumatic stress disorder. *American Journal of Psychiatry, 146*, 866–870.

Ozonoff, S. (2001). Advances in the cognitive neuroscience of autism. In C. A. Nelson & M. Luciana (Eds.), *Handbook of developmental cognitive neuroscience* (pp. 537–548). Cambridge, MA: MIT Press.

Paquette, V., Levesque, J., Mensour, B., Leroux, J. M., Beaudoin, G., Bourgouin, P., & Beauregard, M. (2003). "Change the mind and you change the brain": Effects of cognitive–behavioral therapy on the neural correlates of spider phobia. *NeuroImage, 18*, 401–409.

Paris, J. (1997). Childhood trauma as an etiological factor in the personality disorders. *Journal of Personality Disorders, 11*(1), 34–49.

Parker, J. G., & Herrera, C. (1996). Interpersonal processes in friendship: A comparison of maltreated and nonmaltreated children's experiences. *Developmental Psychology, 32*, 1025–1038.

Patrick, M., Hobson, R. P., Castle, D., Howard, R., & Maughan, B. (1994). Personality disorder and the mental representation of early social experience. *Development and Psychopathology, 6*, 375–388.

Patterson, G. R., Reid, J. B., & Dishion, T. J. (1992). *Antisocial boys*. Eugene, OR: Castalia.

Pears, K. C., & Fisher, P. A. (2005). Emotion understanding and theory of mind among maltreated children in foster care: Evidence of deficits. *Development and Psychopathology, 17*, 47–65.

Pellmar, T. C., & Eisenberg, L. (Eds.). (2000). *Bridging disciplines in the brain, behavioral, and clinical sciences*. Washington, DC: National Academy Press.

Perlman, S. B., Kalish, C. W., & Pollak, S. D. (2008). The role of maltreatment experience in children's understanding of the antecedents of emotion. *Cognition and Emotion, 22*, 651–670.

Plomin, R., & Crabbe, J. (2000). DNA. *Psychological Bulletin, 126*, 806–828.

Plomin, R., DeFries, J. C., McClearn, G. E., & McGuffin, P. (2001). *Behavior genetics*. New York: Worth.

Plomin, R., & Rutter, M. (1998). Child development, molecular genetics, and what to do with genes once they are found. *Child Development, 69*, 1223–1242.

Pollak, S. D. (2008). Mechanisms linking early experience and the emergence of emotions: Illustrations from the study of maltreated children. *Current Directions in Psychological Science, 17*, 370–375.

Pollak, S. D., Cicchetti, D., Hornung, K., & Reed, A. (2000). Recognizing emotion in faces: Developmental effects of child abuse and neglect. *Developmental Psychology, 36*, 679–688.

Pollak, S. D., Cicchetti, D., & Klorman, R. (1998). Stress, memory, and emotion: Developmental considerations from the study of child maltreatment. *Development and Psychopathology, 10*, 811–828.

Pollak, S. D., Cicchetti, D., Klorman, R., & Brumaghim, J. (1997). Cognitive brain event-related potentials and emotion processing in maltreated children. *Child Development, 68*, 773–787.

Pollak, S. D., & Kistler, D. (2002). Early experience alters categorical representations for facial expressions of emotion. *Proceedings of the National Academy of Sciences, USA, 99*, 9072–9076.

Pollak, S. D., Klorman, R., Thatcher, J. E., & Cicchetti, D. (2001). P3b reflects maltreated children's reactions to facial displays of emotion. *Psychophysiology, 38*, 267–274.

Pollak, S. D., & Sinha, P. (2002). Effects of early experience on children's recognition of facial displays of emotion. *Developmental Psychology, 38*, 784–791.

Pollak, S. D., & Tolley-Schell, S. A. (2003). Selective attention to facial emotion in physically abused children. *Journal of Abnormal Psychology, 112*, 323–338.

Posner, M. I., Rothbart, M. K., Farah, M., & Bruer, J. (2001). The developing human brain [Special issue]. *Developmental Science, 4*, 253–287.

Post, R. M. (1992). Transduction of psychosocial stress into the neurobiology of recurrent affective disorder. *American Journal of Psychiatry, 149*, 999–1010.

Post, R. M., Weiss, S. R. B., & Leverich, G. S. (1994). Recurrent affective disorder: Roots in developmental neurobiology and illness progression based on changes in gene expression. *Development and Psychopathology, 6*, 781–814.

Post, R. M., Weiss, S. R. B., Leverich, G. S., George, M., Frye, M., & Ketter, T. (1996). Developmental neurobiology of cyclic affective illness: Implications for early therapeutic interventions. *Development and Psychopathology, 8*, 273–305.

Pribor, E. F., & Dinwiddie, S. H. (1992). Psychiatric correlates of incest in childhood. *American Journal of Psychiatry, 149*, 52–56.

Prichard, J. W. (1996). MRS of the brain-prospects for clinical application. In I. R. Young & H. C. Charles (Eds.), *MR Spectroscopy: Clinical applications and techniques* (Vol. 1–25). London: Livery House.

Putnam, F. W. (2003). Ten-year research update review: Child sexual abuse. *Journal of the American Academy of Child and Adolescent Psychiatry, 43*, 269–278.

Putnam, F. W., & Trickett, P. K. (1993). Child sexual abuse: A model of chronic trauma. *Psychiatry, 56*, 82–95.

Putnam, F. W., Trickett, P. K., Helmers, K., Dorn, L., & Everett, B. (1991). Cortisol abnormalities in sexually abused girls. Paper presented at the 144th annual meeting of the American Psychiatric Association.

Quinton, D., & Rutter, M. (1988). *Parenting and breakdown: The making and breaking of intergenerational links*. Aldershot, England: Avebury.

Rakic, P. (1988a). Intrinsic and extrinsic determinants of neocortical parcellation: A radial unit model. In P. Rakic & W. Singer (Eds.), *Neurobiology of neocortex* (pp. 5–27). New York: John Wiley & Sons.

Rakic, P. (1988b). Specification of cerebral cortex areas. *Science, 241*, 170–176.

Rakic, P. (1996). Development of the cerebral cortex in human and nonhuman primates. In M. Lewis (Ed.), *Child and adolescent psychiatry: A comprehensive textbook* (pp. 9–30). Baltimore: Williams & Wilkins.

Rende, R., & Waldman, I. (2006). Behavioral and molecular genetics and developmental psychopathology. In D. Cicchetti & D. Cohen (Eds.), *Developmental psychopathology: Vol. 2. Developmental neuroscience* (2nd ed., pp. 427–464). Hoboken, NJ: John Wiley & Sons.

Repetti, R., Taylor, S., & Seeman, T. (2002). Risky families: Family social environments and the mental and physical health of offspring. *Psychological Bulletin, 128*, 330–366.

Reynolds, A. J., Mathieson, L. C., & Topitzes, J. W. (2009). Do early children interventions prevent child maltreatment? A review of research. *Child Maltreatment, 14,* 182–206.

Reynolds, A. J., & Robertson, D. (2003). School-based early intervention and later child maltreatment in the Chicago Longitudinal Study. *Child Development, 74*, 3–26.

Richters, J. E. (1997). The Hubble hypothesis and the developmentalist's dilemma. *Development and Psychopathology, 9*, 193–229.

Rieder, C., & Cicchetti, D. (1989). Organizational perspective on cognitive control functioning and cognitive-affective balance in maltreated children. *Developmental Psychology, 25*, 382–393.

Robins, L. (1966). *Deviant children grow up*. Baltimore: Williams & Wilkins.

Robins, L., & Rutter, M. (Eds.). (1990). *Straight and devious pathways from childhood to adulthood*. New York: Cambridge University Press.

Robins, R. W., John, O. P., Caspi, A., Moffitt, T. E., & Stouthamer-Loeber, M. (1996). Resilient, overcontrolled, and undercontrolled boys. *Journal of Personality and Social Psychology, 70*, 157–171.

Rodier, P. M. (2002). Converging evidence from brain stem injury in autism. *Development and Psychopathology, 14*, 537–557.

Rogeness, G. A. (1991). Psychosocial factors and amine systems. *Psychiatry Research, 37*, 215–217.

Rogeness, G. A., & McClure, E. B. (1996). Development and neurotransmitter-environmental interactions. *Development and Psychopathology, 8*, 183–199.

Rogosch, F. A., & Cicchetti, D. (1994). Illustrating the interface of family and peer relations through the study of child maltreatment. *Social Development, 3*, 291–308.

Rogosch, F. A., & Cicchetti, D. (2004). Child maltreatment and emergent personality organization: Perspectives from the five-factor model. *Journal of Abnormal Child Psychology, 32*, 123–145.

Rogosch, F. A., Cicchetti, D., Shields, A., & Toth, S. L. (1995). Parenting dysfunction in child maltreatment. In M. H. Bornstein (Ed.), *Handbook of parenting* (Vol. 4, pp. 127–159). Hillsdale, NJ: Erlbaum.

Romer, D., & Walker, E. (2007). *Adolescent psychopathology and the developing brain: Integrating brain and prevention science*. New York: Oxford University Press.

Rosello, J., & Bernal, G. (1999). The efficacy of cognitive-behavioral and interpersonal treatments for depression in Puerto Rican adolescents. *Journal of Consulting & Clinical Psychology, 67*, 734–745.

Rosenbaum, M., & Bennett, B. (1986). Homicide and depression. *American Journal of Psychiatry, 143*, 367–370.

Rothbart, M. K., & Bates, J. E. (1998). Temperament. In W. Damon (Ed.), *Handbook of child psychology: Vol. 3. Social, emotional, and personality development* (5th ed, pp. 105–176). New York: John Wiley & Sons.

Rothbart, M. K., Posner, M. I., & Hershey, K. L. (1995). Temperament, attention, and developmental psychopathology. In D. Cicchetti & D. J. Cohen (Eds.), *Developmental Psychopathology: Vol. 1. Theory and method* (pp. 315–340). New York: John Wiley & Sons.

Rutter, M. (1986). Child psychiatry: The interface between clinical and developmental research. *Psychological Medicine, 16*, 151–160.

Rutter, M. (1989). Pathways from childhood to adult life. *Journal of Child Psychology and Psychiatry, 30*, 23–51.

Rutter, M. (1990). Psychosocial resilience and protective mechanisms. In J. Rolf, A. S. Masten, D. Cicchetti, K. Nuechterlein, & S. Weintraub (Eds.), *Risk and protective factors in the development of psychopathology* (pp. 181–214). New York: Cambridge University Press.

Rutter, M. (1994). Beyond longitudinal data: Causes, consequences, changes, and continuity. *Journal of Consulting and Clinical Psychology, 62*, 928–940.

Rutter, M. (1995). Relationships between mental disorders in childhood and adulthood. *Acta Psychiatrica Scandinavica, 91,* 73–85.

Rutter, M. (1999). Social context: Meanings, measures and mechanisms. *European Review, 7*, 139–149.

Rutter, M. (2005). Multiple meanings of a developmental perspective on psychopathology. *European Journal of Developmental Psychology, 2,* 221–252.

Rutter, M. (2006). *Genes and Behavior: Nture-Nurture Interplay Explained.* Malden, MA: Wiley-Blackwell.

Rutter, M. (2007). Gene–environment interdependence. *Developmental Science, 10,* 12–18.

Rutter, M. (2009). Understanding and testing risk mechanisms for mental disorders. *Journal of Child Psychology and Psychiatry, 50,* 44–52.

Rutter, M., & Garmezy, N. (1983). Developmental psychopathology. In E. M. Hetherington (Ed.), *Handbook of child psychology* (4th ed., Vol. 4, pp. 774–911). New York: John Wiley & Sons.

Rutter, M., Kim-Cohen, J., & Maughan, B. (2006). Continuities and discontinuities in psychopathology between childhood and adult life. *Journal of Child Psychology and Psychiatry, 47,* 276–295.

Rutter, M., & Quinton, D. (1984). Parental psychiatric disorder: Effects on children. *Psychological Medicine, 14*, 853–880.

Rutter, M., & Sroufe, L. A. (2000). Developmental psychopathology: Concepts and challenges. *Development and Psychopathology, 12*, 265–296.

Ryan, R., Deci, E. L., & Grolnick, W. (1995). Autonomy, relatedness, and the self: The relation to development and psychopathology. In D. Cicchetti & D. Cohen (Eds.), *Developmental psychopathology: Theory and methods* (Vol. 1, pp. 618–655). New York: John Wiley & Sons.

Sack, W. H., & Mason, R. (1980). Child abuse and conviction of sexual crimes: A preliminary finding. *Law & Human Behavior, 4*, 211–215.

Salzinger, S., Feldman, R. S., Hammer, M., & Rosario, M. (1993). The effects of physical abuse on children's social relationships. *Child Development, 64*, 169–187.

Sameroff, A. J. (1983). Developmental systems: Contexts and evolution. In P. Mussen (Ed.), *Handbook of child psychology* (Vol. 1, pp. 237–294). New York: John Wiley & Sons.

Sameroff, A. J. (1989). Models of developmental regulation: The environtype. In D. Cicchetti (Ed.), *Rochester symposium on developmental psychopathology: The emergence of a discipline* (Vol. 1, pp. 41–68). Hillsdale, NJ: Erlbaum.

Sameroff, A. J. (2000). Developmental systems and psychopathology. *Development and Psychopathology, 12*, 297–312.

Sameroff, A. J., & Chandler, M. J. (1975). Reproductive risk and the continuum of caretaking casualty. In F. D. Horowitz (Ed.), *Review of child development research* (Vol. 4, pp. 187–244). Chicago: University of Chicago Press.

Sameroff, A. J., Seifer, R., Barocas, R., Zax, M., & Greenspan, S. (1987). Intelligence quotient scores of 4-year-old children: Social-environmental risk factors. *Pediatrics, 79*, 343–350.

Sánchez, M. M., McCormack, K. M., & Maestripieri, D. (in press). Ethological case study: Infant abuse in rhesus macaques. In C. Worthman, P. Plotsky, D. Schechter, & C. Cummings (Eds.), *Formative experiences: The interaction of caregiving, culture, and developmental psychobiology.* New York: Cambridge University Press.

Sánchez, M. M., Noble, P., Lyon, C., Plotsky, P., Davis, M., Nemeroff, C., et al. (2005). Alterations in diurnal cortisol rhythm and acoustic startle response in nonhuman primates with adverse rearing. *Biological Psychiatry*, *57,* 373–381

Santostefano, S. (1978). *A biodevelopmental approach to clinical child psychology*. New York: John Wiley & Sons.

Santostefano, S., & Baker, H. (1972). The contribution of developmental psychology. In B. Wolman (Ed.), *Manual of child psychopathology* (pp. 1113–1153). New York: McGraw-Hill.

Sapolsky, R. M. (1992). *Stress, the aging brain, and the mechanisms of neuron death.* Cambridge, MA: MIT Press.

Sapolsky, R. M. (1994). Individual differences and the stress response. *Seminars in the Neurosciences, 6*, 261–269.

Sapolsky, R. M. (1996). Stress, glucocorticoids, and damage to the NS: The current state of confusion. *Stress, 1*, 1–19.

Scarr, S., & McCartney, K. (1983). How people make their own environments: A theory of genotype-environment effects. *Child Development, 54*, 424–435.

Schmidt, L. A., & Fox, N. A. (1998). Fear-potentiated startle responses in temperamentally different human infants. *Developmental Psychobiology, 32*, 113–120.

Schneider-Rosen, K., & Cicchetti, D. (1991). Early self-knowledge and emotional development: Visual self-recognition and affective reactions to mirror self-image in maltreated and nonmaltreated toddlers. *Developmental Psychology, 27*, 481–488.

Schulenberg, J., Sameroff, A., & Cicchetti, D. (2004). The transition from adolescence to adulthood [Special issue]. *Development and Psychopathology, 16*(4).

Schulenberg, J., Wadsworth, K. N., O'Malley, P. M., Bachman, J. G., & Johnston, L. D. (1996). Adolescent risk factors for binge drinking during the transition to young adulthood: Variable- and pattern-centered approaches to change. *Developmental Psychology, 32,* 659–674.

Schwartz, J.. Stoessel, P. W., Baxter, L. R., Martin. K. M., & Phelps, M. E. (1996). Systematic changes in cerebral glucose metabolic rate after successful behavior modification treatment of obsessive-compulsive disorder. *Archives of General Psychiatry. 53.* 109–113.

Senn, M. (1975). Insights on the child development movement. *Monographs of the Society for Research in Child Development, 40*, 3–4.

Serafica, F. C., & Vargas, L. A. (2006). Cultural diversity in the development of child psychopathology. In D. Cicchetti & D. Cohen (Eds.), *Developmental psychopathology* (2nd ed., Vol. 1, pp. 588–626). Hoboken, NJ: John Wiley & Sons.

Serbin, L. A., & Karp, J. (2004). The intergenerational transfer of psychosocial risk: Mediators of vulnerability and resilience. *Annual Review of Psychology, 55,* 333–363.

Shackman, J., Shackman, A., & Pollak, S. D. (2007). Physical abuse amplifies attention to threat and increases anxiety in children. *Emotion, 7,* 838–852.

Shenton, M. E., Frumin, M., McCarley, R. W., Maier, S. E., Westin, C.-F., Fischer, I. A., et al. (2001). Morphometric magnetic resonance imaging studies: Findings in schizophrenia. In D. D. Dougherty & S. L. Rauch (Eds.), *Psychiatric neuroimaging research: Contemporary strategies* (pp. 1–60). Washington, DC: American Psychiatric Publishing.

Sher, K. (1994). Individual-level risk factors. In R. Zucker, J. Howard, & G. Boyd (Eds.), *The development of alcohol problems: Exploring the biopsychosocial matrix of risk* (pp. 77–108). Rockville, MD: National Institute on Alcohol Abuse and Alcoholism.

Shields, A., & Cicchetti, D. (1998). Reactive aggression among maltreated children: The contributions of attention and emotion dysregulation. *Journal of Clinical Child Psychology, 27*, 381–395.

Shields, A., & Cicchetti, D. (2001). Parental maltreatment and emotion dysregulation as risk factors for bullying and victimization in middle childhood. *Journal of Clinical Child Psychology, 30*, 349–363.

Shields, A., Cicchetti, D., & Ryan, R. M. (1994). The development of emotional and behavioral self regulation and social competence among maltreated school-age children. *Development and Psychopathology, 6*, 57–75.

Shields, A., Ryan, R. M., & Cicchetti, D. (2001). Narrative representations of caregivers and emotion dysregulation as predictors of maltreated children's rejection by peers. *Developmental Psychology, 37*, 321–337.

Shirk, S. (Ed.). (1988). *Cognitive development and child psychotherapy.* New York: Plenum Press.

Shonk, S. M., & Cicchetti, D. (2001). Maltreatment, competency deficits, and risk for academic and behavioral maladjustment. *Developmental Psychology, 37*, 3–14.

Shonkoff, J. P. (2000). Science, policy, and practice. Three cultures in search of a shared mission. *Child Development, 71*, 181–187.

Sidman, R. L., & Rakic, P. (1973). Neuronal migration, with special reference to developing human brain: A review. *Brain Research, 62,* 1–35.

Sidman, R. L., & Rakic, P. (1982). Development of the human central nervous system. In W. Haymaker & R. D. Adams (Eds.), *Histology and histopathology of the nervous system* (pp. 3–145). Springfield, IL: Thomas.

Sigel, I. E. (2006). Research to practice redefined. In K. A. Renninger & I. E. Sigel (Eds.), *Handbook of child psychology: Vol. 4. Child psychology in practice* (6th ed., pp. 1017–1023). Hoboken, NJ: John Wiley & Sons.

Sigel, I. E., & Renninger, K. A. (Eds.). (1998). Preface. In *Handbook of child psychology: Vol. 4. Child psychology in practice* (5th ed., pp. xxi–xxiii). New York: Wiley.

Silverman, A. B., Reinherz, H. Z., & Giaconia, R. M. (1996). The long-term sequelae of child and adolescent abuse: A longitudinal community study. *Child Abuse & Neglect, 20*, 709–723.

Simeon, D., Guralnik, O., Schmeidler, J., Sirof, B., & Knutelska, M. (2001). The role of childhood interpersonal trauma in depersonalization disorder. *American Journal of Psychiatry, 158,* 1027–1033

Smetana, J. G., Daddis, C., Toth, S. L., Cicchetti, D., Bruce, J., & Kane, P. (1999). Effects of provocation on maltreated and nonmaltreated preschoolers' understanding of moral transgressions. *Social Development, 8*, 335–348.

Smith, C. A., & Thornberry, T. (1995). The relationship between child maltreatment and adolescent involvement in delinquency. *Criminology, 33*, 451–481.

Soloff, P. H., Lynch, K. G., & Kelley, T. M. (2002). Childhood abuse as a risk factor for suicidal behavior in borderline personality disorder. *Journal of Personality Disorders, 16,* 201–214.

Spear, L. P. (2000). The adolescent brain and age-related behavioral manifestations. *Neuroscience and Behavioral Reviews, 24*, 417–463.

Spear, L. P. (2003). Neurodevelopment during adolescence. In D. Cicchetti & E. F. Walker (Eds.), *Neurodevelopmental Mechanisms in Psychopathology* (pp. 62–83). New York: Cambridge University Press.

Sroufe, L. A. (1979). The coherence of individual development: Early care, attachment, and subsequent developmental issues. *American Psychologist, 34*, 834–841.

Sroufe, L. A. (1983). Infant-caregiver attachment and patterns of adaptation in preschool: The roots of maladaptation and competence. In M. Perlmutter (Ed.), *Minnesota Symposium on Child Psychology* (Vol. 16, pp. 41–83). Hillsdale, NJ: Erlbaum.

Sroufe, L. A. (1989). Pathways to adaptation and maladaptation: Psychopathology as developmental deviation. In D. Cicchetti (Ed.), *Rochester Symposium on Developmental Psychopathology: Vol. 1. The emergence of a discipline* (pp. 13–40). Hillsdale, NJ: Erlbaum.

Sroufe, L. A. (1990). Considering normal and abnormal together: The essence of developmental psychopathology. *Development and Psychopathology, 2*, 335–347.

Sroufe, L. A. (1997). Psychopathology as an outcome of development. *Development and Psychopathology, 9*, 251–268.

Sroufe, L. A. (2007). The place of development in developmental psychopathology. In A. Masten (Ed.), *Minnesota Symposia on Child Psychology: Vol. 34. Multilevel dynamics in developmental psychopathology pathways to the future.* (pp. 285–299). Mahwah, NJ: Erlbaum.

Sroufe, L. A., Carlson, E. A., Levy, A. K., & Egeland, B. (1999). Implications of attachment theory for developmental psychopathology. *Development and Psychopathology, 11*, 1–13.

Sroufe, L. A., Egeland, B., & Kreutzer, T. (1990). The fate of early experience following developmental change: Longitudinal approaches to individual adaptation in childhood. *Child Development, 61*, 1363–1373.

Sroufe, L. A., & Jacobvitz, D. (1989). Diverging pathways, developmental transformations, multiple etiologies, and the problem of continuity in development. *Human Development, 32*, 196–203.

Sroufe, L. A., & Rutter, M. (1984). The domain of developmental psychopathology. *Child Development, 55*, 17–29.

Staudinger, U. M., Marsiske, M., & Baltes, P. B. (1995). Resilience and reserve capacity in later adulthood: Potentials and limits of development across the life span. In D. Cicchetti & D. Cohen (Eds.), *Developmental psychopathology: Risk, disorder, and adaptation* (Vol. 2, pp. 801–847). New York: John Wiley & Sons.

Stein, J. A., Leslie, M. B., & Nyamathi, A. (2002). Relative contributions of parent substance use and childhood maltreatment to chronic homelessness, depression, and substance abuse problems among homeless women: Mediating roles of self-esteem and abuse in adulthood. *Child Abuse and Neglect, 26*, 1011–1027.

Stein, M. B., Yehuda, R., Koverola, C., & Hanna, C. (1997). Enhanced dexamethasone suppression of plasma cortisol in adult women traumatized by childhood sexual abuse. *Biological Psychiatry, 42*, 680–686.

Steingard, R. J., & Coyle, J. T. (1998). Brain development. In N. E. Alessi, J. T. Coyle, S. I. Harrison, & S. Eth (Eds.), *Handbook of child and adolescent psychiatry* (pp. 97–107). New York: John Wiley & Sons.

Sternberg, K., Lamb, M., Greenbaum, C., Cicchetti, D., Dawud, S., Cortes, R., et al. (1993). Effects of domestic violence on children's behavior problems and depression. *Developmental Psychology, 29*, 44–52.

Stokes, D. E. (1997). *Pasteur's quadrant: Basic science and technological innovation*. Washington, DC: Brookings Institution.

Susman, E. J. (2006). Psychobiology of persistent antisocial behavior: Stress, early vulnerabilities and the attenuation hypothesis. *Neuroscience and Biobehavioral Reviews, 30*, 376–389.

Susman, E. J., Dockray, S., Schiefelbein, V. L., Herwehe, S., Heaton, J. A., & Dorn, L. D. (2007). Morningness/eveningness, morning-to-afternoon cortisol ratio, and antisocial behavior problems during puberty. *Developmental Psychology, 43*, 811–822.

Tarullo, A. R., & Gunnar, M. R. (2006). Child maltreatment and the developing HPA axis. *Hormones and Behavior, 50*, 632–639.

Taylor, A., & Kim-Cohen, J. (2007). Meta-analysis of gene–environment interactions in developmental psychopathology. *Development and Psychopathology, 19*, 1029–1037.

Teicher, M. H., Dumont, N., Ito, Y., Vaituzis, A. C., Giedd, J., & Andersen, S. (2004). Childhood neglect is associated with reduced corpus callosum area. *Biological Psychiatry, 56*, 80–85.

Teisl, M., & Cicchetti, D. (2008). Physical abuse, cognitive and emotional processes, and aggressive/disruptive behavior problems. *Social Development, 17*, 1–23.

Thelen, E., & Smith, L. B. (1998). Dynamic systems theories. In W. Damon & R. Lerner (Eds.), *Handbook of child psychology: Vol. 1. Theoretical models of human development* (pp. 563–634). New York: John Wiley & Sons.

Thomas, K., & Cicchetti, D. (2008). Imaging brain systems in normality and psychopathology [Special issue]. *Development and Psychopathology, 20*.

Thompson, R., Briggs, E., English, D. J., Dubowitz, H., Lee, L. C., Brody, K., et al. (2005). Suicidal ideation among 8-year-olds who are maltreated and at risk: Findings from the LONGSCAN Studies. *Child Maltreatment, 10*, 26–36.

Thompson, R. A., & Nelson, C. A. (2001). Developmental science and the media: Early brain development. *American Psychologist, 56*, 5–15.

Toth, S. L., & Cicchetti, D. (1993). Child maltreatment: Where do we go from here in our treatment of victims? In D. Cicchetti & S. L. Toth (Eds.), *Child abuse, child development, and social policy* (pp. 399–438). Norwood, NJ: Ablex.

Toth, S. L., & Cicchetti, D. (1996a). The impact of relatedness with mother on school functioning in maltreated youngsters. *Journal of School Psychology, 3*, 247–266.

Toth, S. L., & Cicchetti, D. (1996b). Patterns of relatedness and depressive symptomatology in maltreated children. *Journal of Consulting and Clinical Psychology, 64*, 32–41.

Toth, S. L., & Cicchetti, D. (1999). Developmental psychopathology and child psychotherapy. In S. Russ & T. Ollendick (Eds.), *Handbook of psychotherapies with children and families* (pp. 15–44). New York: Plenum Press.

Toth, S. L., Cicchetti, D., & Kim, J. E. (2002). Relations among children's perceptions of maternal behavior, attributional styles, and behavioral symptomatology in maltreated children. *Journal of Abnormal Child Psychology, 30*, 478–501.

Toth, S. L., Cicchetti, D., Macfie, J., & Emde, R. N. (1997). Representations of self and other in the narratives of neglected, physically abused, and sexually abused preschoolers. *Development and Psychopathology, 9*, 781–796.

Toth, S. L., Cicchetti, D., Macfie, J., Maughan, A., & VanMeenan, K. (2000). Narrative representations of caregivers and self in maltreated preschoolers. *Attachment and Human Development, 2*, 271-305.

Toth, S. L., Manly, J. T., & Cicchetti, D. (1992). Child maltreatment and vulnerability to depression. *Development and Psychopathology, 4*, 97–112.

Toth, S. L., Manly, J. T., & Nilsen, W. J. (2008). From research to practice: Lessons learned. *Journal of Applied Developmental Psychology, 29*, 317–325.

Toth, S. L., Maughan, A., Manly, J. T., Spagnola, M., & Cicchetti, D. (2002). The relative efficacy of two interventions in altering maltreated preschool children's representational models: Implications for attachment theory. *Development and Psychopathology, 14*, 777–808.

Toth, S. L., Rogosch, F. A., Manly, J. T., & Cicchetti , D. (2006). The efficacy of toddler-parent psychotherapy to reorganize attachment in the young offspring of mothers with major depressive disorder. *Journal of Consulting & Clinical Psychology, 74*, 1006–1016.

Toth, S. L., Rogosch, F. A., Sturge-Apple, M., & Cicchetti, D. (2009). Maternal depression, children's attachment security, and representational development: An organizational perspective. *Child Development, 80,* 192–208.

Townsend, J., Courchesne, E., & Egaas, B. (1997). Slowed orienting of covert visual-spatial attention in autism: Specific deficits associated with cerebellar and parietal abnormality. *Development and Psychopathology, 8,* 563–584.

Trickett, P. K., McBride-Chang, C., & Putnam, F. (1994). The classroom performance and behavior of sexually abused females. *Development and Psychopathology, 6*, 183–194.

Tsuang, M. T., Wollson, R. F., & Fleming, J. A. (1979). Long-term outcome of major psychoses, I: Schizophrenia and affective disorders compared with psychiatrically symptom-free surgical conditions. *Archives of General Psychiatry, 39,* 1295–1301.

U.S. Department of Health and Human Services. (2000). Child maltreatment 1998: Reports from the States to the National Child Abuse and Neglect Data System. Washington, DC: U.S. Government Printing Office.

von Bertalanffy, L. (1968). *General system theory*. New York: Braziller.

Vondra, J., Barnett, D., & Cicchetti, D. (1989). Perceived and actual competence among maltreated and comparison school children. *Development and Psychopathology, 1*, 237–255.

von Eye, A., & Bergman, L. R. (2003). Research strategies in developmental psychopathology: Dimensional identity and the person-oriented approach. *Development and Psychopathology, 15*, 553–580.

Vythilingam, M., Heim, C., Newport, J., Miller, A. H., Anderson, E., Bronen, R., et al. (2002). Childhood trauma associated with smaller hippocampal volume in women with major depression. *American Journal of Psychiatry, 159*, 2072–2080.

Waddington, C. H. (1957). *The strategy of genes*. London: Allen & Unwin.

Wakefield, J. C. (1992). The concept of mental disorder: On the boundary between biological facts and social values. *American Psychologist, 47*, 373–388.

Wakefield, J. C. (1997). When is development disordered? Developmental psychopathology and the harmful dysfunction analysis of mental disorder. *Development and Psychopathology, 9*, 269–290.

Walker, E. F., Davis, D. M., & Gottlieb, L. A. (1991). Charting the developmental trajectories to schizophrenia. In D. Cicchetti & S. L. Toth (Eds.), *Rochester Symposium on Developmental Psychopathology: Vol. 3. Models and integrations* (pp. 185–205). Rochester, NY: University of Rochester Press.

Walker, E. F., & DiForio, D. (1997). Schizophrenia: A neural diathesis-stress model. *Psychological Review, 104*, 1–19.

Wapner, S., & Demick, J. (1998). Developmental analysis: A holistic, developmental systems-oriented perspective. In W. Damon (Ed.), *Handbook of child psychology* (5th ed., pp. 761–806). New York: John Wiley & Sons.

Watson, C., & Gametchu, B. (1999). Membrane-initiated steroid actions and the proteins that mediate them. *Proceedings of the Society for Experimental Biology and Medicine, 220*, 9–19.

Watson, J. D., Hopkins, N. H., Roberts, J. W., Steitz, J. A., & Weiner, A. M. (1987). *Molecular Biology of the Gene.* Benjamin/Cummings.

Watt, N. (1971). Developmental changes in semantic interpretation of ambiguous words. *Journal of Abnormal Psychology, 77*, 332–339.

Watt, N., Anthony, E. J., Wynne, L., & Rolf, J. (Eds.). (1984). *Children at risk for schizophrenia: A longitudinal perspective*. New York: Cambridge University Press.

Weaver, T., & Clum, G. (1993). Early family environments and traumatic experiences associated with borderline personality disorder. *Journal of Consulting and Clinical Psychology, 61*, 1068–1075.

Weinberger, D. R. (1987). Implications of normal brain development for the pathogenesis of schizophrenia. *Archives of General Psychiatry, 44*, 660–669.

Weiss, P. A. (1961). Deformities as cues to understanding development of form. *Perspectives in Biology and Medicine, 4*, 133–151.

Weisz, J. R., & Hawley, K. M. (2002). Developmental factors in the treatment of adolescents. *Journal of Consulting and Clinical Psychology, 70,* 21–43.

Werner, H. (1948). *Comparative psychology of mental development*. New York: International Universities Press.

Werner, H., & Kaplan, B. (1963). *Symbol formation*. New York: John Wiley & Sons.

Westen, D. (1994). The impact of sexual abuse on self structure. In D. Cicchetti & S. L. Toth (Eds.), *Rochester Symposium on Developmental Psychopathology* (Vol. 5, pp. 223–250). Rochester, NY: University of Rochester Press.

Whaley, A. L., & Davis, K. E. (2007). Cultural competence and evidence-based practice in mental health services: A complementary perspective. *American Psychologist, 62*, 563–574.

Widom, C. S. (1989). The cycle of violence. *Science, 244*, 160–166.

Widom, C. S., & Morris, S. (1997). Accuracy of adult recollections of childhood victimization, Part 2: Childhood sexual abuse. *Psychological Assessment, 9*, 34–46.

Widom, C. S., & Shephard, R. L. (1996). Accuracy of adult recollections of childhood victimization: Part 1. Childhood physical abuse. *Psychological Assessment, 8*, 412–421.

Wilden, A. (1980). *System and structure*. London: Tavistock.

Wolfe, D. A. (1993). *Child abuse: Implications for child development and psychopathology* (2nd ed.). Thousand Oaks, CA: Sage.

Wolfe, D. A., & Jaffe, P. (1991). Child abuse and family violence as determinants of child psychopathology. *Canadian Journal of Behavioural Science, 23*, 282–299.

Wolfe, D. A., & Wekerle, C. (1993). Treatment strategies for child physical abuse and neglect: A critical progress report. *Clinical Psychology Review, 13*, 501–540.

Youngstrom, E., Meyers, O., Youngstrom, J. K., Calabrese, J. R., & Findling, R. L. (2006). Diagnostic and measurement issues in the assessment of pediatric bipolar disorder: Implications for understanding mood disorder across the life cycle. *Development and Psychopathology, 18*, 989–1021.

Zanarini, M. C. (2000). Childhood experiences associated with the development of borderline personality disorder. *Psychiatric Clinics of North America, 23*, 89–101.

Zanarini, M. C., Gunderson, J. G., Marino, M. F., Schwartz, E. O., & Frankenburg, F. R. (1989). Childhood experiences of borderline patients. *Comprehensive Psychiatry, 30*, 18–25.

Zanarini, M. C., Skodol, A. E., Bender, D., Dolan, R., Sanislow, C., Schaeffer, E., et al. (2000). The Collaborative Longitudinal Personality Disorders Study: Reliability of Axis I and II diagnoses. *Journal of Personality Disorders, 14,* 291–329.

Zanarini, M. C., Williams, A. A., Lewis, R. E., Reich, R. B., Vera, S. C., Marino, M. F., et al. (1997). Reported pathological childhood experiences associated with the development of Borderline Personality Disorder. *American Journal of Psychiatry, 154*, 1101–1106.

Zeanah, C. H., Nelson, C. A., Fox, N. A., Smyke, A. T., Marshall, P. M., Parker, S. W., et al. (2003). Designing research to study the effects of institutionalization on brain and behavioral development: The Bucharest Early Intervention Project. *Development and Psychopathology, 15*, 885–907.

Zigler, E. (1969). Developmental versus defect theories of mental retardation and the problem of motivation. *American Journal of Mental Deficiency, 73*, 536–556.

Zigler, E. (1973). The retarded child as a whole person. In D. Routh (Ed.), *The experimental study of mental retardation*. Chicago: Aldine.

Zigler, E. (1998). A place of value for applied and policy studies. *Child Development, 69*, 532–542.

Zigler, E., & Glick, M. (1986). *A developmental approach to adult psychopathology*. New York: John Wiley & Sons.

Zingraff, M. T., Leiter, J., Myers, K. A., & Johnsen, M. C. (1993). Child maltreatment and youthful problem behavior. *Criminology, 31*, 173–202.

Zucker, R. (2006). Alcohol use and the alcohol use disorders: A developmental-biopsychosocial systems formulation covering the life course. In D. Cicchetti & D. Cohen (Eds.), *Developmental psychopathology: Vol. 3. Risk, disorder, and adaptation* (2nd ed., pp. 620–656). Hoboken, NJ: John Wiley & Sons.

Zucker, R. A., Fitzgerald, H. E., & Moses, H. D. (1995). Emergence of alcohol problems and the several alcoholisms: A developmental perspective on etiologic theory and life course trajectory. In D. Cicchetti & D. Cohen (Eds.), *Developmental psychopathology: Vol. 2. Risk, disorder, and adaptation* (pp. 677–711). New York: John Wiley & Sons.

Zuravin, S. J. (1991). Research definitions of child abuse and neglect: Current problems. In R. Starr & D. Wolfe (Eds.), *The effects of child abuse and neglect: Issues and research* (pp. 100–128). New York: Guilford Press.

CHAPTER 15

Developing Civic Engagement within a Civic Context

JONATHAN F. ZAFF, DANIEL HART, CONSTANCE A. FLANAGAN, JAMES YOUNISS, and PETER LEVINE

Engaging in civic activities benefits both the individual and the individual's family, community, and country. That is, civic engagement is associated with other positive outcomes of individual development, such as educational achievement and social competencies, and with societal benefit, such as having an active citizenry that participates in democracy and contributes in other ways to the greater good, such as through volunteering in the community or protesting against unfair labor practices (Calabrese & Schumer, 1986; Lerner, 2004; Levine & Youniss, 2006; Moore & Allen, 1996; Morgan & Streb, 2000; Youniss, McLellan, Su, & Yates, 1999; Zaff & Michelsen, 2002). This bidirectional relationship of the community and the individual is consistent with developmental systems theories (Lerner, 2002, 2006). Scholars in all advanced Western nations are concerned about engaging their citizenry in civic activities due to low levels of involvement, the need to revitalize democracy as older generations are replaced, the perceived neglect of civic engagement in schools throughout the world, and the erosion of a civic infrastructure in communities.

In this chapter, we define civic engagement, examine trends over the past 30 years, consider the developmental process within a developmental systems framework (what we call a *civic context*), and provide an illustration of this developmental process for non–college-attending youth, a group at high risk for not engaging in civic activities. We conclude with implications for the practice community as well as next steps for research. Although we take a life-span perspective in this chapter, we are mostly resigned to focus on development from childhood through the transition to adulthood. The empirical literature on the continued development of civic engagement among older adults is unfortunately thin and life-span data ranging from childhood into older adulthood is even thinner.

Civic engagement encapsulates civic behaviors, civic skills, civic connections, and civic commitment. Thus, civic engagement is best understood in terms of these distinctions as enduring and necessarily dependent on the individual's view of self. The following are essential to civic engagement: (1) knowledge and exercise of rights and responsibilities, (2) some sense of concern for the state and shared fate with one's fellow citizens, and (3) a subjective identification with other citizens. Citizens must accept these roles and responsibilities and maintain identification with fellow citizens over time if a society is to endure.

Civic engagement goes beyond participation in a civic act. Being substantively engaged includes the integration of behavioral, emotional, and cognitive components (Zaff, Boyed, Li, Lerner, & Lerner, 2010), such that civic behaviors, civic skills, civic connections, and civic commitment are all considered part of the civic engagement construct. That is, civic engagement is more than civic behaviors, although civic behaviors are essential components of civic engagement. This multidimensional idea of civic engagement construct is rooted in Erikson's ego identity theory (involving a search for a sense of self that reflects a role meeting both individual and societal needs) (Erikson, 1963; Marcia, 1980) and in German "action" theories (Baltes, 1987; Baltes, Lindenberger, & Staudinger, 2006; Freund & Baltes, 2002); these latter conceptions note that adaptive development involves mutually beneficial relations between the actions of the individual on the context (e.g., engagement with or contributions to the institutions of civil society) and the actions of the context (e.g., involving constraining or promoting individual behavior) on the individual (Brandtstädter, 1998, 2006).

Erikson and German action theorists posit that cognitive processes and overt (and implicit) behaviors are inherently interconnected. For instance, in action theory, behaviors are intertwined with motivations and goal orientations toward specific tasks. This theory is not necessarily presenting a cause (motivation)/effect (task) dynamic. Instead, the cognitive, emotional, and behavioral are part of the intraindividual developmental system, pieces that are inseparable in the developmental process. Action theorists might hypothesize that civic engagement is expressed as a connection to one's community, a commitment to improving that community, and the act of helping one's community. Actions that enhance the community in this way will likely feed back to the individual, providing a context with the resources to support his/her positive development (Lerner, 2004; Lerner, Alberts, & Bobek, 2007). Consistent with these theories, Youniss (2006) has argued for a developmental theory of political-civic engagement that integrates cognitive processes with actions that take place within a collectively shared structure.

Civic participation has many facets. In the United States, as noted earlier, *voting* is often considered to be the most important of civic duties, and voting, as well as other roles in the electoral process, are frequently viewed as core components of political participation (e.g., Conway, 2000). Political scientists and sociologists have also emphasized the importance of community service as essential for the well-being of civic life in the United States (e.g., Putnam, 2000). In addition, and unlike voting and much of community service, political and civil activism, such as protesting, boycotting, or buycotting is typically conducted apart from government agencies and in defiance of the government. With the myriad ways that an individual can engage with her or his community, we might suggest that free citizens define their roles as citizens in various ways from activism to voting, from the violent revolution of George Washington to the nonviolent resistance of Martin Luther King, Jr.

In this chapter, we do not discuss broader forms of contribution, such as to the family. Although these behaviors, attitudes, and skills are important for the health and well-being of the recipients of the contributions, and are related to positive developmental outcomes of the individual (Lerner, 2004), our focus is on civic contributions; that is, actions that benefit the broader and more distal community and/or the polity.

TRENDS IN CIVIC ENGAGEMENT

With the preceding definition for civic engagement we examine the trends in civic engagement over the past three decades, which is when data on various aspects of civic involvement were initially collected.

Voting

Voting is the best documented form of civic engagement, and the trend in young Americans voting turnout tells a meaningful story that we can also observe in some other variables. There was a smooth downward trend from the first year when late adolescents were eligible to vote, 1972, until 2000, broken only by a spike in 1992. During this period, there was no decline in turnout among Americans

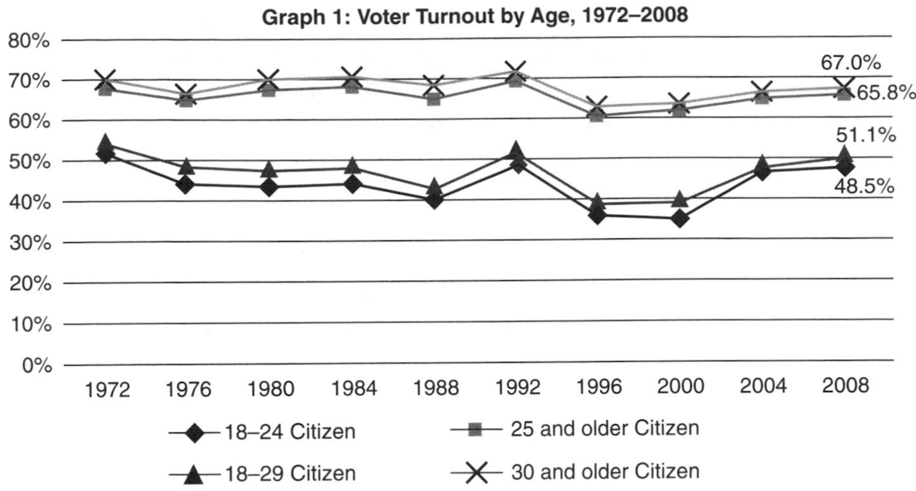

Figure 15.1 Voter turnout by age, 1972–2008.

over the age of 25 (see Figure 15.1). The decline in overall voter participation appeared to be strictly a youth phenomenon, with the trend for older Americans staying relatively stable (Levine & Lopez, 2002). However, there have been significant increases in youth voting in two consecutive presidential elections. Given that the declining rates of civic participation among youth are developmentally more interesting than the stable rates of older Americans, we focus more so on youth in this section.

Trends in the average levels of participation for all youth over time put an emphasis on generational differences, but people who are born at the same time may have very different experiences, contributing to very different levels of engagement. In particular, social class is a well-documented correlate of civic engagement (Verba, Schlozman, & Brady, 2000). If we operationalize social class for young adults in a simple way, as attending or not attending college for any amount of time, we divide the population into roughly equal groups. Each group has witnessed declines in many forms of civic engagement since the 1970s, and large gaps between these groups remain (see Figures 15.2 and 15.3) (Flanagan, Levine, & Settersten, 2008). The only exception is volunteering for those young adults who have attended at least 1 year of college.

When we do observe declines in the rate of civic engagement for young people (or for young people of a particular demographic category), at least two interpretations can be offered. One is that the desirable behavior is declining by generation, with lasting detrimental effects for democracy. The other is that people are delaying their entry into civic engagement, much as they are delaying child-bearing and lengthening their years of education. The decline in voting

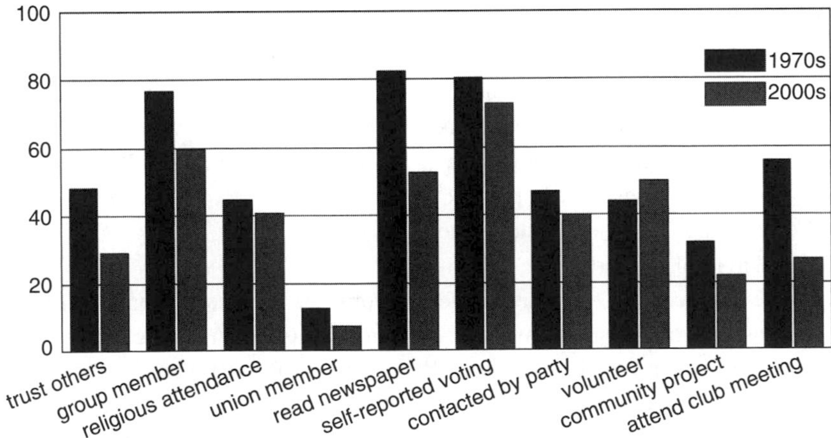

Figure 15.2 Civic engagement among 20- to 29-year-olds with at least one year of college experience, 1970s and 2000s.

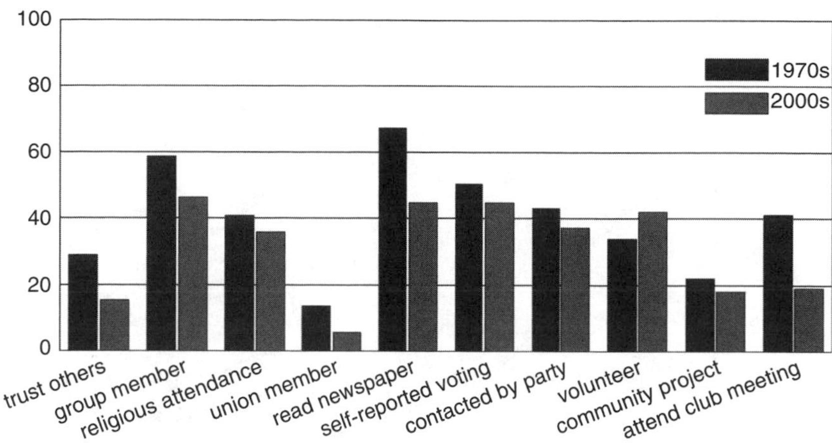

Figure 15.3 Civic engagement among 20- to 29-year-olds with no college experience, 1970s and 2000s.

from 1972 to 2000 may be more a matter of delay. Each cohort began with a lower turnout rate than its predecessors but narrowed the gap as it moved toward age 30.

Volunteering

On the other hand, volunteering has been rising in recent years. Among American 12th graders in the Monitoring the Future survey, there has been a steady increase in the rate of those who had volunteered at least once in the past 12 months, rising from 65.3% in 1976 to 75.9% in 2005 (Lopez & Marcelo, Lopez, & Kirby, 2007a). Data have not been collected as long for 10th graders, but a similar trend exists, rising from 67.9% in 1990 to 70.6% in 2005. For eighth graders, there had been an initial increase, but then a decrease in 2005 to the 1990 benchmark of approximately 65%. The 10th- and 12th-grade trends are similar to those from the Higher Education Research Institute's (HERI) freshman survey, showing an increase in the percentage of freshman reporting having volunteered at least once in high school, from 66% in 1989 to 83% in 2005. However, when looking at regular volunteering (i.e., at least once per month), the trends are much lower and flatter: for 12th graders, ranging from 7.8% in 1976 to 13.2% in 2005; for 10th graders, flat at approximately 10%; and for 8th graders, a slight decline from 10% to 9%. According to the Current Population Survey, administered by the U.S. Census, there has been a large increase in volunteering among the population aged 16 years and older,[1] rising more than 30% between 1989 and 2008, from approximately 20 to 27%. This increase has been most apparent for 16- to 19-year-olds (26% in 2008), 45 to 64-year-olds (29.4%), and those 65 years old and older (23.5%).

Civic Activism

Contemporary American youth are, in general, less likely to be engaged in traditional forms of political activism—demonstrations, rallies, protests, and so on—than were youth of the 1960s (Galston, 2001). Evidence for this claim is based upon the Roper Survey of Political and Social Attitudes data set, which contains survey responses from representative samples of Americans questioned each year between 1974 and 1994. Each year, the Roper organization asked Americans whether in the past year they had participated in any of twelve political activities such as "attended a political rally or speech," "served on a committee for some local organization," "attended a public meeting on town or school affairs," "been a member of some group like the League of Women Voters, or some other group interested in better government," "worked for a political party," and so on. For each of the activities, the trend is clear for 18- to 24-year-olds between 1974 and 1994: Participation declines with historical time. Youth near the close of the century were much less likely to report political participation—50% less likely in some instances—than were youth just 20 years earlier. While data are not available for the 15 years since, there is little reason to imagine that youth political activism as measured in the Roper Survey has increased (see Figure 15.4).

[1] Data accessed on August 1, 2009, available at: http://www.volunteeringinamerica.gov/national.

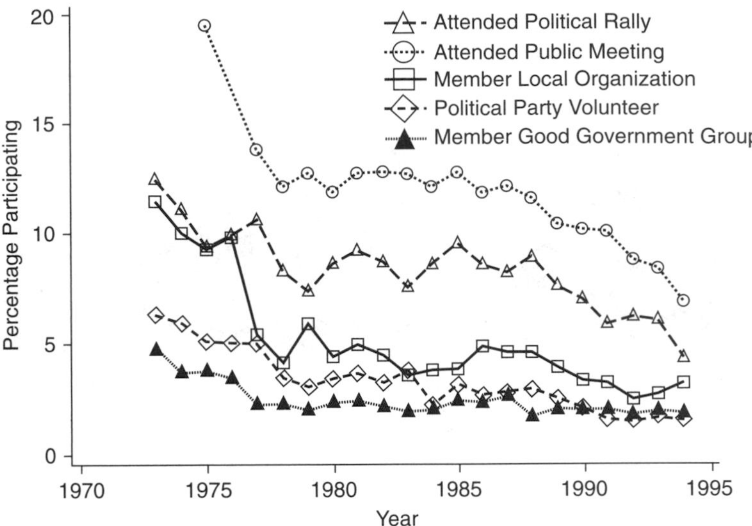

Figure 15.4 MSCivic participation among 18- to 24-year-olds, 1974–1994.

In addition, using the Roper data set, Hart and colleagues (2007) found that political activism in 1974 was more tightly connected to educational attainment and family social class than it was in 1994. For example, family income was positively correlated with political activity for youth in 1974 (i.e., as family income increases, so does the number of political activities), but there was virtually no association between family income and political activity in 1994. Similarly, the association of educational attainment with political activism was stronger in 1974 than in 1994.

Between the 1960s and the 1990s, there was a striking decline in the frequency of protests, especially involving young people. According to data collected by Soule and Earl (2005) from newspaper archives, the United States saw more than twice as many protest events per year between 1964 and 1974 than during the 1980s. In 1970, more than half of all protests were initiated by youth, whereas only 10 to 20% had youth leaders in the eighties. In other words, youth protests were an important part of the national political scene in 1970 but either rare or unnoticed 15 years later.

On college campuses, the rate of demonstrations fell by two-thirds between 1967 and 1978, but it almost fully recovered by 1997 (Levine & Cureton, 1998). Some of the means of political expression that have become increasingly common among college students (such as email petitions, lawsuits, and media campaigns) could be considered difficult for non-college youth to manage, since they do not have the institutional infrastructure from which to become active nor the close-knit communities of civically motivated peers. Meanwhile, strikes have become much less frequent, both on campus and in the workforce. The general trend is away from protests, pickets, strikes, and disruptions and toward sophisticated "white-collar" forms of politics. This raises the question, as posed by some, such as Skocpol (2000) about the practical relevance of certain types of activities (e.g., email petitions) and whether these activities should be considered civic.

Aside from the Roper survey, protesting and other forms of civic activism have not been systematically tracked overtime. In addition, even in the Roper survey, the way that the questions are asked do not necessarily resonate with the respondents. For instance, young African-American males in low-income urban centers might be more likely than high-income youth attending preparatory schools to participate in civic actions against government entities, such as the police and the schools that they perceive to be underserving or mistreating them. Thus, these hypothetical acts might be considered to be civic and appropriate for their context, but would not necessarily be assessed through typical survey research; especially surveys funded and/or fielded by the federal government, which do not contain such measures. Thus, it is important to consider that the trends presented and the differences seen by race/ethnicity, gender, and generation, do not provide a full picture of the types of civic behaviors in which some groups might be more involved than others.

News Consumption

The long and deep decline in youth voting between 1972 and 2000 was accompanied by a similar decline in news consumption. HERI surveys of incoming college freshmen (Pryor et al., 2006) found that the proportion who considered it "important" or "essential" to "keep up-to-date with political affairs" fell from 60% in 1966 to about 30% in 2000, although it recovered by six points between 2000 and 2005 (while turnout also rose). Likewise, in the National Election Studies, the percentage of Americans between the ages of 18 and 25 who consistently followed the news fell from 24% in 1960 to 5.1% in 2000, but popped up to 9.6% in 2004. Newspaper readership among young people was cut in half between 1975 and 2002, according to the General Social Survey, although again there was some recovery in 2004.

This downward trend is not confined to younger Americans. According to the biennial news consumption survey conducted by the Pew Center for People and the Press (2008), newspaper readership declined from 58% in 1994 to 34% in 2008. Similar decreases are seen in radio news, local TV news, and morning and nighttime network news. There were slight increases in regularly watching cable TV news or online news, from 33% in 2002 to 39% in 2008, and in viewing online news three or more days per week, from 2% in 1995 to 37% in 2008. These upward trends have not been enough to offset the other declines. In addition, there was an increase in the percentage of all Americans, 18 years and older, who reported not viewing any news the previous day.

To make matters worse, it does not seem to be the case that people are delaying their interest in the news until later in their lives, and then catching up with previous generations. On the contrary, several careful studies of the historical data show that each recent generation has entered adulthood with less interest in the news than its predecessors had, and has never closed the gap. For example, those who were young adults in 1982 have remained about 20 percentage points behind the children of the 1960s in news consumption as the two cohorts have moved through their lives (see Figures 15.5 and 15.6).

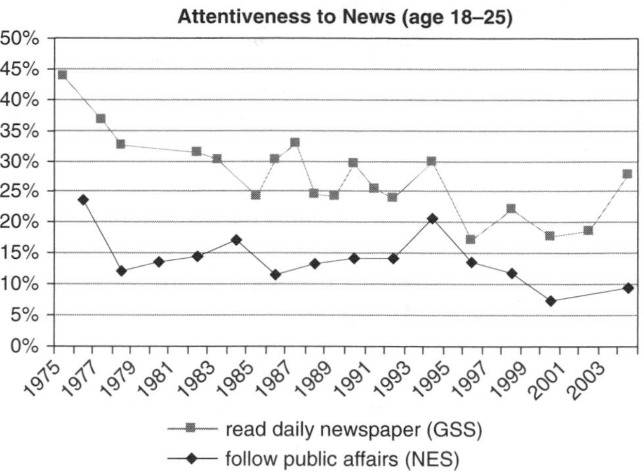

Figure 15.5 MSAttentiveness to news among 18- to 25-year-olds.

Social Connections

Social connections, whether through clubs, civic associations, or formal or informal community dialogues, create social capital and support and promote civic activity participation among members (e.g., see Putnam, 2000, for a discussion of social capital and civic organizations). In 1975, according to the General Social Survey, two-thirds of young people (aged 18 to 25) belonged to at least one group. (Respondents were prompted to think of several kinds of associations, including church groups, unions, and sports clubs, and were also given the opportunity to say that they belonged to a kind that had not been listed.) In 1994 and 2004, only half said that they belonged to any group at all. In DDB Lifestyle surveys conducted during the 1970s, 40 to 50% of young people said that they had attended a club meeting at least once within the previous year (see Figure 15.7). In the same survey conducted between 2000 and 2006, only 15 to 22% of young people recalled attending a club meeting.[2]

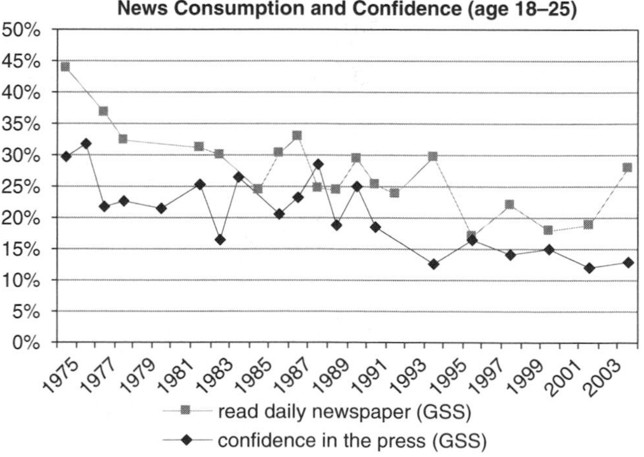

Figure 15.6 MSNews consumption and confidence among 18- to 25-year-olds.

[2] Authors' tabulations.

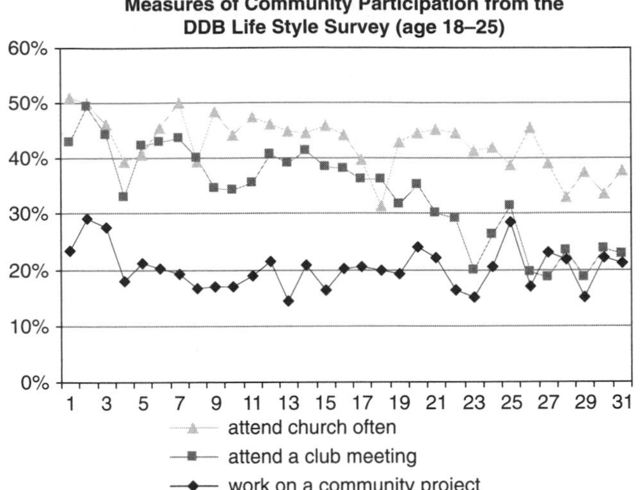

Figure 15.7 Measures of community participation for 18- to 25-year-olds.

Attitudes and Values

Attitudes toward others and values about social and economic issues can facilitate both a civil discourse to move forward on social and economic problems in a country or a community, or a derisive discourse between parties with competing views. In addition, such attitudes and values can help to define the civic quality of a given generation.

Only 4% of young Americans (age 18 to 25) say that they favor segregated neighborhoods. That is down from about 25% in the 1970s, and is lower than the rate among people over age 25. This change is almost entirely attributable to the arrival of new generations: again, individuals do not seem to change much over their lifetimes.[3] However, this change in values has not accompanied a big change in behavior. More than half of young churchgoers still say that their congregations have members of only one race/ethnicity—the same rate as among older people, and not much different since 1975. In the Social Capital Benchmark Survey (Saguaro Seminar, 2001), 66% of young white people who belonged to participatory groups said that all the other members were also white. This rate was not much different for older whites. In the same survey, just 20% of young people claimed that they had invited a friend of another race/ethnicity to their house—better than the 6% rate among adults over age 56, but still not so common. We do not know whether tolerant answers to survey questions will translate into real social change if people remain quite segregated in their daily lives.

A similar pattern is evident in attitudes toward allowing an "admitted homosexual teacher" to speak (see Figure 15.8). People born before 1906 were extremely unfavorable when

[3] General Social Survey, authors' tabulations.

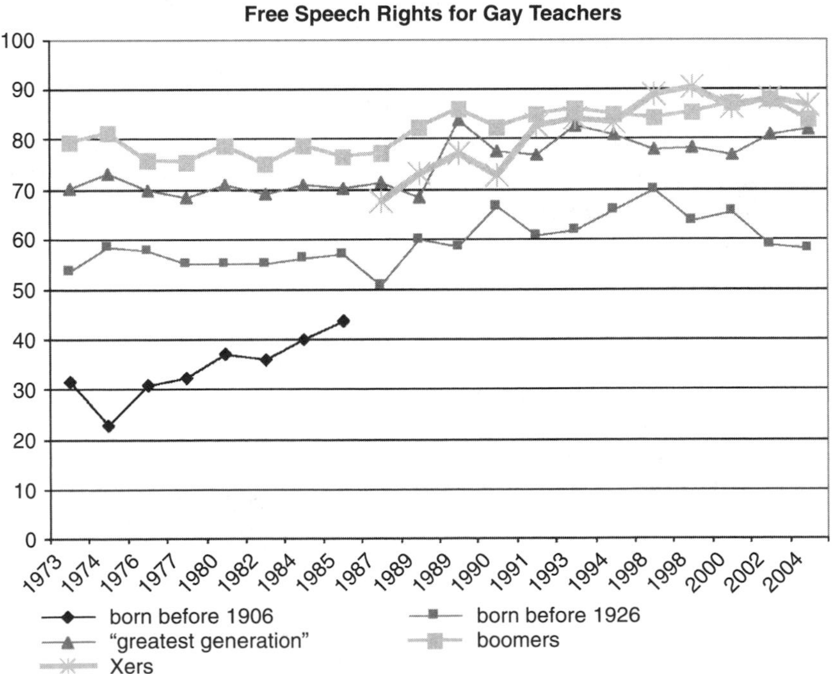

Figure 15.8 MSAttitudes toward free-speech rights for gay teachers, 1970–2004.
Source: General Social Survey.

they were first asked the question in 1973, but some became more tolerant as they aged. The subsequent generations have changed less, but in the same direction. Each generation is more favorable than the older ones.

Young Americans are also highly patriotic and idealistic (Rahn & Transue, 1998). Many believe that they can and should make the world better, especially by directly serving their fellow human beings. However, there have been some disturbing trends in values over the past 20 years. For example, there has been a 50% decline in the proportion of young people who trust others. Rahn and Transue (1998) explain the erosion of young people's social trust as a result of "rapid rise of materialistic value orientations that occurred among American youth in the 1970s and 1980s" (p. 548). Uslaner and Brown (2005) explain trust as a function of optimism. People who believe that the world will get better (that there will be more public goods for all) are willing to trust others and cooperate. People who believe that the pie is shrinking adopt a zero-sum, "me-first" approach (Ostrom, 1999). Whatever the cause, a decline in trust is a caution for civil society, since trust correlates with participation in voluntary associations.

Overall, Americans want to make the world a better place, with a focus on community service. These attitudes can be seen in the higher rates of volunteering, but decreasing rates of political engagement. In addition, although the populace is more tolerant of their fellow citizens, these attitudes are accompanied by a decreasing level of trust.

CIVIC ENGAGEMENT IN AN ECOLOGICAL MODEL OF DEVELOPMENT

Several theoretical frameworks have been used to examine the development of civic engagement. In this section, we discuss the prevailing theories and present a theoretical framework that captures the multidimensionality of the development of civic engagement and how a civic context promotes civic engagement. In recent years, the most prevalent framework has been the political socialization model. This model stresses the importance of familial and school-based influences on future engagement, especially political participation, which is often measured in terms of voting rates, and refer to those practices whereby citizens are incorporated as full members of the polity or public sphere of society (Flanagan & Gallay, 1995). Although individuals are guaranteed rights by virtue of their status as citizens, it is through the exercise of those rights that they assume membership and have a voice in defining the polity and through their civic engagement sustain their rights (Walzer, 1989).

Interest in the psychological mechanisms underlying political stability motivated early political socialization studies in the aftermath of World War II. Political scientists and developmental psychologists in this tradition focused on the early years as formative of political loyalties and held that maturation in later adolescence "crystallizes and internalizes patterns established during the preadolescent period" (Dawson & Prewitt, 1969, p. 51). According to this theory, loyalty to civic leaders and the polity they represented flowed from the young child's sense of basic trust in the benevolence of those leaders—that is, his or her belief that they ruled with the child's best interests in mind (Easton & Dennis, 1969). Knowledge about the specifics would come later but was based on this affective foundation.

A critique of political socialization theory concerns its emphasis on the social integration of younger generations into an extant political system and their assimilation of system norms (Hyman, 1959). In this vertical model it was assumed that adult agents passed on to the younger generation a set of principles that sustained the system. Relatively little attention was paid to the interaction between the socialization process and context within which the process takes place, in the inherent strength of youth and adults, or in the life-span development of the individual: for example, politics as a contestation of views, the reasons why marginalized groups would buy into a system in which they might feel excluded, or the role of peers in political development. In fact, change—whether in individuals or in society—was given short shrift. The focus on childhood eclipsed attention to the adolescent and adult years and the ways in which growth in understanding the political system might also be related to an increase in political cynicism. The active role of younger generations in interpreting the principles of their social order—of stabilizing the system by making those principles their own—was not part of the models of human development in that period. Instead, political socialization drew from a replication model in which older generations passed an intact system on to younger generations. As generational replacement theorists have subsequently shown, engagement of younger generations and replacement of their elders in the political process is a source of political change (Delli Carpini, 1989).

This theory also did not account for how the cognitive processes of civic engagement are plastic and influenced by the culture of the individual's political ethos. Despite an increase in hypothetical reasoning, pessimism about the possibilities of eliminating social problems such as poverty or crime increased with age (Leahy, 1983). Although late adolescents were aware that social systems could be changed, they were not very adept at imagining alternatives to the status quo. However, this may reflect more about the average adolescent's exposure to alternative political systems than about their capacities. One recent study comparing the political views of adolescents in four security-based societies in which the state plays a major social welfare role, with their peers in two opportunity-based societies in which individuals shoulder more responsibility for their basic needs concluded that normative beliefs about the proper relationship between states and citizens reflect the social contracts to which the youth are accustomed (Flanagan & Campbell, in press). Other work suggests that exposure to alternative systems can broaden adolescents' political perspectives. Using a simulation exercise, Torney-Purta (1992) has demonstrated that adolescents' schemas about international politics accommodate when they assume the roles of different nations and share perspectives on political issues as seen from different nations' points of view.

To account for these influences, the generational perspective of civic engagement concentrated on the role of historical events in distinguishing generations and on young people as actors engaged in rather than merely reacting to social change. Theorists in this tradition contended that the late adolescent and early adult period was a watershed in the development of a political ideology. Drawing from Mannheim (1952), they held that this was a stage when an individual was not yet saddled with social roles and could view society from a fresh perspective. At this stage of transition to adulthood, many young people are in settings away from their families where they are exposed to different lifestyles, norms, and perspectives on social issues and would potentially form new reference groups (Alwin, Cohen, & Newcomb, 1991). For example, longitudinal comparisons of high school seniors who attended college in the late 1960s with their peers who did not attend college revealed that political attitudes were shaken up by the college experience, but that once crystallized, the attitudes of those who went to college were more stable thereafter (Jennings, 1993).

Consolidating political views is part of the process of consolidating identity. Thus, the way an individual grapples with and resolves the salient social issues of the period when he or she comes of age becomes an integral part of personality thereafter (Stewart & Healy, 1989). In fact, longitudinal work shows that it is not the historical events per se but the way that different generational units deal with those events that predicts their subsequent political positions (Jennings, 2002). Notably, it is not simple exposure or even interest in the salient political issues during one's coming of age but rather how actively one grapples with and is affected by those issues that are formative of identity thereafter.

By focusing on the transition to adulthood as a politically defining period, less attention was paid in generational theory to the formative role of family values in the development of political views. Longitudinal studies that followed students of the 1960s and their parents showed that the political positions of activists and their parents were more liberal than were those of their age-mates during the height of student activism as well as 15 years later (Dunham & Bengston, 1992). Likewise, a study conducted in the 1990s found that college students' attitudes toward the Persian Gulf War were similar to the attitudes that the students' parents had held toward the Vietnam War in their college years (Duncan & Stewart, 1995). Not surprisingly, concordance of political attitudes is higher in those families in which political issues are salient topics of discussion and action (Jennings, 2002).

Neither the political socialization nor the generational theories that attended to the developmental antecedents of politics in adulthood were grounded in the everyday lives of adolescents. However, many of the skills and motivations associated with adult political engagement are learned in the formative years. Moreover, political views, like other aspects of social cognition, are rooted in social relations. Among other things, they concern the way we think about our membership in society, our rights, responsibilities, and relationships with others in society. Such views are formulated as adolescents theorize about society and their role in it and as significant adults in their lives share their views of the world and the values that matter to them. For example, in a study of 434 11- to 18-year-olds, Flanagan & Tucker (1999) found significant associations between adolescents' personal and family values and beliefs and their theories about inequality: Those who held individuals accountable for being poor, unemployed, or homeless were more likely to believe that America was a fair society where opportunities were equally distributed, and were more likely to endorse materialist values and believe ardently in self-reliance. In contrast, youth who attributed these problems to systemic or structural causes were more likely to endorse compassion and altruist values. In another study, adolescents' descriptions of the personal meaning that democracy holds for them showed consistent relationships with their personal and family values: Youth for whom civic equality was the most meaningful aspect of democracy were more likely than their peers for whom individual rights were the most meaningful to espouse environmental values and less likely to espouse materialist values or social mistrust toward other people. The youth who espoused equality also were more likely than their peers for whom representative rule defined democracy to endorse values of social responsibility (Flanagan et al., 2005).

To resolve the dichotomy between individual attributes and external influences, a growing number of civic engagement scholars and practitioners have moved toward embracing a developmental model—one they believe to be more holistic and explanatory of civic participation across the life span. Based on the dialectical relationship between individual and contextual factors that is described by developmental systems theories (Bronfenbrenner & Ceci, 1993; Lerner, 1991), an emerging theory of civic development recognizes that factors which exist both in the youth, such as values, and external to the youth, such as socializing agents, work in concert to encourage or deter civic engagement. This composite of individual and social contextual variables can be considered to comprise a civic context. Further, consistent with Erikson (1966) and developmental systems theorists (e.g., Bronfenbrenner & Ceci, 1993; Eccles et al., 1993; Vygotsky, 1978), an age-appropriate civic context should be in place throughout childhood in order to encourage the summative development of civic knowledge, skills, engagement, and eventual identity. The following are tenets of the developmental model that we use to frame the intraindividual and contextual factors that encourage civic engagement. In other words, developmental systems theories provide a useful and appropriate framework for understanding the interconnecting factors within and external to the individual that promote civic engagement (Zaff, Youniss, & Gibson, 2009).

- *Assumes that civic skills and behaviors are acquired over time*. Developmental theorists believe that sustained civic participation—or civic identity—is a process that evolves throughout childhood and into adulthood. Civic identity does not suddenly emerge at age 18 with voting eligibility or with an AmeriCorps experience after college. Rather, civic identity is developed through multiple experiences during childhood and adolescence that predispose young people to take advantage of opportunities as they emerge throughout the life span.
- *Addresses a wide and diverse array of proximal factors that influence young people's civic development* such as families, communities, faith traditions, peer groups, the media, schools, out-of-school activities, public events, and others—rather than from one school, course, or family.
- *Views all young people as capable of becoming civically engaged* but understands that this potential must be sparked by adequate resources and opportunities. In short, when the proper conditions are in place, the developmental processes will kick in.
- *Recognizes the importance of societal and community-level factors in influencing civic development.* Poverty, social disorganization, isolation, and lack of access to political systems can be as influential in influencing civic engagement as familial or school-related factors. Communities with a civic infrastructure that includes nonprofits, faith-based institutions, and voluntary groups are more likely to promote sustained and active participation, while communities without these elements may hinder it.
- *Believes that interventions, programs, and/or events intended to increase youth civic engagement should be implemented long before young people reach college* and even prior to high school—a conclusion that education reformers also have reached.[4] While civic development can and does occur during adulthood to remediate civic deficits in childhood and adolescence, starting earlier leads to longer-term and more substantial results later.

Thus, civic engagement is deeply embedded in psychological, social, and political contexts. The consequence is that adolescent activism is relatively common in some historical periods, in some strata of youth, and in some with particular attributes, but rare in other periods, other cohorts, and in some types of adolescents. Without considering these variables together, an incomplete picture of the development of civic engagement will emerge.

INTRAINDIVIDUAL FACTORS RELATED TO CIVIC INVOLVEMENT

Stability/Trajectories of Civic Behaviors

Civic attitudes remain relatively stable across the life course. In fact, across more than 30 years, Jennings and Stoker (2002, 2004) found that stability is more a norm

[4] This is based on the exponential increase in funding for early childhood education and pre-K initiatives over the past decade, as well as the strong focus of No Child Left Behind on elementary schools.

than change with regard to political attitudes. Although the content of the issues might differ by generation (e.g., gay rights for more recent generations compared to the Vietnam War for older generations), the stability in attitudes about the content tends to remain the same. This stability has been found to be more pronounced among those who were more active earlier in life than those who were less active. Importantly, and consistent with the notion that the emerging adult years are a particularly pertinent time in civic engagement development, stability in political attitudes is lower during young adulthood and increases during subsequent developmental periods (Alwin & Krosnick, 1991).

The stability of political involvement is suggested by the political behaviors of former student activists (Fendrich & Lovoy, 1988). Data were collected in 1986 from 85 adults who had been assessed 25 years earlier concerning their political activism. The researchers found that the ex-student radical activists and institutional activists participated in a wide range of local political activities (e.g., community activism, party and campaign work, political communication) 25 years later.

The developmental trajectories of the sense of membership and of rights are quite surprising in that both seem to emerge at very young ages. For example, Barrett, Wilson, and Lyons (2003) demonstrated that English school children distinguished between British citizens and those of America and Germany as young as 5 years of age. Moreover, even young children preferred citizens of their own nations to those of others (for further evidence of in-group preference see Abrams, Rutland, & Cameron, 2003). Barrett and colleagues (2003) found that the importance of their national identities increased over the course of childhood, with older children judging nationality to be more important to them than gender and age identities. In comparing their results to those of other researchers, Barrett et al. concluded that there is considerable variation in findings across countries and that developmental trajectories are yet to be fully identified.

With respect to cognitive capacities, optimal levels of abstract reasoning and reflective thinking are attained in the early adult years. Typically, it is not until late in the second or early in the third decade of life that people genuinely integrate different points of view as they form opinions. Although adolescents can deal with abstract concepts and viewpoints, it is usually in the early adult years that they can coordinate several abstract systems together and appreciate the subtleties in abstract relations, including understanding themselves and others. Young adults are more capable than adolescents of understanding the implications of their own (as well as states' or corporations') actions on abstract "others." They also understand the consequences of their own and others' actions over time. Thus twenty-somethings are better than teens at understanding the lifetime impact of passive smoking on a nonsmoking spouse or of hydrocarbons on the ozone layer. Young adults appreciate principled reasoning and can separate another person's political views from their friendship with that individual. They should, therefore, be able to passionately debate political issues without personalizing the differences. Compared to adolescents and to their own parents, young adults are more committed to civil liberties and are more tolerant of points of view that differ from their own. Young adulthood is an optimal time for reflective thinking, for examining the bases of ideas and opinions. However, that capacity is more likely to develop when ideas are challenged by opposing information or points of view (Fisher, Yan, & Stewart, 2003). In other words, any undergraduate student should have the innate capacity for reflective judgment. However, it is in the context of Socratic dialogue, where ideas that are taken for granted are examined, or in encounters with heterogeneous groups, where different views are aired, that reflective judgment is likely to reach an optimal level.

Demographic Differences

Multiple studies have found that females are more likely to participate in civic activities than males, although this difference varies by country. For instance, among high school seniors in the United States (Johnston, Bachman, & O'Malley, 1999), females (33.6%) were found to participate in community affairs or volunteer activities more than males (28.3%). Using cross-sectional data, Flanagan and colleagues (1998) found that, in five countries (United States, Australia, Hungary, Bulgaria, and Russia) females were more likely than males to report having engaged in community service. In the Czech Republic and Sweden, there were no gender differences. European-American youth are more likely to vote and to volunteer in community service than African-American and Hispanic-American youth (Johnston, Bachman, & O'Malley, 1999). African-American youth are well ahead of whites on several measures of civic engagement: regular volunteering, raising money for charity, persuading other people about elections, displaying signs and buttons, donating money to parties and candidates, belonging to political groups, contacting the print and broadcast media, and canvassing (Marcelo, Lopez, & Kirby, 2007b). The electoral turnout of African-American youth has been very close to that of whites in most recent federal elections, even though black youth have less education on average, and even though an estimated 1.4 million African-American men (of all ages) are blocked from voting because of felony convictions (The Sentencing Project, 2008). As seen in the trends presented earlier in this chapter, there are disparities in various aspects of civic engagement by socioeconomic status, whether measured by income or educational level. We describe the contextual factors that explain these differences later in this chapter, but we note that the disparities are apparent across the life course (Tang, 2008).

Age can have important implications for understanding civic engagement. For instance, older adults (aged 60 years and older) have a greater sense of civic duty than younger generations. However, these older groups are not necessarily more likely to be engaged in civic activities (Dalton, 2006). In addition, older adults have stronger political party identification than younger cohorts (Alwin & Krosnick, 1991) and they have a stronger reliance on voluntary organizations to take part in volunteer activities (Tang, 2008). Thus, levels of aspects of civic engagement (e.g., duty) might vary by the age of individuals and engagement might be promoted in different ways (e.g., through voluntary organizations). However, as described previously, other components of civic engagement, such as attitudes toward one's community and the greater polity remain relatively stable over time. Internal assets, such as functional ability, relates to service dependent on age, such that older adults are more likely to volunteer for organizations if they have higher levels of functional ability, whereas the effect is not necessarily apparent in younger cohorts (Tang, 2006).

Sociopsychological Factors

A collection of sociopsychological factors increase the likelihood that youth and adults will participate in civic actions, including values and motivations, civic knowledge, trust, a sense of belonging, and an assortment of personality characteristics.

Values and Motivations

From a psychological perspective, it is important to think about the extent to which a nation's values are subsumed in the citizenry, as well as the nature of the values that are subsumed. A nation's valuing of free market forces over regulation does not, for example, mean that the citizenry adopts the same values. Groups within a society attempt to drive national values, while national values attempt to drive citizens. It is of interest here to note that certain human values such as the right to life, liberty, and the pursuit of happiness are seen universally to manifest either in formal documents or in attempts to resist oppression of those most basic values (see, e.g., Turiel, 2003). Developing an ideology comprised of values and motivations enables youth to organize and manage the vast array of choices the world presents. Political ideologies are forming in adolescence when personal values, worldviews, and political attributions appear to be highly concordant (Flanagan & Tucker, 1999).

Collectivist and altruistic ideologies, that is, a motivation to act for the greater good, in early adolescence predict civic engagement among older adolescents and adults (Avrahami & Dar, 1993; Batson & Shaw, 1991; Colby & Damon, 1995; Omoto & Snyder, 1995; Perkins, Brown, & Taylor, 1996). There has been little research on individual values as a contributing factor to civic engagement, although having a moral commitment to community service has been linked to participating in civic activities (Colby & Damon, 1995; Flanagan & Faison, 2001; Hart, Yates, Fegley, & Wilson, 1995; Serow & Dreyden, 1990). Research also suggests that social contextual variables promote the acquisition of the types of values that predict civic engagement, such as parents, peers, and siblings (e.g., Eisenberg, 2003; Hoffman, 1975; Pratt, Arnold, Pratt, & Diessner, 1999; Volling, 2003).

Two main types of motivation for community service participation that have been found for adults are collectivistic motivations and individualistic motivations (Omoto & Snyder, 1995; Perkins, Brown, & Taylor, 1996; Perkins et al., 1990). Data from one study of Israeli adolescents support this finding. Avrahami and Dar (1993) examined the collectivistic and individualistic motivations of community service volunteers among 415 kibbutz youth in Israel (192 boys and 223 girls). A total of 465 youth, matched to the age of the other cohort who chose to go directly to the army, were also assessed. The results revealed a range of motivations for volunteering, going from more individualistic motives to collectivistic motives.

Other types of motivation may exist for adolescents, as well. In one study, Johnson, Beebe, Mortimer, and Snyder (1998) examined a longitudinal panel sample of adolescents in St. Paul, Minnesota. One thousand ninth graders were selected for inclusion in the study and subsequently followed over a 4-year period; 933 participants remained in the fourth year of the study. Analyses indicated that 13 to 19% of the students volunteered during each year of the data collection, with over 40% of the participants volunteering at least once over the 4 years of the study.

On average, the students participated in these activities for approximately 4 to 5 hours per week. Regarding predictors of volunteering, ninth graders with higher educational plans, aspirations, and grade point averages, and an intrinsic motivation toward school had a greater likelihood of volunteering in grades 10 through 12. Thus, intrinsic motivation works in conjunction with other factors that define healthy developmental trajectories to promote civic engagement. More specifically for girls, having higher academic achievement and positive self-esteem and overall well-being, and lower self-derogation were related to a greater likelihood of volunteering.

Importantly, research suggests that motivations and attitudes directed toward engagement are derived from involvement in activities (Penner, 2002; Reinders & Youniss, 2006). We discuss the effect of program participation later in this chapter. What is not necessarily known is whether there is an interaction between motivations and attitudes before a civic experience and the civic experience. For example, involvement in a service activity to help the homeless for an individual who already feels empathy for the homeless might have a greater impact on that individual's future attitudes and behaviors than an individual who did not have that empathy when entering the service experience. On the contrary, there might be a more sustained, transformative impact on an individual who did not have such empathy before the experience, but gains a deep appreciation for the homeless while participating in the service activity.

Individuals need to have the opportunity to help, not just the motivation. Research with adults suggests that a desire to participate (i.e., their motivation) combined with their knowledge of and accessibility to volunteer opportunities is associated with participation in youth prevention programs (Kauffman & Poulin, 1994; Poulin & Kauffman, 2006). These results were derived from data collected from 1,019 adults (50.9% male with a slight oversampling of high socioeconomic status [SES]) in one study and 250 participants (51% male and 66.7% European American coming primarily from middle- to lower-SES families) in the second study.

Civic Knowledge

Civic knowledge is important, as well. Civic knowledge is associated with political participation and respect for rights (Galston, 2001). Indeed, the association of civic knowledge with civic engagement is foundational for most civics curricula, based on the assumption that those who know will do, although this assumption is not as well-substantiated as many proponents of civics education imagine (Hart, Donnelly, Youniss, & Atkins, 2007). Civic knowledge includes information on government functioning, current political issues, and community needs. Such information can be obtained through interactions at home and with friends, participation in community service, reading newspapers and magazines, listening to news on the radio or television, and courses taught in school. As Niemi and Junn (1998, p. 1) point out, "political knowledge has frequently been considered one of the most important qualifications for self-governance."

Research consistently demonstrates that civic knowledge is related to civic participation (for a review, see Galston, 2001). For example, using data from the National Election Studies (NES), Delli Carpini and Keeter (1996) found that 90% of citizens in the top decile of political knowledge voted in the 1988 presidential election, while only 20% of the least-knowledgeable individuals (bottom decile) went to the polls. This trend held up even after controlling for demographic factors, efficacy, and political engagement. Other research has found weaker associations between knowledge and action. In an analysis by Hart and colleagues (2007), the association of high school civic knowledge with voting in young adulthood is positive and stable, but the magnitude is very small. In addition, after accounting for demographic factors, community service, and extracurricular participation, young adults who were one standard deviation apart in civic knowledge in high school were almost equally likely to vote. Moreover, the relation of high school coursework in the social sciences to civic knowledge was surprisingly weak.

Thus, a review of the existing literature on civic knowledge indicates that increased civic knowledge does not guarantee youth involvement in political or civic action and that other factors must also be considered when attempting to promote youth social engagement. In particular, *belonging* and *trust* in governmental institutions are crucial in fostering traditional political action. This means, for instance, that youth with a sense of connection to their communities and social institutions and a high level of trust would be more engaged and interested in the political process and less likely to report intent to take part in illegal or risky political activities.

Trust

Social trust—the expectation that others are fair, trustworthy, and helpful rather than out for their own gain—is the cornerstone in the psychological foundation of citizenship (Flanagan, 2003). Adults high in trust participate in civic life to a much greater degree than do those who lack trust (Putnam, 2000). Similarly, adolescents who are high in trust report more conventional civic engagement, and more intended civic engagement in adulthood, than adolescents who lack trust in political institutions (Hart & Gullan, in press). One recent longitudinal study following more than 1,000 early, middle, and late adolescents over 2 years found that social trust is more malleable in early adolescence and tends to crystallize by late adolescence. Further, controlling for levels of social trust at Time 1, the authors found that students' reports of school solidarity and democratic climates for learning at their school boosted levels of social trust at Time 2 over and above those at Time 1 (Flanagan & Stout, in press). This is important because it suggests that young people's faith in humanity can be affected by their experiences. In contrast, most of the research on adults suggests that social trust is rarely affected by adults' involvement in community organizations, with the possible exception of groups that are highly diverse and those that engage in charitable work (Uslaner, 2002).

There is abundant evidence to indicate that generalized trust is associated with interpersonal contexts (Flanagan, 2003) as well as economic indicators such as poverty and income inequality (Kawachi, Kennedy, Lochner, & Prothrow-Stith, 1997). Together these mean that, for instance, harmonious family life complemented by a flourishing national economy would contribute to high levels of trust. In an analysis of IEA Civics Study data, Hart and colleagues (2007) found that political trust is a predictor of political activity. The results of these analyses suggest that political trust is a predictor of both forms of political activity, although in the case of illegal protest, the association was negative, with high levels of political trust predictive of low levels of illegal protest. Second, civic knowledge was also predictive of both forms of political activity. Of particular importance for our purposes in this chapter are the interactions among political trust, civic knowledge, child saturation, and voice and accountability. In particular, adolescents' endorsement of items in the illegal protest scale suggest that this form of political activism reflects the interplay of individual-level characteristics (political trust, civic knowledge) with the political and demographic qualities of the country. In short, endorsement of illegal protest is facilitated by low levels of political trust combined with low levels of civic knowledge, country-level acceptance of political dissent, and high levels of child saturation. Certainly the last two qualities were characteristic of the United States during the 1960s. Furthermore, trust in political institutions is positively associated with the forms of political activism that societies traditionally aim to foster and negatively associated with illegal forms of political protest. Widespread youth support for illegal protest probably requires a confluence of forces that include low trust, high child saturation, and a society accepting of political dissent.

Belonging

From a peer relations perspective, the need to belong seems to be a primary motivator for many people, leading to even greater acceptance of negative behavior when it is a norm in the group in which membership is desired (Duffy & Nesdale, 2009). It is likely that individuals also feel a need to belong to a nation, even in childhood (Bennett, 2004). The extent to which a need to belong to a nation will affect one's civic identity is unclear, although a sense of belonging is certainly related to the formation of a national versus ethnic identity (Berry, Phinney, Sam, & Vedder, 2006).

The need to belong may be a universal human motivation (Baumeister & Leary, 1995), and there is considerable evidence that when adolescents feel like they belong and feel connected to social institutions, not only are they more likely to make healthy decisions and avoid risky ones, they also are more likely in early adulthood to vote (Smith, 1999). Adolescents who feel a sense of belonging or solidarity with their school and the students and teachers therein also are more likely than peers who do not to say that they would intervene to stop a fellow peer from an act that would pose harm to fellow members of the school community (Syvertsen, Flanagan, & Stout, 2009).

Erikson (1968) captured the developmental imperatives that youth face to belong when he described the key psychosocial tasks of these years as exploring and consolidating an identity. This entails seeking purpose, deciding on beliefs and commitments, and linking to others (in organizations, religious traditions, or social causes) who share such commitments.

Personality

Many sociologists posit an indirect association and suggest that personality traits lead to actions that put people in contexts in which they are recruited for volunteering. For example, extraversion may lead to volunteering because extraverted individuals are more likely to join the organizations that provide opportunities for volunteering (Wilson, 2000). However, other researchers claim a direct association of personality to volunteering and assert that prosocial personality traits such as empathy lead some to volunteer in order to help others. In a study of AIDS organization volunteers, Penner and Finkelstein (1998) found that prosocial characteristics such as concern for others in need predicted volunteering. Proponents of this direct association of personality to volunteering have also emphasized that motivations for volunteering may not be strictly prosocial but may also include instrumental factors (Clary, Snyder, & Stukas, 1996). For example, an ambitious high school student, knowing that college admission committees look favorably on community service, may volunteer to tutor children in an after-school program—a decision that would reflect achievement motivation but not necessarily a prosocial personality (Friedland & Morimoto, 2005).

Using inverse factor analysis and cluster analysis to analyze personality data, researchers have found that most individuals can be classified into one of three personality prototypes based on their distinct patterns of scores on the personality instruments. The three most common patterns, or personality types, to emerge have been labeled *resilient, overcontrolled*, and *undercontrolled* (Asendorpf & van Aken, 1999; Caspi & Silva, 1995; Chang Weir & Gjerde, 2002; Hart, Hofmann, Edelstein, & Keller, 1997; Robins et al., 1996). Resilients are high in emotional regulation, are socially skilled, and tend toward positive emotionality. In contrast, the undercontrolled and overcontrolled types have difficulty with emotional regulation. Individuals characterized as undercontrolled have low levels of impulse control and tend to have difficulty maintaining successful social interactions due to externalizing behaviors such as hyperactivity. Individuals characterized as overcontrolled are shy, timid, anxious, and also have problems in social interactions.

Longitudinal analyses of the National Longitudinal Survey of Youth (NLSY) conducted by Hart, Atkins, and Fegley (2003) suggest that children categorized as resilient possess a pattern of prosocial traits that one would also expect to find in individuals likely to volunteer. For example, emotional regulation and positive emotionality are associated with prosocial behavior (Eisenberg, 2000; Eisenberg & Fabes, 1998). Hart and colleagues (2003) found that resilient children exhibited higher levels of emotional regulation and positive emotionality than their overcontrolled and undercontrolled counterparts. They found that these characteristics were also associated with prosocial behavior such as sharing.

Empathy, or the disposition to be emotionally responsive to others' emotions, has also been identified in the literature as being associated with prosocial behaviors such as volunteering (Davis et al., 1999; Eisenberg, 2000). Similarly, Penner, Fritzsche, Craiger, and Freifeld (1995) identified two personality dimensions, labeled other-oriented empathy and helpfulness, and found that these two dimensions were predictive of volunteering. These characteristics are also consistent with the personality typology discussed above; for example, Hart and colleagues (2003) found that undercontrolled children had lower levels of empathic concern than resilient and overcontrolled children. Most volunteering is motivated by prosocial values; however, prosocial concerns are not solely responsible for volunteering. Instrumental factors, such as an interest in gaining new skills or a desire to engage in an activity looked upon favorably by society, have also been found to contribute to volunteering (Clary, Snyder, & Stukas, 1996). Resilient children are probably more likely to volunteer for these reasons than are children characterized as overcontrolled and undercontrolled. For example, resilients have been found to perform better academically than their overcontrolled and undercontrolled counterparts (Hart et al., 1997). This finding suggests that resilients are attached to the institution of school and consequently may be likely to seek out opportunities within the context of school that develop competence or participate in activities regarded favorably by school personnel. A cocurricular activity such as community-service volunteering is one example. It is possible that the relation of personality to volunteering is a result of personality's influence on joining social organizations. For example, Wilson (2000) suggested that extraversion might lead individuals to social organizations from which they are recruited to volunteer. The magnitude of personality in the prediction of volunteering is substantial. We can estimate that children characterized as resilient in early childhood are 50% more likely than undercontrolled children and 29% more likely than overcontrolled children to volunteer in adolescence. Moreover, the results suggest that the personality types, assessed in early childhood, were established prior to volunteering. Consequently, it appears that personality type led to volunteering, rather than participation in volunteering shaping personality type.

Genetics

Children and adolescents vary in their propensity to participate in civic life, and new research suggests that to some extent *genetic* factors may play a role in producing these individual differences. The general argument that genes are important for understanding individual differences in childhood is not a new one. For example, Turkheimer (2000) has suggested that many (if not most) psychological characteristics are influenced by genes. In fact, behavioral geneticists have argued that the resemblance of children to their parents is more attributable to genes than it is to parents' systematic behavior toward children (Turkheimer, 2000).

Two lines of research are evident in the study of the genetic roots of civic life. The first of these uses behavioral genetic evidence, generally from examining patterns of similarity among monozygotic (MZ) and dizygotic (DZ) twins. The assumption is that if there is greater similarity in a civic quality between MZ twins (who are genetically identical) than observed between DZ twins (who share about 50% of the same genes), then genetic factors are operative. MZ twins are more similar than DZ twins in voting (Fowler, Baker, & Dawes, 2008) and strength of party affiliation (Alford, Funk, & Hibbing, 2005). Indeed, the authors of these studies suggest that genetic factors outweigh the influence of family environment in shaping political attitudes and political behavior. For our purposes in this chapter, the findings of behavioral genetics are cautionary. Until research is done on the influence of parents on adopted, biologically unrelated children—in which case parents do not share genes with their children—then it is impossible to be certain that parenting patterns, not genes, influence civic development.

A second line of research has looked for gene–environment interactions. The emphasis in this work has been to examine the effects that different versions of genes have in varying environments. A great deal of work in this tradition has been done in the study of psychopathology. For example, Caspi et al. (2003) in a widely cited paper reported that children with one version of a gene regulating serotonin, a neurotransmitter affecting mood, were particularly likely to develop depression in adulthood if—and only if—they were exposed to abuse in childhood and adolescence. This is an example of a gene–environment interaction, with the gene only predictive of a particular outcome in a particular environment (abusive). Fowler and Dawes (2008) reported that a gene–environment interaction predicted voting, with one variant of MAOA, a gene involved in the regulation of serotonin and consequently mood, associated with an increased likelihood of voting particularly if the individual regularly attended religious services. Such findings are provocative and interesting—that voting is in part motivated by biological processes that are activated by social institutions—but very much in need of replication. Indeed, Caspi et al.'s findings described above that were so influential in driving research on gene–environment interactions have not been replicated (Risch et al., 2009). While work on genes and civic development will surely continue—and continue to fascinate—it seems safest to conclude at this point that it should be viewed as a direction of work with much promise but few well-established facts.

In summary, longitudinal and cross-sectional research, while minimal, suggests several tentative conclusions. Numerous individual factors potentially contribute to the development of civic engagement. Although demographic differences have emerged in some cases (i.e., regarding gender), more interesting findings emerge for internal attributes such as motivation, personality, empathy, and feelings of trust and belonging. There does not appear to be one particular motivation or personality that matters. Rather, several different motivations and personality attributes may drive the same behavior, but with a different rationale for that behavior. Gene–environment interactions comprise an emerging, but still nascent field within civic engagement, which provides an intriguing line of research to complement the others.

THE ROLES OF VARIOUS CONTEXTS IN DEVELOPING CIVIC ENGAGEMENT

Considering the variety of activities that comprise civic engagement, antecedent activities are most likely not consistent across activity type. Colby and Damon's moral socialization theory (1995) operationalizes these experiences by noting that parents, peers, culture, and society socialize individuals to have a sense of moral commitment to various goals and behaviors; for instance, with a moral commitment to helping others or improving the state of society. In this section, we explore more deeply the contextual factors that encourage the development of civic engagement.

Other relationships, such as positive relationships with peers, also predict civic behaviors (Wentzel & McNamara, 1999; Yates & Youniss, 1998; Green, Gerber, & Nickerson, 2003), although the long-term effects of these relationships are unknown. Participation in religious activities is also related to a greater likelihood of participating in community service activities (Serow & Dreyden, 1990; Youniss, McLellan, Su, & Yates, 1999). These associations are consistent with the theories of social capital in which social connections and social organizations create norms and an infrastructure to support civic engagement (Putnam, 2000).

Race/Ethnicity/Immigration

Ethnic and racial diversity among citizens poses some potential challenges for encouraging civic engagement. Putnam (2000) has reported that increasing racial and ethnic diversity is often accompanied by decreases in social capital. Ethnic and racial diversity may undermine social capital because citizens of different races and ethnicities can view themselves in competition with each other (Perlmutter, 2002), the consequences of which can be increased bias favoring those who share the same racial and ethnic identities and derogation of those who do not. Social capital, according to Putnam, is created through social networks characterized by reciprocity and trustworthiness. Those who have access to more social capital tend to be healthier, wealthier, and happier. Most importantly, with regard to civic engagement, social capital is positively associated with civic participation (Kahne & Sporte, 2008). There is evidence that this occurs even in countries that are known for their tolerance of others, such as the Nordic nations (Pred, 2000). However, other lines of research indicate that preference and affection for one's group does not equate to disdain for other groups (Brewer, 1999) and, in fact, a strong ethnic identity may be an important step toward tolerance of others (Phinney, Ferguson, & Tate, 1997) since a comfort with one's own culture provides a comfort with oneself and thus a base from which to interact with those from other cultures. Personal experiences of prejudice and social exclusion are likely a factor in the civic motivation and action of ethnic minorities. Not only do ethnic minorities report more instances of prejudice than their majority peers, but those experiences also are positively related to their ethnic identity awareness. Ethnically aware youth and African-American youth in particular, are more likely than others to say that they want to be politically active by advocating for the rights of their ethnic group and by working to improve race relations. But African Americans are less likely than other ethnic minorities or their ethnic majority peers to believe that the government is responsive to the average citizen (Flanagan et al., 2009). Contrary to prevailing stereotypes, immigrant youth are not less civically engaged than their native-born peers, once other social background factors are controlled. Furthermore, compared to native-borns, immigrant youth display their civic commitments in a wide variety of forms, including many that benefit their extended community of fellow immigrants (see Jensen & Flanagan, 2008). Although the research is inconclusive, the current findings provide for an important discussion about the intersection of race, ethnicity, diversity, and civil society.

National and Political Influences on Civic Engagement

Civic engagement is also likely to be the product of political climate. For instance, civic engagement is likely to be different in societies characterized by repression of dissenting views than it is in societies open to a variety of competing perspectives. For example, Hart and Gullan (in press) have suggested that the emergence of political activism is influenced by the openness of a society to political protest. In a related vein, the absence of explicit political activism does not imply satisfaction or complicity in the state of affairs of a nation, but may simply reflect the acknowledgment of the danger of activism in a society closed to opposition (Turiel, 2003). Torney-Purta, Wilkenfeld, and Barber (2008) found that political efficacy, which may influence civic engagement, was actually lower in countries in which more political rights and civil liberties are accorded to citizens.

One study by Sears and Valentino (1997) helps to illustrate how societal level factors may influence the development of civic engagement. The researchers investigated how a political event (in this case, the 1980 Wisconsin presidential primary) can socialize youth to be politically active. The researchers used three longitudinal waves of data taken from a probability sample of Wisconsin families (second wave n = 501 pairs, third wave n = 366 pairs), with youth aged 10 to 17 years. Surveys were taken before the Wisconsin presidential primary (January to March 1980), after the election, and 1 year after the end of the election. Before the election, the youth did not have a concrete political identity; making partisan statements without knowing facts or having deep thoughts about the topics. During the campaign, youth partisan attitudes became more concrete, with an increase in knowledge of the candidates and their political parties. However, at the 1-year follow-up, most political identity gains had dissipated.

The constituents of civic engagement are connected to social realities. Participation, membership, and support for rights are all linked to demographic and political characteristics of countries. In the United States, political scientists such as Skocpol (2000) have theorized that the decreasing rate of political engagement has resulted from a political infrastructure that has evolved from one that was influenced by civic associations to one influenced by professional advocates and lobbyists and other political elites. The power of political elites, and thus the weakening strength of the average citizen, possibly acts as a disincentive to engage in the political process because of reduced self-efficacy in the process. Similarly, participation, membership, and support are predicted by the interaction of trust, an individual level characteristic, with political voice measured at the level of country. The nature of the interaction is that scores for participation, membership, and support for rights are highest among those with high levels of trust residing in countries characterized by high levels of voice. Finally, child saturation was positively associated with conventional participation and patriotism. In addition, according to a synthesis by Yates and Youniss (1998), there are several nations (e.g., Israel and Canada, among others) that have mandatory service requirements, whether in the social service sector or military. The authors suggest that such policies create a national ethos of service and possibly result in a deeper national identity among its citizens than in countries without such national service policies.

Family

Parents who act as role models, who reinforce volunteering behavior in their children, and who participate in general activities with their children have children who are more likely to be involved in volunteering activities (Dunham & Bengston, 1992; Flanagan et al., 1998; Fletcher, Elder, & Mekos, 2000; Hashway, 1998). Parents can act as socializing agents for civic engagement among youth, either by reinforcing adolescents' actions or by modeling civic behaviors. Several small, cross-sectional studies have revealed a relationship between parenting (i.e., reinforcement, modeling, warmth, and support) and adolescent civic engagement (e.g., Kasser, Ryan, Zax, & Sameroff, 1995). In a cross-sectional, cross-cultural study, Flanagan and colleagues (1998) examined civic commitment among 5,579 12- to 18-year-old adolescents living in seven countries (United States, Australia, Sweden, Hungary, Czech Republic, Bulgaria, and Russia). The researchers sought to identify variables that were associated with a future commitment to contribute to one's country and to improve one's society. A consistent finding across all seven countries was that a family ethic of social responsibility was associated with civic commitment.

Fewer longitudinal or experimental studies have been conducted on parental influences on civic engagement. In one example, Fletcher, Elder, and Mekos (2000) analyzed data from the Iowa Youth and Families Project, a longitudinal study of 451 European-American families from several rural counties in north central Iowa. Using data from the 9th- and 10th-grade waves, they sought to determine whether parental influence predicts adolescent involvement in community service (e.g., Sunday school teacher, Future Farmers of America) and other community-level activities (sports, academic activities, etc.). Overall, it appears that parental modeling of participation, parental warmth, and parental reinforcement of adolescent behavior is associated with extracurricular activity participation, including community service. Parental reinforcement of youth involvement is most predictive when the parents are not themselves involved in community service activities. Using data from the Maryland Adolescence in Context Study, Zaff and colleagues (Zaff, Malanchuk, & Eccles, 2008) analyzed data from a diverse sample of 1,000 youth followed from middle school into young adulthood. The authors found that parental socialization of civic behaviors and ethnic/cultural norms encouraged the sustained civic participation of the youth.

In a nationally representative, longitudinal study of volunteering behavior, Hart, Atkins, and Ford (1999) investigated the development of volunteering behavior among adolescents. Using the National Longitudinal Survey of Youth, Child Sample, the researchers studied the reasoning behind volunteer service (what the researchers consider to be a contributor to the development of moral identity) of 421 males and 407 females. This nationally representative sample was comprised of adolescents born to mothers who were 14 to 21 years old in 1979, and therefore are the children of younger mothers who tend to be disadvantaged. Average age of the adolescents was 16 at the time of the survey. The results suggest that cognitively and socially stimulating family environments and parent–child activity participation predicts greater volunteer service.

It should also be noted that children can potentially affect the civic engagement of their parents. For example, McDevitt and colleagues (McDevitt & Chaffee, 2000; McDevitt, Chaffee, & Saphir, 2001; McDevitt & Kiousis, 2006) have tested their "trickle up" model in which they theorize that increased youth civic knowledge acts as a catalyst for political discussions with parents. This, in turn, would result in increased parental civic knowledge. Results of their analysis of 5th through 12th graders and their parents found that student exposure to a civics curriculum (in this case, through a program called Kids Voting USA) predicted higher levels of parent–student discussion about civic topics (e.g., a presidential election), which was significantly related to higher levels of parent civic knowledge.

Overall, there is evidence to suggest that parents can influence the civic engagement of youth, and youth have the potential of influencing at least the civic knowledge of their parents. More specifically, parents who act as role models, who reinforce volunteering behavior in their children, and who participate in general activities with their children have children that are more likely to be involved in volunteering activities.

Program Participation

Civic engagement researchers have hypothesized that civic activities are formative contexts that develop a youth's civic identity (Youniss, McLellan, Su, & Yates, 1999) and sustained civic participation. In addition, activities that are not explicitly civic in nature, such as sports or the arts, could serve as microcosms of public life, thus providing the social capital and opportunities for social skill building that are related to later civic engagement. To examine this theory with regard to civic engagement, researchers have focused on whether participation in civic and non-civic activities leads to a civic identity, using civic engagement as a rough proxy for civic identity (Glanville, 1999; Zaff, Moore, Papillo, & Williams, 2003; Hahn, Leavitt, & Aaron, 1994; Youniss, McLellan, Su, & Yates, 1999). Researchers have found that it is important to engage youth in the specific activities we would like to see in the future (Youniss & Yates, 1999; Zaff & Moore, 2002). Researchers have theorized that programs to promote civic engagement should begin with an opportunity for adolescents to participate in civic activities, such as community service or political volunteering. By performing service, a participant may become personally involved with political issues, rather than thinking about them abstractly (Youniss & Yates, 1997). Involvement in community service also provides a network of people with whom to discuss civic issues (Crystal & DeBell, 2002). In performing community service, people may also become familiar with social problems of which they were previously unaware (Eyler & Giles, 1999). This last point, about specific activity participation, is important since there appears to be a disconnect in increased national trends in the United States in volunteering rates and flat or decreasing rates of political activity. This disparity is possibly the result of volunteering that is typically focused on non-political activities (e.g., tutoring or working in a soup kitchen) instead of activities with a more political valence (Wilson & Musick, 1999). In their analysis of two national longitudinal U.S. data sets, McFarland and Thomas (2006) report that involvement as a youth in voluntary associations that entail community service, public speaking, debate, and performance, and religious affiliations are the strongest predictors of political involvement in young adulthood. After controlling for multiple social background and selection factors, they conclude that "youth organizations that demand time commitments and that concern service, political activity, and public performance have the most significant positive relation to long-term political participation" (p. 416). In addition, active involvement in addressing social problems during youth is predictive of long-term civic engagement. This relationship has been found for involvement in civil rights (e.g., Fendrich, 1993; McAdam, 1988), anti-war (e.g., Jennings, 2002), and feminist (e.g., Stewart, Settles, & Winter, 1998) movements. Although the typical service activities of high school students do not equate directly with participation in the above movements, they can be seen as a form of "proto-activism" in which young people take steps toward more intense engagement (Jennings, 2002). Special note is taken of the fact that school-based required service was found to be as efficacious as voluntary service in predicting subsequent civic engagement.

Civic Engagement Programs

Overall, research has demonstrated relatively strong associations between being engaged in civic activities in middle and high school and later civic involvement. Smith (1999) analyzed the 1988 National Education Longitudinal Study (NELS) data to attempt to determine the association of engagement in activities in high school and political participation in adulthood. Smith found that previous extracurricular voluntary participation was most predictive of future political participation (e.g., registering to vote, voting, and volunteering in political organizations). Using data from the National Longitudinal Study of the High School Senior Class of 1972, Hanks (1981) explored the relationship between youth participation in voluntary activities and participation by those adolescents in adulthood. He found that extracurricular activity participation during the senior year of high school was related, 2 years later, to more political campaign participation, to more discussion of political issues, and to a higher likelihood of voting. This finding remains after controlling for social class, academic performance, and self-esteem. The strength of the association is greatest for participation in activities that are a means to an end (e.g., honorary clubs, vocational education clubs, school newspaper), as opposed to activities that are an end in themselves (e.g., athletic teams). This finding has been replicated in an analysis of Monitoring the Future (combining data from 1988 to 1993), a cross-sectional and nationally representative data set of high school seniors (Youniss, McLellan, Su, & Yates, 1999). After controlling for several background variables such as religion, gender, socioeconomic status, and minority status, the researchers found that frequency of community service was strongly and significantly related to participation in conventional political activities (whether seniors had voted or were likely to vote, work on a political campaign, contribute money to a political campaign, or write a letter to an office holder) and unconventional political activities (whether seniors had or were likely to boycott some organizations or participate in a public demonstration for some cause). A similar finding came from a study using High School and Beyond data (Glanville, 1999). Using data from the first wave (1980) and third follow-up (1986) of this nationally representative survey of high school seniors, Glanville found that extracurricular participation in activities that have some tangible outcome as the goal, such as student government, debate, and the school newspaper, was predictive of working for a campaign, attending a political gathering, and contributing money to a campaign as a young adult. The association remained after accounting for several individual-level variables (locus of control, sociability, political interest, and community leadership), church attendance, and demographics. However, an association with voting disappeared once the individual level variables were included in the model.

When youth in low-income communities participate in community service, their participation tends to be mediated by local churches, rather than by a wide set of community-based nonprofit organizations that typically attract more college-bound youth and are also able to offer a wider-ranging and more diverse set of service experiences. This means that youth from these neighborhoods have less of a "buffet" from which to choose how and where they will do their service and tend to have lower rates of participation in such opportunities (Harvard Family Research Project, 2007).

There are some bright spots in this picture. Some after-school programs, especially those that focus on at-risk youth, have been able to combine academic and social enrichment with recreation and opportunities for community service (Allen, Philliber, Herrling, & Kuperminc, 1997; Philliber, Williams, Herrling, & West, 2002). Quantum Opportunities, Teen Outreach Project, and Across Ages are examples of programs that have had at least a modest impact on current community service, as well as on academic and social outcomes that lead to more positive outcomes during adolescence (Allen, Philliber, Herrling, & Kuperminc, 1997; Hahn, 1994; LoSciuto, Rajala, Townsend, & Taylor, 1996). Other programs, such as service-learning programs funded through the Learn-and-Serve federal grant program, have had mixed results. Here we present findings from programs that illustrate the potential of programs to promote civic engagement.

One program that experimentally evaluated civic engagement at program follow-up is the Quantum Opportunity Program (QOP), a multiservice, 4-year, year-round demonstration project that was conducted in five cities (San Antonio, Philadelphia, Milwaukee, Saginaw, and Oklahoma City). The program was designed to serve disadvantaged youth by giving youth a supervised and safe place after school in which to do homework, learn to use computers, take field trips to museums, hear speakers on various health topics, and participate in volunteer activities. Learning life skills is also part of the curriculum. An older mentor was paired with the youth to mentor them during the 4-year period that started in ninth grade and continued through high school. Students were given a small stipend for participating in program services and given bonuses for completing program segments.

By aggregating across sites (n = 25 participants per site), and using a randomly assigned experimental/control group design, Hahn, Leavitt, and Aaron (1994) were able to determine the effectiveness of the program, including post–high school effectiveness. Along with a plethora of positive academic impacts (e.g., increased rates of high school graduation and postsecondary education, reduced rates of high school dropouts, and increased number of students with the attitude of being "hopeful about the future"), the experimental group donated significantly more time than the control group to a nonprofit, charitable, school, or community group, in the 6 months after leaving the program. There was not, however, a follow-up beyond the 6-month one, so longer-term impacts are not known. The impacts were also mainly driven by a subset of the communities, so the universality of the program's effectiveness is not conclusive.

A national quasi-experimental evaluation of Learn and Serve America's service-learning programs funded by the Corporation for National and Community Service (CNCS) was conducted by the Center for Human Resources at Brandeis University (1999). CNCS is a government entity created to fund programs that support school and community-based efforts to promote national and community service. The Learn and Serve evaluation covered the 1994–1997 period and consisted of an ethnically and socioeconomically diverse sample. The programs were selected through a structured sampling process from a group of 210 randomly selected sites. Although there was variation among program characteristics, all of the programs chosen for the evaluation had been in operation for at least 1 year, reported higher-than-average service hours of participants, reported regular use of student written and oral reflection, and were school-based and linked to a formal curriculum. Across the sites, students provided, on average, 70 hours of direct service, such as working as a tutor, in a nursing home or homeless shelter. Over 75% of participants had face-to-face contact with those they were serving, such as meeting with students or senior citizens. This service also generally involved both individual and group projects. Very importantly, 80% of the program participants felt that they had made a contribution to their community, and over 60% said that their service involved real responsibilities, a chance to do things themselves, and opportunities for discussion. Post-program results demonstrated short-term effectiveness. Aside from educational implications (e.g., school engagement, higher school grades) high school participants had significantly higher service leadership attitudes and civic attitudes than the comparison group. Program participants were also significantly more likely to have volunteered for and spent more time doing community service. Middle school participants, aside from having better social studies grades and fewer arrests and instances of pregnancy, were also significantly more likely than controls to have volunteered, but then did not volunteer significantly more hours.

Participants were also evaluated 1 year after the program to determine longer-term associations with positive outcomes. Of the original 1,000 participants, 764 were involved in the follow-up (460 program participants and 304 comparison participants). The only effect that remained for middle school students was a marginally significant difference on number of arrests in the previous 6 months (i.e., participants having fewer arrests). High school participants provided almost twice as many hours of volunteer service as comparison students, but this effect was only marginally significant. Service leadership was significantly greater for participants, but the size of the effect decreased over the past year. Also, these longer-term associations may be confounded by individual characteristics. For instance, those who continued to be involved in community service after the end of the program were significantly more likely to volunteer and have college aspirations, and less likely to consume alcohol than those who did not continue to be involved in community service.

These programs suggest that a well-designed extension of schooling into the community can increase achievement (see meta-analysis by Durlak & Weissberg, 2006, for additional program examples). A host of other service-based programs targeting higher-risk youth show that they have a significant, although modest, impact on academic, behavioral, and labor market outcomes, but either do not show any impact on civic participation or were not evaluated to test for that outcome (see Michelson, Zaff, & Hair, 2002, for a review). Moreover, although some of these programs are directed toward youth from disadvantaged backgrounds, they still tend to reach only a relatively small number of this population. The availability of these opportunities is not necessarily equitable across socioeconomic status. According to the Harvard Family Research Project (2007), youth from higher-income families are still significantly more likely to participate in virtually all out-of-school programs and activities—sports, clubs, arts, and so on—than youth from lower-income families, with the exception of the latter receiving more tutoring as part of compensatory education.

There are data available that suggest particular program attributes of which program designers should be aware. For instance, Conrad and Hedin (1982), in an evaluation of 27 experiential education programs, found that the presence of seminars that occur at least once per week was the strongest variable predicting student positive citizenship. Also, engaging youth in the formation of service-learning programs has been suggested as an important program characteristic. Such interactive classroom time allows for reflection and makes for an explicit connection between the service and the learning (Katula, 2000). Other factors that have been found to be effective components of service-learning programs include the length of the program and the number of experiences (i.e., program intensity) (Conrad & Hedin, 1982). Providing opportunities for interesting activities in which adolescents feel appreciated for their work and they can see the impact that they have on their communities may help to make the experience a positive one for youth. Research findings also suggest that students should be involved in the formation of the programs. In other words, youth should be given a voice in deciding the types of activities in which to participate and the curriculum in school (Garvey, McIntyre-Craig, & Myers, 2000; Katula, 2000; Morgan & Streb, 2000). Garvey and colleagues (2000) made several suggestions for how to give youth a voice. They suggest allowing adolescents to assess their community's needs for programs, making sure to engage adolescents in discussion during class time, sharing program planning responsibilities, letting youth help with determining the budget and funds needed for the program, allowing youth to apply what they have learned in the classroom to the implementation and eventual evaluation of the program, and celebrating the impact that they and the program have had on the community.

Evidence suggests that community service performed during adolescence is related to later civic participation. Astin, Sax, and Avalos (1999) analyzed longitudinal data from college students with outcome measures collected 9 years after college graduation. They found that volunteering in college positively predicted volunteering 9 years after graduation. For example, 44% of people who were very involved in volunteering in college and also volunteered shortly after college were volunteers 9 years after graduation, while only 19% of people who neither volunteered during college nor shortly after college were volunteers 9 years later. Similarly, Wilson and Musick (1997) found in their analysis of the Americans' Changing Lives panel survey that volunteering in adulthood was predictive of volunteering 3 years later and Smith (1999), analyzing data from the National Education Longitudinal Study (NELS), found that students who did service in their last year of high school were higher 2 years later on a composite measure of civic participation (combining volunteering and voting) than were peers who had not done service in their senior year.

Experiences during emerging adulthood also appear to be important for encouraging civic engagement. For example, Americorps is the national service program funded by CNCS. Americorps has two components. The state and national program engages participants in substantive service work with public and non-profit organizations throughout the country. The National Citizen Community Corps (NCCC), a team-based residential program for 18- to 24-year-olds in which participants live with their teams at regional campuses and are deployed to time-limited projects throughout their region. The projects range from environmental preservation and low-income housing to youth development and disaster relief. An 8-year follow-up in a quasi-experimental evaluation of national/state and NCCC programs found multiple effects on participants' civic measures (Corporation for National and Community Service, 2008). The comparison group was comprised of individuals who had explored applying to the program but decided against joining. Propensity scores were used to control for differences between the program and comparison groups. Participation in community affairs, such as community meetings, and employment with a public service organization were significantly higher for Americorps participants, as were several civic attitudes, such as efficacy to lead a community-based initiative and to positively impact a community. Similar findings were found for the NCCC participants, except that they did not have significantly higher rates of participating in community affairs, but they did have significantly higher rates of volunteering behaviors. Overall, considering the long-term nature of this study, it is impressive that civic effects were sustained, suggesting that the experiences in Americorps support the development of civic engagement and that the effects might differ based on the Americorps experience. Two important caveats, however, temper the results. First, although propensity scores were used, the scores did not include specific measures of motivation to participate. Thus, it could be that the program group was comprised of individuals with higher levels of civic motivation before entering the program than the comparison group. Also, the response rate at the 8-year follow-up, as compared to the baseline assessment, was only 58%, leaving open the possibility that those who responded to the follow-up were more exceptional in their civic attitudes and behaviors than those who did not respond.

The benefits of community service for civic development may depend on whether it is *required* or *voluntary*. A number of commentators have suggested that requiring community service of students—either as a condition of high school graduation or as part of a class—produces unthinking, possibly resented, activity that cannot deepen students' commitment to the civic good (e.g., Stukas, Snyder, & Clary, 1999). Chapman (2002, p. 12) has asked rhetorically, "Does a student who learns that almost anything counts toward the service requirement [for a school]—so long as he doesn't get paid—develop a keen sense of civil calling? Or does he hone his skill at gaming the system?" Friedland and Morimoto (2005) has found that "resume padding" such as for college admissions is a possible driving force for participation in civic actions, although the authors do not have data to support their contention that the motivation to participate has any effect on the civic activities in which the students participate.

On the other hand, there is some evidence that required service is linked to later volunteering. Metz and Youniss (2003) studied a high school prior to, and following, the introduction of a community service requirement. This allowed them to compare students who were voluntarily involved in community service with those whose community service was mandated. Metz and Youniss (2003) found that those whose service was required evidenced the same gains in civic interest and behavior evident in the volunteers following the service activities.

Other research (Hart, Donnelly, Youniss, & Atkins, 2007) has shown that being required to perform community service in high school is associated with higher rates of voting in adulthood, not lowered civic engagement. Those who participated frequently in community service in high school were more likely to volunteer than were those whose community service was nonexistent or infrequent. Extracurricular involvement in high school was also a statistically significant predictor of civic volunteering, and there were important differences among types of extracurricular activities. Leadership in high school instrumental extracurricular activities is associated with the highest levels of civic volunteering in adulthood.

Bennett (2003), Finn and Vanourek (1995), and others have hypothesized that mandated service might prove to de-motivate young people because they are forced to help others and address social problems. Stukas, Snyder, and Clary (1999) made a similar conjecture based on the notion that adolescents who are striving for autonomy might be especially averse to forced service. Findings from Hart et al. (2007) should allay such concerns, as they show that mandated service can motivate high school students' civic engagement. Why is service, even when mandated, effective, and why might its effects persist through the onset of adulthood? One explanation is that community service shapes identity. Many students do service at sites that are managed by non-profit organizations and social service agencies that respond to social problems, such as homelessness, and provide assistance to people in need of food, shelter, and the like (Raskoff & Sundeen, 1999). These organizations offer assistance in the name of explicit value systems that are communicated to their clients as well as volunteer personnel. For example, Allahyari (2000) describes how administrators at a Salvation Army Mission and soup kitchen run by the Catholic Workers educate clients and volunteers in their philosophies of conversion-reform and respect with dignity for the poor, respectively. These philosophies provide rationales for service that volunteers can incorporate into their self-concepts as they come to see themselves as persons capable of contributing to the common good (Hart, 2005; Penner, 2002; Piliavin, Grube, & Callero, 2002). In this regard, young people are not only doing service, but also doing it as representatives of a particular value tradition as they serve in the name of a specific tradition. Because organizations and their founding philosophies persist over time, individuals have a referent point to which they can relate as they move ahead in the life cycle. These organizations are an anchoring point for personal as well as social identity (Erikson, 1968). Moreover, because service is done at these sites, students may become members of networks with other persons with whom they did service collectively. Thus, individuals find themselves connected to organizations and networks that afford them lasting resources for civic involvement (McAdam, 1988).

The mechanisms underlying the long-term civic impact of organizational involvement in one's youth are not well delineated but several come to mind. First is a selection effect: Joiners in youth become joiners in adulthood. As research on voluntarism suggests, their personalities may differ: Volunteers are more likely than non-volunteers to exhibit positive emotions and social skills including openness, agreeableness, and extraversion (Matsuba, Hart, & Atkins, 2007).

Second, once in an organization, an individual is likely to get recruited into other organizations and civic activities (Verba, Schlozman, & Brady, 1995). Thus, engagement as a youth sets one on a recruitment trajectory, that is, involvement in one group increases the likelihood of recruitment into others.

Third, although social rewards are the reason that most youth initially join organizations, over time they are likely to develop an affinity and identification with the organization and its mission, and feel a sense of coherence between their own values and views and those of others in the organization (Erikson, 1968). The public or collective identity that they are forging is a necessary foundation for sustained civic action insofar as such action benefits the community, not just the self. We are more likely to forego individual gain on behalf of the good of a group if we feel a sense of solidarity with the group. Solidarity or identification with a group or organization is related to a fourth reason why organizational engagement in youth is related to civic engagement in adulthood. By working with a group to achieve a goal, particularly if they succeed, they may experience a sense of collective efficacy, that is, a belief in the capacity of the group to achieve something together. Since political goals are typically achieved through collective action, this is an important constituent for sustaining their engagement.

Organizing and Activism

Youth organizing has been another way to bridge school and community toward encouraging civic participation. The importance of institutions and social relationships in contemporary youth activism permeates research reports on the topic. Kirshner (2007, p. 370) noted that "activism groups typically embody cross-age collaborations in which young adults (usually in their twenties) play critical roles as organizers and advisers." Kirshner (2007) also discussed the development of adolescent activism as a process akin to apprenticing, with adults playing a crucial role in transmitting skills and attitudes. Pearce and Larson (2006) studied intensively a youth activism group and found that the adult leader played a crucial role in maintaining group cohesion and in organizing the group's activities. When youth participate in programs that encourage them to take action in addressing problems of immediate interest to their lives (e.g., promoting neighborhood safety, school reform, etc.), they feel connected to the work and show capabilities for collaboration with their peers. Both of these, in turn, contribute to effective collective action among groups of young people. Additionally, youth demonstrate competence in establishing relationships with officials such as school administrators, police, or legislators (Ginwright, 2007; Larson & Hansen, 2005; Hart & Kirshner, 2009).

McAdam (1988) has argued that engaging in intense political activism during the transition to adulthood transforms identity in fundamental ways. He compared young adults who participated in the Mississippi Freedom Summer voter registration drives with a group of their peers who volunteered to go but in the end did not participate. Although the period of time was short, the actions in which these volunteers were engaged were highly contested and their lives were on the line. According to McAdam, these facts, combined with the collective identity they experienced as part of a group powerfully committed to a cause, fundamentally transformed their identities and also disrupted subsequent life trajectories.

Paige's (1971) work reveals similarities between rioters in Newark and participants in Freedom Summer, suggesting that the various *actions* that are subsumed in everyday notions of political activism are related to each other. For example, the twelve forms of legal political action included in the Roper survey, described earlier, are associated with each other (these analyses are available from the authors). This means that individuals who report attending political rallies are more likely than those who did not attend rallies to be members of committees, signing petitions, and so on. Moreover, the various political actions all show the same general historical declines. While McAdam's (1986) caution against assuming all forms of political activism are identical in function and motivation is well made, the tendency of different types of activist behavior to co-occur, combined with at least broad similarities evident in the psychology of disparate lines of activism such as Freedom Summer participation and rioting, suggest that political activism might be usefully considered as a single phenomenon (while simultaneously recognizing the value of investigations aiming to explicate the unique features of any single incident of youth activism).

In important respects, the focus on individual and social characteristics of activists, particularly those prominent in the United States during the last half of the 20th century, distorts our understanding of youth activism. This is so because the very same characteristics that were linked to political activism in youth of this era and in this political context might not result in political activism in a different context. Consider, for example, the long tradition in the United States of encouraging and protecting political expression. The historical record is replete with examples in which political expression has been repressed in the United States; nonetheless, in comparison to other countries in the same time period—for example, China or the USSR—the social and legal climate of the United States was relatively supportive of the forms of expression characteristic of political activism. It is unlikely that the wave of activism characteristic of American youth in the 1960s could have occurred in countries with traditions of active repression of political dissent.

Extracurricular Activities

There is also the possibility that simply being consistently engaged in any kind of activity as an adolescent is associated with being engaged in positive citizenship activities in young adulthood. Extracurricular activities provide students with opportunities to learn civic and leadership skills, such as giving speeches, coordinating efforts with others, influencing others, writing formal documents, and holding meetings (Kirlin, 2003a, 2003b; Youniss & Yates, 1997). Extracurricular activities also may serve as a forum for interactions with people from various backgrounds and with adults who may serve as role models or mentors. These discussions may promote civic knowledge and civic engagement (Zaff, Moore, Papillo, & Williams, 2003). There is some evidence that involvement in extracurricular activities in high school increases the likelihood of future civic engagement. Analyzing the NELS data, Zaff et al. (2003) found that, compared to individuals who only occasionally participated in extracurricular activities, individuals who regularly participated in at least one extracurricular activity in the 8th, 10th, and 12th grades had higher levels of both voting and volunteering 2 years after high school. In a review of the literature, Kirlin (2003a) concluded that the effects of participation in extracurricular activities on civic engagement might depend on the type of activity. For adult organizations, *instrumental activities* have been defined as activities in which the primary objective is to "maintain or to create some normative condition or change…to attain goals that lie outside of the organizations themselves," whereas *expressive activities* are groups which provide activities for members as their primary objective (Gordon & Babchuk, 1959, p. 25). These definitions of adult organizations also have been applied to extracurricular activities in school. Instrumental activities typically include student government, student newspaper, yearbook, debate club, political clubs, and vocational clubs. Expressive activities encompass athletics, cheerleading, academic clubs, band, chorus, drama, and hobby clubs. Some research findings suggest that in comparison to expressive activities, instrumental activities are more likely to increase civic engagement. For example, in analyzing the High School and Beyond database, Glanville (1999) found that after controlling for demographic, personality, and political variables, individuals who participated in instrumental activities as seniors were more likely to participate in politics 6 years after high school than youth who participated in expressive activities. In fact, individuals in the expressive group were no more likely to participate in politics than individuals who were involved in no activities as seniors in high school. Similarly, Hanks (1981) found in his analyses of the National Longitudinal Study of the High School Senior Class of 1972 that involvement in instrumental activities predicted higher levels of political participation 1 to 2 years later than did involvement in expressive activities. Another potential predictor of civic engagement is leadership of an extracurricular activity (Kirlin, 2003a). Leadership typically involves giving speeches, persuading others, organizing people, and knowledge of larger issues. Youth who are leaders of activities may be more prepared to engage civically in the future. There is evidence that participation in student government, a prominent leader position, does lead to increased civic participation (e.g., Glanville, 1999).

Community Context: Youth Bulges

Youth bulge refers to a cohort of youth between the ages of 16 and 25 that is unusually large relative to the adult population in a society. Historical research has linked youth bulges to revolutions in 17th-century England, 18th-century France, and 20th-century Indonesia (Goldstone, 2002; Moller, 1968); to political activism in Western and Middle Eastern countries (Huntington, 1996); and to the prevalence of warfare throughout the world (Mesquida & Wiener, 1999; Urdal, 2002). The associations of youth bulges to activism, revolution, and warfare—the latter two are particularly likely in societies experiencing simultaneous economic difficulties (Huntington, 1996)—leads national security analysts (e.g., Helgerson, 2002) and the popular press (e.g., Zakaria, 2001) to classify countries with disproportionately large cohorts of youth as at risk for the emergence of political extremism. Hart and colleagues (2004) have hypothesized that the extraordinary willingness to participate in political transformation that is characteristic of youth in a youth bulge is a consequence, in part, of community influences on civic development. Countries with youth bulges have many communities in which children and adolescents make up a large fraction of the population. Communities affect civic knowledge and civic participation through social influence. Knowledge, attitudes, and behaviors are shaped in daily interactions with other people (Latané et al., 1995). Compared with other communities, child-saturated communities have fewer adults with high levels of civics expertise that can be transmitted through informal contact to children and adolescents. Consequently, youth living in child-saturated communities could know less about the political system than youth living in adult-saturated communities. Child-saturated communities are consequently more likely to offer models of involvement in volunteer activities than are adult-saturated ones.

Social influence theory explains the positive contribution of child saturation (an increase in volunteering) on civic development, a finding not easily deduced from other theories. For example, theoretical accounts of youth bulges that focus on the poor economic prospects of members of youth bulges (e.g., Huntington, 1996) and the predilection of young men in youth bulges to violence (e.g., Mesquida & Wiener, 1999) cannot readily accommodate findings concerning the benefits of child saturation for volunteering. Hart and colleagues (2004) have offered a second explanation for the relation of youth bulges to warfare and activism. These authors suggest that the economic theory neglects the consequences of growing up from birth to adolescence in large cohorts of similarly aged individuals. Hart et al. suggest that those who grow up in communities and societies with large cohorts of children (child-saturated contexts) are less influenced by adults than are children who develop in communities and societies in which adults constitute large majorities (adult-saturated contexts). They hypothesized that growing up in adult-saturated contexts results in the transmission from adults to children knowledge of, and respect for, the culture and society. This transmission is possible because in adult-saturated contexts many of a child's interactions will naturally involve adults, who typically possess knowledge about society and culture. In contrast, in child-saturated contexts, children interact frequently with other children, and less transmission of cultural information can take place because children typically have little information about their societies. Hart et al. demonstrated that children living in child-saturated communities in the U.S. have less civic knowledge than do children living in adult-saturated communities, and showed as well that children in child-saturated countries possess less civic knowledge than do children in adult-saturated countries. Hart et al. suggested, but have not proved, that those who possess little civic knowledge are more likely to become involved in radical political and social activism than are those who possess more civic knowledge. In summary, then, Hart et al. argue that members of youth bulges have less civic knowledge than youth of the same age who were not socialized in large cohorts of children, and that a deficit in civic knowledge can lead to participation in extremist political activities.

Adolescents should be more likely to volunteer in communities in which many other people volunteer in child-saturated communities than in communities in which volunteering is less common (adult-saturated communities). In one analysis, Hart and colleagues (2007) found that in low-poverty neighborhoods, the rate of participation in community service was nearly twice as high in neighborhoods with a child-saturation quotient of 0.4 as in neighborhoods with a child-saturation quotient of 0.2. In moderate-poverty neighborhoods, child saturation had little effect on participation in community service. Extremely poor neighborhoods with a child-saturation quotient of 0.4 had extremely low rates of participation in community service. As predicted, child saturation was negatively associated with civic knowledge. From the regression equation, it was estimated that adolescents in a community with a child-saturation quotient of 0.2 could be expected to be about 0.2 SD higher in civic knowledge than equivalent adolescents in a community with an extreme child-saturation quotient of 0.4.

Together, the findings suggest that the age structure of communities and of countries influences the civic development of youth. Other factors, such as other individual and family-level factors cannot account for the pattern.

Classrooms

Conventional wisdom in political science has held until recently that course-based civic education had little effect on the civic development of students. However, based on several large, empirical studies conducted since the 1980s, positive correlations have been consistently found between taking a class on civics, government, or American history, on one hand, and possessing civic knowledge, confidence, and attitudes, on the other (Comber, 2003). These studies include the National Assessment of Education Progress (NAEP) Civics Assessment (a test-like instrument created by the federal government and taken by 20,000 students); the IEA Civic Education Study (a detailed survey of 14-year-olds conducted simultaneously in the United States and in 27 foreign countries); and several polls of young adults that ask them about their own civic education as well as their current civic activities.

For example, Niemi and Junn (2000) carefully analyzed the NAEP Civics Assessment, which measures factual knowledge and cognitive skills (such as interpreting political speeches and news articles). They found that course-taking has a positive relationship with knowledge and skills even after other factors were controlled. Using their own Metro Civic Values Survey (conducted in Maryland in 1999–2000), Gimpel and colleagues found that taking a government course raised students' habits of discussing politics by 5%, their political knowledge by 3%, and their "internal efficacy" by 2%. (Internal efficacy is a person's confidence in his or her own political skills.) Taking a government course lowered students' confidence in the responsiveness of government by about 2% (Gimpel, Lay, & Schuknecht, 2003).

But civil climates for learning in which teachers encourage a respectful exchange of opinions, respect students' diverse opinions, and intervene to stop acts of social exclusion or intolerance are positively and significantly related to ethnic minority (African-, Arab-, and Latino-American) and ethnic majority (European-American) students' beliefs that America is a just society and the motivations that these students hold about being contributing members of that society (Flanagan, Cumsille, Gill, & Gallay, 2007).

Perhaps the strongest evidence supports civil, balanced discussions of controversial events in classrooms, with evidence suggesting that such discussions increase students' interest in politics and their knowledge of it (Hess, 2009). Some research finds that the whole positive impact of civics or government classes on civic engagement is due to the discussions that happen in these courses. Promoting discussion in class can also send off interesting ripples, such as such discussions contributing to conversations at home and thereby increasing parents' political awareness (McDevitt & Kiousis, 2006).

These discussions need to be moderated, which is a skill. It is especially challenging for younger teachers to moderate current events discussions today, because the examples that we see on television tend to be shouting matches, and few of today's teachers experienced discussion in their own schools back in the 1980s and 1990s. By that time, the once popular high school class called "Problems of American Democracy," which involved reading newspapers and debating issues, had largely disappeared from the curriculum.

At the same time, we need to change reward structures so that teachers can promote discussion of current events. Skills and knowledge related to current events are not measured on tests. And controversial discussions can get teachers into hot water. They need support from administrators and leaders outside the schools.

Unfortunately, we tend to offer class discussions and all the other engaging forms of civic education to our most successful students, not to their less advantaged peers. As Mills College researchers Joseph Kahne and Ellen Middaugh have found, within a given high school, it is usually the college-bound students who report service learning, classroom discussions of issues, field trips, visiting speakers, and other challenging and inspiring civic experiences. These students tend to come from more privileged backgrounds.

Furthermore, when we compare suburban schools to urban and rural schools, or schools with high and low average test scores, we find that the more privileged schools are the ones that offer interactive civic education.

Data, in fact, substantiate this rationale, indicating that when service is connected conceptually to civics instruction—what many call service learning—it can lead to long-term involvement in volunteering and voting (Beane, Turner, Jones, & Lipka, 1981; Hanks & Eckland, 1987; Hart & Kirshner, 2009; Yates & Youniss, 1998). By providing students with opportunities to address community problems or issues, lead those initiatives, and reflect on their experiences, young people are able to build social and civic competencies that equip them for life-long civic participation.

There is a disparity, however, between opportunities in high- and low-poverty schools. A recent analysis of Current Population Survey data shows a 7-point disparity in service-learning opportunities between high- and low-poverty schools (27 vs. 20%, respectively), as well as in schools that recognize students' civic actions (72% for low-poverty vs. 62% for high-poverty), and arrange civic activities for students (61% for low poverty and 54% for high poverty) (Spring, Dietz, & Grimm, 2007).

Our study builds upon several decades of research that demonstrates that civic knowledge, extracurricular participation in high school, and volunteering are related to civic participation in adulthood (e.g., Delli Carpini & Keeter, 1996; Kirlin, 2003a; Krampen, 2000).

PUTTING IT ALL TOGETHER: NON–COLLEGE-BOUND YOUTH AS AN EXAMPLE

As emerging adults, non–college-attending youth face more challenges than their college-bound peers, not only in their everyday lives but also in opportunities for civic participation. Many continue to live in neighborhoods with weak civic infrastructures. Most employment available to them is part-time with little or no prospect of having health or other benefits—a stark contrast to jobs available to former generations, especially those with strong unions that historically served as social and civic centers for blue-collar workers and new immigrants. A lower level of job and financial security impedes buying a first home and, therefore, developing strong attachments to a broader community. And there are few, if any, ready-made programs or initiatives such as those that college-bound youth have available to them on their college campuses to "get involved" in civic or political affairs.

In short, what was the standard series of life events for emerging adults has dissembled into diverse patterns, with particular implications for non–college-bound youth (NCBY). First, the events that had traditionally been important in connecting emerging adults to their families, communities, fellow workers, and country are no longer reliable in helping to fuel civic participation. Second, the lack of strong civic associations and infrastructure in communities where NCBY grow up and live as emerging adults suggests that there will be little incentive or interest in participating over the long term.

This generational change in engagement with civically reinforcing institution has resulted in a civic gap between college-attending youth and their non–college-attending counterparts. Increases in voting, volunteering, and other forms of civic engagement are driven disproportionately by young people from higher-income families and communities, as well as youth who are college bound or already enrolled in secondary institutions. In contrast, low-income and NCBY are lagging far behind in their levels of civic participation—a gap that threatens the health of a democracy that depends on the full participation of everyone, not just some.

Ample data underscore the stark differences in the civic and political engagement of college-bound and NCBY in the United States:

- Nearly 60% of 18- to 24-year-old college students voted in the 2004 presidential election, while only one-third of non–college-attending youth (aged 18 to 24) voted (Lopez, Kirby, & Sagoff, 2005). That disparity also emerged during the 2008 primaries, with college students nearly four times more likely to have voted than students not attending college (25 vs. 7%) (Marcelo & Kirby, 2008).
- The gap between college-educated and NCBY continued during the 2008 presidential election. Although just 57% of U.S. citizens under 30 have ever attended college, 70% of all young voters in the 2008 election had gone to college (Marcelo & Kirby, 2008).
- The same disproportion emerged in young people without a high school diploma. Although the latter make up 14% of the general population, only 6% of young voters in the 2008 presidential election had no high school diploma (Marcelo & Kirby, 2008).
- According to the Current Population Survey, 8.3% of 19- to 25-year-old NCBY volunteered in 2006, down from 10.6% the previous year. In contrast, in 2006, nearly one in three college students (31%) volunteered (Marcelo et al., 2007a). Similar education-related disparities were reported for all adults aged 16 years and older (Foster-Bey, 2008).
- A recent survey found that college-bound youth had higher rates of civic involvement across 16 of 19 indicators of civic participation, including voting, volunteering, canvassing, boycotting, and "buycotting" (Lopez et al., 2006).

Traditional measures of civic engagement for non-college youth have declined substantially since the 1970s, when unions, churches, and other religious congregations, social movements, and voluntary associations provided more opportunities for NCBY to attend meetings, work on community projects, belong to groups, and meet political officials (National Conference on Citizenship, 2006). Whether musical culture or new forms of association that use the Internet can compensate is still a question.

Today, 40% of the entire youth population under the age of 18 come from low-income backgrounds (American Community Survey, 2008), and are underexposed (or in some cases, have no exposure whatsoever) to high-quality civic education. They also lack opportunities to assume leadership roles in their schools and communities and to participate in civic activities, school-led or otherwise (Hart & Kirshner, 2009; Kahne & Middaugh, 2008; McFarland & Starrmans, 2007).

Low-income youth or youth whose parents never attended college also are less likely to attend postsecondary institutions where much attention to youth civic engagement occurs. The average educational attainment of those growing up in poverty, for example, is less than a high school diploma (Duncan, Kalil, & Ziol-Guest, 2008), and approximately 40 to 50% of students from low-income families drop out before graduation (Kauffman, Alt, & Chapman, 2004).

This is a particularly severe problem in high-poverty school districts (Neild & Balfanz, 2006). Conservative estimates show that nearly half of young people from low-income families do not attend college (Horn & Nunez, 2000), although the rate is most likely lower in urban centers.

While civic knowledge among young people overall continues to sag, it is particularly low among young people who are less likely to go to college. The National Assessment of Educational Progress (NAEP) civics test, which is periodically administered to 8th- and 12th-grade American students, found that students whose parents had, at most, a high school diploma, scored 30 points or more below students whose parents achieved higher levels of education. Only 10% of students with parents with high school degrees or less were assessed as being proficient (Lutkus & Weiss, 2007).

Using the civic engagement framework that has guided this chapter and the research base we have presented, we describe the contextual civic opportunities available to NCBY.

Family

Family is important in the cultivation of civic behaviors and civic identity, whether through transmission of cultural norms or modeling of behaviors and attitudes (Dunham & Bengston, 1992; Flanagan et al., 1998; Fletcher, Elder, & Mekos, 2000; Zaff, Malanchuk, & Eccles, 2008).

Data consistently show that adults with lower educational attainment have lower rates of voting and volunteering, suggesting that young people in those families may not be receiving adequate civic socialization within their family system. Lower numbers of NCBY also report having fewer political discussions with parents, which is a strong predictor of civic knowledge (McIntosh et al., 2007).

Schools

Schools are obvious vehicles for conveying civic knowledge and stoking political interest and have, in many cases, helped to compensate for parents' lack of familiarity with the political system, such as students of parents who have emigrated from non-democratic settings.

Research, though, shows that students in high schools where the majority of young people are not headed for college are at a distinct disadvantage when it comes to having access to civic education, which, in an environment of scarce resources, is often viewed as less important than core subjects such as math and reading. A recent study of California public high schools, for example, reported a direct correlation between the number and quality of civics classes and the socioeconomic status of students these schools served, with higher levels of poverty having fewer civics classes (Kahne & Middaugh, 2008).

Teachers are also often reluctant to embrace civic education because they see it as "yet another add-on" to an already packed curriculum focused on science, math, and reading. Standards and testing regulations only add to that pressure to "teach to the test."

Teachers interested in civic education are often left to their own devices when trying to incorporate it into their classrooms, and there are few opportunities for these educators to obtain substantive training and support. When there are civics classes, these classes are less likely to involve democratic procedures such as teachers encouraging civil discussion of serious issues (Niemi & Junn, 1998).

It is not just civic classes that are frequently missing in high schools serving NCBY, but an array of enriching supplements that can facilitate learning and make civic-related content interesting to young people (Kahne & Middaugh, 2008). Among these are opportunities to discuss controversial issues, community service projects, participation in simulated political processes, and use of technology, among others (Gibson & Levine, 2003).

High schools serving NCBY also are less likely than high schools serving college-bound youth to have student governments, participation in which has been shown to increase the likelihood of civic engagement later in life (Hanks & Eckland, 1987; Verba, Schlozman, & Brady, 1995). Students in NCBY-predominant schools are also less likely (or be asked) to participate in helping to create school policy or rules. Students, for example, may be permitted to raise funds for the senior prom, but they are unlikely to partake in decisions regarding disciplinary issues that may emerge during that event (McFarland & Starrmans, 2007).

An analysis of New York City high schools underscores the sharp divisions between institutions serving NCBY and those serving college-bound youth (Devine, 1996).[5] In NCBY schools, classroom-based academic learning is formally segregated from the civic life occurring in public spaces inside and outside the school building.

While classroom instruction is managed by administration and teachers, the rest of the school environment is usually under the control of a non-teaching security force that monitors students' behavior and enforces disciplinary codes. Students tend to have little, if any, say regarding the disciplinary codes, and frequently find themselves at odds with a set of rules they perceive as arbitrary, impersonal, and unrelated to "real life."

This split between teaching functions and discipline offers young people few, if any, opportunities to integrate civic practice and learning into everyday social behavior. It also results in a woefully deficient civic atmosphere (Devine, 1996; Fine, 1994).

Thus, when the connection is made between practice and learning, it is hardly surprising that NCBY perform well. When NCBY are given opportunities to participate in school reform, they are able to focus on a host of issues that would improve the educational context, such as fair application of the disciplinary code, effective dealing with sexual harassment, and limiting the use of high-stakes tests that often penalize these students (Larson & Hansen, 2005; Sherman, 2002).

Neighborhood and System-Level Factors

"Place"—and the conditions place provides for civic development—has been relatively overlooked as an important factor contributing to civic socialization. Neighborhood wealth or poverty, the quality of municipal governance and services, and whether systems are functional or dysfunctional can and do encourage or impede civic engagement.

A study of the Baltimore-Washington region across several congressional districts, for example, revealed surprising

[5] The distinction between NCBY and CBY institutions was made by calculating the proportion of students who score highly on achievement scores and go on to college.

differences in young people's political knowledge and involvement in politics (Gimpel, Lay, & Schuknecht, 2003). Districts were compared according to the degree of competition in recent elections, which has been shown to be directly associated with socioeconomic status.

Areas with a preponderance of less-wealthy and less-educated citizens tended to have fewer contested elections, that is, many districts have long-serving, unchallenged elected officials, and are more prone to gerrymandering that ensures re-election of incumbents. Less electoral competition was associated with less knowledge about and involvement in politics. Young people living in less-competitive districts also had less interest in discussing political issues with family members, teachers, and peers.

Another factor associated with NCBY and lower SES is an unfavorable distribution of adults relative to children. In areas highly saturated with children, political knowledge among youth tends to suffer, compared to areas with higher proportions of adults (Hart & Kirshner, 2009). While one reason may be the lack of attention schools in low-income neighborhoods tend to pay to civic education, another is that the relative absence of adults, especially politically knowledgeable adults, diminishes opportunities for discussion of issues and political processes, including elections and campaigns (McIntosh, Youniss, & Hart, 2007).

In civic-deficient environments such as those prevalent in low-income areas, government and governmental institutions are often seen as uninviting and fraught with tension. Elected officials may feel safe enough in incumbency so as not to invite citizen participation. City workers representing the municipal government tend to act bureaucratically or impersonally, rather than respectfully, to community residents, whether the focus is motor vehicle registration or garbage collection. Police treatment of community residents—perceived or actual—can also influence whether and how people participate in civic life (Gimpel & Pearson-Merkowitz, 2009; Bourgoise, 1995; Hagedorn, 1988).

Work and Income

"Churn" was already common for young adults in the 1970s. However, for men, the decade between age 30 and age 40 has changed substantially; job "churn" is now much more common. This means that obtaining a lasting, full-time job—a traditional marker of full adulthood, at least for men—now lies far in the future or may not seem possible at all for Americans in their 20s.

If obtaining a stable job is delayed or never occurs, younger generations may be less likely to become stakeholders in local communities, owning property and sending their children to local schools. That could suppress political and civic engagement, or it could mean that the life cycle/local stakeholder model of political engagement will be outdated and that younger generations will get engaged in politics for causes or interest groups or via the Internet—and likely more episodically.

Rosch, Brinson, and Hassel, (2008) presented some sobering statistics about the growing numbers of 18- to 24-year-olds who are disconnected from society and its institutions. In 2003, 8% in this age group, 1.9 million, held no degree beyond high school, had no job, and was not enrolled in school. According to the report, this rate had increased to 8.7%, approximately 2.1 million young people, by 2006.

This is particularly pertinent considering the shift of the labor market—from middle to lower incomes, from career track to career dead-ends, from full benefits to few or no benefits, and from union to non-union jobs. This has had profound effects on whether and to what extent NCBY are able to connect to civic institutions.

Today, many NCBY have to take multiple jobs just to meet basic needs, making civic participation an implausible luxury (Gauthier & Furstenburg, 2005). Lack of a college degree carries a larger income penalty today than in the recent past. During the past three decades, the average hourly wage of high school dropouts declined by 16%.

Also, the income disparity between high school and college graduates grew from 1.5:1 to 2:1 (Heckman & Krueger, 2003). And, high school graduates' incomes have been hit harder than college graduates by periodic recessions (Hacker, 2008). As a result, many NCBY become part of the "working poor" whose top priorities are putting food on the table and a roof over their heads, rather than participating in community and national issues.[6]

The economic picture for communities of color is even more dire. Among African-American and Hispanic 18- to 24-year-olds, nearly 25% live in poverty. Less than 60% of African Americans ages 20 to 24 are employed (Current Population Survey, 2007). These income disparities present

[6] The distinction between NCBY and CBY institutions was made by calculating the proportion of students who score highly on achievement scores and go on to college.

even more daunting barriers to civic participation among African-American and Hispanic NCBY.

The national decline in union membership has been especially debilitating to NCBY's opportunities for civic engagement. Historically, unions have done more than guarantee living wages and benefits; they have created common bonds among members that often led to shared political goals and activities (Verba, Schlozman, & Brady, 1995). The demise of unions in traditional employment sectors and their nonexistence in other parts of the labor force has diminished these kinds of opportunities for employees to connect with one another, as well as with their employers, and thus, make them less likely to feel a sense of civic belonging.

Military

NCBY enlist in the military in far greater numbers than their college-bound peers. Today, more than 90% of recruits across branches are NCBY (Kane, 2006). Since its inception in 1973, the all-voluntary military has been attractive to NCBY for several reasons. It offers useful employment in contrast to working on and off in a series of dead-end jobs. It provides job training in mechanical, electronic, culinary, and other fields that can help lead to more lucrative employment (Bachmann, Freedman-Doan, & O'Malley, 2000). And it offers opportunities for enlistees to earn GEDs and college stipends.

The military also might be a particularly promising milieu in which to encourage civic engagement among NCBY. Civic lessons, for example, are part of the Initial Entry Training required of every enlistee and, thus, have the potential to be compensatory for NCBY who either dropped out of high school or attended schools with no civics classes (e.g., Kahne & Middaugh, 2008).

The effects of this training have not yet been proven definitively, but some studies suggest that they may be effective in enhancing civic participation. Enlistees also are provided with an introduction to what Boyte (2005) and others call "civic work"—work that requires action in service to one's community and country.

These and other opportunities can help lead to the likelihood of more civic engagement after active service. Moskos and Butler (1996), for example, report that African-American veterans have higher rates of marriage, employment, and income—the very factors that enhance civic attachment—than non-veterans. Teigen (2006) has found consistently higher rates of voting by veterans compared to non-veterans.

Integration into Community Life: Homeownership and Organizational Affiliations

Establishing permanent residency often leads to caring about and being involved in community-related issues (such as the quality of local schools and safety) (DiPasquale & Glaeser, 1998). While some residential mobility is expected during emerging adulthood, significant disparities exist between NCBY and college-bound youth regarding homeownership, and these disparities continue to grow (Gyourko & Linneman, 1997).

Communities of color, in particular, have substantially lower rates of homeownership than white households. Only 26% of African-American and 36% of Hispanic 25- to 34-year-olds own their homes, compared to 53% of whites in the same age group.

One of the central concerns about recent generations of emerging adults, especially NCBY, is their aversion to membership in traditional value-bearing institutions such as churches, affinity groups, social movements, and the like that play important roles in inculcating civic engagement (Settersten, Furstenburg, & Rumbaut, 2005).

Churches, in particular, have experienced membership declines among emerging adults who shy away from denominational "truths" they find exclusionary and, instead, gravitate toward what they believe are more inclusionary spiritual practices and beliefs (Arnett, 2005; Roof, 1993; Smith, 2007). Young adults, especially those who are NCBY, also are less likely to attend religious services on a regular basis,[7] further weakening their ties with these kinds of community institutions.

Continuity in service engagement during the young adult years shows a positive and significant relationship with the likelihood that youth, including those from economically disadvantaged families, will make educational progress over a 4-year period. Finlay and Flanagan (2009) conducted secondary analyses of a national study of young people who participated in AmeriCorps programs and their peers who investigated the program but did not join AmeriCorps. They found that over the 4 years of the study, those youth who increased their educational attainment were more likely than their peers who made no progress to have consistently engaged in service, whether in AmeriCorps or not.

---

[7] Based on original analysis of Monitoring the Future data by staff at Child Trends. For more information, see http://www.childtrendsdatabank.org.

Technology and New Media

Some believe that focusing on declining participation in traditional institutions fails to account for new civic venues to which emerging adults are gravitating, most notably, Internet-based forms of social life. Today, emerging adults are using cell phones, websites, Facebook/MySpace, and other media tools to connect with peers and the world around them.

Among college- and non–college-attending youth, there were smaller gaps in certain forms of online engagement. For example, 57% of young adults with college experience, and 52% of young adults without college experience, said that they had used social networking sites such as MySpace or Facebook to address social issues. On six measures of online engagement, college youth were ahead of non-college youth, but these gaps were notably smaller than the gaps in traditional forms of engagement that were observed in the same survey (see Figure 15.9). Use of social media is already extremely high and this usage crosses racial/ethnic and socioeconomic lines. Thus, the Internet holds a potential path for all Americans to be involved in the democratic process, even when traditional avenues for such participation are not as clearly marked or open to all.

These forms of interaction are, in turn, driving changes in the way people communicate, stay connected, and obtain information. A "digital divide," however, still exists. Only 59% of those with a high school diploma and 36% of those with less have access to any form of the Internet at home (Pew Research Center for the People and the Press, 2008).

These groups also are less likely to have broadband access—34 and 21%, respectively (Horrigan & Smith, 2008). And while some reports conclude that Internet access at schools is helping to close this gap among primary and secondary school students (DeBell & Chapman, 2003), there is still no indication that non-school time with computers and the Internet will be focused on academic or civic-related activities.

For those who do have Internet access, there are increasing venues through which to engage in civic or political efforts—for example, Causes on Facebook, Change.org, Razoo, and political blogs, as well as cell phones and texting. Young people, for example, used online social networks and tools to "engage in one of the most contentious techno-political issues today, with more than 17,000 of them signing up as 'friends of network neutrality on MySpace'" (Rheingold, 2007; Montgomery, 2007). The thousands of young people who left their offices and schools in early 2006 to participate in immigration marches were fueled less by formal organizations and more by the buzz created among peers using cell phones, text messaging, and blogs (Fine, 2006).

Moreover, young people's participation through technology is highly interactive, with more than 50% of today's teenagers creating their own digital media through blogs, wikis, RSS, tagging, mashups, podcasts, videoblogs, and virtual communities (Rheingold, 2007; Lenhart & Madden, 2006). This penchant for media production, some argue, can and should be used to generate more political and civic involvement, but it will require the cooperation of traditional institutions such as schools to facilitate this process

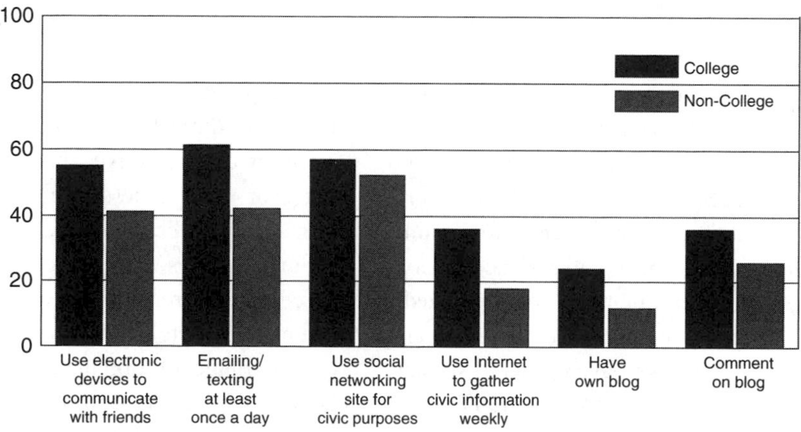

Figure 15.9 Online civic engagement, 18- to 30-year-olds.

since the latter are where the majority of young people learn about democracy and other political processes.

Given that NCBY are less likely to have access to new technologies in schools—especially those that allow for self-expression—and/or curricula and programs that encourage the use of these technologies, there are serious questions about whether and to what extent NCBY will be able to engage as fully as they might through the relatively low-cost and accessible venues that these tools provide (Rheingold, 2007).

Others maintain that the jury is still out about whether these new media have enhanced (or have the potential to replace) traditional avenues of engagement for young people in general, or whether they will continue to be used primarily for socializing with friends and others (Fine, 2008). There are also questions as to whether these social media will attract only the "usual suspects," that is, emerging adults who are already predisposed to political engagement (Stolle & Hooghe, 2005; Levine, 2007) and who are more likely to be college-bound youth.

Agency and Opportunity for College Attenders

Among NCBY, many perceive the political system and politics to be profoundly irrelevant and unresponsive to their needs and to those of their communities. A recent nationally representative study, for example, showed that two-thirds of NCBY surveyed said they believed they could "make little difference in politics," compared to only one-third of college-bound youth. Fewer NCBY than college-bound youth also considered voting to be important or a duty (Lopez, Kirby, & Sagoff, 2005). The result is a circular problem: NCBY are not tapped for political participation so they are less likely to be involved or vote. In turn, the political parties and other political organizations are much less likely to engage NCBY because they are less inclined to vote. The mutually reinforcing set of institutions (e.g., family, schools, workplace, churches, civic organizations, and informal community networks) that used to help instill a sense of civic identity has become fractured for NCBY. Family ties have weakened. Schools have pared down curricula to convey basics, neglecting the civics curriculum and opportunities for service-learning experiences. Jobs increasingly have become impermanent, non-unionized, and low paying. Membership in voluntary associations has waned. And, informal networks have clustered so that NCBY interact more narrowly with one another rather than being extended outward to people with more resources.

On the other hand, for those who are in college, they are more likely to be in settings where (1) they accrue resources (knowledge about issues and the wherewithal to take action); (2) they are recruited (someone asks them to join an organization or invites them to a community meeting); and (3) there are normative pressures to participate in community affairs (because others around them are participating). But the growing social class divide in civic participation in recent years is due in part to the loss of institutions where members of the working class get recruited into political action. In young adulthood it is more incumbent on individuals to identify those opportunities; and for those who do not go on to 4-year colleges, there are fewer institutions where they can garner resources and get recruited.

Importantly, it is not the mere fact of being in college that produces civic benefits but rather the exposure to different perspectives and the pressure to come to grips with them that helps youth crystallize their own views. As social movement literature has documented, for civic engagement in one's youth to have lifelong effects, one has to actively wrestle with the issues rather than watch from the sidelines. Citizenship figures prominently in most college mission statements and, in recent years, courses with a community service component have been on the rise. At the same time, universities have enacted policies that restrict the range of backgrounds and perspectives their students will naturally encounter. For example, computer matching services to help new students find roommates who are similar to them are now common practice. To improve their standing with peer institutions, universities seek students with high standardized test scores and attract them by increasing the proportion of merit versus need-based scholarships and providing small "honors" colleges within the larger public university.

Nonetheless, being in college (or other institutional settings such as work, faith-based organizations, etc.) enhances the likelihood of recruitment into civic activity. Verba, Schlozman, and Brady (1995) show that variation in civic participation among American adults can be explained by three factors: the fact that citizens who have *resources* can be active, those who are *engaged* are motivated or want to be active, and those who are *recruited* often say yes when asked. College plays a role in at least two and perhaps all three of these: Youth with more resources are more likely to attend college, and additional political contacts and resources accrue with education. A wide range of organizations, clubs, and associations also are a typical part of student life, and participation in such groups has both social and civic pay-offs. Student members of organizations are likely to get recruited into community volunteer work or political activity even if the primary purpose of their organization is social. Civic skills and dispositions may accrue as a consequence of their volunteer work. It is less clear that college attendance impacts the motivation for civic participation. However, college attendance does seem to sustain the civic engagement of the highly motivated by offering structured opportunities for staying engaged.

CONCLUSIONS

There are several points to consider from the available research on the development of civic engagement. The available literature suggests that there are associations between civic engagement and individual, parental, and societal-level factors. Also, programs that are effective, at least in the short term, use multiple strategies. Therefore, programs should consider using strategies that address the multiple contexts of an adolescent's environment in order to maximize effectiveness. Examples of points of intervention could be adolescents' motivation to act as positive citizens, adolescents' values, adolescents' role models, and adolescents' socialization (i.e., the community and culture in which youth are raised). A firm appreciation for an individual's cultural context is important to ensure that the programs are relevant to the individual's life and therefore more likely to engage the individual substantively.

Individuals need to feel engaged in activities. Having youth who are placed into boring volunteer positions will inevitably ensure that they probably will not want to volunteer again. Allowing youth to be part of the planning process of programs and providing ongoing input into the workings of organizations is one strategy that research suggests helps to engage youth. In addition, providing youth (and adults) with easy opportunities to become involved appears to increase greatly the likelihood that they will become involved.

Programs should continue over the long term. Encouraging civic engagement is not a "one-shot deal." The intensity and duration of programs is important, as well—not just how many hours per week, but also how many weeks or months of participation.

Basic measurements of civic engagement need to be developed that capture the breadth of behaviors, attitudes, and skills that represent all backgrounds. There is no consensus on how to define or measure civic engagement for all individuals. For this chapter, we focused on volunteering/community service, political participation, and activism as broad indicators of political engagement and community service. However, the quality of these broad indicators might very well vary based on an individual's context and personal values. For instance, the peaceful activism of Martin Luther King, Jr. and Mahatma Gandhi is just as civic as the violent revolution of George Washington or the force used by Winston Churchill. Even within categories of civic engagement, definitions and measurement can be an issue. Community service, for instance, can include playing within a given system, such as working with schools to improve the educational instruction, or can include playing against the system, such as youth from low-income communities voicing their opposition to the way that schools are treating them. Both provide an important service to a given community, but the latter is often neglected in civic measurement.

Non-participation in civic activities can deepen the cycle of civic exclusion. For example, considerable data indicate that when parents don't vote, their children are much less likely to vote (Plutzer, 2002), resulting in a cycle of voter apathy unless intentional efforts are made to bring young people into the booth. If, for instance, NCBY do not become civically involved now, there is a high likelihood that their children will not be involved later.

Youth is a critical period for civic and political socialization. Although the ages of 16 to 24 are not the only time period during which political and civic identities are shaped, they are a particularly fertile window in which lifelong civic habits are formed (Mannheim, 1952; Flanagan & Faison, 2001). If this developmentally opportune moment is missed, it is highly likely that compensatory steps will need to be taken to ensure the same results. Starting even earlier with age-appropriate programs, such as in the elementary and middle school years, could provide a strong base for later involvement. More research is needed to understand how such early experiences benefit later civic engagement.

Civic engagement opportunities contribute to youth development overall. Much research indicates that young people will not achieve their full potential as adult citizens if they are not given the support and opportunities needed to encourage their civic and political participation during childhood and adolescence (Lerner, 2002). Disadvantaged environments are often unable to provide or support firsthand experiences in public discussion of community issues, meeting with public officials, participation in student government, or having one's views sought out by municipal officials. In the United States, for example, African-American youth have lower average levels of income and education than their white counterparts;

yet, they surpass whites on most measures of civic engagement, due, at least in some part, to traditions, norms, and institutions that promote participation in the black community (Lopez et al., 2006; Levine, 2007). Research could provide a deeper understanding about how these civic experiences further promote positive developmental trajectories.

Data resources need to be developed that enable a more robust longitudinal analysis across the life span. Aside from a select few studies (e.g., Jennings, 1993), there are few studies on civic engagement development that have followed youth from adolescence into later adulthood. Even fewer, or none, have consistently tracked the contexts and civic development across time. Without such data sources, researchers are left with a piecemeal picture of the developmental process. We do not know, for instance, why there is a decrease in a generational gap in civic involvement once cohorts reach their 30s. Having such studies across nations would enable analyses that could start to disentangle national-level effects on individual engagement.

More rigorous experimental studies are needed on the impact of civic engagement interventions, especially for NCBY and non–college-attending youth and adults. As seen in this chapter, there is much known about the factors that predict the development of civic engagement. There is not, however, a firm understanding about converting these predictors into actionable programs, especially programs that address the unique needs of groups at a higher risk for not becoming civically engaged. For any program evaluation, we recommend for long-term follow-ups since the effects of most programs that we mention in this chapter dissipate after relatively short periods, such as a 1-year post-program. Following program participants over time would also enable researchers to understand whether the effects have fully dissipated or whether there is a civic moratorium at certain developmental periods, possibly followed by an upswing in civic activity.

REFERENCES

Abrams, D., Rutland, A., & Cameron, L. (2003). The development of group dynamics: Children's judgments of normative and deviant in-group and out-group individuals. *Child Development, 74,* 1840–1856.

Alford, J. R., Funk, C. L., & Hibbing, J. R. (2005). Are political orientations genetically transmitted? *American Political Science Review, 99,* 153–167.

Allahyari, R. A. (2000). *Visions of charity: Volunteer workers and moral community.* Berkeley: University of California Press.

Allen, J., Philliber, P., Herrling, S., & Kuperminc, G. P. (1997). Preventing teenage pregnancy and academic failure. *Child Development, 64,* 729–742.

Alwin, D. F., Cohen, R. L., & Newcomb, T. M. (1991). *Political attitudes over the life span: The Bennington Women after fifty years.* Madison: University of Wisconsin Press.

Alwin, D. F., & Krosnick, J. A. (1991). Aging, cohorts, and the stability of sociopolitical orientations over the life span. *American Journal of Sociology, 97,* 169–195.

Arnett, J. (2005). *Emerging adulthood: The winding road from the late teens through the twenties.* New York: Oxford University Press.

Asendorpf, J. B., & van Aken, M. A. G. (1999). Resilient, overcontrolled, and undercontrolled personality prototypes in childhood: Replicability, predictive power, and trait-type issue. *Journal of Personality and Social Psychology, 77,* 815–832.

Astin, W. A., Sax, L. J., & Avalos, J. (1999). Long-term effects of volunteerism during the undergraduate years. *Review of Higher Education, 22,* 187–202.

Avrahami, A., & Dar, Y. (1993). Collectivistic and individualistic motives among kibbutz youth volunteering for community service. *Journal of Youth and Adolescence, 22,* 697–714.

Bachmann, J. G., Freedman-Doan, P., & O'Malley, P. M. (2000). Should U.S. military recruits write-off the college-bound? *Armed Forces and Society, 27,* 461–476.

Baltes, P. B. (1987). Theoretical propositions of life-span developmental psychology: On the dynamics between growth and decline. *Developmental Psychology, 23,* 611–625.

Baltes, P. B., Lindenberger, U., & Staudinger, U. M. (2006). Life span theory in developmental psychology. In R. M. Lerner & W. Damon (Eds.), *Handbook of Child Psychology: Vol 1. Theoretical models of human development* (6th ed., pp. 569–664). Hoboken, NJ: John Wiley & Sons.

Barrett, M., Wilson, H., & Lyons, E. (2003). The development of national in-group bias: English children's attributions of characteristics to English, American, and German people. *British Journal of Developmental Psychology, 21,* 193–220.

Batson, C., & Shaw, L. (1991). Encouraging words concerning the evidence for altruism. *Psychological Inquiry, 2,* 159–168.

Baumeister, R. F., & Leary, M. R. (1995). The need to belong: Desire for interpersonal attachments as a fundamental human motivation. *Psychological Bulletin, 117,* 497–529.

Beane, J., Turner, J., Jones, D., & Lipka, R. (1981). Long-term effects of community service programs. *Curriculum Inquiry, 11,* 143–155.

Bennett, D. (2003). Doing disservice: The benefits and limits of volunteerism. *The American Prospect, 14.* Available at: http://www.prospect.org.

Bennett M., Barrett, M., Karakozov, R., Kipiani, G., Lyons, E., Pavlenko, V., & Riazanova, T. (2004). Young children's evaluations of the ingroup and of outgroups: A multi-national study. *Social Development, 13,* 124–141.

Berry, J. W., Phinney, J. S., Sam, D. L., & Vedder, P. (2006). Immigrant youth: Acculturation, identity, and adaptation. *Applied Psychology: An International Review, 55,* 303–332.

Bourgeois, P. (1995). *In search of respect: Selling crack in el barrio.* New York: Cambridge University Press.

Boyte, H. (2005). *Everyday politics: reconnecting citizens and public life.* Philadelphia: University of Pennsylvania Press.

Brandtstädter, J. (1998). Action perspectives on human development. In R. M. Lerner (Ed.), *Handbook of child psychology.* Vol. 1: *Theoretical models of human development* (5th ed., pp. 807-863). Editor in chief: W. Damon. New York: John Wiley & Sons.

Brandtstädter, J. (2006). Action perspectives on human development. In R. M. Lerner & W. Damon (Eds.), *Theoretical models of human development: Vol. 1. Handbook of child psychology* (6th ed., pp. 516–568). Hoboken, NJ: John Wiley & Sons.

Brewer, M. B. (1999). The psychology of prejudice: Ingroup love or outgroup hate. *Journal of Social Issues, 55*, 429–444.

Bronfenbrenner, U., & Ceci, S. J. (1993). Heredity, environment, and the question "how?": A first approximation. In R. Plomin & G. E. McClearn (Eds.), *Nature, nurture & psychology* (pp. 313–324). Washington, DC: American Psychological Association.

Calabrese, R., & Schumer, H. (1986). The effects of service activities on adolescent alienation. *Adolescence, 21,* 675–687.

Caspi, A., & Silva, P. (1995). Temperamental qualities at age three predict personality traits in young adulthood: Longitudinal evidence from a birth cohort. *Child Development, 66,* 486–498.

Caspi, A., Sugden, K., Moffitt, T. E., Taylor, A., Craig, I. W., Harrington, H. L., et al. (2003). Influence of life stress on depression: Moderation by a polymorphism in the 5-HTT gene. *Science 301,* 386–389.

Center for Human Resources. (1999). Summary report national evaluation of Learn and Serve America. Waltham, MA: Brandeis University Center for Human Resources.

Chang Weir, R., & Gjerde, P. F. (2002). Preschool personality prototypes: Internal coherence, cross-study replicability, and developmental outcomes in adolescence. *Personality and Social Psychology Bulletin, 28,* 1229–1241.

Chapman, B. (2002). A bad idea whose time is past: The case against universal service. *The Brookings Review, 20,* 10–13.

Clary, E. G., Snyder, M., & Stukas, A. (1996). Volunteers' motivations: Findings from a national survey. *Nonprofit and Voluntary Sector Quarterly, 25,* 485–505.

Colby, A., & Damon, W. (1995). The development of extraordinary moral commitment. In M. Killen & D. Hart (Eds.), *Morality in everyday life: Developmental perspectives* (pp. 342–370). New York: Cambridge University Press.

Comber, M. K. (2003). Civic curriculum and civic skills. *CIRCLE Fact Sheet.* Medford, MA: Center for Information and Research on Civic Learning and Engagement.

Conrad, D., & Hedin, D. (1982). The impact of experimental education on adolescent development. *Child and Youth Services, 4,* 57–76.

Conway, M. M. (2000). *Political participation in the United States* (3rd ed.). Washington, DC: CQ Press.

Crystal, D. S., & DeBell, M. (2002). Sources of civic orientation among American youth: Trust, religion, valuation, and attributions of responsibility. *Political Psychology, 23*, 113–132.

Current Population Survey. (2007). Table 1. Reported Internet usage for households, by selected householder characteristics: 2007. Washington, DC: U.S. Census Bureau. Available at: http://www.census.gov/population/www/socdemo/computer/2007.html.

Dalton, R. J. (2006). *Citizenship norms and political participation in America: The good news is ... the bad news is wrong*. Occasional Paper 2006–01. Washington, DC: Center for Democracy and Civil Society, Georgetown University.

Davis, M., Mitchell, K., Hall, J., Lothert, J., Snapp, T., & Meyer, M. (1999). Empathy, expectations, and situational preferences: Personality influences on the decision to participate in volunteer helping behaviors. *Journal of Personality, 67,* 469–503.

Dawson, R. E., & Prewitt, K. (1969). *Political socialization*. Boston: Little, Brown.

DeBell, M., & Chapman, C. (2003). Computer and Internet use by children and adolescents in 2001. Washington, DC: National Center for Educational Statistics, U.S. Department of Education.

Delli Carpini, M. (1989). Age and history: Generations and sociopolitical change. In R. S. Sigel (Ed.), *Political learning in adulthood* (pp. 11–55). Chicago: University of Chicago Press.

Delli Carpini, M. X., & Keeter, S. (1996). *What Americans know about politics and why it matters*. New Haven, CT: Yale University Press.

Devine, J. (1996). *Maximum security: The culture of violence in inner-city schools*. Chicago: University of Chicago Press.

DiPasquale, D., & Glaeser, E. L. (1998). Incentives and social capital: Are homeowners better citizens? Working Paper 6363. Cambridge, MA: National Bureau of Economic Research.

Duffy, A. L., & Nesdale, D. (2009). Peer groups, social identity, and children's bullying behavior. *Social Development, 18,* 121–139.

Duncan, L. E., & Stewart, A. J. (1995). Still bringing the Vietnam war home: Sources of contemporary student activism. *Personality and Social Psychology Bulletin, 18,* 147–158.

Duncan, G. J., Kalil, A., & Ziol-Guest, K. M. (2008). *Economic costs of early childhood poverty*. Washington, DC: Partnership for Success.

Dunham, C. C., & Bengtson, V. L. (1992). The long-term effects of political activism on intergenerational relations. *Youth & Society, 24,* 31–51.

Durlak, J. A., & Weissberg, R. P. (2006). *The impact of after-school programs that seek to promote personal and social skills*. Chicago: Collaborative for Academic, Social, and Emotional Learning. Available at: http://www.casel.org.

Easton, D., & Dennis, J. (1969). *Children in the political system*. New York: McGraw-Hill.

Eccles, J. S., Midgley, C., Wigfield, A., Buchanan, C. M., Reuman, D., Flanagan, C., & Iver, D. M. (1993). Development during adolescence: The impact of stage-environment fit on young adolescents' experiences in schools and in families. *American Psychologist, 48,* 90–101.

Eisenberg, N. (2000). Emotion, regulation, and moral development. *Annual Review of Psychology, 51,* 665–697.

Eisenberg, N. (2003). Empathy, sympathy and prosocial behaviors. In M. Bornstein, C. Keyes, K. Moore, & L. Davidson (Eds.), *Well-being: Positive development across the lifespan* (pp. 253–265). Mahwah, NJ: Erlbaum.

Eisenberg, N., & Fabes, R. (1998). Prosocial development. In N. Eisenberg (Ed.), *Handbook of child psychology: Vol. 3. Social, emotional, and personality development* (pp. 701–778). New York: John Wiley & Sons.

Erikson, E. H. (1963). *Childhood and society*. New York: W. W. Norton.

Erikson, E. H. (1966). Eight ages of man. *International Journal of Psychiatry, 2*, 281–300.

Erikson, E. H. (1968). *Identity: Youth and crisis*. New York: W. W. Norton.

Eyler, J., & Giles, D. E., Jr. (1999). *Where's the learning in service-learning?* San Francisco: Jossey-Bass Publishers.

Fendrich. J. M. (1993). *Ideal citizens: The legacy of the civil rights movement*. Albany: State University of New York Press.

Fendrich J. M., & Lovoy, K. L. (1988). Back to the future: Adult political behavior of former student activists. *American Sociological Review, 53,* 780–784.

Fine, A. (2006). Allison Fine, interview, June 21, 2006.

Fine, A. (2008). *Social citizens, beta*. Washington, DC: Case Foundation.

Fine, M. (1994). *Charting urban school reform: Reflections on public high schools in the midst of change*. New York: Teachers College Press.

Finlay, A., & Flanagan, C., (2009). Making educational progress: Links to civic engagement during the transition to adulthood. CIRCLE Working Paper. Medford, MA: Center for Information and Research on Civic Learning and Engagement.

Finn, C. E., & Vanourek, G. (1995). Charity begins at school. *Commentary, 100,* 46–53.

Fisher, K., Yan, Z., & Stewart, J. (2003). Adult cognitive development: Dynamics in the developmental web. In J. Valsiner & K. J. Connolly (Eds.), *Handbook of developmental psychology*. Thousand Oaks, CA: Sage.

Flanagan, C. (2003). Trust, identity, and civic hope. *Applied Developmental Science 7,* 165–171.

Flanagan, C. A., Bowes, J., Jonsson, B., Csapo, B., & Sheblanova, E. (1998). Ties that bind: Correlates of adolescents' civic commitments in seven countries. *Journal of Social Issues, 54,* 457–475.

Flanagan, C. A., & Campbell, B. (in press). Social class and adolescents' beliefs about justice in different social orders. *Journal of Social Issues.*

Flanagan, C., Cumsille, P., Gill, S., & Gallay, L. (2007). School and community climates and civic commitments: Processes for ethnic minority and majority students. *Journal of Educational Psychology, 99,* 421–431.

Flanagan, C., & Faison, N. (2001). *Youth civic development.* Policy Report. Ann Arbor, MI: Society for Research in Child Development.

Flanagan, C., & Gallay, L. (1995). Reframing the meaning of "political" in research with adolescents. *Perspectives on Political Science, 24,* 34–41.

Flanagan, C. A., Gallay, L. S., Gill, S., Gallay, E., & Nti, N. (2005). What does democracy mean? Correlates of adolescents' views. *Journal of Adolescent Research, 20,* 193–218.

Flanagan, C., Levine, P., & Stettersten, R. (2008). *Civic engagement and the changing transition to adulthood.* Medford, MA: The Center for Information and Research on Civic Learning and Engagement, Jonathan M. Tisch College of Citizenship and Public Service, and Tufts University.

Flanagan, C. A., & Stout, M. (in press). Developmental patterns of social trust between early and late adolescence: Age and school climate effects. *Journal of Research on Adolescence.*

Flanagan, C., A., Syvertsen, A. K., Gill, S., Gallay, L. S., & Cumsille, P. (2009). Ethnic awareness, prejudice, and civic commitments in four ethnic groups of American adolescents. *Journal of Youth and Adolescence, 38,* 500–518.

Flanagan, C. A., & Tucker, C. J. (1999). Adolescents' explanations for political issues: Concordance with their views of self and society. *Developmental Psychology, 35,* 1198–1209.

Fletcher, A., Elder, G., & Mekos, D. (2000). Parental influences on adolescent involvement in community activities. *Journal of Research on Adolescence, 10,* 29–48.

Foster-Bey, J. (2008). *Do race, ethnicity, citizenship and socio-economic status determine civic engagement?* CIRCLE Working Paper #62. Medford, MA: Center for Information and Research on Civic Learning and Engagement.

Fowler, J. H., Baker, L. A., & Dawes, C. T. (2008). The genetic basis of political participation. *American Political Science Review, 102,* 233–248.

Fowler, J. H., & Dawes, C. T. (2008). Two genes predict voter turnout. *Journal of Politics, 70,* 579–594.

Freund, A. M., & Baltes, P. B. (2002). Life-management strategies of selection, optimization and compensation: Measurement by self-report and construct validity. *Journal of Personality and Social Psychology, 82,* 642–662.

Friedland, L. A., & Morimoto, S. (2005). The changing lifeworld of young people: Risk, resume-padding, and civic engagement. Working Paper 40. Medford, MA: Center for Information and Research on Civic Learning and Engagement. Available at: http://www.civicyouth.org/PopUps/WorkingPapers/WP40Friedland.pdf.

Galston, W. A. (2001). Political knowledge, political engagement, and civic education. *Annual Review of Political Science, 4,* 217–234.

Garvey, J., McIntyre-Craig, C., & Myers, C. (2000). Youth voice: The essential element of service-learning. In C. Myers, & M. Bellener (Eds.), *Embedding service-learning into teacher education: Issue briefs*. Indianapolis, IN: Center for Youth as Resources.

Gauthier, A. H., & Furstenberg, F. F., Jr. (2005). Historical trends in patterns of time use among youth in developed countries. In R. A. Settersten, F. F. Furstenberg, Jr., & R. G. Rumaut (Eds.), *On the frontier of adulthood* (pp. 150–176). Chicago: University of Chicago Press.

Gibson, C., & Levine, P. (2003). *The civic mission of schools.* Report for Carnegie Corporation. New York: Carnegie Corporation.

Gimpel, J. G., Lay, C., & Schuknecht, J. E. (2003). *Cultivating democracy: Civic environments and political socialization in America.* Washington, DC: Brookings Institution Press.

Gimpel, J. G., & Pearson-Merkowitz, S. (2009). Policies for civic engagement beyond the schoolyard. In J. Youniss & P. Levine (Eds.), *Engaging young people in civic life.* Nashville, TN: Vanderbilt University Press.

Ginwright, S. A. (2007). Black youth activism and the role of critical social capital in black community organizations. *American Behavioral Scientist, 51,* 403–418.

Glanville, J. (1999). Political socialization of selection? Adolescent extracurricular participation and political activity in early adulthood. *Social Science Quarterly, 80,* 279–290.

Goldstone, J. A. (2002). Population and security: How demographic change can lead to violent conflict. *Journal of International Affairs, 56,* 3–23.

Gordon, C. W., & Babchuk, N. (1959). A typology of voluntary associations. *American Sociological Review, 24,* 22–29.

Green, D. P., Gerber, A. S., & Nickerson, D. W. (2003). Getting out the vote in local elections: Results from six door-to-door canvassing experiments. *Journal of Politics, 65,* 1083–1096.

Gyourko, J., & Linneman, P. (1997). The changing influence of education, income, family structure and race on homeownership by age over time. *Journal of Housing Research, 8,* 1–25.

Hacker, J. S. (2008). Income volatility: Jacob Hacker responds to the CBO. *Economist's View*, January 19, 2008.

Hagedorn, J. M. (1988). *People and folks: gangs, crime, and the underclass in a rust belt city.* Chicago, IL: Lakeview Press.

Hahn, A. (1994). Extending the time of learning. In D.J. Besharov (Ed.), *America's disconnected youth: Toward a preventative strategy* (pp. 233–266). Washington, DC: CWLA Press and American Enterprise Institute for Public Policy Research.

Hahn, A., Leavitt, T., & Aaron, P. (1994). *Evaluation of the quantum opportunities program: Did the program work?* Waltham, MA: Brandeis University.

Hanks, M. (1981). Youth, voluntary associations and political socialization. *Social Forces, 60,* 211–223.

Hanks, R., & Eckland, B. K. (1987). Adult voluntary associations. *Sociology Quarterly, 19,* 481–490.

Hart, D. (2005). The development of moral identity. In G. Carlo & C. P. Edwards (Eds.), *Nebraska Symposium on Motivation.* Vol. 51: *Moral motivation through the lifespan* (pp. 165–196). Lincoln: University of Nebraska Press.

Hart, D., Atkins, R., & Fegley, S. (2003). Personality and development in childhood: A person-centered approach. *Monographs of the Society for Research in Child Development, 68* (1, Serial No. 272). Ann Arbor, MI: Society for Research in Child Development.

Hart, D., Atkins, R., & Ford, D. (1999). Family influences on the formation of moral identity in adolescence: Longitudinal analyses. *Journal of Moral Education, 28,* 375–386.

Hart, D., Atkins, R., Markey, P., & Youniss, J. (2004). Youth bulges in communities: The effects of age structure on adolescent civic knowledge and civic participation. *Psychological Science, 15,* 591–597.

Hart, D., Donnelly, T. M., Youniss, J., & Atkins, R. (2007). High school community service as a predictor of adult voting and volunteering. *American Educational Research Journal, 44,* 197–219.

Hart, D., & Gullan, R. (in press). The sources of adolescent activism: Historical and contemporary findings. In L. Sherrod, J. Torney-Purta, & C. Flanagan (Eds.), *Handbook of research and policy on civic engagement in youth.* Hoboken, NJ: John Wiley & Sons.

Hart, D., Hofmann, V., Edelstein, W., & Keller, M. (1997). The relation of childhood personality types to adolescent behavior and development: A longitudinal study. *Developmental Psychology, 33,* 195–205.

Hart, D., & Kirshner, B. (2009). "Promoting civic participation and development among urban adolescents." In J. Youniss & P. Levine (Eds.), *Engaging young people in civic life.* Nashville, TN: Vanderbilt University Press.

Hart, D., Yates, M., Fegley, S., & Wilson, G. (1995). Moral commitment in inner-city adolescents. In M. Killen & D. Hart (Eds.), *Morality in everyday life* (pp. 371–407). New York: Cambridge University Press.

Harvard Family Research Project. (2007). Findings from HFRP's study of predictors of participation in out-of-school time activities: Fact sheet. Cambridge, MA: Harvard Graduate School of Education.

Hashway, R. (1998). *Assessment and evaluation of developmental learning: Qualitative individual assessment and evaluation models.* Westport, CT: Praeger.

Heckman, J.J., & Krueger, A. (2004). *Inequality in America: What role for human capital policies?* Cambridge, MA: MIT Press.

Helgerson, J. L. (2002). The national security implications of global demographic change: Proposed remarks to the Denver World Affairs Council and the Better World Campaign, Denver, CO, April 30. Available at: http://www.dni.gov/nic/speeches_demochange.html.

Hess, D. (2009). *Controversy in the classroom: The democratic power of discussion.* New York: Routledge.

Hoffman, M. L. (1975). Moral internalization, parental power, and the nature of the parent–child interaction. *Developmental Psychology, 11,* 228–239.

Horn, L., & Nu–ez, A. M. (2000). *Mapping the road to college: First-generation students' math track, planning strategies, and context of support.* Washington, DC: National Center for Education Statistics.

Horrigan, J., & Smith, A. (2008). *Home broadband adoption, 2008.* Washington, DC: Pew Internet and American Life Project.

Huntington, S. (1996). *The clash of civilizations and the remaking of world order.* New York: Simon & Schuster.

Hyman, H. H. (1959). *Political socialization: A study of the psychology of political behavior.* Glencoe, NY: Free Press.

Jennings, K. M. (1993). Education and political development among young adults. *Politics & the Individual, 3,* 1–24.

Jennings, M. K. (2002). Generation units and the student protest movement in the United States: An intra- and inter-generational analysis. *Political Psychology, 23,* 303–324.

Jennings M. K., & Stoker, L. (2002). Generational change, life cycle processes, and social capital. Paper prepared for a workshop on Citizenship on Trial: Interdisciplinary Perspectives on the Political Socialization of Adolescents. McGill University, Montreal, Canada.

Jennings, M. K., & Stoker, L. (2004). Social trust and civic engagement across time and generations. *Acta Politica, 39,* 342–379.

Jensen, L. A., & Flanagan, C. A. (2008). Immigrant civic engagement: New translations. *Applied Developmental Science, 12,* 55–56.

Johnson, M., Beebe, T., Mortimer, J., & Snyder, M. (1998). Volunteerism in adolescence: A process perspective. *Journal of Research on Adolescence, 8,* 309–331.

Johnston, L. D., Bachman, J. G., & O'Malley, P. M. (1999). *Monitoring the future: Questionnaire responses from the nation's high school seniors.* Ann Arbor, MI: University of Michigan Institute for Social Research.

Kahne, J., & Middaugh, E. (2008). Democracy for some: The civic opportunity gap in high school. Working Paper. 59. College Park: Center for Information and Research in Civic Learning and Engagement, University of Maryland.

Kahne, J. E., & Sporte, S. E. (2008). Developing citizens: The impact of civic learning opportunities on students' commitment to civic participation. *American Educational Research Association Journal.* Article 10.3102. Available at: http://www.aerj.aera.net.

Kane, T. (2006). *Who are the recruits? The demographic characteristics of U.S. military enlistment.* Washington, DC: Heritage Foundation.

Kasser, T., Ryan, R., Zax, M., & Sameroff, A. (1995). The relations of maternal and social environments to late adolescents' materialistic and prosocial values. *Developmental Psychology, 31,* 907-914.

Katula, M. C. (2000). Successful characteristics of service-learning: Results from the field. In C. Meyers & M. Bellner (Eds.), *Embedding service-learning into teacher education: Issue briefs.* Indianapolis, IN: The Center for Youth as Resources.

Kauffman, P., Alt, M., & Chapman, C. (2004). *Dropout rates in the U.S.* Washington, DC: U.S. Department of Education, National Center for Education Statistics.

Kauffman, S., & Poulin, J. (1994). Citizen participation in prevention activities: A path model. *Journal of Community Psychology, 22,* 359–374.

Kawachi, I., Kennedy, B. P., Lochner, K., & Prothrow-Stith, D. (1997). Social capital, income inequality, and mortality. *American Journal of Public Health, 87,* 1491–1498.

Kirlin, M. K. (2003a). *The role of adolescent extracurricular activities in adult political engagement.* Medford, MA: Center for Information and Research on Civic Learning and Engagement. Available at: http://www.civicyouth.org.

Kirlin, M. K. (2003b). *The role of civic skills in fostering civic engagement.* Medford, MA: Center for Information and Research on Civic Learning and Engagement. Available at: http://www.civicyouth.org.

Kirshner, B. (2007). Introduction: Youth activism as a context for learning and development. *American Behavioral Scientist, 51,* 367–379.

Krampen, G., (2000). Transition of adolescent political action orientations to voting behavior in early adulthood in view of a social-cognitive action theory model of personality. *Political Psychology, 21,* 277–297.

Larson, R., & Hansen, D. (2005). The development of strategic thinking: Learning to impact human systems in a youth activism program. *Human Development, 48,* 327–349.

Latané, B., Liu, J. H., Nowak, A., Benevento, M., & Zheng, L. (1995). Distance matters: Physical space and social impact. *Personality and Social Psychology Bulletin, 21,* 795–805.

Leahy, R. L. (1983). Development of the conception of economic inequality: II. Explanations, justifications, and concepts of social mobility and change. *Developmental Psychology, 19,* 111–125.

Lenhart, A., & Madden, M. (2006). Teen content creators and consumers. Washington, DC: Pew Internet and American Life Project. Available at: http://www.pewinternet.org/pdfs/PIP_Teens_Content_Creation.pdf.

Lerner, R. M. (1991). Changing organism–context relations as the basic process of development: A developmental contextual perspective. *Developmental Psychology, 27,* 27–32.

Lerner, R. M. (2002). *Concepts and theories of human development* (3rd ed.). Mahwah, NJ: Erlbaum.

Lerner, R. M. (2004). *Liberty: Thriving and civic engagement among American youth*. Thousand Oaks, CA: Sage.

Lerner, R. M. (2006). Editor's introduction: Developmental science, developmental systems, and contemporary theories. In R. M. Lerner (Ed.), *Handbook of child psychology: Vol 1. Theoretical models of human development* (6th ed., pp. 1–17). Hoboken, NJ: John Wiley & Sons.

Lerner, R. M., Alberts, A. E., & Bobek, D. (2007). Thriving youth, flourishing civil society: How positive youth development strengthens democracy and social justice. In Bertelsmann Stiftung (Ed.), *Civic engagement as an educational goal* (pp. 21–35). Guterslöh, Germany: Verlag Bertelsmann Stiftung.

Levine, A., & Cureton, J. S. (1998). Student politics: The new localism. *Review of Higher Education, 21,* 137–150.

Levine, P. (2007). *The future of democracy: Developing the next generation of American citizens*. Medford, MA: Tufts University Press.

Levine, P., & Lopez, M. H. (2002). *Youth voter turnout has declined by any measure*. Medford, MA: Center for Information and Research on Civic Learning and Engagement.

Levine, P., & Youniss, J. (2006). Youth and civic participation: Introduction. In P. Levine & J. Youniss (Eds.), *Youth Civic Engagement: An Institutional Turn*. Circle Working Paper 45 (pp. 3–6). Baltimore, MD: Center for Information and Research on Civic Learning and Engagement.

Lopez, M. H., Kirby, E., & Sagoff, J. (2005). The youth vote 2004. CIRCLE Fact Sheet. Medford, MA: Center for Information and Research on Civic Learning and Engagement.

Lopez, M., Levine, P., Both, D., Kiesa, A., Kirby, E., & Marcelo, K. (2006). *The 2006 civic and political health of the nation: A detailed look at how youth participate in politics and communities*. Medford, MA: Center for Information and Research on Civic Learning and Engagement.

Lopez, M. H, & Marcelo, K. B. (2007). Volunteering among young people. CIRCLE Fact Sheet. Medford, MA: Center for Information and Research on Civic Learning and Engagement.

LoSciuto, L., Rajala, A. K., Townsend, T. N., & Taylor, A. S. (1996). An outcome evaluation of across ages. *Journal of Adolescent Research, 11,* 116–129.

Lutkus, A. D., & Weiss, A. R. (2007). *The nation's report card: Civics 2007 (NCES 2007–476)*. U.S. Department of Education, National Center for Education Statistics. Washington, DC: U.S. Government Printing Office.

Mannheim, K. (1952). The problem of generations. In P. Kecshevich (Ed.), *Essays on the sociology of knowledge* (pp. 276–322). London: Routledge & Kegan Paul [1928].

Marcelo, K. B., & Kirby, E. H. (2008). The youth vote in the 2008 Super Tuesday states. CIRCLE Fact Sheet. Medford, MA: Center for Information and Research on Civic Learning and Engagement.

Marcelo, K. B., Lopez, M. H., & Kirby, E. H. (2007a). Civic engagement among young men and women. CIRCLE Fact Sheet. Medford, MA: Center for Information and Research on Civic Learning and Engagement.

Marcelo, K. B., Lopez, M. H., & Kirby, E. H. (2007b). Civic engagement among minority youth. CIRCLE Fact Sheet. Medford, MA: Center for Information and Research on Civic Learning and Engagement.

Marcia, J. E. (1980). Identity in adolescence. In J. Adelson (Ed.), *Handbook of adolescent psychology*. New York: John Wiley & Sons.

Matsuba, J. K., Hart, D., & Atkins, R. (2007). Psychological and social–structural influences on commitment to volunteering. *Journal of Research in Personality, 41,* 889–907.

McAdam, D. (1986). Recruitment to high–risk activism: The case of freedom summer. *American Journal of Sociology, 92,* 64.

McAdam, D. (1988). *Freedom summer*. New York: Oxford University Press.

McDevitt, M., & Chaffee, S. (2000). Closing gaps in political communication and knowledge: Effects of a school intervention. *Communication Research, 27,* 259–292.

McDevitt, M., Chaffee, S., & Saphir, M. (2001). Student-initiated discussion as a catalyst to citizenship: Kids voting in Lubbock. Miami, FL: John S. and James L. Knight Foundation.

McDevitt, M., & Kiousis, S. (2006). *Experiments in political socialization: Kids Voting USA as a model for civic education reform*. College Park, MD: The Center for Information & Research on Civic Learning & Engagement.

McFarland, D. A., & Starrmans, C. (2007). Student government and political socialization. *Teachers College, 111,* 27–54.

McFarland, D. A., & Thomas, R. J. (2006). Bowling young: How youth voluntary associations influence adult political participation. *American Sociological Review, 71* (June), 401–425.

McIntosh, H., Youniss, J., & Hart, D. (2007). The influence of family political discussion on youth civic development. *PS: Politics & Political Science, 40,* 495–500.

Mesquida, C. G., & Wiener, N. I. (1999). Male age composition and severity of conflicts. *Politics and the Life Sciences, 18,* 181–189.

Metz, E., & Youniss, J. (2003). A demonstration that school-based required service does not deter but heightens volunteerism. *PS: Political Science and Politics, 36,* 281–286.

Michelson, E., Zaff, J. F., & Hair, E. C. (2002). *Civic engagement programs and youth development: A synthesis*. Washington, DC: Child Trends.

Moller, H. (1968). Youth as a force in the modern world. *Comparative Studies in Sociology and History, 10,* 238–260.

Montgomery, K. (2007). Youth and digital democracy: Learning how digital media can engage youth. In L. Bennett (Ed.), *Civic life online: Learning how digital media can engage youth*. The John D. and Catherine T. MacArthur Foundation Series on Digital Media and Learning. Cambridge, MA: MIT Press.

Moore, C., & Allen, J. (1996). The effects of volunteering on the young volunteer. *Journal of Primary Prevention, 17,* 231–258.

Morgan, W., & Streb, M. (2000). *Effecting efficacy through service learning*. Chicago: Midwest Political Science Association Conference.

Moskos, C., & Butler, J. S. (1996). *All that we can be*. New York: Basic Books.

National Conference on Citizenship. (2006). *America's civil health index: Broken engagement*. Washington, DC: National Conference on Citizenship.

Neild, R. C., & Balfanz, R. (2006). Unfulfilled promise: The dimensions and characteristics of Philadelphia's dropout crisis, 2000–2005. Philadelphia, PA: Project UTurn.

Niemi, R. G., & Junn, J. (1998). *Civic education: What makes students learn*. New Haven, CT: Yale University Press.

Omoto, A., & Snyder, M. (1995). Sustained helping without obligation: Motivation, longevity of service, and perceived attitude change among AIDS volunteers. *Journal of Personality and Social Psychology, 68,* 671–686.

Ostrom, E. (1999). Coping with tragedies of the commons. *Annual Review of Political Science, 2,* 493–535.

Paige, J. M. (1971). Political orientation and riot participation. *American Sociological Review, 36,* 810–820.

Pearce, N. J., & Larson, R. W. (2006). How teens become engaged in youth development programs: The process of motivational change in a civic activism organization. *Applied Developmental Science, 10,* 121–131.

Penner, L. (2002). Dispositional and organizational influences on sustained volunteerism: An interactionist perspective. *Journal of Social Issues, 58,* 447–467.

Penner, L. A., & Finkelstein, M. (1998). Dispositional and structural determinants of volunteerism. *Journal of Personality and Social Psychology, 74,* 525–537.

Penner, L. A., Fritzsche, B. A., Craiger, J. P., & Freifeld, T. R. (1995). Measuring the prosocial personality. In J. Butcher & C. D. Spielberger (Eds.), *Advances in personality assessment* (Vol. 10, pp. 147–163). Hillsdale, NJ: Erlbaum.

Perkins, D., Brown, B., & Taylor, R. (1996). The ecology of empowerment: Predicting participation in community organizations. *Journal of Social Issues, 52,* 85–110.

Perkins, D. D., Florin, P., Rich, R. C., Wandersman, A., & Chavis, D. M. (1990). Participation and the social and physical environment of residential blocks: Crime and community context. *American Journal of Community Psychology, 18,* 83–116.

Perlmutter, P. (2002). Minority group prejudice. *Society, 39,* 59–65.

Pew Research Center for the People and the Press. (2008). Pew Research Center biennial news consumptions survey. Washington, . DC: Pew Research Center for the People and the Press.

Philliber, S., Williams, K., Herrling, S., & West, E. (2002). Preventing pregnancy and improving health care access among teenagers: An evaluation of the Children's Aid Society-Carrera Program. *Perspectives on Sexual and Reproductive Health, 34,* 244–251.

Phinney, J. S., Ferguson, D. L., & Tate, J. D. (1997). Intergroup attitudes among ethnic minority adolescents: A causal model. *Child Development, 68,* 955–969.

Piliavin, J. A., Grube, J. A., & Callero, P. L. (2002). Role as resource for action in public service. *Journal of Social Issues, 58,* 469–485.

Plutzer, E. (2002). Becoming a habitual voter: Inertia, resources, and growth in young adulthood. *American Political Science Review, 96,* 41–56.

Poulin, J., & Kauffman, S. (2006). Citizen participation in prevention activities: Path model II. *Journal of Community Psychology, 23,* 234–249.

Pratt, M. W., Arnold, M. L., Pratt, A. T., & Deissner, R. (1999). Predicting early adolescent moral reasoning from family climate: A longitudinal study. *Journal of Early Adolescence, 19,* 148–175.

Pred, A. R. (2000). *Even in Sweden: Racisms, racialized spaces, and the popular geographical imagination*. Berkeley, CA: University of California Press.

Pryor, J. H., Hurtado, S., Saenz, V. B., Lindholm, J. A., Korn, W. S., & Mahoney, K. M. (2006). *The American freshman: National norms for fall 2005*. Los Angeles: Higher Education Research Institute, University of California.

Putnam, R. (2000). *Bowling alone: The collapse and revival of American community*. New York: Simon and Schuster.

Rahn, W., & Transue, J. E. (1998). Social trust and the value change: The decline of social capital in American youth. *Political Psychology, 19,* 545–566.

Raskoff, N., & Sundeen, R. (1999). Community service programs in high schools. *Law and Contemporary Problems, 64,* 73–111.

Reinders, H., & Youniss, Y. (2006). School-based required community service and civic development in adolescents. *Applied Developmental Science, 10,* 2–12.

Rheingold, H. (2007). Using participatory media and public voice to encourage civic engagement. In L. Bennett (Ed.), *Civic life online: Learning how digital media can engage youth*. The John D. and Catherine T. MacArthur Foundation Series on Digital Media and Learning. Cambridge, MA: MIT Press.

Risch, N., Herrell, R., Lehner, T., Liang, K. Y., Eaves, L., Hoh, J. et al. (2009). Interaction between the serotonin transporter gene (5-HTTLPR), stressful life events, and risk of depression: A meta-analysis. *Journal of the American Medican Association, 301,* 2462–2471.

Robins, R. W., John, O. P., Caspi, A., Moffitt, T. E., & Stouthamer-Loeber, M. (1996). Resilient, over-controlled, and under-controlled boys: Three replicable personality types. *Journal of Personality and Social Psychology, 70,* 157–171.

Roof, W. C. (1993). *Generation of seekers: The spiritual journeys of the Baby Boom generation*. San Francisco: Harper San Francisco.

Rosch, J., Brinson, D., & Hassel, B. (2008). *Youth at high risk of disconnection.* Baltimore, MD: Annie E. Casey Foundation.

Saguaro Seminar (2001). *Social capital community benchmark survey executive summary.* Cambridge, MA: Author. Available at: http://www.cfsv.org/communitysurvey/results.html.

Sears, D., & Valentino, N. (1997). Politics matters: Political events as catalysts for pre-adult socialization. *American Political Science Review, 91,* 45–65.

Sentencing Project (2008). *Felony disenfranchisement laws in the United States*. Available at: http://www.sentencingproject.org/doc/publications/fd_bs_fdlawsinus.pdf.

Serow, R., & Dreyden, J. (1990). Community service among college and university students: Individual and institutional relationships. *Adolescence, 25,* 553–556.

Settersten, R. A., Furstenberg, F. F., & Rumbaut, R. G. (2005). *On the frontier of adulthood: Theory, research, and public policy*. Chicago: University of Chicago Press.

Sherman, R. F. (2002). Building young people's lives: one foundation's strategy. In B. Kirshner, J. L. O'Donoghue, & M. McLaughlin, (Eds.), *Youth participation: Improving institutions and communities* (pp. 47–64). San Francisco: Jossey-Bass.

Skocpol, T. (2000). *The missing middle: Working families and the future of American social policy*. New York: W. W. Norton.

Smith, C. (2007). Getting a life: The challenge of emerging adulthood. *Christianitytoday.com*. Available at: http://www.christianitytoday.com/bc/2007/2.10.html.

Smith, E. S. (1999). The effects of investments in social capital on political and civic behavior in young adulthood: A longitudinal analysis. *Political Psychology, 20,* 553–80.

Soule, S. A., & Earl, J. (2005). A movement society evaluated: Collected protest in the United States, 1960–1986. *Mobilization: An International Quarterly, 10,* 345–364.

Spring, K., Dietz, N., & Grimm, R. (2007). *Leveling the path to participation: Volunteering and civic engagement among youth from disadvantaged circumstances*. Policy Report. Washington, DC: Corporation for National & Community Service.

Stewart, A. J., & Healy, J. M. (1989). Linking individual development and social changes. *American Psychologist, 44,* 30–42.

Stewart, A. J., Settles, I. H., & Winter, N. J. G. (1998). Women and the social movements of the 1960s: Activists, engaged observers, and nonparticipants. *Political Psychology, 19,* 63–94.

Stolle, D., & Hooghe, M. (2005). Shifting inequalities: patterns of exclusion and inclusion in new forms of political participation. Paper presented at annual meeting of American Political Science Association, Washington, DC, September 1.

Stukas, A., Snyder, M., & Clary, E. (1999). The effects of "mandatory volunteerism" on intentions to volunteer. *Educational Horizons, 77,* 194–201.

Syvertsen, A. K., Flanagan, C. A., & Stout, M. (2009). Breaking the code of silence: How school climate influences students' willingness to intervene in a peer's dangerous plan. *Journal of Educational Psychology, 101,* 219–232.

Tang, F. (2006). What resources are needed for volunteerism? A life course perspective. *Journal of Applied Gerontology, 25,* 375–390.

Tang, F. (2008). Socioeconomic disparities in voluntary organization involvement among older adults. *Nonprofit and Voluntary Sector Quarterly, 37,* 57–75.

Teigen, J. M. (2006). Enduring effects of the uniform: Previous military experience and voting turnout. *Political Research Quarterly, 59,* 601–607.

Torney-Purta, J. (1992). Cognitive representations of the political system in adolescents: The continuum from pre-novice to expert. In H. Haste & J. Torney-Purta (Eds.), *The development of political understanding: A new perspective.* (pp. 11–25). San Francisco: Jossey-Bass.

Torney-Purta, J., Wilkenfeld, B., & Barber, C. (2008). How adolescents in 27 countries understand, support, and practice human rights. *Journal of Social Issues, 64,* 857–880.

Turiel, E. (2003). Morals, motives and actions. *BJEP Monograph Series II, No. 2: Development and Motivation, 1,* 29–40. Leicester: British Psychological Society.

Turkheimer, E. (2000). Three laws of behavior genetics and what they mean. *Current Directions in Psychological Science, 9,* 160–164.

Urdal, H. (2002, March). The devil in the demographics: How youth bulges influence the risk of domestic armed conflict. Paper presented at the annual meeting of the International Studies Association, New Orleans, LA. Available at: http://www.prio.no/publications/papers/YouthBulgesUrdal.pdf.

Uslaner, E. M. (2002). *The moral foundations of trust.* New York: Cambridge University Press.

Uslaner, E. M., & Brown, M. (2005). Inequality, trust and civic engagement. *American Politics Research, 33,* 868–894.

Verba, S., Schlozman, K. L., & Brady, H. E. (1995). *Voice and equality: Civic volunteerism in American politics.* Cambridge, MA: Harvard University Press.

Verba, S., Schlozman, K. L., & Brady, H. E. (2000). Rational activity and political activity. *Journal of Theoretical Politics, 12,* 243–268.

Volling, B. L. (2003). Sibling relationships. In M. H. Bornstein, L. Davidson, C. L. M. Keyes, & K. A. Moore (Eds.), *Well-being: Positive development across the life course* (pp. 205–220). Mahwah, NJ: Erlbaum.

Vygotsky, L. S. (1978). *Mind and society: The development of higher mental processes.* Cambridge, MA: Harvard University Press.

Walzer, M. (1989). Citizenship. In T. Ball, J. Farrand, & R. Hanson, (Eds.), *Political innovation and conceptual change* (pp. 211–219). Cambridge: Cambridge University Press.

Wentzel, K., & McNamara, C. (1999). Interpersonal relationships, emotional disturbance and prosocial behavior in middle school. *Journal of Early Adolescence, 19,* 114–125.

Wilson, J. (2000). Volunteering. *Annual Review of Sociology, 26,* 215–240.

Wilson, J., & Musick, M. (1997). Who cares? Toward an integrated theory of volunteer work. *American Sociological Review, 62,* 694–713.

Wilson, J., & Musick, M. A. (1999). Attachment to volunteering. *Sociological Forum, 14,* 243–272.

Yates, M., & Youniss, J. (1998). Community service and political identity development in adolescence. *Journal of Social Issues, 54,* 495–512.

Youniss, J. (2006). Reshaping a developmental theory for political-civic development. In P. Levine & J. Youniss (Eds.), *Youth civic engagement: An institutional turn.* Medford, MA: Center for Information and Research on Civic Learning and Engagement.

Youniss, J., McLellan, J., Su, Y., & Yates, M. (1999). The role of community service in identity development. *Journal of Adolescent Research, 14,* 248–261.

Youniss, J., & Yates, M. (1997). *Community service and social responsibility in youth.* Chicago: University of Chicago Press.

Youniss, J., & Yates, M. (1999). Youth service and moral-civic identity: A case for everyday morality. *Educational Psychology Review, 11,* 361–376.

Zaff, J.F., Boyd, M. L., Li, Y., Lerner, R. M., & Lerner, J. V. (2010). Active and engaged citizenship: Multi-group and longitudinal factor analysis of an integrated construct of civic engagement. *Journal of Youth and Adolescence,* www.10.1007/310964–010–9541–6.

Zaff, J. F., Malanchuk, O., & Eccles, J. S. (2008). Predicting positive citizenship from adolescence to young adulthood: The effects of a civic context. *Applied Developmental Science, 12,* 38–53.

Zaff, J. F., & Michelsen, E. (2002). *Background for community-level work on positive citizenship in adolescence: A review of antecedents, programs, and investment strategies.* Report prepared for the John S. and James L. Knight Foundation. Washington, DC: Child Trends.

Zaff, J. F., & Moore, K. A. (2002). *Promoting well-being among America's teens.* Report prepared for the John S. and James L. Knight Foundation. Washington, DC: Child Trends.

Zaff, J. F., Moore, K. A., Papillo, A. R., & Williams, S. (2003). Implications of extracurricular activity participation during adolescence on positive outcomes. *Journal of Adolescent Research, 18,* 599–630.

Zaff, J. F., Youniss, J., & Gibson, C. M. (2009). *An inequitable invitation to citizenship: Non-college-bound youth and civic engagement.* Denver, CO: Philanthropy for Active Civic Engagement.

Zakaria, F. (2001). The politics of rage: Why do they hate us? *Newsweek,* p. 22.

CHAPTER 16

Religious and Spiritual Development across the Life Span[1]

A Behavioral and Social Science Perspective

W. GEORGE SCARLETT and AMY EVA ALBERTS WARREN

DEFINING RELIGIOUS AND SPIRITUAL DEVELOPMENT

Our task is to explain religious and spiritual (R-S) development across the life span—in the light of research from the behavioral and social sciences. This task is formidable for several reasons. First, in recent years the number of publications devoted to R-S development has increased significantly. Second, the research on R-S development comes from a wide variety of disciplines and subdisciplines, including developmental psychology, neuroscience, sociology, anthropology, linguistics, clinical psychology, and psychiatry (Lerner, Roeser, & Phelps, 2008, pp. 1–2; Roehlkepartain, King, Wagener, & Benson, 2005). Third, even though there has been a great deal of recent research concerning religion and spirituality, there

[1] The authors are indebted to David Henry Feldman, Richard M. Lerner, Michael E. Lamb, and Alexandra M. Freund for their advice and support throughout this project.

are still gaps in the overall database, making it difficult to construct a coherent picture of R-S development across the life span.

However, the most critical challenge may well be to provide adequate definition of the central terms used to explain R-S development, in particular, the terms *religion, religious, spiritual*, and *development*. These terms have no agreed upon meaning, and so there is often confusion about what is being studied and explained. We begin, then, with the problem of definition, not only because it needs to be solved if we are to understand the scientific contribution of particular research studies but also because doing so provides a way to frame the discussion throughout this chapter.

The problem of definition may be addressed by making explicit the main meanings given to the central terms, and also by showing that different meanings yield different types of studies and ways to think about R-S development. To illustrate how different meanings of the central terms yield different types of studies, each with its own contribution, we begin with a comparison of two main types of studies. The first type uses a conventional way of defining *religion, religious*, and *development*—in terms of beliefs, institutions, and general adaptation or functioning. Therefore, we will call this first type a *belief-institution* way of defining R-S development.

The second type uses a less conventional way of defining *religion, religious*, and *development*, at least less conventional within the behavioral and social sciences. This second type looks within the experience of the faithful themselves and within the ongoing cumulative traditions surrounding them to explain how faith and the cumulative traditions together explain R-S development. While this second type is also concerned with general adaptation or functioning, it often focuses on the quality and pattern of faith itself and on how faith changes the way an individual experiences being in the world. We will call this second type a *faith-tradition* way of defining.

Belief-Institution Ways of Defining Religious Development

Two studies will serve to explain what we mean by a belief-institution way of defining. Furthermore, they will illustrate how ways of defining reveal an overall approach—thus also revealing how defining central terms is crucial to how research on R-S development is conducted and for what purposes. When it comes to defining the central terms for explaining R-S development, differences in definition are not "merely semantic."

The first example is a study by Regnerus and Elder (2003) who set out to determine whether adolescents' involvement in local religious institutions (here that meant churches) would prove to be a protective factor for adolescents from high-risk neighborhoods. Specifically, the study investigated whether adolescents from high-risk neighborhoods would be more likely to "stay on track" in school if they were involved in their family's church.

What Regnerus and Elder found was that church attendance, but not "religious salience" (saying religion is important in one's life), positively correlated with staying on track in school, more so for the adolescents from high-risk neighborhoods than for the adolescents from low-risk neighborhoods. They concluded:

> The ritual action of attending worship services or ceremonies, in contrast with theological differences that mark distinct religious affiliations and beliefs, appears to be a process that operates independently of particular belief systems and organizational affiliations. Church attendance may constitute—even by accident—a form of social integration that has the consequence of reinforcing values conducive to educational achievement and goal setting. (p. 645)

They go on to say,

> The ritual practice of rising and going to church or mass, and so forth, whether compelled by one's own faith or one's parents' demands—commits a youth to a practice and routine, a skill that translates into tools needed for academic success. Measures of private religiosity, on the other hand, do not operate similarly. Indeed, even the most religious students can still suffer academic difficulties since schooling success taps talents and tools that may have little to do with how religious one considers oneself. Private religiosity (or measures of religious salience or importance) may indirectly influence educational success, but the effect is very likely mediated. (p. 646)

These quotes reveal what Regnerus and Elder mean by *religion, religious*, and *development*. For them, religion has to do with religious institutions (churches, synagogues, mosques, etc.) and with sets of beliefs and practices that define Christianity, Judaism, Buddhism, and other religions.

Here, there is the assumption that the terms *Christian religion, Jewish religion, Buddhist religion*, and so on have a definite meaning that can be taken for granted when conducting research on R-S development. From this point of view, while the religions themselves differ from one another in their sets of beliefs and practices, what defines them as religions is that they have sets of beliefs and practices *which are religious and not secular*. In this way of defining, religion is a domain distinct from the secular—as illustrated by the distinction that Regnerus and Elder make between the "ritual act" of going to church and staying on track in school.

Finally, although Regnerus and Elder recognize that there is personal, "inner" religion or faith, their not going deeply into its nature indicates that for them, faith is not a significant independent variable for explaining general functioning, nor does it need to be a main focus in answering the question, "What develops?" Put another way, the study and its authors indicate that development has to do with general adaptation and functioning in the larger society, not with qualitative or quantitative changes in inner religious experience or faith.

In contrast to Regnerus and Elder's focus on outward behavior and religious institutions, Inzlicht, McGregor, Hirsh, and Nash (2009) focused on inner activity in the brain and on religious beliefs and the emotional response to beliefs that define whether individuals have or do not have religious convictions. Their aim was to shed light on how religious conviction may function to help a person psychologically. By assessing the brain activity of people from various religious traditions and with varying degrees of religious conviction, they showed that religious conviction is associated with reduced activity in the anterior cingulated cortex (ACC), a cortical system involved in self-regulation and managing anxiety. In short, they showed that developing strong religious convictions interacts with brain functioning to make it easier to cope with anxiety and error—although they add that the same changes in coping with anxiety could come from the development of non-religious convictions.

At first glance, this second study appears to differ in kind from the first—by its focusing on the inner spiritual lives of "the religious" rather than on outward, more easily measured behavior such as church attendance. However, on closer inspection, we find that this study and the first study share the same way of defining, that is, both are examples of the same belief-institutional type.

In this second study, conviction is defined as emotional investment in beliefs, and the research subjects are identified by their membership in some religion: "39% Christian, 21% Muslim, 14% Hindu, 11% Buddhist, and 15% other (including non-religious)" (Inzlicht et al., 2009, p. 9). Furthermore, the main focus of the study is not on the development of faith but, rather, on the development of self-regulation—a central process involved in general adaptation and functioning. In their own words, "Many people derive peace of mind and purpose in life from their belief in God...[and the results of the study] suggest that religious conviction...[acts] as a buffer against anxiety and minimizing the experience of error" (p. 2).

Certainly there is value in these belief-institutional ways of defining *religion, religious*, and *development*. We see the value in how the definitions set up research questions and measures that yield important facts—such as the fact that church attendance can be a protective factor for adolescents in high-risk neighborhoods and the fact that religious convictions can make it easier to manage anxiety and error. But for many, especially for the religiously faithful being studied, there is something essentially alien about these belief-institution ways of defining. To the religious themselves, these studies come from an outsider's view of religion and religious development.

We do not have to go far to get evidence of how the faithful view things differently, because Regnerus and Elder include in their introduction a quote from a young woman from a high-risk neighborhood in a study by Anderson (1999), a quote revealing her explanation for why she and her mother were functioning despite their circumstances. She said, "We have a strong relationship with God. God is our support. I don't know...it comes from within. We don't have too many supports" (p. 60).

What this young woman was saying was that the reason she and her mother were functioning was not because of their beliefs, emotions, or institutional affiliation. The reason they were functioning, she said, was because of their faith, a faith expressed in the form of their particular faith tradition.

Faith-Tradition Ways of Defining Religious Development

Faith-tradition ways of defining see *religion*, *religious*, and *development* as terms referring to *faith* and not necessarily to beliefs—as well as to *faith traditions* that are cumulative traditions and not necessarily religious institutions identified by their organized sets of beliefs and practices. In these ways of defining, faith becomes the fundamental religious category, and the category itself refers to a person's development and not simply or mainly to the acquisition of strong religious beliefs. As such, faith-tradition ways of defining implicitly or explicitly adopt Wilfred Cantwell Smith's (1998a) way of defining faith as:

> a quality of the person ... an orientation of the personality, to oneself, to one's neighbor, to the universe;

> a total response; a way of seeing whatever one sees and of handling whatever one handles; a capacity to live at a more than mundane level; to see, to feel, to act in terms of, a transcendent dimension. (p. 12)

Christian Smith and Melinda Denton provide a clear example of a faith-tradition way of defining *religion, religious*, and *development*. They are sociologists, but in their major study, *Soul Searching: The Religious and Spiritual Lives of American Teenagers* (2005), they show that they have familiarized themselves with information, concepts, and distinctions found in major works on religious history, comparative religious studies, and theology. They also show that they have integrated these concepts and distinctions into their own research on the R-S development of American teenagers. Put another way, in contrast to the previously mentioned researchers, Smith and Denton define *religion, religious*, and *development* more in keeping with the way "insiders" define or use these terms.

Nowhere do we see this more clearly than in their implicit distinction between faith and belief and between cumulative faith traditions and static institutions (implied in such terms as *Christianity, Judaism*, and *Buddhism*). In their writing we see that they have listened to and accepted what so many scholars from historical studies, comparative religious studies, and theology have been saying for decades, namely, that faith, personal faith, means much more than having a set of beliefs, and that religion and developing religiously mean much more than religious institutions and internalizing the beliefs espoused by religious institutions.

Throughout history and from the point of view of the faithful themselves, faith has meant a way of being in the world, an identity formed as a response not to static institutions with sets of beliefs but to ever changing, dynamic, faith traditions with their symbols, that is, their stories, music, dances, pictures, prayers, and yes, creeds and beliefs. The key to understanding R-S development is not to understand beliefs and convictions so much as it is to understand individuals' total response to a tradition's symbols or, as Wilfred Cantwell Smith (1998a) put it:

> To live religiously is not merely to live in the presence of certain symbols, but to be involved with them or through them in a quite special way—a way that may lead far beyond the symbols, that may demand the totality of a person's response, and may affect one's relation not only to them but to everything else: to oneself, to one's neighbor, and to the stars. It is that special involvement that pleads to be elucidated. (p. 3)

From this point of view, to be religious is less about attending religious services and subscribing to religious beliefs than it is about living one's faith everywhere and at all times. Where the belief-institution way of defining treats religion as a domain separated off from secular, everyday life (going to school, raising children, holding a job, etc.), the faith-tradition way adopts a more developmental systems way of defining, one that overcomes the split conception (cf. Overton, 2006) of religious versus secular life. We see this in the way that Smith and Denton go about conducting their study and analyzing their results.

In short, Smith and Denton have put to use an understanding of R-S development quite different from the understanding conveyed in the previous studies discussed. Furthermore, their use makes clear that individual religiosity or faith and faith traditions dynamically interact over the life span to determine what exactly develops (or fails to develop)—interacting not only with one another but with the historical times and immediate context, that is, with all the levels of the dynamic, developmental system (Brandtstädter, 2006; Lerner, 2002). From this understanding of R-S development, to be a Christian, Jew, Buddhist, or member of some other faith tradition in the 21st century is to interact with a tradition that has changed time and time again over the course of thousands of years and will continue to change—as a result of the faith-driven work of individuals but also as a result of larger social forces that characterize a particular time in history. For example, to be a Jew in 1932 is not the same as to be a Jew in 2009. The Nazi experience and especially the Holocaust forever make the meaning of being a Jew different than before the Nazi experience and the Holocaust.

The same can be said for anyone identifying with the Christian faith tradition, with the Buddhist faith tradition, with any religious faith tradition—the character of one's faith identity and the meaning of R-S development will inevitably change with the times and with historical issues. As another example, to be black, American, and Christian is apt to make Christianity mean something quite different than it does if one is white, American, and Christian—since being faithful in a Christian sort of way has, for so many black Americans, been tied to the experience or memory of slavery and Jim Crow. Smith and Denton clearly understand this, and their understanding works to design their methodology and evaluate their results—results which show that the faith of their adolescent subjects reflects a dynamic interaction not simply between their subjects and religious traditions but also between their subjects and the culture and times they live in. In the 21st century, to be involved in a faith tradition, especially one from one of the Abrahamic faith traditions, is apt to mean confronting issues around diversity that were not such powerful issues for the faithful in previous centuries, and in particular, the issue of how to counter over-investment in

> the value of doctrinal truth with another value…: the moral value of acceptance of other men. (Oxtoby, 1976, p. 3)

Smith and Denton's highly interactionist—faith-focused—perspective on religion and being religious provides them with their framework for interviewing teenagers about their faith. It drives them to go beyond adolescents' superficial statements about whether religion matters to them so as to get at the character of their interviewees' faith. As a result, these two social scientists were able to unearth startling findings about the R-S development of many, if not most American teenagers.

For our purposes, their most relevant finding is that beneath the surface and largely on an unconscious level, many American teenagers have a faith quite different from the faith espoused by the faith traditions to which they say they belong. That faith has the following creed:

1. A God exists who created and orders the world and watches over human life on earth.
2. God wants people to be good, nice, and fair to each other, as taught in the Bible and by most world religions.
3. The central goal of life is to be happy and to feel good about oneself.
4. God does not need to be particularly involved in one's life except when God is needed to resolve a problem.
5. Good people go to heaven when they die (pp. 162–163).

Smith and Denton contrast this faith with the pattern of faith more closely aligned with the Christian tradition. They write:

> This is not a religion of repentance from sin, of keeping the Sabbath, of living as a servant of a sovereign divine, of building character through suffering, of basking in God's love and grace, of spending oneself in gratitude and love for the cause of social justice, etcetera, etcetera. Rather, what appears to be the actual dominant religion among U.S. teenagers is centrally about feeling good, happy, at peace. (pp. 163–164)

In addition,

> When teenagers talked in their interviews about grace, they were usually talking about the television show *Will and Grace*, not God's grace. When teenagers discussed honor, they were almost always talking about taking honors courses or making the honor role at school, very rarely, about honoring God with their lives. When teens mentioned being justified, they almost always meant having a reason for doing something behaviorally questionable, not having their relationship with God made right. (pp. 167–168)

What Smith and Denton found, then, was a widespread faith among American teenagers, one that is hidden under the teenagers' claim that they are Christian, Jewish, Muslim or whatever, and one that reflects American culture in the 21st century more than it reflects one of the historical faith traditions.

Furthermore, and as any reader may have already realized, Smith and Denton do more than describe their interviewees' hidden faith. They evaluate this faith as being largely superficial, inadequate, and immature. This is especially clear in their calling it a "parasitic faith" and in their naming it "Moralistic Therapeutic Deism," because it is a faith that treats God as

> something like a combination Divine Butler and Cosmic Therapist: he is always on call, takes care of problems when they arise, professionally helps his people to feel better about themselves, and does not become too personally involved in the process. (p. 165)

We see, then, that for Smith and Denton, religious development has to do with the development of faith, and not simply or even mainly with undifferentiated religiosity's connection to general adaptive functioning. They conclude as follows:

> [I]t appears that only a minority of U.S. teenagers are naturally absorbing by osmosis the traditional substantive content and character of the religious traditions to which they claim to belong. For, it appears to us, another popular religious faith, Moralistic Therapeutic Deism, is colonizing many historical religious traditions and, almost without noticing, converting believers in the old faiths to its alternative religious vision of divinely underwritten personal happiness and interpersonal niceness. (p. 171)

Smith and Denton's focusing on faith's development and problems in faith's development does not mean they are concerned only with faith patterns such that they ignore overall adaptive functioning. They are concerned with both. However, they differ from the behavioral and social scientists carrying out the studies described in the opening two examples by their seeing overall adaptive functioning in spiritual and moral terms and by their linking faith development to *character* and *finding positive meaning in living*. For them, the problem with Moralistic Therapeutic Deism is that it places individuals in a "morally insignificant universe" where "moral commitments, decisions, obligations, and actions have little if any larger meaning, purpose, significance, or consequence; that universe is, in short, a morally empty reality" (p. 156).

In contrast, a "morally significant universe," a universe described in one way or another by many faith traditions, is

> a larger, morally meaningful order that provides significant direction and purpose to one's thoughts, feelings, and actions. Such a universe provides weight and gravity to living. It impregnates life's choices, commitments, and moral actions with purpose… Its significance is not derived from one's own life. Significance rather emanates to selves from the very order of things, the creation, the cosmos, the human story, or the light and force of history. One's own single life finds significance not in relation to itself, but by becoming connected to this larger moral order, by living a life in tune with and reflecting that order. (pp. 156, 157)

We see in this last quote just how their faith-tradition way of defining leads them to focus on something far broader than belief and religious practices. We see how it leads them to focus on a person's way of understanding and experiencing being human, being situated in the universe, and being in relation to what is divine or transcendent.

The Two Ways of Defining Compared

In reflecting on these two types of studies, how they differ in the way that they define R-S development and in what they choose to focus on, it is tempting to say that the first type sticks to being objective and scientific whereas the second type goes beyond science by becoming involved in the ways of valuing and perceiving that characterize particular faith traditions. However, in reality, both types express ways of valuing and perceiving that go beyond being objective and scientific. After all, it is as much a value choice to take staying on track in school as what develops as it is to take experiencing oneself as living in a morally significant universe as what develops.

Furthermore, by ignoring disciplines such as theology and comparative religious studies, behavioral and social scientists leave themselves vulnerable and as likely to distort reality as are behavioral and social scientists carrying out studies of the second type. As an example, Inzlicht and colleagues (2009) report that a significant percentage of their sample were Buddhists, and yet they define religious convictions in terms of belief in God. In doing so, they unwittingly apply the concept of God to a faith tradition in which the term *God* has little or no meaning, or at least a very different meaning than that given in the Abrahamic, that is, the Christian, Jewish, and Muslim faith traditions. The point here is that studies of the first type can ask important questions, be methodologically sound, come up with significant findings, and at the same time be limited by their having discounted the experience of the faithful and the work of scholars outside the behavioral and social sciences, particularly work in the disciplines of history, comparative religious studies, and theology.

As for studies of the faith-tradition type, they too can be scientific and yield significant findings yet still be limited by their own particular biases. Who is to say, for example, whether Smith and Denton's pejorative label for the underlying faith of their adolescent subjects is a fair assessment of the R-S development of American teenagers? It is possible that Smith and Denton's knowledge and valuing of their own Christian faith tradition has made it difficult for them to be open to the possibility that Moralistic Therapeutic Deism, rather than being a parasitic faith, is, in actuality, a transition faith, one that helps adolescents cope until, as adults, they come to master life's complexities enough to adopt a mature faith, one that is more in line with some historical faith tradition. Put another way, Smith and Denton focus on faith, but they do not do so in a sufficiently developmental way, one that not only describes and evaluates but also explains fully how new patterns of faith emerge over time. We will have more to say about this in the next section where we discuss developmental systems thinking.

And so, neither the belief-institution nor the faith-tradition ways of studying R-S development are free from bias. Each tends toward a different kind of bias, and when considered together, each can have a corrective influence on the other. More important, each may contribute to the puzzle and task of constructing an overall picture and model of how persons develop, or fail to develop, as faith-full persons over the life span—as the rest of this chapter will attempt to explain.

Defining *Spiritual*

We turn now to the term *spiritual*. In the behavioral and social science literature on R-S development, the consensus seems to be that being religious and being spiritual are conceptually, if not entirely empirically, distinct (Dowling et al., 2004; Oser, Scarlett, & Bucher, 2006; H. Reich, Oser, & Scarlett, 1999). But why the separation today, since for most of history, spirituality has been viewed as a religious phenomenon? And what significance does this recent separation have for conducting research on R-S development?

One answer to the question of why the recent separation is that it is the outcome of a largely North American and European late 20th-century disenchantment with religious institutions and a corresponding rise in interest in cultivating personal, non-religious spirituality. However, a more considered answer may be that the recent separation is the outcome of a much longer process that began with the beginning of the Enlightenment in 18th-century Europe when, not coincidentally, the concept of faith was beginning to be equated with belief. That is, the present day belief-institution type of research and the present day distinction between being religious and being spiritual have their roots in the Enlightenment.

Furthermore, we see here implications for answering the second question about the significance of separating off spirituality from being religious. Doing so follows naturally from transforming the meaning of faith as referring to a quality of living into faith as referring to believing. When faith or being religious refers to believing and participating in religious institutions, religion loses much of its original meaning and value; it no longer represents a living, moving, dynamic developmental system. Rather, when faith refers to believing, religion is fragmented into a collection of distinct beliefs and religious institutions. Here is Wilfred Cantwell Smith (1998a) saying essentially the same thing when explaining the transformation in faith's meaning that occurred during the Enlightenment:

> Belief became...the category of thought by which sceptics, reducing others' faith to manageability, translated that faith into mundane terms. They substituted for an interest in it as faith an interest rather in the exotic mental processes and conceptual framework of those whose lives had been sustained and enriched by it...What had been a relation between the human and something external and higher...was transformed by the new thinking into a self-subsistent, mundane operation of the mind....To imagine that religious persons "believe" this or that is a way of dominating intellectually, and comfortably, what in fact one does not truly discern. (p. 144)

We see, then, that by equating faith with belief and being religious with participating in religious institutions, today's dominant, belief-institution way of defining religion and being religious leaves out lots having to do with cultivating spirituality, including efforts to connect the self to sacred principles, to attain desirable states of consciousness, to form more caring relationships with others, to feel more connected to nature, and, in general, to find positive meaning, even noble purpose in living. Put another way, when religion and being religious are defined in terms of belief and participation in an institution, the leftovers (spirituality) appear to be much better than the original meal (religion), and so in at least some of the behavioral and social science literature on spiritual development one can detect a distinction, albeit subtle, between bad (or not as good) religiosity and good (or better) spirituality.

However, leaders in the psychology of religion have cautioned against making too sharp a distinction between being religious and being spiritual, and especially against making the distinction between bad religion and good spirituality. As Hill et al. (2000, p. 72) point out, "Characterizing religiousness and spirituality as incompatible opposites and rejecting conventional or traditional expression of faith and worship contradicts the experiences of many who appear to integrate both constructs into their lives." For example, in one oft-quoted study, about three-quarters of those surveyed identified themselves as being both R-S (Zinnbauer et al., 1997).

More important, throughout history all the main faith traditions have made it their business to value and nurture spirituality, not simply or mainly to support general adaptive functioning (better health, etc.) but also to support an overall positive way of being in the world, a way characterized by W. C. Smith (1998a) as:

> a quality of human living. At its best it has taken the form of serenity and courage and loyalty and service: a quiet confidence and joy which enable one to feel at home in the universe, and to find meaning in the world and in one's life...Men and women of this kind of faith face catastrophe and confusion, affluence and sorrow, unperturbed...The opposite of faith in this sense is nihilism: a bleak inability to find either the world around one, or one's life, significant... (pp. 12–13)

At the very least, then, the terms *religious* and *spiritual* are overlapping constructs, not true dichotomies. Furthermore, both have to do with what we are calling faith.

Another major problem has been the overly vague and broad way that the term *spiritual* has been used. At times, spiritual has been used to refer to specific practices such as meditation and yoga—without specifying what makes them spiritual practices. At other times, the term has been used to refer to feelings such as awe and wonder, without specifying what makes these spiritual feelings. At still other times, spiritual has referred to almost anything that individuals are passionate about—including gardening and football. As Hill et al. (2000) write, "when the term *spirituality* is invoked to describe ideologies or lifestyles that do not invoke notions of the sacred..., they are not spiritualities at all, just strongly held ideologies and highly elaborated lifestyles" (p. 64). Without an agreed upon focus, then, the term *spiritual* becomes a useless term for the researcher needing a definite and reasonable focus.

To solve this last problem, several scholars have suggested limiting the meaning of the term *spiritual* to the phenomenon of subordinating the self to something considered to be sacred, a higher power, or something greater than the self and deserving of devotion. Using this referent as the meaning of *spirituality*, we see spirituality and noble purpose being treated as almost identical.

However, noble purpose, by itself, does not exhaust the meaning of spirituality (cf. Mariano & Damon, 2008), since spirituality entails linking noble purpose to the experience of transcendence and to the human drama as having meaning, usually an ethical meaning, not captured in the materialist meanings offered by science (Farnham & Kellert, 2002). Therefore, not even good works carried out over long periods of time should define spirituality unless there is a specifically spiritual interpretation given to tie good works to some conception of and devotion to whatever may be considered to be sacred and transcendent—some essentially spiritual interpretation that provides the motivation and "engine" for the good works and that sets up a special relationship between person and transcendence, a relationship we refer to as faith. Put another way, good works are simply good works without some form of faith that explains the spiritual meaning of good works as well as the devotion to doing good works.

Religious examples of this kind of interpreting are easy to find—such as when John Muir, in his efforts to preserve areas of the wilderness, referred to mountains as "God's cathedrals" (Cronon, 1997) and when Mother Teresa in caring for the destitute of Calcutta referred to the destitute as "Christ in his distressing disguise" (Kwilecki, 1999). In both examples we see more than love of nature and humanitarianism, and in Mother Teresa's case especially, we see "the religious capacity to look beyond appearances, to detect the Most High in the most wretched" (p. 18).

However, the most common example of giving spiritual meaning to something that does not have such meaning for everyone may be the least researched by behavioral and social scientists. The most common example may be when in the lives of individuals, a book becomes sacred scripture—a book not just to read but to be responded to so as to lead good lives. The Qur'an, the Bible, the Bhagavad-Gita, all of the major examples of sacred scripture are not sacred and linked to some understanding of transcendence without individuals making them so—in actions and not just in believing (Smith, 1971). We see this phenomenon operating at the individual level but also at the cultural level. History tells us that the Qur'an, the Bible, and other texts have had very different influence and meaning, depending on historical era—and that their meaning is tied to this phenomenon of individuals treating a text as being a sacred text, a window onto the transcendent, and a motive and framework for action.

Non-religious examples of developing spiritually through making something sacred and linked to some notion of transcendence include making principles and ideals into organizing, sacred principles and ideals. We see this in Lincoln's making the U.S. Declaration of Independence's "All men are created equal" statement into a sacred principle and ideal imbuing that ideal with the spirituality of the transcendentalist movement of his time (Scarlett, 1999; Wills, 1992). Today, we see a similar phenomenon in the ecology movement led by individuals, many identifying themselves as scientists, who not only treat the natural world as sacred but also engage in talk and action that have all the markings of faith (cf. Dewitt, 2002; Goodenough, 1998; Kellert & Farnham, 2002).

In this discussion, we will follow the lead of scholars who limit the meaning of the term *spiritual* to this phenomenon of subordinating the self to something considered to be sacred. But we do so emphasizing that "subordinating the self" is another way of saying "becoming committed and devoted," that is, becoming faith-full. In defining spirituality this way, we will discuss the literature on how imaginative construal of what is sacred and what is transcendent comes to organize lives so as to help individuals develop spiritually. And we will show that faith is the central concept for understanding spiritual development as well as for understanding religious development—since faith need not refer to religious faith. For example, classical Greece and Rome provided a secular faith, which is, says Smith (1998a):

> a living tradition with its own metaphysical underpinning, its own great champions and even martyrs, its own institutions, its own apprehension of or by transcendence, and ... its own type of faith. (p. 134)

In sum, whether we speak of religious or spiritual development, the focus remains, or should remain, on faith.

Defining *Development*

This is not the place to review the lengthy and complex discussions within the behavioral and social sciences that have taken place over the past half-century about the meaning of the concept of development (Harris, 1957; Kaplan, 1983a; Kuhn, 1995; Lerner, 2002). Our focus is much narrower. Our focus is on the meanings of development as they have been applied to religiosity and spirituality. Since the belief-institution versus faith-tradition distinction does not always help differentiate one way of defining development from another, we need an additional distinction to capture the main differences in the meaning of development. Here, that additional distinction will be between *functional-adaptation* and *stage-structural* meanings of development.

Functional-Adaptation Meanings of Development

Within the literature on R-S development, most studies now adopt a functional-adaptation meaning of development, a meaning that portrays development as developing the knowledge, skills, and ways of acting needed to adapt and function well in one or more *domains*. We see this in many of the belief-institution ways of studying R-S development—as in the opening example of Regnerus and Elder's (2003) study, where the behaviors and experience involved in regularly attending religious services are linked to the behaviors needed to stay on track in school.

However, a functional-adaptation way of defining development can also be found in faith-tradition ways of studying R-S development. For example, in Susan Kwilecki's study (1999) of poor, devout (i.e., faith-full), and poorly educated adults in the American South, she makes clear that for her, development is about developing strong faith that can prove to be highly functional or adaptive—even when the form, structure, or character of the faith itself seems primitive or immature. Reminiscent of W. C. Smith's observation about faith leading to serenity, courage, and a quiet confidence, Kwilecki writes the following about one of her subjects:

> Thus, destitute in an indifferent world, Charles invested his only resource—energy and time—toward ends accessible solely through imagination. He thereby survived the worst conditions—scarcity, futility, degradation—with the best qualities—gentleness, hope, virtue. It made quite a picture, I thought: an adult absorbed in a realm with the same empirical status as Oz and ennobled by it! The religious, I surmised, were at once escapist and heroic, foolish and grand. (p. 16)

In both of these examples, we see the concept of development tied not to qualitative changes in faith but to religious beliefs or faith evaluated solely in terms of strength (salience) and adaptive functioning.

Stage-Structural Meanings of Development

In contrast to functional-adaptation ways of defining development, other ways define development more in terms of the structure of faith itself or the structure of some religious practice such as prayer—and in terms of how different structures form some sequence defining development. The focus in these stage-structural ways of defining development is on qualitative changes or differences that often are referred to as stages. We have seen this way of defining development in the Smith and Denton (2005) study—where Moralistic Therapeutic Deism was treated as an immature faith largely on the basis of its being qualitatively different from the orthodox faith of historic faith traditions and by its not providing a clear enough differentiation between faith and culture. Stage and structure, then, have to do with something other than content—as in the content being a set of beliefs. Furthermore, subsumed under the concept of structure is the concept of form and the presumption that stage development is usually, but not always, tied to better functioning. We need, then, to be clear about how content, form, structure, and stage are used together to define a stage-structural way of defining development.

To illustrate distinctions between content, form, structure, and function and how these distinctions figure into defining R-S development, we use the phenomenon of personal prayers (Scarlett & Perriello, 1991). Personal prayers, as distinct from impersonal group prayers said during religious services, offer a reasonable way to illustrate these distinctions, because personal prayers are both widespread and religious in nature and because, with age, personal prayers not only change, they develop—as indicated by a number of accepted criteria. We focus mostly on petitionary personal prayers because of all the various types of prayers (confessions, thanksgivings, etc.), they are the most common.

Prayer's content refers to the specific themes, ideas, and beliefs contained in prayer. Prayer may be about healing, avoiding danger, hoping for success—almost anything and everything. It may be about gods, ancestors, or patron saints. It may be about something as small and petty as finding a parking space or as large and noble as achieving world peace. The variety of contents found in personal prayers shows how prayer provides a window on what is on an individual's mind, and on how an individual may be thinking in ways characteristic of his or her family, community, and culture.

However, the variety in content limits its value for defining development. How, for example, should we distinguish developmentally between prayer directed to a single divinity and prayer directed to gods or ancestors? Given that there are no agreed upon criteria, we should not. Furthermore, although there have been attempts to distinguish the content of children's prayers as self-centered or self-serving compared to the more altruistic and "noble purpose" prayers of adults, on closer inspection, the distinction seems to have little or no empirical support. And even if there were age differences such that adult prayers are more likely to be about altruism and noble purpose, it is possible to see even self-serving and seemingly petty prayers as expressing something quite positive and adaptive—as when Susan Kwilecki (1999) saw in the prayers of her adult subjects (e.g., prayers to find decaffeinated coffee in the kitchen, a new head gasket for a Toyota, etc.) the positive experience of having a close, personal relationship with God.

Better indicators of developmental differences have been differences in *form* and *structure*. For example, a petitionary prayer containing "If it be your will,..." may indicate a more mature understanding of the relationship between the person praying and the agency to whom the prayer is directed—since there is no egocentric assumption that the will of the person and that of the divine agency are one in the same.

Attending to prayers' functions can also assist in efforts to define what develops. By definition, petitionary prayers serve the function of making requests. However, a closer inspection reveals that requests may differ from one another in ways that have implications for evaluating developmental status. For example, a child and an adult may both pray for a sick relative to get well. However, the adult may also pray for personal strength to give support to the sick relative and add something about not knowing what to do if things turn out for the worse. This request for personal strength and the added comment about not knowing what to do if things turn out for the worse suggest that prayer sometimes serves the added functions of helping the person praying to take responsibility for actions (not leaving it up to God alone), and of helping the person figure out, puzzle, or search for ways to better understand or frame something so mysterious as death. These functions of gaining personal strength and searching for ways to better understand and frame are hardly ever found in children's prayers, which provides one justification for using them to help define what develops in the development of prayer.

Therefore, by analyzing and evaluating separately the content, form, structure, and functions of R-S phenomena such as prayer, we often gain a better way of defining R-S development. However, in doing so, we still are not able to define how persons develop religiously and spiritually. For this we need the concept of *stage*.

The concept of stage offers an indispensable means for defining the R-S development of persons. It does so first in the way it organizes content, form, structures, and functions to reveal the full meaning of the R-S life. Attending to content, form, structures, and functions separately or in sequence can lead to overlooking the central characteristics that define the development of persons as faith-full persons.

The stage concept also offers a means to describe the transformational nature of R-S development. In the previously cited example of adding functions to petitionary prayer, we see a transformation in the self's structured way of being in the world—from being in the world as a self depending on some divine power to resolve crises to being in the world as a self acting in concert with a divine power. The change from one to the other is significant because it has profound implications for adaptation, which is a major reason why we judge the second way of structuring to be more developed.

The neo-Kantian philosopher, Ernst Cassirer (1955), provides an example of how stage-structural analysis can be indispensable in defining and evaluating the R-S development of persons. For Cassirer, at the lower stages of R-S development, individuals live in a mytho-poetic world where symbol and referent are fused and where there is no distinction between meaning and existence. Cassirer distinguishes a mytho-poetic way of being in the world with a higher, more developed, "religious" way or stage. Furthermore, while the two stages are distinct (discontinuous), they are also inseparable. He writes:

> If we attempt to isolate and remove the basic mythical components from religious belief, we no longer have religion in its real, objectively historical manifestation;

> all that remains is a shadow of it, an empty abstraction. And yet, although the contents of myth and religion are inextricably interwoven, their form [structure] is not the same. And the particularity of the religious form is disclosed in the changed attitude which consciousness here assumes toward the mythical image world. It cannot do without this world, it cannot immediately reject it; but seen through the medium of the religious attitude this world gradually takes on a new meaning.
>
> The new ideality, the new spiritual dimension, that is opened up through religion not only lends myth a new signification but actually introduces the opposition between meaning and "existence" into the realm of myth. Religion takes the decisive step that is essentially alien to myth: in its use of sensuous images and signs it recognizes them as such—a means of expression which, though they reveal a determinate meaning, must necessarily remain inadequate to it, which "point" to this meaning but never wholly exhaust it. (p. 239)

In Cassirer's account, we see how important stage-structural differences can be for defining what is essential in R-S development. For Cassirer, it is the transformation from living in a mytho-poetic world to living in a world where the myths and poetry of faith traditions become symbols pointing to truths and ideals to live by. Others who engage in stage-structural analysis find different ways to characterize what is essential. However, whatever the ways, the effort is the same, namely, to define what develops when we say a person develops religiously or spiritually.

One additional thought about this distinction between functional-adaptational and stage-structural ways of defining development: Here, we are making essentially the same distinction as that made by Overton (2006) between variational and transformational change. Variational change (e.g., attending church more or less) defines one type of change that may be used to define what develops. Transformational change (e.g., going from a mytho-poetic to a "religious," in Cassirer's sense, way of being in the world) defines another type of change that also defines what develops.

Aims of Development

While the main distinctions here for defining development are between functional-adaptation and stage-structural ways of defining development, we need to make one additional distinction to adequately capture differences in how the term *development* is used in the literature on R-S development. The additional distinction has to do with the purported *aim* of development—not as subjectively experienced by individuals but as objectively defined by scholars using principles or rules, such as Werner's (1957) orthogenetic principle for defining development, namely, increasing differentiation and hierarchic integration. After all, "The question is what one would possibly describe if one did not understand development as tending toward some specific end?" (Overton, 2006, p. 26).

Functional-adaptation ways of defining development usually do so by assuming the aim of development is to *cope* or *mature*. What develops need not be rare. What develops is what we often find among adults. Stage-structural ways of defining development may also have coping and maturing as the aim, but often stage-structural ways employ a different aim, namely, *perfection*. Here, we need to explain the differences between these different aims and show how they manifest themselves in studies of R-S development.

When the aim of development is seen as coping or maturing, to develop religiously and spiritually is seen as attaining or maintaining something valued and hoped for, but not something that is rare. We see this aim in how the term *development* is used in the majority of recent studies on R-S development but also in many of the classics. For example, Jung (1968) saw religious development as potentially useful for supporting the integration of parts of the psyche that often remain hidden, thereby effecting a more integrated self. For Jung, then, the aim of R-S development had to do with maturing.

Development as perfecting defines development as approximating some *ideal end point*. In doing so, development is treated as "a movement toward perfection, as variously as that idea may be constructed" (Kaplan, 1983a, p. 59). Using perfection as the aim of development, models of development are not necessarily meant to be used to describe change over time. Rather, models of development as perfecting are meant to provide extended definitions of development and ways to evaluate where anyone is at any given time—thus helping with the ongoing task of identifying and explaining individual differences but also with practical tasks such as providing adequate religious education and pastoral counseling.

As one example of development defined as movement toward perfection, William James in his monumental work, *The Varieties of Religious Experience* (1958 [1902]) gives us a composite picture of saintliness—intended to describe and define the ideal end point of R-S development. In so doing, James provides a definition of what it means to develop religiously or spiritually. For James, it mattered little whether many actually reach sainthood. What mattered is that we can conceive of sainthood or religious-spiritual perfection, and in so conceiving, we can better define and evaluate R-S development.

One further point about this aim of perfection: When developmental theories use an ideal end point to define development, they do not mean to say that everyone *should* become perfect or that all of us who fall short of perfection (and that is all of us) are defective, deficient, or otherwise unacceptable in how we really are. In James's (1958 [1902]) own words:

> Let us be saints … if we can … But … each of us must discover for himself the kind of religion and the amount of saintship which best comport with what he believes to be his powers and feels to be his truest mission and vocation. (p. 290)

Summary: Defining Religious and Spiritual Development

To summarize, when defining R-S development, we have found it useful to distinguish between two major ways of defining *religion, religious*, and *spiritual*, two ways of defining *development*, and two ways of defining the aims of development. Table 16.1 provides a summary of these distinctions and how they relate to one another.

In defining key terms and in making these distinctions, we have implied that faith (as defined by more than belief) is the central concept for understanding both religious and non-religious spiritual development, and that the development of faith involves a transformation in the self whereby individuals come to subordinate themselves to whatever they take to be sacred, transcendent, and worthy of lifelong devotion. Finally, we have implied that the development of faith is as worthy a focus for research as is the focus on general adaptation and functioning. With this introduction completed, we turn now to discussing theories that work to do more than define R-S development by their also explaining the various causes and combinations of causes that push, pull, and support R-S development—and by their working to explain the emergence of novel forms and structures.

Table 16.1 Key Terms and Distinctions for Defining R-S Development

Key Terms	Ways of Defining	Aims of Development
Religion/Religious/ Spiritual	Belief-Institution	Maturity/Coping
	Faith-Tradition	Maturity/Coping/ Perfection
Development	Functional-Adaptation	Maturity/Coping
Stage Structural		Maturity/Coping/ Perfection

THEORIES: EXPLAINING RELIGIOUS-SPIRITUAL DEVELOPMENT

How should we explain what causes R-S development and how novel expressions of religiosity and spirituality emerge in the lives of so many? Here, we focus on some of the major theories of the past century to show how R-S development has usually been explained using *organismic* models, models that treat humans as organized systems and development as the emergence of new forms or systems, ones that more closely approximate some telos or developmental end point (Lerner, 2002, p. 58). In organismic models of development, context (family, culture, historic period, etc.) may support or impede development, but context does not define development. What defines development is the sequence of qualitative changes in the human organism. Organismic models of R-S development can be found in a wide range of theories. Here, we give just a sampling—to show how organismic-developmental theories have contributed to our understanding of R-S development but also to show their limitations.

We have already explained the usefulness of defining development in terms of a sequence of stages with the highest stage providing a telos or end point. However, used as a way to explain development, organismic stage theories have their limitations. One limitation is that development conceived as a march toward maturity or perfection fails to explain the incredible variety we find in human development, that is, the multiple pathways leading to multiple end points—with any given pathway and end point needing its own separate explanation. It also fails to explain the losses that often accompany gains and that are part of what should be meant by development.

To address these and other limitations in organismic developmental theories, present day theories are more apt to conceive of development not as a march toward a single, universal end point, but as water flooding a hillside, or as a branching bush, or as some other analogy that better captures the fact that development occurs along multiple pathways leading to multiple end points (Harris, 2000). Furthermore, present day developmental theories are apt to include loss in their explanations of what develops (Baltes, 1997).

However, the main limitation of organismic developmental theories is that they fail to give adequate explanations of how new stages emerge. To address this limitation, today's developmental theories are apt to apply developmental systems ways of thinking. Developmental systems thinking (DST)[2] shifts the focus from the individual to multiple intraindividual and contextual systems and to how these multiple systems dynamically interact. When development is so conceived,

> the person is not biologized, psychologized, or sociologized. Rather, the individual is "systematized"—that is, his or her development is embedded within an integrated matrix of variables derived from multiple levels of organization, and development is conceptualized as deriving from the dynamic relations among the variables within this multitiered maxtrix. (Lerner, 1998, p. 1)

Developmental systems thinking promises to provide a more detailed and fuller account of R-S development across the life span. So far, that promise has yet to be realized, in large part, we think, because too few have adopted a faith-tradition way of conceptualizing R-S development. However, already developmental systems thinking allows us to reinterpret organismic developmental theories as well as to link recent empirical studies on aspects of R-S development (e.g., brain functioning) so as to begin to piece together a more complete account of R-S development and the emergence of novel stages. Later on, we will give examples. For now, we need to focus on organismic developmental theories of R-S development—their contributions and limitations.

Organismic Developmental Theories of Religious and Spiritual Development

This discussion involves just a sampling of organismic theories of R-S development, a sampling that focuses on some of the better known and more influential theories. We begin with William James's experiential theory of R-S development, as explained in his monumental work, *The Varieties of Religious Experience* (1958 [1902]).

William James's Experiential Theory of Religious-Spiritual Development

The *Varieties* is arguably the single most influential book in the psychology of religion. Even after a century since it was written, readers find in it insights that are directly relevant to our times. However, the *Varieties* is not normally thought of as a text on R-S development. For one thing, there is hardly any mention of children. For another, it gives us religious types, but the types themselves seem ordered more along a horizontal plane than along a vertical, developmental one. This seems especially true of James's two major types: "The Healthy-Minded" or "once-born" and the "Sick Soul" or those who feel themselves in need of being reborn. Nevertheless, a closer reading of the *Varieties* shows James to be very much a developmentalist.

James saw the sick soul as having a more mature grasp of reality than the healthy minded—and a greater potential for developing spiritually. He shows this developmental ordering of the two types when he turns from writing about the "once-born," healthy-minded to writing about the sick soul.

> Let us then resolutely turn our backs on the once-born and their sky-blue optimistic gospel; let us not simply cry out, in spite of all appearances, "Hurrah for the Universe!—God's in his Heaven, all's right with the world." Let us see rather whether pity, pain, and fear, and the sentiment of human helplessness may not open a profounder view and put into our hands a more complicated key to the meaning of the situation. (p. 118)

James goes on to explain how the sick soul does indeed have a profounder view providing the sick soul with opportunity to develop further.

For James, R-S development occurs not simply or mainly when the individual tries harder but also when the individual stops trying. For the sick soul, the experience is that of surrender followed by grace. James gives a more psychological account—of the individual giving over to unconscious processes that, in turn, lead to a shifting of feelings and attitudes until spiritual emotions become central. In James's own words:

> There is a state of mind, known to religious men, but to no others, in which the will to assert ourselves and hold our own has been displaced by the willingness to close our mouths and be as nothing in the floods and waterspouts of God. In this state of mind, what we most dreaded has become the habitation of our safety, and the hour of our moral death has turned into our spiritual birthday. (p. 53)

---

[2] We say developmental systems thinking rather than developmental systems theory to indicate that we are talking about a meta-theoretical way of thinking, a heuristic for generating adequate explanations (theories) of religious and spiritual development.

And what might this "spiritual birthday" produce? Later on, James gives us the answer when he discusses saintliness. After a second, spiritual birth, the previously sick soul is more sensitive to the world's contingencies. This is essential for development, and the development made possible by a second birth is development toward "saintliness."

James's concept of saintliness is not the everyday concept of a moral exemplar couching morality in religious language. Rather, James's concept of saintliness is essentially religious or spiritual, not moral. To be a saint is to have "a feeling of being in a wider life than that of this world's selfish little interests; and a conviction, not merely intellectual, but as it were sensible, of the existence of an Ideal Power" (p. 216). He follows this description with the added comment that the saint has "a sense of the friendly continuity of the ideal power with our own life, and a willing self-surrender to its control" (p. 217). For James, then, religious and spiritual emotions are central. Morality is a by-product.

The stage of saintliness is itself defined in terms of interacting component parts that include the following:

1. Strength of soul as through adopting noble purpose so that personal motives become insignificant
2. Asceticism and finding positive pleasure in sacrifice
3. Purity or the cleansing of existence from brutal and sensual elements
4. Charity or tenderness toward fellow creatures

For James, saintliness is an ideal end point not for structural reasons but because saintliness bears "fruits." He wrote (1958 [1902]),

> The highest flights of charity, devotion, trust, patience, bravery to which the wings of human nature have spread themselves have been flown for religious ideals. (p. 207)

In other words, saintliness is an ideal end point because it produces great good.

James' theory is a faith-tradition type of theory, although he focuses mostly on the development of individuals' faith in relative isolation from faith communities and cumulative faith traditions, a significant limitation for some (e.g., Taylor, 2002), but also a limitation in many organismic theories of R-S development.

One further point about James' organismic developmental theory of R-S development: If the defining experience of saintliness is a person's having "a feeling of being in a wider life than that of this world's selfish little interests" and "a sense of the friendly continuity of the ideal power with our own life, and a willing self-surrender to its control," then certain individuals should be considered saints for their non-religious spirituality. This is implied in James's linking the extraordinary phenomenon of religious saintliness to the more ordinary phenomenon of experiencing something sacred and transcendent when experiencing nature. The example he gave was of Thoreau writing about an experience he had at Walden Pond,

> Every little pine-needle expanded and swelled with sympathy and befriended me. I was so distinctly made aware of the presence of something kindred to me, that I thought no place could ever be strange to me again. (p. 218)

Presumably, if individuals cultivate a Thoreau-like feeling and experience of Nature so that this feeling and experience becomes central in their everyday living, then they too must qualify as saints, albeit in a non-religious sort of way.

Jane Goodall (Goodall, 1999; Goodall & Bekoff, 2002; Peterson, 2008) provides one well-known example of a naturalist living out a saintly life—as James defined a saintly life. From very early on, Goodall cultivated a deep interest in and identification with non-human animals and the natural world. In her adult years, that interest and identification made it possible for her to sit patiently in the wild until she cultivated relationships with chimpanzees, thus bridging a gap between human and non-human animals that had been assumed, incorrectly, to be a gap made by God. In the following is the description (2002) of her first such relationship with a chimpanzee, a chimp she named David Greybeard. (Naming the subjects in her research underscored her experiencing chimps as having a moral and spiritual connection to humans.)

> As I sat near him, I saw the ripe red fruit of an oil nut palm lying on the ground. I picked it up and held it toward David on my palm. He turned his head away. I moved my hand closer. He turned, gazed directly into my eyes, took and dropped the nut, then very gently pressed my hand with his fingers. This is how chimpanzees reassure each other. His message was clear. He did not want the nut, but he understood I meant well. I had communicated with David in an ancient language that predated words, a language that we had inherited—the human and the chimpanzee—from some common ancestor who had walked Earth millions of years before. (pp. 42–43)

During her adult years, Goodall's identification with non-human animals and the natural world transformed into a full-blown faith, as she tirelessly proselytized for the cause of helping everyone develop a similar identification so as to extend the ethic of justice and care not just to human animals, but to non-human animals as well. She wrote (2002):

> We have a highly sophisticated way of communicating with words. This has led, in the Western world, to a belief that humans stand in glorious isolation apart from the rest of the animal kingdom. We have placed the great apes on the next rung down, then monkeys, cetaceans, dogs, and so on until we get to insects, mollusks, and sponges. The worst part about this way of thinking is the conviction that we are superior to the rest of the animal kingdom. With our big brains and advanced technology, we have been able to dominate other life forms. And all those raised in the Judeo-Christian belief system have taken it for granted that Earth and all its riches, including animals, were created for our benefit. (p. 19)

In contrast to the pattern of faith found in the Book of Genesis, a pattern that places humans above nature and having dominion over nature, Goodall gives us a different pattern of faith, one that places humans in the middle of nature—and she demonstrated this pattern of faith on a continual basis—which qualifies her as a saint, albeit one fashioned more from spiritual experiences of nature and from coming to know nature through the disciplines required of a scientist, such as close observation and measurement, than from spiritual experiences of God and from coming to know God through the disciplines required of the religiously faithful, such as prayer and worship.

Psychoanalytic Theories of Religious-Spiritual Development

Psychoanalytic theories share a common assumption that the most important aspects of human motivation are rooted in unconscious, intrapsychic conflicts having to do with basic human longings and fears, such as the longing to be independent and competent (autonomy) versus the longing to be protected and securely connected to others (intimacy). The most important intrapsychic conflicts are life-long conflicts—so that the most we can expect from individuals is that they adequately *cope* with their anxieties. How well any given individual copes defines, to a large extent, how healthy that individual is, psychologically speaking.

Psychoanalytic theories also share a common developmental perspective, one that sees human development in terms of increasing ability to cope with anxiety and manage impulses without the external supports provided in the early years—through the introduction of more advanced defense mechanisms for coping and managing, such as sublimation (Freud, 1937), and also through the development of ego strength or capacity to assess and coordinate inner reality (longings and fears) with external reality (interpersonal relations and cultural and contextual opportunities and constraints (Erikson, 1963).

While psychoanalytic theories focus primarily on the inner lives of children, adolescents, and adults, they focus also on the "ego" supports provided (or not provided, as the case may be) by the immediate environment, particularly supports from significant caregivers. Ego supports have to do with helping individuals cope with anxiety and manage impulses so that individuals can make good decisions based on both inner and outer reality.

Psychoanalytic theory has proven invaluable in clinical work, and many of the theory's core concepts (unconscious motivation, defense mechanisms, managing intrapsychic conflict, etc.) are still widely used in the clinical treatment of children, adolescents, and adults diagnosed with psychiatric disorders. However, psychoanalytic theory has fallen on hard times among research-oriented developmental scientists, because of the difficulties measuring what the theory deems important to measure and because of what the theory presents in the place of testable hypotheses, namely, interpretations of unconscious processes.

All this is to say that while psychoanalytic theories have provided plausible accounts of R-S development (cf. Erikson, 1958, 1969), they have not lent themselves to measurement or scientific methods for assessing the validity of their conclusions. That said, the question is not whether psychoanalytic theory has been useful for explaining R-S development—it has and will continue to be useful. The question is in what special ways can psychoanalytic theory contribute by focusing on what might be overlooked, undervalued, or inaccessible to alternative theoretical perspectives.

We believe that the single most useful contribution of psychoanalytic theory may be its focusing on religious and spiritual *imagination* or what the analytically minded refer to as *illusion-making*. The Freudian origins of psychoanalytic theory looked unkindly on illusion-making—as being a child-like defense that should, over time, be discarded for more adult-like ways of coping with anxiety. Here is Freud (1961) making this argument to an imagined opponent:

> I must contradict you when you go on to argue that men are not completely unable to do without the consolation of the religious illusion, that without it they could not bear the troubles of life and the cruelties of reality...Men cannot remain children for ever; they must in the end go out into "hostile life." We may call this "*education to reality.*" (p. 81)

Certainly, no one doubts that religious imagination may serve to soothe, comfort, and for some, at least, enable a life-long propensity to remain childishly dependent and immature. However, what Freud overlooks is the fact that religious imagination may also serve to enable individuals to pursue noble purpose and take on the most challenging and life-threatening problems. History shows us this has often been the case, as is evident in the lives of spiritual exemplars such as Gandhi, M. L. King Jr., and Mother Teresa. But we need not go to spiritual exemplars to show how religious imagination can work to support positive development—as Susan Kwilecki reminds us in the previously cited quote about ordinary religious adults who are "absorbed in a realm with the same empirical status as Oz and ennobled by it!"

Of course, the opposite can also be true. Religious imagination can lead to negative development, even to evil—as when Hitler took Jesus as a model by selectively focusing on the image of Jesus throwing out the money-changers (for Hitler, a symbol of "the Jews") in the temple (Hitler, 1953, p. 586; Scarlett, 2009). Religious imagination is, then, not all the same; its worth is ultimately to be measured by its "fruits," whether it supports noble purpose, generally accepted moral values and principles, and ability to remain steadfast in the face of adversity. Therefore, the question is not whether religious imagination is "rational" but whether it supports positive development and the "good life."

Here is a biographical account by the well-known psychoanalytic theorist of religious development, Paul Pruyser, making this same distinction about religious imagination and how certain types of religious imagination are more supportive of positive development than others. Pruyser (1991) writes,

> I attended a denominational school...that stood for much greater Calvinist orthodoxy than did my family. Thus, home and school presented me with two different religious and emotional worlds. The first was mellow, optimistic, and forgiving; the second strict, somber and punitive—both equally taking recourse to scripture... There is nothing like such an upbringing to convince a young boy that religion is what you make it, that all of it is what I now call "illusionistic." Fortunately, home won over school, undoubtedly because of its deeper roots in my childhood practicing of the transitional sphere. The hand of God, much talked about in school, was closer to my mother's tender-and-firm hand than to the threatening and often slapping extremities of my teachers. (p. 180)

In other words, for Pruyser—and for many trained in the psychoanalytic object relations tradition—the decisive step in R-S development is adopting or developing positive imaginings. For Pruyser, the gentler, nurturing imagery promoted in Pruyser's religious education at home seemed healthier to Pruyser than the more punitive imagery promoted at school.

There are, then, distinctions to be made between religious-spiritual imagination, distinctions between better and worse, good and bad, healthy and unhealthy—although making such distinctions is always difficult and requires reasoning. This is essentially the same point made by the theologian H. Richard Niebuhr (1941):

> The heart must reason; the participating self cannot escape the necessity of looking for pattern and meaning in its life and relations. It cannot make a choice between reason and imagination but only between reasoning on the basis of adequate images and thinking with aid of evil imaginations. (p. 80)

In sum, psychoanalytic theories of R-S development still have much to teach us about R-S development—primarily in the way they shed light on the meaning and significance of religious-spiritual imagination. They do so because theories from other theoretical traditions have usually focused elsewhere—and because imagination has so often been treated as a "lesser," more primitive form of thinking than reasoning. Furthermore, they do so because in focusing on imagination, they show how the categories Christian, Jew, Muslim, Buddhist, and so on often fail miserably to capture the underlying faith pattern of individuals. To truly understand those faith patterns, we have to understand the way individuals imagine.

One word of caution: If we are to follow psychoanalytic theory's suggestion that we attend more closely to religious and spiritual imagining so as to understand the lives of the faithful and how the faithful develop, we are in for methodological problems that have long plagued scholars who focus on imagination to uncover and explain. As the anthropologist Clifford Geertz (1971, p. 109) has pointed out, to get at an individual's religious imagination, one has to get at religious experience, the kind of experience that occurs during intense moments of personal prayer. Using interviews and other research methods can distort rather than illuminate what actually occurs in moments of religious-spiritual imagining.

This brief overview suffices to explain what we mean by psychoanalytic theories and their contribution to explaining R-S development. We turn, now, to another group of theories that have figured centrally in discussions of R-S development, namely, to constructivist stage theories.

Constructivist Stage Theories of Religious-Spiritual Development

The theories to be discussed here are in the constructivist tradition associated with the work of Jean Piaget. Because Piaget's theory focused on epistemology and cognitive development, constructivist stage theories of R-S development are often criticized for being too cognitive. Critics assume that any offshoot of Piaget's theory is bound to be too cognitive. Take the following comment by David Hay (1998) as an example:

> The cumulative feeling I am left with after reviewing what we know about childhood spirituality is an uneasiness about the adequacy of developmental theory [meaning constructivist stage theory] to give an account of it...The major problem [with constructivist stage theories] is their narrowness, coming near to dissolving religion into reason and therefore childhood spirituality into nothing more than a form of immaturity and inadequacy. (pp. 50–51)

However, Piaget's early reflections on R-S development show his own theory of R-S development to involve much more than the development of reason.

From his late teens until his early thirties, Piaget preoccupied himself with the question of how one can believe in God and remain objective (Reich, 2005). His questioning led to his distinguishing between a transcendent and immanent God. For Piaget, God initially meant the God of conservative theology—a transcendent and mysterious God whose laws must be followed slavishly. Over time and in the context of actively debating and discussing, Piaget developed a very different meaning of God, so that eventually God, for him, went inward. In rejecting transcendence in favor of immanence, Piaget came to identify God with the heart, with the norms of reason, and with the internalized example of Jesus. Based on this personal experience of development, Piaget constructed an incipient theory of R-S development.

Piaget's theory centered on a presumed transformation from transcendent to immanent meanings of divinity. For Piaget, this transformation was far more than a cognitive transformation and certainly more than developing faith in reason. To be sure, reason was there in his theory, but so too was the heart and a faith tradition. He makes this clear in a lecture he gave in 1929, to members of the Swiss Christian Students Association (1930):

> [I]f, beyond men, one examines the currents of thought that propagate from generation to generation, immanentism appears as the continuation of the impulse of spiritualization that characterizes the history of the notion of divinity. The same progress is accomplished from the transcendental God endowed with supernatural causality to the purely spiritual God of immanent experience, as from the semi-material God of primitive religions to the metaphysical God. Now—and this is the essential point—to this progress in the realm of intelligence corresponds a moral and social progress, that is, ultimately an emancipation of inner life. (p. 10)

Piaget never developed a research program to test his theory of R-S development. Whatever the reasons may be for Piaget's abandoning his public reflections on R-S development, his early discussions clearly indicate that a true Piagetian approach to R-S development demands much more than attending to cognition and reasoning.

However, in the early 1960s, when Piaget's cognitive developmental theory was eclipsing all other theories of cognitive development, his early reflections on R-S development were forgotten or overlooked entirely. The result was an application of Piaget that was not at all Piagetian and that was indeed overly cognitive. The clearest example is the work of Ronald Goldman.

In Goldman's (1964) influential study, *Religious Thinking from Childhood to Adolescence*, he argued that, "Religious thinking is not different in mode and method from non-religious thinking. Religious thinking is...the activity of thinking towards religion" (p. 3). Using Piaget's "methode clinique," Goldman interviewed children and adolescents on their understanding of well-known stories in the Bible (e.g., the story of Moses and the burning bush). From the interviews, he constructed the following stages of religious thinking, which, as can be seen in Table 16.2, parallel Piaget's stages of cognitive development.

From this summary table, we see that Goldman conceptualized mature religious thinking as moving beyond the "childish and immature religious ideas of children" (p. 67) so that individuals come to see the symbolic-metaphorical structure of religious language in general and Biblical language in particular (aim of maturity).

Table 16.2 Stages of Piaget and Goldman Compared

Piaget	Goldman	Example
Pre-operational	Intuitive religious thought	Religious contents comprehended unsystematically, fragmentarily, frequently in a magical way; God represented anthropomorphously; frequent transductive conclusions: *"Why did Moses not go to the bush?"—"Because there was a sign saying 'Keep off the Grass.'"*
Concrete operational	Concrete religious thought	Magical and animistic elements receding; religious concepts presented in a more coherent and objective way—though their symbolic-metaphorical nature not yet apprehended: *"The burning bush had a fire behind it; it only seemed to be burning."*
Formal operational	Abstract religious thought	Religious contents now reflected in a hypothetical-deductive manner with symbols recognized as symbols: *"The burning bush is a symbol that God is there."*

Goldman inspired an abundance of studies replicating his work (Hyde, 1990; Slee, 1986). Other psychologists of religion also made use of the semi-clinical interview (Elkind, 1964), and they too applied Piaget's cognitive stages to religious concepts. The overall picture painted was that, with increasing age, concrete modes of thinking recede and are replaced by more abstract religious thinking (Tamminnen, 1976).

Probably as a reaction to Goldman's overestimation of the role of reasoning in R-S development, the first empirically based and broad constructivist theory of R-S development was James Fowler's (1981) faith developmental theory. Fowler's focus was broad because his view of faith was broad. Following the lead of theologians Paul Tillich, H. Richard Niebuhr, and Wilfred Cantwell Smith, Fowler defined faith as a universal quality of persons and the way persons orient themselves within the cosmos and, at higher stages, within an ideal, yet-to-be-achieved or experienced ultimate environment (aim of perfection). In Judeo-Christian thinking, this ultimate environment is defined as the "kingdom of God," the end point of human history. Faith so defined is reflected in how individuals make or find meaning, what they take to be centers of value and power, and how they adopt symbols and stories to reveal or express their faith.

Fowler's theory was also broad because he was intent on capturing the overall psychological development of persons. His theory borrows heavily from Erikson, Piaget, and Kohlberg, and to a lesser extent from Sullivan, Stern, Rizzuto, and Kegan. His stages take into consideration an individual's development with respect to major developmental tasks, including identity achievement, cognitive development, moral judgment, symbol formation, social perspective taking, and locus of control. For Fowler, the development of faith and the development of persons are so intertwined as to be to a large extent, one in the same.

At the heart of Fowler's view of faith development is the issue of individuation within a pluralistic society. From this view, the central challenge for individuals is that of being true to oneself—one's feelings, intuitions, beliefs, and understandings—while at the same time maintaining or constructing ethical, positive relationships with increasingly diverse communities. At first, this challenge is played out in the family and with one's inherited extra-familial community and faith tradition, then with self-consciously adopted communities and faith traditions, and ultimately with the community of humankind. Fowler's stages of faith development were tested using semi-structured interviews. Table 16.3 provides a brief overview of the stages.

After conducting his study in the 1970s, Fowler focused more on making faith developmental theory useful for practitioners, particularly practitioners in the fields of pastoral counseling and religious education. However, he continued to modify the theory in response to criticisms, especially criticisms concerning gender bias and over-emphasis on autonomy issues and criticisms concerning cultural bias and his not emphasizing enough the power of specific cultural contexts to foster or impede development.

Another influential constructivist stage theory of R-S development is Fritz Oser and Paul Gmunder's (Oser, 1991; Oser & Gmunder, 1991) developmental theory of religious judgment and reasoning. Goldman's research was on judgment and reasoning about religious content and concepts. Oser and Gmunder's research was on religious judgment and reasoning about unspecified content. The distinction is important. In Goldman's theory, judgment and reasoning is the issue, and religion is the content. In Oser and Gmunder's theory, religiousness is the issue, and judgment

Table 16.3 Fowler's Stages of Faith Development

Stage One: Primal Faith (Infancy)	Pre-linguistic faith defined by the trust developing between infants and their caregivers and by the psychological bonds created through affect attunement.
Stage Two: Intuitive-Projective Faith (Early Childhood)	Faith defined by the images created to represent both threatening and protective powers, by representations of God that derive from experience with significant caregivers, by the awakening of moral standards, and by continued reliance on and referencing to caregivers.
Stage Three: Mythic-Literal Faith (Elementary School Years)	Faith defined by widening sources of authority to include those outside the family so as to create a community of like minds, by the appreciation of myths and narratives taken literally and valued for their ability to explain and express faith, and by anthropomorphic images/conceptions of God.
Stage Four: Synthetic-Conventional Faith (Adolescence and Adulthood)	Faith defined by the development of a world-view derived from conventionally or consensually sanctioned authorities, by self-identity forming a synthesis of the perceptions of others so that identity is defined in terms of belonging (to family, ethnic group, sex role, religion) and/or possessing, and by undeveloped ability to understand and identify with groups with world views different from one's own.
Stage Five: Individuative-Reflective Faith (Late Adolescence to Adulthood)	Faith defined by the self-conscious, explicit examination of commitments, beliefs, and values leading to critical examination of the individual's faith heritage and a self-conscious choosing of the faith tradition and community to which the individual belongs. Faith at this stage indicates the individual takes charge of his/or life in defining self and commitments—often limiting the individual's ability to connect to faith-based groups and faith traditions and to take the perspective of alternative groups.
Stage Six: Conjunctive Faith (Average Age: About 30)	Faith defined as self-conscious commitment to ethical action based on fully internalized principles and to a vision of meaning, coherence, and value that fully accepts the limitations of the self to understand fully and act purely. Faith at this stage is maintained without the props of external authority and may be described as paradoxical faith inasmuch as commitments are made in the context of self-doubt and despair that allows for appreciation of alternative perspectives but threatens passivity and inability to act.
Stage Seven: Universalizing Faith (Average Age: Minimum about 40)	Faith defined as overcoming paradox through identifying with the ultimate conditions of existence ("kingdom of God").

and reasoning are means to understanding religiousness. In Oser and Gmunder's theory, then, religious judgment and reasoning are treated as a "mother structure" or way of thinking that cannot be reduced to some other way of thinking.

Because religious judgment and reasoning constitute judgment and reasoning about something, the question arises as to what religious judgment and reasoning are about. The answer varies. For Oser and Gmunder, religious judgment and reasoning are most apt to be about resolving ambiguities elicited by *contingency* situations, those situations that beg the question, "Who is in control?"—such as when unexpected good or bad fortune happens. What can be revealed at those times is how individuals understand their relationship to God or whatever they take to be *Ultimate* (Oser and Gmunder's word for transcendence). Reminiscent of Piaget's transcendent to immanent meanings of divinity, the direction of development in Oser and Gmunder's sequence of stages is toward an intimate, integrated relationship between self and God (the Ultimate) such that God (the Ultimate) becomes expressed through the actions of the self.

Table 16.4 lists the stages of religious judgment and provides brief descriptions. These stages were developed and tested using hypothetical dilemmas for eliciting religious judgments—similar in form to Kohlberg's hypothetical dilemmas for eliciting moral judgments. Though they were developed and tested as stages of religious judgment, the term *spiritual* may also apply.

Research coming mainly from Oser's lab in Fribourg, Switzerland has shown how these stages shed light on individual differences in (1) involvement in religious communities (Kager, 1995; Zondag & Belzen, 1999), (2) interpretations of religious texts (Zondag & Belzen, 1999), and (3) coping with adversity (Gnos, 2003).

Criticisms of Constructivist Stage Theories of Religious-Spiritual Development Constructivist stage theories of development, in general, and R-S development,

Table 16.4 Oser and Gmunder's Stages of Religious Judgment

Stage 1	Orientation of religious heteronomy—deus ex machina. God (the Ultimate) is understood as active and as intervening unexpectedly in the affairs of the world; persons are conceived as mostly reactive to God's (the Ultimate's) power and interventions.
Stage 2	Orientation of do est des—"Give so you may receive." God (the Ultimate) is understood to be external, all-powerful, and intervening; however, God (the Ultimate) now can be influenced through promises and deeds.
Stage 3	Orientation of ego autonomy and one-sided responsibility. The influence of God (the Ultimate) is consciously reduced. The individual is conceived of as responsible for his or her own life. The Ultimate Being (if accepted as real) has a separate and hidden existence and responsibility/function.
Stage 4	Orientation of mediated autonomy. God (the Ultimate) is mediated through immanence—as in developing faith in a divine plan and living life accordingly. Social engagement becomes a form of religious/spiritual expression.
Stage 5	Orientation of unconditional religiosity. The individual feels that he or she is always and unconditionally related to the Ultimate Being—so that each moment is or can have a religious/spiritual dimension.

in particular, have come under attack for several reasons. The main reasons have to do with concerns over:

- The emphasis on cognition, judgment, and reasoning
- The linear treatment of development
- The normative treatment of development and the emphasis on presumed universals to the exclusion of individual and cultural differences
- The mostly positive/optimistic view of structural development that overlooks loss and problems at higher stages

A fair assessment of constructivist stage theories must, then, address these concerns.

We have already addressed the first concern when discussing Piaget's own theory of R-S development—and concluded that while overemphasis on cognition, judgment and reasoning is a fair criticism of Goldman's theory, it is not so for Piaget's. As for the theories of Fowler and Oser and Gmunder, several points apply. Fowler, as well as Oser and Gmunder, include in their descriptions of stages many issues, conflicts, and concerns that are social and emotional in nature. For example, the descriptions place at the center of R-S development, not the ability to think logically or abstractly, but the ability to coordinate conflicts between individuation and making positive connections to God (the Ultimate) and to communities of diverse believers. Furthermore and following Piaget's lead, Oser and Fowler assumed that emotion provides a functional "motor" for the transition from one stage to another. This seems to be particularly the case for transitions between the upper stages (Rollett & Kager, 1999).

As for the second and third concerns, David Wulff (1993) expresses these concerns as follows:

> The positing of religious development, especially in the form of progressive and irreversible stages, requires the assumption of religion-specific dispositions or structures as well as of particular end-states representing the fullest realization of the inborn potential. It is difficult to say, however, of what these rarely observed end-states consist. Furthermore, the construction of these states requires the imposition of certain philosophical and theological views, thus undermining any claims for universality. (p. 182)

Those who object to the linear treatment of constructivist stage theories usually do so because they see development as having to do with change over time. They are, then, quick to point out that constructivist stage theories of R-S development fail to capture the many different ways that individuals change over time in how they express being religious or spiritual—as indicated by Fowler, Oser, and Gmunder's own findings that their stage sequences do not capture changes over time among their older adolescent and adult subjects. Furthermore, very few subjects attained stages six and seven in Fowler's model and stage five in Oser and Gmunder's.

However, if the concept of development is distinguished from the concept of change over time, as we think it should be, then the linear nature of constructivist stage theories can be seen for its essential worth, namely, for providing useful *definitions* of R-S development and for contributing to our ability to *evaluate* any given pattern of faith—both essential if we are to engage mindfully in supporting R-S development and if we are to conduct research on the significance of developing religiously or spiritually. Linear, constructivist stage theories of R-S development need not, then, describe age changes across the life span for them to be useful (Kaplan, 1983a).

Furthermore, when R-S development is conceived of as a non-universal domain, it becomes much more reasonable to think in terms of invariant sequences of stages even though we know these sequences do not apply to everyone (or even to the majority). As David Henry Feldman (2008) has put it,

> "Nonuniversal" sequences share with universal ones the feature that the sequence from beginning or novice states to "master" or advanced states is invariant. They do not share the feature that they are inevitable, nor do they share the feature that everyone who embarks on the journey from novice to master will (or can) reach the end of the sequence. (p. 178)

As for the third concern, the concern that because constructivist stage theories are normative and posit ideal end points, they are biased, there has been one long-standing reply. While stage sequences and ideal end points do indeed reveal the value biases of the stage theorists themselves, the theorists almost always have reasonable arguments for ordering stages and defining end points as they do. For example, it is reasonable to say that having convictions while being tolerant of others (prominent in theories such as Fowler's) is higher and more developed than having convictions and being intolerant or not having convictions. One can argue whether convictions and tolerance should be central in defining development or some ideal end point, but the issue is at least arguable and open for anyone to challenge.

For constructivist stage developmentalists, then, what appears to be a weakness (showing biases) should be considered a strength—since they, at least, make explicit their values when defining development whereas others who may share their values, refuse to do so in the name of being objective and sensitive to cultural differences. This is not a new argument. Here is how Bernard Kaplan put it over a quarter of a century ago (1983b):

> The major problem with this attempt to achieve a non-normative, nonethnocentric characterization of human development is … the failure on the part of those pursuing the facts to realize that *facts* are not data … [F]acts are not given but made, and their making involves categories and methods that are of parochial provenance, and thereby inherently ethnocentric. Ingredient in the very language of the outsiders who do the investigating, no matter how much they seek to be insiders, are value distinctions … alien to the scenes in which the insiders live. (p. 103)

As for the fourth concern, namely, that constructivist stage theories are overly positive/optimistic, our own view is that this concern is justified. With development, there are losses as well as gains, and content matters, particularly with respect to whether an individual's or group's images and beliefs support or undermine an ethical life. Clearly, some individuals functioning at lower stages in constructivist stage models may show more enthusiastic faith through their not having doubts and clearly they may show more compassion than many who function at higher stages as defined by structural criteria only. Put another way, there are spiritual problems at all stages—as we will discuss later on in this section and in the final section dealing with problems of a religious and/or spiritual nature, such as the problem of religiously inspired terrorism. There is, then, a need for research in this area, to document and explain the nature of problems at every stage of R-S development.

One final note about criticisms of constructivist stage theories of R-S development: Constructivist stage theories are apt to be vague about the transitions from one stage to another. Mentioning unconscious processes, disequilibrium and emotions does not suffice to give a proper scientific account of how a structured whole (a stage) can transform into an altogether different structured whole (new stage). Therefore, developmental systems thinking is sorely needed to provide accounts of just how and why individuals move from one stage of R-S development to another. We turn, then, to how developmental systems thinking can contribute to our understanding of R-S development.

Developmental Systems Thinking

Developmental systems thinking (Gilbert & Sarkar, 2000; Griffiths & Gray, 2005; Keller, 2005; Lerner, Roeser, & Phelps, 2008; Lewis, 2000) provides ways to improve on organismic developmental and purely contextual (e.g., socialization) explanations of R-S development. It does so by offering better ways to explain the emergence of novel forms and functions not easily explained by organismic and contextual theories—by assuming the following (Thelen & Smith, 2006, p. 258):

1. Development can only be understood as the multiple, mutual, and continuous interaction of all the levels of the developing system, from the molecular to the cultural.
2. Development can only be understood as nested processes that unfold over many timescales from milliseconds to years.

Using this framework, we come to understand development not in terms of reductionistic, static, and linear ways of explaining novelty but in terms of emerging novel forms and systems rooted in the interactions among abilities, processes, and systems located both within and outside the organism.

In this discussion, our aim is not to provide a comprehensive overview of studies carried out using developmental systems thinking. Rather, our aim is to provide examples to show how this way of thinking can enrich our understanding of R-S development. Specifically, our aim is to explain how developmental systems thinking can shed light on the ways that R-S development can be explained in terms of interacting *abilities, triggers, processes, and systems.*

Abilities and Religious-Spiritual Development

Thelan and Ulrich's (1991) research on the emergence of infants' first steps provides an example of the usefulness of developmental systems thinking for explaining development in terms of previously acquired skills or abilities that at some point in time work together to create new functions and abilities. In their research, they show that prior to infants taking their first step (a new ability), infants acquire at different times, different abilities which, once they have all been acquired, work together as a dynamic system out of which comes an infant's first steps. In the case of first steps, those different abilities include the following:

1. Ability to maintain balance made possible by the development of a better center of gravity occurring when the head-to-body proportion changes with growth
2. Ability to move toward a goal—an important motivational component
3. Ability to maintain erect posture made possible by the development of visual, vestibular, and somatosensory perception
4. Ability to create a step-like movement (which happens before actual stepping) made possible by the flexions and extensions of various joints (hip, knee, and ankle joints) moving nearly synchronously

By isolating these abilities and showing the asynchrony of their development as components in the system involved in walking, Thelan and Urlich provide a much richer account of infants' first steps than that provided by previous linear, static, and single-cause theories.

How might this way of thinking be applied to R-S development? One example comes from recent studies (Boyer & Walker, 2000; Harris, 2000, 2003; Woolley, 2000) of how children acquire beliefs in supernatural agencies (e.g., Gods, ghosts, ancestors), agencies who behave both the same and different from ordinary human beings. Faith is not belief, and so acquiring beliefs in supernatural agencies is not the same as developing faith. However, belief in supernatural agencies is central in a great many faith traditions, and so ability to believe in supernatural agencies can be considered a component ability among other abilities needed for explaining emerging faith.

What follows is a paraphrase of Harris's (2003, p. 96) summary of the findings about how children acquire beliefs in supernatural agencies (gods, ghosts, ancestors):

1. By age 3 or 4, young children have developed intuitive theories of physics, biology, and psychology based on their own direct experience with the world.
2. Between age 3 and 5 they develop ability to understand that knowledge depends on one's access to information and not simply on what is actually true.
3. After having developed an intuitive psychology (e.g., understanding that human agents cannot be in more than one place at one time) and after having realized that others may have access to information they do not have (theory of mind), young children are highly interested in the counterintuitive beliefs taught to them by trusted caregivers, beliefs about supernatural agencies (e.g., agencies who can be in more than one place at one time).
4. Because caregivers are trusted and come across as serious in their beliefs about the reality of religious-spiritual supernatural agencies (in contrast to when caregivers tell about supernatural agencies in fairy tales), young children come to believe in religious-spiritual supernatural agencies.
5. Because beliefs in religious-spiritual supernatural agencies do not upset ongoing beliefs acquired through direct experience, children are able to keep a "double booking"—with beliefs acquired through direct experience kept on one side of the ledger and beliefs acquired through the testimony of trusted caregivers kept on the other side. This is in contrast to scientific concepts (e.g., the concept of evolution), which require individuals to radically change the "common sense" acquired through direct experience (e.g., the common sense that the natural world is divided into fixed and separate species).

Later on, in adolescence, the ability to believe in religious-spiritual supernatural agencies is there to combine with adolescents' newfound ability to think "beyond the present...[and commit] to possibilities" (Piaget, 1958, p. 339), especially to possibilities that are "meaningful to the self and...to the world beyond the self" (Mariano & Damon, 2008).

In Mariano and Damon's surveys and interviews, they found "few young people today are choosing [long-term] purposes of religious faith and spirituality, at least not as central objects worthy of their dedication" (p. 215). However, they also found that religion and spirituality often influence adolescents' long-term purposes either as guides to finding a purpose (e.g., to become a teacher), or as imbuing some purpose with religious-spiritual meaning (e.g., feeling oneself as meant to be a teacher), or as promoting good character out of which comes some purpose to contribute to society, or as motivation to become immersed in a religious community that reinforces individual purpose. In other words and as developmental systems thinking predicts, the patterns emerging from combining ability to believe in a supernatural religious agent (e.g., God) with ability and motivation to adopt a long-term purpose are to be explained not in terms of some single track theory of development but in terms of unique combinations of abilities, processes, and systems that characterize the situation of any given adolescent and that explain any given course of development. We give this as but one example of how abilities acquired at different times can help explain the emergence of new forms of spirituality and faith later on.

Triggers, Processes, Systems, and Religious-Spiritual Development

New systems (stages), including new systems or patterns of faith, sometimes emerge as the result of a trigger that puts into motion dynamic interactions among processes both within individuals and between individuals and outside systems. To show how this dynamic developmental systems way of thinking works to explain the R-S development of a person, we provide the example of Mother Teresa. In doing so, we highlight two fundamental points made by developmental systems thinking, namely, that novelty emerges from the dynamic interactions of processes and systems and that what emerges cannot always be predicted because development occurs along multiple pathways and toward multiple end points, depending on differences found at every level of organization (biological, emotional, social, cultural, etc.).

The Case of Mother Teresa

Mother Teresa is universally recognized as a religious and spiritual exemplar—as indicated by her receiving a Nobel prize for her work with the poor but also as indicated by her being a European Catholic nun given a state funeral in a mostly Hindu country, India. In using her to illustrate developmental systems thinking applied to R-S development, we adopt the tactic suggested by William James (1958 [1902]) when he wrote,

> It would profit us little to study [the] second-hand religious life. We must make search rather for the original experiences which were the pattern-setters ... These experiences we can only find in individuals for whom religion exists not as a dull habit, but as an acute fever rather. (p. 24)

Mother Teresa is also a good choice because she developed a powerful faith whose pattern fits within both organismic and contextual models and at the same time, does not fit—a pattern of faith that also fits within the Catholic faith tradition and, at the same time, shows unique and uncommon features.

The life of Mother Teresa also provides occasions to illustrate just how developmental systems thinking can help explain otherwise puzzling phenomena related to R-S development. How did it come about that already, at age 12, she had developed the long-term purpose of devoting her life to God? By what processes did she try to discern God's will when trying to decide, at age 18, whether to become a nun and at age 36, when deciding to leave the convent and devote herself entirely to serving the poor? Most perplexing, how did it happen that throughout her decades of heroic work with the poor, she suffered from chronic doubt and feelings of abandonment by God?

The first question takes us to the circumstances surrounding the upbringing of Mother Teresa, then Agnes Bojaxhiu. In 1910, Agnes was born to a well-to-do family in Skopja, Yugoslavia. Skopja had a mostly Muslim population. The Bojaxhiu family belonged to a small, close-knit community of Albanian Catholics who used their parish both for religious purposes and to preserve their culture. Within the family, religion was a daily presence. Each morning, the children were taken to Mass, and at night, the family prayed together. Furthermore, Agnes's extremely religious mother, Drana, regularly took the children to help her distribute food and money to the local poor. When she was 9, her father, then a city counselor active in a movement to have Skopje annexed to Albania, died. The strong suspicion was that he was poisoned by communist authorities opposed to his politics. At 12, she listened to Jesuit missionaries visiting her church tell about their work in India, and this, she said, elicited in her a strong desire to become a missionary and dedicate her life to God.

Using developmental systems thinking, a number of observations can be made that bring out the significance of these facts and that suggest a way to explain Mother Teresa's precocious interest in dedicating her life to God. There is, first of all, the obvious, namely, that her precocity and the nature of her long-term purpose had to do with her coming from an extremely religious family and community—so that she was socialized, early on, to think and act as a religious person. However, so too were her siblings and so too are millions of children from highly religious families and communities, and yet very few show the same desire, at 12, to dedicate their lives to God. To use these facts in a more powerful way, we need to view them together as suggesting that something unusual, powerful, and complex was going on in the time leading up to Agnes's adopting this long-term, purely religious purpose. We begin with what is the most extraordinary fact mentioned, namely, the death of Agnes's father when she was 9 years old.

Compared to the general population, eminent historical figures are about three times more likely to suffer the death of a parent in childhood (Eisenstadt, 1978; Ochse, 1990; Simonton, 1994, p. 136; Sulloway, 1996). One reason given is that death of a parent creates insecurity and hardship that, if mastered, can leave an individual better equipped and more motivated to take on some long-term purpose and stick to it.

Based on the facts we know, such as her family struggling financially following the death of her father and about her mother's keeping the family a devout Catholic family, we can assume that the death of her father triggered in young Agnes a heightened sense of vulnerability (insecurity) and dependence on God. It is not too much of a stretch, then, to imagine Agnes using her faith to master her insecurities by adopting the well-researched tactic of gaining control by giving up control to God (Baugh, 1988). In short, we can assume that the death of her father set in motion cognitive and affective processes that led to her gaining control by adopting the long-term purpose of giving up control and dedicating her life to God.

Evidence for this interpretation comes from the many instances throughout her life when Mother Teresa linked dedication to God with placing control entirely in his hands—as when she left the convent to serve the poor without a detailed plan and later on when she refused to fundraise for the "Missionaries of Charity," the organization she founded to aid the poor. "Money," she said, "I never think of it. It always comes. The Lord sends it. We do his work. He provides the means. If he does not give us the means, that shows that he does not want the work. So why worry?" (Teresa, 1985, p. 32).

Ceding control to God and following His will requires that one discern God's will, and so another life-long characteristic of Mother Teresa's faith was her constant puzzling to discern God's will. This was particularly evident around the time when she decided to become a nun. According to her own account (Teresa, 1985), she asked her confessor, "How can I know if God is calling me and for what he is calling me?," and he replied, "If you are happy with the idea that God calls you to serve him and your neighbor, this will be proof of your vocation." Later on, she reported that while "praying…and singing in my heart, full of joy inside, when I took the life decision to wholly devote myself to God through religious life." This was one of several incidents where, early in her religious career, she used her positive feelings to assess God's will and sustain her faith and purpose.

The situation was quite different at age 36, when she was contemplating leaving the relative security of the convent to go out into the streets to serve the poor. At this time, and while on a train to Darjeeling, she experienced a direct call to leave the convent and serve the poor. She would have other such experiences, but during the next 2 years leading up to her gaining permission from her superiors to leave the convent, she felt abandoned by God. In one of her confessions at this time, she wrote (Kolodiejchuk, 2007):

> I am told God loves me—and yet the reality of darkness and coldness and emptiness is so great that nothing touches my soul. Did I make a mistake in surrendering blindly to the Call of the Sacred Heart? (p. 171)

Paradoxically, this feeling of spiritual abandonment became the basis for a new, more profound pattern of faith, one that emerged in the course of her work with the poor. Aided by the suggestion of one of her spiritual mentors, Mother Teresa was able to shift from using her positive feelings as guides to ascertain God's will and instead use her work with the poor as her only guide. Furthermore, she reframed her feeling of being abandoned as her experiencing the abandonment Christ felt on the Cross. By so doing, she transformed what normally is thought to be an experience that undermines faith into one that supported a powerful and strangely pure pattern of faith, one characterized by absolute dependence on God, a faith unmoored from the usual supports for faith, namely, happiness and security, as happiness and security are normally defined. This radical form of faith powered her work with the poor who became, for her, "Christ in his terrible disguise."

Again, we give this example to show how R-S development can follow pathways not captured by purely organismic and purely contextual theories—and not captured by belief-institution ways of explaining. For any given individual, we need to explain how triggers, processes, and systems—the various levels of the developmental system—combine to give that individual's development its own special character. We also give this example to demonstrate why, in order to explain R-S development, we need to explain the emergence of new forms of faith.

DEVELOPMENTAL TASKS AND RELIGIOUS-SPIRITUAL DEVELOPMENT

We turn now to perspectives on how identity and moral development interface with R-S development. Outside the research community, these two developmental tasks are often assumed to have an intimate connection to R-S development. However, within today's community of empirical researchers, this is not generally the case. Here, we explain why and show how a faith-tradition perspective helps better to understand the connections.

We begin with one of the most enduring explanatory concepts in developmental psychology, namely, the concept of identity formation, how individuals develop positive identities over the course of their lifetime. While discussions of identity formation usually give special attention to late adolescence and early adulthood, this discussion makes clear that identity formation is a life-long process, especially when there are threats or challenges to maintaining a positive identity—as occurs among members of groups that have been historically marginalized and groups undergoing dramatic changes.

Identity and Religious-Spiritual Development

Concern about identity and identity development is central to all faith traditions—because faith traditions are themselves responses to the ultimate identity question, "Who are we?" This central concern often gets lost among other concerns surrounding religion and faith. For example, the famous 1925 Scopes trial that pitted Darwinian evolutionary theory against Biblical accounts of creation was not simply about the concern and question of, "Who is right, science or religion?" It was also about the concern and question, "Who are we?" (Ruthven, 2004). Are we brutes among other brutes and thus free to adopt an ethic of survival of the fittest? Or are we "made in the image of God," thus having a moral responsibility to care for one another and the natural world? While the majority today do not see social Darwinism as the necessary outcome of believing in evolutionary theory, many at the time of the Scopes trial and many today do see it this way. For them, the issue was and is about identity.

Wherever we find faith traditions, we find this same focus on the question "Who are we?" and the traditions themselves can be defined as different answers to this question. Among the variety of Hindu faith traditions, one common answer refers to a hidden spiritual self or identity found within individuals which, if experienced deeply enough, becomes a way for individuals to identify with a universal self or Atman (Renou, 1962; Roeser, 2005; Smith, 1995). In the Confucian tradition, the answer refers to a social self or identity found within relationships and loyalties (Smith, 1995). The answers are varied, but from one tradition to another the question remains the same.

Most belief-institution studies miss or ignore the fact that R-S development is at least partly defined by how individuals respond to this ultimate identity question, "Who are we?" And if it is not ignored, the assumption is that it is those in positions of institutional authority, not the community of the faithful, that defines the response to this and related identity questions.

If, however, we look at how people actually behave and respond, we find a lot more variation than is predicted by institutional beliefs. Furthermore, we find that the faithful themselves experience themselves as carriers of their faith tradition—sometimes in agreement but sometimes in opposition to the beliefs of the faith-based institutions to which they belong. Faith traditions belong, then, as much to individuals as they do to those in power positions within institutions.

Throughout this discussion, the results of empirical literature will make both of these points clear—that there are tremendous within group differences in response to identity questions having to do with faith traditions and that individuals and not just institutions are carriers of and contributors to the ongoing development of faith traditions. Moreover, we see in this discussion how a faith-tradition way of conceptualizing R-S development instantiates developmental systems thinking and provides a more detailed and fuller account of R-S development across the life span.

The Behavioral and Social Sciences, Identity, and Religious-Spiritual Development

The behavioral and social sciences have a long history linking R-S development to identity development. Well-known examples include works by William James (1890, 1958 [orig. 1902]), Erik Erikson (1958, 1963, 1964, 1965, 1969), Gordon Allport (1950, 1955, 1963, 1967), Carl Jung (1969), Abraham Maslow (1970, 1971), and Carl Rogers (1961). More recently, the focus has been on spirituality and identity development (Benson, 1997; Benson, Roehlkepartain, & Rude, 2003; Kiesling, Sorell, Montgomery, & Colwell, 2006; Lerner, Alberts, Anderson, & Dowling, 2006; Lerner et al., 2008; Roeser et al., 2008; Templeton & Eccles, 2006).

Erikson is perhaps the best-known scholar linking identity to R-S development—especially for his writings on adolescence (Erikson, 1963, 1965, 1968) and for his groundbreaking books on Martin Luther and Mohandas (Mahatma) Gandhi (Erikson, 1958, 1969). Erikson focused on adolescence not only as a time when identity issues come to the forefront but also as a time when religious ideologies and religious institutions often play an important role in adolescents' identity development. According to Erikson (1968), ideologies provide the developing individual with a basis for "fitting in" and "a geographic-historical world image as a framework for the young individual's budding identity" (p. 188). Furthermore, for Erikson, religious institutions and ideological systems represent two potentially important contexts where adolescents explore their identity. That exploration (or moratorium) may lead adolescents to adopt temporary, negative identities—as was the case with Martin Luther in his early years as a monk and as is the case for some who join cults. From an Eriksonian perspective, such temporary identities, even though negative, may be necessary transitions from outworn identities formed in childhood to more positive and individualized identities allowing individuals to thrive in adulthood.

The work linking R-SR-S development to identity development has also focused on religious institutions and faith traditions offering young people models (exemplars) to emulate. The founders of faith traditions (the Buddha, Christ, Mohammad, etc.) are themselves held up as models—although their special status and nature make them difficult to imitate. In addition to the founders, we find myriad lesser figures who the faithful, at times, identify with and attempt to emulate. Robert Coles (1990) provides a charming example, in his writing about "Connie," an eight-year-old, feisty and rebellious Catholic patient who identified with the (even more) feisty and rebellious St. Bernadette of Lourdes and Joan of Arc, so as to maintain a positive identity. In addition to the spiritual models found in the myths and teachings of faith traditions, religious communities offer potential role models in the persons of congregational leaders and fellow worshippers (King, 2003).

As for empirical work, James Marcia (1993) was among the first to systematically explore the link between religion and identity formation (Kiesling et al., 2006). Marcia's four categories defining different types of "identity status"—diffusion, foreclosure, moratorium, and achievement—have proven useful for making important distinctions in how identity links to R-S development. For example, identity achievement has been associated with intrinsic (Allport, 1963) forms of religiousness (Fulton, 1997; Markstrom-Adams & Smith, 1996) and with higher rates of religious attendance. In contrast, identity diffusion has been associated with lower rates of religious attendance (Markstrom-Adams, Hofstra, & Dougher, 1994).

In other empirical studies, religion has been shown to predict commitment and purposefulness in identity (Tzuriel, 1984) and to give interpretive value to life experiences such that identity development is enhanced (Youniss, McLellan, Su, & Yates, 1999). In their research on extraordinary moral commitment, Colby and Damon (1992, 1995) found that religion acted as a unifying construct in the lives of individuals who possess a salient moral identity. That is, for many of these moral exemplars, faith enabled the integration of personal goals and moral concerns, a central feature of identity achievement.

Taken together, these data point to living, cumulative faith traditions as distinct contexts for identity formation. In the following discussions, we will narrow our focus to examine the variegated role of religion and spirituality in the development of three key domains of identity: gender, ethnic, and sexual identity.

Gender Identity, Faith, and Faith Traditions

Many scholars concerned with the religious context for the formation of gender identity have approached the topic through an examination of *gender doctrine* (e.g., Goldman & Isaacson, 1999; Plaskow, 1991; Stark, 1996). In doing so, they have focused on "patterned definitions of femininity and masculinity embedded in every religion's overall doctrine…[that delimit] gender differences, the nature of deity(ies), the division of labor, interpersonal bonds, sexuality, and procreation" (Goldman & Isaacson, 1999, p. 411). By focusing on doctrines, these scholars have adopted a belief-institution way of defining R-S development—a way that treats religion as a fixed part of "the masculinist power structure within which social relations become gendered" (Winter, 2006, p. 93) and identities become formed. Conclusions about religion's effect on gender identity are typically derived from scholarly (usually feminist) interpretations of sacred texts (e.g., Ali, 2006; Barlas, 2002; Sechzer, 2004; Stitzlein, 2008) and variable-centered analyses (e.g., Baker & Terpstra, 1986; Burn & Busso, 2005; Colaner & Giles, 2008) guided by skepticism about the meaning and practice of religion in women's lives (McGinty, 2007).

As an example of the gender doctrine approach, in their study of female Evangelical college students, Colaner and Giles (2008) examined the impact of Evangelical gender role ideologies on mothering and career aspirations. The authors noted that this population of women is subject to poignant messages concerning their potential role in society. To make their case, the authors went on to reference several passages in the Bible that point to the subordinate status of women. They wrote,

> [There is an] extensive literature on gender roles within Evangelical subcultures wherein a myriad of books, articles, workshops, and sermons encourage conformity to specific gender role ideologies. (p. 527)

These ideologies represent "ideals based on perceived truth concerning all women and men that can be supported through the Bible" (p. 527).

In this study, a convenience sample of women from two colleges in the United States responded to closed-ended survey items comprising the three scales (variables) of interest: Evangelical gender role ideology, career aspirations, and mothering aspirations. The Evangelical gender role ideology scale taps the two ends of a continuum of gender ideology, as defined by the Council on Biblical Manhood and Womanhood (1988) and the non-profit organization, Christians for Biblical Equality (1989), respectively: complementarianism and egalitarianism. The conservative complementarian position holds that men and women have unequal roles, where men have ultimate authority and responsibility. On the other end of the continuum, the liberal egalitarian position deems marital partners as equals, who together exercise authority and responsibility. It was hypothesized that mothering and career aspirations could be predicted by participants' degree of identification with the two positions. Indeed, as expected, mothering aspirations were predicted by the Evangelical gender role ideology.

In this variable-centered study, religion is portrayed as a fixed entity, one that is external to and passively absorbed (to varying degrees) by its adherents. From this vantage point, Evangelical women are especially susceptible to the "unidirectional" influences of gender doctrine, given the volume of this material in the Evangelical church. Moreover, the answer to the question, "What develops?" is mothering and career aspirations; religion is cast as a factor in that development. At no point do we hear the voices of the women, the faithful and how they dynamically interact with gender doctrine to arrive at an understanding of self or why they might value family over career.

Complementing this approach is one that situates the effect of religion on gender identity in the lives of the faithful themselves (Ali et al., 2008; Chen, 2005; Dufour, 2000; Ewing & Allen, 2008; Kikoski, 2001; McGinty, 2007; Predelli, 2004; Ramji, 2007; Ringel, 2007; Smith, Faris, Denton, & Regnerus, 2003; Yadgar, 2006). Implicit in this body of work is the idea that "religions are not fixed entities existing in some eternally abstract space untouched by humans but [rather] are dynamic...vehicle[s] through which power and hierarchy can be challenged, subverted, overthrown, or modified" (Winter, 2006, p. 93).

This research that examines men and women's own interpretations of patriarchal teachings reveals the rich, complex, and contradictory nature of religion's effect on gender identity. For example, Chen (2005) found that "women as religious agents *use religion to do gender* in their everyday lives" (italics added). (p. 341)

> Religions are multifaceted systems of meaning that in and of themselves, do not determine individual behaviors. In one instance, an actor may use religion to maintain traditional familial and gender structures. The very same religion may inspire actors to break from these traditions. (p. 341)

Feminist ethnography (Abu-Lughod, 1990; Kikoski, 2001) and narrative analysis (Ewing & Allen, 2008; McGinty, 2007; Ramji, 2007) have become favored approaches for those behavioral and social scientists trying to understand women's subjective experiences of religion. Semi-structured interview questions are typically used "to facilitate and thicken the natural flow of the narrative" (Kikoski, 2001, p. 139). The objective here is to replace presumptions about the female experience with a grounded, faith-tradition understanding of what it means to be a woman.

Using these qualitative methodologies, a growing number of studies have revealed the unexpected and empowering ways in which religiously conservative women interpret what appear to be patriarchal teachings (Bartkowski, 2001; Pevey, William, & Ellison, 1996; Stacey & Gerard, 1990). For example, in their study of Southern Baptist women, Pevey, William, and Ellison (1996) found that these women redefined the doctrine of wifely submission in ways that diminished its constraining effect. Similarly, Griffith (1997) found that evangelical Christian women use the doctrine of womanly submission to critique gender norms, thereby empowering themselves. This research is in accord with Stacey and Gerard's (1990) finding that many Christian women in the United States use contemporary evangelicalism as a flexible resource "for renegotiating gender and family relationships, and not exclusively in reactionary or masculinist directions" (p. 99).

In their extensive interview study of evangelicals, Smith and Lundquist (2000) found a much more nuanced approach toward gender and marriage than would be predicted from looking just at church doctrine. While the majority were not committed egalitarians ideologically, most of those interviewed were

> very comfortable thinking about marriage as an equal partnership. They stress the need for mutual respect and participation in the relationship. They conspicuously avoid talk of wifely submission and take great pains to stress that husbands may not rule their families as superiors. Indeed, when most evangelicals discuss the meaning of [male] headship, it has little to do with male privilege or domination, but instead means, for husbands, extra responsibility for, accountability to, and sacrifice on account of their wives and children. And when they describe their lived experiences of marriage, their practices tend to sound more egalitarian than patriarchal. (p. 189)

In contrast to feminist critiques of gender roles within the ultra-Orthodox Jewish community, scholars such as Bonnie Morris (1995) and Shoshana Ringel (2007) listened to the voices of ultra-Orthodox Jewish women to learn of their own views on gender. Several respondents addressed the negative perceptions of Orthodox women, in particular, the perception that women in the Orthodox community are regarded as less valuable than men:

> Non-religious Jews think that Orthodox women have a second place. They're not important and they're shoved in the back and that kind of thing, and it's such a misconception, I don't feel any less important than my husband. (Ringel, 2007, p. 36)

Respondents noted that gender roles are distinct and different, yet of equal value. One woman told a story of a seemingly patriarchal marriage, of an occasion when the couple entertained some guests. The husband sat, enjoyed his meal, and entertained the guests, while the wife ran around tending to him. At first, the guests thought that the husband should be ashamed of himself for not helping his wife. However, they came to appreciate the harmony within their marriage and the function of complementary roles. The respondent continued:

> At first they don't see what she gets out of it and so it looks a little bit slavish, but then when they see, they see the two of them and they see their shining faces and they see the children feeling so secure knowing that they have two very distinctive, different types of supports. (Ringel, 2007, p. 35)

The respondents were explicit that their current lifestyle was a preferred choice and superior to the secular lifestyle that many had experienced and intentionally left behind. One participant, who grew up secular, lamented that no one told her as a child that "being a woman has its own specialness to it and that instead of saying that what women do is secondary and no good, we should try to be what men are, that we should value the beauty of what we do" (Ringel, 2007, p. 39). It was not until she began to engage her faith tradition that she realized how empowered women could be:

> Being religious has ... empowered me as a mother and a wife and reinforced the values that I already had ... I feel like Judaism understands much better than our mainstream culture about empowering women and who women are. (Ringel, 2007, p. 39)

Although outsiders may think of ultra-Orthodox women as universally subject to a constrictive paradigm for women's lives, these data portray a paradigm for self-actualization, one that is tied to spiritual, familial, and communal achievements as opposed to individual and professional aspirations.

In a similar vein, several researchers have shown how Muslim women have used religious teachings in emancipatory ways (Bartkowski & Ghazal Read, 2003; McGinty, 2007; Predelli, 2004). For example, McGinty (2007) drew on the life stories of two female Muslim converts to discuss feminist approaches to Islam. For these women, Islam provides a salient framework for resistance to patriarchal ideas and ways of defining women's roles. Thus, the Muslim religious identity lies *not necessarily* in the realm of patriarchy, as assumed by many Western feminists and scientists who have been criticized by "Third World" feminists for their portrayal of (often Muslim) woman as hopelessly oppressed and without agency or voice (Mohanty, 2003). In the words of Cecilia, a female convert to Islam (McGinty, 2007, p. 483):

> If there is anything I wonder about I will look and search through thousands of books until I find the answer. And if my husband says anything different I throw the book in his face saying: "NO, this is how it is!" Then he has to accept that he has learned.
>
> Interviewer: So you use the Qur'an to support your arguments?
>
> Cecilia: Oh, yes!…I am who I am and I don't accept whatever. Instead I look things up.
>
> To Cecilia, "religion is not so much a set of fixed rules and beliefs … as a flexible resource for interpreting gender relations." (Predelli, 2004, p. 473)

As a flexible resource, religion serves to legitimize a range of views and practices—both liberating and oppressive—among its adherents. This range is illustrated well in Ramji's (2007) research on the dynamic relationship between religion and gender identity among British Muslims. Through in-depth interviews with the participants, she found that men and women mobilize religion as a "power resource" to form their gender identity, as well as to legitimize (often starkly different) gender-related viewpoints. Common among the male participants was the mobilization of Islam as a form of capital that legitimates the domination of men and the subordination of women. For example, a 21-year-old male respondent used Islam to rationalize a gendered division of labor:

> What do women need a degree for anyway? They're not allowed out to work. They can only work inside the home. I certainly won't let my wife work … She'll have to observe *purdah*. (Ramji, 2007, p. 1178)

Similarly, a 28-year-old male respondent rooted his gendered beliefs in Islam:

> Women can't work as hard as men. Our religion recognizes this and there isn't the expectation that women should work. Their real role is in the family and Islam makes sure that they can concentrate their efforts here by giving them specific modesty roles. (Ramji, 2007, p. 1177)

In contrast, common among the female participants was the mobilization of Islam to challenge conventional gender roles. In the words of a 29-year-old medical doctor:

> The inequality between [Muslim] men and women that people just accept has no foundation in the Qur'an. It is actually a very un-Islamic practice. Islam is about all believers being equal. (Ramji, 2007, p. 1182)

Similarly, another female participant spoke to the flexible and dynamic nature of Islam:

> All Muslims are required to practice modesty, but how this is interpreted in clothing styles is not compulsory at all. It is left to the piety and taste of the individual. Modesty is not just about a freedom from vanity and showiness. It is decency and moderation in speech, manner, dress and total attitude and behaviour towards life. (Ramji, 2007, p. 1184)

These data reveal religion as a flexible, variegated resource for the development of gender identity. While the men in this study used the Qur'an to rationalize their social dominance, the women used it to justify their more egalitarian views and practices.

Ethnic Identity, Faith, and Faith Traditions

Ethnic identity is a complex construct defined by multiple components (for a review of the components of ethnic identity, see Phinney & Ong, 2007; see also Umaña-Taylor, Yazedjian, & Bámaca-Gómez, 2004). Forming an ethnic identity is a dynamic process involving movement from an unexamined stage or the absence of understanding about the role of ethnicity in one's life, to a period of exploration or questioning and information-seeking about the role of ethnicity in one's life, to achievement or adoption of a clear and committed understanding of the ways in which ethnicity contributes to one's identity (French, Seidman, Allen, & Aber, 2006; Phinney, 1989; Seaton, Scottham, & Sellers, 2006). Ethnic identity is regarded as an important part of one's overall development, especially for ethnic-minority youth (Waters, 1999) who are subject to prejudice, discrimination, and stereotypes that may prompt ethnic-minority youth to adopt negative identities or at least to become chronically ambivalent (Garc'a Coll et al., 1996). Juang and Syed (2008) have characterized ethnic identity as an important feature of positive development.

Research has indicated the intrapersonal benefits to ethnic minorities of possessing a strong and positive ethnic identity, for example, by fostering greater self-esteem and lower levels of depression (J. Phinney, 2003, 2006; Quintana, 2007), as well as interpersonal benefits such as becoming politically and civically engaged (Gutierrez, 1990; Zimmerman, 1995).

Religious organizations have a long history of providing cultural support for the development and maintenance of ethnic identity (Juang & Syed, 2008). In communities where cultural supports are limited, ethnic churches may be the sole context—outside of the family—for ethnic identity formation. For example, historically, the African-American church was the one institutional setting that offered a place to commune, even during the days of slavery. Jagers (1997) depicted the church as a source of emotional, spiritual, and instrumental support for African-American parents and their children. Sometimes regarded as an extended family, the church has been a source of social as well as financial, support (Chatters, Taylor, Lincoln, & Schroepfer, 2002; Taylor, Chatters, & Levin, 2004). For African-American adults, indicators of religious identity have been linked to many positive outcomes, including better health through religious coping, increased life satisfaction, decreased alcohol consumption, and fewer depressive symptoms (Steffen, Hinderliter, Blumenthal, & Sherwood, 2001).

However, despite the centrality of the church in African-American history and in the lives of African-American youth (Donahue & Benson, 1995; Wallace, Forman, Caldwell, & Willis, 2003), very little research has focused specifically on the intersection of religion and African-American youth (Taylor et al., 2004). Social scientists who have studied this intersection typically do so from a belief-institution vantage point, that is, by examining racial differences in patterns of religiousness (e.g., patterns of church attendance and prayer) (Mattis, Ahluwalia, Cowie, & Kirkland-Harris, 2006). While revealing some group differences in certain features of religious and spiritual experience, these studies do little to explicate the substantive role of religion in the ethnic development of a given group.

The few studies that have focused on the role of religion in the lives of African-American youth are primarily concerned with the deterrence of problem behaviors, not with the promotion of positive identity. For example, Johnson, Jang, Li, and Larson (2000) found that indicators of religiousness were associated with decreased delinquent behavior in African-American youth living in at-risk communities. Cook (2000) proposed that churches provide youth with positive role models that function to deter delinquency. Research that has touched upon the issue of promotion of positive identity has shown religion and spirituality are rich resources for the development of self-concept and ethnic identity, especially among African-American youth (Chae, Kelly, Brown, & Bolden, 2004; Fukuyama & Sevig, 2002; Paranjpe, 1998; Spencer, Fegley, & Harpalani, 2003; Stanczak, 2006; Stewart, 2002). Nevertheless, "we know little of how youth *synthesize* ethnicity and religion/spirituality to arrive at a unique, coherent sense of self" (italics added) (Juang & Syed, 2008, p. 271).

Juang and Syed (2008) point to research on immigrant adaptation as one body of work providing insight into the importance of religion for understanding ethnic identity development (e.g., Ajrouch, 2004). Individuals who move from one context to another may find their ethnic identities spotlighted and challenged. Therefore, "immigrants are an ideal group in which to study the intersection of ethnic and religious identities" (Juang & Syed, 2008, p. 267), as migration forces individuals to redefine personal and group identities (Williams, 2000). Religious communities often play a vital role during this transition, supporting immigrants in numerous ways. In particular, religious communities provide refuge and serve as a source of psychological (Hirschman, 2004), social (Min, 2000), and instrumental (Hirschman, 2004) support. For example, in her study of Korean immigrants, Min (2000) examined the functional role of Korean ethnic churches. She found that these churches provide fellowship, social services, and social status for Korean immigrants, as well as help to maintain the Korean cultural tradition.

Religious communities can serve as "a familiar anchor in the midst of novel and challenging experiences associated with adaptation to a new country" (Juang & Syed, 2008, p. 268). As a context in which traditional cultural values are passed from one generation to the next, ethnic churches can provide immigrants with some semblance of the cultural community they left behind and, thus, with a ripe context for ethnic identity development (Bankston & Zhou, 1995; Min, 2000). Bankston (2000) argued that the maintenance and development of a strong ethnic identity is afforded through participation in a religious community that practices cultural customs and traditions.

Bankston and Zhou's (1995) study of Vietnamese-American adolescents illustrates this link between religion and ethnic identity. Religious participation (i.e., frequency of church attendance) was shown to facilitate a stronger ethnic identity, as indicated by Vietnamese language usage, commitment to marry someone Vietnamese, self-identification as Vietnamese, and friendship circles comprised of Vietnamese. In fact, religious participation had a stronger effect on ethnic identification than did family.

Although relevant to an understanding of religion's role in ethnic identity development, Bankston and Zhou's (1995) study failed to capture the dynamic, developmental processes involved. The study, like others on this topic (e.g., Min, 2000), employed a belief-institution way of defining religiosity, where religion is portrayed as a fixed entity external to and passively absorbed by its adherents (in this case, through church attendance). However, there is a complementary endeavor underway, one that employs integrative theoretical frameworks and qualitative methodologies for defining religion from a faith-tradition standpoint (e.g., Spencer et al., 2003; Stanczak, 2006; Stewart, 2002).

For example, Ethnic Identity in Everyday Experiences Study (conducted by M. Syed, L. P. Juang, and M. Azmitia) is an ongoing, multisite investigation of ethnic identity in emerging adulthood. Juang and Syed (2008) presented findings from this study for a sample of 354 (69% female) ethnically and socioeconomically diverse emerging adults (age in years: m = 19.26; sd = 1.11). Their presentation was informed by a narrative approach to identity development, which is concerned with the subjective construction of identity through the process of life narrative (McAdams, 2001). Narratives afforded a developmentally situated account of how emerging adults perceive the intersection of ethnicity and religion.

Juang and Syed (2008) examined participant responses to two open-ended questions: "Are there other social groups (e.g., gender, social class, religion, sexuality, sports, etc.) that you feel are more important or as important to who you are than your race/ethnicity?" and "Do you feel that you are similar to other members of your racial/ethnic group in your values?" Both questions involved follow-up probes so that participants would elaborate on their yes/no responses. These questions were chosen given their likelihood for generating responses pertaining to the intersection of religion/spirituality and ethnic identity.

In their responses to the first question, some emerging adults made explicit the link between their ethnicity and religion. For example, one 22-year-old woman wrote:

> My religion, my faith in being a Catholic is just as important as my identification with being Filipino. I honor my Catholic upbringing and feel that being a Catholic is important in my life not only for spiritual guidance but also as a connection with my family's past roots. (p. 274)

In a similar vein, a 19-year-old Mexican-American woman wrote:

> My religion forms a great part of who I am. At the same time it is a great part of my racial group as well. Ever since I was a little girl my mom brought me up with all sorts of religious beliefs that now it forms a great part of me. (p. 274)

Juang and Syed (2008) concluded that, for these emerging adults, religion and ethnicity are inextricably intertwined and cannot be discussed in isolation. They go on to write that for certain young people, such as Jewish adolescents, religion and ethnicity are in fact synonymous.

Responses to the second question also illustrated the intersection of ethnicity and religion. For some emerging adults, religion was shown to elicit feelings of closeness, as well as distance, regarding their ethnic group. For example, one 19-year-old woman wrote:

> I feel that I am very similar to those in my race because a majority of Filipinos are Catholic, so our religious views are typically the same. Filipinos are known to be very religious, and I believe I fall into that category. (p. 275)

In contrast, a 22-year-old white, Latino man wrote in response to the question, "Do you feel that you are similar to other members of your racial/ethnic group in your values?":

> Usually not, because most Latinos are Catholic and very religious. They have very strong values that coincide with the morals and values of the church. I am spiritual, but I do not go to church. I have strong values, but they are not defined by the church. (p. 275)

Taken together, these data reveal the dynamic relationship between religion and ethnicity, a relationship brought to life by the voices of the faithful themselves.

Sexual Identity, Faith, and Faith Traditions

For many individuals, religion and sexuality are inextricably intertwined, as nearly every religion tries to regulate the sexual behavior of its membership and promotes values regarding sexuality. Religiously inspired "moral convictions regarding sexual orientations, values, needs, or behaviors can have significant consequences for sexual identity development...regarding the levels of exploration and commitment that one may exhibit in defining one's sexuality" (Worthington, Savoy, Dillon, & Vernaglia, 2002, pp. 507–508). As such, religious systems have been regarded as powerful contexts for sexual identity formation, contexts with the potential to affirm (Love, Bock, Jannarone, & Richardson, 2005) as well as to oppress (Henrickson, 2007; Jeffries, Dodge, & Sandfort, 2008; Miller, 2007; Rosario, Yali, Hunter, & Gwadz, 2006). Here, we will focus on sexual orientation as a clear example of how religion and sexual identity interface.

Virtually all social scientific literature regarding sexual identity is intended to elucidate lesbian, gay, bisexual, and/or transgender (LGBT) issues (see Wilcox, 2007, for a review of the history of terminological shifts; but see Eliason, 1995, Sullivan, 1998, and Worthington et al., 2002, for work on heterosexual identity development). Cass (1979) is recognized as the first to formulate and widely disseminate a model of gay and lesbian sexual identity development. However, more recently, McCarn & Fassinger (1996) reinterpreted her model as one depicting the *coming-out process*, rather than identity development per se. Since the introduction of Cass's (1979) model, a number of authors have forwarded models of sexual minority identity development (for a review, see Reynolds & Hanjorgiris, 2000). Despite these advancements in the field, contextual factors (e.g., religion) have typically been ignored (Worthington et al., 2002). As a result, research on religion and spirituality among LGBT individuals is quite limited (Heermann, Wiggins, & Rutter, 2007).

Notably, anthropology was one of the earliest fields to acknowledge the global diversity of sexual practices and definitions of gender (Wilcox, 2007). Yet this field's focus on the intersection of religion and LGBT issues is limited, with the exception of two published studies of LGBT congregations in the United States (Primiano, 1993, 1995; Shokeid, 1995). Both studies identified a similar theme: Gay men (it was typically men, not women) who attended these LGBT congregations came in search of a space in which to explore and integrate their sexual and religious identities (Wilcox, 2007). Most members had begun this process of identity formation individually and then, once comfortable with the idea of joining a group, had approached the religious community most reflective of their upbringing and current beliefs (Shokeid, 1995). These trends have been replicated and expanded upon by ethnographic studies of LGBT religious communities (Comstock, 1996; Thumma, 1991; Thumma & Gray, 2004; Warner, 1995; Yip, 1997).

The psychology of religion has produced just a handful of articles on LGBT issues over the past several decades (most recently Mahaffy, 1996; Rodriguez & Ouellette, 2000). Wilcox (2007) noted in her review of these studies that most concern identity negotiation and internalized oppression. Notably, these studies reveal no direct relationship between religion and internalized oppression. Furthermore, they show no significant differences in self-esteem among those who attend LGBT-specific religious organizations, those who attend other religious organizations, and those who attend none at all.

The developmental sciences have also begun to reveal the LGBT-affirming, as well as LGBT-oppressing, aspects of various religious systems. Love (1997) found that religion was a source of strength for gay students attending a religiously affiliated liberal arts college. To further elucidate the function of religion in this context, Love et al. (2005) undertook a qualitative, faith-tradition approach to examine the intersection between religion and sexual minority identity within a college-age sample. They found that young adult LGB individuals with a strong religious upbringing were better able to reconcile any dissonance between their religious and sexual identities. In contrast, young adult LGB individuals with little or no religious background tended to lack various intrapersonal and interpersonal supports—for example, the language, traditions, and community—that may enable development of an integrated spiritual and sexual identity. Love et al. (2005) concluded that for LGBT individuals, a strong religious background may provide resources that become useful during identity crises.

In their study, Love et al. (2005) identified three categories of reconciliation: *undeveloped*, *unreconciled*, and *reconciled*. Undeveloped students were passive or active in their rejection of religious and spiritual issues, while unreconciled students were engaged in religious practice but had not yet reconciled any dissonance between their religiosity and sexual identity. For example, it was common among unreconciled individuals to keep secret their sexual orientation. Those participants who displayed the most developed, reconciled identity had several things in common. Prior to reaching reconciliation, these students tended to deemphasize one of their conflicting identities (e.g., sexual) in order to focus on the other (e.g., religious). Reconciliation came only after an extended period of conflict. However, once reconciled, these students drew on spirituality as a source of strength and demonstrated an integrated spiritual and sexual identity and a strong sense of self-awareness (Love et al. 2005). Among other things, reconciliation was fostered by having experienced a loving religious environment.

In contrast, participation in non-affirming religious congregations can have negative consequences for the mental health of LGBT individuals (Ritter & Terndrup, 2002; Rodriguez & Ouellette, 2000). The condemning messages, heterosexist biases, and punitive stances on homosexuality of non-affirming religious congregations are associated with increased internalized homonegativity (i.e., negative attitudes toward one's own homosexuality) (Shidlo, 1994), which has been shown to be negatively correlated with psychological health (Lease, Horne, & Noffsinger-Frazier, 2005). Many of these individuals perceive a dichotomous choice between their religion and their sexual identity (Barret & Barzan, 1996; Bartoli & Gillem, 2008); many end up choosing the latter (Lease et al., 2005), especially following negative faith-group experiences (Beckstead, 2001; Goodwill, 2000). Those who do work to reconcile their religious context and sexual identity may experience depression, guilt, shame, cognitive distress, internalized homonegativity, and suicidal ideation (Rodriguez & Ouellette, 2000; Schuck & Liddle, 2001). These findings are particularly salient for ethnic minority LGBT individuals, many of whom grew up with a significant level of involvement in and social connection to their faith communities (Jeffries et al., 2008; Miller, 2007; Moore, 2008; Rosario, Scrimshaw, & Hunter, 2004; Margaret Rosario et al., 2006; Ward, 2005).

The diversity of these findings—that some LGBT individuals are empowered by their faith, while others are oppressed by it—reveals, yet again, the need for a dynamic developmental investigation of the relationship between faith and sexual identity. These dynamic interactions are touched upon within Yip's (2002) quantitative and qualitative study of the persistence of faith among nonheterosexual Christians. He found that human reason and biblical understanding, within the framework of lived experiences, were stronger factors in respondents' sexual identity formation than religious doctrine and authority structures. Respondents were asked to rank, in order of importance, four items that, in their opinion, constituted the referential framework of their Christian faith. The majority of respondents ranked "personal experience" the most important, and "church authority" the least important ("human reason" and "the Bible" ranked in the middle). In her justification of this rank ordering, a Catholic lesbian respondent said:

> The reason I put personal experience on the top is that any Christian will tell you that their relationship is about their personal experience of God. That's the same with me. When people talk to me about Christianity, the only way I can relate it to them is to talk about my own personal experience of God, and how my life has changed as a result of coming into contact with God. That would never have happened by the church authority telling me God existed. Having encountered God, my own reasoning told me that there was God. The Bible, in a sense also backs up what I have experienced. So yes, it is my reasoning and my reading of the Bible, in relation to my experience, not what the church has to say. (Yip, 2002, p. 206)

The vast majority of respondents described their faith as a dynamic developmental process:

> I think it is important to use the Bible, to historically look back and see what various people are saying about what has happened at the time. I just don't think you should look at the Bible as the be all and end all. I think it is [in] relation of experiences that you can [do this]. It's like a reference text. It should be interpreted based on our reasoning and experiences. (Yip, 2002, p. 207)

The voice of a Roman Catholic gay respondent illustrates the dynamic relationships among culture, faith, and sexuality:

> I personally wouldn't take on board everything that the gay community has to offer. Some of it, like mindless casual sex is definitely beyond me. My Christian conscience wouldn't allow that … In conducting my life, I have to look within myself. I wouldn't do everything my flesh wants to do though. It has to be OK with my Christian faith. (Yip, 2002, p. 208)

One salient theme was clearly illustrated by these data—the primacy of the self in the construction of sexual identity. Yip (2002) concluded that "the basis of [respondents'] Christian faith was predicated on the employment of *their* own human reason in *their* interpretation of the Bible, within the framework of *their* personal experience, in the fashioning of *their* Christian faith and living" (p. 207). Religious affiliation does not necessarily mean conformity to and compliance with religious doctrine. Indeed, many of the respondents' reinterpreted Christian doctrine. Given that sexual identities are constructed within a dynamic, developmental system, the impact of religious doctrine on the lives of individuals is not uniform and permanent; diversity in views and practices is inevitable. The inevitability of diversity underscores the importance of faith-tradition ways of defining religion and spirituality.

Conclusions: Dynamic Faith-Tradition Interactions and Identity Formation

This brief overview of identity formation and R-S development suggests the following: First, for many, involvement in faith traditions and religious communities is important, sometimes centrally important to their identity development. Second, within any given faith tradition, negative identity messages not withstanding, there is ample opportunity for individuals to use faith to foster a positive identity. Third, for marginalized groups or groups facing particular challenges to maintain their cultural identity, faith traditions and religious communities can provide islands of continuity and support for individuals to effectively cope and master their own specific culture- and ethnicity-related identity issues.

Belief-institution ways of defining R-S development predominate in current research about the relation between religion and identity. Basic religious variables tend to be used, such as church attendance, religious activities, and beliefs (King, 2003). If religion is a fixed entity, prescribed, packaged, and "handed down" to its adherents (as it is often caricatured both inside and outside the behavioral and social sciences), then belief-institution ways of defining R-S development might suffice. However, as we have seen in the discussions above, there is tremendous "within-group" diversity indicating that religion is not a fixed entity but rather a fluid expression of dynamic person–context interactions. Given such diversity, we would be remiss to define religion simply in terms of beliefs, institutions, and institutional affiliations. Studies in the faith-tradition type begin to capture this diversity and, thereby, enable us to situate religion and identity within a dynamic developmental system.

Moral and Religious-Spiritual Development

One of the more perplexing realities in the behavioral and social science literature on moral development is the absence of much discussion on religion and spirituality. We see this in the absence of chapters on religion and spirituality in major handbooks on moral development (cf. Killen & Smetana, 2006). We see it too in the absence of any extended discussion on R-S development in major reviews of moral development (cf. Turiel, 2006), prosocial development (cf. Eisenberg, Fabes, & Spinrad, 2006), and character education (cf. Lapsley & Narvaez, 2006). Why is this so? Why is it that the community of behavioral and social scientists conducting research on moral development and related subjects generally treats religion and R-S development as largely irrelevant when faith traditions and the general public (Walker, Pitts, Hennig, & Matsuba, 1995; Walker & Reimer, 2006) have treated religious, spiritual, and moral development as bound together in unique and powerful ways?

One answer brings us back, once again, to the distinction between belief-institution and faith-tradition ways of defining religion, religious, and spiritual. The dominant, belief-institution ways lead naturally to treating moral development as independent of R-S development. The minority, faith-tradition ways do not. The following discussion makes this clear. It also makes clear that present-day discussions of moral development are still heavily influenced by the legacy of Lawrence Kohlberg, even though Kohlberg himself understood full well how a faith-tradition way of understanding R-S development can lead to a better understanding of how moral and R-S development interrelate. We begin, then, with Kohlberg, so as to provide the framework that has encouraged thinking about moral development as a domain independent of R-S development, but also to show that Kohlberg's later thinking about morality and faith is today virtually ignored.

Kohlberg, Moral Development, and Religious-Spiritual Development

For over two decades, Lawrence Kohlberg (1967, 1980) labored to have moral development considered as a separate, autonomous domain—with the main engine of moral development before adulthood being mundane conflicts that confront children and adolescents on a daily basis, conflicts that, with help from adults, stimulate thinking about what is just and caring. In doing so, Kohlberg argued against divine command theory and all those who believe that morality derives from "transmission" models of education in general (DeVries & Kohlberg, 1990; Kohlberg & Lickona, 1990). His arguments were based not simply on philosophy. They were based also on the empirical evidence from belief-institution studies, all saying the same thing, namely, that religiosity as defined by religious beliefs and institutional affiliation does not differentiate the religious from the non-religious on moral issues. Furthermore, for most of his career, Kohlberg saw religion as having a potential retarding effect because of those times when "divine command" theory (saying something is right or wrong because the Bible, Qur'an, or some other religious authority says that it is right or wrong) suppresses the individual's taking an active role in puzzling about right and wrong.

However, in time and influenced by the writings of theologians, including Paul Tillich (1957), philosophers, including Steven Toulmin (1950), and psychologists, including James Fowler (1981), Kohlberg developed an appreciation of the function of religion and spirituality for helping individuals respond to the essentially religious-spiritual, meta-ethical question, "Why be moral in an immoral world?" and for sustaining moral action even in the face of injustice and misfortune.

Kohlberg came to believe that the primary function of religious structures is to validate and support being moral by integrating morality into an overall faith in a cosmic order or "the way things are." Reminiscent of William James's writing about sick souls gradually making spiritual feelings central, Kohlberg wrote about individuals feeling despair when first taking a cosmic perspective on death and misfortune—then shifting to a perspective centering on faith. He wrote (1981):

> It is when we begin to see our lives as finite from some more infinite perspective that we feel despair. The meaninglessness of our lives in the face of death is the meaninglessness of the finite from the perspective of the infinite. The resolution of the despair… represents a continuation of the process of taking a cosmic perspective whose phase is despair. In despair, we are the self seen from the distance of the cosmic or infinite. [In the state beyond despair] we identify ourselves with the cosmic or infinite perspective itself; we value life from its standpoint. At such a time, what is ordinarily background becomes foreground and the self is no longer figure to the ground. We sense the unity of the whole and ourselves as part of that unity. This experience of unity, often mistakenly treated as a mere rush of mystic feelings, is … associated with a structure of ontological and moral conviction. (p. 345)

While Kohlberg never conducted research on this connection between morality and faith, he did provide examples of individuals who successfully grounded their morality in a faith in a cosmic order—thereby helping them function morally under extremely adverse circumstances.

For Kohlberg, then, moral development was a necessary but not sufficient condition for faith development. Early studies investigating the necessary but not sufficient condition hypothesis produced mixed results and were limited in important ways—prompting Day and Naedts (1999) to implement a carefully designed study comparing subjects' responses on tests for moral (Gibbs, Basinger, & Fuller, 1992) and religious (Oser & Gmunder, 1991) judgment. The results provided only weak support for the necessary but not sufficient condition hypothesis—indicating that the relation between moral and religious judgment has yet to be fully defined.

Besides this necessary-but-not-sufficient condition way of looking at the moral-faith development connection, Kohlberg also came to see that when faith and morality are integrated at the highest levels, together the two can produce a moral-spiritual exemplar. This is precisely the way that more recent studies have described moral exemplars (Colby & Damon, 1992; Walker, 2003), and it is the way that we described Mother Teresa when she turned to serving the poor.

If "moral fortitude" or some equivalent concept is admitted into this discussion, then there is evidence suggesting that ordinary people use faith to show moral fortitude in the way that they cope with adversity. For example, Dillon and Wink (2007), while drawing on the data collected from longitudinal studies dating back to the 1920s and carried out by several generations of researchers at the University of California-Berkeley's Institute of Human Development, posed a life-span developmental psychology kind of question (cf. Baltes, 1997), "Does R-S development help offset the losses associated with aging?" From analyzing the data, they concluded that it does.

> [T]he study participants who were in poor physical health [in late adulthood and old age]…and who were not religious were the most depressed or unhappy and the least satisfied with their lives…Remarkably, the study participants who [in late adulthood and old age] were in poor physical health were as well satisfied with their lives and as positive in outlook as their nonreligious peers who enjoyed good physical health. (p. 186)

Much in Kohlberg's theory of moral development remains central to today's discussions, however, today's discussions usually leave out Kohlberg's comments about faith's connection to morality. A clear example is discussions within the major outgrowth of Kohlberg's theory, namely moral domain theory.

Moral Domain Theory and Religious-Spiritual Development

Kohlberg's linear model had moral principles replacing social conventions as the bases for moral judgments. The model assumed that children do not differentiate the truly moral (issues of justice, rights, and welfare) from conventions (how one should eat in public, how children should address elders, etc.). However, from the mid-1970s to the present, studies have shown children do make this differentiation between the moral and the conventional (Nucci, 2001; Turiel, 1975, 2006). And so the focus has been on examining moral development defined by issues of justice, rights, and welfare (harm). Moral domain theory thereby went beyond Kohlberg's theory but left in tact the central premise that moral knowledge is an autonomous domain and that moral development occurs "in the trenches [meaning] moral development occurs in the context of dealing with events that include social problems, conflicts, and struggles" (Turiel, 2006, p. 30).

The argument is that religion does not define for individuals what is moral or immoral, and moral development itself occurs "in the trenches" of everyday living, rather than when engaged with religion. For example, Nucci (2003) in his debate with Kunzman, points out that the statement "God is good" implies the speaker knows about God and knows about what is good. He goes on to say that both have to be known separately in order to be able to put them together. In other words, the good is not defined by knowing God. More to Nucci's point, evidence from his own and others' studies suggests that the religious and non-religious define moral and immoral in virtually identical ways (Nucci & Turiel, 1993).

We come now to how differences in the meaning of "being religious" and "having faith" figure into differences in how moral domain theorists have construed the relationship between religious, spiritual, and moral development. The argument over the autonomy of the moral domain is not simply an empirically based argument. It is also a philosophically based argument over the meaning of "being moral" and "being religious." For example, in the debate just mentioned between Robert Kunzman (2003) and Larry Nucci (2003), Kunzman took the position that, for the religious, morality is not totally independent of religion because religion functions to provide motivation to act morally and because the meaning of "being moral" is, for the religious (at least those from Abrahamic traditions), inextricably bound up with having a relationship with God.

Nucci responded that Kunzman had conflated functional relationships with moral knowledge and in so doing, he had failed to understand that moral knowledge (of the good) is independent of religious knowledge (e.g., of divine commands)—as evidenced by the fact that, in his interviews with children, both religious and non-religious subjects understood what is moral and immoral in essentially the same ways.

However, in one comment, Nucci shows that his position and that of Kunzman are not so far apart as they might at first appear to be and that their differences turn mainly on whether religious motivation, religious concepts, and moral knowledge are seen as what W. C. Smith (1998b) calls "conflict dualities" (this vs. that) or as "complement dualities." In the latter case, dualities fit together like yin and yang, their meaning being co-determined by one another. Nucci (2003) writes:

> What Kunzman can offer correctly…is that the child's motivation to care about morality in a particular situation may be affected by that child's concern to act in accordance with the precepts of her religion… The dialogue that would ensue between the [child's] own understanding of morality and an examination of the precepts of his or her religion would undoubtedly be an important element in the construction of the moral self…Such a dialogue, however, is predicated on more than a [child's] morality, and includes a host of religious and cultural assumptions… (pp. 268, 269)

Nucci's reference to "precepts" is one indicator of his adopting a belief-institution understanding of religion. According to this understanding, engaging in religious practices is mostly about following the beliefs and precepts of an institution—as opposed to becoming engaged in the kind of reflection and struggle that characterizes thinking in the "moral trenches," to paraphrase Turiel. But do the faithful engage in religious practices this way—or is there some better description?

Religious Practices and Moral Development

Belief-institution ways of defining R-S development often imply that religious practices are fairly uniform within any given religious community and that the religious carry out practices in ways prescribed by the institution. However, this is not the case—as the following discussion will indicate. Here, we will discuss two common religious practices, namely, reading sacred texts and engaging in personal (private) prayer.

Belief-institution ways of referring to religious practices (see the Regnerus and Elder example at the very beginning of this chapter) often imply that for the religious, reading sacred texts is for the purpose of discerning the beliefs and divine commands that define their religion—as if sacred texts are spiritual and moral dictionaries. However, the evidence suggests that this is not generally the way sacred texts are used, even among so-called conservative groups that outsiders assume use sacred texts this way. A better description is that most individuals interpret sacred texts for their "relevance"—with the full understanding that their interpretations are just that, interpretations. Dictionaries do not need interpreting. Sacred texts do—as seen in how most of the faithful actually use them. Here is one anthropologist saying essentially the same thing—about a Bible study group for fathers from an Evangelical church:

> [M]uch of Evangelical Bible reading pursues questions of personal application, not questions of textual meaning. This "search for relevance" assumes the form of a guarantee, where there is the distinct certainty that the Bible will always be appropriate, relevant, and applicable to the readers' own circumstances...When multiple interpretations occur, the experience is not one of the Bible's being obtuse but of the Bible's having different messages for different individuals and for the same individual under different circumstances,...a "natural" outcome of multiple readers approaching the same text, rather than a challenge to the Bible's stability. (Bielo, 2008, pp. 16, 17)

The term *messages* could be interpreted to mean the same thing as *answers, divine commands*, or *precepts*, but given Bielo's description of the active discussions going on during these Bible study meetings, the meaning of the term is closer to that of *insights*, as in insights following discussions or periods of reflection.

Lest this single example be taken as an example rooted only in western democratic traditions where individuals are apt to be highly schooled, here is another example, this time from an anthropologist's research on Seventh-Day Adventist Bible study in a rice-farming village on the east coast of Madagascar. The people of the village enthusiastically engage in studying the Bible, both in and out of church, even when their reading skills are quite poor. They do so as a way to question and reflect about small and great problems—both alone and together. Here is the anthropologist, Eva Keller (2006), describing how Bible study goes when village members gather for "Sabboth school":

> The purpose of Sabbath school is to exchange ideas, opinions, and interpretations of what everyone has read over the week at home, and to possibly develop in group discussion a common understanding of the past week's chapter. The members of the church are encouraged to reflect and ponder and to form their own opinion on a given matter...Adventist Bible study is not a matter of the truth being taught by some to others; and this includes the pastor, whose office per se does not authorize his interpretations of the biblical text. Rather, it is a matter of everyone discovering the truth contained in the Bible for themselves by way of study, reflection, and discussion. The goal of such discussions is not to establish one correct answer... The main purpose of Sabbath schools, as of Bible study at home, is to enable the discussion to take place. (p. 282)

If we can generalize from these examples, ordinary individuals do not approach a sacred text asking what are the beliefs and precepts of their religion. Rather, they approach a sacred text asking how it relates to them, to their lives and particularly to their struggles to live good lives. Often they go away from their reading not with answers but with some feeling of empowerment to take on their struggles in the "moral trenches." Furthermore, rather than thinking of alternative interpretations as somehow wrong or dangerous, they see alternative interpretations as the natural outcome of different people experiencing life differently and having to make different uses of scripture to help guide and support them.

Put another way, rather than describing the practice of reading sacred scripture as a means to discern divine commands, the practice is better described as a support for constructing personal narratives. There is something here akin to what Bruner (1986) referred to as a narrative mode of thought and explanation. There are situations where scientific methods, references to evidence, and logic work best to provide explanations of causes and prescriptions for addressing problems. However, when there is ambiguity, we resort to constructing stories. Biblical stories, stories of the prophet Mohammad, stories of the Buddha, and all sacred stories are available to the faithful to help them with this process of constructing the right stories to explain their own lives and arrive at good ways to address problems, including moral problems. This way of describing how sacred texts are read is a far cry from the descriptions of sacred texts as spiritual and moral dictionaries or as receptacles of a religion's set of beliefs and divine commands. Even for the self-proclaimed fundamentalist, the assumption is not that the sacred text is to be taken literally but that the sacred text is to be taken as relevant, useful, and (hopefully) an inspiration to understand, through interpretation and reflection, life's dramas, both big and small.

As for personal prayer, from a belief-institution way of defining R-S development, one might imagine personal prayer as being mostly ritual prayer, such as Roman Catholics saying the rosary or Muslims saying the five daily prayers that make up the second "pillar"—and one might imagine a solitary individual petitioning God to heal a sick relative, save a business from bankruptcy, improve an unsatisfying marriage, or otherwise intervene to do some job that the individual can't do or feels he or she can't do. In both images, the person praying is neither reflecting nor puzzling, that is, the person is not "in the moral trenches."

However, a closer inspection reveals, once again, that the faithful, while praying, reflect and puzzle much more than these images suggest. For example, in a study referred to earlier (Scarlett & Perriello, 1991), the young adolescent subjects gave prayers that asked God to intervene to do some job or change some unsatisfactory situation. In contrast, the older adolescent and young adult subjects more often prayed for strength and wisdom to carry out some difficult task or figure out a way to manage some complex situation having a moral dimension. The older but not the younger subjects indicated that they had no clear idea of God's will and therefore no clear idea of God's commands. Rather, they indicated that through prayer they might come to know God's will and thereby be better equipped to cope with and take responsibility for difficult situations. William James (1958 [1902]) said something similar about this kind of prayer when he wrote:

> [T]he belief is, not that particular events are tempered more toward…us by a superintending providence, as a reward for our reliance, but that by cultivating the continuous sense of our connection with the power that made things as they are, we are tempered more towardly for their reception. The outward face of nature need not alter, but the expressions of meaning in it alter. (p. 359)

In sum, what we find in many of the prayers of the faithful is an indication that the faithful are struggling to figure out God's will so as to take responsibility for their own actions. For them, there is mystery rather than clarity about divine commands and God's will so that the task at hand is to use prayer to reflect and puzzle. Again, religious practice places the individual inside, not outside, the spiritual-moral trenches.

Sacred Values, Sacred Principles, and Sacred Order

The Kohlberg legacy also keeps separate the moral from the sacred—at least this is the impression given in discussions of the moral domain, discussions that emphasize the role of reason and judgment. However, occasionally one finds individuals treating some value, maxim, or principle not as a mere value, maxim, or principle but as something sacred to which they owe their allegiance. This experience of values, maxims, and principles as sacred can be what transforms a morality into a full-blown faith.

Gibbs et al. (2009) find in the following passage from Piaget what might be a precursor to this phenomenon of individuals turning a value, maxim or principle into something sacred—the moment when individuals come to realize there is an ideal world or way of being in the world:

> [The child's] concern with reciprocity leads [him or her] beyond ... short-sighted justice.... The child begins by simply practicing reciprocity, in itself not so easy a thing as one might think. Then, once one has grown accustomed to this form of equilibrium in his action, his behavior is altered from within, its form reacting, as it were, upon its content. What is regarded as just is no longer merely reciprocal action, but primarily behavior that admits of indefinitely sustained reciprocity. (Piaget, 1964 [1932], pp. 323–324)

That is, experiencing reciprocity as an ideal way of being in the world can be seen as just another instance of developing moral knowledge or a precursor for imbuing reciprocity with a sense of what is sacred (e.g., "Do unto others…"). If the latter, devotion to ideal reciprocity can become what organizes a pattern of faith.

History gives us plenty of examples of individuals coming to see reciprocity or some moral principle as a way to organize a pattern of faith. For example, more than one historian (Charnwood, 1996; Wills, 1992) has suggested that Lincoln experienced such a transformation during the turbulent 1850s—when the U.S. legal and political systems were working toward permanently institutionalizing slavery. This disturbing trend led him to reexamine and make sacred the great principle of equality that framed the country's Declaration of Independence and to use that principle to organize and energize a faith in a democratic way of creating and maintaining a just, caring, and diverse community. Here is an excerpt from his Springfield, Illinois speech in 1857 following the infamous Dred Scott Supreme Court ruling, an excerpt that gives his interpretation that the Founding Fathers meant the principle of equality to be not simply a moral principle, but an article of faith to live and die for. Lincoln interpreted the intent behind the principle of equality to be:

> a standard maxim for free society, which could be familiar to all, and revered by all; constantly looked to, constantly labored for, and even though never perfectly attained, constantly approximated, and thereby constantly spreading and deepening its influence, and augmenting the happiness and value of life to all people of all colors everywhere. (Basler, 1969, p. 360)

As for experiencing the order of things (the universe) as being itself sacred, there is evidence that this phenomenon of rooting morality in a sacred cosmic order and using faith to support and motivate moral conduct is more common than the collection of studies on moral development might lead one to believe. It is not uncommon for individuals to organize their thoughts about morality around religious concepts such as karma (Hindu), agape (Christian), covenant (Jewish), dharma (Buddhist), and surrender (Islam). What is moral, then, becomes a matter of conceiving "the good life" in a religious or spiritual way—much as what Richard Shweder and his colleagues describe as "the ethic of divinity"—where individuals organize themselves around the metaphor of a sacred world (Shweder, Much, Hahapatra, & Park, 1997, pp. 147–150).

Character Education, Community Service, and Religious-Spiritual Development

Moral development involves much more than judgment and reasoning. It also involves action. Action, in turn, is the measure of character and service. We need, then, to understand what connections there are between character, service, and R-S development.

While there is a great deal written about character and character education (cf. Damon, 2002; Lapsley & Narvaez, 2006), there is not much empirical evidence linking character development to R-S development. Nevertheless, progress in the field of character education allows for making several generalizations.

The main progress has been in coming to see character development as having to do with conduct and how individuals "align personal goals with moral ones, [and] identify the actual self with ideal representations" (Lapsley & Narvaez, 2006, p. 267). This perspective contrasts with other perspectives that see character development has having to do with teaching core values and providing risk-and-prevention programs. Thinking of character development as a process of aligning personal goals with moral goals and as identifying with ideal representations provides a more positive approach and better captures what it takes for individuals to equip themselves to live moral lives.

Progress has also been made by incorporating developmental systems thinking into thinking about what it takes to support character development. Increasingly, character development is being located not in the individual but in the dynamic interactions between individual and context. Nowhere is this more clearly shown than in the positive youth development approach (Lerner, Dowling, & Anderson, 2003) to character development, an approach that emphasizes supporting and building up developmental *assets* both within individuals and within communities.

Programs adopting a positive youth development approach may not describe themselves as character education programs, because talk about virtues, values, and prevention is not central to the programs. What is central is involving youth in important tasks that have a moral dimension—and giving youth real responsibility and responsibility for leading—so as to ensure that they become not just committed but also competent to live moral lives.

We see this positive youth development approach clearly illustrated in service learning programs for youth, and in a few studies, we gain glimpses of how service learning connects moral and R-S development. A number of studies have demonstrated positive outcomes following involvement in community service sponsored by religious institutions. For adolescents, community service sponsored by religious institutions seems to have a different and more positive meaning than does community service sponsored by other institutions, such as schools. For example, Donnelly, Matsuba, Hart, and Atkins (2005) found that adolescents doing community service within the context of religious institutions as compared to those doing community service in other contexts are more likely to do community service later on in their post–high school, adult lives.

Why is this so? The research of Youniss, McLellan, Su, and Yates (1999) suggests at least two reasons. They found that church-sponsored community service made it more likely that youth would adopt the religious rationale behind doing service—a rationale that presumably they could use in the future to motivate them to continue to do service. Furthermore, and in keeping with a developmental systems perspective, they underscored the importance of religious institutions (e.g., churches) often providing both volunteer programs and programs for those in need. That is, religious institutions often provide a better overall person–context system for doing service than that provided by other institutions overseeing volunteer work. In their own words:

> Churches are involved at both ends of the process, as the professionals who deliver services and as the organizations from which volunteers are recruited. There is, then, a structure behind voluntary services that is superordinate to personality and individual proclivities. Members of established community organizations are likely to be accorded opportunities for service either because these organizations provide services or because they are targets for recruiters. (p. 244)

Furthermore, they add that high school students who valued religion and who were deeply involved in community service were not the service nerds some might assume them to be. Rather, they were "vibrantly engaged in their schooling, the betterment of their communities, and the development of identities which presage healthy lives" (p. 252).

In sum, although there is not much research linking character development and service to R-S development, there is enough to suggest the links are there. Character development and commitment to a lifetime of service link naturally to developing oneself religiously and spirituality—so that at times it is difficult to say what is being observed, character or R-S development, the two can seem so intertwined.

Conclusions

The answer to the opening question about why behavioral and social scientists largely ignore R-S development when discussing moral development seems to be that belief-institution approaches set one up for missing the way that the faithful reflect and struggle to figure out how their faith can guide and motivate them morally. This is a very different characterization of the faithful than that given by references to divine command theory and ritual practices. Once we gain a close-up of the faithful puzzling over how to proceed with their lives in the light of sacred texts or from praying, we find incredible diversity—even among groups assumed to derive what is "good" from the divine commands and revealed truth found in their religion's sources of authority. In addition, once we move from viewing moral development as being mostly about moral judgment and learning core values to being more about showing character in being of service to others, then, we see how those who are both engaged with their religious communities and engaged in community service are those likely to continue to show character through serving.

Of course, this generalization does not describe all who are faithful. There are obviously those among the faithful who use their religion to do harm to themselves and/or to others. In other words, R-S development sometimes leads to problems—the subject of the next and final section.

PROBLEMATIC RELIGIOUS-SPIRITUAL DEVELOPMENT

The preceding sections have shown how spirituality and religiousness may be associated with positive development across the life span. The term *religion*, however, also elicits images of September 11, 2001, and of Jonestown, Guyana, where several hundred people from a religious cult committed or were forced to commit suicide. We need, then, to also understand the problems associated with R-S development. However, before doing so, we begin by discussing the negative biases against religion that, in the behavioral and social sciences, have impeded progress in sorting out negative from positive. These negative biases are marked by a failure to recognize within-group diversity and as well as a failure to employ a dynamic systems—faith-tradition—approach to the study of problematic R-S development.

With respect to R-S development, the history of both psychological research and clinical practice has been a history of negative bias and prejudice. That bias and prejudice persists today but has lessened considerably—both because of a new tolerance for cultural diversity and because of empirical research that has challenged old negative stereotypes, including research presented in this chapter. Nevertheless, we begin with a brief discussion of the most obvious negative biases and prejudices because their persistence presents a significant roadblock to understanding problematic R-S development.

Negative bias is particularly evident in stereotyping, that is, in collapsing meaningful distinctions into a single negative category. A collapse of meaningful distinctions—the failure to recognize within-group diversity—is the hallmark of belief-institution ways of defining religion and spirituality. An overview of the literature reveals the predominance of this belief-institution approach when discussing central religious concepts such as *belief* and *revelation*, which are assumed to have one meaning only. And yet, there are many different meanings for these concepts, and the differences matter.

With regard to the concept of belief, research psychologists and clinicians have customarily equated the meaning of religious belief with the meaning of belief as it is used when speaking of, say, belief in trees and dogs (Blackstone, 1963). With regard to the concept of revelation, research psychologists and clinicians have generally given one single meaning to revelation when, in fact, there are several, including meanings that acknowledge diverse interpretations of sacred texts and religious experience (Dulles, 1994).

Without making important distinctions that reveal the diverse meanings of these and other central religious concepts, we blunt the meaning of religion; religion becomes irrational belief and dogmatic, childish denial that truth is a matter of interpretation and argument, and nothing more. Add a quantitative dimension to the discussion, and such negative views of religion often turn into pathologizing religion whenever religion is taken seriously. One is reminded of Albert Ellis's (1980) remark, "The less religious (people) are, the more emotionally healthy they will tend to be" (p. 637).

The failure to make meaningful distinctions, then, has been one problem. Making false distinctions has been another. Perhaps the most obvious example of making a false distinction is the distinction between science and religion, such that one is split from the other. This split conception often goes unchallenged despite the fact that the majority of religious persons who are also scientists find no contradiction in being both, and despite the fact that only a small minority of the religious believe in unscientific theories such as creationism (Gould, 2003).

Research psychologists and clinicians have been particularly harsh on fundamentalist groups. Fundamentalists are routinely lumped together to form a negative stereotype consisting of character traits such as *immature, dogmatic, rigid*, and *prejudiced*. There is evidence to support the claim that religious fundamentalism is indeed associated with higher levels of prejudice and an "us versus them" mentality (Altemeyer, 2003). However, there is also evidence suggesting that prejudice is not confined to any one group and that groups of so-called healthy, quest-orientated individuals are also prejudiced, especially toward fundamentalists (Goldfried & Miner, 2002).

Fundamentalist movements are reactions to problems of modernity. They have in common several features, including the following: negative reactions to the secular, modern world, dualistic thinking (e.g., good vs. evil), selective reading of sacred texts for the purpose of bolstering positions on specific issues, and, for many, millennialism or the belief that God will triumph in the end and establish his kingdom on earth (Herriot, 2007).

For scholars embracing the values of the Enlightenment, this composite picture of fundamentalism can make fundamentalism seem pathological or at least pathogenic. However, faith-tradition approaches to studying fundamentalist groups often reveal a much more nuanced overall picture than that painted by negative stereotypes derived from belief-institution approaches. Recall Susan Kwilecki's conclusion about one of her case studies of a man who could be described as a religious fundamentalist: "an adult absorbed in a realm with the same empirical status as Oz and ennobled by it!" (Kwilecki, 1999, p. 16). Therefore, whether or not fundamentalism supports problematic behavior is determined not by the pattern of faith but by a combination of the faith pattern, circumstances, and interconnecting systems.

In pointing out the diversity among the religious, especially among religious fundamentalists, our intent is not to downplay those very real instances of problematic R-S development. We need not go to the opposite extreme. The point here is that in the history of psychology and psychiatry there has been persistent negative bias against religion, a bias perpetrated through belief-institution approaches to the study of R-S development. Indeed, R-S development is a complex phenomenon, so complex as to require a more nuanced approach, one afforded by dynamic systems thinking and faith-tradition ways of defining. Pathology is real and does not reside in the eyes of the diagnostician, but pathology, as a concept, needs to be understood as embedded within the dynamic developmental system.

Having cleared away some of the brush that has impeded progress in the past, we can turn now to recent research on problematic R-S development. We will discuss, in turn, the subjects of prejudice, bad cults, mental disorders, and religiously inspired violence—all subjects that deal problematic R-S development.

Prejudice

Perhaps the best researched problem associated with R-S development has been that of prejudice. Allport (1966; Allport & Ross, 1967), in his well-known work on the multiple causes of prejudice and discrimination, examined the role of religion and, in particular, of religious doctrine. He detailed how the doctrine of *election*, which undergirds such concepts as "God's chosen people," can manifest as divinely sanctioned ethnocentrism in that it "divides the ins from the outs with surgical precision" (p. 450). He continued, "Since God is for the ins, the outs must be excluded from privileges, and in extreme cases eliminated by sword or by fire."

However, given the theoretical paradox that religion both "makes" and "unmakes" prejudice (Allport, 1966), and given empirical findings about the curvilinear relationship between church attendance and prejudiced attitudes (Allport & Ross, 1967), Allport did not simply designate religion as the taproot of prejudice. Rather, he distinguished between two types of religious orientations: *extrinsic* and *intrinsic* (Allport, 1963). People with an extrinsic religious orientation regard religion as strictly instrumental and utilitarian. That is, religion is a means to a personal end, such as security, status, and self-justification. Allport and Ross (1967) argued that the functional significance of extrinsic religion and prejudice is identical and, therefore, individuals dependent on the supports of one will likely be dependent on the supports of the other.

In contrast, people with an intrinsic religious orientation regard faith as an end in and of itself. Religion is not an instrumental device, a method of conformity, a bid for status, or a sedative. Intrinsic religious individuals have internalized their religion, including its values of humility, compassion, and unlimited love (Post, 2003). These individuals are "oriented toward a unification of being, [take] seriously the commandment of brotherhood, and [strive] to transcend all self-centered needs" (p. 455). Such faith "floods the whole life with motivation and meaning" and, unlike the extrinsic form of religious sentiment, is not "limited to [a] single segments of self-interest" (p. 455). Indeed, Allport (1966; Allport & Ross, 1967) demonstrated that people with an extrinsic religious orientation were significantly more prejudiced than people with an intrinsic religious orientation.

Earlier work by Allport and Kramer (1946), which linked church attendance and intolerance for ethnic minorities, spawned a series of studies exploring the relationship between religion and prejudice. Rosenblith (1949) replicated most of Allport and Kramer's (1946) findings based on three New England colleges in her study of Southern, rural colleges. She found ethnic prejudice to be highest among Catholics, veterans, disciplinarians, and those who conceive of the world as evil. Kirkpatrick (1949) found religious people to be less humanitarian than nonreligious people, as indicated by more *severe* attitudes toward criminals, delinquents, prostitutes, homosexuals, and individuals in need of psychiatric treatment. In turn, in a review of empirical research on the structure of belief systems, Rokeach (1960) found nonbelievers to be consistently less dogmatic, less authoritarian, and less ethnocentric than believers.

Here again we see the predominance of belief-institution approaches to the study of problematic spirituality and religiousness. Such group comparative analyses do little to explicate within-group diversity, which exceeds the diversity between groups. Again, in pointing out this diversity, our intent is not to downplay those very real instances of religiously sponsored prejudice. For example, certain fundamentalist groups find in the Bible grounds for considering homosexuality a sin. Rather, our intent is to note the limitations of belief-institution approaches to the study of problematic R-S development.

Bad Cults

Historically, the term *cult* has had a neutral meaning—both within faith traditions and within the sociology of religion. However, since the 1960s and especially since the Jonestown and Waco tragedies, the term has been defined by the media and certain government agencies (and, in turn, by many behavioral and social scientists) as referring to a particular kind of group, one with a self-appointed, dogmatic, and charismatic leader who promotes deceptive-coercive recruitment practices to ensnare individuals to join a totalitarian community organized to solicit funds and secure favors that benefit neither the group's members nor society (Barrett, 2001). The media often adds terms such as "brainwashing" to characterize the socialization of cult members.

This negative definition of cults works well as an "ideal type" for identifying harmful cults, but unfortunately, the definition has been applied indiscriminately and to religious groups that do not fit the definition. As a result, discussions of cults are often polemical and divided into "cult critics" and "cult sympathizers"; neither of these absolute positions recognize the extraordinary diversity among and within cults and occultist practices.

Cult sympathizers are more likely to use the terms "new religious movements" and "alternative religions" instead of "cult," although these terms too have their problems. Certain groups considered by most to be cults are not new, and in some contexts would not be alternatives to the mainstream. The International Society for Krishna Consciousness, otherwise known as the Hare Krishna, is an example (Daner, 1976). Nevertheless, new religious movements or alternative religions have become accepted terms. Cult sympathizers point out, tongue in cheek, that the difference between a cult and a religion is about a million members (Barrett, 2001). There is also misunderstanding about the average age of cult members. Cults are associated with "youth religions," which came into greater prominence in the 1970s; however, the average age of cult members is estimated to be between 25 and 40 (Schmitz & Friebe, 1992). For those in the Bhagwan Shree Rajneesch, living in Oregon, the average age is 34 years (Richardson, 1995).

Available evidence suggests that cult members generally are no more pathological than are non-members (Barrett, 2001). In explaining why and how a person comes to join a cult, a more dynamic systems, and less organismic, approach may work best—because each level of the organism's developmental system plays a decisive role. Using

Barrett's (2001) example, a newly arrived freshman at college may, along with other freshman, feel lonely and disoriented and adjust without joining a cult, but if that freshman happens to meet and talk with a cult member, he or she may well end up joining a cult.

Of particular relevance to life-span developmental psychology are the reasons why individuals join cults. Several clinical studies conducted mostly with persons who had left cults, established that many had serious family and non-family problems before joining cults (Klosinski, 1996). By some accounts, life before joining a cult was characterized by a history of poor relationships with both parents and peers (Silverstein, 1988). In her sample, Rollett (1996) too found that young people with a high exposure to crises tended more strongly toward joining cults. Others have characterized those who join cults as persons who have suffered from the absence of a father during childhood and who have difficulty dealing with the complexities of life (Ullman, 1982). This is consistent with the finding of one study that showed that new converts to cults held stronger authoritarian values than did non-converts (Shaver, Leneuaer, & Sadd, 1980).

Popular scientific accounts often deliver the blanket judgment that cults rob their members of freedom, individuality, and wealth. These accounts accuse cults of fostering dislocation from reality, thought paralysis, and regression (Lademann-Priemer, 1998). The doctrines of many cults do seem to operate on lower developmental stages—as when cults divide humanity into groups of those who are "good" and who are "saved," from the great majority who are "bad" and "lost" (Brickerhoff & MacKie, 1986). As another example, the Krishnas, who consider a doll to be the Divine itself, seem to collapse the distinction between a religious symbol and its referent (Cassirer, 1955; Fowler, 1981).

However, negative characterizations of those joining cults may well be the result of interviewing mostly those who have left cults because they were dissatisfied. The research, then, may be biased toward having a negative view inasmuch as the sample of former cult members is a biased sample (Richardson, van der Lans, & Derks, 1985).

As for the effects of joining cults, in the worst case, the results can be fatal, as was the case in 1974 for 74 members of the Solar Temple Order founded by Luc Jouret. Fatal or otherwise harmful effects may happen, especially in cases when cult members engage in occultist practices.

However, some researchers have shown positive effects of cults. Salzman (1953) found that cults sometimes have positive effects by helping members to cope. In a survey of 517 members of the Unification Church and of Ananda Marga, Kuner (1981) showed that long-term membership produced "resocializing" and "therapeutic" effects, and Schibilsky (1976) found that joining cults helped members cope with developmental tasks such as forming an identity and developing self-discipline. As another example of positive effects, Wicca groups have been described as empowering women and helping them to heal wounds inflicted on them in societies where women, especially lesbians, have been disempowered and hurt by homophobia (Warwick, 1995).

This positive view of the effects of cults is sometimes accompanied by the observation that cults help individuals make a transition. People often belong to cults on a temporary basis and perceive them as protective spaces and "havens" (Hood, Spilka, Hunsberger, & Gorsuch, 1996). In his thorough meta-analysis of clinical studies on the psychic effects of joining new religious groups such as "the Rajneeshees" and "Hare Krishna," Richardson (1995) concluded that membership is often therapeutic instead of harmful (Latkin, 1995).

In addition to contextualizing problematic spirituality and religiousness, some researchers have also demonstrated a greater sensitivity to issues of development. What may at first appear to be psychopathology of a religious or spiritual nature, on closer inspection, can turn out to be a means for spiritual growth. For example, Streib (1999), in reporting on groups of European adolescents engaged in occult practices that he calls "off-road religion," characterized these practices in terms of their experimental, uncommitted, and adventurous nature for the individuals involved—the implication being that this kind of activity is developmentally appropriate.

Also with regard to occult practices, and contrary to popular and negative views, the overwhelming majority of studies have shown that only a minority of teenagers regularly perform occult practices, and most do so out of sheer curiosity and not out of existential engagement (Streib, 1996, 1999). Rollet (1992) demonstrated that Catholic youth are more attracted to occultism than are youth without any religious denomination. Bucher (1994) showed that adolescents at stage two of religious judgment according to Oser and Gmünder (1991) (see Table 16.4) consider occult practices as being plausible more so than do adolescents at stage three. Occult practices can, therefore, be expressions of religious stage.

With respect to cults, then, the main conclusions are the following:

1. We need to distinguish harmful cults from those new religious movements that do no harm. In doing so, we can apply criteria such as deception, manipulation, and coercion but not without a careful examination of the evidence.
2. We need to develop reliable measures to evaluate cults in terms of short- versus long-term functioning.

Mental Disorders and Mental Health

As used here, the concept of a mental disorder is the same as used in major classification systems such as the American Psychiatric Association's Diagnostic and Statistical Manual (DSM). These classification systems have a number of conceptual and practical advantages over dimensional approaches (Cantwell & Rutter, 2002). However, they also have disadvantages. Professionals agree, then, that classification systems should be used in conjunction with dimensional approaches so as to correct for their inherent deficiencies. With this cautionary point made, we can proceed to discuss how the current literature treats R-S development with respect to mental disorders as defined by classification systems, particularly by DSM-IV.

First, with regard to DSM-IV itself, the revised form includes a V-code for "other conditions"—those conditions that occasionally warrant a clinician's help but which do not constitute mental disorders. Medication-induced movement disorder is one example. "Religious or spiritual problem" is another.

Including the V-Code "religious or spiritual problem" marks a step forward—because it openly says that problems with a religious or spiritual content should not be automatically pathologized. However, some have argued that the inclusion of R-S problems as one of several "other conditions" marginalizes these problems when, in certain cases, they should not be marginalized (Scott, Garver, Richards, & Hathaway, 2003).

As for the other categories defining mental disorders, the picture is more complex. Perhaps the best overall characterization of the research is that with these other categories (psychotic disorders, mood disorders, etc.), religiosity and spirituality can define the content of the disorders (e.g., having delusions with religious content), but there is no evidence that religiosity and spirituality cause these disorders. For example, the frequency of religious delusions in groups of psychotic individuals varies considerably depending on the group sampled—as much as between 7 and 45% (Kingdom, Siddle, & Rathod, 2001)—suggesting that psychotic individuals use whatever content is available in their context and culture to construct their delusions.

A further point about complexity is made with regard to individuals with the same diagnosis but who differ from one another in their religiosity. For example, when accompanied by a strong religious faith, depression may have a different and more positive meaning with respect to ability to function than depression without faith (Stone, 2000).

Of course, mental disorders are not all there is to psychopathology. Clinicians and researchers have always taken on a number of psychological problems that do not meet the criteria for mental disorders. Here, the discussion turns to dimensional and developmental-contextual approaches to mental health and psychopathology. In doing so, the question becomes not "Does this individual have such and such a diagnosis?" but "To what degree and in what context and at what stage in life does a person have problems that many if not most of us experience on occasion?"

For example, religious attributions (Spilka & McIntosh, 1995) can further self-esteem and psychic equilibrium, but they can also weaken them. In particular, a person's ability to cope can be impeded when critical events in life are attributed to the punishment of God, which traditional religious instruction used to encourage. Not only do feelings of anger appear, but also feelings of helplessness, shame, and fear (Pargament, Ensing, & Falgout, 1990). For example, 13% of the cardiac patients, interviewed by Croog and Levine (1972), convinced themselves that their illness was a punishment for earlier sins; this damaged their ability to cope, because their recovery time was longer, and their sense of well-being was poorer than for those without these negative religious attributions.

An avenging God, predominant at the lower stages of religious judgment, brings about guilt feelings, and can drive the self into punishing itself if it perceives itself to be disobedient in the eyes of God (Hood, 1992, p. 118). On the basis of clinical studies, Frielingsdorf (1992) described shocking examples of casuistry, where people lost all self-respect on account of demonic images of God, felt themselves to be "like dirt," and filled with fear. He found that these people were often unwanted and neglected as children.

Religiously Inspired Acts of Violence

The subject of religiously inspired acts of violence invariably brings into discussion religious fundamentalism. However, given what has already been said about negative stereotyping and the evidence showing that fundamentalism does not invariably breed problems, we need to understand religiously inspired violence among fundamentalists in a more dynamic and developmental systems way. A good example is religiously inspired terrorist groups.

Similar to what was said about cults, what constitutes a terrorist group depends on one's vantage point. Those identifying with or participating in such groups define the groups very differently than outsiders—as aggrieved victims of violent injustice (Silke, 2003). For them, the group is all about justice and freedom, not what is implied by the term "terrorist group." Also, becoming a member of a terrorist group can be seen and experienced as entirely natural and normal—akin to joining the army or police (Silke, 2003). Furthermore, terrorists, on average, have no appreciable psychopathology and are average with respect to level of education and socioeconomic status (Atran, 2003).

It seems, then, that terrorism is more a group phenomenon than it is an individual phenomenon—and should be studied as such. For example, Scot Atran (2003) has found that religiously inspired suicide bombers often come from small groups of men living away from home but connected to Internet sites where they feel in touch with the worldwide Muslim community, and where their anger is fueled by images and slogans portrayed on Muslim websites. Under such conditions, their reading of the Qur'an is apt to become increasingly selective—focusing more and more on the Qur'an's war surahs and on the first pillar of Islam (confession of faith in Allah) and deemphasizing less and less the counter-balancing surahs and the other four pillars such as the pillar of charity.

This example of religiously inspired terrorist groups suggests that religiously inspired violence is not the direct product of fundamentalism—as a belief-institution approach might lead one to believe—but rather is a product of the dynamic interaction between patterns of faith and particular systems and conditions such as being isolated in a foreign country, watching inflammatory video on the Internet, living in a world with negative stereotyping and injustice, and so forth. With respect to religiously inspired violence, then, the main conclusions seem to be the following:

1. We need to focus on changing the social and political conditions that lead essentially normal individuals to join terrorist groups.
2. We need to focus on educating the general public about those social and political conditions so as to minimize the demonizing that continues the cycle of violence.
3. We need to prevent violent groups from forming in the first place by countering the selective interpretations of sacred texts with more balanced interpretations.

Conclusions

This brief overview of problematic spirituality and religiousness begins to reveal the extraordinary diversity in seemingly invariant concepts (such as religiously inspired violence) and how such problems are a fluid expression of dynamic interactions among the faithful, their cumulative faith traditions, and circumstances. When we acknowledge this diversity, we must also acknowledge the limitations associated with belief-institution approaches to the study of problematic R-S development. These approaches pin the problem on religious doctrine and, even, on whole religions, rather than teasing apart the dynamic interactions that precipitate problematic spirituality and religiousness. Reducing spiritual problems to psychological, sociological, or biological problems will not suffice. To build an adequate research base, we need to develop more nuanced—faith-tradition—approaches to the study of problematic R-S development.

There are, for example, conceptual reasons to distinguish among different forms of problematic faith. For example, there is structurally immature faith, preventing individuals from decentering and benefiting from reflection through discussion, and there is structurally developed faith whose content (corrupt images of divinity, humanity, and nature) may promote evil (Scarlett, 2008, 2009). We need more research to establish whether these or other distinctions can be used scientifically to further our understanding of problematic R-S development.

CONCLUDING REMARKS

Our aim has been to show that understanding R-S development is central to understanding human development. At issue also is how best to support identity and moral development and how best to prevent serious problems related to religion. Science can contribute a great deal, but only if those doing science first adequately define the nature of the phenomenon under investigation. The phenomenon of R-S development is only poorly grasped in terms of beliefs and institutions. It is better grasped in terms of faith and cumulative faith traditions. Furthermore, it is better grasped when the faithful themselves are understood in terms of the complexities of interacting systems, when their development is seen not as a matter of acquiring institutional beliefs but as a matter of responding to their faith traditions, to their context, to their culture, and to virtually everything central and important in their lives.

REFERENCES

Abu-Lughod, L. (1990). Can there be a feminist ethnography? *Women and Performance: A Journal of Feminist Theory, 5,* 7–27.

Ajrouch, K. J. (2004). Gender, race, and symbolic boundaries: Contested spaces of identity among Arab-American adolescents. *Sociological Perspectives, 47,* 371.

Ali, K. (2006). *Sexual ethics in Islam: Feminist reflections on Qur'an, hadith, and jurisprudence.* Oxford: Oneworld Publications.

Ali, S. R., Mahmood, A., Moel, J., Hudson, C., & Leathers, L. (2008). A qualitative investigation of Muslim and Christian women's views of religion and feminism in their lives. *Cultural Diversity and Ethnic Minority Psychology, 14,* 38–46.

Allport, G. W. (1950). *The individual and his religion: A psychological interpretation.* New York: Macmillan.

Allport, G. W. (1955). *Becoming: Basic considerations for a psychology of personality.* New Haven, CT: Yale University Press.

Allport, G. W. (1963). Behavioral science, religion, and mental health. *Journal of Religion and Health, 2,* 187–197.

Allport, G. W. (1966). The religious context of prejudice. *Journal for the Scientific Study of Religion, 5,* 448–451.

Allport, G. W., & Kramer, B. M. (1946). Some roots of prejudice. *Journal of Psychology, 22*(9–39).

Allport, G. W., & Ross, J. (1967). Personal religious orientation and prejudice. *Journal of Personality and Social Psychology, 5,* 432–443.

Anderson, E. (1999). *Code of the street: Decency, violence, and the moral life of the inner city.* New York: W. W. Norton.

Atran, S. (2003). Genesis of suicide terrorism. *Science Magazine, 299*(March), 1534–1539.

Baker, D. D., & Terpstra, D. E. (1986). Locus of control and self-esteem versus demographic factors as predictors of attitudes toward women. *Basic and Applied Social Psychology, 7,* 163.

Baltes, P. (1997). On the incomplete architecture of human ontogeny: Selection, optimization, and compensation as foundation of developmental theory. *American Psychologist, 52,* 366–380.

Bankston, C . L. (2000). Sangha of the south: Laotian Buddhism and social adaptation in rural Louisiana. In M. Zhou & J.V. Gatewood (Eds.), *Contemporary Asian America: A multidiciplinary reader.* (pp. 357–371). New York: New York University Press.

Bankston, C. L., & Zou, M. (1995). Religious participation, ethnic identification, and adaptation of Vietnamese adolescents in an immigrant community. *Sociological Quarterly, 36,* 525–534.

Barlas, A. (2002). *"Believing women" in Islam: Unreading patriarchal interpretations of the Qur'an.* Austin: University of Texas Press.

Barret, R., & Barzan, R. (1996). Spiritual experience of gay men and lesbians. *Counseling and values, 41,* 4–15.

Barrett, D. (2001). *The new believers: A survey of sects, cults, and alternative religions.* London: Cassell.

Bartkowski, J. P. (2001). *Remaking the godly marriage: Gender negotiation in evangelical families.* New Brunswick, NJ: Rutgers University Press.

Bartkowski, J. P., & Ghazal Read, J. (2003). Veiled submission: Gender negotiation among evangelical U.S. Muslim women. *Qualitative Sociology, 26,* 71–92.

Bartoli, E., & Gillem, A. R. (2008). Continuing to depolarize the debate on sexual orientation and religion: Identity and the therapeutic process. *Professional Psychology: Research and Practice, 39,* 202.

Basler, R. (Ed.). (1969). *Abraham Lincoln: His speeches and writings.* New York: World Publishing Co.

Baugh, J. R. (1988). Gaining control by giving up control: Strategies for coping with powerlessness. In I. W. R. Miller & J. E. Martin (Eds.), *Behavior therapy and religion* (pp. 125–138). Newbury Park, CA: Sage.

Beckstead, L. (2001). Cures versus choices: Agendas in sexual reorientation therapy. *Journal of Gay and Lesbian Psychotherapy, 5,* 87–115.

Benson, P. L. (1997). Spirituality and the adolescent journey. *Reclaiming Children and Youth, 5,* 206–209.

Benson, P. L., Roehlkepartain, E. C., & Rude, S. P. (2003). Spiritual development in childhood and adolescence. *Applied Developmental Science, 7,* 204–212.

Bielo, J. (2008). On the failure of "meaning": Bible reading in the anthropology of Christianity. *Culture and Religion, 9,* 1–21.

Blackstone, W. (1963). *The problem of religious knowledge.* Englewood Cliffs, NJ: Prentice-Hall.

Boyer, P., & Walker, S. (2000). Intuitive ontology and cultural input in the acquisition of religious concepts. In C. Rosengren, C. Johnson, & P. L. Harris (Eds.), *Imagining the impossible* (pp. 130–156). New York: Cambridge University Press.

Brickerhoff, M. B., & MacKie, M. (1986). The applicability of social distance for religious research. *Review of Religious Research, 28,* 151–167.

Bruner, J. (1986). *Actual minds, possible worlds.* Cambridge, MA: Harvard University Press.

Bucher, A. (1994). Ist Okkultismus die neue Jugendreligion? Eine empirische Untersuchung an 650 Jugendli-chen. *Archiv für Religionspsychologie, 21*(248–266).

Burn, S. M., & Busso, J. (2005). Ambivalent sexism, scriptural literalism, and religiosity. *Psychology of Women Quarterly, 29,* 412.

Cantwell, D., & Rutter, M. (2002). Classification: Conceptual issues and substantive findings. In S. B. Thielman (Ed.), *Child and adolescent psychiatry*, 4th ed. (pp. 3–19). Cambridge, MA: Blackwell Science.

Cass, V. C. (1979). Homosexual identity formation: A theoretical model. *Journal of Homosexuality, 4,* 219–235.

Cassirer, E. (1955). *The philosophy of symbolic forms.* Vol. 2: *Mythical thought.* New Haven, CT: Yale University Press.

Chae, M. H., Kelly, D. B., Brown, C. F., & Bolden, M. A. (2004). Relationship of ethnic identity and spiritual development: An exploratory study. *Counseling and values, 49,* 15–26.

Charnwood, G. R. (1996). *Abraham Lincoln: A Biography.* Lanham, MD: Madison Books.

Chatters, L. M., Taylor, R. J., Lincoln, K. D., & Schroepfer, T. (2002). Patterns of informal support from family and church members among African Americans. *Journal of Black Studies, 33,* 66–85.

Chen, C. (2005). A self of one's own: Taiwanese immigrant women and religious conversion. *Gender & Society, 19,* 336–357.

Christians for Biblical Equality. (1989). Statement on men, women, and Biblical equality. Available at: http://www.cbeinternational.org/.

Colaner, C. W., & Giles, S. M. (2008). The baby blanket or the briefcase: The impact of evangelical gender role ideologies on career and mothering aspirations of female evangelical college students. *Sex Roles, 58*(7–8), 526.

Colby, A., & Damon, W. (1992). *Some do care: Contemporary lives of moral commitment.* New York: Free Press.

Colby, A., & Damon, W. (1995). The development of extraordinary moral commitment. In M. Killen & D. Hart (Eds.), *Morality in everyday life: Developmental perspectives* (pp. 343–369). Cambridge: Cambridge University Press.

Coles, R. (1990). *The spiritual lives of children*. Boston: Houghton-Miflin.

Comstock, G. D. (1996). *Unrepentant, self-affirming, practicing: Lesbian/gay/bisexual people within organized religion*. New York: Continuum.

Cook, K. V. (2000). "You have to have somebody watching your back, and if that's God, then, that's mighty big." The church's role in the resilience of inner-city youth. *Adolescence, 35*, 717–730.

Council on Biblical Manhood and Womanhood. (1988). The Danvers Statement. Wheaton, IL. Available at: http://www.cbmw.org/about/danvers.html.

Cronon, W. (1997). *John Muir: Nature writings*. New York: Penguin Putnam.

Croog, S., & Levine, S. (1972). Religious identity and response to serious illness: A report on heart patients. *Social Science and Medicine, 6*(17–32).

Damon, W. (Ed.). (2002). *Bringing in a new era in character education*. Stanford, CA: Hoover Institutional Press.

Daner, F. (1976). *The American children of Krsna: A study of the Hare Krsna movement*. Stanford, CA: Stanford University Press.

Day, J., & Naedts, M. (1999). Moral and religious judgment research. In R. Mosher, D. Youngman, & J. Day (Eds.), *Human development across the life span*. Westport, CT.: Praeger.

DeVries, R., & Kohlberg, L. (1990). *Constructivist early education: Overview and comparison with other programs*. Washington, DC: National Association for the Education of Young Children.

Dewitt, C. (2002). Spiritual and religious perspectives of creation and scientific understanding of nature. In S. Kellert & T. Farnham (Eds.), *The good in nature and humanity: Connecting science, religion, and spirituality with the natural world*. Washington, DC: Island Press.

Dillon, M., & Wink, P. (2007). *In the course of a lifetime: Tracing religious belief, practice, and change*. Berkeley: University of California Press.

Donahue, M. J., & Benson, P. L. (1995). Religion and the well-being of adolescents. *Journal of Social Issues, 51*, 145–160.

Donnelly, T., Matsuba, M. K., Hart, D., & Atkins, R. (2005). The relationship between spiritual development and civic development. In E. C. Roehlkepartain, P. E. King, L. M. Wagener, & P. L. Benson (Eds.), *Handbook of spiritual development in childhood and adolescence*. Thousand Oaks, CA: Sage.

Dowling, E., Gestesdottir, S., Anderson, P., von Eye, A., Almerigi, J., & Lerner, R. M. (2004). Structural relations among spirituality, religiosity, and thriving in adolescence. *Applied Developmental Science, 8*, 7–16.

Dufour, L. R. (2000). Sifting through tradition: The creation of Jewish feminist identities. *Journal for the Scientific Study of Religion, 39*, 90–106.

Dulles, A. (1994). *Models of revelation*. Maryknoll, NY: Orbis Books.

Eisenberg, N., Fabes, R., & Spinrad, T. (2006). Prosocial development. In W. Damon & R. Lerner (Eds.), *Handbook of child psychology* (Vol. 3). New York: John Wiley & Sons.

Eisenstadt, J. M. (1978). Parental loss and genius. *American Psychologist, 33*, 211–223.

Eliason, M. J. (1995). Accounts of sexual identity formation in heterosexual students. *Sex Roles, 32*, 821–834.

Elkind, D. (1964). Piaget's semiclinical interview and the study of the spontaneous religion. *Journal for the Scientific Study of Religion, 4*, 40–46.

Ellis, A. (1980). Psychotherapy and atheistic values: A response to A.E. Bergin's "Psychotherapy and religious values." *Journal of Consulting and Clinical Psychology, 48*, 635–639.

Erikson, E. (1958). *Young man Luther: A study in psychoanalysis and history*. New York: W. W. Norton.

Erikson, E. (1963). *Childhood and society (*2nd ed.). New York: Norton.

Erikson, E. (1964). *Insight and responsibility*. New York: Norton.

Erikson, E. (1965). Youth: Fidelity and diversity. In E. Erikson (Ed.), *The challenges of youth* (pp. 1–28). Garden City, NY: Anchor.

Erikson, E. (1968). *Identity: Youth and crisis*. New York: Norton.

Erikson, E. (1969). *Gandhi's truth: On the origins of militant nonviolence*. New York: W. W. Norton.

Ewing, J., & Allen, K. R. (2008). Women's narratives about god and gender: Agency, tension, and change. *Journal of Systemic Therapies, 27*, 96–113.

Farnham, T., & Kellert, S. (2002). Building the bridge: Connnecting science, religion, and spirituality with the natural world. In S. Kellert & T. Farnham (Eds.), *The good in nature and humanity: Connecting science, religion, and spirituality with the natural world*. Washington, DC: Island Press.

Feldman, D. H. (2008). The role of developmental change in spiritual development. In R. M. Lerner, R. Roesser, & E. Phelps (Eds.), *Positive youth development and spirituality*. West Conshohocken, PA: Templeton Foundation Press.

Fowler, J. (1981). *Stages of faith: The psychology of human development and the quest for meaning*. New York: Harper and Row.

French, S. E., Seidman, E., Allen, L., & Aber, J. L. (2006). The development of ethnic identity in adolescence. *Developmental Psychology, 42*, 1–10.

Freud, A. (1937). *The ego and the mechanisms of defence*. London: The Institute of Psycho-Analysis.

Freud, S. (1961). The future of an illusion. In J. Strachey (Ed.), *The standard edition of the complete works of Sigmund Freud* (Vol. 21, pp. 1–56). London: Hogarth Press and the Institute of Psychoanalysis.

Frielingsdorf, K. (1992). *Dämonische Gottesbilder: Ihre Entstehung, Entlarvung und Überwindung*. Mainz, Germany: Grunewald.

Fukuyama, M. A., & Sevig, T. (2002). Spirituality in counseling across cultures. In P. Pedersen, J. Draguns, W. Lonner, & J. Trimble (Eds.), *Counseling across cultures* (5th ed., pp. 273–295). Thousand Oaks, CA: Sage.

Fulton, A. S. (1997). Identity status, religious orientation, and prejudice. *Journal of Youth and Adolescence, 26*, 1–11.

Garc'a Coll, C., Crnic, K., Lamberty, G., Wasik, B. H., Jenkins, R., Garcia, H. V., et al. (1996). An integrative model for the study of developmental competencies in minority children. *Child Development, 67*, 1891–1914.

Geertz, C. (1971). *Islam observed: Religious development in Morocco and Indonesia*. Chicago: University of Chicago Press.

Gibbs, J., Basinger, K. S., & Fuller, D. (1992). *Moral maturity: Measuring the development of sociomoral reflection*. Hillsdale, NJ: Erlbaum.

Gibbs, J., Moshman, D., Berkowitz, M., Basinger, K., & Grime, R. (2009). Taking development seriously: Critique of the 2008 *JME* special issue on moral functioning. *Journal of Moral Education, 38*, 271–282.

Gilbert, S., & Sarkar, S. (2000). Embracing complexity: Organicism for the 21st century. *Developmental Dynamics, 219*, 1–9.

Gnos, C. (2003). *Bewältigungsverhalten, religiöses urteil und werthaltungen*. Unpublished master's thesis, University of Freiburg, Freiburg.

Goldman, M. S., & Isaacson, L. (1999). Enduring affiliation and gender doctrine for Shiloh sisters and Rajneesh Sannyasins. *Journal for the Scientific Study of Religion, 38*, 411–422.

Goldman, R. (1964). *Religious thinking from childhood to adolescence*. New York: Seabury.

Goodall, J. (1999). *Reason for hope: A spiritual journey*. New York: Warner Books.

Goodall, J., & Bekoff, M. (2002). *The ten trusts: What we must do to care for the animals we love*. New York: HarperCollins.

Goodenough, U. (1998). *The sacred depths of nature*. New York: Oxford University Press.

Goodwill, K. A. (2000). Religion and the spiritual needs of gay Mormon men. *Journal of Gay and Lesbian Social Services: Issues in Practice, Policy & Research, 11*, 23–37.

Gould, S. J. (2003). *The hedgehog, the fox, and the magister's pox: Mending the gap betwen science and the humanities*. New York: Harmony Books.

Griffith, R. M. (1997). *God's daughters: Evangelical women and the power of submission*. Berkeley: University of California Press.

Griffiths, P., & Gray, R. (2005). Discussion: Three ways to misunderstand developmental systems theory. *Biology and Philosophy, 20*, 417–425.

Gutierrez, L. M. (1990). Working with women of color: An empowerment perspective. *Social Work, 35*, 149–153.

Harris, D. B. (1957). *The concept of development: An issue in the study of human behavior*. Minneapolis: University of Minnesota Press.

Harris, P. L. (2000). On not falling down to earth: Children's metaphysical questions. In K. S. Rosengren, C. N. Johnson, & P. L. Harris, (Eds.), *Imagining the impossible: magical, scientific, and religious thinking in children*. Cambridge: Cambridge University Press.

Harris, P. L. (2003). Les dieux, les ancêtres et les enfants (Gods, ancestors and children). *Terrain, 40*, 81–98.

Hay, D., & Nye, R. (1998). *The spirit of the child*. London: Fount.

Heermann, M., Wiggins, M. I., & Rutter, P. A. (2007). Creating a space for spiritual practice: Pastoral possibilities with sexual minorities. *Pastoral Psychology, 55*, 711.

Henrickson, M. (2007). Lavender faith: Religion, spirituality and identity in lesbian, gay and bisexual New Zealanders. *Journal of Religion & Spirituality in Social Work, 26*, 63.

Herriot, P. (2007). *Religious fundamentalism and social identity*. New York: Routledge.

Hill, P., Pargament, K., Hood, R., McCullough, M., Swyers, J., Larson, D., et al. (2000). Conceptualizing religion and spirituality: Points of commonality, points of departure. *Journal for the Theory of Social Behavior, 30*, 51–77.

Hirschman, C. (2004). The role of religion in the origins and adaptation of immigrant groups in the United States. *International Migration Review, 38*, 1206–1233.

Hitler, A. (1953). *Hitler's secret conversations*. New York: Farrar, Straus, & Young.

Hood, R. W. (1992). Sin and guilt in faith traditions: Issues of self-esteem. In J. Schumaker (Ed.), *Religion and mental health* (pp. 110–121). New York: Oxford University Press.

Hood, R. W. J., Spilka, B., Hunsberger, B., & Gorsuch, R. (1996). *The psychology of religion: An empirical approach*. New York and London: Guilford Press.

Hyde, K. (1990). *Religion in childhood and adolescence*. Birmingham, AL: Religious Education Press.

Inzlicht, M., McGregor, I., Hirsh, J. B., & Nash, K. (2009). Neural markers of religious conviction. *Psychological Science, 20*, 385–392.

Jagers, R. (1997). Afrocultural integrity and the social development of African American children: Some conceptual, empirical and practical considerations. *Journal of Prevention and Intervention in the Community, 16*, 7–31.

James, W. (1890). *The principles of psychology*. New York: Holt.

James, W. (1958 [1902]). *The varieties of religious experience*. New York: The American Library.

Jeffries, W., Dodge, B., & Sandfort, T. G. M. (2008). Religion and spirituality among bisexual Black men in the USA. *Culture, Health & Sexuality, 10*, 463–477.

Johnson, B. R., Jang, S. J., Li, S. D., & Larson, D. (2000). The "invisible institution" and black youth crime: The church as an agency of local social control. *Journal of Youth and Adolescence, 29*, 479–498.

Juang, L., & Syed, L. M. (2008). Ethnic identity and spirituality. In R. M. Lerner, E. Phelps, & R. W. Roeser (Eds.), *Positive youth development and spirituality: From theory to research* (pp. 262–284). West Conshohocken, PA: Templeton Foundation Press.

Jung, C. G. (1968). Concerning the archetypes, with special reference to the anima concept. In G. Adler, M. Fordham, & H. Read (Eds.), *The collected works of C.G. Jung*, Vol. 9 (pp. 54–72). Princeton, NJ: Princeton University Press.

Jung, C. G. (1969). *Psychology and religion* (Vol. 11). Princeton, NJ: Princeton University Press.

Kager, A. (1995). Die stufen des religiösen urteils in ordensgemeinschaften. Eine pilotstudie. Unveröffentliche Magisterarbeit an der Universität Wien.

Kaplan, B. (1983a). Genetic-dramatism: Old wine in new bottles. In S. Wapner & B. Kaplan (Eds.), *Toward a holistic developmental psychology*. Hillsdale, NJ: Erlbaum.

Kaplan, B. (1983b). Reflections on culture and personality from the perspective of genetic-dramatism. In S. Wapner & B. Kaplan (Eds.), *Toward holistic developmental psychology* (pp. 95–110). Hillsdale, NJ: Erlbaum.

Keller, E. (2006). Scripture study as normal science: Seventh-Day Adventist practice on the east coast of Madagascar. In F. Cannell (Ed.), *The anthropology of Christianity*. Durham, NC: Duke University Press.

Keller, E. F. (2005). DDS: Dynamics of developmental systems. *Biology and Philosophy, 20*, 409–416.

Kellert, S., & Farnham, T. (Eds.). (2002). *The good in nature and humanity: Connecting science, religion, and spirituality with the natural world*. Washington, DC: Island Press.

Kiesling, C., Sorell, G. T., Montgomery, M. J., & Colwell, R. K. (2006). Identity and spirituality: A psychosocial exploration of the sense of spiritual self. *Developmental Psychology, 42*, 1269–1277.

Kikoski, C. K. (2001). Feminism in the Middle East: Reflections on ethnographic research in Lebanon. *Journal of Feminist Family Therapy, 11*, 131–146.

Killen, M., & Smetana, J. (Eds.). (2006). *Handbook of moral development*. Mahwah, NJ: Erlbaum.

King, P. E. (2003). Religion and identity: The role of ideological, social, and spiritual contexts. *Applied Developmental Science, 7*, 197–204.

Kingdom, D., Siddle, R., & Rathod, S. (2001). Spirituality, psychosis, and the development of "normalising rationales." In I. Clarke (Ed.), *Psychosis and spirituality* (pp. 177–198). London: Whurr.

Kirkpatrick, C. (1949). Religion and humanitarianism: A study of institutional implications. *Psychological Monographs, 63*(9), 304–324.

Klosinski, G. (1996). *Psychokulte. Was Sekten fur Jugendliche so attraktiv macht*. München: Beck.

Kohlberg, L. (1967). Moral and religious education and the public schools: A developmental view. In T. Sizer (Ed.), *Religion and public education* (pp. 164–183). Boston: Houghton Mifflin.

Kohlberg, L. (1980). Stages of moral development as a basis for moral education. In B. Munsey (Ed.), *Moral development, moral education, and Kohlberg*. Birmingham, AL: Religious Education Press.

Kohlberg, L., & Lickona, T. (1990). Moral discussion and the class meeting. In R. DeVries & L. Kohlberg (Eds.), *Constructivist early education: Overview and comparison with other programs.* Washington, DC: National Association for the Education of Young Children.

Kohlberg, L., & Power, C. (1981). Moral development, religious thinking, and the question of a seventh stage. In L. Kohlberg (Ed.), *Essays on moral development: The philosophy of moral development* (Vol. 1). San Francisco: Harper and Row.

Kolodiejchuk, B. (Ed.). (2007). *Mother Teresa: Come by my light—The private writings of the saint of Calcutta.* New York: Doubleday.

Kuhn, D. (Ed.). (1995). *Development and learning: Reconceptualizing the intersection* (Vol. 38). New York: S. Karger.

Kuner, W. (1981). Jugendsekten: Ein Sammelbecken fur Verr¸ckte? *Psychologie Heute, 8,* 53–61.

Kunzman, R. (2003). Religion, ethics, and the implications for moral educaton: A critique of Nicci's morality and religious rules. *Journal of Moral Education, 32,* 251–261.

Kwilecki, S. (1999). *Becoming religious.* Cranbury, NJ: Associated University Press.

Lademann-Priemer, G. (1998). *Warum faszinieren Sekten? Psychologische Aspekte des Religionsmissbrauchs.* München: Claudius.

Lapsley, D., & Narvaez, D. (2006). Character education. In W. Damon & R. Lerner (Eds.), *Handbook of child psychology* (Vol. 4). Hoboken, NJ: John Wiley & Sons.

Latkin, C. A. (1995). New directions in applying psychological theory to the study of new religions. *The International Journal for the Psychology of Religion, 5,* 177–180.

Lease, S. H., Horne, S. G., & Noffsinger-Frazier, N. (2005). Affirming faith experiences and psychological health for Caucasian lesbian, gay, and bisexual individuals. *Journal of Counseling Psychology, 52,* 378–388.

Lerner, R., Alberts, A., Anderson, P., & Dowling, E. (2006). On making humans human: Spirituality and the promotion of positive youth development. In E. Roehlkepartain, P. King, L. Wagener, & P. Benson (Eds.), *The handbook of spiritual development in childhood and adolescence* (pp. 60–72). Thousand Oaks, CA: Sage.

Lerner, R., Dowling, E., & Anderson, P. (2003). Positive youth development: Thriving as the basis of personhood and civil society. *Applied Developmental Science, 7,* 172–180.

Lerner, R., Roeser, R., & Phelps, E. (Eds.). (2008). *Positive youth development and spirituality: From theory to research.* West Conshohocken, PA.: Templeton Foundation Press.

Lerner, R. M. (1998). Theories of human development: Contemporary perspectives. In R. M. Lerner (Ed.), *Handbook of child psychology: Theoretical models of human development,* (5th ed., Vol. 1, pp. 1–24). New York: John Wiley & Sons.

Lerner, R. M. (2002). *Concepts and theories of human development* (3rd ed.). Mahwah, NJ: Erlbaum.

Lerner, R. M., Roeser, R. W., & Phelps, E. (2008). Positive development, spirituality, and generosity in youth: An introduction to the issues. In R. M. Lerner, R. W. Roeser, & E. Phelps (Eds.), *Positive youth development and spirituality: From theory to research.* West Conshohocken, PA: Templeton Foundation Press.

Lewis, M. (2000). The promise of dynamic systems approaches for an integrated account of human development. *Child Development, 71,* 36–43.

Love, P. G. (1997). Contradiction and paradox: Attempting to change the culture of sexual orientation at a small Catholic college. *Review of Higher Education, 20,* 381–398.

Love, P. G., Bock, M., Jannarone, A., & Richardson, P. (2005). Identity interaction: Exploring the spiritual experiences of lesbian and gay college students. *Journal of College Student Development, 46,* 193–209.

Mahaffy, K. A. (1996). Cognitive dissonance and its resolution: A study of lesbian Christians. *Journal for the Scientific Study of Religion, 35,* 392–402.

Marcia, J. E. (1993). The ego identity status approach to ego identity. In J. E. Marcia, A.S. Waterman, D. R. Matteson, S. L. Archer, & J. L. Orlofski (Eds.), *Ego identity: A handbook for psychological research.* New York: Springer-Verlag.

Mariano, J., & Damon, W. (2008). The role of spirituality and religious faith in supporting purpose in adolescence. In R. Lerner, R. Roeser, & E. Phelps (Eds.), *Positive youth development and spirituality: From theory to research.* West Conshohocken, PA: Templeton Foundation Press.

Markstrom-Adams, C., Hofstra, G., & Dougher, K. (1994). The ego virtue of fidelity: A case for the study of religion and identity formation in adolescence. *Journal of Youth and Adolescence, 23,* 453–469.

Markstrom-Adams, C., & Smith, M. (1996). Identity formation and religious orientation among high school students from the United States and Canada. *Journal of Adolescence, 19,* 247–261.

Maslow, A. H. (1970). *Religions, values, and peak experiences.* New York: Viking Press.

Maslow, A. H. (1971). *The farther reaches of human nature.* New York: Penguin.

Mattis, J. S., Ahluwalia, M. K., Cowie, S. E., & Kirkland-Harris, A. M. (2006). Ethnicity, culture, and spiritual development. In E. C. Roehlkepartain, P. E. King, L. M. Wagener, & P. L. Benson (Eds.), *The handbook of spiritual development in childhood and adolescence* (pp. 283–296). Thousand Oaks, CA: Sage.

McAdams, D. P. (2001). The psychology of life stories. *Review of General Psychology, 5,* 100–122.

McCarn, S. R., & Fassinger, R. E. (1996). Revisioning sexual minority identity. *The Counseling Psychologist, 24,* 508–524.

McGinty, A. M. (2007). Formation of alternative femininities through Islam: Feminist approaches among Muslim converts in Sweden. *Women's Studies International Forum, 30,* 474–485.

Miller, R. L., Jr. (2007). Legacy denied: African American gay men, AIDS, and the Black church. *Social work, 52,* 51.

Min, P. G. (2000). The structure and social functions of Korean immigrant churches in the United States. In M. Zhou & J. V. Gatewood (Eds.), *Contemporary Asian America: A multidisciplinary reader* (pp. 372–390). New York: New York University Press.

Mohanty, C. (2003). *Feminism without borders: Decolonizing theory, practicingsolidarity.* Durham, NC: Duke University Press.

Moore, D. (2008). Guilty of sin: African-American denominational churches and their exclusion of SGL sisters and brothers. *Black Theology, 6,* 83–97.

Morris, B. (1995). Agents or victims of religious ideology? Approaches to locating Hasidic women in feminist studies. In J. Belcove-Shalin (Ed.), *New world Hasidim* (pp. 161–181). Albany, NY: SUNY Press.

Niebuhr, H. R. (1941). *The meaning of revelation.* New York: Macmillan.

Nucci, L. (2001). *Education in the moral domain.* Cambridge: Cambridge University Press.

Nucci, L. (2003). Morality, religion, and public education in pluralist democracies: A reply to Kunzman. *Journal of Moral Education, 32,* 263–270.

Nucci, L., & Turiel, E. (1993). God's word, religious rules, and their relation to Christian and Jewish concepts of morality. *Child Development 64,* 1475–1491.

Ochse, R. (1990). *Before the gates of excellence.* New York: Cambridge University Press.

Oser, F. (1991). The development of religious judgment. In F. Oser & W. G. Scarlett (Eds.), *Religious development in childhood and adolescence.* San Francisco: Jossey-Bass.

Oser, F., & Gmunder, P. (1991). *Religious judgement: A developmental approach*. Birmingham, AL: Religious Education Press.

Oser, F., Scarlett, W. G., & Bucher, A. (2006). Religious and spiritual development throughout the life span. In W. Damon & R. M. Lerner (Eds.), *Handbook of child psychology: Theoretical models of human development* (6th ed., Vol. 1). Hoboken, NJ: John Wiley & Sons.

Overton, W. (2006). Developmental psychology: Philosophy, concepts, methodology. In R. Lerner (Ed.), *Handbook of child psychology* (6th ed., Vol. 1.) Hoboken, NJ: John Wiley & Sons.

Oxtoby, W. (Ed.). (1976). *Religious diversity: Essays by Wilfred Cantwell Smith*. New York: Harper & Row.

Paranjpe, A. C. (1998). *Self and identity in modern psychology and Indian thought*. New York: Plenum Press.

Pargament, K. I., Ensing, D. S., & Falgout, K. (1990). God help me: Religious coping effects as predictors of the outcomes of significantnegative life events. *American Journal of Community and Psychology, 18*, 793–824.

Peterson, D. (2008). *Jane Goodall: The woman who redefined man*. New York: Houghton Mifflin.

Pevey, C., William, C. L., & Ellison, C. G. (1996). Male God imagery and female submission: Lessons from a Southern Baptist ladies' bible class. *Qualitative Sociology, 19,* 173–193.

Phinney, J. (2003). Ethnic identity and acculturation. In K. Chun, P. Organista, & G. Marin (Eds.), *Acculturation: Advances in theory, measurement, and applied research* (pp. 63–81). Washington, DC: American Psychological Association.

Phinney, J. (2006). Ethnic identity exploration in emerging adulthood. In J. Arnett & J. L. Tanner (Eds.), *Coming of age in the 21st century: The lives and contexts of emerging adults* (pp. 117–134). Washington, DC: American Psychological Association.

Phinney, J. S. (1989). Stages of ethnic identity development in minority group adolescents. *The Journal of Early Adolescence, 9,* 34–49.

Phinney, J. S., & Ong, A. (2007). Conceptualization and measurement of ethnic identity: Current status and future directions. *Journal of Counseling Psychology, 54*, 271–281.

Piaget, J. (1930). Immanentisme et foi religieuse. Paper presented to Le Groupe romand des Anciens Membres de l'Asscociation Chretienne d'Etudiants, Geneva.

Piaget, J. (1932/1964). *Moral judgment of the child* (M. Gabain, trans.) New York: Free Press.

Piaget, J. (1958). *The growth of logical thinking from childhood to adolescence*. New York: Basic Books.

Plaskow, J. (1991). *Standing again at Sinai: Judaism from a feminist perspective*. San Francisco: Harper.

Post, S. G. (2003). *Unlimited love: Altruism, compassion, and service*. West Conshohocken, PA: Templeton Foundation Press.

Predelli, L. N. (2004). Interpreting gender in Islam: A case study of immigrant Muslim women in Oslo, Norway. *Gender & Society, 18,* 473.

Primiano, L. N. (1995). Vernacular religion and the search for method in religious folklife. *Western Folklore, 54*, 37–56.

Primiano, L. N. (1993). "I would rather be fixated on the Lord": Women's religion, men's power, and the "dignity" problem. *New York Folklore, 19*(1–2), 89–99.

Pruyser, P. B. S. N. Y., Oxford University Press. (1991). Forms and functions of the imagination in religion. In M. Newton & B. Spilka (Eds.), *Religion in psychodynamic perspective: The contributions of Paul W. Pruyser*. New York: Oxford University Press.

Quintana, S. M. (2007). Racial and ethnic identity:Developmental perspectives and research. *Journal of Counseling Psychology, 54,* 259–270.

Ramji, H. (2007). Dynamics of religion and gender amongst young British Muslims. *Sociology, 41,* 1171–1189.

Regnerus, M., & Elder, G. (2003). Staying on track in school: Religious influences in high- and low-risk settings. *Journal for the Scientific Study of Religion, 42,* 633–649.

Reich, H. (2005). Jean Piaget's views on religion. Unpublished manuscript. Fribourg: University of Fribourg.

Reich, H., Oser, F. K., & Scarlett, W. G. (1999). Spiritual and religious development: Transcendence and transformations of the self. In K. H. Reich, F. O. Oser, & W. G. Scarlett (Eds.), *Psychological studies on spiritual and religious development: being human: The case of religion*. Scottsdale, AZ: Pabst Science Publishers.

Renou, L. (Ed.). (1962). *Hinduism*. New York: George Braziller.

Reynolds, A. L., & Hanjorgiris, W. F. (2000). Coming out: Lesbian, gay, and bisexual identity development. In R. M. Perez, K. A. DeBord, & K. Bieschke (Eds.), *Handbook of counseling and psychotherapy with lesbian, gay, and bisexual clients* (pp. 35–55). Washington, DC: American Psychological Association.

Richardson, J. T. (1995). Clinical and personality assessment of participants in new religions. *The International Journal for the Psychology of Religion, 5*, 145–170.

Richardson, J. T., van der Lans, J., & Derks, F. (1985). Leaving and labeling: Voluntary and coerced disaffiliation from new religious movements. *Social Movements, Conflict, and Change, 8*, 385–393.

Ringel, S. (2007). Identity and gender roles of Orthodox Jewish women: Implications for social work practice. *Smith College Studies in Social Work, 77*, 25–.

Ritter, K. Y., & Terndrup, A. I. (2002). Handbook of affirmative psychotherapy with lesbians and gay men. *Handbook of affirmative psychotherapy with lesbians and gay men.* New York: Guilford Press.

Rodriguez, E. M., & Ouellette, S. C. (2000). Gay and lesbian Christians: Homosexual and religious identity integration in the members and participants of a gay-positive church. *Journal for the Scientific Study of Religion, 39*, 333–347.

Roehlkepartain, E. C., King, P. E., Wagener, L., & Benson, P. (Eds.). (2005). *The handbook of spiritual development in childhood and adolescence*. Thousand Oaks, CA: Sage.

Roeser, R. W. (2005). An introduction to Hindu India's contemplative psychological perspective on motivation, self, and development. In M. L. Maehr & S. Karabenick (Eds.), *Advances in motivation and achievement* (pp. 297–345). Amsterdam: Elsevier.

Roeser, R. W., Issac, S. S., Abo-Zena, M., Brittian, A., & Peck, S. C. (2008). Self and identity processes in spirituality and positive youth development. In R. M. Lerner, R. W. Roeser, & E. Phelps (Eds.), *Positive youth development and spirituality: From theory to research* (pp. 74–105). West Conshohocken, PA: Templeton Foundation Press.

Rogers, C. R. (1961). *On becoming a person*. Boston: Houghton-Mifflin.

Rokeach, M. (1960). *The open and closed mind: Investigations into the nature of belief systems and personality systems*. New York: Basic Books.

Rollett, B. (1992). *Religiöse Entwicklung und Interesse an Jugendsekten*. Forschungsbericht Universität Wien: Abteilung für Entwicklungspsychologie und Pädagogische Psychologie.

Rollett, B. (1996). Religiöse Entwicklung im Jugendalter. In H. M. Trautner (Ed.), *Entwicklung im Jugendalter* (pp. 205–215). Göttingen: Hogrefe.

Rollett, B., & Kager, A. (1999). Post-modern religiousness: A prerogative of the "New Religious?" Religious emotions and religious development. Findings of a pilot study. In H. Reich, F. Oser, & W. G. Scarlett (Eds.), *Psychological studies on spiritual and religious development: Being human: The case of religion* (Vol. 2). Lengerich, Germany: Pabst Science Publishers.

Rosario, M., Scrimshaw, E. W., & Hunter, J. (2004). Ethnic/racial difference in the coming-out process of lesbian, gay, and bisexual youths: A comparison of sexual identity development over time. *Cultural Diversity and Ethnic Minority Psychology, 10,* 215–228.

Rosario, M., Yali, A. M., Hunter, J., & Gwadz, M. V. (2006). Religion and health among lesbian, gay, and bisexual youths: An empirical investigation and theoretical explanation. In A. M. Omoto & H. S. Kurtzman (Eds.), *Sexual orientation and mental health: Examining identity and development in lesbian, gay, and bisexual people* (pp. 117–140). Washington, DC: American Psychological Association.

Rosenblith, J. F. (1949). A replication of "Some roots of prejudice." *Journal of Abnormal and Social Psychology, 44*, 470–489.

Ruthven, M. (2004). *Fundamentalism: The search for meaning*. Oxford: Oxford University Press.

Salzman, L. (1953). The psychology of religious and ideological conversion. *Psychiatry, 16*, 177–187.

Scarlett, W. G. (1999). Spiritual development: Lessons from Lincoln. In H. Reich, F. Oser, & W. G. Scarlett (Eds.), *Psychological studies on spiritual and religious development: the case of religion* (pp. 25–49). Langerich: Pabst Science Publishers.

Scarlett, W. G. (2008). Spirituality and positive youth development: The problem of transcendence. In R. Lerner, R. Roeser, & E. Phelps (Eds.), *Positive youth development and spirituality: From theory to research*. West Conshohocken, PA.: Templeton Foundation Press.

Scarlett, W. G. (2009). Spiritual pathology: The case of Adolf Hitler. Medford, MA: Tufts University, unpublished manuscript, 1–28.

Scarlett, W. G., & Perriello, L. (1991). The development of prayer in adolescence. In F. Oser & W. G. Scarlett (Eds.). *Religious development in childhood and adolescence*. San Francisco: Jossey-Bass.

Schibilsky, M. (1976). *Religi^se Erfahrung und Interaktion. Die Lebenswelt jugendlicher Randgruppen*. Stuttgart: Kohlhammer.

Schmitz, E., & Friebe, S. (1992). Die Neuen Jugendreligionen"—öffentliche Akzeptanz und Konversionsmotive. In I. E. Schmitz (Ed.), *Religionspsychologie* (pp. 235–262). Gottingen: Hogrefe.

Schuck, K. D., & Liddle, B. J. (2001). Religious conflicts experiences by lesbian, gay, and bisexual individuals. *Journal of Gay and Lesbian Psychotherapy, 5,* 63–82.

Scott, S., Garver, S., Richards, J., & Hathaway, W. (2003). Religious issues in diagnosis: The V-Code and beyond. *Mental Health, Religion and Culture, 62*, 160–173.

Seaton, E. K., Scottham, K. M., & Sellers, R. M. (2006). The status model of racial identity development in African American adolescents: Evidence of structure, trajectories, and well-being. *Child Development, 77 (5)*, 1416–1426.

Sechzer, J. A. (2004). "Islam and woman: Where tradition meets modernity": History and interpretations of Islamic women's status. *Sex Roles, 51*, 263–272.

Shaver, P., Leneuaer, M., & Sadd, S. (1980). Religiousness, conversion, and subjective well-being: The "healthy-minded" religion of modern American women. *American Journal of Psychiatry, 137*, 1563–1568.

Shidlo, A. (1994). Internalized homophobia: Conceptual and empirical issues in measurement. In B. Greene & G. M. Herek (Eds.), *Lesbian and gay psychology: Theory, research and clinical application* (pp. 176–205). Thousand Oaks, CA: Sage.

Shokeid, M. (1995). *A gay synagogue in New York*. New York: Columbia University Press.

Shweder, R. A., Much, N. C., Hahapatra, M., & Park, L. (1997). The "big three" of morality (autonomy, community, and divinity) and the "big three" explanations of suffering. In A. Brandt & P. Rozin (Eds.), *Morality and health* (pp. 119–169). Standford, CA: Stanford University Press.

Silke, A. (2003). Becoming a terrorist. In E. Salib (Ed.), *Terrorists, victims, and society: Psychological perspectives on terrorism and its consequences*. Southern Gate, England: John Wiley & Sons.

Silverstein, S. M. (1988). A study of religious conversion in North America. *Genetic, Social, and General Psychology Monographs, 114*, 261–305.

Simonton, D. K. (1994). *Greatness: Who makes history and why*. New York: Guilford Press.

Slee, N. (1986). Goldman yet again: An overview and critique of his contribution to research. *British Journal of Religious Education, 8*, 84–33.

Smith, C. (2000). *Christian America? What evangelicals really want.* Berkeley: University of California Press.

Smith, C., & Denton, M. (2005). *Soul searching: The religious and spiritual lives of American teenagers*. New York: Oxford University Press.

Smith, C., Faris, R., Denton, M. L., & Regnerus, M. D. (2003). Mapping American adolescent subjective religiosity and attitudes of alienation toward religion: A research report. *Sociology of Religion, 64*, 111–123.

Smith, H. (1995). *The world's religions*. San Francisco: Harper.

Smith, W. C. (1971). The study of religion and the study of the Bible. *Journal of the American Academy of Religion, 39*, 131–140.

Smith, W. C. (1998a). *Faith and belief: The difference between them.* Oxford: Oneworld Publications.

Smith, W. C. (1998b). *Patterns of faith around the world.* Boston: Oneworld Publications.

Spencer, M. B., Fegley, S. G., & Harpalani, V. (2003). A theoretical and empirical examination of identity as coping: Linking coping resources to the self processes of African American youth. *Applied Developmental Science, 7,* 181–188.

Spilka, B., & McIntosh, D. N. (1995). Attribution theory and religious experience. In R. W. Hood Jr. (Ed.), *Handbook of religious experience: Theory and practice* (pp. 421–445). Birmingham, AL: Religious Education Press.

Stacey, J., & Gerard, S. E. (1990). "We are not doormats": The influence of feminism on contemporary evangelicals in the United States. In F. Ginsburg & A. L. Tsing (Eds.), *Uncertain terms: Negotiating gender in American culture* (pp. 98–117). Boston: Beacon.

Stanczak, G. C. (2006). Strategic ethnicity: The construction of multi-racial/multi-ethnic religious community. *Ethnic and Racial Studies, 29,* 856–881.

Stark, R. (1996). *The rise of Christianity: A sociologist reconsiders history*. Princeton, NJ: Princeton University Press.

Steffen, P. R., Hinderliter, A. L., Blumenthal, J. A., & Sherwood, A. (2001). Religious coping, ethnicity, and ambulatory blood pressure. *Psychosomatic Medicine, 63*, 523–530.

Stewart, D. L. (2002). The role of faith in the development of an integrated identity: A qualitative study of black students at a white college. *Journal of College Student Development, 43,* 579–596.

Stitzlein, S. M. (2008). Private interests, public necessity: Responding to sexism in Christian schools. *Educational Studies: Journal of the American Educational Studies Association, 43,* 45–57.

Stone, M. (2000). Psychopathology: Biological and psychological correlates. *The American Academy of Psychoanalysis, 28,* 203–235.

Streib, H. (1996). *Entzauberung der Okkultfaszination. Magisches Denken und Handeln in der Adoleszenz als Herausforderung an die Praktische Theologie*. Kampen: Kok Pharos.

Streib, H. (1999). Off-road religion? A narrative approach to fundamentalist and occult orientations of adolescents. *Journal of Adolescence, 22*, 255–267.

Sullivan, P. (1998). Sexual identity development: The importance of target or dominant group membership. In R. L. Sanlo (Ed.), *Working with lesbian, gay, bisexual, and transgender college students: A handbook for faculty and administrators* (pp. 3–12). Westport, CT: Greenwood.

Sulloway, F. (1996). *Born to rebel*. New York: Pantheon.

Tamminnen, K. (1976). Research concerning the development of religious thinking in Finnish students. *Character Potential, 7,* 206–219.

Taylor, C. (2002). *Varieties of religion today: William James revisted.* Cambridge, MA: Harvard University Press.

Taylor, R. J., Chatters, L. M., & Levin, J. S. (2004). *Religion in the lives of African Americans: Social, psychological and health perspectives.* Newbury Park, CA: Sage.

Templeton, J. L., & Eccles, J. S. (2006). The relation between spiritual development and identity processes. In E. C. Roehlkepartain, P. E. King, L. M. Wagener, & P. L. Benson (Eds.), *The handbook of spiritual development in childhood and adolescence* (pp. 252–265). Thousand Oaks, CA: Sage.

Teresa, M. (1985). *My life for the poor: Mother Teresa of Calcutta*. San Francisco: Harper & Row.

Thelen, E., & Ulrich, B. D. (1991). *Hidden skills: A dynamic systems analysis of treadmill stepping during the first year*. Chicago: University of Chicago Press.

Thelen, E., & Smith, L. (2006). Dynamic systems theories. In R. M. Lerner (Ed.), *Handbook of Child Psychology* (Vol. 1, pp. 258–312). Hoboken, NJ: John Wiley & Sons.

Thumma, S. (1991). Negotiating a religious identity: The case of the gay evangelical. *Sociological Analysis, 52,* 333–347.

Thumma, S., & Gray, E. (Eds.). (2004). *Gay religion: Innovation and tradition in spiritual practice*. Walnut Creek, CA: Alta Mira.

Tillich, P. (1957). *Dynamics of faith*. New York: Harper.

Toulmin, S. (1950). *An examination of the place of reason in ethics*. Cambridge: University Press.

Turiel, E. (1975). The development of social concepts: Mores, customs, and conventions. In J. M. Foley & D. J. DePalma (Eds.), *Moral development: Current theory and research* (pp. 7–38). Hillsdale, NJ: Erlbaum.

Turiel, E. (2006). *The development of morality* (6th ed., Vol. 3). Hoboken, NJ: John Wiley & Sons.

Tzuriel, D. (1984). Sex role typing and ego identity in Israeli, Oriental, and Western adolescents. *Journal of Personality and Social Psychology, 46*, 440–457.

Ullman, C. (1982). Cognitive and emotional antecedents of religious conversion. *Journal of Personality and Social Psychology, 43,* 183–192.

Umaña-Taylor, A. J., Yazedjian, A., & Bámaca-Gómez, M. (2004). Developing the ethnic identity scale using Eriksonian and social identity perspectives. *Identity, 4,* 9–38.

Walker, L. (2003). Morality, religion, spirituality: The value of saintliness. *Journal of Moral Education, 32,* 373–384.

Walker, L., Pitts, R., Hennig, K., & Matsuba, M. K. (1995). Reasoning about morality and real-life problems. In M. Killen & D. Hart (Eds.), *Morality in everyday life: Developmental perspectives* (pp. 371–407). Cambridge: Cambridge University Press.

Walker, L., & Reimer, K. (2006). The relationship between moral and spiritual development. In E. Roehlkepartain, P. King, L. Wagener, & P. Benson (Eds.), *The handbook of spiritual development in childhood and adolescence*. Thousand Oaks, CA: Sage.

Wallace, J. M., Jr., Forman, T. A., Caldwell, C. H., & Willis, D. S. (2003). Religion and U.S. secondary school students: Current patterns, recent trends, and sociodemographic correlates. *Youth and Society, 35*, 98–125.

Ward, E. G. (2005). Homophobia, hypermasculinity and the US black church. *Culture, Health & Sexuality, 7,* 493–504.

Warner, R. S. (1995). The metropolitan community churches and the gay agenda: The power of Pentecostalism and essentialism. In M. J. Neitz & M. S. Goldman (Eds.), *Sex, lies, and sanctity: Religion and deviance in contemporary North America* (pp. 81–108). Greenwich, CT: JAI Press.

Warwick, L. (1995). Feminist Wicca: Paths to empowerment. *Women and Therapy, 16*, 121–133.

Waters, M. C. (1999). *Black identities: West Indian immigrant dreams and American realities*. Cambridge: Harvard University Press.

Werner, H. (1957). The concept of development from a comparative and organismic point of view. In D. B. Harris (Ed.), *The concept of development: An issue in the study of human behavior*. Minneapolis: University of Minnesota Press.

Wilcox, M. M. (2007). Outlaws or in-laws? Queer theory, LGBT studies, and religious studies. *Journal of Homosexuality, 52,* 73–100.

Williams, R. B. (2000). Asian Indian and Pakistani religions in the United States. In J. V. Gatewood (Ed.), *Contemporary Asian America: A multidisciplinary reader* (pp. 392–407). New York: New York University Press.

Wills, G. (1992). *Lincoln at Gettysburg*. New York: Simon & Schuster.

Winter, B. (2006). The social foundations of the sacred: Feminists and the politics of religion. In K. Davis, M. Evans, & J. Lorber (Eds.), *Handbook of gender and women's studies* (pp. 92). Thousand Oaks, CA: Sage.

Woolley, J. (2000). The development of beliefs about direct mental-physical causality on imagination, magic, and religion. In R. S. Rosengren, C. N. Johnson, & P. L. Harris (Eds.), *Imagining the impossible: Magical, scientific, and religious thinking in childhood* (pp. 99–129). Cambridge: Cambridge University Press.

Worthington, R. L., & Mohr, J. J. (2002). Theorizing heterosexual identity development. *Counseling Psychologist, 30,* 491.

Worthington, R. L., Savoy, H. B., Dillon, F. R., & Vernaglia, E. R. (2002). Heterosexual identity development: A multidimensional model of individual and social identity. *Counseling Psychologist, 30,* 496.

Wulff, D. (1993). On the origins and goals of religious development. *The International Journal for the Psychology of Religion, 3,* 181–186.

Yadgar, Y. (2006). Gender, religion, and feminism: The case of Jewish Israeli traditionalists. *Journal for the Scientific Study of Religion, 45,* 353–370.

Yip, A. K. T. (1997). *Gay male Christian couples: Life stories*. Westport, CT: Praeger.

Yip, A. K. T. (2002). The persistence of faith among nonheterosexual Christians: Evidence for the neosecularization thesis of religious transformation. *Journal for the Scientific Study of Religion, 41,* 199–212.

Youniss, J., McLellan, J. A., Su, Y., & Yates, M. (1999). Religion, community service, and identity in American youth. *Journal of Adolescence, 22,* 243–253.

Zimmerman, M. A. (1995). Psychological empowerment: Issues and illustrations. *American Journal of Community Psychology, 23,* 581–599.

Zinnbauer, B., Pargament, K., Cole, B. Rye, M., Butter, E., Belavich, T., et al. (1997). Religion and spirituality: Unfuzzying the fuzzy. *Journal for the Scientific Study of Religion, 36,* 549–564.

Zondag, H. J., & Belzen, J. A. (1999). Between reduction of uncertainty and reflection: The range and dynamics of religious judgment. *The International Journal for the Psychology of Religion 9*, 63–81.

Author Index

Subject Index